AF819989

NATIONAL TESTING AGENCY (NTA)

UGC NET / JRF / SET PSYCHOLOGY

SOLVED PAPERS
2024-2012

Compiled by
Apoorva Adhikari
Kezia

arihant
SUCCESS AND NOTHING LESS

arihant
SUCCESS AND NOTHING LESS

ARIHANT PUBLICATIONS (INDIA) LIMITED

Administrative & Production Offices

Regd. Office

'Ramchhaya' 4577/15, Agarwal Road, Darya Ganj, New Delhi -110002
Tele: 011- 47630600, 43518550

Head Office

Kalindi, TP Nagar, Meerut (UP) - 250002
Tel: 0121-7156203, 7156204

Sales & Support Offices

Agra, Ahmedabad, Bengaluru, Bareilly, Chennai, Delhi, Guwahati, Hyderabad, Jaipur, Jhansi, Kolkata, Lucknow, Nagpur & Pune.

PRICE ₹575.00

PO No : TXT-XX-XXXXXXX-X-XX

Published by Arihant Publications (India) Ltd.

For further information about the books published by Arihant, log on to www.arihantbooks.com or e-mail at info@arihantbooks.com

Book Available at
amazon Flipkart

PREFACE

NTA UGC NET examination is a highly prestigious and competitive examination conducted by NTA. The purpose of this exam is selection of candidates for Junior Research Fellowship and Assistant Professor.

Keeping in mind the importance of such exam, Arihant Publications presents **NTA UGC Solved Paper Series** – The only series that contains 100% detailed solution for each question.

This book **Psychology Previous Years' Solved Papers** contains all question papers from 2024-2012.

Salient Features of the Books

- 100% detailed & authentic explanations.
- All the facts and data have been provided with latest information.
- 5 Practice Sets also have been provided exactly based on the latest pattern of the examination for practice.

We have taken utmost care in preparing this book and put our best efforts to make it a perfect study resource for the aspirants, still we request all the respected teachers and the aspirants to provide us their valuable feedback or suggestions or reviews whatsoever you want to say about the book.

We assure you that we will try to incorporate all those points in the further edition of the book.

Authors

About the

UGC NET

NTA UGC NET

On behalf of UGC, National Testing Agency (NTA) conducts National Eligibility Test (NET) for determining the eligibility of Indian Nationals for the eligibility for Assistant Professorship or Junior Research Fellowship or both in Indian Universities and Colleges.

NTA will conduct NET in 84 subjects at 91 selected NET Examination cities spread across the country.

CONDITIONS OF ELIGIBILITY

- For General category 55% marks in Master degree, for SC / ST / OBC category 50% marks in Master degree.
- Candidates who have appeared OR will be appearing at the qualifying Master's degree (final year) examination and whose result is still awaited or candidates whose qualifying examination have been delayed may also apply for this test.
- The Ph.D degree holders whose master's level examination had been completed by 19th September 1991 (irrespective of date of declaration of result) shall be eligible for a relaxation of 5% in aggregate marks (i. e. from 55% to 50%) for appearing in NET.

AGE LIMIT & RELAXATION

- **Junior Research Fellowship:** Not more than 30 years. A relaxation up to 5 years is provided to the candidates belonging to OBC (Non creamy layer, as per the central list of OBC available on website).
- **Assistant Professor:** There is no upper age limit for applying for eligibility for Assistant Professor exemption (Eligibility for assistant professor).

EXAMINATION SCHEDULE

NATIONAL ELIGIBILITY TEST (NET)

Sec./Paper	Marks	Number of Questions
First I	100	50 Questions & all are Compulsory
Second II	200	100 Questions & all are Compulsory

CONTENTS

PRACTICE SETS

UGC-NET
PSYCHOLOGY
SOLVED PAPER 2024 (August)

PAPER II

1 Hull's approach to theory construction is called
1 Hypothetical deductive
2 Hypothetical inductive
3 Hypothetical intuitive
4 Hypothetical tautology

Ans. (1)

Exp. Hull's approach to theory construction is based on the hypothetical deductive method, which involves formulating hypotheses derived from theoretical principles and then testing them through empirical observation. This method emphasises the deduction of predictions from general theories and using experiments to validate or refute those predictions.

2 Place the components of 'Broaden-and-Build Model of Positive Emotion' in correct sequence.
A. Building Enduring Personal Resources
B. Positive Emotions
C. Enhanced Health Fulfillments
D. Novel Thoughts, Activities, Relationships

Choose the correct answer from the options given below.
1 B, D, A, C
2 B, A, D, C
3 D, B, A, C
4 D, A, B, C

Ans. (1)

Exp. The correct sequence is B, D, A, C.

In the Broaden-and-Build model of Positive Emotion proposed by Barbara Fredrickson, the sequence of components is as follows

Positive Emotions The model starts with the experience of positive emotions, which serve as the foundation for broadening an individual's thought processes and actions.

Novel Thoughts, Activities, Relationships These positive emotions lead to the expansion of cognition, encouraging individuals to explore new ideas, engage in novel activities and build relationships.

Building Enduring Personal Resources As people engage in new experiences, they build lasting personal resources, such as skills, knowledge and social connections.

Enhanced Health Fulfillments Ultimately, these resources contribute to better health, well-being and life satisfaction.

3 Cognitive psychologists and survey researchers have acknowledged that answering survey questions can be a complex cognitive task. Research suggests that when people answer survey questions, they go through four stages. Arrange the stages in order.
A. Comprehension
B. Judgement
C. Response communication
D. Retrieval

Choose the correct answer from the options given below.
1 A, D, B, C
2 A, B, D, C
3 B, A, D, C
4 B, C, A, D

Ans. (1)

Exp. The correct order is A, D, B, C.

When answering survey questions, respondents typically go through the following four stages in order

Comprehension The respondent first interprets and understands the question being asked, ensuring they grasp its meaning.

Retrieval After comprehending the question, the respondent retrieves relevant information or memories from their memory to formulate an answer.

Judgement The respondent then makes a judgement based on the retrieved information, evaluating how it relates to the question.

Response Communication Finally, the respondent communicates their answer, which may involve choosing from multiple options or providing a written response.

4 **Who is the Personality Theorist who believed that individuals are in the process of 'becoming' and nothing is predetermined?**
1 Sigmund Freud
2 Alfred Adler
3 Carl Jung
4 BF Skinner

Ans. (2)

Exp. Alfred Adler believed that individuals are in the process of 'becoming' and nothing is predetermined. His theory, known as Individual Psychology, emphasised the importance of social factors, birth order, and individual striving for superiority in shaping personality. Unlike Freud, Adler believed that humans are not solely driven by biological instincts but also by social and environmental factors.

5 **Read the following situations. Then order them in the sequence of nominal, ordinal, equal interval and ratio.**
A. Eggs in the supermarket are graded as small, medium, large and jumbo
B. Employees are assigned identification numbers
C. Achievement motivation of hockey players
D. Players' height

Choose the correct answer from the options given below.
1 B, C, D, A   2 B, A, C, D
3 A, B, D, C   4 A, C, B, D

Ans. (2)

Exp. The correct order is B, A, C, D.

Employees are assigned identification numbers (Nominal) This is a nominal scale because the identification numbers are used to label employees without any inherent order or ranking.

Eggs in the supermarket are graded as small, medium, large, and jumbo (Ordinal) This represents an ordinal scale as the sizes can be ranked in order (from small to jumbo), but the differences between the sizes are not uniform or measurable.

Achievement motivation of hockey players (Equal Interval) This situation can be treated as an equal interval scale because it assesses motivation, which can be measured on a continuous scale, allowing for meaningful comparisons of differences in levels of motivation.

Players' height (Ratio) Height is a ratio scale since it has a true zero point (no height) and allows for comparisons using multiplication and division (e.g., one player can be twice as tall as another).

6 **Advaita Vedanta asserts that sensory knowledge is**
A. Illusionary
B. Absolutely false
C. Possible in a transcendental state
D. Relatively true, but not absolutely true

Choose the correct answer from the options given below.
1 C, D only   2 A, B only   3 A, D only   4 B, C only

Ans. (1)

Exp. Advaita Vedanta, a non-dualistic school of thought in Hindu philosophy, asserts that sensory knowledge has certain limitations

Possible in a transcendental state Advaita Vedanta acknowledges that sensory knowledge can be valid within certain contexts or experiences, particularly when individuals reach a higher or transcendental state of awareness. In this state, one's perception may align more closely with ultimate reality.

Relatively true, but not absolutely true This reflects the idea that while sensory knowledge can provide useful information and insight about the world, it is ultimately not the complete or absolute truth. According to Advaita Vedanta, the ultimate reality (Brahman) transcends sensory experiences, making them only relatively true in comparison to the absolute truth.

7 **Following are the steps that should be followed to enhance critical thinking. Arrange them in sequential order.**
A. Adopt the attitude of a critical thinker
B. Evaluate information sources
C. Recognise and avoid critical thinking hindrances
D. Identify and characterise arguments
E. Evaluate arguments

Choose the correct answer from the options given below.
1 A, C, D, B, E   2 A, B, C, E, D
3 B, A, C, E, D   4 C, A, B, E, D

Ans. (1)

Exp. The correct sequential order is A, C, D, B, E.

Adopt the attitude of a critical thinker This foundational step involves cultivating a mindset that values questioning, open-mindedness, and a willingness to engage in reflective thinking.

Recognise and avoid critical thinking hindrances After adopting a critical thinking attitude, it's important to identify potential barriers (like biases, emotions, or preconceived notions) that could obstruct clear thinking and to actively work to avoid them.

Identify and characterise arguments Once hindrances are recognised, the next step is to analyse the arguments presented. This involves identifying claims, supporting evidence and understanding the structure of the arguments.

Evaluate information sources Critical thinkers should assess the credibility, reliability, and relevance of the information sources to ensure the arguments are based on sound evidence.

Evaluate arguments Finally, with a clear understanding of the arguments and the sources, the critical thinker evaluates the strengths and weaknesses of the arguments, leading to well-reasoned conclusions.

8 The distribution, which is skewed to the left, has one high point and has many high scores is called

1 Evenly distributed distribution
2 Platykurtic distribution
3 Negatively skewed distribution
4 Positively skewed distribution

Ans. **(3)**

Exp. A negatively skewed distribution (or left-skewed distribution) is characterised by a longer tail on the left side of the distribution graph. This means that the bulk of the data points (including high scores) are concentrated on the right, with fewer low scores pulling the mean to the left. In such a distribution, there is typically one high point (the mode) that represents the most frequently occurring score, while many high scores contribute to the overall shape of the distribution.

Some characteristics of a negatively skewed distribution:

The mean is usually less than the median.

The distribution has a large tail of small values.

The distribution is the opposite of a positively skewed distribution.

9 Match List-I with List-II.

List-I		List-II
A. Synthetic skill	I.	Decisions about how to deploy the skills available to a person
B. Analytic skill	II.	To see problem with new points of view and get rid of conventional thinking
C. Practical contexual skill	III.	To recognise which idea are worth pursuing and which are not
D. Thinking styles	IV.	To know how to persuade others regarding one's ideas

Choose the correct answer from the options given below.

	A	B	C	D		A	B	C	D
1	II	IV	III	I	2	II	III	IV	I
3	I	II	IV	III	4	IV	III	I	II

Ans. **(2)**

Exp. The correct matching is A-II, B-III, C-IV, D-I.

Synthetic skills involve the ability to combine information and ideas creatively, which helps in viewing problems from new perspectives and overcoming conventional thought patterns.

Analytic skills allow individuals to critically evaluate information, helping them discern valuable ideas from less relevant ones.

Practical contextual skills are about applying knowledge effectively in real-world scenarios, including the ability to persuade others of one's ideas based on context.

Thinking styles refer to the preferred ways in which individuals approach problems and make decisions, which involves strategic deployment of their skills.

10 The functions of Gamma-Aminobutyric Acid GABA can be described in terms of

1 Excitatory or inhibitory, involved in arousal, attention, memory
2 Mainly excitatory, involved in arousal and mood
3 Majorly inhibitory involved in sleep and inhibitory movement
4 Inhibitory neural regulation, involved in pain relief

Ans. **(3)**

Exp. Gamma-Aminobutyric Acid (GABA) is the primary inhibitory neurotransmitter in the central nervous system. Its main functions include

Inhibitory Action GABA helps to reduce neuronal excitability throughout the nervous system, leading to a calming effect on brain activity.

Involvement in Sleep GABA plays a crucial role in promoting sleep by inhibiting wakefulness and facilitating the onset of sleep stages.

Inhibitory Movement It is essential for regulating motor control.

11 Match List-I with List-II.

List-I	List-II
A. Krodha	I. Disgust
B. Bhaya	II. Wonder /Astonishment
C. Jugupsa	III. Anger
D. Vismaya	IV. Fear

Choose the correct answer from the options given below.

	A	B	C	D		A	B	C	D
1	III	IV	I	II	2	I	IV	II	III
3	II	IV	I	III	4	IV	III	II	I

Ans. **(1)**

Exp. The correct matching is A-III, B-IV, C-I, D-II.

Krodha translates directly to anger, representing one of the primary emotions or states of mind in Bharata's classification.

Bhaya corresponds to fear, reflecting the emotional response associated with anxiety or apprehension.

Jugupsa refers to disgust, an emotion that arises from aversion to something perceived as unpleasant or offensive.

Vismaya signifies wonder or astonishment, capturing the feeling of surprise or amazement.

12 Peterson and Seligman carried out their famous work on strengths, virtues and character. This work is referred as

1 Characters in Action Project
2 Strength in Action Project
3 Virtues in Action Project
4 Values in Action Project

Ans. **(4)**

➲ **Exp.** The Values in Action (VIA) project, initiated by psychologists Martin Seligman and Christopher Peterson, focused on identifying and categorising human strengths and virtues. The project aimed to create a framework that could be used to understand and promote positive traits in individuals, emphasising the importance of character in fostering well-being and resilience. The VIA classification includes 24 character strengths grouped under six overarching virtues, providing a comprehensive model for studying and enhancing human potential. The 6 virtues include wisdom, courage, humanity, justice, temperance and transcendence, and each virtue is supported by specific character strengths (e.g., kindness, bravery, gratitude).

13 Arrange the following behaviours of a University professor in a hierarchical order as per Maslow's theory of motivation.

A. Buys a two-bedroom flat
B. Attends at least one refresher course in his discipline every year
C. Applies regularly for various awards
D. Tries to maintain close relationship with the students

Choose the correct answer from the options given below.

1 A, D, C, B
2 D, A, B, C
3 D, C, B, A
4 A, B, D, C

Ans. (1)

➲ **Exp.** The correct order is A, D, C, B.

According to Maslow's hierarchy of needs, behaviours can be organised based on the level of needs they address, from basic physiological needs to higher-order psychological needs

Buys a two-bedroom flat This behaviour addresses the safety and physiological needs (shelter) at the foundational level of Maslow's hierarchy.

Tries to maintain close relationships with the students This behaviour relates to social needs (belongingness and love), where the professor seeks connections and relationships, fulfilling the need for interpersonal interactions.

Applies regularly for various awards This behaviour is linked to the esteem needs, reflecting the professor's desire for recognition, respect and accomplishment within their professional field.

Attends at least one refresher course in his discipline every year This behaviour addresses the self-actualisation needs, where the professor seeks personal growth, development and the realisation of their full potential in their academic discipline.

14 Richardson's Resilience model refers to which of the following?

A. Reintegration with a loss
B. Resistance index
C. Biopsychospiritual homeostasis
D. Disruption
E. Outcome index

Choose the correct answer from the options given below.

1 B, C, E only
2 C, D, E only
3 A, C, D only
4 B, C, D only

Ans. (3)

➲ **Exp.** The correct answer is A, C, D only.

Richardson's (2002) model states that people experience:

Biopsychosocial Homeostasis (physical, mental, spiritual balance) This means that at beginning people are in their comfort zone of body, mind, and spirit. They have adapted to their situation, whether good or bad.

Disruption: Next, a disruption occurs when a person does not have sufficient protective factors to buffer them from stressors. This can be a trauma, abuse, accident or a perceived stressor.

After a while, adjustment and one of four types of reintegration results:

Resilient reintegration – healthy outcome that results in development of more protective factors)

Homeostatic reintegration – return to "comfort zone" of homeostasis, without developing protective factors; just get past it)

A. **Reintegration with loss** – loss of protective factors results in a lower level of homeostasis

Dysfunctional reintegration – significant inability to cope with stressors results in selfdestructive behavior (e.g., substance abuse)

15 Which of the following are not true about the differences between simple regression and multiple regression?

A. The number of predictors
B. The number of criteria
C. Coefficient of determination
D. Sample size

Choose the correct answer from the options given below.

1 A, C, D only
2 A, B, D only
3 B, C, D only
4 A, B, C only

Ans. (3)

➲ **Exp.** Options B, C and D are not true about simple and multiple regression.

The number of criteria Both simple regression and multiple regression typically involve one criterion (dependent variable). The difference lies in the number of predictors (independent variables), not the number of criteria.

Coefficient of determination The coefficient of determination (R^2) is used in both simple and multiple regression to indicate how well the independent variables explain the variance in the dependent variable. Therefore, this is not a distinguishing factor between the two.

Sample size While larger sample sizes are generally recommended for multiple regression to ensure reliability, this is not an inherent difference between simple and multiple regression. Both types of regression can be performed with varying sample sizes.

In contrast, the number of predictors is the main difference between simple regression (with one predictor) and multiple regression (with two or more predictors). Therefore, this option is true.

16 Some casual factors occurring relatively early in life may not show their effects for many years that may contribute to a predisposition to develop a disorder. These would be considered as

1 Proximal risk factors
2 Distal risk factors
3 Fixed risk factors
4 Concomitant risk factors

Ans. **(2)**

Exp. Distal risk factors are those causal factors that occur early in life and may not have immediate effects but contribute to a predisposition for developing a disorder later on. They often include factors such as early childhood experiences, genetic predispositions, or environmental influences that shape an individual's development over time.

17 The leading neuroscience theories of intelligence is called

1 Parieto-Frontal interpolated theory
2 Frontal-Occipital integration theory
3 Parieto-Frontal integration theory
4 Frontal-Parietal symbolic theory

Ans. **(3)**

Exp. The Parieto-Frontal Integration Theory (PFIT) of intelligence posits that intelligence arises from the interactions between the parietal and frontal lobes of the brain. This theory suggests that cognitive processes related to intelligence, such as problem-solving, reasoning and planning, involve the integration of information across these two regions.

The parietal lobe is associated with functions like spatial awareness, mathematical reasoning, and attention, while the frontal lobe is involved in higher-order functions such as decision-making, impulse control and abstract thinking.

The PFIT model emphasises that intelligence is not solely localised in one area but emerges from the dynamic interplay between these brain regions, supporting the idea that both structural and functional connectivity is critical for cognitive performance. This theory has been influential in understanding the neurological basis of intelligence and cognitive abilities.

18 Which of the following softwares can be more helpful for analysis in qualitative research by a psychologist?

A. SPSS B. AMOS
C. NVIVO D. ATLAS
E. R

Choose the correct answer from the options given below.

1 A, B only 2 B, D only
3 C, D only 4 B, D, E only

Ans. **(3)**

Exp. NVIVO and ATLAS are both qualitative data analysis software specifically designed to help researchers analyse unstructured data, such as interviews, focus groups, open-ended survey responses and other qualitative data sources.

NVIVO NVIVO is a Qualitative Data Analysis (QDA) computer software package used across a diverse range of fields, including social sciences such as anthropology, psychology, communication, sociology, human geography as well as fields such as forensics, tourism, criminology and marketing. This software allows researchers to organise, analyse, and visualise qualitative data efficiently. It offers tools for coding, theming and querying data, making it easier to identify patterns and insights.

ATLAS Similar to NVIVO, ATLAS provides a platform for qualitative analysis that supports data coding, memo writing, and network visualisation, enabling researchers to explore complex relationships within the data.

19 Which of the following methods can be used to determine the number of factors to be extracted in Exploratory Factor Analysis?

A. Liserel analysis B. Scree test
C. Eigen value criteria D. Rotation

Choose the correct answer from the options given below.

1 A, B only 2 B, C only
3 C, D only 4 A, D only

Ans. **(2)**

Exp. The correct answer is B and C.

In Exploratory Factor Analysis (EFA), determining the number of factors to be extracted is crucial for proper data interpretation. The following methods are commonly used

Scree Test This graphical method involves plotting the eigen values of the factors and looking for a point where the slope of the curve levels off (the 'elbow'). This point indicates the number of factors that should be retained for analysis.

Eigen value Criteria This method uses the eigen values obtained from the correlation matrix. A common criterion is to retain factors with eigen values greater than 1 (Kaiser Criterion), as these factors are considered to explain more variance than a single observed variable.

However, Liserel analysis and rotation are not methods for determining the number of factors to extract.

Liserel analysis is primarily used for structural equation modeling and is not specifically aimed at determining the number of factors in EFA.

Rotation (such as varimax or oblimin rotation) is a technique used after factors have been extracted to improve interpretability and is not used to determine how many factors should be retained.

20 Arrange the following literary works on different facets of 'Yoga' in chronological order.

A. 'Anashshakti Yoga' by Mahatma Gandhi
B. 'Gitarahasya' by BG Tilak
C. 'Gatha' by Tukaram
D. 'Upadesha' by Raman Maharishi

Choose the correct answer from the options given below.

1 C, D, B, A
2 C, B, D, A
3 B, C, D, A
4 B ,C, A, D

***Ans.* (2)**

Exp. The correct chronological order is C, B, D, A.

'Gatha' by Tukaram Written in the 17th century, Tukaram was a prominent Marathi saint and poet who focused on the devotional aspects of Yoga and spirituality through his Abhanga poetry.

'Gitarahasya' by BG Tilak Published in 1915, this work interprets the teachings of the Bhagavad Gita, emphasising the concept of Karma Yoga, which integrates action with spirituality.

'Upadesha' by Raman Maharishi Although the teachings of Raman Maharishi date back to the early 20th century, 'Upadesha' was compiled and published later, focusing on self-enquiry and the nature of consciousness, both key elements in the practice of Yoga.

'Anashshakti Yoga' by Mahatma Gandhi Written in 1950, this work reflects Gandhi's interpretation of the Gita's teachings, particularly the practice of non-attachment in action (Karma Yoga), which he termed 'Anashakti Yoga'.

21 According to which theory of emotion the physiological reaction and the emotion are assumed to occur simultaneously?

1 James-Lange Theory
2 Cannon-Bard Theory
3 Cognitive-Arousal Theory
4 Cognitive-Mediational Theory

***Ans.* (2)**

Exp. The Cannon-Bard Theory of emotion, proposed by Walter Cannon and Philip Bard, suggests that emotions and physiological responses (like increased heart rate) occur simultaneously, rather than one causing the other. According to this theory, when an emotional event happens, the brain sends signals simultaneously to the body (producing physiological reactions) and the mind (producing the conscious experience of emotion).

This challenges earlier theories, like the James-Lange Theory, which proposed that emotions are a result of physiological changes.

22 One behavioural scientist is developing a questionnaire to assess the attitude towards workplace support. Which of the following will be the best way to establish construct validity of the questionnaire?

1 Croanbach Alpha
2 Inter-item Correlation
3 Factor Analysis
4 Kuder-Richardson Formula

***Ans.* (3)**

Exp. The correct answer is factor analysis because it is a statistical method used to establish construct validity, which refers to how well a test or questionnaire measures the theoretical construct it's intended to measure.

In the case of the workplace support questionnaire, factor analysis can help determine whether the questions group together logically under dimensions of workplace support, thus confirming the questionnaire's ability to assess the construct it's designed to measure.

23 Which of the following are community based protective factors for resilience among children?

A. Ties to pro-social organisations
B. Authoritative parenting
C. Organised home environment
D. Neighbourhood with high collective efficacy
E. Effective schools

Choose the correct answer from the options given below.

1 A, C, D only
2 A, D, E only
3 C, D, E only
4 B, C, D only

***Ans.* (2)**

Exp. The correct answer is A, D, E Only because these are community-based protective factors that promote resilience among children, focusing on the external environment beyond the family.

- Ties to pro-social organisations (like clubs or community groups) provide social support, positive role models, and opportunities for developing social skills, which are key to resilience.
- Neighborhood with high collective efficacy refers to communities where residents trust each other, share common values, and work together to support children's well-being, creating a safe and supportive environment.
- Effective schools provide a positive educational environment, support for emotional and social development, and access to resources, helping children build resilience.

The other options (B and C) are more related to family-based factors: Authoritative parenting and Organised home environment are internal family influences, not community-based factors.

24 One organisational psychologist wanted to verify the efficacy of a group based development intervention. For this purpose he undertook an Action Research. Suggest the correct sequence of the following components of his research.

A. Acting through the intervention
B. Observation
C. Planning about the intervention
D. Reflection

Choose the correct answer from the options given below.

1 B, C, D, A
2 C, B, A, D
3 C, A, B, D
4 B, C, A, D

Ans. (3)

Exp. The correct sequence follows the typical cycle of action is C, A, B, D.

Research, which is a reflective, iterative process aimed at solving a problem while simultaneously contributing to knowledge.

Planning about the intervention The first step is to plan the intervention based on the problem or development need identified.

Acting through the intervention After planning, the intervention is implemented to address the problem.

Observation During or after the intervention, the psychologist observes the outcomes and gathers data to evaluate the effectiveness of the intervention.

Reflection The final step is reflecting on the process and outcomes, drawing insights to refine future interventions.

25 Spreading rumours behind someone's back can most appropriately be referred as

1 Social aggression
2 Relation aggression
3 Indirect aggression
4 Physical aggression

Ans. (3)

Exp. Indirect aggression refers to behaviours intended to harm someone without direct confrontation. Spreading rumors behind someone's back is a classic example of indirect aggression, as it aims to damage the person's reputation or social standing in a subtle or covert way, without face-to-face conflict.

26 Which of the following refer to the theories of Health Behaviour?

A. Reflection-Action Theory
B. Protective Motivation Theory
C. Dialectical Behavioural Theory
D. Precaution Adoption Process Model
E. Organismic Integration Theory

Choose the correct answer from the options given below.

1 A, C, D only
2 B, C, D only
3 A, C, E only
4 B, D, E only

Ans. (4)

Exp. The theories of health behaviour that explain how individuals adopt, maintain, or change health-related behaviours.

Protective Motivation Theory This theory explains how people are motivated to protect themselves from threats by assessing the perceived severity, vulnerability, response efficacy and self-efficacy.

Precaution Adoption Process Model This model outlines the stages individuals go through in adopting a new precautionary behaviour, from being unaware of an issue to taking action.

Organismic Integration Theory A sub-theory of Self-Determination Theory, it describes the process of integration through which extrinsically motivated behaviours becomes autonomous.

27 Which of the following statements are correct?

A. Internal locus of control enhances the perception of stress.
B. Stress functions as a motivator.
C. The behavioural indicators of stress in children are seen in cognitive abilities, social competence and academic performance.
D. In resistance stage of General Adaptation Syndrome GAS, the physiological arousal peaks upto the all time high.
E. Neglect, victimisation, physical assault constitute toxic stress for children.

Choose the correct answer from the options given below.

1 A, C, E only
2 B, C, E only
3 A, C, D only
4 C, D, E only

Ans. (2)

Exp. Statements B, C and E are correct regarding stress and its effects on individuals, particularly children.

Stress can act as a motivator, especially in moderate amounts, prompting individuals to take action and perform better under pressure (e.g., eustress).

Stress in children often manifests in difficulty concentrating, changes in social interactions, and declines in academic performance.

Neglect, victimisation, physical assault are examples of toxic stress, which involves prolonged exposure to adversity without adequate support, leading to harmful long-term effects on a child's development.

The other statements are incorrect.

An internal locus of control often reduces stress, as individuals feel they have control over their situations.

The resistance stage is characterised by a stabilisation of physiological arousal, not a peak; the peak occurs in the initial alarm stage.

28 Match List-I with List-II.

List-I		List-II
A. Premek Principle	I.	The rapid change in performance level as the size of reinforcement is varied
B. Zeigarnik Effect	II.	Reinforcement strengthens the neighbouring response in addition to the response that it produced
C. Crespi Effect	III.	The opportunity to engage in frequently occurring activity can be used to reinforce a less frequently occurring activity
D. Spread of Effect	IV.	The tendency to remember incomplete tasks longer than complete ones

Choose the correct answer from the options given below.

	A	B	C	D		A	B	C	D
1	II	I	IV	III	2	I	III	II	IV
3	IV	III	I	II	4	III	IV	I	II

Ans. (4)

Exp. The correct matching is A-III, B-IV, C-I, D-II.

The Premack Principle states that a more frequently occurring activity can be used to reinforce a less frequently occurring one. For example, allowing a child to play (high-frequency behaviour) can reinforce their homework completion (low-frequency behaviour).

The Zeigarnik Effect is the tendency to remember incomplete or interrupted tasks better than completed ones. This occurs because unfinished tasks create cognitive tension, making them more memorable.

The Crespi Effect refers to the rapid change in performance levels when the size of reinforcement is varied. For instance, increasing the size of a reward can lead to a sudden improvement in performance.

The Spread of Effect suggests that reinforcement not only strengthens the specific response it produces but also strengthens neighbouring or related responses.

29 In the equation for linear regression $Y = a + bX$, b stands for

1 Y intercept on X
2 Regression coefficient
3 X intercept on Y
4 Constant

Ans. (2)

Exp. In the linear regression equation $Y = a + bX$, b represents the regression coefficient, which indicates the slope of the line. It shows the amount of change in the dependent variable (Y) for every one-unit change in the independent variable (X). Essentially, b tells the strength and direction (positive or negative) of the relationship between X and Y.

30 Match List-I with List-II.

List-I	List-II
A. Dukha	I. Suffering is a part of life
B. Dukha-Samudaya	II. Suffering has an end
C. Dukha-Nirodha	III. Suffering has a cause
D. Dukh-Nirodha Marga	IV. There is a way to end suffering

Choose the correct answer from the options given below.

	A	B	C	D		A	B	C	D
1	I	II	IV	III	2	II	I	III	IV
3	III	I	II	IV	4	I	III	II	IV

Ans. (4)

Exp. The correct matching is A-I, B-III, C-II, D-IV.

This matching corresponds to the Four Noble Truths of Buddhism, which explain the nature of suffering (Dukha) and the path to its cessation.

Dukha The first noble truth, 'Dukha', teaches that suffering (or dissatisfaction) is an inherent part of human existence.

Dukha-Samudaya The second noble truth, 'Samudaya', explains that suffering arises from causes, mainly desire, attachment, and ignorance.

Dukha-Nirodha The third noble truth, 'Nirodha', states that it is possible to end suffering by eliminating its causes.

Dukha-Nirodha Marga The fourth noble truth, 'Marga', represents the path (the Noble Eightfold Path) that leads to the cessation of suffering.

31 Five ways to be proactive includes the following.

A. Predict
B. Prevent
C. Program
D. Plan
E. Participate

Choose the correct answer from the options given below.

1 A, B, C, E only
2 B, C, D, E only
3 A, B, D, E only
4 A, B, C, D only

Ans. (3)

Exp. The correct answer is A, B, D and E.

Predict Being proactive involves anticipating potential challenges or opportunities before they arise. By predicting future scenarios, individuals can prepare themselves and make informed decisions.

Prevent Proactivity also means taking steps to prevent problems before they occur. This could involve risk management, setting safeguards, or addressing issues early.

Plan Planning is a critical proactive strategy. It involves setting clear goals, outlining steps to achieve them, and preparing for possible obstacles along the way.

Participate Engaging actively in processes, discussions, or activities contributes to a proactive approach.

32 Which of the following are included in Bruner's theory of cognitive development?

A. Enactive
B. Echoic
C. Iconic
D. Symbolic
E. Deontic

Choose the correct answer from the options given below.

1 A, B, C only
2 A, C, D only
3 A, C, E only
4 A, B, E only

Ans. (2)

Exp. The correct answer is A, C and D.

Bruner's theory of cognitive development is a constructivist theory that focuses on how children actively construct their understanding of the world through their interactions with it. Bruner proposed three modes of representation that children go through as they develop

Enactive This is the earliest stage of development, where children learn through actions and physical exploration. They understand the world by doing things and experiencing them directly.

Iconic As children develop, they begin to use mental images and symbols to represent objects and ideas. This allows them to think about things that are not physically present.

Symbolic At this stage, children are able to use language and abstract symbols to represent ideas and concepts. They can think about things in a more abstract and symbolic way.

33 Match List-I with List-II.

List-I	List-II
A. Taysach disorder	I. The 23rd Pair is actually missing an X
B. Down's syndrome	II. Fatal neurological disorder
C. Klinefelter's syndrome	III. An extra chromosome in What normally be the 21st Pair
D. Turner's syndrome	IV. The 23rd set of sex chromosomes is XXY

Choose the correct answer from the options given below.

	A	B	C	D		A	B	C	D
1	III	IV	II	I	2	II	III	IV	I
3	IV	I	III	II	4	I	III	II	IV

Ans. (2)

Exp. The correct matching is A-II, B-III, C-IV, D-I.

Taysachs is a genetic disorder caused by a deficiency of the enzyme hexosaminidase A, leading to the accumulation of GM2 gangliosides in the brain, resulting in severe neurological deterioration and death, typically in early childhood.

Down's syndrome, also known as Trisomy 21, occurs when there is an extra copy of chromosome 21, leading to developmental and intellectual disabilities.

Klinefelter's syndrome is a genetic condition in males resulting from an extra X chromosome, giving them an XXY chromosomal pattern. This can lead to various physical and developmental features, including infertility.

Turner syndrome occurs in females who have only one X chromosome (XO), leading to various developmental issues and physical characteristics.

34 Pineal Gland

A. helps increase the blood calcium level
B. secretes a hormone called 'melatonin'
C. is located in epithalamus
D. Secretes hormones called 'parathormone' and 'calcitonin'
E. Is used to be known as the 'Third eye'

Choose the correct answer from the options given below.

1 A, D, E only
2 B, C, E only
3 C, D only
4 A, B, C, E only

Ans. (2)

Exp. The correct answer is B, C and E.

The pineal gland is primarily known for producing and secreting melatonin, a hormone that regulates sleep-wake cycles (circadian rhythms) and is influenced by light exposure.

The pineal gland is located in the epithalamus, near the center of the brain, between the two hemispheres, tucked in a groove where the two halves of the thalamus join.

The pineal gland has been referred to as the 'third eye' in various philosophical and spiritual traditions due to its location in the brain and its connection to light *via* the circadian rhythm and melatonin secretion.

35 A psychologist was interested to conduct a study on gamblers. Identifying the gamblers, even with the help of police, is a challenging task. Which of the following sampling technique will be more appropriate to take up the study?

1 Quota sampling
2 Cluster sampling
3 Snowball sampling
4 Stratified sampling

Ans. (3)

Exp. Snowball sampling is a non-probability sampling method where study participants recruit other people they know to participate in a study. The sample grows like a snowball, with each wave of participants recruiting the next. It is often used in qualitative research to study populations that are hard to reach, such as those with specific traits, sensitive topics, or those that are small, geographically dispersed, or stigmatised. It can also be used to locate hidden populations.

36 Which of the following is one of the non-parametric counterpart of ANOVA?

1 Kruskal-Wallis Test
2 Mann-Whitney Test
3 Kendell's Test
4 Wilcox"s Test

Ans. (1)

Exp. The correct answer is Kruskal-Wallis Test because it serves as the non-parametric counterpart to the one-way ANOVA (Analysis of Variance) when comparing three or more independent groups.

37 In the disease called Multiple Sclerosis MS

1 The myelin sheath is destroyed.
2 The myelin sheath is thick.
3 The myelin shows bumps in some places.
4 The electrical signals jump.

Ans. (1)

Exp. Multiple Sclerosis (MS) is an autoimmune disease that affects the central nervous system.

In MS, the immune system attacks the myelin sheath, the protective covering that surrounds nerve fibers. This damage can disrupt the electrical signals that travel through the nerves, leading to a variety of symptoms such as numbness, weakness, vision problems, and fatigue.

38 The multitrait-multimethod design does not provide which one of the following?
1 Predictive evidence validity
2 Discriminant evidence validity
3 Convergent evidence validity
4 Reliability

Ans. (1)

Exp. The multitrait-multimethod design does not provide predictive evidence validity. Predictive evidence validity refers to the ability of a measure to accurately forecast outcomes or behaviours in the future.

The multitrait-multimethod design is a framework used in psychological and social sciences to evaluate the validity of constructs by examining how different traits are measured through various methods.

39 Arrange the following cognitive points sequentially to explain helping behaviour as suggested by Darley and Latane.
A. Taking responsibility
B. Defining an emergency
C. Taking action
D. Noticing
E. Planning a course of action

Choose the correct answer from the options given below.
1 B, D, E, A, C
2 B, E, D, A, C
3 D, A, B, E, C
4 D, B, A, E, C

Ans. (4)

Exp. The correct sequential order is D, B, A, E, C.

As proposed by Darley and Latané in their model of bystander intervention, the sequence of steps involved in helping behaviour are as follows

Noticing The first step is to notice that something is happening, which is crucial in determining whether a person perceives a situation as needing intervention.

Defining an emergency After noticing a situation, the next step is to interpret it as an emergency that requires help. This involves assessing the severity of the situation.

Taking responsibility Once the situation is defined as an emergency, the individual must feel a sense of personal responsibility to act. This is influenced by the number of bystanders present (the more by standers, the less likely any one individual feels responsible).

Planning a course of action After deciding to take responsibility, the person must consider how to help and what action to take.

Taking Action Finally, the individual must execute the planned course of action to provide help.

40 While Carkhuff's Model describes communication skills as pre-processing skills, Ivey and Ivey call it a ....
1 Basic communication skills
2 Life skill model
3 Micro skill approach
4 DASIE model

Ans. (3)

Exp. The correct answer is Micro-Skill approach because Ivey and Ivey's framework emphasises the importance of specific communication skills that are essential for effective helping relationships, particularly in counseling and therapy.

41 Reality Therapy in counselling
A. is based on principles of choice
B. emphasises self-evaluation
C. focuses on the way we live and exist
D. views empowerment from a strength-based perspective
E. follows the stages of Wants, Direction, Evaluation and Planning WDEP

Choose the correct answer from the options given below.
1 A, B, E only
2 A, C, E only
3 A, B, D only
4 C, D, E only

Ans. (1)

Exp. The correct answer is A, B and E.

Developed by William Glasser, the core principles and techniques of Reality Therapy in counselling include

Is based on principles of choice Reality Therapy emphasises the concept of personal choice, asserting that individuals have the power to make choices that shape their lives. It encourages clients to take responsibility for their actions and decisions.

Emphasises self-evaluation A key aspect of Reality Therapy is helping clients assess their behaviours and the effectiveness of those behaviours in meeting their needs. This self-evaluation process allows clients to identify discrepancies between their current behaviours and their goals.

Follows the stages of Wants, Direction, Evaluation and Planning (WDEP) The WDEP system is a structured approach within Reality Therapy that guides clients through identifying their wants, setting goals (direction), evaluating their current behaviours, and planning new strategies to achieve their desired outcomes.

42 Match List-I with List-II.

List-I	List-II
A. Eros Love	I. Treating love as a game
B. Ludos Love	II. Treating love as a friendship
C. Storge Love	III. Loving an ideal person
D. Agape Love	IV. Selfless love

Choose the correct answer from the options given below.

	A	B	C	D
1	II	III	I	IV
2	I	II	IV	III
3	III	I	II	IV
4	IV	I	III	II

Ans. (3)

➲ *Exp.* The correct matching is A-III, B-I, C-II, D-IV.

Eros Love is often characterised by passionate and romantic love, typically associated with a deep desire and longing for an idealised partner.

Ludos Love refers to playful and fun love, where relationships are often seen as lighthearted and not taken too seriously. This type of love is about enjoyment and entertainment, akin to a game.

Storge Love represents affectionate love that develops from familiarity and friendship. It is characterised by a sense of companionship and emotional connection.

Agape Love is often described as unconditional, selfless love that prioritises the well-being of others over oneself. It is a deep, spiritual love that is not dependent on any conditions or expectations.

43 Match List-I with List-II.

List-I		List-II
A. Phenomenology	I.	Indepth detailed examination of an entity in real world context
B. Case study	II.	Application of inductive reasoning
C. Ethnography	III.	Lived experiences
D. Grounded theory	IV.	Description of peoples and culture

Choose the correct answer from the options given below.

	A	B	C	D		A	B	C	D
1	III	II	I	IV	2	II	I	III	IV
3	III	I	IV	II	4	I	III	IV	II

Ans. (3)

➲ *Exp.* The correct matching is A-III, B-I, C-IV, D-II.

Phenomenology is a qualitative research approach focused on understanding and describing individuals' lived experiences and how they perceive and make sense of their experiences.

A **case study** involves a comprehensive and detailed exploration of a specific instance, individual, or group within its real-world context, providing rich insights into the subject matter.

Ethnography is a qualitative research method that involves immersing oneself in a community or culture to understand its practices, beliefs, and social dynamics. It emphasises the researcher's observations and interactions with the participants in their natural setting.

Grounded theory is a qualitative research method that develops theories grounded in data collected from participants. It involves application of inductive reasoning, where patterns and themes emerge from the data, leading to the formulation of theories.

44 The area responsible for interaction between frontal, temporal and motor areas in order to produce speech is called

1 Primary Auditory Cortex
2 Broca's Area
3 Spery's Area
4 Wernicke's Area

Ans. (2)

➲ *Exp.* Broca's Area of the brain is crucial for speech production and is involved in the coordination of language-related activities.

Broca's Area is located in the frontal lobe, typically in the left hemisphere of the brain (in right-handed individuals). It plays a vital role in the production of speech and language processing.

This area is responsible for the planning and execution of movements required for speaking and is involved in grammatical processing, which is essential for forming coherent sentences.

45 Arrange the early schools of psychology in order.

A. Structuralism B. Functionalism
C. Behaviourism D. Humanistic

Choose the correct answer from the options given below.

1 B, A, C, D
2 B, C, A, D
3 A, B, C, D
4 A,C, B, D

Ans. (3)

➲ *Exp.* The correct order is A, B, C, D.

Structuralism Founded by Wilhelm Wundt in the late 19th century, structuralism is considered the first formal school of psychology. It aimed to analyse the structure of the mind by breaking down mental processes into their most basic components through introspection.

Functionalism Emerging in the early 20th century, functionalism was influenced by the work of Wundt but focused more on the purpose of mental processes and behaviour. Prominent figures like William James emphasised the function of consciousness and how mental processes help individuals adapt to their environments.

Behaviourism This school arose in the early 20th century, primarily through the work of John B. Watson and later BF Skinner. Behaviourism shifted the focus away from the internal mental processes studied by structuralism and functionalism to observable behavior and the environmental factors that influence it.

Humanistic Psychology Developed in the mid-20th century, humanistic psychology was a response to both structuralism and behaviourism. Pioneered by figures like Carl Rogers and Abraham Maslow, this approach emphasises individual potential, selfactualisation, and the importance of personal experiences in understanding human behaviour.

46 Asking for a small commitment and after gaining compliance, asking for a bigger commitment is known as

1 Foot-in-the-door technique
2 Low-ball technique
3 Progressive ball technique
4 Door-in-the-face technique

Ans. (1)

Exp. Foot-in-the-Door technique is based on the principle of commitment and consistency. By initially asking for a small commitment, the requester establishes a relationship or sense of obligation. Once the individual agrees to the small request, they are more likely to comply with a subsequent, larger request because they want to maintain a consistent self-image and avoid cognitive dissonance.

For example, if a salesperson first asks a potential customer if they would consider trying a free sample and the customer agrees, they may be more likely to buy the product after having experienced it.

47 Match List-I with List-II.

List-I		List-II
A. Principle of Closure	I.	Tendency to complete incomplete experiences to make them more meaningful
B. Principle of Polarity	II.	Learned material is most performed in the same direction in which it was originally learned
C. Principle of Parsimony	III.	Choosing the simple one out of two equally effective theories
D. Principle of Falsification	IV.	In order for theory to be scientific, it must make risky prediction if not confirmed would refute the theory

Choose the correct answer from the options given below.

	A	B	C	D
1	I	II	III	IV
2	II	I	IV	III
3	III	I	II	IV
4	II	III	I	IV

***Ans.* (1)**

Exp. The correct matching is A-I, B-II, C-III, D-IV.

Principle of Closure refers to the tendency of individuals to perceive incomplete figures or experiences as complete by filling in gaps in their perception. It relates to Gestalt psychology, where people tend to organise visual elements into groups or unified wholes, making them more meaningful.

Principle of Polarity suggests that for any given phenomenon, there are opposing forces or states. It emphasises the idea that things often exist in dualities, like good versus evil or pleasure versus pain.

Principle of Parsimony often known as Occam's Razor, this principle states that when presented with competing hypotheses or theories, one should select the one that makes the fewest assumptions. Essentially, it favors simplicity and efficiency in explanations.

Principle of Falsification proposed by philosopher Karl Popper, this principle asserts that for a theory to be considered scientific, it must be testable and capable of being proven false through observation or experimentation. A theory that cannot be falsified lacks scientific credibility.

48 Which of the following terms are associated with Gestalt approach?

A. Molar
B. Nativistic
C. Atomistic, elementistic
D. Cognitive, phenomenological
E. Objective

Choose the most appropriate answer from the options given below.

1 A, C, D only
2 A, B, D, E only
3 B, C, D, E only
4 A, B, D only

***Ans.* (4)**

Exp. The correct answer is A, B and D.

Molar The Gestalt approach emphasises 'molar' perspectives, focusing on the whole and how different parts integrate to form a complete experience. This is in contrast to a 'molecular' perspective, which would break experiences down into smaller, discrete elements.

Nativistic This term refers to the idea that certain perceptual processes or cognitive abilities are innate or pre-wired in individuals. Gestalt psychology often supports the notion that our understanding and perception of the world are influenced by innate structures in our minds.

Cognitive, Phenomenological The Gestalt approach incorporates cognitive processes and phenomenological perspectives, focusing on subjective experiences and the meaning individuals derive from their perceptions.

However, Atomistic, Elementistic terms are not associated with the Gestalt approach. Instead, they refer to the breaking down of experiences into their constituent parts, which is contrary to the holistic perspective of Gestalt psychology.

While Gestalt psychology acknowledges the importance of subjective experience, it is more associated with a subjective, holistic understanding of perception rather than strictly objective measurements.

49 The situation of conflict arising upon allocation of funding to different groups is an example of conflict arising over issues of

1 interest
2 values
3 growth
4 demand characteristics

***Ans.* (1)**

Exp. As the situation of conflict over the allocation of funding to different groups typically arises from competing interests among those groups.

Conflicts of interest occur when different parties seek to maximise their own benefits or resources. In this scenario, various groups are competing for limited funding, leading to conflicts over how the funds should be distributed to serve their respective goals and objectives. Each group has its own interests in mind, which creates a competitive environment.

50 The disorder where an extra sex chromosome in the 23rd pair resulting in XXY producing a male with reduced masculine characteristics resulting in enlarged breasts, obesity and excessive height is called

1 Phenylketonuria PKU
2 Turner's syndrome
3 Tay-sachs disorder
4 Klinefelter's syndrome

***Ans.* (4)**

Exp. The correct answer is Klinefelter's syndrome.

Klinefelter's syndrome is a genetic condition that occurs in males who have an extra X chromosome, resulting in a chromosomal pattern of XXY instead of the typical XY. This disorder is associated with various physical and developmental characteristics, including: Reduced masculine characteristics (e.g., decreased testosterone production), Enlarged breasts (gynecomastia), Obesity and increased height (often above average).

51 Which of the following attribute, according to Mahatma Gandhi as well as Patanjali, is an essential condition for practicing non-violence?

1 Dukha
2 Vairagya
3 Krodha
4 Utsaha

***Ans.* (2)**

Exp. Vairagya, which translates to 'detachment' or 'non-attachment', is emphasised by both Mahatma Gandhi and Patanjali as a crucial quality for practicing non-violence (ahimsa). In this context, it refers to the ability to remain unaffected by desires, passions, or material possessions, which can lead to conflicts and violence.

Dukha means suffering and is not directly related to the practice of non-violence as a condition for achieving it.

Krodha translates to anger, which is contrary to the principles of non-violence. Utsaha means enthusiasm or zeal, which, while important in many aspects of life, is not specifically cited by Gandhi or Patanjali as an essential condition for practicing non-violence.

52 People living on railway platforms, crowded market area on the main roads with heavy traffic are likely to experience

1 Energetic stress
2 Ergonomic stress
3 Anthropogenic stress
4 Tropical stress

***Ans.* (3)**

Exp. The correct answer is Anthropogenic stress.

Anthropogenic stress refers to stress resulting from human activity and environmental factors created by humans. In this context, people living in crowded and noisy environments, such as railway platforms or busy market areas, are likely to experience stress due to the high levels of noise, pollution and general chaos that come from human activities.

53 A key element in all therapeutic process is the development of an effective

1 challenging
2 personal integration
3 advanced empathy
4 working alliance

***Ans.* (4)**

Exp. A working alliance refers to the collaborative relationship and bond formed between the therapist and the client. It is crucial for the success of any therapeutic process because it fosters trust, open communication, and mutual understanding, which are essential for effective therapy.

54 Match List-I with List-II.

List-I	List-II
A. Material form	I. Vedana
B. Feeling of sensation	II. Vinnana
C. Perception	III. Rupa
D. Reason or intelligence	IV. Sana

Choose the correct answer from the options given below.

	A	B	C	D
1	III	I	IV	II
2	II	I	III	IV
3	I	IV	II	III
4	III	II	I	IV

***Ans.* (1)**

Exp. The correct matching is A-III, B-I, C-IV, D-II.

In Buddhist philosophy, **'Rupa'** refers to physical matter or form.

'Vedana' signifies the sensations or feelings that arise from our experiences.

'Sana' (or 'Sanna') refers to the mental process of perception, which involves recognising and categorising experiences.

'Vinnana' refers to consciousness or awareness, which includes reasoning and cognitive processes.

55 Which of the following are components of hardiness?

1 Control, coherence, challenge
2 Challenge, constructivity, confidence
3 Control, commitment, challenge
4 Commitment, collaboration, control

***Ans.* (3)**

Exp. Hardiness is a psychological construct that reflects an individual's resilience and ability to cope with stress. The three main components of hardiness are

Control This refers to the belief in one's ability to influence events and outcomes in their life. Individuals with a high sense of control feel empowered to make decisions and take action in challenging situations.

Commitment This component involves a strong sense of purpose and dedication to one's goals and values. Hardy individuals are more likely to engage fully in their activities and relationships, even in the face of adversity.

Challenge This reflects the perception of stressors as opportunities for growth rather than threats. People with a hardy personality view challenges as a normal part of life and are more willing to embrace change and take risks.

56 Which of the following statements are correct?

A. Emotionally arousing stimuli have also been seen to lead to amnesia.

B. Some cognitive processing must occur before an individual can experience an emotional response to an event.

C. Repression is a form of motivated forgetting.

D. Functional Magnetic Resonance Imaging FMRI and Position Emission Topography PET are invasive scanning techniques of studying the brain functioning.

E. Theories of emotions have not changed much over the years.

Choose the correct answer from the options given below.

1 A, B, C only
2 A, B, D only
3 B, C, D, E only
4 A, B, D, E only

Ans. (1)

➲ ***Exp.*** Statements A, B and C are correct.

Emotionally charged experiences can lead to memory impairment or amnesia, particularly if the emotional response is intense and traumatic.

Cognitive appraisal is an important step in the process of emotion; it involves evaluating a situation before an emotional response can occur.

Repression refers to the unconscious blocking of unwanted memories or feelings, which is a type of motivated forgetting, where an individual avoids recalling distressing thoughts.

57 Match List-I with List-II.

List-I	List-II
A. Drive-Reduction Theory	I. Yerkes and Dodson
B. Personality and Nach	II. Richard Ryan and Edward Deci
C. Arousal Theory	III. Carol Dweck
D. Self-Determination Theory	IV. Hull

Choose the correct answer from the options given below.

	A	B	C	D
1	IV	I	II	III
2	IV	III	I	II
3	II	III	IV	I
4	I	IV	II	III

Ans. (2)

➲ ***Exp.*** The correct matching is A-IV, B-III, C-I, D-II.

The **Drive-Reduction Theory**, proposed by Clark Hull, suggests that physiological needs create an unpleasant state of tension (a drive) and motivation is aimed at reducing this drive to achieve homeostasis.

The concept of **Need for Achievement (Nach)** relates to personality and was extensively discussed by Carol Dweck, who explored how beliefs about oneself can influence motivation and achievement.

The Yerkes-Dodson Law describes the relationship between arousal and performance, indicating that there is an optimal level of arousal for best performance, which relates to the **Arousal Theory of motivation.**

Richard Ryan and Edward Deci developed the **Self-Determination Theory**, which emphasises the role of intrinsic motivation and the importance of psychological needs in driving behaviour.

58 Match List-I with List-II.

List-I	List-II
A. Standard scores always has a mean of 50 and SD of 10	I. Percentile
B. Standard scores change the unit of measurement	II. Z-score
C. Standard with a mean of zero and SD of 1	III. T-score
D. Units in testing that help to evaluate a person's performance in comparison with others who took the same test	IV. Standard score

Choose the correct answer from the options given below.

	A	B	C	D
1	III	II	I	IV
2	II	III	I	IV
3	III	I	II	IV
4	IV	III	I	II

Ans. (3)

➲ ***Exp.*** The correct matching is A-III, B-I, C-II, D-IV.

The **T-score** is a type of standard score that is specifically designed to have a mean of 50 and a standard deviation (SD) of 10. This makes it easier to interpret individual scores relative to the average performance.

The **percentile rank** transforms raw scores into a relative standing within a population, changing the unit of measurement by indicating the percentage of scores that fall below a particular score.

The **Z-score** is a standard score that indicates how many standard deviations a data point is from the mean. It has a mean of zero and a standard deviation of 1.

The term **standard score** encompasses various types of scores (like T-scores, Z-scores, and percentile ranks) that allow for comparison of an individual's performance to that of a normative group.

59 Which of the following is not included in Sullivan basic modes theory?

1 Prototaxic mode
2 Pretaxic mode
3 Parataxic mode
4 Syntaxic mode

Ans. (2)

➲ ***Exp.*** Pretaxic mode is not included in Sullivan basic modes theory.

Prototaxic mode This is the earliest mode of experience, characteristic of infants. It involves immediate, fragmented experiences without a coherent narrative or meaning. Sensations and feelings occur but are not yet organised into a structured understanding of the world.

Parataxic mode In this mode, individuals begin to make associations between experiences and events, but these associations may be illogical or based on personal feelings rather than objective reality. It reflects a pre-logical way of thinking, often seen in children.

Syntaxic mode This is the most advanced mode, where individuals use logical and coherent thought processes. It involves the ability to communicate and understand concepts in a more sophisticated manner, reflecting the use of shared language and cultural norms.

60 The first psychology department in India was formally started in 1916 by

1 Girindra Shekhar Bose 2 NN Sengupta
3 MV Gopalaswami 4 SM Mohsin

Ans. (2)

Exp. NN Sengupta is credited with establishing the first formal psychology department in India at the University of Calcutta in 1916. He played a pivotal role in introducing psychology as a scientific discipline in the country.

61 The four phases of forgiveness according to Enright, Freedman and Rique includes

1 Undercovering, Contemplation, Work and Recovering
2 Uncovering, Decision, Work and Deepening
3 Uncovering, Covering, Contemplating, Recovering
4 Understanding, Balming, Generosity, Recovering

Ans. (2)

Exp. According to the model proposed by Enright, Freedman, and Rique, the four phases of forgiveness are as follows:

Uncovering The first step in the forgiveness process is to acknowledge and understand the anger and resentment you feel towards the person who has wronged you. This involves exploring the impact of the offence on your thoughts, emotions and behaviours.

Decision The next step is to make a conscious decision to forgive the person who has wronged you. This decision is not made lightly but is based on a desire to let go of negative emotions and move towards healing.

Work Forgiveness is a process that takes time and effort. It involves working through your feelings of anger and resentment and replacing them with compassion and understanding towards the offender. This may involve seeking support from others, practising empathy and engaging in forgiveness exercises.

Deepening The final step in the forgiveness process is to discover the meaning and purpose behind the offence and release the negative emotions associated with it. The emotional relief and newfound meaning may lead to increased compassion for self and others. This allows you to move forward with a sense of peace and closure.

62 The process by which one person tries to change the belief, opinion, position or course of action of another person through argument, pleading or explanation is an example of

1 Social influence 2 Deindividuation
3 Persuasion 4 Prosocial behaviour

Ans. (3)

Exp. Persuasion is the process through which one individual attempts to change another person's beliefs, opinions, attitudes, or behaviours. This can occur through various means, such as logical arguments, emotional appeals and explanations. The goal of persuasion is to convince the other person to adopt a specific viewpoint or to take a particular action.

63 Who among the following is not considered as a reinforcement theorist?

1 Thorndike 2 Gutherie 3 Hull 4 Skinner

Ans. (2)

Exp. The correct answer is Guthrie.

Guthrie, proposed a theory of learning based on contiguity rather than reinforcement. He believed that learning occurs through the association of stimuli and responses, and that the frequency of a behaviour is determined by its direct experience, not by reinforcement or punishment. Thus, Guthrie is not classified as a reinforcement theorist.

While Edward L. Thorndike, Clark Hull and BF Skinner are all considered reinforcement theorists, as their work revolves around the concepts of reinforcement and behaviour modification.

64 Which of the following are methods used in challenging in counselling as per the Developmental model of Egan?

A. Reviewing better times
B. Asocial response
C. Identification of models
D. Immediacy
E. Self-disclosure

Choose the correct answer from the options given below.

1 B, D, E only 2 A, C, D only
3 A, D, E only 4 C, D, E only

Ans. (1)

Exp. In the Developmental model of counselling by Egan, the methods used in challenging typically include

Asocial response This method involves highlighting the client's social interactions and encouraging them to reflect on how these interactions affect their behaviour and emotional responses.

Immediacy This involves addressing the current feelings and thoughts in the therapeutic relationship, encouraging the client to explore what is happening in the moment, and creating an authentic connection.

Self-disclosure The counsellor shares their own relevant experiences or feelings to build trust, normalise the client's feelings, or provide perspective.

65 Which of the following are included in the steps of Eye Movement Desensitisation Reprocessing EMDR therapy?

A. Assessment
B. Cognitive restructuring
C. Installation
D. Skill acquisition
E. Body scan

Choose the correct answer from the options given below.

1 A, C, D only
2 A, C, E only
3 B, D, E only
4 B, C, D only

Ans. (2)

Exp. Eye Movement Desensitisation and Reprocessing (EMDR) therapy is a structured therapy that encourages the patient to briefly focus on the trauma memory while simultaneously experiencing bilateral stimulation (typically eye movements), which is associated with a reduction in the vividness and emotion associated with the trauma memories. It involves several structured phases, and the relevant steps include

Assessment This initial phase involves the therapist and client discussing the client's history and identifying specific targets for EMDR processing, including distressing memories and associated negative beliefs.

Installation This step involves the client focusing on a positive belief that they want to associate with the traumatic memory. The goal is to strengthen the positive belief while desensitising the negative memory.

Body scan In this phase, the therapist asks the client to notice any residual tension or discomfort in their body associated with the memory, helping to process any lingering physical responses to the trauma.

66 Arrange the following in a sequence as per the health belief model where an individual.

A. Reads about the various factors related to cancer
B. Stops smoking
C. Feels that since his father died of cancer he is likely to be genetically disposed
D. Understands that if he continues to smoke there is higher possibility of his suffering from cancer

Choose the correct answer from the options given below.

1 C, D, A, B
2 D, A, C, B
3 A ,C, D, B
4 D ,C, A, B

Ans. (3)

Exp. The correct sequence is A, C, D, B.

The Health Belief Model (HBM) suggests that individuals are more likely to engage in health-promoting behaviours if they believe they are susceptible to a health problem, believe that the problem has serious consequences, believe taking a specific action would reduce their susceptibility to or severity of the problem, and believe the benefits of taking that action outweigh the costs or barriers.

Reads about the various factors related to cancer This step involves gathering information about cancer, which lays the groundwork for understanding personal risk factors.

Feels that since his father died of cancer he is likely to be genetically disposed This represents an increased perceived susceptibility based on familial health history, making the individual more aware of their risk.

Understands that if he continues to smoke there is a higher possibility of his suffering from cancer This is the individual's recognition of the specific behaviour (smoking) contributing to the perceived threat of cancer.

Stops smoking This is the health-promoting behaviour that follows the recognition of risk and the understanding of consequences, leading to the decision to change behaviour for better health outcomes.

67 Which of the following are measures of dispersion?

A. Standard deviation
B. Quartile deviation
C. Mode
D. Variance
E. Range

Choose the correct answer from the options given below.

1 A, B, E only
2 B, C, D only
3 A, B, D, E only
4 A, B, C, D only

Ans. (3)

Exp. The correct answer is A, B, D, E.

Measures of dispersion provide information about the spread or variability of a dataset. The following options are recognised measures of dispersion

Standard Deviation This is a widely used measure that quantifies the amount of variation or dispersion in a set of values. A low standard deviation indicates that the values tend to be close to the mean, while a high standard deviation indicates that the values are spread out over a wider range.

Quartile Deviation Also known as the semi-interquartile range, this measure describes the spread of the middle 50% of the data. It is calculated as the difference between the third quartile (Q3) and the first quartile (Q1), divided by 2.

Variance This measure quantifies how far each number in the dataset is from the mean and is the square of the standard deviation. Variance provides a measure of how data points differ from the average.

Range This is the difference between the maximum and minimum values in a dataset, giving a simple measure of how spread out the values are.

However, Mode is not a measure of dispersion. It is a measure of central tendency that identifies the most frequently occurring value in a dataset.

68 Match List-I with List-II.

List-I (Parts of Nervous System)	List-II (Function)
A. Hypothalamus	I. Fear responses and memory of fear
B. Hippocampus	II. Regulates body Temperature, thirst, hunger
C. Amygdala	III. Forms long-term declarative memories
D. Cingulate cortex	IV. Selective attention, working memory

Choose the correct answer from the options given below.

	A	B	C	D
1	III	IV	I	II
2	II	I	III	IV
3	II	III	I	IV
4	I	III	IV	II

***Ans.* (3)**

Exp. The correct matching is A-II, B-III, C-I, D-IV.

The **hypothalamus** plays a crucial role in maintaining homeostasis in the body. It regulates various autonomic functions, including body temperature, hunger, thirst and circadian rhythms.

The **hippocampus** is essential for the formation of long-term memories, particularly declarative memories, which involve facts and events.

The **amygdala** is primarily involved in processing emotions, especially fear and pleasure. It plays a key role in fear responses and the memory of fear-related experiences.

The **cingulate cortex** is involved in various cognitive functions, including attention and emotional regulation. It plays a role in selective attention and working memory processes.

69 Which one of the following is correct with regard to PASS model developed by JP Das and his associates?

1 Planning, Arousal, Successive and Simultaneous processing
2 Programming, Attentive, Sequencing and Simultaneous processing
3 Processing, Awakening, Simultaneous and Successive processing
4 Planning, Attention, Arousal, Simultaneous and Successive processing

***Ans.* (4)**

Exp. The PASS (Planning, Attention, Simultaneous and Successive) model of intelligence is a theory developed by J.P. Das, Jack Naglieri, and Kirby in 1994. Following are the terms with regard to PASS model.

Planning This involves the ability to set goals, strategise, and make decisions about how to approach tasks and solve problems.

Attention This component refers to the ability to focus on specific stimuli or tasks while ignoring distractions. It is crucial for effective cognitive processing.

Arousal Arousal relates to the level of alertness and responsiveness of an individual, which affects cognitive performance. It plays a role in how information is processed based on an individual's emotional and physical state.

Simultaneous and Successive processing These terms refer to two different ways in which information can be processed. Simultaneous processing involves understanding and integrating multiple pieces of information at once. Successive processing refers to the sequential processing of information, where one piece of information is processed after another.

70 Which of the following are characteristics of a good hypothesis?

A. Affirmative statement
B. Interrogative statement
C. Falsifiability
D. Conjectural
E. Concludes relationship between variables

Choose the correct answer from the options given below:

1 B, D, E only
2 A, C, D only
3 B, C, D only
4 A, C, E only

***Ans.* (2)**

Exp. The correct answer is A, C and D

A good hypothesis should have the following characteristics

Affirmative Statement A hypothesis should be stated positively, asserting a relationship or effect rather than posing a question. It expresses what the researcher believes to be true based on prior knowledge or theory.

Falsifiability A hypothesis must be falsifiable, meaning it can be tested and potentially disproven through experimentation or observation. This is crucial for scientific inquiry, as it allows researchers to confirm or reject their hypotheses based on empirical evidence.

Conjectural A hypothesis is often conjectural, representing an educated guess or prediction about the relationship between variables. It is based on previous knowledge and research and guides the direction of the study.

71 In order to interpret individual test scores and to calculate confidence interval, which of the following is important and necessary?

1 Pearson product moment correlation
2 Test variance
3 Spearman-Brown formula
4 Standard error of measurement

***Ans.* (4)**

Exp. The Standard Error of Measurement (SEM) is crucial for interpreting individual test scores and calculating confidence intervals.

SEM provides an estimate of the amount of error associated with an individual's test score.

It reflects the variability in scores that could occur if the same person took the test multiple times under the same conditions. This understanding is vital for assessing the reliability of the test score. SEM is used to calculate confidence intervals around a test score. A confidence interval gives a range within which the true score (the score that would be obtained if there were no measurement error) is likely to fall. This is essential for making informed decisions based on individual test scores, as it accounts for the inherent uncertainty in those scores.

72 Match List-I with List-II.

List-I	List-II
A. Entropy	I. Comparative assessment of facilitating and restraining forces in the environment
B. Decay Curve	II. A sudden downward drop in the curve of health behaviour
C. Force Field Analysis	III. Ginzberg's theory of career development
D. Fantasy, Tentative, Realistic	IV. A gradual progressive decline in the health behaviour curve

Choose the correct answer from the options given below.

	A	B	C	D		A	B	C	D
1	II	IV	I	III	2	IV	III	II	I
3	III	II	I	IV	4	I	III	IV	II

Ans. (1)

Exp. The correct matching is A-II, B-IV, C-I, D-III.

Entropy refers to a state of disorder or randomness in a system. In the context of health behaviour, a sudden drop in the curve could be due to a significant shift in forces (such as a negative event), aligning with this analysis.

The **Decay Curve** illustrates the gradual decline in health behaviours over time, showing how behaviours can weaken or deteriorate without consistent reinforcement or motivation.

Force Field Analysis, developed by Kurt Lewin, is a method for analysing the driving and restraining forces affecting a situation or change. It emphasises the balance between these forces.In the context of systems theory, it can represent the comparative assessment of forces that facilitate or restrain change, aligning with the idea that higher entropy indicates more disorder.

Ginzberg's theory outlines the stages of career development: **Fantasy** (childhood aspirations), **Tentative** (adolescence), and **Realistic** (adulthood). These stages represent the progression from imaginative career choices to more grounded, realistic decisions.

73 The different states of consciousness like wakefulness, dream, deep sleep as well as extraordinary state turiya avastha are described in

1 Mandukya Upanishad
2 Katha Upanishad
3 Svetasvatara Upanishad
4 Mimamsa

Ans. (1)

Exp. The Mandukya Upanishad is one of the principal Upanishads of Hindu philosophy and specifically addresses the nature of reality and consciousness. It explores the concept of four states of consciousness:

Wakefulness (Jagrat) The state of being alert and aware of the external world.

Dream (Svapna) The state of consciousness where one experiences dreams, representing an internal reality.

Deep Sleep (Sushupti) The state of deep, dreamless sleep, where consciousness is in a latent form.

Turiya The extraordinary or transcendent state, which represents the ultimate reality beyond the three common states of consciousness. It signifies a state of pure awareness or bliss.

The Mandukya Upanisad uses these states to explain the relationship between the self (Atman) and the ultimate reality (Brahman), emphasising the significance of understanding these states for spiritual awakening and enlightenment.

74 Match List-I with List-II.

List-I	List-II
A. Gestalt Therapy	I. Five universal human needs
B. Reality Therapy	II. You are the architect of your life
C. Existentialism	III. Empty chair technique
D. Solution Focused Therapy	IV. Steve de Shazer and Insoo Kim Berg

Choose the correct answer from the options given below.

	A	B	C	D		A	B	C	D
1	II	I	IV	III	2	I	II	III	IV
3	IV	I	II	III	4	III	I	II	IV

Ans. (4)

Exp. The correct matching is A-III, B-I, C-II, D-IV.

Gestalt Therapy employs techniques like the empty chair technique, where clients engage in a dialogue with an empty chair representing a person or aspect of themselves. This method helps clients explore emotions and conflicts by externalising their thoughts.

Reality Therapy developed by William Glasser, focuses on helping individuals meet their five universal human needs: survival, love and belonging, power, freedom, and fun. It emphasises personal responsibility and making choices that fulfill these needs.

Existentialism philosophical approach asserts that you are the architect of your life, emphasising personal freedom and responsibility in shaping one's own existence and meaning.

Solution-focused Therapy's therapeutic approach, developed by Steve de Shazer and Insoo Kim Berg, centers on identifying solutions and leveraging existing resources, rather than focusing on problems. It aims to empower clients to envision and achieve their desired outcomes.

75 Which one of the following are the reasons for forgetting?

A. The information is not attended to and fails to be encoded.

B. Information accessed repeatedly decays.

C. Older information in memory interfers with the learning of new information.

D. Never information interfers with the retrieval of older information.

E. Information attended and perception is poor.

Choose the correct answer from the options given below:

1 A, C, D only
2 A, B, C, D only
3 A, B, D only
4 B, C, D, E only

Ans. (1)

Exp. Statements A, C and D are correct.

The information is not attended to and fails to be encoded This reason highlights that if information is not actively processed or attended to, it is unlikely to be encoded into memory, leading to forgetting.

Older information in memory interferes with the learning of new information This refers to proactive interference, where previously learned information disrupts the ability to learn new information. For example, learning a new phone number might be hindered by remembering an old one.

Newer information interferes with the retrieval of older information This is known as retroactive interference, where new information makes it difficult to recall older memories. For instance, if you learn a new address, you might forget your previous address.

Statements II and V are incorrect.

Information accessed repeatedly decays This statement is not accurate because repeated access typically strengthens memory rather than causes decay.

Information attended and perception is poor While poor perception can affect memory, this option does not directly relate to forgetting as it does not specifically indicate a recognised reason for forgetting.

76 Kohlberg's stages of moral development follows

A. being a moral person in the eyes of others

B. makes moral choices based on beliefs

C. behaves appropriately to avoid punishment

D. conflicts with moral principles and individual rights

E. makes choices based on what is right-behaviour

Choose the correct answer from the options given below.

1 C, E, A, B, D
2 D, E, B, A, C
3 A, D, C, E, B
4 B, E, C, D, A

Ans. (1)

Exp. The correct answer is C, E, A, B, D.

Kohlberg's stages of moral development consist of three main levels.

Stage 1 Behaves appropriately to avoid punishment. At this stage, moral reasoning is based on direct consequences for oneself.

Stage 2 Makes choices based on what is right behaviour, which often reflects a more individualistic perspective of morality, focusing on self-interest.

Conventional Level:

Stage 3 Being a moral person in the eyes of others. This stage emphasises conforming to social norms and expectations to be viewed positively by others.

Stage 4 Makes moral choices based on beliefs. This stage involves following rules and laws to maintain social order and uphold societal values.

Post-conventional Level

Stage 5 Conflicts with moral principles and individual rights. Here, individuals begin to consider abstract principles of justice and the rights of others, even if it conflicts with laws or social conventions.

77 Arrange the following behaviours of the child as per Piaget's stages of cognitive development.

A. The child says the volume of water in a long glass is same even when it is poured into flat bowl.

B. The child looks for an object in the same place where it was hidden earlier.

C. The child says that the clay ball in round shape is smaller than that the one flattened right in front of her.

D. The child argues that cycling gives a better exercise to hip muscles than bending exercises by citing reasons.

Choose the correct answer from the options given below.

1 B, C, A, D
2 B, A, C, D
3 A, C, B, D
4 C, A, B, D

Ans. (1)

Exp. The correct order of behaviours, according to Piaget's stages of cognitive development is B, C, A, D.

- **Sensorimotor Stage** (0-2 years): The child looks for an object in the same place where it was hidden earlier.

- **Preoperational Stage** (2-7 years): The child says that the clay ball in round shape is smaller than the one flattened right in front of her.
- **Concrete Operational Stage** (7-11 years): The child says the volume of water in a long glass is the same even when it is poured into a flat bowl.
- **Formal Operational Stage** (11 years and up): The child argues that cycling gives a better exercise to hip muscles than bending exercises by citing reasons.

78 The theory which is used to compare judgements or the decisions we make under uncertain conditions is called
1 Subliminal perception theory
2 Signal detection theory
3 Judgemental process theory
4 Decision processing theory

***Ans.* (2)**

Exp. Signal Detection Theory (SDT) is a framework used to understand how decisions are made under conditions of uncertainty. It provides a method for measuring the ability to differentiate between signal (the presence of a stimulus) and noise (the absence of a stimulus) when making judgments.

79 One psychologist has developed a tool on nature connectedness. What would be correct sequence of the following psychometric activities?
A. Carrying out Exploratory Factor Analysis
B. Establishing Percentile Norm
C. Examining Croanbach Alpha
D. Verifying Predictive Validity
E. Establishing Content Validity
Choose the correct answer from the options given below.
1 E, C, A, D, B
2 E, C, A, B, D
3 C, A, E, B, D
4 C, E, A, D, B

***Ans.* (4)**

Exp. The correct sequence is C, E, A, D, B.

The following sequence outlines the typical steps in the development and validation of a psychometric tool

Examining Cronbach's Alpha This step assesses the internal consistency of the test items, which is essential in establishing the reliability of the scale. A high Cronbach's Alpha indicates that the items measure the same underlying construct.

Establishing Content Validity After ensuring reliability, content validity is assessed to confirm that the items represent the construct of interest comprehensively. This often involves expert reviews to evaluate whether the items are relevant and appropriate.

Carrying out Exploratory Factor Analysis (EFA) EFA is performed to identify the underlying structure of the data. It helps determine whether the items group together as expected and how many factors exist within the data.

Verifying Predictive Validity Once the factor structure is confirmed, predictive validity is assessed to see if the tool can accurately predict relevant outcomes or behaviors. This is a critical aspect of establishing the tool's utility in real-world applications.

Establishing Percentile Norm Finally, after the tool is validated, percentile norms can be established to provide benchmarks against which individual scores can be compared, facilitating interpretation of the results.

80 The five sheaths Pancha Koshas theory is explained in
1 Katha Upanishad
2 Mandukya Upanishad
3 Prasna Upanishad
4 Taittiriya Upanishad

***Ans.* (4)**

Exp. The Taittiriya Upanishad describes human-being to be having a five sheaths personality (Pancha Kosha) comprising of the material or gross body (Anamaya Kosha), the vital or instinctual component (Pranamaya Kosha), the mental or psychological component (Manomaya Kosha), the intellectual component (Vigyanmaya Kosha) and the fifth aspect of pure bliss and happiness (Anandmaya Kosha).

81 In addition to tripartite system of working memory, Baddeley, Allen and Hitch 2011 added a fourth component which is called
1 Iconic Sketchpad
2 Storage Rehearsal
3 Phonological loop
4 Episodic buffer

***Ans.* (4)**

Exp. The episodic buffer serves as a temporary storage system that can hold and integrate information from the phonological loop, visuospatial sketchpad and long-term memory. It combines information from different sensory modalities and from long-term memory to form a coherent representation of a scene or event. The episodic buffer is thought to operate with a larger capacity than the other components, thereby improving the overall flexibility and functionality of working memory.

82 Which of the following refer to Advanced Empathy as per the Developmental Model of Counselling?
A. Confrontive challenging
B. Theme identification
C. Connecting islands
D. Making the implicit explicit
E. Fortune telling
Choose the correct answer from the options given below.
1 A, B, E only
2 C, D, E only
3 B, C, D only
4 B, D, E only

***Ans.* (3)**

Exp. The correct answer is B, C and D.

In the Developmental Model of Counselling, Advanced Empathy refers to the counsellor's ability to go beyond basic understanding and reflect deeper meanings and themes in the client's communication.

Theme identification This involves recognising underlying themes or patterns in what the client is expressing. It helps the counsellor understand the broader context of the client's experiences and emotions.

Connecting islands This refers to linking different aspects of the client's narrative or feelings that may seem disconnected. By connecting these 'islands', the counsellor helps the client see how various experiences relate to one another.

Making the implicit explicit This means bringing out feelings, thoughts, or themes that the client may not have articulated directly. By doing so, the counsellor helps the client gain insights into their experiences, making them more aware of their emotions and motivations.

83 A famous study called the 'Robber's Cave' conducted by Sherif in 1961 demonstrated the social behaviour known as

1 Social comparison
2 Equal status contact
3 Self-fulfilling prophecy
4 Reciprocity of liking

Ans. (2)

Exp. The correct answer is Equal status contact.

The Robber's Cave study, conducted by Muzafer Sherif and colleagues in 1961, explored how intergroup conflict and cooperation impact social behaviour. The study involved two groups of boys at a summer camp who initially competed against each other, leading to hostility and conflict. However, when researchers introduced situations that required both groups to work together towards common goals—such as fixing a water supply issue—cooperation emerged, reducing hostility and fostering positive intergroup relations.

84 Arrange the following stages of therapy advocated by Adler.

A. Building therapeutic relationship
B. Gathering information
C. Developing new skill
D. Gaining insight

Choose the correct answer from the options given below.

1 B, A, D, C 2 A, B, D, C 3 B, A, C, D 4 A, C, B, D

Ans. (2)

Exp. The correct order is A, B, D, C.

In Adlerian therapy, the stages typically follow this sequence

Building therapeutic relationship Establishing a strong rapport between the therapist and the client is the first step. This creates a safe and supportive environment for the client to explore their issues.

Gathering information Once the therapeutic relationship is established, the therapist gathers relevant information about the client's life, experiences, and psychological dynamics. This helps in understanding the client's lifestyle and patterns of behaviour.

Gaining insight After gathering information, the focus shifts to helping the client gain insight into their thoughts, feelings, and behaviours. This involves exploring underlying beliefs and motivations that influence their current issues.

Developing new skill The final stage involves helping the client develop new skills and strategies to cope with their challenges and make positive changes in their life.

85 Which one of the following is not a component of creativity according to Torrance?

1 Flexibility 2 Elaboration
3 Abstractness of titles 4 Verification

Ans. (4)

Exp. Verification is not considered a component of creativity according to Torrance. Instead, verification involves assessing and confirming the validity of ideas, which is more aligned with the evaluation phase rather than the creative process itself.

Torrance's model of creativity emphasises the following components that contribute to creative thinking and expression

Flexibility The ability to produce a variety of ideas or solutions, demonstrating adaptability in thinking.

Elaboration This involves expanding on ideas by adding details and depth, showcasing how well a person can develop a concept.

Abstractness of titles This refers to the ability to create abstract or imaginative titles that reflect the essence of the ideas generated.

86 Match List-I with List-II.

	List-I		List-II
A.	Non-maleficence	I.	Response to stress
B.	HPA Axis	II.	Encountering paradoxes of life
C.	Art Therapy	III.	Counselling ethics
D.	Existentialism	IV.	Intervention for emotional release

Choose the correct answer from the options given below.

	A	B	C	D		A	B	C	D
1	II	III	I	IV	2	IV	II	III	I
3	III	I	II	IV	4	III	I	IV	II

Ans. (4)

Exp. The correct matching is A-III, B-I, C-IV, D-II.

Non-maleficence This principle is a key aspect of counselling ethics, which emphasises the importance of not causing harm to clients.

HPA Axis The HPA Axis (Hypothalamic-Pituitary-Adrenal Axis) is crucial for the body's response to stress. It involves a complex set of interactions among the hypothalamus, pituitary gland and adrenal glands, playing a significant role in stress response.

Art Therapy This therapeutic approach is designed for emotional release, using creative processes to help individuals express and process their emotions.

Existentialism This philosophical perspective often involves encountering paradoxes of life, focusing on individual existence, freedom, and the inherent challenges and absurdities of life.

87 **Which one of the following is the preferred method for determining item bias?**

1 Item difficulty level
2 Item discrimination index
3 Item characteristic curve
4 Inter item correlation matrix

Ans. (3)

Exp. The Item Characteristic Curve (ICC) is a graphical representation used in Item Response Theory (IRT) to assess the relationship between a test item and the latent trait it is measuring.

The ICC provides insights into how well an item differentiates between respondents with different levels of the trait. It helps identify whether an item functions differently for different groups, indicating potential bias.

88 **According to social identity theory, formation of a person's identity within a particular social group is explained by the sequential process of ....**

1 Social categorisation, social identity and social comparision
2 Social identity, social categorisation and social comparision
3 Social comparision, social identity and social categorisation
4 Social comparision, social categorisation and social identity

Ans. (1)

Exp. According to social identity theory, developed by Henri Tajfel and John Turner, the formation of a person's identity within a particular social group occurs through the following sequential process

Social Categorisation Individuals categorise themselves and others into different social groups (e.g., based on ethnicity, nationality, gender, etc.).

This categorisation helps individuals define themselves in relation to others.

Social Identity Once individuals categorise themselves within a group, they adopt the identity associated with that group.

This identity becomes a significant part of their selfconcept, influencing their behaviors, attitudes, and beliefs.

Social Comparison Finally, individuals compare their group (the ingroup) with other groups (outgroups) to establish a sense of superiority or inferiority.

This comparison reinforces the importance of their social identity and can lead to in-group favoritism or outgroup prejudice.

89 **In case of normal probability curve, the graph/ curve is plotted for**

1 scores and respective frequencies
2 scores and respective deviations
3 'z' scores and respective relative frequencies
4 'z' scores and respective standard deviations

Ans. (3)

Exp. In the context of the normal probability curve (or normal distribution), the graph is specifically plotted using 'z' scores and their corresponding relative frequencies. 'Z' scores are standardised scores that indicate how many standard deviations a particular score is from the mean of the distribution. 'Z' scores allow for comparison of scores from different distributions by converting them into a common scale. Relative Frequencies refers to the proportion of occurrences of each z-score in the dataset relative to the total number of observations. When plotted, the relative frequency shows how often each z-score occurs within the context of the normal distribution.

The resulting graph forms the classic bell-shaped curve associated with normal distributions, where most data points cluster around the mean, and the probabilities taper off symmetrically toward the extremes. This characteristic allows statisticians and researchers to make inferences about population parameters based on sample statistics.

90 **Arrange the following in the sequence of personality development propounded by psychoanalytic theory.**

A. Children refuse to defecate in the toilet, while some hold back the feces
B. Children enjoy breast feeding by mother and put everything in mouth
C. Children develop interest in opposite sex
D. Children are found to play with their genital organs

Choose the correct answer from the options given below.

1 A, C, D, B
2 B, C, D, A
3 B, A, D, C
4 D, A, B, C

Ans. (3)

Exp. The correct sequential order is B, A, D, C.

In psychoanalytic theory, particularly the stages of psychosexual development proposed by Sigmund Freud, the sequence of personality development is organised into distinct stages.

Children enjoy breast feeding by mother and put everything in mouth This behaviour is associated with the oral stage (0-1 year), where the infant's pleasure centers around the mouth. Activities like breastfeeding and oral exploration are crucial for this stage.

Children refuse to defecate in the toilet, while some hold back the feces This behaviour relates to the anal stage (1-3 years), where the focus of pleasure shifts to controlling bladder and bowel movements. Toilet training is a significant part of this stage, leading to conflicts around control and independence.

Children are found to play with their genital organs This behaviour pertains to the phallic stage (3-6 years), where children become aware of their bodies and develop interest in their genitals. It's also the stage where they start to identify with their same-sex parent and form the basis for sexual identity.

Children develop interest in opposite sex This behaviour is characteristic of the genital stage (puberty onwards) which follows after a period of latency stage. Here the focus shifts to developing mature sexual relationships and interests, particularly toward the opposite sex.

Directions (Q. Nos. 91-95) *Read the passage carefully and answer the following questions that follows.*

The researchers assumed that older adults are different from younger adults in their suicidal ideation and in their reasons for thinking about committing suicide because of differences in life experiences and coping competence. Hence, they used cross-sectional research and recruited 150 older adults 60-95 years who were matched with 150 younger adult 17-34 years on gender ethnicity, religion and self-reported health status. Beck's scale for suicidal ideation was used to measure suicidal ideation. They used 't' test for comparison of variables and found no significant difference. According to Siegler, neither cross-sectional nor longitudinal study provide much information about how those changes occur over time. He discussed a method that involves carefully observing behaviour during periods when rapid change is occurring and collecting both quantitative and qualitative information.

91 What is the method Siegler discussed for studying the process of change?

1 Macrogenetic method
2 Exogenetic method
3 Chromogenetic method
4 Microgenetic method

Ans. (4)

Exp. The microgenetic method is an approach used in cognitive developmental research which allows obtaining detailed data about changes in a particular competence at the moment the change is actually taking place. This approach is characterised by three key properties:

- observations encompass the entire period of change, starting before the change begins and continuing until the competence has reached a relatively stable state,
- the density of observations is high relative to the rate of change of the competence under study, and
- observations are analysed intensively on an individual and trial-by-trial basis as to understand the process that gives rise to both qualitative and quantitative aspects of change.

92 What is the df for the 't' test used here?

1 297 2 296 3 294 4 298

Ans. (4)

Exp. In this case, a 't' test is used to compare two independent groups (older adults and younger adults). The formula to calculate the degrees of freedom (df) for an independent samples 't' test is

df = N1 + N2 - 2, where:

N1 is the sample size of the first group (older adults).

N2 is the sample size of the second group (younger adults).

Given that both groups have 150 participants: df = 150 + 150 - 2 = 298

So, the degrees of freedom (df) for this 't' test would be 298.

93 The combination of cross-sectional and longitudinal research is called

1 Time series research
2 Correlational research
3 Sequential research
4 Thematic research

Ans. (3)

Exp. Sequential research is a type of research design that blends both cross-sectional and longitudinal approaches to study changes over time. It involves collecting data from different groups (cohorts) at multiple time points. This design allows researchers to observe developmental trends and changes within individuals (like a longitudinal study) while also comparing different groups at a single point in time (like a cross-sectional study).

94 A potential problem with cross-sectional research is that there may be other variables that are confounded with age. This problem is called

1 Habitat effect
2 Cohort effect
3 Interrupted effect
4 Protective effect

Ans. (2)

Exp. The cohort effect refers to differences between groups (or cohorts) in a cross-sectional study that arise not because of age, but due to shared experiences or environmental factors unique to a particular group based on their historical or cultural context. In cross-sectional research, different age groups (e.g., younger adults *vs.* older adults) are compared at the same point in time. However, these groups may differ not just in age, but in other important ways that could influence the outcome. For example: Older adults might have experienced different societal conditions (e.g., wars, economic challenges) that shaped their attitudes, behaviours and coping strategies.

95 When null hypothesis is false and we are accepting it then we make

1 Type I error
2 Type II error
3 Error of falsifiability
4 Acceptance error

Ans. (2)

Exp. A Type II error occurs when the null hypothesis is false, but we mistakenly fail to reject it (or 'accept' it). In other words, there is a real effect or difference in the population, but the statistical test does not detect it, leading to a wrong conclusion that no effect exists.

Directions (Q. Nos. 96-100) *Read the passage carefully and answer the questions that follows.*

Motivation is the driving force behind human activities. Researchers identified three components of motivation. Motivation originates externally or internally, are defined action or non-action and can be categorised as extrinsic, identified, intrinsic or introjected. One of the causes of flow motivation is "just because an approach or method worked for someone else does not mean that it will work for you". Self-determination theory is built on the idea that people are actively motivated to persue their goals.

96 Self-determination theory is developed by
1 Shelley E. Taylor
2 Deci and Ryan
3 Barbara Frederick
4 Seligman and Lubomirsky

Ans. (2)

Exp. Self-determination theory (SDT) was developed by Edward Deci and Richard Ryan. SDT identifies three basic psychological needs that are essential for promoting well-being and motivation i.e., Competence, Relatedness, Autonomy.

97 What are the three components of motivation ?
1 Need, persistence, goal
2 Activation, persistence and intensity
3 Intensity, identification, drive
4 Activation, intensity and goal

Ans. (2)

Exp. The three components of motivation are activation, persistence and intensity, which help explain how motivation drives behaviour

- Activation is the initial decision or action to begin a behavior or task. It reflects the process of starting a specific activity or goal. For example, deciding to sign up for a class or start a project is an act of activation.
- Persistence refers to the continued effort toward a goal despite challenges, obstacles, or setbacks. It represents the determination to keep going until the goal is achieved. For instance, a student who continues studying for an exam despite feeling tired demonstrates persistence.
- Intensity refers to the level of effort and focus someone puts into pursuing a goal. It highlights how hard a person works to reach their objective. For example, two individuals may both be studying, but one might study with more focus and concentration, showing higher intensity.

98 What are the components of intrinsic motivation?
1 Autonomy, competence, tendency
2 Competence, mastery, purpose
3 Mastery, tendency, competence
4 Autonomy, mastery and purpose

Ans. (4)

Exp. The components of intrinsic motivation are autonomy, mastery and purpose.

Autonomy refers to the need to have control over one's actions and decisions. When people feel autonomous, they engage in activities because they choose to, not because they are pressured or coerced.

Mastery is the desire to improve and develop skills. People are intrinsically motivated when they are working toward becoming better at something that challenges them.

Purpose refers to the sense that one's activities are aligned with meaningful and larger goals or values. When individuals see the significance of what they are doing, they are more likely to feel intrinsically motivated.

99 Introjected motivation is
1 a negative internalised motivation.
2 a positive externalised motivation.
3 a negative externalised motivation.
4 a positive internalised motivation.

Ans. (1)

Exp. Introjected motivation is negative internalised motivation. Introjected motivation is when individuals engage in activities to avoid guilt or anxiety, or to gain approval from others, rather than for their own genuine interest. This form of motivation is somewhat internalised, but it is still driven by external pressures or expectations. People act to meet internalised standards, often feeling they 'should' or 'must' do something, rather than truly wanting to.

100 "Just because an approach or method worked for someone else does not mean that it will work for you" refers to
1 one size fits all
2 absurd function approach
3 there is no common approach for all
4 the approach will work for me

Ans. (3)

Exp. "Just because an approach on method worked for someone else does not mean that it will work for you" refers to there is no common approach for all.

This statement emphasises that individuals are different, and what works for one person may not work for another.

It highlights that there isn't a universal solution or method that fits everyone, as people have unique circumstances, needs, and responses to various approaches.

Therefore, personalised or tailored methods are often more effective.

UGC-NET
PSYCHOLOGY
SOLVED PAPER 2023 (December)

PAPER II

1 According to Piaget's theory a cognitive process in which a schema is modified as a response to feedback from environment.

1 Operation 2 Assimilation
3 Conservation 4 Accommodation

***Ans.* (4)**

➲ ***Exp.*** According to Piaget's theory, accommodation refers to the cognitive process of modifying existing schemas or creating new ones in response to feedback from the environment.

2 Which of the following is a disease not related to Cardiovascular system?

1 Atherosclerosis 2 Angina Pectoris
3 Crohn's Disease 4 Aneurysm

***Ans.* (3)**

➲ ***Exp.*** Crohn's Disease is a type of Inflammatory Bowel Disease (IBD) that primarily affects the gastrointestinal tract, specifically the intestines. It does not involve the cardiovascular system and is associated with symptoms such as abdominal pain, diarrhea and weight loss. In contrast, atherosclerosis, angina pectoris, and aneurysm are all conditions related to the cardiovascular system, involving the heart and blood vessels.

3 Zeigarnik effect explains

1 the translation of learning into behaviour.
2 behaviour directed toward some goal.
3 the tendency to remember uncompleted tasks longer than completed ones.
4 a number of interrelated individual memory traces.

***Ans.* (3)**

➲ ***Exp.*** Zeigarnik effect explains the tendency to remember uncompleted tasks longer than completed ones. The Zeigarnik effect, named after Russian psychologist Bluma Zeigarnik, suggests that people have a better memory for tasks that are interrupted or left unfinished compared to those that are completed.

4 Autoclitic behaviour refers to

1 a grammatical framework for verbal behaviour
2 a person who works alone
3 behaviour for the benefit of oneself
4 behaviour exhibited when one meets a specified objective

***Ans.* (1)**

➲ ***Exp.*** Autoclitic behaviour refers to a grammatical framework for verbal behaviour. Autoclitic behaviour, a concept from BF Skinner's analysis of verbal behaviour, refers to verbal behaviours that modify the meanings of other verbal behaviours by providing additional context or clarification.

5 Statutory rape refers to

1 The husband forcing the unwilling wife for sexual intercourse
2 Forcibly having sexual intercourse with a resisting minor
3 Forcibly having sexual intercourse with a resisting person from the same gender
4 Violence in sexual intercourse by a husband or wife legally married

***Ans.* (2)**

➲ ***Exp.*** Statutory rape, in many jurisdictions, is a non-forced sexual relation between an adult and an individual, who legally is not old enough to consent to the behaviour.

6 Name the psychologist who has proposed and suggested that the declarative memory can either be Episodic or Semantic.

1 Tulving 2 Lockhart
3 Craik 4 Warrington

***Ans.* (1)**

➲ ***Exp.*** Endel Tulving is known for his significant contributions to the understanding of memory, particularly the distinction between episodic and semantic memory. He proposed that declarative memory, which involves the conscious recollection of information, can be divided into these two categories: episodic memory refers to the recall of personal experiences and specific events, while semantic memory involves general knowledge and facts about the world. Tulving's work has been foundational in cognitive psychology, influencing how researchers study and categorise different types of memory.

7 **The increased accessibility or retrievability of information stored in memory produced by the prior presentation of relevant cues is called**

1 Priming　　2 Primacy
3 Cue　　4 Acquisition

Ans. (1)

Exp. Priming refers to the phenomenon where exposure to a stimulus influences the response to a subsequent stimulus, enhancing the retrieval of related information from memory. When relevant cues are presented prior to a task, they activate related memories, making them more accessible and easier to recall. This mechanism underlies many cognitive processes, including perception, memory recall, and even decision-making, highlighting the interconnectedness of stored information in the brain.

8 **One psychologist while collecting data from gamblers, first identified one gambler and from him traced out three more and through these three further more. He continued like this. This is an example of ....**

1 Quota sampling　　2 Stratified sampling
3 Snowball sampling　　4 Accidental sampling

Ans. (3)

Exp. Snowball sampling method is used in qualitative research when the population is hard to access or identify, such as gamblers in this case. The initial participant (the first gambler) helps the researcher find additional participants (the three more gamblers), and this process continues as each new participant refers more individuals. Snowball sampling is particularly useful for exploring hidden or marginalised populations, as it relies on the social networks of existing members to identify further subjects for study.

9 **Parameter : Population : : .... : Sample.**

1 Dispersion　　2 Inference
3 Statistic　　4 Operation

Ans. (3)

Exp. In research terminology, a parameter refers to a measurable characteristic of a population (like the mean or variance), while a statistic refers to a characteristic calculated from a sample. Essentially, parameters describe the entire population, whereas statistics provide estimates based on a subset of that population.

10 **Which of the following is considered to be error component in ANOVA?**

1 Between mean square
2 Within mean square
3 Interaction mean square
4 Total mean square

Ans. (2)

Exp. In ANOVA (Analysis of Variance), the within mean square represents the variation of observations within each group. This variation is considered the error component because it reflects the differences among individuals in the same treatment group that are not attributed to the treatment effects. In contrast, the between mean square measures the variation between group means, which is influenced by the treatments applied. Thus, the within mean square helps assess the random error present in the data.

11 **Which of the following software is used extensively for analysis of qualitative data by researchers in psychology ?**

1 SPSS　　2 AMOS
3 N-VIVO　　4 LISEREL

Ans. (3)

Exp. N-VIVO is specifically designed for qualitative data analysis, enabling researchers to organise, analyse and visualise unstructured data such as interviews, focus groups and open-ended survey responses. It provides tools for coding and thematic analysis, making it highly suitable for psychologists and researchers who need to interpret qualitative information. In contrast, SPSS, AMOS and LISREL are primarily used for quantitative data analysis and structural equation modeling.

12 **To calculate the correlation between a genuinely dichotomous variable and a continuous variable we have to use**

1 Bi-serial 'r'　　2 Point '.' Biserial 'r'
3 Tetrachoric 'r'　　4 Phi coefficient

Ans. (2)

Exp. Point Biserial correlation is specifically used to measure the relationship between one dichotomous variable (which has two categories) and one continuous variable. This method is appropriate when the dichotomous variable represents two distinct groups (e.g., yes/no, male/female) and allows for the assessment of how these groups differ on the continuous variable. In contrast, the other options serve different purposes for different types of data.

13 **Attitude which is conscious and easy to report is called**

1 Implicit attitude　　2 Explicit attitude
3 Unconscious attitude　　4 Intrinsic attitude

Ans. (2)

Exp. Explicit attitudes are those that individuals are consciously aware of and can easily articulate when asked. They reflect a person's deliberate evaluations and beliefs about a particular object, person, or issue, making them straightforward to report in surveys or discussions. In contrast, implicit attitudes are automatic and may not be readily accessible to conscious thought.

14 **A theory which advocates prejudice stems, at least in part, from economic competition between social groups is**

1 Contact Hypothesis
2 Social Identify Theory
3 Realistic Conflict Theory
4 Repulsion Hypothesis

Ans. (3)

➲ *Exp.* Realistic conflict theory, developed by Muzafer Sherif, it posits that prejudice arises from competition over limited resources, such as jobs or housing, between different social groups. When groups perceive that their interests are in conflict, it can lead to hostility and negative attitudes towards one another. This economic competition creates an environment where prejudice and discrimination are more likely to emerge as groups strive to secure their own advantages.

15 If members in a group are performing additive tasks, then
1 social loafing will be less.
2 social loafing will be more.
3 social loafing will not exist.
4 level of social loafing cannot be decided.

Ans. (2)

➲ *Exp.* Social loafing will be more because, in additive tasks, the contributions of individual group members are combined to achieve a common goal. This can lead individuals to exert less effort, thinking that their individual input is less critical to the overall outcome. As a result, they may rely on others to carry the workload, increasing the likelihood of social loafing, where individuals reduce their effort in a group setting compared to when they work alone.

16 The psychological state characterised by reduced self-awareness brought on by external conditions is known as
1 Exhaustion
2 Entitativity
3 Deindividuation
4 Discrimination

Ans. (3)

➲ *Exp.* Deindividuation refers to a psychological state where individuals lose their self-awareness and feel less accountable for their actions, often due to being part of a group or under external influences. This state can lead to impulsive or atypical behaviour, as the individual feels less like an independent entity and more like a member of a collective, diminishing personal responsibility and self-monitoring.

17 Although she likes to wear gold ear-ring very much, Tanmaya removed the same when she joined a school where gold ornaments are not allowed.
This social influence is example of ....
1 compliance
2 conformity
3 symbol influence
4 pluralistic ignorance

Ans. (2)

➲ *Exp.* The social influence described here is an example of conformity because Tanmaya's decision to remove her gold earrings reflects her alignment with the school's rules and social norms. Conformity involves changing one's behaviour or beliefs to match those of a group or to adhere to societal expectations, even if it contradicts personal preferences. In this case, her action demonstrates a desire to fit in with the school's regulations.

18 The two specific objectives of Watson's Behaviourism are 'not'
1 to predict the response by knowing the stimulus and to predict the stimulus by knowing the response.
2 to predict the behaviour of the learner and to modify the behaviour.
3 to control the behaviour of the learner and vary the experimental condition to bring about the change.
4 to study the learner in a controlled laboratory environment and to examine the effect of reinforcement.

Ans. (4)

➲ *Exp.* Watson's behaviourism emphasises observable behaviours rather than studying learners in controlled environments or examining reinforcement effects. Watson believed in focusing on measurable behaviours and their relationship with stimuli, rejecting introspection and the influence of internal mental states, making the study of reinforcement less central to his objectives.

19 The ability of brain to adopt to the environment and to replace function following damage is known as
1 Neuroplasticity
2 Accommodation
3 Assimilation
4 Hemispherical coordination

Ans. (1)

➲ *Exp.* The ability of brain to adopt to the environment and to replace function following damage is known as Neuroplasticity. It refers to the brain's ability to reorganise itself by forming new neural connections throughout life. This adaptability allows the brain to compensate for injury or damage by reorganising and adjusting its functions, enabling recovery and the replacement of lost abilities.

20 Temporal Lobe epilepsy results in
1 Docile behaviour
2 Aggressive behaviour
3 Antisocial behaviour
4 Prosocial behaviour

Ans. (2)

➲ *Exp.* Temporal lobe epilepsy (TLE) can lead to aggressive outbursts due to its effects on the limbic system, which regulates emotions. Seizure activity in this region can cause intense emotions, resulting in aggressive behaviour during episodes.

21 Socrates questioning is a
1 philosophical questioning.
2 technique for self understanding.
3 psychoanalytical technique.
4 technique in which counsellor asks the questions to the client.

Ans. (2)

➲ **Exp.** Socratic questioning is a powerful technique for self-understanding and critical thinking. It involves asking a series of probing questions that encourage individuals to examine their beliefs, assumptions and values more deeply.

This method helps in clarifying thoughts and revealing underlying motivations or inconsistencies in one's reasoning. Socratic questioning is often used in education, therapy and philosophical discussions to promote self-awareness and understanding.

22 **Studies on weight loss programmes in a follow up study revealed that**

1 weight gain was more for those practicing drug therapy.
2 weight gain was more for those practicing behaviour modification therapy.
3 weight loss was less for those practicing drug therapy.
4 those practicing behaviour modification therapy were able to maintain their body weight.

Ans. (4)

➲ **Exp.** Behaviour modification therapy promotes sustainable lifestyle changes, enabling individuals to maintain their weight after losing it. In contrast, drug therapy often leads to temporary weight loss without fostering lasting behavioural changes.

23 **Homeostatic temperature in the body is regulated by**

1 changes in the external environment.
2 drive reduction.
3 preoptic region of the hypothalamus.
4 electrical activities in the brain.

Ans. (3)

➲ **Exp.** The preoptic region of the hypothalamus is crucial for thermoregulation, sensing changes in body temperature and triggering appropriate physiological responses, such as sweating or shivering, to maintain homeostasis. This area integrates information about the body's temperature and helps to balance heat production and loss.

24 **Which of the following is not true of structuralism?**

1 It provided strong scientific impetus.
2 It provided a through test of classical introspective method.
3 It emphasised on basic conscious elements.
4 It provided a strong and clear orthodoxy against which other schools resisted.

Ans. (4)

➲ **Exp.** Statement (4) is not true about structuralism. While structuralism did establish a framework for psychology, it was criticised for its rigid methodology and reliance on introspection, leading to resistance and the emergence of alternative schools of thought.

25 **Which of the following is not a technological system designed to aid, enhance or inspire learning?**

1 Python
2 Logo
3 Squeak
4 Boxer

Ans. (1)

➲ **Exp.** Python is a general-purpose programming language primarily used for software development, data analysis, and web development, rather than being specifically designed as a technological system to aid, enhance, or inspire learning.

26 **According to Watson, Conscious mentalism refer to**

1 wakeful state of mind.
2 knowledge about mental activities.
3 reasoning ability.
4 attention to thinking activities.

Ans. (4)

➲ **Exp.** According to Watson, Conscious mentalism refers to attention to thinking activities. Conscious mentalism emphasises the active awareness and focus on one's own cognitive processes, such as thinking and reasoning. This perspective prioritises observable behaviour over introspective analysis, highlighting the importance of being attentive to one's thoughts as part of the conscious experience.

27 **A decrease in sensitivity to leptin is found to be a factor contributing to**

1 weight gain
2 weight loss
3 maintaining homeostasis
4 loss of appetite

Ans. (1)

➲ **Exp.** A decrease in sensitivity to leptin, a hormone that regulates hunger and energy balance, leads to an inability to recognise when the body is full. This reduced sensitivity can result in increased food intake and, consequently, weight gain as the body's mechanisms for signaling satiety are impaired.

28 **On the basis of which criterion, the tests are classified into 'Verbal Tests' and 'Non-verbal Tests'?**

1 Criterion of purpose
2 Criterion of contents of items
3 Criterion of scoring
4 Criterion of time limits

Ans. (2)

➲ **Exp.** Criterion of contents of items because verbal tests focus on language-based items that assess verbal abilities, such as reading and comprehension, while non-verbal tests consist of items that do not require language skills, such as pattern recognition and spatial reasoning.

29 The Bender Visual-Motor Gestalt Test Bender 1938 has

1 six designs
2 seven designs
3 eight designs
4 nine designs

Ans. (4)

Exp. The Bender Visual-Motor Gestalt Test, developed by Lauretta Bender in 1938, consists of nine geometric figures that assess visual-motor integration and perceptual abilities. Participants are asked to reproduce these designs, providing insight into their cognitive and motor functions.

30 Which one of the following is not intrinsic factor affecting reliability?

1 Group variability
2 Length of the test
3 Range of total scores
4 Homogeneity of items

Ans. (1)

Exp. Group variability it is an extrinsic factor that relates to the characteristics of the sample being tested rather than the test itself. Intrinsic factors affecting reliability are typically related to the test design, such as its length, range of scores and item homogeneity, which directly influence the consistency of test results.

31 Which scale of measurement has absolute zero?

1 Nominal 2 Ordinal 3 Interval 4 Ratio

Ans. (4)

Exp. The ratio scale has an absolute zero or character of origin, the zero point represents the absence of the attribute being measured. Example distance, time, weight, etc.

32 Wechsler Adult Intelligence Scale WAIS published in 1955 has

1 5 Verbal and 5 Performance
2 5 Verbal and 6 Performance
3 6 Verbal and 5 Performance
4 6 Verbal and 6 Performance

Ans. (3)

Exp. The Wechsler Adult Intelligence Scale (WAIS), first introduced by David Wechsler in 1955, indeed has 11 subtests divided into two major categories:

1. **Verbal Scale (6 tests)** Information, Comprehension, Arithmetic, Similarities, Vocabulary and Digit Span.
2. **Performance Scale (5 tests)** Picture Completion, Picture Arrangement, Block Design, Object Assembly and Digit Symbol.

The verbal tests measure a person's ability to use and understand language, memory and general knowledge. The performance tests assess non-verbal reasoning, spatial processing and problem-solving skills.

33 Sigmund Freud was born on

1 23rd September, 1939
2 6th May, 1939
3 23rd September, 1856
4 6th May, 1856

Ans. (4)

Exp. Sigmund Freud, an Austrian neurologist and the founder of psychoanalysis, was born on 6th May, 1856 in Freiberg, Moravia (today Príbor, Czech Republic) to a family of Jewish wool merchants.

34 Which one of the following is not among the twenty needs listed by Murray, 1938 ?

1 Succorance
2 Sentience
3 Sex
4 Safety

Ans. (4)

Exp. Henry Murray developed a theory of personality based on human needs, identifying 20 psychogenic needs that drive human behaviour. These include Sentience: Enjoying sensuous experiences, Sex : Engaging in erotic relationships and Succorance: Seeking help and protection from others. Safety is not a part of this list. The concept of safety is more prominently discussed in Maslow's hierarchy of needs, where it is a primary, foundational need.

35 'Foreign Hull' is the concept coined by

1 Kurt Lewin
2 Alfred Adler
3 Erik Erikson
4 Abraham Maslow

Ans. (1)

Exp. **Foreign Hull is a part of Kurt Lewin's Field Theory**, which he used to explain human behaviour in terms of interactions between an individual and their environment. The foreign hull refers to aspects of the environment that are outside of the individual's life space but still exert some influence on the person. The life space in Lewin's theory consists of the psychological environment or the total set of influences affecting an individual's behaviour. It includes everything a person is consciously aware of or experiences directly.

36 Which of the following is not a source of work related stress?

1 Responsibility for others
2 Lack of support from co-workers
3 Conflict with family members
4 Unpleasant work environment

Ans. (3)

Exp. Conflict with family members because it is a personal stressor that arises from one's home life and interpersonal relationships outside of work. Unlike the other options, which are directly related to job demands or the work environment, conflicts with family do not originate from workplace conditions or responsibilities.

37 The concept of 'collective unconscious' is one of the most powerful, original and controversial features of

1 Adler's Personality Theory
2 Jung's Personality Theory
3 Freud's Personality Theory
4 Fromm's Personality Theory

Ans. (2)

Exp. The concept of 'collective unconscious' is one of the most powerful, original and controversial features of Jung's Personality Theory. Carl Jung introduced the concept of the collective unconscious as a part of his analytical psychology.

38 Brainstorming is technique in Gerard Egan's problem management approach to helping. Which of the statements given below is not a characteristics feature of brainstorming ?

1 Develop 'wild' possibilities
2 Suspend judgement
3 Use one idea as a takeoff point for another
4 Set of time frame

Ans. (4)

Exp. Set of time frame is not a characteristic feature of brainstorming because, while brainstorming encourages free-flowing ideas and creativity, it typically does not impose strict time constraints on the generation of ideas. The focus is on generating a large quantity of ideas without immediate judgement, allowing for more expansive thinking rather than limiting it with a specific timeframe.

39 The number of cases of a disease, injury or disability at a given point of time which can be expressed as the number of new cases or the number of existing cases is called

1 Mortality
2 Prevalence
3 Morbidity
4 Incidence

Ans. (3)

Exp. Morbidity refers to the presence of illness or disease in an individual or population. It is expressed in terms of prevalence (the total number of cases in a population at a given time) or incidence (the number of new cases that occur in a specified time period).

40 'Miracle Question' is a technique used in

1 Narrative therapy
2 Solution focused brief therapy
3 Feminist therapy
4 Reality therapy

Ans. (2)

Exp. The 'miracle question' is a popular intervention in solution-focused brief therapy. It asks the client to imagine and discuss a possible world where problems are removed and issues addressed. The question may take various forms, such as asking the client, "Assume your problem has been solved. What is different?" Or, "Assume your problem is gone. What does this mean to you?" and many more.

41 Which of the following comes under divergent thinking ?

A. Fluency B. Flexibility
C. Elaboration D. Preparation
E. Verification

Choose the correct answer from the options given below.

1 B, C, D only 2 A, C, E only
3 A, B, C only 4 B, C, E only

Ans. (3)

Exp. Divergent thinking refers to the ability to generate creative ideas by exploring many possible solutions.

The key components of divergent thinking include

Fluency is the ability to generate numerous ideas or solutions.

Flexibility is the capacity to think about different categories or approaches to a problem.

Elaboration is the skill of expanding on an idea by adding details.

42 Which are the major components of Emotional Intelligence by Goleman 1995?

A. Recognising the purpose in life
B. Knowing our own emotions
C. Recognising the emotions of others
D. Handling relationship
E. Understanding meaning of life

Choose the correct answer from the options given below.

1 A, B, D only 2 B, C, D only
3 A, B, C, E only 4 A, C, D, E only

Ans. (2)

Exp. The correct answer is B, C and D.

According to Goleman (1995), the major components of Emotional Intelligence include:

Knowing our own emotions (self-awareness) The ability to recognise and understand our own emotions.

Recognising the emotions of others (empathy) The ability to sense and understand the feelings of others.

Handling relationships (social skills) Managing interpersonal interactions effectively.

43 The components of 'Type A' pattern of personality encompasses

A. Happy-go-lucky
B. Prosocial
C. Emotion-focused
D. Competitive striving for achievement
E. Sense of time urgency

Choose the correct answer from the options given below.

1 A and B only 2 C and D only
3 D and E only 4 A, C and E only

Ans. (3)

Exp. The Type A personality is characterised by traits such as:

- Competitive striving for achievement Individuals are highly driven and motivated to succeed.
- Sense of time urgency They tend to feel pressure to do things quickly and efficiently.

Hostility and impatience can also be associated with Type A personalities.

Happy-go-lucky, prosocial, and emotion-focused traits do not align with the characteristics of the Type A personality pattern.

44 Scientifically sound test must possess which of the following?

A. Objectively
B. Norms
C. Time limit
D. Reliability
E. Validity

Choose the correct answer from the options given below.

1 A, B, C, D only
2 A, B, D, E only
3 A, B, C, E only
4 E, D, C, B only

Ans. (2)

Exp. For a test to be scientifically sound, it must include:

Objectivity The test should be free from personal biases or subjective judgement.

Norms Standardised norms provide a basis for interpreting individual test scores.

Reliability Consistency in the test results over time or across different situations is essential.

Validity The test must measure what it is intended to measure.

45 Study of Values prepared by all port, Vernon and lindzey has some basic areas which of the following areas are included in it?

A. Moral
B. Aesthetic
C. Cognitive
D. Religions
E. Economic

Choose the correct answer from the options given below.

1 A, B, C only
2 B, C, D only
3 B, D, E only
4 A, D, E only

Ans. (3)

Exp. The Study of Values by Allport, Vernon, and Lindzey focuses on six primary value areas, three of which are:

Aesthetic Concerned with artistic appreciation and beauty.

Religious Related to spiritual and religious beliefs.

Economic Focuses on material gain and practical benefits.

Moral and Cognitive are not among the six values outlined in the study, which also includes theoretical, political and social values.

46 Factors covered by the General Aptitude Test Battery GATB are

A. Verbal aptitude
B. Form perception
C. Mechanical reasoning
D. Motor coordination
E. Clerical perception

Choose the correct answer from the options given below.

1 A, B, C, D only
2 B, C, D, E only
3 C, D, E, A only
4 A, B, D, E only

Ans. (4)

Exp. The General Aptitude Test Battery (GATB) covers the following factors:

- Verbal Aptitude: Measures the ability to understand and use words.
- Form Perception: Measures the ability to perceive details in objects.
- Motor Coordination: Assesses coordination of fine motor movements.
- Clerical Perception: Involves attention to detail in clerical tasks, like proofreading.
- Mechanical Reasoning is not a factor in the GATB.

47 What is true about retrospective studies?

A. Data are often collected with the help of narrative methods.
B. It is also known as naturalistic inquiry.
C. Collected data can be analysed through.
D. It is same as quasi-experiment.
E. Biographical research is a good example of retrospective study.

Choose the correct answer from the options given below.

1 A, B, D only
2 B, C, D only
3 A, C, E only
4 B, C, E only

Ans. (3)

Exp. Option (3) A, C and E are true about Retrospective Studies.

- Retrospective studies often use narrative methods to collect data, especially when analyzing past events, experiences, or behaviours.
- The data from retrospective studies can be analyzed through various methods, depending on the research question and data type.
- Biographical research is indeed a form of retrospective study, as it involves looking back on an individual's life experiences.

48 Which is correct explanation about Rene Descartes?

A. The mind controls the body both in animals and human beings.
B. He postulated that the mind the body were governed by different laws.
C. The mind was free and possessed only by humans.
D. The duality of mind and body.

Choose the correct answer from the options given below.

1 A, C, D only
2 B, C, D only
3 A, B, C only
4 A, B, D only

Ans. (2)

Exp. Statements B, C and D are correct about Rene Descartes. Rene Descartes is best known for his dualism philosophy, which distinguishes between the mind and body as two separate entities governed by different principles.

- Descartes proposed that the mind and body were governed by different laws, with the body following physical laws and the mind having free will.
- He believed the mind was unique to humans and separate from the physical body.
- The duality of mind and body is central to Descartes' theory, known as Cartesian dualism.

49 Which best explains about 'Paradigm'?

A. It is the study of intact, meaningful mental events.

B. A viewpoint regarding physical reality as we perceive.

C. A point of view shared by a substantial number of scientists that provides a general framework for empirical research.

D. It is usually more than just one theory and corresponds more closely to what is called a school of thought.

Choose the correct answer from the options given below.

1 B and D only   2 C and D only
3 A and D only   4 A and C only

Ans. (2)

Exp. C and D best explains 'Paradigm'. The term 'paradigm' in the context of science refers to a widely accepted framework or model that guides research and practice within a scientific community.

- A paradigm provides a general framework for empirical research, representing a widely held set of beliefs or assumptions.
- A paradigm often involves more than one theory and is closely related to what we call a school of thought, encompassing various concepts and methodologies shared by many scientists.

50 Egan's developmental model of counselling mentions the following distinct steps in its three stages.

A. Possibilities, Commitment

B. Best fit, Leverage

C. Blindspot, Focusing

D. Leverage, Confronting

E. Agenda, Commitment

Choose the correct answer from the options given below.

1 A, B, D only   2 A, B, E only
3 A, B, C only   4 A, B, C, E only

Ans. (2)

Exp. Egan's developmental model of counseling, also known as the Skilled Helper Model, consists of three main stages that focus on helping clients develop solutions and make decisions. These stages include:

- Exploration of the current scenario (Stage 1)
- Development of possibilities and commitment to change (Stage 2)
- Implementing the best fit strategy and sustaining commitment (Stage 3)

The correct steps are Possibilities, Commitment, Best fit, Leverage, and Agenda, Commitment—align with the stages of exploring options, choosing the best strategy, and maintaining progress, whereas other options (like 'Blindspot' and 'Confronting') do not fit the distinct structure of Egan's model.

51 Which of the following are true method of Appreciative Inquiry?

A. Inquiry begins with appreciation.

B. It is not collaborative.

C. It is not proactive.

D. Inquiry is applicable.

Choose the correct answer from the options given below

1 A and D only   2 B and C only
3 C and D only   4 A and B only

Ans. (1)

Exp. Statements A and D are true method of Appreciative Inquiry. Appreciative Inquiry (AI) is a collaborative, strengths-based approach to change in organisations and other human systems. It begins with an appreciation, focusing on identifying and amplifying strengths, successes and positive aspects within an organisation or group.

Appreciative Inquiry is applicable in various contexts, such as organisational development, team building and community engagement, making it a versatile method.

Statements B and C are false. Appreciative Inquiry is inherently collaborative, involving collective participation to explore and build on what works well.

Appreciative Inquiry is proactive, focusing on envisioning and creating positive futures rather than simply reacting to problems.

52 According to Psychophysical School, which of the following statements are true?

A. Weber's ratio increases as the stimulus intensity increases.

B. DL increases proportionately to the changes in the stimulus intensily.

C. Limens determines the perception of sensory stimulus.

D. Weber's ratio and Techner's law are contradictory in nature.

Choose the correct answer from the options given below

1 A and B only   2 B and C only
3 A and D only   4 A and C only

Ans. (2)

Exp. Statements B and C are true.

The Difference Limen (DL), or the just noticeable difference, tends to increase proportionately with changes in stimulus intensity, reflecting a direct relationship between the intensity of the stimulus and the perceived difference.

Limens (thresholds) indeed determine the perception of sensory stimuli, as they represent the minimum levels of stimulus intensity required for detection.

Statements A and D are false. Weber's ratio (the constant ratio of the change in stimulus to the original stimulus) does not increase with stimulus intensity; rather, it remains constant across different levels of intensity.

Weber's law and Fechner's law are not contradictory; they are related concepts in psychophysics, with Weber's law serving as the foundation for Fechner's law.

53 What is true about multiple regression ?

A. There can be more than two criterion.
B. There can be more than two predictors.
C. It indicates linear relation between one predicator and one criterion.
D. The equation for regression line contains partial regression coefficients.

Choose the correct answer from the options given below.

1 A and B only
2 B and C only
3 B and D only
4 A and D only

Ans. (3)

➲ ***Exp.*** B and C are true about multiple regression. Multiple regression can include more than two predictors (independent variables) to explain the variability in the dependent variable (criterion).

The equation for the regression line in multiple regression includes partial regression coefficients, which represent the unique contribution of each predictor to the criterion while controlling for the effects of other predictors.

54 Which of the following can faster prejudice ?

A. Threats to self-esteem
B. Competition for resources
C. Social categorisation
D. Social recategorisation

Choose the correct answer from the options given below.

1 A, C, D only
2 A, B, C only
3 A, B, D only
4 B, C, D only

Ans. (2)

➲ ***Exp.*** Threats to self-esteem can increase prejudice as individuals may react defensively and negatively toward others to protect their self-image and enhance their self-worth.

Competition for resources fosters prejudice, as groups or individuals vying for limited resources may develop negative attitudes towards each other, leading to in-group favoritism and out-group discrimination.

Social categorisation is a cognitive process where individuals classify themselves and others into groups. This can lead to prejudice as it promotes in-group bias and stereotypes against out-groups.

55 Resistance to persuasion may be increased

A. reactance
B. emotional appeal
C. forewarning
D. selective avoidance

Choose the correct answer from the options given below.

1 A, B only
2 B, C only
3 A, B, D only
4 A, C, D only

Ans. (4)

➲ ***Exp.*** Options A, B and D are correct.

Reactance This occurs when people feel that their freedom to choose is being threatened, leading them to resist persuasion. Reactance can cause individuals to hold onto their original beliefs more strongly when they perceive an attempt to persuade them.

Forewarning When individuals are forewarned about an attempt to persuade them, they can prepare counterarguments in advance, which can increase their resistance to the persuasive message.

Selective avoidance This refers to the tendency of individuals to avoid information or messages that conflict with their existing beliefs or attitudes. By selectively avoiding contrary information, individuals bolster their resistance to persuasion.

56 Which of the following are the influencing skills of counselling?

A. Self disclosure
B. Information giving
C. Confrontation
D. Smart-goals

Choose the correct answer from the options given below.

1 D only
2 A, B, D only
3 B, C, D only
4 A, B, C only

Ans. (4)

➲ ***Exp.*** The influencing skills of counselling are A, B, and C.

Self disclosure This is a counselling skill where the counsellor shares personal experiences or feelings to build rapport and encourage clients to open up, fostering a trusting relationship.

Information giving Providing relevant information is crucial in counselling to help clients understand their situation, options, and potential solutions, thus empowering them to make informed decisions.

Confrontation This skill involves gently challenging a client's thoughts, behaviours, or feelings that may be maladaptive or inconsistent. It is used to help clients gain insight and promote self-awareness.

Smart-goals, while they are a useful framework for setting goals (specific, measurable, achievable, relevant, time-bound), are not inherently a skill of counselling; rather, they are a technique or guideline used within the counselling process.

57 Which of the following statements are true for a panic disorder?

A. Recurrent bouts of intense and extreme fear
B. Sensation of shortness of breath or smothering
C. Persistent worry or concern about having additional attacks
D. An episode of panic attack followed by the use of a drug or medication

Choose the correct answer from the options given below.

1 A, B, C only 2 B, C, D only
3 B, D only 4 A, C, D only

Ans. (1)

Exp. Statements A, B and C are true regarding panic disorder.

Panic disorder is characterised by recurrent bouts of intense and extreme fear, known as panic attacks, which can occur unexpectedly.

During a panic attack, individuals often experience physical symptoms such as shortness of breath or a sensation of smothering, which contribute to their fear and distress.

Individuals with panic disorder frequently experience persistent worry or concern about having additional attacks, which can significantly impact their daily lives and lead to avoidance behaviours.

58 Which of the following are the identity statuses of James Marcia's Theory ?

A. Identity achievement
B. Identity foreclosure
C. Identity diffusion
D. Identity crisis
E. Identity moratorium

Choose the correct answer from the options given below.

1 A, B, C, E only 2 A, B, C, D only
3 B, C, D, E only 4 C, D only

Ans. (1)

Exp. The recognised identity statuses in Marcia's theory include A, B, C, and E.

Identity achievement This status reflects individuals who have explored various options and have made firm commitments to their identity.

Identity foreclosure This status describes individuals who have made commitments without experiencing a period of exploration, often adopting the values and beliefs of parents or authority figures.

Identity diffusion This status pertains to individuals who have not made any commitments and are not actively exploring options; they may feel apathetic about their identity.

Identity moratorium This status refers to individuals who are actively exploring options but have not yet made commitments; they are in a state of crisis.

59 Which of the following are the stages in the transtheoretical model of behaviour change?

A. Maintenance B. Intention
C. Contemplation D. Action

Choose the correct answer from the options given below.

1 A, B, C only 2 A, C, D only
3 B, C, D only 4 B, C only

Ans. (2)

Exp. The recognised stages in the transtheoretical model of behaviour change include A, C, and D.

Maintenance This stage involves sustaining the behaviour change over time and working to prevent relapse.

Contemplation In this stage, individuals are aware of the benefits of change and are considering taking action but have not yet made a commitment.

Action This stage is where individuals actively modify their behaviour and implement changes to achieve their goals.

60 Which of the following are not the components of Yama as per Astanga Yoga?

A. Ahimsa B. Shoucha C. Asteya D. Tapas

Choose the correct answer from the options given below.

1 A, C only 2 A, B only 3 B, D only 4 B, C only

Ans. (3)

Exp. Shoucha and Tapas are not the components of Yama as per Astanga Yoga. Shoucha refers to purity and cleanliness but is not one of the five Yamas; it is associated with the Niyama component of Ashtanga Yoga.

Tapas represents self-discipline and austerity, but it is also categorised under the Niyama, not Yama. Asteya is also a component of Yama, referring to non-stealing or respect for others' possessions. Ahimsa is a fundamental component of Yama, representing non-violence and compassion toward all living beings.

61 How type II error can be reduced while testing hypothesis ?

A. Decreasing the chosen level of significance
B. Increasing the chosen level of significance
C. Decreasing the sample size
D. Increasing the sample size

Choose the correct answer from the options given below.

1 A, D only 2 B, D only 3 A, C only 4 B, C only

Ans. (2)

Exp. The correct options is B and D.

Increasing the chosen level of significance This can help reduce Type II error. By increasing the significance level (e.g., moving from 0.01 to 0.05), you make it easier to reject the null hypothesis, thus reducing the chance of committing a Type II error.

Increasing the sample size This is a correct method for reducing Type II error. Larger sample sizes increase the power of the test, making it more likely to detect an effect when there is one.

Decreasing the chosen level of significance This action would not help in reducing Type II error. In fact, it could increase Type II error because lowering the significance level (e.g., from 0.05 to 0.01) makes it harder to reject the null hypothesis when it is false.

Decreasing the sample size This would not reduce Type II error; it would likely increase it. A smaller sample size reduces the statistical power of the test, making it less likely to detect a true effect when one exists.

62 Which of the following statements are correct about 'assimilation'?

A. A kind of matching between the cognitive structures and the physical environment.

B. Learning that one event leads to another.

C. It can be roughly equated with recognition or knowing.

D. Studying a phenomenon as 'it occurs naturally in the environment'.

Choose the correct answer from the options given below.

1 A, B, C only
2 A, D only
3 A, C only
4 A, C, D only

***Ans.* (3)**

Exp. Statements A and C are correct.

Assimilation, according to Piaget's theory of cognitive development, involves integrating new information into existing cognitive structures or schemas, thereby matching or adapting them to the physical environment.

Assimilation can be associated with recognising and understanding new information based on prior knowledge, which is akin to 'knowing'.

63 Which of the following statements are correct about Gestalt Psychology?

A. Gestalt approach is dementistic.

B. Gestalt psychology has sometimes been called phenomenology.

C. Gestalt psychology can be thought of as an attempts to apply field theory from physics.

D. Gestalt psychologists believed that whatever happens to a person influences everything else about the person.

Choose the correct answer from the options given below.

1 A, B, D only
2 A, C, D only
3 A, B, C only
4 B, C, D only

***Ans.* (4)**

Exp. Statements B, C and D are correct.

Gestalt psychology emphasises understanding human perception and experience from a subjective point of view, which aligns with phenomenological approaches.

Gestalt psychologists were influenced by field theory, which posits that behaviour is a function of the individual's environment and the relationships between various elements within it.

Gestalt psychology emphasises that perception and experience are holistic, meaning that every part is interconnected and influences the whole.

64 The theoretical positions about personality whose development have been heavily dependent on factor analysis are

A. RB Cattell
B. Spearman
C. HJ Eysenck
D. JP Guilford
E. Howard Gardner

Choose the correct answer from the options given below.

1 A, C, E only
2 B, D, E only
3 A, C, D only
4 A, C, D, E only

***Ans.* (3)**

Exp. The correct option is A, C and D.

RB Cattell Cattell is known for his work in personality psychology and developed the 16 Personality Factor Questionnaire (16PF) using factor analysis. He believed that personality traits could be identified through the analysis of observable behaviours.

HJ Eysenck Eysenck utilised factor analysis to develop his model of personality, which includes three dimensions: extraversion, neuroticism, and psychoticism. His research contributed significantly to the understanding of personality traits as measurable dimensions.

JP Guilford Guilford's work focused on the structure of intellect and creativity, and he also applied factor analysis to explore different dimensions of intelligence. However, his primary contributions were not specifically in personality theory.

65 Frend believed that at times Ego is unable to control impulses of ID so uses various defense mechanism such as

A. fixation
B. repression
C. rationalisation
D. displacement
E. projection

Choose the correct answer from the options given below.

1 A, B, C, D only
2 B, C, D, E only
3 C, D, E, A only
4 D, E, A, B only

***Ans.* (2)**

Exp. Options B, C, D and E are correct.

Repression is a defense mechanism where the ego pushes unacceptable thoughts and desires into the unconscious mind. It is a way of keeping distressing thoughts from becoming conscious.

Rationalisation involves providing logical or reasonable explanations for behaviours or feelings that are actually driven by irrational impulses. The ego defends against the anxiety that comes from facing the true motives.

Displacement occurs when an individual shifts emotional responses from the true object of their feelings to a safer or more acceptable target. For example, someone might take out their frustrations on a family member instead of confronting the actual source of their stress.

Projection defense mechanism involves attributing one's own unacceptable thoughts or feelings to someone else. For instance, if someone feels insecure, they may accuse others of being insecure.

66 Match List-I with List-II.

List-I	List-II
A. Implicit Memory	I. The kind of memory that underlies perceptual and cognitive skills
B. Working Memory	II. A vivid and relatively permanent record of the circumstances in which one learned of an emotionally charged, significant event
C. Long-term Memory	III. Stored for only a few records
D. Flashbulb Memory	IV. Semi-permanent memory

Codes

	A	B	C	D		A	B	C	D
1	I	III	IV	II	2	I	II	IV	III
3	II	III	IV	I	4	III	IV	II	I

Ans. (1)

Exp. The correct matching is A-I, B-III, C-IV, D-II.

Implicit memory refers to the type of memory that influences our thoughts and behaviours without conscious awareness, underpinning perceptual and cognitive skills such as riding a bike or playing an instrument.

Working memory is a short-term storage system that holds information temporarily for processing and manipulation. It typically retains information for a few seconds to minutes, which refers to memories stored for only a few records.

Long-term memory involves the storage of information over extended periods, potentially for a lifetime by indicating a more permanent or semi-permanent storage of information.

Flashbulb memories are vivid, detailed memories of significant emotional events, often retaining the circumstances under which they were learned. It mentions a vivid and relatively permanent record of such experiences.

67 Match List-I with List-II.

List-I	List-II
A. Associationism	I. Wundt
B. Structuralism	II. Lashley
C. Functionalism	III. Ebbinghaus
D. Behaviourism	IV. Stanley Hall

Codes

	A	B	C	D		A	B	C	D
1	II	III	IV	I	2	IV	II	I	III
3	III	I	IV	II	4	II	IV	III	I

Ans. (3)

Exp. The correct matching is A-III, B-I, C-IV, D-II.

Associationism Hermann Ebbinghaus is best known for his pioneering research on memory and learning, specifically his studies on how associations are formed and forgotten. He conducted experiments using nonsense syllables to understand the nature of memory, which aligns with the principles of associationism.

Structuralism Wilhelm Wundt is often referred to as the father of modern psychology and is credited with founding the school of structuralism. He focused on breaking down mental processes into their basic components, emphasising introspection as a method for studying the structure of the mind.

Functionalism Although more widely known for his contributions to developmental psychology and education, Hall's work aligns with functionalist principles by emphasising the adaptive functions of psychological processes. His focus on child development and the impact of social and cultural factors on behaviour reflects the functionalist perspective that psychology should study the purpose of mental processes.

Behaviourism While not exclusively a behaviourist, Karl Lashley's research in the mid-20th century emphasised the importance of understanding behaviour through observable actions rather than introspection. His work on learning and memory, particularly the search for the "engram" (the physical trace of memory in the brain), aligns with behaviourist principles of studying behaviour as a response to environmental stimuli.

68 Match List-I with List-II.

List-I	List-II
A. Perception	I. Vinnana
B. Consciousness	II. Vedana
C. Feelings	III. Sanna
D. Body	IV. Rupa

Codes

	A	B	C	D		A	B	C	D
1	II	I	IV	III	2	III	I	II	IV
3	IV	II	III	I	4	III	IV	II	I

Ans. (2)

Exp. The correct matching is A-III, B-I, C-II, D-IV.

Perception corresponds to Sanna, which refers to the process of recognising and interpreting sensory information.

Consciousness relates to Vinnana, representing awareness and the mental state of being aware of one's thoughts and experiences.

Feelings are associated with Vedana, which involves the experience of sensations and emotional responses to stimuli.

Body corresponds to Rupa, which refers to physical form or matter in Buddhist philosophy.

69 Match List-I with List-II.

List-I	List-II
A. Secondary Trait	I. Traits that dominate an individual's entire personality
B. Cardinal Trait	II. Key dimensions of personality that underline many other traits
C. Central Traits	III. A bunch of traits that best describes an individual's personality
D. Source Traits	IV. Traits that exert relatively specific and weak effects on behaviour

Codes

	A	B	C	D		A	B	C	D
1	I	II	III	IV	2	II	III	IV	I
3	III	IV	I	II	4	IV	I	III	II

Ans. (4)

Exp. The correct matching is A-IV, B-I, C-III, D-II.

Secondary traits are traits that exert relatively specific and weak effects on behaviour. These traits may influence behaviour in certain situations but are not dominant.

Cardinal traits refers to traits that dominate an individual's entire personality. These are the traits that are defining characteristics of a person.

Central traits are a bunch of traits that best describe an individual's personality. These traits are fundamental and consistent, forming the core of a person's personality.

Source traits correspond to key dimensions of personality that underline many other traits. These are deeper-level traits that provide the foundation for more observable behaviours.

70 Match List-I with List-II.

List-I	List-II
A. Autonomy	I. Fault
B. Industry	II. Shame and Doubt
C. Initiative	III. Stagnation of progress
D. Productivity	IV. Inferiority

Choose the correct answer from the options given below.

	A	B	C	D		A	B	C	D
1	II	IV	I	III	2	II	III	IV	I
3	I	II	III	IV	4	III	II	IV	I

Ans. (1)

Exp. The correct matching is A-II, B-IV, C-I, D-III.

Autonomy This stage is associated with shame and doubt. It refers to the period when children develop a sense of personal control over physical skills and a sense of independence, typically occurring in early childhood.

Industry This stage is related to inferiority. In this stage, children learn to work hard and become competent in various tasks. If they succeed, they feel industrious; if they fail, they may feel inferior.

Initiative This stage is connected to guilt. Children in this stage assert themselves more frequently and initiate activities. If they are successful, they feel a sense of initiative; if not, they may develop guilt over their needs and desires.

Productivity This stage is aligned with Stagnation. It refers to the concern for the next generation and a desire to contribute to society, contrasting with stagnation, where individuals feel unproductive.

71 Match List-I with List-II.

List-I	List-II
A. Coefficient of Dispersion	I. Standard deviation as a percentage of mean
B. Standard Deviation	II. Mean of squared deviations of individual scores from mean
C. Coefficient of Variation	III. Variance in terms of mean
D. Variance	IV. Positive square root of variance

Codes

	A	B	C	D		A	B	C	D
1	IV	III	I	II	2	III	IV	II	I
3	III	IV	I	II	4	IV	II	III	I

Ans. (3)

Exp. The correct matching is A-III, B-IV, C-I, D-II.

Coefficient of Dispersion refers to the measure of relative variability and is defined as the variance in terms of the mean.

Standard Deviation is the positive square root of variance.

Coefficient of Variation is the ratio of the standard deviation to the mean. Hence it is expressed as a percentage of the mean.

Variance This is the mean of squared deviations of individual scores from the mean.

72 Match List-I with List-II.

List-I	List-II
A. Theory of planned behaviour	I. Tajfel and Turner
B. Theory of causal attribution	II. Petigrew
C. Social identity theory	III. Ajzen and Fishbein
D. Contact hypothesis	IV. Kelley

Codes

	A	B	C	D
1	II	I	IV	III
2	I	II	III	IV
3	III	IV	I	II
4	III	IV	II	I

Ans. (3)

Exp. The correct matching is A-III, B-IV, C-I, D-II.

Theory of planned behaviour This theory, developed by Icek Ajzen and Martin Fishbein, posits that an individual's behaviour is influenced by their intention to perform the behaviour, which is in turn influenced by attitudes, subjective norms and perceived behavioural control.

Theory of causal attribution Harold Kelley is known for his work on attribution theory, particularly the covariation model, which explains how individuals determine the causes of their own and others' behaviours based on consistency, distinctiveness and consensus.

Social identity theory This theory was developed by Henri Tajfel and John Turner and explains how individuals derive a sense of identity and self-esteem from their social group memberships, leading to in-group favoritism and out-group discrimination.

Contact hypothesis The contact hypothesis, associated with Gordon Allport and later extended by Thomas Pettigrew, suggests that under certain conditions, increased contact between groups can reduce prejudice and improve relations.

73 Match List-I with List-II.

List-I	List-II
A. Obedience orientation	I. Moral reasoning based on winning the approval of others
B. Interpersonal norms	II. Moral reasoning based on moral principles that apply to all
C. Social contract	III. Moral reasoning based on the belief that adults know what is right or wrong
D. Universal ethical principles	IV. Moral reasoning is based on the belief that laws are for the good of all members of society

Codes

	A	B	C	D		A	B	C	D
1	III	IV	I	II	2	III	I	IV	II
3	I	IV	II	III	4	I	II	IV	III

***Ans.* (2)**

Exp. The correct matching is A-III, B-I, C-IV, D-II.

Obedience orientation Moral reasoning based on the belief that adults know what is right or wrong. This substage reflects a focus on obeying authority figures and following rules to avoid punishment, based on the belief that adults possess the knowledge of right and wrong.

Interpersonal norms Moral reasoning based on winning the approval of others. This substage emphasises conformity and the desire to gain approval from peers or significant others, focusing on maintaining good relationships.

Social contract Moral reasoning is based on the belief that laws are for the good of all members of society. At this stage, individuals recognise that laws are based on mutual agreements and are intended to benefit society as a whole, allowing for a more flexible interpretation of laws in light of social needs.

Universal ethical principles Moral reasoning based on moral principles that apply to all. This highest stage reflects moral reasoning that transcends laws and social agreements, emphasising universal ethical principles such as justice, dignity, and equality that apply to all individuals.

74 Match List-I with List-II.

List-I	List-II
A. Passive euthanasia	I. The doctor ends a suffering of a patient's life at his/her request by administering a lethal dose of a drug.
B. Voluntary active euthanasia	II. The doctor helps the patient take his/her life by enabling the patient swallow or inject a lethal dose of drug
C. Assisted suicide	III. The doctor ends a suffering of a patient by administering a lethal dose of drug without the patients consent or permission.
D. Involuntary active euthanasia	IV. The doctor withholds or withdraws treatment by permitting the patient to die naturally, on the request of the patient

Codes

	A	B	C	D		A	B	C	D
1	IV	I	II	III	2	IV	II	III	I
3	I	II	III	IV	4	I	II	IV	III

***Ans.* (1)**

Exp. The correct matching is A-IV, B-I, C-II, D-III.

Passive euthanasia occurs when medical treatment is withheld or withdrawn, allowing the patient to die naturally. This aligns with the description provided, as it involves not taking action to prolong life.

In **voluntary active euthanasia**, a physician actively ends the life of a patient who has requested it, typically by administering a lethal dose of medication.

Assisted suicide involves the physician providing the means for the patient to end their own life, such as prescribing medication that the patient then self-administers.

Involuntary active euthanasia occurs when a physician actively ends a patient's life without their consent, typically due to the belief that the patient is suffering.

75 Match List-I with List-II.

List-I	List-II
A. Gestalt psychology	I. Believing that one has various horrible disease conditions
B. Hypochondriacal delusions	II. Emphasis on personal growth and self-direction
C. Humanistic existential therapy	III. Whole in more than the sum of its parts
D. Existential neurosis	IV. Feeling of alienation meaninglessness and apathy

Codes

	A	B	C	D
1	III	IV	I	II
2	III	I	II	IV
3	II	I	IV	III
4	II	I	III	IV

***Ans.* (2)**

Exp. The correct matching is A-III, B-I, C-II, D-IV.

Gestalt psychology Gestalt psychology emphasises that the human mind perceives objects as organised wholes rather than as separate, individual parts. This perspective is foundational to Gestalt theory, which asserts that our experiences are shaped by the configuration and relationships of components rather than by the components alone.

Hypochondriacal delusions Hypochondriacal delusions involve an individual's persistent belief that they are suffering from serious illnesses, despite medical evidence to the contrary.

Humanistic existential therapy Humanistic existential therapy focuses on the individual's experience, personal growth, and self-actualisation. It emphasises the importance of self-direction and the subjective experience of individuals.

Existential neurosis Existential neurosis refers to a psychological condition characterised by feelings of alienation, meaninglessness, and a sense of apathy. This condition arises from a lack of purpose and connection to one's existence.

76 Csikszentmihalyi 1996 observed that the creative process normally takes five steps. Arrange those steps in order.

A. Preparation
B. Evaluation
C. Incubation
D. Elaboration
E. Insight

Choose the correct answer from the options given below.

1 A, B, D, E, C
2 A,C, B, D, E
3 A, C, E, B, D
4 A, B, E, C, D

***Ans.* (3)**

Exp. The sequential order of the five steps in the creative process as observed by Csikszentmihalyi is A, C, E, B, D.

Preparation This is the initial stage where an individual gathers information and resources related to the problem or idea. It involves learning, researching, and understanding the subject matter.

Incubation After preparation, the individual allows the information to percolate unconsciously. This stage may involve stepping away from the problem to give the mind time to process the information.

Insight This step involves the moment of clarity or the 'aha' moment when a creative idea or solution suddenly emerges. It's the realisation or understanding of the problem after the incubation period.

Evaluation Once insight is achieved, the individual evaluates the idea or solution. This step involves assessing the feasibility and potential impact of the creative solution.

Elaboration Finally, the individual develops and refines the idea into a workable form. This stage includes putting the creative idea into action and further developing it through additional work.

77 Arrange the following sentences in sequential order according to classical conditioning.

A. A stimulus such as food is presented to an organism which is called Unconditioned Stimulus US.
B. The neutral stimulus light alone is provided which makes the organism to salivate.
C. A neutral stimulus such as light is presented to the organism just prior to the presentation of US.
D. Another neutral stimulus tone is provided prior to light.
E. The neutral stimulus tone above is provided which makes the organism to salivate.

Choose the correct answer from the options given below.

1 A, C, D, B, E
2 A, B, D, C, E
3 A, C, B, D, E
4 A, C, B, E, D

***Ans.* (3)**

Exp. The correct order is A, C, B, D, E.

A stimulus such as food is presented to an organism which is called unconditioned stimulus (US): This is the starting point where the unconditioned stimulus (US), which naturally elicits a response (like salivation), is introduced.

A neutral stimulus such as light is presented to the organism just prior to the presentation of US: The neutral stimulus (NS) is introduced just before the unconditioned stimulus (US), setting the stage for conditioning.

The neutral stimulus light alone is provided which makes the organism to salivate: After repeated pairings of the neutral stimulus (light) with the unconditioned stimulus (food), the neutral stimulus now elicits a conditioned response (salivation). Another neutral stimulus (tone) is provided prior to light: A new neutral stimulus (tone) is introduced before the existing neutral stimulus (light) to see if it can also elicit a response.

The neutral stimulus (tone) above is provided which makes the organism to salivate: Finally, after conditioning, the new neutral stimulus (tone) is presented alone and successfully elicits the conditioned response (salivation) from the organism. This sequence illustrates the classical conditioning process, where an organism learns to associate a neutral stimulus with an unconditioned stimulus, leading to a conditioned response.

78 Arrange the following important works of psychology in ascending chronological order.

A. Intelligence test developed by Binet and Simon in France.
B. The first psychology laboratory established by James in Leipzig.
C. First psychology course in the United States by James.
D. American Psychological Association APA was founded by Stanley Hall.
E. Pavlov wins the Nobel Prize for his work on digestive system.

Choose the correct answer from the options given below.

1 A, B, D, C, E
2 B, C, D, E, A
3 C, B, D, E, A
4 D, B, C, A, E

***Ans.* (3)**

Exp. The correct chronological order is C, B, D, E, A.

First psychology course in the United States by James William James offered the first psychology course at Harvard University in 1875. This marks one of the early formalisations of psychology as a discipline in the U.S.

The first psychology laboratory in Leipzig by Wundt Wilhelm Wundt established the first official psychology laboratory in Leipzig, Germany, in 1879, which is considered the formal beginning of psychology as an experimental and scientific field.

American Psychological Association (APA) was founded by Stanley Hall The APA was founded in 1892 by G. Stanley Hall and others, establishing a professional organisation for psychologists in the United States.

Pavlov wins the Nobel prize for his work on the digestive system Ivan Pavlov was awarded the Nobel Prize in Physiology or Medicine in 1904 for his research on the digestive system, which later led to his famous work on classical conditioning.

Intelligence test developed by Binet and Simon in France The Binet-Simon intelligence test was developed in 1905 and was the first practical intelligence test, designed to identify students in need of educational assistance.

79 **According to Astanga Yoga, arrange the stages in the correct sequence.**

A. Dhyana **B. Asana**
C. Samadhi **D. Pranayama**

Choose the correct answer from the options given below.

1 B, D, A, C 2 A, C, D, B 3 D, B, C, A 4 C, A, B, D

Ans. (1)

Exp. The correct sequence is B, D, A, C.

Asana The practice of physical postures is the foundation of Ashtanga Yoga. It helps in preparing the body for the subsequent stages by building strength, flexibility and stability.

Pranayama After mastering the asanas, practitioners move on to pranayama, which involves breath control. This stage helps regulate energy within the body and deepens the connection between the mind and body.

Dhyana Dhyana refers to meditation, where the practitioner focuses inward, cultivating a deep state of concentration and mindfulness. This stage is essential for developing mental clarity and emotional stability.

Samadhi The final stage is samadhi, which represents a state of transcendence or blissful union with the universe. It is characterised by profound peace and insight, resulting from the practices of the previous stages.

80 **Arrange the following in correct sequence of HPA axis response to stress and consequences.**

A. Adrenal glands get stimulated
B. Release of cotricotropin, releasing factor
C. Release of cortisol, epinephrine and nor epinephrine
D. Release of glucose from liver and muscle
E. Release of adrenocorticotropic hormone

Choose the correct answer from the options given below.

1 A, B, C, E, D **2 A, C, B, E, D**
3 B, E, A, C, D **4 E, B, A, C, D**

Ans. (3)

Exp. The correct sequence is B, E, A, C, D.

Release of corticotropin releasing factor When the body perceives a stressor, the hypothalamus releases corticotropin-releasing factor (CRF). This initiates the stress response.

Release of adrenocorticotropic hormone CRF then stimulates the anterior pituitary gland to release adrenocorticotropic hormone (ACTH) into the bloodstream.

Adrenal glands get stimulated ACTH travels through the bloodstream to the adrenal glands, where it stimulates them to produce and release stress hormones.

Release of cortisol, epinephrine and norepinephrine The adrenal glands release cortisol, epinephrine (adrenaline) and norepinephrine (noradrenaline) in response to ACTH. These hormones are crucial for the body's 'fight or flight' response.

Release of glucose from liver and muscle Cortisol and the catecholamines (epinephrine and norepinephrine) promote the release of glucose from the liver and muscles to provide energy to the body, which is essential for responding to the stressor.

81 **In one Exploratory sequential design, what would be the correct sequence?**

A. Quantitative Data Collection
B. Qualitative Data Collection
C. Quantitative Data Analysis
D. Qualitative Data Analysis
E. Interpretation

Choose the correct answer from the options given below.

1 A, B, C, D, E **2 B, A, D, C, E**
3 A, C, B, D, E **4 B, D, A, C, E**

Ans. (4)

Exp. The correct sequence is B, D, A, C, E.

Exploratory sequential design is a mixed methods research design that involves collecting and analysing qualitative data first, followed by quantitative data.

Qualitative Data Collection This is the first step in an exploratory sequential design, where qualitative methods (like interviews, focus groups, or open-ended surveys) are used to gather in-depth insights about a phenomenon. This helps researchers understand the context, perspectives and experiences of participants.

Qualitative Data Analysis After collecting qualitative data, researchers analyse it to identify themes, patterns, and insights. This analysis helps to clarify the issues and inform the next phase of the study.

Quantitative Data Collection Following the qualitative phase, researchers develop a quantitative phase based on insights gained. This may involve creating surveys or structured instruments to measure specific variables identified in the qualitative analysis.

Quantitative Data Analysis Once quantitative data is collected, it is analysed statistically to test hypotheses, compare groups, or determine relationships between variables.

Interpretation Finally, researchers interpret the results by integrating findings from both the qualitative and quantitative phases, drawing comprehensive conclusions about the research question.

82 **One psychologist developed a questionnaire on employee 'Green behaviour',what would be the correct sequence in the context of this tool develpment.**

A. Identifying the discrimination index of the items
B. Calculation of Cronbach alpha
C. Developing a standard score norm
D. Confirmatory factor analysis
E. Exploratory factor analysis

Choose the correct answer from the options given below.

1 C, A, B, D, E 2 C, B, A, D, E
3 A, E, B, C, D 4 A, B, E, D, C

Ans. (4)

Exp. The correct sequence is A, B, E, D, C.

Identifying the discrimination index of the items This is the initial step where the psychologist evaluates how well each item (question) on the questionnaire differentiates between respondents who exhibit 'behaviour' and those who do not. A high discrimination index indicates that the item is effective in distinguishing between different levels of the behaviour being measured.

Calculation of Cronbach's alpha Once the items are identified, the next step is to assess the internal consistency of the questionnaire. Cronbach's alpha measures how closely related a set of items are as a group. A higher alpha (generally above 0.7) indicates good internal consistency.

Exploratory Factor Analysis After establishing the reliability of the items, exploratory factor analysis can be conducted to identify the underlying relationships between the items. This helps in understanding how items group together and the factors that influence employee 'Green behaviour'.

Confirmatory Factor Analysis Following exploratory analysis, confirmatory factor analysis is performed to test the hypothesis that the data fits a specific factor structure derived from the exploratory analysis. This validates the theoretical model of the questionnaire.

Developing a standard score norm Finally, once the validity and reliability of the questionnaire are established, norms can be created. This involves establishing standard scores that allow comparison between different respondents or groups based on their 'Green behaviour' scores.

83 Arrange the stages of group development as suggested by Tuckman.

A. Storming B. Performing
C. Forming D. Adjourning
E. Norming

Choose the correct answer from the options given below.

1 C, A, B, E, D 2 C, A, E, B, D
3 A, C, E, B, D 4 A, C, B, E, D

Ans. (2)

Exp. The correct answer is C, A, E, B, D.

The stages of group development as proposed by Bruce Tuckman are

1. **Forming** This is the initial stage where group members get to know each other. They establish ground rules, and the team is formed, but members are often polite and may avoid conflict.
2. **Storming** In this stage, conflicts and competition arise as group members begin to assert their individual personalities. Disagreements about tasks and goals can lead to tension and challenges within the group.
3. **Norming** After overcoming initial conflicts, the group begins to establish norms and standards for collaboration. Members develop a sense of unity and establish more effective communication and cooperation.
4. **Performing** At this stage, the group is functioning at a high level, with members collaborating effectively to achieve their goals. The focus shifts from interpersonal relationships to task completion and performance.
5. **Adjourning** This final stage occurs when the group disbands after achieving its objectives. Members reflect on their accomplishments and experiences, and the team's work comes to an end.

84 Development of psychoanalysis is marked by four phases namely antecedent analysis who were associated with each phase sequentially.

A. Breuer B. GT Fechner
C. Sullivan D. Adler

Choose the correct answer from the options given below.

1 B, A, D, C 2 A, B, C, D
3 C, B, A, D 4 D, C, B, A

Ans. (1)

Exp. The correct sequence is B, A, D, C.

GT Fechner Fechner's work in psychophysics laid the groundwork for understanding the connection between the mind and physical sensations, influencing later psychological theories, including those of Freud.

Breuer Josef Breuer was an influential figure in the early development of psychoanalysis. He introduced techniques such as catharsis and the talking cure, which were fundamental to the formation of psychoanalytic theory.

Adler Alfred Adler was initially part of Freud's circle but later developed his own theories, including the concept of individual psychology. He emphasised social interest and the importance of striving for superiority, which expanded the framework of psychoanalysis beyond Freud's original theories.

Sullivan Herbert 'Harry' Stack Sullivan was an American Neo-Freudian psychiatrist and psychoanalyst who held that 'personality can never be isolated from the complex interpersonal relationships in which a person lives' and that 'the field of psychiatry is the field of interpersonal relations under any and all circumstances in which such relations exist'.

85 The Programmer Evaluation Model of a community health programme has 4 steps arranged the following in sequences.

A. Outcome evaluation
B. Identifying goals and desired outcomes
C. Process evaluation
D. Impact evaluation

Choose the correct answer from the options given below.

1 B, C, A, D 2 B, C, D, A 3 C, B, D, A 4 C, D, B, A

Ans. (1)

Exp. The correct sequence is B, C, A, D.

Identifying goals and desired outcomes This is the foundational step in any evaluation model. Before assessing a programme, it's crucial to establish what the programme aims to achieve. Defining clear goals and desired outcomes sets the stage for all subsequent evaluations.

Process evaluation After identifying goals, the next step involves evaluating the implementation of the programme. Process evaluation examines whether the programme is being delivered as intended, including fidelity to the design, participant engagement, and the effectiveness of the strategies employed.

Outcome evaluation Once the programme has been implemented, outcome evaluation assesses the immediate effects of the programme on participants. This step measures whether the desired changes or benefits have been achieved.

Impact evaluation Finally, impact evaluation looks at the long-term effects and broader implications of the programme. This step assesses whether the programme has made a meaningful difference in the community and if the goals were met sustainably.

86 Given below are two statements, one is labelled as Assertion (A) and the other is labelled as Reason (R).

Assertion (A) One psychometrician used Cronbach's alpha to verify relibility of a general knowledge test with answers in True/False format.

Reason (R) Cronbach's alpha estimates the internal consistency of a test.

In the light of the above statements, choose the most appropriate answer from the options given below.

1 Both A and R are true and R is the correct explanation of A.
2 Both A and R are true, but R is not the correct explanation of A.
3 A is true, but R is false.
4 A is false, but R is true.

Ans. (4)

Exp. A is false, but R is true.

Cronbach's alpha is typically used for estimating the internal consistency of tests with continuous or Likert-scale data (e.g., ratings or multiple-choice questions with more than two options). However, it is not the best measure for binary items, such as True/False format tests, where other reliability measures like Kuder-Richardson Formula 20 (KR-20) are more appropriate. Cronbach's alpha does indeed estimate the internal consistency of a test, indicating how well the items in a test measure the same underlying construct.

87 Given below are two statements, one is labelled as Assertion (A) and the other is labelled as Reason (R).

Assertion (A) Allostasis is a process of adaptation to acute stress by releasing stress hormones in the event of challenge with a goal to restore the homeostasis.

Reason (R) HPA axis gets activated in the event of stress.

In the light of the above statements, choose the correct answer from the options given below.

1 Both A and R are true and R is the correct explanation of A.
2 Both A and R are true, but R is not the correct explanation of A.
3 A is true, but R is false.
4 A is false, but R is true.

Ans. (1)

Exp. Both A and R are true and R is the correct explanation of A.

Allostasis is indeed a process of adaptation to acute stress. It involves the release of stress hormones, such as cortisol, to help the body cope with and respond to challenges, aiming to restore stability or homeostasis. The hypothalamic-pituitary-adrenal (HPA) axis gets activated during stress, leading to the release of stress hormones, like cortisol, which play a key role in the allostatic process. Since the activation of the HPA axis directly explains how allostasis functions by releasing stress hormones to restore homeostasis.

88 Given below are two statements, one is labelled as Assertion (A) and the other is labelled as Reason (R).

Assertion (A) The researcher manipulating one or more variables is called an experiment.

Reason (R) A research design is one in which a variable is manipulated with a goal of identifying the causes of events is called experimental design.

In the light of the above statements, choose the correct answer from the options given below.

1 Both A and R are true and R is the correct explanation of A.
2 Both A and R are true, but R is not the correct explanation of A.
3 A is true, but R is false.
4 A is false, but R is true.

Ans. (2)

Exp. Both A and R are true, but R is not the correct explanation of A.

An experiment is a research process in which the researcher manipulates one or more variables to observe their effect on other variables, which defines experimental research. An experimental design involves manipulating variables with the goal of identifying causal relationships between events. However, the assertion simply defines what an experiment is (manipulation of variables), while the reason elaborates on the broader concept of experimental design, which is not directly explaining the assertion itself.

89 Given below are two statements, one is labelled as Assertion (A) and the other is labelled as Reason (R).

Assertion (A) Tabooed words are difficult to recognise.

Reason (R) Perception of the tabooed words is dependent or knowledge about sociocultural factors.

In the light of the above statements, choose the correct answer from the options given below.

1 Both A and R are true and R is the correct explanation of A.
2 Both A and R are true, but R is not the correct explanation of A.
3 A is true, but R is false.
4 A is false, but R is true.

Ans. (2)

Exp. Both A and R are true, but R is not the correct explanation of A.

Tabooed words can indeed be difficult to recognise due to emotional, cognitive, and psychological factors such as social discomfort or inhibition, which may interfere with quick recognition. The perception of taboo words is influenced by sociocultural factors, such as norms, values, and taboos within a society, which shape how people react to or process such words. However, the difficulty in recognising tabooed words is more likely due to emotional inhibition or cognitive interference rather than just the sociocultural knowledge about the words.

90 Given below are two statements, one is labelled as Assertion (A) and the other is labelled as Reason (R).

Assertion (A) Sexual derive is one of the physiological need.

Reason (R) Human beings cannot live without gratifying sexual drive.

In the light of the above statements, choose the correct answer from the options given below.

1 Both A and R are true and R is the correct explanation of A.
2 Both A and R are true, but R is not the correct explanation of A.
3 A is true, but R is false.
4 A is false, but R is true.

Ans. (3)

Exp. A is true, but R is false. Sexual drive is indeed considered one of the physiological needs in Maslow's hierarchy of needs, as it relates to biological functions essential for species survival. While sexual need is a natural drive, human beings can live without gratifying it. Unlike other physiological needs like food or water, which are essential for individual survival, sexual gratification is not necessary for sustaining life, but rather for reproduction.

Directions (Q. Nos. 91-95) *Read the passage and answer the questions that follows.*

Jeevan, a twelve year old boy was brought to the psychologist because he hated school. When the teacher was contacted she informed that Jeevan was unpopular in the class because of his show-off behaviour that even disrupled the class. Apparently, the parents at home used to find such behavioural entertaining and laughed and enjoyed it. The psychologist drew out a programme to bring a change in Jeevan's behaviour. She first helped the parents to understand what is show off behaviour and what is not. His parents were instructed by the psychologist to avoid paying attention to Jeevan's show off behaviour the teacher was instructed to praise other children whenever anyone helped a classmate in any way. The psychologist also added that each time Jeevan manifested show-off behaviour, the loud noise of bore-well digging be played him by the teacher. In fact, the psychologist used therapeutic interventions.

91 Teaching the parents to understand which is show off behaviours and which is not, is helping them with

1 discrimination
2 deactivation
3 generalisation
4 discretion

Ans. (1)

Exp. The correct answer is discrimination because the psychologist is helping Jeevan's parents differentiate between show-off behaviour and acceptable behaviour. Discrimination refers to the ability to recognise and distinguish between different types of behaviours.

92 By instructing the parents not to pay attention to Jeevan's show off behaviour at home the psychologist aimed at

1 punishment
2 stimulus discrimination
3 extinction
4 stimulus generalisation

Ans. (3)

Exp. The correct answer is extinction because the psychologist is instructing the parents to stop reinforcing Jeevan's show-off behaviour by not giving it attention. Extinction occurs when a behaviour decreases or disappears because it is no longer reinforced. By ignoring the behaviour, the psychologist aims to reduce and eventually eliminate Jeevan's show-off behaviour, as it no longer receives the positive reinforcement (attention) it previously did.

93 By instructing the teacher to praise those children whenever anyone helped their classmates the psychologist applied the factor of

1 positive reinforcement for Jeevan
2 modelling for Jeevan
3 reinforcement substitution for Jeevan
4 classical conditional for Jeevan

Ans. (2)

Exp. The psychologist applied the factor of modelling for Jeevan because praising the students who help their classmates provides a positive example for Jeevan to observe. This approach encourages Jeevan to imitate or model the prosocial behaviours of his peers, learning through observation how appropriate behaviours receive positive attention and reinforcement.

94 By instructing the teacher to play the loud noise of bore-well digging the psychologist introduced
1 Aversion therapy 2 Implosive therapy
3 Response shaping 4 Rogerian therapy

Ans. (1)

Exp. The correct answer is aversion therapy because the psychologist is introducing an unpleasant stimulus (the loud noise of bore-well digging) each time Jeevan displays show-off behaviour. Aversion therapy involves pairing an unwanted behaviour with an unpleasant or uncomfortable stimulus in order to reduce or eliminate that behaviour.

95 The approach of the psychologist in handling the problem of Jeevan can be summarised as
1 Gestalt therapy 2 Reality therapy
3 Behaviour therapy 4 Client-centered therapy

Ans. (3)

Exp. The correct answer is behaviour therapy because the psychologist's approach focuses on modifying Jeevan's problematic behaviours through specific interventions such as extinction (ignoring show-off behaviour), positive reinforcement (praising helpful behaviour), and aversion therapy (introducing a loud noise for undesirable behaviour). behaviour therapy aims to change maladaptive behaviours using learning principles like reinforcement, punishment, and conditioning, which is what the psychologist is applying in Jeevan's case.

Directions (Q. Nos. 96-100) *Read the passage carefully and answer the questions that follows.*

A researcher studied the variables that determined the Post Tracematic Growth PTG in the husbands of breastcancer surviours. The existing literature identified a number of factors such as emotional support, quality of marital relationship , exposure to individual with PTG, as important determinants of PTG in women. No information was available on PTG of the husbands of the patients. The researcher investigated the same factors influencing their husbands.

96 What is the design used by the researcher?
1 Correctional design
2 Quasi-experimental design
3 ABBA design
4 Single group pre and post test design

Ans. (2)

Exp. The study used a quasi-experimental design because it investigates the PTG in husbands of breast cancer survivors without any random assignment to treatment or control groups. The researcher focuses on pre-existing relationships and examines how factors like emotional support, marital quality and exposure to individuals with PTG influence the husbands' growth. The influence of these variables are studied in a natural context, rather than manipulating them or implementing an experimental treatment, which is characteristic of quasi-experimental designs.

97 What type of statistical analysis should be used by the researcher address his objective ?
1 One way ANOVA 2 't' test
3 Regression analysis 4 Chi-Square

Ans. (3)

Exp. Regression analysis is used in this study to examine the relationships between multiple independent variables (like emotional support and marital quality) and the dependent variable (PTG levels in husbands). It allows the researcher to determine how much each factor contributes to PTG while controlling for others, identifying significant predictors and providing insights into their interactions in a non-experimental context.

98 What is the criterion variable in this study?
1 Gender 2 Social context factor
3 Post-traumatic growth
4 Quality of marital relationship

Ans. (3)

Exp. A criterion variable is the outcome, result, or effect that researchers try to predict or explain in a study. Post-Traumatic Growth (PTG) is the criterion variable in this study because it represents the outcome that the researcher aims to predict based on the predictor variables such as emotional support, marital quality and exposure to PTG.

99 There are different domains of PGT. Which one of the following does not come under them?
1 Personal strength 2 Spiritual change
3 Relationship with others 4 Creativity

Ans. (4)

Exp. Creativity is not traditionally considered a domain of Post-Traumatic Growth (PTG). PTG is defined as a positive change in certain areas of life as an aftermath of trauma. A positive psychological change can happen in (at least) one of the following domains: (1) interpersonal relationships, (2) new possibilities, (3) personal strength, (4) spiritual change and (5) appreciation of life.

100 Which of the following will be correct hypothesis for the study?
1 The emotional support, quality of marital relationship and exposure to individual modelling of PTG will all contribute husband's experience of PTG.
2 PTG of the husbands will be different from that of wives.
3 The social context factors of husbands and the social context factors of wives will correlate.
4 The emotional support, quality of marital relationship and exposure to individuals modelling PTG will correlate.

Ans. (1)

Exp. Statement (1) is the correct hypothesis because it aligns with the study's aim to investigate whether emotional support, marital relationship quality and exposure to individuals with PTG contribute to the husband's experience of PTG, based on established factors influencing PTG in women.

UGC-NET
PSYCHOLOGY
SOLVED PAPER 2023 (June)

PAPER II

1 .... Vidya is the disciplined and systematic knowledge of the self and the environment attained through precise observation and critical reasoning.

1 Adhibhoulika 2 Adhyatmika
3 Bhoutika 4 Atmika

Ans. (2)

Exp. Adhyatmika, which refers to the knowledge or understanding of the inner self or spiritual reality. In Indian philosophical traditions, Adhyatma Vidya relates to the study and knowledge of one's inner consciousness and the metaphysical aspects of existence, emphasising self-awareness, self-realisation and the pursuit of spiritual wisdom.

2 The Bhagavad Gita has 18 Chapters (Adhyaya) named after some form of Yoga. Which is not the correct Adhyaya out of the following?

1 Dhyana Yoga 2 Aksara-Brahma Yoga
3 Purusottama Yoga 4 Jagrata Yoga

Ans. (4)

Exp. Jagrata Yoga is not the correct Adhyaya. The Bhagavad Gita consists of 18 Chapters, each focusing on different paths of Yoga or spiritual practices. Among the listed options, Dhyana Yoga (meditation), Aksara-Brahma Yoga (imperishable Brahman) and Purusottama Yoga (the supreme person) are legitimate chapters in the Gita.

3 Paedocentrecism is

1 Show the path of knowledge and guide the child to get knowledge
2 Centre on child's skill and behaviour
3 Involve child's behaviour with parents and teachers
4 Focus how the child works and the progress he/she makes

Ans. (1)

Exp. Paedocentrecism shows the path of knowledge and guide the child to get knowledge.

Paedocentrecism is an educational philosophy that places the child at the center of the learning process.

4 There are three types of post-modern therapies, which out of the following is not a part of post-modern therapy?

1 Solution focused therapy 2 Field based therapy
3 Narrative therapy 4 Collaborative therapy

Ans. (2)

Exp. Field based therapy is not a part of post-modern therapy.

Post-modern therapies focus on subjective experiences and socially constructed realities. Common types include

Solution-focused therapy concentrates on finding solutions to problems rather than focusing on the problems themselves.

5 To conduct a study on Anganwadi workers, the researcher randomly selected five districts out of 30 districts of a state and collected data from each and every Anganwadi worker from these five districts. This is an example of....

1 Stratified sampling 2 Cluster sampling
3 Quota sampling 4 Convenient sampling

Ans. (2)

Exp. This is an example of cluster sampling.

In cluster sampling, the population is divided into clusters (in this case, districts), and then a random selection of these clusters is made. After that, data is collected from every individual within the selected clusters.

6 One sports psychologist wanted to carry out a biographical study by writing and recording the experiences of a hockey legend. This is an example of ...... approach.

1 Phenomenology 2 Ethnography
3 Narrative study 4 Grounded theory approach

Ans. (3)

Exp. This is an example of Narrative study.

Researchers use narrative analysis to understand how research participants construct story and narrative from their own personal experience. In this case, the sports psychologist is focusing on writing and recording the life experiences of a hockey legend, making it a narrative approach.

7 "The present article describes a qualitative study of the career development of 16 prominent, highly achieving Indian women across six occupational fields. Our overall aim was to explore critical influences on the career development of these women particularly those related to their attainment of professional success".

The above mentioned purpose statement indicates a ……….

1 Phenomenological study
2 Grounded theory study
3 Ethnographic study
4 Case study

Ans. (2)

➲ ***Exp.*** Grounded theory is a systematic qualitative research method that collects empirical data first, and then creates a theory 'grounded' in the results. In this case, the study seeks to explore critical influences on the career development of highly achieving women, which aligns with the goal of generating a theory grounded in the data collected from the participants.

8 Standard deviation of sampling distribution is known as ……… .

1 Effect size 2 Sampling error
3 Parameter 4 Transitivity

Ans. (2)

➲ ***Exp.*** The standard deviation of the sampling distribution is referred to as the sampling error. It represents the variability or spread of sample statistics around the true population parameter, indicating how much the sample estimates are expected to vary from the actual population values due to chance.

9 The test requires someone to demonstrate his/her tailoring ability is best classified as

1 Self-report test
2 Standardised test
3 Test of maximal performance
4 Objective test

Ans. (3)

➲ ***Exp.*** A test of maximal performance requires individuals to demonstrate their ability or skill by performing tasks to the best of their ability. These assess the individual's ability to perform effectively under standard conditions. In this case, the person is required to show their tailoring ability, making it a performance-based test where their maximum skill level is assessed.

10 A basic set of beliefs that guide action is called

1 Axiology 2 Paradigm
3 Rhetorical 4 Ontology

Ans. (2)

➲ ***Exp.*** The collection of beliefs and concepts is known as a paradigm, which is a set of theories, assumptions and ideas that contribute to your world view or create the framework from which you operate every day.

11 A researcher carried out an analysis in which he looked for underlying theoretical structures in his construct.

Which one of the following design he used?

1 Linear regression
2 Analysis of variance
3 Exploratory factor analysis
4 Confirmatory factor analysis

Ans. (3)

➲ ***Exp.*** Exploratory Factor Analysis (EFA) is a statistical method used to identify underlying relationships between observed variables by grouping them into fewer factors. It helps researchers uncover patterns and structures in data, making it valuable for scale development and understanding complex relationships in various fields, including psychology and social sciences.

12 The formula used to estimate how many homogeneous test questions should be added to a test to raise its reliability to the described level is

1 Coefficient alpha
2 Spearman Brown formula
3 Pearson product moment correlation
4 KR-20

Ans. (4)

➲ ***Exp.*** KR-20 (Kuder-Richardson Formula 20) is a specific method used to estimate the reliability of a test that consists of dichotomous items (e.g. true/false, yes/no). It provides a measure of internal consistency reliability, indicating how well the items on the test measure the same underlying construct. The KR-20 formula can also be used to determine how many additional homogeneous items (questions) need to be added to the test to achieve a desired level of reliability, making it particularly useful for test development and evaluation.

13 Which parts of the brain are connected by the cerebral aqueduct?

1 Third and fourth ventricles of the brain
2 Lateral ventricles of the brain
3 Left and right frontal lobe
4 Frontal and parietal lobe

Ans. (1)

➲ ***Exp.*** Third and fourth ventricles of the brain are connected by the cerebral aqueduct. It also known as the aqueduct of Sylvius, is a narrow channel in the brain that connects the third ventricle to the fourth ventricle. It plays a crucial role in the flow of Cerebrospinal Fluid (CSF) between these two ventricles, helping to maintain proper pressure and provide nutrients to the brain. Any obstruction in the cerebral aqueduct can lead to conditions such as hydrocephalus, where there is an accumulation of CSF in the ventricles.

14 A unipolar neuron found in the soma to sensory system are sensitive to

1 Visual sensations 2 Auditory sensations
3 Tactile sensations 4 Olfactory sensations

Ans. (3)

➲ *Exp.* Unipolar neurons are a type of sensory neuron commonly found in the soma to sensory system are sensitive to tactile sensations. They are characterised by having a single process that splits into two branches: one that extends to the periphery (skin, muscles, etc.) and another that extends to the spinal cord. These neurons are primarily responsible for transmitting tactile sensations, such as touch, pressure and pain, from the skin and other sensory receptors to the central nervous system. This makes them essential for processing tactile information and contributing to the sense of touch.

15 Amygdala, part of the Limbic system, is specifically responsible for one of the following functions

1 Thinking 2 Leaming 3 Memory 4 Emotion

Ans. (4)

➲ *Exp.* The amygdala is a key structure in the limbic system of the brain, primarily involved in processing and regulating emotions. It plays a crucial role in the perception of emotions such as fear, anger, and pleasure and is essential for the formation of emotional memories. The amygdala helps to evaluate emotional significance in stimuli and triggers appropriate emotional responses, making it integral to our ability to respond to emotionally charged situations.

16 Which one of the following areas is not located in the Temperal Lobe?

1 Area for perception of body sensations such as, heat, cold, touch, pressure and pain
2 Area for perception of movements and recognition of faces
3 Broca's speech area
4 Primary auditory area

Ans. (1 & 3)

➲ *Exp.* The correct answers are 1 and 3.

Area for perception of body sensations such as, heat, cold, touch, pressure, and pain: This area is actually located in the parietal lobe. It's responsible for processing sensory information from the body, including touch, temperature and pain.

Broca's speech area: While Broca's area is involved in speech production, its primarily located in the frontal lobe, specifically in the inferior frontal gyrus. It plays a crucial role in formulating and expressing language.

17 What is meant by stroboscopic motion?

1 We perceive an object is in motion whenever its image moves across our retina
2 Loss in sensitivity to motion
3 Tracking objects only in darkness
4 Tracking only the upward motion of objects

Ans. (1)

➲ *Exp.* The correct answer is 'we perceive an object is in motion whenever its image moves across our retina'.

Stroboscopic motion refers to the phenomenon where we perceive continuous motion from a series of static images that are displayed in rapid succession. This effect is commonly seen in animation and movies, where still images are shown in quick succession to create the illusion of movement.

18 What is Thorndike's law of effect?

1 Behaviour that operates on the environment producing consequences
2 Behaviours followed by favourable consequences become more likely and that behaviours followed by unfavourable consequences become less likely to occur
3 Learning that certain events occur together
4 Behaviour that occurs as an automatic response to some stimulus

Ans. (2)

➲ *Exp.* Thorndike's Law of Effect is behaviours followed by favourable consequences become more likely, and that behaviours followed by unfavourable consequences become less likely to occur.

19 When a lighting flashes nearby, we wince and start to prepare ourselves for the thunder to follow. This response to impending thunder is known as

1 Unconditioned stimulus
2 Unconditioned response
3 Conditioned stimulus
4 Conditioned response

Ans. (4)

➲ *Exp.* This response to impending thunder is known as Conditioned response. When we see a flash of lightning, we automatically prepare for the thunder, which is the conditioned response.

20 Which among the following is true about process of extinction of behaviour in classical conditioning?

1 Increase in magnitude of CR
2 Gradual diminishing of CR
3 CS and UCS develop strong association
4 UCS follows CS

Ans. (2)

➲ *Exp.* In classical conditioning, extinction occurs when the Conditioned Stimulus (CS) is repeatedly presented without the Unconditioned Stimulus (UCS), leading to a gradual decrease in the Conditioned Response (CR). This process demonstrates how learned behaviours can fade when the reinforcement that established the association is removed.

21 What is meant by Stroop Effect?

1 The tendency to focus on a superficial feature of the problem at hand
2 Automaticity of the reading process
3 Planning before acting
4 Role of silence in language

Ans. (2)

Exp. The Stroop Effect refers to the difficulty people experience when trying to name the colour of the ink used to print a word when the word itself spells a different colour (e.g., the word 'red' printed in blue ink). This occurs because reading is an automatic process, and the brain automatically processes the meaning of the word, interfering with the task of naming the ink colour. The Stroop Effect demonstrates how the automaticity of reading can conflict with other cognitive tasks, making it harder to override this automatic response.

22 Which of the following is not a meta cognitive activity?

1 Wondering how one could have been mistaken
2 Reflecting on our own thinking process
3 Theory of mind
4 Communicating one's present postal address

Ans. (4)

Exp. Communicating one's present postal address is not a metacognitive activity. Metacognitive activities involve thinking about one's own thinking, such as reflecting on or regulating cognitive processes. Examples include self-awareness of thought patterns, evaluating mistakes and understanding others' mental states (theory of mind). Communicating one's postal address, however, is a straightforward act of recalling information, not involving reflection on the thought process, making it unrelated to metacognition.

23 Which of the following is true about the concept of heritability?

1 The heritability of a trait refers to differences in percentages of a trait within an individual
2 Heritability refers to a population, not to individual
3 The heritability of a trait is a single and fixed number
4 Heritability tells us about the source of mean differences between groups

Ans. (2)

Exp. Statement (2) is true about the concept of heritability.
Heritability is a statistic used in the fields of breeding and genetics that estimates the degree of variation in a phenotypic trait in a population that is due to genetic variation between individuals in that population. It does not apply to individuals but rather to the differences among people in a group.

24 Which of the following is not a chromosomal disorder characterised by subaverage intellectual functioning?

1 Down syndrome 2 Fragile X syndrome
3 Cerebral palsy 4 Trisomy 13

Ans. (3)

Exp. Cerebral palsy is a neurological disorder caused by brain damage that occurs before or during birth or in early infancy. It primarily affects motor skills, muscle tone and movement, but it is not a chromosomal disorder. In contrast, Down syndrome, Fragile X syndrome and Trisomy 13 are all genetic or chromosomal disorders that can be associated with intellectual disabilities. Therefore, cerebral palsy differs in that it is not directly related to chromosomal abnormalities.

25 As per Values in Action (VIA), classification of character strengths and virtues are as under

1 Character strengths - 20; Virtues - 06
2 Character strengths - 24; Virtues - 06
3 Character strengths - 18; Virtues - 06
4 Character strengths - 24; Virtues - 04

Ans. (2)

Exp. According to Values in Action (VIA) classification, there are 24 character strengths organised under 6 broad virtues. It is given by Christopher Peterson and Martin Seligman. These virtues represent core aspects of good character, and the strengths are traits that people exhibit to achieve these virtues.

26 Three stage model of chronic stress formulated by Hans Selye is called

1 GAS - General Adjustment Syndrome
2 GAS - General Adjustment System
3 GAS - General Adaptation System
4 GAS - General Adaptation Syndrome

Ans. (4)

Exp. Hans Selye's General Adaptation Syndrome (GAS) is a three-stage model that explains the body's physiological response to chronic stress.

27 The emergence of the Oedipus and Castration complexes are the chief events of which stage of development in the Freudian theory?

1 Oral stage 2 Anal stage
3 Phallic stage 4 Genital stage

Ans. (3)

Exp. In Freud's psychosexual development theory, the phallic stage occurs between the ages of 3 and 6.

28 Who is the author of the book "Escape from Freedom"?

1 Fromm 2 Sullivan 3 Adler 4 Horney

Ans. (1)

Exp. Erich Fromm is the author of the book "Escape from Freedom" (1941). In the book, Fromm explores humanity's shifting relationship with freedom, how individual freedom can cause fear, anxiety, and alienation and how many people seek relief by relinquishing freedom.

29 Women are likely to gain more number of valued positions during the time of crisis. This is referred as ....

1 Glass ceiling effect 2 Glass-cliff effect
3 Tokenism 4 Singlism

Ans. (2)

Exp. The glass-cliff effect refers to the phenomenon where women (and other underrepresented groups) are more likely to be promoted to leadership positions during the times of crisis or instability, when the risk of failure is higher.

30 Efforts to cope with the knowledge that we will die is known as ....

1 Magical Thinking 2 Terror Management
3 Planning Fallacy 4 Availability Heuristics

Ans. (2)

Exp. Terror Management Theory (TMT) explains that humans cope with the fear of death by developing psychological mechanisms to manage this terror. People create and maintain cultural world views, beliefs and self-esteem to give life meaning and a sense of permanence, which helps them cope with the knowledge of their mortality. This process involves efforts to mitigate existential anxiety that arises from the awareness of death.

31 Which therapeutic approach to counselling is based on the premise 'You are the architect of your life'?

1 Gestalt 2 Existential 3 Adlerian 4 Reality

Ans. (2)

Exp. The existential therapeutic approach emphasises individual responsibility and the idea that people have the freedom to shape their own lives and create meaning. The premise "You are the architect of your life" aligns with the core tenets of existential therapy, which focus on helping individuals confront their existence, make authentic choices and embrace the responsibility that comes with those choices. This approach encourages clients to explore their values, beliefs and the search for meaning in life, ultimately empowering them to design their own paths.

32 Late adulthood often involves a gradual withdrawal from the world on physical, psychological and social levels. Which theory supports this?

1 Disengagement theory
2 Activity theory
3 Continuity theory
4 Selective isolation theory

Ans. (1)

Exp. Late adulthood often involves a gradual withdrawal from the world on physical, psychological and social levels. This was formulated by Cumming and Henry in 1961 in the book Growing Old.

33 Simple skills develop in infants separately and independently and later develop into more complex skills.
Which governing principle of growth is applied here?

1 Proximodistal principle
2 Cephalocaudal principle
3 Principle of hierarchical integration
4 Principle of independence of the systems

Ans. (3)

Exp. The principle of hierarchical integration states that simple skills typically develop separately and independently, but that these simple skills are integrated into more complex ones.

34 Which of the following is not correct about REBT?

1 REBT aims to help individuals think clearly, feel appropriately and act effectively.
2 REBT uses the A-B-C theory of personality to identify client's problems.
3 The focus of the therapist is on the feelings and behaviour of the individual rather than on the incident that induced the negative feelings.
4 REBT aims at a combination of philosophical change with cognitive emotional and behavioural strategies.

Ans. (3)

Exp. Statement (3) is not correct about REBT.
In Rational Emotive Behaviour Therapy (REBT), the therapist focuses not just on the individual's feelings and behaviours but also on the incidents or beliefs that lead to those feelings and behaviours. It emphasises that emotional disturbances often arise from irrational beliefs about events and therefore, understanding and challenging these beliefs is crucial for therapeutic progress. The goal is to help clients recognise and change the underlying beliefs that contribute to negative emotions and behaviours.

35 Which of the following is correct about the impact of stress on immune system of an individual?

1 The immune system is weakened because of an increase in the blood pressure in the face of stress.
2 Increased release of glucose from the liver during stress neutralises the immune functioning of the WBC.
3 Increased level of ACTH in blood destroys the T cells.
4 Increased level of cortisol ill blood destroys the T cells.

Ans. (4)

Exp. In the context of stress, the release of Adrenocorticotropic Hormone (ACTH) from the pituitary gland stimulates the adrenal glands to produce cortisol, a hormone that can have immunosuppressive effects. While it is true that increased levels of cortisol negatively affect immune functioning, the statement about ACTH directly destroying T cells reflects an aspect of how stress hormones impact the immune system.

36 Which of the following contributes to maintaining a health risk behaviour?

1 Lack of knowledge and the health risk behaviour helping the individual in avoidance of pain
2 The incentive ingrained in health risk behaviour and availability of leisure time
3 Avoidance of pain and need to spend money
4 Avoidance of pain and high self-efficacy

Ans. (1)

Exp. Maintaining health risk behaviours often stems from a lack of knowledge regarding the potential negative consequences of those behaviours. Individuals may engage in unhealthy behaviours (like smoking or overeating) because they believe these actions help them avoid emotional or physical pain (e.g. stress relief or temporary comfort).

37 Which of the following describes resilience?

1 Individuals at risk whose performance is better than expected
2 Individuals in enriched environment excelling in performance
3 Individuals with very good performance sliding down following a traumatic experience
4 Individuals who avoid risks and are happy with their average performance

Ans. (1)

Exp. Resilience refers to the ability of individuals to withstand or recover from difficult conditions or adversity. It is often characterised by individuals at risk (due to factors such as socio-economic challenges, trauma or other stressors) who perform better than what might be anticipated given their circumstances. This positive adaptation and successful functioning in the face of challenges demonstrate resilience, highlighting their ability to overcome difficulties and thrive despite adverse situations.

38 Which of the following does not come under Cardiovascular Disease (CVD)?

1 Myocardial infarction 2 Crohn's disease
3 Angina pectoris 4 Cardiomyopathy

Ans. (2)

Exp. Crohn's disease does not come under Cardiovascular disease (CVD). Crohn's disease is a type of inflammatory Bowel Disease (IBD) that primarily affects the gastrointestinal tract, leading to symptoms such as abdominal pain, diarrhea and weight loss. It is not classified as a cardiovascular disease.

39 Which one of the following is not a principal characteristic of the REM sleep?

1 EEG desynchrony (Rapid Irregular Waves)
2 Lack of muscle tonus
3 Lack of genital activity
4 Dreams

Ans. (3)

Exp. Lack of genital activity is not a principal characteristic of the REM sleep.

During REM (Rapid Eye Movement) sleep, several principal characteristics are observed

- **EEG desynchrony** (Rapid Irregular Waves) The brain exhibits a pattern similar to wakefulness, with rapid and irregular brain waves.
- **Lack of muscle tonus** There is significant muscle atonia or lack of muscle tone during REM sleep, which prevents the body from acting out dreams.
- **Dreams** REM sleep is strongly associated with vivid dreaming.

40 Which of the following behaviours is not a stage of observational learning?

1 Be motivated to reproduce the behaviour
2 Remember what was observed
3 Exploring the environment
4 Pay attention to the model's behaviour

Ans. (3)

Exp. Exploring the environment, while it can be a part of learning in general, is not a specific stage of observational learning. It does not directly pertain to the process of learning through observation of others, making it the correct choice in this context. In the context of observational learning, which was primarily studied by Albert Bandura.

41 The basic aspects of the philosophy of early Buddhism fall into

I. Theory of Knowledge
II. Theory of Society
III. Theory of Reality
IV. Theory of Perception

Choose the most appropriate answer from the options given below.

1 I and IV 2 I, II and III 3 I, III and IV 4 II and IV

Ans. (2)

Exp. Options I, II and III are correct.

The basic aspects of the philosophy of early Buddhism can be grouped into the following areas

Theory of Knowledge Early Buddhism emphasises understanding and insight, particularly through the Four Noble Truths and the Eightfold Path, which guide individuals toward enlightenment and wisdom.

Theory of Society Early Buddhism addresses ethical conduct and the nature of human relationships within society, promoting compassion, non-attachment and the importance of community.

Theory of Reality Early Buddhist philosophy explores the nature of existence, impermanence and the concept of anatta (non-self), which challenges conventional views of reality.

However, Theory of Perception, while relevant in broader philosophical contexts, is not a central aspect of early Buddhist philosophy.

42 Existentialism is associated with which of the following names?

I. Soren Kierkegaard II. Vlademier
III. Friedrich Nietzsche IV. Husserl

Choose the most appropriate answer from the options given below.

1 I and II 2 I, II and III
3 I, III and IV 4 I, II and IV

Ans. (3)

Exp. Options I, III and IV are correct.

Existentialism is a philosophical movement that focuses on individual freedom, choice and the meaning of existence. The key figures associated with existentialism include

Soren Kierkegaard Often considered the father of existentialism, Kierkegaard emphasised personal choice, faith and the individual's subjective experience.

Friedrich Nietzsche Nietzsche is known for his exploration of themes such as the 'will to power,' the idea of eternal recurrence, and the rejection of absolute truths, all of which are central to existentialist thought.

Edmund Husserl Although Husserl is primarily known as the founder of phenomenology, his work on consciousness and experience has influenced existentialist thinkers.

However, Vlademier does not appear to be a widely recognised figure in existential philosophy.

43 Which of the following should be assured before going for parametric Analysis of Variance?

I. Independence of scores of the subjects
II. Categorical dependent variable
III. Random assignment of subjects to the treatments
IV. Homogeneity of variance of the subjects' scores

Choose the most appropriate answer from the options given below.

1 I, II, III and IV
2 I, II and III
3 I, III and IV
4 II, III and IV

Ans. (3)

Exp. Statements I, III and IV are correct.

Before conducting a parametric Analysis of Variance (ANOVA), certain assumptions must be met to ensure the validity of the results

Independence of scores of the subjects This means that the scores of one subject should not influence the scores of another. Each subject's response must be independent.

Random assignment of subjects to the treatments Randomly assigning subjects to different treatment groups helps to control for biases and ensures that groups are comparable.

Homogeneity of variance of the subjects' scores This assumption requires that the variances among the groups being compared are approximately equal. It is important for the robustness of the ANOVA results.

However, categorical dependent variable is not a requirement for parametric ANOVA. Instead, ANOVA requires a continuous dependent variable.

44 Which of the following are true about multiple regression?

I. It is linear regression.
II. There are more than one criterion.
III. There are more than one predictor.
IV. It doesn't have intercept constant.

Choose the most appropriate answer from the options given below.

1 II and III 2 I and III
3 I, II and IV 4 II, III and IV

Ans. (2)

Exp. Statements I and III are correct.

Multiple regression is a statistical technique that models the relationship between multiple predictor variables and a single outcome (criterion) variable.

Multiple regression is a form of linear regression that extends the concept to include multiple predictors.

Multiple regression involves two or more predictor variables used to predict the outcome variable.

45 Which of correct about Multitrait - Multimethod design?

I. Investigates construct validity
II. Associates with Coombs and Holladay
III. Associates with Campbell and Fiske
IV. Investigates composite reliability

Choose the most appropriate answer from the options given below.

1 I and II 2 I and III
3 II and III 4 II and IV

Ans. (2)

Exp. Options I and III are correct.

The Multitrait-Multimethod (MTMM) design is a framework used in psychology and social sciences to assess the construct validity of a measure.

The MTMM design is specifically used to evaluate construct validity by examining the relationships between different traits measured by various methods.

The MTMM approach was introduced by Donald T. Campbell and DW. Fiske in their seminal work in 1959, making it closely linked to their research on validity.

46 In the context of formula for Cohen's Kappa

I. $K = \dfrac{f_0 - f_c}{N - f_c}$ II. f_0 = observed frequency
III. f_c = expected frequency
IV. N = Overall total of data points in the frequency matrix

Choose the most appropriate answer from the options given below.

1 I and II 2 I and III
3 I, II and III 4 I, II, III and IV

Ans. (4)

Exp. The correct answer is I, II, III and IV.

In the context of Cohen's Kappa, which is a statistical measure used to assess the level of agreement between two raters or evaluators, the following statements are true

- $K = (f_0 - f_c) / (N - f_c)$: This formula represents Cohen's Kappa, where f_0 is the observed frequency of agreement, fa is the expected frequency of agreement under the assumption of random chance, and N is the total number of observations.
- f_0 refers to the observed frequency of agreements between the raters.
- f_c represents the expected frequency of agreement that would occur by chance.
- N is the total count of all data points being analysed.

47 A specific brain region can be destroyed by some of the following methods. Choose the correct answers.

I. Immunocytochemical method
II. Radio frequency lesion method
III. Excitotoxic lesion method
IV. Fluorogold method
V. Experimental ablation method

Choose the most appropriate answer from the options given below.

1 II, III and V 2 I, II and III
3 III, IV and V 4 I, IV and V

Ans. (1)

➲ ***Exp.*** Options II, III and V are correct.

The following methods are commonly used to destroy specific brain regions in research

Radio frequency lesion method This technique uses high frequency radio waves to generate heat, effectively destroying targeted brain tissue.

Excitotoxic lesion method This method involves the use of excitatory amino acids (like kainic acid) to selectively damage and destroy neurons in a specific area by overstimulating them, leading to cell death.

Experimental ablation method This general approach involves surgically removing or damaging a specific brain area to study its functions and effects on behaviour or physiology.

However, the other methods are

Immunocytochemical method This is used to visualise specific proteins or antigens in brain tissue, not to destroy brain regions.

Fluorogold method This method involves using a fluorescent tracer to label neurons and track their connections, but it does not destroy brain tissue.

48 Which of the following is true about negative reinforcement?

I. It strengthens a response.
II. It works by reducing or removing something undesirable or unpleasant.
III. Fastening a seat belt in car to turn off beeping sound is an example of negative reinforcement.
IV. It weakens a response.
V. It works by increasing desirability and pleasantness of a stimulus.

Choose the most appropriate answer from the options given below.

1 IV and II 2 I, II and III
3 I and V 4 IV, II and III

Ans. (2)

➲ ***Exp.*** Statements I, II and III are true about negative reinforcement.

Negative reinforcement increases the likelihood of a behaviour by following it with the removal of an aversive stimulus.

Negative reinforcement involves taking away an unpleasant stimulus to enhance the desired behaviour.

In this example, the act of fastening the seatbelt removes the unpleasant beeping sound, reinforcing the behaviour of buckling up.

49 Which of the following are true about perceptual constancy?

I. It applies to perception of size and colour only.
II. Many visual illusions may be explained by the various constancies.
III. Constancies occur in all sensory modalities.
IV. It keeps the appearance of objects the same in spite of large variations in the initial representation of the stimuli received by the sense organs that are engendered by various environmental factors.

Choose the most appropriate answer from the options given below.

1 I, II and IV 2 II, III and IV
3 I and II 4 Only IV

Ans. (2)

➲ ***Exp.*** Statements II, III and IV are true about perceptual constancy.

Perceptual constancies can help explain how and why certain visual illusions occur, as they illustrate how our brain maintains a stable perception of objects despite changes in viewing conditions.

While the term is often discussed in the context of visual perception, constancies can also occur in other sensory modalities, such as hearing (e.g., pitch constancy) and touch.

Perceptual constancy allows us to perceive objects as stable and unchanging in size, shape and colour, even when the sensory input changes due to distance, angle, lighting or other environmental factors.

50 What is meant by theory of mind?

I. People's idea about feelings perceptions and thoughts of self and others and the behaviour these might predict.
II. A term first coined by Daniel Goleman.
III. People's ideas about their own and other's mental states.
IV. By the age of six months, children worldwide display an advanced level of theory of mind acquisition.
V. People with autism are said to have an impaired theory of mind.

Choose the most appropriate answer from the options given below.

1 I and III 2 I, III and V 3 I and II 4 III and V

Ans. (2)

➲ ***Exp.*** Statements I, III and V are correct about theory of mind.

People's idea about feelings, perceptions and thoughts of self and others and the behaviour these might predict : This statement accurately captures the essence of theory of mind, which involves understanding that others have their own thoughts, feelings, and beliefs that may differ from one's own.

People's ideas about their own and others' mental states : This statement is also true and aligns with the concept of theory of mind, emphasising the understanding of one's own and others' mental states.

People with autism are said to have an impaired theory of mind : Individuals with Autism Spectrum Disorder (ASD) often struggle with understanding others' perspectives, thoughts and feelings, which is a key aspect of theory of mind.

51 Which of the following is true about a Phoneme?

I. It refers to the disrupted language of a patient with aphasia.
II. Every language has its own set of phonemes.
III. A phonema is a category of speech sounds.
IV. It is the smallest twit of language that carries meaning.

Choose the most appropriate answer from the options given below.

1 Only I 2 II and IV 3 II and III 4 Only IV

***Ans.* (3)**

Exp. Statements II and III are correct.

A phoneme is the smallest unit of sound in a language that can distinguish one word from another. Each language has its own unique set of phonemes. For example, the phoneme /p/ distinguishes pat from bat in English.

A phoneme represents a category of similar speech sounds that are perceived to be the same within a language. Different phonetic realisations of the same phoneme are called allophones.

52 Self-determination theory of Deci and Ryan focused on following basic needs to explain well-being.

I. Creativity
II. Engagement
III. Competence
IV. Relatedness
V. Autonomy

Choose the most appropriate answer from the options given below.

1 I, II and III
2 III, IV and V
3 II, IV and V
4 I, III and IV

***Ans.* (2)**

Exp. Options III, IV and V are correct.

Self-Determination Theory (SDT) by Deci and Ryan identifies three basic psychological needs that are essential for promoting well-being and motivation.

Competence The need to feel effective in interacting with the environment and achieving desired outcomes. It is the desire to experience mastery and success.

Relatedness The need to establish meaningful relationships and feel connected to others. This involves feeling cared for and having a sense of belonging.

Autonomy The need to feel in control of one's own behaviours and goals. It refers to the sense of being the agent of one's own life, making choices according to one's values.

However, creativity and engagement are important for well-being but are not part of the three core needs defined in SDT. Creativity might be an outcome of fulfilling the need for autonomy and competence and engagement can result from satisfying these psychological needs, but they are not primary components of SDT.

53 The structural components of the collective unconscious (lung) are called by different names.

I. Archetypes
II. Imagoes
III. Creative ego
IV. Libido
V. Dominants

Choose the most appropriate answer from the options given below.

1 I, V and III
2 II, III and IV
3 I, II, III and V
4 I, II and V

***Ans.* (4)**

Exp. Options I, II and V are correct.

In Carl Jung's theory of the collective unconscious, the structural components are often referred to by various terms. The most important components are

Archetypes These are universal, inherited symbols or patterns of behaviour found in the collective unconscious. Archetypes represent fundamental human experiences, such as the hero, the mother and the shadow.

Imagoes These are idealised images or figures that exist in the collective unconscious, often related to relationships (e.g. the idealised image of a parent or partner).

Dominants Jung used the term dominants to describe powerful forces within the collective unconscious, which could be archetypes that influence an individuals thoughts and behaviours.

54 In late adulthood, retirement from job follows specific stages, as per Atchley (1982).

I. Honeymoon
II. Disenchantment
III. Craving for money
IV. Reorientation
V. Social withdrawal

Choose the most appropriate answer from the options given below.

1 I, II and V
2 II, III and IV
3 III, IV and V
4 I, II and IV

***Ans.* (4)**

Exp. Options I, II and IV are correct.

According to Atchley's model of retirement (1982), retirement typically follows a series of psychological stages

Honeymoon This is the initial stage after retirement, where individuals often feel excited and free, enjoying their newfound leisure time and freedom.

Disenchantment After the honeymoon phase, some retirees may experience disenchantment, realising that retirement may not be as fulfilling or exciting as they had imagined. This can lead to feelings of disappointment or restlessness.

Reorientation In this stage, retirees begin to reassess their situation and start to adapt to their new lifestyle. They may find new activities or ways to gain a sense of purpose and satisfaction, leading to a more fulfilling retirement.

55 As indicated by reflexes, a new born baby responds to touch around the area of

I. Head, neck and mouth II. Belly, foot and neck
III. Mouth, calf and head IV. Mouth and foot
V. Palm

Choose the most appropriate answer from the options given below.

1 I and II 2 II and III 3 III and II 4 IV and V

Ans. (4)

Exp. Options IV and V are correct.

Newborn babies display reflexes that are essential for survival and early development, responding to stimuli in certain areas of their body

Mouth and foot : Newborns have strong reflexes around the mouth (such as the rooting reflex, where the baby turns their head toward a touch on the cheek or mouth) and foot (such as the Babinski reflex, where the toes fan out when the foot is stroked). These reflexes are critical for feeding and basic motor responses.

Palm : Newborns also respond to touch on their palm, which triggers the grasp reflex, causing them to close their hand around an object placed in it. The other combinations (head, neck, belly, calf) are not primary areas where newborn reflexes are typically triggered.

56 Etiological models of psychopathology includes

I. Nervous system going awry II. Social conflicts
III. Intrapsychic conflicts
IV. Learning dysfunctional behaviour
V. Indulgence in religion.

Choose the most appropriate answer from the options given below.

1 I, II and III 2 II, III, IV and V
3 I, III and IV 4 I, III, IV and V

Ans. (3)

Exp. Options I, III and IV are correct.

Etiological models of psychopathology aim to understand the causes (etiology) of psychological disorders.

Nervous system going awry This option refers to biological or neurological factors that can lead to psychopathology. Issues in the nervous system, such as neurotransmitter imbalances or brain structure abnormalities, are significant in understanding certain mental disorders.

Intrapsychic conflicts This relates to psychological models, particularly psychodynamic theories, which emphasise internal conflicts within the mind (such as unconscious desires and feelings) that can lead to psychological distress.

Learning dysfunctional behaviour This aligns with behavioural models, which suggest that maladaptive behaviours are learned through conditioning or reinforcement processes. This perspective focuses on how behaviours can develop and be maintained through environmental interactions.

While the other two options social conflicts and indulgence in religion, can contribute to psychological issues, they do not typically relate to the core etiological models of psychopathology.

57 Conflicts are readily kindled and fueled by

I. Competition II. Conciliation
III. Cooperation IV. Misperception
V. Social dilemma

Choose the most appropriate answer from the options given below.

1 I, II and III 2 II, III and IV
3 III, IV and V 4 I, IV and V

Ans. (4)

Exp. Options I, IV and V are correct.

Conflicts can often be ignited and intensified by the following factors

Competition When individuals or groups are in competition for limited resources, it can lead to conflict. Competition often heightens tensions and creates an adversarial atmosphere.

Misperception Conflicts can be fueled by misunderstandings or misperceptions about intentions, beliefs, or actions of others. When people misinterpret each other's motives, it can lead to unnecessary conflict and escalation.

Social Dilemmas Social dilemmas arise when individuals face a choice between their own interests and the common good. This can create conflicts, particularly when individuals prioritise their own needs over the collective interests of a group, leading to tension and strife.

However, conciliation and cooperation typically serve to reduce conflict rather than fuel it. Conciliation involves negotiation and compromise, while cooperation emphasises working together towards mutual goals.

58 What is meant by bottom-up processing?

I. It always distorts our observations.
II. Sensory analysis that starts at the entry level.
III. When our experience and expectations guide our perception.
IV. Higher level mental processes are involved.
V. Helps to detect the lines, angles and colours.

Choose the most appropriate answer from the options given below.

1 I and II 2 I, III and IV
3 II and V 4 III and V

Ans. (3)

Exp. II and V are correct.

Bottom-up processing refers to the way sensory information is processed starting from the basic sensory input to build up to a final perception.

Sensory analysis that starts at the entry level : This statement accurately describes bottom-up processing. It begins with the raw sensory data that is gathered from the environment, which is then processed to form a perception.

Helps to detect the lines, angles, and colours : This statement is also true for bottom-up processing. It involves recognising basic visual elements like lines, angles, and colours as part of the initial sensory input that contributes to overall perception.

59 Robert Sternberg proposed a triarchic theory of following intelligence types

I. Creative II. Analogical III. Analytical
IV. Emotional V. Practical

Choose the most appropriate answer from the options given below.

1 I, III and V
2 I, II and IV
3 I, II and III
4 I, III and IV

***Ans.* (1)**

Exp. Options I, III and V are correct.

Robert Sternberg's Triarchic Theory of Intelligence identifies three main types of intelligence

Creative Intelligence This type refers to the ability to generate new ideas, think outside the box and use novel approaches to solve problems. It involves creativity and the capacity to adapt to new situations.

Analytical Intelligence This type involves the ability to analyse, evaluate and compare information. It is often what is measured by traditional intelligence tests and relates to problem-solving and critical thinking skills.

Practical Intelligence This type refers to the ability to apply knowledge to real-world situations. It involves common sense and practical skills to navigate everyday challenges effectively.

60 Which of the following is/are related to developmental screening tests?

I. Gesell Developmental Schedule
II. Denver Developmental Screening Test
III. Holland Developmental Schedule
IV. Bruner Developmental Screening Test

Choose the most appropriate answer from the options given below.

1 I and III
2 II and IV
3 I and II
4 III and IV

***Ans.* (3)**

Exp. I and II are correct.

Developmental screening tests are tools used to assess a child's developmental progress and identify potential delays or disabilities.

The Gesell Developmental Schedules are a standardised way to evaluate a child's development from one month to five years old. The schedules were developed by Dr. Arnold Gesell, an American pediatrician and child psychologist, and his colleagues. The schedules are based on observation and measure a child's development in five areas: Gross motor, fine-motor, language, personal-social and adaptive.

The Denver Developmental Screening Test (DDST) was introduced in 1967 to identify young children, up to age six, with developmental problems. The tests address four domains of child development: personal-social (for example, waves bye-bye), fine motor and adaptive (puts block in cup), language (combines words) and gross motor (hops). The other two options are not recognised as developmental screening tests.

61 Human personality is analysed into five factors as viewed by Buddhism. Choose the correct factors included in personality.

I. Material, Perception, Feeling
II. Disposition, Consciousness
III. Thinking, Belief, Intelligence
IV. Memory, Attention

Choose the most appropriate answer from the options given below.

1 I and II
2 II and III
3 III and IV
4 I and IV

***Ans.* (1)**

Exp. I and II are correct.

In the context of Buddhism, personality is often analysed through a framework that encompasses various factors contributing to an individual's experience and behaviour. The relevant factors include

Material, Perception, Feeling are related to the concept of the Five Aggregates (Pañca Khandha), which are crucial in Buddhist philosophy. They consist of form (material), sensation (feeling), perception, mental formations and consciousness. The aggregates help explain how individuals construct their experience and personality.

Disposition can relate to an individual's tendencies or character traits, while consciousness is a fundamental aspect of personal experience in Buddhism. These elements reflect the mental processes that contribute to one's personality.

62 Which of the following is true about stimulus generalisation?

I. People's emotional reactions to one stimulus generalise to similar stimuli.
II. With repeated exposure and reinforcement dogs can differentiate between types of sounds.
III. Normally desirable foods such as cakes and pastries are unappealing when shaped to resemble dog's feces.
IV. Sudden appearance of forgotten response.

Choose the most appropriate answer from the options given below.

1 I and IV
2 I and III
3 I and II
4 II and IV

***Ans.* (2)**

Exp. I and III are correct.

Stimulus generalisation refers to the phenomenon where a response learned in the presence of a specific stimulus occurs in the presence of similar stimuli. Here's a breakdown of each statement

People's emotional reactions to one stimulus generalise to similar stimuli. This statement accurately reflects the concept of stimulus generalisation, where feelings or responses to a specific stimulus can extend to similar stimuli. For example, if someone has a fear of dogs, they may also react fearfully to other animals that resemble dogs.

Normally desirable foods, such as cakes and pastries, are unappealing when shaped to resemble dog's feces. This statement illustrates how generalisation can affect perception and desire; the negative association with the appearance of feces can generalise to affect the desirability of food shaped similarly.

63 Which of the following does not come under the matrix reasoning subtest of WAIS IV ?

I. Visuospatial reasoning II. Psychomotor speed
III. Abstract reasoning IV. Visual organisation
V. Ability to follow directions

Choose the most appropriate answer from the options given below.

1 I, II and III 2 I, III and IV
3 II, III and IV 4 I, II, III and IV

***Ans.* (*)**

➲ ***Exp.*** **This Question has been dropped by UGC.**

64 Identify the components of the 'Ethical Decision Making.

I. Moral awareness II. Moral anxiety
III. Moral intent IV. Moral judgement
V. Moral context

Choose the most appropriate answer from the options given below.

1 I, II and III 2 II, III and IV
3 III, IV and V 4 I, III and IV

***Ans.* (4)**

➲ ***Exp.*** I, III and IV are correct.

Ethical decision making involves a structured process where individuals consider moral principles and values when making decisions. The key components include

Moral awareness The ability to recognise that a situation involves ethical issues. This is the first step in the ethical decision-making process.

Moral intent This refers to the intention to act in a morally appropriate manner, reflecting the commitment to make ethical decisions.

Moral judgement The ability to evaluate the ethicality of different actions or choices, weighing the moral implications of potential decisions.

65 Informed consent, as suggested by Diener and Crandall includes the components.

I. Voluntarism II. Researcher's competence
III. Information IV. Comprehension

Choose the most appropriate answer from the options given below.

1 I and III 2 I, II and III
3 I, III and IV 4 II, III and IV

***Ans.* (3)**

➲ ***Exp.*** I, III and IV are correct.

Informed consent, as outlined by Diener and Crandall, involves several key components that ensure participants fully understand and voluntarily agree to take part in research. These components include

Voluntarism Participation must be voluntary, meaning that individuals choose to participate without any form of coercion or undue pressure.

Information Participants must be given clear and adequate information about the study, including its purpose, procedures, risks and benefits, to make an informed decision.

Comprehension Participants must fully understand the information provided to them. This ensures that they are making a truly informed decision about their involvement in the research.

66 Match List-I with List-II.

List-I	List-II
A. Samacariya	I. Transformation wholeness
B. Tanha	II. Desire
C. Satori	III. Healthy virtuous
D. Sammadithhi	IV. Thinking

Choose the correct answer from the options given below.

	A	B	C	D		A	B	C	D
1	III	I	II	IV	2	IV	I	II	III
3	III	II	I	IV	4	II	III	I	IV

***Ans.* (3)**

➲ ***Exp.*** The correct matching is A-III, B-II, C-I, D-IV.

Samacariya refers to ethical or virtuous behaviour, which aligns with the concept of being healthy and virtuous in one's actions.

Tanha means craving or desire in Buddhist teachings, particularly the desire that leads to suffering.

Satori is a term in Zen Buddhism that refers to sudden enlightenment or a profound transformation leading to wholeness and spiritual awakening.

Sammadithhi refers to 'right view' or 'right understanding' in the Buddhist Eightfold Path, which is related to correct thinking or perception of reality.

67 Match List-I with List-II.

List-I	List-II
A. Grounded Theory	I. Lives of individual studied and retold to develop a chronology
B. Phenomoenological Research	II. Studying intact cultural group in national setting.
C. Narrative Research	III. Deriving a general abstract theory through views of participants
D. Ethnography	IV. Understanding lived experiences of a small member of participants

Choose the correct answer from the options given below.

	A	B	C	D		A	B	C	D
1	III	I	IV	II	2	II	IV	I	III
3	II	I	IV	III	4	III	IV	I	II

***Ans.* (4)**

➲ ***Exp.*** The correct matching is A-III, B-IV, C-I, D-II.

Grounded Theory Grounded theory involves developing a general theory based on data collected from participants, often through interviews or other qualitative methods.

Phenomenological Research Phenomenological research focuses on understanding and describing the lived experiences of individuals, usually through in-depth exploration of a small group.

Narrative Research Narrative research involves studying the stories or life histories of individuals and retelling them to form a detailed chronology or narrative of their experiences.

Ethnography Ethnography is a research method focused on studying the behaviours, customs and practices of an intact cultural group in their natural environment, typically through observation and participation.

68 **Match List-I with List-II.**

List-I	List-II
A. Preferred method for determining item bias	I. Slope
B. Coefficient for correlating two absolutely dichotomous variables	II. Intercept
C. The place where the regression line crosses the y-axis	III. Phi coefficient
D. The expected change in Y for every one unit change in X on the regression line	IV. Item characteristic curve

Choose the correct answer from the options given below.

	A	B	C	D
1	IV	III	II	I
2	III	IV	II	I
3	I	III	II	IV
4	I	II	IV	III

Ans. (1)

Exp. The correct matching is A-IV, B-III, C-II, D-I.

Preferred method for determining item bias The Item Characteristic Curve (ICC) is used in Item Response Theory (IRT) to detect item bias, as it shows how the probability of a correct response varies with the ability level.

Coefficient for correlating two absolutely dichotomous variables The Phi coefficient is a measure of association for two binary (dichotomous) variables. It is similar to a correlation coefficient but is specifically designed for dichotomous data.

The place where the regression line crosses the y-axis The intercept is the point where the regression line crosses the y-axis, representing the expected value of the dependent variable (Y) when the independent variable (X) is zero.

The expected change in Y for every one unit change in X on the regression line The slope of the regression line represents the change in the dependent variable (Y) for each one-unit change in the independent variable (X).

69 **Match List-I with List-II.**

List-I	List-II
A. Effortful Processing	I. Associates new and old information and solves problem
B. Spacing Effect	II. Encoding of space, time and word meanings
C. Working Memory	III. Remembering the concepts of psychology
D. Automatic Processing	IV. Better long-term retention through distributed practice

Choose the correct answer from the options given below

	A	B	C	D
1	I	II	III	IV
2	II	III	I	IV
3	III	IV	I	II
4	IV	II	III	I

Ans. (3)

Exp. The correct matching is A-III, B-IV, C-I, D-II.

Effortful Processing Effortful processing involves active, conscious efforts to encode information, such as studying and remembering complex material like psychological concepts.

Spacing Effect The spacing effect refers to the phenomenon that information is better retained over the long-term when practice or learning sessions are spaced out over time rather than crammed.

Working Memory Working memory is responsible for holding and manipulating information temporarily, allowing the brain to solve problems by associating new information with existing knowledge.

Automatic Processing Automatic processing refers to the unconscious encoding of information such as space, time, frequency and the meanings of words, without needing conscious effort.

70 **Match List-I with List-II.**

List-I	List-II
A. Young-Helmholtz theory	I. Colour perception
B. Place theory	II. High pitches
C. Touch sensations	III. Rubber-hand illusion
D. Gate control theory	IV. Pain

Choose the correct answer from the options given below

	A	B	C	D
1	IV	III	II	I
2	I	II	III	IV
3	II	I	III	IV
4	III	IV	I	II

Ans. (2)

Exp. The correct matching is A-I, B-II, C-III, D-IV.

Young-Helmholtz theory The Young-Helmholtz theory, also known as the trichromatic theory, explains colour perception by proposing that the retina contains three types of cones sensitive to red, green, and blue, which combine to produce the perception of colour.

Place theory Place theory suggests that high pitches are detected based on the specific location on the basilar membrane of the cochlea where sound waves peak. Different frequencies activate different areas along the membrane.

Touch sensations The Rubber-hand illusion is a phenomenon that illustrates how the brain integrates visual and tactile sensations to create a sense of body ownership, showing how touch sensations can be manipulated by visual cues.

Gate control theory The Gate control theory of pain suggests that the spinal cord contains a 'gate' mechanism that either blocks or allows pain signals to pass to the brain, thereby regulating the sensation of pain.

71 **Match List-I with List-II.**

List-I	List-II
A. Sigmund Freud	I. Genetic view
B. B.F. Skinner	II. Psychoanalytic view
C. Carl Rogers	III. Behavioural view
D. Hans Eysenck	IV. Humanistic view

Choose the correct answer from the options given below.

	A	B	C	D		A	B	C	D
1	IV	I	II	III	2	II	III	I	IV
3	II	III	IV	I	4	I	II	III	IV

***Ans.* (3)**

➲ ***Exp.*** The correct matching is A-II, B-III, C-IV, D-I.

Sigmund Freud Freud is the founder of the psychoanalytic view, which emphasises unconscious processes, childhood experiences and instincts in shaping personality and behaviour.

B.F. Skinner Skinner is associated with the behavioural view, which focuses on observable behaviour and the influence of the environment, particularly through reinforcement and punishment (operant conditioning).

Carl Rogers Rogers is a prominent figure in the humanistic view, which emphasises personal growth, self-actualisation, and the innate goodness of individuals.

Hans Eysenck Eysenck is known for his genetic view of personality, particularly his focus on the biological and genetic bases of personality traits such as extraversion and neuroticism.

72 **Match List-I with List-II.**

List-I	List-II
A. Manic Disorder	I. Frontal-striatal region of the brain implicated
B. Panic Disorder	II. Elevated expansive mood and increased energy
C. Schizophrenia	III. Heightened awareness of emotion specific stimulus
D. ADHD	IV. Delusion, hallucination, incoherent speech

Choose the correct answer from the options given below.

	A	B	C	D		A	B	C	D
1	II	III	IV	I	2	I	IV	II	III
3	III	II	I	IV	4	IV	III	II	I

***Ans.* (1)**

➲ ***Exp.*** The correct matching is A-II, B-III, C-IV, D-I.

Manic Disorder Manic disorder, often associated with bipolar disorder, is characterised by an elevated, expansive mood, increased energy and sometimes risky behaviour.

Panic Disorder Panic disorder involves sudden and intense episodes of fear, often triggered by specific emotional stimuli, and can lead to heightened physiological and emotional responses.

Schizophrenia Schizophrenia is marked by severe symptoms such as delusions hallucinations, and incoherent speech, reflecting a disconnect from reality.

ADHD ADHD (Attention-Deficit/Hyperactivity Disorder) is associated with dysfunctions in the frontal-striatal region of the brain, which affects attention, impulse control and executive function.

73 **Match List-I with List-II.**

List-I	List-II
A. Object Permanence	I. Pre operation
B. Abstract thinking	II. Sensory motor
C. Ego centrism	III. Concrete operation
D. Conservation	IV. Formal operation

Choose the correct answer from the options given below.

	A	B	C	D		A	B	C	D
1	II	IV	III	I	2	II	IV	I	III
3	II	I	IV	III	4	IV	III	II	I

***Ans.* (2)**

➲ ***Exp.***The correct matching is A-II, B-IV, C-I, D-III.

Object Permanence Object permanence is the understanding that objects continue to exist even when they cannot be seen. This concept develops during the sensory motor stage (birth to about 2 years) in Piaget's theory of cognitive development.

Abstract thinking Abstract thinking involves the ability to think about concepts and ideas that are not physically present. This ability emerges during the formal operational stage (around 12 years and up), where individuals develop advanced reasoning skills.

Ego centrism Egocentrism is the inability to see a situation from another person's perspective, which is typical in the pre-operational stage (ages 2 to 7) of cognitive development.

Conservation Conservation refers to the understanding that certain properties of objects remain the same despite changes in their form or appearance. This concept is developed during the concrete operational stage (ages 7 to 11).

74 **Match List-I with List-II.**

List-I	List-II
A. Rosenstock	I. Protective Motivation Theory
B. Rogers	II. Health Belief Model
C. Fishbein	III. Self-Regulation Model
D. Leventhal	IV. Theory of Reasoned Action

Choose the correct answer from the options given below.

	A	B	C	D		A	B	C	D
1	II	I	IV	III	2	II	III	I	IV
3	II	IV	I	III	4	II	I	III	IV

***Ans.* (1)**

➲ ***Exp.*** The correct matching is A-II, B-I, C-IV, D-III.

Rosenstock Irwin Rosenstock is known for developing the Health Belief Model, which explains health behaviours based on individuals' beliefs about health conditions, perceived benefits of action, and barriers to action.

William Rogers Rogers contributed to the Protective Motivation Theory, which focuses on how individuals are motivated to protect themselves from threats through the evaluation of perceived severity and vulnerability.

Martin Fishbein Fishbein is one of the key figures associated with the Theory of Reasoned Action, which posits that individual behaviour is determined by their intention to perform that behaviour, influenced by attitudes and subjective norms.

Howard Leventhal Leventhal developed the Self-Regulation Model, which emphasises the role of self-regulation and personal agency in managing health behaviours and coping with health-related issues.

75 **Match List-I with List-II.**

List-I	List-II
A. Pratyahara	I. Concentration
B. Dharana	II. Attaining Oneness or Integration
C. Dhyana	III. Control over thoughts
D. Samadhi	IV. Meditation

Choose the correct answer from the options given below

	A	B	C	D		A	B	C	D
1	II	I	IV	III	2	III	II	I	IV
3	III	I	IV	II	4	II	I	III	IV

***Ans.* (3)**

Exp. The correct matching is A-III, B-I, C-IV, D-II.

Pratyahara Pratyahara is the practice of withdrawing the senses and controlling one's thoughts and distractions, which is essential for deeper meditation practices.

Dharana Dharana refers to the practice of focused concentration, where the mind is directed towards a single point or object, preparing for meditation.

Dhyana Dhyana is the practice of meditation itself, characterised by sustained attention and awareness, leading to a deep state of meditation.

Samadhi Samadhi is the final stage in yoga practice, where the practitioner experiences a state of oneness or integration with the object of meditation, often described as a deep connection or unity with all.

76 **Arrange Erik Eriksons stages of psychosocial development and basic strengths.**

I. Trust *vs* mistrust
II. Initiative *vs* guilt
III. Industriousness *vs* inferiority
IV. Autonomy *vs* doubt and shame

Choose the correct answer from the options given below.

1 I, IV, II, III
2 I, III, II, IV
3 I, II, IV, III
4 II, III, I, IV

***Ans.* (1)**

Exp. The correct order of Erik Erikson's stages of psychosocial development along with their basic strengths is I, IV, II, III.

Trust *vs* Mistrust This is the first stage (infancy, 0-1 year) where the basic strength developed is hope. Infants learn to trust their caregivers and the environment.

Autonomy *vs* Doubt and Shame This is the second stage (early childhood, 1-3 years) where the basic strength developed is will. Children learn to become independent and develop a sense of personal control over physical skills and a sense of independence.

Initiative *vs* Guilt This is the third stage (preschool age, 3-6 years) where the basic strength developed is purpose. Children begin to initiate activities and interact with other children, developing a sense of initiative while facing the potential for guilt over misdeeds.

Industry *vs* Inferiority This is the fourth stage (school age, 6-12 years) where the basic strength developed is competence. Children learn to work with others and develop a sense of pride in their accomplishments and abilities.

77 **Prepare the steps involved in Action Research in correct sequence with reference to behavioural science.**

I. Action
II. Observation
III. Plan
IV. Reflection

Choose the correct answer from the options given below.

1 I, II, III, IV
2 II, III, I, IV
3 III, I, II, IV
4 III, II, IV, I

***Ans.* (3)**

Exp. The correct sequence of steps involved in Action Research with reference to behavioural science is III, I, II, IV.

Plan The first step involves identifying a problem or area of focus and developing a plan for action. This includes setting objectives and deciding on the methods to be used for research.

Action After planning, the next step is to implement the action based on the developed plan. This is where the actual intervention or change is applied in the context of the research.

Observation Following the action, researchers observe the effects of the intervention. This step involves collecting data and monitoring the outcomes of the action taken.

Reflection The final step is to reflect on the results of the action and observations. This involves analysing the data, considering what worked, what didn't, and planning for further action or research.

78 **Arrange the following statements in the correct sequence of the movement of ions during the action potential.**

I. Na^+ channels open, Na^+ begins to enter cell.
II. K^+ continues to leave cell, causes membrane potential to return to resting level.
III. K^+ channels open, K^+ begins to leave cell.
IV. K^+ channels close, Na^+ channels reset.

V. Na^+ channels become refractory, no more Na^+ enters the cell.

Choose the correct answer from the options given below.

1 I, II, III, IV, V 2 I, III, V, II, IV
3 I, V, III, IV, II 4 IV, V, I, III, II

Ans. (2)

Exp. The correct sequence of statements representing the movement of ions during an action potential is I, III, V, II, IV.

Na^+ channels open, Na^+ begins to enter cell This is the initial phase of the action potential, where the opening of sodium channels allows Na^+ ions to flow into the neuron, causing depolarisation.

K^+ channels open, K^+ begins to leave cell As the action potential reaches its peak, potassium (K^+) channels open. This allows K^+ to exit the cell, starting the repolarization phase.

Na^+ channels become refractory, no more Na^+ enters the cell After depolarisation, the sodium channels become refractory, meaning they cannot open again immediately. This prevents additional Na^+ from entering and helps in the reset of the action potential.

K^+ continues to leave cell, causes membrane potential to return to resting level The continued exit of K^+ ions helps restore the resting membrane potential by repolarising the neuron.

K^+ channels close, Na^+ channels reset Finally, the potassium channels close, and the sodium channels reset to their original state, preparing the neuron for the next action potential.

79 Correctly arrange the components of emotion as explained in the two-factor theory of Schachter and Singer, 1962.

I. Stimulus
II. Cognitive appraisal of arousal
III. General physiological arousal
IV. Subjective experience of emotion

Choose the correct answer from the options given below.

1 I, II, III, IV 2 I, III, II, IV
3 IV, I, III, II 4 III, II, IV, I

Ans. (2)

Exp. In the two-factor theory of emotion proposed by Schachter and Singer in 1962, emotions are the result of both physiological arousal and cognitive appraisal. The correct sequence of the components of emotion according to this theory is I, III, II, IV.

Stimulus The process begins with a stimulus in the environment that triggers an emotional response. This can be an event, object, or situation that elicits a reaction.

General physiological arousal Following the stimulus, there is a physiological response or arousal (such as increased heart rate, sweating, etc.) that occurs in reaction to the stimulus.

Cognitive appraisal of arousal The next step involves cognitive appraisal, where the individual interprets and evaluates the physiological arousal in the context of the stimulus, which helps to determine the specific emotion experienced.

Subjective experience of emotion Finally, this cognitive appraisal leads to the subjective experience of emotion, where the individual feels and labels the emotion (e.g., fear, happiness, anger) based on the interpretation of the arousal.

80 What would be the correct order of the steps involved in prosocial behaviour?

I. Accept the responsibility for helping
II. Noticing something unusual
III. Decision about possession of required knowledge or skills
IV. Interpreting the event as emergency
V. Deciding to actually help

Choose the correct answer from the options given below.

1 I, III, II, IV, V 2 II, IV, I, III, V
3 II, IV, III, I, V 4 V, II, IV, III, I

Ans. (2)

Exp. The correct order of the steps involved in prosocial behaviour is II, IV, I, III, V.

Noticing something unusual The first step is recognising that something is out of the ordinary. This can be any event that may require assistance, such as a person in distress or an emergency situation.

Interpreting the event as an emergency After noticing something unusual, the individual must interpret the situation as needing urgent help. This interpretation is crucial for motivating a prosocial response.

Accept the responsibility for helping Once the event is identified as an emergency, the person must accept personal responsibility to help. This step is influenced by social dynamics, such as the bystander effect, where individuals may feel less responsible if others are present.

Decision about possession of required knowledge or skills At this point, the individual evaluates whether they have the necessary knowledge or skills to effectively help in the situation. This assessment can influence whether they decide to take action.

Deciding to actually help Finally, after assessing the situation and their own abilities, the individual makes the decision to help or take action.

81 Arrange the following in sequence as per development model of counselling.

I. Identification of blind spots
II. Brain storming
III. Developing possibilities
IV. Force-field analysis

Choose the correct answer from the options given below.

1 I, III, II, IV 2 II, III, I, IV
3 I, III, IV, II 4 I, II, IV, III

Ans. (1)

Exp. The correct sequence is I, III, II, IV.

In the development model of counselling, the steps can be arranged in the following sequence

Identification of blind spots The first step involves helping clients recognise areas in their lives or thinking patterns that they may be unaware of, which can hinder their progress. This sets the stage for further exploration.

Developing possibilities Once blind spots are identified, the next step is to explore and develop possible options or solutions for the issues at hand. This is about generating ideas for change or improvement.

Brainstorming After identifying possibilities, brainstorming can be employed to expand on those options. This step encourages creativity and helps clients think of multiple ways to address their concerns.

Force-field analysis Finally, this step involves analysing the forces that support or hinder change. This helps clients understand the dynamics affecting their decisions and the factors they need to consider to move forward.

82 Arrange the following physiological response to stress sequentially.

I. Release of Adrenocorticotropin hormone from pituitary gland
II. Release of CRF from hypothalamus
III. Perception of stress
IV. Suppression of immune system functioning
V. Glurcocorticoid release from Adrenal gland

Choose the correct answer from the options given below.

1 II, III, V, I, IV 2 III, II, I, V, IV
3 I, III, IV, II, V 4 V, IV, III, I, II

Ans. (2)

Exp. The correct sequence of physiological responses to stress is III, II, I, V, IV.

Perception of stress The process begins when an individual perceives a stressor, which can be any event or situation that triggers a stress response.

Release of CRF from hypothalamus In response to the perception of stress, the hypothalamus releases Corticotropin-Releasing Factor (CRF), which is a key hormone in the stress response pathway.

Release of Adrenocorticotropin hormone from pituitary gland The CRF then stimulates the pituitary gland to release Adrenocorticotropic Hormone (ACTH) into the bloodstream.

Glucocorticoid release from adrenal gland ACTH prompts the adrenal glands to release glucocorticoids, primarily cortisol, which plays a crucial role in the stress response by mobilising energy and regulating various bodily functions.

Suppression of immune system functioning Finally, the increased levels of glucocorticoids lead to the suppression of immune system functioning as part of the body's response to stress, which helps prioritise immediate survival but can have negative long-term effects on health.

83 Arrange 'Pancha Kosha' in order.

I. Annamaya Kosha II. Manomaya Kosha
III. Vijnanamaya Kosha IV. Pranamaya Kosha
V. Anandamaya Kosha

Choose the correct answer from the options given below.

1 I, V, II, IV, III 2 I, IV, II, III, V
3 I, II, IV, III, V 4 I, III, II, V, IV

Ans. (2)

Exp. The correct chronological order is I, IV, II, III, V.

Annamaya Kosha This is the food sheath, representing the physical body and the material aspects of existence, including the physical structure and processes.

Pranamaya Kosha This is the vital sheath, which encompasses the life force or prana. It involves the physiological processes related to breath and energy flow in the body.

Manomaya Kosha This is the mental sheath, representing the mind and its functions, including thoughts, emotions, and sensory perceptions.

Vijnanamaya Kosha This is the wisdom sheath, associated with higher mental functions, intelligence and awareness. It includes the ability to discern and understand deeper truths.

Anandamaya Kosha This is the bliss sheath, representing the innermost layer associated with spiritual bliss, happiness and the ultimate state of being beyond suffering.

84 Arrange the emergence of following leadership approaches in a chronological order.

I. Behavioural approach
II. Transformational approach
III. Trait approach
IV. Contingency Approach

Choose the correct answer from the options given below.

1 I, III, II, IV 2 I, III, IV, II
3 III, I, II, IV 4 III, I, IV, II

Ans. (4)

Exp. The correct chronological order of the emergence of the leadership approaches is III, I, IV, II.

Trait approach This approach emerged first, primarily in the early to mid-20th century. It focuses on identifying specific characteristics or traits that effective leaders possess, suggesting that certain inherent qualities make a good leader.

Behavioural approach Following the trait approach, the behavioural approach gained prominence in the 1940s and 1950s. This approach shifted the focus from inherent traits to observable behaviours of leaders, examining what leaders do rather than who they are.

Contingency Approach This approach emerged in the 1960s and 1970s, emphasising that effective leadership depends on the context and situation. It suggests that different leadership styles may be more effective in different circumstances.

Transformational approach This approach emerged later, in the late 20th century, particularly in the 1970s and 1980s. Transformational leadership focuses on inspiring and motivating followers to achieve extraordinary outcomes and foster personal development.

85 Sequentially arrange the sections of the vertebrae of the spinal column from top to bottom.

I. Thoracic vertebrae II. Sacral vertebrae
III. Cervical vertebrae IV. Lumbar vertebrae

Choose the correct answer from the options given below.

1 I, IV, II, III
2 III, I, IV, II
3 I, III, II, IV
4 II, I, IV, III

***Ans.* (2)**

Exp. The correct sequential arrangement of the sections of the vertebrae of the spinal column from top to bottom is III, I, IV, II.

Cervical vertebrae These are the topmost vertebrae in the spinal column, consisting of seven vertebrae (C1 to C7) located in the neck region.

Thoracic vertebrae Below the cervical vertebrae are the thoracic vertebrae, which consist of twelve vertebrae (T1 to T12). They are located in the upper and mid-back region and articulate with the ribs.

Lumbar vertebrae Following the thoracic vertebrae are the lumbar vertebrae, which consist of five vertebrae (L1 to L5). They are located in the lower back and are larger to support more weight and movement.

Sacral vertebrae Finally, the sacral vertebrae consist of five fused vertebrae (S1 to S5) that form the sacrum, connecting the spine to the pelvis. This section is located at the base of the spinal column.

86 Given below are two statements, one is labelled as Assertion (A) and the other is labelled as Reason (R).

Assertion (A) There are five universal human needs according to reality therapy.

Reason (R) These needs are - survival, love and belonging, power, freedom and fun.

In the light of the above statements, choose the most appropriate answer from the options given below.

1 Both A and R are true and R is the correct explanation of A.
2 Both A and R are true, but R is not the correct explanation of A.
3 A is true, but R is false.
4 A is false, but R is true.

***Ans.* (1)**

Exp. Both A and R are true and R is the correct explanation of A.

Reality therapy, developed by William Glasser, identifies five basic human needs that motivate human behaviour.

'These needs are - survival, love and belonging, power, freedom and fun.'

87 Given below are two statements, one is labelled as Assertion (A) and the other is labelled as Reason (R).

Assertion (A) To eliminate the impact of an extraneous independent variable, the researcher can choose participants who are homogeneous on that independent variable.

Reason (R) Matching is one of the method to control extraneous variance.

In the light of the above statements, choose the most appropriate answer from the options given below.

1 Both A and R are true and R is the correct explanation of A.
2 Both A and R are true, but R is not the correct explanation of A.
3 A is true, but R is false.
4 A is false, but R is true.

***Ans.* (2)**

Exp. Both A and R are true, but R is not the correct explanation of A.

By selecting participants who are similar (homogeneous) on certain extraneous variables, researchers can reduce the variability that these variables might introduce into the study's results. Matching involves pairing participants based on certain characteristics (like age, gender or other relevant traits) to ensure that those characteristics do not confound the results.

88 Given below are two statements, one is labelled as Assertion (A) and the other is labelled as Reason (R).

Assertion (A) Monozygotic twins are called fraternal twins, who share half of their genes. Both members of the twins may be males or females.

Reason (R) Dizygotic twins develop from two different eggs and share the genes like a brother and sister. One of the twins may be a male and the other one may be a female.

In the light of the above statements, choose the most appropriate answer from the options given below.

1 Both A and R are true and R is the correct explanation of A.
2 Both A and R are true, but R is not the correct explanation of A.
3 A is true, but R is false.
4 A is false, but R is true.

***Ans.* (4)**

Exp. A is false, but R is true.

Monozygotic twins, also known as identical twins, develop from a single fertilised egg that splits into two embryos, resulting in twins that share 100% of their genes. Fraternal twins (dizygotic twins), on the other hand, develop from two different eggs fertilised by two different sperm, sharing about 50% of their genes. Monozygotic twins can be either both male, both female, or one of each, but the statement incorrectly refers to them as fraternal twins.

Dizygotic twins do develop from two different eggs fertilised by two different sperm cells. They share approximately 50% of their genetic material, similar to any other siblings. It is also true that one twin can be male while the other can be female.

89 Given below are two statements, one is labelled as Assertion (A) and the other is labelled as Reason (R).

Assertion (A) Project Head Start and other preschool quality programme boost children's chances of success in future by increasing their school readiness.

Reason (R) Genes and experience together determine cognitive and social skills.

In the light of the above statements choose the most appropriate answer from the options given below.

1 Both A and R are true and R is the correct explanation of A.
2 Both A and R are true, but R is not the correct explanation of A.
3 A is true, but R is false.
4 A is false, but R is true.

Ans. (1)

Exp. Both A and R are true and R is the correct explanation of A.

Programmes like Project Head Start are designed to provide early childhood education, health, nutrition and parental involvement services to low-income children and families, which indeed enhance school readiness and can contribute to long-term academic success.

Both genetic factors (nature) and environmental factors (nurture) play significant roles in shaping cognitive and social skills. This understanding aligns with the nature-nurture debate in psychology, highlighting that neither genes nor experience alone is responsible for development.

90 Given below are two statements.

Statement (I) Motivation is a condition that energizes behaviour but gives no direction.

Statement (II) Motivational States arise only from external incentive factors.

In the light of the above statements, choose the most appropriate answer from the options given below.

1 Both Statement I and Statement II are correct.
2 Both Statement I and Statement II are incorrect.
3 Statement I is correct, but Statement II is incorrect.
4 Statement I is incorrect, but Statement II is correct.

Ans. (2)

Exp. Both Statement I and Statement II are incorrect.

Motivation not only energizes behaviour but also provides direction. Motivation can be understood as the driving force that prompts individuals to take action toward achieving specific goals. While external incentives (like rewards, praise or money) can certainly influence motivation, motivational states can also arise from internal factors, such as intrinsic motivation (e.g., personal satisfaction, interest, or passion for an activity).

Directions (Q. Nos 91-95) *Read the passage carefully and answer the questions that follows.*

A study was conducted to find out whether participation in meditation influences well-being in children.

Hence a group of children who have not participated ill meditation before but are now planning to begin participating in meditation were given a well-being scale before they began meditation. The children were administered the same test again after 2 months of meditation. The well- being was measured on an internal scale, with higher scores indicating higher well-being. The scores on the scale were normally distributed. The scores are given below.

Before	After
4	6
8	5
10	11
12	10
14	15
16	17
18	16

91 What is the degrees of freedom for the test?

1 10 2 11 3 6 4 5

Ans. (3)

Exp. The correct answer is 6. The study described is a paired-sample t-test (also known as a dependent t-test), as the same group of children is measured twice-before and after meditation. The degrees of freedom (df) for a paired-sample t-test are calculated using the formula: $df = n - 1$, where n is the number of paired observations (i.e., the number of children in this case).

92 What statistical test should be used to analyse the data?

1 Mann-Whitney U test
2 Wilcoxon signed Rank test
3 Correlated 't' test
4 Independent 't' test

Ans. (3)

Exp. The correlated t-test (also known as the paired-sample t test) is the appropriate statistical test for this situation.

93 Rejection of null hypothesis indicates

1 Participation in meditation leads to significant difference in well-being scores
2 Participation in meditation leads to just above the well-being score after meditation
3 Participation in meditation leads to lower well being scores
4 Participation in meditation has no significant effect

Ans. (1)

Exp. In this context, rejection of the null hypothesis implies that the change in well-being scores is statistically significant, meaning that participation in meditation has led to a significant difference in the well-being scores of the children.

94 Which of the following is correct about directional hypothesis?

1 Meditation has effect on well-being
2 Meditation has positive effect on well-being
3 Meditation has both positive and negative effect on well-being
4 Meditation has direction for well-being

Ans. (2)

➲ *Exp.* Statement (2) is correct about directional hypothesis.

A directional hypothesis is a specific type of hypothesis that predicts not only that there will be an effect, but also the direction of the effect (positive or negative).

95 Which of the following is correct about interval scale?

1 Identity, magnitude equal unit size and absolute zero are the properties of this scale.

2 Identity and equal unit size are its properties

3 Identity, magnitude and equal unit size are its properties

4 Identity and magnitude are the properties of this scale

Ans. (3)

➲ *Exp.* Statement (3) is correct about interval scale.

An interval scale is a level of measurement that has the following properties

Identity Each value on the scale has a unique meaning.

Magnitude Values can be ordered meaningfully based on their size (i.e., a higher number represents more of the property being measured).

Directions (Q. Nos 96-100) *Read the passage carefully and answer the questions that follows.*

Lev S. Vygotsky developed a theory of cognitive development. He explained that experienced adults help children with innate basic capabilities to attain more complex and higher order cognitive capabilities. To describe and assess this potential, he proposed the notion of ZPD. Based on Vygotskian thinking, all instructional process was developed in which the more knowledgeable partner adjusts the amount and type of support he offers to fit with the child's learning needs over the course of interaction. According to Vygotsky psychological tools and signs facilitate and direct thinking process.

96 The theory of Vygotsky is called

1 Cultural theory of cognitive development

2 Social theory of cognitive development

3 Social cultural theory of cognitive development

4 Bio social cultural theory of cognitive development

Ans. (3)

➲ *Exp.* Vygotsky believed cognitive development is influenced by cultural and social factors. He emphasised the role of social interaction in the development of mental abilities e.g., speech and reasoning in children.

97 The ZPD stands for

1 Zone of Postnatal Development

2 Zone of Proximal Development

3 Zone of Proximodistal Development

4 Zone of Proximal Distance

Ans. (2)

➲ *Exp.* The ZPD stands for Zone of Proximal Development. It is the difference between what a learner can do without help and what they can do with guidance and encouragement from a skilled partner.

98 ZPD is defined by Vygotsky as

1 the region of sensitivity for learning characterised by the difference between the developmental level when the child is working alone and the level he/she is capable of reaching with the aid of an adult.

2 the region of difference between inability to use a known dung and benefit from the use of such a strategy.

3 the region of learning what a child has learnt from experience and knows about the world in general.

4 the region of ability to fit into change and choose environments that best fulfill the child's needs and desires to learn from society and culture.

Ans. (1)

➲ *Exp.* ZPD is the region of sensitivity for learning characterised by the difference between the developmental level when the child is working alone and the level he/she is capable of reaching with the aid of an adult.

99 The instructional process in which the more knowledgeable partner adjusts the amount and type of support he offers to fit with the child's learning needs over the course of interaction is called

1 Tacit knowledge

2 Social referencing

3 Pragmatics

4 Scaffolding

Ans. (4)

➲ *Exp.* Scaffolding refers to the instructional process in which a more knowledgeable partner (such as a teacher or parent) provides tailored support to a learner based on their individual needs.

100 The psychological tools and signs such as language, counting, mnemonics, algebric symbols, art and writing that facilitate and direct thinking process is called by Vygotsky as

1 Moderators

2 Mediators

3 Confounders

4 Facilitators

Ans. (2)

➲ *Exp.* In Vygotsky's theory, mediators are the psychological tools and signs, such as language, symbols, and other cultural artifacts, that facilitate and direct cognitive processes. Instead of acting in a direct, unmediated way in the social and physical world, our contact with the world is indirect or mediated by signs.

Solved Paper

2022

UGC-NET
PSYCHOLOGY
SOLVED PAPER 2022 (October)

PAPER II

Direction *This paper contains* ***hundred*** *(100) objective type questions of* ***two*** *(2) marks each. All questions are compulsory.*

1 In Weber's Law, $\frac{\Delta I}{I} = K$, ΔI stands for?

1 Noticeable difference
2 Point of subjective equality
3 Constant proportion
4 Differential threshold

Ans. (2)

Exp. In Weber's Law, $\frac{\Delta I}{I} = K$, ΔI stands for point of subjective equality. In Weber's Law ΔI (Delta I) represents the difference threshold I represents the initial stimulus intensity and k signifies that the proportion on the left side of the equation remains constant despite variations in the I term. Weber's Law states that the just noticeable difference in stimulus intensity may affect the production of sensations proportionally.

According to Weber's Law, the size of noticeable differences in stimuli may affect the increase in production of the census. This can be denoted by Delta S. $dS = K * S$, where S is the reference stimuli and K is constant.

2 Rational concept is that which involves

1 a combination of several attributes
2 relationship among elements in a situation
3 at least one element from a number of elements
4 All of the above

Ans. (2)

Exp. Rational concept is that which involves relationship among elements in a situation.

An approach in psychology emphasising philosophy, deductive reasoning and logic as insightful sources into the underlying principles of the mind is rational psychology. It attempts to address problems in the client using logic to understand the principles of the workings of the mind.

3 What will happen with the continuous stress?

1 Stage of exhaustion
2 Body resources drained
3 Stress hormones depleted
4 All of the above

Ans. (4)

Exp. With continuous stress, body resources will be drained. There will be a stage of exhaustion and stress hormones get depleted.

When a person has long-term (chronic) stress, continued activation of the stress response causes wear and tear on the body.

Physical, emotional and behavioral symptoms develop. Studies have found many health problems related to stress. Stress seems to worsen or increase the risk of conditions like obesity, heart disease, Alzheimer's disease, diabetes, depression, gastrointestinal problems and asthma.

4 What percentage of participants fully obeyed the experimenter's command to deliver a 450-volt shock to the learner in the experiment conducted by Psychologists of Yale University?

1 5%
2 20%
3 35%
4 65%

Ans. (4)

Exp. 65% of the participants will fully obey the experimenter's command to deliver a 450-volt shock to the learner in the experiment conducted by psychologists of Yale University.

The experiment found, unexpectedly, that a very high proportion of subjects would fully obey the instructions, with every participant going up to 300 volts, and 65% going up to the full 450 volts. The Milgram experiment(s) on obedience to authority figures were a series of social psychology experiments conducted by Yale University psychologist Stanley Milgram.

They measured the willingness of study participants, 40 men in the age range of 20 to 50 from a diverse range of occupations with varying levels of education, to obey an authority figure who instructed them to perform acts conflicting with their personal conscience.

5 Which of the following neurons of cortex produce most EEG?

1 Pyramidal 2 Cuboidal
3 Tubular 4 Cylindrical

Ans. (1)

➲ *Exp.* Pyramidal neurons of the cortex produce most EEG. Pyramidal cells, or pyramidal neurons, are a type of multipolar neuron found in areas of the brain including the cerebral cortex, the hippocampus and the amygdala.

Pyramidal neurons are the primary excitation units of the mammalian prefrontal cortex and the corticospinal tract. Pyramidal neurons in fifth layer are major projection neurons from the neocortex.

6 According to Kohlberg .... and ..... are the major reasons of moral behaviour during the stage of conventional morality.

1 gaining acceptance; getting rewards
2 avoiding censure by others; achieving justice
3 gaining acceptance; avoiding censure by others
4 avoiding censure by others; achieving justice

Ans. (3)

➲ *Exp.* According to Kohlberg gaining acceptance and avoiding censure by others are the major reasons of moral behaviour during the stage of conventional morality. According to him "Performing an act and doing something because others approve it", represents the Conventional stage of morality as the reason for moral behavior of a child during this stage is 'gaining acceptance and avoiding censure by others'. Conventional Morality is a stage of morality in which Children make decisions to please others. Children try to maintain interpersonal relations.

Children make efforts to get the approval of others.

7 Who is known for the development of the drive theory?

1 Clark Hull 2 Dweck
3 Susan Harter 4 Piaget

Ans. (1)

➲ *Exp.* Clark Hull is known for the development of the drive theory. He was the first psychologist to produce a theory of motivation that was widely accepted and called his theory drive theory. He said that people were motivated to reduce the tension caused by such things as hunger and thirst. In other words, people want to satisfy their urges.

He also states that we engage in behaviour to diminish a biological drive, like hunger, sexual desire, or a need for warmth. These drives create an unpleasant state and Hull suggested that's what motivates us to engage in behaviours that reduce them.

8 Implicit thinking involves mainly

1 motor activity 2 sensory activity
3 reflex activity 4 glandular activity

Ans. (1)

➲ *Exp.* Implicit thinking involves mainly motor activity. Implicit cognition refers to unconscious influences such as knowledge, perception or memory, that influence a person's behaviour.

Implicit cognition is everything one does and learns unconsciously or without any awareness that one is doing it. There are many processes in which implicit memory works, which include learning, our social cognition, and our problem-solving skills.

9 Working memory involves which of the following?

1 Storage capacity and Biographical information.
2 Semantic information and Processing capacity.
3 Storage capacity and Processing capacity.
4 Biographical information and Semantic information.

Ans. (3)

➲ *Exp.* Working memory involves Storage capacity and Processing capacity. It is the small amount of information that can be held in mind and used in the execution of cognitive tasks, in contrast with long-term memory, the vast amount of information saved in one's life.

Working memory is one of the most widely-used terms in psychology. It facilitates planning, comprehension, reasoning and problem-solving. It has often been connected or related to intelligence, information processing, executive function, comprehension, problem-solving and learning, in people ranging from infancy to old age and in all sorts of animals.

10 Which famous psychologist applied Gestalt principles to explain his theory of personality?

1 Kurt Lewin 2 Abraham Maslow
3 Freud 4 Guildford

Ans. (1)

➲ *Exp.* Kurt Lewin was famous psychologist who applied Gestalt principles to explain his theory of personality.

"The whole is other than the sum of the parts." The human eye and brain perceive a unified shape in a different way to the way they perceive the individual parts of those shapes. Gestalt Principles are principles/laws of human perception that describe how humans group similar elements, recognise patterns and simplify complex images when we perceive objects. Designers use the principles to organise content on websites and other interfaces so it is aesthetically pleasing and easy to understand.

11 What is 'Supra mentalisation' in integral Yoga?

1 Realisation of enlightenment
2 Realisation of the supermind
3 Realisation of illumination
4 All of the above

Ans. (4)

➲ *Exp.* 'Supra mentalisation' in integral Yoga is realisation of enlightenment, realisation of the supermind and realisation of illumination.

Integral yoga, sometimes also called supramental yoga, is the yoga-based philosophy and practice of Sri Aurobindo and The Mother (Mirra Alfassa).

Yoga is a rapid and concentrated evolution of being, which can take effect in one life-time, while unassisted natural evolution would take many centuries or many births.

12 In instrumental conditioning

1 reinforcement is given irrespective of the production of an appropriate response.
2 reinforcement is given before the onset of the response.
3 appropriate response is immediately followed by reinforcement.
4 reinforcement is not given.

Ans. (3)

➲ *Exp.* In instrumental conditioning, appropriate response is immediately followed by reinforcement. Instrumental conditioning (also called operant conditioning) is a procedure in which a reinforcement, such as food, is delivered contingent upon a response, although it may also be contingent upon the time of occurrence of a previous stimulus or reinforcement.

For example, if a student is rewarded with praise every time she raises her hand in class, she becomes more likely to raise her hand again in the future. If she is also scolded when she speaks out of turn, she becomes less likely to interrupt the class

13 Mental images

1 represent abstract ideas
2 consist entirely of unconscious information
3 have a picture like quality
4 always prototype

Ans. (3)

➲ *Exp.* Mental images have a picture-like quality. The mental image or mental representation is defined as what an individual can feel, hear, see or taste in one's own mind. A mental image is a mental picture or representation of an object or event.

People form mental images of many different objects—faces of familiar people, the lay-out of the furniture in their homes, the letters of the alphabet, a graduation or religious ceremony.

14 Who said, "psychology has a long past but only a short history"?

1 Hermann Ebbinghaus 2 Skinner
3 Aristotle 4 Watson

Ans. (1)

➲ *Exp.* In 1908, Hermann Ebbinghaus wrote that "Psychology has a long past, but only a short history". The use of the term psychology predates both the experimental and the systematic empirical psychologies of the 18th century.

15 Which of the following factors influence developmental process?

1 Normative influences
2 Education and Training
3 Hereditary factors
4 All of the above

Ans. (4)

➲ *Exp.* Normative influences, Education and Training and Hereditary factors influence the developmental process. Psychological development, the development of human beings' cognitive, emotional, intellectual and social capabilities and functioning over the course of a normal life span, from infancy through old age.

It is the subject matter of the discipline known as developmental psychology. A development process has following stages such as ideation, research, planning, prototyping, sourcing, costing and commercialisation.

16 With the help of classical conditioning, emotional responses

1 are learned best
2 are equal to other responses
3 are learned very slowly
4 are learned only when US (Unconditioned Stimulus) is powerful

Ans. (4)

➲ *Exp.* With the help of classical conditioning, emotional responses are learned only when the US (Unconditioned Stimulus) is powerful. Discovered by Russian psychologist Ivan Pavlov, classical conditioning is a type of unconscious or automatic learning.

This learning process creates a conditioned response through associations between an unconditioned stimulus and a neutral stimulus. Classical conditioning involves placing a neutral stimulus before a naturally occurring reflex.

17 Who discovered a new device pupilometrics?

1 Wundt 2 Eckhard Hess
3 Friensen 4 Engen

Ans. (2)

➲ *Exp.* Eckhard Hess discovered a new device pupilometrics. It is the psychological study of the effects of emotional and other influences on the pupil of the eye. The pupilometer is a hand-held instrument which provides quantitative pupillary measurements by taking 30 pictures per second of the pupil's response to light stimulus.

18 According to George Polya problem solving means

1 finding way around an obstacle.
2 it is specific achievement of intelligence.
3 attaining an aim that was not immediately understandable.
4 All of the above

Ans. (4)

➲ *Exp.* According to Geogre Polya, problem solving means finding a way around an obstacle. It is a specific achievement of intelligence and attaining an aim that was not immediately understandable. Polya created his famous four-step process for problem solving, which is used all over to aid people in problem solving. These are

Step 1 : Understand the problem

Step 2 : Devise a plan (translate).

Step 3 : Carry out the plan (solve).

Step 4 : Look back (check and interpret).

19 We are more likely to experience which of the following during adolescence than at any other time in our lives?

1 Moodiness 2 Parent-child conflicts

3 Risky behaviour 4 All of these

Ans. (4)

➲ *Exp.* We are more likely to experience Moodiness, Parent-child conflicts and risky behaviour during adolescence than at any other time in our lives. Adolescence is the phase of life between childhood and adulthood, from ages 10 to 19.

It is a unique stage of human development and an important time for laying the foundations of good health. Adolescents experience rapid physical, cognitive and psycho-social growth.

20 A network of associated facts and concepts that make out general knowledge of the world is referred to as

1 episodic memory

2 explicit memory

3 implicit memory

4 semantic memory

Ans. (4)

➲ *Exp.* A network of associated facts and concepts that make out general knowledge of the world is referred to as semantic memory.

Semantic memory refers to our general world knowledge that encompasses memory for concepts, facts, and the meanings of words and other symbolic units that constitute formal communication systems such as language or math. For instance, semantic memory might contain information about what a cat is, whereas episodic memory might contain a specific memory of petting a particular cat.

21 Which ligand is introduced in body during PET scan?

1 Chlorine-4 2 Helium-20

3 Fluorine-18 4 All of these

Ans. (3)

➲ *Exp.* Flourine-18 is introduced in the body during PET Scan. It can be used to make a radioactive form of glucose that is readily taken up by cancer cells and other cells. Using nuclear imaging it can be used to detect tumours, map brain function and detect other illnesses.

A Positron Emission Tomography (PET) scan is an imaging test that can help reveal the metabolic or biochemical function of your tissues and organs. The PET scan uses a radioactive drug (tracer) to show both normal and abnormal metabolic activity.

22 Social psychology focuses on .... and their ....

1 individuals; feelings 2 groups; experiences

3 people; feelings 4 people; thoughts

Ans. (4)

➲ *Exp.* Social psychology focuses on people and their thoughts.

Social psychology is the study of your mind and behavior with other people. Social psychology looks at your personality, interpersonal relationships and group behaviour. Social psychology focuses on three main areas: social thinking, social influence and social behaviour.

23 Which of the following is an application of operant conditioning?

1 Aversive conditioning

2 Behaviour modification

3 Systematic desensitisation

4 Transfer of learning

Ans. (2)

➲ *Exp.* Behaviour modification is an application of operant conditioning. Operant behaviour is behaviour 'controlled' by its consequences.

In practice, operant conditioning is the study of reversible behaviour maintained by reinforcement schedules. Operant conditioning relies on a fairly simple premise: Actions that are followed by reinforcement will be strengthened and more likely to occur again in the future. If you tell a funny story in class and everybody laughs, you will probably be more likely to tell that story again in the future.

24 Match List I with List II.

List I (Psychologist)	List II (Contributions)
A. Viktor Frankl	I. Shadow
B. Rollo May	II. Logotherapy
C. Fritz Pearls	III. Paradoxical intentions
D. Carl Rogers	IV. Gestalt therapy

Codes

	A	B	C	D		A	B	C	D
1	I	II	III	IV	2	II	III	IV	I
3	III	II	IV	I	4	III	I	II	IV

Ans. (2)

➲ *Exp.* The correct matching is A-II, B-III, C-IV, D-I.

Viktor Frankl was an Austrian neurologist and psychologist who founded what he called the field of 'Logotherapy', which has been dubbed the 'Third Viennese School of Psychology'.

Rollo May introduced existentialism and paradoxical intentions to American psychologists, and has remained the best known proponent of this approach in America.

Trained in a fairly traditional format as a psychoanalyst, May considered the detachment with which psychoanalysts approached their patients as a violation of social ethics.

Fritz Perls was a German-born psychiatrist, psychoanalyst and psychotherapist. Perls coined the term 'Gestalt therapy' to identify the form of psychotherapy.

Carl Rogers is esteemed as one of the founders of humanistic psychology. He developed the person-centered, also known as client-centered, approach to psychotherapy and developed the concept of unconditional positive regard.

25 Consider the following statements.

I. The semi-interquartile range measures the spread of the middle 50% of scores.

II. Standard deviation is the measure of dispersion of results from the mean result.

Which of the statements given above is/are correct?

1 Only I
2 Only II
3 Both I and II
4 None of these

Ans. (3)

Exp. Both the statements I and II are correct.

The semi-interquartile range (SIR) (also called the quartile deviation) is a measure of spread. It tells you something about how data is dispersed around a central point (usually the mean). The semi-interquartile range is half the interquartile range. When the data set is small, it is simple to identify the values of quartiles.

A standard deviation (or s) is a measure of how dispersed the data is in relation to the mean. Low standard deviation means data are clustered around the mean, and high standard deviation indicates data are more spread out.

26 Arrange in order the scientific thoughts according to their emergence.

I. Rationalism
II. Positivism
III. Critical research
IV. Post-positivism

Codes

1 I, II, III, IV
2 IV, I II, III
3 I, II, IV, III
4 II, I, IV, III

Ans. (3)

Exp. I, II, IV, III is the correct order of the scientific thoughts according to their emergence.

The order of their emergence is rationalism, positivism, post-positivism and at last critical research. These schools are explained individually below :

Rationalism is a method of thinking that is marked by being a deductive and abstract way of reasoning. In ordinary usage rationalism is a basic sense of respect for reason or to refer to the idea that reason should play a large role in human life.

Positivism is the name for the scientific study of the social world. Its goal is to formulate abstract and universal laws on the operative dynamics of the social universe. Critical thinking is objective and requires you to analyse and evaluate information to form a sound judgement.

27 Abstract, idealised representation that captures an average or typical member of a category of things is referred to as

1 Exemplar
2 Prototype
3 Concept
4 Schemes

Ans. (2)

Exp. Abstract, idealised representation that captures an average or typical member of a category of things is referred to as prototype.

Prototype means typical, this approach is used to determine what the abstract representation of a 'typical' member of a category would be. Linguistic constructs, such as syntactic and lexical categories, also display prototype effects. The application of prototype theory to the study of parts of speech and syntactic constructions has been especially fruitful.

28 Who among the following presented decisive experimental evidence for exploration and curiosity to be motivational concepts?

1 Fantz
2 Lorenz
3 Gibson
4 Harlow

Ans. (4)

Exp. Harlow presented decisive experimental evidence for exploration and curiosity to be motivational concepts.

Curiosity is defined as the intrinsic desire to know, to see, or to experience something, which motivates information seeking behaviour.

29 In the present era of competitive marketing some of the companies are offering door-to-door sales services. In such case which kind of reinforcement schedule is practiced by the company for their sales executives?

1 Fixed-ratio schedule
2 Fixed-interval schedule
3 Variable-ratio schedule
4 Variable-interval schedule

Ans. (3)

Exp. In the present era of competitive marketing some of the companies are offering door-to-door sales services. In such a case, variable-ratio schedule is a kind of reinforcement schedule practiced by the company for their sales executives.

In operant conditioning, a variable-ratio schedule is a partial schedule of reinforcement in which a response is reinforced after an unpredictable number of responses. Gambling and lottery games are good examples of a reward based on a variable-ratio schedule.

30 Which of the following is most effective in conditioning?

1 Backward conditioning
2 Delayed conditioning
3 Simultaneous conditioning
4 Trace conditioning

Ans. (2)

➲ *Exp.* Delayed conditioning is most effective in conditioning. In classical conditioning, a procedure in which the conditioned stimulus is presented, and remains present, for a fixed period (the delay) before the unconditioned stimulus is introduced.

After repeated exposure to such pairings, a conditioned response develops. If the delay is long enough, inhibition of delay may be observed, also called delayed conditioning.

31 Out of the following, which approach used in assessment of intelligence, is oldest one?

1 Psychometric Approach
2 Biological Approach
3 Culture Fair
4 Chronometric Analysis

Ans. (4)

➲ *Exp.* Chronometric Analysis is the used in assessment of intelligence, is oldest one. The chronometric analysis is a method that is used for evaluation of an unknown sample with reference to the known colours. It is basically a technique of evaluation by comparing a sample with a standard colour. The analysis is used in a variety of industries to test the quality of the products, processes and raw materials.

32 Ruby was listening to a tape recording of a famous speech that was played backward. She just heard gibberish until a classmate said the phrase 'meet me in St Louis' was clearly spoken. The tape was rewound and as Ashlynn listened this time, she also clearly heard the same phase. Ruby's ability to detect the phrase the second time through the tape illustrates

1 the opponent-process model of perception
2 the top-down processing model of perception
3 the bottom-up processing model of perception
4 the electric model of perception

Ans. (2)

➲ *Exp.* Ruby's ability to detect the phrase the second time through the tape illustrates the top-down processing model of perception.

In top-down processing, perceptions begin with the most general and move toward the more specific. These perceptions are heavily influenced by our expectations and prior knowledge. Put simply, your brain applies what it knows to fill in the blanks and anticipate what's next. Top-down processing is how knowledge, expectations or past experiences shape the interpretation of sensory information.

33 The DSM-IV-TR definition of mental disorder is perhaps the best current definition because

1 it includes information about both violation of social norms and dysfunction.
2 it includes many components none of which can alone account for mental disorder.
3 it is part of the current diagnostic system.
4 it recognises the limits of our current understanding.

Ans. (2)

➲ *Exp.* The DSM-IV-TR definition of mental disorder is perhaps the best current definition because it includes many components none of which can alone account for mental disorder.

DSM-IV-TR notes that mental disorders are associated with distress, disability, or a significantly increased risk of suffering death, pain, disability, or an important loss of freedom. It also gives an example of distress and defines disability as impairment in one or more important areas of functioning.

34 Milly generally likes to go home to visit her family during vacation. How, after her father tells her she must be home during spring vacation, Milly decides to remain at college. We can probably best understand Milly's behaviour in terms' of

1 reaction formation
2 regression
3 psychological reactance
4 self-serving bias

Ans. (3)

➲ *Exp.* We can probably best understand Milly's behaviour in terms of psychological reactance.

Reactance is an unpleasant motivational arousal that emerges when people experience a threat to or loss of their free behaviours. It serves as a motivator to restore one's freedom. The amount of reactance depends on the importance of the threatened freedom and the perceived magnitude of the threat.

35 Arrange the following steps involved in test construction in chronological order.

I. specifying construct of interest
II. evaluating reliability and validity of test
III. choosing a method
IV. deciding test's function
V. designing item content

Codes

1 I, IV III, V, II
2 I, III, IV, V, II
3 I, IV, III, II, V
4 I, III, IV, II, V

Ans. (1)

➲ *Exp.* The correct chronological order is I, IV III, V, II.

Test development or test construction refers to the science and art of planning, preparing administering, scoring, statistically analysing and reporting results of tests. Steps involved in Test Construction are arranged in a chronological order are as follows:

Step 1: Specifying construct of interest
Step 2: Deciding test's function
Step 3: Choosing a method
Step 4: Deciding test's function
Step 5: Evaluating reliability and validity of test.

36 Which of the following statements is/are correct?

I. Women are easier to convince.
II. Referent informational influence is a concept derived of social identity theory.
III. Social identity theory does not give rise to inter-group discrimination.
IV. Henri Tajfel proposed social identity theory.

Select the correct answer using the codes given below.

1 I and II 2 II and III
3 III and IV 4 II and IV

Ans. (4)

Exp. Statements II and IV are correct.

Referent informational influence theory explains group polarisation as conformity, through self-categorisation, to a local in-group norm that is polarised as a result of the in-group being located toward an extreme of the salient comparative context or social frame of reference.

Social identity theory proposed by Tajfel and Turner (1986) suggests that individuals experience collective identity based on their membership in a group, such as racial/ethnic and gender identities.

37 Arrange the phases of Cooperative Inquiry in sequence of their occurrence.

I. Experiences leading to new fields
II. Reframe
III. Reflection
IV. Action

Codes

1 I, II, III, IV 2 IV, III, II, I
3 III, IV, I, II 4 I, III, II, IV

Ans. (3)

Exp. The order of action in which a co-operative inquiry is conducted is: reflection, action, experiences leading to new fields and reframe.

Co-operative inquiry is a way of working with other people who have similar concerns and interests to yourself, in order to understand your world, make sense of your life and develop new and creative ways of looking at things learn how to act to change things you may want to change and find out how to do things better.

38 Match List I with List II.

List I (Concept)	List II (Researchers)
A. Flashbulb memory	I. Broadbent
B. Organisation as in library	II. Brown and Kulik
C. VLTM	III. Bahrick and Bahrick
D. STM	IV. Wickens

Codes

	A	B	C	D		A	B	C	D
1	II	I	IV	III	2	II	I	III	IV
3	I	II	III	IV	4	IV	I	III	II

Ans. (2)

Exp. The correct matching is A- II, B-I, C- III, D- IV.

Flashbulb Memory phenomenon is defined as the vivid recollection one has of striking events because of the high level of surprise and emotional arousal these events create. It was given by Brown and Kulik in 1977.

Library organisation is essential for day-to-day operations under the financial and policy oversight of the Board of Trustees. Library activities have been classified and divided into manageable jobs and allocated to staff through established salary classifications and position descriptions. It was given by Broadbent.

Very Long-Term Memory Experiment Bahrick and Bahrick, and Wittinger (1975) investigated what they called Very Long Term Memory (VLTM). Participants were asked to list the names they could remember of those in their graduating class in a free recall test.

Short-Term Memory Experiment Wickens demonstrated that marked interference in Short-term Memory was obtained with as few as three proactive items when the test item on the fourth trial and the proactive items were from the same class of materials, namely, consonant trigrams or three-digit numbers.

39 Depending upon the task characteristics, there is a gradual transition from simpler forms of learning to the level of higher complex ones. These different forms are

I. Establishment of simple S-R relationships
II. Acquiring motor and verbal skills
III. Concept formation
IV. Problem-solving

The correct order of learning sequence is

1 I, IV, II, III 2 I, II, III, IV
3 II, IV, I, III 4 II, III, IV, I

Ans. (2)

Exp. The correct order in which the learning process takes place is establishment of simple S-R relationships, acquiring motor and verbal skills, concept formation and problem-solving.

A learning sequence is an ordering of student's learning activities.

In the design literature one may find two basic sorts of instructional design models. Those that focus on materials, i.e. resources arranged to form an organisation of learning-flow content. Sequence learning is inherent to human ability because it is an integrated part of conscious and non-conscious learning as well as activities.

40 "The most important thing a psychologist can study is how a behaviour or thought helps a person navigate the world, rather than how that thought comes to be or what it is made of." This viewpoint probably comes from somebody who believes in what historical theoretical approach?

1 Structuralism 2 Functionalism
3 Gestalt 4 Psychoanalysis

Ans. (2)

➲ *Exp.* Functionalism viewpoint comes from somebody who believes in what historical theoretical approach. Functionalism, in social sciences, theory based on the premise that all aspects of a society—institutions, roles, norms, etc. — serve a purpose and that all are indispensable for the long-term survival of the society. The approach gained prominence in the works of 19th-century sociologists.

41 Consider the following statements.

I. Guilford classify mental abilities the same way chemical element classified in periodic table.

II. Mednick said that true creativity is the ability to think a remote idea.

Which of the statements given above is/are correct?

1 Only I   2 Only II
3 I and II   4 None of these

Ans. (3)

➲ *Exp.* Statements I and II are correct.

According to Guilford's Structure of Intellect (SI) theory (1955), an individual's performance on intelligence tests can be traced back to the underlying mental abilities or factors of intelligence.

Mednick defined the process of creative thinking as the forming of associative elements into new combinations which either meet specific requirements or are in some way useful. The more mutually remote the elements of the new combination, the more creative the process or solution.

42 Match List I with List II and select the correct answer by choosing from the codes given below.

List I (Books)	List II (Authors)
A. Toward a Psychology of Being	I. May
B. A Way of Being	II. Maslow
C. Man's Search for Meaning	III. Rogers
D. Love and Will	IV. Frankl

Codes

	A	B	C	D		A	B	C	D
1	I	II	III	IV	2	II	III	IV	I
3	III	II	I	IV	4	IV	I	II	III

Ans. (2)

➲ *Exp.* The correct matching is A-II, B-III, C-IV, D-I.

Toward a Psychology of Being by Maslow addresses two gaps he saw in the behaviourist and psychoanalytic psychologies of his time.

A profound and deeply personal collection of essays, **A Way of Being** by renowned psychologist Carl Rogers. The late Carl Rogers, founder of the humanistic psychology movement, he believed that children learn through unconditional acceptance and understanding.

Man's Search for Meaning is a 1946 book by Viktor Frankl chronicling his experiences as a prisoner in Nazi concentration camps during World War II, and describing his psychotherapeutic method, which involved identifying a purpose in life to feel positive about, and then immersive imagining that outcome.

Love and Will (1969) is a book by American existential psychologist Rollo May, in which he articulates the principle that an awareness of death is essential.

43 Sanam has just finished a long exhausting 6 mile run. She and her friend Jamal are gasing at a hill they need a climb to get back to their car. Jamal asks Sanam, "Gee how steep do you think that hill is"? Based on research by Proffitt and his colleagues Sanam is likely to

1 make a reasonably accurate estimate of the hill's slant, as most people do.
2 underestimate the hill's slant, as most people do.
3 overestimate the hill's slant, but to a lesser degree then she would have before her exhausting run.
4 overestimate the hill's slant to an even greater degree than she would have before her exhausting run.

Ans. (4)

➲ *Exp.* Based on research by Proffitt and his colleagues Sanam is likely to overestimate the hill's slant to an even greater degree than she would have before her exhausting run. William Proffitt's research focuses on understanding the identities and lived experiences of Black boys with and without disability labels and those with whom Black boys co-construct the world.

44 Read each of the following two statements labelled as Assertion (A) and Reason (R) and indicate your answer using the codes given below.

Assertion **(A) Both, context dependent memory and state dependent retrieval refer to the ease with which one can recall information in a similar context or state as when it was acquired.**

Reason **(R) According to encoding specificity principle retrieval of information is successful to the extent that the retrieval cues match the cues the learner used during the learning phase.**

Codes

1 Both A and R are true and R is the correct explanation of A.
2 Both A and R are true, but R is not the correct explanation of A.
3 A is true, but R is false.
4 A is false, but R is true.

Ans. (1)

➲ *Exp.* Both Assertion (A) and Reason (R) are true and Reason (R) is the correct explanation of Assertion (A). Context-dependent memory describes the phenomenon in which recall is stronger when a subject is present in the same environment in which the original memory was formed (Halbach et al, 2008).

The encoding specificity principle is the general principle that matching the encoding contexts of information at recall assists in the retrieval of episodic memories. It provides a framework for understanding how the conditions present while encoding information relate to memory and recall of that information.

45 **Consider the following statements.**

I. Median is preferred method for highly systematic distributions.

II. The mode is the most used measure of central tendency.

Which among the above is/are correct?

1 Only I
2 Only II
3 Both I and II
4 None of these

Ans. (1)

Exp. Only statement I is correct.

Median is the preferred method for highly systematic distributions. In a symmetric distribution, the mean and median both are the central measures of tendency. They are approximately equal, and both are valid measures of central tendency.

The median is the most informative measure of central tendency for skewed distributions or distributions with outliers. For example, the median is often used as a measure of central tendency for income distributions, which are generally highly skewed.

46 **Which of the following is not a consequence of Spearman's Theory?**

1 The correlation between different measures of intelligence will be positive.
2 The correlation between measures of intelligence will be equal to $r_{1g} \times r_{2g}$, where 1 and 2 represent the two different measures and g represents general factor.
3 The correlation between to measures of intelligence will be equal to $r_{1g} + r_{2g}$, where 1 and 2 represent the two different measures and g represents general factor.
4 The law of tetrad difference will mold for four measures of intelligence.

Ans. (2)

Exp. The correlation between measures of intelligence will be equal to $r_{1g} + r_{2g}$ where 1 and 2 represent the two different measures and g represents a general factor that is not a consequence of Spearman's Theory. General intelligence, also known as g factor, refers to a general mental ability that, according to Spearman, underlies multiple specific skills, including verbal, spatial, numerical and mechanical.

47 **Arrange the steps in order in Pavlov's experiment**

I. Selecting stimulus and response

II. Establishing classical conditioning

III. Testing for Conditioning

Codes

1 I, II, III
2 III, I, II
3 II, I, III
4 I, III, II

Ans. (1)

Exp. I, II, III is the correct sequence of steps in order in Pavlov's experiment. According to the experiment, Pavlov's conditioning first selects the stimulus and response, then classical conditioning is administered and lastly the conditioning is tested. According to Pavlov, conditioning does not involve the acquisition of any new behaviour, but rather the tendency to respond using the learned ways to a new stimuli. This explanation is called the stimulus- substitution theory of conditioning.

48 **Match List I with List II.**

List I	List II
A. Preparation	I. Ideas are ascertained, checked and reassured by themselves and by other confirming the validity of their hypothesis.
B. Incubation	II. 'Happy thoughts' do not occur to lazy persons; they arise in well prepared and well stocked minds.
C. Illumination	III. The climax of the process of creative thinking dawns the saving-guiding idea, which is the forerunner of the final solution.
D. Verification	IV. The 'hatching' period in creative thought process us characterised by restlessness and poorly coordinated activity accompanied by a feeling of unease and frustration through unconscious thought processes.

Codes

	A	B	C	D
1	II	III	IV	I
2	I	III	IV	II
3	III	II	I	IV
4	III	IV	I	II

Ans. (1)

Exp. The correct matching is A- II, B- III, C-IV, D- I.

These are the five steps using which an individual's creative processes develop. The order of the development of a creative process are preparation, concentration, incubation, illumination and verification.

Preparation is the first step where the problematic part of the whole is ruled out and defined. Second step is concentration where all the attention is paid to solving the problem. Third step is incubation in which the subconscious mind equips itself with the idea and lastly illumination i.e. the very moment the idea comes up. The last step is verification where the practicality and functionality of the idea is tested.

49 **Which of the following sets of stage models of health behaviour is in correct chronological order?**

I. People are unaware of health issues.

II. People are aware of the issue but never thought about adopting the precaution.

III. People decide against adopting the.

IV. People act on their decision.

Codes

1 I, II, III, IV
2 I, II, IV, III
3 II, I, III, IV
4 II, I, IV, III

Ans. (1)

➲ *Exp.* The most-often used theories of health behaviour are Social Cognitive Theory, the Transtheoretical Model/Stages of Change, the Health Belief Model and the Theory of Planned Behaviour.

The most-often mentioned theoretical model that has not been fully applied in research and practice is the Social Ecological Model.

50 What is considered statistically 'abnormal' for a person to score in an IQ Test?

1 Below 55
2 Above 145
3 Both 1 and 2
4 None of the above

Ans. (3)

➲ *Exp.* Below 55 and above 145 is considered statistically 'abnormal' for a person to score in an IQ Test.

If an individual scores below 55 on an IQ test are considered statistically 'abnormal' for a person. IQ tests are made to have an average score of 100. Psychologists revise the test every few years in order to maintain 100 as the average. Most people (about 68%) have an IQ between 85 and 115. Only a small fraction of people have a very low IQ (below 70) or a very high IQ (above 130).

51 Muller-Lyer illusion exists in cultures in which there are

1 more men than women
2 more women than men
3 lots of trees
4 buildings with lots of corners

Ans. (4)

➲ *Exp.* The Muller-Lyer illusion exists in cultures in which there are buildings with lots of corners. It is one of the most famous optical illusions in psychology.

It consists of two sticks, one framed by closed fins and one framed by open fins. After seeing the illusion, viewers usually estimate that the stick with two open fins is longer, even though the sticks are actually the same length.

52 Functionalism influenced which two major areas in psychology?

1 Emotion and cognition
2 Thinking and reasoning
3 Learning and motivation
4 Perception and learning

Ans. (3)

➲ *Exp.* Functionalism influenced learning and motivation, areas in psychology. Functionalism is a theory about the nature of mental states.

According to functionalists, mental states are identified by what they do rather than by what they are made of. Functionalism is the most familiar or 'received' view among philosophers of mind and cognitive science.

53 Perceived fairness of the amount and rewards among individuals refers to while perceived fairness of the ways used for rewards and pays refers to

1 organisational justice; distributive justice
2 equity justice; organisational justice
3 distributive justice; procedural justice
4 procedural justice; distributive justice

Ans. (3)

➲ *Exp.* Perceived fairness of the amount and rewards among individuals refers to distributive justice while perceived fairness of the ways used for rewards and pays refers to procedural justice.

Distributive justice refers to the perceived fairness of an allocation or, more broadly, to how people judge what they receive.

It was probably the first type of justice to gain the attention of organisational justice scholars and continues to receive wide attention.

Perceived justice has three dimensions (i) procedural justice, which refers to the perceived equity of policies (ii) procedures and criteria used by decision-makers when arriving at the outcome of a dispute or negotiation (iii) interactional justice, which refers to the way people are treated during the conflict resolution process.

54 Consider the following statements.

I. A set of source can be summarised by a set of central tendency (or average) of the scores.
II. A measure of dispersion (or spread) are the scores located around the mean.

Which of the statements given above is/are correct?

1 Only I
2 Only II
3 Both I and II
4 None of these

Ans. (3)

➲ *Exp.* Both I and II are correct statements.

A measure of central tendency is a single value that attempts to describe a set of data by identifying the central position within that set of data.

Standard deviation (SD) is the most commonly used measure of dispersion. It is a measure of spread of data about the mean. SD is the square root of sum of squared deviation from the mean divided by the number of observations.

55 Charles Darwin proposed that natural selection leads to the development of characteristics most suited to the survival and reproduction of a species.

His theory has most influenced which branch of psychology?

1 Humanism
2 Evolutionary psychology
3 Cognitive psychology
4 Behaviourism

Ans. (2)

➲ *Exp.* Charles Darwin theory has the most influential contribution to the evolutionary branch of Psychology. Evolutionary psychology is the study of behaviour, thought and feeling as viewed through the lens of evolutionary biology.

56 **To be an accurate eyewitness, a person must pass the following stages. Arrange the following in chronological order.**

I. Acquisition II. Retrieval
III. Storage

Codes

1 I, II, III 2 II, I, III
3 I, III, II 4 III, I, II

Ans. *(3)*

➲ *Exp.* I, III, II is the correct chronological order.

Eyewitnesses can provide very compelling legal testimony, but rather than recording experiences flawlessly, their memories are susceptible to a variety of errors and biases. They can make errors in remembering specific details and can even remember whole events that did not actually happen. But to make a compelling eyewitness testimony an individual must acquire, decode, retrieve and then reproduce the information accurately.

57 **The fact that cultural groups with less exposure to carpentered buildings are less susceptible to the Muller-Lyer illusion suggests that**

1 not all cultures test perceptual hypothesis.
2 people in technologically advanced cultures are more gullible.
3 optical illusions can be experienced only by cultures that have been exposed to the concept of optical illusions.
4 perceptual inferences can be shaped by experience.

Ans. *(4)*

➲ *Exp.* The fact that cultural groups with less exposure to carpentered buildings are less susceptible to the Muller-Lyer illusion suggests that perceptual inferences can be shaped by experience. The Muller-Lyer illusion exists in cultures in which there are buildings that have lot of corners.

The Muller-Lyer illusion is one of the most famous optical illusions in psychology. It consists of two sticks, one framed by closed fins and one framed by open fins. After seeing the illusion, viewers usually estimate that the stick with two open fins is longer, even though the sticks are actually the same length.

58 **Match List I with List II.**

List I (Measures)	List II (Objectives)
A. Mode	I. Purpose of the test
B. Quartile deviation	II. Consistency of test scores
C. Reliability	III. Measure of variability
D. Validity	IV. Measure of central tendency

Codes

	A	B	C	D
1	III	IV	II	I
2	IV	III	II	I
3	III	IV	I	II
4	IV	III	I	II

Ans. *(2)*

➲ *Exp.* The correct matching is A- IV, B-III, C-II, D-I.

Mode is helpful in presenting a brief picture of data. It helps in giving a brief description of the main feature of the entire data.

Quartile deviation helps to examine the spread of a distribution about a measure of its central tendency, usually the mean or the average.

Reliability determines the failure rate, the mean life, and the reliability of components, equipment, and systems and their associated confidence limits at desired confidence levels.

Validity tells you if the characteristic being measured by a test is related to job qualifications and requirements. Validity gives meaning to the test scores.

59 **In 'Signal Detection Theory', which of the following determinants are assumed?**

I. Observer's sensitivity
II. Sensory threshold
III. Response bias
IV. Decision bias

Codes

1 Only I 2 I and III
3 I, III and IV 4 II and III

Ans. *(2)*

➲ *Exp.* In 'Signal Detection theory', observer's sensitivity and Response bias determinants are used.

Signal detection theory is a method of differentiating a person's ability to discriminate the presence and absence of a stimulus (or different stimulus intensities) from the criterion the person uses to make responses to those stimuli Signal detection theory (SDT) is used when psychologists want to measure the way an individual makes decisions under conditions of uncertainty.

60 **Consider the following statements.**

I. According to Jensen, 'Intelligence' is essentially another activity or function of the individual like blood pressure, temperature, etc.
II. Intelligence test provides accurate results.

Which of the statements given above is/are correct?

1 Only I 2 Only II
3 Both I and II 4 Neither I nor II

Ans. *(3)*

➲ *Exp.* Both the statements I and II are correct. According to Jensen, 'Intelligence' is essentially another activity or function of the individual like blood pressure, temperature, etc. Thus as a sphygmomanometer and a thermometer give us measures of blood pressure or body temperature, intelligence tests also give us a measure of intelligence, and therefore there is no need to multiply the same.

According to Jensen, there are two factors of intelligence-breadth and altitude. The former includes general information, vocabulary, etc., which are directly dependent on a person's experience, exposure and opportunities which a person has had.

61 Arrange the following steps of decision- making in order.

I. Developing and weighing the options
II. Plan and execute
III. Take follow up action
IV. Choosing lest possible option

Codes

1 I, II, III, IV   2 II, III, IV, I
3 I, IV, II, III   4 IV, II, III, I

Ans. (3)

Exp. The correct order of decision making steps is I, IV, II, III.

The decision-making process is a tool that is used to effectively make decisions effectively and productively. The decision-making process allows for the exploration of all alternatives in order to solve a problem, and it ensures that the best solution is found. The decision-making process includes the following steps: define, identify, assess, consider, implement, and evaluate.

62 The relative apparent motion of object in the visual field as the viewer moves the head is called

1 Image retina system
2 Accommodation
3 Motion parallax
4 The eye-head system

Ans. (3)

Exp. The relative apparent motion of an object in the visual field as the viewer moves the head is called Motion Parallax. Motion parallax is a type of depth perception cue in which objects that are closer appear to move faster than objects that are further. Motion parallax is a monocular depth cue arising from the relative velocities of objects moving across the retina of a moving person.

63 The chronological age that most typically corresponds to a given level of performance is called

1 Intelligence Quotient   2 Maturation
3 Mental age   4 None of these

Ans. (3)

Exp. The chronological age that most typically corresponds to a given level of performance is called Mental age.

Mental age is the age level of an individual's mental ability. It is based on the age in which it takes an average individual to reach that same level of mental attainment. Mental age is usually measured by standardised intelligence tests. To calculate the IQ level of an individual the chronological age is divided by the mental age and the whole score is multiplied by 100.

$$IQ = CA / MA \times 100$$

64 Which one of the following statistical measure is used for assessing the test-item bias?

1 Item-remainder correlation
2 Differential item functioning
3 Construct validity
4 Multidimensional scaling

Ans. (2)

Exp. Differential item functioning statistics are used for assessing the test-item bias. Differential item functioning (DIF) occurs when groups (such as defined by gender, ethnicity, age or education) have different probabilities of endorsing a given item on a multi-item scale after controlling for overall scale scores.

65 Patients with damage to the frontal lobes behave as if they lack control systems that monitor their processing resources appropriately. They are said to suffer from

1 Gertsman Syndrome   2 Dysexecutive Syndrome
3 Korsakoff's Syndrome   4 None of these

Ans. (2)

Exp. Patients with damage to the frontal lobes behave as if they lack control systems that monitor their processing resources appropriately.

They are said to suffer from Dysexecutive Syndrome. The term 'dysexecutive syndrome' refers to a dysregulation of executive functions and is strictly associated to frontal lobe damage.

Dysexecutive syndrome typically encompasses emotional, motivational and behavioural symptoms, as well as cognitive deficits.

66 Which of the following is not a standard physiological measure of sleep?

1 Electrooculogram   2 Electromyogram
3 Electrocardiogram   4 Electroencephalogram

Ans. (3)

Exp. Electrocardiogram is not a standard physiological measure of sleep. An Electrocardiogram (ECG) is a simple test that can be used to check your heart's rhythm and electrical activity.

Sensors attached to the skin are used to detect the electrical signals produced by your heart each time it beats. Many different heart conditions can show up on an ECG, including a fast, slow or abnormal heart rhythm, a heart defect, coronary artery disease, heart valve disease or an enlarged heart.

67 In heightened emotional states, the following functions are not triggered by sympathetic Nervous System activity.

I. Perspiration   II. Heightened pulse rate
III. Digestion   IV. Pupillary dilation

Codes

1 Only III   2 III and IV
3 I, II and III   4 I, III and IV

Ans. (1)

➲ *Exp.* In heightened emotional states, only Digestion functions are not triggered by sympathetic Nervous System activity.

Sympathetic nervous system is best known for its role in responding to dangerous or stressful situations. In situations like these, the sympathetic nervous system activates to speed up your heart rate, deliver more blood to areas of your body that need more oxygen or other responses to help an individual get out of danger.

68 Arrange the following tests with respect to their ability to elicit projective responses from low to high.

I. Sentence Completion Test
II. Rorschach Inkblot Test
III. Rosenzweig Picture Frustration Study
IV. Thematic Apperception Test

Codes

1 II, IV, III, I
2 I, III, IV, II
3 IV, II, I, III
4 II, I, IV, III

Ans. (2)

➲ *Exp.* I, III, IV, II is the correct sequence of given tests with respect to their ability to elicit projective responses from low to high. Sentence Completion Test (SCT) is a projective test used widely by clinicians and psychologists to explore the needs, inner conflicts, fantasies, attitudes, aspirations, adjustment difficulties and sexual abuse in the children and adolescents.

Rorschach Inkblot Test was designed to look for patterns of thought disorder in schizophrenia and has evolved to include other areas, like personality, emotional disorders and intelligence.

Rosenzweig Picture Frustration Study is a projective test administered to assess personality characteristics, in which the subject is shown scenes depicting moderately frustrating situations and asked what the frustrated person depicted would probably do, or how the subject would react in such situations.

Thematic Apperception Test, or TAT, is a projective test that involves having people explain what is happening in ambiguous scenes.

69 When the action potential reaches the end of the axon terminals, it causes the release of

1 an electric spark that sets off the next neuron.
2 positively charged ions that excite the next cell.
3 negatively charged ions that inhibit the next cell.
4 neurotransmitters that excite or inhibit the next cell.

Ans. (4)

➲ *Exp.* When the action potential reaches the end of the axon terminals, it causes the release of neurotransmitters that excite or inhibit the next cell.

The neurotransmitter can either help (excite) or hinder (inhibit) neuron B from firing its own action potential. In an intact brain, the balance of hundreds of excitatory and inhibitory inputs to a neuron determines whether an action potential will result.

70 An interval scale of measurement contains

I. properties of normal and ordinal scales.
II. true zero point.
III. comparable differences between different intervals of the scale.
IV. a minimum requirement for use of parametric tests.

Codes

1 I, II, III and IV
2 I and II
3 I, II and IV
4 I, III and IV

Ans. (4)

➲ *Exp.* An interval scale of measurement contains properties of nominal and ordinal scales, comparable differences between different intervals of the scale and a minimum requirement for use of parametric tests.

The interval scale is a quantitative measurement scale where there is order, the difference between the two variables is meaningful and equal, and the presence of zero is arbitrary. It measures variables that exist along a common scale at equal intervals.

71 Which of the following are not nuclei of Thalamus?

I. Internal lamina
II. Anterior nucleus
III. Ventromedial nucleus
IV. Paraventricular nucleus

Codes

1 I and II
2 II and III
3 III and IV
4 I and III

Ans. (3)

➲ *Exp.* The Ventromedial nucleus and Paraventricular nucleus are not nuclei of Thalamus.

The thalamic nuclei are the clusters of densely packed neuronal cell bodies that comprise the thalamus. The thalamus is an ovoid, paired gray matter structure, found in the center of the brain, just superior to the brainstem.

72 The theories of intelligence appeared in which one of the following orders?

1 Binet-Simon, Thurstone, RB Cattell, Spearman
2 Binet-Simon, Spearman, Thurstone, RB Cattell
3 Spearman, Binet-Simon, Thurstone, RB Cattell
4 RB Cattell, Binet-Simon, Thurstone, Spearman

Ans. (3)

➲ *Exp.* The theories of intelligence appeared in Spearman, Binet-Simon, Thurstone, RB Cattell order.

General intelligence, also known as *g* factor, refers to a general mental ability that, according to Spearman, underlies multiple specific skills, including verbal, spatial, numerical and mechanical.

Binet Simon created the concept of a mental age, or how well an individual performs intellectually relative to the average performance at that age.

Thurstone (1938) challenged the concept of a *g*-factor.

The Cattell-Horn (1966) theory of fluid and crystallised intelligence suggests that intelligence is composed of a number of different abilities that interact and work together to produce overall individual intelligence.

73 .... makes neurons stand out visibly depicting which neurons are active, whereas .... uses antibodies attached to a dye to identify cellular component such as receptors, neurotransmitters or enzymes.

1 Immunocytochemistry; Autoradiography
2 Autoradiography; Immunocytochemistry
3 Myelin staining; Nissl Staining
4 Nissl Staining; Myelin Staining

Ans. *(1)*

➲ *Exp.* Immunocytochemistry makes neurons stand out visibly depicting which neurons are active, whereas Immunocytochemistry is used to detect proteins in isolated cells.

Autoradiography is an imaging technique that uses radioactive sources contained within the exposed sample. Autoradiography uses antibodies attached to a dye to identify cellular components such as receptors, neurotransmitters or enzymes.

74 Which of the following scaling methods have been developed by Thurstone?

I. Method of paired comparison
II. Method of summated ratings
III. Method of successive intervals
IV. Equal appearing intervals method

Codes

1 Only II
2 II and III
3 I, II and IV
4 II, III and IV

Ans. *(2)*

➲ *Exp.* Method of summated ratings and Method of successive intervals scaling methods have been developed by Thurstone.

Method of summated ratings is a type of assessment instrument comprising a series of statements measuring the same construct or variable to which respondents indicate their degree of agreement or disagreement. The method of successive intervals is a psychological scaling procedure in which stimuli are classified into successive intervals according to the degree of some defined attribute which they are judged to possess.

75 Given below are two statements, one is labelled as Assertion (A) and the other labelled as Reason (R).

Assertion (A) **Subliminal perception implies detection of a stimulus with a magnitude for below the absolute threshold.**

Reason (R) **Receptors always receive information and that is always perceived.**

Codes

1 Both A and R are true and R is the correct explanation of A.
2 Both A and R are true, but R is not the correct explanation of A.
3 A is true, but R is false.
4 A is false, but R is true.

Ans. *(3)*

➲ *Exp.* Assertion (A) is true, but Reason (R) is false.

Subliminal perception is the perception of a series of stimulus which the person is not consciously aware of and gets under the influence involuntarily, in addition to the perception with the five sense organs. Subliminal perception occurs when a stimulus is too weak to be perceived yet a person is influenced by it.

76 Out of the following theories of intelligence which one is regarded as latest one?

1 Sternberg's theory
2 Mayer and Salovey theory
3 Jensen's theory
4 Cattell's theory

Ans. *(1)*

➲ *Exp.* Sternberg's theory is regarded as the latest theory of intelligence.

Sternberg's Theory of Intelligence contends that intelligent behaviour arises from a balance between analytical, creative and practical abilities, and that these abilities function collectively to allow individuals to achieve success within particular socio-cultural contexts.

77 Which of the following do not belong to laws of perceptual grouping?

I. Law of figure and ground
II. Law of good continuation
III. Law of common fate
IV. Law of closure
V. Law of proximity

Codes

1 I and V   2 II and IV
3 III and V   4 I and III

Ans. *(4)*

➲ *Exp.* Law of figure and ground and Law of common fate do not belong to laws of perceptual grouping. Proposed by the Gestalt psychologists in the early 20th century, the Gestalt laws of grouping involve a set of principles that account for such natural manner of perception. These include six categories namely: similarity, proximity, good form, closure, common fate and continuation.

78 Which of the following is/are correct in Rogerian therapy?

I. The therapist is supportive and non-directive.
II. It is the client and not the therapist who best understands the problem and in what direction the therapy should proceed.

III. The therapist can sense the client's tensions and incongruent feelings and reflect them back to the client.

Codes

1 Only I
2 I and II
3 I and III
4 I, II and III

Ans. (4)

Exp. Statements I, II and III are correct in Rogerian Therapy.

Rogerian therapy is a type of counseling in which the therapist is non-directive but supportive, allowing the client to direct the course of each therapy session. The counselor's expertise is secondary to the patient's ability to solve his or her problems.

This type of therapy diverged from the traditional model of the therapist as expert and moved instead toward a non-directive, empathic approach that empowers and motivates the client in the therapeutic process.

79 Identify the correct concepts related with Cattell's theory of personality.

I. Dynamic Lattice
II. Specification Equation
III. Orthogonal Rotation
IV. Ergs

Codes

1 II, III and IV
2 I, II and IV
3 II and IV
4 I, II, III and IV

Ans. (2)

Exp. Dynamic Lattice, Specification Equation and Ergs are the correct concepts related with Cattell's theory of personality.

According to Cattell, traits and types are not fundamentally different, but rather opposite extremes of the same statistical measures. The fundamental, underlying traits are known as source traits. Source traits often combine and/or interact in ways that appear, on the surface, to indicate a single trait.

80 Which of the following tests are considered to be culture-fair tests of intelligence?

I. Cattell's Culture-Fair Test of Intelligence
II. Raven's Progressive Matrices
III. Wechsler's Intelligence Scale for Children
IV. Goodenough-Harris Test

Codes

1 Only I
2 I and II
3 I, II and III
4 I, II and IV

Ans. (4)

Exp. I, II and IV tests are considered to be culture-fair tests of intelligence.

Culture fair test is a test that is equally fair to all cultural groups. Fairness is related to a lack of bias in the interpretation or use of a test to classify or diagnose. In a culture fair test, the validity of the interpretation is similar across different cultural groups. An example of culture fair intelligence tests are Raven's Progressive Matrices.

81 Given below are two statements, one is labelled as Assertion (A) and the other labelled as Reason (R). Choose your answer using the codes given below.

Assertion (A) Algorithm is a logical rule that guarantees solving a particular problem.

Reason (R) One can find the solution even to complex problems by following step by step procedure.

Codes

1 Both A and R are true and R is the correct explanation of A.
2 Both A and R are true, but R is not the correct explanation of A.
3 A is true, but R is false.
4 A is false, but R is true.

Ans. (2)

Exp. Both Assertion (A) and Reason (R) are true, but Reason (R) is not the correct explanation of Assertion (A).

Algorithm is a logical rule that guarantees solving a particular problem. An algorithm is a defined set of step-by-step procedures that provides the correct answer to a particular problem.

By following the instructions correctly, you are guaranteed to arrive at the right answer.

82 Match List I with List II.

List I (Design)	**List II** (Full forms)
A. ANOVA	I. Multivariante Analysis of Variance
B. MANOVA	II. Analysis of Variance
C. ANCOVA	III. Analysis of Covariance

Codes

	A	B	C
1	I	II	III
2	II	I	III
3	I	III	II
4	II	III	I

Ans. (2)

Exp. The correct matching is A-II, B-I, C-III.

Analysis of Variance (ANOVA) is a family of statistical tests that are useful when comparing several sets of scores. A common application of ANOVA is to test if the means of three or more groups are equal. The basic idea behind ANOVA is a comparison of the variance between the groups and the variance within the groups.

Multivariate Analysis of Variance (MANOVA) is a statistical analysis used when a researcher wants to examine the effects of one or more Independent Variables (IVs) on multiple Dependent Variables (DVs).

The Analysis of Covariance (ANCOVA) is a method for testing the hypothesis of the equality of two or more population means, ideally in the context of a designed experiment.

83 In an experiment the stimuli were presented to the subjects in a certain order and after the presentation of stimuli their order was disturbed. In the test phase the subjects were needed to set them in the presented order. Which of the following methods was used in this experiment?

1 Recognition 2 Relearning
3 Reconstruction 4 Recall

Ans. (3)

Exp. Reconstruction methods was used in the given experiment.

Reconstruction in psychology memory is the process of remembering conceived as involving the recreation of an experience or event that has been only partially stored in memory. When a memory is retrieved, the process uses general knowledge and schemas for what typically happens in order to reconstruct the experience or event.

84 Given below are two statements, the first labelled as Assertion (A) and the other labelled as Reason (R). Indicate your answer using the codes given below.

Assertion (A) Resolution of Oedipus complex is the main reason for the development of Super Ego.

Reason (R) Resolution of Oedipus complex involves a child's identification with the same gender parent.

Codes

1 Both A and R are true and R is the correct explanation of A.
2 Both A and R are true, but R is not the correct explanation of A.
3 A is true, but R is false.
4 A is false, but R is true.

Ans. (1)

Exp. Both Assertion (A) and Reason (R) are true and Reason (R) is the correct explanation of Assertion (A).

Resolution of Oedipus complex is the main reason for the development of Super Ego.

Resolution of Oedipus complex involves a child's identification with the same gender parent. Freud attributed the Oedipus complex to children of about the ages three to five. He said the stage usually ended when the child identified with the parent of the same sex and repressed its sexual instincts.

85 Choose the right sequence of endocrine system.

1 Hypothalamus → Cortico releasing hormone → Pancreas → Insulin.
2 Pituitary gland → Adenocorticotrophic hormone → Adrenal gland → Epinephrine.
3 Hypothalamus → Adenocorticotrophic hormone → Gonads → Androgens.
4 Thyroid gland → Cortico releasing hormone → Hypothalamus → Thyroxin.

Ans. (2)

Exp. The endocrine system is a complex network of glands and organs. It uses hormones to control and coordinate your body's metabolism, energy level, reproduction, growth and development, and response to injury, stress and mood. The most integral parts of the endocrine system is the Hypothalamus.

86 Match List I with List II.

List I (Strategies)	List II (Concepts)
A. Heuristic	I. Step by step
B. Algorithm	II. Sudden occurrence
C. Trial and Error	III. Rule of thumb
D. Insight	IV. Multiple attempts

Codes

	A	B	C	D		A	B	C	D
1	III	I	II	IV	2	II	IV	I	III
3	III	I	IV	II	4	II	IV	III	I

Ans. (3)

Exp. The correct matching is A- III, B- I, C- IV, D- II. **Heuristics** is an approach to problem-solving in which the objective is to produce a working solution within a reasonable time frame.

The **Algorithm Strategy** is a collection of methods or techniques to solve problems, in order to achieve the specified, which in this case the description of the method or technique is stated in a sequence of correct computational steps in solving the problem.

Trial and error is a fundamental method of Problem solving. It is characterised by repeated, varied attempts which are continued until success, or until the agent stops trying. Until getting the right answer the problem is repeated through various steps.

Insight Strategy is an insight driven consultancy that helps businesses build and refine their brand and marketing strategies.

87 Match List I with List II and choose your answer using the codes given below.

List I (Neurotransmitter)	List II (Location)
A. Acetylcholine	I. Mid brain
B. Serotonin	II. Autonomic nervous system
C. Adrenalin	III. Brain stem
D. Dopamine	IV. Neuromuscular Junction

Codes

	A	B	C	D
1	I	II	III	IV
2	IV	III	II	I
3	III	II	I	IV
4	II	IV	I	III

Ans. (2)

Exp. The correct matching is A- IV, B- III, C- II, D- I.

Within the brain, **Acetylcholine** has involvement in memory, motivation, arousal and attention. Acetylcholine originates from two major places in the brain: 1) basal forebrain and 2) the mesopontine tegmental area.

Serotonin is a chemical that carries messages between nerve cells in the brain and throughout your body. **Serotonin plays** a key role in such body functions as mood, sleep, digestion, nausea, wound healing, bone health, blood clotting and sexual desire.

The adrenal (suprarenal) glands secreted **Adrenalin** are located at the top of both kidneys. They produce hormones that regulate the immune system, blood pressure, metabolism, and the stress response.

Dopamine is a type of monoamine neurotransmitter. It's made in your brain and acts as a chemical messenger, communicating messages between nerve cells in your

88 Read each of the following statements Assertion (A) and Reason (R) and choose your answer using codes given below.

Assertion (A) Pre-operational child is incapable of performing operations.

Reason (R) Pre-operational child cannot mentally re-arrange a sequence of events into reverse order.

Codes

1 Both A and R are true and R is the correct explanation of A.
2 Both A and R are true, but R is not the correct explanation of A.
3 A is true, but R is false.
4 A is false, but R is true.

Ans. (1)

Exp. Both Assertion (A) and Reason (R) are true and Reason (R) is the correct explanation of Assertion (A).

Pre-operational child is incapable of performing operations. A toddler hits the pre-operational stage between 18 to 24 months when they start to talk.

As they build up their experiences of the world around them, they move towards the stage where they can use logical thought and imagine things. They also develop memory and imagination, which allows them to understand the difference between past and future, and engage in make-believe.

89 Experience of failure followed by .... cognitions lead to depression. Choose your answer using the codes given below.

I. Internal attributions
II. Feeling of controllability
III. Hopelessness
IV. Stable attributions
V. Specific attributions

Codes

1 I, III and IV
2 I, II and IV
3 II, III and V
4 III, IV and V

Ans. (2)

Exp. Experience of failure followed by internal attributions, feeling of controllability and stable attributions cognitions lead to depression.

Depression is a mood disorder that causes a persistent feeling of sadness and loss of interest. Also called major depressive disorder or clinical depression, it affects how you feel, think and behave and can lead to a variety of emotional and physical problems.

90 Match List I with List II and choose your answer with the help of the codes given below.

List I	List II
A. Multi-store Model	I. Craik and Lockhart
B. Neural Network Model	II. Atkinson and Shiffrin
C. Levels of Processing Model	III. McClleland and Rumelhart
D. Encoding Specificity Principle	IV. Tulving

Codes

	A	B	C	D
1	IV	I	III	II
2	I	II	IV	III
3	III	IV	II	I
4	II	III	I	IV

Ans. (2)

Exp. The correct matching is A-II, B- III, C- I, D- IV.

The **multi-store model** is an explanation of memory proposed by Atkinson and Shiffrin which assumes there are three unitary (separate) memory stores, and that information is transferred between these stores in a linear sequence.

A **Neural Network** (NN) modal is a technique for stimulating the neuronal changes in the brain that underpin cognition and perception that involves connecting a large number of basic hypothetical neural units. It was proposed by McClleland and Rumelhart.

Levels of Processing model, created by Fergus IM Craik and Robert S Lockhart in 1972, describes memory recall of stimuli as a function of the depth of mental processing. This model explains how deeper levels of analysis produce more elaborate, longer-lasting, and stronger memory traces than shallow levels of analysis.

Encoding Specificity Model Endel Tulving and Donald Thomson introduced the Encoding Specificity Principle in the early 1970s. The Encoding Specificity Principle is the general principle that matching the encoding contexts of information at recall assists in the retrieval of episodic memories.

Direction *(Q. Nos. 91-95) Read the passage given below and answer the following questions.*

One of the first experimental demonstrations of the effects of stimulus uncertainly in choice RT was provided by Merkel continue as a single paragraph.

The result reflected an interesting regularity in the nature of RT, but the general applicability of this regularity did

not become fully apparent until. Hick realised that the uncertainty produced by variations in the number of stimulus alternatives could be viewed in information theory terms by expressing the number of alternatives in bits. Consequently, he repeated Merkel's experiment using one to ten lamps arrayed in an irregular circle.
Hick found that in the language of information theory, RT was proportional to stimulus uncertainty. By and of itself, this was not a new discovery on Hick's part, it was merely a confirmation of Merkel's earlier finding , using a different scale for expressing the number of stimulus alternatives. However, by introducing the information metric into this problem, Hick made it possible to map a variety of ways of manipulating stimulus uncertainty into a common scale.

91 Who provided the first experimental demonstrations of the effects of stimulus uncertainty on choice RT?

1 Merkel 2 Hick 3 Piter 4 Schlosberg

Ans. (1)

➲ *Exp.* Merkel provided the first experimental demonstrations of the effects of stimulus uncertainty on choice RT. By and of itself, this was not a new discovery on Hick's part, it was merely a confirmation of Merkel's earlier finding, using a different scale for expressing the number of stimulus alternatives.

92 Which numerical is found in the stimuli?

1 Arabic 2 English
3 Roman 4 Arabic and Roman

Ans. (4)

➲ *Exp.* Arabic and Roman are found in the stimuli. In a typical choice RT paradigm, a set of stimuli is associated with a set of responses, usually with a one-to-one mapping of stimuli onto responses. A stimulus is presented on each trial and the task is to choose the corresponding response, with correct RT serving as the primary dependent measure.

93 Who repeated Merkel's experiment?

1 Hick 2 Molber
3 Rojer 4 Miller

Ans. (1)

➲ *Exp.* Hick repeated Merkel's experiment. His work was merely a confirmation of Merkel's earlier finding, using a different scale for expressing the number of stimulus alternatives.

However, by introducing the information metric into this problem, Hick made it possible to map a variety of ways of manipulating stimulus uncertainty into a common scale.

94 In which procedure Hick repeated Merkel's experiment?

1 One to five lamps arranged in a regular circle
2 One to ten lamps arranged in an irregular circle
3 One to five lamps arranged in an irregular circle
4 One to ten lamps arranged in regular circle

Ans. (2)

➲ *Exp.* In One to ten lamps arranged in an irregular circle procedure Hick repeated Merkel's experiment. One of the first experimental demonstrations of the effects of stimulus uncertainly in choice RT was provided by Merkel. The result reflected an interesting regularity in the nature of RT.

95 Hick found that in the arrangement information theory RT was proportionary to

1 stimulus uncertainly 2 stimulus certainly
3 locus uncertainly 4 locus certainly

Ans. (1)

➲ *Exp.* Hick found that in the arrangement information theory RT was proportionary to stimulus uncertainly.

Hick's law reflects a combination of associative interference during retrieval from declarative memory and occasional savings for stimulus–response repetitions due to non-retrieval.

Direction *(Q. Nos. 96-100) Read the passage given below and answer the following questions.*

A researcher hypothesised that a given drug would adversely affect the reaction to forty subjects were tested for discriminatory reaction time. Each subject was then given a prescribed drug dosage (5 mg/kg body weight) and after appropriate time gap, the subject was retested for discriminatory reaction time.
The time-interval between a ready signal and actual presentation of the stimulus was randomly varied from half a second to three seconds. For evaluating the mean difference on the reaction time, the researcher considered various statistical options like the test, analysis of variance, chi-square test, etc., and employed the appropriate techniques.
The mean difference was statistically significant (Mean without drug condition = 240 ms, SD = 20 and mean with drug condition = 210 ms, SD = 18). The statistical examination further revealed that the difference between the two standard deviations was insignificant. During the course of research, the researcher suspected that the effect of drug dosage would be different for discriminatory and simple reaction times.
For this purpose, researcher considered the different experimental designs options such as matched two group design, factorial design, analysis of covariance, variance design, quasi-experimental design etc. Finally, researcher selected the appropriate design to carry out the new investigation.

96 On the basis of above passage, what would you conclude about the variance?

1 The two conditions have homogeneity of variance.
2 The two conditions have heterogeneity of variance.
3 We cannot conclude about the homogeneity of variance from the above data.
4 It is necessary to apply an additional test to infer about homogeneity of variance.

Ans. (4)

➲ *Exp.* On the basis of above passage, it is necessary to apply an additional test to infer about homogeneity of variance. Homogeneity of variance is an assumption underlying both T tests and F tests (analyses of variance, ANOVAs) in which the population variances (i.e., the distribution, or 'spread,' of scores around the mean) of two or more samples are considered equal.

97 For studying whether the effect of drug would be different for discriminatory and simple reactions, the appropriate design would be

1 quasi-experimental design
2 matched two-group design
3 analysis of covariance design
4 factorial design

Ans. *(1)*

➲ *Exp.* For studying whether the effect of drug would be different for discriminatory and simple re-actions, the appropriate design would be quasi-experimental design. Quasi-experimental design attempts to establish a cause-and-effect relationship by using criteria other than randomisation.

98 For evaluating the mean differences, which of the following techniques would be appropriate?

I. T-test for independent samples
II. Repeated measures ANOVA
III. Chi-square test
IV. Paired samples test

Select the correct answer using the codes given below.

1 Only IV
2 II and IV
3 I, II and III
4 II, III and IV

Ans. *(3)*

➲ *Exp.* T-test for independent samples, Repeated measures ANOVA and Chi-square test are used for evaluating the mean differences. The mean difference (more correctly, 'difference in means') is a standard statistic that measures the absolute difference between the mean value in two groups in a clinical trial.

It estimates the amount by which the experimental intervention changes the outcome on average compared with the control.

99 On the basis of above information, what can you conclude about the researcher's hypothesis?

1 The researcher's hypothesis is rejected
2 The researcher's hypothesis is partially verified
3 The researcher's hypothesis is accepted
4 The data are inadequate to evaluate the researcher's hypothesis

Ans. *(2)*

➲ *Exp.* On the basis of above information, it can be concluded that the researcher's hypothesis is partially verified. A researcher hypothesised that a given drug would adversely affect the reaction to forty subjects were tested for discriminatory reaction time.

100 Which of the following variable is/are not controlled variables?

I. Drug to body weight ratio
II. Foreperiod
III. Type of reaction
IV. Reaction time

Select the correct answer using the codes given below.

1 Only IV
2 I and IV
3 II and IV
4 I, II and IV

Ans. *(2)*

➲ *Exp.* Foreperiod and Reaction time are not controlled variables. A control variable is any variable that's held constant in a research study. It's not a variable of interest in the study, but it's controlled because it could influence the outcomes.

UGC-NET PSYCHOLOGY

SOLVED PAPER 2021 (November)

PAPER II

1 Which theory determines poverty as a psychological problem of separated classes in society?

1 Attribution theory
2 Depletable self–control theory
3 Distancing theory
4 Multiple factor theory of poverty

Ans. *(3)*

Exp. Distancing theory determines poverty as a psychological problem of separated classes in society.

According to this theory, distancing is the dominant response to poor people on the part of those who are not poor and that distancing, separation, exclusion and devaluing operationally define discrimination Such responses, together with stereotypes and prejudice, define classism. There are three types of distancing: cognitive distancing, institutional distancing (in education, housing, health care, legal assistance politics and public policy) and interpersonal distancing.

2 A person's chronological age is 20 years and mental age is 16 years. What would be his IQ?

1 120   2 100
3 80   4 110

Ans. *(2)*

Exp. A person's chronological age is 20 years and mental age is 16 years. His IQ will be 100.

The equation used to calculate a person's IQ score is Mental Age / Chronological Age x 100.

According to Stern, the chronological age for any age above 16 is automatically calculated as 16. Therefore, maximum chronological age is taken as 16 years. Therefore, the IQ will be 16/16 x 100 = 100.

3 Match List I with List II.

List I (Tests)		List II (Psychologists)	
A.	Creative Achievement Questionnaire	I.	Carson-Peterson-Higgins
B.	Ideational Behaviour Scale	II.	Runco
C.	Preference for Active Divergence Scale	III.	Basadur
D.	Consensual Assessment Technique	IV.	Amabile

Choose the correct answer from the options given below :

	A	B	C	D
1	I	II	III	IV
2	II	I	IV	III
3	III	IV	I	II
4	IV	III	II	I

Ans. *(1)*

Exp. The correct matching is A-I, B-II, C-III, D-IV.

Creative Achievement Questionnaire was proposed by Carson-Peterson-Higgins. It is a new self-report measure of creative achievement that assesses achievement across 10 domains of creativity. A three-factor solution identified Expressive, Scientific and Performance factors of creative achievement. A two-factor solution identified an Arts factor and a Science factor.

Ideational Behaviour Scale was proposed by Runco. It a self-report survey and was constructed to assess individual ideational behaviour as an interchangeable term for thinking disposition or creative ideation.

Preference for Active Divergence Scale was proposed by Basadur. It is a six-item 'preference for ideation in problem solving' scale was used to measure the 'active divergence in problem solving' attitude.

Consensual Assessment Technique was proposed by Amabile. It is a method of judging creativity derives from a simple operational definition of creativity. Products or responses are considered creative to the extent that the appropriate observers (experts in the field) consider them creative.

4 Match List I with List II.

List I (Theoretical Perspective)		List II (Explanation)	
A.	Encoding Specificity Hypothesis	I.	Does not endorse different memory storage
B.	Retrieval Induced Forgetting	II.	Suppress unwanted memories

C. Schema Theory of Memory	III. Superiority of recognition over recall
D. Level of Processing Theory	IV. Effect of meaning and knowledge on memory

Choose the correct answer from the options given below :

Codes

	A	B	C	D		A	B	C	D
1	II	IV	I	III	2	III	II	IV	I
3	I	II	III	IV	4	IV	I	II	III

Ans. *(2)*

Exp. The correct matching is A-III, B-II, C-IV, D-I.

Encoding Specificity Hypothesis refers to the superiority of recognition over recall. It is the principle that retrieval of memory is optimal when the retrieval conditions (such as context or cues) duplicate the conditions that were present when the memory was formed. The effects of the relation between list cues and target items on recognition and recall of target words was studied. The results suggested that recall superiority over recognition was reversed by the use of unrelated word pairs in the study list.

Retrieval Induced Forgetting refers to suppression of unwanted memories. It is a memory phenomenon where remembering causes forgetting of other information in memory. It involves suppressing memories that become active but are not relevant for a given situation.

Schema Theory of Memory refers to the effect of meaning and knowledge on memory. Schema theory is a branch of cognitive science concerned with how the brain structures knowledge. The schema allows specific stimuli to be encoded as abstractions to be stored as meaning without details.

Level of Processing Theory does not endorse different memory storage. It focuses on the depth of processing involved in memory and predicts that the deeper information is processed, the longer a memory trace will last. It changed the direction of memory research and showed that encoding was not a simple, straightforward process. This widened the focus from seeing long-term memory as a simple storage unit to seeing it as a complex processing system.

5 Which of the following are features of Metacognition?

I. Encoding II. Regulation
III. Monitoring IV. Evaluation

Choose the most appropriate answer from the options given below :

1 I, II and III
2 I and II
3 III and II
4 II, III and IV

Ans. *(4)*

Exp. The correct codes are II, III and IV.

The features of Metacognition are as follows

Regulation: It refers to the regulation of cognition and learning experiences through a set of activities that help people control their learning.

Monitoring: It refers to one's awareness of comprehension and task performance.

Evaluation: It refers to appraising the final product of a task and the efficiency at which the task was performed. This can include re-evaluating strategies that were used.

6 Young adults who return after leaving home for some period, to live in their middle aged parents home are known as

1 Sandwich children 2 Benevolent children
3 Boomerang children 4 Compliant children

Ans. *(3)*

Exp. Young adults who return after leaving home for some period, to live in their middle aged parents home are known as Boomerang children.

Boomerang children are young adults or other adult children who move back in with their parents after living independently. Often, Boomerang children return to their parents for economic reasons such as low wages, low savings, high debt or unemployment, or global financial crisis.

7 Behaviour is a direct result of behavioural intentions, this is explained by which of the following?

1 Theory of Reasoned Action
2 Theory of Social Impact
3 Equity Theory
4 Correspondent Inference Theory

Ans. *(1)*

Exp. Behaviour is a direct result of behavioural intentions, this is explained by Theory of Reasoned Action.

The Theory of Reasoned Action (TRA) suggests that a person's behaviour is determined by their intention to perform the behaviour and that this intention is, in turn, a function of their attitude toward the behaviour and subjective norms.

The best predictor of behaviour is intention or instrumentality (belief that the behaviour will lead to the intended outcome). Instrumentality is determined by three things: their attitude toward the specific behaviour, their subjective norms, and their perceived behavioural control. The more favourable the attitude and the subjective norms and the greater the perceived control, the stronger the person's intention to perform the behaviour.

8 Memory that is thought to contain knowledge, facts, information, ideas that can be recalled or described in words, pictures, or symbols is called

1 Procedural memory
2 Episodic memory
3 Semantic memory
4 Declarative memory

Ans. *(4)*

Exp. Memory that is thought to contain knowledge, facts, information, ideas that can be recalled or described in words, pictures, or symbols is called Declarative memory.

Declarative or explicit memory is devoted to processing of names, dates, places, facts, events and so forth. These are entities that are thought of as being encoded symbolically and that thus can be described with language. In terms of function, declarative memory is specialised for fast processing and learning.

9 Match List I with List II.

List I (Type of communication in family therapy)	List II (Description)
A. Congruent	I. Carries an air of self-importance
B. Placating	II. Placing others above oneself
C. Blaming	III. Seeing the world with a lens of objectivity and coolness
D. Super reasonable	IV. Reasonably flexible with a sense of connection

Choose the correct answer from the options given below :

	A	B	C	D		A	B	C	D
1	III	I	II	IV	2	II	III	I	IV
3	IV	II	I	III	4	IV	I	II	III

Ans. (3)

Exp. The correct matching is: A-IV, B-II, C-I, D-III.

Congruent Communication in family therapy states that one needs to reasonably flexible with a sense of connection. Congruence is a state of internal and external harmony. It is a sense of calmness, wholeness, peace and tranquility. Congruence is a state therapists are encouraged to be in during their therapy sessions. It is a sense of empowerment, which means that the individual is not controlled or triggered negatively by the outside world, but responds to the world from a state of internal harmony with one's deepest Self, as well as with others and within the context of the situation.

Placating Communication in family therapy refers to placing others above oneself. Clients, who use the placating stance as their way of coping under stress, can easily be reached through their feelings. Clients like this are often depressed, see themselves as victims and feel helpless and hopeless. By relating to the client through their feelings, rapport is built and therapy can begin.

Blaming Communication in family therapy states that one carries an air of self-importance. Clients, who use the blaming stance as their way of coping under stress, can easily be reached through their expectations. The therapist focuses on what the client wants instead of how he feels. By doing this, rapport can be built quickly and easily.

Super Reasonable Communication in family therapy refers to seeing the world with a lens of objectivity and coolness. Clients, who use the super-reasonable stance as their way of coping under stress, can easily be reached through their perceptions. These clients seem to be in their heads, rational, reasonable, logical, factual and poorly connected with their feelings. To engage these clients beyond their super-reasonable stance, the therapist might first explore their body reactions and their expectations before they can connect with their feelings.

10 A woman who learns that she has been deprived of promotion to a higher job in a company, may storm into her boss's office and have temper tantrum. It exemplifies

1 Sublimation
2 Rationalisation
3 Reaction Formation
4 Regression

Ans. (4)

Exp. A woman who learns that she has been deprived of promotion to a higher job in a company, may storm into her boss's office and have temper tantrum. It exemplifies Regression.

Regression refers to a return to a prior, lower state of cognitive, emotional, or behavioral functioning. This term is associated particularly with psychoanalytic theory, denoting a situation in which the individual reverts to immature behaviour or to an earlier stage of psychosexual development when threatened with overwhelming external problems or internal conflicts.

11 As per Socrate's Greek Philosophy, which of the following is not true about eudaimonia?

1 It means living well or flourishing
2 It is more than merely attaining pleasure
3 Being virtuous is almost identical to eudaimonia
4 Being virtuous does not guarantee eudaimonia

Ans. (4)

Exp. As per Socrate's Greek Philosophy, being virtuous does not guarantee eudaimonia is not true about eudaimonia.

One important move in Greek philosophy to answer the question of how to achieve eudaimonia is to bring in another important concept in ancient philosophy, 'virtue'. Aristotle says that the eudaimon life is one of 'virtuous activity in accordance with reason'; even Epicurus, who argues that the eudaimon life is the life of pleasure, maintains that the life of pleasure coincides with the life of virtue. So, the ancient ethical theorists tend to agree that virtue is closely bound up with happiness.

12 The person's failure to respond to the second stimulus while continuing to respond to the first stimulus is because of

1 Event Related Potential (ERP)
2 Psychological Refractory Period (PRP)
3 Priming effect
4 Excessive mental effort

Ans. (2)

Exp. The person's failure to respond to the second stimulus while continuing to respond to the first stimulus is because of Psychological Refractory Period (PRP).

Psychological Refractory Period (PRP) is the period after response to a stimulus during which response to a second stimulus, presented shortly after the first, is delayed. Reaction time for the second task is increased when the stimulus for it occurs immediately (i.e., within one fourth of a second) after the stimulus for the first task. This PRP effect has been attributed to a response-selection bottleneck.

13 Pattern of familial transmission of intelligence from one generation to other is investigated in which of the following?

1 Linkage analysis studies
2 Adoption studies
3 Association studies
4 Segregation analysis studies

Ans. *(1)*

Exp. Pattern of familial transmission of intelligence from one generation to other is investigated in Linkage analysis studies.

Linkage analysis is based on identifying recombination events between genetic markers and trait loci and inferring whether a trait and marker alleles are traveling in close proximity on the same chromosome or are farther away or on different chromosomes. More recently, a genome-wide linkage scan of IQ has been reported in a sample consisting of sibling pairs from Australian and Dutch families. One region, on chromosome 2q, yielded significant evidence of linkage to Performance IQ. A second region, on chromosome 6p, met criteria for suggestive evidence of linkage to Full Scale IQ.

14 Give the sequence of Identity Formation in Adolescents.

I. Consolidation II. Exploration
III. Rapprochement IV. Differentiation

Choose the correct answer from the options given below :

1 II, IV, III, I 2 IV, II, I, III
3 IV, II, III, I 4 III, I, II, IV

Ans. *(3)*

Exp. The correct sequence of Identity Formation in Adolescents is IV, II, III, I.

Margaret Mahler defines Separation- Individuation as the process by which internal maps of the self and of others are formed. The process can be broken down into four sub-phases :

Differentiation : It is called hatching where the adolescent differentiactes out of symbolic unit.

Exploration : It represents a shift to a more autonomous functioning. During exploration, the adolescents checks back to emotionally refuel and use the parent/caregiver as a secure base.

Rapproachement : It is characterised behaviourally but an active approach back to the parent/caregiver. These behaviours reflect the adolescent's simultaneous need for autonomy and need for support.

Consolidation : It involves all aspects of previous stages. There are advances in cognition and individual achieves an identity with stable internal representation of self and others.

15 Give the correct sequence of stages in the relationship maintenance as suggested by Thibaut and Kelly (1959) in their Social Exchange Theory.

I. Bargaining
II. Commitment
III. Sampling
IV. Institutionalisation

Choose the correct answer from the options given below.

1 I, III, II, IV 2 III, I, II, IV
3 II, IV, I, III 4 III, II, IV, I

Ans. *(2)*

Exp. The correct sequence is III, I, II, IV.

The correct sequence of stages in the relationship maintenance as suggested by Thibaut and Kelly (1959) in their Social Exchange Theory is described as follows:

Sampling : This is the pre-relationship stage where the individual considers the potential costs and benefits of the relationship and other relationships in comparison.

Bargaining : The phase at the beginning of a relationship where a person has chosen to commit to the relationship by both giving and receiving rewards. This is the stage where individuals are simply tasting and trying out the relationship first in order to work out whether the relationship will benefit them in the future and satisfy their needs.

Commitment : This is stage where both partners in the relationship become more intimate with one another and the costs become lower. That would explain why people tend to give more gifts at the start of a relationship than any later stages.

Institutionalisation : The most serious stage of a relationship where both partners agree on a set of established norms and values that allow both parties to gain from the relationship. This phase is concerned with both partners trying to bring balance to their relationship.

16 Ethological approach to motivation mainly explains

I. biological aspects of behaviour.
II. evolutionary history of behaviour.
III. causation of behaviour in terms of stimulus, hormonal and neurobiological events.
IV. proximal determinants of behaviour.

Choose the most appropriate answer from the options given below :

1 I and II 2 III and IV
3 I, II and III 4 II, III and IV

Ans. *(3)*

Exp. The correct codes are I, II and III.

Ethological approach to motivation mainly explains the following

Biological aspects of behaviour: The ethological theory believes that motivation is linked to biological structure. It generally aims to utilise a neo-Darwinian principle by applying his theory in studying biological structures and behaviour under the perspective of ecology.

Evolutionary history of behaviour: The study of behaviour in ethology is based on two principles: changes in behaviour to survive and heritable behavioral traits. Clearly, Charles Darwin's work about evolution has become the foundation of this very theory. Darwin proposed that organismal traits and behaviour are adapted to their natural environment in order to determine who will survive.

Causation of behaviour in terms of stimulus, hormonal and neurobiological events: Ethologists define motivational state as aroused by specific stimuli that give rise to behaviour and cellular/molecular factors like neurotransmitters, hormones, biochemical and neurobiological events.

17 Discovery and understanding of our own abilities brings happiness but also brings fear of new responsibilities and duties. It is called

1 Fear of failure
2 Jonah complex
3 Motives conflict
4 Fear of success

Ans. (2)

Exp. Discovery and understanding of our own abilities brings happiness but also brings fear of new responsibilities and duties. It is called Jonah complex.

The Jonah complex is the fear of success or the fear of being one's best. This fear prevents self-actualisation, or the realisation of one's own potential. It is the fear of one's own greatness, the evasion of one's destiny, or the avoidance of exercising one's talents. As the fear of achieving a personal worst may serve to motivate personal growth, likewise the fear of achieving a personal best may hinder achievement.

18 "When individuals believe that moral choices are not dependent on close ties to others and that rules must be enforced in the same manner for everyone and each person should uphold them". The following statement is characteristic of which stage of Moral Development according to Kohlberg?

1 Social contract orientation
2 Morality of Interpersonal Cooperation
3 Social order maintaining orientation
4 Universal Ethical principle orientation

Ans. (3)

Exp. "When individuals believe that moral choices are not dependent on close ties to others and that rules must be enforced in the same manner for everyone and each person should uphold them". The statement is characteristic of Social order maintaining orientation stage of Moral Development according to Kohlberg.

It is the orientation to 'doing duty' and to showing respect for authority and maintaining the given social order or its own sake. In this stage, laws and social order reign supreme. Rules and regulations are to be followed and obeyed.

19 Which of the following nerves carry the sensory messages from skin, eyes and ears to Central Nervous System?

1 Efferent
2 Afferent
3 Cranial
4 Peripheral

Ans. (2)

Exp. Afferent nerves carry the sensory messages from skin, eyes and ears to Central Nervous System.

The afferent nerves are the messenger neurons that bring the information from different parts of the body to the Central Nervous System (CNS). The afferent nerves are defined as the projections of axons that carry the stimulus from the peripheral organs like skin, eyes and ears to the Central Nervous System.

20 When a target is defined by just one distinctive feature which is available on its feature map and it calls attention to itself is known as

1 Binding effect
2 Pop-out effect
3 Conjunction effect
4 Orienting effect

Ans. (2)

Exp. When a target is defined by just one distinctive feature which is available on its feature map and it calls attention to itself is known as Pop-out effect.

The Pop-out effect (also known as Pop-out phenomenon) occurs when a visual stimulus that is comprised of differing components has mostly similar looking objects but one differing object that 'pops-out' or stands out very noticeably from the other objects in the visual field.

21 Given below are two statements, one is labelled as Assertion (A) and the other labelled as Reason (R).

Assertion (A) Lewin asserted that avoidance – avoidance conflicts are relatively more stable.

Reason (R) Opposing forces tend to remain in a state of disequilibrium.

In the light of the above statements, choose the most appropriate answer from the options given below :

1 Both (A) and (R) are correct and (R) is the correct explanation of (A).
2 Both (A) and (R) are correct but (R) is not the correct explanation of (A).
3 (A) is correct but (R) is not correct.
4 (A) is not correct but (R) is correct.

Ans. (3)

Exp. (A) is correct but (R) is not correct.

Lewin asserted that avoidance – avoidance conflicts are relatively more stable. This is true as when tension, valence and distance are equally strong, the conflict is not easy to solve, making it so that such conflicts can be relatively stable over time.

This occurs when each of the competing alternatives possesses negative consequence that is they are equally repulsive. Avoidance-avoidance conflict is one of the three major types of conflict described by psychologist Kurt Lewin in 1931. This conflict involves choosing between undesirable alternatives or outcomes in which a person tends to avoid.

Opposing forces tend to remain in a state of disequilibrium. This is false as in this situation, the individual is both attracted and repelled by the same goal. This is known as an Approach-avoidance conflict situation which produces stable equilibrium. As the individual nears the goal, the strength of avoidance increases more rapidly than that of approach, pushing him from the goal; at this point the strength of approach is higher than the avoidance tendency. In this manner, the person is brought back to the original point of equilibrium.

22 Which one of the following is usually not considered an example of the evaluative dimension of the Osgood Semantic Differential?

1 Clean – Dirty
2 Slow – Fast
3 Good – Bad
4 Kind – Cruel

Ans. (2)

Exp. Slow – Fast is usually not considered an example of the evaluative dimension of the Osgood Semantic Differential.

Slow – Fast represents activity dimension of Osgood Semantic Differential.

Osgood Semantic Differential (SD) is a type of a rating scale designed to measure the connotative meaning of objects, events and concepts. The connotations are used to derive the attitude towards the given object, event or concept. Using factor analysis of large sets of semantic differential data, Osgood found three recurring attitudes that people used in assessing words and phrases: evaluation (such as 'good/bad'), potency (such as 'strong/weak'), and activity (such as 'passive/active').

The following represent evaluative dimension of Osgood Semantic Differential: Clean – Dirty, Good – Bad, and Kind – Cruel.

23 Some people are able to draw an object, match similar objects and describe the component parts but they fail to recognise the objects that they had just seen or drawn. Which of the following describes this phenomena?

1 Associative Agnosia
2 Apperceptive Agnosia
3 Visual Neglect
4 Form Agnosia

Ans. (1)

Exp. Some people are able to draw an object, match similar objects and describe the component parts but they fail to recognise the objects that they had just seen or drawn. Associative Agnosia describes this phenomenon.

Associative agnosia refers to the inability to recognise objects, despite apparently intact perception of the object. In associative agnosia, the patient is able to perceive objects as objects, but cannot name them or demonstrate their use. It is a failure to understand the meaning of an object.

24 Integration of cognitive aspects of learning with the emotional aspects of experience and learning is known as

1 Integrated approach to learning
2 Confluent Education
3 Feeling class approach to education
4 Motivational approach to learning

Ans. (2)

Exp. Integration of cognitive aspects of learning with the emotional aspects of experience and learning is known as Confluent Education.

Confluent Education (CE) refers to a process of holistic learning, involving multiple aspects of the learner, including his or her emotions, spirit, and ideation (Shapiro, 1995, 1997). Rather than focusing on simply memorising facts or learning particular skills, Confluent Education (CE)seeks to engage the 'whole learner' in a process of personal, as well as academic or professional growth. To do this, the course or program must be open to providing education through a variety of methods and styles, engage each unique individual in the classroom, and focus as much on helping the students learn about themselves and others, as on the traditional subject matter or skills.

25 Which one of the following is a nearest parametric alternative to Kruskal–Wallis test?

1 Independent samples test
2 Paired samples t-test
3 One–way ANOVA for independent groups
4 One–way ANOVA for repeated measures

Ans. (3)

Exp. One–way ANOVA for independent groups is a nearest parametric alternative to Kruskal–Wallis test.

Kruskal–Wallis H test is a non-parametric method for testing whether samples originate from the same distribution. It is used for comparing two or more independent samples of equal or different sample sizes. The parametric equivalent of the Kruskal–Wallis test is the one-way analysis of variance for independent groups (ANOVA). One-way ANOVA is a parametric technique that can be used to compare whether two samples means are significantly different or not.

26 **Which of the following is correct for the Pheromones?**

1 Biochemicals found within the brain which effect a person's behaviour.
2 Biochemials which play an important role in transmitting information from neuron to neuron.
3 Chemical messengers found in the Central Nervous System.
4 Chemical substances emitted by the person into the environment affecting the behaviour of others.

Ans. (4)

Exp. Pheromones are chemical substances emitted by the person into the environment affecting the behaviour of others.

A Pheromone is a secreted or excreted chemical factor that triggers a social response in members of the same species. Pheromones are chemicals capable of acting like hormones outside the body of the secreting individual, to affect the behaviour of the receiving individuals. There are alarm pheromones, food trail pheromones, sex pheromones and many others that affect behaviour or physiology.

27 **Which of the following tactics for gaining compliance are based on reciprocity?**

I. The Door–in–the–face technique
II. That's - Not–All Approach
III. Playing hard to get
IV. Foot–in–the Door Technique

Choose the correct answer from the options given below:

1 I and II
2 I and III
3 II and IV
4 III and IV

Ans. (1)

Exp. The correct codes are I and II.

The tactics for gaining compliance are based on reciprocity are described as follows:

The Door–in–the–face technique : It is a compliance method whereby the persuader attempts to convince the respondent to comply by making a large request that the respondent will most likely turn down. This technique works due to the principle of reciprocity. Saying 'no' to a large request may make the person feel they owe the other person who made the request a favour.

That's – not–All Approach: That's-not-all (TNA) compliance-gaining technique offers a product at an initial price and then improves the deal by either lowering the price or adding an extra product before the target responds to the final and adjusted offer. The effectiveness of this tactic may be in part due to the norm of reciprocity. Playing hard to get is based on the principle of scarcity. It means something that is perceived as scarce or hard to obtain is considered valuable.

Foot–in–the Door Technique works on the principle of consistency. People prefer not to contradict themselves in both actions and beliefs. This means that as long as the request in consistent with or similar in nature to the original small request, the technique will work.

28 **According to Master and Johnson, which of the following is correct sequence of Sexual Response?**

I. Excitement II. Desire
III. Plateau IV. Orgasm
V. Resolution

Choose the correct answer from the options given below :

1 I, III, IV, V 2 II, I, IV, V
3 II, I, III, IV 4 I, II, III, IV

Ans. (1)

Exp. The correct sequence is I, III, IV, V.

According to Master and Johnson, following is correct sequence of Sexual Response:

Excitement: The first phase, excitement, refers to the initial physiological sexual arousal response as characterised by increased heart rate, respiration and blood pressure. In addition, myotonia (an increase in muscle tension), vasocongestion (engorgement of blood vessels) and nipple hardening or erection occur.

Plateau: The plateau phase intensifies the responses from the excitement phase—breathing, blood flow and heart rate continue to increase and stabilise. Muscle tension increases and may extend to hands, feet, face and other areas of the body.

Orgasm: The orgasm phase represents the peak or sexual climax of excitement, though not all men and women necessarily reach this stage. Orgasm is marked by involuntary, rhythmic muscle contractions throughout the body as well as a sense of euphoria and a feeling of tension relief.

Resolution: The last phase is resolution, marked by a return to baseline. Muscles relax, blood pressure drops and respiration returns to the prearousal state. Blood flow to the genital region decreases and erectile tissues return to normal.

29 **Match List I with List II.**

List I (Social Concepts)	List II (Explanations)
A. Elaboration Likelihood Model	I. Gender stereotypes
B. Realistic Conflict Theory	II. Central and peripheral route to persuasion
C. Glass Cliff	III. Idealogical change in core aspect of a group
D. Schism	IV. Intergroup competition as a source of prejudice

Choose the correct answer from the options given below :

	A	B	C	D		A	B	C	D
1	I	III	II	IV	2	III	IV	I	II
3	II	I	IV	III	4	II	IV	I	III

Ans. (4)

Exp. The correct matching is A-II, B-IV, C-I, D-III.

Elaboration Likelihood Model involves central and peripheral route to persuasion. The Elaboration Likelihood Model (ELM) of persuasion is a dual process theory describing the change of attitudes. The ELM proposes two major routes to persuasion-the central route and the peripheral route. Under the central route, persuasion will likely result from a person's careful and thoughtful consideration of the true merits of the information presented in support of an advocacy. Under the peripheral route, persuasion results from a person's association with positive or negative cues in the stimulus or making a simple inference about the merits of the advocated position.

Realistic Conflict Theory involves intergroup competition as a source of prejudice. Realistic conflict theory is a social psychological model of intergroup conflict. The theory explains how intergroup hostility can arise as a result of conflicting goals and competition over limited resources and it also offers an explanation for the feelings of prejudice and discrimination toward the outgroup that accompany the intergroup hostility.

Glass Cliff involves gender stereotypes. The glass cliff is the phenomenon of women in leadership roles, such as executives in the corporate world and female political election candidates, being likelier than men to achieve leadership roles during periods of crisis or downturn, when the risk of failure is highest.

Schism involves idealogical change in core aspect of a group. Schism is the process by which a religious body divides to become two or more distinct, independent bodies. The division takes place because one or each of the bodies has come to see the other as deviant, as too different to be recognised as part of the same religious brotherhood.

30 Arrange the following correlations in ascending order in terms of their strength of relationship

I. −0.75 II. −0.30
III. 0.40 IV. 0.68

Choose the correct answer from the options given below :

1 II, III, IV, I
2 II, I, III, IV
3 I, II, III, IV
4 IV, III, II, I

Ans. (1)

Exp. The correct order is II, III, IV, I.

Arranging the correlations in ascending order in terms of their strength of relationship, we get – 0.30, 0.40, 0.68, – 0.75.

The strength of relationship is measured from -1.00 to +1.00. The correlation coefficient, often expressed as *r*, indicates a measure of the direction and strength of a relationship between two variables. When the *r* value is closer to +1 or -1, it indicates that there is a stronger linear relationship between the two variables. The closer the correlation is to 0, the weaker it is, while the closer it is to +/-1, the stronger it is.

31 Vouyerstic and exhibitionistic disorders are included in which of the following in DSM-5?

1 Sexual dysfunctions
2 Paraphillic disorders
3 Other conditions that focus on clinical attention
4 Disruptive impulse control and conduct disorders

Ans. (2)

Exp. Vouyerstic and exhibitionistic disorders are included in Paraphillic disorders in DSM-5.

Paraphilias are sexual interests in objects, situations, or individuals that are atypical. The American Psychiatric Association, in its Diagnostic and Statistical Manual, Fifth Edition (DSM-5), draws a distinction between paraphilias (which it describes as atypical sexual interests) and paraphilic disorders (which additionally require the experience of distress or impairment in functioning).

According to DSM-5, the most common symptoms of Voyeuristic Disorder are experiencing intense sexual fantasies and urges or getting sexual gratification from watching a person naked with or without the consent of the target.

The DSM-5 states that the behaviours associated with Exhibitionistic Disorder will have occurred over a period of six months, are recurrent and result in intense sexual arousal from the exposure of one's genitals to a stranger or unsuspecting individual.

32 Which of the following describes the enduring facilitation of synaptic transmission that occurs following activation of synapses by high intensity and high frequency stimulation of pre-synaptic neurons?

1 Action potential
2 Absolute refractory period
3 Relative refractory period
4 Long term potentiation

Ans. (4)

Exp. Long term potentiation describes the enduring facilitation of synaptic transmission that occurs following activation of synapses by high intensity and high frequency stimulation of pre-synaptic neurons.

Long-term potentiation (LTP) is the enhancement of synaptic transmission, which can last for weeks, caused by repeated brief stimulations of one nerve cell that trigger stimulation of a succeeding cell. The capacity for potentiation has been best shown in hippocampal tissue. LTP is studied as a model of the neural changes that underlie memory formation, and it may be a mechanism involved in some kinds of learning.

33 The components of 'Working Memory' are

I. Acoustic unit
II. Semantic unit
III. Central executive
IV. Episodic buffer

Choose the correct answer from the options given below :

1 I and II 2 I and III
3 II and IV 4 III and IV

Ans. *(4)*

Exp. The correct codes are III and IV.

The components of 'Working Memory' are described as follows:

Central Executive: It is a component that manages the activities of the phonological loop and visuospatial sketchpad. In coordinating the numerous processes of working memory, the central executive thus performs such varied functions as manipulating material held within the loop and sketchpad, focusing attention on and switching attention between different tasks, dividing attention between simultaneous tasks and initiating long-term memory encoding and retrieval.

Episodic Buffer: It is a temporary multimodal store that combines information from the phonological loop and visuospatial sketchpad subsystems of working memory with information about time and order to form and maintain an integrated, detailed representation of a given stimulus or event that can then be deposited into long-term memory as necessary. It is 'episodic' in the sense that it holds integrated episodes or scenes and a 'buffer' in the sense of providing a limited capacity interface between systems using different representational codes.

34 What are the characteristics of 'Emerging persons' in Rogerian approach?

I. Honest and open
II. Indifferent to material comforts and rewards
III. Caring
IV. Having profound trust in authority

Choose the most appropriate answer from the options given below :

1 I and II 2 III and IV
3 I, II and III 4 II, III and IV

Ans. *(3)*

Exp. The correct codes are I, II and III.

Emerging persons are the people of the future whose interpersonal relationships are characterised by honesty, cooperation and concern for others; who avoid sham, facades and hypocrisy; and who welcome change and opt for growth even when it is painful to do so.

The characteristics of 'Emerging persons' in Rogerian approach are:

1. They are honest and open.
2. They are indifferent to material comforts and rewards.
3. They are caring persons.
4. They have a deep distrust of cognitively based science and a technology that uses that science to exploit and harm nature and people.
5. They have a trust in their own experience and a profound distrust of all external authority.

35 Which of the following are considered as projective tests of personality?

I. Thematic Apperception Test (TAT)
II. Rotter's Incomplete Sentences Blank (RISB)
III. Guttman's Scalogram Analysis
IV. Kent–Rosenoff Free Association Test

Choose the correct answer from the options given below :

1 I and IV 2 I, II and III
3 I, II and IV 4 I, II, III and IV

Ans. *(3)*

Exp. The correct codes are I, II and IV.

The following are considered as projective tests of personality :

Thematic Apperception Test (TAT): It is a projective test, developed by Henry Alexander Murray and his associates, in which participants are held to reveal their attitudes, feelings, conflicts and personality characteristics in the oral or written stories they make up about a series of ambiguous black-and-white pictures.

Rotter's Incomplete Sentences Blank (RISB): It is a projective psychological test developed by Julian B. Rotter. It comes in three forms (for different age groups) and comprises 40 incomplete sentences usually only 1–2 words long, such as 'I regret ..' and 'Mostly girls ...'. As with other sentence completion tests, the subject is asked to complete the sentence.

Kent–Rosenoff Free Association Test: It is a popular word-association test consisting of 100 nouns, adjectives and verbs selected by the US Psychologist Grace H. Kent (1875–1973) and the Russian-born US Psychologist Aaron J. Rosanoff (1878–1943) and published in the American Journal of Insanity in 1910. The words are all emotionally neutral, unlike some other word-association tests and norms obtained by counting and classifying the associations given by 1,000 normal respondents are supplied.

Guttman's Scalogram Analysis : It is not a projective test of personality. It is a technique to examine whether a set of items is consistent, in the sense that they all measure the same thing. If all items measure the same thing, they are said to be One-dimensional, that is, they have a single dimension.

36 The evolution of the various explanations or models of memory occur in the following sequence.

I. Multistore
II. Working memory
III. Level of processing
IV. Interference

Choose the correct answer from the options given below :

1 IV, I, III, II
2 IV, III, II, I
3 I, II, III, IV
4 II, III, IV, I

Ans. (1)

Exp. The correct sequence is IV, I, III, II.

The evolution of the various explanations or models of memory occur in the following sequence:

Interference: There are many aspects of memory that operate on a basic and unconscious level. Some of these involve the encoding, storage and retrieval of relatively simple contingencies that fall under the heading of 'conditioning.' This was the domain of the behaviourists. Often what researchers were doing was looking at the effects of interference of prior learning on new learning. Issues of interference continue to be of interest to memory researchers.

Multistore: According to multistore view, memory is not a unitary thing. Instead, it has several different subcomponents. Each subcomponent has evolved, as a result of selection pressures, to handle a different job. The standard model of memory, or the modal model (Atkinson and Shiffrin, 1968), is a heuristic guide for understanding how memory works. This model has four primary components: (1) the sensory registers, (2) short-term store, (3) long-term store and (4) control processes

Level of processing: The levels of processing model (Craik and Lockhart, 1972) focuses on the depth of processing involved in memory and predicts the deeper information is processed, the longer a memory trace will last.

Working memory : Working memory is a cognitive system with a limited capacity that can hold information temporarily. Working memory is important for reasoning and the guidance of decision-making and behaviour.

37 It is possible to accept the world as it is, without experiencing dissatisfaction. This is related to which of the following in Buddhism?

1 Right thought in eight–fold path
2 Right mindfulness in eight-fold path
3 Elimination of craving
4 Existence of satisfaction/dissatisfaction

Ans. (3)

Exp. It is possible to accept the world as it is, without experiencing dissatisfaction. This is related to Elimination of craving in Buddhism.

There is a noble truth about the cessation of suffering. It is the complete fading away and cessation of this craving [tanha]; its abandonment and relinquishment; getting free from and being independent of it. Cessation of tanha can be obtained by following the Noble Eightfold Path. In Theravada Buddhism, the cessation results from the gaining of true insight into impermanence and non-self. The 'insight meditation' practice of Buddhism, states Kevin Trainor, focuses on gaining 'right mindfulness' which entails understanding three marks of existence - *dukkha* (suffering), *anicca* (impermanence) and *anatta* (non-self). The understanding of the reality of non-self, adds Trainor, promotes non-attachment because 'if there is no soul, then there is no locus for clinging'. Once one comprehends and accepts the non-self doctrine, there are no more desires, i.e. tanha ceases.

38 Which of the following in learning environment are considered to be true about school success?

I. The self-image is vital to learning.
II. Very high goal setting is necessary to motivate and study.
III. Success experience is a function of challenge more than repetition.
IV. Child's spiritual identity is vital to learning.

Choose the correct answer from the options given below :

1 I and IV
2 II and III
3 I, III and IV
4 II, III and IV

Ans. (3)

Exp. Statement I, III and IV are considered to be true about school success.

The following in learning environment are considered to be true about school success:

The self-image is vital to learning: In today's world characterised by changed systems of values and materialism, pedagogy should emphasise education for a positive self-image, especially in the contemporary school, whose educational goals are freedom, independence and individuality.

Success experience is a function of challenge more than repetition: Rote repetition — simply repeating a task — will not by itself improve performance. Deliberate practice involves attention, rehearsal and repetition and leads to new knowledge or skills that can later be developed into more complex knowledge and skills and ultimately leads to success experience.

Child's spiritual identity is vital to learning: Through spiritual development, children learn to be aware of and comfortable with qualities such as respect, responsibility and reverence for self and others. They learn to be capable of acknowledging differences between people without feeling fear. They develop a love for the Earth and take action to protect it.

Statement II is not true as very high goal setting and unattainable goals often end in failures and how people react to failure varies greatly. This may not be necessary to motivate and study.

39 In the two group design with a continuous dependent variable, which of the following measures of effect size can be employed?

I. Cohen's D
II. Point biserial correlation
III. Eta square
IV. Partial Eta Squared

Choose the most appropriate answer from the options given below :

1 Only I 2 II and III
3 I, II and III 4 I, II and IV

***Ans.** (3)*

Exp. The correct codes are I, II and III.

In the two group design with a continuous dependent variable, the following measures of effect size can be employed:

Cohen's D: Cohen's D is the appropriate effect size measure if two groups have similar standard deviations and are of the same size.

Point biserial correlation : The point biserial correlation is a useful measure of effect size, that is, statistical magnitude, of the difference in means between two groups. It is based on Pearson's product moment correlation.

Eta square : Eta-squared describes the ratio of variance explained in the dependent variable by a predictor while controlling for other predictors, making it analogous to the r^2.

40 Arrange the first five elements of 'Flow' in correct sequence.

I. Clarity of Goals
II. Immediate Feedback of Actions
III. Balance between challenges and skills
IV. Merger of awareness and actions
V. Exclusion of distractions from consciousness

Choose the correct answer from the options given below :

1 I, II, III, IV, V 2 I, III, II, IV, V
3 II, III, I, V, IV 4 III, II, I, IV, V

***Ans.** (1)*

Exp. The correct sequence is I, II, III, IV, V.

The first five elements of 'Flow' in correct sequence are described as follows:

Clarity of Goals: The activity must have clear goals and progress. This establishes structure and direction.

Immediate Feedback of Actions: The task must provide clear and immediate feedback. This helps to negotiate any changing demands and allows adjusting performance to maintain the flow state.

Balance between challenges and skills: Good balance is required between the perceived challenges of the task and one's perceived skills. Confidence in the ability to complete the task is required.

Merger of awareness and actions: Complete involvement creates a state in which there is no room for worry, fear, distraction or self-conscious rumination. Performers do not feel separated from their actions; they are one with their performance. This feeling of unity can expand to a person's surroundings (nature) as well as to a whole group of people working together (team flow).

Exclusion of distractions from consciousness: High levels of concentration narrows our attention excluding any unnecessary distractions. Because we are absorbed in the activity, we are only aware of what is relevant to the task at hand and we do not think about unrelated things.

41 Which of the following statements describe the term 'Diffusion of Responsibility?

1 People help others in order to reduce their emotional discomfort.
2 Greater the number of witnesses to an emergency, the less likely the victims are to receive help.
3 Helping others is a means of increasing one's own status and reputation.
4 Prosocial acts are motivated solely by the desire to help someone in need.

***Ans.** (2)*

Exp. The statement 'Greater the number of witnesses to an emergency, the less likely the victims are to receive help' describe the term 'Diffusion of Responsibility'.

Diffusion of Responsibility refers to the fact that as the number of bystanders increases, the personal responsibility that an individual bystander feels decreases. As a consequence, so does his or her tendency to help. Assumption of responsibility tends to decrease when the potential helping group is larger, resulting in little aiding behaviour demonstrated by the bystander(s).

42 Which among these is correct for Cyber bullying?

I. It involves disinhibition
II. Lesser role of Bystanders
III. Ability of targets to retaliate is more
IV. No evidence left behind

Choose the correct answer from the options given below :

1 I and II 2 I, II and III
3 II, III and IV 4 I, II and IV

***Ans.** (2)*

Exp. The correct codes are I, II and III.

The following are correct for Cyber bullying:

It involves disinhibition: Online disinhibition effect is the lack of restraint one feels when communicating online in comparison to communicating in-person. Online disinhibition plays a role in the act of cyberbullying.

Lesser role of Bystanders: There have been only a few studies focusing on bystanders in Cyber bullying. A study in Belgium found that the majority of bystanders tended to ignore cyberbullying (54.1%), followed by those who would intervene (41.7%) and those who would join in (4.2%). If bystanders help the victims or intervene to stop the cyberbullying, it can prevent reoccurrences of cyberbullying.

Ability of targets to retaliate is more: The active strategies called confrontation and retaliation were less helpful for cyberbullying victims and were more often effective in stopping the aggressors in cases of less severe online harassment. The explanation might be that compared to bullies, those who harass online are not so determined to cause harm, or even do not perceive and intend their behaviour as malevolent.

43 Arrange the following as per the Yogic Concept of Cognition.

I. Sensorial transformation is attended by manas
II. Reaction by budhi to the object of cognition
III. Registration of external object on mind
IV. Assimilation and discrimination by manas
V. Information to Ahamkara

Choose the correct answer from the options given below :

1 III, I, V, II, IV
2 III, I, IV, V, II
3 I, III, IV, V, II
4 III, I, II, IV, V

Ans. (2)

Exp. The correct codes are III, I, IV, V, II.

The following are arranged as per the Yogic Concept of Cognition:

Registration of external object on mind: The sense mind chooses an external object through the peripheral sense organs.

Sensorial transformation is attended by manas: The sensory system reaches out to the objects and takes on the form of the object.

Assimilation and discrimination by manas: The perceptual process in the manas attends to the sensory content by assimilation and discrimination.

Information to Ahamkara: The Ahamkara appropriates the processed content giving rise to the ownership of the content as belonging to the person engaged in the perceptual act.

Reaction by budhi to the object of cognition: The budhi further distils the inputs received, makes the final determination of the object, what it means by localising it, i.e. placing it in the time-space matrix and primes the person to act.

44 Match List I with List II.

List I (Variable type)	List II (Examples)
A. Artificially discrete variable	I. Reaction time
B. Continuous behavioural variable	II. Gender
C. Continuous organismic variable	III. Selection test result interms of selected, not selected, on waiting list
D. Dummy variable	IV. Height

Choose the correct answer from the options given below :

	A	B	C	D		A	B	C	D
1	III	I	IV	II	2	III	IV	I	II
3	II	IV	I	III	4	I	III	II	IV

Ans. (1)

Exp. The correct matching is A-III, B-I, C-IV, D-II.

An example of an *Artificially discrete variable* is selection test result in terms of selected, not selected, on waiting list. An artificially discrete variable is one that falls into separate categories with no intermediate values possible by the researcher itself.

An example of a *Continuous behavioural variable* is reaction time. A Continuous behavioural variable can take on an unlimited number of values between the lowest and highest points of measurement with respect to the behaviour or action of the individual.

An example of a *Continuous organismic variable* is height. A continuous organismic variable is any relatively stable physical characteristic of an organism which can take on an unlimited number of values.

An example of a *Dummy variable* is Gender. A dummy variable is one that takes only the value 0 or 1 to indicate the absence or presence of some categorical effect that may be expected to shift the outcome.

45 Visuospatial sketch pad is a component of which of the following?

1 Long-term memory
2 Short-term memory
3 Working memory
4 Sensory memory

Ans. (3)

Exp. Visuospatial sketch pad is a component of Working memory.

Working memory is a cognitive system with a limited capacity that can hold information temporarily. In 1974, Baddeley and Hitch introduced the multicomponent model of working memory. The theory proposed a model containing three components: the central executive, the phonological loop and the visuospatial sketchpad with the central executive functioning as a control centre of sorts, directing info between the phonological and visuospatial components. The visuospatial sketchpad, stores visual and spatial information. It can be used, for example, for constructing and manipulating visual images and for representing mental maps.

46 In which schools of Indian thought about yoga, 'Prakrti' remains isolated as a principle of ultimate reality into self and is active only in the presence and service of 'Purusa'?

1 Integral yoga philosophy
2 Vedanta
3 Samkhya
4 Sahaj yoga

Ans. (3)

Exp. In Samkhya school of Indian thought about yoga, 'Prakrti' remains isolated as a principle of ultimate reality into self and is active only in the presence and service of 'Purusa'.

Samkhya is a dualistic astika school of Indian philosophy, regarding reality human experience as being constituted by two independent ultimate principles, purusa a ('consciousness' or spirit) and prakrti, (cognition, mind and emotions. Purusa is the witness-consciousness.

It is absolute, independent, free, imperceptible, unknowable through other agencies, above any experience by mind or senses and beyond any words or explanations. Unmanifest prakrti is the primordial matter. It is inactive and unconscious, and consists of an equilibrium of the three gunas ('qualities, innate tendencies'), namely *sattva*, *rajas and tamas*.

47 Given below are two statements.

Statement I Edwards Personality Preference Schedule (EPPS) uses forced choice format.

Statement II The forced choice format is presumed to prevent socially desirable responding.

In the light of the above statements, choose the most appropriate answer from the options given below :

1 Both Statement I and Statement II are correct
2 Both Statement I and Statement II are incorrect
3 Statement I is correct, but Statement II is incorrect
4 Statement I is incorrect, but Statement II is correct

Ans. (1)

Exp. Both Statement (I) and Statement (II) are correct.

Edwards Personality Preference Schedule (EPPS) uses forced choice format. Developed by psychologist and University of Washington professor Allen L. Edwards, the Edwards Personal Preference Schedule (EPPS) is a forced choice, objective, non-projective personality inventory. This is a forced choice instrument involving the choice of one of the two paired statements with 225 such pairs in all comprising the test.

The forced choice format is presumed to prevent socially desirable responding. The forced-choice method has been proposed as a viable strategy to prevent Socially Desirable Responding (SDR) on self-report non-cognitive measures. The ability of the method to eliminate SDR stems from matching items that are perceived as equally desirable into forced-choice item-blocks.

48 After being robbed by a boy recently the shopkeeper says 'beware of teenagers in our community'.

Which of the following explains his reactions?

1 Algorithm
2 Availability Heuristic
3 Representative Heuristic
4 Gambler's fallacy

Ans. (3)

Exp. After being robbed by a boy recently the shopkeeper says 'beware of teenagers in our community'. Representative Heuristic explains his reactions.

It is a strategy for making categorical judgements about a given person or target based on how closely the exemplar matches the typical or average member of the category. For example, given a choice of the two categories teenage boys and thieves, it is likely for the shopkeeper to assign teenage boys to the former category of thieves; however, the much greater frequency of teenagers in the population means that such a person is more likely to be a thief.

49 Which of the following are true regarding Broca's area?

I. It is located in the frontal lobe.
II. Its function is speech production.
III. Understanding and processing aspects of language are associated with it.
IV. It helps people using sign language.

Choose the correct answer from the options given below :

1 I and II
2 III and IV
3 I, II and III
4 I, II, III and IV

Ans. (1)

Exp. The correct codes are I and II.

The following are true regarding Broca's area:

It is located in the frontal lobe: Broca's area is an area of the lateral frontal lobe in the dominant hemisphere concerned with the production of speech.

Its function is speech production: Broca's area, located in the left hemisphere, is associated with speech production and articulation. Our ability to articulate ideas, as well as use words accurately in spoken and written language, has been attributed to this crucial area.

Wernicke's area is a critical language area responsible for understanding and processing aspects of language are associated with it. It helps people using sign language.

50 The tendency to believe that a task will take less time than it really will, is known as

1 Magical Thinking
2 Planning Fallacy
3 Optimistic Bias
4 Fundamental Attribution Error

Ans. (2)

Exp. The tendency to believe that a task will take less time than it really will is known as Planning Fallacy.

The Planning Fallacy is a phenomenon in which predictions about how much time will be needed to complete a future task display an optimism bias and underestimate the time needed. This phenomenon sometimes occurs regardless of the individual's knowledge that past tasks of a similar nature have taken longer to complete than generally planned.

51 Which among the following does not refer to Social Referencing?

I. Intentional search for information about other's feelings, to help explain the meaning of uncertain circumstances and events.

II. It occurs around the age of 2 – 3 years.

III. Infants make use of facial expressions in social referencing.

IV. Infants need to understand the significance of other's behaviour within the context of a specific situation.

Choose the most appropriate answer from the options given below :

1 Only II 2 I and III
3 II and III 4 I and IV

Ans. (1)

Exp. Statement II does not refer to Social Referencing.

Social Referencing is intentional search for information about other's feelings, to help explain the meaning of uncertain circumstances and events.

Infants make use of facial expressions in social referencing. Infants need to understand the significance of other's behavior within the context of a specific situation.

It does not occur around the age of 2–3 years. Social referencing starts between eight and ten months of age while infants use visual information obtained from their parent's or caregiver's faces to help them understand different situations.

52 Which of the following categories were given by Skinner for different verbal responses in terms of how they are reinforced?

I. Mand

II. Tact

III. Echoic Behaviour

IV. Autoclitic Behaviour

Choose the correct answer from the options given below :

1 I and II
2 III and IV
3 I, II and III
4 I, II, III and IV

Ans. (4)

Exp. The correct codes are I, II, III and IV.

The following categories were given by Skinner for different verbal responses in terms of how they are reinforced:

Mand: It is verbal behaviour where a speaker asks for something that he or she wants. Mands occur when there is a Motivating Operation (MO) for something and the reinforcement is the acquisition of that thing directly related to that MO.

Tact: These are verbal operant where the speaker labels things in the environment. Tacts occur when a non-verbal stimulus is presented which becomes a discriminative stimulus (Sd) via discrimination training.

Echoic Behaviour: It is a verbal operant that is present when a person verbally repeats what another person says. It is a point-to-point correspondence meaning that the verbal stimulus and response products match in entirety.

Autoclitic Behaviour is a verbal behaviour that modifies the functions of other verbal behaviours. These are verbal responses that modify the effect on the listener of the primary operants.

53 Projective measures, particularly inkblot tests, index, which of the following?

1 Novelty context of creativity
2 Meaning context of creativity
3 Domain specific creativity
4 General creative potential

Ans. (2)

Exp. Projective measures, particularly inkblot tests, index meaning context of creativity.

Psychometric measures of creativity are considered to tap novelty context, whereas projective tests, particularly inkblot techniques are taken to index meaning context of creativity. Similarly, verbal and non-verbal measures of intelligence are taken to be indices of crystallised and fluid intelligences respectively.

54 Jensen's Level I and Level II abilities can be best understood in terms of which of the following?

I. Difficulty and complexity of tasks

II. SES Differences

III. Racial Differences

IV. Gender Differences

Choose the most appropriate answer from the options given below :

1 I and II 2 III and IV
3 I, II and III 4 II, III and IV

Ans. (3)

Exp. The correct codes are I, II and III.

Jensen's Level I and Level II abilities can be best understood in terms of Difficulty and complexity of tasks, SES differences and Racial differences.

Difficulty and complexity of tasks: In Jensen's theory there is an important conceptual distinction between difficulty and complexity. Complexity implies the need for more mental manipulation and transformation of the input. If a task is more difficult, there is lower probability of success.

SES Differences: Different Socio Economic Status (SES) and racial groups tend to obtain equal average scores on Level I, whereas middle SES and white groups obtain higher scores on tests of Level II, on average, than groups of low SES and black individuals.

Racial Differences: A greater white-black difference in tasks predicts from the hypothesis that the magnitude of racial differences should be a function of the degree to which Level II predominates in the cognitive demands of the particular test.

55 New Mood Therapy

I. is a cognitive therapy
II. is meant for treatment of depression
III. involves many behavioural interventions
IV. was originated by Ellis
V. is action commitment therapy

Choose the correct answer from the options given below :

1 I, II and V
2 I, II and III
3 II and V
4 II, III and IV

Ans. *(2)*

Exp. New Mood Therapy is a cognitive therapy, meant for treatment of depression and involves many behavioural interventions.

New Mood Therapy is proposed by David D. Burns who popularised Albert Ellis's and Aaron T. Beck's Cognitive Behavioural Therapy (CBT) when his books became bestsellers during the 1980s.

It is a form of psychotherapy based on the concept that emotional and behavioural problems in an individual are, at least in part, the result of maladaptive or faulty ways of thinking and distorted attitudes toward oneself and others. The objective of the therapy is to identify these faulty cognitions and replace them with more adaptive ones, a process known as cognitive restructuring.

56 If a person's distinctive social category makes him or her vulnerable to stereotyping, it is referred to as

1 Token integration
2 Neosexism
3 Ingratiation
4 Token bias

Ans. *(1)*

Exp. If a person's distinctive social category makes him or her vulnerable to stereotyping, it is referred to as Token integration.

It is the practice of making only a perfunctory or symbolic effort to be inclusive to members of minority groups, especially by recruiting people from underrepresented groups in order to give the appearance of racial or gender equality within a workplace or educational context. The effort of including a token individual in work or school is usually intended to create the impression of social inclusiveness and diversity (racial, religious, sexual, etc.)

57 Given below are two statements, one is labelled as Assertion (A) and the other labelled as Reason (R).

Assertion (A) In fixed interval schedule of reinforcement behaviour is reinforced in a fixed time period.

Reason (R) When students get feedback intermittently their level of performance increases.

In the light of the above statements, choose the most appropriate answer from the options given below :

1 Both (A) and (R) are correct and (R) is the correct explanation of (A).
2 Both (A) and (R) are correct, but (R) is not the correct explanation of (A).
3 (A) is correct, but (R) is not correct.
4 (A) is not correct but (R) is correct.

Ans. *(2)*

Exp. Both (A) and (R) are correct but (R) is not the correct explanation of (A).

In fixed interval schedule of reinforcement behaviour is reinforced in a fixed time period. This is true as in case of fixed interval schedule, the first response that occurs after a set interval of time has elapsed is reinforced.

When students get feedback intermittently their level of performance increases. This is true as in case of intermittent reinforcement, the delivery of a reward is at irregular intervals. It is a method that has been determined to yield the greatest effort from the subject. The subject does not receive a reward each time they perform a desired behaviour or according to any regular schedule but at seemingly random intervals.

58 Which of the following characteristics are applicable to emotions that are considered to occur as a result of interaction among subjective and environmental factors and neural and hormonal processes?

I. Emotions give rise to hedonic experiences.
II. Emotions stimulate to generate cognitive explanations.
III. Emotions trigger variety of internal neurobiological changes.
IV. Emotions always elicit rewarding behaviour.

Choose the most appropriate answer from the options given below :

1 I and II
2 II and III
3 I, II and III
4 II, III and IV

Ans. *(3)*

Exp. Statement I, II and III are correct.

Emotions give rise to hedonic experiences. Although core affect is ubiquitous, there are individual and group differences in the degree to which people characterise their experience in terms of pleasure and displeasure. Individuals who are sensitive to the evaluative properties of their surroundings implicitly emphasised the hedonics of their experience.

Emotions stimulate to generate cognitive explanations. The mental representations of emotion routinely involve amore dorsal medial prefrontal system that may support the cognitive processes involved with generating at least some of these contents, specifically conceptualisations of situational cause.

Emotions trigger variety of internal neurobiological changes. The experiences of emotion are content-rich events that emerge at the level of psychological description, but are instantiated by neurobiological processes.

Statement IV is not true as the emotions elicits behaviours when the objects or events are helpful or harmful, rewarding or threatening, calling for acceptance or rejection.

59 In which phase of Enright's model of psychological forgiveness, individual gains a cognitive understanding of the offender in a new light that brings a positive change in view about the offender, self and the relationship?

1 Uncovering phase
2 Decision phase
3 Work phase
4 Deepening phase

Ans. *(3)*

Exp. In Work phase of Enright's model of psychological forgiveness, individual gains a cognitive understanding of the offender in a new light that brings a positive change in view about the offender, self and the relationship.

The Work Phase involves actually working on forgiving. In this phase, a person "gains a cognitive understanding of the offender and begins to view the offender in a new light, resulting in positive change in affect about the offender, about the self and about the relationship." Concrete actions in this phase commonly begin with working toward an accurate understanding of the offender. This reframing may involve rethinking the offensive situation or seeing the offender from a new perspective, as "a person who is, in fact, a human being and not evil incarnate".

60 Multivariate Analysis of Variance (MANOVA) is best suited for making groupwise comparisons for several dependent variables. Which of the following are these?

1 Uncorrelated
2 Moderately correlated
3 Very highly correlated
4 Either uncorrelated or have small negative correlations

Ans. *(2)*

Exp. Multivariate Analysis of Variance (MANOVA) is best suited for making groupwise comparisons for several dependent variables which are moderately correlated.

MANOVA is used to determine whether there are any differences between independent groups on more than one continuous dependent variable. The assumption of using MANOVA includes that there is no multicollinearity. Ideally, the dependent variables are to be moderately correlated with each other. If the correlations are low, it is better to run separate one-way ANOVAs, and if the correlation(s) are too high (greater than 0.9), there are chances of multicollinearity. This is problematic for MANOVA and needs to be screened out.

61 Match List I with List II.

List I (Depth Cues)	List II (Explanations)
A. Motion Parallax	I. Both eyes fixate on the same point in space
B. Texture Gradient	II. Partial occlusion of a far object by a near object
C. Interposition	III. Graded variation in the shape, size and density of the surface elements
D. Convergence	IV. Movement in one part of the image relative to another

Choose the correct answer from the options given below

	A	B	C	D		A	B	C	D
1	III	II	IV	I	2	IV	III	II	I
3	I	IV	III	II	4	II	I	III	IV

Ans. *(2)*

Exp. The correct matching is A-IV, B-III, C-II, D-I.

Motion Parallax is the movement in one part of the image relative to another. Motion parallax is a monocular depth cue arising from the relative velocities of objects moving across the retinae of a moving person. The term parallax refers to a change in position. Thus, motion parallax is a change in position caused by the movement of the viewer.

Texture Gradient is the graded variation in the shape, size and density of the surface elements. Texture gradient is the distortion in size which closer objects have compared to objects farther away. It also involves groups of objects appearing denser as they move farther away.

Interposition is the partial occlusion of a far object by a near object. Interposition is a monocular depth cue occurring when two objects are in the same line of vision and the closer object, which is fully in view, partly conceals the farther object.

Convergence is when both eyes fixate on the same point in space. Convergence is the rotation of the two eyes inward toward a light source so that the image falls on corresponding points on the foveas. Convergence enables the slightly different images of an object seen by each eye to come together and form a single image. The muscular tension exerted is also a cue to the distance of the object from the eyes.

62 Which of the following are correct for the Biopsychosocial Model of health?

I. Close interaction between body and mind, though they are separate entities
II. Active participation of the patient

III. Health and illness are on the same continuum
IV. Treatment process involves medication, surgery and radiation

Choose the most appropriate answer from the options given below :

1 I, II and III
2 I, II and IV
3 II, III and IV
4 I, II, III and IV

Ans. (4)

Exp. Statement I, II, III and IV are correct for the Biopsychosocial Model of health.

The Biopsychosocial model states that the workings of the body, mind, and environment all affect each other. According to this model, none of these factors in isolation is sufficient to lead definitively to health or illness—it is the deep interrelation of all three components that leads to a given outcome.

Biopsychosocial model empowers patients as persons, who actively participate in managing their illnesses.

Health is defined as a positive state of physical, mental and social well-being not simply the absence of injury or disease that varies over time along a continuum. At the wellness end of the continuum, health is the dominant state. At the other end of the continuum, the dominant state is illness or injury, in which destructive processes produce characteristic signs, symptoms or disabilities.

A biopsychosocial approach to treatment planning focuses on meeting patients' behavioural health needs and promoting their biopsychosocial functioning from a comprehensive holistic perspective. From a biological standpoint, this approach involves medication, surgery and radiation as treatment process.

63 Which one of the following is considered as a culture-fair test?

1 Bhatia's Battery of Intelligence
2 Kaufman's Intelligence Tests
3 Wechsler's Adult Intelligence scale
4 Naglieri Non-verbal Ability Test

Ans. (4)

Exp. Naglieri Non-verbal Ability Test is considered as a culture-fair test.

The Naglieri Non-verbal Ability Test is 'a brief, culture-fair, non-verbal measure of school ability' (Naglieri, 1996) that is group-administered and timed. The NNAT is divided into seven levels: Level A for Kindergarten, Level B for Grade 1, Level C for Grade 2, Level D for Grades 3-4, Level E for Grades 5-6, Level F for Grades 7, 8, 9, and Level G for Grades 10, 11, 12. Each level has 38 items. For this study archival data were only available for Levels D and F. Grades 3-5 were administered under Level D, while Grade 8 was administered under Level F.

64 Match List I with List II.

	List I (Concept)		List II (Description)
A.	Situational Poverty	I.	Not equipped with tools to move out
B.	Generational Poverty	II.	Not able to meet the average standard of society
C.	Relative Poverty	III.	Scarcity of necessities like shelter, running water and food
D.	Absolute Poverty	IV.	Caused by environmental disasters, divorce and other issues like poor health etc

Choose the correct answer from the options given below :

	A	B	C	D		A	B	C	D
1	I	III	IV	II	2	III	I	IV	II
3	IV	I	II	III	4	IV	II	I	III

Ans. (3)

Exp. The correct matching is A-IV, B-I, C-II, D-III.

Situational Poverty is caused by environmental disasters, divorce and other issues like poor health etc. Situational poverty is a period wherein an individual falls below the poverty line because of a sudden event. Situational poverty can be caused by a range of factors, such as: a divorce, death of the family head, illness, a natural disaster or loss of job.

Generational Poverty is not equipped with tools to move out. Generational poverty is a term applied to families who have experienced poverty for at least two generations. Generational poverty persist mostly because of internal psychological factors, although financial issues are the external force that create these psychological barriers. It's a combination of hopelessness, scarcity mindset and toxic stress.

Relative Poverty is when an individual is not able to meet the average standard of society. Relative poverty is the condition in which people lack the minimum amount of income needed in order to maintain the average standard of living in the society in which they live. Relative poverty is considered the easiest way to measure the level of poverty in an individual country.

Absolute Poverty is scarcity of necessities like shelter, running water and food. Absolute poverty refers to when a person or household does not have the minimum amount of income needed to meet the minimum living requirements needed over an extended period of time. In other words, they cannot meet their basic needs. When an individual goes below this threshold their survival is threatened.

65 Cattell proposed his theory of fluid and crystallised intelligences on the basis of which of the following?

1 First order factors of abilities
2 Second order factors of abilities
3 Third order factors of abilities
4 Higher order factors of abilities

Ans. (2)

Exp. Cattell proposed his theory of fluid and crystallised intelligences on the basis of second order factors of abilities.

Second-Order Abilities include Fluid Intelligence (Gf), Crystallised Intelligence (Gc), Short-Term Memory (Gsm), Long-Term Memory (Glr), Processing Speed (Gs), Visual Processing (Gv), Auditory Processing (Ga), and Quantitative Knowledge (Gq).

66 Match List I with List II.

List I (Indices)	List II (Test)
A. Universal Index	I. OATB
B. Disclosure Index	II. MCMI
C. True Response	III. MMPI Inconsistency
D. Coping Deficit Index	IV. Rorschach Inkblot Test

Choose the correct answer from the options given below :

	A	B	C	D
1	I	II	III	IV
2	II	I	IV	III
3	III	IV	I	II
4	IV	III	II	I

Ans. (1)

Exp. The correct matching is A-I, B-II, C-III, D-IV.

Universal Index is associated with OATB. Comprehensive battery of tests is called 'Objective Analytic Test Battery' (OATB). Of the 16 factors indexed by 16 PF, 12 show considerable similarity with factors from L-Data and 4 appear to be unique to Q–Data.

Disclosure Index is associated with MCMI. The MCMI is a psychological assessment tool intended to provide information on personality traits and psychopathology, including specific psychiatric disorders outlined in the DSM-5. The Disclosure scale measures whether the person was open in the assessment, or if they were unwilling to share details about his/her history.

True Response is associated with MMPI Inconsistency. TRIN or True Response Inconsistency scale in Minnesota Multiphasic Personality Inventory-2 (MMPI-2) includes 23 pairs of items that are semantically inconsistent. High scores, 13 or more, have responded to the MMPI in a 'yea-saying' test set, responding mostly 'True'. This can be also be High due to severe psychopathology. Low scores of 5 or less responded with a "nay-saying" test set, responding mainly 'False.'

Coping Deficit Index is associated with Rorschach Inkblot Test. The Coping Deficit Index (CDI) is an empirically derived set of variables generated as a by-product of the Depression Index. An elevated CDI (CDI = 4) indicates a persistent personality style causing difficulties in social adjustment and is associated with maladaptive development.

67 Which of the following is involved in Type 'a' processes of thinking as described by Wertheimer?

1 Grouping and reorganisation
2 Assimilation and conditioning
3 Blind trial and error
4 Partially productive methods

Ans. (1)

Exp. Grouping and reorganisation is involved in Type 'a' processes of thinking as described by Wertheimer.

Wertheimer criticised the current educational emphasis on traditional logic and association, arguing that such problem-solving processes as grouping and reorganisation, which dealt with problems as structural wholes, were not recognized in logic but were important techniques in human thinking. Related to this argument was Wertheimer's concept of Pragnanz ('precision') in organization; when things are grasped as wholes, the minimal amount of energy is exerted in thinking. To Wertheimer, truth was determined by the entire structure of experience rather than by individual sensations or perceptions.

68 Which of the following statements is incorrect?

1 Body's requirement of sleep varies with age
2 Tertiary prevention is action taken to identify and treat an illness or injury early with an aim of stopping or reversing the problem
3 Endorphins are released during exercise
4 Excessive alcohol consumption leads to shrinking of frontal lobe of the brain.

Ans. (2)

Exp. Statement 2 is incorrect.

Tertiary prevention seeks to reduce the impact of established disease by eliminating or reducing disability, minimising suffering, and maximising potential years of quality life. In epidemiological terms, tertiary prevention aims to reduce the number and/or impact of complications.

69 Arrange the Nafs (Self in Sufism) from lower to higher self.

I. The self pleasing to God
II. The Pure self
III. Inspired self
IV. Serene self
V. The Pleased self

Choose the correct answer from the options given below :

1 V, III, I, II, IV
2 III, IV, V, I, II
3 III, V, I, IV, II
4 II, III, V, IV, I

Ans. (2)

Exp. The correct sequence is III, IV, V, I, II

The Nafs (Self in Sufism) from lower to higher self are arranged as follows :

Inspired self : The Inspired or balanced self marks the beginning of genuine spiritual integration and a release of the self from the tyranny of physical instincts and the desires of the ego.

Serene self : The serene self, tranquil self or self at peace, as its name implies, has attained a degree of detachment from worldly concerns and an increasing awareness of the Presence of God in all things.

The Pleased self : The Pleased, fulfilled or satisfied self is the initial merging or union of the individual with God.

The self pleasing to God: The self-pleasing, fulfilling or satisfying self, also described as the self of total submission, is the merging of God with the individual.

The Pure self : The pure, perfected and complete self is the state of total union with God and the attainment of universal consciousness.

70 Communication of the understanding of the 'internal frame of reference' to client by a therapist pertains to which type of counselling skills?

1 Reflection
2 Focusing
3 Empathy
4 Social influencer

Ans. (1)

Exp. Communication of the understanding of the 'internal frame of reference' to client by a therapist pertains to Reflection.

Reflecting a client's emotions is often useful for heightening the client's awareness of and ability to label their own emotions. It is important that counselors have a wide emotional vocabulary, so they can tailor their word choice to match a level of emotional intensity that is congruent with a client's experience. Although this may seem a very simple skill, reflecting back what the client is bringing provides the ideal opportunity for them to confirm or refute our understanding.

71 Given below are two statements, one is labelled as Assertion (A) and the other labelled as Reason (R).

Assertion (A) Chances of inheriting the dominant genes are twice in females as compared to males.

Reason (R) Females in comparison to males have two 'X' chromosomes.

In the light of the above statements, choose the most appropriate answer from the options given below :

1 Both (A) and (R) are correct and (R) is the correct explanation of (A)
2 Both (A) and (R) are correct but (R) is not the correct explanation of (A)
3 (A) is correct but (R) is not correct
4 (A) is not correct but (R) is correct

Ans. (1)

Exp. Both (A) and (R) are correct and (R) is the correct explanation of (A).

Chances of inheriting the dominant genes are twice in females as compared to males. This is true as in X-linked dominant inheritance, the gene responsible for the disease is located on the X-chromosome, and the allele that causes the disease is dominant to the normal allele in females.

Females in comparison to males have two 'X' chromosomes. This is true and explains the chances of inheriting the dominant genes are twice in females as compared to males because females have twice as many X-chromosomes as males, females tend to be more frequently affected than males in the population.

72 Who of the following emphasised nomothetic approach in personality research?

1 Allport
2 Eysenck
3 Jung
4 Galton

Ans. (2)

Exp. Eysenck emphasised nomothetic approach in personality research.

The term 'nomothetic' comes from the Greek word 'nomos' meaning 'law'. Psychologists who adopt this approach are mainly concerned with studying what we share with others (i.e. similarities between people). Therefore, the nomothetic approach involves establishing laws or generalisations that apply to all people. The psychometric approach to the study of personality compares individuals in terms of traits or dimensions common to everyone.

Eysenck used the nomothetic approach. He tested a large group of people and used their data to divide them into personality types such as 'introverted-neurotic' or 'extroverted-neurotic'. This method allows personality to be easily and quickly sorted into a universal personality test.

73 Arrange in correct sequence, the first five intelligences given by Gardner.

I. Linguistic Intelligence
II. Logico-mathematical Intelligence
III. Spatial Intelligence
IV. Kinesthetic Intelligence
V. Natural intelligence

Choose the correct answer from the options given below :

1 I, II, III, IV, V
2 II, I, III, V, IV
3 III, II, I, IV, V
4 IV, III, V, II, I

Ans. (1)

Exp. The correct sequence is I, II, III, IV, V.

The correct sequence of the first five intelligence given by Gardner is as follows :

Linguistic Intelligence : People with high verbal-linguistic intelligence display a facility with words and languages. They are typically good at reading, writing, telling stories and memorising words along with dates. Verbal ability is one of the most g-loaded abilities.

Logico-mathematical Intelligence : This area has to do with logic, abstractions, reasoning, numbers and critical thinking. This also has to do with having the capacity to understand the underlying principles of some kind of causal system.

Spatial Intelligence : This area deals with spatial judgement and the ability to visualise with the mind's eye. Spatial ability is one of the three factors beneath g in the hierarchical model of intelligence.

Kinesthetic Intelligence : The core elements of the bodily-kinesthetic intelligence are control of one's bodily motions and the capacity to handle objects skillfully. Gardner elaborates to say that this also includes a sense of timing, a clear sense of the goal of a physical action, along with the ability to train responses.

Natural intelligence : This area has to do with nurturing and relating information to one's natural surroundings. Examples include classifying natural forms such as animal and plant species and rocks and mountain types. This ability was clearly of value in our evolutionary past as hunters, gatherers, and farmers; it continues to be central in such roles as botanist or chef.

74 Who among the following proposed that different emotional stimuli induce different patterns of ANS activity and that these different patterns produce different emotional experiences?

1 James–Lange 2 Cannon–Bard
3 Singer–Schachter 4 Plutchik

Ans. (1)

Exp. James–Lange proposed that different emotional stimuli induce different patterns of ANS activity and that these different patterns produce different emotional experiences.

The basic premise of the theory is that physiological arousal instigates the experience of emotion. Instead of feeling an emotion and subsequent physiological (bodily) response, the theory proposes that the physiological change is primary, and emotion is then experienced when the brain reacts to the information received via the body's nervous system. It proposes that each specific category of emotion is attached to a unique and different pattern of physiological arousal and emotional behavior in reaction due to an exciting stimulus.

75 Match List I with List II.

List I	List II
A. Cognitive Assessment System	I. Dass
B. Hold and Don't Hold Tests	II. Wechsler
C. Cognitive Assessment Battery	III. Cattell
D. Differential Ability Test	IV. Elliot

Choose the correct answer from the options given below :

	A	B	C	D		A	B	C	D
1	I	II	III	IV	2	II	I	IV	III
3	III	IV	I	II	4	IV	III	II	I

Ans. (1)

Exp. The correct matching is A-I, B-II, C-III, D-IV.

Cognitive Assessment System was proposed by Dass. The Das–Naglieri Cognitive Assessment System (CAS) test is an individually administered test of cognitive functioning for children and adolescents ranging from 5 through 17 years of age that was designed to assess the planning, attention, simultaneous and successive cognitive processes as described in the PASS theory of intelligence.

Hold and Don't Hold Tests was proposed by Wechsler. These are tests that in comparison to each other are thought to be either relatively resistant to aging or cognitive impairment associated with brain dysfunction or relatively sensitive to the same processes.

Cognitive Assessment Battery was proposed by Cattell. It consists of six short tests covering the cognitive domains of speed/attention, episodic memory, visuospatial functions, language and executive functions.

Differential Ability Test was proposed by Elliot. It measures a variety of cognitive abilities including verbal and visual working memory, immediate and delayed recall, visual recognition and matching, processing and naming speed, phonological processing, and understanding of basic number concepts.

76 Match List I with List II.

List I (Concept)	List II (Description)
A. Turiyavastha	I. Transcognitive realisation
B. Aparvidya	II. Highest state of consciousness
C. Paravidya	III. Transcendental knowledge
D. Nididhasan	IV. Empirical knowledge

Choose the correct answer from the options given below :

	A	B	C	D		A	B	C	D
1	I	III	II	IV	2	II	III	IV	I
3	II	I	III	IV	4	III	II	IV	I

Ans. (*)

Exp. The correct matching is A-II, B-III, C-IV, D-I.

Turiyavastha is associated with highest state of consciousness. The turiyavastha is the highest state of consciousness in which the essential nature of the Atma is experienced.

Aparvidya is associated with Transcendental knowledge. The lower knowledge consists of all textual knowledge - the four Vedas, the science of pronunciation etc., the code of rituals, grammar, etymology, metre and astrology.

Paravidya is associated with Empirical knowledge. The higher knowledge is by which the immutable and the imperishable Atman is realized, which knowledge brings about the direct realization of the Supreme Reality, the source of All.

Nididhasan is associated with Transcognitive realisation. It means understanding the meaning of the scriptures on the basis of the relation between the words and the sense in which they are expressed.

77 Which of the following are the correct differences between Parkinson's disease and Huntington's disease?

I. Parkinson's disease is a disorder of middle and old age while Huntington's disease is a disorder of young.

II. Parkinson's disease is a movement disorder while Huntington's disease is an emotional disorder.

III. Unlike Parkinson's disease, Huntington's disease has a strong genetic base.

IV. Parkinson's disease is not associated with severe dementia while Huntington's disease is.

Choose the correct answer from the options given below:

1 I and II
2 III and IV
3 I, III and IV
4 II, III and IV

Ans. (2)

Exp. The correct codes are III and IV only.

Unlike Parkinson's disease, Huntington's disease has a strong genetic base. Huntington's disease is an inherited condition resulting from genetic changes that pass down from parent to child. Conversely, experts believe that a combination of environmental and genetic factors contributes to Parkinson's disease.

Parkinson's disease is not associated with severe dementia while Huntington's disease is. Cognitive decline or dementia can also occur in both. However, severe dementia can be found in Huntington's disease.

Huntington's disease typically develops between the ages of 30 and 50. Parkinson's disease typically starts around age 70, though it can begin earlier. Therefore, Parkinson's disease is not a disorder of middle and old age while Huntington's disease is a disorder of young.

There is some overlap between Parkinson's and Huntington's, in that they both affect movement. Therefore, Parkinson's disease is not a movement disorder alone. Huntington's is a movement disorder as well along with an emotional disorder.

78 Mayer-Salovey-Caruso Emotional Intelligence Test (MSCEIT) measures

I. Perceiving emotions

II. Using emotions to facilitate thought

III. Understanding emotions

IV. Implicit motivation

Choose the correct answer from the options given below :

1 I and II
2 III and IV
3 I, II and III
4 II, III and IV

Ans. (3)

Exp. Mayer-Salovey-Caruso Emotional Intelligence Test (MSCEIT) measures perceiving emotions, using emotions to facilitate thought and understanding emotions.

Perceiving emotions is the ability to perceive emotions in oneself and others as well as in objects, art, stories, music, and other stimuli.

Using emotions to facilitate thought is the ability to generate, use, and feel emotion as necessary to communicate feelings or employ them in other cognitive processes.

Understanding emotions is the ability to understand emotional information, to understand how emotions combine and progress through relationship transitions, and to appreciate such emotional meanings.

79 Loftus and Pickrell (1995) asked people to read and think about events which had happened to them in childhood and also instructed to write a description of one event which was actually fictitious. About one third of the participants described the fictitious events as having really happened to them.

This is called

I. Eyewitness memory

II. False memory

III. Flash bulb memory

IV. Autobiographical memory

Choose the correct answer from the options given below :

1 I and II
2 Only II
3 II and III
4 Only I

Ans. (2)

Exp. Loftus and Pickrell (1995) asked people to read and think about events which had happened to them in childhood and also instructed to write a description of one event which was actually fictitious. About one third of the participants described the fictitious events as having really happened to them. This is called False memory.

A False memory is a phenomenon where someone recalls something that did not happen or recalls it differently from the way it actually happened. Suggestibility, which is the activation of associated information, the incorporation of misinformation, and source misattribution have been suggested to be several mechanisms underlying a variety of types of false memory.

80 Persons inclined to be verbally aggressive have

1 low threshold for Behaviour Activation system
2 low threshold for Flight–Fight system
3 high threshold for Behaviour Inhibition system
4 high threshold for Behaviour Activation system

Ans. (1,2,3)

Exp. Persons inclined to be verbally aggressive have low threshold for Behaviour Activation system, low threshold for Flight-Fight system and high threshold for Behaviour Inhibition system.

The Behavioural Activation/Approach System (BAS) is an appetitive–motivational system that is activated by reward consumption and conditioned signals of reward or non-punishment, triggering approach behaviour.

81 Which of the following characterises Cognitive Dissonance?

I. Dissonance often occurs in situations involving forced compliance.
II. Attempts to resolve dissonance are reflected in increased cortical activity.
III. Dissonance cannot be reduced directly but only by adding cognitions that justify our behaviours.
IV. Dissonance is stronger when we have little justification for our attitude–inconsistent behaviour.

Choose the correct answer from the options given below :

1 I, II and III
2 I, II and IV
3 II, III and IV
4 I, II, III and IV

Ans. *(2)*

➲ *Exp.* Statement I, II and IV characterises Cognitive Dissonance.

Dissonance often occurs in situations involving forced compliance. When someone is forced to do (publicly) something they (privately) really don't want to do, dissonance is created between their cognition (I didn't want to do this) and their behaviour (I did it).

Its attempts to resolve dissonance are reflected in increased cortical activity. A link between individual neural dynamics (long-range temporal correlations) of the frontocentral cortices during rest and follow-up neural and behavioural effects of cognitive dissonance.

Dissonance is stronger when we have little justification for our attitude – inconsistent behaviour. Little justification for our attitudes lead to more significant dissonance. A substantial disparity between conflicting and harmonious beliefs will result in more dissonance.

Statement III is incorrect as Dissonance can be reduced directly by adding cognitions that justify our behaviours. The central thesis of cognitive dissonance theory is that when two beliefs are inconsistent, individuals experience negatively arousing cognitive conflict (called dissonance). The individuals are therefore motivated to reduce the conflict by justifying the decision they have made.

82 Which of the following are the performance subtests of WAIS?

I. Digit span
II. Similarities
III. Digit symbol
IV. Object assembly

Choose the correct answer from the options given below :

1 I and III
2 III and IV
3 II, III and IV
4 I, III and IV

Ans. *(2)*

➲ *Exp.* Digit symbol and Object assembly are the performance subsets of WAIS.

The following are the performance subtests of WAIS are:

Digit symbol: It is a paper-and-pencil cognitive test presented on a single sheet of paper that requires a subject to match symbols to numbers according to a key located on the top of the page. The subject copies the symbol into spaces below a row of numbers.

Object assembly: It assesses the ability of the participant to construct an object from component pieces that only fit together properly if joined in the correct sequence.

83 Given below are two statements, one is labelled as Assertion (A) and the other labelled as Reason (R).

Assertion (A) Cattell incorporated factors Q_1, Q_2, Q_3 and Q_4 in 16 PF.

Reason (R) Some factors appeared only in *L*–data not in *Q* and *T*-data.

In the light of the above statements, choose the most appropriate answer from the options given below.

1 Both (A) and (R) are correct and (R) is the correct explanation of (A)
2 Both (A) and (R) are correct but (R) is not the correct explanation of (A)
3 (A) is correct, but (R) is not correct
4 (A) is not correct, but (R) is correct

Ans. *(2)*

➲ *Exp.* Both (A) and (R) are correct but (R) is not the correct explanation of (A).

Cattell incorporated factors Q_1, Q_2, Q_3 and Q_4 in 16 PF. This is true as the four factors were added in 16 PF which are Openness to Change Q_1, Self-Reliance Q_2, Perfectionism Q_3, and Tension Q_4.

Some factors appeared only in L–data not in Q and T-data. This is true as L-data deals with the individual's actual everyday situations. It is life record data such as school grades, absence from work, etc. Cattell analysed the list of 4500 adjectives and organized the list of adjectives into fewer than 171 items and asked subjects to rate people whom they knew on each of the adjectives on the list (an example of L-data because the information was gathered from observers). This allowed Cattell to narrow down to 35 terms and factor analysis in 1945, 1947 and 1948 revealed a 11 or 12 factor solution.

84 Which of the following correctly described influences of Behaviourism?

I. Watson's scientific psychology was designed to predict and control human behaviour.
II. Mary Cover Jones studied the effectiveness of counter conditioning.

III. Skinner claimed to have introduced the term 'Behaviour therapy' and is also credited for it.
IV. Lazarus emphasised the extension of Thorndike's Law of effect.

Choose the correct answer from the options given below :

1 I and IV
2 II and III
3 I and II
4 III and IV

Ans. (3)

Exp. Statement I and II are correct.

The following are correctly described influences of Behaviourism:

Watson's scientific psychology was designed to predict and control human behaviour. Watson believed that psychology should primarily be scientific observable behavior. He is remembered for his research on the conditioning process. Watson is also known for the Little Albert experiment, in which he demonstrated that a child could be conditioned to fear a previously neutral stimulus.

Mary Cover Jones studied the effectiveness of counter conditioning. Mary Cover Jones was the first to show the effectiveness of the counter conditioning process in her rabbit experiments. She was able to eliminate the fear of rabbits from a young boy. The boy was allowed to touch the rabbit and then was able to eat his food to reduce the nervousness touching the rabbit induced.

85 Which of the following type of inversion is observed in reaction formation?

I. Implicit
II. Explicit
III. Conscious
IV. Unconscious

Choose the correct answer from the options given below :

1 I and IV
2 II and III
3 II and IV
4 I and III

Ans. (3)

Exp. The correct codes are II and IV only.

The following type of inversion is observed in reaction formation:

Explicit : More recent studies have continued to provide evidence for reaction formation. For example, in a 2012 study, Weinstein and her colleagues used a test to measure participants' implicit sexual orientation and asked them to identify their sexual orientation explicitly. The researchers found that when there was a discrepancy between participants' implicit and explicit sexual orientation, they were more likely to regard those who identified as gay with hostility.

Unconscious : Reaction formation is a defense mechanism in which a person unconsciously replaces an unwanted or anxiety-provoking impulse with its opposite, often expressed in an exaggerated or showy way.

86 Which of the following is/are correctly associated with Plato's idea of 'Chariot that is pulled by two horses'?

I. Desiring soul is the charioteer
II. Rational soul is located in the head
III. Rational soul is governed by restraint and modesty
IV. Spirited soul knows the honour

Choose the correct answer from the options given below :

1 Only III
2 I and II
3 II and IV
4 I, III and IV

Ans. (3)

Exp. Statement II and IV are correctly associated with Plato's idea of 'Chariot that is pulled by two horses'.

In Plato's idea rational soul is located in the head. The rational part corresponds to the guardians in that it performs the executive function in a soul just as it does in a city.

Also, this idea conclude that spirited soul knows the honour. The spirited part corresponds to the military or auxiliary forces because it is expected to display the virtue of courage.

87 Qualities such as calmness, tolerance, sociability, love of comfort and easy goingness depict, which of the following?

1 Viscertonia
2 Somatotonia
3 Cerebrotonia
4 Ectomorphia

Ans. (1)

Exp. Qualities such as calmness, tolerance, sociability, love of comfort and easy goingness depict, Viscertonia.

According to Sheldon's constitutional theory of personality, it is the personality type that is associated with an endomorphic physique and is characterised by a tendency toward love of comfort, food, relaxation, and sociability.

88 Attitudes can be classically conditioned even without our awareness by which of the following?

I. Subliminal conditioning
II. Observational learning
III. Mere exposure
IV. Social networks

Choose the correct answer from the options given below :

1 I and II
2 II and III
3 I and III
4 II and IV

Ans. (3)

Exp. Attitudes can be classically conditioned even without our awareness by Subliminal conditioning and Mere exposure.

Subliminal conditioning: Subliminal Conditioning (of attitudes) is classical conditioning of attitudes by exposure to stimuli that are below the threshold of conscious awareness.

Mere exposure: The mere exposure effect is a psychological phenomenon by which people tend to develop a preference for things or people that are more familiar to them than others.

89 Arrange in a sequence the Stop-start Relapse Cycle of Internet Addiction.

I. Regret
II. Rationalisation
III. Relapse
IV. Abstinence

Choose the correct answer from the options given below

1 I, IV, II, III 2 II, I, IV, III
3 IV, I, III, II 4 I, II, IV, III

Ans. (2)

Exp. The correct sequence is II, I, IV, III.

The Stop-start Relapse Cycle of Internet Addiction is arranged in the correct sequence as follows:

Rationalisation : The addict rationalises that the Internet serves as a treat after a long, hard day of work, often making a statement such as "I work hard, I deserve it"; "just a few minutes won't hurt:' "I can control my Internet use"; "The computer relaxes me"; or "With the stress I've been under, I deserve this". The addict justifies the need to look at a few adult sites, chat for a few minutes with an online lover or play game with friends, only to discover that the behavior is not so easily contained.

Regret : After the Internet experience, the addict experiences a period of deep regret. Turning off the computer, the addict realizes that work is piling up and feels guilty for the behavior, making statements such as "I know this is hurting my job"; "I can't believe I wasted all this time"; "or I am a horrible person for what I just did."

Abstinence: The addict views the behavior as a personal failure or willpower and promises never to do it again, so a period of abstinence follows. During this time, he or she engages in healthy patterns of behavior, works diligently, resumes interests in old hobbies, spends more time with his or her family, exercises, and gets enough rest.

Relapse : The addict craves the online high or experience as temptations to return to the Internet emerge during stressful or emotionally charged moments. The addict recalls the self-medicating effects of being online and its associated relaxation and excitement. The addict remembers how good it felt to be online and forgets how bad it felt afterward. The rationalization period started again, and the availability of the computer starts the cycle anew.

90 Interscorer reliability is relevant in

I. projective tests of personality
II. achievement tests with short answers
III. achievement tests with essay type questions
IV. self-report personality inventories

Choose the correct answer from the options given below :

1 I and II
2 I and III
3 I, II and III
4 II, III and IV

Ans. (3)

Exp. The correct codes are I, II and III.

Inter-scorer reliability is the degree of agreement among independent observers who rate, code, or assess the same phenomenon. Interscorer reliability is relevant in:-

(A) projective tests of personality
(B) achievement tests with short answers
(C) achievement tests with essay type questions

It is not used in self-report personality inventories where objective and standardised scoring is required.

Directions (Q. Nos. 91-95) *Read the following paragraph and answer the five questions that follow :*

A psychologist was interested in developing English Language Usage test for HSSC students. She wrote 120 questions trying to cover several areas of the language usage. Each question had five alternatives out of which only one was right.

The draft version of the test was given to a sample of 200 students. The test items were analysed in two ways carrying out item-remainder correlation and discrimination index for each item.

For the purpose of computing item discrimination index, she labelled those who had a total score below P_{27} as low scorers. and those who had a total score above P_{73} as high scorers. (Assume that P_{27} and P_{73} had non fractional. i.e. full integer values). The statistical significance of the discrimination index of each item was evaluated by appropriate test. Ninety items were retained in item analysis.

The Ninety-item version was administered to a fresh sample of 400 subjects. Cronbach alpha was computed. The psychologist also wondered if she could compute Kuder Richardson (K-R) reliability for her test. Since the Cronbach alpha was pretty high i.e 947 and the test was quite long she decided to develop the two parallel forms each of 45 items. She randomly assigned the items to two halves, labelling them as Form A and Form B. For each form, she assessed average inter-item correlation mean, standard deviation and Cronbach alpha. The two forms satisfied the criteria for parallel forms.

91 Item I was passed by 30 subjects in Low scoring group and by 56 subjects in High scoring group. What would be the discrimination index for item I?

1 0.241 2 0.481
3 0.556 4 0.796

Ans. (2)

Exp. Item I was passed by 30 subjects in Low scoring group and by 56 subjects in High scoring group. The discrimination index for item I would be 0.481.

92 Which one of the following test can be used for evaluating statistical significance of the discrimination index?

1 Chi-square test 2 T-test
3 F test 4 Mann-Whitney U test

Ans. (1)

Exp. Chi-square test can be used for evaluating statistical significance of the discrimination index.

The chi-square statistic compares the observed values to the expected values. This test statistic is used to determine whether the difference between the observed and expected values is statistically significant.

93 Give below are two statements, one is labelled as Assertion (A) and the other labelled as Reason (R).

Assertion (A) It is not possible to compute K-R reliability for the above test, since each item has five alternatives.

Reason (R) K-R reliability can be computed, when the items can be dichotomously scored.

In the light of the above statements, choose the most appropriate answer from the options given below :

1 Both (A) and (R) are correct and (R) is the correct explanation of (A)
2 Both (A) and (R) are correct, but (R) is not the correct explanation of (A)
3 (A) is correct, but (R) is not correct
4 (A) is not correct, but (R) is correct

Ans. (4)

Exp. (A) is not correct but (R) is correct.

It is not possible to compute K-R reliability for the above test, since each item has five alternatives. This is not true as in this case where the code for each multiple-choice question is 1 for a correct answer and 0 for an incorrect answer.

K-R reliability can be computed, when the items can be dichotomously scored. This is true as The Kuder and Richardson Formula 20 test checks the internal consistency of measurements with dichotomous choices. It is equivalent to performing the split-half methodology on all combinations of questions and is applicable when each question is either right or wrong. A correct question scores 1 and an incorrect question scores 0.

94 What is the expected Cronbach alpha for the Form A?

1 .474 2 .899 3 .913 4 .947

Ans. (2)

Exp. The expected Cronbach alpha for the Form A is 0.899.

The formula for calculating the Cronbach alpha is:

rfull = 2 (rhalf) / 1 + rhalf, where rfull = 0.947.

Putting the values, we get rhalf as 0.899.

95 For computing inter-item correlations, which one of the following is suitable?

1 Point biserial correlation
2 Biserial correlation
3 Rank difference correlation
4 Phi-coefficient

Ans. (4)

Exp. For computing inter-item correlations, Phi-coefficient is suitable.

The phi correlation coefficient (phi) is one of a number of correlation statistics developed to measure the strength of association between two variables. The phi is a nonparametric statistic used in cross-tabulated table data where both variables are dichotomous.

Directions (Q. Nos. 96-100) *Read the following paragraph and answer the five questions that follow :*

An experimental psychologist wanted to test two hypotheses. The first hypothesis proposed that stress would adversely affect the rate of serial learning. The second hypothesis proposed that the type of material (meaningless vs. meaningful) would moderate the effect of stress. The Psychology formed six groups by manipulating stress (A) at three levels—Low, Moderate and High and Type of material (B) at two levels. The subjects were randomly assigned to these groups from an initial pool of subjects. The list of 15 CVC trigrams constituted meaningless material and the list of 15 three-lettered meaningful words constituted meaningful material. The number of trials required to learn the list was the dependent variable. The data were analysed by suitable analysis of variance. Following are the selected findings.

1. The ratio of largest to smallest standard deviations for the six groups was reasonably close to one.
2. The degrees of freedom for error variance was 135.
3. The F ratio for the effect of stress was 0.95.
4. The effect sizes for each effect were calculated both the obtaining *eta* square and partial *eta* square.

96 Which one of the following F ratio would be used to evaluate second hypothesis?

1 $F = MS_A / MS_E$
2 $F = MS_B / MS_E$
3 $F = MS_{A\times B} / MS_E$
4 $F = MS_A / (MS_{A\times B} + MS_E)$

Ans. (3)

Exp. $F = MS_{A\times B} / MS_E$ ratio would be used to evaluate second hypothesis.

97 The above data indicates

1 that the assumption of homogeneity of variance is satisfied
2 that the assumption of homogeneity of variance is not satisfied
3 the absence of information related to the assumption of homogeneity of variance
4 the formal test of homogeneity of variance needs to be carried out

Ans. (1)

Exp. The above data indicates that the assumption of homogeneity of variance is satisfied.

The assumption of homogeneity of variance is an assumption of the independent samples t-test and ANOVA stating that all comparison groups have the same variance.

98 The above findings indicate that the post-hoc comparisons are

1 Necessary for the effect of stress
2 Necessary for the effect of type of material
3 Necessary both for the effect of stress and type of material
4 Neither necessary for the effect of stress nor the type of material

Ans. (4)

Exp. The above findings indicate that the post-hoc comparisons are neither necessary for the effect of stress nor the type of material.

99 The above results indicate that

1 the first hypothesis is verified
2 the first hypothesis is rejected
3 the first hypothesis is partially verified
4 the inadequate information for evaluating the first hypothesis

Ans. (2)

Exp. The above results indicate that the first hypothesis is rejected.

100 The above design can best be labelled as

1 Randomised 3 × 2 balanced factorial design
2 Randomised 3 × 2 balanced factorial design with a covariate
3 Randomised 3 × 2 unbalanced factorial design
4 Randomised block design

Ans. (3)

Exp. The above design can best be labelled as Randomised 3× 2 unbalanced factorial design.

UGC-NET
PSYCHOLOGY

SOLVED PAPER 2020 (September)

PAPER II

1 Which one of the following branches of philosophy of science deals with the question of existence?

1 Post-positivism 2 Structuralism
3 Ontology 4 Scientific realism

Ans. *(3)*

Exp. Ontology is a discipline that deals with the question of existence. It studies the nature of existence. It combines the words, 'onto,' which means 'being,' and the word 'logia,' which refers to a logical discourse.

Ontology also deals with the concepts of reality, being, and becoming.

2 Which one of the following terms denotes that there are qualities of experience that cannot be explained in terms of combinations of traditional kinds of sensations?

1 Zeitgeist 2 Tropism
3 Gestalt Qualitaten 4 Conarium

Ans. *(3)*

Exp. 'Gestalt Qualitaten' refers to gestalt qualities. It refers to qualities that cannot be explained by the integration of the traditional types of senses. It is a concept that was given by Christian von Ehrenfels.

In Gestalt theories, the whole is always the primary quality. For instance, a melody is something that is understood as a whole. It sounds the same when played in any key. This cannot be explained in the terms of traditional senses. Therefore, they are understood when taken as a whole rather than the sum of their parts. Other concepts include marriage and war, among others.

3 A researcher is studying group process of software startup developers by staying with them and line them for six months. Which of the following is used by her?

1 Grounded Theory
2 Ethnography
3 Narrative analysis
4 Phenomenological research

Ans. *(2)*

Exp. In the given case, the researcher is using Ethnography. Ethnography is referred to as the study of different kinds of human societies. In this type of study, the researcher tends to immerse themselves among the people whom they are studying. For instance, they immerse themselves with their everyday life and their culture.

Similarly, when a researcher is studying a group whilst they are developing a software by completely immersing herself with the group and being a part of their day-to-day activities, she is conducting an Ethnographic study.

4 Testing the scientific hypothesis is impossible due to the need of auxiliary assumptions. What is this associated with?

1 Occam's razor 2 Logical empiricism
3 Duhem-Quine thesis 4 Incommensurability

Ans. *(3)*

Exp. Testing the scientific hypothesis is impossible due to the need of auxiliary assumptions. It is associated with Duhem-Quine thesis.

Duhem-Quine thesis is also referred to as the Duhem-Quine problem, which deals with the impossibility of testing a given hypothesis in isolation because any empirical investigation of a hypothesis would involve certain background assumptions, which are known as auxiliary assumptions. For instance, if one has to disprove that the functions of the right side of the body are not controlled by the left cerebral hemisphere, one has to test this hypothesis against the process of information from the right visual field not being processed in the left cerebral hemisphere, or test it against some other such kind of a bodily function. It was given by Pierre Duhem and Willard Van Orman Quine.

5 Making decisions by the use of mental shortcuts that focus on one aspect of a problem, while ignoring others refers to which one of the following?

1 Framing 2 Belief perseverance
3 Heuristics 4 Mental set

Ans. *(3)*

Exp. Heuristics refers to making decisions by the use of mental shortcuts that focus on one aspect of a problem, while ignoring others

Heuristics are mental shortcuts that help people in solving problems at a faster pace. However, they do not always guarantee a desirable outcome. One shortcoming of a heuristic is that it concentrates only on one aspect of the problem rather than taking all the aspects into consideration.

One mental shortcut generally used is to utilise the same method of solving a problem in case it has worked in the past. For instance, consider that a student was able to correctly solve a simple interest (SI) problem by using the SI formula. Then, when he encounters a compound interest (CI) problem, he would try to solve it using the SI formula as the problem would seemingly have all the components of a SI problem, therefore, the student ignores the information that differentiates one from another. In doing so, he makes a mistake.

6 A group of sixty newly diagnosed diabetic patients were tested for anxiety using a standardised inventory. They were retested for anxiety again after months using the same inventory. The mean difference in anxiety was evaluated by a suitable *t*-test. The degrees of freedom associated with the *t*-test would be

1 120 2 118 3 59 4 58

Ans. (3)

Exp. In this case, the degrees of freedom associated with the *t*-test would be 59.

Degrees of Freedom (DF) are the number of independent values that are allowed to vary. For instance, consider one has 7 pairs of shoes and can wear a different one pair every day of the week. For the first 6 days, one has a choice of picking from other pairs. However, on the 7th day, one can only pick the one that is left. Therefore, variance is allowed for the 6 pairs of shoes, but not for the 7th one.

Typically, the DF for *t*-test is calculated using the formula (N-1), where N stands for the number of subjects. In an experimental design involving 60 subjects in each group, the DF will be 60 – 1, which is 59.

7 In depth perception, what kind of images are used?

1 Uni-dimensional image
2 Two-dimensional images
3 Three-dimensional images
4 Four-dimensional images

Ans. (3)

Exp. In depth perception, three-dimensional images are used.

Depth perception is considered as the ability to perceive the world in three dimensions, therefore it can perceive the depth, distance, and size. Depth perception can take place through one eye (monocular) as well as both the eyes (binocular). Consequently, three-dimensional images are used for the purpose of depth perception. For instance, in a painting, the artist makes use of several cues that allow one to perceive depth in an image. Consider a painting involve two people of the same height. The painter places one of the persons a little further away from the other so that they produce a smaller image on the retina of the eye than the one who is comparatively closer.

8 Total cholesterol is determined by adding which of the following values?

1 HDL + LDL
2 HDL + LDL + 30% OF VLDL
3 HDL + LDL + 10% OF VLDL
4 HDL + LDL + 20% of Triglycerides

Ans. (4)

Exp. Total cholesterol is determined by using the formula, HDL + LDL + 20% of Triglycerides.

Cholesterol is a lipid that is present in the blood. Some types of cholesterol, good cholesterol or high density lipoprotein (HDL), are important for the body as they help in cell building and hormone production. However, high amount of bad cholesterol or low-density lipoprotein (LDL) is bad for the body as they can settle in the arteries, and clog them. This can lead to different health conditions including heart attacks.

Total cholesterol refers to the overall amount of cholesterol present in the blood. It is calculated using the formula:

HDL + LDL + 20% of Triglycerides

Triglycerides are a type of fat. They are included in the formula because people with high triglycerides also tend to have high cholesterol, which is high LDL and low HDL.

9 Which approach focussed on the nature of a task and its influence on a person's ability in solving problems?

1 Associationist approach
2 Information processing approach
3 Gestalt approach
4 Behaviourist approach

Ans. (3)

Exp. Gestalt approach focussed on the nature of a task and its influence on a person's ability in solving problems

When it comes to the Gestalt approach to problem-solving, the theorists tended to focus on the nature of the task, and the impact it has upon a person's ability to solve problems. For instance, Max Wertheimer proposed two types of thinking:

1. *Productive thinking* : This refers to the quick and creative response to situations.
2. *Reproductive thinking* : It refers to a type of problem-solving that is done on the basis of prior experiences.

Both of these patterns of thinking are dependent on the nature of the task, and the impact it has on a person which leads to these types of thinking.

In another theory, Kohler proposed 'insight,' which refers to a way of solving certain problems that begins with not having any idea to suddenly gaining an insight, or understanding into how to solve the problem.

10 Pavlov while discussing the strong/weak nervous system believed that the point of 'transmarginal inhibition' is the point beyond which

1 the magnitude of response decreases as stimulus intensity decreases.
2 the magnitude of response increases as stimulus intensity decreases.
3 the magnitude of response increases irrespective of stimulus intensity decrease/increase.
4 the magnitude of response decreases irrespective of stimulus intensity decrease/increase.

Ans. (4)

Exp. Ivan Pavlov while discussing the strong/weak nervous system believed that the point of 'transmarginal inhibition' is the point beyond which the magnitude of response decreases irrespective of stimulus intensity decrease/increase.

Ivan Pavlov gave the concept of Transmarginal Inhibition (TMI). He said that as the magnitude of a Conditioned Stimulus (CS) increases, the Conditioned Response (CR) also increases, but only upto a certain extent, after which it tends to decrease.

TMI explains the body's response to overwhelming stimuli. For instance, a person may lose their consciousness in case they are tortured for too long. This happens so as to help the person avoid enduring the pain for too long. TMI happens after a certain threshold is reached. In people with a weak nervous system, who according to Pavlov are introverted people, this threshold is reached at a lower intensity itself. Therefore, TMI can be referred to as decrease in the magnitude of response irrespective of the increase/decrease in the intensity of the stimulus after a certain point.

11 In multiple approach-avoidance conflict, one has to choose between which of the following?

1 Two goals possessing both negative and positive aspects.
2 More than two goals; each having both positive and negative aspects.
3 More than two goals; one having negative aspects and others having positive valences.
4 More than two goals; at least one having positive aspects while others may have negative aspects.

Ans. (2)

Exp. In multiple approach-avoidance conflict, one has to choose between more than two goals; each having both positive and negative aspects.

Multiple approach – avoidance conflict describes a method of approaching a conflict wherein one has to weigh two options, both of which have their positive and negative elements. For instance, when buying a car, one must choose between a car that gives great mileage and is easy to maintain, and another car which looks good, has all the fancy equipment, but is highly expensive to maintain.

12 Which one of the following models proposes that there are three major functional units of the brain; focussing on sustaining attention; receiving and storing information and planning and self-monitoring?

1 PASS Model
2 Kar and Parrila's Model
3 Atkinson and Shiffrin Model
4 Hunt's Model

Ans. (1)

Exp. PASS Model proposes that there are three major functional units of the brain; focussing on sustaining attention; receiving and storing information and planning and self-monitoring.

PASS Model is a model of intelligence that was put forth by Alexander Luria. PASS model purports that the brain comprises of separate functional systems, which are interdependent. The three cognitive processes take place within these systems. These are:

1. *Attention*: It refers to directing the focus towards certain information. Selective attention refers to focusing only on the information that is relevant, while tuning out the irrelevant ones.
2. *Planning* : It refers to the development or selection of strategies that help in solving a given problem.
3. *Simultaneous and Successive Processing* : It requires the receiving and storing of information. Simultaneous processing takes place when the brain integrates all the parts of information it receives, and constructs a whole. Successive processing takes place when the information received requires to be stored and remembered in a serial order, one after the other.

13 For an intelligence test in an educational setting, which of the following difficulty value shows maximum discrimination?

1 0.8 2 0.6 3 0.5 4 0.3

Ans. (3)

Exp. For intelligence tests used in educational setting, 0.5 difficulty value shows maximum discrimination.

In educational setting, intelligence tests are used to assess the Intelligence Quotient (IQ) of potential students. This has several uses, such as a good IQ is a predictor of academic success.

Intelligence tests consist of several items that a test-taker must respond to. The difficulty index of an item refers to the proportion of the test-takers who are able to respond to it correctly, while discrimination index refers to how well an item is able to differentiate between test-takers who are intelligent or knowledgeable and those who are not. Generally, an item with a difficult index of 0.5 is considered to be a good item as it indicates that 50% of the test-takers have been able to respond to it accurately. This in turn also shows that the item is able to appropriately segregate between those who are knowledgeable and those who are not as well.

14 What do you call the attention that is drawn automatically to a stimulus without the intention of the participant?

1 Divided attention
2 Shadowing
3 Endogenous attention
4 Exogenous attention

Ans. (4)

Exp. Exogenous attention is the attention that is drawn automatically to a stimulus without the intention of the participant.

It is the attention that is captured by a prominent or salient stimulus—for example, in the peripheral visual field—rather than deliberately applied or focused by the individual. It is also called involuntary attention. This can have something to do with the properties of the stimulus that attract one's attention towards it. For instance, they can be physical properties like brightness.

15 Jensen put forward the 'Regression' argument to account for which of the following?

1 To understand inter-generation changes in intellegence.
2 To understand intra-generation changes in intelligence.
3 To understand group differences in intelligence.
4 To understand the role of genetics in intelligence.

Ans. (4)

Exp. Jensen put forward the 'Regression' argument to account to understand the role of genetics in intelligence. Jensen put forth a theory of intelligence which purported that genes were the primary factors involved in intelligence where he gave genetic interpretation of racial differences in intelligence. It was found that the regression effects for IQ are compatible with genetic influences on intelligence.

In one of his most controversial works, "How Much Can We Boost IQ and Scholastic Achievement?" he said that the programmes designed to boost the IQ of African-Americans had failed. He put forth the Regression argument in favour of his assessment. That is, regression effects may be predicted to differ for whites and blacks if there really are any genetic differences in intelligence between the two races. Therefore, it can be said that he used the Regression argument to understand the genetic differences in intelligence.

16 What is the retention without conscious recollection of skills and dispositions called?

1 Iconic memory
2 Implicit memory
3 Explicit memory
4 Semantic memory

Ans. (2)

Exp. Retention without conscious recollection of skills and dispositions is called Implicit memory.

It is also referred to as the Non-declarative memory. It is the type of memory that happens to be unconscious and unintentional, that is, it exists outside the awareness of a person. Procedural memory is categorised as implicit memory; it refers to the memory pertaining to the performance of a task. For instance, riding a scooter is implicit, procedural memory. One does not consciously remember how to do it, but the skill is, however, retained in one's memory.

17 Who among the following is credited with proposing the investment theory of creativity?

1 Gatzels and Jackson
2 Kaufman
3 Wallach and Kogan
4 Sternberg

Ans. (4)

Exp. The investment theory of creativity was proposed by Robert Sternberg, in collaboration with Todd Lubart.

Investment theory of creativity purports that when creative people come up with novel ideas and try to propagate or sell them, they may be 'buying low' because at the time these ideas may come across as being very novel or even slightly absurd. However, once their ideas begin to become accepted and gain prominence, they 'sell high' as they are reaping the benefits of a fine idea.

18 Client : (Silent and shifting nervously in her chair. She is facing the counsellor, but her eyes scan anxiously about).
Counsellor : It must be difficult for you to decide what you going to do here with me.

This response is an example of

1 dealing with content speculated to be motivating for non-verbal behaviour by the counsellor.
2 encourages to deal with non-verbal behaviour.
3 encourages to understand the feelings.
4 reflection of feelings.

Ans. (1)

Exp. The given response is an example of dealing with content speculated to be motivating for non-verbal behaviour by the counsellor.

Non-verbal behaviour communicates information in a non-verbal manner, such as eye-contact, body language, facial expressions, etc. In the given situation, the counsellor is dealing with content that could be a motivating factor for the non-verbal behaviour of the client. That is, the client is visibly nervous and fidgety.

This could imply that the client is actually anxious about the therapy session, and the anxiety is driving this behaviour. Therefore, the therapist tries to address the reason for her uneasy behaviour by asking her whether she is finding it difficult to comprehend what would go on in the therapy session.

19 In Bronfenbrenner's Model, which one of the following systems is independent of cultural bias?

1 Micro system
2 Meso system
3 Exo system
4 Macro system

Ans. (4)

Exp. Macro system from Bronfenbrenner's model is said to be independent from any cultural bias.

Urie Bronfenbrenner gave the ecological systems theory which aims to explain the way in which a child's development is influenced by the surrounding environment. Macro system is a component that focuses on the way in which the cultural elements of child's environment, such as, their ethnicity, wealth or poverty, socio-economic status, impact their development. It focuses on how the culture that a child grows up in, whatever it is, impacts their development.

Cultural bias is a criticism often levied against intelligence testing, where it is said to favour the whites or Western culture. However, this (Macro system) component of Bronfenbrenner's theory can be said to be free of any cultural bias as it refers to any culture that a child can grow up in, and not just the culture of the West.

20 A harsh father always restricts the curiosity motive of his son and the son develops a general hostility towards his superiors. Which of the following is correct about this?

1 The father represses the curiosity.
2 Such change is permanent.
3 It is the most modifiable response.
4 It is conditioned hostility.

Ans. (4)

Exp. The given case illustrates conditioned hostility.

Classical conditioning takes place when a neutral stimulus is associated with an unconditional stimulus, and therefore becomes the conditioned stimulus, eliciting a conditioned response. Unconditional stimulus being the one that naturally elicits a response.

The impact of classical conditioning can be seen in anger or hostility. In the given case, a superior is a neutral stimulus. However, a harsh father restricting his son's curiosity makes the son develop a hostility towards him. This hostility gets transferred to a previously neutral stimulus, such as any superior, therefore, the son develops a hostility towards his superiors as well. This happens because a superior is closely associated with the father, who happens to be a superior figure in his son's life. Therefore, this can be said to be a case of conditioned hostility.

21 Which of the following principles is violated when a psychologist intentionally misrepresents his research results?

1 Beneficence
2 Fidelity and responsibility
3 Integrity
4 Confidentiality

Ans. (3)

Exp. Integrity is the ethical principle that is violated when a psychologist intentionally misrepresents his research results.

The American Psychological Association (APA) has put forth general ethical principles which all the psychologists are required to follow. One of the principles is 'integrity,' which requires the psychologists to be honest and transparent in all their practices, and therefore, they must not take part in any behaviour that can be seen as being dishonest, malicious, or exploitative. Consequently, if a psychologist intentionally misrepresents the results of his research, he is engaging in behaviour that is dishonest and deceptive. Therefore, he is violating the principle of integrity.

22 According to Lazarus, what comes between the stimulus and emotional response to that stimulus to mediate?

1 Physiological reactions
2 Labeling
3 Social and situational cues
4 Cognitive appraisal

Ans. (4)

Exp. Cognitive appraisal comes in between stimulus and emotional response, as per the Richard Lazarus's theory of emotion.

In Lazarus's theory, the sequence of events leading to the experience of an emotion first involve the stimulus, followed by a cognitive appraisal of the stimulus, which then leads to the emotional response. Cognitive appraisal refers to how a person appraises the stimulus. For instance, one spots a snake, they appraise it as a threatening stimulus, therefore, they feel fear.

23 Vaibhasika and Sautrantika are associated with which of the following?

1 Theravada
2 Cetasikas
3 Madhyamikavada
4 Sarvastivadin

Ans. (4)

Exp. Vaibhasika and Sautrantika are associated with Sarvastivadin.

The Sarvastivadin was one of the early Buddhist schools established around the reign of Ashoka (third century BCE). It refers to the realist school of Buddhism. This approach states that all the states of experience, whether they are material, mental, or otherwise, tend to exist. The Vaibhasika is a sub-school which held that dharmas of the three times all exist and that only present dharmas have 'efficacy', thus they were able to explain how the present seems to function differently than the past or future.

The Sautrantika ("those who uphold the sutras"), also known as Darstantikas (who may or may not have been a separate but related group), did not uphold the Mahavibhasa Sastra, but rather emphasized the Buddhist sutras as being authoritative.

24 In the famous experiment by Schachter and Singer involving epinephrine, what was found to govern the emotions?

1 Perceptual cues only
2 Social appraisal only
3 Both cognitive appraisal and physiological arousal
4 Both cognitive and social appraisal

Ans. (3)

Exp. As per Schachter and Singer, both, cognitive appraisal and physiological arousal were found to govern the emotions.

Schachter and Singer felt that physiological arousal was crucial to the experience of emotion. However, in their experiments with epinephrine, a hormone involved in the fight-or-flight response to stress/threat/danger, they felt that only physiological arousal was not enough to experience emotion. This arousal must be cognitively labelled for one to feel emotion. For instance, one spots a snake, they experience an increase in heart rate, breathing rate, and begin to tremble. This is the physiological arousal that the person experiences, and they must attribute this experience to the feeling of fear. Therefore, they feel fear.

25 Which of the following is the correct response pattern for the semantic differential test to measure a trait 'active'?

1 I am active : SA A N D SD
2 I am active : True/False
3 Choose one : Active-Trusting
4 Active…Neutral…Passive

Ans. (4)

Exp. Active…Neutral…Passive is the correct response pattern for semantic differential tests to measure a trait, 'active.'

Semantic differential tests are tests that seek to measure the literal, cultural, and emotional meaning of concepts, objects, can be used to measure traits, attitudes, etc. The rating is based on adjectives in pairs, such as good-bad, strong-weak, or active-passive. The active – neutral – passive refers to the activity factor. That is, it indicates whether the traits measured are 'active.'

26 Which one of the following is the correct description of old fashioned racism?

1 A contemporary form of antagonism towards a racial based on prejudice and values rather than on self-interest.
2 Beliefs in which racial superiority, segregation and formal discrimination.
3 Attitude towards a racial group, combining egalitarian social values and negative emotion resulting in avoidance of that group.
4 Well learned sets of association that can be automatically activated, uncontrollable and unintentional.

Ans. (2)

Exp. Old fashioned racism refers to the belief in racial superiority, segregation, and formal discrimination. For instance, imperialism is based on the racial superiority of the whites. An instance of segregation is when the blacks in the USA were separated from the whites.

Racism is the prejudice, discrimination, and the antagonism of a person on the basis of their race.

27 Which of the following is an attitude measure that places a single adjective in the centre of an even number of numerical values?

1 Edward Scale
2 Thurstone Scale
3 Stapel Scale
4 Semantic Differential Scale

Ans. (3)

Exp. Stapel Scale is an attitude measure that places a single adjective in the centre of an even number of numerical values.

Stapel Scale is a kind of rating scale that utilizes a single adjective, that is close-ended. This scale is used to collect information regarding a test-taker's insight regarding a certain subject or event. It places an adjective at the centre of numerical values. For instance, consider measuring the attitude of a class towards a class teacher, the Stapel scale will be as follows: +3, +2, +1, Supportive, -1, -2, -3.

28 Which one of the following is considered as correct for poverty gap?

1 Gap between rich and poor.
2 Gap between developed and developing nations.
3 Difference between poverty line and actual income level of all those living below that line.
4 Gap in the infrastructure facilities between developed nations.

Ans. (3)

Exp. Poverty gap is the difference between poverty line and the actual income level of all those living below the poverty line.

Poverty gap refers to the ratio by which the average income of those who are poor falls below the poverty line. Poverty line refers to the least amount of income that is considered to be adequate in a certain country. Therefore, poverty gap can be said to be the difference between the poverty line and the income level of those people living below this poverty line.

29 Who among the following conducted one of the most famous and controversial experiments in the area of obedience?

1 Sherif 2 Asch 3 Milgram 4 Cialdini

Ans. (3)

Exp. Stanley Milgram conducted one of the most famous and the controversial experiments in the area of obedience.

He wanted to test the extent to which people could go in obeying an authority figure. Therefore, these experiments involved an authority figure asking participants to deliver shocks to the learners, and they were led to believe that the shocks would help them in their learning. The shocks were of increasing intensity, which could have been fatal.

However, in reality, the shocks were fake, but the participants did not know about this. Considering this, it was shocking when the results found that a very high proportion of the participants were willing to obey the authority figure in the delivery of the shocks.

30 Immediately after an action potential, the cells do not produce another action potential due to

1 absolute refractory period
2 relative refractory period
3 resting state
4 active state

Ans. (1)

Exp. Immediately after an action potential, the cells do not produce another action potential because of absolute refractory period.

An action potential refers to the rise and fall of the membrane potential (or voltage) across the cellular membrane of a neuron or a muscle cell. An adequate amount of current is required for an action potential to fire. This action potential helps in the transmission of messages from one neuron or muscle cell to the next.

Following an action potential, there is an interval during which the cells do not give rise to another action potential. This is known as the absolute refractory period, which refers to the period when a second action potential cannot commence.

31 Which one of the following attitude scaling methods is especially unsuitable for scaling a large number of attitude statements?

1 Paired comparison
2 Equal appearing intervals
3 Summated ratings
4 Successive intervals

Ans. (1)

Exp. Paired comparison attitude scaling method is considered to be unsuitable for scaling a large number of attitude statements.

In Paired comparison attitude scaling method, the test-taker is presented with two objects, and is asked to choose one based on certain criteria. The information gathered is ordinal, which uses numerical data for the designation of a certain place, like ranks. This type of scaling method is not particularly useful when it comes to scaling more number of attitude statements as it involves comparison between two statements.

32 The 'Door in the Face Technique' is based on which tactics of compliance?

1 Tactics based on reciprocity.
2 Tactics based on commitment or consistency.
3 Tactics based on friendship or liking.
4 Tactics based on scarcity.

Ans. (1)

Exp. 'Door in the Face Technique' is based on tactics of reciprocity. It involves making a very big request of someone, which is sure to be denied, and then that is followed by a smaller one, which one is most likely to comply to.

'Door in the Face Technique' follows the rule of reciprocity, which refers to the obligation one has towards someone who does something for them. It uses the method of reciprocal concession.

That is, the first request seems so large, and consequently, the second request seems like a concession. By making a smaller request, the person feels like the person requesting has offered them a concession, therefore, in exchange, they are obligated to do something for them. Hence, they comply to their request.

33 Which neurotransmitter is helpful in synaptic plasticity?

1 Acetylcholine
2 Glutamate
3 GABA
4 Dopamine

Ans. (2)

Exp. The neurotransmitter helpful in synaptic plasticity is Glutamate.

Synaptic plasticity refers to the ability of the synapses to either strengthen or weaken based on the respective increases or decreases in their activity.

Glutamate is released by neurons sending messages to one another. When neurotransmitters like glutamate bind to the receptor NMDA, it leads to the opening ion channels, allowing the flow of ions such as Na+, K+, and even some amount of Ca2+. The flow of Ca2+ is considered to be very important in the formation of synaptic plasticity.

34 Which technique of studying the brain involves injecting the patient with radioactive glucose?

1 EEG
2 MRI
3 PET
4 CT

Ans. (3)

Exp. Positron Emission Tomography (PET) scan is a brain imaging technique that involves injecting the patient with radioactive glucose.

It is highly useful in detecting any brain disorders. For instance, for the diagnosis of conditions like epilepsy or tumour, some amount of radioactive glucose is injected into the vein of a person. Then, the PET scanner develops an image regarding which area of the brain is utilising most of the glucose. Based on this, a diagnosis is made.

35 What does 'Absolute Poverty' mean?

1 Poverty in terms of absolute number of people.
2 Poverty in terms of prevailing price level.
3 Poverty in terms of absolute level of unemployment.
4 Basic minimum calorie requirement.

Ans. (4)

Exp. 'Absolute Poverty' refers to a condition wherein a person's or a family's income is so low that even the basic requirements, such as minimum calorie intake, are not being met. For instance, an absolute poverty measurement would involve a certain percentage of population eating lesser food than is required for the body to sustain itself, and this is based on the number of calories consumed in a day, that is, approximately 2,000 – 2,500 calories per day.

36 What do you call the neurological procedure involving the implantation of a medical device under the skin in the chest that sends electrical impulses to electrodes surgically placed in the specific location in the brain?

1 Deep Brain Stimulation (DBS)
2 Repetitive Transmagnetic Stimulation (rTMS)
3 Electroconvulsive Therapy (ECT)
4 Vagus Nerve Stimulation (VNS)

Ans. (1)

➲ *Exp.* Deep Brain Stimulation (DBS) is a surgical intervention wherein a device is implanted under the skin in the upper chest region, and this transmits messages to the electrodes which have been surgically implanted into certain brain regions. These electrodes, in turn, give rise to impulses that help in controlling abnormal brain activities.

DBS can help in controlling the symptoms of a myriad of conditions such as epilepsy, essential tremor, obsessive-compulsive disorder, and Parkinson's disease, among others.

37 Antiduretic Hormone (ADH) is released by which of the following?

1 Adrenal Convex
2 Adrenal Medulla
3 Anterior Pituitary
4 Posterior Pituitary

Ans. *(4)*

➲ *Exp.* Antidiuretic Hormone (ADH) is released by the Posterior pituitary gland.

Hormones are chemical messengers that are present in the body. Antidiuretic Hormone (ADH) is a hormone that helps the kidneys in controlling the amount of water present in the body.

ADH is created by the hypothalamus, and is stored in the posterior pituitary gland, which also releases it. In case of ADH dysregulation, conditions like excessive urination and excessive thirst are experienced. Diabetes insipidus is also caused by ADH deficiency.

38 Which of the following is the correct explanation of "An intolerance for weakness, a punitive attitude and submissive respect for their in-group authorities as reflected in their agreement"?

1 Social Dominance Orientation
2 Ethnocentrism
3 Conformity
4 Inequality

Ans. *(2)*

➲ *Exp.* Ethnocentrism is correct explanation of "An intolerance for weakness, a punitive attitude and submissive respect for their in-group authorities as reflected in their agreement".

Ethnocentricism refers to the belief in the superiority of one's own ethnic or cultural group, and it is also marked by a disdain for other groups. Ethnocentricism comprises 9 traits, 3 of which are mentioned below:

1. *Power and toughness* : It is characterised by division of people into weak and strong, and an intolerance for weakness.
2. *Authoritarian aggression* : It is characterised by a punitive attitude towards those who violate the norms.
3. *Authoritarian submission* : It is characterised by a very submissive respect for authority figures of their group as is reflected in their agreement regarding obedience being the most important of all virtues.

39 Who believed that meaning in life can be uncovered by creative, experiential and attitudinal values?

1 Rollo May
2 Viktor Frankl
3 Friedrick Nietzsche
4 Jean Paul Sartre

Ans. *(2)*

➲ *Exp.* Victor Frankl said that meaning of life can be uncovered by creativity, experiences, and attitudinal values. He wrote the widely acknowledged and revered book, 'Man's Search for Meaning.' It refers a positive outlook towards one's life by finding a purpose to it, and then immersing oneself imagining the consequence of achieving that purpose.

40 Who among the following has laid emphasis on examining the relationship of culturally specific practices with development?

1 Piaget
2 Fodor
3 Vygotsky
4 Kohlberg

Ans. *(3)*

➲ *Exp.* Vygotsky laid emphasis on examining the relationship of culturally specific practices with development. Lev Vygotsky gave the sociocultural theory of development, which purports that the learning is a social process that affects one's intelligence, and has its roots in one's society and culture. He said that human social interactions play a vital role in cognition, and by that extension, in intelligence as well. In doing so, he emphasized the importance of culture in the overall development of a person.

41 Which of the following are considered in favour of scientific realism?

I. Corroboration
II. Empiricism
III. Miracle argument
IV. Selective optimism

Choose the correct answer from the options given below.

1 I and II
2 II and IV
3 II and III
4 I, III and IV

Ans. *(4)*

➲ *Exp.* Corroboration, Miracle argument, and Selective optimism are in favour of scientific realism.

Scientific realism refers to the belief in the observable and the unobservable phenomena supported by science. The concepts in favour of scientific realism are:

1. *Corroboration* : It refers to providing evidence that confirms or supports a theory or phenomenon. For instance, if a phenomenon is detected by different modes of detection, and these detections can be corroborated by several means, such as different observations, then it lends credence to the supposition that something does in fact, exist, or is true.
2. *Miracle argument* : It is also known as the 'no miracle argument.' It favours scientific realism by stating that the success of science is not based on a miracle. That is,

if a given theory is far from the truth, its success would be a miracle. However, the predictive success of science is based on the premise that it is not even remotely close to being a miracle.

3. *Selective optimism* : With unobservable phenomena, most of the theories are widely accepted as being false. However, there may be certain aspects of these theories that are true or closer to the truth. Therefore, one has to be selectively optimistic about these aspects that are most epistemically noteworthy.

42 In the independent groups' design, selective subject loss occurs because of which of the following?

I. Subject are lost differently across conditions.
II. Subject characteristics are responsible for subject loss.
III. Subject are lost uniformly across conditions.
IV. Subject characteristics are independent of subject loss.

Choose the correct answer from the options given below.

1 I and II 2 I and III 3 II and IV 4 III and IV

Ans. (1)

Exp. Statement I and II are correct.

Independent groups design refers to an experimental design involving different conditions, and different participants are assigned to different conditions.

Subject loss or subject attrition refers to subjects leaving an experiment or study. Selective subject loss refers to the tendency of subjects to quit experiments. In independent groups design, selective subject loss or attrition takes place when subjects are lost in different patterns across different conditions, or when the presence of certain subject characteristics lead to the loss of subjects. For instance, some people may lose motivation to carry on with the experiment, some may fall ill, or some may even pass away.

43 Which one of the following personality test/s employs a 'Lie scale'?

I. Rotter's Locus of control scale.
II. Eysenck Personality Profiler
III. Minnesota Multiphasic Personality Inventory-2
IV. Edwards Personal Preference Schedule

Choose the correct answer from the options given below.

1 Only III 2 II and III
3 I, II and IV 4 II, III and IV

Ans. (2)

Exp. Eysenck Personality Profiler and Minnesota Multiphasic Personality Inventory-2 employ a 'Lie scale'.

Lie scales are used in personality questionnaires or inventories to assess whether the test-taker is answering the given items truthfully. If test-takers are answering the items in a way to portray themselves in a more positive or negative light, then the responses to those items on the lie scale will be inconsistent.

Eysenck Personality Profiler and Minnesota Multiphasic Personality Questionnaire-2 are instances of personality inventories that do have a lie scale. Eysenck Personality Profiler measures two pervasive, independent dimensions of personality, Extraversion-Introversion and Neuroticism-Stability, which account for most of the variance in the personality domain. Each form contains 57 "Yes-No" items with no repetition of items. The inclusion of an 18-item falsification scale (lie scale) provides for the detection of response distortion. The Minnesota Multiphasic Personality Inventory (MMPI) is a standardized psychometric test of adult personality and psychopathology.

The first major revision of the MMPI was the MMPI-2, which was standardized on a new national sample of adults in the United States and released in 1989. It contains four validity scales designed to measure a person's test-taking attitude and approach to the test. One of them is a Lie (L) scale which is intended to identify individuals who are deliberately trying to avoid answering the MMPI honestly and in a frank manner.

44 Which of the following are involved in decreased food intake and weight loss?

I. Insulin II. Leptin
III. Cholecystokinin IV. Orexin

Choose the correct answer from the options given below.

1 I and II 2 I, II and III
3 I, II and IV 4 II, III and IV

Ans. (2)

Exp. Insulin, Leptin, and Cholecystokinin are involved in decreased food intake and loss of weight.

Insulin is a hormone produced by the pancreas. It helps the body utilize glucose to produce energy. If one intakes a highly carbohydrate-rich food, the pancreas release high amount of insulin. Therefore, this is related to weight gain. The key to weight loss is to control insulin levels.

Leptin is a hormone produced by adipose cells in order to control the balance of energy by reducing hunger. It helps in restricting the intake of food, and thereby helps in weight loss.

Cholecystokinin is a peptide hormone. It is responsible for the digestion of both, proteins and fat. While the effects of excess cholecystokinin are unknown, it has been observed that in people with obesity, very low levels of cholecystokinin are present. This may contribute to reduced feelings of satiety, thereby making losing weight very difficult.

45 Which of the following character strengths are included in the VIA classification of strengths?

I. Creativity II. Forgiveness
III. Resilience IV. Prudence

Choose the correct answer from the options given below.

1 I, II and III 2 IV, III and I
3 I, II and IV 4 I and III

Ans. (3)

Exp. Creativity, Forgiveness, and Prudence are the character strengths involved in the Values in Action (VIA) classification of strengths. VIA classification involves the classification of positive traits present in people. Positive traits involve character strengths which are as follows:

1. *Creativity* : It is a strength categorized under wisdom. It refers to the ability to look at a given problem from all possible angles, and coming up with new ways of solving a problem.
2. *Forgiveness* : It is a strength categorized under temperance. It refers to being able to pardon somebody who has done harmed a person in some manner.
3. *Prudence* : It is a strength categorized under temperance. It refers to the quality of being careful with one's choices, and choosing to think before acting.

46 Which of the following internal roadblocks to effective listening is exemplified by the statement "We have never done it that way before"?

I. Resistance to change
II. Halo Effect
III. Stereotyping
IV. Hearing only, not feeling

Choose the correct answer from the options given below.

1 Only I   2 I and II
3 I, II and III   4 I, II, III and IV

Ans. (1)

Exp. The internal roadblocks as is showcased in the statement, "We have never done it that way before," is resistance to change.

Change management is "the practice of applying a structured approach to transition an organization from a current state to a future state to achieve expected benefits." It uses tools and techniques, like strategic planning, project management and organizational development, to help people within the organization adopt the change and function in the desired state.

Even though humans are resilient, they still may be reluctant to change, especially if they lack specific behavioural traits that help them adapt to evolving circumstances. Resistance to change may be explicit or implicit. For instance, people may outright reject a certain method of doing something. Considering transitioning from written correspondence to email in companies, people may outright resist it by saying, "We have never done that way before."

47 Adult neurons rely heavily on which of the following?

I. Glucose   II. Protein
III. Potassium   IV. Sodium

Choose the correct answer from the options given below.

1 Only I   2 I and II
3 III and IV   4 I, III and IV

Ans. (1)

Exp. Neurons in adults are heavily dependent on Glucose. In an adult brain, neuron tend to have a very high energy requirement. Therefore, they heavily depend on glucose as it provides adenosine triphosphate (ATP) for their actions. ATP is a molecule that carries energy, and this energy-carrying molecule provides the fuel for neuronal functions.

48 Which of the following were considered to be appropriate for psychological study by Wundt?

I. Analysis of cultural products
II. Higher mental processes
III. The totality of psychological phenomena
IV. Self-observation
V. Physiological type of experimentation

Choose the correct answer from the options given below.

1 II, III and IV   2 II, III, IV and V
3 I, IV and V   4 I, III, IV and V

Ans. (3)

Exp. Analysis of cultural products, Self-observation and physiological type of experimentation were considered to be appropriate for psychological study by Wundt.

Analysis of cultural products : Wilhem Wundt's work, 'Volkerpsychologie,' is considered to be a milestone in cultural psychology. In this work, he investigated different cultural elements and dynamics from the perspective of psychological principles.

Self-observation : Wilhelm Wundt proposed that the mental states one is aware of can be studied by using the method of introspection, which is looking inward or a self-examination. Since this method involves self-examination, it can be said that it is a form of self-observation.

Physiological type of experimentation : Wundt founded the first psychological laboratory in the world. This helped mark psychology as an independent field. He conducted many experiments in this laboratory, which is considered to be a physiological type of experimentation as he strived to project the same type of rigour into his experiments.

49 The cognitive theory contends dependency behaviours to be arising, from and being maintained by cognitive distortions and maladaptive thought processes. Which of the following are associated with cognitive distortions?

I. Availability
II. Hindsight bias
III. Flexible attribution
IV. Illusion of control

Choose the correct answer from the options given below.

1 I, II, III and IV   2 I, II and III
3 II, III and IV   4 III and IV

Ans. (1)

Exp. Availability, Hindsight bias, Flexible attribution, and illusion of control are associated with cognitive distortions.

Cognitive distortions refer to the ways of thinking that are not accurate or have a negative bias to them. It is the tendency to view reality incorrectly. Certain reasons for cognitive distortions are:

1. *Availability* : It refers to the cognitive distortion wherein one tends to overestimate the probability of an event based on its higher availability in memory. For instance, one remembers cases of shark attacks more vividly. Therefore, one tends to think they are more common than they actually are.
2. *Hindsight bias* : It refers to the tendency of people to look back at a certain event and think that it was foreseeable, when in reality, it was not.
3. *Flexible attribution* : It is an attributional bias wherein one tends to emphasize internal factors for someone else's undesirable behaviour, for instance, their character or personality, and when one tends to emphasize external factors for one's own undesirable behaviour.
4. *Illusion of control* : It refers to the tendency of people to overestimate their control over events, when in reality, they have little to no control.

50 Which of the following is true about Hypovolemia?

I. It causes thirst.
II. It increases the blood pressure.
III. Angiotensin is released during this condition.
IV. The volume of blood increases.
V. Blood pressure reduces.

Choose the correct answer from the options given below.

1 I, II and III
2 I, III and V
3 I, IV and V
4 II, III and IV

Ans. (2)

Exp. Hypovolemia is a condition wherein there is a decrease in the volume of blood present in the body. It either leads to blood loss or loss of other bodily fluids. The symptoms of hypovolemia involve:

1. Increase in thirst.
2. Reduced blood pressure.
3. Release of Angiotensin, which is a protein hormone that constricts blood vessels in order to maintain blood pressure and sustain other fluids in the body, thereby preventing their loss.

51 Which of the following are the parts of mental logic theories of reasoning?

I. A set of interference schemas
II. Accumulation of concepts
III. A reasoning program
IV. A set of pragmatic principles

Choose the correct answer from the options given below.

1 I, II and III   2 I, II and IV
3 I, III and IV   4 II, III and IV

Ans. (3)

Exp. The parts of mental logic theories of reasoning are a set of inference schemas, a reasoning program, and a set of pragmatic principles.

Mental logic theory refers to the inference rules akin to the ones developed by the logicians in the field of propositional calculus. Therefore, mental logic theory of reasoning involves:

1. *Inference schemas* : Schemas refer to the mental framework that helps in the organization and interpretation of information. Inference schemas are those that help in making inferences from the information present.
2. *Reasoning programme* : It is one that utilizes the inference schemas in terms of reasoning, either directly or indirectly.
3. *Pragmatic principles* : These principles suggest that the meaning of every logic present in the inferences is justified by the inference schemas.

52 Which is true about coefficient alpha?

I. It is a lower bound of a test of parallel items.
II. It is an upper bound of a test of parallel items.
III. It is an average of all combination of split-half reliabilities.
IV. It is independent of inter-item correlations.

Choose the correct answer from the options given below.

1 Only III   2 I and II   3 I and III   4 III and IV

Ans. (3)

Exp. Among the given statements regarding coefficient alpha, Statements I and III are correct.

Coefficient alpha is also known as Cronbach's alpha. It is a statistical measure of internal consistency of a test, that is, it seeks to measure how closely the items in a test are related to one another. It is considered to be a reliability scale.

It is a lower bound of a test of parallel items. Coefficient alpha is the most common lower bound in terms of the reliability of a test. Lower bound is a value that is either less than or equal to each element present in a data set.

It is an average of all combination of split-half reliabilities. It is a measure of internal consistency regarding the scores of a test, where the items are split into two halves, and the scores on both the halves are correlated with one another.

53 Which of the following statements are true about Unity Thema?

I. It is a compound of interrelated needs linked to press.
II. It is a compound of conflicting needs linked to press.

III. It operates largely as an unconscious force.
IV. It operates largely as a conscious force.

Choose the correct answer from the options given below.

1 I, II and III 2 I and III
3 I and IV 4 II and IV

Ans. (1)

Exp. Among the given statements regarding Unity Thema, Statements I, II, and III are correct.

Unity thema is a concept given by Henry Alexander Murray. It is considered to be a compound of all the needs related to one another, and the origin of these needs can be traced all the way back to one's childhood years.

Unity thema operates on an unconscious level, and it is both, a compound of inter-related and conflicting needs. For instance, one may have a unity thema of both, rebellion and martyrdom.

54 What comprises haptic perception?

I. Shape II. Size
III. Volume IV. Identity

Choose the correct answer from the options given below.

1 I, II and III 2 I, III and IV
3 II, III and IV 4 I, II and IV

Ans. (4)

Exp. Haptic perception comprises shape, size, and identity.

Haptic perception is brought about by the touch and the deliberate exploration of objects. It emerges during the period of infancy itself and continues to adolescence. For instance, an infant frequently places objects in its mouth so as to learn more about them.

Haptic perception involves the tactile perception of an object's shape, size, and identity. For instance, the sensory nerve cells convey the messages to the brain from one's hand or mouth regarding the shape, size, and other identifying aspects of the object, such as its texture.

55 Which of the following are the components of Metacognition?

I. Metacognitive knowledge
II. Metacognition experience
III. Metacognition control
IV. Metacognition regulation

Choose the correct answer from the options given below.

1 I and II 2 I and IV
3 I, II and III 4 I, II and IV

Ans. (2)

Exp. Metacognitive knowledge and Metacognition regulation are the components of metacognition.

Metacognition is a cognitive process pertaining to thinking about the process of thinking. For instance, it involves deliberation of how one thinks or learns. It involves the following components:

Metacognitive knowledge : It involves knowledge regarding the way in which people learn and process information. It involves knowledge pertaining to tasks, such as its nature and the demands it places on a person. It also involves knowledge pertaining to strategies, such as the cognitive strategies employed in completing given tasks, or problem-solving, for instance.

Metacognitive regulation : It refers to the ability to control thinking in order to enable learning. For instance, metacognitive regulation abilities are involved when choosing learning strategies most suitable to a task, or adapting strategies to the demands of the task.

56 Which of the following are associated with the path in Sufism?

I. Establishing self and assertion
II. Repentance
III. Renunciation
IV. Poverty
V. Annihilation

Choose the correct answer from the options given below.

1 II, III and V 2 I, II and IV
3 I, II, III and IV 4 II, III, IV and V

Ans. (4)

Exp. The path to Sufism involves repentance, renunciation, poverty, and annihilation.

Sufism is an islamic belief wherein people strive for the truth of divine love, and obtain knowledge through a direct experience with God. The following are the concepts associated with the path to Sufism:

1. *Repentance* : It is described as the return to God.
2. *Renunciation* : It refers to giving up worldly things and pleasures, purifying the soul, and contemplating on the nature of God.
3. *Poverty* : It is interpreted as a lack of interest in anything else apart from God.
4. *Annihilation* : It refers to the annihilation of one's personal qualities, and taking on the qualities associated with God.

57 Which of the following is useful for testing univariate normality of distribution?

I. Q-Q Plot II. Shapiro-Wilk Test
III. Jarque-Bera Test IV. Scatter Plot

Choose the correct answer from the options given below.

1 I and II 2 II and IV
3 I, II and IV 4 I, II and III

Ans. (4)

Exp. The tests that are useful in testing the univariate normality of distributions are Q-Q plot, Shapiro-Wilk test, and Jarque-Bera test.

A normal distribution is a type of probability distributions that is symmetrical about the mean. In this type of distribution, the mean and median are the same. The common values cluster around the mean, and the less common ones are farther away from the mean. A univariate normal distribution refers to the probability distribution involving one variable.

Q-Q Plot : The univariate Quantile-Quantile (Q-Q) plot is a well-known graphical tool for examining whether two data sets are generated from the same distribution or not. It is also used to determine how well a specified probability distribution fits a given sample.

Shapiro-Wilk Test : It is a test of normality in frequentist statistics. The Shapiro–Wilk test tests the null hypothesis that a sample x1, ..., xn came from a normally distributed population.

Jarque-Bera Test : It is a goodness-of-fit test of whether sample data have the skewness and kurtosis matching a norma distribution. The test statistic is always non-negative. If it is far from zero, it signals the data do not have a normal distribution.

58 Johnson-Laird (1995) has some contengencies in the scientific study of logic, which comprise

I. relational inferences II. propositional inferences
III. focus gambling IV. syllogisms

Choose the correct answer from the options given below.

1 I, II and III 2 I, II and IV
3 I, III and IV 4 II, III and IV

Ans. *(2)*

Exp. Johnson-Laird (1995) has some contengencies in the scientific study of logic, which comprise relational inferences, propositional inferences, and syllogisms.

Johnson-Laird has been analysing people's ability to reason, which is the scientific study of logic. As per him, the contingencies in the study of logic are:

1. *Propositional inferences* : They refer to propositions and the relations between them. A propositional inference is made on the basis of these propositions and the relationship between them.
2. *Relational inferences* : They are the same as propositional inferences, however, it allows one to compute new relations than the ones that are already known. Based on these relations, relational inferences are made.
3. *Syllogisms*: It involves drawing inferences based on two given propositions. These propositions can also be assumptions.

59 Which of the following are comprised in executive functions?

I. Planning II. Attention
III. Set shifting IV. Declarative memory

Choose the correct answer from the options given below.

1 I, II and III 2 I, II and IV
3 I, III and IV 4 II, III and IV

Ans. *(1)*

Exp. Planning, Attention and Set shifting are comprised in executive functions.

Executive function refers to the cognitive skills that help in the management of one's life. They involve:

Attention : It refers to directing one's concentration towards some information, phenomenon, or other stimuli.

Planning : It refers to the ability to predict the right way of going about a task in order to reach one's goal.

Set-shifting : It refers to the ability to shift one's attention between tasks without any conscious awareness.

60 Mr 'A' is very good at discriminating between progressive and regressive ways of behaviour. His choices are clearly perceived by him and adequately symbolised.

According to Rogers, these are the characteristics of which of the following?

I. Individual tendency towards 'growth'.
II. Tendency to 'self actualise'.
III. His constructive creativity.
IV. His self-affirmation.

Choose the correct answer from the options given below.

1 I and III 2 I, III and IV
3 I and II 4 Only II

Ans. *(3)*

Exp. As per Carl Rogers, Mr. 'A' possesses a individual tendency towards 'growth' and 'self-actualization.'

Carl Rogers purported that all people have an actualizing tendency, wherein one seeks to fulfil their full potential, and people are oriented towards growth, autonomy, and independence from all forms of external control.

Being able to differentiate between progressive behaviour and regressive behaviour, and making clear choices by differentiating between the ones that are progressive and the ones that are regressive, symbolises self-actualization and a tendency of making choices related to one's growth.

61 The Psychosocial stage of Intimacy v/s Isolation is preceded and succeeded by which of the following?

I. Generativity v/s Stagnation
II. Identity v/s Identity Confusion
III. Industry v/s Diffusion

Choose the correct answer from the options given below.

1 Only I 2 I and III 3 I and II 4 II and III

Ans. *(3)*

Exp. Among the eight stages of psychosocial development proposed by Erik Erikson, Intimacy Vs. Isolation is the sixth stage. It is preceded by Identity Vs. Identity Confusion, which is the fifth stage, and it is followed by Generativity Vs. Stagnation, which is the seventh stage.

1. *Identity Vs. Identity Confusion* takes place during one's adolescent years. During this stage, people explore different roles, and develop a sense of identity. Failure to do so would result in confusion.

2. *Intimacy Vs. Isolation* takes place during one's early adulthood years. During this stage, people seek to form long-term friendships and intimate, romantic relationships. Failure to do so would lead to isolation.
3. *Generativity Vs. Stagnation* takes place during one's middle adulthood years. During this stage, people seek to create and nurture something that would outlast them, and positively contribute towards other people and the society. Failure to do so would lead to feelings of stagnation.

62 Which of the following characterise the hardy person?

I. He is high on sense of commitment.
II. He is more likely to act to 'cover-up'.
III. He doesn't avoid problems, yet he is often angry.
IV. He is always under the control of his life and events.

Choose the correct answer from the options given below.

1 I and III
2 I and IV
3 I and II
4 I, II and IV

Ans. *(2)*

Exp. A hardy person is high on sense of commitment and is always in control of his life events.

A hardy person is one who has the personality trait of hardiness. This personality trait is described as one of resilience and an effective ability to cope with stress. The characteristics of a hardy person are:

- A hardy person is high on commitment. Their resilience helps them stay committed to life and different goals despite adverse and stressful circumstances. This is what allows them to persist their goals and stay engaged with life.
- A hardly person is high on personal control in terms of life and other events. In the face of challenges, they seek to master and overcome them. Even when mastery over every dimension is not possible, they find certain aspects that they can control.

63 Which of the following dimensions are essential to be mastered in multicultural counselling, as per McFadden's transcultural perspective?

I. Cultural-Historical
II. Historical Hostility Management
III. Scientific-Ideological
IV. Minority Identity Management
V. Social

Choose the correct answer from the options given below.

1 I, V and II
2 II, IV and I
3 II, IV and V
4 I, III and V

Ans. *(4)*

Exp. As per Mcfadden's transcultural perspective, Cultural-Historical, Scientific-Ideological, and Social dimensions are required to be mastered in multicultural counselling.

Dr. John McFadden proposed the transcultural model of counselling, which seeks to provide counselling and work with clients from within one's culture and across different cultures. Certain dimensions that are required to be mastered in this form of counselling are:

Cultural-Historical : It refers to understanding the culture of the client and how their history evolved over a period of time.

Scientific-Ideological : It refers to the client's immediate experience, which is the situation that they are trying to seek counselling for.

Social : It pertains to the dynamics of the client's social interactions among the people of their culture, and outside of their culture.

64 Several types of heuristics have been identified by researchers. Which of the these are included in it?

I. Lexicographic Strategy
II. Satisficing Strategy
III. Mental Set
IV. Elimination by Aspects

Choose the correct answer from the options given below.

1 I, II and III
2 I, II and IV
3 I, III and IV
4 II, III and IV

Ans. *(2)*

Exp. Heuristics are mental shortcuts that people use in problem-solving. They help quicken the process of problem-solving, however, they do not always guarantee a desired outcome. Certain types of heuristics are:

Lexicographic Strategy : This strategy towards heuristics involves inspection of all the information in a sequential manner, and making the decision based on the first piece of information one encounters.

Satisficing Strategy : In this type of heuristic, one tends to sift through all the alternatives present till an acceptable threshold is reached. This is usually done when the most suitable alternative cannot be identified.

Elimination by Aspects : In this type of heuristic, one sifts through a given set of alternatives, and eliminates them one by one when they do not have a certain attribute. This goes on till the only one good alternative remains.

65 A teacher engages students in hands-on, inquiry-based and relevant learning activities in his class. What does this illustrate?

I. Application of the law of exercise.
II. Application of the law of effect.
III. Creating intrinsic motivation.
IV. Creating extrinsic motivation.

Choose the correct answer from the options given below.

1 Only II 2 II and III
3 I and III 4 Only III

Ans. (2)

Exp. When a teacher enables her student to partake in learning activities that are hands-on and inquiry based, it is an illustration of application of law of effect and creating intrinsic motivation.

Law of effect : This principle suggests that when certain behaviours lead to contentment tend to become attached with the situation, and are likely to recur if the situation is repeated. Therefore, when a teacher engages in hands-on and inquiry-based learning, students may feel engaged, active, and satisfied as opposed to only listening to a lecture. Consequently, they tend to perform better. Therefore, when this situation is repeated, their performance also increases.

Creating intrinsic motivation : Intrinsic motivation is one that comes from within the person. A teacher can make academics intrinsically motivating by making it more exciting. One of the ways to do it is by engaging her students in hands-on and inquiry-based learning. This motivates students to engage and perform in the class as the motivation for it comes from within.

66 **Match List I with List II.**

List I	List II
A. Cancer that originates in the blood-forming cells such as stem cells	I. Carcinoma
B. Cancer of the epithelial tissue, cells that line the outer and inner surface of the body such as skin, stomach etc.	II. Sarcoma
C. Cancer that arises from the cells in connective tissue such as bone, muscles	III Leukaemia
D. Cancer of the sympathetic system which is one of the rare types of cancer	IV Lymphoma

Choose the correct answer from the options given below.

	A	B	C	D		A	B	C	D
1	II	III	I	IV	2	I	II	IV	III
3	IV	II	III	I	4	I	II	III	IV

Ans. (*)

Exp. The correct matching is A–III, B–I, C –II, D–Neuroblastoma (not mentioned).

Leukaemia is the cancer that originates in the blood-forming cells such as the stem cells. It leads to the production of a very high number of white blood cells, which impede the ability of bone marrow to give rise to red blood cells and platelets.

Carcinoma refers to the cancer that originates from the epithelial tissue, which is present in the internal and external lining of the body such as the skin, stomach etc. It is a type of cancer that starts in cells that make up the skin or the tissue lining organs, such as the liver or kidneys. Like other types of cancer, carcinomas are abnormal cells that divide without control.

Sarcoma is the type of cancer that arises out of the connective tissue present in the body, such as nerves, blood vessels, muscles, and fats. Sarcoma is the general term for a broad group of cancers that begin in the bones and in the soft (also called connective) tissues (soft tissue sarcoma). Soft tissue sarcoma forms in the tissues that connect, support and surround other body structures.

Neuroblastomas refer to the cancers that originate in the nerve cells of the sympathetic nervous system. They begin in the abdominal region, perhaps an adrenal gland or in other sympathetic nerve ganglia.

67 **Match List I with List II.**

List I (Sources of Personal Efficacy by Bandura)	List II (Therapeutic Processes)
A. Performance accomplishment	I. Live models, symbolic modelling
B. Vicarious experiences	II. Attribution, relaxation biofeedback, symbolic desensitisation
C. Verbal persuasion	III. Participant modelling, performance exposure
D. Emotional arousal	IV. Suggestion, exhortation, self-instruction

Choose the correct answer from the options given below.

	A	B	C	D		A	B	C	D
1	III	II	IV	I	2	I	III	II	IV
3	II	III	I	IV	4	III	I	IV	II

Ans. (4)

Exp. The correct matching is A – III, B – I, C – IV, D – II.

The therapeutic processes related to *Performance accomplishment* are participant modelling and performance exposure. It is amongst the strongest sources of self-efficacy. This source of efficacy information is especially influential because it is based on personal mastery experiences.

The therapeutic processes related to *Vicarious experiences* are live models and symbolic modelling. It refers to observing other people succeed through their sustained performance, which serves as an inspiration to do the same.

The therapeutic processes related to *Verbal persuasion* are suggestion, exhortation, and self-instruction. It attempts to influence human behaviour, verbal persuasion is widely used because of its ease and readily availability.

The therapeutic processes related to *Emotional arousal* are attribution, relaxation biofeedback, symbolic desensitisation. Stressful situations generally elicit emotional arousal that, depending on circumstances, might have informative value concerning personal competency. Therefore, emotional arousal is another constituent source of information that can affect perceived self-efficacy in coping with threatening situations.

68 Match List I with List II.

List I (Types of Reliability)	List II (Source of Error Variance)
A. Test-Retest	I. Content heterogeneity
B. Alternate Form (delayed)	II. Inter-scorer differences
C. Coefficient alpha	III. Time sampling
D. Cohen's Kappa	IV. Content sampling and time sampling

Choose the correct answer from the options given below.

	A	B	C	D		A	B	C	D
1	IV	II	I	III	2	IV	I	II	III
3	III	IV	I	II	4	III	IV	II	I

Ans. *(3)*

Exp. The correct matching is A – III, B – IV, C – I, D – II.

The source of error variance in *test-retest reliability* is time sampling. Test-retest reliability is when there is consistency in the results of a test when it is repeated on the same sample at different points in time. Time sampling is collecting information by recording behaviour when it takes place.

The source of error variance in *alternate form (delayed) reliability* is content sampling and time sampling. Alternate-form reliability refers to the consistency in results among different tests that are equivalent forms of a test. Content sampling is an error when an irrelevant variable enters the scores because of unexpected factors related to the content of the items.

The source of error variance in *Coefficient alpha* is content heterogeneity. In coefficient alpha, error variance is because of content heterogeneity. Coefficient alpha measures the consistency based on the inter-relatedness of items in a test.

The source of error variance in *Cohen's kappa* is inter-scorer differences. The inter-scorer differences refer to the differences in the subjective evaluation of the reviewers. Cohen's Kappa is a measure used in inter-rater reliability, that is, consistency in the decisions of two independent reviewers.

69 Match List I with List II.

List I	List II
A. Pratibha	I. Samkhya Philosophy
B. Prajma	II. Nyaya-Vaisheshika
C. Vak	III. Tantrik Tradition
D. Bhavas	IV. Patanjali Yoga System

Choose the correct answer from the options given below.

	A	B	C	D
1	I	II	IV	III
2	II	IV	I	III
3	II	IV	III	I
4	I	IV	II	III

Ans. *(3)*

Exp. The correct matching is A – II, B – IV, C – III, D – I.

Pratibha belongs to Nyaya-Vaisheshika. Nyaya and Vaisheshika are orthodox systems in the Indian philosophy. Nyaya refers to justice, rules, or even logic, while Vaisheshika attests that the tools of knowledge are perception and inferences.

Prajma belongs to the Patanjali Yoga System. Patanjali Yoga System classifies Ashtanga yoga as the classic yoga. It refers to the eight limbs (ashtanga) which are the basis for self-awareness and freedom.

Vak belongs to the Tantrik tradition. A tantrik is someone who is enlightened regarding themselves as well as the visible world.

Bhavas belongs to the Samkhya philosophy, which is an Indian philosophy that attests that experience is made up of two separate realities, consciousness and cognition.

70 Match List I with List II.

List I	List II
A. Efficacy	I. Response activated when drugs bind with a receptor
B. Tolerance	II. Repeated exposure with less activation of receptors
C. Down regulation	III. Compensatory reduction in receptor availability
D. Withdrawal	IV. Unpleasant physiological responses

Choose the correct answer from the options given below.

	A	B	C	D
1	II	I	III	IV
2	I	II	III	IV
3	III	IV	II	I
4	IV	I	II	III

Ans. *(2)*

Exp. The correct matching is A – I, B – II, C – III, D – IV.

Efficacy refers to the response activated when drugs bind with a receptor. A drug efficacy refers to the highest response that can be achieved by a drug.

Tolerance refers to repeated exposure with less activation of receptors. When there is repeated exposure to a drug, albeit with lower activation of the receptors. Drug tolerance develops when regular consumption of the drug leads to reduce in the effect of the drug, and the drug no longer gives rise to the same response as it used to.

Down regulation refers to the compensatory reduction in receptor availability. It is the reduction in the availability of receptors on the surface of the cell, leading to lower sensitivity to drugs or other substances.

Withdrawal refers to the unpleasant physiological responses. Withdrawal takes place upon the cessation of a drug/other substances, and it leads to unpleasant symptoms like nausea, dizziness, or other illnesses.

71 **Match List I with List II.**

List I	List II
A. Happiness results from experiences of personal expressiveness	I. Rayan and Deci
B. Happiness is self-realisation, meaning the expression and fulfilment of inner potentials	II. Diener
C. Happiness reflects an individual's own judgement about the quality of his or her life	III. Aristotle
D. Happiness result from the fulfilment of three basic psychological needs : autonomy, competence and relatedness	IV. Waterman

Choose the correct answer from the options given below.

	A	B	C	D		A	B	C	D
1	I	II	III	IV	2	III	IV	I	II
3	IV	III	II	I	4	II	I	IV	III

Ans. *(3)*

Exp. The correct matching is A – IV, B – III, C –II, D – I.

Alan Waterman said that happiness results from experience of personal expressiveness. In his study, he found that personal expressiveness was positively correlated to hedonic enjoyment.

Aristotle purported that happiness is self-realisation, meaning the expression and fulfilment of inner potentials. He said that happiness is dependent on oneself.

Ed Diener purported that happiness reflects an individual's own judgement about the quality of his or her life. It comes from a person's reflection and evaluation on the quality of their life.

Ryan and Deci said that happiness results from the fulfiment of three basic psychological needs: autonomy, competence and relatedness. Autonomy is the need to feel ownership of one's behaviour. Competence is the need to produce desired outcomes and to experience mastery. Relatedness is the need to feel connected to others.

72 **Match List I with List II.**

List I	List II
A. Aggression	I. Aggression that is permissible according to the norms of the individual's social group
B. Anti-social Aggression	II. Aggressive acts that support commonly accepted social norms
C. Pro-social Aggression	III. Any action intended to hurt another person
D. Sanctioned Aggression	IV. Aggressive acts that violate commonly accepted social norms

Choose the correct answer from the options given below.

	A	B	C	D		A	B	C	D
1	IV	II	III	I	2	III	IV	I	II
3	I	II	III	IV	4	II	I	III	IV

Ans. *(2)*

Exp. The correct matching is A –III, B – IV, C – I, D – II.

Aggression refers to any behaviour that is intended towards causing harm to another person. For instance, physical aggression, where one intends to physically injure another person.

Anti-social aggression refers to the acts of aggression that violate the social norms. For instance, when one physically hits someone, it is a violation of the social rules of the society.

Pro-social aggression refers to acts of aggression that are permissible as per the norms of the social group the person belongs to. For instance, aggressive acts one commits in order to defend themselves, like in self-defence.

Sanctioned aggression refers to acts of aggression that are in support of the established norms. For instance, aggressive behaviour in contact sport, such as wrestling, boxing, karate etc.

73 **Match List I with List II.**

List I (Description)	List II (Type of Reinforcement)
A. A reinforcement that reinforces a response at unpredictable time intervals	I. Fixed-ratio schedule
B. A reinforcement that reinforces a response only after a specified time has lapsed	II. Variable-ratio schedule
C. A reinforcement that reinforces a response after an unpredictable number of responses	III. Fixed-interval schedule
D. A reinforcement that reinforces a response only after a specified number of responses	IV. Variable-interval schedule

Choose the correct answer from the options given below.

	A	B	C	D
1	I	II	III	IV
2	II	III	IV	I
3	III	IV	I	II
4	IV	III	II	I

Ans. *(4)*

Exp. The correct matching is A –IV, B –III, C – II, D – I.

Variable-interval schedule is a type of reinforcement schedule that reinforces a desirable response after unpredictable time period has passed. For instance, a supervisor appreciating a worker's work at any given points in time in a day.

Fixed-interval schedule is a type of reinforcement schedule that reinforces a desirable response after a fixed time period has passed. For instance, an employee receiving incentives for hitting the target every month.

Variable-ratio schedule is a type of reinforcement schedule that reinforces a desirable response after unpredictable number of desirable responses have been made. For instance, in gambling, one may receive a reward after unpredictable number of tries.

Fixed-ratio schedule is a type of reinforcement schedule that reinforces a desirable response after a fixed number of desirable responses have been made. For instance, a cat receiving milk after pushing the level every five times.

74 Match List I with List II.

List I		List II
A. The theory that an individual's self-concept is driven partly from membership in a group	I.	Realistic group conflict theory
B. The theory that prejudice arises from a real conflict of interest between groups	II.	Social Dominance theory
C. The theory that all societies are organised in group hierarchies and sustained through discrimination	III.	Social identity theory
D. The most important social perspective in social psychology	IV.	Interdependence theory

Choose the correct answer from the options given below.

	A	B	C	D
1	II	III	I	IV
2	III	IV	II	I
3	I	II	III	IV
4	III	II	IV	I

***Ans.* (*)**

Exp. The correct matching is A – III, B – I, C – II, D – IV.

Social identity theory states that an individual's self-concept is driven partly from membership in a group. It is a conceptual perspective on group processes and intergroup relations that assumes that groups influence their members' self-concepts and self-esteem, particularly when individuals categorize themselves as group members and identify strongly with the group.

Realistic group conflict theory states that prejudice arises from a real conflict of interest between groups. It purports that prejudice and discrimination develop when different groups are in competition with each other for limited essential resources.

Social Dominance theory states that all societies are organised in group hierarchies and sustained through discrimination. This theory attests that societies seek to minimise conflict by giving rise to consensus on ideologies that support and encourage the superiority of one group over the others.

Interdependence theory is the most important social perspective in social psychology. It states that interpersonal relationships are characterised by interpersonal interdependence, and that social interactions have impact people's experiences.

75 Match List I with List II.

List I (Description)		List II (Concept)
A. A laboratory device for testing depth in infants and young animals	I.	Perceptual adaptation
B. Refer to differences in two eyes location of corner angles	II.	Horizontal disparity
C. Refer to two points which fall on non-corresponding retinal positions one nearer and the other farther	III.	Vertical disparity
D. Perceptional adaptability to adjust to an artificially displaced visual field	IV.	Visual cliff

Choose the correct answer from the options given below.

	A	B	C	D
1	I	II	III	IV
2	II	III	IV	I
3	III	IV	I	II
4	IV	III	II	I

***Ans.* (4)**

Exp. The correct matching is A –IV, B – III, C – II, D – I.

Visual cliff is a laboratory device that is used to test the sense of depth in infants and young animals. It is an instrument that has a seeming but not a real drop from one surface to the next. The assumption is that infants and young animals able to perceive depth would refuse to crawl through the apparent drop.

Vertical disparity refers to the difference in the two eyes regarding the location of corner angles. It pertains to the alignment of the eyes that helps provide information regarding distance.

Horizontal disparity refers to the two points that fall on non-corresponding retinal positions, one nearer and one farther. It leads to a single perception stemming from slightly different images from both eyes. It helps in providing information on distance.

Perceptual adaptation refers to the perceptual adaptability to adjust to an artificially displaced visual field. It helps in ignoring the distractions. For instance, someone who lives close to an airport is able to tune out the noise as a result of this adaptation.

76 Which is the correct sequence of speech and language development according to Vygotsky?

I. Naive II. Primitive
III. Egocentric IV. Ingrowth

Choose the correct from the options given below.

1 I, II, III, IV 2 II, I, III, IV
3 I, II, IV, III 4 II, I, IV, III

***Ans.* (2)**

Exp. The correct chronological order for the sequence of speech in language development as per Vygotsky is – II, I, III, IV.

Lev Vygotsky gave stages in which language development takes place. They are as follows:

1. *Primitive* : This stage is from birth to 2 years. In this stage, the child begins to talk by imitating others' speech, mostly words, and by responding socially and emotionally, that is, either by laughing or crying, respectively.
2. *Naive* : This stage takes place from 2 years to 4 years. In this stage, the child realizes that words are symbols, and that they refer to or signify objects.
3. *Egocentric* : This stage takes place from 4 years to 7 years. In this stage, children speak their thoughts out loud as they perform tasks.
4. *Ingrowth* : This stage begins from 8 years onwards. During this stage, children begin to internalize many tasks they have learnt. For instance, they count in their minds. Private speech, or the things spoken to oneself, also begins to decline during this stage.

77 In cognitive therapy by Elis, arrange the sequence of the following after recognising the activating event.

I. Discriminating the new emotional/behavioural consequences.
II. Recognising the emotional/behavioural consequences of belief.
III. Understanding the corresponding beliefs.
IV. Challenging and counteracting these beliefs.
V. Recognising new feelings.

Choose the correct from the options given below.

Codes

1 II, III, I, V, IV   2 III, II, IV, I, V
3 III, II, I, V, IV   4 II, III, IV, I, V

Ans. *(2)*

Exp. The correct chronological order in the cognitive therapy as given by Albert Elis is – III, II, IV, I, V.

In ABC model, the cognitive therapy given by Elis, the sequence of stages after identifying the activating event, which is an event taking place around a person, is as follows:

1. *Understanding the corresponding belief* : These are beliefs pertaining to the activating event.
2. *Recognising the emotional/behavioural consequences of belief* : Identifying the outcomes, both emotionally and behaviourally, with regards to that belief. For instance, an irrational belief may lead to unhealthy consequences.
3. *Challenging and counteracting these beliefs* : The beliefs that happen to be problematic or negative are challenged and counteracted.
4. *Discriminating the new emotional/behavioural consequences* : In this, the irrational belief is replaced by a more rational and a healthy one.
5. *Recognising new feelings* : It involves understanding the positive consequences that the new rational and healthy beliefs have led to.

78 What is the correct sequence of decision-making perspective of pro-social behaviour to help a person in distress?

I. Taking personal responsibility
II. Weighing the cost and benefits
III. Perceived a need
IV. Deciding how to help

Choose the correct from the options given below.

1 I, III, II, IV   2 II, I, III, IV
3 I, II, III, IV   4 III, I, II, IV

Ans. *(4)*

Exp. The correct chronological order of decision-making from the perspective of pro-social behaviour is – III, I, II, IV.

Pro-social behaviours are geared towards helping/benefitting others. The decision-making process while engaging in pro-social behaviour to help a person in distress is:

1. *Perceived a need* : It involves a person's judgement regarding the requirement of a certain service.
2. *Taking personal responsibility* : It involves the responsibility towards the person in distress in terms of helping them is taken.
3. *Weighing the cost and benefits* : It involves the way in which their prosocial behaviour is going to cost them, and how it benefits the person in distress is evaluated. The benefits must outweigh the costs.
4. *Deciding how to help* : It involves a plan of action is chosen and executed.

79 Arrange the following in sequence as per the Extinction Transfer Theory of Aggression.

I. Frustration   II. Residual Arousal
III. Arousing Events   IV. Increased Arousal
V. Arousal attributed to Frustration

Choose the correct from the options given below.

1 I, III, II, IV, V   2 IV, II, III, I, V
3 III, IV, II, I, V   4 I, III, IV, II, V

Ans. *(3)*

Exp. The correct chronological order as per the Extinction Transfer Theory of Aggression is – III, IV, II, I, V.

Extinction Transfer Theory of Aggression suggests that the aggression pertaining to one event can fester and intensify the aggression taking place in the following unrelated events. The following is the sequence in which this takes place:

1. *Arousing events* : It involves the event(s) that give rise to aggression.
2. *Increased arousal* : It involves the emotional arousal following the arousing events.
3. *Residual arousal* : It involves the remnant of the frustration from the previous arousing event(s).
4. *Frustration* : It involves the experience of the emotion.
5. *Arousal attributed to frustration* In this, when the emotional arousal experienced is recognised as stemming from frustration.

80 Arrange in sequence what Yerkes described commonly takes place in "insight learning".

I. Sharpening and frequent recurrent attention to the goal
II. Trial
III. Survey/Inspection
IV. Attitude of concentrated attention
V. Critical point

Choose the correct from the options given below.

1 II, III, I, IV, V   2 II, IV, III, I, V
3 III, IV, II, I, V   4 II, III, I, V, IV

Ans. (3)

Exp. The correct chronological order for the way in which Yerkes's "insight learning" takes place is – III, IV, II, I, V.

Yerkes said that insight learning is a type of learning in which learning takes place when one tends to suddenly grasp information. It is akin to a flash of understanding regarding the solution to a problem. Insight learning takes place in the following sequence:

1. *Survey/Inspection* : In this, the problem is surveyed and inspected.
2. *Attitude of concentrated attention*: In this, there is a focus of one's attention on the problem at hand.
3. *Trial* : In this, the solution of the problem is found using trial and error.
4. *Sharpening and frequent recurrent attention to the goal-* If one is not able to solve the problem at hand, one frequently returns to it with increased and sharper focus or attention.
5. *Critical point* : In involves Point of insight, wherein one suddenly grasps the solution to the problem.

81 The enhancement of dominant responses is strongest when people think they are being evaluated. What is the correct sequence of this theory?

I. Evaluation apprehension
II. Well learned
III. Presence of other
IV. Increased arousal
V. Social facilitation

Choose the correct from the options given below.

1 II, I, III, IV, V   2 III, IV, I, II, V
3 I, II, III, IV, V   4 I, III, IV, II, V

Ans. (2)

Exp. The correct chronological order in social facilitation is – III, IV, I, II, V.

Social facilitation refers to the condition in which performance becomes better for simple or well-learned tasks in the presence of other people. Cottrell suggested that the dominant responses are enhanced and become strongest when one feels that they are being judged. This take place in the following order

1. *Presence of other*: It refers to the presence of other people, like an audience.
2. *Increased arousal*: It refers to the physiological changes taking place when other people are present. For instance, heart beats faster, breathing rate increases, and so on.
3. *Evaluation apprehension*: It refers to the concern arising out of the perception of being judged.
4. *Well learned* : It refers to the task-related responses that are well-learned, or the dominant responses.
5. *Social facilitation* : It refers to the tendency to perform a simple or well-learned task better in the presence of other people.

82 What is the correct sequence of transformation in integral yoga?

I. Transformation of physical
II. Transformation of subconscient
III. Transformation of mind
IV. Transformation of vital
V. Transformation of inconscient

Choose the correct from the options given below.

1 III, IV, I, II, V   2 I, III, IV, II, V
3 I, IV, III, II, V   4 III, I, IV, II, V

Ans. (1)

Exp. The correct chronological order of transformation in integral yoga is – III, IV, I, II, V.

Integral yoga is a practice based on the teachings of Sri Aurobindo. In integral yoga, the aim is to look and move inward towards the self, and discover the psychic being. As this takes place, the physical nature is transformed into divine nature. The transformation takes place as follows:

1. *Transformation of the mind-* It refers to the cognitive mind.
2. *Transformation of vital* : It refers to refers to the life force, but also to the various passions, desires, feelings, emotions, affects, compulsions, and likes and dislikes.
3. *Transformation of the physical* : It refers to both the physical body and the body's consciousness.
4. *Transformation of the subconscient* : It refers to the aspects that are submerged, like notions, habits, impressions, and associations.
5. *Transformation of the inconscient* : It refers to the spirit. The inconscient is the same as the western psycho-analytic unconscious mind, while the subconsciousness is another layer of consciousness.

83 In which sequence, according to Piaget, the following cognitive milestones are achieved?

I. Object permanence   II. Reversibility
III. Abstraction   IV. Centration

Choose the correct from the options given below.

1 I, II, III, IV   2 III, I, II, IV
3 IV, I, II, III   4 I, IV, II, III

Ans. (4)

Exp. The correct chronological order of the cognitive milestones as per Jean Piaget is – I, IV, II, III.

Cognitive development involves achieving cognitive milestones. These milestones are age-related. The sequence is as follows:

1. *Object permanence* : It refers to the child's ability to understand that objects do not cease to exist even if they are no longer visible or audible. It takes place between 4 and 7 months of age.
2. *Centration* : It is the tendency to focus only on one aspect of a given problem. It takes place between the ages of 4 and 7 years.
3. *Reversibility* : It refers to the ability to reverse the order of events in order to restore something to its initial state. It develops between the ages of 7 and 12 years.
4. *Abstraction* : It refers to a higher order form of thinking wherein common features of a given problem are identified or abstracted. It takes place between the ages of 11 and 16 years.

84 Arrange the pairings of US and CS in classical conditioning in terms of onset of US in relation to CS starting from the earliest.

I. Backward
II. Simultaneous
III. Delayed
IV. Trace

Choose the correct from the options given below.

1 I, II, III, IV   2 IV, II, III, I
3 III, IV, II, I   4 IV, III, I, II

Ans. *(1)*

Exp. The correct chronological order of pairings between the Unconditioned Stimulus (US) and Conditioned Stimulus (CS) from the onset of the US in relation to the CS is – I, II, III, IV.

In classical conditioning, US is the one that naturally elicits a response. When this is frequently associated with a neutral stimulus, an organism makes an association between the two, and the neutral stimulus begins to elicit a response known as the conditioned response. The neutral stimulus, therefore, becomes the conditioned stimulus (CS). From the onset of US in relation to the CS, the pairings between the both of them in classical conditioning are as follows:

1. *Backward* : It refers to when US is presented before the CS.
2. *Simultaneous* : This type of conditioning takes place when US and CS are presented at the same time.
3. *Delayed* : This type of conditioning takes place when a significant time gap is introduced between the respective presentation of CS and US.
4. *Trace* : This type of conditioning refers to the separate presentation of US and CS with a significant time or trace interval in between.

85 Arrange the stages of personality development in the theory given by Rollo May.

I. Innocence
II. Rebellion
III. Ordinary consciousness of self
IV. Creative consciousness of self

Choose the correct from the options given below.

1 I, III, II, IV   2 I, II, III, IV
3 II, III, I, IV   4 II, III, IV, I

Ans. *(2)*

Exp. The correct chronological order of the stages in personality development as given by Rollo May is I, II, III, IV.

Rollo May suggested that personality development takes place in the following manner:

1. *Innocence* : It is a pre-egoic stage, and takes place during infancy, wherein an infant does only what they are supposed to do.
2. *Rebellion* : This stage is characterized by a wish for freedom, however, the understanding of the responsibility that comes with freedom is still not present.
3. *Ordinary consciousness of self* : This takes place when an adult first learns responsibility, finds it tedious, and therefore, seeks to take refuge in conforming to traditional values.
4. *Creative consciousness of self* : This stage is an authentic adult stage, where the person strives for self-actualisation. In this stage, the person is accepting of responsibility, destiny, and ready to face challenges that may come their way.

86 Given below are two statements one is labelled as Assertion (A) and the other is labelled as Reason (R).

Assertion (A) Shertzer and Stone (1974) specified that acceptance requires respect for the individual as a person of warmth.

Reason (R) Therapists relate to their patients/clients in a non-judgemental, non-critical and non-punitive way.

In the light of the above statement, choose the correct answer from the options given below

Codes

1 Both (A) and (R) are true and (R) is the correct explanation of (A)
2 Both (A) and (R) are true, but (R) is not the correct explanation of (A)
3 (A) is true, but (R) is false
4 (A) is false, but (R) is true

Ans. *(1)*

Exp. Both (A) and (R) are true and (R) is the correct explanation of (A).

Counselling is a form of therapy in which the therapist assists their clients in dealing with their problems. Shertzer and Stone (1974) said that counselling must involve the acceptance of the client and their emotions without any judgment or criticism. This helps make counselling successful.

In order to convey or show their acceptance of the client, therapists behave in a manner that is non-judgemental, non-critical, and non-punitive. For instance, unconditional positive regard is a counselling technique that unconditionally accepts a person the way they are, regardless of their feelings or behaviour.

87 Given below are two statements one is labelled as Assertion (A) and the other is labelled as Reason (R).

Assertion (A) Obtained t-valve will follow theoretical t-distribution if underlying assumptions are fulfilled.

Reason (R) The application of t-test makes an assumption of heterogeneity of variance.

In light of the above statement, choose the correct answer from the options given below

Codes

1 Both (A) and (R) are true and (R) is the correct explanation of (A)
2 Both (A) and (R) are true, but (R) is not the correct explanation of (A)
3 (A) is true, but (R) is false
4 (A) is false, but (R) is true

Ans. *(3)*

Exp. (A) is true, but (R) is false.

Some of the underlying assumptions when using t-test as a statistical measure are random sampling, normal distribution of the data, adequate sample size, and a presence of equality in variance when it comes to standard deviation. If these underlying assumptions are fulfilled, then the value obtained from the t-test follows a theoretical t-distribution. T-distribution is a probability distribution that is similar to the normal distribution, wherein most of the common scores are clustered around the mean, while the extreme ones are farther away from the mean.

From the above, it can be said that t-test does not assume the presence of heterogeneity in variance. In fact, it assumes equality in variance.

88 Given below are two statements one is labelled as Assertion (A) and the other is labelled as Reason (R).

Assertion (A) According to Classical Test Theory (CTT), total variance is equal to the sum of true variance and error variances.

Reason (R) Error variance and true variance are independent of each other as per CTT.

In light of the above statement, choose the correct answer from the options given below

Codes

1 Both (A) and (R) are true and (R) is the correct explanation of (A)
2 Both (A) and (R) are true, but (R) is not the correct explanation of (A)
3 (A) is true, but (R) is false
4 (A) is false, but (R) is true

Ans. *(1)*

Exp. Both (A) and (R) are true and (R) is the correct explanation of (A).

Classical Test Theory (CTT) purports that when it comes to psychological testing, every person has a true score which can be obtained if there are no errors in measurement. True score refers to the person's expected score over several or even infinite administrations of the test. As per this theory, error refers to everything apart from the true score of the test. Consequently, the total variance as per CTT is the sum of true score variance and error variance.

In CTT, the total variance is the product of the sum of true score variance and error variance because true score variance and error variance are independent of each other as true score refers to the expected score of the person over infinite administrations of the psychological test, and error refers to everything other than the true score.

89 Given below are two statements one is labelled as Assertion (A) and the other is labelled as Reason (R).

Assertion (A) The NEO-PI-R does not have a response style scale.

Reason (R) NEO-PI-R developers argued that adjustment of social desirability leads to a reduction in a validity.

In light of the above statement, choose the correct answer from the options given below

1 Both (A) and (R) are true and (R) is the correct explanation of (A)
2 Both (A) and (R) are true, but (R) is not the correct explanation of (A)
3 (A) is true, but (R) is false
4 (A) is false, but (R) is true

Ans. *(1)*

Exp. Both (A) and (R) are true and (R) is the correct explanation of (A).

The NEO-PI-R scale is a personality questionnaire that examines the Big Five personality traits, which are openness to experience, conscientiousness, extroversion, agreeableness, and neuroticism. This scale does not have a response style scale. Response styles are errors that take place when test-takers give answers not on the basis of the meaning of the respective item, but on content-irrelevant matters.

NEO-PI-R scale does not have a response style scale as if any adjustments were made in terms of social desirability, then it may lead to a reduction in the validity of the scale, which is the quality of the scale to examine what it intends to examine.

90 **Given below are two statements, one is labelled as Assertion (A) and the other is labelled as Reason (R).**

Assertion (A) Many companies now enable their employees to share profits or even to participate in company ownership.

Reason (R) Worker's productivity boosts rewards from employers.

In light of the above statement, choose the correct answer from the options given below

Codes

1 Both (A) and (R) are true and (R) is the correct explanation of (A)
2 Both (A) and (R) are true, but (R) is not the correct explanation of (A)
3 (A) is true, but (R) is false
4 (A) is false, but (R) is true

Ans. *(1)*

Exp. Both (A) and (R) are true and (R) is the correct explanation of (A).

Many companies allow for their employees to share profits or even participate in the ownership of the company. For instance, owning shares or stakes in the company. In many companies, this is provided to employees who have served the company best and have stayed with the company for a long time.

The reason for companies allowing employees to share profits or even participate in the ownership of the company is for it to serve as a reward, thereby boosting their productivity and performance. This happens because these rewards serve as reinforcements, and increase the desired behaviour, which is productivity and performance.

Directions (Q. Nos. 91-95) *Read the following paragraph and answer the five questions which as follows.*

A researcher wanted to predict academic achievement using Intelligence Test-A (IT-A), Intelligence Test-B (IT-B), Type of school (rural/urban), and conscientiousness as predictors. She used multiple regression analysis. She collected data on 200 students on all variables. The OLS estimator was used.

The F = 8.9, P < 0.1 for the entire model. In individual predictor analysis, IT-B was the insignificant predictor. The suitable test indicated homoscedasticity. The model $R^2 = 6.64$ and adjusted $R^2 = 0.59$. Both intelligence tests are significantly correlated with the criterion variable with each other.

91 **Which of the following is df for F for the entire model?**

1 4 ; 195 2 4 ; 199
3 4 ; 195 4 3 ; 199

Ans. *(1)*

Exp. df for F for the entire model is 4; 195.

df stands for degrees of freedom, which are the number of values in a given measurement that are allowed to vary.

The formula for df for different groups: df = k – 1, where k is the number of variables.

In this case, k = 5. Therefore, df = 5-1 = 4.

The formula for df within samples: df = n – k, where n = number of participants and k = number of groups.

In this case, n = 200, k = 5. Therefore, df = 200-5 = 195.

Consequently, the df for overall F will be 4; 195.

92 **Which of the following is correct about residual variance in the passage?**

1 It is correlated with predictor variable.
2 It is correlated with criterion variable.
3 It is systematically distributed.
4 It is randomly distributed.

Ans. *(4)*

Exp. Residual variance refers to unexplained variance. It is a part of the total variance in the regression line. It is what is left over when the variance due to regression is subtracted from the total variance. In the given study, the residual variance is randomly distributed.

93 **What kind of a variable is 'type of school' in the passage?**

1 Moderator variable 2 Mediator variable
3 Dummy variable 4 Quasi-continous variable

Ans. *(3)*

Exp. In the given study, the 'type of school,' which may be either rural or urban is a dummy variable. In regression analysis, a dummy variable is one that requires the values of either 0 or 1 to indicate its absence or presence, respectively. That is, if the participants belong to either of the two schools, it will be marked as 1, otherwise, it will be marked as 0.

94 **Which of the following is the reason for the insignificance of IT-B?**

1 Heteroscedasticity 2 Poor predictive power
3 Small sample size 4 Multicolinearity

Ans. *(4)*

Exp. The reason for insignificance of IT-B in the given study is because of multicolinearity. In regression analysis, multicolinearity takes place when two independent variables are highly correlated. In this study,IT-A and IT-B were the independent variables, and given that they are highly correlated to one another, it means they are not independent of one another, and in fact, are very similar to each other. This renders IT-B insignificant or inconsequential.

95 **What is indicated by R^2 in the passage?**

1 64% variance is explained
2 80% variance is explained
3 32% variance is explained
4 36% variance is explained

Ans. (4)

➲ *Exp.* Variance is equal to the percentage of the square of R or R^2. In the given study, the total variance is: 6.64 + 0.59 = 7.32.

Therefore, 36% of the variance is explained.

Directions (Q. Nos. 96-100) *Read the following paragraph and answer the five questions which as follows.*

A psychologist developed a scale for measuring warmth and competence dimensions. As a part of scale development, she factor analysed 25 items to retain 20-items. She chose Exploratory Factory Analysis (EFA). The Bartlett's test = 237.8, $p < .001$.

The overall, Kaiser-Meyer-Olkin test (KMO) is 0.89. The Principal Components Analysis (PCA) was used to extract components. The first eight eigenvalues were 9.9, 6.5, 1.00, 0.85, 0.82 and 0.79. She retained factors on the basis of scree plot and rotated them using varimax criteria. Three items showed cross-loadings, eighteen items loaded on only one of the factors, and remaining items did not load on any factors.

96 Which of the following is correct in case of three items having cross-loading?

1 They have excellent validity
2 They are conceptually sound items
3 The scale has poor reliability
4 They should not be retained in the final scale

Ans. (4)

➲ *Exp.* Factor loading takes place when the variance in a certain factor is explained by a given variable. When a variable is found to have more than one significant loading, it is referred to as cross-loading. This is highly problematic as it becomes difficult to differentiate and label the factors. Therefore, when three items have cross-loading, they must not be retained in the final scale.

97 In the above example, what percentage of the variance would be explained by the first unrotated factor?

1 9.9 2 39.6
3 65.6 4 72.0

Ans. (2)

➲ *Exp.* In the given study, the researcher retained the factors only after rotations. Therefore, the first un-rotated factor may not have been retained. Given this, it explains 39.6% of the variance as the rest may be explained by the rotated factors.

98 The Bartlett's test results in the above study suggested that

1 population correlation matrix is not an identity matrix.
2 population correlation matrix is an identity matrix.
3 sample correlation matrix is not an identity matrix.
4 sample correlation matrix is an identity matrix.

Ans. (1)

➲ *Exp.* Bartlett's test of sphericity tests whether the correlation matrix is an identity matrix. This would mean that variables are not related, and are, therefore, not suitable for the identification of any structure. The Bartlett's test results in the given study, however, indicate that the population correlation is not an identity matrix.

99 Using the Kaiser-Guttman criterion, how many factors would be retained in the above study?

1 4 2 8
3 2 4 –3

Ans. (1)

➲ *Exp.* Kaiser-Guttman criterion dictates that as many number of factors that are given by the number of eigen values that are greater than one, must be retained. In the given study, the first eight eigen values are 9.9, 6.5, 1.00, 0.85, 0.82, and 0.79. Based on the Kaiser-Guttman criterion, the number of eigen values greater than 1 are two (9.9 and 6.5). The general rule is to retain the factors accounting for 80% - 90% of the variance. Hence, 4 factors must be retained.

100 Which of the following is correct for the Kaiser-Meyer-Olkin test?

I. It is a test of sampling adequacy.
II. Chi-square test is used to test the significance.
III. Values smaller than 0.5 are desirable.
IV. Smaller partial correlation leads to high KMO.

Choose the correct answer from the options given below.

1 Only I
2 I and II
3 I and IV
4 II, III and IV

Ans. (3)

➲ *Exp.* The KMO measures how suitable is a data set for the performance of factor analysis. This test:

- Measures sample adequacy. If KMO values fall between 0.8 and 1, sampling is adequate.
- KMO values closer to zero indicate large partial correlations. Therefore, smaller partial correlations lead to high KMO values.

UGC-NET
PSYCHOLOGY

SOLVED PAPER 2019 (December)

PAPER II

1 Phi-Phenomenon is best seen between which of the following time intervals?

1 50 to 350 milliseconds
2 110 to 320 milliseconds
3 30 to 200 milliseconds
4 215 to 375 milliseconds

Ans. *(3)*

Exp. Phi-Phenomenon is best visible between the time intervals of 30 to 200 milliseconds.

Phi-phenomenon is an optical illusion which takes place when two stationary objects seem to be in motion if they are shown to rapidly appear and disappear one after the other. Consider blinking lights, it seems that one light tends to move rapidly between the two points. However, in reality, these are two distinct lights that are blinking one after the other, and not one light that is moving between the points.

2 Dr. 'X' as a therapist felt a sense of complete understanding towards a father client, whose children behaved exactly the way his own children used to behave. This is

1 empathy
2 jumping to conclusion
3 warmth and genuineness
4 sympathy

Ans. *(4)*

Exp. When Dr. 'X' is able to completely understand the client as his children behave in the same manner, it shows that Dr. 'X' experiences sympathy.

In psychotherapy, 'sympathy' refers to an understanding of the client's emotion, and this triggers an emotional response, such as feelings of concern or sorrow towards the client.

3 Which of the following would be the best method for studying the relative contribution of heredity and environment?

1 Comparing identical and fraternal twins reared together.
2 Comparing identical and fraternal twins reared apart.
3 Comparing siblings reared together and reared apart.
4 Comparing identical and fraternal twins: half of whom have been reared apart.

Ans. *(4)*

Exp. The best method for studying the relative contribution of heredity and environment would be comparing identical and fraternal twins, half of whom have been reared together and half of whom have been reared apart.

Twin studies involve the study of both, identical and fraternal twins. Identical twins share 100% of the genetic material, while fraternal twins share 50%. Similarities between twins enable the researchers to understand how the influences of shared genetics and shared environment, while differences also help enable the researchers to understand the influences of differences in genetics and environment shape a person.

4 Which of the following is the most common anti-obesity hormone?

1 Leptin
2 Orexin
3 Insulin
4 Ghrelin

Ans. *(1)*

Exp. The hormone, 'Leptin' is considered to be the most common anti-obesity hormone.

Obesity is a physical condition/disease that is characterised by excessive fat. 'Leptin' is known as the anti-obesity hormone as it activates certain centres in the brain in order to decrease a person's appetite. This helps to control obesity as one of the reasons for obesity is excessive eating.

5 'Y' has 'concrete experience' and a 'reflective observation' as dominant learning abilities, views concrete situations from different viewpoints, has broad cultural interests and is imaginative and emotional. His experiential learning style is

1 assimilating style
2 diverging style
3 converging style
4 accommodating style

Ans. *(2)*

Exp. 'Y' has a diverging experiential learning style.

Kolb put forth in different learning styles. One of them is characterised by the actions of feeling and watching. Kolb referred to this learning style as the 'diverging learning style.' People with this learning style tend to imaginative, have wide interests, gather information, and tend to look at a given concept from all the different perspectives. They are also very cooperative and are open to feedback. Therefore, they have both, 'concrete experiences' and 'reflective observation'. Given this, it can be said that 'Y' has a diverging experiential learning style.

6 Which of the following problem solving techniques, involves the analysis of difference between the current situation and the desired set goal, then doing something to reduce this difference?

1 Heuristics 2 Subgoals
3 Means ends analysis 4 Brain storming

Ans. (3)

Exp. 'Means ends analysis' is a problem-solving technique wherein a person first imagines the end, or the final goal, and then comes up and executes the best strategy in order to reach the final goal.

For instance, consider one wants to travel from Bombay to Goa in the least amount of time as is possible. They would first envision the least amount of time as possible that is required to make this journey, and choose the route that helps one cover this distance, taking into consideration all conditions, such as the traffic and weather.

7 Using Hull's theory, Taylor conceptualised that anxiety is an emotionally based drive and therefore, high anxious subjects on Taylor's Manifest Anxiety Scale (MAS) should be conditioned faster than the low anxious subjects. The study verified the hypothesis. This provides evidence for

1 Concurrent validity of MAS
2 Construct validity of MAS
3 Convergent validity of MAS
4 Lack of validity for MAS

Ans. (2)

Exp. Taylor's study provides evidence for construct validity of MAS.

Validity helps in demonstrating whether a test is measuring what it is purporting to measure. Constructs refer to concepts or ideas. A given assessment is said to have construct validity when it is closely linked with or based on a certain theoretical concept.

In the given instance, Taylor uses Hull's theory to define anxiety as an emotion-based drive, and therefore, those who score high in Taylor's Manifest Anxiety Scale (MAS) will be conditioned faster than the ones who score low. In doing so, he is devising a way to assess and understand based on the theory given by Hull. Hence, it provides evidence for construct validity.

8 Imaginal disputation by using the ability of client to imagine is a method of

1 REBT
2 Existential Confrontation
3 Gestalt Therapy Confrontation
4 Mindfulness

Ans. (1)

Exp. Imaginal disputation by using the ability of client to imagine is a method used in Rational-Emotive Behaviour Therapy (REBT) that helps in cognitive reorganisation. After a client describes the situation that is disturbing them, in this method, they are asked to imagine a scenario in order to contemplate different dimensions of the situation that is disturbing to the client. When one is able to do that, it gives them insight into new perspectives, therefore, they can accordingly change their responses to the situation.

9 What of the following was described by RB Cattell using S-Technique of Factor Analysis?

1 Differential effects of stimulus situations on personality
2 Group formation
3 Social interactions
4 Individual differences among people

Ans. (3)

Exp. Social interactions was described by RB Cattell using S-Technique of Factor Analysis.

Factor analysis is a statistical method used to reduce a large number of variables into smaller sets by extracting the commonality in variances among them. S-technique is a technique used to identify different kinds of people.

R.B. Cattell gave the 16 personality factors. He used Factor Analysis for the identification of the 16 personality factors. In doing so, he explained why people behaved the way that they did. In his explanation of extroverted people, he said that they were strengthened by social interactions. Consequently, social interactions used the S-technique of factor analysis as it helped to identify people who were strengthened by them.

10 A psychological currency that permits deviation from the group is called

1 conformity 2 obedience
3 idiosyncracy credit 4 compliance

Ans. (3)

Exp. A psychological currency that allows deviation from the group is referred to as idiosyncracy credit.

It is a concept in social psychology that refers to a group member's acceptable deviation from the expectations of their group. These credits are earned whenever a member conforms to the expectations of the group, and they are deducted from their quota whenever they deviate from the expectations of their group. Idiosyncracy credit model is an explanation of the leniency that groups sometimes display when high-status members violate group norms. This model assumes that such individuals, by contributing to the group in significant ways and expressing loyalty to it, build up idiosyncrasy credits, which they "spend" whenever they make errors or deviate from the group's norms. So, as long as their actions do not completely deplete their supply of credits, their infractions will not undermine their status in the group.

11 In a newly developed adjustment inventory using 'Yes/No' format, there were some positively worded items ('Yes' response indicating adjustment) and some negatively worded items ('No' response indicating adjustment). Test developers follow this practice to offset the effects of

1 Acquiescence
2 Faking
3 Random responding
4 Socially desirable responding

Ans. (1)

Exp. Test developers follow this practice to offset the effects of Acquiescence.

Acquiescence effect refers to the tendency of participants to certain statements even if it is not the true reflection of their attitude towards it or their behaviour. This usually happens in inventories that require statements to be answered with opposing pairs, such as True/False or Yes/No. Consequently, when some positive and negative statements indicative of Yes/No are included in an adjustment inventory, the practice of offset involved is the effect of acquiescence.

12 Which of the following is the explanation of Premack Principle?

1 A primary reinforcement is thought of being related to an organism's survival.
2 A secondary reinforcer acquires reinforcing value because of pairing with primary reinforcer.
3 All responses are potential reinforcers.
4 More frequently occurring activity can be used to reinforce the activity that occurs less often.

Ans. (4)

Exp. According to Premack Principle, more frequently occurring activity can be used to reinforce the activity that occurs less often.

Premack Principle is a theory pertaining to reinforcement. It purports that a less appealing behaviour can be reinforced provided an opportunity to engage in a highly desired behaviour is provided. For instance, if one is allowed to watch T.V. for 30 minutes provided they complete their homework, the more desired opportunity of watching T.V. enables one to complete their homework, which is a less appealing prospect.

Therefore, in other words, it can be said that an activity that takes place more frequently can be used to reinforce an activity that takes place less often.

13 Which part of brain is responsible for transferring information from short-term memory to long-term memory?

1 Amygdala
2 Hypothalamus
3 Hippocampus
4 Cerebellum

Ans. (3)

Exp. Hippocampus plays an important role in the transfer of information from the short-term memory to the long-term memory. This means that the information is going to be retained for longer periods of time, or even permanently. This process is known as memory consolidation.

The Hippocampus plays a vital role in memory consolidation as it helps in the formation of memories pertaining to personal events and facts, which are held in the long-term memory store. Damage to this area of the brain can make a person unable to develop new memories, and can even affect the older memories that have not been completely consolidated.

14 According to definition theory, for the development of a concept of an "OFFICE", one must

1 construct an ideal office.
2 visit various offices.
3 list all essential features of an office.
4 transform a room into office.

Ans. (3)

Exp. According to definition theory, for the development of the concept of an 'OFFICE,' one must list all the essential features of an office.

'Definition Theory' is used to explain the meaning of a concept by listing all the essential features. Consequently, in explaining the idea of an office, listing all its features helps in understanding what an office actually means. The concept of an office is defined as "a room(s) or a building that is used as a place to conduct professional, bureaucratic, or commercial work." In doing so, the definition is listing all the important features of an office.

15 Read the conversation and choose the best option.
X-What time is it?
Y-I think it is about 9:30 AM. This is

1 adult-adult transaction
2 adult-adult complimentary transaction
3 child-adult complimentary transaction
4 child-adult transaction

Ans. (2)

Exp. The given conversation exemplifies adult-adult complimentary transaction.

A complimentary transaction involves the same ego state in each of the persons involved. In an adult-adult complimentary transaction, the Person X, who is an adult, may be inquisitive about something. In this case, X is inquisitive about the time. Therefore, they ask the Person Y, who is also an adult, hoping to get an answer. Person Y replies in kind, which is, in this case, mentioning the time (9:30 AM).

16 Feminist theory helped in

1 dealing with gender inequality.
2 understanding sexual preferences.
3 human growth and development.
4 gender issues.

Ans. (3)

Exp. Feminist theory helps in human growth and development.

Feminist theory is derived from feminism, which is a movement that helps in fighting for equality between both the sexes. Feminist theory helps in analysing gender inequality, which are the distinctions that are made between men and women on the basis of biology, psychology, and other social factors such as cultural norms. In doing so, it helps in understanding gender inequality, and devising the ways of reducing it, thereby contributing towards human growth and development as it helps in giving rise to equality between both the sexes.

17 Which of the following is excluded from Berkowitz's frustration-aggression hypothesis?

1 Frustration always leads to aggression.
2 Social rules may inhibit aggression.
3 Frustration may result in other behaviour than aggression.
4 Cognitive factors can overside aggression.

Ans. (1)

Exp. Berkowtiz's frustration-aggression hypothesis excludes the claim that frustration always leads to aggression.

Berkowitz revised the earlier version of frustration-aggression hypothesis given by John Dollar and his colleagues which purported that aggression always stems from frustration. In his revised version, Berkowitz said that frustration does not always lead to aggression, but aggression is more likely to be displayed if relevant cues are present. For instance, if weapons are present while someone is in a state of frustration, it can lead to acts of aggression.

18 Eleven rural, eleven semi-urban and eleven urban students were thoroughly interviewed and they were ranked (using a pooled sample of N = 33) for their communication skills. Which one of the following statistical technique would be appropriate to explore group-wise difference in communication skills?

1 Friedman's Test
2 Kruskal Wallis H-Test
3 Rank Difference correlation
4 One-way ANOVA for independent samples

Ans. (2)

Exp. The Kruskal-Wallis H-test is the most appropriate technique that can be used to explore group-wise differences in communication skills.

The Kruskal-Wallis H-test is a non-parametric substitute for one-way ANOVA test. The H-test is generally used when there is no normality in distribution, that is, when the medians the groups being tested are going to be different. Therefore, when a pooled sample of 33 urban, semi-urban, and rural students were tested on their communication skills and ranked, the H-test is used as it cannot be assumed that there will be normality in distribution, and that most scores will cluster around the mean.

19 The bipolar adjectives scale 'Fast-slow' in Osgood semantic differential would belong to

1 evaluative factor
2 potency factor
3 general factor
4 activity factor

Ans. (4)

Exp. The bipolar adjectives scale 'Fast-slow' in Osgood semantic differential belong to activity factor as it defines the speed factor of activity. It indicates whether the traits are active or not.

Semantic differential test by Osgood seeks to measure the literal, cultural and emotional meaning of concepts, objects, and events. They can be used to measure traits, attitudes, etc. The rating is based on adjectives in pairs, such as fast-slow, good-bad, or strong-weak.

20 In quota sampling, the probability of each element of population being included in the sample

1 is equal to sampling fraction.
2 can be specified in advance.
3 cannot be specified in advance.
4 is $\frac{1}{K}$ where K is the number of strats.

Ans. (3)

Exp. In quota sampling, the probability of each element of population being included in the sample cannot be specified in advance.

Quota sampling is a very tailored technique that does not specify the probability of every element possible being included in the sample. It is a type of sampling where a population is divided into sub-groups, and the sample is chosen to meet a certain quota. In this form of sampling, the sample chosen is in proportion to the characteristic/condition under study.

It is a non-probability sampling technique, wherein the probability of any member being included in the sample cannot be specified. Therefore, it does not mention the probability of every element possible being included in the sample.

21 Which of the following school of Buddhism focuses on collective freedom from suffering and feeling the ways of enlightenment?

1 Nirvana
2 Theravada Buddhism
3 Mahayana Buddhism
4 Vajrayana Buddhism

Ans. (3)

Exp. The school of Buddhism that focuses on collective freedom from suffering and feeling the ways of enlightenment is referred to as Mahayana Buddhism.

Mahayana Buddhism is one of the major Buddhist traditions, which base its philosophies on the teachings of Siddartha Guatama, more commonly referred to as the Buddha. Mahayana Buddhism is both a philosophy and a way of life that aspires to nirvana. Nirvana is a state of enlightenment that comes with the recognition that the ego, or the thing we think of as our self, is an illusion that causes us pain and suffering. Mahayana Buddhism emphasises sunyata, or the emptiness that comes with enlightenment. It embraces the letting go of all phenomena as aspects of illusion. It believes that the right path will lead towards the redemption of all the people. Buddhism believes that while life is full of suffering, good behaviour, physical and spiritual hard work, and meditation can lead one towards enlightenment.

22 The three psychologists who illustrated the diversity of approaches to functional psychology at Columbia were

1 Harvey Carr, James Mckeen Cattell and EL Thorndike
2 James Angell, Harvey Carr and James Mckeen Cattell
3 EL Thorndike, RS Woodworth and James Angell
4 James Mckeen Cattell, EL Thorndike and RS Woodworth

Ans. (4)

➲ *Exp.* The three psychologists who demonstrated the diversity of approaches towards functional psychology at Columbia were James McKeen Cattell, Edward Thorndike, and RS Woodworth.

Cattell used quantification methods and statistical measures that helped in the development of psychology as an experimental science discipline.

Edward Thorndike conducted experiments to test how reinforcements and punishments contributed to the strengthening and weakening of observed behaviours.

RS Woodworth gave the Stimulus-Organism-Response (SOR) formula of behaviour. This formula suggests that stimulus is an impulse, and an organism responds to the stimulus.

23 Which one of the following statements is true regarding the relationship of test length with reliability and validity?

1 As test length increases, only reliability improves.
2 As test length increases, only validity improves.
3 As test length increases, neither reliability nor validity improves.
4 As test length increases, both reliability and validity improve.

Ans. (4)

➲ *Exp.* Statement 4 is true regarding the relationship of test length with reliability and validity.

Test length refers to the total number of possible points that can obtained on a given test. As test length increases, reliability and validity improve as well.

Reliability refers to the consistency of a given test. As test length increases, the reliability will improve as well. That is, the more points obtained in a given area, the more reliable are the scores.

Validity refers to whether a test measures what it purports to measure. As test length increases, the validity also improves.

24 According to Decision Stage Model, how many stages are comprised in taking a decision?

1 Three   2 Four
3 Five   4 Six

Ans. (3)

➲ *Exp.* The Decision Stage Model purports that there are five stages involved in taking a decision.

In the 1980s, psychologist Leon Mann and colleagues developed a decision-making process called GOFER. The process was based on extensive earlier research conducted with psychologist Irving Janis. GOFER is an acronym for five decision-making steps:

1. *Goals clarification* : It involves surveying values and objectives.
2. *Options generation* : It involves considering a wide range of alternative actions.
3. *Facts-finding* : It involves searching for information.
4. *Consideration of Effects* : It involves weighing the positive and negative consequences of the options.
5. *Review and implementation* : It involves planning how to review the options and implement them.

25 Which among the following are the levels of processing proposed by Craik and Lockhart?

1 Symbolic, Semantic and Acoustics
2 Physical, Behavioural and Acoustics
3 Behavioural, Acoustics and Semantic
4 Physical, Acoustics and Semantic

Ans. (4)

➲ *Exp.* Craik and Lockhart proposed the three levels of processing involved in memory, which are Physical or Structural, Acoustic, and Semantic.

The levels of processing model (Craik & Lockhart, 1972) focuses on the depth of processing involved in memory, and predicts the deeper information is processed, the longer a memory trace will last. We can process information in 3 ways :

1. *Physical or Structural processing* : It is based on physical appearance which occurs when we encode only the physical qualities of something. E.g. the typeface of a word or how the letters look.
2. *Acoustic or Phonemic processing* : It occurs when we encode its sound.
3. *Semantic processing* : It happens when we encode the meaning of a word and relate it to similar words with similar meaning. For example, giving words a meaning or linking them with previous knowledge.

26 Which device is used for the expression of different letters of a word?

1 Acoustics   2 Acronyms
3 Key word system   4 Clustering

Ans. (2)

➲ *Exp.* Acronym is a mnemonic device that uses the expression of different letters of a word.

An acronym is a type of abbreviation in which the first letters or syllables of a group of words is condensed into a smaller word.

Acronyms can either be novel words that are pronounced as a word (NATO: North Atlantic Treaty Organization), words made up of syllables (Interpol: International Criminal Police Organization), or words pronounced as a series of letters (APA: American Psychological Association, CIA: Central Intelligence Agency).

27 Which of the following explains the tendency of traits that are encoded on the same chromosome to be inherited together?

1 Mitosis 2 Meiosis
3 Linkage 4 Gene expression

Ans. *(3)*

Exp. Genetic linkage explains the tendency of traits that are encoded on the same chromosome to be inherited together.

Gene linkage is the tendency for genes or genetic markers that are located physically close to each other on a chromosome to be inherited together. Linkage data can provide high-risk family members with estimates of their individual risk for the disease or condition conveyed by the gene.

28 'Confrontation' in Gestalt therapies involves

1 what and why questions.
2 what and how questions.
3 how and why questions.
4 what, how and why questions.

Ans. *(2)*

Exp. 'Confrontation' in Gestalt therapies involves what and how questions.

Confrontation is a part of the client-therapist relationship in the Gestalt framework. Yontef advocates for an 'empathic inquiry' focused on awareness when this method is used. It can be an invitation for clients to examine their behaviors, attitudes, and thoughts, and to notice incongruities between their verbal and nonverbal expressions.

A gestalt therapist focuses on what is happening in the moment and finding solutions in the present time. For example, rather than discuss why something happened in the past, the therapist will encourage the client to re-enact the moment and discuss how it feels right now. In other words, the client will be asked to experience their feelings, rather than simply talk about them. The therapist will ask questions like, "What's going on in this moment?" or "How does this make you feel now?"

29 Descartes argued that body and mind interact. According to him, which is the site for this interaction?

1 Pancreas Gland 2 Pineal Gland
3 Pituitary Gland 4 Adrenal Gland

Ans. *(2)*

Exp. Descartes said that the site of interaction for body and mind is the Pineal gland.

Rene Descartes put forth the theory of 'dualism,' which says that mind and body are entities that are independent of each other.

This theory says that human beings have both, physical (body) and non-physical (mind) characteristics present in them. Descartes said that the mind controls the body at the point of their interaction, which is the Pineal gland.

30 "Value of behaviour to the organism, its evolutionary history, and its causation in terms of stimulus, hormonal and neurological events" has been area of study of which of the following?

1 Evolutionary psychology 2 Psychoanalysis
3 Ethology 4 Instinct psychology

Ans. *(3)*

Exp. "Value of behaviour to the organism, its evolutionary history, and its causation in terms of stimulus, hormonal and neurological events" has been area of study of Ethology.

Ethology considers behaviour to be a change in the hormonal and neurological activity of the animal, taking place in response to a stimulus. Ethology is the study of animal behaviour. This field considers it important to study animal behaviour because it believes that behaviour of animals is fundamental to understanding whether the animal will survive and procreate. This helps in fully understanding the nature and history of evolution.

31 Which part of neuron is covered by Myelin sheath?

1 Whole of Axon
2 Parts of Axon
3 Whole of Dendrite
4 Parts of Dendrites

Ans. *(2)*

Exp. Myelin sheath is an insulating layer that is present around parts of an axon.

It is made of protein and fatty substances. It helps in the faster conduction of an impulse, and also protects the axon from harm. However, not all axons have a myelin sheath. The ones that do are known as myelinated axons.

32 If you move a book from your desk to a shelf, you know the form of book is not changing. It may be because of which of the following?

1 Linear perspective
2 Relative size
3 Shape constancy
4 Size constancy

Ans. *(3)*

Exp. Shape constancy is a phenomenon in which the perception of the shape of an object (book) remains the same in spite of the changes taking place in the object's (book) image on the retina of the eyes. Therefore, when one moves a book from the desk to a shelf, the shape of the book's image on the retina of the eye changes, however, the perception of the shape of the book remains the same despite the changes.

33 Beta endorphin is mobilised from pituitary gland during stress in approximately same quantities as

1 Adreno Corticotropic Hormone (ACTH)
2 Corticotropin Releasing Factor (CRF)
3 Epinephrine
4 Dopamine

Ans. (1)

Exp. During stressful situations, Beta endorphin is mobilised from the pituitary gland during stress in almost the same quantities as the Adreno Corticotropic Hormone (ACTH). Beta endorphin is a substance that blocks pain, and is released during times of stress, while ACTH stimulates the production of cortisol, which is also a stress-related hormone. Both of these substances help in combating stress.

34 The phenomenon where by-standers assume that nothing is wrong in an emergency as no one looks concerned is called

1 diffusion of responsibility
2 pluralistic ignorance
3 pro-social behaviour
4 by-stander effect

Ans. (2)

Exp. The phenomenon where by-standers assume that nothing is wrong in an emergency as no one looks concerned is called pluralistic ignorance.

By-standers demonstrate pluralistic ignorance when they assume nothing is wrong even during an emergency. Pluralistic ignorance is a phenomenon in social psychology where majority of the people privately dismiss a norm, however, they follow it because they mistakenly happen to assume that it is accepted by other people. So, when by-standers think that nothing is wrong even in case of an emergency because nobody else present looks concerned, they are demonstrating pluralistic ignorance.

35 Client: "I really don't have much to say (tapping foot)".
Counsellor: "Do you know you are tapping your foot".
Client: "No I guess I am feeling some impatience (pause) even more some confused _______________".

Here the counsellor is

1 trying to create awareness in client.
2 being a little too harsh.
3 making an effort to understand client's behaviour at deeper level.
4 trying to create both awareness and deeper understanding.

Ans. (4)

Exp. Here, the counsellor is trying to create both, awareness and deep understanding.

In terms of body language, when someone taps their feet, it indicates nervousness, frustration, or even a lie. Consequently, when the therapist notes that the client is tapping their feet, they are making the client aware of a behaviour, they think is contrary to what they are saying. In doing so, they are enabling the client to gain some insight into themselves.

36 For becoming a good basketball player, one must use

1 Algorithms
2 Heuristics
3 Concepts
4 Prototypes

Ans. (1)

Exp. If one wants to become a good basketball player, they must use algorithms.

Algorithms are a definite set of sequential steps, or instructions, that are to be followed in order to get to a goal or solve problems. Therefore, if one's goal is to be a good basketball player, then they have to follow a set of well-defined steps or stages that would help them become a good basket ball player.

37 Which of the following consists of Elaborative rehearsal?

1 Remembering of information to maintain it in STM.
2 Transferring information from STM to LTM.
3 Holding information for brief period of time while being used.
4 Ability to focus on only stimulus.

Ans. (2)

Exp. Elaborative rehearsal helps in transferring information from STM to LTM.

Rehearsal involves repeating information in order to commit it to memory. Elaborative rehearsal is a type of rehearsal wherein connections are made between the new information and already existing one. This helps in memorising information, and transferring it from Short-Term Memory (STM) to Long-Term Memory (LTM). In Short-Term Memory, information is retained only for few seconds. However, if information is transferred and stored in the Long-Term Memory, it is retained for a lengthy duration of time, and sometimes, even permanently.

38 Choose the odd one for pattern of sympathetic activation during emotions.

1 Increased heart rate
2 Pupil constriction
3 Increased breathing rate
4 Lowered skin resistance

Ans. (2)

Exp. Pupil constriction is the odd one out when it comes to sympathetic activation during times of emotion.

Sympathetic nervous system helps the body in combating during times of great emotion, such as stress. Sympathetic nervous system activation leads to increased heart rate, increased breathing rate, reduced skin resistance, and pupil dilation, but not pupil constriction.

39 In terms of Psychoanalytic Therapy, the means of keeping the unconscious conflict intact; thereby impeding any attempts to probe into real sources of personality problems is known as

1 repression
2 suppression
3 denial
4 resistance

Ans. (4)

Exp. In terms of Psychoanalytic Therapy, the means of keeping the unconscious conflict intact; thereby impeding any attempts to probe into real sources of personality problems is known as resistance.

In psychoanalysis, resistance refers to oppose any source that seeks to threaten the unconscious defences that are set up by the ego, thereby lowering them. In doing so, any conflict in the unconscious remains in the unconscious itself, and is never brought to the conscious in order to address it, and deal with the real issues that lead to problems in one's personality and life.

40 Which of the following norms suggest people that they ought to behave?

1 Social Responsibility Norms
2 Reciprocity Norms
3 Prescriptive Norms
4 Proscriptive Norms

Ans. (3)

Exp. Prescriptive norms suggest the way people must behave. They are also referred to as injunctive norms. They are the moral and societal standards for behaviours. In simple words, they differentiate right from the wrong, and dictate how one ought to behave as they establish the behaviour that is considered to be good and appropriate in a given society.

41 Generational-digital or Gen-D factor

I. pertains to reversal of power hierarchy in terms of digital technology.
II. pertains to imparting knowledge downward to younger generation.
III. calls for psychoeducation of parents and caregivers on digital technology usage.
IV. calls for the adolescent psychoeducation on digital technology usage.

Choose the correct option.

1 Only I
2 Only II
3 Both I and III
4 Both II and IV

Ans. (3)

Exp. Generational-digital or Gen-D factor pertains to reversal of power hierarchy in terms of digital technology and calls for psychoeducation of parents and caregivers on digital technology usage.

The Digital Generation (Gen-D) is comprised of technologically savvy consumers comfortable using all types of devices and apps. Generational-digital or Gen-D is the generation that has grown up with very easy access to technology, and it believes that digital technology can be a force for good. It pertains to reversal of power hierarchy in terms of digital technology, where the parents and caregivers are given psychoeducation on digital technology usage.

42 According to Goleman, 'Management of Emotions' component of emotional intelligence includes

I. handling feelings, so that they are appropriate.
II. ability to soothe oneself.
III. ability to shake off rampant anxiety, gloom or irritability.
IV. recognising feeling as it happens.

Choose the correct option.

1 I, II and IV
2 II, III and IV
3 I, II and III
4 I, II, III and IV

Ans. (3)

Exp. Among the given statements regarding the 'Management of Emotions' component of emotional intelligence, statement I, II and III are correct.

Daniel Goleman specified certain dimensions of emotional intelligence. Among them, 'Management of Emotions' involves the ability to regulate one's feelings so that one's behaviour is appropriate. It also involves the ability to soothe oneself, and the ability to control one's impulses and manage one's emotions so that they can shake off irritability, rampant anxiety, or gloom, all of which help in preventing one from acting out in a rash manner.

43 Double standards of mental health with regard to adult females

I. depicted adult female behaviour as less socially desirable and healthy.
II. had set up barriers against the advancement of women in non-traditional roles.
III. pertain to the changing dual personality of women in the current scenario.
IV. pertain to the identification of the general standards of healthy behaviour with men only.

Choose the correct option.

1 Only IV is correct
2 Only III is correct
3 Only I and II are correct
4 I, II and III are correct

Ans. (4)

Exp. Among the given statements, pertaining to double standards of mental health with regards to adult females, statements I, II, and III are correct.

There are double standards of mental health when it comes to adult females. Some of them are:

1. *Depicted certain female behaviour as being less socially desirable* : Some characteristics considered to be positive in males are not the same when it comes to females. For instance, assertiveness.

2. *Set up barriers against the advancement of women in non-traditional roles* : For instance, many theories consider a mother to be a child's primary caregiver. This perspective hinders women from building careers for themselves and expects them to stay home and take care of their children.
3. *Found in changing dual roles of women in current scenarios* : Nowadays, women are getting to be a force at work and a force at home. However, some mental health standards may consider these dual roles to be very challenging and stressful to women, leading to burn out. Again, this standard is restrictive towards women.

44 Which of the following are the two major symptoms of Alzhiemer's disease?

1 Neurofibrilliary tangles and Amyloid plaques
2 Collateral sprouting and cerebral ischemia
3 Amyloid plaques and cerebral ischemia
4 Neurofibrilliary tangles and collateral sprouting

Ans. (1)

Exp. Neurofibrillary tangles and Amyloid plaques are the two major symptoms of Alzheimer's disease. Alzheimer's disease is a progressive neurological condition which leads to the shrinking and death of the brain cells. This leads to a decline in different cognitive abilities. The most prominent symptoms of this disorder are described as follows :

- *Neurofibrillary tangles* are the aggregates of tau protein which are the microtubule-associated protein, considered to be a biomarker for Alzheimer's disease.
- *Amyloid plaques* are aggregates of proteins that are misfolded, and are found in the spaces present between nerve cells. They tend to develop first in the regions of the brain associated with different cognitive functions.

45 Read the following conversation and choose the correct option.
X: "I am so hungry! I am like way starving".
Y: "You might consider a small nutritional snack to suppress your appetite". This is

1 adult-adult and child-child interaction respectively.
2 complimentary transactions
3 child-child and adult-adult, crossed transactions respectively.
4 child-adult and adult-child crossed transactions respectively.

Ans. (3)

Exp. In the given case, the transaction is a child-child and adult-adult, crossed transactions, respectively.

Ego states are a place from which communications take place. Child, parent, adult are examples of ego states. Crossed transactions take place when a person says something from a certain ego state, and receives a response that they were not expecting, and one that they may not like.

In the given scenario, when Person 'X' say that they are starving, they are coming from a child ego state. Person 'Y' responds by telling them to have a small snack in order to curb their appetite. Person 'Y' is coming from an adult ego state. Person 'Y's response is not something that Person 'X' may be expecting. If they were complaining about starving, it is general to wish for the other person to respond in kind, and provide them with a meal. Therefore, the resulting transaction is a child-child and adult-adult, cross transactions, respectively.

46 According to 'Social Impact Theory', the effect of majority on minority rests on three of following factors.

I. Majority's strength II. Minority's will
III. Immediacy IV. Number of persons

Choose the correct option.

1 I, II and III 2 I, III and IV
3 II, III and IV 4 II, IV and I

Ans. (2)

Exp. According to 'Social Impact Theory', the effect of majority on minority rests on the three following factors: Majority's strength, Immediacy, and Number of persons.

Social Impact Theory seeks to explain that the amount of influence that a minority person experiences from the majority depends upon:

1. *Majority's strength* : It refers to the power or social status of the majority.
2. *Immediacy* : It refers to the physical and psychological proximity.
3. *Number of persons* : It refers to the number of people present in the majority group.

47 Which of the following correctly describe "Nafs" (Self or ego) in Sufism?

I. It can be viewed along a continuum.
II. It is not meant to please the God.
III. It refers to negative traits only.
IV. It has a potential to function from grossest to highest level.

1 I and III are correct 2 II and III are correct
3 II and IV are correct 4 I and IV are correct

Ans. (4)

Exp. Among the given statements pertaining to 'Nafs' in Sufism, statement I and IV are correct.

Sufism is an Islamic belief system wherein people seek to understand the truth of divine love from direct experience with God. In Sufism, the self or the ego is referred to as "Nafs." It is meant to please the God. Sufic psychology identifies seven levels of the nafs, which have been identified in the Quran. The process of growth depends on working through these levels. These are: tyrannical self, regretful self, inspired self, serene self, pleased self, pleasing self and the pure self.

"Nafs" (Self or ego) in Sufism can be viewed along a continuum and has a potential to function from grossest to highest level.

In Sufism, "Nafs" is that dimension of the psyche that can be viewed in terms of a continuum and has the capability of functioning from grossest to the highest level. At the base level, it is brimming with negative traits, and is under the control of needs, feelings, and pleasure. At the highest level, it is completely pure. Therefore, it does not refer to negative traits only.

48 The core emphasis of developmental psychology is represented by which of these sets of pairs?

1 Individual v/s shared and stability v/s change
2 Young v/s old and stability v/s change
3 Individual v/s shared and young v/s old
4 Cross-sectional v/s longitudinal and self esteem v/s self doubt

Ans. (1)

Exp. Developmental psychology is represented by individual v/s shared and stability v/s change.

Developmental psychology is a sub-field in psychology that seeks to understand the way in which people develop and change all through their life. The core emphasis in this field is whether development is unique to every individual, or whether there are shared features in development that are common to all people.

Meanwhile, stability in developmental psychology refers to the perspective that personality traits that manifest themselves during infancy remain stable throughout one's life. On the other hand, the change perspective believes that personality goes through modifications during the course of one's life as it is impacted by the environment, ranging from family, friends, peers, to cultures.

49 Which of the following are the advantages of fMRI over PET scan?

I. Nothing has to be injected into the body.
II. Provides both structural and functional information of the same image.
III. Produces three dimensional images of activity over the entire brain.

Choose the correct option.

1 Only I and II
2 Only I and III
3 Only II and III
4 I, II and III

Ans. (4)

Exp. Among the given statements with regards to the advantages of fMRI over PET scan, Statement I, II, and III are correct.

Positron Emission Tomography (PET) scan is a brain imaging technique. It is highly useful in detecting any brain. However, in order to conduct a PET scan, some amount of radioactive glucose has to be injected into the vein of a person.

However, with fMRI (Functional Magnetic Resonance Imaging), this is not the case, it works by determining the changes in blood oxygenation and flow that take place in response to neural activity. It does not require anything to be injected into the body. Additionally, it provides both, the structural and the functional information in the same image itself, which is not the case with PET. fMRI also produces 3D images of activity taking place all over the brain.

50 Which of the following are the main biases in attribution process?

I. Fundamental attribution error
II. Actor-observer effect
III. Situational influence
IV. Self-serving bias

Choose the correct option.

1 I, II and III
2 I, II and IV
3 II, III and IV
4 I, III and IV

Ans. (2)

Exp. Fundamental attribution error, Actor-observer effect, and Self-serving bias are the main biases in attribution process.

1. *Fundamental attribution error* : It refers to people's tendency of overestimating the role of internal factors whilst explaining the behaviour of other people. In doing so, they also underestimate the role of external factors in other people's behaviours, the ones that are beyond their control.
2. *Actor-observer effect* : It refers to people's tendency to attribute other people's behaviours to internal factors, such as their personality or disposition. At the same time, people also have a tendency to attribute their behaviours to external factors, ones that are beyond their control.
3. *Self-serving bias* : It refers to people's general tendency of taking credit for positive outcomes, while blaming external factors in case of negative outcomes.

51 Which of the following are the elements of language acquisition process?

I. Phonemes
II. Morphemes
III. Syntax
IV. Pragmatics

Choose the correct option.

1 I, III and IV
2 II, III and IV
3 I, II and III
4 I, II and IV

Ans. (3)

Exp. Phonemes, Morphemes and Syntax are the different elements involved in language acquisition process. It involves the understanding and grasping of the following elements:

- *Phonemes* are basic units of sound which help in distinguishing one word from the other. For instance, 'b' and 'c' are distinct sounding, therefore, 'bat' is distinguished from 'cat' on the basis of the differences in sound between them.
- *Morphemes* are the smallest meaningful units of speech, and cannot be shortened any further as this would make the word meaningless. For instance, in restart, 're' and 'start' are morphemes, and further shortening of any of these words would deprive them of any meaning.
- *Syntax* is the sequential arrangement of words in order to form legible sentences or phrases.

52 There are many mnemonic devices to help a person to memorise the lists of words and vocabulary items. Identify the correct device series.

I. Categorical Clustering
II. Interactive Images
III. Recognition
IV. Pegword System
V. Method of Loci

Choose the correct option.

1 I, II and III
2 II, III and IV
3 III, IV and V
4 I, II, IV and V

Ans. *(4)*

Exp. Categorical clustering, interactive images, Peg-word system, Method of loci are the mnemonic devices that help in memorising list of vocablary items or words.

Mnemonic devices help increase the ability to remember certain things like list of items. Some of them are:

1. *Categorical clusters* : This involves organising information into related groups, and placing similar/related items into the same category. This helps improve recall.
2. *Interactive imagery* : In this mnemonic, images of the items on the list are pictured in one's head. Then, each image is associated with the following one by having an interaction with it. For instance, if the words to remember are "tomato" and "carrot." Then, an interactive image would have a huge carrot hitting the tomato as if it were a ball.
3. *Peg-word system*: It can be used to recall lists. Pegs are objects/images associated with numbers. For instance, 1 stands for sun, 2 for shoe, and so on. Now, if one wants to remember the sequential order of items in a recipe, one can associate each item with the image. For instance, carrot can be associated with the sun by picturing a huge carrot whacking the sun. This type of imagery helps to remember the list better.
4. *Method of loci* : It involves visualising familiar spatial environments to help improve recall of information. For instance, consider a house with all its rooms. Each of these locations forms a locus. So, while remembering a list of items, each item is associated with one locus. If the first item on the list is 'milk,' imagine a huge milk packet lying on the bed of one's bedroom. If the next item is "corn," imagine a huge corn 'bob' hiding in the closet present in the same bedroom.

53 Consider the three types of investigation in psychological research written in alphabetical order:

I. Controlled laboratory experiments
II. Ex post facto studies
III. Field experiments.

Arrange them in descending order in terms of their ability to control secondary variance usually.

1 I, III, II
2 I, II, III
3 III, I, II
4 II, III, I

Ans. *(1)*

Exp. The correct descending order of different psychological research techniques being able to control secondary variance is I, III, and II.

In research, secondary variance is a consequence of external factors exerting an influence over the Dependent Variable (DV), and one that the experiment has no control over. From the given options, the descending order of the research techniques that are able to control secondary variance are:

Controlled Laboratory Experiments are conducted in a lab where the experimenter can manipulate the independent variable whilst controlling the external factors as well.

Field Experiments are conducted in field settings. In this type of experiment, not all external factors can be controlled. For instance, disturbance cannot be controlled.

Ex Post Facto Studies consist of groups with pre-existing qualities which are compared to some other dependent variable.

54 During 1960s, Hoffman and others criticised the college entrance examination and other nationally administered educational tests, and argued that

I. these favour shrewd and nimble witted.
II. these are over concerned with quality of thought behind it and the expression of skill than answer.
III. these favour subtle, creative and more profound persons.
IV. these carry a bad effect in recognition of merit.

Choose the correct option.

1 Only I is correct
2 I and IV are correct
3 Only III is correct
4 III and IV are correct

Ans. *(2)*

Exp. During 1960s, Hoffman and others criticised the college entrance examination and other nationally administered educational tests, and argued that these favour shrewd and nimble witted and these carry a bad effect in recognition of merit.

According to them, these tests do not tap the integrative, imaginative and original quality of mind, while favor "the candidates who read rapidly and are quick witted and superficially brilliant".

55 That is the reason of negative voltage of a neuron during resting potential. (Sodium = Na^+; Potassium = K^+; Chloride = Cl^-; Organic Anions = A^-)

1 Na^+ and Cl^- ions outside the membrane have more negative charge than K^+ and A^- ions inside.
2 Na^+ and Cl^- ions outside the membrane have more negative charge than K^+ and A^- ions inside.

3 Na^+ and A^- ions outside the membrane have more negative charge than K^+ and Cl^- ions inside.
4 Na^+ and A^- ions outside the membrane have more negative charge than K^+ and Cl^- ions inside.

Ans. (2)

Exp. The Na^+ and Cl^- ions outside the membrane have more negative charge than K^+ and A^- ions present inside the membrane, thereby contributing to the negative voltage of a neuron during resting potential. Resting potential of a neuron results from the imbalance between the electrical charge present in the interior of the neuron and its surroundings. The resting potential is around -70mV.

56 Suler's (2004) concept of 'Online Disinhibition Effect' is characterised by

I. anonymity
II. accessibility
III. hierarchies negation
IV. easy escape consequences

Choose the correct option.

1 I and II only
2 I, II and III
3 I, III and IV
4 I, II and IV

Ans. (3)

Exp. Suler's (2004) concept of 'Online Disinhibition Effect' is characterised by anonymity, negation of hierarchies, and easy escape consequences.

Online disinhibition effect is the lack of restraint one feels when communicating online in comparison to communicating in-person. People feel safer saying things online which they would not say in real life because they have the ability to remain completely anonymous and invisible behind the computer screen. It is characterised by :

1. *Anonymity* : Anonymity can make a person feel safe online, like a different person, one might even take on a new persona. It can also make one feel like doing or saying anything is possible because one will most likely not be reprimanded in real life.
2. *Negation of hierarchies* : On the internet, status and social classes are ambiguous and social hierarchies based on age, experience, respect, fame, expertise, etc., mean little (in most contexts) unless they are particularly relevant to an online post.
3. *Easy escape consequences* : If we combine the opportunity to easily escape or dissociate from what happens online with the psychological process of creating imaginary characters, we get a somewhat different force that magnifies disinhibition.

57 Which are the two basic features of Schema?

I. Influencing memory
II. Promoting forgetting
III. Resisting change
IV. Promoting change

Choose the correct option.

1 I and II
2 I and III
3 I and IV
4 II and III

Ans. (2)

Exp. The two basic features of Schema are that they have an impact on memory and are resistant to change.

Schema is a collection of basic knowledge about a concept or entity that serves as a guide to perception, interpretation, imagination, or problem solving. It is a cognitive structure representing a person's knowledge about some entity or situation, including its qualities and the relationships between these. Schemas refer to the mental framework that helps in the organisation and interpretation of information.

The basic features of schema are described as follows :

1. *Influencing memory* : Schemas also affect the way in which memories are encoded and retrieved, supporting the theory that our memories are reconstructive. Using schemas, we are able to develop an understanding of the objects around us based on characteristics that we have encountered in similar objects in the past.
2. *Resisting change* : When a schema is strong, it resists change. Individuals who have a strong schema have been shown to resist learning new information when it is more specific than, not applicable to, or discrepant with their current schema.

58 Creativity has been conceptualised in terms of which of the following?

I. As a person
II. As a potential
III. As a process
IV. As a perseverance

Choose the correct option.

1 I, II and III
2 II, III and IV
3 I, III and IV
4 I, II, III and IV

Ans. (1)

Exp. The conceptualisation of creativity can be done in terms of a person, as a potential, as a process. Creativity has been conceptualised in following three ways :

1. *As a person* : When creativity is conceptualised in terms of a person, it refers to the personal attributes of a creative person.
2. *As a potential* : When creativity is conceptualised in terms of a potential, it refers to a latent ability to be creative, however, this ability needs fostering.
3. *As a process* : When creativity is conceptualised in terms of a process, it refers to the ability to look at a problem/situation from all the different perspectives and coming up with novel ways of solving a problem or dealing with a situation.

59 The Eudemonic view of subjective well-beings holds that

I. true happiness is found in expression of virtue.
II. well being refers to 'striving for perfection'.

III. subjective well-being focuses on bodily pleasures like focus on appetite and self-interests.

IV. well-being consists of fulfilling its 'true-self'.

Choose the correct option.

1 Only III
2 III and IV
3 I, II and IV
4 Only I

Ans. (3)

Exp. Among the given statements regarding the Eudemonic view of subjective well-being, Statement I, II, and IV are correct.

Eudemonic view of subjective well-being can be found in the works of Aristotle, who dismissed the idea that happiness comes from the fulfilment of one's desires. While it may bring pleasure, it does not bring wellness. Well-being comes from living a life that is virtuous and fulfilling one's full potential.

The Eudemonic view of subjective well-beings holds that:

1. True happiness is found in expression of virtue. Aristotle thought that true happiness is found by leading a virtuous life and doing what is worth doing. He argued that realising human potential is the ultimate human goal.
2. Well-being refers to 'striving for perfection'. Eudaimonia implies a positive and divine state of being that humanity is able to strive for and possibly reach towards perfection.
3. Well-being consists of fulfilling its 'true-self'. Aristotle was the originator of the concept of eudaimonia (from daimon–true nature). Daimon refers to potentialities of each person, realisation of which leads to the greatest fulfilment. Efforts to live in accordance with one's daimon, the congruence between this and people's life activities, lead to the experience of eudaemonia.

60 Which of the following are the motivators for helping others?

I. Attitudes
II. Empathy
III. Personal distress
IV. Norms and values

Choose the correct option.

1 I, II and III
2 I, II and IV
3 I, III and IV
4 II, III and IV

Ans. (4)

Exp. Empathy, personal distress and norms and values are motivators for helping others.

The behaviour that is geared towards helping others and for the benefit of others are referred to as prosocial behaviour. Prosocial behaviour requires motivators for them to be performed.

The motivators are as follows :

1. *Empathy* : It is the ability to understand others. Being empathetic allows one to help others as it gives rise to understanding and compassion towards others' plight.
2. *Personal distress* : It refers to the apprehension regarding something negative that might happen to oneself if they do not help others. This also allows people to help others.
3. *Norms and values* : They provide knowledge regarding what behaviours are considered as good and appropriate. Helping others is considered to be a good behaviour. Therefore, people follow norms and values and help others.

61 In the context of marginalisation it is suggested to adopt 'Social Empowerment Model' while dealing with LGBTs because

I. it increases this group's collective and personal self advocacy.

II. they learn that they can lead "fulfilling and satisfying" lives.

III. concerns about LGBTs are social concerns and not the concern for individual.

IV. they realise that being gay or lesbian is not a pathological condition.

Choose the correct option.

1 I, II and III are correct
2 I and IV are correct
3 II and III are correct
4 I, II and IV are correct

Ans. (4)

Exp. Among the given statements regarding the utilization of 'Social Empowerment Model' while dealing LGBT issues, Statement I, II, and IV are correct.

'Social Empowerment Model' says that people feel worthless/helpless as a result of oppression, and is geared towards helping people achieving a sense of control. In the context of marginalisation it is suggested to adopt 'Social Empowerment Model' while dealing with LGBTs because :

1. It increases this group's collective and personal self advocacy. Community, or collective, empowerment is one way for LGBTs to support and help each other deal with distress politically as a group. To increase self-advocacy of LGBT clients, a logical goal would be to promote empowerment. This includes the elimination of the entire system of heterosexism, forming coalitions with other marginalized groups of people.
2. They learn that they can lead "fulfilling and satisfying" lives. They can learn to lead fulfilling, productive lives, or participate in stable primary relationships.
3. They realise that being gay or lesbian is not a pathological condition. Psychologists are encouraged to avoid attributing a client's non-heterosexual orientation to arrested psychosocial development or psychopathology.

62 Jensen's Level I and Level II abilities can be best understood in terms of which of the following?

I. Difficulty and complexity of tasks
II. Socio-economic differences
III. Racial differences
IV. Geographical differences

Choose the correct option.

1 I, III and IV
2 I, II and III
3 II, III and IV
4 I, II, III and IV

Ans. *(2)*

Exp. Jensen's Level I and Level II abilities can be best understood in terms of Difficult and complexity of tasks, Socio-economic Differences and Racial differences.

Jensen divides intelligence into two different sets of abilities:

Level I : They involve abilities of memory and simple associative learning.

Level II : They involve abstract reasoning and conceptual thought.

From his research, Arthur Jensen inferred that while Level I abilities are equally distributed amongst all the races, Level II abilities are more evident in whites and Asian people. They are considered to be more crucial for success in academics, thereby placing white and Asian students at an advantage.

Consequently, the Level I and II abilities can be understood in the complexity of the given tasks, they can also be understood in terms of socio-economic and racial differences as Level II does not appear to be equally distributed among all races as per Jensen. While there is racial difference, there can also be said to be socio-economic differences as those children who come from wealthy backgrounds tend to receive more advantages and mental stimulation when compared to those who come from impoverished backgrounds, thereby contributing towards their intelligence.

63 Which of the following statements are correct?

I. Dilthey opposed reductionism.

II. Dilthey opposed psychophysical parallelism.

III. Dilthey rejected the positivistic approaches to experimental psychology.

IV. Dilthey rejected the idea of description.

Choose the correct option.

1 I, II and IV are correct
2 I, III and IV are correct
3 II and IV are correct
4 I, II and III are correct

Ans. *(4)*

Exp. Among the given statements, Statement I, II and III are correct.

Dilthey opposed reductionism. Reductionism is the practice of describing something complicated in simple terms. According to him, description of human perception, experience, and action is narrative rather than reductive, and it respects ambiguity as sometimes inherent to the subject matter rather than as a deficient account.

Dilthey opposed psychophysical parallelism. He believed that no metaphysical formulation can have more than relative validity because it attempts to arrive at a totalization that transcends experience.

Dilthey rejected the positivistic approaches to experimental psychology. Positivism being an approach that relies mainly on scientific evidence. He urged that psychology become a rigorous and systematic science, a model for all the Geisteswissenschaften (the disciplines of mind, spirituality, and human affairs). He argued against the new discipline modeling itself on the highly successful disciplines of time, mathematics, and the natural sciences.

Dilthey did not reject the idea of description. According to him, the human science psychology differentiates itself from positivistic traditions by drawing on broad hermeneutic traditions and/or phenomenological descriptions of persons as always being in relation to the world, always temporally on the way from and toward, and on existential extensions of those descriptions of persons as always being in relation to lived body and to the social world, and as inevitably participating in making meaning and choices no matter how constrained.

64 The teacher had marks for 50 students in his class. He computed their mean and standard deviation, considering that the evaluation was too strict, he gave five grace marks to each student. This would

I. increase mean by five.

II. alter standard deviation in an unpredicted way.

III. change the rank order of the students.

IV. change the skewness of the distribution.

Choose the correct option.

1 Only I
2 I and II
3 I, II and III
4 I, III and IV

Ans. *(4)*

Exp. After computing the mean and standard deviation, and finding the evaluation to be very strict, if the teacher awarded 5 grace marks to every student, it would:

1. *Increase the mean by 5* : Mean refers to average, which is the sum of all the marks divided by the total number of students. Therefore, if each of the students' marks was increased by 5, then the mean would increase by 5 as well.
2. *Change the rank order of the students* : In schools, every rank requires a certain number of marks. For instance, a student may require minimum of 90 marks to receive A+ rank and 75 to receive A rank. Therefore, if 5 marks is awarded to every student, some students may move from A to A+ ranks. Therefore, their rank order would change.
3. *Change the skewness of the distribution* : In a given distribution, skewness refers the degree of variation from a normal distribution where most scores are clustered around the mean. If every student is awarded 5 grace marks, the skewness may change as scores may move away from the mean as there is an increase in the marks.

65 Which of the following are true as per Brentano's concept of Phenomenology?

I. Outer objects can be perceived only.
II. Mental experiences can be perceived only.
III. Feelings and willing be combined in one category.
IV. Outer objects can be both perceived and experienced.

Choose the correct option.

1 III and IV are correct
2 I and III are correct
3 II, III and IV are correct
4 I and II are correct

Ans. (3)

Exp. Among the given statements regarding Brentano's concept of Phenomenology, Statements II, III, and IV are correct.

Phenomenology is a description of experiences, and Franz Brentano said that phenomenology involves an understanding the subject matter of awareness in a way that it sheds light on the differences between the mental and the non-mental. He said that:

1. Mental experiences can only be perceived.
2. Feeling and willing should be combined in one category as they are placed on a spectrum, where the feeling (of sadness) is on one end on the spectrum and the willingness (desire) to act is on the other end of the spectrum. Influence takes place as a result of the relation between feeling and willing.
3. Outer objects (non-mental) can be both, perceived and experienced.

66 Match the given concepts in List I with description given in List II.

List I	List II
A. Turiyavastha	I. The state of normal consciousness concerned with material world
B. Prajnavastha	II. Subconscious faculty concerned with the subtler aspects of human knowledge and experience
C. Swapnavastha	III. State of super consciousness when dichotomy between grossness and subtlety disappears
D. Jagrathavastha	IV. Steady state of consciousness when essential nature of atman is experienced

Codes

	A	B	C	D		A	B	C	D
1	III	II	I	IV	2	IV	III	II	I
3	III	IV	II	I	4	I	III	II	IV

Ans. (2)

Exp. The correct matching is A–IV, B– III, C–II, D–I.

Turiyavastha is a steady state of consciousness when essential nature of the atman is experienced. It is a pure and tranquil in which all the discriminating attributes (gunas) transcend and dissolve.

Prajnavastha is a state of super consciousness when the dichotomy between the grossness and subtlety disappears. It is a transcendental state where all the desires are sublimated into spiritual experience.

Swapnavastha is a subconscious faculty concerned with the subtler aspects of human knowledge and experience. It is a dream state where the identification and the inkling of the experience of divinity take place.

Jagrathavastha is the state of normal consciousness concerned with the material world. This state consists of 19 aspects of empirical knowledge which leads one to desire for the pleasures that come with the material world.

67 Match the following concepts with the corresponding bodily states.

List I	List II
A. Rebound Phenomenon	I. REM sleeps
B. Phantom Limb	II. Pain
C. Scotopic Process	III. Vision
D. Apoptosis	IV. Cell death

Choose the correct option from those given below.

	A	B	C	D		A	B	C	D
1	I	II	III	IV	2	II	I	IV	III
3	I	IV	III	II	4	IV	I	III	II

Ans. (1)

Exp. The correct matching is A – I, B – II, C – III, D – IV.

Rebound phenomenon takes place during the REM (Rapid Eye Movement) stage of sleep. It is known as REM rebound wherein there is an increase in the length and the frequency of the time one spends in the REM stage of sleep. It follows a period of sleep deprivation.

Phantom Limb is connected to the experience of phantom limb pain. Phantom limb is a perception of the limb that is no longer there as it may have been amputated. Phantom limb pain refers to the ability to experience pain in the limb that is no longer present.

Scotopic Process is related to Vision. Scotopic vision refers to the vision under low-light conditions. In these conditions, scotopic process involves the use of rod cells to see. It means that objects do tend to be visible, but they only appear in black and white.

Apoptosis refers to Cell death. It is a programmed cell death. It takes place during early developmental stages where the cells that are not required are removed. In adults, it involves removing those cells that are completely damaged.

68 Match the following types of aggression with their description.

List I	List II
A. Hostile Aggression	I. An instinctual drive involving aggressive actions towards death
B. Emotional Aggression	II. Injury in which the goal is to obtain something of value
C. Instrumental Aggression	III. An act stemming from feelings of anger and aimed at inflicting pain
D. Thanatos	IV. Injury or harm that is carried out for the explicit goal of hurting someone

Choose the correct option from those given below.

Codes

	A	B	C	D		A	B	C	D
1	I	II	III	IV	2	II	III	IV	I
3	III	IV	I	II	4	III	IV	II	I

Ans. *(4)*

Exp. The correct matching is A–III, B–IV, C–II, D–I.

Hostile Aggression is an act stemming from feelings of anger, and is aimed at inflicting pain. It is impulsive and reactionary. For instance, getting into a fight with a stranger at a bar.

Emotional Aggression refers to injury/harm that is carried out for the explicit goal of hurting someone. It stems from intense negative emotions. For instance, lashing out at one's partner.

Instrumental Aggression refers to inflicting injury as the goal is to obtain something of value. It is generally well planned. For instance, injuring someone while robbing them so that they can obtain their money.

Thanatos is an instinctual drive involving aggressive actions towards one's death. This drive makes one engage in behaviours that can be risky or destructive.

69 Match the given concepts with relevant description.

List I	List II
A. Bottom up	I. Happiness due to circumstances tends to be temporary because we generally adjust fairly soon to new circumstances
B. Top down	II. Life circumstances influence happiness
C. Happiness set point	III. Happiness begins in ourselves
D. Hedonic adaptation	IV. Happiness levels are fixed and stable across time

Codes

	A	B	C	D		A	B	C	D
1	II	I	IV	III	2	II	III	I	IV
3	III	II	IV	I	4	II	III	IV	I

Ans. *(4)*

Exp. The correct matching is A–II, B– III, C–IV, D–I.

Bottom-up happiness refers to when life circumstances have an impact on happiness. Bottom-up theory says that overall happiness is the sum of its parts (life circumstances).

Top-down happiness refers to when happiness begins within ourselves. Top-down theory states that overall happiness depends on one's personality traits and other fixed genetic patterns.

Happiness set point refers to when happiness levels are fixed and stable across time. It is a general level of happiness that happens to be unique to every individual.

Hedonic adaptation takes place when happiness due to circumstances tends to be temporary because we generally adjust fairly soon to new circumstances. For instance, after being promoted, the happiness is momentary as one becomes used to their new position, and therefore, it no longer remains new and exciting for one to derive happiness out of it.

70 Match the following diseases with their corresponding descriptions.

List I	List II
A. Parkinson's Disease	I. Movement disorder associated with cognitive deficits
B. Huntington's Disease	II. Progressive motor disorder associated with severe dementia
C. Alzheimer's Disease	III. Progressive decline in memory starting with selective forgetting
D. Korsakoff's Syndrome	IV. A form of dementia which is caused by deficiency of vitamin Thiamine

Codes

	A	B	C	D		A	B	C	D
1	II	I	IV	III	2	I	IV	III	II
3	I	II	III	IV	4	II	III	IV	I

Ans. *(3)*

Exp. The correct matching is A–I, B–II, C–III, D–IV.

Parkinson's Disease is a movement disorder associated with cognitive deficits. It is characterised by tremors in the hand and also causes the slowing down and stiffness of movement.

Huntington's Disease is a progressive motor disorder associated with severe dementia. It is characterised by stumbling and clumsiness, mood swings, irritability, and other cognitive declines.

Alzheimer's Disease is a progressive decline in memory starting with selective forgetting. It also affects the behavioural and social skills of a person, thereby impeding their ability to function independently.

Korsakoff's Syndrome is a form of dementia which is caused by deficiency of Vitamin Thiamine. It affects the memory system, and may be caused by substance abuse, eating disorders, prolonged vomiting, or even chemotherapy.

71 **Match the following elements of Immune System with their respective functions.**

List I		List II	
A.	Neutrophils	I.	Field Marshals
B.	Immunoglobins	II.	Cytoxic Action
C.	NK (Natural Killer) Cells	III.	Phagocytic Action
D.	CD_4	IV.	Antibody Action

Choose the correct option.

	A	B	C	D		A	B	C	D
1	IV	II	III	I	2	III	I	II	IV
3	III	IV	II	I	4	II	IV	I	III

Ans. *(3)*

Exp. The correct matching is A–III, B–IV, C–II, D–I.

Neutrophils are responsible for Phagocytic action. Neutrophils are a kind of white blood cells that are phagocytic. That is, they appear at any wound cites and consume the bacteria, thereby destroying them.

Immunoglobins are responsible for Antibody action. Immunoglobins, also referred to as antibodies, recognize antigens (bacteria, viruses) in the body, bind to them, attack them, and destroy them.

Natural Killer (NK) cells are responsible for Cytotoxic action. They are lymphocytes that take action against infected cells and are also responsive towards tumours. They bring about the death of cells that are damaged beyond repair (apoptosis).

CD_4 are Field marshals. CD_4 or cluster of differentiation 4 is a glycoprotein that serves as a co-receptor for the T-cell receptor (TCR). They are white blood cells, also known as T-cells, that play an important role in fighting infection. These are referred to as field marshals as the army of CD_4 cells is responsible for precision and coordination of immune cells.

72 **Match the following leadership styles with their characteristics.**

List I		List II	
A.	Directive	I.	Leader consults subordinates thereby permitting them to participate in decision making
B.	Supportive	II.	Leader sets challenging goals and seeks improvement in performance
C.	Participative	III.	Leader provides specific guidance by establishing work schedules and rules
D.	Achievement oriented	IV.	Leader establishes good relations with subordinates and satisfies their needs

Choose the correct option from the given below.

	A	B	C	D		A	B	C	D
1	I	II	III	IV	2	II	III	IV	I
3	III	IV	I	II	4	IV	I	II	III

Ans. *(3)*

Exp. The correct matching is A–III, B–IV, C–I, D–II.

Directive leader is one who provides specific guidance by establishing work schedules and rules. For instance, they define tasks, set the deadlines, and strictly enforce rules.

Supportive leader is one who establishes good relations with subordinates and satisfies their needs. They emphasise the well-being of their subordinates are approachable and supportive. They also treat their subordinates with dignity and respect.

Participative leader is one who consults with their subordinates, thereby permitting them to participate in decision-making. For instance, if a new policy is being enforced, they take every subordinate's point of view into consideration.

Achievement-oriented leader is one who sets challenging goals and seeks improvement in performance. They tend to show high faith in their subordinates' abilities and expect only the highest level of performance from them.

73 **Match the following types of memories with their features.**

List I		List II	
A.	Non-declarative memory	I.	Type of declarative memory containing general knowledge of language and information
B.	Echoic memory	II.	Type of declarative memory containing personal information not readily available with others
C.	Semantic memory	III.	Type of LTM for skills, procedures, habits etc.
D.	Episodic memory	IV.	Auditory sensation lasting only for 2 to 4 seconds

Choose the correct option from those given below.

Codes

	A	B	C	D
1	I	II	III	IV
2	II	III	IV	I
3	III	IV	I	II
4	IV	III	II	I

Ans. *(3)*

Exp. The correct matching is A–III, B–IV, C–I, D–II.

Non-declarative memory is a type of LTM (Long-Term Memory) that is required for the performance of skills, procedures, habits, etc. It is also known as implicit memory and does not require conscious effort for recall. For instance, procedural memory involves memory about bodily movements and how to use objects. While balancing a bike, one knows how to do it because of procedural memory, but it does not require conscious recall.

Echoic memory is an auditory sensation lasting for only 2 – 4 seconds. It is a part of the sensory register and is a very short storage of the sounds one hears.

Semantic memory is a type of declarative memory containing general knowledge, of language and information. It is an explicit form of LTM that requires conscious recall. For instance, to remember the meaning of a word, one has to consciously try to remember it.

Episodic memory is a type of declarative memory containing personal information that is not readily available for others. It is an explicit form of LTM that stores memories of personal events. It requires conscious recall.

74 Match the waves with the corresponding frequencies.

	List I		List II
A.	Alpha Waves	I.	4-7 Hz
B.	Beta Waves	II.	14-30 Hz
C.	Theta Waves	III.	8-13 Hz
D.	Delta Waves	IV.	0-3 Hz

Codes

	A	B	C	D		A	B	C	D
1	III	II	I	IV	2	II	III	I	IV
3	III	II	IV	I	4	III	II	IV	I

Ans. *(1)*

Exp. The correct matching is A–III, B–II, C–I, D–IV.

Alpha Waves are brain waves that have a frequency of 8-13 Hz. They are considered to be linked with attention, and are required for filtering out distractions.

Beta Waves are brain waves that have a frequency of 14-30 Hz. They are involved in conscious and logical thinking patterns.

Theta Waves are brain waves that have a frequency of 4-7 Hz. They are considered to play a role in behavioural activations and inhibitions.

Delta Waves are brain waves that have a frequency of 0-3 Hz. They play a role in deep relaxation and restorative sleep.

75 Match the following intelligence/ability tests with the associated features.

	List I		List II
A.	Naglieri Non-Verbal Ability Test	I.	Provides deviation IQ
B.	Raven's Progressive Matrices (Standard)	II.	Open-ended Test
C.	Torrance Test of Creative Thinking	III.	Suitable for Children
D.	Wechsler Adult Intelligence Scale	IV.	Adult Culture Fair Test

Codes

	A	B	C	D		A	B	C	D
1	III	IV	II	I	2	IV	II	I	III
3	IV	III	II	I	4	III	IV	I	II

Ans. *(1)*

Exp. The correct matching is A – III, B – IV, C – II, D – I.

Naglieri Non-Verbal Ability Test is suitable for children. It helps in assessing children's learning abilities without requiring them to speak, read or write.

Raven's Progressive Matrices (Standard) are Adult Culture-Fair tests. They are non-verbal tests that help in assessing general intelligence and abstract reasoning skills. They contain matrices that involve a missing part, and the test-taker is required to choose an alternative that completes the pattern.

Torrance Test of Creative Thinking is an open-ended test. It helps in determining the creative thinking patterns in children. It is administered to children in order to determine advance placements or it is given during entrance examinations.

Wechsler Adult Intelligence Scale provides deviation IQ. It is a scale used to assess intelligence and mental abilities. It provides deviation IQ, which is a measure of how far a person deviates from the mean on a given IQ test.

76 Arrange the following in temporal sequence.

I. Establishment of Psychology Department in Mysore
II. Establishment of Psychology Department in Calcutta
III. Establishment of Psychology Department in Madras
IV. Establishment of Psychology Department in Pune
V. First Indian Journal of Psychology

Choose the correct option.

1 II, I, III, V, IV
2 II, I, V, III, IV
3 II, III, I, IV, V
4 I, II, V, III, IV

Ans. *(2)*

Exp. The correct chronological order in temporal sequence is II, I, V, III, IV.

1. The establishment of Psychology Department in Calcutta University took place in the year, 1916. It was established by Sen Gupta.
2. The establishment of Psychology Department in Mysore University took place in the year, 1924. It was established by Charles Spearman.
3. The first official journal of Psychology in India, known as the Indian Journal of Psychology, was published in the year, 1925. The editor was Sen Gupta.
4. The establishment of Psychology Department in Madras University took place in the year, 1943. It was established by Dr. G. D. Boaz.
5. The establishment of Psychology Department in Pune University took place in the year, 1950. It was established by Professor V. K. Kothurkar, an experimental psychologist.

77 Arrange the following in sequences as per Atkinson and Shiffrin's Model of memory when the information is processed.

I. Short term memory
II. Elaborative rehearsal
III. Long term memory
IV. Attention
V. Sensory memory

1 IV, V, I, II, III 2 V, I, IV, II, III
3 V, IV, I, II, III 4 IV, V, I, II, III

Ans. (3)

Exp. The correct chronological order for information processing as per Atkinson and Shiffrin Model of memory is V, IV, I, II, III.

Sensory memory : In the sensory memory store, information arrives from the 5 senses such as sight (visual information), sounds and touch. The sensory memory store has a large capacity but a very brief duration, it can encode information from any of the senses and most of the information is lost through decay.

Attention : It is the first step in remembering something, if a person's attention is focused on one of the sensory stores then the data is transferred to STM.

Short-term memory : The STM store has a duration of up to 30 seconds, has a capacity of 7+/-2 chunks and mainly encodes information acoustically. Information is lost through displacement or decay.

Elaborative rehearsal : If the information is given meaning (elaborative rehearsal) it is passed on to the LTM. Elaborative rehearsal involves the process of linking new information in a meaningful way with information already stored in long-term memory. For example, you could learn the lines in a play by relating the dialogue and behavior of your character to similar personal experiences you remember.

Long-term memory : The LTM has unlimited capacity and duration and encodes information semantically. Information can be recalled from LTM back into the STM when it is needed.

78 Involvement of frontal lobe in intelligence can be understood in terms of which of the following sequences.

1 Frontal lobe → focusing attention internally → working memory → general reasoning
2 Frontal lobe → focusing attention internally → response selection → general reasoning
3 Frontal lobe → short term storage → working memory → general reasoning
4 Frontal lobe → response selection → working memory → general reasoning

Ans. (1)

Exp. The correct chronological order in terms of the involvement of frontal lobe in intelligence is: Frontal lobe → focusing attention internally → working memory → general reasoning.

These are described as follows :

1. *Frontal lobe* : It is known to play a very important role in attention and memory. We need lateral prefrontal cortex when learning something new. When something is new, those who recruit lateral prefrontal cortex most often perform best.
2. *Attention* : It is necessary even during memory retrieval. Therefore, focusing one's attention internally towards the retrieval of a memory will help bring it from long-term memory to the working memory. Focusing on information held in mind for several seconds might as easily be called keeping your attention focused on those mental contents for several seconds.
3. *Working memory* : It involves the manipulation of the stored information, and it is the memory that is required to perform a given task. It involves holding information in mind and mentally working with it (or said differently, working with information no longer perceptually present.
4. *General reasoning* : Reasoning would not be possible without working memory as it critical to our ability to see connections between seemingly unrelated things and to pull apart elements from an integrated whole, and hence to creativity because creativity involves disassembling and recombining elements in new ways. WM also enables us to bring conceptual knowledge and not just perceptual input to bear on our decisions, and to consider our remembered past and future hopes in making plans and decisions. Working memory is highly crucial for general reasoning, which is an aspect of intelligence.

79 Arrange in sequence, the scoring categories for 'Motive to Avoid Success' as given below.

I. Non-contingent negative consequences
II. Interpersonal engagement
III. Relief
IV. Absence of instrumental conditioning
V. Absence of others

Which of the given below sequence is correct?

Codes

1 I, II, IV, III, V 2 I, II, III, IV, V
3 II, I, III, V, IV 4 III, IV, V, II, I

Ans. (2)

Exp. The correct chronological order for the scoring categories for 'Motive to Avoid Success' is – I, II, III, IV, V.

The scoring categories for MAS, as given by Homer, are as given below :

1. *Non-Contingent : Negative Consequences*: When negative consequences come from external forces, such as external events. The scoring is (+2).
2. *Interpersonal Engagement* : When two people are involved with one another. The scoring is (+2).
3. *Relief* : When a certain tension is instantly alleviated. The scoring is (+1).

4. *Absence of Instrumental Activity*: Instrumental activity refers to when some actions are being taken towards the attainment of a goal. Absence of it is a lack of any such actions. The scoring is (+1).
5. *Absence of others*: When no other people are involved. The scoring is (-2).

Motive to Avoid Success (MAS) is a concept proposed by Homer, and it says that there's a motivation to avoid success because of the fear of negative outcomes that are related with success, such as, social rejection. Women tend to score high on MAS as success is viewed as not being associated with feminity by the society. Based on the scoring, MAS ranges from -2 to +8.

80 Arrange the following stages of moral development in sequence of their emergence as an individual grows up.

I. Morality of interpersonal cooperation
II. Universal ethical principle orientation
III. Social order maintaining orientation
IV. Instrumental purpose orientation

Choose the correct option.

1 IV, I, II, III
2 IV, I, III, II
3 I, II, IV, III
4 II, III, IV, I

***Ans.* (2)**

Exp. The correct chronological order of the stages of moral development is IV, I, III, II.

The following are the stages in the sequence of their emergence when it comes to moral development:

1. *Instrument purpose orientation* : It is the second stage. Behaviour is dependent on outcomes. During this stage, a person focuses on attaining rewards and satisfying personal desires.
2. *Morality of interpersonal cooperation* : It is the third stage. Behaviours and decisions are made on the basis of the judgment from other people's perspective. During this stage, a person desires to be viewed in a positive light by others.
3. *Social order maintaining orientation* : It is the fourth stage. Behaviours and moral decisions are made taking into consideration the rules of the society in order to preserve law and order.
4. *Universal ethical principle orientation*: It is the sixth and the highest stage of moral development. During this stage, behaviours and moral decisions are based on one's own ethical principles that have their roots in one's conscience.

81 In what sequence the social combination rules are followed for group success?

1 Additive, disjunctive, compensatory, conjunctive
2 Additive, compensatory, disjunctive, conjunctive
3 Disjunctive, compensatory, conjunctive, additive
4 Compensatory, conjunctive, disjunctive, additive

***Ans.* (1)**

Exp. The correct chronological order for social combination rules followed for group success is as follows :

1. *Additive* : It allows the members of the group to make individual contributions, all of which are combined together in order to put forth a greater group output.
2. *Disjunctive* : It allows all the members of the group to come up with a single method/solution for a given task that applies to the entire group.
3. *Compensatory* : It allows the members of the group to give their individual recommendations, and an average is created.
4. *Conjunctive* : It allows the members of the group to collectively contribute towards the completion of a task.

82 Arrange the ego strengths in correct sequence according to Erikson's stages of ego development.

1 Hope → Purpose → Competence → Fidelity → Love → Care → Wisdom → Will
2 Will → Hope → Purpose → Competence → Fidelity → Care → Wisdom → Love
3 Hope → Will → Purpose → Competence → Fidelity → Love → Care → Wisdom
4 Purpose → Hope → Will → Fidelity → Competence → Care → Wisdom → Love

***Ans.* (3)**

Exp. The correct chronological order of ego strengths as per Erikson's stages of ego development is Hope → Will → Purpose → Competence → Fidelity → Love → Care → Wisdom.

1. *Hope* : This is the outcome of the first psychosocial stage of development, which is Trust vs. Mistrust.
2. *Will* : This is the outcome of the second psychosocial stage of development, which is Autonomy vs. Shame/Doubt.
3. *Purpose* : This is the outcome of the third psychosocial stage of development, which is Initiative vs. Guilt.
4. *Competence* : This is the outcome of the fourth psychosocial stage of development, which is Industry vs. Inferiority.
5. *Fidelity* : This is the outcome of the fifth psychosocial stage of development, which is Identity vs. Role Confusion.
6. *Love* : This is the outcome of the sixth psychosocial stage of development, which is Intimacy vs. Isolation.
7. *Care* : This is the outcome of the seventh psychosocial stage of development, which is Generativity vs. Stagnation.
8. *Wisdom* : This is the outcome of the eighth and last psychosocial stage of development, which is Integrity vs. Despair.

Erikson believed that the successful completion or mastery of every stage leads to an ego strength. Ego strength helps in giving rise to a sense of competence that allows one to excel in different areas of life.

83 Escalation of commitment involves following sequence of steps.

I. Occurrence of loss
II. Self-Justification

III. Strengthening by external factor
IV. Rational expectation of positive outcome

Choose the correct option.

1 IV, I, III, II
2 IV, I, II, III
3 I, II, III, IV
4 I, II, IV, III

Ans. (2)

Exp. The correct chronological order for escalation of commitment is IV, I, II, and III.

Escalation of commitment is a behavioural pattern in which a person/group who face adverse consequences from an action or a decision continue with the same behavior instead of modifying it. It happens in the following sequence :

1. *Rational expectation of a positive outcome* : Many researchers believe that the need to escalate resources is linked to expectancy theory. According to such a viewpoint, decision makers assess the probability that additional resource allocations will lead to goal attainment, as well as the value of goal attainment (i.e., rewards minus costs), and thereby generate a subjective expected utility associated with the decision to allocate additional resources.
2. *Occurrence of loss* : It is the negative consequence. It seems that the reasonable thing to do when our decisions result in unfavorable outcomes would be to face the consequences and learn how to make better choices for next time. However, this is not always what actually occurs. When our behavior has negative consequences, we often change our attitudes towards the outcome.
3. *Self-justification* : The next phase of the escalation process is self-justification and rationalizing if the decision the leader made used resources well, if the resources being used were used to make positive change, and assuring themselves that the decision they chose was right.
4. *Strengthening by external factor* : If external factors, such as other peers or society, buy into the justification, then the behaviour continues and strengthens. Otherwise, an alteration in the behavioural pattern may be seen.

84 Choose the correct sequence of events following prolonged stress.

I. Corticotropin releasing factor
II. Adrino-corticotrophic hormone
III. Cortisol
IV. Immune suppression

Choose the correct option.

1 I, II, III, IV
2 IV, III, I, II
3 I, III, IV, II
4 II, III, I, IV

Ans. (1)

Exp. The correct chronological order for events following prolonged stress is I, II, III, IV.

Following prolonged stress, the following events take place :

1. *Corticotropin releasing factor* (CRF) : It is a neuropeptide that plays a major role in mediating stress, and induces immune activation or suppression. It activates the synthesis and production of Adreno-corticotropic Hormone (ACTH).
2. *Adrenocorticotropic hormone* (ACTH) : It stimulates the production of cortisol, which is a stress hormone.
3. *Cortisol* : It is a steroid hormone which is prepared by adrenal glands. It is a stress hormone that plays a role in the regulation of protein and glucose, metabolism of lipids, maintenance of the body's blood pressure, and in suppressing the immune system's response.
4. *Immune suppression* : It takes place when the body's immune system is not working properly. It reduces the body's defences, making it vulnerable to infections and diseases. It is an effect of prolonged stress, brought about by increased cortisol.

85 Arrange in sequence, the network of auditory pathways.

I. Auditory Nerve
II. Cochlear Nuclei
III. Superior Olives
IV. Lateral Leminiscus
V. Inferior Colliculus
VI. Medial Geniculate Nuclei
VII. Primary Auditory Cortex

Choose the correct sequence.

1 I, III, II, IV, V, VII, VI
2 I, II, III, IV, V, VI, VII
3 II, I, IV, III, VII, V, VI
4 VI, VII, V, IV, III, II, I

Ans. (2)

Exp. The correct chronological order of the network of auditory pathway is I, II, III, IV, V, VI, and VII.

The auditory pathway plays a role in the sense of hearing. Its network is as follows :

1. *Auditory Nerve* : It connects the inner ear with the brain.
2. *Cochlear Nuclei* : These are the receptors in the inner ear which are carried by the auditory nerve.
3. *Superior Olive* : It is the collection of the brain stem nuclei that plays a role in different aspects of hearing.
4. *Lateral Leminiscus* : These are the axons in the brainstem that carry sound from the cochlear nuclei to different brainstem nuclei.
5. *Inferior Colliculus* : It is the part of the midbrain that acts as a major auditory centre for the body, and is the channel for auditory signals.
6. *Medial Geniculate Nuclei* : It is the part of the thalamus and acts as a relay centre for auditory signals between the inferior colliculus and auditory cortex.
7. *Primary Auditory Cortex* : This is where the sound signals finally reach for the conscious perception of sound.

86 Given below are two statements one is labelled as Assertion (A) and the other is labelled as Reason (R).

Assertion (A) MRI provides images of brain activity rather than brain images.

Reason (R) Results in MRI are obtained from the measurement of waves that hydrogen atoms emit when they are activated by radio-frequency waves in a magnetic field.

In the light of the above two statements, choose the correct option.

1 Both (A) and (R) are true and (R) is the correct explanation of (A)
2 Both (A) and (R) are true, but (R) is not the correct explantion of (A)
3 (A) is true, but (R) is false
4 (A) is false, but (R) is true

***Ans.* (4)**

Exp. (A) is false, but (R) is true.

Magnetic Resonance Imaging (MRI) only gives a static image of the brain, but not the brain activity.

MRI helps one see inside the body with great detail. It uses magnetic fields and radio waves in order to assess the amount of water present in different body tissues. Using the location of the water, it gives a detailed image. Water consists of two hydrogen atoms and one oxygen atom (H_2O). In MRI, the results are obtained from the measurement of waves that these hydrogen atoms emit when they are activated by the radio-frequency waves present in the magnetic field.

87 Given below are two statements one is labelled as Assertion (A) and the other is labelled as Reason (R).

Assertion (A) Sensitivity to targets reflects the placement of a flexible criterion and is measured in terms of 'hits minus false alarms'.

Reason (R) When the consequences of making a Miss are very grave, we lower the criterion for considering something as a Hit.

In the light of the above two statements, choose the correct option.

1 Both (A) and (R) are true and (R) is the correct explanation of (A)
2 Both (A) and (R) are true, but (R) is not the correct explantion of (A)
3 (A) is true, but (R) is false
4 (A) is false, but (R) is true

***Ans.* (1)**

Exp. Both (A) and (R) are true and (R) is the correct explanation of (A).

Signal detection theory states that the detection of a stimulus (target) depends upon the intensity of the stimulus as well as the physical and mental state of the person. This theory states that there are four consequences:

1. *Hit* : When a stimulus is present and it is identified.
2. *Miss* : When a stimulus is present but it is not identified.
3. *False alarm* : When a stimulus is not present but is determined as being present.
4. *Correct rejection* : When a stimulus is absent and is identified as not being present.

The sensitivity towards the presence of a certain stimulus (target) is based on a certain flexible criterion and is measured in terms of hits minus false alarms. If the consequences of missing (Miss) a stimulus even when it is present are very serious, then the criterion to consider something as a 'Hit' is lowered so that the chances of a 'Miss' is less. Consequently, the sensitivity towards a target is measured in terms of hits minus false alarms. If one is more sensitive, there is a less chance of a false alarm.

88 Given below are two statements one is labelled as Assertion (A) and the other is lablled as Reason (R).

Assertion (A) High sensation seekers are inclined to get involved in variety of thrill seeking activities.

Reason (R) Engagement in thrill seeking behaviour triggers the release of epinephrine.

In the light of above two statements, choose the correct option.

1 Both (A) and (R) are true and (R) is the correct explanation of (A)
2 Both (A) and (R) are true, but (R) is not the correct explantion of (A)
3 (A) is true, but (R) is false
4 (A) is false, but (R) is true

***Ans.* (3)**

Exp. (A) is true, but (R) is false.

High sensation seekers are those who are very sensitive to experiences, and select those experiences that provide them with the highest stimulation. They deliberately pursue experiences, and in order to gain maximum stimulation, they engage in highly thrill-seeking experiences.

Thrill-seeking does not trigger the release of epinephrine. In fact, when thrill-seeking is involved, the amygdala identifies a risk that may be present and releases adrenaline, dopamine, and other endorphins that help protect the body against any harm that may entail the risk.

89 Given below are two statements one is labelled as Assertion (A) and the other is labelled as Reason (R).

Assertion (A) Culture encompasses life styles, values, practices and goals which provide distinct identities to the people and community.

Reason (R) Culture always acts as a constraint in the growth of a community.

In the light of the above two statements, choose the correct option.

1 Both (A) and (R) are true and (R) is the correct explanation of (A)
2 Both (A) and (R) are true, but (R) is not the correct explantion of (A)
3 (A) is true, but (R) is false
4 (A) is false, but (R) is true

Ans. (3)

Exp. (A) is true, but (R) is false.

Culture is a social factor that is encompassing of the values, practices, lifestyles, goals of the people that are distinct to those who belong to a certain culture.

Culture does not always act as a constraint in the growth of a community. For instance, in collectivistic cultures, importance is given to the family and society rather than the individual. In doing so, the culture encourages cooperation with others that helps in the growth of a community.

90 Given below are two statements one is labelled as Assertion (A) and the other is labelled as Reason (R).

Assertion (A) Philosophically the word pragmatism emphasises results rather than methods.

Reason (R) A pragmatic view of science accepts methodological approaches to knowledge.

In the light of above two statements, choose the correct option.

1 Both (A) and (R) are true and (R) is the correct explanation of (A)
2 Both (A) and (R) are true, but (R) is not the correct explantion of (A)
3 (A) is true, but (R) is false
4 (A) is false, but (R) is true

Ans. (2)

Exp. Both (A) and (R) are true, but (R) is not the correct explanation for (A).

Pragmatism is a philosophical approach refers to the evaluation of theories and beliefs in terms of their successful practical applications. Therefore, in philosophical terms, pragmatism can be considered to place more emphasis on the outcomes rather than on the methods used.

Pragmatic view refers to dealing with things in a realistic and practical manner. Therefore, a pragmatic view of science accepts methodological approaches to knowledge.

From the above, it can be said that while both, A and R are correct, they deal with two different aspects of pragmatism, and R is not the explanation for A.

Directions (Q. Nos. 91-95) *Read the following paragraph and answer the questions which are as follows.*

The experimental psychologist wanted to explore whether the noise adversely affects the Reaction Time (RT). She also wanted to explore whether the stress level would moderate the effect of noise. She varied noise at three levels-Low (30 decibels), Moderate (60 decibels) and High (90 decibels). She varied stress at two levels-low and high. From the initial pool of college students, subjects were randomly assigned to different groups. However, a few subjects could not turn up to the laboratory due to vacation. In all, two hundred and ninety seven subjects participated in the experiments. Each subject, in each group, was tested for simple RT, disjunctive RT, and choice RT.

The theory and preliminary analyses indicated the three types of RT were moderately correlated. The covariance matrices, showing the covariances among the three types of RTs, were found to be quite similar for all the groups. The Multivariate Analysis of Variance (MANOVA) results were computed to explore the group differences in means. As the most common practice is, four test criteria (Pillai's Criterion. Wilks' Criterion, Hotelling's Criterion and Roy's Criterion) were obtained. Among the different results obtained in this work, one interesting finding was that the stress moderated the effect of noise level on reaction time.

91 Which one of the following reasons best justifies the application of MANOVA in the present work?

1 There are several groups and more than one Independent Variable (IV).
2 More than one Dependent Variables (DV) have been employed.
3 More than one Dependent Variables with moderate inter-correlations, have been employed.
4 The moderating effect of stress on the effect of noise on RT can be demonstrated only through MANOVA.

Ans. (3)

Exp. The best justification for using Multivariate Analysis of Variance (MANOVA) is that there are more than one Dependent Variables with inter-correlations being tested in the given study.

MANOVA is used to test the difference in the means of three or more groups. It is used instead of ANOVA when there are multiple continuous dependent variables present. In the given study, the experimenter wanted to test whether noise adversely impacts reaction time, and whether stress moderates the effect of noise. The two dependent variables are reaction time and effect of noise, therefore, MANOVA is used.

92 The design employed in the above study can best be labelled as

1 randomised six group design with single factor.
2 balanced factorial design.
3 unbalanced factorial design.
4 unbalanced factorial design with a covariate.

Ans. (3)

➲ *Exp.* The design employed in the given study can be labelled as 'unbalanced factorial design.'

When there are different groups for the same independent variable, and each of the groups has an unequal number of observations, it is referred to as an unbalanced factorial design. In the given experiment, there were a total of 297 participants who were randomly assigned to three groups. In this case, every group cannot have the same number of participants, therefore, the number of observations will be unequal.

One of the reasons this may happen is because of missing observations, which in this case is because few subjects not being able to be present for the experiment.

93 The above information suggests that

1 the assumption of homogeneity of covariance matrices is not satisfied.
2 the assumption of homogeneity of covariance matrices is satisfied.
3 covariance among Dependent Variables (DVs) are zero.
4 the assumption of homogeneity of variances is not tenable.

Ans. (2)

➲ *Exp.* The above information suggests that the assumption of homogeneity of covariance matrices is satisfied.

Homogeneity of covariance is concerned with the covariance matrices when multiple dependent variables are involved, as is in the case of MANOVA. For instance, if there are three dependent variables, then it tests for six covariances for the purpose of equality across groups. In the given study, the covariances among three types of reaction times–simple, disjunctive, and choice, were tested and found to be similar across all groups. Therefore, the assumption of homogeneity of covariance matrices was satisfied.

94 Which of the following test criterion is more appropriate than the others?

1 Roy's Criterion
2 Wilk's Criterion
3 Hotelling's Criterion
4 Pillai's Criterion

Ans. (4)

➲ *Exp.* For the given experiment, Pillai's Criterion is more appropriate than the others. It is used as a test statistic in MANOVA, and ranges from 0 to 1. Increasing values means that null hypothesis can be rejected. Pillai's criterion is a good choice to use when there are uneven cell sizes, which in this experiment is the case as there are 297 participants randomly assigned to 3 groups. Therefore, the cell sizes will not be even for all the groups .

95 Which one of the following conclusions can be confidently drawn from the above study?

1 Main effect of noise is significant.
2 Main effect of stress is significant.
3 Noise × stress interaction is significant.
4 The main effects of noise, stress and interaction effect are significant.

Ans. (3)

➲ *Exp.* The conclusion that can confidently be drawn from the given experiment is that the Noise x Stress interaction is significant.

The experimenter wanted to test whether noise has a negative impact on reaction time, and whether stress levels moderate the effect of noise. The outcome that the given experiment yielded was stress moderated the effect of noise level on reaction time, thereby proving that there was a significant interaction between noise and stress.

Directions (Q. Nos. 96-100) *Read the following paragraph and answer the five questions which are as follows.*

A leading business school in the city had a view that its students must have a good proficiency in English language usage. As an initial step, the school authorities decided to develop a brief language usage test.

The project incharge wrote 30 items. Each item had five alternative answers, one of which was correct. He administered these 30 items to a sample of 250 students. For item analysis, item-remainder correlations were computed. The item analysis retained 25 items.

The twenty-five item version was administered to a fresh sample of 300 students. Three reliability coefficients were computed split half reliability coefficient. Kuder-Richardson (K-R) reliability coefficient, and Cronbach alpha were computed. The Cronbach alpha was found to be 0.7. The test-retest reliability was also computed with a time-interval of eight weeks in two administrations, using the same sample.

The test retest correlation was found to be 0.26, significant at .001 level. The school authorities, pleased with the efforts of the project incharge, asked him to add similar items and develop a 75 item version.

96 Which one of the following correlations is most suitable for computing item-remainder correlations?

1 Tetrachoric Correlation
2 Phi-Coefficient
3 Contingency Coefficient
4 Point bi-serial Correlation

Ans. (4)

➲ *Exp.* Point bi-serial correlation is most suitable for computing item-remainder correlations.

Item-remainder correlation refers to the correlation of each item with the sum of the other remaining items. The outcome is the test score without the item being tested. In this type of correlation, point bi-serial correlation is highly suitable as it tests the correlation between the scores on the item being correlated with the remaining items by correlating the score on the given item and adding up the scores of the remaining items, which is the essence of item remainder correlation.

97 Given below are two statements one is labelled as Assertion (A) and the other is labelled as Reason (R).

Assertion (A) The computation of (K-R) reliability is questionable in the above study.

Reason (R) K-R reliability is suitable for tests with dichotomous items.

In the light of the above two statements, choose the correct option.

1 Both (A) and (R) are true and (R) is the correct explanation of (A).
2 Both (A) and (R) are true but (R) is not the correct explantion of (A).
3 (A) is true, but (R) is false.
4 (A) is false, but (R) is true.

Ans. (4)

Exp. (A) is false, but (R) is true.

Kuder-Richardson (K-R) reliability can be used for binary items where there is a possibility of only one correct answer, for instance, right or wrong. Hence, the computation of it is not questionable in the given test as each item involves 5 alternatives out of which only one is correct, and any other alternative is marked as wrong.

Kuder-Richardson (K-R) reliability measures the reliability for a test involving dichotomous items. For instance, multiple-choice items that have only one distractor among the possible answers, besides the one that is correct.

98 The above information provides an evidence for

I. unsatisfactory test-retest reliability
II. satisfactory test-retest reliability
III. acceptable internal consistency reliability
IV. unacceptable internal consistency reliability

Choose the correct option.

1 I and III
2 I and IV
3 II and III
4 II and IV

Ans. (1)

Exp. The above information provides evidence for unsatisfactory test-retest reliability and acceptable internal consistency reliability.

Test-retest reliability is a measure of reliability obtained by administering the same test twice over a period of time to a group of individuals. The scores from Time 1 and Time 2 can then be correlated in order to evaluate the test for stability over time. In the given paragraph, the test-retest reliability was computed within a time-interval of eight weeks in two administrations, using the same sample. It was found to be 0.26, which is a low correlation. Therefore, it provides an evidence for unsatisfactory test-retest reliability.

Internal consistency is a method of reliability in which we judge how well the items on a test that are proposed to measure the same construct produce similar results. It is typically a measure based on the correlations between different items on the same test (or the same subscale on a larger test). In the given paragraph, the Cronbach's alpha was found to be 0.70, which is a good correlation. Therefore, it provides an evidence for acceptable internal consistency reliability.

99 Consider the three reliability coefficients :

I. Split-half reliability coefficient;
II. K-R reliability coefficient
III. Cronbach alpha computed in the above study.

Which one of the following is true in the above context?.

1 All the three reliability coefficients would be same.
2 All the three reliability coefficients would be different.
3 II and III would be same, but I can be different.
4 I and III would be same, but II can be different.

Ans. (3)

Exp. In the above mentioned test, the K-R reliability coefficient and Cronbach's alpha would be the same, however, split-half reliability coefficient would be different.

K-R reliability can be used to measure the reliability of items in a test that involve only one possible correct answer, and measures the test's overall reliability. Cronbach's alpha is used to measure the internal consistency of a given test, to see how related the items are with each other as a group. If the test is reliable overall, there is a possibility that it will be internally consistent as well. Consequently, K-R reliability and Cronbach's alpha would be the same since the test is high on internal consistency (0.7).

Split-half reliability measures the extent to which all the parts of given test equally contribute to the concept being measured. For this, the scores of one half of the test are split from the other half to see whether they yield same results. However, this can vary as not all items on the test might equally contribute to the concept being measured, and there is no indication of it either.

100 The project incharge developed a 75-item version by adding similar items, what would be the expected Cronbach alpha?

1 0.700
2 0.824
3 0.875
4 0.931

Ans. (3)

Exp. Cronbach's alpha can increase up to 0.875, if a 75-item version of the test involving similar items was prepared.

Cronbach's alpha is used to measure the internal consistency of a given test, to test how related the items are with one other as a collective. For the given test of 25 items, the Cronbach's alpha was 0.7, which is the minimum desired value. With increasing items, the Cronbach's alpha can increase as well. So, if it were to increase from 25 to 75, and there is high inter-correlatedness given there is adding of similar items, Cronbach's alpha can increase up to 0.875.

UGC-NET
PSYCHOLOGY

SOLVED PAPER 2019 (June)

PAPER II

1 A competent and a well-performing female middle-level manager did not consider herself suitable for the position of senior manager thinking that females are not suitable for such high positions. This is a typical example of which of the following?

1 Glass-ceiling phenomenon
2 Low motivation to approach success
3 Gender discrimination
4 High motivation to avoid failure

Ans. (1)

Exp. The given case is an example of the Glass-ceiling phenomenon.

Glass-ceiling phenomenon refers to a situation where a qualified and deserving person, hoping to advance to a higher level within an organisation is stopped from doing so, and is kept at a lower level because of the sex-based discrimination that is present in the organisation.

Therefore, in the given case, when a competent middle-level manager who is a female does not consider herself to be suitable for a position at the senior management level on the basis of females not being suitable for that position, it is an illustration of Glass-ceiling phenomenon.

2 Mr. 'A' approached the therapist for anger management. After Mr. 'A' narrated an incident in which he experienced anger, which of the following is the most appropriate way of further questioning at initial level?

1 Could you please tell me why did you get angry?
2 Could you please explain what made you angry?
3 Please help me understand whom did you get angry at.
4 Please explain how did you feel when you were angry.

Ans. (2)

Exp. "Could you please tell me what made you angry?" is the most appropriate way of further questioning at the initial level of anger management.

Anger management is a therapeutic process wherein people learn to control their anger and deal with tense situations in a positive and constructive manner. During the initial stages of anger management, clients are encouraged to identify or recognise what is it that triggers or give rise to anger. Hence, in the given case, when the client, Mr. 'A', narrates an incident wherein he experienced anger, the therapist asking the client, "Could you please tell me what made you angry?" is the most appropriate way to ask the follow-up question as it allows the client to examine what made him angry.

3 According to Jung, what is made up of all the archetypes taken together?

1 Personal unconscious
2 Collective unconscious
3 Mandala
4 Shadow

Ans. (2)

Exp. According to Jung, Collective unconscious comprises all the archetypes taken together.

Carl Jung gave the concept of Collective unconscious. As per Jung, archetypes taken together form a part of Collective unconscious, which one inherits from their ancestors. Archetypes refer to universal images or patterns that exist in all cultures, and have throughout history. For instance, the archetype of a hero is that of a brave knight in a shining armour, who performs deeds of great courage.

4 In Cattell's theory, Dynamic Lattice shows the relationship among which of the following?

1 Ergs, sentiments and ability traits
2 Ergs, attitudes and temperamental traits
3 Sentiments and ergs
4 Ergs, sentiments and attitudes

Ans. (4)

Exp. In Cattell's theory, the Dynamic Lattice shows the relationship between ergs, sentiments and attitudes.

Raymond B. Cattell gave his theory of personality, where the dynamic lattice helps to understand how personality evolves. It is a pattern involving subsidisation wherein attitudes are considered to be subsidiary to sentiments, which in turn are subsidiary to ergs. Therefore, dynamic lattice shows the relationship between these three dynamic traits of personality.

They are as described below:

Ergs – They are physiologically based drives that involve hunger, curiosity, fear, pugnacity, acquisitiveness, sex, narcissistic sex, self-assertion, and parental protection.

Sentiments – They are social objects which one acquires by the process of learning, and are considered to be the sub-goals leading to the path of the final goals -the ergs.

Attitudes – Cattell defined attitude as the desire to act in a specific way in response to a specific situation. Attitudes are interconnected within the dynamic lattice.

5 According to Adler, which of the following is used by the neurotic to escape from the problems?

1 Depreciation
2 Self-accusation
3 Distancing
4 Safeguarding strategies

Ans. *(3)*

Exp. According to Adler, distancing is used by the neurotic to escape from problems.

Alfred Adler said that people experiencing neurosis tend to use 'distancing' in order to escape from their problems. Different manifestations of distancing can be seen when it is used. For instance, people tend to move backward or behave in a childish manner in order to escape or gain control. They can also simply stay still, not doing anything, thereby avoid failure by not even attempting to solve the problem or task. Distancing can also be manifested in the form of hesitation or becoming engrossed in other diversions till it becomes too late to deal with the problem at hand.

6 Positive emotions are expressed as a result of activation of which of the following?

1 Frontal areas of right hemisphere
2 Pre-frontal areas of right hemisphere
3 Frontal areas of left hemisphere
4 Pre-frontal areas of left hemisphere

Ans. *(4)*

Exp. Positive emotions are expressed as a result of activation of pre-frontal areas of left hemisphere. Researchers, using a variety of techniques, have found that the left prefrontal cortex participates with other structures in a circuit that may be important for certain types of positive emotion. Activation patterns in the right prefrontal cortex, by contrast, are more associated with certain types of negative affect accompanied by increased vigilance to threat-related cues, a symptom that often occurs with certain types of anxiety.

7 Jung identified eight personality types on the basis of which of the following?

1 Two attitudes and four functions
2 Four attitudes and two functions
3 Four attitudes and four functions
4 Two attitudes and six functions

Ans. *(1)*

Exp. Jung identified eight personality types on the basis of two attitudes and four functions. The personality theory given by Carl Jung was based on two attitudes and four functions. The two attitudes are :

1. *Introversion*: It refers to the personality theory of persons whose psyche energy only limits their own thoughts and feelings. They thinks always about themselves. Introverts are considered as shy person. They always focus on their own thoughts. They do not want opinions from other persons in the world.
2. *Extroversion* : It refers to the personality theory type of people. It is the opposite of introversion. The psyche energy flows towards the outer world and other people. These types of persons are very sociable and very open-minded.

Their outgoing, vibrant nature draws people to them, and they have a hard time turning away the attention. They thrive off the interaction.

The four functions are :

1. *Sensation* : It refers to the gathering of information from one's senses.
2. *Intuition* : It refers to the ability to comprehend something without any conscious reasoning.
3. *Feeling* : It refers to the ability to emphasise more on one's emotions.
4. *Thinking* : It refers to the ability to use logic and reasoning instead of focusing on emotions.

8 Which of the following is a step in transformative change where unpredictable and often affective experience occurs?

1 Integration
2 Preparation
3 Inspiration
4 Organic inquiry

Ans. *(3)*

Exp. Inspiration is a step in transformative change where unpredictable and often affective experience takes place.

Organic inquiry is an approach to research, wherein research is considered to be almost sacred. In this type of research, the fundamental aspect is to tell or listen to a story.

Organic researchers employ a three-step model of transformative change, of which inspiration is one. In this step, one steps out of their ego, that is, their conscious information, and move towards the space of the subconscious mind. In order to access their subconscious mind, organic researchers use guided imagery, meditation, dance, and other techniques.

9 When acetylcholine links up on the post-synaptic side, it generates a depolarisation. What do you call it?

1 Inhibitory postsynaptic potential
2 Excitatory postsynaptic potential
3 End-plate potential
4 End-plate potential and inhibitory postsynaptic potential

Ans. *(3)*

Exp. When acetylcholine (ACh) links up on the post-synaptic side, it generates depolarisation, which is known as End-plate potential.

ACh is a neurotransmitter which is released by the motor neuron. It binds with the receptors on the post-synaptic side of the neuron, the motor end-plate. This process generates depolarisation, which is referred to as the end-plate potential. Depolarisation takes place when there is a reduction in the voltage difference inside and outside the nerve cell/neuron. The depolarisation caused by the end-plate potential then spreads along the myolemma (cell membrane), which creates an action potential. The action potential then moves along the entirety of the cell membrane, thereby creating a wave of depolarisation.

10 An observer watches the video in which the speaker's lips form the sound 'ga-ga' while the sound trace provides speech that is normally perceived as 'ba-ba'. The conjunction of these conflicting sources produces the perception of 'da-da' which integrates these information and results in which illusion?

1 Cross-model illusion
2 Size illusion
3 Muller-Lyer illusion 4 Visual illusion

***Ans.** (1)*

Exp. The integration of the given information gives rise to the Cross-model illusion.

Cross-model illusion, also known as the McGurk effect, is an illusion that takes place when the incoming information from distinct senses (sight and sound) happens to be conflicting. It takes place when the auditory component of a sound is linked with the visual component of another sound, thereby giving rise to the perception of a different third sound.

For instance, in the given case, the two senses involved are sight and hearing. The observer watches the speaker's lips move so as to form the words "ga-ga," while the trace of the sound gives rise to speech that is perceived as "ba-ba." Conjunction of these conflicting information from the senses of sight and sound (eyes and ears) takes place, thereby giving rise to the perception of "da-da." This illustrates the cross-model illusion.

11 A 30 year-old man identified as Mr. K.C. suffered a serious motorcycle accident. Mr. K.C. remembers many things but cannot everything. Mr. K.C. seems to have which memory loss?

1 Semantic
2 Episodic
3 Procedural
4 Working memory

***Ans.** (2)*

Exp. Mr. K.C. seems to have Episodic memory loss.

Episodic memory refers to the memory of personal events. The hippocampus and other surrounding structures present in the temporal lobe are responsible for episodic memory. Episodic memory loss takes place when people tend to remember several events, but not all of them. In the given case, Mr. K.C. seems to be suffering from episodic memory loss after the accident as he is able to remember several things, but not all of them.

12 Projective measures, particularly inkblot tests, index which of the following?

1 Novelty context of creativity
2 Meaning context of creativity
3 Domain-specific creativity
4 Everyday creativity

***Ans.** (2)*

Exp. Projective measures, particularly the inkblot tests, index the meaning context of creativity.

Psychometric measures of creativity are considered to tap novelty context, whereas projective tests, particularly inkblot techniques are taken to index meaning context of creativity. Alfred Binet also experimented with the idea of using inkblots as a way to test creativity and originally planned to include inkblots in his intelligence tests.

Meaning context of creativity refers to context-specific creativity which is the ability to arrive at a solution to a specific kind of issue or problem. Since inkblot tests involve obscure stimuli, the responses to them can be viewed as a measure of divergent thinking ability, which has been regarded as a good estimate of creativity.

13 Hold a pencil at arm's length and look at it first with one eye then with the other. There is a little difference between the two views relative to the background. Now bring the pencil just six inches away from your face and try the same thing. This time you will perceive a great difference between the two views. Which one is the correct answer of above example?

1 Monocular cue 2 Binocular cue
3 Top-down processing 4 Bottom-up processing

***Ans.** (2)*

Exp. Binocular cue is the correct choice for the given example.

Binocular cues involve the use of both the eyes, and they help in depth perception. Parallax is a binocular cue that refers to the difference in the relative positions of a given object when they are seen from different perspectives.

So, when one holds a pencil at an arm's length and looks at it separately from both the eyes, the difference between two views is little. However, when the pencil is held only 6 inches away from the eye, and the same action is repeated, then a great difference between the two views can be perceived.

This happens because of parallax. Parallax helps in determining the distance, that is, if the angle between the two relative positions from different perspectives is narrow, the object is farther away, however, if it is wide, then the object is close.

14 The major function of parathyroid is to maintain the level of

1 calcium in blood 2 proteins in blood
3 vitamin D in blood 4 gluco-corticoids in blood

Ans. (1)

Exp. The major function of the parathyroid is to maintain the level of calcium in the blood.

Parathyroid glands are located behind the thyroid glands. They produce the parathyroid hormone whose main function is to regulate the calcium level in the blood.

Enlargement of parathyroid glands leads to too much of parathyroid hormone being produced, which gives rise to a condition known as hyperthyroidism. This leads to high amount of calcium in the blood. Another condition known as secondary hyperthyroidism leads to low amount of calcium in the blood. Both of these conditions have detrimental effects on the health of a person.

15 Which one of the following is NOT a characteristic of attention?

1 Processing capacity and selectiveness
2 Automatic processing
3 Initial detection of stimuli
4 Control

Ans. (2)

Exp. Automatic processing is not a characteristic of attention.

Automatic processing is any involuntary processing of information that takes place without deliberation, intention, or control on part of the person. For instance, well-practiced activities such as reading, driving, seeing, etc, come under automatic processing.

Automatic processing is not a characteristic of attention as attention is required when conscious and intentional processing of information takes place. It helps in the detection and processing of the stimuli as it involves the direction of one's focus towards the same.

16 Which of the following is true about Radio Immunological Assays?

1 These are methods to measure hormones
2 These methods were discovered by Jay Tepperman
3 These are anatomical methods
4 These measure brain structures

Ans. (1)

Exp. Radio-Immunological Assays are methods to measure hormones.

Radio-Immunological Assays (RIA) are in-vitro techniques wherein the concentration of antigens present in the body are measured by utilising the antibodies that work against these antigens. For the measurement of hormone (antigens), an RIA employs an antibody which is directed against the radio-labelled form of the specific hormone.

17 Skills that are operated automatically and without thinking are stored in which memory?

1 Implicit memory
2 Explicit memory
3 Flashbulb memory
4 Autobiographical memory

Ans. (1)

Exp. Skills that are operated automatically and without thinking are stored in the Implicit memory.

Implicit memory tends to influence one's behaviour without the need for any conscious retrieval. For instance, implicit memory involves procedural memory, which is memory pertaining to the skilled movements of the body or the way in which objects are to be used.

Balancing a bike is a type of procedural memory. One does not require to consciously recall how they perform this skill, however, the memory of the same influences their actions.

18 Torrance used the term 'creatively handicapped' for whom?

1 Students very high in creativity but low in academic achievement
2 Students high in intelligence but low in creativity
3 Students average in both intelligence and creativity
4 Students with low levels of both intelligence and creativity

Ans. (1)

Exp. Torrance used the term 'creatively handicapped' for students very high in creativity but low in academic achievement.

Ellis Paul Torrance created the Torrance Tests of Creative Thinking (TTCT) which measured creativity, divergent thinking, and other skills related to problem-solving. TTCT employed 4 scales, which are:

1. *Fluency* : It refers to the overall number of meaningful and relevant ideas developed in response to a given stimulus.
2. *Flexibility* : It refers to the different categories the relevant ideas can be placed under.
3. *Originality* : It refers to the rarity of the ideas.
4. *Elaboration* : It refers to the detail present in the ideas.

There were some students who scored high in TTCT, however, academically, their performance was low. These students were referred to as being "creatively handicapped" by Torrance.

19 The interaction of sensory impulses indicates the complexity of stimulation and therefore the difficulties in predicting behaviour. Behaviour is seldom a function of only one stimulus rather it is a function of many stimuli. The above explanation is based on which learning theory?

1 Guthrie's theory
2 Pavlov's theory
3 Hull's theory
4 Tolman's theory

Ans. (3)

Exp. The given explanation is based on Hull's theory.

Clark Leonard Hull developed a learning theory that states that a Stimulus (S) has an effect on the Organism (O), and the response depends upon the characteristics of 'S' as well as 'O'. In simple terms, Hull was interested in analysing the intervening variables that affected behaviour, which involved drives, incentives, previous training, and even inhibitors. Therefore, he said that behaviour was not the function of just one stimulus, but many stimuli. Hence, the difficulty in predicting behaviour.

20 Psychometric tests of creativity like Torrance Tests of Creative Thinking Index, measure creativity in terms of

1 person 2 product
3 process 4 persuasion

Ans. (3)

Exp. Psychometric tests of creativity, like Torrance Tests of Creative Thinking Index, measures creativity in terms of a process.

Creativity is referred to as the ability to look at a given situation/problem from different perspectives and come up with a novel idea to solve the situation/problem. Ellis Paul Torrance created the Torrance Tests of Creative Thinking (TTCT) which measured the process of creativity by using 4 scales to measure the processes involved in creativity:

1. *Fluency* : It refers to the overall number of meaningful and relevant ideas developed in response to a given stimulus.
2. *Flexibility* : It refers to the different categories the relevant ideas can be placed under.
3. *Originality* : It refers to the rarity of the ideas.
4. *Elaboration* : It refers to the detail present in the ideas.

21 Which attention is shifted without moving the eyes, commonly referred to as seeing something out of the corner of one's eye?

1 Covert attention 2 Overt attention
3 Divided attention 4 Span of attention

Ans. (1)

Exp. Covert attention is the type of attention that is shifted without moving the eyes, and is commonly referred to as seeing something out of the corner of one's eye.

In this type of attention, the brain attends to information without moving the eyes. Therefore, attention is taken place, but in a way that is not visible to other people. For instance, while driving, one's eyes are on the road however, some other things, like a movie poster, may catch their attention and they may look at without taking their eyes off the road.

22 A 12-year-old boy started showing a gradual onset of jerky, uncontrolled movements in limbs with clumsiness, frequent falling, slurred speech and drooling caused by HTT mutation. What disorder is he suffering from?

1 Ataxia 2 Huntington's
3 Dystonia 4 Essential tremors

Ans. (2)

Exp. The 12-year-old boy is suffering from Huntington's disease.

Huntington's disease is a rare and progressive genetic disorder caused by HTT mutation. It is characterised by the degeneration of nerve cells present in the brain. This disease tends to adversely affect a person's abilities to function, giving rise to cognitive, psychiatric, and movement disorders. For instance, a person may exhibit some jerky movements that are involuntary, have problems with their posture and balance that they tend to be clumsy and stumble, and even frequently fall. There may be problems with speech and swallowing. Typically, Huntington's disease starts at the age of 30 or 40 years. However, if it develops before the age of 20 years, it is known as juvenile Huntington's disease.

23 While conducting an experiment, the researcher manipulates the independent variable within a pre-decided range. Which of the following describes this type of research?

1 Quasi-experiment 2 Random-effect model
3 Fixed-effect model 4 Mixed-method approach

Ans. (3)

Exp. The given type of research is known as the Fixed-effect model.

In a Fixed-effect model, the experimenter manipulates the independent variable within a pre-decided range. These fixed-effect variables tend to be constant over a period of time. For instance, age, sex, ethnicity are certain examples of these type of independent variables.

24 Limbic system, basal ganglia and corpus striatum are parts of which section of brain?

1 Midbrain 2 Hindbrain
3 Telencephalon 4 Diencephalon

Ans. (3)

Exp. Limbic system, basal ganglia and corpus striatum are parts of the Telencephalon of the brain.

The Telencephalon is also known as the cerebrum. It is a very greatly developed part of the brain, and consists of right and left cerebral hemispheres. In the Telencephalon, the limbic system, basal ganglia and corpus striatum are located. The limbic system is responsible for emotional and behavioural responses, especially those behavioural responses that are linked with survival. Basal ganglia are subcortical nuclei. They play a role in motor learning, executive functioning, emotional behaviours, and are also responsible for addictive behaviours or habits as they play a role in reinforcements. Corpus striatum refers to the caudate and lentiform nuclei that are located within the basal ganglia.

25 Who gave the statement that the nature and frequency of human aggressive behaviour varies tremendously across human societies and likely to occur in some than others?

1 Borowitz 2 Freud
3 Dollard and Miller 4 Lorenz

Ans. (1)

Exp. Borowitz said that the nature and frequency of human aggressive behaviours tend to vary greatly across different human societies and are more likely to take place in certain societies than the others.

According to him, people in different cultures strongly differ in their support for aggressive or confrontational responses. Those in individualistic cultures such as the United States tend to support aggressive responding more than those in collectivistic cultures such as China, Turkey, or Ghana.

26 On a Wechsler type Adult Intelligence Scale, having normally distributed scores, the subject had a percentile rank of 84. His deviation IQ would be

1 84 2 85
3 115 4 120

Ans. (3)

Exp. The subject's deviation IQ would be 115.

In the Wechsler's Adult Intelligence Scale (WAIS), a deviation IQ is the absolute measure of how a person deviates from the mean on a given IQ test. In WAIS, a percentile rank refers to the percentage of scores that are lower than the person's obtained score. For instance, if the subject's percentile rank in the given case is 84th, then their score is higher than the scores obtained by 84% of the population on whom the test has already been administered. The corresponding Z-score to the 84th percentile is +0.99. The formula for transforming a Z-score into a Deviation IQ score is as follows: $100 + 15(z)$.

Deviation IQ $= 100 + 15(0.99) = 100 + 14.85 = 114.85 \sim 115$.

Therefore, the deviation IQ would be 115.

27 Which of the following endeavours to revalue the unique qualities associated with womanhood and feminity?

1 Cultural feminism
2 Liberal feminism
3 Radical feminism
4 Socialistic feminism

Ans. (1)

Exp. Cultural feminism endeavours to revalue the unique qualities associated with womanhood and feminity. Cultural feminism is a perspective which believes that there is a 'unique female essence,' and therefore, seeks to revalue the unique qualities associated with being a woman. For instance, it seeks to highlight the differences, especially biological, in males and females. The reproductive capacity of a woman is especially considered to have a superior, distinctive virtue. It also says that women share a perspectives and have a shared identity, which gives rise to feelings of 'sisterhood.'

28 First make a small request, when the person complies, make another large request. This concept is based on which compliance technique?

1 Foot-in-the-door 2 Door-in-the-face
3 Lowball 4 That's not all

Ans. (1)

Exp. The given concept of compliance is based on 'Foot-in-the-door' technique.

Foot-in-the-door technique is a compliance technique wherein getting someone to agree to a small request makes it more likely for them to agree to a bigger one. The underlying idea behind this is that once a person agrees to a small request, they find it difficult to refuse a bigger one. For instance, if one wants to borrow a certain amount of money from an acquaintance, they begin by borrowing a small sum, and then proceed to request a larger sum.

29 Mrs. 'B' has attained the level of 'self' in that she now takes genuine pleasure in prayer, meditation and other spiritual activities. Which type of 'self' is this in Sufism?

1 Serene self 2 Inspired self
3 Pleased self 4 Pure self

Ans. (2)

Exp. Mrs. 'B' has attained the 'Inspired self' in Sufism.

Sufism is an Islamic belief and practice wherein people seek to understand divine knowledge and love through a direct experience with God.

There are 7 stages of self in Sufism, one of which is the Inspired self. When one attains this self, one gains pleasure in prayer and other related spiritual activities. They also find joy in their spiritual experiences. Additionally, they are driven by ideals pertaining to moral values, compassion, and service. Therefore, it can be said that Mrs. 'B' has attained 'Inspired self'.

30 "When people are pressurised to admit guilt, but privately continue to believe in their own innocence".

Choose the correct answer of above statement.

1 Voluntary false confession
2 Coerced-compliant false confession
3 Coerced-internalised false confession
4 Character evidences

Ans. (2)

Exp. The given statement is 'Coerced-compliant false confession.'

Coerced-compliant false confession is given in cases where a potential suspect is subjected to aversive type of interrogation, and therefore, admits their guilt despite believing themselves to be innocent in order to escape the aversive situation.

Coerced-compliant false confession is also given when a potential suspect hopes to gain some implied reward. For instance, when subjected to aversive interrogation and they see no way out of it, if the interrogators promise to decrease their punishment or prison time, they tend to admit guilt despite believing in their innocent in order to escape a greater punishment.

31 What is theoretical approach called which attempts to explain completely the phenomenon of one field of study in terms of the dynamics of a more basic field?

1 Interactionism 2 Reductionism
3 Pragmatism 4 Comfiant solution

Ans. (2)

Exp. Reductionism is the theoretical approach that attempts to explain the phenomenon of one field of study in terms of the dynamics of a more basic field.

It is the practice of analysing complicated phenomena in terms of simpler or basic components, that is, it reduces complex phenomenon into simple components.

For instance, in an attempt to explain the workings of the brain and its impact on behaviour, reductionism seeks to analyse the way in which each part of the brain works, and how each part of the brain impacts behaviour.

32 The cognitive approach of prejudice arises from which theory that an individual's self-concept derives partly from membership in an 'in-group'?

1 Realistic group conflict theory
2 Scapegoat theory
3 Frustration aggression theory
4 Social identity theory

Ans. *(4)*

Exp. The cognitive approach to prejudice arises from the Social identity theory.

Social identity theory was given by Henri Tajfel. He stated that people desired to have a positive social identity by having the group that they belonged to (in-group) maintain its favourable social standing in comparison to other related out-groups. This favouritism towards one's in-group leads to discrimination against the out-groups, thereby giving rise to prejudice.

33 Which of the following explains the theory's ability to organise and explain several otherwise disjointed observations?

1 Heuristic function
2 Synthesising function
3 Principle of verification
4 Scientific function

Ans. *(2)*

Exp. Synthesising function helps to explain the theory's ability to organise and explain several otherwise disjointed observations.

In this function, several disjointed images or ideas are combined and brought together in order to form meaningful whole. Synthesising is the combination of parts, or elements, in order to form a more complete view or system. The coherent whole that results is considered to show the truth more completely than would a mere collection of parts.

34 Choose the correct answer for leadership style, low task, low relationship style

1 Participating style
2 Selling style
3 Delegating style
4 Telling style

Ans. *(3)*

Exp. Delegating style is a leadership style that is characterised by low task and low relationship style.

In this leadership style, the leader empowers people by providing them with autonomy, and trusting them to deliver the required results. However, this style only works best when the person who is entrusted with a certain task is competent and confident.

35 Which of the following is degenerative disease accompanied by Amnesia caused by frontotemporal lobular degeneration and depression?

1 Alzheimer's disease
2 Parkinson's disease
3 Pick's disease
4 Huntigton's disease

Ans. *(3)*

Exp. Pick's disease is a degenerative disease accompanied by Amnesia, and is caused by frontotempora lobular degeneration and depression. It is a kind of dementia that is akin to Alzheimer's diseases, however, it is rarer in comparison. Pick's disease affects several parts of the brain that moderate emotions, personality, behaviours, and language. It gives rise to depression, withdrawal, mood swings, irritability, and other related symptoms.

36 The vicious circles that maintain depression, loneliness and shyness can be broken by social skill training by positive experience that after self-perception by changing negative thought patterns. This is the description of which social-psychological approach to treatment?

1 Social skill training
2 Explanatory style therapy
3 Internal attribution
4 Social influence

Ans. *(1)*

Exp. The given description is of Social skill training approach to treatment.

The vicious circles that maintain depression, loneliness, and shyness, can be broken down by Social skills training. Many times, the psychological disorders or conditions adversely impact people's social lives. With people being social beings, they thrive, in part, on social interactions with other people. Without these interactions, the effects of depression and loneliness can lead to further detrimental effects. Therefore, Social skills training is geared towards providing people with social skills that help people in their social interactions, thereby becoming powerful tools in psychotherapy.

37 Which of the following is NOT true?

1 At the time of birth, the brain is not fully lateralised rather it is plastic
2 Though the left hemisphere is broadly associated with, language development, yet if it is injured during first few years, other regions take over language functions to attain the normal language competence
3 Damage to the left frontal lobe areas usually yields language comprehension problems
4 Broca's area supports grammatical processing and language production

Ans. *(3)*

Exp. Statement 3 is not true as damage to the left frontal lobe does not usually yields to language comprehension problems.

The left frontal lobe is a place where the Broca's area is located. Broca's area is responsible for speech production and fluency in speech. Therefore, damage to this area gives rise to problems with speech/language production, but not comprehension of language/speech. Language comprehension takes place in the Wernicke's area, which is located in the left temporal lobe.

38 The inferential technique that 'A' borrowed his father's car during a college vacation and smashed it after the party 'A' attended. Expected reaction of his father runs through A's mind and generates several possibilities. It is the example of which heuristic?

1 Availability heuristic
2 Representativeness heuristic
3 Conjunction error
4 Simulation heuristic

Ans. (4)

Exp. The given case is an example of Simulation heuristic.

In Simulation heuristic, the person imagines all the possible simulations, also referred to as alternative outcomes, in reaction to the event they encounter. It takes place after the person has gone through an event in their life. Consequently, in the given scenario, after 'A' borrows and crashes his father's car, him imagining all the expected reactions of his father is a demonstration of the Simulation heuristic.

39 Who has proposed a three componential theory of wisdom explaining cognitive, affective and reflective wisdom?

1 Sternberg 2 Baltes
3 Chandler 4 Ardelt

Ans. (4)

Exp. Monika Ardelt has given the three componential theory of wisdom, which explains cognitive, affective and reflective wisdom.

Ardelt says that wisdom has three dimensions, which are described as follows :

1. *Cognitive* : It refers to the understanding of one's life and the quest to learn the truth. It involves the comprehension of meaning and significance of different happenings in one's life, especially those pertaining to intrapersonal and interpersonal matters.
2. *Reflective* : It refers to the understanding of the events in one's life from all different perspectives. It involves self-awareness, self-insight, and self-examination.
3. *Affective* : It refers to being sympathetic and understanding towards other people.

40 The quotation, "People believe good things should happen to good people and bad things to bad people", represents

1 Blank-out hypothesis 2 Just world hypothesis
3 Karma-hypothesis 4 Retribution hypothesis

Ans. (2)

Exp. The given quotation represents the 'Just world hypothesis.'

Just world hypothesis is a cognitive bias that tends to assume that people get what they are deserving of. Hence, when people believe that good things happen to those people who are good, and bad things happen to those people who are bad, it is a reflection of the 'Just world hypothesis.'

41 Repeated presentation of negative events in mass-media may lead to increase in the occurrence of such negative events because of

1 Wither effect 2 Contagion effect
3 Frequency effect 4 Crespi effect

Ans. (2)

Exp. Repeated presentation of negative events in the mass-media may lead to an increase in the occurrences of negative events because of the Contagion effect.

Contagion effect is a social psychological phenomenon which refers to the inclination of certain behaviours being imitated by certain observers. The motive to emulate these behaviours comes from the desire to escape the restraints imposed upon people by the norms and society. Therefore, when there is a repeated presentation of negative events in the media, it may lead to an increase in negative events taking place in the world as a consequence of the contagion effect.

42 What is the term given to 'autonomy or being self-determining, independent and able to resist social pressures to think and act in certain ways'?

1 Emotional well-being
2 Social well-being
3 Psychological well-being
4 Physical well-being

Ans. (3)

Exp. The term 'Psychological well-being' refers to the 'autonomy or being self-determining, independent, and able to resist social pressures to think and act in certain ways'.

Well-being is a dynamic concept that includes subjective, social, and psychological dimensions as well as health-related behaviours. The Ryff Scales of Psychological Well-Being is a theoretically grounded instrument that specifically focuses on measuring multiple facets of psychological well-being. These facets include the following: self-acceptance, the establishment of quality ties to other, a sense of autonomy in thought and action, the ability to manage complex environments to suit personal needs and values, the pursuit of meaningful goals and a sense of purpose in life, and a continued growth and development as a person.

43 Who proved this observation that cyclists seemed to ride faster when they raced against other cyclist than when they raced alone?

1 Zajone 2 Allport
3 Baron 4 Norman Triplett

Ans. (4)

Exp. Normal Triplett proved the observation that cyclists seemed to ride faster when they raced against other cyclist than when they raced alone. This experimentation led to the discovery of the 'social facilitation effect,' which refers to either the increase or decrease in a person's performance when they tend to work with others as compared to when they tend to work alone.

44 Which one of the following is the correct answer of the experiment conducted in University of California at Santa Barbara; individuals running on jogging path speed up as they came upon a woman seated on the grass facing them rather than sitting with her back turned?

1 Distraction conflict
2 Presence of co-actor
3 Evaluation apprehension
4 Free riders

Ans. (3)

Exp. Evaluation apprehension is the correct choice for the experiment conducted in the University of California at Santa Barbara.

Evaluation apprehension is defined as the discomfort that arises out of the fear of being judged or evaluated by others. It is especially experienced by the participants of an experiment wherein they seek to be judged favourably by the experimenter or other observers. Therefore, when the participants sped up as they came upon a woman sitting on the grass facing them rather than when she was sitting with her back turned towards them, it is because of evaluation apprehension.

45 Which of the following is correct explanation of 'out-group homogeneity effect'?

1 Members of an in-group assume that other in-group members show their attitudes and values
2 Perception that members of out-group are more similar to each other than members of in-group are to each other.
3 The tendency to give more favourable evaluation and greater rewards to members of out-group.
4 People are arbitrarily classified into group than, allowed to allocate reward to each other.

Ans. (2)

Exp. A perception of the members of the out-group being more similar to each other than the members of the in-group are to each other is the description of the 'Out-group homogeneity effect.' Therefore, it refers to when people view the group they belong to (in-group) as being more diverse than the other relevant groups they do not belong to (out-groups). For instance, while Italians view themselves as being different from one another, Americans view Italians as being very similar to one another.

46 Multiple sclerosis is

I. Demyelinating disorder
II. An autoimmune disease
III. Always accompanied by amnesia and cognitive disorder
IV. Known to lead io jerky movements

Select the correct option

1 I and II
2 I, II and III
3 I, II and IV
4 I and IV

Ans. (3)

Exp. Multiple sclerosis is a demyelinating disorder, an autoimmune disease and is known to lead to jerky movements.

It is a demyelinating disorder in which the myelin sheath of neurons is damaged. In multiple sclerosis, insulating covers of nerve cells in the brain and spinal cord are damaged. This damage disrupts the ability of parts of the nervous system to transmit signals, resulting in a range of signs and symptoms, including physical, mental, and sometimes psychiatric problems. It is an autoimmune disorder that develops from an interaction of the individual's genetics and as yet unidentified environmental causes. Damage is believed to be caused, at least in part, by attack on the nervous system by a person's own immune system.

It is known to lead to jerky movements and can cause problems with movement, balance and coordination, including loss of balance, tremors, unstable walking (ataxia), giddiness (vertigo), clumsiness of a limb, lack of coordination, muscle weakness, tightness, stiffness or 'pull' of muscles (spasticity), and involuntary muscle spasms.

It is not always accompanied by amnesia and cognitive disorder. About half of people with multiple sclerosis have some cognitive problems, including memory loss or amnesia, often these problems are mild and don't interrupt a person's daily life.

47 Consideration of mental health needs of persons with cancer will have positive effects on

I. quality of life
II. emotional well-being
III. positive biological changes
IV. killing carcinogenic cells

Select the correct option

1 I and II
2 III and IV
3 I, II and III
4 II, III and IV

Ans. (3)

Exp. Consideration of mental health needs of persons with cancer will have positive effects on quality of life, emotional well-being, and positive biological changes.

When a person is affected with cancer, it leads to a myriad of physical effects. However, it can adversely impact the mental health of the person as well. For instance, they can experience anxiety, depression, fear of death, and other related conditions.

Therefore, when consideration is given to the psychological requirements of the person affected with cancer, and adequate therapy and social support is provided to the person, it helps facilitate their emotional well-being and increases their quality of life as well. This positive impact can bring about positive changes in the body as well.

48 Which of the following are steps of problem solving cycle?

I. Problem identification
II. Problem definition
III. Organisation
IV. Allocation of resources

Select the correct option :

1 I and II
2 III and IV
3 II, III and IV
4 I, II, III and IV

Ans. (4)

Exp. Problem identification, Problem definition Organisation and Allocation of resources are steps of problem solving cycle.

The steps of problem solving cycle are as follows :

I. *Problem identification* : This involves recognising the problem that requires solving. In cases of multiple problems, it requires prioritising.
II. *Problem definition* : This refers to defining the problem that is required to be solved.
III. *Organisation* : This refers to organising the different pieces of information in a problem in order to make them fit together.
IV. *Allocation of resources* : This refers to considering and deciding upon the time, effort, and money, among others, one is required to put towards solving the problem.

49 Which of the following are characteristics of post-trauma growth?

I. Relationships are strengthened or enhanced
II. Self-views become more positive
III. Life philosophies become ambiguous
IV. Greater acceptance of personal limitations

Select the correct option

1 I, II and III
2 I, II and IV
3 II, III and IV
4 I, III and IV

Ans. (2)

Exp. Among the given statements regarding the characteristics of post-trauma growth, statements I, II, and IV are correct.

Post-traumatic growth is a theory that seeks to explain the ways in which people transform after having experienced something traumatic in their lives. The characteristics of post-trauma growth are :

1. People develop a new understanding or insight into themselves, which makes them more accepting of their weaknesses or shortcomings.
2. People also understand the way they relate to other people, which may lead to an improvement or strengthening of their relationships with significant others in their lives.
3. They may also have an understanding of the future they may have, and an understanding into the way in which they must lead their lives hereon, which may give rise to ambiguity in their life philosophies.

50 Marked impairments in establishing social interactions and living in their own worlds, repetitive behaviour patterns and non-existent or poor language skills are three major characteristics of which disorder/s?

I. Autism
II. Obsessive-compulsive disorder
III. Catatonic schizophrenia
IV. Apraxia

Select the correct option:

1 Only I
2 Only II and III
3 Only IV
4 Only I and IV

Ans. (1)

Exp. Autism is a disorder that is characterised by impairments in developing social interactions and living in their own worlds, exhibition of repetitive behavioural patterns, and poor or non-existent language skills. Autism is a condition that is related to brain development, which leads to all the aforementioned problems. It is often referred to as 'Autism Spectrum Disorder,' with the spectrum referring the symptoms ranging from mild to severe.

51 Which of the following theorists used the ideographic approach to personality?

I. Allport
II. Kelley
III. Cattell
IV. Eysenck

Select the correct option

1 Only I and II
2 Only I and III
3 Only III and IV
4 Only I, III and IV

Ans. (1)

Exp. Allport and Kelly used the idiographic approach to personality.

The ideographic approach to personality suggests that every person has a psychological makeup that is unique to them. Therefore, their personality possesses certain traits or combination of traits that are unique to them alone. Gordon Allport's Trait Theory of Personality and George Kelly's Personal Construct Theory, both, emphasise the uniqueness of people's personalities.

52 Which among the following are the assumptions on which Binet developed his first test of intelligence?

I. Mental competence increases over the childhood years.
II. Child's relative standing in mental development compared to his age group will remain constant as the child grows.
III. Child's relative standing in mental development compared to his age group increases as the child grows.
IV. Mental competence decreases over the childhood years.

Select the correct option

1 I and II 2 I and III
3 II and III 4 II and IV

Ans. (1)

Exp. Among the given statements regarding the assumptions on the basis of which Binet developed his first test of intelligence, only statements I and II are correct.

Alfred Binet developed his first intelligence test that measured people's intelligence (IQ) in the year 1916 in order to assess the children who may face difficulties in academics, and may require special assistance as a consequence. He based his intelligence test on the following two assumptions :

1. Mental competence of children increases during their childhood years.
2. Child's relative standing in mental development in comparison to their age group will remain constant as the child grows.

53 Which of the following is/are true about rhodopsin?

I. It is a rod pigment that enables vision in low light.
II. It is a cone pigment that enables vision in bright light.
III. It is a G-protein coupled receptor.
IV. It is a cone pigment and G-protein coupled receptor.

Select the correct option:

1 Only I 2 I, III and IV
3 Only II 4 I and III

Ans. (4)

Exp. Among the given statements regarding rhodopsin, only statements I and III are true.

Rhodopsin is a light-sensitive protein that converts light into an electrical signal. It is a rod pigment which is present in the rod photoreceptor cells, and facilitates vision in dim light conditions. It is a G-protein coupled receptor, which means that it binds to extracellular substances, and transmits the signals from these extracellular substances to an intracellular molecule that is referred to as the G-protein.

54 In Torrance Test of Creative Thinking (figural), picture construction activity is scored for which of the following?

I. Fluency II. Flexibility
III. Originality IV. Elaboration

Select the correct option

1 Only I and II 2 Only III and IV
3 Only II, III and IV 4 I, II, III and IV

Ans. (2)

Exp. In Torrance Test of Creative Thinking (TTCT), picture construction activity is scored for Originality and Elaboration.

Ellis Paul Torrance created the Torrance Tests of Creative Thinking (TTCT) which measured creativity. The TTCT had 4 scales, and the picture construction activity was scored for the following two :

1. *Originality* – The rarity of the ideas.
2. *Elaboration* – The detail present in the ideas.

55 Fill in the blanks by choosing the right sequence

In the upside-down and reversed-image projection process on_____, the _____ bends the rays entering the eye and the light rays from the top of an object are projected onto _____ at the bottom of_____ .

Select the correct option

1 receptors, lens, retina, retina
2 lens, retina, receptors, retina
3 retina, lens, receptors, retina
4 retina, lens, retina, receptors

Ans. (3)

Exp. In the upside-down and reversed-image projection process on the retina, the lens bends the rays entering the eye and the light rays from the top of an object are projected onto the receptors at the bottom of the retina. The images on the retina are projected in an upside-down manner, and the retina sees everything in reverse (backwards), however, the brain is involved in reorienting the images.

56 Which of the following are the behaviours identified by Maslow that lead to self-actualisation?

I. Growth choices II. Use of Ego defence
III. Self-awareness IV. Concentration

Select the correct option

1 I, II and III only 2 I, III and IV only
3 III and IV only 4 I, II and IV only

Ans. (2)

Exp. Growth choices, Self-awareness and Concentration are the behaviours identified by Abraham Maslow as leading towards self-actualisation.

As per Maslow, self-actualisation is the highest need which is geared towards reaching one's full potential. The behaviours that facilitate self-actualisation are:

1. *Growth Choices* : These refer to choosing the choices related to growth rather than regression, and making progressive choices in one's life leads towards self-actualisation.
2. *Self-awareness* : It refers to the consciousness about one's thinking patterns, emotions, and other sensations help in achieving self-actualisation.
3. *Concentration* : It refers to focusing and experiencing life like a child, with full absorption.

57 Retrieval is more commonly explained as the basis of which generation recognition theory?

I. Information Processing
II. Iconic Image
III. Sensory Register
IV. Primary Effect

Select the correct option.

1 I, II and III only
2 Only I
3 II and III only
4 Only II and IV

Ans. (1)

Exp. Retrieval is more commonly explained on the basis of Iconic image, Sensory register, and Information processing.

In memory, iconic image and sensory register are those concepts that allow memory to be stored in its original state. However, it lasts only for a fraction of a second in this state. Encoding allows this information to be processed, and stored in the short-term memory, and further, in the long-term memory.

Retrieval is the third stage of Information Processing. It involves recalling information for the purpose of utilising it for some task or another.

For retrieval to take place, information from iconic image and sensory register ought to be processed, which happens via information processing.

58 Which of the following are true for bootstrapping?

I. It involves large number of sub-samples.

II. It does not rely on assumptions about population.

III. It is applicable in case of nonmetric data only.

IV. It is based on sample data only.

Select the correct option

1 Only I and II
2 Only I, II and III
3 Only I, II and IV
4 Only II, III and IV

Ans. (3)

Exp. Among the given statements regarding bootstrapping, statements I, II, and IV are true.

Bootstrapping is a concept in statistics wherein new samples are generated from already existing samples. So, if bootstrapping is done 100 times, 100 new samples are generated. With regards to bootstrapping, the following are true:

It involves a large number of sub-samples. The bootstrap sample is taken from the original by using sampling with replacement, so, assuming N is sufficiently large, for all practical purposes there is virtually zero probability that it will be identical to the original 'real' sample. This process is repeated a large number of times (typically 1,000 or 10,000 times), and for each of these bootstrap samples, we compute its mean (each of these is called bootstrap estimates).

It does not rely on any presumptions regarding the population. It is often used as an alternative to statistical inference based on the assumption of a parametric model when that assumption is in doubt, or where parametric inference is impossible or requires complicated formulas for the calculation of standard errors.

It is done only on the basis of the sample data. The basic idea of bootstrapping is that inference about a population from sample data (sample $\rightarrow$ population) can be modelled by resampling the sample data and performing inference about a sample from resampled data (resampled $\rightarrow$ sample).

Statement III is incorrect as it is not applicable in case of non-metric data only, rather there are three different ways of obtaining and evaluating bootstrap estimates: non-parametric, parametric, and semi-parametric. In practice, because non-parametric intervals make parametric assumptions, this division is rather arbitrary. Whilst these terms may provide some insight, they are not very useful classification.

59 According to self-determination theory, which of the following form the bases of intrinsic motivation?

1 Experience, Competence
2 Competence, Autonomy
3 Competence, Novelty Seeking
4 Novelty Seeking, Sensation Seeking

Ans. (2)

Exp. As per the self-determination theory, Competence and Autonomy form the bases of intrinsic motivation.

Self-determination theory purports that people are driven towards growth by the innate needs of autonomy, competence and connection. They become self-determined when these three needs are met.

Intrinsic motivation, which is the motivation that arises from within, is based on:

1. *Autonomy* : People have a need to be in control and responsible for their own behaviours and goals.
2. *Competence* : People have an innate need to gain mastery over skills and tasks.

60 Mechanistic view of motivation can be characterised by which of the following?

I. S-O-R

II. Direction is determined by S-R bonds.

III. Probability of habits depends on prior reinforcement contingencies.

IV. Persistence of behaviour

Select the correct option

1 Only I, II and III
2 Only I, II and IV
3 Only II, III and IV
4 I, II, III and IV

Ans. (3)

Exp. Among the given statements regarding the characteristics of mechanistic view of motivation, statements II, III, and IV are correct.

Mechanistic approach assumes that psychological needs and behaviours can be explained the same way as the physiological ones. It uses the metaphor of a machine to explain these. The mechanistic view characterises motivation as:

1. Being directed by the Stimulus-Response (S-R) bonds.
2. The likelihood of habits is dependent upon the prior reinforcement contingencies.
3. Persistence of behaviour.

61 Mayer-Salovey-Caruso Emotional Intelligence Test (MSCEIT) measures which of the following?

I. Perceiving emotions
II. Using emotions to facilitate thought
III. Understanding emotions
IV. Self-motivation

Select the correct option

1 I and II
2 III and IV
3 I, II and III
4 II, III and IV

Ans. (3)

Exp. Mayer-Salovey-Caruso Emotional Intelligence Test (MSCEIT) measures:

1. Perceiving emotions
2. Utilising emotions for the purpose of facilitating thinking
3. Understanding emotions

The Mayer-Salovey-Caruso Emotional Intelligence Test is an ability test that is designed to test Emotional Intelligence (EI) as purported by Mayer and Salovey. It consists of 141 test items, and takes approximately 30-45 minutes to complete.

62 Given below are two statements, one labelled as Assertion (A) and other labelled as Reason (R). Read the statements.

Assertion (A) A 3 to 4 year-old will readily handover a blanket to another individual who is rubbing hands and shivering a lot.

Reason (R) In sensitive face-to-face communication, infants connect emotionally with their caregivers, this experience is believed to be foundation for empathy.

Choose the correct answer from the options given below

1 Both (A) and (R) are true and (R) is the correct explanation of (A)
2 Both (A) and (R) are true but (R) is not the correct explanation of (A)
3 (A) is true, but (R) is false
4 (A) is false, but (R) is true

Ans. (2)

Exp. Both (A) and (R) are true but (R) is not the correct explanation of (A).

A 3 to 4 years-old child will hand over their blanket to another person who is feeling cold and shivering a lot. This is because at 3-4 years of age, children are able to relate to other people if they share the same perspective. Since 3-4-years-old child does understand how severe cold can be an unpleasant feeling, they empathise with the other person, and therefore, hand over a blanket to them.

Infants are able to connect with their caregivers through face-to-face communication, and this is the foundation of empathy.

While both the above mentioned statements are true, Reason (R) is not the correct explanation of Assertion (A) as the former is speaking about infants, while given Assertion pertains to empathy in early childhood years.

63 Given below are two statements, one labelled as Assertion (A) and other labelled as Reason (R). Read the statements.

Assertion (A) Method of calculating IQ in terms of $\frac{MA}{CA} \times 100$ as such does not work with adults.

Reason (R) Intelligence does not increase linearly with age past childhood.

Choose the correct answer from the options given below

1 Both (A) and (R) are true and (R) is the correct explanation of (A)
2 Both (A) and (R) are true, but (R) is not the correct explanation of (A)
3 (A) is true, but (R) is false
4 (A) is false, but‘ (R) is true

Ans. (1)

Exp. Both (A) and (R) are true and (R) is the correct explanation of (A)

The method of calculating IQ in terms of Mental Age (MA) / Chronological Age (CA) x 100 does not work when it comes to adults.

This is because the above mentioned method of calculating IQ only helps to explain the linear growth of IQ of a child, as to how they are doing for their age. However, IQ does not grow in linear direction past one's childhood years. Generally, it is said to stabilise around the age of 10 years. Therefore, this method is not useful when it comes to adults' IQ.

64 Given below are two statements, one labelled as Assertion (A) and other labelled as Reason (R). Read the statements.

Assertion (A) Intelligent teachers select information that is relevant for their pedagogical purpose.

Reason (R) Selective combination involves determining which elements in a set of information are relevant for a given purpose.

Choose the correct answer from the options given below

1 Both (A) and (R) are true and (R) is the correct explanation of (A)
2 Both (A) and (R) are true, but (R) is not the correct explanation of (A)
3 (A) is true, but (R) is false
4 (A) is false, but (R) is true

Ans. (3)

Exp. (A) is true, but (R) is false

Intelligent teachers tend to select information that is relevant for their pedagogical purpose which refers to an activity of learning that helps benefit students more than just delivering the content required to be learnt.

Selective combination refers to the identification of a problem by analysing its different components, and combining them together in order to form meaningful wholes. However, it does not pertain to identifying which elements in given information are relevant for a given purpose.

65 Given below are two statements, one labelled as Assertion (A) and other labelled as Reason (R). Read the statements.

Assertion (A) Clients must be allowed complete freedom to discuss in their natural manner to communicate respect and acceptance.

Reason (R) Completely suspending the judgement and expressing positive regard are Rogers' core therapeutic conditions.

Choose the correct answer from the options given below

1 Both (A) and (R) are true and (R) is the correct explanation of (A)
2 Both (A) and (R) are true, but (R) is not the correct explanation of (A)
3 (A) is truc, but (R) is false
4 (A) is false, but (R) is true

Ans. (1)

Exp. Both (A) and (R) are true and (R) is the correct explanation of (A).

In a therapeutic setting, clients must be given a platform wherein they can speak and discuss their problems in a direct and natural manner so as to communicate respect and acceptance.

This is crucial because Carl Rogers says that unconditional positive regard is complete acceptance of a client without judgement, and this forms the core of a therapy. That is, if clients are made to feel they are accepted and respected without any judgement on the part of the therapist, only then will they be able to discuss their problems without hesitation. Otherwise, they tend to hold back, and this is detrimental for the purpose and progress of psychotherapy.

66 Given below are two statements, one labelled as assertion (A) and other labelled as Reason (R). Read the statements.

Assertion (A) Mental stress may cause cardiac ischemia.

Reason (R) Stress unfavourably affects the balance between cardiac demand and supply.

Choose the correct answer from the options given below

1 Both (A) and (R) are true and (R) is the correct explanation of (A)
2 Both (A) and (R) are true, but (R) is not the correct explanation of (A)
3 (A) is true, but (R) is false
4 (A) is false, but (R) is true

Ans. (1)

Exp. Both (A) and (R) are true and (R) is the correct explanation of (A).

Mental stress may lead to cardiac ischemia.

The above happens because stress adversely impacts the balance between cardiac demand and supply, which leads to cardiac ischemia. That is, cardiac ischemia happens because of decreased oxygen and blood flow the heart, which is among the physiological effects of stress.

67 Given below are two statements, one labelled as Assertion (A) and other labelled as Reason (R). Read the statements.

Assertion (A) If children watch programmes with violent and aggressive contents, they themselves take recourse to violent and aggressive behaviour.

Reason (R) Children learn aggressive behaviour from media through observational learning, where the observed behaviour need not be positively reinforced.

Choose the correct answer from the options given below

1 Both (A) and (R) are true and (R) is the correct explanation of (A)
2 Both (A) and (R) are true, but (R) is not the correct explanation of (A)
3 (A) is true, but (R) is false
4 (A) is false, but (R) is true

Ans. (1)

Exp. Both (A) and (R) are true and (R) is the correct explanation of (A).

When children watch aggressive and violent behaviours on media, they tend to imitate the same.

The above happens because of observational learning wherein people learn behaviours by watching others and replicating the same in the future. This type of learning does not require the observed behaviour to be reinforced. It happens because of symbolic modelling, wherein real or fictional characters in live/print media facilitate observational learning.

68 Given below are two statements, one labelled as Assertion (A) and other labelled as Reason (R). Read the statements.

Assertion (A) According to classical theory of test scores, total variance is equal to true variance plus error variance.

Reason (R) Classical theory of test scores assumes significant but low positive correlation between true scores and error scores.

Choose the correct answer from the options given below

1 Both (A) and (R) are true and (R) is the correct explanation of (A)
2 Both (A) and (R) are true, but (R) is not the correct explanation of (A)
3 (A) is true, but (R) is false
4 (A) is false, but (R) is true

Ans. *(3)*

Exp. (A) is true, but (R) is false.

The classical test theory purports that every person has a true score that can be obtained if there were no errors in measurement. Therefore, it suggests that total variance in scores is equal to true variance plus error variance.

Classical test theory does not assume significant but low positive correlation between true scores and error scores. In fact, the classical test theory actually assumes that errors are uncorrelated with the true score.

69 Given below are two statements, one labelled as Assertion (A) and other labelled as Reason (R). Read the statements.

Assertion (A) Focus group involves unstructured interview.

Reason (R) Focus group involves interaction among participants moderated by the researcher, as a source of data.

Choose the correct answer from the options given below

1 Both (A) and (R) are true and (R) is the correct explanation of (A)
2 Both (A) and (R) are true, but (R) is not the correct explanation of (A)
3 (A) is true, but (R) is false
4 (A) is false, but (R) is true

Ans. *(4)*

Exp. (A) is false, but (R) is true.

Focus group refers to a group interview involving a small group of people who demographically resemble one another. However, in a focus group, the interview does not happen to be unstructured.

Focus group involves a group interview of a group of participants, and it also involves interaction among the participants that is regulated by the researcher, and in this way, the interactions serve as a source of data for their research.

70 Given below are two statements, one labelled as Assertion (A) and other labelled as Reason (R). Read the statements.

Assertion (A) Changing client's perception requires persuasive skills and direction from the counsellor and such input is known as 'lead'.

Reason (R) Counsellor should make minimum verbal responses and maintain silence so that clients feel some pressure to continue; and will choose to continue with minimum input from the counsellor; thus counsellor taking a good lead.

Choose the correct answer from the options given below

1 Both (A) and (R) are true and (R) is the correct explanation of (A)
2 Both (A) and (R) are true, but (R) is not the correct explanation of (A)
3 (A) is true, but (R) is false
4 (A) is false, but (R) is true

Ans. *(3)*

Exp. (A) is true, but (R) is false.

In therapy, when the perspective of the client requires to be changed so as to facilitate their healthy functioning, the therapist is required to use their persuasive skills and direction in order to help their client in doing so. This input from the counsellor is referred to as 'lead.'

In therapy, counsellor is not always required to maintain silence or give only minimum of verbal responses. Therapy involves a two-way communication, and therefore, the counsellor must respond when required.

For instance, reflective statements from the counsellor help communicate understanding and empathy towards the client. Maintaining silence or giving few verbal responses is not an indication of a good lead on part of the counsellor.

71 Given below are two statements, one labelled as Assertion (A) and other labelled as Reason (R). Read the statements.

Assertion (A) Tolman's purposive behaviourism was considered to be a major advancement in the field of Psychology.

Reason (R) Pre-Tolman behaviourism excessively emphasised S-R relations and ignored cognitive processes.

Choose the correct answer from the options given below

1 Both (A) and (R) are true and (R) is the correct explanation of (A)
2 Both (A) and (R) are true, but (R) is not the correct explanation of (A)
3 (A) is true, but (R) is false
4 (A) is false, but (R) is true

Ans. *(1)*

Exp. Both (A) and (R) are true and (R) is the correct explanation of (A).

As per Edward Tolman's purposive behaviourism, an organism learns when they are in pursuit of a certain goal. This theory was considered to be a major advancement in the field of Psychology.

Tolman's purposive behaviourism was considered to be a major advancement in the field of Psychology because prior to his theory, learning was said to take place as a consequence of associations between stimulus and response. It ignored the cognitive aspect of learning entirely. However, when Tolman said that learning happens when the organism is pursuing a certain goal they had in mind, it reflected the importance of cognition in learning as well.

72 Given below are two statements one labelled as Assertion (A) and other labelled as Reason (R). Read the statements.

Assertion (A) According to Freud, painful memories are the target of Repression.

Reason (R) Repression can be primal i.e. innately part of the Id or Proper i.e , unacceptable derivates of original Id impulses.

Choose the correct answer from the options given below

1 Both (A) and (R) are true and (R) is the correct explanation of (A)
2 Both (A) and (R) are true, but (R) is not the correct explanation of (A)
3 (A) is true, but (R) is false
4 (A) is false, but (R) is true

Ans. *(2)*

Exp. Both (A) and (R) are true, but (R) is not the correct explanation of (A).

As per Sigmund Freud, people tend to repress memories that are painful. This is referred to as 'repression.' Repressed memories are the content of the unconscious mind, and they tend to influence one's personalities and behaviours.

As per Freud, repression is innate part of the Id, and it happens to be unacceptable derivations of the original Id impulses.

While both of the above statements are true, the fact that repressed memories are unacceptable derivations of the original impulses of the Id, it does not explain why they are painful and why they are repressed. The reason painful memories are repressed is because their awareness is threatening to the ego.

73 Given below are two statements, one labelled as Assertion (A) and other labelled as Reason (R). Read the statements.

Assertion (A) According to Rogers, all people, are capable of growth and personal development.

Reason (R) Positive change is a natural and expected progression.

Choose the correct answer from the options given below

1 Both (A) and (R) are true and (R) is the correct explanation of (A)
2 Both (A) and (R) are true, but (R) is not the correct explanation of (A)
3 (A) is true, but (R) is false
4 (A) is false, but (R) is true

Ans. *(1)*

Exp. Both (A) and (R) are true and (R) is the correct explanation of (A).

As per Carl Rogers, all people have an actualising tendency. That is, all people have a tendency towards realising and achieving their full potential. One of the ways this happens is when people make choices pertaining to growth. Therefore, all people have a tendency towards growth as they have internal resources for personal growth.

Rogers says that growth happens because positive change is natural in organisms, and is an expected part of progression.

74 Given below are two statements one labelled as Assertion (A) and other labelled as Reason (R). Read the statements.

Assertion (A) If all the assumptions are ful-filled, addition of any predictor in the Multiple Regression Analysis will increase the value of coefficient of determination.

Reason (R) Correlation of criterion variables with the predictor variables can be positive or negative.

Choose the correct answer from the options given below

1 Both (A) and (R) are true and (R) is the correct explanation of (A)
2 Both (A) and (R) are true, but (R) is not the correct explanation of (A)
3 (A) is true, but (R) is false
4 (A) is false, but (R) is true

Ans. *(1)*

Exp. Both (A) and (R) are true and (R) is the correct explanation of (A).

If all the required assumptions are fulfilled, then any predictor in the Multiple Regression Analysis tends to increase the value of coefficient of determination. Coefficient of determination (R2) explains how the differences in one variable can be explained by differences in others.

The above happens because the correlation of criterion variables with the predictor variables can either be positive or negative. Therefore, any addition of predictor variables can increase the value of coefficient of determination.

75 Given below are two statements, one labelled as Assertion (A) and other labelled as Reason (R). Read the statements.

Assertion (A) In simple regression analysis, if the value of one regression coefficient (b_{xy}) is less than 1.00, the value of second regression coefficient (b_{yx}) has to be less than 1.00.

Reason (R) The correlation between two variables and is equal to the geometric mean between the two regression coefficients (b_{xy} and b_{yx}).

Choose the correct answer from the options given below

1 Both (A) and (R) are true and (R) is the correct explanation of (A)
2 Both (A) and (R) are true, but (R) is not the correct explanation of (A)
3 (A) is true, but (R) is false
4 (A) is false, but (R) is true

Ans. *(4)*

Exp. (A) is false, but (R) is true.

In simple regression analysis, if the value of one regression coefficient (b_{xy}) is less than 1.00, the value of second regression coefficient (b_{yx}) has to be less than 1.00. This is false as in simple regression analysis, if the value of one regression coefficient is less than 1.00, it is not necessary that the value of the second regression coefficient must also be less than 1.00. However, if one regression coefficient is greater than unit (1.00), then the other must be less than unit (1.00) but not vice versa. ie. both the regression coefficients can be less than unity but both cannot be greater than unity, ie. if $b1>1$ then $b2<1$ and if $b2>1$, then $b1<1$.

The correlation between two variables and is equal to the geometric mean between the two regression coefficients (b_{xy} and b_{yx}). The coefficient of correlation is the geometric mean of two regression coefficient. The formula for calculating correlation coefficient, $r = \sqrt{b_{xy} \times b_{yx}}$.

76 Given below are two statements, one labelled as Assertion (A) and other labelled as Reason (R). Read the statements.

Assertion (A) The likelihood that fetal alcohol syndrome will occur depends on the social environment.

Reason (R) Social influences also act upon developing, the brain and mind.

Choose the correct answer from the options given below

1 Both (A) and (R) are true and (R) is the correct explanation of (A)
2 Both (A) and (R) are true, but (R) is not the correct explanation of (A)
3 (A) is true, but (R) is false
4 (A) is false, but (R) is true

Ans. *(4)*

Exp. (A) is false, but (R) is true

If a woman drinks during pregnancy, the baby is likely to develop fetal alcohol syndrome. Therefore, the likelihood of fetal alcohol syndrome is not dependent on the social environment, but the environment of the mother's womb. Social influences tend to have a role to play in the development of the mind and the brain. For instance, when children are mentally stimulated, it positively impacts the development of their mind and brain.

77 Which of the following sequences of decision making perspectives of prosocial behaviour is correct?

1 Perceived need → taking personal responsibility → weighing the cost and benefits → deciding how to help → help is given
2 Taking personal responsibility → deciding how to help → help is given → weighing the cost and benefits → perceived need
3 Weighing the cost and benefits → perceived need →deciding how to help → help is given → taking personal responsibility.
4 Perceived need → weighing the cost and benefits → deciding how to help → taking personal responsibility → help is given

Ans. *(1)*

Exp. The correct sequences of decision making perspectives of prosocial behaviours is:

Perceived need → taking personal responsibility → weighing the cost and benefits → deciding how to help → help is given.

Pro-social behaviours are geared towards helping/benefitting others. The decision-making process while engaging in pro-social behaviour to help a person in distress is:

1. *Perceived a need* : A person's judgement regarding the requirement of a certain service.
2. *Taking personal responsibility* : It involves taking personal responsibility towards the person in distress in terms of helping them.
3. *Weighing the cost and benefits* : Evaluating the way in which their prosocial behaviour is going to cost them, and how it benefits the person in distress. The benefits must outweigh the costs.
4. *Deciding how to help* : Choosing a plan of action and executing it.
5. *Help is given* : After deciding how to help, help is provided to the person in need.

78 Arrange the following in correct sequence of development of emotional expressions

I. Self-conscious emotions emerge but depend on monitoring and encouragement of adults.
II. Expression of happiness increases while interacting with familiar people.
III. Anger and fear increase in frequency and intensity.
IV. Self-conscious emotions are clearly linked to self-evaluation.

Select the correct option.

1 II, I, III, IV　　2 II, III, I, IV
3 II, III, IV, I　　4 III, II, I, IV

Ans. *(2)*

Exp. The correct chronological order for the development of emotional expression is II, III, I, and IV.

When it comes to the development of emotional expressions in a person, the order for the same happens as follows:

1. First, the emotional expression of happiness develops. It tends to increase when one is interacting with familiar people. The foundation for this is laid when the infant develops a bond with their caregiver who happen to be familiar to them.
2. Following happiness, the emotional expression for anger and fear develop.
3. Self-conscious emotions, such as embarrassment, emerge later on, however, they depend on the monitoring of the adults. For instance, Erik Erikson explains that in the second stage of psychosocial development (Autonomy vs. Shame), children tend to feel shame when they are shamed by their parents for not being able to control their bodily functions, such as bowel movements.
4. Self-conscious emotions are linked to self-evaluation. For instance, when people tend to feel shame or embarrassed, it is attributed to negative evaluation of themselves.

79 Which of the following sequences of Bandura's observational learning is correct?

1 Attention process → retention → production → motivation

2 Retention → attention process → production → motivation

3 Attention process → motivation → retention → production

4 Attention process → retention → motivation → production

Ans. (1)

Exp. The correct chronological order of Bandura's observational learning is:

Attention process → retention → production → motivation.

As per Albert Bandura, observational learning is a form of learning wherein people acquire behaviours by observing others engaging in them, and repeating the same.

Observational learning takes place in four steps:

1. *Attention process* : This refers to focussing on the behaviour a person/people are engaging in.
2. *Retention* : This refers to committing the information one has observed to memory.
3. *Production* : This refers to reproducing or performed the observed behaviour.
4. *Motivation* : This refers to the motivation involved that enables the repetition of the observed behaviour.

80 Match List I with List II.

List I (Concept)	List II (Description)
A. Impairment	I. Any loss or abnormality of psychological, physiological or anatomical structure or function
B. Disability	II. Any restriction or lack of ability to perform an activity in age appropriate manner
C. Handicap	III. Perception and assessment of one's abilities to be lower relative to others
D. Disadvantage	IV. Inability to perform with expected norms

Codes

	A	B	C	D		A	B	C	D
1	I	II	III	IV	2	II	IV	I	III
3	III	I	IV	II	4	IV	III	II	I

Ans. (1)

Exp. The correct matching is A–I, B–II, C–III, D–IV.

Impairment refers to any loss or abnormality of psychological, physiological, or anatomical structure or function. For instance, speech impairments can give rise to problems in production and comprehension of speech.

Disability refers to any restriction or lack of ability to perform an activity in age appropriate manner. For instance, dyslexia is a reading disability wherein people are unable to exhibit the level of reading skills that is expected of their age.

Handicap refers to a perception and assessment of one's abilities to be lower in relation to others.

Disadvantage refers to the inability to perform with expected norms. For instance, people from impoverished backgrounds may not have access to education, therefore, they are at a disadvantage and may not be able to perform as per the norms pertaining to academics.

81 Match List I with List II.

List I (Psychologist)	List II (Concept)
A. Carol Ryff	I. Psychological well-being
B. Seligman	II. Signature strength
C. Victor Frankl	III. Post-traumatic growth
D. Suler	IV. Online inhibition effect

Codes

	A	B	C	D		A	B	C	D
1	I	II	III	IV	2	II	IV	I	III
3	III	I	IV	II	4	IV	III	II	I

Ans. (1)

Exp. The correct matching is A–I, B–II, C –III, D–IV

Carol Ryff said that psychological well-being comprised 6 dimensions, namely, self-acceptance, personal growth, autonomy, environmental mastery, purpose in life, positive interpersonal relations.

Martin Seligman gave the concept of Signature strength, and said that signature strengths were those characteristics that a person possesses, celebrates, and exhibits frequently.

Victor Frankl gave the concept of Post-traumatic growth, which seeks to explain the ways in which people's lives transforms after they have undergone something traumatic.

Suler gave the concept of online disinhibition effect, which explains how virtual communication facilitates the lack of restraint in people's communications with one another.

82 **Match List I with List II.**

List I (Concept)	List II (Description)
A. Savouring	I. Applying conscious awareness to enjoyment of experiences
B. Hedonic adaptation	II. Happiness due to circumstances tends to be temporary
C. Type-A behaviour	III. Hurry syndrome behaviour
D. Undoing hypothesis	IV. Positive emotions lead to a quick recovery from detrimental effects

Codes

	A	B	C	D		A	B	C	D
1	I	II	III	IV	2	II	IV	I	III
3	III	I	IV	II	4	IV	III	II	I

Ans. *(1)*

➲ *Exp.* The correct matching is A–I, B– II, C–III, D–IV.

Savouring refers to applying conscious awareness to enjoyment of experiences. For instance, a voracious reader consciously enjoys their reading experiences, savouring the moments they spend reading.

Hedonic adaptation refers to the happiness due to circumstances which tends to be temporary. This phenomenon describes the way in which people return to their stable state of happiness after they have experienced either positive or negative changes in their lives.

Type-A behaviour is the hurry syndrome behaviour. That is, it is characterised by an intense sense of urgency, impatience, competitive behaviours, and even aggressiveness and hostilities.

Undoing hypothesis refers to the theory that positive emotions lead to a quick recovery from detrimental effects. That is, this hypothesis posits that positive emotions facilitate faster recovery from the physiological response to stressful events.

83 **Match List I with List II**

List I (Concept)	List II (Explanation)
A. Mental representation	I. Building schemas through direct interaction with environment
B. Operations	II. Using current schemas to interpret the external world
C. Adaptation	III. The ability to remember and copy the behaviour of models who are not present
D. Assimilation	IV. Mental representation of actions they obey using logical rules.

Codes

	A	B	C	D		A	B	C	D
1	IV	III	I	II	2	IV	II	I	III
3	III	IV	I	II	4	II	I	IV	III

Ans. *(3)*

➲ *Exp.* The correct matching is A–III, B –IV, C–I, D–II.

Mental representation refers to the ability to remember and copy the behaviour of models who are not present. It refers to the thought or memory of a behaviour that one has observed.

Operations refer to the mental representation of actions individuals obey using logical rules. For instance, while performing arithmetic operations in mind, one relies on the mental representation of digits and other numerical functions in order to perform them.

Adaptation refers to building schemas through direct interaction with the environment. Schemas are mental concepts that organise information into categories, and they are acquired through experience of the world.

Assimilation refers to the use of current schemas to interpret the existing world. Fitting in new information with the schemas is referred to as assimilation. For instance, if one's schema of a horse involves one of white colour, when they come across a black horse, they fit it into their schema of the horse.

84 **Match List I with List II.**

List I (Concept)	List II (Description)
A. Reward power	I. Potential to deliver threats and punishment to others
B. Coercive power	II. Authority of a person by virtue of certain characteristics
C. Referent power	III. Positive reinforcement to produce change
D. Legitimate power	IV. Power to influence others

Codes

	A	B	C	D		A	B	C	D
1	III	II	IV	I	2	IV	III	II	I
3	III	I	IV	II	4	I	II	IV	III

Ans. *(3)*

➲ *Exp.* The correct matching is A–III, B–I, C–IV, D–II.

Reward power refers to the application of positive reinforcement in order to produce change. For instance, using rewards to make employees perform better and follow the rules of the organisation.

Coercive power refers to the potential to deliver threats and punishments to others. For instance, a manager can get an employee to follow their orders by threatening them with dire consequences.

Referent power refers to the power to influence others. For instance, a leader can influence others by winning the respect and admiration of their followers.

Legitimate power refers to the authority of a person by the virtue of certain characteristics. For instance, the power derived by the CEO of a company based on their position in the organisation.

85 Match List I with List II

List I (Psychologist)	List II (Concept)
A. Kelly	I. Constructive alternativism
B. Eysenck	II. Hedonic tone
C. Cattell	III. Hypothetico deductive spiral
D. Hull	IV. Response hierarchies

Codes

	A	B	C	D		A	B	C	D
1	I	III	II	IV	2	II	IV	I	III
3	I	II	III	IV	4	II	I	IV	III

Ans. (3)

Exp. The correct matching is A–I, B–II, C –III, D–IV.

George Kelly gave the concept of Constructive alternativism. It refers to the phenomenon wherein different perceptions of a given reality are experienced despite there being only one reality.

Hans Eysenck gave the concept of Hedonic tone, which refers to one's ability to experience pleasure. Low hedonic tone leads to a lowered experience of pleasure, while a high hedonic tone refers to the increased experience of pleasure.

Raymond Cattell gave the concept of Hypothetico-deductive spiral. It refers to the method of scientific inquiry which involves empirical observation, proposal of a rough hypothesis, experimenting to test the hypothesis, using the data to develop a more precise hypothesis, and testing this precise hypothesis by conducting more experiments.

Clark Hull gave the concept of Response hierarchies. It refers to the sequence of responses in the order of which they are more likely to be elicited.

86 Match List I with List II.

List I (Type of Skin Receptors)	List II (Sensory Function)
A. Meissner's corpuscles	I. Cold
B. Pacinian corpuscles	II. Pain
C. Krause's end bulbs	III. Touch
D. Free nerve ending	IV. Pressure

Codes

	A	B	C	D		A	B	C	D
1	II	IV	III	I	2	III	IV	I	II
3	IV	I	II	III	4	IV	II	I	III

Ans. (2)

Exp. The correct matching is A–III, B–IV, C–I, D–II

Meissner's corpuscles are the skin receptors that play a role in the sensation of touch. They are also known as Tactile corpuscles.

Pacinian corpuscles are the skin receptors that play a role in sensing pressure. They also detect vibrations.

Krause's end bulbs are thermoreceptors that play a role in sensing cold.

Free nerve endings play a role in sensing pain. A certain type of free endings, known as nociceptors, are the receptors that sense pain.

87 Match List I with List II

List I (Concept)	List II (Description)
A. Naturalistic intelligence	I. Skill critical and important for archaeologists and botanists
B. Cognitive processing speed	II. Ability to execute easy and highly overlearned cognitive tasks
C. Meta-components	III. Mental processes individuals use effectively to guide their problem-solving efforts
D. Motivating oneself	IV. Delaying gratification and stifling impulsiveness

Codes

	A	B	C	D		A	B	C	D
1	I	II	III	IV	2	II	I	IV	III
3	III	IV	I	II	4	IV	III	II	I

Ans. (1)

Exp. The correct matching is A – I, B – II, C – III, D – IV.

Naturalistic intelligence is a skill critical and important for archaeologists and botanists. It is the ability to recognise and classify the patterns prevalent in the natural world. People high on such type of intelligence tend to have an appreciation for nature.

Cognitive processing speed refers to the ability to execute easy and the highly overlearned cognitive tasks. It can be said to be the time it takes for person to perform a mental task. For instance, recognising the words that they read.

Meta-components refer to the mental processes, people use in order to effectively guide their problem-solving efforts. These may involve the information regarding strategies of problem-solving, the use of those strategies, and monitoring these strategies.

Motivating oneself involves delaying gratification and stifling impulsiveness. For instance, in order to pursue a long-term goal, one has to give up on instant gratifications and other impulsive behaviours. This requires motivating oneself in persisting towards their goals.

88 Match List I with List II.

List I (Concept)	List II (Description)
A. Big-C creativity	I. Creativity of eminence
B. Little-C creativity	II. Creativity of everyday life recognised by other
C. Mini-C creativity	III. Subjective and personal form of day-to-day creativity
D. Pro-C creativity	IV. Professional creativity which has not attained status of eminence

Codes

	A	B	C	D		A	B	C	D
1	I	II	III	IV	2	II	I	IV	III
3	III	IV	I	II	4	IV	III	II	I

Ans. (1)

Exp. The correct matching is A–I, B–II, C–III, D–IV.

Big-C creativity refers to the creativity of eminence. It is the creativity that can be found in world-changing works or masterpieces. For instance, da Vinci's Mona Lisa is an example of Big-C creativity.

Little-C creativity refers to the creativity of everyday life that is recognised by others. For instance, it involves the production of novel and useful ideas.

Mini-C creativity refers to subjective and personal form of day-to-day creativity. It involves the creation of new and meaningful interpretations of one's experiences, events, and other actions.

Pro-C creativity refers to professional creativity that has not yet attained the status of eminence. It is generally associated with the creativity of the professionals or other experts who have gained mastery in a certain field.

89 **Match List I with List II.**

List I (Schools of Psychology)	List II (Concept)
A. Psychoanalysis	I. Elements of conscious experience
B. Behaviourism	II. Self-actualisation
C. Structuralism	III. Unconscious processes
D. Transpersonal Psychology	IV. S-R relations

Codes

	A	B	C	D
1	III	I	IV	II
2	III	IV	I	II
3	I	IV	II	III
4	I	II	IV	III

Ans. (2)

Exp. The correct matching is A–III, B–IV, C–I, D–II.

Psychoanalysis studies unconscious processes. This school of psychology purports that the mind is divided into conscious and unconscious. The unconscious mind is the reservoir of painful memories, and they tend to have an impact on one's behaviours.

Behaviourism studies S-R (stimulus-response) relations. As per this school of psychology, all behaviours can be understood in terms of a response to a stimulus. For instance, on seeing food, the dog salivates. Here, the food is the stimulus, and the salivation is the response exhibited in reaction to the stimulus.

Structuralism studies the elements of conscious experiences. It employs the method of 'introspection,' which involves looking inwards and relating one's subjective experiences they are aware of.

Transpersonal Psychology studies self-actualisation. It is also known as spiritual psychology. Self-actualisation refers to realising and achieving one's full potential.

90 **Match List I with List II.**

List I (Psychologist)	List II (Definition)
A. Binet and Simon	I. The power of good response from the perspective of truth or fact
B. Terman	II. The capacity to judge, understand and reason well
C. Thorndike	III. The capacity to form concepts and grasp their significance
D. Eysenck, M.W.	IV. Error-free transmission of information through the cortex

Codes

	A	B	C	D		A	B	C	D
1	IV	III	I	II	2	I	II	III	IV
3	II	III	I	IV	4	III	II	IV	I

Ans. (3)

Exp. The correct matching is A–II, B– III, C–I, D–IV.

Binet and Simon defined intelligence as the ability to judge, understand, and reason well. Binet and Simon (1905) defined intelligence in terms of judgment, practical sense, initiative, and adaptability.

Lewis Terman defined intelligence as the capacity to develop concepts and grasp their significance. It involves abstract thinking. Terman defined intelligence as "the ability to carry on abstract thinking" and used the label IQ or Intelligence Quotient.

Edward Thorndike defined intelligence as the power of good responses from the perspective of truth or facts. The law of effect principle developed by Edward Thorndike suggested that "responses that produce a satisfying effect in a particular situation become more likely to occur again in that situation, and responses that produce a discomforting effect become less likely to occur again in that situation."

M.W. Eysenck defined intelligence in terms of error-free transmission of information to the cortex. He conceptualised intelligence in terms of cerebral efficiency, which enables faster processing of information.

Directions (Qs, No. 91-95) *Read the following paragraph and answer the questions which follow :*

A psychologist wanted to develop an achievement test in Chemistry for SSC students of central schools. For this purpose, he wrote 110 items having multiple-choice format. He administered this draft version to a sample of 300 subjects. Item analysis was carried out by computing item-remainder correlations. The item analysis retained 80 items. The eighty-item version was administered to a fresh sample of 400 subjects which yielded a mean of 40.00 and standard deviation of 8.00.

The scores were found to be normally distributed. Cronbach alpha for eighty-item version was found to be 0.94. The psychologist also computed odd-even reliability and Kuder-Richardson (K-R) reliability for this version. On this version, one of the subjects Manas, had a score of 32. Since the eighty-item version was considered long for administration, two forms, Form A and Form B were prepared by randomly assigning 40 items to each form.

91 For computing item-remainder correlations, which one of the following correlations would be suitable?

1 Phi-coefficient
2 Contingency coefficient
3 Point-biserial correlation
4 Tetrachoric correlation

Ans. (3)

Exp. Point-biserial correlation is most suitable for computing item-remainder correlations.

Item-remainder correlation refers to the correlation of each item with the sum of the other remaining items. The outcome is the test score without the item being tested. In this type of correlation, point bi-serial correlation is highly suitable as it tests the correlation between the scores on the item being correlated with the remaining items by correlating the score on the given item and adding up the scores of the remaining items, which is the essence of item remainder correlation.

92 In the above study, the psychologist computed three reliability coefficients

I Cronbach's alpha
II Split-half reliability coefficient
III Kuder-Richardson (K-R) reliability coefficient

Which one of the following expectations is true?

1 I, II and III would be the same
2 I and III would be the same, but II can be different
3 II and III would be the same but I would be different
4 I, II and III, all three would be different

Ans. (2)

Exp. In the above mentioned test, the K-R reliability coefficient and Cronbach's alpha would be the same, however, Split-half reliability coefficient would be different.

K-R reliability can be used to measure the reliability of items in a test that involve only one possible correct answer, and measures the test's overall reliability. Cronbach's alpha is used to measure the internal consistency of a given test, to see how related the items are with each other as a group. If the test is reliable overall, there is a possibility that it will be internally consistent as well. Consequently, K-R reliability and Cronbach's alpha would be the same since the test is high on internal consistency (0.94).

Split-half reliability coefficient measures the extent to which all the parts of given test equally contribute to the concept being measured. For this, the scores of one half of the test are split from the other half to see whether they yield same results. However, this can vary as not all items on the test might equally contribute to the concept being measured, and there is no indication of it either.

93 The expected Cronbach's alpha for Form A would be

1 0.47
2 0.89
3 0.62
4 0.94

Ans. (2)

Exp. Cronbach's alpha can decrease up to 0.89 for Form A if the items were reduced from 80 to 40.

Cronbach's alpha is used to measure the internal consistency of a given test, to test how related the items are with one other as a collective. For the given test of 80 items, the Cronbach's alpha was 0.94, which is a highly desired value. With decreasing items, the Cronbach's alpha can decrease as well. So, if it were to decrease from 80 to 40, and there is high degree of inter-correlatedness among the items, Cronbach's alpha can decrease up to 0.89.

94 The score of 32 (score obtained by Manas on eighty-item version) would correspond to percentile rank

1 16
2 32
3 80
4 84

Ans. (1)

Exp. The score of 32 would correspond to 16th percentile rank.

Percentile rank refers to the comparison between a certain score and the scores of the rest of the group. So, if the mean is 40 with a standard deviation of 8, and the given score of 32, then percentile rank is derived by subtracting the score from the mean and computing the z-score, which refers to the number of standard deviations away from the mean the given score is. Using the z-score chart, the analysis would lead to the score of 32 corresponding to 16th percentile rank.

95 The 95% confidence interval for the true score of 32 would be

1 32 ± 0.94
2 32 ± 1.96
3 32 ± 6.00
4 32 ± 3.84

Ans. (4)

Exp The 95% confidence interval for the true score of 32 would be 32 + or – 3.84.

Confidence interval refers to the uncertainty present in a certain statistic. Therefore, a 95% confidence interval, in simple terms, means that 95 out of 100 confidence intervals will have true mean value. It is computed using the formula:

$$CI = \bar{x} \pm z\frac{8}{\sqrt{n}}$$

Consequently, in this case, 95% confidence interval for the true score of 32 would be 32 + or – 3.84.

Directions (Qs. No. 96-100) *Read the following paragraph and answer the five questions which follow*

A researcher wanted to study the effect of organisation of material (A) on recall. She expected that retention interval (B) would moderate the effect of organisation of material. She varied A at three levels—Low organisation. Moderate organisation, and High organisation. She varied B at two levels—Short retention interval and Long retention interval. The subjects were randomly assigned to the different groups. Each subject received the list of words with specified level of organisation. Each of them learnt the list upto one errorless trial and was tested after the specified retention interval. All the subjects had also received the intelligence test.

The number of items, recalled by the subject, was the dependent variable. The data were analysed by the appropriate ANOVA, treating intelligence as a covariate. The partial results are given here—(i) the sum of squares for organization of material (A) was 255.00; (ii) the degrees of freedom for error variance was 115; (iii) the F ratio for interaction (A × B) was 0.95. The obtained results were appropriately interpreted.

96 How many subjects have been employed in this study?

1 116
2 120
3 121
4 122

Ans. (3)

Exp. The number of subjects in this study were 121.

Given that the degrees of freedom for error is 115, it can be deduced that the number of subjects employed in this study were 121.

97 The design in the above study can be best labelled as

1 Randomised single-factor six-group design with a covariate significant
2 Randomised balanced 3 × 2 factorial design with a covariate
3 Randomised unbalanced 3 × 2 factorial design with a covariate
4 Randomised 3 × 2 blocked factorial design with a covariate .

Ans. (3)

Exp. The design of the given study can be best labelled as randomised unbalanced 3 × 2 factorial design with a covariate.

In this given study, there were two variables, organistion of material (A) and retention interval (B). 'A' was varied at three levels, while 'B' was varied at 2 levels. The subjects were randomly assigned to either different groups. Consequently, this design would be a randomised unbalanced 3 × 2 factorial design with a covariate, as the covariate here is the intelligence level.

98 The 'mean square' for organisation of material would be

1 42.50
2 127.50
3 85.00
4 255.00

Ans. (2)

Exp. The 'mean square' for organisation of material would be 127.50.

The sum of squares for organization of material, labelled as 'A', is 255.00. Therefore, the 'mean square' would be 255.00/2, which is equal to 127.50.

99 What would be the degrees of freedom for covariate?

1 1
2 2
3 5
4 6

Ans. (1)

Exp. The degrees of freedom for the covariate would be 1.

Degrees of freedom refers to the number of values that are free to vary. Here, the covariate is 'intelligence level.' Only one covariate is present, therefore, the degrees of freedom would be 1 itself.

100 From the above results, it can be concluded that

1 main effect of organisation of material is significant
2 main effect of organisation of material is non-significant
3 retention interval does not moderate the effect of organisation of material
4 retention interval moderates the effect of organisation of material

Ans. (3)

Exp. From the given study, it can be concluded that the retention level does not moderate the effect of organisation of material.

The researcher wanted to study whether the retention level 'B' moderates the effect of organisation of material 'A'. The findings of the study revealed that the F-ratio for interaction between A and B is 0.95. However, for the null hypothesis to be rejected, the F-ratio must be greater than 1. It is not so in this case, and therefore, the null hypothesis cannot be rejected.

Consequently, it can be said that the retention level does not moderate the effect of organisation of material.

UGC-NET
PSYCHOLOGY

SOLVED PAPER 2018 (December)

PAPER II

1 A person who tries to increase compliance by inducing an individual to agree first to small request is using the technique known as

1 Door-in-the-face technique
2 Elaboration technique
3 Foot-in-the-door technique
4 Low-ball technique

Ans. *(3)*

Exp. A person who tries to increase compliance by inducing an individual to first agree to a small request is using the 'Foot-in-the-door' technique.

Foot-in-the-door technique is one of the different compliance tactics. As per this technique, getting someone to agree to a small request makes it more likely for them to agree to a bigger one. The underlying idea behind this is that once a person agrees to a small request, they find it difficult to refuse a bigger one. For instance, if one wants to borrow a certain amount of money from an acquaintance, they begin by borrowing a small sum, and then proceed to request a larger sum.

2 Which one of the following is not one of the Gestalt psychology laws of perception?

1 Closure 2 Continuity
3 Proximity 4 Relative size

Ans. *(4)*

Exp. Among the given options, Relative size does not belong to the Gestalt psychology laws of perception.

Gestalt laws of perception help to explain how the brain interprets information regarding relationships in pictures or designs based on visual cues. Relative size, however, does not belong to this category as it is a perceptual cue that helps in determining the proximity of objects to another object of a known size. For instance, if there are two poles in a picture, and they are of the same size, then it is assumed that the pole that casts a smaller image on the retina of the eye is the one that is farther away.

3 The basic unit in the Human Associative Memory model is

1 Predicate 2 Sentence
3 Proposition 4 Association

Ans. *(3)*

Exp. Proposition is the basic component of the Human Associative Memory model.

Human Associative Memory (HAM) model is a memory network model. The component which is its basic unit is known as 'Proposition.' A proposition can be a representation of something, like the format of a sentence, but not the entire sentence in itself. Propositions can also be relationships between concepts or locations. Every relationship is binary in nature and intertwines two concepts at a given point in time.

4 The basic elements of thought are

I. Concepts II. Propositions
III. Images IV. Intelligence

Choose the correct answer from the codes given below.

1 I and II 2 I and III
3 I and IV 4 I, II and III

Ans. *(4)*

Exp. The basic elements of thought involve Images, Concepts, and Propositions. Thinking is an activity that takes place in the brain.

Thinking allows people to come up with novel ideas or combine ideas together. The mind thinks in the form of visual images that are representative of something. For instance, when one thinks of a 'banana,' the image of the banana comes to their mind. Then comes concept. This refers to a myriad of objects that share one similar characteristic. For instance, the concept of a 'fruit' can be described in words on the basis of several images that may come to one's mind. The other basic element of thinking is proposition, which is the relationship between two concepts. For instance, a relationship between 'bat' and a 'mammal.' After understanding the concept of a 'bat' and a 'mammal', the brain makes a connection between these two concepts, and deciphers that a 'bat' is a 'mammal'.

5 Sensory-specific satiety takes place in

1 Papillae
2 Thalamus
3 Nucleus of solitary tract
4 Insula

Ans. *(3)*

Exp. Sensory-specific satiety takes place in the nucleus of the solitary tract.

The consumption of the same food over and over again tends to reduce its appeal. This phenomenon is referred to as Sensory-Specific Satiety (SSS). SSS takes place in the nucleus of the solitary tract (NST), which is located in the medulla oblongata of the brain.

6 People with high need achievement usually tend to

I. be persistent in their work
II. like to achieve the feedback on how they are doing
III. raise their levels of aspiration in a more realistic way
IV. work even if they have no control on the situation
V. dislike working on moderately challenging situations/tasks that promise success.

Choose the correct answer from the codes given below.

Codes

1 I, II and III are correct; IV and V are incorrect
2 I, III and V are correct; II and IV are incorrect
3 II, III and V are correct; I and IV are incorrect
4 I and II are correct; III, IV and V are incorrect

Ans. *(1)*

Exp. Statement I, II and III are correct; IV and V are incorrect.

The need for achievement is defined as the drive for performance, improvement, and excellence.

People with a high need for achievement are intrinsically motivated by the completion of a given task, therefore, they tend to be persistent with their work. Since they strive for excellence, they seek to complete a given work, thereby persisting at it even when it is difficult. Hence, Statement I is correct.

People with a high need for achievement tend to strive for improvement. Therefore, those with a high need for achievement tend to seek feedback as it is one of the ways to helps build on one's strengths and improve on one's weak points. Hence, Statement II is correct.

People with a high need for achievement tend to give importance to their performance. They typically raise their aspirations in a realistic manner, like aiming for a better performance in comparison to their previous one. Additionally, research says that people who realistically raise their aspirations achieve greater success. Hence, Statement III is correct.

Need for achievement is marked by an affinity for control, and people high on this need prefer to act decisively and claim responsibility for their actions and behaviours. Therefore, they may not prefer to work in a situation where they lack control as they cannot act decisively in such situations. Hence, Statement IV is incorrect.

People with a high need for achievement strive for performance and success. Consequently, they tend to prefer tasks that are moderately difficult or challenging as these tasks help in achieving success and allows one to view themselves as being a competent person. Hence, Statement V is incorrect.

7 Given below are two statements, one labelled as Assertion (A) and the other labelled as Reason (R). Read the statements and choose the correct answer using the codes given below.

Assertion (A) The moderate similarity between original list and interpolated list results in more retroactive interference.

Reason (R) The moderate similarity between original list and interpolated list results in more response competition.

Codes

1 Both (A) and (R) are true and (R) is the correct explanation of (A).
2 Both (A) and (R) are true, but (R) is not the correct explanation of (A).
3 (A) is true, but (R) is false.
4 (A) is false, but (R) is true.

Ans. *(1)*

Exp. Both (A) and (R) are true, and (R) is the correct explanation for (A).

Retroactive interference is a phenomenon in memory where recently learnt information prevents the recall of the information that has been learnt at an earlier stage. Consider an Original list (List I) one has to memorise and recall after a time gap. During this gap, a somewhat similar list, List II (Interpolated list), is memorised. When it is time to recall List I, the moderate similarity between the Original list and the Interpolated list results in more retroactive interference because of increased response competition.

Response competition is a phenomenon wherein one tends to make multiple responses to the same stimulus. For instance, while recalling items from the Original list (List I), one has to respond to a cue. Then, because of response competition, the recall items from List I become blocked because other items from List II become connected to that same cue. This happens because of the similarity between the two items.

8 Motivating potential score comprises of several factors which is determined by

I. Skill variety
II. Intelligence
III. Task identity and task significance
IV. Autonomy and feedback

Choose the correct answer from the codes given below.

Codes

1 I, II and III
2 II, III and IV
3 I, II and IV
4 I, III and IV

Ans. (4)

Exp. Motivating potential score comprises several factors that are determined by skill variety, task identity and task significance, autonomy, and feedback.

Motivating Potential Score (MPS) is a composite score that determines the potential for motivation present in a given job. To have a high MPS, a job must score high on one of the three task-related factors i.e. skill variety, task identity, or task significance, as these factors help in making a job more meaningful. It must also be high on autonomy and feedback, as autonomy helps in providing increased responsibility, while feedback helps gain insight into the effectiveness of their performance.

The formula for MPS is:

MPS=[(Skill variety + Task identity + Task significance)/3] × Autonomy × Feedback

9 Which of the following are correct for Pollyanna principle?

I. Pleasant items are processed more efficiently than unpleasant ones.
II. Pleasant items are processed more accurately than unpleasant ones.
III. Pleasant items are retained for a longer period than unpleasant ones.
IV. Pleasant items are retained for a shorter period than unpleasant ones.

Choose the correct answer from the codes given below

Codes

1 I and II
2 III and IV
3 I, II and III
4 I, II and IV

Ans. (3)

Exp. Statement I, II and III are correct in relation to Pollyanna principle.

Pollyanna principle is also known as positivity bias. The term 'Pollyanna' is derived from Eleanor Porter's novel, "Pollyanna," which is about a girl who is eternally optimistic and focuses on the brighter side of life.

Pollyanna principle says that pleasant items are processed more efficiently and accurately than the unpleasant ones because the human brain tends to be more precise and meticulous in its process of pleasant items when compared to the unpleasant ones. Pollyanna principle also suggests that people tend to remember pleasant items for a longer period because the brain tends to pay more attention to, and retains the positive things better than the negative things.

10 Match List I with List II and select the correct answer using the codes given below.

List I (Function of perception)	List II (Perceptual issue)
A. Attention	I. What does that thing characterise?
B. Localisation	II. What is that thing?
C. Recognition	III. Where is something?
D. Abstraction	IV. Is there something?

Codes

	A	B	C	D		A	B	C	D
1	II	III	I	IV	2	IV	III	I	II
3	IV	III	II	I	4	II	I	III	IV

Ans. (3)

Exp. The correct matching is A-IV, B-III, C-II, D-I.

Attention refers to the ability to focus only on certain details whilst being able to tune out other information. Therefore, attention can be associated with, "Is there something?" as it involves directing one's focus towards only certain details that may indicate the presence of a given object.

Localisation refers to the ability to identify the position of a given object in the context of its environment. For instance, determining the closeness between two objects, knowing where a given object is situated, or determining the direction of moving objects. Therefore, localisation can be associated with, "Where is something?"

Recognition is the ability to identify and correctly interpret a given object. It involves identification of an object by its features, or the relationship between features. Therefore, recognition can be associated with, "What is that thing?" as this issue pertains to the identification and interpretation of a given object.

Abstraction refers to the ability that involves the identification of common characteristics amongst different objects. In the brain, an object is represented only by its quintessential characteristics so that it can be categorised. Therefore, abstraction can be associated with, "What does that thing characterise?"

11 Perceptual processes consist of many things

I. Perceptual learning
II. Motives and needs
III. Personality types
IV. Perceptual cognitive styles

Choose the correct answer from the codes given below.

Codes

1 I, II and III
2 I, III and IV
3 I, II and IV
4 II, III and IV

Ans. (3)

Exp. Among the given options, Perceptual process involves Perceptual learning, Motives and needs, and Perceptual cognitive styles.

Perceptual process signifies the underlying process behind perception, which is the ability to identify, organise, interpret, and respond to incoming information. It helps in understanding one's environment.

Perceptual learning is an increased ability to respond to a given stimulus due to repeated exposure to the same. It helps in discriminating between two stimuli that are otherwise very confusing in nature. For instance, a musician learning to differentiate between very similar sounding notes of 'A' and 'B' after repeated exposure.

Motives and biological needs of a person play a very strong role in perception. A study by Levine et al. in 1942 involved the presentation of certain vague drawings to some students. Students who were hungry perceived food-related objects in those drawings, while those who were not hungry perceived other things. This shows that perception is impacted by needs or motivations.

Perceptual process is affected by cognitive styles. Different cognitive styles help explain why people identify and interpret an object in different ways. For instance, people with a field-independent cognitive style are able to separate details from other information, while people with field-dependent cognitive style are unable to do so.

12 Given below are two statements, one labelled as Assertion (A) and the other labelled as Reason (R). Read the statements and choose the correct answer using the code given below.

Assertion (A) According to Bandura, the behaviour is fully determined by mental images of past experiences.

Reason (R) Information gained from observations is stored symbolically in retentional processes to make it useful.

Codes

1 Both (A) and (R) are true and (R) is the correct explanation of (A).
2 Both (A) and (R) are true, but (R) is not the correct explanation of (A).
3 (A) is true, but (R) is false.
4 (A) is false, but (R) is true.

Ans. *(4)*

Exp. (A) is false, but (R) is true.

According to Albert Bandura, behaviour is not determined by mental images of prior experiences. His social learning theory states that behaviour is learnt by observation and modelling. In fact, Bandura said that people can perform even those behaviours of which they do not have any prior experience.

Retention is the ability to remember information and recall it when required. In observational learning, the information obtained is stored in the form of symbols to increase the competency of the retention process. Symbols are basic units of thinking, such as words that help conjure up an image in one's mind. For instance, the word 'dance' may conjure up an image of a dancing ballerina in one's mind.

13 The tendency to pay attention primarily to the information that affirms existing views refers to

1 Hindsight effect
2 Reasoning
3 Confirmation bias
4 Belief

Ans. *(3)*

Exp. The tendency to pay attention primarily to the information that affirms one's existing views refers to Confirmation bias.

Confirmation bias is a type of cognitive bias wherein one is biased towards the information that confirms their already existing points of view, and consequently, they tend to only focus on that information whilst ignoring the other information that can be contradictory to one's views. For instance, if one person thinks that right-handed people tend to be better at Mathematics than left-handed ones, they focus only on the information that helps affirm this view.

14 A basic difference between decay and interference theories is that

1 Decay theory assumes unlearning
2 Decay theory is a two-factor theory
3 Decay theory assumes autonomous processes
4 Interference theory emphasizes neural consolidation

Ans. *(3)*

Exp. A basic difference between decay and interference theories is that decay theory assumes autonomous processes.

Decay theory gives a physiological explanation for forgetting. This theory suggests that when a person learns something new, a memory trace is formed. Decay theory suggests that people tend to forget because memory tends to fade over a period of time as a result of non-usage. Interference theory suggests that people forget because different memories interfere with the information that one is trying to recall.

The basic difference between the above mentioned two theories is that decay theory suggests that forgetting is autonomous or self-governing, and takes place over a period of time. That is, it happens when a memory trace weakens as a result of not being in use. Whereas, interference theory suggests that forgetting happens when other information interferes with the encoding of a memory, thereby impeding its consolidation.

15 Self-disclosure

I. serves the function of modelling
II. helps in developing a new perspective
III. develops trust through dyadic effect
IV. must be used frequently

Choose the correct answer from the codes given below.

Codes

1 I and II
2 I, III and IV
3 I, II and IV
4 I, II and III

Ans. *(4)*

Exp. Self-disclosure serves the function of modelling, helps in developing a new perspective, and develops trust through the dyadic effect.

Self-disclosure refers to the process of relaying information pertaining to oneself to another person whether or not one intends to do it. Modelling is a process in which a person observes another person engaging in a behaviour, and imitates the same. Self-disclosure can serve the function of modelling. For instance, a counsellor may disclose some personal information if it helps the client model their behaviour after theirs.

Self-disclosure can enable the development of a new perspective. For instance, when two people hold different viewpoints, and one discloses personal experiences that led them to holding a certain viewpoint, another person may gain a new perspective with regards to that viewpoint.

Dyadic effect takes place when self-disclosure becomes a medium for building a relationship between two people on the basis of trust. If one person reveals something personal about themselves, the other person reciprocates this by sharing something related to themselves. This happens because when people disclose intimate information about themselves, feelings of trust begin to develop.

16 Which of the following are correct for latent learning?

I. Latent learning is not translated into performance.
II. Latent learning remains dormant for a considerable length of time.
III. Reinforcement is not important for latent learning.
IV. Latent learning is complete in one trial.

Choose the correct answer from the codes given below.

Codes

1 I and II　　2 II and III
3 I, II and III　　4 I, II, III and IV

Ans. (3)

Exp. Statement I, II and III are correct in relation to latent learning.

Latent learning is not translated into performance, it remains dormant for a considerable length of time, and does not require reinforcement.

Latent learning refers to hidden learning that only manifests itself once when an incentive is provided to display it.

Latent learning is not necessarily translated into performance as learning is not the same as performance. Learning is the acquisition of knowledge. Only when learning is converted into a learned behaviour that can be performed, it can be considered as a performance.

Latent learning can remain hidden or dormant for a considerable period of time before it gives rise to a behaviour. That is, if an incentive to demonstrate a learnt behaviour is not provided for a lengthy period of time, latent learning may never be manifested.

Latent learning can take place even when people do not receive any immediate reinforcement for the behaviour. Latent learning only manifests itself when a reinforcement/incentive is provided, however, for the process of latent learning itself, no reinforcement is required.

Statement IV is not correct as Latent learning cannot be completed in one trial.

17 Match List I with List II and select the correct answer using the codes given below.

List I (Part of Nervous System)	List II (Response)
A. Sympathetic nervous system	I. Calmness
B. Parasympathetic nervous system	II. Emergency reactions
C. Pituitary gland	III. Arousal
D. Somatic nervous system	IV. ACTH

Codes

	A	B	C	D		A	B	C	D
1	III	I	IV	II	2	I	III	II	IV
3	IV	II	III	I	4	II	III	IV	I

Ans. (1)

Exp. The correct matching is A-III, B-I, C-IV, D-II.

Sympathetic nervous system is a division of the autonomic nervous system that leads the adrenal glands to release stress hormones like adrenaline and noradrenaline, increases heart rate and blood pressure, and puts the body in a state of arousal. This happens in times of crisis, or during a stressful/threatening event.

Parasympathetic nervous system is a division of the autonomic nervous system that is involved in calming the body after a stressful/threatening event or a crisis has been dealt with. It restricts the release of adrenaline or noradrenaline, and lowers the heart rate and blood pressure. Therefore, it helps restore the body to a state of calm.

Pituitary gland, a small gland present at the base region of the brain, prepares the adrenocorticotropic hormone (ACTH), which controls the production of cortisol. Cortisol is a hormone that responds to stress, combats infections, and controls blood sugar, blood pressure, and metabolism. Controlling cortisol is important because distorted cortisol levels can lead to serious health issues.

Somatic nervous system controls voluntary and some involuntary movements. It controls emergency reactions, such as reflex actions or reflexes. These are involuntary movements regulated by the reflex arc present in the spinal cord. For instance, immediately withdrawing one's hand after touching a very hot object.

18 Match List I with List II and select the correct answer using the codes given below.

List I (Indice)	List II (Test)
A. Work interference	I. MCMI
B. Fake bad profiles	II. MMPI-II
C. Capacity for status	III. MMPI-A
D. Immaturity scale	IV. CPI

Codes

	A	B	C	D		A	B	C	D
1	I	II	III	IV	2	II	I	IV	III
3	III	IV	I	II	4	IV	III	II	I

Ans. *(2)*

Exp. The correct matching is A-II, B-I, C-IV, D-III.

Work Interference Scale belongs to MMPI-II (Minnesota Multiphasic Personality Inventory-II) and consists of 33 items. It pertains to those attitudes that contribute towards poor work performance. A high score on this scale indicates work pressure, conflicts with authority figures, attentional difficulties, anxiety, tension, and low initiative, among others.

Faking bad profiles refers to deliberately choosing those options or answers that make one look bad. This is often done when one wants to be exempt from something, for instance, a criminal trial. Therefore, they give answers that make them seem incompetent. MCMI (Million Clinical Multiaxial Inventory) has scales that detect faking bad profiles.

Capacity for status is a scale that belongs to the CPI (California Psychological Inventory). It pertains to the personal characteristics and qualities that help in attaining a status or other symbols associated with achievement.

The *Immaturity Scale* (IMM) is a supplementary scale that is associated with MMPI-A (Minnesota Multiphasic Personality Inventory-Adolescent). It consists of 43 items and helps assess immaturity in one's self-awareness, interpersonal style, cognitive complexity, judgement ability, and impulse control.

19 Given below are two statements, one labelled as Assertion (A) and the other labelled as Reason (R). Read the statements and choose the correct answer using the codes given below.

Assertion (A) Though meager in number, but women in India have also started avoiding having children.

Reason (R)Women decide not to have a baby because the sum of negative and positive valence of having a baby is lower than the sum of valence for pursuing a career.

Codes

1. Both (A) and (R) are true and (R) is the correct explanation of (A).
2. Both (A) and (R) are true, but (R) is not the correct explanation of (A).
3. (A) is true, but (R) is false.
4. (A) is false, but (R) is true.

Ans. *(1)*

Exp. Both (A) and (R) are true and (R) is the correct explanation for (A).

In psychology, a positive valence indicates the quality of an object, situation, or event that makes it good or appealing. On the other hand, negative valence indicates the quality of an object, situation, or event that makes it bad or aversive. The positive valence is indicated by a (+) sign, while the negative valence is indicated by a (-) sign.

In India, a small number of women are deciding to not have children because the sum total of both, positive and negative valences of birthing/raising a baby is lower than that of pursuing a career. This signifies that having a baby is less appealing than pursuing a career to these women.

20 Guilford initially started his work on SOI extending Thurstone's theory of primary abilities but later on diverged on the grounds

I. Obtained factors were not primary (independent) rather related to each other.
II. Thurstones factor analysis was mainly oriented to get simple structure.
III. It was found difficult to name the abilities/factors found in data.
IV. Like Thurstone, Guilford found second order and higher-order factors.

Choose the correct answer from the codes given below.

Codes

1 I and II	2 III and IV
3 I, II and III	4 II, III and IV

Ans. *(3)*

Exp. Guilford diverged from Thurstone's theory of primary abilities because the obtained factors were not independent of each other, factor analysis was directed towards getting a simple structure, and that factors/abilities present in the data were difficult to name.

Guilford's Structure of Intellect is a highly complicated three-dimensional model of intelligence which involves dimensions of content, operations, and products. It is based on factor analysis.

Guilford diverged from Thurstone's theory on the basis that primary abilities of verbal comprehension, word fluency, number facility, spatial visualisation, perceptual speed, associative memory, and reasoning were related to one another rather than being independent of each other, making them highly similar.

He also purported that Thurstone's use of factor analysis was directed towards simplifying the structure of his theory, while Guilford's was highly complicated. In his collection of data, he found the factors/abilities present were difficult to name.

21 Using the notions Chronological Age (CA), Educational Age (EA), and Mental Age (MA), the Accomplishment Quotient (AQ) is computed as

1 100 (MA/CA)	2 100 (EA/MA)
3 100 (EA/CA)	4 100 (MA/EA)

Ans. *(3)*

Exp. The formula of Accomplishment Quotient (AQ) is 100 (EA/CA).

Accomplishment Quotient (AQ), also known as Achievement Quotient, is defined as the measure of a student's academic ability. It is the score obtained, first, by dividing the Educational Age (EA) by their Chronological Age (CA), and then multiplying the resulting value by 100. EA is a certain value or a measure that students are expected to score at a certain age, their CA. For instance, if a 6-year-old scores at a level that is consistent with an 8-year-old, then their EA is two years more than their CA. So, the AQ for this 6-year-old would be:

100 (8/6), which is 1.3 multiplied by 100 equals 130, which is AQ.

22 The improvement in performance following a rest after cessation of practice is called

1 Reminiscence effect 2 Spontaneous recovery
3 Incremental learning 4 Crespi effect

Ans. (1)

Exp. Reminiscence effect is defined as the improvement of performance following a rest after cessation of practice.

Reminiscence effect is a phenomenon that explains the improvement in performance after a period of rest following repeated practice. For instance, consider that an experiment involves swinging a heavy rope till it hits a target. Practicing to hit the target involves a lot of muscular work, which gives rise to fatigue in the subjects. This lowers their performance. Following a period of rest/stoppage of practice leads to increased performance as it gives time for the subjects to recover their expended energy.

23 According to Piaget, which of the following explains the concept of Cognitive Equilibration?

1 Tendency to integrate structures into higher order systems
2 Individual seeking to stabilise his or her cognitive structures
3 Tendency to modify structure in order to incorporate new information
4 Fact that every structure has its origin in earlier structures

Ans. (2)

Exp. According to Piaget, individual seeking to stabilise his or her cognitive structures explains the concept of Cognitive Equilibration.

Jean Piaget said that Cognitive Equilibration is the effort to stabilise one's cognitive structures. Cognitive structures were integral to Piaget's theory. They are actions such as mental organisations of information, known as schemes. Piaget said that behaviour is regulated by these schemes, which help in the interpretation of one's environment, thereby giving rise to a response. Cognitive equilibration refers to the drive to maintain consistency between the schemes and one's environment. For instance, a girl seeing a cat in a book. Following this, she sees the animal in person and associates it with the image she had seen earlier, and identifies it as a cat.

24 Match List I with List II and select the correct answer using the codes given below.

List I (Concept)	List II (Description)
A. Cerebral Palsy	I. Hereditary condition in which the brain's nerve cells break down to affect physical movements, emotions and cognitive abilities
B. Phenylketonuria	II. Group of disorders that affect muscle movement
C. Down Syndrome	III. Rare genetic condition that causes amino acids to build up in the body
D. Huntington's disease	IV. Most common genetic cause of intellectual disability

Codes

	A	B	C	D		A	B	C	D
1	I	III	IV	II	2	II	I	IV	III
3	III	II	IV	I	4	II	III	IV	I

Ans. (4)

Exp. The correct matching is A-II, B-III, C-IV, D-I.

Cerebral Palsy is a group of disorders that affect muscle movement. It is a set of non-progressive movement and posture disorders that results from trauma to the brain occurring prenatally, during the birth process, or before the age of 5. Symptoms include spasticity, uncontrolled movements, paralysis, unsteady gait, and speech abnormalities but may be accompanied by disorders of any other brain function, resulting in cognitive changes, seizures, visual defects, tactile impairment, hearing loss, and intellectual disability.

Phenylketonuria (PKU) is a rare genetic condition that causes amino acids to build up in the body. It is a genetic disorder that leads to the build-up of phenylalanine (an amino acid) in the body. Phenylalanine is a building block of proteins, and untreated PKU can increase its levels to such an extent that it can give rise to intellectual disabilities and other severe health problems.

Down's Syndrome is the most common genetic cause of intellectual disability. It is a condition in which a child is born with a trisomy on their 21st chromosome, that is, they have an extra copy of that chromosome. It can also lead to other physical and mental disabilities, and developmental delays.

Huntington's disease is a hereditary condition in which the brain's nerve cells break down to affect physical movements, emotions and cognitive abilities. It is a progressive hereditary disease associated with degeneration of nerve cells, particularly in the caudate nucleus of the basal ganglia and in the cerebral cortex. It is characterized by abnormalities of gait and posture, motor incoordination, and involuntary jerking motions (chorea) as well as dementia, mood disturbances, and personality and behavioural changes.

25 The pattern of excitation and inhibition that constitutes the activity of the cortex at any given moment, is called

1 Sensitisation
2 Squandrels
3 Cortical Mosaic
4 Neuroplasticity

Ans. (3)

Exp. Cortical Mosaic is the term used to describe the pattern of excitation and inhibition activities taking place in the cortex.

Ivan Pavlov coined the term 'Cortical Mosaic' to the pattern of excitation and inhibition that is a characteristic of the cortex at any given point in time. Pavlov said that excitation takes place when an unconditioned/conditioned stimulus causes excitation and produces a response. For instance, if an insect comes near one's eye, the eye naturally blinks (response). Inhibition takes place when an unconditioned/conditioned stimulus causes inhibition, thereby stopping a response. For instance, when one is walking and spots a snake. They immediately stop moving to avoid the snake.

26 Given below are two statements, one labelled as Assertion (A) and the other labelled as Reason (R). Read the statements and choose the correct answer using the codes given below.

Assertion (A) We recall information accurately if it is processed at deep level rather than at shallow level.

Reason (R) Processing at deep level involves elaboration and distinctiveness.

Codes

1 Both (A) and (R) are true and (R) is the correct explanation of (A).
2 Both (A) and (R) are true, but (R) is not the correct explanation of (A)
3 (A) is true, but (R) is false.
4 (A) is false, but (R) is true.

Ans. (1)

Exp. Both (A) and (R) are true and (R) is the correct explanation of (A).

Deep processing involves understanding the meaning of the item one is trying to memorise, and therefore, is retained for a longer time than shallow processing. Shallow processing involves rehearsal of the item without understanding its meaning, and therefore, is not retained for longer periods.

Deep processing involves distinctiveness and elaboration. Distinctiveness refers to understanding how an item is different from others. It is highly useful when it comes to understanding the differences between different items. Elaboration, meanwhile, involves rich processing in terms of meaning. For instance, understanding the meaning of an item, and associating the idea of it with the already existing knowledge of other items.

27 The Lock-and-Key theory explains

1 Colour vision
2 Depth perception
3 Olfaction
4 High frequency sounds

Ans. (3)

Exp. Olfaction is explained by the Lock-and-Key theory.

Olfaction is the process of smell. The process of smell begins when odour molecules enter the nose and get dissolved in the mucous substance present in the olfactory epithelium. Olfactory epithelium has odour receptors, which are the sensory receptors of smell.

The odour molecules are of a certain shape, and represent the key. When they get dissolved in the olfactory epithelium, they bind with a specifically shaped odour receptor, the lock. When specific shapes of odour molecules bind with their specific receptors, they excite the receptor, thereby giving rise to different types of smells.

28 Agoraphobias

I. Usually onset during early adulthood
II. Are dominantly found amongst women
III. Can onset at any age but mostly during early childhood
IV. Are dominantly prevalent amongst men
V. Share more kinship with panic disorders than phobic disorders

Choose the correct answer from the codes given below

Codes

1 I, IV and V
2 I, II and V
3 I, III and V
4 III IV and V

Ans. (2)

Exp. Statement I, II and V are correct in relation to Agoraphobias.

Agoraphobia is an anxiety disorder that is characterised by fear and avoidance of open spaces as they trigger panic, or make one feel trapped, helpless, or embarrassed.

It usually has an onset during early adulthood. Agoraphobia can begin in childhood, but usually starts in the late teen or early adult years—usually before age 35—but older adults can also develop it.

It is dominantly found amongst women. Agoraphobia is more commonly found in women than in men, and its onset generally takes place during the early childhood years.

It shares more kinship with panic disorders than phobic disorders. Agoraphobia is more similar to panic disorder as it usually develops after the experience of a panic attack. The panic attack makes people fear having another one, and therefore, begin to avoid open spaces in case it happens again.

29 Arrange in sequence the stages of personality development according to Rollo May.

1 Dependence → Innocence → Rebellion → Ordinary consciousness of self → Creative consciousness of self
2 Innocence → Dependence → Rebellion → Creative consciousness of self → Ordinary consciousness of self
3 Dependence → Innocence → Ordinary consciousness of self → Rebellion → Creative consciousness of self
4 Innocence → Rebellion → Dependence → Ordinary consciousness of self → Creative consciousness of self

Ans. (1)

Exp. Rollo May gave the stages of personality development that take place in the following order:

1. *Dependence* : It takes place during infancy, where the infant is dependent on their caregiver for every need.
2. *Innocence* : It takes place during infancy. It is characterised as being neither good or bad, where an infant simply does what they have to.
3. *Rebellion* : It takes place during childhood through adolescence. During this stage, a person strives for freedom but does not fully understand the responsibility that comes with freedom.
4. *Ordinary consciousness of self* : It takes place during early adulthood, where one understands the responsibility that comes with freedom, but finds it to be tedious. Therefore, they simply conform to tradition and cultural values.
5. *Creative consciousness of self* : This stage takes place when an adult is willing to realise their full potential (self-actualisation). It transcends their ego, wherein they are fully accepting of their destiny, and are ready to face every situation with courage.

30 Match List-I with List-II and select the correct answer using the codes given below.

List I	List II
A. Electromyography	I. Procedure for measuring muscular tension
B. Electrooculography	II. Technique for recording eye movements
C. Plethysmography	III. Technique for measuring volume of blood in a particular part of the body
D. Stereotactic surgery	IV. Technique in which devices are precisely positioned in the depth of brain

Codes

	A	B	C	D
1	III	II	I	IV
2	I	II	III	IV
3	II	III	I	IV
4	I	II	IV	III

Ans. (2)

Exp. The correct matching is A-I, B-II, C-III, D-IV.

Electromyography (EMG) is a procedure for measuring muscular tension. It is the recording (via an instrument called an electromyograph) of the electrical activity of muscles through electrodes placed in or on different muscle groups. This procedure is used in the diagnosis of neuromuscular diseases, such as Myasthenia gravis or Amyotrophic lateral sclerosis.

Electrooculography (EOG) is a technique for recording eye movements. It is the process of recording the electric potential that exists between the front and back of the eye as fixation moves between two points.

Plethysmography is a technique for measuring volume of blood in a particular part of the body. It is the process of recording and measuring volume or volume changes in organs or body tissues, such as the blood supply flowing through an organ. The instrument used in this process is called a Plethysmograph.

Stereotactic surgery is a technique in which devices are precisely positioned in the depth of brain. It is a surgical procedure where lesion, frequently a brain tumor, is removed with assistance of image guidance, that is previously obtained images (usually an MRI) are used to guide the surgeon to the exact location of the lesion to facilitate as accurate a pathway through the brain and safe removal of as much abnormal tissue as possible while leaving normal, healthy brain relatively intact.

31 Match List I with List II and select the correct answer using the codes given below.

List I	List II
A. Mental models	I. The impact of past experience on present problem solving through better alternatives
B. Heuristics	II. Knowledge structures that guide our interactions with objects and events around us
C. Availability heuristics	III. Mental rules of thumb that permit us to make decisions and judgements in a rapid manner
D. Mental set	IV. A cognitive rule of thumb in which the probability of various events is judged on the basis of how quickly they come to mind

Codes

	A	B	C	D
1	I	II	III	IV
2	II	III	IV	I
3	II	III	I	IV
4	III	IV	I	II

Ans. (2)

Exp. The correct matching is A-II, B-III, C-IV, D-I.

Mental models are knowledge structures that guide our interactions with objects and events around us. They direct one's interactions with objects or events, and the way in which things work in the world. For instance, the concept of reinforcements and their effect on behaviour helps the employer understand that incentives can make an employee work hard.

Heuristics are mental rules of thumb that permit us to make decisions and judgements in a rapid manner. These are mental shortcuts that help one solve problems quickly, but may not always guarantee the desired results. For instance, always purchasing expensive products instead of cheaper products assuming them to be of high quality, while that may not always be the case.

Availability heuristic is a cognitive rule of thumb in which the probability of various events is judged on the basis of how quickly they come to mind. It is a mental shortcut wherein one judges the probability of something based on how quickly they can remember them. For instance, one might assume that plane crashes are more common than they are because of their extensive media coverage.

Mental set is the impact of past experience on present problem solving through better alternatives. It refers to the tendency to apply the same solutions that have worked in the past despite better alternatives. For instance, a compound interest problem may seem similar to a simple interest one. Therefore, the student may try the simple interest formula and fail to solve it.

32 Which of the following are associated with haptic memory?

I. Sensory memory
II. Related with touch stimuli
III. Parietal lobe
IV. It involves cutaneous and kinesthetics

Choose the correct answer from the codes given below.

Codes

1 I and II 2 I, II and III
3 I, III and IV 4 I, II, III and IV

***Ans.** (4)*

Exp. Statements I, II, III and IV are associated with haptic memory.

Sensory memory is associated with haptic memory. Haptic memory is the form of sensory memory specific to touch stimuli. It is used regularly when assessing the necessary forces for gripping and interacting with familiar objects. It may also influence one's interactions with novel objects of an apparently similar size and density.

Haptic memory is related with touch stimuli. It is related to the sense of touch. It can include sensations like pressure, pain, itching, or something that feels good.

Parietal lobe is associated with haptic memory. Several distinct areas of the parietal lobe are responsible for contributing to different aspects of haptic memory. Memory for the properties of stimuli such as roughness, spatial density, and texture involves activation of the parietal operculum. Properties of stimuli such as size and shape, as detected by touch receptors in the skin, are stored in the anterior part of the parietal lobe. Memory for spatial information such as the location of stimuli involves the right superior parietal lobule and temporoparietal junction.

Haptic memory involves cutaneous and kinesthetics. It involves at least two subsystems; cutaneous, or everything skin related, and kinesthetic, or joint angle and the relative location of body.

33 Key issues in the study of heredity-environment effects on intelligence are

I. Reaction range
II. Proximal and distal causation
III. Collinearity
IV. Environment sphere

Choose the correct answer from the codes given below.

Codes

1 I and II 2 III and IV
3 I, II and III 4 II, III and IV

***Ans.** (3)*

Exp. The key issues in the study of heredity-environment effects on intelligence involve Reaction range, Proximal and distal causation, and Collinearity.

Reaction range : It refers to the upper and lower limits placed on one's intelligence by their genes. However, the environment decides where one's IQ will lie within the constraints of these limits.

Proximal and distal causation : In terms of intelligence, the environment allows the genes to be manifested. Therefore, while studying heredity-environment effects on intelligence, one must consider which of the proximal causes of intelligence, which are generally environmental. One must also consider the distal causes of intelligence, which are both, genetic and environmental.

Collinearity : It refers to the extent to a high degree of correlation between the causes and their consequences in terms of intelligence. This makes it difficult to determine whether intelligence is mostly inherited or environmental. Certain variables may be considered as environmental, however, they might be genetic.

34 In group counselling, there is a typical order of various stages.

I. Norming II. Performing
III. Forming IV. Storming

Choose the correct answer from the codes given below.

Codes

1 III, I, II, IV
2 III, II, I, IV
3 III, IV, I, II
4 III, I, IV, II

***Ans.** (3)*

Exp. Group counselling takes place in the following order of stages:

1. *Forming* : This is the orientation stage. The leader sets the length of the counselling period, discusses the norms pertaining to confidentiality and attendance, and sets the rules of participation.

2. *Storming* : It is marked by transition. During this stage, people may either be open to sharing about themselves or shy. Conflict may also develop among participants because they may openly disagree with one another.
3. *Norming* : It is marked by cohesion. During this phase, the participants come together, feel more comfortable or open to discussing their deeper issues. It is marked by self-disclosure, trust, balance, and safety.
4. *Performing* : It is the performance stage. Here, the participants work with one another, and for themselves. The group becomes more egalitarian.

35 Match List I with List II and select the correct answer using the codes given below.

List I (Concept)	List II (Description)
A. Cataplexy	I. Non-REM sleep
B. Apnoea	II. REM sleep
C. Dreams	III. Waking up as one stops breathing
D. Night terrors	IV. Symptom of narcolepsy

Codes

	A	B	C	D
1	I	III	II	IV
2	IV	III	I	II
3	IV	III	II	I
4	I	II	IV	III

Ans. (3)

Exp. The correct matching is A-IV, B-III, C-II, D-I.

Cataplexy is a symptom of narcolepsy, wherein one feels sudden weakness in their muscles whilst awake. Narcolepsy is a sleep disorder that is characterised by intense daytime drowsiness and sudden sleep attacks.

Sleep apnoea is a sleep disorder wherein one experiences frequent stoppage of breathing whilst asleep. They have to wake up in order to start breathing again.

Dreams involve imagery, sensations, and other emotions. They are experienced during the REM (Rapid eye movement) stage of sleep. Brain is highly active whilst one is dreaming, and its activity resembles that of wakefulness.

Night terrors take place during the deepest stage (Stage 4) of Non-REM sleep. Night terrors are characterised by intense fear, screaming, and thrashing while one is still asleep. They can also lead to sleepwalking.

36 The disruptive effect that occurs when a novel stimulus is presented along with an already established conditioned stimulus is called

1 External inhibition
2 Response inhibition
3 Counter conditioning
4 Stimulus inhibition

Ans. (1)

Exp. The disruptive effect that takes place when a new stimulus is presented along with an already established Conditioned Stimulus (CS) is called External inhibition.

External inhibition is a phenomenon wherein there is a decrease in response when another stimulus that was not a part of the original conditioning procedure is introduced with a CS that has already been established. For instance, when Ivan Pavlov conditioned the dog to salivate to the sound of tuning fork, it was observed that whenever a loud truck passed by during the sounding of the fork, the dog tended to salivate less as it got distracted by the sound of the truck.

37 Match List I with List II and select the correct answer using the codes given below.

List I	List II
A. Night Terror	I. Disturbance in sleep-wake cycle
B. Restless Leg Syndrome	II. Cramps in calf and foot muscles
C. Nocturnal Leg Cramps	III. Sensations in legs causing movements and loss of sleep
D. Circadian Rhythm Disorder	IV. Extreme agitation

Codes

	A	B	C	D
1	I	II	III	IV
2	IV	III	II	I
3	I	III	II	IV
4	IV	II	III	I

Ans. (2)

Exp. The correct matching is A-IV, B-III, C-II, D-I.

Night Terror is a sleep disorder that is characterised by fear, screaming, and extreme agitation whilst one is still asleep. It takes place during the deep stages of non-REM sleep.

Restless Legs Syndrome is characterised by an intense urge to move one's legs because of uncomfortable sensations. It generally occurs during the evening time or night time hours when one is either in a sitting or sleeping, thereby leading to sleep deprivation.

Nocturnal Leg Cramps are characterised by painful spasms in one's legs when they are lying in their bed. The cramps generally take place in the calf, thigh, or foot muscles in the leg.

Circadian Rhythm Disorders are characterised by disturbances that take place when the sleep-wake cycle of the body is not in tune with one's environment. Circadian Rhythms are internal clocks that control different activities of the body, including the sleep-wake cycle. They keep the body in step with the day and night cycle of their environment.

38 Match List I with List II and select the correct answer using the codes given below.

List I (Style)	List II (Description)
A. Directive autocrat	I. Makes decision participatively and gives latitude to subordinates in carrying out their job
B. Directive democrat	II. Makes decision unilaterally and gives subordinates latitude in carrying out their work
C. Permissive autocrat	III. Making decisions participatively by close supervision of subordinates
D. Permissive democrat	IV. Making decisions unilaterally, but closely supervising subordinates

Codes

	A	B	C	D		A	B	C	D
1	I	II	III	IV	2	IV	III	II	I
3	II	III	IV	I	4	II	I	III	IV

Ans. (2)

Exp. The correct matching is A-IV, B-III, C-II, D-I.

Directive autocrats make decisions unilaterally, but closely supervise subordinates. These are leaders who single-handedly make decisions, without consulting with their employees. They closely supervise the works of their employees to check that the assigned tasks are being completed.

Directive democrats make decisions participatively by close supervision of subordinates. These are those leaders who take the input of their employees before taking any decisions. They also closely supervise the works of their employees to check that the tasks are being completed.

Permissive autocrats make decision unilaterally and gives subordinates latitude in carrying out their work. These are those leaders who single-handedly make decisions. However, they allow their employees some flexibility in determining how they are going to carry out their day-to-day work or tasks.

Permissive democrats make decision participatively and gives latitude to subordinates in carrying out their job. These are those leaders who consult with their employees beforemaking any decisions and also allow them flexibility in determining how they are going to carry out their everyday tasks or work.

39 Which of the following neurotransmitters is/are found throughout the central nervous system?

I. GABA II. Glycine
III. Dopamine IV. Serotonin

Choose the correct answer from the codes given below

Codes

1 Only I
2 I and III
3 III and IV
4 II, III and IV

Ans. (1)

Exp. GABA is the neurotransmitter that is found throughout the Central Nervous System.

GABA stands for gamma-aminobutyric acid. It is an amino acid that functions as a neurotransmitter in the brain. That is, it is a chemical messenger that carries messages from one neuron to the others. The function of GABA is to produce a calming effect, therefore, it is highly helpful in reducing emotions like stress, fear, or anxiety. It also helps in reducing seizures. It is found throughout the central nervous system.

40 What is a toddler experiencing who is occupied with pointing at things and asking what they are?

1 The naming explosion
2 Prelinguistic vocables
3 Multilinguistic awareness
4 An overactive Language Acquisition Device (LAD)

Ans. (1)

Exp. A toddler who is pointing at things and asking what they are is experiencing the naming explosion.

By the time babies reach their toddlerhood years, their vocabulary grows from 50 words to 200 words. This happens because they experience a vast growth in their language development, which is known as 'the naming explosion.' Many of the words they know at this stage are nouns. They acquire it by pointing at people, places, or things, and enquiring as to what they are,

41 Given below are two statements, one labelled as Assertion (A) and the other labelled as Reason (R). Read the statements and choose the correct answer using the codes given below.

Assertion (A) Reasoning is often influenced by emotion-laden beliefs.

Reason (R) Powerful beliefs come face-to-face with logical arguments.

Codes

1 Both (A) and (R) are true and (R) is the correct explanation of (A).
2 Both (A) and (R) are true, but (R) is not the correct explanation of (A)
3 (A) is true, but (R) is false.
4 (A) is false, but (R) is true.

Ans. (1)

Exp. Both (A) and (R) are true and (R) is the correct explanation of (A).

Reasoning is often influenced by emotion-laden beliefs. Reasoning involves the interpretation of information in order to reach conclusions. It is a logic-based process. However, emotional states influence reasoning processes. These are often misattributed to focal objects, distort beliefs in an assimilative fashion, disrupt self-control when intensely negative, but do not necessarily increase risk-taking. Emotions seem to promote social and moral behaviour.

Powerful beliefs come face-to-face with logical arguments. A strong argument is a non-deductive argument that succeeds in providing probable, but not conclusive, logical support for its conclusion. Reasoning is oftentimes affected by emotion when very strong beliefs encounter logical arguments. So, the reason explains why reasoning is influenced by emotion-laden beliefs.

42 Match List I with List II and select the correct answer using the codes given below.

List I (Type of Test/Construct)	List II (Example)
A. Forced-choice test	I. Allport, Vernon and Lindzey's Study of Values
B. Ipsative scores	II. Edwards Personality Preference Schedule
C. Projective test	III. Balanced Inventory of Desirable Responding
D. Self-deception/Impression management	IV. Rosenzweig PF Study

Codes

	A	B	C	D		A	B	C	D
1	I	II	IV	III	2	III	IV	I	II
3	II	I	IV	III	4	II	IV	I	III

Ans. *(3)*

Exp. The correct matching is A-II, B-I, C-IV, D-III.

Forced choice tests involve choosing between two alternatives based on which one is more desirable to them. An instance of this type of test is the 'Edwards Personality Preference Schedule,' which is a personality inventory involving 15 needs that are assessed by the forced-choice method.

Ipsative scoring is done on tests that require the test-taker to choose between different alternatives based on their desirability. They help compare a person with themselves and highlight their strengths and weaknesses. Allport, Vernon, and Lindzey's Study of Values involves Ipsative scoring; it measures personal values.

Projective tests assess one's personality based on their responses to ambiguous stimuli, such as images or patterns. Rosenzweig PF study is an instance of a projective test that involves 24 cartoon images, and the test-takers' personality is assessed on their responses to them.

Self-deception involves the belief in false things about themselves, while *Impression management* is a manner in which people affect others' perceptions about themselves. Both of these are associated with social desirability, and the Balanced Inventory of Desired Responding tests deliberate socially desirable responses.

43 Given an opportunity to choose, what should be the order of preference from ideally most appropriate to the least appropriate method to be used for the school students?

I. Counseling
II. Psychoeducation
III. Psychotherapy
IV. Identifying and improving work goals

Choose the correct answer from the codes given below.

Codes

1 I, IV, II, III   2 II, IV, I, III
3 IV, II, I, III   4 IV, I, II, III

Ans. *(2)*

Exp. The correct sequence is II, IV, I, III.

The order of preference from most appropriate to least appropriate methods to be used on students is as follows:

1. *Psychoeducation* : It involves providing information about mental health and treatments in cases of problems. It is also emotional and motivating, which allows students to gain an insight into mental health, cope with it, and follow the treatment when required.
2. *Identifying and improving work goals* : Assessment helps in identifying or setting goals. When goals are set, one can identify the areas where they need to improve to reach these goals.
3. *Counseling* : It involves the provision of professional assistance that may help a student resolve their psychological and other problems.
4. *Psychotherapy* : It involves therapy for treating mental health problems and disorders. It involves taking the student to a psychologist, psychiatrist, or other mental health professionals in order to treat the psychological problems or disorders they may be suffering from.

44 Which of the following are the sources which lead to prejudice?

I. Direct intergroup conflict
II. In group and out group
III. Social learning
IV. Parent's degree of prejudice

Choose the correct answer from the codes given below.

Codes

1 II and III   2 I, II and IV
3 II, III and IV   4 I, II, III and IV

Ans. *(4)*

Exp. Prejudice can arise from direct intergroup conflict, in-group and out-group, social learning, and parent's degree of prejudice.

Prejudice is negative, preconceived beliefs about others, and has no basis in one's own experiences. Different sources give rise to prejudice, and some of them are:

1. *Direct intergroup conflict* : These are disagreements that exist within the members of a group. For instance, members of the same group can hold different opinions, thereby resulting in conflicts. These conflicts can lead to prejudiced feelings against those members.
2. *In-group and out-group* : In-group is a group that one identifies with, and is a member of. Out-group is one that a person may not identify with. One is generally biased towards their in-group, and this bias can lead to prejudiced feelings against the out-group.
3. *Social learning* : This involves learning through the observation of other people's behaviours. If people observe others around them behaving in a prejudiced manner against other people, they may also develop prejudiced feelings towards those people.
4. *Parent's degree of prejudice* : It can be explained by social learning. Children tend to observe and imitate the behaviour of their parents. When children observe their parents displaying prejudice, it may give rise to feelings of prejudice in children as well.

45 Which of the following are true about attribution?

I. Internal attributions ascribe the causes of behaviour to personal dispositions and traits.

II. Internal attributions ascribe the causes of behaviour to individual abilities and feelings.

III. External attributions ascribe the causes of behaviours to situational demands.

IV. External attributions are always unstable.

V. Internal attributions are always stable.

Choose the correct answer from the codes given below.

Codes

1 I, II and III are correct; IV and V are incorrect
2 I and III are correct; II, IV and V are incorrect
3 I and II are correct; III, IV and V are incorrect
4 IV and V are correct; I, II and III are incorrect

***Ans.** (1)*

Exp. Statement I, II and III are correct; IV and V are incorrect.

Internal attribution is when people ascribe personal reasons for a behaviour instead of ascribing it to external reasons. For instance, if a student gets a good grade on a test, they attribute it to their diligent study. Hence, Statement I is correct.

Internal attributions take place when people ascribe personal reasons to their abilities or feelings instead of attributing them to external reasons. For instance, if one is good at piano, they may attribute it to their ability in music. Hence, Statement II is correct.

External attributions take place when people ascribe the reasons for their behaviour to external factors like situational demands. For instance, if one rebukes their child, they may attribute the reason for their anger to the child's unruly behaviour (situational demand). Hence, Statement III is correct.

External attributions may not always be unstable. For instance, if a student is always attributing their failure in exams to bad fortune, then it is a stable external attribution. Hence, Statement IV is incorrect.

Internal attributions may not always be stable. For instance, if a student may attribute their failure to them not studying well sometimes, or they may attribute it to their inability at other times. Hence, Statement V is incorrect.

Directions (Qs. No. 46-50) *Read the following paragraph and answer the questions which follow* :

A sport psychologist wanted to study the effect of a specific type of steroids. She hypothesized that the consumption of steroid would temporarily improve the running rate. Seventy athletes in the age range of 25 to 30 years were employed in this work. Two Groups, A and B, of equal size were formed by random assignment.

The examination of the two groups revealed that the two groups had similar genderwise composition. Group A athletes received the drug dosage, adjusted for the body weight. Group B athletes received the placebo. Twenty-five minutes (time required to manifest the steroid effects) after, the athletes were required to run a specific track. The mean time to run the track was calculated for each group. The mean time required to run the track was I80 seconds and 145 seconds respectively for Group A and Group B. The mean difference was evaluated by appropriate statistical test.

46 Which of the following statistical tests can be used to analyse the data in the above experiment?

I. Independent samples t-test

II. Paired samples t-test

III. One-way analysis of variance

IV. Mann-Whitney U test

Choose the correct answer from the codes given below.

Codes

1 Only I
2 II and III
3 I and IV
4 I, III and IV

***Ans.** (4)*

Exp. Independent samples t-test, One-way analysis of variance (ANOVA), and Mann-Whitney U test can be used to calculate the mean difference between two groups.

Independent samples t-test is a statistical measure used to analyse the mean difference between two independent groups. In the given experiment, the performance of one group is not dependent on the other. Hence, independent samples t-test can be used to analyse the mean difference between them.

One-way ANOVA can be used to analyse whether there is any statistically significant difference between the performance of two independent groups. Hence, it can be used to analyse the mean differences between groups A and B mentioned in the experiment.

Mann-Whitney U test can be used in the given experiment to compare the differences between A and B groups as the dependent variable, in this case, the performance, is ordinal and continuous. Ordinal refers to gender differences in performance, and continuous can be performances based on other attributes of athletes, like their age or fitness levels.

47 The hypothesis of the above study can be best labelled as

1 Directional hypothesis
2 Null hypothesis
3 Non-directional hypothesis
4 Non-causal hypothesis

Ans. (1)

Exp. The hypothesis of the above study can be said to be Directional hypothesis.

A directional hypothesis is a prediction made by the experimenter with regards to a positive or negative change in the relationship between the Independent Variable (IV) and the Dependent Variable(DV). Here, the experimenter hypothesises that intake of steroids (IV) enhances athletic performance (DV). This indicates that independent variable affects a positive change in dependent variable. Hence, the hypothesis is directional.

48 The researcher's hypothesis in the above study

1 has been verified
2 has been rejected
3 has been partially verified
4 could not be verified due to inadequate data

Ans. (2)

Exp. The researcher's hypothesis in the above study has been rejected.

The experimenter hypothesised that intake of steroids would improve performance. In the experiment, Group A was given the steroids, while Group B received a placebo, which is a fake treatment that did not consist of any steroids. Placebo may lead to participants believing they have received steroids, which may impact their performance. Their performance on the track indicated that Group A took an average of 180 seconds to run the track, while Group B took an average of 145 seconds. Group B, the group that did not receive the steroid, ran faster than Group A, indicating that steroids did not improve performance. Hence, the hypothesis must be rejected.

49 In the context of the above experiment, match List I with List II and select the correct answer using the codes given below.

List I (Type of variable)	List II (Actual varaible)
A. Independent variable	I. Age
B. Dependent variable	II. Drug dosage
C. Controlled variable	III. Gender
D. Dummy variable	IV. Time required to run

Codes

	A	B	C	D
1	IV	II	I	III
2	II	IV	III	I
3	II	IV	I	III
4	I	III	II	IV

Ans. (2)

Exp. The correct matching is A-II, B-IV, C-III, D-I.

Independent Variable (IV) is one that an experimenter can manipulate, and has an impact on the Dependent Variable (DV). Here, drug dosage is the independent variable as steroids are given to some participants and not given to others, and they are hypothesised to improve performance (DV).

Dependent Variable is the one that is being tested in an experiment. It is dependent on the independent variable. Here, the time required to run the track is considered to be Dependent variable as it is being measured, and is hypothesised to be impacted by the steroids (IV).

Controlled Variable is the one that is controlled or held constant by the experimenter.

Here, the composition of the two groups, A and B, are equalised in terms of gender. That is, gender differences are controlled, or made constant.

Dummy variables are numerical and can be representative of sub-groups in an experiment. Here, age is a numerical variable, and the ages between 25 and 30 years can be further divided into sub-groups, and the performance levels based on age can also be analysed.

50 Given below are two statements, one labelled as Assertion (A) and the other labelled as Reason (R). In the context of the above experiment, read the statements and choose the correct answer using the codes given below.

Assertion (A) In the above experiment, subjects have been randomly allotted to two groups.

Reason (R) Random allotment, makes the groups reasonably comparable in terms of individual differences.

Codes

1 Both (A) and (R) are true and (R) is the correct explanation of (A).
2 Both (A) and (R) are true, but (R) is not the correct explanation of (A).
3 (A) is true, but (R) is false.
4 (A) is false, but (R) is true.

Ans. (1)

Exp. Both (A) and (R) are true and (R) is the correct explantion of (A).

Random assignment or allotment is used to reduce personal differences between two groups in a study/experiment. In random assignment, every participant of the study stands an equal chance to be in either of the two groups. In the given experiment, participants were randomly assigned to either Group A or Group B to minimise differences.

One of the ways random assignment helped in reducing differences was minimising gender differences. That is, both the groups resembled each-other, genderwise.

51 Given below are two statements, one labelled as Assertion (A) and the other labelled as Reason (R). Read the statements and choose the correct answer using the codes given below.

Assertion (A) Rogers contends that ideal condition for the development of healthy self-concept and movement towards becoming fully functioning is unconditional regard.

Reason (R) Unconditional positive regard can generate incongruence between true-self and experience.

Codes

1 Both (A) and (R) are true and (R) is the correct explanation of (A).
2 Both (A) and (R) are true, but (R) is not the correct explanation of (A).
3 (A) is true, but (R) is false.
4 (A) is false, but (R) is true.

Ans. (3)

Exp. (A) is true, but (R) is false.

Rogers contends that ideal condition for the development of healthy self-concept and movement towards becoming fully functioning is unconditional regard. Carl Rogers contends that for the development of a healthy self-concept and for a person to become a fully functioning individual, that is, someone who realises and work towards their full potential, requires Unconditional Positive Regard (UPR).

Unconditional positive regard can generate incongruence between true-self and experience. UPR is complete acceptance and support of the true-self of a person, as and how they are. Since UPR is unconditional, there are no conditions for worth, and this leads to the healthy development of a self-concept. Therefore, UPR leads to congruence between true-self and the experience of one's true self, and not incongruence.

52 The tendency of working hard for the 'fun of it' creatively and for the satisfaction that comes from the mastery and deep understanding of a problem comes from

I. Exploration needs
II. Curiosity
III. Effectance motivation
IV. Internal locus of control

Choose the correct answer from the codes given below.

Codes

1 Only I and II are correct
2 Only I and IV are correct
3 Only III is correct
4 Only I, II and III are correct

Ans. (4)

Exp. The tendency of working hard for the 'fun of it' creatively and for the satisfaction that comes from the mastery and deep understanding of a problem comes from exploration needs, curiosity, and effectance motivation.

Curiosity is the impulse or desire to investigate, observe, or gather information, particularly when the material is novel or interesting. Curiosity is considered to be the desire for knowledge.

It leads to effectance motivation, which is the motivation to effectively interact with one's environment, investigate matters deeply, and master skills or techniques. Curiosity and effectance motivation are prerequisites for exploration, which refers to the activities that help in collecting information regarding one's environment. Consequently, these three factors are required when it comes to enjoying hard work, or mastery and deep understanding of problems as one must be curious, which is central to effectance motivation, and these two lead to exploratory behaviours.

53 Patterns of familial transmission of intelligence from one generation to other is investigated in

1 Linkage analysis studies
2 Adoption studies
3 Association studies
4 Segregation analysis studies

Ans. (1)

Exp. Patterns of familial transmission of intelligence from one generation to another are investigated in Linkage analysis studies.

Linkage analysis studies refer to the studies that aim to establish linkage between different genes. Linkage refers to genes being inherited together because of them being situated near one another on chromosomes. Genome-wide linkage analyses have been conducted to determine the regions in chromosomes containing genes that influence intelligence, and these studies have involved the analysis of more than a hundred families to determine the pattern of transmission of intelligence.

54 **Reciprocal determinism is an interaction between which of the following?**

1 Person and his environment
2 Person and his behaviour
3 Person's behaviour and his environment
4 Person, his behaviour and his environment

Ans. (4)

Exp. Reciprocal determinism is an interaction between a person, his behaviour, and his environment.

Reciprocal determinism is a concept proposed by Albert Bandura. He says that three factors play a role in influencing behaviour : the person, his environment, and his behaviour itself. For instance, consider a child in a school environment. If the child does not like going to school, they may indulge in unruly behaviour. This leads to their teacher admonishing them, which only increases their unruly behaviour. Here, the child, the school environment, and their unruly behaviour is determining the increase in their unruly behaviour.

55 **Given below are two statements, one labelled as Assertion (A) and the other labelled as Reason (R). Read the statements and choose the correct answer using the codes given below.**

Assertion (A) The information processing approach is rooted in structuralism.

Reason (R) It attempts to identify the basic capacities and processes that one uses in cognition.

Codes

1 Both (A) and (R) are true and (R) is the correct explanation of (A).
2 Both (A) and (R) are true, but (R) is not the correct explanation of (A).
3 (A) is true, but (R) is false.
4 (A) is false, but (R) is true.

Ans. (1)

Exp. Both (A) and (R) are true and (R) is the correct explanation of (A).

Structuralism is a school of psychology that is geared towards breaking down mental processes into the basic components. Information processing approach is a cognitive approach that refers to the deciphering, manipulation, and regulation of information. It seeks to understand the way in which information is processed by understanding the basic components like thinking and memory. Therefore, it can be said that it aims to identify the basic components or processes that are involved in cognition, which is the processing of information.

56 **Given below are two statements, one labelled as Assertion (A) and the other labelled as Reason (R). Read the statements and choose the correct answer using the codes given below.**

Assertion (A) While scaling the attitude items (statements) by the method of equal appearing intervals, median is often used as the measure of scale values.

Reason (R) The distribution of categories, assigned by the judges, is skewed for several items.

Codes

1 Both (A) and (R) are true and (R) is the correct explanation of (A).
2 Both (A) and (R) are true, but (R) is not the correct explanation of (A).
3 (A) is true, but (R) is false.
4 (A) is false, but (R) is true.

Ans. (1)

Exp. Both (A) are (R) are true and (R) is the correct explanation of (A).

While scaling the attitude items (statements) by the method of equal appearing intervals, median is often used as the measure of scale values. Equal-appearing interval, also known as Thurstone scale, is used to measure attitudes. In this scale, attitudes are scored from1 to 11, 1 being extremely unfavourable and 11 being extremely unfavourable.

Then, the median is computed for each item. Median refers to the middle number in a list arranged from ascending order to descending order. The median value of each scale item represents the weight to be used for aggregating the items into a composite scale score representing the construct of interest.

The distribution of categories, assigned by the judges, is skewed for several items. The reason why median is used is because the distribution of categories as per the judges often appears to be skewed or distorted. The resulting scores of equal appearing interval scale strongly skew judges' scores and lead to persistent mark inflation. Therefore, median rank works well with skewed scores as median ranks control measurement error than other measurements.

57 **Given below are two statements, one labelled as Assertion (A) and the other labelled as Reason (R). Read the statements and choose the correct answer using the codes given below.**

Assertion (A) Concepts are used to solve problems as well as to think creatively.

Reason (R) Concepts are useful for identifying objects and saving us from learning the same thing time and again.

Codes

1 Both (A) and (R) are true and (R) is the correct explanation of (A).
2 Both (A) and (R) are true, but (R) is not the correct explanation of (A).
3 (A) is true, but (R) is false.
4 (A) is false, but (R) is true.

Ans. (1)

Exp. Both (A) are (R) are true and (R) is the correct explanation of (A).

Concepts are used to solve problems as well as to think creatively. Concept refers to the idea/knowledge of something (an object). Creative thinking involves understanding a problem in all possible ways, and coming up with new ways to solve problems. For instance, when one understands the concept of a puzzle, one can identify a puzzle, and an understanding of a puzzle helps one look at it from all possible angles, and think of creative ways to solve it.

Concepts are useful for identifying objects and saving us from learning the same thing time and again. Concepts help us in identifying an object and save people from the prospect of having to learn the same thing repeatedly, and therefore, can be used in creative thinking. The reason is correct and explains why the concepts are used to solve problems and to think creatively.

58 Given below are two statements, one labelled as Assertion (A) and the other labelled as Reason (R). Read the statements and choose the correct answer using the codes given below.

Assertion (A) New employees in organisations generally lack quality threshold performance.

Reason (R) The confusion and disorientation is experienced by many newcomers to an organisation.

Codes

1 Both (A) and (R) are true and (R) is the correct explanation of (A).
2 Both (A) and (R) are true, but (R) is not the correct explanation of (A).
3 (A) is true, but (R) is false.
4 (A) is false, but (R) is true.

Ans. *(1)*

Exp. Both (A) are (R) are true and (R) is the correct explanation of (A).

New employees in organizations generally lack quality threshold performance. Threshold for quality refers to establishing norms or criteria. When one does not completely understand the norms, it is inevitable that their performance is lacking quality threshold.

The confusion and disorientation is experienced by many newcomers to an organisation. Confusion, also referred to as disorientation, is experienced by employees when they newly enter an organisation. This is because they do not have a full understanding of the norms and workings of the organisation yet, and it requires some getting used to. Therefore, they lack quality threshold performance. The reason is correct and explains the assertion.

59 Self-actualisers can be characterised as

I. Having more efficient perception of reality.
II. Showing greater acceptance of themselves, others and nature.
III. Having tendency to be more concerned with understanding tasks that will benefit themselves.
IV. Recognising their own weaknesses but do not being so anxious of them.

Choose the correct answer from the codes given below.

Codes

1 I and II are correct, III and IV are incorrect.
2 III and IV are correct, I and II are incorrect.
3 I, II and III are correct, IV is incorrect.
4 I, II and IV are correct, III is incorrect.

Ans. *(4)*

Exp. Statement I, II and IV are correct, III is incorrect.

Self-actualisers are those who have reached their full potential. Self-actualisers have an acute sense of realism. They are able to view life in terms of logic and rationalism. Hence, Statement I is correct.

One of the aspects of self-actualisation is the acceptance of oneself. Therefore, self-actualisers are highly accepting of themselves. They also possess a very democratic view of the world, therefore, they are accepting of others and the world around them as well. Hence, Statement II is correct.

Self-actualisers recognise their weaknesses, however they are not very anxious about them as they accept themselves as they are, inclusive of their flaws. Hence, Statement IV is correct.

Self-actualisers have a tendency to achieve tasks whose benefits are far and wide, that is, beyond themselves. For instance, humanitarians can be said to come under this category. Hence, Statement III is incorrect.

60 In which kind of bureaucracy, operating core is considered as the dominant group?

1 Adhocracy
2 Professional bureaucracy
3 Machine bureaucracy
4 Divisionalised structure

Ans. *(2)*

Exp. In a Professional bureaucracy, the operating core is considered as the dominant group.

Professional bureaucracy is one in which the major work is done by professionals who are highly trained experts. They are known as the operating core, and professional bureaucracy affords them a high degree of control over their own work. Hence, they become the dominant group in this system.

61 Which of the following are correct according to "levels of processing approach"?

I. Recall of words with visual characteristics is better than words with semantic characteristics.
II. Recall of words with self-reference is better than words with sematic characteristics.
III. Recall of words with semantic characteristics is better than words with self-reference.
IV. Recall of words with semantic characteristics is better than words with acoustic characteristics.

Choose the correct answer from the codes given below.

Codes

1 I and II 2 II and III
3 III and IV 4 II, III and IV

Ans. (3)

Exp. Statement III and IV are correct according to "levels of processing approach".

The levels of processing approach suggests that the deeper the processing of information, the longer-lasting is the memory trace (physically stored memory). Deep processing involves understanding the meaning of words (semantic processing). Understanding the semantics of a word helps better remember it when compared to self-reference or simply remembering it on the basis of the way it sounds (acoustic).

Recall of words with semantic characteristics is better than words with self-reference. Levels of processing have been an integral part of learning about memory. The self-reference effect describes the greater recall capacity for a particular stimulus if it is related semantically to the subject. This can be thought of as a corollary of the familiarity modifier, because stimuli specifically related to an event in a person's life will have widespread activation in that person's semantic network. For example, the recall value of a personality trait adjective is higher when subjects are asked whether the trait adjective applies to them than when asked whether trait adjective has a meaning similar to another trait.

Recall of words with semantic characteristics is better than words with acoustic characteristics. Words that had been encoded semantically were better remembered than those encoded visually or acoustically. Semantic encoding involves a deeper level of processing than the shallower visual or acoustic encoding.

62 Match List I with List II and select the correct answer using the code given below.

List I (Attachment theory)	List II (Attachment related behaviour)
A. Psychoanalytic theory	I. Caregiver's responsiveness to infant's hunger and other basic needs
B. Learning theory	II. Feeding and responsiveness to infant's needs
C. Cognitive development theory	III. Infant discriminates between caregiver and stranger
D. Ethological theory	IV. Infants have characteristics that elicit attachment from caregivers

Codes

	A	B	C	D		A	B	C	D
1	II	I	IV	III	2	I	II	III	IV
3	I	III	II	IV	4	II	III	IV	I

Ans. (2)

Exp. The correct matching is A-I, B-II, C-III, D-IV.

The attachment related behaviour associated with the *Psychoanalytic theory* is caregiver's responsiveness to infant's hunger and other basic needs. Psychoanalytic theory suggests that development of attachment happens when the needs of the infant are satisfied by the caregiver. This theory was given by Sigmund Freud.

The attachment related behaviour associated with the *Learning theory* is feeding and responsiveness to infant's needs. Learning theory suggests that all behaviour is learnt, and infant forms attachment with the caregiver via classical or operant conditioning. This takes place when the infant learns to associate the caregiver with feeding and being responsive towards their basic needs.

The attachment related behaviour associated with the *Cognitive development* theory is when infant discriminates between caregiver and stranger. Cognitive development theory suggests that attachment develops when an infant learns to recognise and differentiate the caregiver from other strangers. Therefore, attachment involves cognitive processes like attention and memory.

The attachment related behaviour associated with the *Ethological theory* is when infants have characteristics that elicit attachment from caregivers. Ethological theory suggests that behaviour has a survival value. Therefore, this theory suggests that infants display behaviours that help form attachment with caregivers. This is because attachment helps attend to survival and safety needs.

63 Match List I with List II and select the correct answer using the codes given below.

List I (Concept)	List II (Description)
A. Fetishism	I. Sexual urges and arousing fantasies involving cross-dressing
B. Necrophilia	II. Sexual arousal or fantasies about or actual use of non-living objects
C. Frotteurism	III. Sexual urges involving touching or rubbing a non-consenting person
D. Transvestic fetishism	IV. Sexual obsession with corpses

Codes

	A	B	C	D		A	B	C	D
1	I	III	II	IV	2	II	IV	III	I
3	II	IV	I	III	4	II	I	III	IV

Ans. (2)

Exp. The correct matching is A-II, B-IV, C-III, D-I.

Fetishism involves sexual arousal or fantasies about or actual use of non-living objects. It is a type of paraphilia in which inanimate objects—commonly undergarments, stockings, rubber items, shoes, or boots—are repeatedly or exclusively used in achieving sexual excitement. Objects designed for use in stimulating the genitals (e.g., vibrators) are not considered to be involved in Fetishism.

Necrophilia involves sexual obsession with corpses. It is a behaviour in which one derives sexual pleasure by engaging in sexual activities with dead people or corpses.

Frotteurism involves sexual urges involving touching or rubbing a non-consenting person. It is a sexual urge in which one touches or rubs their genitals against an individual who has not given their consent to do so. In doing so, they derive sexual pleasure.

Transvestic fetishism involves sexual urges and arousing fantasies involving cross-dressing. It is a paraphilia characterized by the wearing of female clothes by a heterosexual male for the purpose of achieving sexual excitement and arousal.

64 Creative thinking is a combination of _______ in thinking and ________ in understanding to produce _______ ideas and _________ .

1 reorganisation, flexibility; new, solutions
2 flexibility, reorganisation; innovative, solutions
3 flexibility, reorganisation; novel, solutions
4 flexibility, reorganisation; abstract, solutions

Ans. *(2)*

➲ *Exp.* Creative thinking is a combination of flexibility in thinking and reorganisation in understanding to produce innovative ideas and solutions.

Creative thinking involves looking at a problem from all possible angles, and coming with novel ways to solve them. Therefore, the defining aspect of creative thinking is flexibility in thinking, which makes it possible for the reorganisation of one's understanding and experiences in order to create innovative ideas and solutions.

65 The rapid changes in performance level as the size of reinforcement is varied is called

1 Spread of effect
2 Crespi effect
3 Reminiscence effect
4 Instinctual drift

Ans. *(2)*

➲ *Exp.* Crespi effect refers to the rapid changes in performance levels as the size of the reinforcement is varied.

Crespi effect is a phenomenon in conditioning wherein there is an increase or a decrease in behaviour that is not in proportion to the reinforcement provided. This effect takes place when there are sudden changes in the reinforcement. For instance, if a behaviour is being reinforced by 1 gm of food, and suddenly it has been increased to 5 gms, the performance of that behaviour will be higher than if it were being continuously reinforced only by 5 gms of food.

66 The following are all involved in hunger and eating process

I. Lateral hypothalamus
II. Ventral hypothalamus
III. Amino acids

In what sequence do these act?

1 III, I, II 2 I, III, II 3 I, II, III 4 III, II, I

Ans. *(2)*

➲ *Exp.* Lateral hypothalamus, Amino acids, Ventral hypothalamus are involved in hunger and eating process.

The sequence in which the different parts act when it comes to hunger is as follows:

Lateral hypothalamus responds to internal or external factors that make one feel hungry.

The levels of *amino acids* in the blood as well as the brain are important indicators when it comes to the feeling full after one has eaten. This helps in controlling appetite and body weight.

Ventral hypothalamus is the satiety centre in the brain. Through indicators, like levels of amino acids, it facilitates the determination of satiety, that is, the state of being fed to contentment. In doing so, it relieves hunger after one has eaten.

67 Given below are two statements, one labelled as Assertion (A) and the other labelled as Reason (R). Read the statements and choose the correct answer using the codes given below.

Assertion (A) Spearman proposed the existence of general mental ability (g factor) in his two-factor theory.

Reason (R) Spearman found positive manifolds in the intercorrelations matrix of ability tests.

Codes

1 Both (A) and (R) are true and (R) is the correct explanation of (A).
2 Both (A) and (R) are true, but (R) is not the correct explanation of (A).
3 (A) is true, but (R) is false.
4 (A) is false, but (R) is true.

Ans. *(1)*

➲ *Exp.* Both (A) and (R) are true and (R) is the correct explanation of (A).

Spearman proposed the existence of general mental ability (G factor) in his two-factor theory. Charles Edward Spearman proposed his two-factor theory of intelligence in 1904.

He was the first who introduced the concept of general intelligence called the"g" factor. . He proposed that intelligence consists of two factors, i.e., the 'g' factor (General ability) and the 's' factor (Specific ability), where the 'g' factor is involved in every general mental ability task of the person, and the 's' factor is responsible for only the specific intellectual abilities of the person.

Spearman found positive manifolds in the intercorrelations matrix of ability tests. Charles Spearman administered different tests to assess cognitive abilities. He found that there were positive correlations between all these tests, which he referred to as 'positive manifold.' For instance, scores on verbal test positively correlate with scores on reasoning test. This indicates the presence of a general factor (g-factor) of intelligence, which is a wide-ranging mental capacity that impacts the performance on different cognitive abilities.

68 Humanistic approach to personality is characterised by

I. Emphasis on personal responsibility
II. No denial to importance of past, but more focus on present
III. Description of naturally striving persons
IV. Description of individual differences along some dimensions

Choose the correct answer from the codes given below.

Codes

1 I and II are correct; III and IV are incorrect.
2 III and IV are correct; I and II are incorrect.
3 I, II and IV are correct; III is incorrect.
4 I, II and III are correct; IV is incorrect.

Ans. (4)

Exp. Statement I, II and III are correct; IV is incorrect.

Humanistic approach to personality considers a person as a whole, and focuses on qualities such as free will and self-actualisation (fulfilment of one's potential). Consequently, it emphasises personal responsibility. Hence, Statement I is correct.

Humanistic approach does not view personality as being determined entirely by one's past. It places certain importance on people's pasts, however, it focuses more on the present. Hence, Statement II is correct.

Humanistic approach to personality says that people have a natural tendency to strive, which is to sustain, actualise, and improve the quality of one's experiences. Hence, Statement III is correct.

Humanistic approach considers a person as a whole, and in doing so, it emphasises their uniqueness on the whole as well, and not just along certain dimensions. Hence, Statement IV is incorrect.

69 Match List I with List II and choose the correct answer using the codes given below.

List I	List II
A. Moon illusion effect	I. Monocular cue
B. Aerial perspective	II. Relative size hypothesis
C. Ponzo effect	III. Binocular cue
D. Convergence	IV. Optical illusion

Codes

	A	B	C	D		A	B	C	D
1	I	II	III	IV	2	II	III	IV	I
3	II	I	IV	III	4	III	I	II	IV

Ans. (3)

Exp. The correct matching is A-II, B-I, C-IV, D-III.

Moon illusion effect indicates that the moon appears to be larger when it is close to the horizon. Relative size hypothesis purports that the perceived size of an object is dependent on its immediate environment. With moon illusion, the size of objects in its immediate environment make it appear larger.

Aerial perspective refers to distant objects appearing blurred and less detailed. It helps in judging how far away objects are. It is a monocular cue, which indicates that it can be perceived with only one eye.

Ponzo effect is an optical illusion that takes place when two horizontal lines of the same size are placed on two vertical converging lines. On viewing, it appears that the horizontal line close to where the vertical lines are converging is smaller than the horizontal line which is far from where the lines are converging. In reality, they are both of the same size.

Convergence is a cue that provides information regarding distance. As objects move farther away, they appear to converge (like railway tracks). It is a binocular cue, which means that it requires two eyes to be perceived.

70 'Vacillation of thought and behaviour' is associated with the following types of conflicts

1 Approach-approach and approach-avoidance
2 Approach-approach, approach-avoidance and multiple approach-avoidance
3 Approach-avoidance and avoidance-avoidance.
4 Avoidance-avoidance, approach-avoidance and multiple approach-avoidance

Ans. (4)

Exp. 'Vacillation of thought and behaviour' is associated with Avoidance-avoidance, approach-avoidance and multiple approach-avoidance types of conflicts.

Vacillation of thought and behaviour refers to going back and forth when faced with conflicting situations. For instance, consider when a person is attracted towards another. They consider approaching them, but they may also feel shy. In doing so, they show vacillation in terms of thought and behaviour.

Vacillation of thought and behaviour is evident in three types of conflict-related behaviours:

1. *Avoidance-avoidance* : This style is seen when one is faced with two negative situations, and seeks to avoid them both.
2. *Approach-avoidance* : This style is seen when a situation has its benefits and disadvantages at the same time. One approaches it, and one may seek to avoid it as well.
3. *Multiple approach-avoidance* : This style is seen when a person is faced with a number of alternatives, and each has its pros and cons. They may approach some and avoid some.

71 Interpersonal justice refers to judgements concerning the _____ and _____ individuals are shown by parties responsible for distributing available to members of a group.

1 considerateness, courtesy, incentives
2 courtesy, considerateness, rewards
3 considerateness, courtesy, rewards
4 courtesy, considerateness, incentives

Ans. (3)

Exp. Interpersonal justice refers to judgements concerning the considerateness and courtesy individuals are shown by parties responsible for distributing available rewards to members of a group.

Interpersonal justice refers to the perceived fairness in terms of how employees are treated by those in authority. It refers to treating employees with respect, courtesy, and dignity. It involves judgements concerning the considerateness and courtesy that is shown to people by those responsible for distributing the rewards to members of a given group.

72 Given below are two statements, one labelled as Assertion (A) and the other labelled as Reason (R). Read the statements and choose the correct answer using the codes given below.

Assertion (A) Frankl described death as a boundary situation, an urgent experience that forces a person to deal with an existential situation.

Reason (R) The boundary situation provides deep meaning for the individual.

Codes

1 Both (A) and (R) are true and (R) is the correct explanation of (A).
2 Both (A) and (R) arc true, but (R) is not the correct explanation of (A).
3 (A) is true, but (R) is false.
4 (A) is false, but (R) is true.

Ans. *(1)*

Exp. Both (A) and (R) are true and (R) is the correct explanation of (A).

Frankl described death as a boundary situation, an urgent experience that forces a person to deal with an existential situation. Boundary situations are those that touch the boundary of one's existence. They represent difficulties that appear to be insurmountable, but the desire to overcome them may lead one to realise their true authentic self. Viktor Frankl described death to be a boundary situation as it existential threat (touching the boundary of one's existence), and forcing a person to face and deal with it.

The boundary situation provides deep meaning for the individual. Prototypical boundary situations are death, suffering, struggle, guilt, and chance. Boundary situations are opaque and inevitable. Boundary situation may help to become conscious of the loneliness and suspiciousness of being and to risk the leap from an possible to a true existence in freedom. Therefore, the reason explains the assertion.

73 The best home environment for intellectual development is one in which

I. Child is encouraged to work out problems with guidance and support from parents.
II. Parents tell the child what to do.
III. Child is left on his or her own.
IV. Child is facilitated more than required.

Choose the correct answer from the codes given below.

Codes

1 Only I
2 I and II
3 III and IV
4 I, II, III and IV

Ans. *(1)*

Exp. The best home environment for intellectual development is one in which child is encouraged to work out problems with guidance and support from parents.

Children require mental stimulation in their home environment which can lead them to learn many things. The best home environment is one where children are able to solve problems on their own with support and guidance from their parents. For instance, when it comes to solving a puzzle, a child must be allowed to solve it on their own. If they are stuck at one step in the puzzle, parents must only provide guidance that allows them to solve it rather than solving it for them. In this way, children develop intellectually.

74 Neurons make up only about ______ per cent of the brain's cells and other ______ per cent are glia cells.

1 80 per cent; 20 per cent
2 10 per cent; 90 per cent
3 20 per cent; 80 per cent
4 90 per cent; 10 per cent

Ans. *(2)*

Exp. Neurons make up only about 10 per cent of the brain's cells and other 90 per cent are glia cells.

Neurons or nerve cells are the basic functioning unit of the brain. They help in the transmission of signals. However, they make up only 10% of the cells in the brain. The rest 90% are glia or glial cells. Glia are of three types – astrocytes, oligodendrocytes, and microglial cells. They help in providing support (like providing nutrients) to the neurons and are also involved in protecting them.

75 In matched two-group design with 30 subjects per group, the 't' test would be based on ______ degrees of freedom.

1 29 2 30 3 58 4 59

Ans. *(1)*

Exp. Degrees of freedom (DF) are the number of independent values that are allowed to vary. For instance, if one has 7 dresses and can wear a different one every day of the week, for the first 6 days, one has a choice of picking from all the dresses. However, on the 7th day, one can only pick the one that is left. Therefore, variance is allowed for the 6 dresses, but not for the 7th one.

Typically, the DF is calculated using the formula (N-1), where N stands for the number of subjects. In a matched two-group design with 30 subjects in each group, the DF will be 30 – 1, which is 29.

76 Given below are two statements, one labelled as Assertion (A) and the other labelled as Reason (R). Read the statements and choose the correct answer using the codes given below.

Assertion (A) Electrical stimulation of brain is considered to be a more important research tool than lesion method.

Reason (R) Electrical stimulation elicits a few behavioural effects which are easy to record.

Codes

1 Both (A) and (R) are true and (R) is the correct explanation of (A).
2 Both (A) and (R) are true, but (R) is not the correct explanation of (A).
3 (A) is true, but (R) is false.
4 (A) is false, but (R) is true.

Ans. (3)

Exp. (A) is true, but (R) is false.

Electrical stimulation of the brain is an important research tool as it helps in determining neural connections in the brain. For instance, when a certain region of the brain is electrically stimulated, and this elicits an electrical response in some other region of the brain, it can be understood that these two regions are connected in some manner. A lesion is the destruction of a particular brain tissue due to injury and damage.

Studying the behavioural effects of lesions can be complicated because many functions are distributed throughout the brain, and localised lesions cannot be used to study all the effects. Therefore, electrical stimulation is a more viable research tool as any area of the brain can be studied.

The behavioural effects brought about by electrical stimulation may not be easy to record. For instance, electrical stimulation of lateral hypothalamus, an area involved with feeding behaviour, does not give rise to an immediate increase in eating. The increase may happen slowly.

77 The basic rules of language used for learning and communication comprise of

I. Phonemes II. Morphemes
III. Syntax IV. Speech

Choose the correct answer from the codes given below.

Codes

1 I, II and III 2 I, III and IV
3 II, III and IV 4 I, II and IV

Ans. (1)

Exp. The basic rules of language used for learning and communication are :

1. *Phonemes* are units of sound that help distinguish one word from another. For instance, p and b are distinct sounding, therefore, pat is distinguished from bat on the basis of this difference.
2. *Morphemes* are the smallest meaningful units of speech which cannot be shortened any further. For instance, firehouse. In this fire and house are referred to as morphemes, and shortening either of the words any further would render them meaningless.
3. *Syntax* refers to the arrange words in such a manner so as to form meaningful sentences.

78 In response to questions asked by teachers, Ayan keeps jumping up with a raised hand on his seat till the teacher asks him to get up and answer. He also remains uneasy. Which is the most appropriate way of dealing with Ayan by the teacher?

1 Didactic counselling to explain why this is a bad habit
2 Shaping
3 Response cost form of punishment
4 Extinction

Ans. (1)

Exp. Didactic counselling is the most appropriate way of dealing with Ayan by the teacher.

Didactic counselling is a form of counselling in which concepts are explained, and instructions are provided. This may be most suitable to Ayan because when a professional explains why his hyperactivity and restlessness in a class are bad, he might be more willing to listen than if punished for his behaviour. Additionally, the counsellor also helps in providing instructions or techniques to reduce this behaviour, which Ayan may apply in the class.

79 Match List I with List II and select the correct answer using the code given below.

List I (Content)	List II (Test)
A. Addiction Potential Scale	I. MMPI– A
B. Alcohol Drug Knowledge Scale	II. MMPI–2
C. Self-defeating Scale	III. Rorschach Inkblot Test
D. Economy Index	IV. Million Clinical Multiaxial Inventory

Codes

	A	B	C	D		A	B	C	D
1	I	II	III	IV	2	II	I	IV	III
3	III	IV	I	II	4	IV	III	II	I

Ans. (2)

Exp. The correct matching is A-II, B-I, C-IV, D-III.

Addiction Potential Scale is a scale found in MMPI-2, and measures the personality factors that lead to the development of addictive disorders such as substance dependence. It consists of 39 items.

Alcohol Drug Knowledge Scale is a part of MMPI-A, and it was developed to identify people who abuse drugs or alcohol.

Self-defeating Scale is a part of Million Clinical Multiaxial Inventory (MCMI). It helps in identifying self-defeating behaviours which happen to be masochistic in nature. They may lead to failures, and development of other disorders.

Economy Index is found in Rorschach Inkblot Test. An interpretation of inkblot images present to the client as part of the test helps in understanding their economic perspective.

80 What is Piaget's term for a child's uneven cognitive performance, an inability to solve certain problems even though one can solve similar problems requiring the same mental processes?

1 A-not-B error
2 Invariant developmental sequence
3 Horizontal decalage
4 Representational insight

Ans. (3)

Exp. Horizontal décalage is a term given by Jean Piaget for a child's uneven cognitive performance, an inability to solve certain problems even though one can solve similar problems requiring the same mental processes.

It is usually observed during 7 – 11 years of age wherein a child, after learning to perform a task, is not able to apply the same concept to other similar tasks or functions. For instance, consider conservation, which refers to the understanding that certain properties of an object remain the same despite its physical changes. Children gain an understanding of the conservation of mass at the age of 6-7 years, however, they are not able to apply the same conservation concept when it comes to weight.

81 Super has given the following stages in his theory of career development and counselling. These are

I. Establishment II. Maintenance
III. Decline IV. Exploration
V. Growth

What is the correct sequence of these stages?

Choose the correct answer from the codes given below.

Codes

1 V, IV, I, II, III
2 I, II, IV, V, III
3 IV, I, V, II, III
4 I, IV, V, II, III

Ans. (1)

Exp. The correct sequence is V, IV, I, II, III.

Donald Super gave five stages of career development, which take place in the following sequence :

1. *Growth* takes place between the ages of 0 and 14 years. During this stage, needs self-concept, attitudes, and a general sense regarding work develops.
2. *Exploration* takes place between the ages of 15 and 24 years. During this stage, people explore their hobbies and try out different kinds of work.
3. *Establishment* takes place between the ages of 25 and 44 years. During this stage, people build on their skills and gain a sense of stability through their work.
4. *Maintenance* takes place between the ages of 45 and 64 years. During this stage, people continue to adjust and seek to improve their position at work.
5. *Decline* takes place after age 65 onwards. During this stage, people's work output tends to reduce, and they prepare for retirement.

82 Match List I with List II and select the correct answer using the codes given below.

List I (Term)	List II (Description)
A. Prudence	I. Undergoing hardships for their benefit
B. Justice	II. Controlling disruptive emotions and practicing self-discipline
C. Fortitude	III. Fulfilling obligations to parents and respecting their rights
D. Temperance	IV. Using reason for their benefit

Codes

	A	B	C	D		A	B	C	D
1	I	II	III	IV	2	III	IV	II	I
3	IV	III	I	II	4	IV	III	II	I

Ans. (3)

Exp. The correct matching is A-IV, B-III, C-I, D-II.

Prudence refers to wisdom. It involves using reasoning for one's benefit.

Justice refers to fairness. Hence, people with a sense of justice seek to fulfil their obligations towards their parents and hold respect for their rights. This is because they may find it just to be dutiful towards their parents as their parents were dutiful when it came to nurturing and raising them.

Fortitude refers to displaying courage when faced with adversities. Therefore, fortitude indicates the ability to go through hardships, which may lead towards one's benefit.

Temperance refers to moderation and self-restraint. Therefore, being able to control one's emotions and practice self-discipline indicates temperance.

83 Raphe Nuclei are most closely related to ______ neurotransmitter.

1 Epinephrine 2 Serotonin
3 Norepinephrine 4 Glycine

Ans. (2)

Exp. Raphe Nuclei are most closely related to Serotonin neurotransmitter.

Raphe nuclei are nuclei that are found from the midbrain to the spinal cord regions, and are highly concentrated in the brainstem region. Raphe nuclei are the primary regions involved in the production and the synthesis of the neurotransmitter, Serotonin. Serotonin plays a primary role in the stabilisation of mood, and produces feelings of well-being and happiness. It also plays a role in sleeping, eating, and digestion.

84 Given below are two statements, one labelled as Assertion (A) and the other labelled as Reason (R). Read the statements and choose the correct answer using the codes given below.

Assertion (A) Thurstone labelled his theory of intelligence as theory of primary mental abilities.

Reason (R) Thurstone found more than two first-order factors of intelligence through orthogonal rotation.

Codes

1 Both (A) and (R) are true and (R) is the correct explanation of (A).
2 Both (A) and (R) are true, but (R) is not the correct explanation of (A).
3 (A) is true, but (R) is false.
4 (A) is false, but (R) is true.

Ans. (1)

Exp. Both (A) and (R) are true and (R) is the correct explanation of (A).

Thurstone labelled his theory of intelligence as theory of primary mental abilities. According to Thurstone, there are seven primary mental abilities, namely, verbal comprehension, word fluency, spatial visualisation, number facility, perceptual speed, reasoning, and associative memory.

Thurstone found more than two first-order factors of intelligence through orthogonal rotation. Orthogonal rotation refers to a method in factor analysis that helps minimise the variables that are highly related to one another. In an orthogonal model, the variables involved are not correlated with one another. L.L. Thurstone used this method and found that there were more than two first-order factors in intelligence, that is, neither of them was correlated with the other. This led to him putting forth a theory of intelligence, which purported that intelligence consisted of seven separate primary mental abilities. Therefore, the reason explains the assertion.

85 Given below are two statements, one labelled as Assertion (A) and the other labelled as Reason (R). Read the statements and choose the correct answer using the codes given below.

Assertion (A) In multiple regression, the b or β coefficient associated with a given predictor is sometimes statistically non-significant, although the correlation between the criterion and the given predictor is significant.

Reason (R) In multiple regression, the b or β coefficients are partial regression coefficient.

Codes

1 Both (A) and (R) are true and (R) is the correct explanation of (A).
2 Both (A) and (R) are true, but (R) is not the correct explanation of (A).
3 (A) is true, but (R) is false.
4 (A) is false, but (R) is true.

Ans. (1)

Exp. Both (A) and (R) are true and (R) is the correct explanation of (A).

In multiple regression, the b or β coefficient associated with a given predictor is sometimes statistically non-significant, although the correlation between the criterion and the given predictor is significant. β-coefficients are partial regression coefficients in multiple regression analysis that is used in a causal model. They measure changes in the dependent variable as per the changes occurring in the independent variables, when all other extraneous variables are held constant. However, sometimes, b-coefficients may be statistically non-significant despite a significant correlation between the criterion (dependent variable) and predictor (independent variable). This is because correlation only indicates that the two variables are related to one another, however, it does not indicate a causal relationship between the two. Therefore, b-coefficients can be statistically non-significant despite high correlation as they help measure a casual relationship.

In multiple regression, the b or β coefficients are partial regression coefficient. The partial regression coefficients obtained in a multiple regression measure the change in the average value of 'y' associated with a unit increase in the corresponding 'x', holding constant all other variables. One interpretation of a partial correlation coefficient considers it as a measure of the linear association between the criterion variable and some predictor when both have been adjusted for their linear association with the remaining predictors.

86 _______ such as _______ believe that depth perception is innate.

1 Empiricists, Descartes
2 Nativists, Descartes
3 Empiricists, Berkeley
4 Nativists, Berkeley

Ans. (2)

Exp. Nativists such as Descartes believe that depth perception is innate.

Nativists believe that mental capacities are inborn, and not learnt. Rene Descartes was a nativist who believed that depth perception is innate as human beings are born with natural laws that can help in measuring the angles of the eye, thereby helping in the perception of depth.

87 Match List I with List II and select the correct answer using the codes given below.

List I (Tests)	**List II** (Concept)
A. Block design	I. Perceptual reasoning
B. Similarities	II. Comprehension
C. Matrix task	III. Simultaneous processing
D. Sentence questions	IV. Successive processing

Codes

	A	B	C	D		A	B	C	D
1	I	II	III	IV	2	II	IV	I	III
3	III	I	IV	II	4	IV	III	II	I

Ans. (1)

Exp. The correct matching is A-I, B-II, C-III, D-IV.

Block design test is associated with perceptual reasoning. It is a subtest of perceptual reasoning index of the Wechsler Adult Intelligence Scale IV. The block design test measures spatial perception, visual abstract processing, and problem solving. It is a test that helps in the assessment of intelligence. It involves viewing images of block designs and reproducing the same with the blocks provided.

Similarities is associated with comprehension. It is a subtest that is involved in the assessment of intelligence. It requires test-takers to view images, comprehend, and explain the way in which they are alike or different.

Matrix task is associated with Simultaneous processing. Simultaneous processing involves combining unconnected stimuli for better understanding and interpretation. Raven's progressive matrices is a matrix task that requires simultaneous processing as it involves the identification of missing parts that help complete a pattern.

Sentence questions are associated with Successive processing. Successive processing involves the integration of stimuli in a sequential order for comprehension and interpretation. For instance, the sentence questions task requires successive processing as it involves framing words in a serial order to form meaningful sentences.

88 Match List I with List II and select the correct answer using the codes given below.

List I (Books)	List II (Authors)
A. The Analysis of the Self	I. Maslow
B. Motivation and Personality	II. Kohut
C. Freedom to Learn	III. Rollo May
D. Man's Search for Himself	IV. Rogers

Codes

	A	B	C	D		A	B	C	D
1	I	II	III	IV	2	III	IV	I	II
3	II	I	IV	III	4	IV	III	II	I

Ans. (3)

Exp. The correct matching is A-II, B-I, C-IV, D-III.

The author of the book *The Analysis of the Self* is Kohut. It is the first monograph by the Austrian born American psychoanalyst Heinz Kohut. His biographer Charles B. Strozier has called it a masterpiece. Kohut wrote the book in his late 50's, in the late 1960s and early 1970s. He sent the finished manuscript to his publisher in the spring of 1970. The subject matter of this book concerns the psychoanalytic treatment of narcissistic personality disorders.

The author of the book *Motivation and Personality* is Maslow. It is a book on psychology by Abraham Maslow, first published in 1954. Maslow's work deals with the subject of the nature of human fulfillment and the significance of personal relationships, implementing a conceptualization of self-actualization. The subject matter of this book pertains to human fulfilment, implementation of self-actualisation, and the significance of interpersonal relationships. The author of the book *Freedom to Learn* is Rogers. Carl Rogers presented his theory of learning in Freedom to Learn (1969). The subject matter of this book pertains to the importance of allowing autonomy when it comes to learning, and the importance of freedom in a learning situation.

The author of the book *Man's Search for Himself* is Rollo May. It was published in 1953 where May talks about his experience with his patients and the recurring problems they had in common such as loneliness and emptiness. May looks deeper into this and discusses how humans have an innate need for a sense of value and also how life can often present an overwhelming sense of anxiety. The subject matter of this book pertains to exploring the hidden layer's of one' personality that help in revealing the true nature of oneself.

89 Given below are two statements, one labelled as Assertion (A) and the other labelled as Reason (R). Read the statements and choose the correct answer using the codes given below.

Assertion (A) As one enters a dimly lit room after being exposed to bright light, retinal rods become more sensitive.

Reason (R) Dark adaptation enables a person to see in dim light.

Codes

1 Both (A) and (R) are true and (R) is the correct explanation of (A).
2 Both (A) and (R) are true, but (R) is not the correct explanation of (A).
3 (A) is true, but (R) is false.
4 (A) is false, but (R) is true.

Ans. (1)

Exp. Both (A) and (R) are true and (R) is the correct explanation of (A).

As one enters a dimly lit room after being exposed to bright light, retinal rods become more sensitive. The photoreceptor cells, rods, are highly sensitive to light. So, in dimly lit conditions, they become more sensitive towards light, and help in vision. This is made possible because of the photoreceptor pigment, rhodopsin, which regenerates and increases the sensitivity towards light.

Dark adaptation enables a person to see in dim light. Dark adaptation refers to the ability of the eye to adjust to dimly-lit conditions as a result of increased sensitivity towards light. Dark adaptation is mainly made possible by the photoreceptor cells, rods. The reason correctly explains the assertion.

90 Which of the following are the mnemonic devices?

I. Categorical clusters
II. Peg-word system
III. Method of loci
IV. Heuristic

Choose the correct answer from the codes given below.

Codes

1 I and II
2 I, II and III
3 I, II and IV
4 I, II, III and IV

Ans. (2)

Exp. Categorical clusters, Peg-word system and Method of loci are the mnemonic devices.

Mnemonic devices are tools that help increase the ability to remember certain things. Mnemonic devices include:

1. *Categorical clusters* : This involves organising information into related groups, and placing similar/related items into the same category. This helps improve recall.
2. *Peg-word system* : It can be used to recall lists. Pegs are objects/images associated with numbers. For instance, 1 stands for sun, 2 for shoe, and so on. Now, if one wants to remember the sequential order of items in a recipe, one can associate each item with the image. For instance, tomato can be associated with the sun by picturing it engulfing the sun. This type of imagery helps remember the list better.
3. *Method of loci* : It involves visualising familiar spatial environments to help improve recall of information. For instance, consider a house, and all the rooms one finds in a house. Each of these locations forms a locus. So, while remembering a list of items, each item is associated with one locus. If the first item on the list is 'corn,' imagine a huge corn bob lying on the bed. If the next item is milk, imagine a huge milk packet hiding in the closet.

91 Academic achievement had a multiple correlation of 0.65 with the three predictors-intelligence, achievement, motivation and socio-economic status. How much variance in academic achievement is explained by the three predictors?

1 35.00 per cent
2 42.25 per cent
3 57.75 per cent
4 65.00 per cent

Ans. (2)

Exp. Multiple correlation is denoted by R, which is 0.65 in this case. In multiple correlation, variance is defined as the percentage of $(R)^2$.

The square of 0.65 is 0.4225, the percentage of which is 42.25%. Therefore, it can be said that the combination of intelligence, achievement motivation, and socioeconomic status explain 42.25% of variance in academic achievement.

92 What is the correct sequence of products in Guilford's SOI model?

1 Unit → Class → Relation → System → Implication → Transformation
2 Class → Unit → System → Relation → Transformation → Implication
3 Unit → Class → Relation → System → Transformation → Implication
4 Unit → Relation → Class → System → Transformation → Implication

Ans. (3)

Exp. Guilford's Structure of Intellect (SOI) model purports that intelligence is a function of multiple abilities. He gave three dimensions to intellect, among which, one is the product dimension. There are 6 types of products in the given order :

1. *Unit* : A single item of information
2. *Class* : Set of items with shared attributes
3. *Relation* : Connections between items, such as associations or opposites.
4. *System* : Organisation of items
5. *Transformation* : Conversion, perspective changes, or changes in knowledge. For instance, reversing a word.
6. *Implication* : Drawing inferences from information, making predictions, or anticipating consequences.

93 Which of the following are the methods used in studying verbal learning?

I. Serial learning
II. Paired-associate learning
III. Verbal discrimination learning
IV. Free recall

Choose the correct answer from the codes given below.

Codes

1 I and II
2 I, II and III
3 I, II and IV
4 I, II, III and IV

Ans. (4)

Exp. Serial learning, Paired-associate learning, Verbal discrimination learning and Free recall are the methods used in studying verbal learning.

Verbal learning generally involves memorisation and recall of items from a list. In verbal learning, all of the given methods are used :

1. *Serial learning* : Recalling stimuli in the same order in which they were presented. For instance, memorising a sequential list.
2. *Paired-associate learning* : In this form of learning, every two words from the list are paired together as stimulus-response. For instance, stove (stimulus) – shoe (response). Therefore, whenever the learner is prompted with the stimulus, which is stove, they respond with the word, shoe.
3. *Verbal discrimination learning* : In paired-associate learning, when the stimuli presented are very similar, the discrimination ability reduces. Verbal discrimination learning involves discriminating between stimuli. For instance, discriminating between boat, barge, canoe, which are highly similar.
4. *Free recall* : This involves recalling a list of items in any given order.

94 Myelin Stains and Nissl Stains identify _____ and _________ respectively.

1 Neural pathways; Neural cell bodies
2 Neural pathways; White matter
3 Neural cell bodies; Neural pathways
4 Nuclei; Neural cell bodies

***Ans.** (1)*

Exp. Myelin Stains and Nissl Stains identify Neural pathways and Neural cell bodies respectively.

Myelin is the component of myelin sheath that insulates axons. Myelin stains are used to identify neural pathways. Nissl stains are used for identifying neural cell bodies. It is helpful in measuring the density of the neurons as stained cell bodies can be easily identified and measured.

95 Rules within a language indicating how words can be combined into meaningful sentences refer to

1 Semantic development
2 Phonological development
3 Grammar
4 Babbling

***Ans.** (3)*

Exp. Rules within a language indicating how words can be combined into meaningful sentences refer to Grammar.

Grammar are rules pertaining to the system and structuring of a language. They help in conveying how words can be framed in order to form meaningful sentences. For instance, the grammar rule of subject-verb-object indicates a sentence structure where the subject comes first, followed by the verb, and then by the object. This rule helps in the formation of a meaningful sentence. For instance, Lucy loves painting, where Lucy is the subject, loves is the verb, painting is the object.

Directions (Qs. No. 96-100) *Read the following paragraph and answer the questions which follow* :

A researcher working in the vocational interests surveyed different interest assessment tools and after a careful scrutiny selected 68 scales presumably covering all areas of vocational interests. He administered all these scales to a large sample (N = 750). The researcher correlated every scale with every other scale and obtained 68×68 correlation matrix.

The 68×68 correlation matrix, without altering any of the diagonal elements, was factor analysed and the unrotated factors were extracted.

The Cattell's scree suggested 11 factors, where as Kaiser-Guttman' s root ≥ 1 criterion suggested 14 factors for further rotation.

The eleven factors explained 72 per cent of variance. The eleven factors were varimax-rotated. After examining the results and discussion, the researcher decided to carry out the second-order factor analysis. He, therefore, re-rotated the eleven factors and found that some of the inter-factor correlations were fairly high. The second-order factor analysis suggested three second-order factors which were fairly interpretable.

96 Which of the following factor extraction methods have not been used in the above work while extracting the first-order factors?

I. Principal axes method
II. Principal components method
III. Maximum likelihood method
IV. Generalised least squares method

Choose the correct answer from the codes given below.

Codes

1 I and III	2 II and III
3 III and IV	4 I, III and IV

***Ans.** (4)*

Exp. Principal axes method, maximum likelihood method, and Generalised least squares method are the extraction methods which have not been used in the above work while extracting the first-order factors.

In the above work, the method of Principal components method has been used. In the extraction of first-order factors, Cattell's scree-plot was used. The scree-plot is used to determine the Principal Components to retain in a Principal Component Analysis (PCA). PCA seeks to find the linear combination of variables so that maximum variance can be extracted from the resulting variables. Then, it eliminates the variance in order to seek a second linear combination. This method involves the principal axis method, which results in orthogonal factors, that is, factors unrelated to one other. In this case, 11 factors were extracted. Since scree-plot was used, only the Principal Axes method was considered for the extraction of first-order factors. Consequently, Principal components method, Maximum likelihood method or Generalised least squares method were not used.

97 Given below are two statements, one labelled as Assertion (A) and the other labelled as Reason (R). Read the statements and choose the correct answer using the codes given below.

Assertion (A) In the above work, the researcher preferred Cattell's scree-plot over Kaiser-Guttrnan's root ≥ 1 criterion.

Reason (R) Even with a small number of variables, Kaiser-Guttman's criterion always leads to the extraction of more factors, as compared to Cattell's scree.

Codes

1 Both (A) and (R) are true and (R) is the correct explanation of (A).
2 Both (A) and (R) are true, but (R) is not the correct explanation o(A).
3 (A) is true, but (R) is false.
4 (A) is false; but (R) is true.

***Ans.** (3)*

Exp. (A) is true, but (R) is false.

Cattell's scree-plot suggested 11 factors, whereas Kaiser-Guttman's root ≥ 1 criterion suggested 14 factors. The researcher considered the 11 factors which suggested 72% variance, and considered them for varimax-rotation and re-rotation. Therefore, the researcher preferred Cattell's scree-plot over Kaiser-Guttman's root ≥ 1 criterion.

Kaiser-Guttman's root ≥ 1 criterion does not always lead to the extraction of more variables than Cattell's scree-plot.

98 Given below are two statements, one labelled as Assertion (A) and the other labelled as Reason (R). Read the statements and choose the correct answer using the codes given below.

Assertion (A) In the above work, the researcher preferred Cattell's scree over Kaiser-Guttman's root ≥ 1 criterion.

Reason (R) The angles of separation among varimax-rotated factors are non-ninety.

Codes

1 Both (A) and (R) are true and (R) is the correct explanation of (A).
2 Both (A) and (R) are true, but (R) is not the correct explanation of (A).
3 (A) is true, but (R) is false.
4 (A) is false, but (R) is true.

Ans. (1)

Exp. Both (A) and (R) are true and (R) is the correct explanation of (A).

In the above work, the researcher preferred Cattell's scree over Kaiser-Guttman's root >/ 1 criterion. The researcher preferred Cattell's scree-plot over Kaiser-Guttman's root >/ 1 criterion as only the 11 factors suggested by Cattell's scree-plot were considered for varimax-rotation.

The angles of separation among Varimax-rotated factors are non-ninety. Varimax-rotation helps in clarifying the relationship amongst different factors. In this case, varimax-rotation showed that high correlations among the factors were present. The high correlations among the factors indicate that the angles of separation are non-ninety. That is, they are smaller than 90°, thereby indicating correlation.

99 During re-rotation of the first-order factors, which of the following methods is/are likely to have been used?

I. Oblimin　　II. Promax
III. Quartimax　　IV. Equamax

Choose the correct answer from the codes given below.

Codes

1 Only I
2 I and II
3 III and IV
4 II, III and IV

Ans. (2)

Exp. Oblimin and Promax rotations are oblique rotations which are used in cases when factors are not required to be uncorrelated.

Oblimin rotation is used in factor analysis when two or more factors happen to be correlated. Promax rotation makes for factors to be correlated, and can be calculated faster than oblimin rotation. Therefore, it is likely that these two methods were used as inter-correlations between the 11 factors after re-rotation was found to be very high.

Orthogonal rotation is used when factors are uncorrelated. Quartimax and equamax rotations are both orthogonal rotations. Hence, they are not likely to be used during re-rotations.

100 The three second-order factors would explain ________ of the variance among 68 scales.

1 less than 72 per cent
2 72 per cent
3 more than 72 per cent
4 100 per cent

Ans. (1)

Exp. The three second-order factors would explain less than 72 per cent of the variance among 68 scales.

In the given study, Cattell's scree-plot suggested 11 factors that explained 72 percent of the variance. In a second-order factor analysis, these 11 factors were re-rotated, and the factor analysis suggested that three of the second-order factors were interpretable. So, these three second-order factors will only be able to explain less than 72 per cent of the variance as all 11 factors put together were able to explain the entire 72 per cent of the variance.

UGC-NET PSYCHOLOGY

SOLVED PAPER 2018 (July)

PAPER II

1 In Erikson's theory, which psycho-social crises preceed and succeed Autonomy v/s Shame

1 Basic trust v/s Mistrust and Industry v/s Inferiority.
2 Initiative v/s Guilt and Industry v/s Inferiority.
3 Industry v/s Inferiority and Identity v/s Role confusion.
4 Basic trust v/s Mistrust and Initiative v/s Guilt.

***Ans.* (4)**

Exp. Among the given options, Basic trust v/s Mistrust precedes Autonomy v/s Shame, while Initiative v/s Guilt follows it.

Erik Erikson gave 8 stages of psychosocial development. Each stage is named after a psychosocial conflict, which helps in the development of personality.

The first stage is Basic trust v/s Mistrust. This stage takes place during infancy, where the infant is dependent on caregivers. If the caregivers are able to provide for the infant's needs, the infant develops trust, otherwise, they become mistrusting.

The second stage is Autonomy v/s Shame, which is followed by Initiative v/s Guilt. This stage takes place during one's preschool years. In this stage, children start taking initiative and strive to exercise certain control over their world. For instance, they can control their play behaviour, or control social interactions. Success during this stage helps in giving rise to feelings of initiative, while a failure to do so would give rise to feelings of guilt.

2 Read each of the following statements - Assertion (A) and Reason (R); and indicate your answer using code given below.

Assertion (A) Horner found high level of motive to avoid success or fear of success in females.

Reason (R) As a result of success, the threat of social rejection and fear concerning perceived lack of feminity are aroused in women.

Codes

1 Both (A) and (R) are true and (R) is the correct explanation of (A)
2 Both (A) and (R) are true, but (R) is not the correct explanation of (A)
3 (A) is true, but (R) is false
4 (A) is false, but R is true

***Ans.* (1)**

Exp. Both (A) and (R) are true and (R) is the correct explanation of (A).

M.S. Horner's theory regarding 'Fear of Success' seeks to explain the differences between sexes when it comes to achievement rates. Horner alleges that there is a high disposition among women to avoid success.

She claims that women tend to avoid success in certain areas as it happens to be incongruent with the social norms. For instance, they tend to avoid success in intellectual or academic areas. This is because success in these areas may not align with the societal notion of femininity, thereby giving rise to a fear of being rejected, socially.

3 Match List I with List II and select the correct answer by choosing from codes given below.

	List I (Concept)		List II (Explanation)
A.	Life Space	I.	Unlearned, fixed stereotyped pattern of activity.
B.	Instinctual Behaviour	II.	Psychological reality depicting the totality of facts that determine behaviour at a moment in true. It counts of environment as perceived by the person.
C.	Vacuum Behaviour	III.	Tendency to resume the previously unfinished task during intervening period.
D.	Task Resumption	IV.	Behaviour patterns that appear when the sign stimulus is not identifiable.

Codes

	A	B	C	D
1	I	II	III	IV
2	II	I	IV	III
3	III	IV	I	II
4	IV	III	II	I

***Ans.* (2)**

Exp. The correct matching is A-II, B-I, C-IV, D-III.

Life space is the psychological reality depicting the totality of facts that determine behaviour at a moment in true. It counts of environment as perceived by the person. It is the space that one moves through, and consisting of the overall facts that determine a person's behaviour at a given point in time. It involves the person themselves, their desired goals (positive valence), and avoiding variables that hinder their goals (negative valence). Kurt Lewin gave the concept of life-space.

Instinctual Behaviours are unlearned, fixed stereotyped pattern of activity. These are Fixed Action Patterns (FAP) that take place in response to a certain stimulus. They are innate, hence they are unlearnt. They are displayed by all the members of a given species.

Vacuum Behaviours are behaviour patterns that appear when the sign stimulus is not identifiable. These are Fixed Action Patterns (FAP) that are performed by organisms in the absence of external stimuli that usually give rise to them. These are innate. The concept of vacuum behaviours was first proposed by Konrad Lorenz.

Task Resumption is the tendency to resume the previously unfinished task during intervening period. It is a paradigm that proposes that people show an inclination towards resuming an unfinished task during the intervening period. It refers to the persistence present while pursuing goals.

4 Read each of the following statements Assertion (A) and Reason (R) and indicate your answer using codes given below.

Assertion (A) Perceived fairness of the interpersonal treatment is used to determine organisational outcomes.

Reason (R) People expect informational transparency and respect in organisations.

Codes

1 Both (A) and (R) are true and (R) is the correct explanation of (A)
2 Both (A) and (R) are true, but (R) is not the correct explanation of (A)
3 (A) is true, but (R) is false
4 (A) is false but (R) is true

Ans. (1)

Exp. Both (A) and (R) are true and (R) is the correct explanation of (A).

Organisational justice pertains to the presence of both, justice and fairness, in organisations and other workplaces. One of the components of organisational justice includes "Procedural justice," which was first proposed by Thibaut and Walker in the year, 1975. It is the perception of fairness in different processes, including interpersonal treatment, that play a role in giving rise to organisational outcomes.

When it comes to perceived fairness in interpersonal treatment and other processes, employees expect the organisation to be transparent in their procedures and treat them with respect. That is, even when an outcome happens to be unfavourable towards an employee, they will react to it positively if they believe that the processes involved in determining this unfavourable outcome were just and fair.

5 Match List I with List II and select the correct answer by choosing from codes given below.

List I (Concept)	List II (Explanation)
A. Episodic retrieval	I. Physical environment at retrieval matching that at encoding.
B. Context-dependent retrieval	II. Mood at retrieval matching that at encoding.
C. State-dependent retrieval	III. Retrieval stimulated by hints from the external and internal environment.
D. Cue-dependent retrieval	IV. Subsequent reactivation of stored memory traces.

Codes

	A	B	C	D		A	B	C	D
1	I	II	III	IV	2	II	IV	III	I
3	III	IV	II	I	4	IV	I	II	III

Ans. (4)

Exp. The correct matching is A-IV, B-I, C-II, D-III.

Episodic retrieval pertains to reactivation of stored memory traces. That is, the retrieval of specific past events that are present or stored in the form of memory traces. Memory trace is also known as an engram, which is a memory that is physically stored in the brain.

Context-dependent retrieval refers to an enhanced retrieval of information/events when the contextual cues pertaining to the physical environment in which the memory was encoded are the same as when it is being retrieved. For instance, if a list is memorized underwater, retrieval is better when recall takes place underwater itself.

State-dependent retrieval refers to an enhanced retrieval of information/events when the cues pertaining to the psychological or physical state, such as mood, in which the memory was encoded is the same as when it is being retrieved. Here, the similar state acts as a cue for recall.

Cue-dependent retrieval is the recall of information/events enabled by the cues (or hints) present in the environment, both internal and external. Internal may refer to one's psychological state, while external may refer to one's physical environment.

6 Read each of the following statements - Assertion (A) and Reason (R) and indicate your answer using codes given below.

Assertion (A) Rational persuation refers to the use of logical arguments and facts to persuade others for achieving a desired result.

Reason (R) Managers use several techniques to influence others in organisations.

Codes

1 Both (A) and (R) are true and (R) is the correct explanation of (A)
2 Both (A) and (R) are true, but (R) is not the correct explanation of (A)
3 (A) is true, but (R) is false
4 (A) is false, but R is true

Ans. *(1)*

Exp. Both (A) and (R) are true and (R) is the correct explanation of (A).

Rational persuasion is a technique wherein a well-reasoned argument based on factual and logical arguments is put forth in order to convince others to work towards a desired result.

In organisations, managers use this technique to make an impact on the people working under them. For instance, if a manager thinks that their way of dealing with a task is the best option available, they present a logical argument for the same, thereby convincing others to work towards achieving the desired outcome.

7 Match List I with List II and select the correct answer by choosing from codes given below.

List I (Concept)	List II (Description)
A. Counter-conditioning	I. After conditioning, a new CS(B) when paired with already Conditioned Stimulus CS(A) and presented as a compound stimulus, little or no conditioning occurs to CS(B)
B. Blocking	II. Elimination of undesirable behaviour by pairing CS with US other than the one that originally reinforced that behaviour.
C. Overshadowing	III. Inhibition of conditioned response caused by conditioned emotional response.
D. Conditioned Suppression	IV. While using compound CS where one of its components is more salient than the other, only the salient component is conditioned.

Codes

	A	B	C	D
1	II	I	III	IV
2	II	I	IV	III
3	IV	III	I	II
4	IV	III	II	I

Ans. *(2)*

Exp. The correct matching is A-II, B-I, C-IV, D-III.

Counter-conditioning is the elimination of undesirable behaviour by pairing CS with US other than the one that originally reinforced that behaviour. It is when an undesirable behaviour is reduced/eliminated by associating a Conditional Stimulus (CS) with an Unconditional Stimulus (US) that is different from the one that initially reinforced the undesirable behaviour. For instance, the pairing of a feared object with relaxation techniques help in reducing phobias.

Blocking occurs when a new conditioned stimulus CS(B) is paired with an already conditioned stimulus, CS(A), is presented as a compound stimulus CS(AB), and no conditioning does not take place. This happens because the conditioning response training for CS(A) interferes with the conditioning response acquisition towards CS(B). Therefore, no conditioning response is elicited.

Overshadowing happens while using compound CS where one of its components is more salient than the other, only the salient component is conditioned. It is a phenomenon in classical conditioning wherein when a Compound Stimulus (a stimulus comprising of multiple simple stimuli) is being conditioned, then themore relevant or the salient stimulus is the only one that becomes conditioned, and elicits the conditioned response.

Conditioned Suppression is the inhibition of conditioned response caused by conditioned emotional response. It takes place when there is an inhibition/reduction in the conditioned response which is caused by the display of a conditioned emotional response. This usually happens when the conditioned emotional response is one that is aversive in nature.

8 Match List I with List II and select the correct answer by choosing from codes given below.

List I (Concept)	List II (Explanation)
A. Convergence	I. If you see a distant mountain range on a crystal-clear day, it looks like it was only a few miles away.
B. Frame of reference	II. When the two images are fused into one overall image.
C. Stereoscopic vision	III. When we look at a distant object, the lines of vision from our eyes are parallel. Looking at a nearby object, the eyes turn in.
D. Aerial perspective	IV. An internal perspective relative to which events are perceived.

Codes

	A	B	C	D		A	B	C	D
1	I	II	III	IV	2	III	IV	II	I
3	II	III	IV	I	4	IV	I	III	I

Ans. *(2)*

Exp. The correct matching is A-III, B-IV, C-II, D-I.

Convergence refers to when an object is closer in distance, then the eyes must turn inward. The more inward they turn, the closer the object appears to be. However, if the object is distant, then the eyes are required to turn outward, making the lines of vision parallel. It is a binocular cue pertaining to distance.

Frame of reference refers to the internal perspectives of a person, such as assumptions or attitudes, which colour their perception of events. Sometimes these frames of reference can also distort one's perception, thereby giving rise to prejudice or bias.

Stereoscopic vision refers to the brain's ability to fuse two slightly different images together, thereby enabling the perception of a single overall image. The slight difference is a consequence of different retinal images of the two eyes (binocular disparity).

Aerial perspective is when on a bright and clear day, a distant mountain range is perceived as being only a few miles away. However, in reality, the person could be viewing it from a distance of 50 miles. This is because distant objects appear to be hazy or blurred. Elements like fog, dust, or smog, affect the perception of the distance of an object by adding to it. However, in their absence, the effect of aerial perspective is more apparent.

9 Read each of the following statements Assertion (A) and Reason (R) and indicate your answer using codes given below.

Assertion (A) Perception remains constant although the proximal sensation changes.

Reason (R) Our perceptual system has mechanisms that adjust our perception of the proximal stimulus.

Codes

1 Both (A) and (R) are true and (R) is the correct explanation of (A)
2 Both (A) and (R) are true, but (R) is not the correct explanation of (A)
3 (A) is true, but (R) is false
4 (A) is false, but (R) is true

Ans. *(1)*

Exp. Both (A) and (R) are true and (R) is the correct explanation of (A).

Perceptual constancy is a phenomenon that enables the perceptual response to a proximal stimulus to be the same despite the sensory changes that take place.

Perceptual constancy happens because the human brain has the capacity to be able to adjust one's perceptions of proximal stimulus. Proximal stimulus is one in which the energy pattern belonging to a stimulus directly stimulates the sensory receptors. For instance, consider looking at a coin. When it is viewed from different angles, the shape appears to change. However, one perceives the shape of the coin to be round despite the changes in proximal sensations, such as angles. This happens because the brain enables the adjustments in perceptions of proximal stimuli, thereby bringing about perceptual constancy.

10 Match List I with List II and select the correct answer by choosing from codes given below.

List I (Concept)	List II (Description)
A. Physiological Psychology	I. Studies the psychological effects of brain damage in human patients.
B. Neuropsychology	II. Studies the neural mechanisms of behaviour by manipulating the nervous systems of non-human animals in controlled experiments.
C. Psychophysiology	III. Studies the relation between physiological activity and psychological processes in human subjects by non-invasive physiological recording.
D. Cognitive Neuroscience	IV. Studies the neural mechanisms of human cognition, mainly by using functional brain imaging techniques.

Codes

	A	B	C	D		A	B	C	D
1	I	II	III	IV	2	III	IV	I	II
3	II	I	IV	III	4	IV	III	II	I

Ans. *(*)*

Exp. The correct matching is A-II, B-I, C-III, D-IV.

Physiological Psychology studies the neural mechanisms of behaviour by manipulating the nervous systems of non-human animals in controlled experiments. It studies behaviours in non-human animals, such as rats, by subjecting their neural mechanisms to manipulation. For instance, severing of corpus callosum in non-human animals, and the analysis of its effect on behaviours. It is a subdivision of biological psychology.

Neuropsychology studies the psychological effects of brain damage in human patients. It studies the way in which brain damage can bring about changes in cognition or behaviour as it studies the relationship between the mechanisms of the brain and cognition/behaviour.

Psychophysiology studies the relation between physiological activity and psychological processes in human subjects by non-invasive physiological recording. It studies the relationship between physiological and psychological processes by using non-invasive physiological recording modalities such as electroencephalography, and fMRI, among others. For instance, fMRI is used to study which brain regions are activated during the encoding of information.

Cognitive Neuroscience studies the neural mechanisms of human cognition, mainly by using functional brain imaging techniques. It is a discipline that studies the relationship between the physiological signals in the mind and the body, such as neuralmechanisms, and their effect on cognition. It does so by using functional brain imaging techniques, such as functional magnetic resonance imaging (fMRI).

11 Which of the following explains the Threshold Hypothesis regarding Intelligence-Creativity relationship?

1 There is a positive correlation between intelligence and creativity.
2 There is a positive correlation between intelligence and creativity upto a particular level of intelligence.
3 There is a positive correlation between intelligence and creativity beyond a particular level of intelligence.
4 There is a negative correlation between intelligence and creativity beyond a particular level of intelligence.

Ans. *(2)*

Exp. The Threshold Hypothesis regarding Intelligence-Creativity relationship purports that there is a positive correlation between intelligence and creativity up to a particular level of intelligence.

The Threshold Hypothesis pertaining to the relationship between intelligence and creativity says that greater levels of creativity require above-average levels of intelligence at the very least. That is, it says that above-average intelligence is among the conditions required for greater levels of creativity, but it alone is not sufficient. Therefore, it can be said that the Threshold Hypothesis purports that there is a positive correlation between intelligence and creativity, but only up to a certain level of intelligence.

12 Match List I with List II and select the correct answer by choosing from codes given below.

List I (Concept)	List II (Explanation)
A. Concordance	I. Percentage of cases in which, if specific gene is present, a particular trait, characteristic or disease will actually manifest itself in the fully developed organism.
B. Penetrance	II. Relationship between twins or other family members with respect to a given trait.
C. Prevalence	III. Number of new cases of specific condition or disease that arise during a particular period of time.
D. Incidence	IV. Frequency of occurrence of a given condition among a certain population at a particular point of time.

Codes

	A	B	C	D		A	B	C	D
1	I	II	III	IV	2	III	IV	I	II
3	II	I	IV	III	4	IV	III	II	I

Ans. *(3)*

Exp. The correct matching is A-II, B-I, C-IV, D-III.

Concordance refers to relationship between twins or other family members based on the presence of similar traits. It pertains to the probability that both persons may have a certain characteristic. Identical twins are said to epitomize concordance as they have the same set of genes, therefore, their characteristics tend to be highly similar.

Penetrance refers to the proportion of individuals who possess a certain genetic variant or a geneticmutation, and will thereby display symptoms or signs of a particular trait or disorder. For instance, polydactyly is caused by the presence of a dominant allele (genetic variant). So, if a person possesses this dominant allele, the condition will be expressed.

Prevalence pertains to the frequency of a certain condition occurring in people of a certain population at a specific point in time. For instance, the prevalence of the condition of obesity among people in England is estimated to be 28% (The Health Survey for England, 2019). It is a concept in epidemiology.

Incidence refers to the rate of new cases pertaining to a disease or condition during a specific period in time. For instance, the new cases for strokes in the United Kingdom are estimated to be 113,000 every year. Therefore, the incidence is 113,000. It is a concept in epidemiology.

13 Which of the following significant changes have been incorporated in DSM-5 ?

I. The title of the manual is not DSM-V, but DSM-5, a deliberate shift from traditional Roman numerals used in previous editions toward Arabic numerals.
II. Multiaxial Assessment System - a central feature of DSM since its introduction in DSM - III in 1980, has been dropped altogether from DSM-5.
III. DSM-5 authors have overhauled the manual to emphasise neuropsychological or biological roots of mental disorders.
IV. DSM-5 authors have removed 5 of 10 personality disorders previously included in that section. Dropped disorders are paranoid, schizoid, histrionic, dependent and narcissistic personality disorders.

Codes

1 I, II, III are correct; IV is incorrect
2 II, III and IV are correct; I is incorrect
3 I and II are correct; III and IV are incorrect
4 III and IV are correct; I and II are incorrect

Ans. *(3)*

➲ *Exp.* Among the given statements regarding changes in DSM-5, statements I and II are correct, while statements III and IV are incorrect.

The last few editions of the Diagnostic Statistical Manual of Mental Disorders (DSM) have been titled using the Roman numerals. For instance, the fourth edition was titled 'DSM-IV.' However, DSM-5 does not use Roman numeral. It uses the Arabic numeral for five, and is titled 'DSM-5.'

DSM-5 discarded the previously used multiaxial system. It got rid of Axes I, II, III, IV, and V,and placed all the disorders in Section II (previously, Axes I, II, and III), while significant psychological and contextual features have taken the place of Axis IV. Axis V has been altogether removed.

One among the many criticisms levied against DSM-5 is that it has not spoken anything about the biological/ neuropsychological basis of disorders. There is a lack of emphasis on those.

In the previous edition of DSM, personality disorders were placed in a separate axis. However, now they are listed in the same section as other disorders. All the ten personality disorders have been retained despite calls to remove paranoid, schizoid, narcissistic, histrionic, and dependent personality disorders.

14 Which one of the trait theories/models is/are not based on factor analytic methodology ?

I. Allport's Theory
II. Costa and McCrae's Model
III. Goldberg's Model
IV. Eysenck's Theory

Codes

1 Only I
2 I and III
3 II and III
4 II and IV

Ans. *(1)*

➲ *Exp.* Among the given theories/models, only Allport's Theory is not based on the factor analytic methodology.

Gordon Allport used seminal research to come up with his trait theory of personality, which purports that personality comprises the following traits:

1. *Cardinal Traits* : These traits are rare, but are highly involved in determining one's behaviour.
2. *Central Traits* : These are present among all people, but in different degrees. They impact one's behaviour, but do not determine it.
3. *Secondary Traits* : These traits are present in all people, and only have an impact on behaviour. They are not involved in the determination of a behaviour. They are also highly dependent on the context, therefore, they do not manifest in every given situation.

15 The factors that operate with deep levels of processing are

I. Distinctiveness
II. Sameness
III. Elaboration
IV. Physical contours

Codes

1 I and II
2 II and III
3 II and IV
4 I and III

Ans. *(4)*

➲ *Exp.* Among the given factors, distinctiveness and elaboration operate with the deep levels of processing.

Craik and Lockhart gave the 'Levels of Processing Model,' which purports that the deeper the processing of information, the longer lasting is the memory of it. Factors of deep levels of processing include:

- Distinctiveness refers to the quality of a stimulus to stand apart. It creates stronger memory traces (physically stored memories), thereby making memories last longer. It is especially useful when it comes to understanding the differences among stimuli.
- Elaboration requires a higher level of meaningful analysis. It involves thinking, imagery, and associations, among others. For instance, in order to remember new words, one can associate them with their meaning, or a previously existing concept or instance of the same word.

16 Observation learning involves following processes. Arrange them in the correct sequence

I. Attentional processes
II. Retention processes
III. Production processes
IV. Motivational processes

Codes

1 I, II, III, IV
2 I, IV, II, III
3 IV, I, II, III
4 I, II, IV, III

Ans. *(1)*

➲ *Exp.* The correct chronological order of the processes involved in Observational learning is – I, II, III, IV.

As per Albert Bandura, Observational learning is a form of learning wherein people acquire behaviours by observing others engaging in the behaviours, and repeating the same. Observational learning has the following four processes:

1. *Attentional process* : This refers to focussing on the behaviour a person/people are engaging in.
2. *Retention process* : This refers to committing the information one has observed to memory.
3. *Production process* : This refers to reproducing or performed the observed behaviour.
4. *Motivation process* : This refers to the motivation involved that enables the repetition of the observed behavior.

17 Key issues in the study of environmental effects on intelligence are

I. Reaction Range
II. Proximal and Distal Causation
III. Colinearity
IV. Environment Sphere

Codes

1 I, II and III
2 I, II and IV
3 II, III and IV
4 I, III and IV

Ans. (1)

Exp. Reaction Range, Proximal and Distal Causation, and Colinerality are the key issues in the study of environmental effects on intelligence.

The key issues in the study of environmental effects on intelligence involve:

1. *Reaction Range* : It is the upper limit and the lower limit imposed on intelligence by the genes. However, the environment plays a decisive role in determining where the IQ lies within the constraints of these limits.
2. *Proximal and Distal Causation* : With regards to intelligence, the environment enables the manifestation of genes. Therefore, in determining the environmental effects on intelligence, consideration must be given to its proximal causes, which are generally environmental. Consideration must also be given to its distal causes, which are genetic and environmental.
3. *Colinearity* : It refers to the great degree of correlation between the causes and their outcomes in terms of intelligence. This makes it complicated to understand whether intelligence is mainly inherited or mainly environmental. Certain variables may be considered environmental, however, they might be genetic.

18 Read each of the following statements - Assertion (A) and Reason (R) and indicate your answer using codes given below.

Assertion (A) According to two factor theory, cognitive appraisal of cues in the environment helps the individual label the emotions.

Reason (R) An individual is aroused when he confronts any emotion producing event.

Codes

1 Both (A) and (R) are true and (R) is the correct explanation of (A)
2 Both (A) and (R) are true, but (R) is not the correct explanation of (A)
3 (A) is true, but (R) is false
4 (A) is false, but (R) is true

Ans. (2)

Exp. Both (A) and (R) are true, but (R) is not the correct explanation of (A).

Two factor theory of emotion purports that there are two aspects to emotion, namely, physical arousal and cognitive appraisal. Emotions are experienced as a result of an interaction between the physical arousal and the cognitive appraisal. That is, cognitive appraisal labels the physical arousal, and then the result is the experience of emotion. As per this theory, only experiencing physical arousal is not enough. The two factor theory does say that physical arousal is experienced when one encounters an emotion-producing event, however, it is not enough to explain the experience of emotion.

19 Whether we can be affected by stimuli that remain outside our conscious awareness has been examined by researches using a technique called

1 Cuing
2 Visualisation
3 Imagery
4 Priming

Ans. (4)

Exp. Priming is a technique used by researchers to explain that the people can be affected by stimuli that remain outside of their conscious awareness.

It is a phenomenon in which a person's exposure to a certain stimulus has an impact on their response to another subsequent stimulus. This may take place outside of conscious awareness, that is, a person is not aware of priming actually taking place. For instance, when exposed to the colour, 'yellow,' a person recognizes a banana faster than they can recognize a dog. This happens because the colour and the fruit are closely connected in one's mind.

20 Which of the following sequences depicts Erikson's stages of development correctly ?

1 Oral Sensory → Muscular anal → Locomotor genital → Latency → Adolescence → Adulthood.
2 Muscular anal → Oral Sensory → Locomotor genital → Latency → Adolescence → Adulthood.
3 Oral Sensory → Muscular anal → Latency → Locomotor genital → Adolescence → Adulthood.
4 Muscular anal → Locomotor genital → Oral Sensory → Latency → Adolescence → Adulthood.

Ans. (1)

Exp. The correct chronological order with regards to Erikson's developmental stages is Oral sensory, Muscular anal, Locomotor genital, Latency, Adolescence, and Adulthood.

Erik Erikson gave stages of development. Healthy development takes place when a person successfully completes these stages from infancy to adulthood. The stages are as follows:

1. *Oral Sensory* : During this stage, the infant is highly dependent on the caregivers for fulfilment of needs. If needs are met, trust develops, otherwise, it leads to mistrust.
2. *Muscular Anal* : During this stage, a child begins to gain control over their motor abilities and bowel movements. They set about exploring the world.
3. *Locomotor Genital* : During this stage, the child continues to gain mastery over their sense of the world. They also take the initiative of performing certain basic behaviours on their own.
4. *Latency* : During this stage, the child is more oriented towards play. They become industrious, responsible, try to be good people and do what is right.
5. *Adolescence* : This stage marks the transition from childhood to adulthood. It is a stage of identity crisis, as individuals work towards establishing their identity. Towards the later part of adolescence, individuals explore their sexuality as well.
6. *Adulthood* : During this stage, people begin to form close and intimate relationships. They seek to blend in. During the later part of this stage, people have established their identities, and are ready for making long-term commitments in their relationships with others.

21 Match List I with List II and select the correct answer by choosing from codes given below.

	List I (Concept)		List II (Explanation)
A.	Magnocellular System	I.	Discrimination of fine detail and colour.
B.	Parvocellular System	II.	Specialised for brightness contrast and for movement.
C.	Fourier Analysis	III.	Neurons that fire most when they receive input from both ears at the same time.
D.	Coincidence Detectors	IV.	Analysis of a complex wave into sine wave components.

Codes

	A	B	C	D		A	B	C	D
1	I	II	III	IV	2	III	IV	I	II
3	II	I	IV	III	4	IV	III	II	I

Ans. (3)

Exp. The correct matching is A-II, B-I, C-IV, D-III.

Magnocellular System is a part of visual system that helps in quick perception of movement and receptive to changes in brightness. It stems from the ventral layers of the lateral geniculate nucleus.

Parvocellular System is a part of the visual system that enables the perception of colours, fine details, and greater changes in colours. It stems from the dorsal layers of the lateral geniculate nucleus.

Fourier Analysis can be used to define complex wave in terms of sine wave components. It was introduced by the mathematicians, Jean Baptiste Joseph and Baron de Fourier, and is used to understand waveforms in context of trigonometric functions.

Coincidence Detectors are neurons that fire the most when they receive information from both the ears at the same time. This leads to the receptors detecting simultaneous activation of neurons.

22 Match List I with List II and select the correct answer by choosing from codes given below.

	List I (Concept)		List II (Explanation)
A.	Inductive thought	I.	Thought that is intuitive and haphazard.
B.	Logical thought	II.	Thought that applies a general set of rules to specific situations.
C.	Deductive thought	III.	Drawing conclusions on the basis of principles of learning.
D.	Illogical thought	IV.	Thinking in which a principle is inferred from a series of specific examples.

Codes

	A	B	C	D		A	B	C	D
1	I	II	III	IV	2	II	III	IV	I
3	III	IV	I	II	4	IV	III	II	I

Ans. (4)

Exp. The correct matching is A-IV, B-III, C-II, D-I.

Inductive thought is a part of inductive reasoning, wherein a principle is derived from specific examples. Inductive reasoning takes place when broader generalizations are derived from specific observations.

Logical thought use of principles of learning in order to arrive at conclusions. The principles of learning involved are analysis, critical thinking, and reasoning.

Deductive thought is a part of deductive reasoning that involves the application of general rules to specific situations. Deductive reasoning takes place when specific observations are made from general principles.

Illogical thought involves the use of intuition and is haphazard. It is a form of disordered thinking where critical thinking or reasoning skills do not form the basis of inferences.

23 Which of the following personality questionnaires have a lie scale ?

I. Edward Personality Preference Schedule
II. Eysenck Personality Questionnaire
III. Minnesota Multiphasic Personality Questionnaire-2
IV. Rotter's Locus of Control Scale.

Codes

1 I and II
2 I and III
3 II and III
4 I, II and III

Ans. (3)

Exp. Eysenck Personality Questionnaire and Minnesota Multiphasic Personality Questionnaire-2 are personality questionnaires that do have a lie scale.

Lie scales are used in personality questionnaires or inventories to assess whether the test-taker is answering the given items truthfully. If test-takers are answering the items in a way to portray themselves in a more positive or negative light, then the responses to those items on the lie scale will be inconsistent.

24 Read the following statements and describe which are correct.

I. Archetypes are themes that have existed in all cultures through history.
II. Personal unconscious is the region next to ego which consists of all the forgotten experiences that have lost their intensity.
III. Masculine archetype in men is called animus.
IV. Persona is a compromise between demands of the environment and necessities of individuals.

Codes

1 I, II and III are correct ; IV is not correct
2 II, III and IV are correct ; I is not correct
3 I, II and IV are correct ; III is not correct
4 I, III and IV are correct ; and II is not correct

Ans. (3)

Exp. Among the given statements, only statements I, II, IV are correct, while statement III is incorrect.

Carl Jung gave the concept of archetypes, which are universal images or patterns that form a part of collective unconscious, which one inherits from their ancestors. They exist in all cultures, and have throughout history. For instance, a hero is generally associated with courage.

Carl Jung said that personal unconscious is the region that consists of memories that may be temporarily forgotten, and it may also be a reservoir of repressed thoughts. He also said that ego is the conscious mind, and contains thoughts, feelings, and memories that one is fully aware of.

Jung said that persona is a compromise struck between one's needs and the demands of the environment. He said that persona is the way in which people present themselves to the world, and its literal meaning is 'mask.' For instance, even if one does not like their guests, they behave politely with them as it is what propriety dictates.

As per Carl Jung, animus is not the masculine archetype in men. In fact, animus represents the unconscious masculine qualities possessed by a woman.

25 George Sperling (1960) studied iconic memory using

I. Partial-report procedure
II. Whole-report procedure
III. Self-report procedure
IV. Backward procedure

Codes

1 Only I
2 Only IV
3 I and III
4 II and IV

Ans. (1)

Exp. Partial-report procedure was used in the study of iconic memory by George Sperling.

Iconic memory is a type of sensory memory that lasts only for few milliseconds before it fades away. For instance, an image in the mind that is seen only for a very brief period of time. Sperling was interested in the duration and capacity of iconic memory, therefore, he used the partial-report procedure to test it. Partial-report procedure requires only a part of the total information to be recalled.

In his experiments, he showed his participants few letters only for a fraction of a second, and then they were asked to recall. The results of this experiment showed that the human brain was able to retain this information despite its presentation being very brief. However, not all letters were recalled because iconic memory itself was very brief in nature.

26 Match List I with List II and select the correct answer by choosing from codes given below.

	List I (Sub Test)		List II (Test)
A.	Visual Puzzles	I.	WAIS - IV
B.	Famous people	II.	Kaulfman Adult Intelligence Test (KAIT)
C.	Matrix Task	III.	Cognitive Assessment System (CAS)
D.	Matrix Patterns	IV.	Otis-Lenon Test

Codes

	A	B	C	D
1	I	II	III	IV
2	II	I	IV	III
3	III	IV	I	II
4	IV	III	II	I

Ans. (1)

Exp. The correct matching is A-I, B-II, C-III, D-IV.

In the *Wechsler Adult Intelligence Scale*-IV (WAIS-IV), visual puzzles are among the subtests that help in determining the ability to analyse and integrate abstract stimuli, and also measure non-verbal reasoning ability.

Kaufman Adult Intelligence Test (KAIT) includes a Famous Faces subtest in which 18 famous people are presented, and the test-taker is required to recognize them. It helps in gauging the general knowledge of the test-taker, obtained through experience.

The *Cognitive Assessment System* (CAS) consists of a matrix task which requires the test-taker to fill the missing geometric part of a matrix. It helps in assessing simultaneous processing ability.

The *Otis-Lennon Test* consists of a matrix patterns task that helps in assessing arithmetic reasoning ability. It is a number series test wherein the missing number in the matrix must be identified.

27 Which of the following terms explains the reinforcement which is given only if a specific response is made ?

1 Concurrent Reinforcement
2 Incremental Reinforcement
3 Contingency Contract
4 Contingent Reinforcement

Ans. (4)

Exp. Contingent Reinforcement explains the reinforcement that is provided when the desired response is made.

Reinforcements are pleasant stimuli that help in increasing desired responses/behaviours. In contingent reinforcement, the delivery of the reinforcer is based/contingent on the desired response/behaviour, hence the name. This type of contingent reinforcement is a positive reinforcement. For instance, a child is given their favourite candy only when they clean their room, and not otherwise. In certain circumstances, contingent reinforcement involves the removal of an aversive stimulus on the basis of a desired response. This type of contingent reinforcement is negative reinforcement.

28 Read each of the following statements-Assertion (A) and Reason (R) and indicate your answer using codes given below.

Assertion (A) A person scored high on Hope of Success (as measured by TAT) and high on Fear of Failure (as measured by Mandler and Sarason's TAQ). As per Atkinson's theory, his resultant achievement motivation will be intermediate.

Reason (R) As per Atkinson, the resultant achievement motivation is a product of Hope of Success and Fear of Failure.

Codes

1 Both (A) and (R) are true and (R) is the correct explanation of (A)
2 Both (A) and (R) are true, but (R) is not the correct explanation of (A)
3 (A) is true, but (R) is false
4 (A) is false, but (R) is true

Ans. (3)

Exp. (A) is true, but (R) is false.

As per Atkinson, achievement motivation refers to the need for achievement, which is dependent on two factors:

1. *Hope for Success* : Wishing and hoping for success keeps one motivated to perform certain actions that may lead to achievement.
2. *Fear of Failure* : A fear of failing impedes one from performing certain behaviours that may lead to achievement, but may be risky.

Consequently, as per Atkinson, someone who scores high on the hope of success as per TAT (Thematic Apperception Test) and high on fear of failure as per TAQ (Test Anxiety Questionnaire) will have an achievement motivation that falls in between or intermediate.

As per Atkinson, achievement motivation is a function of hope for success and fear of failure, but not a product. That is, these two opposing factors work together in order to determine the likelihood of performing achievement motivational behaviours.

29 Read each of the following statements - Assertion (A) and Reason (R) and indicate your answer using codes given below

Assertion (A) Personality factors such as D, J, K and P are not incorporated in Cattell's 16 PF test.

Reason (R) Some personality factors appeared only in Life - data (L-data) measures.

Codes

1 Both (A) and (R) are true and (R) is the correct explanation of (A)
2 Both (A) and (R) are true, but (R) is not the correct explanation of (A)
3 (A) is true, but (R) is false
4 (A) is false, but (R) is true

Ans. (1)

Exp. Both (A) and (R) are true and (R) is the correct explanation of (A).

Personality factors like D, J, K, and P are not a part of the 16 PF test developed by Raymond Cattell.

Personality factors like D, J, K, and P were not a part of the 16 PF test because these factors only appeared in the life data measures, which involved information from everyday behaviours and characteristic patterns performed in the real world. Factor analysis was then performed on information collected from life data, experimental data, and questionnaire data, which gave rise to the 16 personality factors involved in the final 16 PF test.

30 During which stage most of the creative thinking occurs ?

1 Preparation
2 Incubation
3 Illumination
4 Evaluation

Ans. (2)

Exp. Most of the creative thinking takes place during the incubation stage.

Creativity involves divergent thinking that involves considering all potential solutions to a problem and coming up with novel and original solutions to a problem.

Creative thinking takes place in stages, and incubation is the second stage. It follows the preparation stage, which involves collection of all information.

During the incubation stage, one contemplates all the solutions and works with the problem. It is a stage where one is also open to all the possible ideas, and even the most absurd ones. Therefore, most of the creative thinking takes place during this stage.

31 Match List I with List II and select the correct answer by choosing from codes given below.

	List I (Concept)		List II (Explanation)
A.	Disjunctive Concept	I.	A class of objects that have two or more features in common.
B.	Prototype	II.	Showing relationship between object and surroundings.
C.	Conjunctive Concept	III.	Showing the presence of at least one of several possible features.
D.	Relational Concept	IV.	An ideal model referring to a particular concept.

Codes

	A	B	C	D		A	B	C	D
1	I	II	III	IV	2	III	IV	I	II
3	II	III	IV	I	4	IV	III	I	II

Ans. (2)

Exp. The correct matching is A-III, B-IV, C-I, D-II.

Disjunctive concept is showing the presence of at least one of several possible features. It involves being in possession of at least one set of attributes/features among the several ones. For instance, an object that is blue or a rectangle is defined by its disjunction. It can either be blue or a rectangle, but not both.

Prototype is an ideal model referring to a particular concept. It refers to the ideal model that is a representation of a certain concept or a certain category. For instance, Rolls Royce is an ideal representation of a car.

Conjunctive Concept is a class of objects that have two or more features in common. It is a concept that is defined by a set of attributes, every member of which must be present for the concept to apply. For example, the concept brother requires the joint presence of the attributes (a) male and (b) sibling, neither of which may be omitted.

Relational concept is a concept that is defined by relationships between objects or surroundings. It classifies objects on the basis of their relationship to something else or by the relationship between features of an object. Larger, above, left, north, and upside down are all relational concepts. For instance, defining a person in relation to another person, such as, C is the son of A and B.

32 Chimpanzee Sarah's one of the most outstanding achievements was the construction of sentences involving

1 Negation
2 Conditional relationship
3 Adult grammar
4 Unprompted questions

Ans. (2)

Exp. Chimpanzee Sarah's most outstanding achievement was the construction of sentences involving Conditional relationships.

Chimpanzee Sarah was an encultured research chimpanzee whose cognitive skills were documented. She was trained to use words, and learnt certain nouns, verbs, adjectives, and prepositions. Training involved the use of plastic objects to represent words, and a sequence of them was used to represent sentences. Among her most outstanding achievements involve conditional relationship in the construction of sentences. A conditional relationship involves promised or plausible, but not definite, relationship between two clauses.

33 In a typical 'Learning' experiment which of the following are used as dependent variables ?

I. Probability of Response
II. Latency
III. Rate of Presentation
IV. Trials to Extinction

Codes

1 I and II
2 II and IV
3 I, II and III
4 I, II and IV

Ans. (4)

Exp. In a typical 'Learning' experiment, Probability of Response, Latency, and Trials to Extinction are the ones that are used as dependent variables.

'Learning' experiments are those in which behaviours are learnt in an experimental condition. In a learning experiment, the dependent variable (DV) is a behaviour or response that can be measured. Consequently, the dependent variables are:

- *Probability of response* : It refers to the likelihood of an increase or decrease in response based on reinforcements and punishments, respectively. The acquisition and probability of response is a learned behaviour that can be tested and measured in learning experiments, therefore, it is a DV.
- *Latency* : In a learning experiment, latency refers to the learning that has taken place but is not manifested immediately. It only manifests itself when a reinforcement is provided. Latency is a learned behaviour that can be tested and measured, therefore, it is a DV.
- *Trials to extinction* : Extinction refers to the gradual elimination of the learned response. This takes place when behaviours are not followed by reinforcements. Therefore, the number of non-reinforced trials leading to extinction is a DV as they are responses that can be measured

34 Explanation of the moon illusion given by is, "The horizon seems more distant than the night sky."

1 Perceptual learning hypothesis
2 Expectancy hypothesis
3 Apparent - distance hypothesis
4 Frame of reference hypothesis

Ans. (3)

Exp. Moon illusion is explained by the Apparent-distance hypothesis.

Moon illusion refers to an optical illusion that explains when moon is on the horizon appears to be farther away when it is in the night sky. This is because the moon on the horizon is surrounded by filled space, while moon in the night sky is not surrounded by anything.

Apparent distance theory explains that the moon on the horizon appears to be larger because it is farther away. The judging of distance is based on the intervening objects that appear to be in the way between the observer and the horizon. However, moon in the night sky appears smaller as there are no intervening objects between the observer and the night sky.

35 Absorptive phase of energy mobilisation involves the following events. Arrange them in the correct sequence.

I. Glucose increases.
II. Parasympathetic activation.
III. Pancreas secretes insulin.
IV. Glucose enters the body cells.
V. Glucose is stored in liver and muscles as glycogen.
VI. Fat stored in adipose cells as triglycerides.

Codes

1 I, II, III, V, IV, VI
2 I, II, III, IV, V, VI
3 I, III, II, IV, VI, V
4 I, IV, II, VI, V, III

Ans. (2)

Exp. The correct chronological order events involved in the absorptive phase of energy mobilisation is – I, II, III, IV, V, VI.

Absorptive phase of energy mobilization takes place after a meal when the body is digesting and absorbing nutrients present in the food. During this phase, absorbed nutrients provide energy.

Absorptive phase takes place in a sequence which first sees an increase in glucose and the activation of parasympathetic nervous system. The rise in glucose levels leads to the secretion of insulin by the pancreatic cells. Insulin leads to the absorption of glucose by the liver, adipose and muscle cells. Following this, glucose is converted into glucose-6-phosphate. In doing so, the glucose in the blood becomes higher than in the body cells, therefore, the glucose enters the body cells. Insulin also triggers the storage of glucose in the liver and muscle cells in the form of glycogen, and this can be used for the energy requirements of the body. If energy is not expended shortly after the meal, then the excess glucose is stored in the form of fat in adipose tissue as triglycerides.

36 In a multiple regression analysis, the three predictors explained 49 per cent variance in the criterion variable. What would be the value of multiple correlation ?

1 0.30 2 0.49 3 0.51 4 0.70

Ans. (4)

Exp. Among the given options, 0.70 would be the value of multiple correlation.

Multiple regression is used to measure the value of a variable on the basis of the values of two or more variables. In multiple regression, a multiple correlation coefficient is the measure of how well a variable can predict other variables. It is denoted as R.

In multiple regression, the formula for variance is R^2. In this case, the variance is 0.49. Therefore, the multiple correlation will be the square root of variance, $\sqrt{0.49}$, is 0.70.

37 Read each of the following statements - Assertion (A) and Reason (R) and indicate your answer using codes given below.

Assertion (A) The analysis of time series designs often involve the problem of auto correlation.

Reason (R) Quasi - experiments, as compared to laboratory experiments, do not control secondary variance efficiently.

Codes

1 Both (A) and (R) are true and (R) is the correct explanation of (A)
2 Both (A) and (R) are true, but (R) is not the correct explanation of (A)
3 (A) is true, but (R) is false
4 (A) is false, but (R) is true

Ans. (2)

Exp. Both (A) and (R) are true, but (R) is not the correct explanation of (A).

Analysis of time-series design involves autocorrelation. Time series design is used in experimental method to investigate the variations among subjects that are dependent on time. Autocorrelation represents the degree of similarity between a given time series and a lagged version of itself over successive time intervals. Autocorrelation measures the relationship between a variable's current value and its past values. When time series design is analysed, it involves autocorrelation as it allows checking the relation between one behaviour and its previous behaviours. This helps in analysing the time dependency between observations. For instance, repeated measurements of a behaviour across time-intervals is a time series design that can be used to investigate the variations in the behaviour among objects in relation to time.

Quasi– experiments, as compared to laboratory experiments, do not control secondary variance efficiently. Quasi-experiments are different from laboratory experiments as they do not involve random assignment. Secondary variance refers to the variances in the dependent variable caused by secondary variables, which are not the independent variable. In quasi-experiments, secondary variance cannot be well controlled as random assignment brings about an equity between the participants, thereby controlling the influence of other variables.

From the above, it can be said that the two concepts are unrelated.

38 Future oriented performance appraisal techniques consist of

I. MBO
II. 360° Appraisal
III. Psychological Appraisal
IV. BARS

Codes

1 I, II and IV 2 I, II and III
3 II, III and IV 4 I, III and IV

Ans. (2)

Exp. Future oriented methods of performance appraisal techniques consist of Management by Objectives (MBO), 360° Appraisal, and Psychological Appraisal.

Future oriented methods of performance appraisal are geared toward assessing future performances. They involve:

1. *Management by Objectives* (MBO): Here, performance is rated on the basis of the achievement of objectives as given by the management. It involves setting of goals and desired outcomes, establishing the standards of performance, comparison of the goals achieved by the employee against the goals set by the management, and setting of new goals and new strategies for the goals not achieved.
2. 360° *Appraisal* : In this technique, appraisal is based on the information regarding performance given by immediate supervisors, members of the team, peers, clients, and also of the self. This type of appraisal is useful in terms of assessing interpersonal skills, team building, and ensuring customer satisfaction.
3. *Psychological Appraisal* : This type of appraisal is oriented towards the employees' potential with regards to future performances. It involves conducting psychological evaluations, in-depth interviews, interactions with supervisors and review of their evaluations.

39 In group counselling, what is the correct sequence of stages of group development ?

I. Forming II. Norming
III. Mourning IV. Storming
V. Performing

Codes

1 II, III, I, V, IV 2 I, IV, II, V, III
3 I, III, V, II, IV 4 IV, I, II, III, V

Ans. *(2)*

➲ *Exp.* The correct chronological order of stages involved in group development is – I, IV, II, V, III.

Group development takes place in the following order of stages:

1. *Forming* : This is the orientation stage. It involves the time period in which the group initially comes together. It is characterized by uncertainty and anxiety.
2. *Storming* : It is marked by transition. During this stage, the group members compete and openly disagree with each other. The dominant members emerge during this stage, while the shy ones tend to keep to their comfort zone.
3. *Norming* : It is marked by cohesion. During this phase, group members come together and become more comfortable with one another. Mutual trust and respect develops.
4. *Performing* : It is the performance stage. Here, the participants work with one another. They bring their talent and skills to the table, and work towards a shared goal.
5. *Mourning* : It is the termination stage. After the goal has been achieved, the group members disperse and set off in their own direction. It is marked by the sadness of not working together anymore.

40 Read each of the following statements - Assertion (A) and Reason (R) and indicate your answer using codes given below.

Assertion (A) Pre-operational child is incapable of performing operations.

Reason (R) Pre-operational child cannot mentally rearrange a sequence of events into reverse order.

Codes

1 Both (A) and (R) are true and (R) is the correct explanation of (A)
2 Both (A) and (R) are true, but (R) is not the correct explanation of (A)
3 (A) is true, but (R) is false
4 (A) is false, but (R) is true

Ans. *(1)*

➲ *Exp.* Both (A) and (R) are true and (R) is the correct explanation of (A).

A child in pre-operational stage cannot perform mental operations. Pre-operational stage is the second stage of cognitive development, taking place between 2 and 7 years of age. During this stage, learning is more symbolic. Mental operations involve functions such as reversibility, which develops between 7 and 12 years of age. Reversibility is reversing an order of events, thereby restoring its final condition to its original condition. Therefore, a Pre-operational child cannot rearrange a sequence involving events in the reverse order, taking it back to its initial stage.

41 Read each of the following statements - Assertion (A) and Reason (R) and indicate your answer using codes given below.

Assertion (A) For extraversion, monozygotic twins correlated more than the dizygotic twins.

Reason (R) Extraversion has genetic basis.

Codes

1 Both (A) and (R) are true and (R) is the correct explanation of (A)
2 Both (A) and (R) are true, but (R) is not the correct explanation of (A)
3 (A) is true, but (R) is false
4 (A) is false, but (R) is true

Ans. *(1)*

➲ *Exp.* Both (A) and (R) are true and (R) is the correct explanation of (A).

Monozygotic twins are those twins that share 100% of the genetic material, while dizygotic twins are those twins that share 50% of the genetic material. Monozygotic and dizygotic twins can generally be said to share the same environment.

Therefore, when monozygotic twins, who share 100% of the genetic material show higher correlation in terms of extraversion when compared to dizygotic twins who share only 50%.

When monozygotic twins show higher correlation in terms of extraversion when compared to dizygotic twins, the greater correlation can be traced to the greater degree of shared genetic material. This indicates that extraversion has a genetic basis

42 During autobiographical recall, we often reveal a ________ , as a consequence, our memory of the past may be _______

1 inconsistency bias; distorted
2 consistency bias; distorted
3 inconsistency bias; enhanced
4 consistency bias; enhanced

Ans. *(2)*

➲ *Exp.* During autobiographical recall, we often reveal a consistency bias, as a consequence, our memory of the past may be distorted.

Autobiographic memory is a memory of events pertaining to one's life. Autobiographic memory is subject to distortion, which refers to the reconstruction of memory in several different ways after the events have taken place.

Therefore, when it comes to autobiographic recall, one generally tends to reveal a consistency bias as autobiographic memory is subject to distortion. Consistency bias refers to mistakenly remembering one's past attitudes or behaviours as being consistent with their present attitudes or behaviours. For instance, one might mistakenly recall being open-minded always. However, it may not actually be the case.

43 Persons with a leison at the ventromedial nucleus are likely to

1 Overeat
2 Undereat
3 Eat normally
4 Eat normally or undereat

Ans. (1)

Exp. Persons with a leison at the ventromedial nucleus are likely to Overeat.

The ventromedial nucleus is a morphological nucleus whose functions involve the termination of hunger, fear, and sexual activity. It identifies the feeling of fullness after having engaged in eating, and gives rise to feelings of satiety. Lesions or damage to this nucleus can cause a person to overeat as identification of fullness or feelings of satiety does not take place. In rats, lesions to the ventromedial nucleus have given rise to obesity.

44 The percepts are based on

I. What we sense
II. What we know
III. What we infer
IV. What we conform

Codes

1 I and II
2 II and III
3 I, II and III
4 I, II and IV

Ans. (3)

Exp. Percepts are based on what we sense, know, and infer.

A percept refers to the stimulus of perception, one that is being perceived. Perception is a sensory experience that involves recognition of the object, and acting in response to the stimulus.

Therefore, a percept involves what we sense. It involves what we know as this information can lead to the recognition of the stimulus. It involves what we infer from the stimulus, as this leads to acting in response to it.

45 Match List I with List II and select the correct answer by choosing from codes given below.

	List I (Concept)		List II (Explanation)
A.	Phrenology	I.	Field that locates areas of the brain responsible for specific aspects of emotional and behaviour functioning.
B.	Selective Breeding	II.	An approach to establish genetic - behaviour relationship through mating of successive generations with a particular trait.
C.	Plasticity	III.	Ability of parts of neurobiological system to change temporarily and for extended period time.
D.	Twin studies	IV.	An approach to establish of genetic - behaviour relationship through the comparison degree of similarity among identical twins, fraternal twins and non-twins siblings.

Codes

	A	B	C	D		A	B	C	D
1	I	II	III	IV	2	II	I	IV	III
3	III	IV	I	II	4	IV	III	II	I

Ans. (1)

Exp. The correct matching is A-I, B-II, C-III, D-IV.

Phrenology is the field that locates areas of the brain responsible for specific aspects of emotional and behaviour functioning. It is a pseudoscience which believes that certain mental traits such as thoughts emotion, and character are located in specific areas of the brain. It is based on the assumption that the brain's areas have specific functions. It was developed by Franz Joseph Gall.

Selective Breeding is an approach to establish genetic - behaviour relationship through mating of successive generations with a particular trait. It is a method in which rats are selected and bred for a certain phenotype, which is done done by mating successive generations with that specific behavioural trait. It is an old and powerful method used in behavioural genetics.

Plasticity is the ability of parts of neurobiological system to change temporarily and for extended period time. It is a special ability of the brain to change for the purpose of adaption, either temporarily or for longer periods of time. For instance, in case of brain damage in rats, the nerve cells close to the damaged area underwent certain changes which allowed them to perform the functions of the damaged area.

Twin studies are an approach to establish of genetic - behaviour relationship through the comparison degree of similarity among identical twins, fraternal twins and non-twins siblings. It include studies in which genetic-behaviour relationship is established by identifying the genetic and environmental impacts on behaviours by comparing the similarities and differences among the different types of twins. They are conducted on identical and fraternal twins.

Directions (Q. Nos. 46 to 50) *Read the following paragraph and answer the five questions which follow.*

A researcher in experimental psychology hypothesised that a particular 'Reward System' for fast reactions would improve the reaction time. To verify this hypothesis, he selected forty subjects in the age range of 25 to 35 years from an organisation. Following the standard reaction time experiment, he measured the simple reaction time without the reward system. While taking each trial in the experiment, the time-interval between the ready signal and the onset of stimulus was randomly varied between two to five seconds. In the second part of the experiment, the reward system was introduced and the simple reaction time was measured again for the same subjects. The mean reaction time before the introduction of reward system was 210 milliseconds and the mean reaction time after the introduction of reward system was 250 milliseconds. The difference between the two means was statistically significant at .01 level.

46 In the above study, the researcher's hypothesis is

1 Correlational hypothesis
2 Directional hypothesis
3 Non-directional hypothesis
4 Null hypothesis

***Ans.** (2)*

Exp. In the above study, the researcher's hypothesis is Directional hypothesis.

Directional hypothesis refers to a prediction with regards to a positive or a negative change or relationship among the different variables. In the above study, the researcher predicts that a certain 'Reward System' for fast reaction will enhance reaction times, indicating a positive change in reaction times. Therefore, it is a directional hypothesis.

47 Which of the following statistical techniques can be used for evaluating the mean differences ?

I. Independent samples t-test
II. Paired samples t-test
III. Mann-Whitney U-test
IV. Repeated measures ANOVA

Codes

1 Only II 2 I and II
3 II and IV 4 I, II and IV

***Ans.** (3)*

Exp. Paired sample t-test and Repeated measures ANOVA can be used for evaluating mean differences.

Paired sample t-test is used to compare the means of two measurements obtained from the same person.

The Repeated measures ANOVA (analysis of variance) compares means pertaining to repeated measures across one or more than one variable. In the given study, the researcher compares the means of the same participants before and after the reward system has been provided. Therefore, both paired sample t-test and repeated measures ANOVA are applicable because the test is being conducted on the same set of participants, and repeated measures have been obtained.

48 Which one of the following conclusions can be drawn on the basis of the above study ?

1 The researcher's hypothesis has been accepted.
2 The researcher's hypothesis has been rejected.
3 The researcher's hypothesis has been partially accepted.
4 Inadequate hypothesis to verify the hypothesis.

***Ans.** (2)*

Exp. In the given study, the hypothesis proposed by the researcher has been rejected.

The researcher hypothesized that a certain kind of reward system provided for fast reaction will enhance the reaction times among people. In this regard, he chose 40 participants, and compared their reaction times on reaction time tasks before and after providing the reward system. The reaction time before the provision of the reward system was 210 milliseconds, and after the introduction of the reward system, it was 250 milliseconds. This shows that the reaction time increased, indicating the reaction time slowed down after the reward system was provided. Consequently, the hypothesis must be rejected.

49 Read each of the following statements - Assertion (A) and Reason (R) and indicate your answer using codes given below.

Assertion (A) In the above study, the foreperiods were randomly varied.

Reason (R) Random variation of the foreperiods reduces the false reactions.

Codes

1 Both (A) and (R) are true and (R) is the correct explanation of (A)
2 Both (A) and (R) are true, but (R) is not the correct explanation of (A)
3 (A) is true, but (R) is false
4 (A) is false, but (R) is true

***Ans.** (1)*

Exp. Both (A) and (R) are true and (R) is the correct explanation of (A).

In the given study, foreperiods were randomly varied. In measuring the participants' reaction times on simple reaction task, the researcher introduced a time-interval between the ready signal and the presentation of the stimulus, to which the participants had to react to. The time-interval refers to the foreperiod. The foreperiods for trials were randomly varied from 2 – 5 seconds.

Foreperiods were randomly varied so as to decrease false reactions, which take place if the foreperiod between the ready signal and the presentation of the stimulus is set. The participant may automatically react after the set time period has passed. That is, their reaction has not got anything to do with the stimulus, but is only based on the time period.

50 In this experiment, reaction time can be labelled as

I. Continuous variable II. Dependent variable
III. Stimulus variable IV. Behavioural variable

Codes

1 Only II 2 I and II
3 I, II and III 4 I, II and IV

***Ans.** (4)*

Exp. In the experiment, reaction time can be labelled as a Continuous variable, Dependent variable and Behavioural variable.

Continuous variable is one whose value can be determined by measuring it. Here, the reaction time is measured, and the average values obtained are 210 milliseconds and 250 milliseconds.

In an experiment, dependent variable is one that is being tested or measured. Here, the effect of the reward system on the reaction time is being tested, and this effect is analysed by measuring the reaction time.

Reaction time refers to the amount of time taken before the perception and reaction to something. This speed at which one reacts to something is a behavioural measure, thereby making it a behavioural variable.

51 In Vertebrates, myelin is produced in the brain and spinal cord by ________ and in rest of nervous system by ________

1 Oligodendrocytes ; Schwann cells
2 Schwann cells ; Oligodendrocytes
3 Astrocytes ; Microglia
4 Microglia ; Astrocytes

Ans. *(1)*

Exp. In Vertebrates, myelin is produced in the brain and spinal cord by oligodendrocytes and in rest of nervous system by Schwann cell.

In the brain and the spinal cord, myelin is produced by the oligodendrocytes, which are large glial cells. Glial cells are mainly involved in supporting the neurons. In the other nervous system, which is the peripheral nervous system, myelin is produced by the Schwann cells. Schwann cells are glial cells of the peripheral nervous system.

Myelin is an insulating layer, and it covers the nerves, even those found in the brain and spinal cord. The myelin sheath found covering the neurons helps in protecting them, and also allows for the faster transmission of signals.

52 Read each of the following statements - Assertion (A) and Reason (R) and indicate your answer using codes given below.

Assertion (A) Algorithm is a logical rule that guarantees solving a particular problem.

Reason (R) One can find the solution even to complex problems by following step by step procedure.

Codes

1 Both (A) and (R) are true and (R) is the correct explanation of (A)
2 Both (A) and (R) are true, but (R) is not the correct explanation of (A)
3 (A) is true, but (R) is false
4 (A) is false, but (R) is true

Ans. *(1)*

Exp. Both (A) and (R) are true and (R) is the correct explanation of (A).

Algorithm is a logical method that guarantees solving a certain problem. It is a procedure or a rule used to solve problems, and involves a definite number of sets.

By following the step-by-step procedure of an algorithm, even the complex problems can be solved efficiently. However, it can be difficult, but it is a sure shot way of solving a problem.

53 Match List I with List II and select the correct answer by choosing from codes given below.

List I (Personality tests)	List II (Dimensions covered)
A. EPQ-R	I. Need for power
B. NEO-PI-3	II. Psychoticism
C. TAT	III. Anxiety as a state
D. STAI	IV. Openness to experience

Codes

	A	B	C	D		A	B	C	D
1	II	IV	I	III	2	IV	II	I	III
3	II	IV	III	I	4	I	IV	III	II

Ans. *(1)*

Exp. The correct matching is A-II, B-IV, C-I, D-III.

Psychoticism is covered in the Eysenck Personality Questionnaire–Revised (EPQ-R). It an aspect of personality characterized by antisocial behaviours, impulsivity, and aggression among others.

Openness to experience is covered in the NEO Personality Inventory–3 (NEO-PI-3). It is a personality dimension characterized by an openness towards trying out and enjoying new things. People high on this dimension are curious, imaginative, and open-minded.

Need for power is determined by the Thematic Apperception Test (TAT), which is designed in a manner so as to reveal people's hidden needs and drives. It is defined as the wish to control other people for the purpose of achieving one's own goals or to achieve one's own goals for the greater good.

State anxiety is measured by the State-Trait Anxiety Inventory (STAI). State anxiety is a temporary emotional state characterized by tension or fear about a certain situation or event.

54 The basic speech sounds are called _______ and the meaningful smallest units of speech are called _______ .

1 Phonemes ; Fixation
2 Phonemes ; Lexigram
3 Morphemes ; Phonemes
4 Phonemes ; Morphemes

Ans. *(4)*

Exp. The basic speech sounds are called Phonemes and the meaningful smallest units of speech are called Morphemes.

Phonemes are basic units of sound which help in distinguishing one word from the other. For instance, b and c are distinct sounding; therefore, bat is distinguished from cat on the basis of the differences in sound between them.

Morphemes are the smallest meaningful units of speech, and cannot be shortened any further as this would make the word meaningless. For instance, in 'restart', 're' and 'start' are morphemes, and further shortening of any of these words would deprive them of any meaning.

55 Which of the following concept/s is/are not found in Freudian Psychoanalysis ?

I. Unconscious motivation

II. Collective unconscious

III. Striving for superiority

IV. Instincts

Codes

1 I and II
2 II and III
3 III and IV
4 I, II and IV

Ans. (2)

Exp. Collective Unconscious and Striving for superiority are not concepts found in Freudian psychoanalysis.

Collective Unconscious is part of the theory given by Carl Jung. It refers to the shared mental concepts present in the unconscious mind that are common to all of mankind. It is inherited. For instance, archetypes, which are universal patterns of people or behaviours, are part of collective unconscious.

Striving for superiority is a concept given by Alfred Adler. It refers to people behaving in a self-centred manner so as to gain superiority over others. It is often done without any consideration for other people or greater good

56 Tests of declarative memory are termed as _______ tests, whereas tests of non-declarative memory are termed as _______ tests.

1 Long term memory ; explicit memory
2 Short term memory ; implicit memory
3 Implicit memory ; explicit memory
4 Explicit memory ; implicit memory

Ans. (4)

Exp. Tests of declarative memory are termed as Explicit memory tests, whereas tests of non-declarative memory are termed as Implicit memory tests.

Long-term memory is divided into explicit memory and implicit memory. Explicit memory is also referred to as declarative memory as it requires conscious effort to retrieve information. For instance, recalling the mathematical table of 5 requires conscious effort. Therefore, tests for declarative memory are known as explicit memory tests.

Implicit memory is also known as non-declarative memory as this type of memory does not require conscious effort when it comes to retrieval or recall of information. It is more automatic in nature. Procedural memory is part of implicit memory, and it is the memory pertaining to the performance of a task, like riding a scooter. Consequently, tests for non-declarative memory are known as implicit memory tests.

57 Which method is used for memorising a poem ?

1 Massed practice
2 Distributed practice
3 Serial memorising
4 Syntactic memorising

Ans. (2)

Exp. In memorising a poem, Distributed practice is highly effective.

Distributed practice is a practice technique wherein a learner distributes the effort they put into studying a given matter, like a poem, over several sessions of study. These study sessions are relatively short in time. Poems, for instance, may be large to memorise everything at one go, therefore, memorising one stanza during one study session is more effective

58 _______ makes neurons stand out visibly depicting which neurons are active; whereas _______ uses antibodies attached to a dye to identify cellular components such as receptors, neurotransmitters or enzymes.

1 Immunocytochemistry ; Autoradiography
2 Autoradiography ; Immunocytochemistry
3 Myelin staining ; Nissl Staining
4 Nissl Staining ; Myelin Staining

Ans. (2)

Exp. Autoradiography makes neurons stand out visibly depicting which neurons are active; whereas Immunocytochemistry uses antibodies attached to a dye to identify cellular components such as receptors, neurotransmitters or enzymes.

Autoradiography are used to trace neurons and neuronal processes. It utilizes the radioactive sources present within the target neurons to expose those neurons which are active. It was developed in the late 1960s.

Immunocytochemistry (ICC) utilizes antibodies to identify certain antigens in given cells. Antibodies are attached to enzymes or a dye, and when they bind to the antigen present in the given cell, the enzyme/dye becomes activated. In this manner, ICC is used to detect and visualise receptors, neurotransmitters, and other enzymes.

59 Which of the following are predictors of good prognosis in Schizophrenia.

I. Positive symptoms

II. Late onset

III. Acute onset

IV. No precipitating factors

Codes

1 I, II and III are correct ; IV is incorrect
2 II, III and IV are correct ; I is incorrect
3 III, IV and II are correct ; I is incorrect
4 I, III and IV are correct ; II is incorrect

Ans. (4)

Exp. Positive symptoms, acute onset, and no precipitating factors are predictors of good prognosis for schizophrenia, while late onset is not.

A good prognosis indicates that there is a good chance for the treatment to be successful. In terms of schizophrenia, statistics reveal that at least 50% of the people have recovered or are capable of working and living on their own. Some factors associated with good prognosis are:

1. *Positive symptoms* They are changes that begin to happen with the development of schizophrenia, and serve as indicators of the disorder. For instance, hallucinations and delusions.
2. *Acute onset* It refers to the sudden and severe onset of schizophrenia, however, it is rare. Rapid onset of these symptoms is associated with good prognosis.
3. *No precipitating factors* Precipitating factors are risk factors, and they include family history, abnormalities in the autoimmune system, and drug abuse, among others. Having no precipitating factors for schizophrenia is associated with good prognosis.

However, late onset of schizophrenia, which is generally defined as the development of schizophrenia after the age of 45 years has not been associated with good prognosis, indicating that recovery is highly difficult.

60 The body's response to danger is triggered by the release of __________ by the __________ glands.

1 Acetylcholine ; adrenal
2 Epinephrine and norepinephrine; adrenal
3 Acetylcholine ; pituitary
4 Epinephrine and norepinephrine; pituitary

Ans. (2)

Exp. The body's response to danger is triggered by the release of Epinephrine and norepinephrine by the adrenal glands.

Epinephrine and norepinephrine are hormones secreted by the adrenal glands. They play a very important role in 'fight-or-flight' response, which takes place when a person is faced with a threatening situation. These hormones increase the blood flow in the body, increase heartrate and breathing rate, and also increase the blood sugar levels in the body so as to provide the body with energy. In performing all these actions, they arouse and prepare the body to face any danger or threat.

61 Which of the following is the characteristic of Mastery-Oriented Students ?

1 They see ability as improvable
2 They feel competent when they succeed
3 They feel worthless when they fail
4 They set unrealistically high goals

Ans. (1)

Exp. Mastery-Oriented Students see their ability as improvable.

Mastery-oriented students seek to increase their comprehension and competence in a given task or skill. In doing so, they seek that every ability can be enhanced, therefore, they put in increasing levels of effort to master a certain task or skill.

Mastery-oriented people tend to choose patterns of learning most suitable to a given task or skill, and this adaptive form of learning can lead to high achievement.

62 A child's cognitive transition from external influences to internal thoughts occurs in four stages. What is the correct order of this transition?

I. Naive Stage
II. Natural / Primitive Stage
III. Ego-centric speech Stage
IV. Ingrowth Stage

Codes

1 I, II, III, IV 2 II, I, III, IV
3 I, II, IV, III 4 II, I, IV, III

Ans. (2)

Exp. The correct chronological order with regards to a child's transition from external influences to internal thoughts is II, I, III, and IV.

1. *Primitive stage* : This takes place from birth to 2 years. During this stage, the child is learning from external influences, like imitating the words or speech they hear.
2. *Naïve stage* : This takes place from 2 to 4 years of age. During this stage, they learn that words can be used to symbolise things. For instance, they learn the names of different objects surrounding them.
3. *Ego-centric speech stage* : This takes place from 4 to 7 years of age. During this stage, children begin to verbalise their thought process when they are conversing with others or even when they are alone.
4. *Ingrowth stage* : This takes place from 8 years onwards. During this stage, children tend to internalise many of the tasks they have learnt. For instance, while counting, instead of using their fingers, they count in their head. In this stage, their tendency to internalise thought also begins to increase as a consequence of having to interact with others.

Therefore, from hereon, people are more influenced by their internal thoughts.

63 Match List I with List II and select the correct answer by choosing from codes given below.

	List I (Psychologist)		List II (Concept)
A.	Bruner	I.	Conservation
B.	Vygotsky	II.	Iconic mode of representation
C.	Sternberg	III.	Scaffolding
D.	Piaget	IV.	Componential Analysis

Codes

	A	B	C	D		A	B	C	D
1	II	III	IV	I	2	IV	II	III	I
3	II	III	I	IV	4	III	II	IV	I

Ans. *(1)*

➲ *Exp.* The correct matching is A-II, B-III, C-IV, D-I.

Iconic mode of representation was given by Jerome Bruner. It refers to an internal visual representation of external symbols, and this takes place in the form of a mental image known as icon.

Scaffolding was given by Lev Vygotsky. It is a method of learning where a person learns more with appropriate assistance from a more knowledgeable other, who can be a parent, teacher, or someone older and experienced.

Componential analysis was given by Robert Sternberg. It involves breaking up intellectual tasks into components of elementary information processes, such as reasoning and planning, among others.

Conservation was given by Jean Piaget. It is the ability to understand that the quantity of an entity remains the same despite changes in its physical appearances, such as its shape.

64 Which of the following issues are addressed in the field of Personality Psychology?

I. Human Universals
II. Individual Differences
III. Uniqueness
IV. Modification of Behaviour

Codes

1 I and II 2 II and III
3 I, II and III 4 II, III and IV

Ans. *(3)*

➲ *Exp.* Human Universals, Individual differences and Modification of behaviours are the issues addressed by Personality Psychology.

Personality psychology studies the development of personality and the way in which it impacts thought and behaviour. The issues addressed by personality psychology are as follows:

1. *Human universals* : They are mental attributes that are shared by almost all people over the world. For instance, the concept of luck.
2. *Individual differences* : Personality is defined as stable and enduring pattern of characteristics that account for each person's distinctive character. Differences in personalities can explain how one person differs from another in terms of their thought or behaviour.
3. *Modification of behaviours* : It is a method which involves altering problematic behaviour. A person's personality can give rise to problematic behaviours such as anxiety, anger, and the like. Understanding the way in which a person's personality is giving rise to these kinds of behaviours helps in modifying them.

65 Match List I with List II and select the correct answer by choosing from codes given below.

	List I (Psychologist)		List II (Concept)
A.	Thorndike	I.	Equipotentiality premise
B.	Pavlov	II.	Cortical Mosaic
C.	Wertheimer	III.	Neural Bond
D.	Seligman	IV.	Isomorphism

Codes

	A	B	C	D		A	B	C	D
1	I	IV	III	II	2	II	III	IV	I
3	III	II	IV	I	4	IV	I	II	III

Ans. *(3)*

➲ *Exp.* The correct matching is A-III, B-II, C-IV, D-I

The concept of *Neural bonds* was given by Edward Thorndike. He believed that neural bonds are connections formed between stimuli and responses through experience.

The term *'Cortical Mosaic'* was coined by Ivan Pavlov. He believed that the cortex in the brain is characterized by both, excitation and inhibition at any given point in time.

Isomorphism is a concept given by Max Wertheimer. Isomorphism refers to the similarity between the objective physiological representation of a certain phenomenon and the subjective experience of that phenomenon.

Equipotentiality was opposed by Martin Seligman. It is a premise which states that any two stimuli can become associated via learning. This implies that any phobia of any object can develop provided it is closely connected to something traumatic. Seligman opposed this premise as he said that certain phobias are linked to survival, and they do not just develop by the association of any object with a trauma, regardless of its nature.

66 In case of visual stimulus "Where" pathways in the brain are mainly responsible for processing

I. Location II. Colour
III. Motion IV. Shape

Codes

1 I and II 2 II and III
3 III and IV 4 I and IV

Ans. *(4)*

➲ *Exp.* In case of visual stimulus.

"Where" pathways in the brain are mainly responsible for processing location and shape.

The processing of visual stimuli involves two streams, the 'what,' which pertains to recognition, and 'where,' which pertains to spatial vision. The where pathway is involved in processing the spatial location of a given visual stimulus and recognizing where the stimulus is located in space. Therefore, it is mainly involved in the processing of information pertaining to the location and shape of the object.

67 Which of the following sequences describes the Cranial Nerves in ascending order?

1 Optic → Trochlear → Abducens → Auditory - Vestibular → Vagus
2 Trochlear → Optic → Auditory-Vestibular → Abducens → Vagus
3 Optic → Abducens → Trochlear → Vagus → Auditory - Vestibular
4 Abducens → Trochlear → Optic → Auditory - Vestibular → Vagus

Ans. (1)

Exp. Cranial nerves are present in pairs, and are responsible for connecting the brain to parts of the head, neck, and the trunk. There are 12 cranial nerves. Among the 6 mentioned, the ascending order is as follows:

1. *Optic nerve* : Sensory nerve which plays a role in vision.
2. *Trochlear nerve* : It controls the superior oblique muscle which is responsible for the inward, outward, and downward movements of the eyes.
3. *Abducens nerve* : It controls the lateral rectus muscle, which is responsible for the outward movement of the eye, especially whilst looking sideways.
4. *Auditory nerve* : It is involved in hearing and the maintenance of balance.
5. *Vestibular nerve* It is a portion in the auditory nerve which is responsible for the rotational and linear movements of the head.
6. *Vagus nerve* It is diverse in nature, and performs both sensory and motor functions. For instance, it is responsible for the sense of taste especially at the root region of the tongue and is also involved in the motor control of the throat muscles, among other functions.

68 Many psychologists played pivotal role in the emergence of the field of Social Psychology. Arrange them in correct chronological sequence.

1 F Allport; William McDougall; Kurt Lewin; Muzafer Sherif
2 Kurt Lewin; William McDougall; Muzafer Sherif; F Allport
3 William McDougall; F Allport; Kurt Lewin; Muzafer Sherif
4 F Allport; William McDougall; Muzafer Sherif; Kurt Lewin

Ans. (3)

Exp. The correct chronological order of the psychologists who played an important role in the emergence of social psychology is as follows:

1. *William McDougall* : He opposed behaviourism, and wrote the book 'An Introduction to Social Psychology' in the year 1908, which was highly important for the development of the field.
2. *Floyd Allport* : He is considered as the founder of social psychology as he worked on many social psychology-related topics such as social facilitation, social influence, and conformity.
3. *Kurt Lewin* : He is known as the father of modern social psychology. He wrote about many topics including field theory, which emphasizes that a person's behaviour is a function of different social interactions, and also group dynamics.
4. *Muzafer Sherif* : He is also known for his contributions to modern social psychology. He developed tools that helped in understanding social processes like those of social norms and social conflict.

69 Kinship Selection Theory suggests that we help others who are related to us because this increases the likelihood that our ________ shall be ________ to future ________ .

1 character; transferred; population
2 genes; transmitted; population
3 genes; transmitted; generation
4 genes; transferred; population

Ans. (3)

Exp. Kinship Selection Theory suggests that we help others who are related to us because this increases the likelihood that our genes shall be transmitted to future generation.

Kinship Selection Theory explains altruism. It purports that living beings engage in altruistic behaviours (such as self-sacrificing behaviours) that favour their kin as it increases the chance of one's genes being transmitted to future generations. The understanding behind is that a person shares 50% of their genes with their parents and siblings. So, if they risk themselves to help their parents or other siblings to survive or reproduce, then they indirectly secure the transmission of their genes to future generations.

70 Read each of the following statements - Assertion (A) and Reason (R); and indicate your answer using codes given below.

Assertion (A) Results of experimental studies of bilateral lesion effects are considered more promising than those of unilateral lesions.

Reason (R) Behaviour effects of bilateral lesions are milder than those of unilateral lesions.

Codes

1 Both (A) and (R) are true and (R) is the correct explanation of (A)
2 Both (A) and (R) are true, but (R) is not the correct explanation of (A)
3 (A) is true, but (R) is false
4 (A) is false, but (R) is true

Ans. (3)

Exp. (A) is true, but (R) is false.

Bilateral lesion is a lesion or damage to both the sides of an organ, especially one in both the cerebral hemispheres of the brain. Bilateral lesions can produce significant damage and impair behaviour.

Unilateral lesions, on the other hand, produces hardly any effect, as the intact side of the organ can perform the functions of the damaged side. Consequently, in experimental settings, it becomes easier to understand the effects of bilateral lesions on behaviours as their impairments are more pronounced. Understanding the effect of bilateral lesions on behaviour also helps in locating the regions of the brain involved in that behaviour. Since unilateral lesions produce hardly any damage, these cannot be studied. Therefore, in experimental conditions, bilateral lesions yield more significant results.

As mentioned above, bilateral lesions cause significant behavioural impairment, while unilateral lesions hardly produce any effect. Therefore, it cannot be said that the behavioural effects of bilateral lesions are milder than the unilateral ones.

71 Which of the following are the basic forms of intelligence in Triarchic Theory?

I. Dimensional II. Componential
III. Contextual IV. Experiential

Codes

1 I, II and III 2 I, II and IV
3 II, III and IV 4 I, III and IV

Ans. *(3)*

Exp. Contextual, Experiential, and Componential are the basic forms of intelligence mentioned in the Triarchic Theory.

Robert Sternberg gave the Triarchic Theory of Intelligence. He broke down the theory in three sub-theories,which are :

1. *Contextual Intelligence* pertains to the manner of functioning in everyday environments, such as, the ability to choose the best environment, adapt to one's environment, and shape one's environment as per one's needs.
2. *Experiential Intelligence* pertains to the ability to deal with novel task or situations and the ease with which one deals with familiar tasks or situations.
3. *Componential Intelligence* pertains to the ability to plan, make decisions and solve problems, and also the ability to acquire new information.

72 In a single factor repeated measures design, the F-ratio, evaluating the effect of independent variable (treatment) is evaluated as

1 MStreatment/MSsubjects
2 MStreatment/MStreatment × subjects
3 MStreatment/(MSsubjects) + (MStreatment×subjects)
4 MStreatment/MStotal

Ans. *(2)*

Exp. Single factor repeated measures design involves one treatment with two or more levels. The participants go through all the different levels. In order to evaluate the effect of the treatment, single factor ANOVA is used, and the formula for F-ratio is :

MStreatment / MStreatment x subjects

73 Match List I with List II and select the correct answer by choosing from codes given below.

List I (Leadership style)	List II (Description)
A. Task Management	I. Less focus on both production and workers
B. Team Management	II. More Focus on both production and workers
C. Impoverished Management	III. Less focus on production but more on workers
D. Country Club Management	IV. More focus on production but less on workers

Codes

	A	B	C	D		A	B	C	D
1	I	II	III	IV	2	IV	III	II	I
3	III	IV	I	II	4	IV	II	I	III

Ans. *(4)*

Exp. The correct matching is A-IV, B-II, C-I, D-III.

Task management style is focussed on the completion of the given tasks in order to meet the goals. Therefore, the emphasis is more on the task, and less on workers.

Team Management style is focussed both, on the production and workers. Here, importance is given to motivating the workers and also their needs. At the same time, emphasis is on the completion of the task in order to meet the goals.

Impoverished Management is a style where the focus is neither on the task nor the workers. It is an ineffective management style as there is no impetus to create a motivating environment nor a productive one that leads to the completion of the task.

Country Club Management is a style where the manager is highly focused on the requirements and feelings of the workers, and not enough on the task(s) at hand. It is a very accommodative management style.

74 Read each of the following statements Assertion (A) and Reason (R) and indicate your answer using codes given below.

Assertion (A) Behaviour therapy helps people to respond to life situations in the way they would like to respond.

Reason (R) Positive therapeutic relationship is a necessary but not sufficient condition for effective behaviour therapy.

Codes

1 Both (A) and (R) are true and (R) is the correct explanation of (A)
2 Both (A) and (R) are true, but (R) is not the correct explanation of (A)
3 (A) is true, but (R) is false
4 (A) is false, but (R) is true

Ans. *(2)*

Exp. Both (A) and (R) are true, but (R) is not the correct explanation of (A).

The goal of behavioural therapy is to remove undesirable behaviours and replace them with desirable ones. This provides the clients with the ability to respond to different life situations in the way they want to. For instance, consider a fear of flying which is an undesirable behaviour. Behavioural therapy seeks to eliminate it by equipping the client with relaxation techniques whenever they are required to fly. This allows them to overcome their fear of flying, and take a flight whenever they are required to.

A positive therapeutic relationship is one that has a bond of trust, mutual respect, and a sense of caring. This is required for a therapy to work as a client will only open up to the therapist if they trust and respect them. However, this relationship alone does not make a behavioural therapy effective. There are other components that are required. For instance, determination and commitment on the part of the client to overcome the undesirable behaviours, skills of the therapist, and social support, among others.

75 Decentration and reversible thought processes are the characteristics of which of the following stage ?

1 Sensory-Motor
2 Pre-Operational
3 Concrete-Operational
4 Formal-Operations

Ans. *(3)*

Exp. Decentration and reversible thought processes are the characteristics of Concrete-Operational stage.

Concrete-Operational stage is the fourth stage of cognitive development as per Jean Piaget. It begins at the age of 7 years and lasts till the age of 11 years. Decentration and reversibility are characteristic of this stage.

Decentration refers to the ability to focus on different attributes of a given object rather than just one. For instance, decentration allows the child to focus on dimensions such as colour, quantity, shape, and size, rather than only one of them.

Reversibility refers to the ability to understand that events and actions can be reversed. Reversibility can be used to restore something from its final state to its original state.

76 Match List I with List II and select the correct answer by choosing from codes given below.

List I (Concept)	**List II** (Explanation)
A. Central executive	I. Helps us in playing videogames, jigsaw puzzles, etc.
B. Visuospatial sketchpad	II. Helps us in solving new problems and plan future activities.
C. Episodic buffer	III. Helps us decide what to do next and what not to do.
D. Phonological loop	IV. Helps us in reading and mathematical calculations.

Codes

	A	B	C	D
1	I	II	III	IV
2	III	I	II	IV
3	IV	III	I	II
4	II	III	IV	I

Ans. *(2)*

Exp. The correct matching is A-III, B-I, C-II, D-IV.

Central executive helps one to decide what to do next and what to not to do. It is a part of working memory that regulates the incoming information, directs attention and prioritizes certain tasks over the others.

Visuospatial sketchpad helps in playing videogames or solving puzzles. It allows people to retain visual and spatial information temporarily. It helps in navigation.

Episodic buffer helps in solving novel problems and planning future activities. It is a back-up store that incorporates information from the working memory store and the long-term memory store.

Phonological loop helps in reading and solving mathematical calculations. It helps in holding spoken and written information, and repeat verbal information. Therefore, it allows one to read. It is also involved in encoding and retaining arithmetic operations.

77 Read each of the following statements Assertion (A) and Reason (R) and indicate your answer using codes given below.

Assertion (A) Working memory is like a workbench where material is constantly being handled, combined and transformed.

Reason (R) Both new material and old material retrieved from long term memory are held in working memory.

Codes

1 Both (A) and (R) are true and (R) is the correct explanation of (A)
2 Both (A) and (R) are true, but (R) is not the correct explanation of (A)
3 (A) is true, but (R) is false
4 (A) is false, but (R) is true

Ans. *(2)*

Exp. Both (A) and (R) are true, but (R) is not the correct explanation of (A).

Working memory is a limited storage capacity memory store where memory is stored and manipulated in order to perform tasks such as reasoning. It is compared to a 'workbench' as information here undergoes constant integration and transformation as it is subject to processing. If memory is not processed, then it is lost.

Working memory holds both, new and old information from long-term memory store. For instance, consider reading comprehension. In order to comprehend what one has read, they have to retrieve information from the long-term memory store to understand the meaning of words. This may either be words one has recently learnt or ones that have been learnt in the past.

78 Read each of the following statements - Assertion (A) and Reason (R) and indicate your answer using codes given below.

Assertion (A) Galton developed anthropometric tests of intelligence.

Reason (R) Psychometric tests were low in reliability and validity.

Codes

1 Both (A) and (R) are true and (R) is the correct explanation of (A)
2 Both (A) and (R) are true, but (R) is not the correct explanation of (A)
3 (A) is true, but (R) is false
4 (A) is false, but (R) is true

Ans. *(3)*

Exp. (A) is true, but (R) is false.

Anthropometric tests measure the composition of the human body. Sir Francis Galton developed anthropometric tests to assess intelligence. He tested intelligence by measuring physical characteristics of noblepersons and tested their reaction time and other sensory characteristics.

Reliability of a psychometric test refers to how consistently it is able to measure a characteristic, while validity refers to how efficiently a psychometric test is able to measure a characteristic. Psychometric tests are standardized. That is, they are instruments whose reliability and validity have been established. Therefore, it cannot be said that they are low on either of these two aspects.

79 Read each of the following statements - Assertion (A) and Reason (R) and indicate your answer using code given below.

Assertion (A) Proprioceptive stimuli result from the firing of the kinesthetic receptors in the muscles, joints and tendons of the body.

Reason (R) A response is conditioned to the stimuli present prior to the ingestion of a primary reinforcer.

Codes

1 Both (A) and (R) are true and (R) is the correct explanation of (A)
2 Both (A) and (R) are true, but (R) is not the correct explanation of (A)
3 (A) is true, but (R) is false
4 (A) is false, but (R) is true

Ans. *(1)*

Exp. Both (A) and (R) are true and (R) is the correct explanation of (A).

Proprioception is referred to as the sense of body position and self-movement. Therefore, proprioceptive stimulus is one which arises from within a person's self, and it is mediated by the kinaesthetic neurons located in the muscles, joints, and tendons.

Proprioceptive stimulus accompanies fraction of a certain response. The reason for this is that the response is conditioned to the stimulus present even before the primary reinforcer is presented. Consequently, every response becomes a fraction of the target.

80 Activation of anterior portions of both hemispheres is associated with the ________ of emotions, while activation of the posterior portions of the hemispheres is associated with ________.

1 expressions; moods
2 valence; arousal
3 intensity; expressions
4 arousal; valence

Ans. *(3)*

Exp. Activation of anterior portions of both hemispheres is associated with the intensity of emotions, while activation of the posterior portions of the hemispheres is associated with expressions.

The activation of the anterior portions of both the cerebral hemispheres is connected with the intensity of emotions. Frontal lobes are present in the anterior regions of these hemispheres. They are considered to be the centre of emotional control. Therefore, activation of them leads to intensity of emotions. On the other hand, activation of the posterior portions of both the cerebral hemisphere leads to the expression of emotions.

81 Signal detection theory identifies two distinct processes in sensory detection

I. sensory process	II. decision process
III. motivational process	IV. response bias

Codes

1 I and II	2 III and IV
3 I and III	4 I and IV

Ans. *(1)*

Exp. Signal detection theory identifies two distinct processes in sensory detection, which are sensory and decision processes.

Signal detection theory is based on the premise that decisions are often required to be taken when there is uncertainty around. It is a technique that emphasizes the role of sensory processes in decision making, in that, the target of the decision-making must be extracted from the background noise. For instance, when it comes to perceiving distance in conditions that are foggy, people often decide the distance of a given object based on the sight of the object that has been impaired by the foggy conditions. Therefore, here, the two processes involved are sensory and decision-making processes. Sensory process involves detecting the object, and decision-making process involves the deciding of distance.

82 Read each of the following statements - Assertion (A) and Reason (R) and indicate your answer using codes given below.

Assertion (A) Visual Simple Reaction Time is more than Auditory Simple Reaction Time.

Reason (R) Visual system involves more complex photochemical processes.

Codes

1 Both (A) and (R) are true and (R) is the correct explanation of (A)
2 Both (A) and (R) are true, but (R) is not the correct explanation of (A)
3 (A) is true, but (R) is false
4 (A) is false, but (R) is true

Ans. (1)

Exp. Both (A) and (R) are true and (R) is the correct explanation of (A).

Simple reaction time refers to the minimum time taken to react to a stimulus. The simple reaction time for a visual stimulus is more than that for an auditory stimulus. A study conducted by Dr. Jaiswal (2016) lends credence to this wherein the mean reaction time for visual stimulus lay between 285.59 milliseconds to 301.15 milliseconds, while the mean reaction time for auditory stimulus lay between 246.88 milliseconds to 250.35 milliseconds.

The reason for this are the complex photochemical processes taking place in the visual system. These processes involve absorption of light by the pigment, rhodopsin. This is then converted into an electrical signal by the brain, which is then interpreted as an image. Whereas, with hearing, the processes are more simple wherein the sound waves from the air travel to the eardrum and are carried towards the auditory centres of the brain, which takes lesser time.

83 Creative thinking is different from routine problem solving in respect of

I. Fluency II. Flexibility
III. Originality IV. Day dreaming

Codes

1 I and II 2 II and III
3 III and IV 4 I, II and III

Ans. (2)

Exp. Creative thinking is different from routine problem-solving in the respect of flexibility and originality.

Everyday involves tasks that require to be solved. Routine problem-solving involves regular ways of solving a problem, which is to identify the problem, plan and choose from the different methods to solve it, and execute the plan.

Creative thinking involves looking at a problem from all the possible angles and coming up with novel ways to solve the problem. In this type of thinking, one is more open to different ideas, even those that are absurd. Therefore, there is a flexibility to creative thinking. Therefore, creative thinking differs from regular problem-solving in terms of originality and flexibility.

84 The Wechsler type deviation IQ of 115 corresponds to which value of percentile rank?

1 68 2 84
3 90 4 9

Ans. (2)

Exp. A deviation IQ is one that is a standard score derived from an IQ test with a mean of 100, with a standard deviation specific to that particular test. Usually, it is 15 or 16. For Wechsler tests, the standard deviation is 15. Therefore, the score one standard deviation higher than 100 will be 115.

Percentile rank refers to the percentage of scores present in a frequency distribution that are either equal or lower to it. For instance, a score of 115 on Wechsler's scales is more than 84% of the scores obtained by people taking those tests, therefore, its percentile rank is 84.

85 Match List I with List II and select the correct answer by choosing from codes given below.

	List I (Term)		List II (Description)
A.	Conformity	I.	Rules indicating how individuals are expected to behave in a specific situation.
B.	Compliance	II.	Social influence involving direct request from other.
C.	Social norms	III.	Social influence wherein individuals change their attitude to go along with existing norms.
D.	Intense indoctorinisation	IV.	Process in which members of extreme group accept the beliefs and rules in unquestioning way.

Codes

	A	B	C	D		A	B	C	D
1	I	II	III	IV	2	II	III	IV	I
3	III	IV	I	II	4	III	IV	II	I

Ans. (*)

Exp. The correct matching is A-III, B-II, C-I, D-IV.

Conformity is a kind of social influence wherein one changes their beliefs or behaviours in order to go along with the existing norms. For instance, despite not liking pink, one may wear pink coloured clothing if others in their group prefer it.

Compliance is a kind of social influence which takes place where one does what another person requires them to do, either in terms of a request or a suggestion.

Social norms are unwritten rules regarding how people must behave in a given situation. For instance, if a person is meeting their superior, the person is supposed to shake hands with them only if the superior initiates the handshake.

Intense indoctrinisation is a kind of process through which people become members of groups with extreme beliefs or ideas, and become accepting and committed to them without even questioning any of these beliefs or ideas

86 Spatial processing of location relies on :

I. Dorsal pathway
II. Inferior temporal cortex

III. Subcortical pathway
IV. Ventral pathway

Codes

1 Only I 2 Only IV 3 II and III 4 I and IV

Ans. (1)

Exp. Spatial processing of location relies on the Dorsal pathway.

Spatial processing of location relies on the "where" pathway, which is the dorsal stream. It is a pathway that stretches from the occipital lobe to the parietal lobe of the brain. It helps in understanding where the target objects are located in the space, and is also involved in assisting actions that help in locating a certain object.

87 Read each of the following statements - Assertion (A) and Reason (R) and indicate your answer using codes given below.

Assertion (A) Jensen has put forward regression argument in favour of his theory.

Reason (R) Children of parents having very high intelligence levels will have below average intelligence scores.

Codes

1 Both (A) and (R) are true and (R) is the correct explanation of (A)
2 Both (A) and (R) are true, but (R) is not the correct explanation of (A)
3 (A) is true, but (R) is false
4 (A) is false, but (R) is true

Ans. (3)

Exp. A is true, but R is false.

Arthur Jensen put forward his theory of intelligence which said that genes were the primary factors involved in intelligence. He believed that genetic makeup influenced most of what a person is. He put forth the regression argument in favour of his theory, which is a statistical method of sorting out which of the variables tend to influence other variables.

If Jensen believed that genetics was the primary factor influencing intelligence, then this shows that heredity plays a role in intelligence. Consequently, children having high intelligence cannot have parents with below average intelligence.

88 Handling feelings appropriately, ability to soothe oneself and ability to shake off rampant anxiety are the characteristics of which of the components of emotional intelligence as proposed by Goleman?

1 Knowing one's emotions 2 Managing emotions
3 Motivating oneself 4 Handling relationships

Ans. (2)

Exp. Emotional intelligence is described as the ability to understand and judge one's own emotions, use emotions to effectively shape thinking, understanding of emotions and knowledge pertaining to emotions, and to be able to efficiently monitor one's emotion in order to facilitate emotional and intellectual development.

Managing emotions is among the components of emotional intelligence given by Daniel Goleman, which refers to the ability to monitor and handle one's emotions, soothe oneself, and deal with feelings of anxiety

89 Which of the following new disorders have been introduced in DSM-5 ?

I. Premenstrual Dysphoric Disorder
II. Mild Neurocognitive Disorder
III. Disruptive Mood Dysregulation Disorder
IV. Road Rage Behaviour Disorder

Codes

1 I, II and III are correct ; IV is incorrect
2 I, II and IV are correct ; III is incorrect
3 I, III and IV are correct ; II is incorrect
4 All I, II, III and IV are correct

Ans. (1)

Exp. Premenstrual Dysphoric Disorder, Mild Neurocognitive Disorder, Disruptive Mood Dysregulation Disorder are the new disorders introduced in Diagnostic and Statistical Manual of Mental Disorders–5 (DSM-5).

Premenstrual Dysphoric Disorder (PMDD) is characterised by extreme irritability, anxiety and depression two to three weeks prior to the start of a period. The symptoms tend to disappear two to three days after the period starts. PMDD was introduced in DSM-5.

Mild Neurocognitive Disorder (MND) pertains to ageing. It is characterized by cognitive decline that require assistance in the form of accommodations and other compensatory strategies that help a person to be independent and perform daily activities. Mild Neurocognitive Disorder was introduced in DSM-5.

Disruptive Mood Dysregulation Disorder (DMDD) is a childhood disorder which is characterized by extreme anger, frustration, and frequent angry outbursts and temper tantrums. DMDD was introduced in DSM-5.

Road rage is a condition that is displayed by those who drive vehicles. It is characterized by extreme anger, and can include insults, threats, and dangerous driving on the road. This behaviour can lead to accidents and even deaths. However, there is no disorder known as Road Rage Behaviour disorder.

90 In selection process, Guilford-Zimmerman Test assesses :

1 Mathematical and Verbal skills
2 Mental and Personal profile
3 Extent of temperamental adaptability
4 Analytical and Verbal Skills

Ans. (3)

Exp. In selection process, Guilford-Zimmerman Test assesses the extent of temperamental adaptability.

Guilford- Zimmerman Temperament Survey (GZTS) is used to assess temperamental adaptability in selection process. This refers to the ease with which people can adjust their temperaments in accordance with the situations. While it is not widely used any longer, it was used by the Italian government to assess military pilots. Its scales include general activity, restraint, ascendance, sociability, emotional stability, objectivity, friendliness, thoughtfulness, personal relations, and masculinity.

91 'Mechanistic Behaviour Analysis' are characterised as

I. Behaviour is instigated by the onset of external or internal stimuli.
II. Direction of behaviour is determined by S-R bonds or habits.
III. Behaviour directed toward the goal persists till the achievement of goal.
IV. Events related to the goal achievement are encoded, categorised, and transformed into a belief.

Codes

1 I and II correct ; III and IV are incorrect
2 II and III correct ; I and IV are incorrect
3 I, II and III are correct ; IV is incorrect
4 II, III and IV are correct ; I is incorrect

Ans. *(3)*

Exp. Among the given statements pertaining to the characterization of 'Mechanistic Behaviour Analysis,' statements I, II, and III are correct, while statement IV is incorrect.

The Mechanistic Behaviour Analysis tends to describe psychological processes in the same way as mechanical or physiological processes are. In doing so, it reduces complicated psychological phenomena into simpler physical ones. According to this analysis:

1. Behaviour is a reaction to external or internal stimulus.
2. Stimulus-Response (S-R) bonds indicate that behaviours are learnt by associations between a stimulus and response, and the direction of these behaviours is determined by the S-R bonds.
3. Behaviour is goal-directed. Therefore, behaviour lasts only till a goal has been achieved.

However, this analysis does not imply that events pertaining to the achievement of a goal can be encoded, categorised, and changed into a belief. This implies a role of cognition in behaviour, which is not addressed by Mechanistic Behaviour Analysis.

92 Guilford (1981) in his modified SOI model mentioned hierarchical structure of intellectual abilities reporting that there are first order factors; second order factors and third order factors.

1 150; 85; 20
2 120; 80; 20
3 150; 85;16
4 180; 75; 18

Ans. *(3)*

Exp. Guilford gave the Structure of Intellect (SOI) model to understand intelligence. He divided intelligence into operations, content, and product. He used the technique of factor analysis, which yielded that the structure of intellect constituted many independent factors of different operations, content, and product combinations, known as first-order factors. These factors can further be correlated, and that will give rise to more factors. Therefore, he came up with first-order factors, second-order factors, and third-order factors.

Guilford reported that there were 150 first-order factors, 85 second-order factors, and 16 third-order factors.

93 Read each of the following statements - Assertion (A) and Reason (R) and indicate your answer using codes given below.

Assertion (A) Children have remarkable ability to create mental representation of the world in the form of language.

Reason (R) Reasoning and problem solving are the ways of manipulating the ideas.

Codes

1 Both (A) and (R) are true and (R) is the correct explanation of (A)
2 Both (A) and (R) are true, but (R) is not the correct explanation of (A)
3 (A) is true, but (R) is false
4 (A) is false, but (R) is true

Ans. *(2)*

Exp. Both (A) and (R) are true, but (R) is not the correct explanation of (A).

Jean Piaget suggested that language is highly crucial for cognitive development of a child. Children have the ability to use language to create mental representations of the world. Language is used for communication, and while communicating, one tends to focus on different attributes in the world, and this has an influence on one's mental representation of the world. Language can also be used as a means of encoding one's perception of the world.

Reasoning refers to the use of rationality and logic in order to make decisions or solve problems. Problem-solving refers to identifying a problem, coming up with a solution, and executing the solution. Both of these processes involve manipulation of ideas.

From the above, it can be understood that both the statements are true, albeit unrelated to each other.

94 Read each of the following statements - Assertion (A) and Reason (R) and indicate your answer using codes given below.

Assertion (A) Forgetting of everyday events in young people is not an indication of a poor memory.

Reason (R) Ineffective encoding due to failure to attend to an event while it is happening results in failure to remember.

Codes

1 Both (A) and (R) are true and (R) is the correct explanation of (A)
2 Both (A) and (R) are true, but (R) is not the correct explanation of (A)
3 (A) is true, but (R) is false
4 (A) is false but (R) is true

Ans. (1)

Exp. Both (A) and (R) are true and (R) is the correct explanation of (A).

Forgetting is not limited only to the elderly, even young people forget things. However, this is not an indication of poor memory.

A failure to pay attention can lead to ineffective encoding, which leads to forgetting. For instance, consider absentmindedness. Consider that one has left their car keys on the couch in a hurry, and then when they needed the keys, they happened to search the entire house in order to find it them they could not remember where they placed the keys. This is because while they were placing the keys on the couch, they were in a hurry, so they did not pay attention to the function of placing the keys on the couch. This led to ineffective encoding, which in turn led to forgetting.

95 Read each of the following statements - Assertion (A) and Reason (R) and indicate your answer using codes given below.

Assertion (A) Premack principle, based on Probability-Differential Hypothesis, states that the opportunity to engage in a frequently occurring activity can be used to reinforce less frequently activity.

Reason (R) According to Probability-Differential Hypothesis, restricted access to a response makes that response reinforcing and excessive access to that response makes that response punishing.

Codes

1 Both (A) and (R) are true and (R) is the correct explanation of (A)
2 Both (A) and (R) are true, but (R) is not the correct explanation of (A)
3 (A) is true, but (R) is false
4 (A) is false, but (R) is true

Ans. (3)

Exp. (A) is true, but (R) is false.

The Premack principle or probability-differential hypothesis states that when there is a chance to engage in more frequently occurring behaviours, it will reinforce the less frequently occurring behaviours. For instance, consider that a child likes watching T.V. and avoids completing their homework. In this case, the highly probable behaviour is watching T.V., while the less probable one is to complete homework. Therefore, if the child is allowed to watch T.V. after the completion of their homework, it reinforces the completion of homework as the chance to watch T.V. acts as a reward.

From the above, it can be understood that the access to one response leads to another. However, it does not say that restricted access makes a response reinforcing or excessive access makes a response punishing, only that one response reinforces another if it is contingent on it.

Directions (Q. Nos. 96-100) *Read the following paragraph and answer the five questions which follow.*

An educational psychologist wanted to develop an achievement test in physics for graduate students. After going through the usual test construction procedure, he retained 100 items; each item having five alternatives, one of them being correct. The psychologist wanted to examine the factor structure of the resulting achievement test. Using a sample of 1,000 subjects, the psychologist obtained the inter-item correlations. He obtained the initial estimates of communality and then decided to factor analyse the inter-item correlations matrix by following the common-factor model. He extracted the unrotated factors and retained the first nine factors for rotation. The nine unrotated factors explained 67.5 per cent of variance. After factor rotation, all the inter-factor correlations were found to be zero. The factor structure of the achievement test of physics was found to be interpretable.

96 The inter-item correlations would be :

1 Biserial correlations
2 Kendall's tau
3 Phi-coefficients
4 Point-biserial correlations

Ans. (3)

Exp. The inter-item correlations will be Phi-coefficients as this is a measure of correlation between binary items. The correlation coefficient ranges from-1 to +1, wherein -1 indicates perfect negative correlation while +1 indicates perfect positive correlation. 0 indicates no correlation.

97 Read each of the following statements - Assertion (A) and Reason (R) and indicate your answer using codes given below.

Assertion (A) For the factor analysis of item scores, Common-Factor model is quite often more suitable.

Reason (R) Item scores are quite often less reliable than the psychometrically measured trait variables.

Codes

1 Both (A) and (R) are true and (R) is the correct explanation of (A)
2 Both (A) and (R) are true, but (R) is not the correct explanation of (A)
3 (A) is true, but (R) is false
4 (A) is false, but (R) is true

Ans. (1)

Exp. Both (A) and (R) are true and (R) is the correct explanation of (A).

Common factor model purports that covariance present in variables being observed can be because of the influence of one or more than one common factors. When a test includes items, each item yields a score. When it comes to the factor analysis of these item scores, common factor model is more appropriate.

The reason for common factor model being more suitable for item scores is because they are not as consistent as psychometrically measured traits are. Psychometric measures are standardized, therefore, they have established reliability, which indicates consistency in the measures. Therefore, any covariance among item scores can be the influence of one or more common factors making common factor model more suitable to them.

98 Which one of the following method of factor extraction, the psychologist would not use in the present study ?

1 Principal axes method
2 Principal components method
3 Psychometric (alpha) factor analysis
4 Maximum likelihood method

Ans. *(2)*

Exp. In the present study, the psychologist would not use the Principal component method.

Principal component method is a statistical method often used to decrease a larger set of variables into a smaller set of variables, which are referred to as principal components. For instance, reducing the number of variables on the basis of the same underlying construct. Instead, in this study, the researcher uses factor analysis to determine the structure of the factors present in the results of the achievement test.

Factor analysis seeks to determine the hidden factors present in the observed data which is vastly difference from principal component method. Principal component method is used to determine the variables that are combinations of the observed variables.

99 Which method/s of rotation has/have most probably been used in the present study ?

I. Oblimin II. Promax
III. Quartimax IV. Varimax

Codes

1 Only I 2 Only III
3 III and IV 4 II, III and IV

Ans. *(3)*

Exp. The methods of rotation most probably used in the study are Quartimax and Varimax rotations.

In the given study, the researcher seeks to analyse inter-item and inter-factor correlations. Therefore, quartimax and varimax rotations are more likely to be used. Varimax rotation seeks to clarify the relationship among different factors, while quartimax rotation seeks to reduce the number of factors required to explain each variable.

100 The second-order factor analysis of the nine rotated factors is not recommended in the present study because

1 there are only nine first-order factors.
2 the interfactor correlations are zero.
3 the factors obtained by common-factor model are not subjected to second-order factor analysis.
4 unrotated factors are more suitable for second-order factor analysis.

Ans. *(2)*

Exp. The second-order factor analysis of the nine rotated factors is not recommended in the present study because the interfactor correlations are zero.

Factor analysis is basically used to reduce large number of variables into smaller factors by finding out the common variance among them. However, given that the inter-factor correlations between the 9 factors are 0, indicating no relationship amongst them, a second-order factor analysis is not required as there would be no common variance among them due to the lack of any relation between them.

UGC-NET PSYCHOLOGY

SOLVED PAPER 2017 (November)

PAPER II

1 Match List I with List II and select the correct answer by choosing from the codes given below.

List I (Concept)	List II (Description)
A. Type	I. Consistent style of behaviour or emotion, a person displays across the situations
B. Trait	II. A cluster of many dispositions
C. System	III. Enduring qualities that define the individual and distinguish individuals from one another
D. Structure	IV. A collection of highly interconnected parts of personality whose overall behaviour reflects them being organised

Codes

	A	B	C	D		A	B	C	D
1	I	II	III	IV	2	II	I	IV	III
3	III	II	I	IV	4	IV	III	II	I

Ans. (2)

Exp. The correct matching is A-II, B-I, C-IV and D-III.

Type is a cluster of many dispositions and traits. The type approach to personality attempts to comprehend human personality by examining certain broad patterns in the observed behavioural characteristics of individuals.

Trait is a consistent style of behavior or emotion, a person displays across the situations which are relatively stable. The trait approach to personality focuses on the specific psychological attributes along which individuals tend to differ in consistent and stable ways.

System is a collection of highly interconnected parts of personality whose overall behaviour reflects them being organised.

Structure is defined as the enduring qualities that define the individual and distinguish individuals from one another.

2 Which of the following is true for Tip of the Tongue (TOT) state?

I. Feeling of knowing

II. Feeling that memory is available

III. Retrievable memory

IV. Maintenance recoding

Codes

1 I and II 2 I and III

3 II and IV 4 III and IV

Ans. (1)

Exp. Feeling of knowing and feeling that memory is available is true for Tip of the Tongue (TOT) state.

It is the phenomenon of failing to retrieve a word from memory, combined with partial recall and the feeling that retrieval is imminent. It means that memory is available but not retrievable.

3 Read each of the following two statements Assertion (A) and Reason (R) and indicate your answer using codes given below.

Assertion (A) Conditioning done using partial reinforcement schedule decreases resistance to change.

Reason (R) Partial reinforcement schedules influence rate of responding.

Codes

1 Both (A) and (R) are true and (R) is the correct explanation of (A)

2 Both (A) and (R) are true, but (R) is not the correct explanation of (A)

3 (A) is true, but (R) is false

4 (A) is false, but (R) is true

Ans. (1)

Exp. Both (A) and (R) are true, and (R) is the correct explanation of (A).

Conditioning done using partial reinforcement schedule decreases resistance to change. This is true as in partial or intermittent reinforcement, the response is reinforced only part of the time making the response more resistant to extinction.

Partial reinforcement schedules influence rate of responding. Learned behaviours are acquired more slowly with partial reinforcement. This type of reinforcement is regarded more powerful in maintaining or shaping behaviour.

4 Arrange the clinical scales of MMPI-II in correct sequence.

1 Depression → Hypochondriasis → Hysteria → Psychopathic Deviate → Masculinity- Feminity → Paranoia → Psychasthenia → Schizophrenia → Hypomania → Social Introversion
2 Hypochondriasis → Depression → Hysteria → Psychopathic Deviate → Masculinity-Feminity → Paranoia → Psychasthenia → Schizophrenia → Hypomania → Social Introversion
3 Social Introversion → Hypomania → Hypochondriasis → Depression → Hysteria → Psychopathic Deviate → Masculinity-Feminity → Paranoia → Psychasthenia → Schizophrenia
4 Social introversion → Schizophrenia → Psychasthenia → Paranoia → Masculinity-Feminity → Psychopathic deviate → Hysteria → Depression → Hypochondriasis

Ans. (2)

Exp. Clinical scales of MMPI - II in correct sequence are:

Hypochondriasis → Depression → Hysteria → Psychopathic Deviate → Masculinity-Feminity → Paranoia → Psychasthenia → Schizophrenia → Hypomania → Social Introversion.

The MMPI-II is designed with 10 clinical scales which assess 10 major categories of abnormal human behaviour. *Hypochondriasis* (Hs) scale tapes a wide variety of vague and non-specific complaints about bodily functioning.

Depression (D) scale measures clinical depression, which is characterized by poor morale, lack of hope in the future, and a general dissatisfaction with one's life.

Hysteria (Hy) scale primarily measures five components — poor physical health, shyness, cynicism, headaches and neuroticism.

Psychopathic Deviate (Pd) scale measures general social maladjustment and the absence of strongly pleasant experiences.

Masculinity/Feminity (Mf) scale measures in a general sense how rigidly a person conforms to very stereotypical masculine or feminine roles.

Paranoia (Pa) scale primarily measures interpersonal sensitivity, moral self-righteousness and suspiciousness.

Psychasthenia (Pt) scale is intended to measure a person's inability to resist specific actions or thoughts, regardless of their maladaptive nature.

Schizophrenia (Sc) scale measures bizarre thoughts, peculiar perceptions, social alienation, poor familial relationships, difficulties in concentration and impulse control, lack of deep interests, disturbing question of self-worth and self-identity, and sexual difficulties.

Hypomania (Ma) scale is intended to measure milder degrees of excitement, characterized by an elated but unstable mood, psychomotor excitement and flight of ideas.

Social Introversion (Si) scale measures the social introversion and extroversion of a person.

5 Allport defined personality as

1 response style
2 social stimulus value
3 intervening variable
4 thinking style

Ans. (2)

Exp. Allport defined personality as social stimulus value.

According to him, "Personality is the dynamic organisation within the individual of those psychophysical systems that determine his unique adjustment to his environment".

6 Read each of the following two statements - Assertion (A) and Reason (R) and indicate your answer using codes given below :

Assertion (A) Increase in synaptic strength is due to the simultaneous stimulation of pre-synaptic and post-synaptic neurons.

Reason (R) Long term potentiation can be induced in the laboratory by stimulating the pre-synaptic neurons with pulses of high frequency of electricity for few seconds.

Codes

1 Both (A) and (R) are true and (R) is the correct explanation of (A)
2 Both (A) and (R) are true, but (R) is not the correct explanation of (A)
3 (A) is true, but (R) is false
4 (A) is false, but (R) is true

Ans. (2)

Exp. Both (A) and (R) are true, but (R) is not the correct explanation of (A).

Increase in synaptic strength is due to the simultaneous stimulation of pre-synaptic and post-synaptic neurons. This is true as synaptic strength is defined as the average amount of current or voltage excursion produced in the postsynaptic neuron by an action potential in the presynaptic neuron.

Long term potentiation can be induced in the laboratory by stimulating the pre-synaptic neurons with pulses of high frequency of electricity for few seconds. This is true as Long Term Potentiation (LTP) is a persistent strengthening of synapses based on recent patterns of activity and stimulations of the presynaptic axons alone is sufficient for LTP induction. However, it does not explain the assertion.

7 Concepts allow us to identify things without ________.

1 learning
2 relearning
3 recognition
4 remembering

Ans. (2)

➲ *Exp.* Concepts allow us to identify things without relearning. Concept involves the following steps:

Categorization→ Better organizing→ Storing information in memory→ Identify things without relearning.

8 Below given are some concepts. Indicate which is the correct sequence in terms of levels of increasing abstraction ? Concepts are

I. Negation concept

II. Alternative denial concept

III. Disjunction concept

Codes

1 I, II, III 2 I, III, II

3 II, I, III 4 III, II, I

***Ans.* (2)**

➲ *Exp.* The correct sequence in terms of levels of increasing abstraction are Negation concept, Disjunction concept and Alternative denial concept.

In logic, negation, also called the logical complement, is an operation that takes a proposition 'p' to another proposition "not p", written p, which is interpreted intuitively as being true when p is false and false when p is true.

The Alternative denial is a truth-functional operator in logic which is equivalent to the English wording "not both" "and". It is used to deny a conjuntion, stating that at least one of the connected propositions is false.

Disjunction (also called alternation) is a combination of two sentences with connective or linking the sentences. The two sentences so combined are called disjuncts (or alternatives).

9 Match List I with List II and select the correct answer by choosing from the codes given below:

List I (Description)	List II (Concept)
A. Transformation of the order of items	I. Non-specific transfer
B. Transformation in contents of items	II. Learning to learn
C. Use of coding devices and mediators	III. Coding
D. Learning how to perform the task	IV. Clustering

Codes

	A	B	C	D		A	B	C	D
1	III	IV	I	II	2	IV	III	II	I
3	II	I	V	III	4	I	II	III	IV

***Ans.* (2)**

➲ *Exp.* The correct matching is A-IV, B-III, C-II and D-I.

Clustering is the transformation of the order of items. It refers to the process of organizing objects into groups whose members are similar with respect to a similarity or distance criterion.

Coding is the transformation in contents of items. It is a process of identifying the content of the passage in the text or other data items (photograph, image), searching and identifying concepts and finding relations between them.

Learning to learn is use of coding devices and mediators. It helps to generate meaning for the new information that is to be learned.

Non-specific transfer is to learn how to perform the task. Non-specific transfer effects refer to improvements in performance on a second task that are independent of the specific content of the tasks.

10 Binocular cues depend on

I. combination of the images in the left and right retinas

II. the way two eyes work together

III. image in either right or left eye

IV. difference between the images in the two eyes

Codes

1 I, II and IV 2 I, III and IV

3 III, I and II 4 II, III and IV

***Ans.* (1)**

➲ *Exp.* Binocular cues depend on combination of the images in the left and right retinas, the way two eyes work together and difference between the images in the two eyes. Binocular cues provide depth information when viewing a scene with both eyes. Animals that have their eyes placed frontally can also use information derived from the different projection of objects into each retina to judge depth.

By using two images of the same scene obtained from slightly different angles, it is possible to triangulate the distance to an object with a high degree of accuracy. Each eye views a slightly different angle of an object seen by the left and right eyes. This happens because of the horizontal separation parallax of the eyes.

11 The correct order of the stages of Master's and Johnson's sexual response cycle is

1 plateau, excitement, orgasm, resolution

2 excitement, plateau, orgasm, resolution

3 excitement, orgasm, plateau, resolution

4 excitement, plateau, orgasm, refractory

***Ans.* (2)**

➲ *Exp.* The correct order of the stages of Master's and Johnson's sexual response cycle is excitement, plateau, orgasm, resolution.

Master's and Johnson's human sexual response cycle consists of four phases which are linear and comes one after the other.

12 Where is Broca's area located?

1 Frontal lobe
2 Occipital lobe
3 Parietal lobe
4 Temporal lobe

Ans. (1)

Exp. Broca's area is located in Frontal lobe. It is located in the lower portion of the left frontal lobe of the brain. Broca examined this part of the brain when dealing with people who had speech impairments to determine that is responsible for the production of words and speech. Broca's area is mainly for speech production and also known as motor-speech area.

13 Read each of the following two statements - Assertion (A) and Reason (R) and indicate your answer using codes given below.

Assertion (A) Generally, performance is optimal when arousal is low.

Reason (R) On easy tasks performance becomes optimal.

Codes

1 Both (A) and (R) are true and (R) is the correct explanation of (A)
2 Both (A) and (R) are true, but (R) is not the correct explanation of (A)
3 (A) is true, but (R) is false
4 (A) is false, but (R) is true

Ans. (4)

Exp. (A) is false, but (R) is true.

The Assertion is false as performance is not optimal when the arousal is low because according to Yerkes-Dodson law, optimum level of arousal is required for an optimum performance. Over- or Under-arousal leads to reduction in task performance.

On easy tasks performance becomes optimal. This is true as in case of simple or well-learned tasks, performance improves as arousal increases.

14 Motivation is best understood as a state that

1 reduces a drive
2 aims at satisfying a biological need
3 energises an organism to act
4 energises and directs behaviour

Ans. (4)

Exp. Motivation is best understood as a state that energises and directs behaviour.

Classical conditioning approach to motivation states that biological responses to associated stimuli energize and direct behaviour. Motivation is an internal state or condition that serves to activate or energise behaviour and give it direction. It is a factor which guide our behaviour towards a goal.

15 Match List I with List II and select the correct answer by choosing from the codes given below.

	List I (Concept)		List II (Phenomenon)
A.	Functional fixedness hypothesis	I.	A kind of set that would make the images of all material almost similar
B.	Functional equivalence hypothesis	II.	Mental manipulation performed on images of objects made to be similar to those that would be performed on actual objects
C.	Functional manipulative hypothesis	III.	A kind of set that would point thoughts in the wrong direction
D.	Functional object imagery	IV.	Mental manipulation performed on images of objects which are very similar to those that would be performed on actual objects

Codes

	A	B	C	D		A	B	C	D
1	I	II	III	IV	2	II	III	IV	I
3	III	IV	II	I	4	IV	II	I	II

Ans. (3)

Exp. The correct matching is A-III, B-IV, C-II and D-I.

Functional fixedness hypothesis is a kind of set that would point thoughts in the wrong direction. It is a cognitive bias that limits a person to using an object only in the way it is traditionally used.

Functional equivalence hypothesis is the mental manipulation performed on images of objects which are very similar to those that would be performed on actual objects.

Functional manipulative hypothesis is the mental manipulation performed on images of objects made to be similar to those that would be performed on actual objects.

Functional object imagery is a kind of set that would make the images of all material almost similar.

16 Match List I with List II and select the correct answer by choosing from the codes given below.

	List I (Concept)		List II (Explanation)
A.	Procedural memory	I.	Memory for facts, words, dates, names of objects.
B.	Declarative memory	II.	Combining several letters, words, phrases into one 'stack' of information.
C.	Episodic memory	III.	Memory for typing, driving, riding a bicycle.
D.	Recoding	IV.	Memory about 'what', 'where' and 'when' of our lives.

Codes

	A	B	C	D		A	B	C	D
1	I	II	III	IV	2	III	I	IV	II
3	IV	III	II	I	4	II	IV	III	I

Ans. (2)

Exp. The correct matching is A-III, B-I, C-IV and D-II.

Procedural memory is usually an implicit memory (unconscious) such as typing, driving and riding a bicycle. It is a part of the long-term memory that is responsible for knowing how to do things such as typing, driving, etc.

Declarative memory (conscious) is usually a memory for facts, words, dates and names of objects. It is memory of facts and events, and refers to those memories that can be consciously recalled.

Episodic memory (conscious) is a type of declarative memory which tells about the events of what, where, when etc. It is the memory of autobiographical events such as times, places, associated emotions and other contextual who, what, when, where, why knowledge, that can be explicitly stated.

Recoding is combining several letters, words and phrases into one "stack" of information. It is when we take knowledge already in our memory and change the format in which it is stored. e.g. chunking, a memory technique in which large sets of information are remembered by grouping or 'chunking' pieces together in more memorable sets.

17 Purposive manipulation of reinforcement contingencies, which encourage desirable behaviour, is called

1 Contingency management
2 Contingency contracting
3 Contingent reinforcement
4 Non-contingent reinforcement

Ans. (1)

Exp. Purposive manipulation of reinforcement contingencies, which encourage desirable behavior, is called as Contingency management.

Contingency management refers generally to the modification of behaviour via the control or manipulation of consequences (contingencies) to the behaviour. In essence, some control is sought over what follows a certain behavior to increase or decrease the frequency or other characteristics (e.g., intensity) of that behaviour. Contingency management is derived from Applied Behaviour Analysis (APA) where an individual is rewarded for their positive behavioural change.

18 Which of the following depth cue is based on muscular feedback?

1 Texture gradients
2 Motion parallax
3 Accommodation
4 Light and shadow

Ans. (3)

Exp. Accommodation is the depth cue which is based on muscular feedback.

It occurs with both eyes, but it is still a monocular cue, because one eye alone would give the same information as would both. Accommodation refers to the feedback we receive from the muscles in the eye that cause the lens to bulge or get thinner. As we focus on distant objects, our lens is made thinner, and as we focus on near objects, our lens is made thicker.

19 Nomothetic approach in personality research was mainly emphasised by

I. Allport	II. Skinner
III. Cattell	IV. Eysenck

Codes

1 I and III	2 I and II
3 II and III	4 III and IV

Ans. (4)

Exp. Nomothetic approach in personality research was mainly emphasized by Cattell and Eysenck.

Nomothetic approach is the study which uses quantitative data of what people have common in with each other. It basically involves large number of data and results in generalization. Idiographic approach to personality is where the study is about indepth of the individuals which mainly uses qualitative data. This approach is mainly supported by Allport and Humanist psychologists.

20 Read each of the following two statements. Assertion (A) and Reason (R) and indicate your answer using codes given below.

Assertion (A) Spearman proposed the existence of specific factor of intelligence.

Reason (R) It was observed that tetrad differences are always equal to zero.

Codes

1 Both (A) and (R) are true and (R) is the correct explanation of (A)
2 Both (A) and (R) are true, but (R) is not the correct explanation of (A)
3 (A) is true, but (R) is false
4 (A) is false, but (R) is true

Ans. (1)

Exp. Both (A) and (R) are true, and (R) is the correct explanation of (A).

Spearman proposed the existence of specific factor of intelligence. This is true as Charles Spearman developed two factor theory using factor analysis. He developed 'g' factor of general intelligence and 's' factor of specific intellectual abilities.

It was observed that tetrad differences are always equal to zero. The tetrad difference, according to Spearman, in all cases comes to zero. The variation in measured intelligence that was not explainable in terms of this General factor or 'g' was attributed by Spearman to Specific factors or 's'.

21 Which theory of emotion implies that every emotion is associated with a unique physiological reaction?

1 James - Lange theory
2 Cannon - Bard theory
3 Two factor theory
4 Opponent - process theory

Ans. (1)

Exp. James - Lange theory of emotion implies that every emotion is associated with a unique physiological reaction. This theory suggests that our emotions are caused by our interpretation of bodily reactions. For example when you encounter a snake in the garden area, your heart starts to palpitate (physiological reaction) and you interpret the emotion as fear.

22 Read each of the following two statements Assertion (A) and Reason (R) and indicate your answer using codes given below.

Assertion (A) Some people perceive wolf as dog.
Reason (R) External features in a category of concepts are associated with each other.

Codes

1 Both (A) and (R) are true and (R) is the correct explanation of (A)
2 Both (A) and (R) are true, but (R) is not the correct explanation of (A)
3 (A) is true, but (R) is false
4 (A) is false, but (R) is true

Ans. (1)

Exp. Both (A) and (R) are true, and (R) is the correct explanation of (A).

Some people perceive wolf as a dog. This is true because it has the external features associated with the concept of dog.

External features in a category of concepts are associated with each other. This is true and explains the assertion as the Feature Detection Theory proposes that the nervous system sorts and filters incoming stimuli to allow the human (or animal) to make sense of the information. This sorting and filtering process result in associations with the prior information.

23 The frequency with which an operant response occurs before it is systematically reinforced, is called

1 Rate of responding
2 Operant level
3 Orienting reflex
4 Autoclitic behaviour

Ans. (2)

Exp. The frequency with which an operant response occurs before it is systematically reinforced, is called Operant level.

BF Skinner created this term to define the control baseline against which to measure learning in instrumental conditioning. It refers to the frequency or form of a performance under baseline conditions before any systematic conditioning procedures are introduced.

24 An important factor which enables one to adapt to inverted vision is

1 orientation
2 active movement
3 new learning
4 frame of reference

Ans. (2)

Exp. An important factor which enables one to adapt to inverted vision is active movement.

Active movement speeds adaptation to a new perceptual environment. Interacting with a new visual world through active movement (self-generated action) is key to rapid adaptation. Inverted vision implies adaptation to complete inversion of visual world is possible.

25 ________ defined intelligence as the ability to 'see relations and to educe correlates'.

1 Binet
2 Spearman
3 Terman
4 Boring

Ans. (2)

Exp. Spearman defined intelligence as the ability to 'see relations and to reduce correlates'.

Spearman's definition of general intelligence focuses on the role of reducing correlates and relations. The ability to reduce relations and correlates is best reflected in reasoning measures.

26 Which of the following statements are true about Eysenck Personality Questionnaire-Revised (EPQ-R) and the NEO - Personality Inventory - 3 (NEO-PI-3) ?

I. Both EPQ - R and NEO - PI - 3 have Extraversion and Neuroticism scales.
II. Eysenckian Psychoticism scale correlates positively with Agreeableness, and negatively with conscientiousness scales of NEO - PI - 3.
III. Eysenckian Psychoticism scale correlates negatively with Agreeableness and conscientiousness scales of NEO - PI - 3.
IV. Only EPQ - R has lie scale; NEO - PI - 3 does not have lie scale.

Codes

1 I and II
2 I and III
3 I, II and III
4 I, III and IV

Ans. (4)

Exp. Statement I, III and IV true about Eysenck personality questionnaire and the NEO-personality inventory.

The NEO-PI-R assesses five major domains of personality: Neuroticism (N), Extroversion (E), Openness to Experience (O), Agreeableness (A) and Conscientiousness (C). The Eysenck Personality Questionnaire (EPQ) measures three large factors: Extraversion, Neuroticism, and Psychoticism. Both the tests have an Extraversion and Neuroticism scale. Although, the first 3 scales were predicted upon a biologically based theory of personality, the fourth scale has not been theoretically specified to the same extent, but it was considered to be conceptually strong to the extent that it would demonstrate the same degree of measurement similarity across cultures. Therefore, Eysenckian psychoticism scale correlates negatively with agreeableness and conscientiousness scales of NEO–PI–3 is true. Only EPQ-R includes L-Lie/Social Desirability Scale.

27 Afferent and Efferent nerves are found in which of the following?

1 Sympathetic Nervous System
2 Para - Sympathetic Nervous System
3 Somatic Nervous System
4 Central Nervous System

Ans. *(3)*

Exp. Afferent and Efferent nerves are found in Somatic Nervous System.

The Somatic Nervous System (SNS or Voluntary Nervous System) is the part of the peripheral nervous system associated with the voluntary control of body movements and skeletal muscles. The Somatic Nervous System consists of afferent nerves or sensory nerves and efferent nerves or motor nerves.

Sensory neurons are also known as afferent neurons. Afferent nerves are responsible for relaying sensation from the body to the Central Nervous System (CNS). Motor neurons are also known as efferent neurons. Efferent nerves are responsible for sending out commands from the CNS to the body, stimulating muscle contraction; they include all the non-sensory neurons connected with skeletal muscles and skin.

28 Match List I with List II and select the correct answer by choosing from the codes given below.

List I (Type of Test)	List II (Example)
A. Forced choice personality inventory	I. Minnesota Multiphasic Personality Inventory (MMPI - 2)
B. Ipsative Scale	II. Rosenzweig Picture Frustration Study
C. Personality inventory with a lie scale	III. Edwards Personal Preference Schedule (EPPS)
D. Projective test	IV. Allport - Vernon - Lindzey's Study of Values

Codes

	A	B	C	D		A	B	C	D
1	IV	III	II	I	2	III	IV	I	II
3	III	I	IV	II	4	IV	II	III	I

Ans. *(2)*

Exp. The correct matching is A-III, B-IV, C-I and D-II.

An example of a *Forced choice personality inventory* is Edwards Personal Preference Schedule (EPPS). Edwards Personal Preference Schedule is a force choice, objective, non-projective personality inventory, derived from the theory of HA Murray, which measures the rating of individuals in fifteen normal needs or motives.

An example of an *Ipsative Scale* is Allport-Vernon-Lindsey's Study of Values. Study of Values is an ipsative scale that means if you score higher on one scale, you must score lower on another scale.

An example of a *Personality inventory with a lie scale* is Minnesota Multiphase Personality Inventory (MMPI-2). Minnesota Multiphasic Personality Inventory (MMPI-2) is a personality inventory that includes lie scale. Lie scale measures honesty by asking questions in several forms and estimating whether they are deliberately attempting to deceive.

An example of a *Projective test* is Rosenzweig Picture Frustration Study. The Rosenzweig Picture Frustration test consists of 24 cartoon pictures, each portraying two persons in a frustrating situation and is a projective test.

29 Which is the correct sequence of parts of ear through which sound travels in the ear?

1 Tymphanic membrane → Stapes → Incus → Malleus → Cochlea
2 Tymphanic membrane → Incus →Stapes → Malleus → Cochlea
3 Malleus → Incus → Stapes → Cochlea → Tymphanic membrane
4 Tymphanic membrane → Malleus → Incus → Stapes → Cochlea

Ans. *(4)*

Exp. Tympanic membrane → Malleus → Incus → Stapes → Cochlea is the correct sequence of parts of ear through which sound travels in the ear.

Sound vibrations are transmitted from the tymphanic membrane (outer layer), across the tymphanic cavity, via the ossicles (malleus, incus, then stapes) – (middle layer) and then Cochlea (inner layer).

30 The 1986 Symposium on intelligence identified the main loci of intelligence

I. Intelligence within the individual
II. Intelligence within the environment
III. Intelligence within the interaction between the individual and environment
IV. Intelligence to be measured by psychometric measures

Codes

1 I and IV
2 III and IV
3 I, II and III
4 II, III and IV

Ans. *(3)*

Exp. The 1986 Symposium on intelligence identified the main loci of intelligence as intelligence within the individual, intelligence within the environment and intelligence within the interaction between the individual and environment.

31 Match List I with List II and select the correct answer by choosing from the codes given below:

List I (Terms)	List II (Explanation)
A. Anorexia nervosa	I. Sudden death occurs as terrified person's parasympathetic nervous system over reacts due to which heart slows down to stop
B. Bulimia nervosa	II. A resting period after orgasm, during which a person cannot achieve another orgasm
C. Refractory period	III. An eating disorder in which a person significantly becomes underweight
D. Voodo Curse	IV. An eating disorder marked by over eating

Codes

	A	B	C	D		A	B	C	D
1	I	II	III	IV	2	II	III	IV	I
3	III	IV	I	II	4	III	IV	II	I

***Ans.** (4)*

Exp. The correct matching is A-III, B-IV, C-II and D-I.

Anorexia nervosa is an eating disorder in which a person significantly becomes underweight. It is an eating disorder characterised by low weight, fear of gaining weight and a strong desire to be thin, resulting in food restriction.

Bulimia nervosa is an eating disorder marked by overeating and involves purging which includes vomiting. It is an eating disorder characterised by binge eating followed by purging. Binge eating refers to eating a large amount of food in a short amount of time. Purging refers to the attempts to get rid of the food consumed.

Refractory period is a resting period after orgasm, during which a person cannot achieve another orgasm. It is usually the recovery phase after orgasm during which it is physiologically impossible for a person to have additional orgasms.

Voodo Curse is sudden death occurs as terrified person's parasympathetic nervous system over reacts due to which heart slows down to stop. It is also known as psychogenic death or psychosomatic death and is the phenomenon of sudden death as brought about by a strong emotional shock, such as fear.

32 The most commonly overlooked and obvious reason for forgetting is

1 encoding specificity
2 encoding failure
3 lack of sleep
4 faulty eating habits

***Ans.** (2)*

Exp. The most commonly over looked and obvious reason for forgetting is Encoding failure.

The inability to retrieve a memory is one of the most common causes of forgetting. The most common reason for this is encoding failure, which refers to the brain's occasional failure to create a memory link. It is also failure to store sufficient information to form a useful memory.

33 Which of the following sequence is correctly arranged ?

1 Incoming information → Rehearsal buffer → Selective attention
2 Rehearsal buffer → Selective attention → Incoming information
3 Selective attention → Rehearsal buffer → Incoming information
4 Incoming information → Selective attention → Rehearsal buffer

***Ans.** (4)*

Exp. Incoming information → Selective attention→ Rehearsal buffer is the sequence which is correctly arranged.

Incoming information : It is transformed or processed as it passes from one stage of memory to the next.

Selective attention : It refers to the learner's ability to select and process certain information while simultaneously ignoring other information. For learning we filter the information and only rehearse the necessary information.

Maintenance rehearsal : It refers to the repetition of information in order to maintain it in STM for some designated period of time.

34 Match List I with List II and select the correct answer by choosing from the codes given below.

List I (Concept)	List II (Explanation)
A. Inattentional blindness	I. Medium point of one's personal frame of reference
B. Habituation	II. Ingrained patterns of organisation and attention
C. Adaption level	III. Failure to perceive a stimulus that is in plain view, but not the focus of attention
D. Perceptual habits	IV. Tendency to respond less to predictable and unchanging stimuli

Codes

	A	B	C	D		A	B	C	D
1	III	IV	I	II	2	II	I	III	IV
3	III	II	V	I	4	IV	III	II	I

Ans. (1)

➲ *Exp.* The correct matching is A-III, B-IV, C-I and D-II.

Intentional blindness is a failure to perceive a stimulus that is in plain view, but not the focus of attention. It is also known as Perceptual blindness. It is a psychological lack of attention that is not associated with any vision defects or deficits. It may be further defined as the event in which an individual fails to perceive an unexpected stimulus that is in plain sight.

Habituation is the tendency to respond less to predictable and unchanging stimuli. It is a form of learning in which an organism decreases or ceases its responses to a stimulus after repeated presentations. Essentially, the organism learns to stop responding to a stimulus which is no longer biologically relevant.

Adaptation level is the medium point of one's personal frame of reference. According to Adaptation-level theory, an individual's behavioral response to stimuli represents modes of adaptation to environmental and organismic forces, i.e., one's personal frame of reference.

Perceptual habits are the ingrained patterns of organization and attention. These are defined as the well established patterns of perceptual organisation and attention.

35 Match List I with List II and select the correct answer by choosing from the codes given below.

List I (Tests)	List II (Authors)
A. Cognitive Assessment Battery	I. Cattell, RB
B. Deviation IQ	II. Terman
C. Cognitive Assessment System	III. Wechsler
D. Stanford - Binet Scales	IV. Naglieri and Das

Codes

	A	B	C	D		A	B	C	D
1	I	II	III	IV	2	II	III	IV	I
3	IV	III	I	II	4	I	III	IV	II

Ans. (4)

➲ *Exp.* The correct matching is A-I, B-III, C-IV and D-II.

Cattell, RB is the author of Cognitive Assessment Battery. The Cattell-Horn-Carroll (CHC) theory of cognitive abilities is the most comprehensive and empirically supported psychometric theory of the structure of cognitive abilities to date. Most recently, it has been used for classifying intelligence and achievement batteries and neuropsychological tests to: (a) facilitate interpretation of cognitive performance; and (b) provide a foundation for organizing assessments for individuals suspected of having a learning disability.

Wechsler is the author of Deviation IQ. David Wechsler, developer of the Wechsler-Bellevue Scale of 1939 popularised the use of 'deviation IQs' as standard scores of IQ tests rather than the 'quotient IQs'.

Naglieri and Das are the author of Cognitive Assessment System. Cognitive Assessment System by Das-Naglieri test is an individually administered test of cognitive functioning for children and adolescents ranging from 5 through 17 years of age that was designed to assess the planning, attention, simultaneous and successive cognitive processes.

Terman has revised the Stanford-Binet scales. The Stanford-Binet intelligence scales (commonly known as the Stanford-Binet) is an individually administered intelligence test that was revised from the original Binet-Simon scale by Lewis M Terman, a psychologists at Stanford University.

36 Read each of the following two statements - Assertion (A) and Reason (R) and indicate your answer using codes given below

Assertion (A) Some persons engage in activities such as collecting things, being good listeners, or being gullible persons.

Reason (R) In Freudian psychoanalysis, it is assumed that fixation at oral stage results in the development of oral incorporative character.

Codes

1 Both (A) and (R) are true and (R) is the correct explanation of (A)
2 Both (A) and (R) are true, but (R) is not the correct explanation of (A)
3 (A) is true, but (R) is false
4 (A) is false, but (R) is true

Ans. (1)

➲ *Exp.* Both (A) and (R) are true, and (R) is the correct explanation of (A).

Some persons engage in activities such as collecting things, being good listeners, or being gullible persons. According to Freud, an adult who is fixated at the early oral stage engages in an abundance of oral activities as eating, drinking, smoking and kissing. This person also engages in activities such as collecting things, being a good listener or a gullible person, i.e. a person who swallows anything he or she hears.

In Freudian psychoanalysis, it is assumed that fixation at oral stage results in the development of oral incorporative character is true and is the correct explanation because if fixation happens at a particular stage it will result in incorporative behaviour. Such a person is called an oral-incorporative character. The oral character can encompass characteristics like optimism, passivity and dependency.

37 A researcher wants to scale nine attitude items by the method of paired comparison. What would be the number of pairs of the attitude items?

1 81   2 72   3 36   4 9

Ans. (3)

➲ *Exp.* A researcher wants to scale nine attitude items by the method of paired comparison and the number of pairs of the attitude items is 36

In a paired comparison task a judge is presented with a pair of objects and asked to state which possesses more of a specified attribute.

Formula is n (n-1)/2 = 9*8/2 = 72/2 = 36

38 **Which of the following are regulated by Sympathetic Nervous System?**

I. Dilation of pupils
II. Decreased activity of Adrenal Gland
III. Digestion is stimulated
IV. Increased heart rate
V. Dryness in mouth

Codes

1 I, II and III
2 II and III
3 I, IV and V
4 I, III, IV and V

Ans. (3)

Exp. Dilation of pupils, increased heart rate and dryness in mouth are regulated by Sympathetic Nervous System. Sympathetic Nervous System is mainly responsible for fight or flight which secrets adrenaline in response to a stressor. It can accelerate heart rate, widen bronchial passages; decrease motility (movement) of the large intestine; constrict blood vessels; increase peristalsis in the oesophagus; cause pupillary dilation, piloerection (goose bumps) and perspiration (sweating) and raise blood pressure. It normalizes functions to produce localised adjustments such as sweating as a response to an increase in temperature and reflex adjustments of the cardiovascular system. SNS dilates pupil, inhibits salivation and inhibits secretion.

39 **Which of the following can cause errors in reasoning?**

I. Premise phrasing manner
II. Foreclosure effects
III. Confirmation bias

Codes

1 I and II
2 I and III
3 II and III
4 I, II and III

Ans. (4)

Exp. Premise phrasing manner, Foreclosure effects and Confirmation bias can cause error in reasoning. Foreclosure effect is the tendency where we fail to consider all possibilities before considering true as a conclusion. Confirmation bias occurs when we assume the outcome before fully considering the premises which leads us to make errors in evaluating the syllogism or to choose statements that will support an expected outcome.

40 **Read each of the following two statements - Assertion (A) and Reason (R) and indicate your answer using codes given below.**

Assertion (A) The names of objects, days of the week, the seasons and other general facts are all quite lasting and we do not forget them.

Reason (R) Most of our basic factual knowledge about the world is almost totally immune to forgetting.

Codes

1 Both (A) and (R) are true and (R) is the correct explanation of (A)
2 Both (A) and (R) are true, but (R) is not the correct explanation of (A)
3 (A) is true, but (R) is false
4 (A) is false, but (R) is true

Ans. (1)

Exp. Both (A) and (R) are true and (R) is the correct explanation of (A)

The names of objects, days of the week, the seasons and other general facts are all quite lasting and we do not forget them because this type of information is tend to be stored as we indulged in elaborative rehearsal from our beginning of our age.

Most of our basic factual knowledge about the world is almost totally immune to forgetting. Semantic memory includes things that are common knowledge, such as the names of colours, sounds of letters and other basic facts. Humans mostly do not forget these types of basic factual information.

41 **According to Skinner, which of the following are the characteristics of 'Respondent Behaviour' ?**

I. It is elicited.
II. It is emitted.
III. It is conditioned.
IV. It is unconditioned.

Codes

1 I and III
2 II and III
3 I, III and IV
4 II, III and IV

Ans. (3)

Exp. The characteristics of 'Respondent Behaviour' are elicited, conditioned and unconditioned.

Respondent behaviour or involuntary reflex behaviour elicited by a known stimulus. Skinner said that some responsive behaviours are automatic (such as jumping at the sound of a loud noise) while others are learned. The learned behaviour is called 'conditioning'. Respondent conditioning occurs when we link or pair a previously neutral stimulus with a stimulus that is not learned or innate, called an unconditioned stimulus.

42 **Read each of the following two statements - Assertion (A) and Reason (R) and indicate your answer using codes given below**

Assertion (A) To use a computer, we must learn to pay attention to specific stimuli, such as icons, commands and signals.

Reason (R) Learning creates perceptual habits that affect our daily experience.

Codes

1 Both (A) and (R) are true and (R) is the correct explanation of (A)
2 Both (A) and (R) are true, but (R) is not the correct explanation of (A)
3 (A) is true, but (R) is false
4 (A) is false, but (R) is true

Ans. *(1)*

➲ *Exp.* Both (A) and (R) are true and (R) is the correct explanation of (A).

To use a computer, we must learn to pay attention to specific stimuli, such as icons, commands and signals. It is true because by directing attention only to important signals or being repeatedly exposed to signals in an important context, our sensory systems learn to process important signals more efficiently than the less-important signals.

Learning creates perceptual habits that affect our daily experience is true and it is the correct explanation because perceptual learning is prevalent and occurs continuously in everyday life. As our perceptual system adapts to the natural world, we become better at discriminating between different stimuli when they belong to different categories than when they belong to the same category.

43 Arrange Thurston's primary abilities in correct sequence

1 Verbal Comprehension; Verbal Fluency; Numerical Ability; Memory; Perceptual Speed; Inductive Reasoning, Spatial Visualisation
2 Verbal Fluency; Verbal Comprehension; Numerical Ability; Memory; Perceptual Speed; Spatial Visualisation; Inductive Reasoning
3 Numerical Ability; Verbal Comprehension; Verbal Fluency; Memory; Inductive Reasoning; Spatial Visualisation; Perceptual Speed
4 Spatial Visualisation; Inductive Reasoning; Memory; Perceptual Speed; Numerical Ability; Verbal Fluency; Verbal Comprehension

Ans. *(*)*

➲ *Exp.* Thurstone's primary abilities in correct sequence are: Verbal Comprehension; Verbal fluency; Numerical Ability; Spatial Visualisation; Memory; Perceptual Speed; Inductive Reasoning.

Thurstone proposed primary mental ability in 1936 where he gave seven unitary factors revealed by factor analysis to be essential components of intelligence. These factors are measured by the Primary Mental Abilities Test.

Verbal Comprehension : Ability to understand word and sentences.

Verbal fluency : Ability to solve arrangement and to find rhythms etc.

Numerical Ability : Ability to make mental and other numerical computations.

Spatial Visualisation : Ability to visvalize a complex shape in varions orientations.

Memory : Ability to recall verbal material, learn pairs of unrelated words etc.

Perceptual speed : Ability to detect visual details quickly.

Inductive Reasoning : Ability to induce a general rule from a few instances.

44 Read each of the following two statements - Assertion (A) and Reason (R) and indicate your answer using codes given below:

Assertion (A) According to the Classical Test Theory (CTT), the true score component and the error component of the observed score are assumed to be uncorrelated.

Reason (R) According to the CTT, the error component is assumed to be distributed with a mean of zero.

Codes

1 Both (A) and (R) are true and (R) is the correct explanation of (A)
2 Both (A) and (R) are true, but (R) is not the correct explanation of (A)
3 (A) is true, but (R) is false
4 (A) is false, but (R) is true

Ans. *(2)*

➲ *Exp.* Both (A) and (R) are true, but (R) is not the correct explanation of (A).

According to the Classical Test Theory (CTT), the true score component and the error component of the observed score are assumed to be uncorrelated. Under Classical Test Theory (CTT), it is assumed that Observed score = true score + error component (uncorrelated). So Assertion statement is correct.

According to the CTT, the error component is assumed to be distributed with a mean of zero. In CTT, we assume that the error is normally distributed, uncorrelated with true score and has a mean of zero. It is also true but not the correct explanation of given Assertion.

45 Arish, on a Wechsler type of scale, has a DIQ (deviation IQ) of 85. His percentile rank would be

1 16 2 34 3 68 4 85

Ans. *(1)*

➲ *Exp.* Arish, on a Wechsler type of scale, has a DIQ (deviation IQ) of 85. His percentile rank would be 16.

Deviation Intelligence Quotient is a way of measuring generalized intelligence. It uses statistics to analyse a person's intelligence relative to their age. Deviation IQ is scored based on how an individual deviates from the average IQ of 100. It measures IQ as a normal distribution with the average IQ being a 100 with a standard deviation of +/- 15. The percentile rank is one of the most widely used means of interpreting pupil performance on standardized measures of ability and achievement. On most standardised tests, an IQ of 100 is at the 50th percentile. IQ tests are standardised with a mean score of 100 and a standard deviation of 15. That means following IQ scores will be roughly equivalent to the following percentiles.

IQ	Percentile	IQ	Percentile
65	01	105	63
70	02	110	75
75	05	115	84
80	09	120	91
85	16	125	95
90	25	130	98
95	37	135	99
100	50		

Directions (Q. Nos. 46-50) *Read the following paragraph and answer the five questions which follow :*

A psychologist, working in the area of Learning and memory hypothesised that a particular drug would adversely affect the learning rate. One hundred and fifty subjects, 75 boys and 75 girls, studying in the first year of a degree college, in the age range of 18 to 20 years, were available for the study. It was ensured that all the subjects were in the DIQ (deviation IQ) range of 85 to 115. Three groups - A, B and C of equal size were formed by random assignment.

Group A received high dosage of drug, Group B received moderate dosage of drug, and Group C received only placebo. A list of 15 CVC trigrams, each having an association value in the range of 50 to 70 was already prepared. Each subject was required to learn the list upto two errorless trials using method of anticipation on a memory drum. The mean trials required to learn the list were 12, 15 and 20 respectively. The intergroup mean differences were statistically significant at .01 level.

46 Which one of the following conclusions can be drawn on the basis of the above study?

1 The researcher's hypothesis has been verified
2 The researcher's hypothesis has been rejected
3 The researcher's hypothesis has been partially accepted
4 Inadequate data to evaluate the hypothesis

Ans. *(1)*

Exp. On the basis of above study, it can be concluded that the researcher's hypothesis has been verified. Hypothesis was the drug would adversely affect the learning rate. The mean trials required to learn the list were 12(high dosage), 15(moderate) and 20(placebo).

47 In the above study, 'association value' can be labelled as

I. continuous variable
II. controlled variable
III. organismic variable
IV. stimulus variable

Codes

1 I and II
2 I and III
3 I, II and III
4 I, II and IV

Ans. *(4)*

Exp. 'Association value' can be labelled as continuous variable, controlled variable and stimulus variable.

Association value is related to the stimulus of CVC words list. 'Association values' is a concept in cognitive psychology and in particular the psychology of human learning and memory. The association value of a stimulus is a measure of its meaningfulness. Association value acts as a link between learning and memory.

Continuous variable is a variable whose value is obtained by measuring, i.e., one which can take on an uncountable set of values.

Controlled variables are the variables that are not changed throughout an experiment, because its unchanging state allows the relationship between the other variables being tested to be better understood. The 'association values' for CVC words are controlled to be in range 50-70.

Stimulus variables are the specific features that make up the context in which behaviour occurs. They represent the factors that have actual or potential effects on the organism's response.

48 Read each of the following two statements - Assertion (A) and Reason (R) and indicate your answer using codes given below

Assertion (A) In the above study, the subjects have been randomly assigned to the three groups.
Reason (R) The independent variable is manipulated more effectively with random assignment of subjects.

Codes

1 Both (A) and (R) are true and (R) is the correct explanation of (A)
2 Both (A) and (R) are true, but (R) is not the correct explanation of (A)
3 (A) is true, but (R) is false
4 (A) is false, but (R) is true

Ans. *(3)*

Exp. (A) is true, but (R) is false.

In the above study, the subjects have been randomly assigned to the three groups is true as it was ensured that all the subjects in the DIQ were in the range of 85 to 115. All the three groups A, B and C were of equal size by random assignment.

The independent variable is manipulated more effectively with random assignment of subjects is false because learning rate is the dependent variable and drug dosage is the independent variable. Effectiveness in varying the drug dosage however does not depend upon the random assignment of the subjects

49 Match List I with List II in the context of above study and select the correct answer by choosing from the codes given below

List I	List II
A. Independent variable	I. Intelligence
B. Dependent variable	II. Drug dosage
C. Controlled variable	III. Gender
D. Discrete variable	IV. Trials required to learn the list

Codes

	A	B	C	D		A	B	C	D
1	IV	II	III	I	2	IV	II	I	III
3	II	IV	III	I	4	II	IV	I	III

Ans. (4)

Exp. The correct matching is A-II, B-IV, C-I and D-III.

An example of an *independent variable* is drug dosage (as it is manipulated). It is a variable in an experiment that is specifically manipulated or is observed to occur before the dependent, or outcome, variable, in order to assess its effect or influence.

An example of a *dependent variable* is trials required to learn the list. It is the outcome that is observed to occur or change after the occurrence or variation of the independent variable in an experiment.

An example of a *controlled variable* is intelligence. It is a variable that is not changed throughout an experiment, because its unchanging state allows the relationship between the other variables being tested to be better understood.

An example of a *discrete variable* is gender. It is a variable that has distinct, discrete values but no precise numerical flow.

50 In the above study, the variance caused by drug dosage can be labelled as

1 primary variance
2 secondary variance
3 controlled variance
4 error variance

Ans. (1)

Exp. In the above study, the variance caused by Drug dosage can be labelled as primary variance.

Here, drug dosage is the main independent variable and the main input hence the variance caused by the drug dosage is primary variance. If the drug has got any impact or affected is called as secondary variance.

PAPER III

1 The act in which people help others without any personal interest, motive, reason is called

1 Altruism
2 Nurturance
3 Prosocial Behaviour
4 Social Obligation

Ans. (1)

Exp. The act in which people help others without any personal interest, motive, and reason is called as Altruism. Altruism refers to a tendency of helping others in order to relieve a person's distress which purely comes out of their own interest and motivation and it has nothing to do with recognition, reciprocity or any rewards.

2 Read each of the following two statements - Assertion (A) and Reason (R) and indicate your answer using codes given below :

Assertion (A) Mean level of fluid intelligence (gf) is higher in young adults than older adults.

Reason (R) Crystallised intelligence increases throughout life span.

Codes

1 Both (A) and (R) are true and (R) is the correct explanation of (A)
2 Both (A) and (R) are true, but (R) is not the correct explanation of (A)
3 (A) is true, but (R) is false
4 (A) is false, but (R) is true

Ans. (2)

Exp. Both (A) and (R) are true; but (R) is not the correct explanation of (A).

Mean level of fluid intelligence (gf) is higher in young adults than older adults. Fluid intelligence is the ability to use knowledge in novel situations without pre-existing conditions which is higher in young adults than older and it starts to decline progressively around the age 30 or 40. Hence, the Assertion is correct.

Crystallised intelligence increases throughout lifespan. Crystallised intelligence is the ability to use knowledge which is acquired through some pre-existing conditions such as education. Crystallized intelligence is maintained or improved around age of 60 or 70 years. Hence the reason is correct but it does not explain the assertion.

3 The multiple correlation ranges between

1 - 0.50 to +0.50
2 -1.00 to +1.00
3 Zero to 1.00
4 There is a fixed range for bivariate correlation, but not for multiple correlation

Ans. (3)

Exp. The multiple correlation ranges between Zero to 1.00. The coefficient of multiple correlation, denoted as R, is a scalar that is defined as the Pearson correlation coefficient between the predicted and the actual values of the dependent variable in a linear regression model that includes an intercept. It measures how well a given variable can be predicted using a linear function of a set of other variables.

The coefficient of multiple correlation takes values between 0 and 1. A higher value indicates a better predictability of the dependent variable from the independent variables, with a value of 1 indicating that the predictions are correct and a value of 0 indicating that no linear combination of the independent variables is a better predictor than is the fixed mean of the dependent variable.

4 Match List I with List II and select the correct answer by choosing from the codes given below :

List I (Concept)		List II (Explanation)
A. Viewer - centered representation	I.	The individual stores a representation of the object, independent of its appearance
B. Structuralist view of perception	II.	The individual builds a cognitive understanding of the object
C. Object - centered representation	III.	The individual stores the way, the object looks to him or her
D. Constructivist view of perception	IV.	Simple sensations constitute the building blocks of perceived form

Codes

	A	B	C	D		A	B	C	D
1	I	II	III	IV	2	III	IV	I	II
3	II	I	IV	III	4	IV	III	II	I

Ans. (2)

Exp. The correct matching is A-III, B-IV, C-I and D-II.

Viewer-centered representation suggests that the individual stores the way, the object looks to him or her. Viewer-centered theory suggests that object-recognition is done based on matching specific views to a set of templates, which requires explicit viewer-specific object representations.

Structuralist view of perception suggests that the simple sensations constitute the building blocks of perceived form. It is the theoretical approach by Wilhelm Wundt who established the psychology laboratory in Leipzig in Germany in 1879.

Object - centered representation suggests that the individual stores a representation of the object, independent of its appearance. Object based representations are shapes of mental images that represent the single dimension general outline of a class of similar objects (dogs, cats etc). It means user stores representation of object independent of its appearance.

Constructivist view of perception suggests that the individual builds a cognitive understanding of the object. Constructivists have largely influenced in directing theories and research of perception. This approach illustrate that individuals build a cognitive understanding of stimuli from the environment.

5 According to Gibson's theory of perception

1. We directly perceive the environment. We do not need the aid of complex thought processes.
2. We do not directly perceive the environment. We need the aid of complex thought processes.
3. We perceive the environment using our intelligence.
4. We do not connect what we perceive, to what we have stored in our mind.

Ans. (1)

Exp. According to Gibson's theory of perception, we directly perceive the environment. We do not need the aid of complex thought processes. He argues that perception is direct and not subject to hypothesis testing.

Gibson's direct perception theory, also known as bottom-up theory, states that perception is an innate mechanism which not involved complex thought processing and he also stated that perception can be determined solely from the environment. He was mainly opposed by Richard Gregory's top-down processing, which states that perception are mainly influenced from past experiences and there are so much hypothesis to be tested to get processed to sensory inputs.

6 According to Bandura, which of the following is the correct sequence of processes involved in observation learning ?

1. Attention → Retention → Cognitive Rehearsal → Corrective Action
2. Attention → Cognitive Rehearsal → Corrective Action → Retention
3. Attention → Corrective Action → Cognitive Rehearsal → Retention
4. Corrective Action → Attention → Cognitive Rehearsal → Retention

Ans. (1)

Exp. According to Bandura, Attention → Retention → Cognitive Rehearsal → Corrective Action is the correct sequence of processes involved in observation learning. Social learning theory was introduced by Albert Bandura.

Attention : Participants or observers must pay attention to the model so that they can replicate the behaviour.

Retention : It is not only necessary to pay attention but the act should also be remembered at some time.

Cognitive Rehearsal is the repetition of information in an attempt to maintain it longer in memory.

Corrective Action ensures correction in prior learning.

7 Read each of the following two statements Assertion (A) and Reason (R) and indicate your answer using codes given below :

Assertion (A) Lewin asserted that avoidance -avoidance conflicts are comparatively more stable.

Reason (R) Opposing forces tend to remain in state of equilibrium.

Codes

1 Both (A) and (R) are true and (R) is the correct explanation of (A)
2 Both (A) and (R) are true, but (R) is not the correct explanation of (A)
3 (A) is true, but (R) is false
4 (A) is false, but (R) is true

Ans. *(1)*

Exp. Both (A) and (R) are true, and (R) is the correct explanation of (A).

Lewin asserted that avoidance-avoidance conflicts are comparatively more stable. In the avoidance-avoidance conflict, the individual is faced with two goals or objectives which are repellant or negative and hence they are relatively more stable. For example, a child is told to mow the lawn or do his homework.

Opposing forces tend to remain in state of equilibrium. The reason is correct because the repelling forces make the individual to get balanced or to attain the equilibrium. For example either a child wants to eat a bottle guard or have to go to bed without supper.

8 Match List I with List II and select the correct answer by choosing from the codes given below.

List I (Concept)	List II (Description)
A. Intrinsic motivation	I. "I am really not feeling too good today. I may not be able to perform well".
B. Achievement motivation	II. "I love to drive very fast, no matter what happens".
C. Self-handicapping	III. "For me, accomplishing difficult tasks and meeting high standards of excellence is the top most priority".
D. Sensation-seeking	IV. "I go for swimming everyday. I just love it. I take out time from my tight study schedule".

Codes

	A	B	C	D
1	I	II	III	IV
2	II	I	IV	III
3	IV	III	I	II
4	III	IV	II	I

Ans. *(3)*

Exp. The correct matching is A-IV, B-III, C-I and D-II.

Intrinsic motivation is the tendency to do something purely out of their own interest and motivation which makes them to be enjoyed. External rewards are not the motivating factor. "I go for swimming every day. I just love it. I take out time from my tight study schedule" is an example of Intrinsic motivation.

Achievement motivation is the tendency to achieve something. "For me, accomplishing difficult tasks and meeting high standards of excellence is the top most priority" comes under Achievement motivation.

Self – handicapping is the tendency to cultivate the barrier to one's own success. "I am really not feeling too good today. I may not be able to perform well" is an example of Self-handicapping.

Sensation – seeking is the personality trait and this concept was developed by Marvin Zuckerman and it is the tendency for the people to achieve varied novel and intense experiences. "I love to drive very fast, no matter what happens" is an example of Sensation seeking.

9 Identity status of individuals who are exploring alternatives in an effort to find values and goals to guide their life is called

1 Identity Diffusion
2 Identity Foreclosure
3 Moratorium
4 Identity Confusion

Ans. *(3)*

Exp. Identity status of individuals who are exploring alternatives in an effort to find values and goals to guide their life are called as Identity Moratorium.

Identity moratorium is a period of identity development that occurs after the adolescent stage of identity diffusion and is generally considered the longest period of that development. It is a period of active searching and exploring alternatives to current situations. This is seen as a time where a person questions their earlier choices; whether or not to change college majors, whether to marry or remain single, exploration of sexual identity, etc. Once these questions are resolved a person finally approaches the stage of identity achievement in which the individual finds their true sense of self.

10 Sex chromosome anomaly (XXY) results into the development of

1 Klinefelter's Syndrome
2 Down Syndrome
3 Turner's Syndrome
4 Phenylketonuria

Ans. *(1)*

Exp. Sex chromosome anomaly (XXY) results into the development of Klinefelter's Syndrome.

It is a condition in which a male is born with an extra copy of X chromosome which usually results in low testosterone levels. Klinefelter's syndrome is a chromosomal condition that affects male physical and cognitive development. Its signs and symptoms vary among affected individuals. It is also known as 47, XXY.

11 Which of the following is associated with memory for emotionally charged events ?

I. Thalamus II. Hypothalamus
III. Amygdala IV. Temporal lobe

Codes

1 I and II 2 Only III
3 II and IV 4 Only IV

Ans. *(2)*

Exp. Amygdala is associated with memory for emotionally charged events.

Amygdala is an almond-sized shape in the brain which is used to regulate emotions such as fear etc. It helps in decision making. The amygdala contains neurons that influence anger, aggression, fear, and rage. Although there are other parts of the brain that influence these emotions, the amygdala may have the most influence. Early studies demonstrated that damaging these areas can turn very aggressive animals into docile, even fearful creatures.

12 "Development is the result of Individual's active participation in the development process in interaction with important environmental influences". This is the assumption of which of the following approaches?

1 Maturational/Biological
2 Psychodynamic
3 Behavioural
4 Cognitive

Ans. *(4)*

Exp. "Development is the result of Individual's active participation in the development process in interaction with important environmental influences". This is the assumption of Cognitive development.

Cognitive development is the growth and maturation of thinking processes of all kinds, including perceiving, remembering, concept formation, problem solving, imagining, and reasoning. Various cognitive developmental theories exist that attempt to explain the mechanisms underlying such growth and maturation. Explanations may be in terms of stages of development in which the changes in thinking are relatively abrupt and discontinuous, or the changes may be viewed as occurring gradually and continuously over time.

13 A person, who reports that he oftenly feels above his physical body. It is an example of

1 Derealisation 2 Depersonalisation
3 Delusion 4 Identity Disorientation

Ans. *(2)*

Exp. A person, who reports that he often feel above his physical body. It is an example of Depersonalisation disorder. It causes significant distress or impairment in functioning especially emotional expression and deficits in perception.

It is a dissociative disorder characterized by one or more episodes of depersonalization severe enough to impair social and occupational functioning.

Onset of depersonalization is rapid and usually manifested in a sensation of self-estrangement, a feeling that one's extremities are changed in size, a sense of being mechanical, a perception of oneself as if from a distance, and, in some cases, a feeling that the external world is unreal (derealization).

14 Humanistic theories of personality are characterised as

I. Having optimistic ideas about human nature.
II. Emphasize personal responsibility.
III. Focus on present than on past.
IV. Believe that fate is an important determinant of human behaviour.

Codes

1 I and II 2 III and IV
3 I, II and III 4 II, III and IV

Ans. *(3)*

Exp. Humanistic theories of personality are characterized as having optimistic ideas about human nature, emphasize personal responsibility and focus on present than on past.

Humanistic approach to personality believes that personal worth of the individual, centrality of human lives and to focus on the present rather dwelling upon past experiences.

15 The following statements represent the work of Noam Chomsky, choose the correct one from the codes given below

I. He called himself a Cartesian linguistic
II. He analysed syntax
III. He wrote about transformational grammar
IV. He developed an artificial language called 'Yerkish'

Codes

1 I, II and III 2 I, II and IV
3 II, III and IV 4 I, III and IV

Ans. *(1)*

Exp. Statement I, II and III represent the work of Noam Chomsky.

In 1950s linguistic school of thought known as transformational-generative grammar received wide acclaim through the works of Noam Chomsky. He called himself a Cartesian linguistic as the word "Cartesian" is the adjective pertaining to René Descartes, a prominent 17th-century philosopher. However, rather than confine himself to the works of Descartes, Chomsky surveys other authors interested in rationalist thought. Chomsky analyzed syntax and postulated a syntactic base of language (called deep structure), which consists of a series of phrase-structure rewrite rules, i.e., a series of (possibly universal). He also wrote about transformational grammar which include rules that generates the underlying phrase-structure of a sentence, and a series of rules (called transformations) that act upon the phrase-structure to form more complex sentences.

16 Which of the following is the evidence that REM sleep specifically enhances consolidation ?

I. REM increases after learning
II. REM deprivation interferes with learning
III. Performance improves following REM sleep

Codes

1 I and II
2 I and III
3 II and III
4 All of these

Ans. *(4)*

Exp. REM increases after learning, REM deprivation interferes with learning and performance improves following REM sleep are the evidences that REM sleep specifically enhances consolidation.

REM sleep is important to your sleep cycle because it stimulates the areas of your brain that are essential in learning and making or retaining memories. Lack of REM sleep may have adverse effects in both physical and mental health.

17 Read each of the following two statements - Assertion (A) and Reason (R) and indicate your answer using codes given below.

Assertion (A) Managers make judgements about employee's dispositions in various situations.

Reason (R) Inferences are drawn on the basis of observations.

Codes

1 Both (A) and (R) are true and (R) is the correct explanation of (A)
2 Both (A) and (R) are true, but (R) is not the correct explanation of (A)
3 (A) is true, but (R) is false
4 (A) is false, but (R) is true

Ans. *(1)*

Exp. Both (A) and (R) are true, and (R) is the correct explanation of (A).

Managers make judgments about employee's dispositions in various situations. It is true and is based on their attribution theory and hence the Assertion is correct.

Inferences are drawn on the basis of observation is also true. It is something we observe within the person is dispositional attribution (internal attribution). Observing a person outside is an example of situation attribution (external attribution). The reason explains the assertion of making judgments about employees' dispositions.

18 Arrange the following correlation coefficients in descending order in terms of their strength of relationship, as defined by common variance.

1 -0.8, 0.7 -0.5, 0.4
2 0.7, 0.4 -0.5, -0.8
3 0.4, -0.5 0.7, -0.8
4 -0.8, -0.5, 0.4, 0.7

Ans. *(1)*

Exp. Correlation coefficients in descending order in terms of their strength of relationship, as defined by common variance are -0.8 > 0.7 > -0.5 > 0.4.

Both negative and positive values indicate the increasing strength of the relationship and the sign indicate the direction of the relationship. So, we should consider only the absolute values of correlation while deciding the strength of relationship. Thus, $|-0.8| > |0.7| > |-0.5| > |0.4|$

19 A mother is telling her child to eat vegetables before getting dessert. It is an example of

1 Reward - Contrast Principle
2 Delay Conditioning
3 Premack Principle
4 Crespi Effect

Ans. *(3)*

Exp. A mother is telling her child to eat vegetables before getting dessert. It is an example of Premack Principle. Engaging in more probable behavior or activity (dessert) will reinforce the less probable behavior (eating vegetables). Premack's principle or the relative theory of reinforcement, states that more probable behaviours will reinforce less probable behaviours. This is a principle of operant conditioning originally identified by David Premack in 1965.

20 Read each of the following two statements- Assertion (A) and Reason (R) and indicate your answer using codes given below

Assertion (A) Teacher's motivating style determines student's motivation for reading.

Reason (R) To enhance student's interest in reading, teacher may offer a reward for reading along with helpful feedback.

Codes

1 Both (A) and (R) are true and (R) is the correct explanation of (A)
2 Both (A) and (R) are true, but (R) is not the correct explanation of (A)
3 (A) is true, but (R) is false
4 (A) is false, but (R) is true

Ans. *(1)*

Exp. Both (A) and (R) are true, and (R) is the correct explanation of (A).

Teacher's motivating style determines student's motivation for reading is correct because teacher acts as a main proponent in cultivating motivation in student's learning.

To enhance student's interest in reading, teacher may offer a reward for reading along with helpful feedback is also correct because helpful feedback is important to make them learning effective and better.

21 The levels of processing proposed by Craik and Tulving follow the specific sequence in progressive order of depth; choose the correct.

1 Acoustic • Semantic • Physical
2 Physical • Acoustic • Semantic
3 Semantic • Physical • Acoustic
4 Acoustic • Physical • Semantic

Ans. *(2)*

Exp. The levels of processing proposed by Craik and Tulving are Physical • Acoustic • Semantic.

Craik and Tulving levels of processing model focuses on the depth of processing involved in memory and predicts that the deeper the information is processed, the longer a memory trace will last.

22 DSM-III is considered qualitatively different and superior to its predecessors, because

I. It is multi-axial

II. It deleted misnomor words

III. It introduced coding system

IV. It used experimental data

Codes

1 I, II and III 2 I, III and IV
3 II, III and IV 4 All of these

Ans. (2)

Exp. DSM-III is considered qualitatively different and superior to its predecessors, because it is multi-axial (five axis), introduced coding system and used experimental data.

The third edition of DSM or DSM-III, which was published in 1980, introduced a system of five axes or dimensions for assessing all aspects of a patient's mental and emotional health. The multi-axial system is designed to provide a more comprehensive picture of complex or concurrent mental disorders.

Here, additional diagnostic categories were added, some were deleted. Throughout the development of DSM III, the omission of the DSM II diagnostic class of Neuroses has been a matter of great concern to many clinicians. The Task Force believed that field trials using drafts of DSM III should be conducted during the development process to identify problem areas in the classification and to try out solutions to these problems. Deletion of misnomor words took place in DSM-III R.

23 According to Jensen what percent (%) of variance in intelligence is explained by genetic factors?

1 20 to 30% 2 55 to 65%
3 80 to 90% 4 40 to 50%

Ans. (3)

Exp. According to Jensen, 80 to 90% of variance in intelligence is explained by genetic factors.

Jensen was an American psychologist and was a proponent of nature vs. nurture debate. He stated that genetics played an important role in behavioural traits such as intelligence and personality. In Jensen's estimation, 80% of the variance in IQ in the population studied was the result of genetic factors and the remainder was due to environmental influences.

24 Read each of the following two statements - Assertion (A) and Reason (R) ; and indicate your answer using codes given below

Assertion (A) Westerners tend to focus mostly on the figure when viewing a scene and much less on the ground whereas East Asians pay greater attention to the overall context.

Reason (R) Culture affects the way we direct our attention to notice or ignore things around us.

Codes

1 Both (A) and (R) are true and (R) is the correct explanation of (A)
2 Both (A) and (R) are true, but (R) is not the correct explanation of (A)
3 (A) is true, but (R) is false
4 (A) is false, but (R) is true

Ans. (1)

Exp. Both (A) and (R) are true, and (R) is the correct explanation of (A).

Westerners tend to focus mostly on the figure when viewing a scene and much less on the ground whereas East Asians pay greater attention to the overall context is true. East Asians promote collectivist culture so they pay greater attention to the overall context whereas Westerners promotes personal autonomy so they pay attention to the particular objects.

Culture affects the way we direct our attention to notice or ignore things around us is true because cultures affect the way people process emotional information in the environment. Hence, culture plays an important role in paying attention to the context, which explains the differences between Westerners and East Asians in viewing a scene.

25 Read each of the following two statements - Assertion (A) and Reason (R) and indicate your answer using codes given below

Assertion (A) Autoshaping involves S - S learning.

Reason (R) Some behaviours are innate responses to a stimulus and because of temporal contiguity between them, they acquire stimulus related properties.

Codes

1 Both (A) and (R) are true and (R) is the correct explanation of (A)
2 Both (A) and (R) are true, but (R) is not the correct explanation of (A)
3 (A) is true, but (R) is false
4 (A) is false, but (R) is true

Ans. (1)

Exp. Both (A) and (R) are true, and (R) is the correct explanation of (A).

Auto shaping involves S - S learning in which a subject has been given reinforcement following a stimulus regardless of its response to that stimulus, consistently performs an irrelevant behavior. Hence, it involves S-S learning (Stimulus-Stimulus learning).

Some behaviors are innate responses to a stimulus and because of temporal contiguity between them, they acquire stimulus related properties is also true. explanation. Temporal contiguity occurs when two stimuli are experienced close together in time and, as a result an association may be formed. The S-S learning asserts that stimuli become associated simply as a result of occurring contiguously in space and time.

26 Emotions can be characterised as

I. Giving rise to affective experiences
II. Stimulating generation of cognitive explanations
III. Triggering a variety of internal neurobiological changes
IV. Always eliciting rewarding behaviour

Codes

1 I, II and III
2 I, III and IV
3 II, III and IV
4 I, II, III and IV

Ans. (1)

Exp. Emotions can be characterized as giving rise to affective experiences, stimulating generation of cognitive explanations and triggering a variety of internal neurobiological changes.

Some theorists place emotions in a more general category of affective states. Some theories on emotions argue that cognitive activity in the form of judgements, evaluations or thoughts is necessary in order for an emotion to occur. Based on discoveries made through neural mapping of the limbic system, the neurobiological explanation of human emotion is that emotion is a pleasant or unpleasant mental state organised in the limbic system of the mammalian brain. An emotion does not always elicit rewarding behaviour.

27 Read each of the following two statements - Assertion (A) and Reason (R) and indicate your answer using codes given below

Assertion (A) Every cigarette packet has a verbal and pictorial warning about negative consequences of smoking.

Reason (R) Inconsistent cognitions have the motivational properties.

Codes

1 Both (A) and (R) are true and (R) is the correct explanation of (A)
2 Both (A) and (R) are true, but (R) is not the correct explanation of (A)
3 (A) is true, but (R) is false
4 (A) is false, but (R) is true

Ans. (1)

Exp. Both (A) and (R) are true, and (R) is the correct explanation of (A).

Every cigarette packet has a verbal and pictorial warning about negative consequences of smoking is true because the pictorial and verbal warning helps to strengthen the motivation to quit.

Inconsistent cognitions have the motivational properties is also true because even though a person who smoke feels positive but seeing a verbal and pictorial warning makes them to feel negative creating a cognitive dissonance.

28 When students study and practice hard with interest and enjoyment, it is called

1 Emotional engagement
2 Cognitive engagement
3 Behavioural engagement
4 Healthy adjustment

Ans. (1)

Exp. When students study and practice hard with interest and enjoyment, it is called as Emotional engagement. Emotional engagement encompasses the affective factors of engagement, including enjoyment, support, belonging and attitudes towards teachers, peers, learning and school in general. It contributes to a student's active involvement in school.

29 If the teacher presents the extrinsic motivator in a controlled way, then

1 It will enhance competence of students
2 It will interfere with autonomy of students
3 It will enhance their overall learning
4 It will enhance the autonomy of students

Ans. (2)

Exp. If the teacher presents the extrinsic motivator in a controlled way, then it will interfere with autonomy of students.

Extrinsic motivation refers to behaviour that is driven by external rewards. Organismic Integration Theory (OIT) suggests that extrinsic motivation affect the autonomy. It is found that offering people extrinsic rewards for behaviour that is intrinsically motivated undermined the intrinsic motivation as they grow less interested in it. Initially intrinsically motivated behaviour becomes controlled by external rewards, which undermined their autonomy.

30 According to the Connectionist view, memories are

1 Abstract concepts
2 Knowledge structures
3 Interconnections among neurons
4 Schemas

Ans. (3)

Exp. According to the Connectionist view, memories are interconnections amount neurons.

Connectionism is a set of approaches in the fields of artificial intelligence, cognitive psychology, cognitive science, neuroscience and philosophy of mind, which models mental or behavioural phenomena as the emergent processes of interconnected networks of simple units.

31 Read each of the following two statements - Assertion (A) and Reason (R) and indicate your answer using codes given below

Assertion (A) The dynamic process of parent - child interaction during Phallic stage leads to the solidification of Ego.

Reason (R) Child's successful resolution of Oedipus complex leads to appropriate gender role identification.

Codes

1 Both (A) and (R) are true and (R) is the correct explanation of (A)
2 Both (A) and (R) are true, but (R) is not the correct explanation of (A)
3 (A) is true, but (R) is false
4 (A) is false, but (R) is true

Ans. (4)

Exp. (A) is false, but (R) is true

The healthy resolution of the oedipal dynamic leads to the solidification of ego. The phallic stage is the third stage of psychosexual development, spanning the ages of three to six years, wherein the infant's libido (desire) centers upon his or her genitalia as the erogenous zone.

Child's successful resolution of Oedipus complex leads to appropriate gender role identification. Resolution of oedipus complex results in girls moving to hetro sexual feminity and boys through competition with father move towards hetrosexual masculinity.

32 A patient in Mental Hospital somehow procured a needle and thread and while sleeping, she tried to stitch her lips together, so that someone does not pour poison in her mouth when asleep. Most probably she suffers from

1 Bipolar Disorder
2 Hebephrenic Schizophrenia
3 Delusional Disorder
4 Borderline Personality Disorder

Ans. (3)

Exp. A patient in Mental Hospital somehow procured a needle and thread, and while sleeping, she tried to stitch her lips together, so that someone does not pour poison in her mouth when asleep. Most probably she suffers from delusional disorder.

Delusional Disorders are a type of psychosis in which the patient experiences persistent false beliefs but can still function reasonably well in society. The delusions are considered "non-bizarre" in that they involve situations that could actually happen in reality, such as being lied to or cheated on by your partner. The types of delusional disorders are erotomanic, grandiose, jealous, persecutory, somatic, and mixed. For example, in the erotomanic type of delusion, the patient may think that another person, often a celebrity or status figure, is in love with them. In the persecutory type, the patient may be convinced that another person is out to get them or do them harm.

33 John, the chess master selects his next move by considering the moves that it would threaten the opponent's queen whilst his opponent, a chess playing computer, selects its next move by considering all possible moves John is using _______ whilst the computer is using ________.

1 Algorithm ; heuristic
2 Prototype ; mental set
3 Mental set ; prototype
4 Heuristic ; algorithm

Ans. (4)

Exp. John is using heuristic whilst the computer is using algorithm.

Heuristics are the shortcut to problem solving but it does not guarantee a correct solution. Algorithm is set of rules which is time consuming but definitely guarantees a correct solution.

34 Today social psychology studies

I. Social cognition
II. Ethnic Diversity
III. Multiculturalism

Codes

1 I and II
2 I and III
3 II and III
4 All of these

Ans. (4)

Exp. Today social psychology studies Social cognition, Ethnic Diversity and Multiculturalism.

Social psychology is about understanding individual behaviour in a social context. Social cognition is a subarea of Social Psychology which exams our ability to gather information about and understand the rules and concepts that govern our social interactions—the ways in which we understand social rules of etiquette, proximity, gestures, inferences, etc.

At its essence, social cognition includes the processes we use to understand the world around us. Ethnic diversity refers to the presence of people from a variety of cultural and ethnic backgrounds or identities. Multiculturalism refers to the co-existence of multiple cultures in close proximity to one another. It usually refers to the demographic makeup of neighborhoods, businesses, schools, cities and even nations. This phenomenon is most clearly seen in the ethnic sections of large cities where immigrants and insular ethnic communities congregate.

35 Read each of the following two statements - Assertion (A) and Reason (R) and indicate your answer using codes given below :

Assertion (A) People perform in accordance to the social positions they hold.

Reason (R) People select relevant information from tremendous amount of social information.

Codes

1 Both (A) and (R) are true and (R) is the correct explanation of (A)
2 Both (A) and (R) are true, but (R) is not the correct explanation of (A)
3 (A) is true, but (R) is false
4 (A) is false, but (R) is true

Ans. (2)

Exp. Both (A) and (R) are true, but (R) is not the correct explanation of (A).

People perform in accordance to the social positions they hold is true. Social position is the position of an individual in a given society and culture. People will perform as per the social positions they hold. Social positions an individual may hold fall into the categories of occupation, profession, hobby etc.

People select relevant information from tremendous amount of social information is also true. Most situations provide a tremendous amount of information. People apply filtering rules, considering whether the information is relevant and representative for the target behaviour.

36 The sequence of different dimensions of Job Characteristics Model are

1 Skill variety, task significance, autonomy, task identity, feedback
2 Skill variety, task identity, task significance, autonomy, feedback
3 Task identity, task significance, autonomy, skill variety, feedback
4 Autonomy, task identity, skill variety, task significance, feedback

Ans. (2)

Exp. The sequence of different dimensions of Job Characteristics Model is Skill variety, task identity, task significance, autonomy, feedback. According to Hackman and Oldham job characteristic model, a job in itself is the key to employer's motivation.

Skill Variety : The degree to which a job requires various activities, requiring the worker to develop a variety of skills and talents.

Task Identity : The degree to which the job requires the jobholders to identify and complete a workpiece with a visible outcome.

Task Significance : The degree to which the job affects other people's lives. The influence can be either in the immediate organization or in the external environment.

Autonomy : The degree to which the job provides the employee with significant freedom, independence, and discretion to plan out the work and determine the procedures in the job.

Feedback : The degree to which the worker has knowledge of results. This is clear, specific, detailed, actionable information about the effectiveness of his or her job performance.

37 Fill in the blank by selecting appropriate alternative.
Harlow's classic studies with baby monkeys and wire or cloth artificial mothers have demonstrated the importance of ______ in the early development.

1 regular feeding
2 classical conditioning
3 freedom to explore
4 physical contact

Ans. (4)

Exp. Harlow's classic studies with baby monkeys and wire or cloth artificial mothers have demonstrated the importance of physical contact in the early development.

In a set of classic studies in the 1950s and 1960s, Harry Harlow and others investigated the nature of attachment in young rhesus monkeys.

In one study, the researchers exposed young monkeys to two artificial mothers, one wrapped in towelling cloth and another made of bare wire, but with a feeding bottle attached to it. The experiment showed that the infants clung to the mother with the towelling cloth for most of the time and would only approach the other mother when in need of food. This showed that close, warm contact is an important part of bonding with a mother.

38 A person with Schizophrenia was found to repeat whatever words the psychiatric social worker was speaking. This behaviour can be labelled as

1 Echopraxia
2 Neologism
3 Word Salading
4 Echolalia

Ans. (4)

Exp. A person with Schizophrenia was found to repeat whatever words the psychiatric social worker was speaking. This behavior can be labelled as Echolalia. Mimicking another person's words is known as Echolalia. Mimicking another person's movement is known as Echopraxia.

39 Which of the following are not Factor Analytically derived personality inventories ?

I. 16 PF
II. Comrey Personality Scales
III. Jenkins Activity Survey
IV. Edwards Personal Preference Schedule

Codes

1 I and II
2 III and IV
3 I, II and III
4 II, III and IV

Ans. (2)

Exp. Jenkins Activity Survey and Edwards Personal Preference Schedule are not Factor Analytically derived personality inventories.

Personality tests which used factor analysis in its construction:

- 16 PF
- Comrey Personality Scales
- NEO Personality Inventory (NEO-PI-R)
- Eysenck Personality Questionnaire (EPQ)
- Guilford Zimmerman Temperament Survey

Important psychologist who developed personality test using factor analysis strategy are Guilford, Cattell, Eysenck.

40 In which parts of brain the feeling of hunger and full are felt ?

1 Hypothalamus ; Cerebral Cortex
2 Lateral hypothalamus ; Ventromedial hypothalamus

3 Lateral hypothalamus ; Cerebral Cortex
4 Cerebral Cortex ; Ventromedial hypothalamus

Ans. (2)

Exp. Lateral hypothalamus is the hunger centre and Ventromedial hypothalamus is the feeling of satiety. The satiety center in animals is located in the ventromedial nucleus of the hypothalamus. Energy homeostasis is controlled mainly by neuronal circuits in the hypothalamus and brainstem, whereas reward and motivation aspects of eating behaviour are controlled by neurons in limbic regions and cerebral cortex. In order to increase the blood glucose levels, the lateral hypothalamus activates the behaviour that each individual has for finding and consuming food.

41 As per Goleman "Motivating Oneself" component of emotional intelligence includes :

I. Marshalling emotions in the service of goal
II. Delaying gratification and stifling impulsiveness
III. Being able to get into 'flow state'
IV. Monitoring feelings from moment to moment

Codes

1 I and II
2 III and IV
3 I, II and III
4 II, III and IV

Ans. (3)

Exp. As per Goleman "Motivating Oneself" component of emotional intelligence includes marshalling emotions in the service of goal, delaying gratification and stifling impulsiveness and being able to get into 'flow state'. The five broad areas of traits in the Goleman (1995) model of EI are knowing emotions, managing emotions, motivating oneself, recognising emotions in others, and handling relationships.

42 Read each of the following two statements - Assertion A and Reason (R) and indicate your answer using codes given below :

Assertion (A) In Time Series Design, auto correlation is a routine feature.

Reason (R) Autocorrelation is efficiently handled by statistical method ARIMA.

Codes

1 Both (A) and (R) are true and (R) is the correct explanation of (A)
2 Both (A) and (R) are true, but (R) is not the correct explanation of (A)
3 (A) is true, but (R) is false
4 (A) is false, but (R) is true

Ans. (1)

Exp. Both (A) and (R) are true and (R) is the correct explanation of (A).

In Time Series Design, auto correlation is a routine feature. It is true as the autocorrelation is intended to measure the relationship between a variable's present value and any past values that one may have access to. Autocorrelation uses the same time series two times: once in its original values, and then again once a few different time periods have occurred.

Autocorrelation is efficiently handled by statistical method ARIMA is true because Autoregressive Integrated Moving Average (ARIMA) model is a generalized model of Autoregressive Moving Average (ARMA). As a process, autocorrelation is also known by a few other names, among them serial correlation, time series correlation and lagged correlation. Regardless of how it's actually being used, autocorrelation is an ideal method for uncovering trends and patterns in time series data that would have otherwise gone undiscovered.

43 An example of Feature Analysis is

1 phonics
2 words
3 context of words
4 meaning of words

Ans. (4)

Exp. An example of Feature Analysis is meaning of words. In feature-analysis we recognise objects by assembling their features to determine what the object is. One of the most important type of feature analysis in comprehension is Semantic Feature Analysis. It is an effective strategy which mimics the neural paths using which brain organises information.

It offers students a visual representation, a matrix, on how terms are alike and different, the students are able to analyse the relationships among the given concepts. That is instead of directly providing the meaning the focus is on contextual information. In addition, SFA supports reading as an interactive process. The reader is characterised as an active participant who interacts with the text to construct meaning. From this perspective, the reader uses prior vocabulary knowledge as a framework to understand the meaning of new concepts and phrases.

44 Read each of the following two statements - Assertion (A) and Reason (R) ; and indicate your answer using codes given below :

Assertion (A) According to Dollard and Miller, observational learning will occur only if organism's overt behaviour is followed by reinforcement.

Reason (R) Copying behaviour involves guiding of one person's behaviour by another person.

Codes

1 Both (A) and (R) are true and (R) is the correct explanation of (A)
2 Both (A) and (R) are true, but (R) is not the correct explanation of (A)
3 (A) is true, but (R) is false
4 (A) is false, but (R) is true

Ans. (2)

Exp. Both (A) and (R) are true, but (R) is not the correct explanation of (A).

According to Dollard and Miller, observational learning will occur only if organism's overt behavior is followed by reinforcement. It is true as Miller and Dollard postulated a drive of imitation based on observational learning. Imitation is a process by which similar actions are performed by two individuals in response to appropriate cues. At the start, imitation is a behaviour, which can be reinforced by the environment, just as other behaviours are.

Copying behaviour involves guiding of one person's behavior by another person. When rewarded regularly, however, it takes on the properties of an acquired drive. Thereafter, the individual is motivated to imitate the behaviour of others to copy their behaviour in order to obtain the same rewards that they receive from their actions.

45 Which of the following is the final destination for much of the brain's information about emotion, before action is taken?

1 Amygdala
2 Anterior Cingulated Cortex
3 Pre-frontal cortex
4 Hypothalamus

Ans. *(3)*

Exp. The final destination for much of the brain's information about emotion, before action is taken is known as Pre-frontal cortex.

The Pre-frontal cortex performs functions of cognitive control, and is prominently –though not exclusively–involved in working memory organization via central executive processes. It is involved in the organization of material prior to encoding, as well as the verification, monitoring, and evaluation of representations that have been retrieved from long-term memory.

46 Read each of the following two statements - Assertion (A) and Reason (R) and indicate your answer using codes given below :

Assertion (A) You can remember vividly what you wore on your first date.

Reason (R) Memories of emotionally significant events cannot be accurate at all.

Codes

1 Both (A) and (R) are true and (R) is the correct explanation of (A)
2 Both (A) and (R) are true, but (R) is not the correct explanation of (A)
3 (A) is true, but (R) is false
4 (A) is false, but (R) is true

Ans. *(3)*

Exp. (A) is true, but (R) is false.

You can remember vividly what you wore on your first date is true because emotionally significant events are important and eventually we will remember it.

Memories of emotionally significant events cannot be accurate at all is false because emotionally significant events are accurate. Flashbulb memory is the memory of emotionally significant events that people often recall with more accuracy and vivid imagery than everyday events.

47 Read each of the following two statements - Assertion (A) and Reason (R) and indicate your answer using codes given below

Assertion (A) Cattell incorporated factors, Q1, Q2, Q3, and Q4 in 16 PF.

Reason (R) Some factors appeared only in L - data, not in Q - data.

Codes

1 Both (A) and (R) are true and (R) is the correct explanation of (A)
2 Both (A) and (R) are true, but (R) is not the correct explanation of (A)
3 (A) is true, but (R) is false
4 (A) is false, but (R) is true

Ans. *(2)*

Exp. Both (A) and (R) are true, and (R) is not the correct explanation of (A).

Cattell incorporated factors, Q1, Q2, Q3, and Q4 in 16 PF. It is true as factors labeled 'Q' (Q1, Q2, Q3, Q4) are so designated because they are reported to be evident only in questionnaire data, rather than in both behavioural and questionnaire realms.

Some factors appeared only in L - data, not in Q – data is true. L-data includes life record rating of behaviours observed in real-life situations such as classroom or office. Q-data includes self-report questionnaire ratings of our characteristics, attitudes and interests. Both the statements are independently true and reason does not explain the assertion.

48 Read each of the following two statements - Assertion (A) and Reason (R) and indicate your answer using codes given below :

Assertion (A) Naturalistic decision making involves decisions as they occur in every day life.

Reason (R) The decisions required in many situations often have serious ramifications for those who make decisions.

Codes

1 Both (A) and (R) are true and (R) is the correct explanation of (A)
2 Both (A) and (R) are true, but (R) is not the correct explanation of (A)
3 (A) is true, but (R) is false
4 (A) is false, but (R) is true

Ans. *(1)*

Exp. Both (A) and (R) are true, and (R) is the correct explanation of (A).

Naturalistic decision making involves decisions as they occur in everyday life. Naturalistic decision making is a means of studying how people make decisions and perform cognitively complex function in demanding, real-world situations. E.g. – firefighters, military commanders, pilots etc.

The decisions required in many situations often have serious ramifications for those who make decisions. The reason is true and is the correct explanation of the assertion as real-life situations require series of decisions to be made, with each decision depending on previous feedback from a potentially changing environment. The consequences of these decisions are serious in many situations.

49 Match List I with List II and select the correct answer by choosing from the codes given below:

List I (Phenomenon)	List II (Explanation)
A. Over-extension	I. The use of single word to represent whole phrase or sentence
B. Under-extension	II. The tendency to apply a word to more objects or actions than it actually represents
C. Holophrastic speech	III. Speech marked by reliance on nouns and verbs, while omitting other parts of speech including articles and propositions
D. Telegraphic speech	IV. The tendency to apply a word to fewer objects or actions than it actually represents

Codes

	A	B	C	D		A	B	C	D
1	I	III	II	IV	2	II	IV	I	III
3	I	IV	II	III	4	II	III	I	IV

Ans. (2)

Exp. The correct matching is A-II, B-IV, C-I and D-III.

Over-extension is the tendency to apply a word to more objects or actions than it actually represents. It is the tendency of very young children to extend the use of a word beyond the scope of its specific meaning, such as by referring to all animals as "doggie."

Under-extension is the tendency to apply a word to fewer objects or actions than it actually represents. It is the incorrect restriction of the use of a word, which is a mistake commonly made by young children acquiring language. For example, a child may believe that the label dog applies only to Fido, the family pet.

Holophrastic speech is the use of single word to represent whole phrase or sentence. In the holophrastic or one-word stage, children use holophrastic speech or one word at a time when speaking. Complex ideas are sometimes expressed with a single word, accompanied by gestures and emphasis. For example, depending on the context and how the word is spoken, milk may mean : That is milk, I want more milk, or I spilled the milk.

Telegraphic speech is the speech marked by reliance on nouns and verbs, while omitting other parts of speech including articles and propositions. It is usually in the form of two-word expressions up to the age of about 24 months (see two-word stage) and thereafter is characterized by short but multiword expressions (e.g., dog eat bone).

50 Which part of Central Nervous System controls much of the Endocrine System by regulating the Pituitary Gland?

1 Amygdala
2 Hypothalamus
3 Hippocampus
4 Medulla

Ans. (2)

Exp. Hypothalamus is the part of the Central Nervous System which controls much of the Endocrine System by regulating the Pituitary Gland.

The Pituitary gland is called the 'master gland' because it controls functions of other endocrine glands. However, it is largely regulated by the hypothalamus.

51 Cognitive structures that represent an organised collection of knowledge about people, events and concepts are called

1 Images
2 Schemas
3 Social influence
4 Disposition

Ans. (2)

Exp. Cognitive structures that represent an organized collection of knowledge about people, events and concepts are called Schemas.

A schema is a cognitive structure that serves as a framework for one's knowledge about people, places, objects, and events. Schemas help people organize their knowledge of the world and understand new information.

52 Which is not the part of Equity Theory?

1 Over payment
2 Under payment
3 Linear payment
4 Equitable payment

Ans. (3)

Exp. Linear payment is not the part of Equity Theory.

Equity theory, popularly known as Adam's equity theory, aims to strike a balance between an employee's input and output in a workplace. If the employee is able to find his or her right balance it would lead to a more productive relationship with the management. Over payment, under payment and equitable payment are the part of equity theory.

53 Match List I with List II and select the correct answer by choosing from the codes given below :

List I (Dimensions)	List II (Behaviour)
A. Delegating	I. High task and high relationship
B. Participating	II. High task and low relationship
C. Selling	III. Low relationship and low task
D. Telling	IV. High relationship and low task

Codes

	A	B	C	D		A	B	C	D
1	I	II	III	IV	2	II	III	IV	I
3	III	IV	I	II	4	IV	III	II	I

Ans. (3)

Exp. The correct matching is A-III, B-IV, C-I and D-II.

Delegating is associated with Low relationship and low task. In this style, the leader allows the group to take responsibility for task decisions. Low task means low task direction of more autonomy.

Participating is associated with High relationship and low task. In this style, the leader emphasizes sharing of ideas and decisions.

Selling is associated with High task and high relationship. In this style, the leader attempts to sell his ideas to the group by explaining task direction in a persuasive manner.

Telling is associated with High task and low relationship. In this style, the leader gives explicit directions and supervises work closely.

54 Match List I with List II and select the correct answer by choosing from the codes given below :

List I (Concept)	List II (Description)
A. Successful Intelligence	I. Ability to cope with the problems of day-to-day life
B. Practical Intelligence	II. Ability to achieve one's goals of life across given cultural contexts, capitalising on strengths and correcting weaknesses to adapt with the environment
C. Mating Intelligence	III. Ability to cope with novel problems and situations
D. Creative Intelligence	IV. Ability to understand the outcomes of mind's reproductive system

Codes

	A	B	C	D		A	B	C	D
1	I	II	III	IV	2	II	I	IV	III
3	III	IV	II	I	4	IV	III	I	II

Ans. (2)

Exp. The correct matching is A-II, B-I, C-IV and D-III.

Successful Intelligence is the ability to achieve one's goals of life across given cultural contexts, capitalizing on strengths and correcting weaknesses to adapt with the environment. A successfully intelligent person accomplishes these goals by figuring out his or her strengths and weakness and then by capitalising on the strengths and correcting or compensating for the weakness.

Practical Intelligence is the ability to cope with the problems of day-to-day life. It is the result of an experimental hands-on operating style that leads to specific learning. It is the ability to thrive in the real world; it involves the ability to understand how to deal with everyday problems.

Mating Intelligence is the ability to understand the outcomes of mind's reproductive system.

Creative Intelligence is the ability to cope with novel problems and situations. It involves going beyond what is given to generate novel and interesting ideas.

55 How many 'three way interactions' can be studied in a 4×3×3 factorial design ?

1 Only 1
2 Only 4
3 Only 12
4 Only 3

Ans. (1)

Exp. Only one 'three way interactions' can be studied in a 4×3×3 factorial design. Order of this number makes no difference and hence we can easily claim as only one three way interaction.

56 In a verbal memory experiment, the two independent variables, 'meaningfulness of material' and 'retention interval' were employed, each varied at three levels. The number of words correctly recalled was the dependent variable. The sum of squares due to meaningfulness of material is 270. The Mean square for the meaningfulness of material would be

1 30.0
2 67.5
3 90.0
4 135.0

Ans. (2)

Exp. We have two variables which is variable one V1 varied at three levels (low, moderate and high) and variable two V2 (low, moderate and high) and degrees of freedom include df=n-1 which is (3-1) (3-1)= 4

The sample variance also referred to as a mean square is obtained by dividing the sum of squares by the respective degrees of freedom. Therefore, the total mean square is MST_T.

$$MST_T = \frac{SST}{dft}$$

Solving this equation we get 270/4 = 67.5

57 In 'Signal Detection Theory', which of the following determinants are assumed ?

I. Observer's sensitivity
II. Sensory threshold
III. Response bias
IV. Decision bias

Codes

1 Only I
2 I and III
3 I, III and IV
4 II and III

Ans. (2)

Exp. Observer's sensitivity and Response bias are the assumed determinants in Signal Detection Theory. According to Signal Detection Theory, performance in such tasks is limited by observer sensitivity, which depends on the degree of overlap between the distributions of a decision variable produced by the stimulus classes.

58 According to Tolman, which among the following are the "Individual Differences" variables which interact with independent variables to produce behaviour

I. Age
II. Heredity
III. Previous Training
IV. Special Endocrine, Drug or Vitamin conditions

Codes

1 I and III
2 I, III and IV
3 II, III and IV
4 I, II, III and IV

Ans. (4)

Exp. Age, heredity, previous training and special endocrine, drug or vitamin conditions are the "Individual Differences" variables which interact with independent variables to produce behaviour.

In his attempts to explain behaviour, Tolman introduced a set of environmental and individual difference variables. Individual difference variables are heredity, age, previous training and special endocrine, drug or vitamin conditions (also called HATE variables).

59 Which of the following theories represent the mechanistic metaphor of motivation ?

I. Psychoanalytic
II. Ethological
III. Sociobiological
IV. Expectancy-value

Codes

1 I, II and III
2 II, III and IV
3 I, III and IV
4 I, II, III and IV

Ans. (1)

Exp. Psychoanalytic, Ethological and Sociobiological theories represent the mechanistic metaphor of motivation.

The mechanistic metaphor presumes that personality is determined with the same external, decisive determinism that propels physical objects through space. Mechanistic view suggests that psychological processes and behaviours ultimately can be understood in the same way that mechanical or physiological processes are understood. Its explanations of human behaviour are based on the model or metaphor of a machine and invoke mechanical causality, reducing complex psychological phenomena to simpler physical phenomena.

60 According to Meichenbaum (1977), the steps involved in cognitive behaviour modification are

1 Covert self instruction → overt external guidance → overt self guidance → cognitive modelling → faded overt self-guidance
2 Cognitive modelling → faded overt self - guidance → overt external guidance → Covert self instruction → overt self-guidance
3 Covert self instruction → faded overt self - guidance → overt external guidance → Cognitive modelling → overt self - guidance
4 Cognitive modelling → overt external guidance → overt self - guidance → faded overt self - guidance → Covert self-instruction

Ans. (4)

Exp. Meichenbaum described five instructional steps to help impulsive children to get attention to a task and reduce errors. These steps are Cognitive modelling → overt external guidance → overt self-guidance → faded overt self-guidance → Covert self-instruction.

Meichenbaum developed a therapeutic technique called Cognitive Behaviour Modification (CBM), which focuses on identifying dysfunctional self-talk in order to change unwanted behaviours. It is a five step instructional program to help impulsive children to use self-control techniques to increase their attention to a task and reduce errors. The five steps are as follows:

(i) *Cognitive modelling* : The instructor performs the task, verbalising each action as it is performed.
(ii) *Overt External Guidance* : The student carries out the same task under the direction of the instructor who whispers each step.
(iii) *Overt Self-guidance* : The student performs the task, verbalizing the instructions for each step.
(iv) *Faded Overt Guidance* : The student performs the task again, whispering the instructions.
(v) *Covert Self-instruction* : The student performs the task, silently talking through each step (private speech).

61 Match List I with List II and select the correct answer by choosing from the codes given below

List I (Concept)	List II (Description)
A. Interactive Images	I. Visualising walking around an area with distinctive landmarks that you know well and link them
B. Acronyms	II. 'One is a bun' 'Two is a shoe'
C. Method of Loci	III. If you have to remember to buy socks, apples and a pair of scissors, you might imagine cutting a socks that has an apple stuffed in it with a pair of scissors
D. Pegword System	IV. Devising a word or expression in which each of its letters stands for a certain other word or concept

Codes

	A	B	C	D
1	I	II	III	IV
2	III	IV	I	II
3	II	III	IV	I
4	IV	III	II	I

Ans. (2)

Exp. The correct matching is A-III, B-IV, C-I and D-II.

An example of *Interactive Images* is "If you have to remember to buy socks, apples and a pair of scissors, you might imagine cutting a socks that has an apple stuffed in it with a pair of scissors." Bower studied the power of interactive imagery by having subjects imagine either adjacent images or interacting images.

Acronyms are devising a word or expression in which each of its letters stands for a certain other word or concept. An acronym is a word or name formed as an abbreviation form the initial components in a phrase or a word, usually individual letters and sometimes syllables. e.g. VIBGYOR (rainbow colours – violet, indigo, blue, green,yellow, orange, red)

An example of *Method of Loci* is visualizing walking around an area with distinctive landmarks that you know well and link them. Method of Loci is the visualization of you in a spatial familiar environment so that it enhances the recall of particular information.

An example of *Pegword System* is 'One is a bun' 'Two is a shoe'. Peg word system is a mnemonic device which involves remembering the list which needs to be in order. Peg-word system is a memory aid that involves linking words with numbers. It is utilised by creating mental associations between items to be remembered and items that are already associated with numbers. One is bun, two is a shoe, three is a pen, four is a pencil etc.

62 Which of the following concept, according to which each mental event has a unique time of ascendency, the plan for which is contained in the organism's gene?

1 Epigenesis
2 Maturation
3 Genotype
4 Phenotype

Ans. (1)

Exp. Epigenesis is the concept according to which each mental event has a unique time of ascendency, the plan for which is contained in the organism's gene.

Maturation refers to the ways in which we grow and develop throughout the lifespan.

Genotype is the part (DNA sequence) of the genetic makeup of a cell.

Phenotype is the composite of an organism's observable characteristics or traits, such as its morphology, development, biochemical or physiological properties, behaviour and products of behaviour.

63 Rollo May's description of personality development can be explained in which of following sequences

1 Innocence → Dependence → Rebellion → Ordinary Consciousness of self → Creative Consciousness of self
2 Dependence → Innocence → Rebellion → Ordinary Consciousness of self → Creative Consciousness of self
3 Innocence → Rebellion → Dependence → Ordinary Consciousness of self → Creative Consciousness of self
4 Dependence → Innocence → Rebellion → Creative Consciousness of Self → Ordinary Consciousness of self

Ans. (2)

Exp. Rollo May's description of personality development can be explained in the following sequence : Dependence →Innocence → Rebellion → Ordinary Consciousness of self → Creative Consciousness of self.

Rollo May gave the stages of personality development that take place in the following order:

1. *Dependence* : It takes place during infancy, where the infant is dependent on their caregiver for every need.
2. *Innocence* : It takes place during infancy. It is characterised as being neither good or bad, where an infant simply does what they have to.
3. *Rebellion* : It takes place during childhood through adolescence. During this stage, a person strives for freedom but does not fully understand the responsibility that comes with freedom.
4. *Ordinary consciousness of self* : It takes place during early adulthood, where one understands the responsibility that comes with freedom, but finds it to be tedious. Therefore, they simply conform to tradition and cultural values.
5. *Creative consciousness of self* : This stage takes place when an adult is willing to realise their full potential (self-actualisation). It transcends their ego, wherein they are fully accepting of their destiny, and are ready to face every situation with courage.

64 Match List I with List II and select the correct answer by choosing from the codes given below :

List I (Test)	List II (Author)
A. Personal Orientation Inventory	I. Rogers
B. Q - sort	II. Maslow
C. House - Tree - Person Test	III. R.B. Cattell
D. Objective Analytic Tests Battery	IV. Buck

Codes

	A	B	C	D
1	I	II	III	IV
2	II	I	IV	III
3	III	IV	II	I
4	IV	III	I	II

Ans. (2)

Exp. The correct matching is A-II, B-I, C-IV and D-III.

Personal Orientation Inventory is developed by Maslow. Personal Orientation Inventory test is based on the concept of the self-actualising person as defined by Maslow. It measures the Attitudes and values of normal to high-functioning adults in terms of the concept of self-actualising.

Q – sort is developed by Rogers. Q-sort is a self-assessment procedure for measuring congruence, a state of internal consistency which Carl Rogers saw as important to healthy personality growth.

House-Tree-Person Test is developed by Buck. The House-Tree-Person test is a projective personality test, a type of exam in which the test taker responds to or provides ambiguous, abstract or unstructured stimuli. Buck believed that drawings of houses and trees could also provide relevant information about the functioning of an individual's personality.

Objective Analytic Tests Battery is developed by Raymond Cattell. Cattell assembled a broad sample of non-questionnaire behaviours and searched the domain for non-questionnaire dimensions of personality to lay down Objective Analytic Tests Battery.

65 Because of the lightning speed, computers can retrieve and manipulate stored data faster than people, but the human brain beats the computer hands down when it comes to

1 Using heuristics
2 Following algorithms
3 Serial processing
4 Simultaneous processing

Ans. (1)

Exp. Because of the lightning speed, computers can retrieve and manipulate stored data faster than people, but the human brain beats the computer hands down when it comes to using Heuristics.

When the nervous system does not dispose of precise rules of information processing or when algorithmic processing needs a very long time, humans must use heuristic processing. This is the feature that differentiates the human brain from the electronic computer that can work only according to some extremely precise rules. The human brain can work according to less precise rules because it can resort to trial and error operations, and because it works according to a form of logic. Computer can use an algorithm, serial processing and simultaneous processing but human brain beats the computer down when it comes to heuristics.

66 Which of the following is the sleep disorder in which the person is physically active during REM sleep ?

1 Narcolepsy
2 Cataplexy
3 Somnambolism
4 REM Sleep Behaviour Disorder

Ans. (4)

Exp. REM Sleep Behaviour Disorder is the sleep disorder in which the person is physically active during REM sleep.

REM Sleep Behavior Disorder is a parasomnia. Parasomnia is the abnormal behaviors that occur during sleep. Nightmares, sleep terrors and sleepwalking are the disorders of parasomnia.

67 Match List I with List II and select the correct answer by choosing from the codes given below :

List I (Technique)	List II (Description)
A. CT	I. Detects increase in oxygen levels during neural activity
B. MRI	II. Measures variations in hydrogen concentration in brain tissue
C. PET	III. Forms 3-D image of brain by combining X-rays of cross sections of brain
D. fMRI	IV. Image produced by emission from injected substances that have been made radioactive

Codes

	A	B	C	D
1	IV	I	III	II
2	III	II	IV	I
3	IV	II	III	I
4	III	I	IV	II

Ans. (2)

Exp. The correct matching is A-III, B-II, C-IV and D-I.

Computerized Tomography or CT forms 3-D image of brain by combining X-rays of cross sections of brain. CT known as Computed Tomography scan, makes use of computer-processed combinations of many X-ray measurements taken from different angles to produce cross-sectional images of specific areas of a scanned object.

Magnetic Resonance Imaging or MRI measures variations in hydrogen concentration in brain tissue. Under normal circumstances, the hydrogen proton bar magnets spin in the body but when the body is placed in a strong magnetic field, such as an MRI scanner, the protons axes all line up.

Positron Emission Tomography or PET produce image by emission from injected substances that have been made radioactive. PET scan is an imaging test which uses a special dye that has radioactive tracers. These tracers are injected into a vein in the arms.

Functional Magnetic Resonance Imaging or fMRI detects increase in oxygen levels during neural activity. FMRI measures brain activity by detecting changes associated with blood flow.

68 Match List I with List II and select the correct answer by choosing from the codes given below

List I (Phenomenon)	List II (Explanation)
A. Just world phenomenon	I. Tendency to have first agreed to a small request and to comply with a larger request
B. Foot-in-door phenomenon	II. A situation where conflicting parties are being caught for protecting self interest
C. Social trap	III. The phenomenon where repeatedly facing novel stimuli increases their liking
D. Mere exposure phenomenon	IV. The belief that world is just and the people get what they deserve to get and vice-versa

Codes

	A	B	C	D
1	I	II	III	IV
2	II	III	IV	I
3	III	II	IV	I
4	IV	I	II	III

Ans. (4)

Exp. The correct matching is A-IV, B-I, C-II and D-III.

Just world phenomenon is the belief that world is just and the people get what they deserve to get and vice–versa. The just world phenomenon is the tendency to believe that the world is just and that people get what they deserve.

Foot-in-door phenomenon is the tendency to have first agreed to a small request and to comply with a larger request. It is based on the principle of consistency. Foot-in the door technique is a compliance tactic that involves getting a person to agree to a large request by first setting them up by having that person agree to a modest request.

Social trap is a situation where conflicting parties are being caught for protecting self interest. Social trap is a situation in which a group of people act to obtain short-term individual gains, which in the long run leads to a loss for the group as a whole.

Mere exposure phenomenon is a phenomenon where repeatedly facing novel stimuli increases their liking. Mere-exposure effect is a psychological phenomenon by which people tend to develop a preference for things merely because they are familiar with them.

69 Organisational behaviour focusses on

I. How to improve productivity
II. Reduce absenteeism and turnover
III. Increase employees job satisfaction and commitment
IV. Increase decision making ability

Codes

1 I, II and IV	2 II, III and IV
3 I, II and III	4 I, III and IV

Ans. (3)

Exp. Organizational Behaviour or Organization Citizen Behavior (OCB) is the concept developed by Dennis Organ. It focuses to improve productivity, reduce absenteeism and turnover and to increase employee's job satisfaction and commitment. There is a relationship (both correlational and predictive) between the use of certain effective behaviours and employee productivity, job satisfaction and organisational commitment.

In the employment context, organisational behaviour is more commonly known as Organisation Citizenship Behaviour (OCB) or organisational commitment. OCB is defined as discretionary employee behaviour that benefits the organisation. The behaviour is not formally recognised or directly related to the employee's job description or performance standards.

70 Fluid general intelligence (gf) includes the abilities:

I. to perceive relationship among stimulus patterns
II. to comprehend implications
III. to draw inferences from relationships
IV. to acquire quantitative knowledge

Codes

1 I and II	2 III and IV
3 I, II and III	4 II, III and IV

Ans. (3)

Exp. Fluid general intelligence (gf) includes the abilities to perceive relationship among stimulus patterns, to comprehend implications and to draw inferences from relationships.

Fluid intelligence or fluid reasoning is the capacity to reason and solve novel problems, independent of any knowledge from the past. It is the ability to analyse novel problems, identify patterns and relationships that underpin these problems and the extrapolation of these using logic.

It is necessary for all logical problem–solving. Fluid reasoning includes inductive and deductive reasoning. Perceiving relationship among stimulus patterns, comprehending implications and drawing inferences from relationships are all related to fluid general intelligence – applying the intelligence to novel or new problems.

Directions (Q.Nos. 71-75) *Read the following paragraph and answer the five questions that follow :*

A personality psychologist wanted to factor analyse the important personality traits. He selected personality scales of 78 important personality traits, presumed to cover most of the important characteristics. These scales were administered to a sample of eight hundred and fifty respondents. The intercorrelations among the 78 traits were computed and the 78×78 correlation matrix was obtained. Retaining unities in the diagonal spaces of the correlation matrix, unrotated factors were extracted. Cattell's scree plot favored fifteen factor solution.

The fifteen factors together condensed 72 percent of variance. The first factor condensed 18 percent variance. The 15 factors were rotated and the inter-factor correlations were examined. Since some of the inter-factor correlations were substantial, the psychologist decided to carry out the second order factor analysis.

71 Which one of the following method of factor extraction has been, most likely, employed in the above study?

1 Maximum likelihood
2 Unweighted least square
3 Principal components method
4 Principal axis method

Ans. (3)

Exp. Since the researcher found intercorrelations among the 78 traits and the 78 x 78 correlation matrix was obtained retaining unities in the diagonal spaces of the correlation matrix, he had employed Principal Components Method.

In Principal Component Analysis (PCA) there are simply geometrical abstractions which may or may not map to real world constructs. All of the observed variance is analyzed in PCA. Only the shared variance is analyzed in FA.

72 What percent of variance would be condensed by the second unrotated factor in the above study?

1 18 percent
2 Less than 18 percent
3 More than 18 percent
4 Inadequate data

Ans. (2)

Exp. Less than 18 percent of variance would be condensed by the second unrotated factor in the above study. Since the first factor condenses 18 percent variance, the remaining 54(72-18) of the 72 percentage variance is accounted by remaining factors. When the factors were arranged in order, the first factor accounts for maximum variance and the second factor will account for variance less than 18 percent.

73 Cattell's scree plot has

1 Order of eigen value on X-axis and actual eigen value on Y-axis
2 Order of eigen value on X- axis and the covariance on Y-axis
3 Actual eigen value on X-axis and order of eigen value on Y-axis
4 Actual eigen value on X-axis and covariance on Y-axis

Ans. (1)

Exp. According to the view of exploratory analysis, Eigen values of PCA are contaminated with error variance. So the Cattell's scree plot has Order of Eigen value on X-axis and actual Eigen value on Y-axis.

74 Out of the following four methods of factor rotation, which method/s has/have, most likely, been used in the above study ?

I. Varimax II. Quartimax
III. Promax IV. Oblimin

Codes

1 I and II 2 I and III
3 II and III 4 III and IV

Ans. (4)

Exp. In the above study since the factors are correlated we have to use oblique rotation methods which include Promax and Oblimin. Orthogonal rotation methods include varimax and quartimax which are mainly used for uncorrelated factor.

75 What percentage of total variance will be explained by the 15 factors after rotation?

1 Less than 72 percent
2 72 percent
3 More than 72 percent
4 Inadequate data

Ans. (2)

Exp. 72 percentage of total variance will be explained by the 15 factors after rotation.

Rotation changes the distribution of the proportion explained by each factor and whatever may be the case the total rotation and variance would remain the same and hence it is 72 percent.

UGC-NET PSYCHOLOGY

SOLVED PAPER 2017 (January)

PAPER II

1 Which among the following are the products in Guilford's Structure of Intellect Model ?

I. Systems
II. Transformation
III. Reasoning
IV. Interpretation

Codes

1 I and II
2 I, II and III
3 I, II and IV
4 I, II, III and IV

Ans. *(1)*

➲ *Exp.* Systems and Transformation are the products in Guilford's Structure of Intellect Model (SOI).

In Guilford's Structure of Intellect (SI) theory, intelligence is viewed as comprising operations, contents, and products. There are 5 kinds of operations (cognition, memory, divergent production, convergent production, evaluation), 6 kinds of products (units, classes, relations, systems, transformations, and implications), and 5 kinds of contents (visual, auditory, symbolic, semantic, behavioral). Since each of these dimensions is independent, there are theoretically 150 different components of intelligence.

Systems refer to as multiple relations interrelated to comprise structures or networks.

Transformations refer to changes, perspectives, conversions, or mutations to knowledge.

2 According to Jung, which of the following is "the deepest and darkest part of collective unconscious and contains all of the animal instincts".

1 Anima
2 Animus
3 Shadow
4 Persona

Ans. *(3)*

➲ *Exp.* According to Jung, "the deepest and darkest part of collective unconscious which contains all of the animal instincts" is Shadow.

According to Carl Jung, 'shadow' or 'shadow aspect' may refer to an unconscious aspect of the personality which the conscious ego does not identify in itself. Shadow is the deepest and darkest part of collective us. One may say that 'the shadow' is roughly equivalent to the whole of the Freudian concept of the unconscious mind. However, contrary to a Freudian definition, the Jungian shadow can include everything outside the light of consciousness, and may be positive or negative.

3 In classical conditioning, progress of conditioning can be examined by indexing Conditioned Response (CR) in terms of

I. Quantity
II. Latency
III. Rate
IV. Density

Codes

1 I, II and IV
2 II, III and IV
3 I, II and III
4 I, III and IV

Ans. *(3)*

➲ *Exp.* In classical conditioning, progress of conditioning can be examined by indexing Conditioned Response (CR) in terms of Quantity, Latency and Rate.

In classical conditioning, the period in which the organism learns the association between the CS and the UCS is the acquisition phase. With each passing trial the CS becomes stronger to elicit CR. The progress of conditioning can be examined by indexing CR in terms of:

Quantity : It is the response magnitude or the amount of CR that increases.

Latency : It is the time gap between the presentation of the CS and the reoccurrence of the CR that decreases.

Rate : It is the rapid rate at which an organism responds.

4 Which of the following intelligence tests are applicable to an illiterate adult ?

I. Wechsler Adult Intelligence Scale
II. Alexander Pass Along Test
III. Coloured Progressive Matrices
IV. Koh's Block Design Test

Codes

1 Only I
2 II and IV
3 I and III
4 II, III and IV

Ans. *(4)*

Exp. Alexander Pass Along Test, Coloured Progressive Matrices and Koh's Block Design Test are some of the intelligence tests which are applicable to an illiterate adult. These tests do not require the use of language, but could be manipulated using figures, pictures, blocks or even other objects. Their advantage is that they can be used for testing subjects who lack language ability.

Alexander Pass Along Test and Koh's Block Design comes under the Bhatia's battery of performance tests which was developed by C.M Bhatia in 1955. Ravens Coloured Progressive Matrices is also a performance test.

Wechsler Adult Intelligence Scale consists of both verbal and performance subsets. It is an individual test which has the unique quality of being simultaneously a verbal as well as a performance scale. The scale consists of eleven sub-tests. Six sub-tests make up the verbal scale and remaining five comprise the performance scale.

5 Match List I with List II and select the correct answer by choosing from the codes given below:

List I (Variable type)	List II (Example)
A. Artificially discrete variable	I. Neuroticism
B. Continuous variable	II. Voice pitch
C. Qualitative variable	III. Gender
D. Real discrete variable	IV. Admission test results in terms of admitted/ not-admitted

Codes

	A	B	C	D		A	B	C	D
1	III	I	II	IV	2	IV	I	II	III
3	IV	II	I	III	4	III	IV	II	I

Ans. *(2)*

Exp. The correct matching is A-IV, B-I, C-II and D-III.

An example of an *Artificially discrete variable* is admission test results in terms of admitted/not-admitted. These variables are the ones which are counted and are artificially divided. They can take a finite number of ranges. Admission test results are in terms of admitted and not-admitted which are categories divided by the researcher.

An example of a *Continuous variable* is Neuroticism. Neuroticism is the trait dimension which can be measured but not counted. Continuous variable is a variable that can take any value between two numbers. It can be measured but not numbered. For example temperature, height, weight etc. It can take any decimals, fractions etc.

An example of a *Qualitative variable* is Voice pitch. A qualitative variable is not measured in numerical form but fits into some category which is not based on logical order (nominal) or fits into some sort of ordering (ordinal). The voice pitch does not fit into numerical form but it can be categorised as high, medium and low voice pitch.

An example of a *Real discrete variable* is Gender. These variables are the ones which are counted and are divided naturally. They can take a finite number of ranges. Gender, i.e., male, female, transgender, etc. fit into the category of real variables that exists naturally and are not divided artificially by the researcher.

6 Length and Intensity of Light wave play an important role in

1 perception of colour and brightness
2 perception of colour and illumination
3 perception of constancy and brightness
4 perception of brightness and illumination

Ans. *(1)*

Exp. Length and Intensity of Light wave play an important role in perception of colour and brightness.

The wavelength of visible light is between about 790 and 390 nanometers. The long wavelength end of the visible light spectrum is perceived as red and at the short end of the spectrum is violet. Waves not only have length, but also have height, or amplitude. The greater the amplitude, the brighter the light.

7 Match List I with List II and select the correct answer by choosing from the codes given below:

List I (Concept)	List II (Explanation)
A. Rods	I. Two optic nerves from two retina join each other for a short distance
B. Cones	II. Do not distinguish colours
C. Blind spot	III. Good detail vision
D. Optic Chiasm	IV. Optic nerves exit the eyes

Codes

	A	B	C	D
1	II	III	I	IV
2	II	III	IV	I
3	III	II	I	IV
4	I	II	III	IV

Ans. *(2)*

Exp. The correct matching is A-II, B-III, C-IV and D-I.

Rods are the photoreceptors which do not distinguish colours. It is located in the human retina which is mainly responsible for vision at dim light (scotopic). These can function in less intense light. Rods are usually found concentrated at the outer edges of the retina and are used in peripheral vision.

Cones are mainly meant for good detail vision. These are the photoreceptors located in the human retina which is mainly responsible for vision at bright light (photopic). These require moderate to bright light for activation, as opposed to retinal rods, which require very little light for activation.

Blind spot is the region where optic nerve exits the eyes. It contains no light sensitive cells. It is the area of the monocular visual field in which stimulation cannot be perceived because the image falls on the site of the optic disk in the eye.

Optic Chiasm are the two optic nerves from two retinas join each other for a short distance. It is located at the base of the brain at which the optic nerves from the two eyes meet.

8 Geeta studied for sociology exam and then studied for psychology exam. Certain concepts and theories are similar in psychology and sociology. While taking sociology exam, she finds that she keeps getting confused with psychology theorists. Geeta's problem is most likely due to

1 decay of memory trace
2 proactive interference
3 retroactive interference
4 encoding failure

***Ans.** (3)*

Exp. While taking sociology exam, Geeta finds that she keeps getting confused with psychology theorists. Geeta's problem is most likely due to retroactive interference. When a newly learnt information (Psychology) interferes with the previously learnt information (Sociology) is known as retroactive interference.

When previously learnt information interferes with newly learnt information is known as proactive interference.

9 Which of the following sequence is correct in case of the curve of forgetting?

1 Percent recall of words is greatest immediately after learning → Percent recall decreases rapidly within the first hour → Percent recall further decreases rapidly after 30 days
2 Percent recall of words is greatest immediately after learning → Percent recall decreases rapidly within the first hour → Forgetting levels off after the first hour
3 Percent recall of words is greatest after two days → Forgetting levels off within 10-15 days → Percent recall decreases further after 30 days
4 Percent recall of words is greatest after 2 days → Percent recall decreases rapidly 20 days → Forgetting levels off after 30 days

***Ans.** (2)*

Exp. The correct sequence in case of the curve of forgetting is :

Percent recall of words is greatest immediately after learning → Percent recall decreases rapidly within the first hour → Forgetting levels off after the first hour.

The forgetting curve describes how the ability of the brain to retain information decreases with time. Hermann Ebbinghaus was the first to study the forgetting behaviour in an experimental, scientific way. He found that forgetting is exponential in nature that means that in the first days the memory loss is biggest, later you still forget but the rate at which you forget is much, much slower.

Humans tend to lose the memory of a studied or learnt knowledge over a period of time unless it is properly and consciously reviewed again and again.

10 Consider the following three types of investigations.

I. Expost facto field studies,
II. Laboratory experiments and
III. Field experiments

Arrange the above three types of investigations in ascending order in terms of researcher's ability to control secondary variance.

1 III, II, I	2 II, III, I
3 II, I, III	4 I, III, II

***Ans.** (4)*

Exp. Three types of investigations in ascending order in terms of researcher's ability to control secondary variance are Expost facto field studies, Field experiments and Laboratory experiments.

Secondary variances are the extraneous factors which are not controlled by the researcher so that it results in affecting the dependent variable.

Expost facto field studies are after-the-fact research studies where the analysis or inquiry starts where the fact have already been occurred without the interference from the researcher. It is also often applied as a substitute for true experimental research to test hypotheses about cause-and-effect relationships or in situations in which it is not practical or ethically acceptable to apply the full protocol of a true experimental design.

Field experiments are done in the everyday (i.e. real life) environment of the participants. The experimenter still manipulates the independent variable, but since its in a real-life setting, controlling the extraneous variables is difficult and at times not possible. These generally occur in natural settings which is high in both external and internal validity but it hard to set up and relatively rare.

Laboratory experiments are scientific study conducted in a laboratory, where the investigator has some degree of direct control over the environment and can manipulate the independent variables. These are conducted in artificial settings and are high in internal validity but low in external validity (generalizability). In laboratory experiments, the researcher has maximum control over the variables and the environment. The researcher can manipulate the conditions to the maximum degree.

11 Read each of the following two statements Assertion (A) and Reason (R) and indicate your answer using codes given below:

Assertion (A) People often attain their visual experiences after many years of blindness.

Reason (R) Most of the knowledge of the world had come to them through the sense of touch.

Codes

1 Both (A) and (R) are true and (R) is the correct explanation of (A)
2 Both (A) and (R) are true, but (R) is not the correct explanation of (A)
3 (A) is true, but (R) is false
4 (A) is false, but (R) is true

Ans. (3)

Exp. (A) is true, but (R) is false.

People often attain their visual experiences after many years of blindness. This is true because they usually develop a spatial representation of the objects and it makes them to encounter the visual experiences after many years of blindness. Hence, the Assertion is true.

Most of the knowledge of the world had come to them through the sense of touch is false because as a human being we strongly depend on all other senses too. Visually impaired people rely on other senses like smell (olfactory), hearing (auditory) and taste (gustatory).

12 In Pavlovian conditioning paradigm the strongest and most rapid conditioning occurs in

1 Simultaneous conditioning
2 Trace conditioning
3 Short-delay conditioning
4 Long-delay conditioning

Ans. (3)

Exp. In Pavlovian conditioning paradigm the strongest and most rapid conditioning occurs in Short-delay conditioning.

In Short-delay conditioning the CS (Conditioned stimulus) is presented and is overlapped by the presentation of the US (Unconditioned stimulus). It is a form of Forward Conditioning, wherein the onset of the CS precedes the onset of the US in order to signal that the US will follow.

13 Read each of the following two statements, Assertion (A) and Reason (R) and indicate your answer using codes given below :

Assertion (A) The information processing approach is rooted in structuralism.

Reason (R) It attempts to identify the basic capacities and processes we use in cognition.

Codes

1 Both (A) and (R) are true and (R) is the correct explanation of (A)
2 Both (A) and (R) are true, but (R) is not the correct explanation of (A)
3 (A) is true, but (R) is false
4 (A) is false, but (R) is true

Ans. (1)

Exp. Both (A) and (R) are true and (R) is the correct explanation of (A).

The information processing approach is rooted in structuralism. This is true because the information processing is based on the idea that humans process the information they receive, rather than merely responding to stimuli.

It attempts to identify the basic capacities and processes we use in cognition. This is true because information processing framework compares computer and human brain and how does it process the information. This explains how the information processing approach is rooted in structuralism.

14 Utilitarianism provided the description of ________ of thought and behaviour.

1 what
2 when
3 why
4 how

Ans. (3)

Exp. Utilitarianism provided the description of why of thought and behaviour.

Utilitarianism is an effort to provide an answer to the practical question 'why ought a man to do?' Its answer is that he ought to act so as to produce the best consequences possible. Utilitarianism relies upon some theory of intrinsic value; something is held to be good in it apart from further consequences, and all other values are believed to derive their worth from their relation to this intrinsic good as a means to an end.

15 Read each of the following two statements, Assertion (A) and Reason (R) and indicate your answer using codes given below:

Assertion (A) Naturalistic observation is a very popular research method in ethological research.

Reason (R) Naturalistic observation is free from observer bias.

Codes

1 Both (A) and (R) are true and (R) is the correct explanation of (A)
2 Both (A) and (R) are true, but (R) is not the correct explanation of (A)
3 (A) is true, but (R) is false
4 (A) is false, but (R) is true

Ans. (3)

Exp. (A) is true, but (R) is false.

Naturalistic observation is a very popular research method in ethological research is true because ethological approach of research in human involves observing the human directly and analysing their behaviours in a natural setting.

Naturalistic observation is free from observer bias is false because naturalistic observation is a type of observational method where researcher observes the participants in a natural setting. Since the researcher observes a person unobtrusively so that person is not aware that he is being studied and a researcher sees what he meant to see.

16 Meaningfulness of verbal material can be indexed in terms of

1 Associative Reaction Time
2 Associative Value
3 Single Response Free Association
4 Single Response Controlled Association

Ans. (2)

Exp. Meaningfulness of verbal material can be indexed in terms of Associative Value.

The Association Value of a stimulus is a measure of its meaningfulness. It is a strong predictor of how easy it is to learn new information about that stimulus, for example to learn to associate it with a second stimulus, or to recall or recognise it in a memory test.

17 Facial Feedback Hypothesis supports

1 Canon-Bard Theory of Emotion
2 James-Lange Theory of Emotion
3 Two-Factor Theory of Emotion
4 Opponent Process Theory of Emotion

Ans. (2)

Exp. Facial Feedback Hypothesis supports James-Lange Theory of Emotion.

The Facial Feedback Hypothesis states that facial movements can influence emotional experience. William James and Carl Lange were two 19th century scholars who independently developed a hypothesis, which later came to be known as James-Lange theory of emotions. The basic premise of the theory is that physiological arousal instigates the experience of emotions. According to this theory, emotions stems from the physiological reactions to the external stimulus or events. For example when you encounter a thief in your garden area you heart might start to palpitate or your blood pressure might increase and therefore you experience the emotion as fear. The external stimulus is the thief, the physiological arousal is the palpitation of heart and increase in blood pressure, and the emotion is fear.

18 Read each of the following two statements , Assertion (A) and Reason (R) and indicate your answer using codes given below:

Assertion (A) In some cases people attempt to reach the goal slowly and hesitantly.

Reason (R) In approach-avoidance conflict, a single goal has positive valence as well as negative valence.

Codes

1 Both (A) and (R) are true, and (R) is the correct explanation of (A)
2 Both (A) and (R) are true, but (R) is not the correct explanation of (A)
3 (A) is true, but (R) is false
4 (A) is false, but (R) is true

Ans. (1)

Exp. Both (A) and (R) are true, and (R) is the correct explanation of (A).

In some cases people attempt to reach the goal slowly and hesitantly are true because they may be attracted by a goal and also feels hesitant to attempt the goal. Kurt Lewin introduced the concept, referring to two competing forces of positive and negative valence that act upon an individual in parallel.

In approach–avoidance conflict, a single goal has positive valence as well as negative valence is true because the person was attracted by a goal and at same time feels hesitant to attempt the goal. For example when a child wants to eat chocolate from the fridge (attracted-positive valence) but at the same time she feels hesitant to eat chocolate from the fridge because when her mother encounters that the chocolate is not in the fridge she will scold her (Hesitant-negative valence).

19 Which of the following are the limitations of the survey method ?

I. Difficulties in obtaining representative samples.
II. Unsuitable for subjects with low educational levels.
III. Socially desirable responding.
IV. Can't be used in longitudinal research.

Codes

1 Only IV	2 II and III
3 I and III	4 I, II and III

Ans. (3)

Exp. Statement I and III are correct with respect to limitations of the survey method.

The limitations of the survey method are:

- *Difficulties in obtaining representative samples*: In conducting a survey research it can be difficult for the researcher to identify the correct representative samples and researcher's bias can influence the choice of sample population.
- *Socially desirable responding*: It is difficult to ensure that the respondent has given a genuine answer and not merely due to social desirability.

20 Read each of the following two statements Assertion (A) and Reason (R) and indicate your answer using codes given below :

Assertion (A) In cross-sectional research to study development process of intelligence, age and cohorts are confounded.

Reason (R) According to Flynn effect, each successive generation of people is more intelligent than the preceding one.

Codes

1 Both (A) and (R) are true, and (R) is the correct explanation of (A)
2 Both (A) and (R) are true, but (R) is not the correct explanation of (A)
3 (A) is true, but (R) is false
4 (A) is false, but (R) is true

Ans. (1)

Exp. Both (A) and (R) are true, and (R) is the correct explanation of (A)

In cross-sectional research to study development process of intelligence, age and cohorts are confounded.

Cross-sectional research involves collection of data from different samples at a given point of time. Participants are usually separated into groups known as cohorts. Age and cohorts are confounded in cross-sectional research to study development process of intelligence because confounded variables are the influencer variables which influence dependent and independent variable and cause a spurious relationship.

According to Flynn effect, each successive generation of people is more intelligent than the preceding one. Flynn did cross-sectional studies to establish that each successive generation of people is more intelligent than the preceding one.

21 Chronometric measurement of intelligence involves the use of which of the following?

1 Reaction time apparatus
2 Flicker-Fusion apparatus
3 ECG Bio-feedback apparatus
4 EMG Bio-feedback apparatus

Ans. (1)

Exp. Chronometric measurement of intelligence involves the use of Reaction time apparatus.

A variety of reaction time measures have been developed and studied as correlates of intelligence. It is now well-established that a strong and significant correlation exists between these chronometric measures of speed of information-processing and performance on standardized IQ tests. Reaction time paradigms hold considerable promise for studies of the nature of human intelligence.

Flicker-Fusion apparatus is an apparatus for testing temporal vision including a target light produced on a portion of a viewing area.

22 Read each of the following two statements, Assertion (A) and Reason (R) and indicate your answer using codes given below :

Assertion (A) The individual is left with little or no energy for cathexis (APM) after satisfying a particular need.

Reason (R) Cathexis is the investment of psyshic energy in the thoughts of objects or processes that will satisfy a need.

Codes

1 Both (A) and (R) are true, and (R) is the correct explanation of (A)
2 Both (A) and (R) are true, but (R) is not the correct explanation of (A)
3 (A) is true, but (R) is false
4 (A) is false, but (R) is true

Ans. (4)

Exp. (A) is false, but (R) is true.

The individual is left with little or no energy for cathexis (APM) after satisfying a particular need is false. After satisfying a particular need, an individual may try to invest their Cathexis to an object, person, desire or wish.

Cathexis is the investment of psychic energy in the thoughts of objects or processes that will satisfy a need is true. Cathexis is usually regarded as an emotional investment. Cathexis, as per Freudian theory, is the investment of psychic energy in the thoughts of objects or processes that will allow an unacceptable repressed thought or desire to get an escape from the unconscious to the sub conscious or the conscious mind. The repressed material keeps finding different ways to seek fulfilment.

23 Network of auditory pathways can be arranged in which of the following sequence

1 Auditory Nerve → Cochlear Nuclei → Superior olives → Lateral Lemniscus → Inferior Colliculi → Medial Geniculate Nuclei → Primary Auditory Cortex
2 Cochlear Nuclei → Auditory Nerve → Lateral Lemniscus → Superior Olives → Inferior Colliculi → Medial Geniculate Nuclei → Primary Auditory Cortex
3 Auditory Nerve → Cochlear Nuclei → Lateral Lemniscus → Inferior Colliculi → Superior Colliculi → Medial Geniculate Nuclei → Auditory Cortex
4 Cochlear Nuclei → Auditory Nerve → Inferior Colliculi → Superior Colliculi → Lateral Lemniscus → Medial Geniculate Nuclei → Auditory Cortex

Ans. (1)

Exp. Network of auditory pathways can be arranged in the following sequence:

Auditory Nerve → Cochlear Nuclei → Superior olives → Lateral Leminiscus → Inferior Colliculi → Medial Geniculate Nuclei → Primary Auditory Cortex

The first relay of the primary auditory pathway occurs in the cochlear nuclei in the brain stem, which receive Type I spiral ganglion axons (auditory nerve); at this level an important decoding of the basic signal occurs: duration, intensity and frequency. The second major relay in the brain stem is in the superior olivary complex: the majority of the auditory fibres synapse there having already crossed the midline.

From the dorsal cochlear nucleus, most fibres cross the midline and ascend in the contralateral lateral lemniscus. Other fibres ascend in the ipsilateral lateral lemniscus. Fibres ascending through the lateral lemniscus from both cochlear nuclei and from the superior olivary nuclei arrive at the inferior colliculus, where all these fibres carrying auditory information converge.

Leaving this relay, a third neuron carries the mesage up to the level of the inferior colliculus (mesencephalus). These two relays play an essential rôle in the localisation of sound.

A last relay, before the cortex, occurs in the medial geniculate body (thalamus); it's here that an important integration occurs: preparation of a motor response (eg vocal response).

The final neuron of the primary auditory pathway links the thalamus to the auditory cortex, where the message, already largely decoded during its passage through the previous neurons in the pathway, is recognised, memorized and perhaps integrated into a voluntary response.

24 The tendency for parallel lines to appear to converge on each other is termed as

1 Motion parallax
2 Ponzo illusion
3 Linear perspective
4 Aerial perspective

Ans. (3)

➲ *Exp.* The tendency for parallel lines to appear to converge on each other is termed as Linear perspective.

Linear perspective is one of the monocular depth cues, arising from the principle that the size of an object's visual image is a function of its distance from the eye. Thus, two objects appear closer together as the distance from them increases, as seen in the tracks of a railroad that appear to converge on the horizon. Linear perspective involves distant objects appear to be closer together than the nearer objects. For example rail tracks, parallel lines appears to converge with the increasing distance with a terminating point at the horizon.

25 In a contingency table, one of the cell has an obtained frequency of 20 and an expected frequency of 30. What would be the contribution of this cell towards the total Chi-square value ?

1 3.33 2 5.00 3 10.00 4 20.00

Ans. (1)

➲ *Exp.* The total contribution of this cell towards the total Chi-square value will be 3.33.

To calculate chi-square, we take the square of the difference between the observed (O) and expected (E) values and divide it by the expected value.

The formula for calculating chi-square is:

$X^2 = \Sigma(O_i - E_i)^2 / E_i$ where O_i = observed value (actual value) and E_i= expected value.

In this case, O_i = 20 and E_i = 30.

Using the formula, X^2 = (20-30^2)/30 = 10^2/30

= 100/30 = 3.33.

26 Match List I with List II and select the correct answer by choosing from the codes given below:

List I (Concept)	List II (Explanation)
A. Analogical reasoning	I. Processes that allow to make predictions about events/objects
B. Deductive reasoning	II. Using inferences to add new knowledge
C. Inductive reasoning	III. Using means-end analysis
D. Physical reasoning	IV. Drawing valid conclusions from premises

Codes

	A	B	C	D		A	B	C	D
1	I	II	III	IV	2	II	III	IV	I
3	III	IV	II	I	4	IV	III	II	I

Ans. (3)

➲ *Exp.* The correct matching is A-III, B-IV, C-II and D-I.

Analogical reasoning involves using means-end analysis. It involves the reasoning between two familiar situations, areas or even domains. The function of mean-end analysis is to reduce the difference between initial state and the goal state by creating sub goals so that is easy for you to achieve the final goal.

Deductive reasoning involves drawing valid conclusions from premises. It starts from general to specific. It is also known as top-down processing.

Inductive reasoning involves using inferences to add new knowledge. It is the form of reasoning in which inferences and general principles are drawn from specific observations and cases. Inductive reasoning is a cornerstone of the scientific method in that it underlies the process of developing hypotheses from particular facts and observations.

Physical reasoning involves processes that allows to make prediction about events/objects. It is the sequence of arguments or proofs used to establish a conclusion in this way.

27 Match List I with List II and select the correct answer by choosing from the codes given below :

List I (Concept)	List II (Explanation)
A. Cortical Mosaic	I. Cortex is constantly being excited or inhibited depending on what the organism is experiencing
B. Dynamic Stereotype	II. Extinction that occurs after a previously excitatory CS is repeatedly presented without reinforcer
C. Conditioned Inhibition	III. Tendency of organisms to attend to and explore novels stimuli that occurs in their environment
D. Orienting Reflex	IV. Events consistently occurring in the environment come to have neurological representation making the responses rapid and autonomic to the familiar environment

Codes

	A	B	C	D		A	B	C	D
1	II	III	I	IV	2	I	IV	II	III
3	III	IV	I	II	4	IV	II	III	I

Ans. (*)

➲ *Exp.* The correct matching is A-I, B-II, C-III and D-IV.

Cortical Mosaic Cortex is constantly being excited or inhibited depending on what the organism is experiencing. It is a term which according to Pavlov refers to the pattern of points of excitation and inhibition that characterises the cortex at any given moment.

Dynamic Stereotype is the extinction that occurs after a previously excitatory CS is repeatedly presented without reinforce. It is to designate a unique aspect that is generated within the system of conditioned reflexes during the life of an organism with intelligent aptitudes.

Conditioned Inhibition is the tendency of organisms to attend to and explore novel stimuli that occurs in their environment. It is a Pavlovian learning phenomenon in which a stimulus that predicts the absence of an otherwise expected outcome comes to control an organism's responding.

Orienting reflex are the events consistently occurring in the environment come to have neurological representation making the responses rapid and autonomic to the familiar environment. An orienting reflex occurs when someone is confronted with a personally significant stimulus. The orienting reflex has its origin with Pavlov and it is described in psychophysiology as a response to novelty; the habituation of the orienting reflex is determined by personal significance.

28 Match List I with List II and select the correct answer by choosing from the codes given below:

List I (Concept)	List II (Explanation)
A. Drive	I. A state of deficiency or excess of something in the organism, the fulfilment or elimination of which is essential for survival and balance
B. Yerkes-Dodsan Law	II. A state of psychological readiness that motivates the organism to act for the fulfilment of need and reduction of tension
C. Power Motive	III. The level of arousal beyond which performance begins to decline
D. Need	IV. Tendency or capacity to produce intended effects on the behaviour or emotions of other persons

Codes

	A	B	C	D
1	I	II	III	IV
2	II	III	IV	I
3	III	IV	I	II
4	IV	III	II	I

Ans. (2)

Exp. The correct matching is A-II, B-III, C-IV and D-I.

Drive is a state of psychological readiness that motivates the organism to act for the fulfillment of need and reduction of tension. It is a generalised state of readiness precipitating or motivating an activity or course of action. Drive is hypothetical in nature, usually created by deprivation of a needed substance (e.g., food), the presence of negative stimuli (e.g., pain, cold), or the occurrence of negative events. Drive is said to be necessary for stimuli or events to serve as reinforcers.

Yerkes-Dodson Law is the level of arousal beyond which performance begins to decline. It is a law stating that the relation between motivation (arousal) and performance can be represented by an inverted U-curve (see inverted-U hypothesis).

Power Motive is the tendency or capacity to produce intended effects on the behaviour or emotions of other persons. It is the desire to have impact on other people, to affect their behaviour or emotions. This broad and general definition includes a whole family of overlapping concepts such as influence, inspiration, nurturance, authority, leadership, control, dominance, coercion, and aggression.

Need is a state of deficiency or excess of something in the organism, the fulfillment or elimination of which is essential for survival and balance. It is a condition of tension in an organism resulting from deprivation of something required for survival, well-being, or personal fulfillment.

29 Match List I with List II and select the correct answer by choosing from the codes given below:

List I (Concept)	List II (Explanation)
A. Syntelity	I. Dynamic source trait with an environmental origin
B. Self-sentiment	II. Description of traits that characterise a group
C. Metaerg	III. Causal relationship between Ergs, sentiments and Attitudes
D. Subsidiation	IV. The most powerful sentiment which organises the entire personality

Codes

	A	B	C	D
1	IV	II	I	III
2	II	IV	I	III
3	IV	III	II	I
4	II	IV	III	I

Ans. (2)

Exp. The correct matching is A-II, B-IV, C-I and D-III.

Syntelity is the description of traits that characterise a group. It is the inferred behavioural tendencies of a group acting as a group that correspond to personality in an individual.

Self-sentiment is the most powerful sentiment which organises the entire personality. Cattell (1957) has defined the self-sentiment as a "factor and system of attitudes centered on the conceived, contemplated self and directed to main- taining its physical, social, and moral integrity as a basis for other sentiment and ergic satisfactions".

Metaerg is the dynamic source trait with an environmental origin. Metaergs are environmental-mold dynamic source traits. These learned motivations can range from the very general, like love of country and esteem of education, to the very specific, like opposition to a particular political candidate.

Subsidiation is the causal relationship between Ergs, sentiments and attitudes. It is the pattern of relationship among motivational drives; how dynamic traits related to one another attitudes serve sentiments, which serve ergs. The subsidisation chain helps determine when specific attitude will produce a specific behaviour.

30 Read each of the following two statements, Assertion (A) and Reason (R) and indicate your answer using codes given below :

Assertion (A) Minor frustrations will add upto produce considerable frustration but not to aggression.

Reason (R) Disruption of goal-directed behaviour usually leads to frustration.

Codes

1 Both (A) and (R) are true, and (R) is the correct explanation of (A)
2 Both (A) and (R) are true, but (R) is not the correct explanation of (A)
3 (A) is true, but (R) is false
4 (A) is false, but (R) is true

***Ans.** (4)*

Exp. (A) is false, but (R) is true.

Minor frustrations will add up to produce considerable frustration but not to aggression is false because Berkowitz's Frustration-Aggression hypothesis states that frustration alone does give direction to aggression. It also depends upon the environmental context and stimuli.

Disruption of goal-directed behaviour usually leads to frustration is true since when our goal or our desire/wish is not fulfilled it always lead to frustration.

31 Which of the following are not nuclei of Thalamus ?

I. Internal Lamina
II. Anterior Nucleus
III. Ventromedial Nucleus
IV. Paraventricular Nucleus

Codes

1 I and II	2 II and III
3 III and IV	4 I and III

***Ans.** (3)*

Exp. Ventromedial nucleus and Paraventricular nucleus are not the nuclei of Thalamus.

Ventromedial nucleus is a nucleus of the hypothalamus. It is involved in feeding, fear, thermoregulation, and sexual activity. This nuclear region is involved with the recognition of the feeling of fullness.

Paraventricular Nucleus is a neuronal nucleus in the hypothalamus. It contains groups of neurons that can be activated by stressful and/or physiological changes.

32 Short-term memory holds information for

I. 50 seconds
II. 30 seconds or less
III. more than 60 seconds
IV. between 50 and 60 seconds

Codes

1 Only III	2 Only I
3 Only II	4 I and IV

***Ans.** (3)*

Exp. Short-term memory holds information for 30 seconds or less.

Short-term memory takes information from sensory memory which can hold information for about 15 to 30 seconds. It may be proceed to long term memory by using proper mnemonic techniques like chunking, peg system etc.

33 Match List I with List II and select the correct answer by choosing from the codes given below :

List I (Concept)	List II (Explanation)
A. Horizontal-Vertical illusion	I. Our eyes turn inward toward one-another in order to see close objects
B. Atmospheric perspective	II. What we perceive often is based more on what goes on in our mind than what is in front of our eyes
C. Convergence	III. Tendency to perceive objects high in our visual field as more distant.
D. Figure-ground	IV. The further away objects are, the less distinctly they are seen

Codes

	A	B	C	D		A	B	C	D
1	I	II	II	IV	2	II	III	IV	I
3	III	IV	I	II	4	IV	I	II	III

***Ans.** (3)*

Exp. The correct matching is A-III, B-IV, C-I and D-II.

Horizontal-Vertical illusion is the tendency to perceive objects high in our visual field as more distant. It is the misperception that vertical lines are longer than horizontal lines when both are actually the same length.

Atmospheric perspective is when the further away objects are, the less distinctly they are seen. It is a cue that aids the perception of depth and distance. Atmospheric perspective is the acquired ability to differentiate near and distant objects on the basis of their clear or indistinct appearance.

Convergence is when our eyes turn inward toward one-another in order to see close objects. It is the rotation of the two eyes inward toward a light source so that the image falls on corresponding points on the foveas. Convergence enables the slightly different images of an object seen by each eye to come together and form a single image.

Figure-ground is what we perceive often is based more on what goes on in our mind than what is in front of our eyes. It is related to the principle that perceptions have two parts: a figure or object that stands out in good contour and an indistinct, homogeneous background.

34 **Read each of the following two statements, Assertion (A) and Reason (R) and indicate your answer using codes given below :**

Assertion (A) Participants of a study were shown novel geometric shapes that served as targets. Then they were shown fragments of these shapes. Participants were quicker to recognise the fragments as part of the original target.

Reason (R) We do not use Gestalt principles in our everyday perception.

Codes

1 Both (A) and (R) are true, and (R) is the correct explanation of (A)
2 Both (A) and (R) are true, but (R) is not the correct explanation of (A)
3 (A) is true, but (R) is false
4 (A) is false, but (R) is true

Ans. *(3)*

Exp. (A) is true, but (R) is false

Participants of a study were shown novel geometric shapes that served as targets. Then they were shown fragments of these shapes. Participants were quicker to recognise the fragments as part of the original target. The assertion is true as people tend to perceive object as completeness rather than seeing the incomplete part. Suppose when encountering a circle we see it as completeness and also seeing a dot of an incomplete circle as complete circle. As per German philosophers who proposed the Gestalt view, perceived objects are always perceived as one and not as assemblages or discrete pieces of sensory information. The total experience is something more than sum of the individual elements.

We do not use Gestalt principles in our everyday perception is false. The reason is incorrect as we tend to follow Gestalt principles in our everyday perception. The Gestalt principles describe when and how our minds see different visual elements as being part of a greater whole.

35 **In problem solving if you follow rules that reduce the number of operations or allow you to take short cuts, you are using**

1 Algorithm
2 Heuristic
3 Strategy
4 Skill

Ans. *(2)*

Exp. In problem solving if you follow rules that reduce the number of operations or allow you to take short cuts, you are using Heuristic. They are mental shortcuts that simplify problem solving by allowing us to skip steps in the process. They are not into step by step solutions so that it cannot guarantee a solution which is predictable or reproducible.

36 **Anticipation method can be used in**

I. Free Recall
II. Serial Learning
III. Verbal Discrimination
IV. Paired Associates Learning

Codes

1 I, II and III
2 I. II, III and IV
3 I and II
4 II and IV

Ans. *(4)*

Exp. Anticipation Method can be used in Serial Learning and Paired Associates Learning.

Anticipation method is a technique that involves learning to associate a stimulus (e.g., an item in a list or series) with a stimulus or response that follows (e.g., the next item in the list or series), so that when subsequently given the stimulus, one can produce the response or recall the next item in the series. This method is frequently used in serial learning and paired-associates learning.

Serial learning is recalling items in the order in which they were presented. For instance, to remember a telephone number, the digits must be correctly sequenced.

Paired-associates learning is a technique used in studying learning in which participants learn syllables, words, or other items in pairs and are later presented with one half of each pair to which they must respond with the matching half.

37 **Gestalt Psychologist Max Wertheimer attempted to train children to think in a logical and systematic way where he used several figures such as**

I. Squares and rectangles
II. Parallelogram
III. Triangles
IV. Circles

Codes

1 I and II
2 II and III
3 III and IV
4 I, II and III

Ans. *(4)*

Exp. Gestalt Psychologist Max Wertheimer attempted to train children to think in a logical and systematic way where he used several figures such as Squares, rectangles, parallelogram and triangles.

Wertheimer pursued research on problem solving, or as he preferred to call it, 'productive thinking.' Wertheimer example of productive thinking involves a child attempting to solve a geometry, problem—the area of a parallelogram. Suddenly the child takes a pair of scissors and cuts a triangle from one end of the figure, turns it and attaches it to the other side forming a rectangle—the problem of the area can now be solved.

Wertheimer referred to this type of learning as 'productive' to distinguish it from 'reproductive' thinking, the simple associative or trial and error learning that involved no insight.

38 Which of the following sequences describes the energy mobilisation in body ?

1 Fasting phase → Absorptive phase → Cephalic phase
2 Cephalic phase → Absorptive phase → Fasting phase
3 Absorptive phase → Fasting phase → Cephalic phase
4 Fasting phase → Cephalic phase → Absorptive phase

Ans. (2)

Exp. The correct sequence of energy mobilisation in body is as follows :

Cephalic phase → Absorptive phase → Fasting phase.

The *Cephalic phase* of gastric secretion occurs even before food enters the stomach, especially while it is being eaten.

Absorptive state is the period in which the gastrointestinal tract is full and the anabolic processes exceed catabolism.

Fasting phase of metabolism is the phase where supplies of glucose are abundant. Most cells live on fatty acids. Glycerol and fatty acids are converted into triglycerides.

39 According to Bandura, which of the following cognitive mechanisms are adopted by a person to act contrary to his or her moral principles without experiencing self-contempt

I. Moral justification
II. Dehumanisation
III. Displacement of Responsibility
IV. Diffusion of Responsibility

Codes

1 I, II and III
2 I, II and IV
3 II, III and IV
4 I, II, III and IV

Ans. (4)

Exp. According to Bandura, Moral justification, Dehumanisation, Displacement of responsibility and Diffusion of responsibility are the cognitive mechanisms that are adopted by a person to act contrary to his or her moral principles without experiencing self-contempt.

Moral justification is a powerful mechanism through which actors interpret their aggressive behaviour as serving a moral purpose, which influences them to consider themselves moral agents who can feel good about themselves (i.e., self-approval) while inflicting harm on others.

Dehumanisation is the process through which a person or group of people is denied 'humanness' or human attributes.

Displacement of responsibility is the distortion of the relationship between actions and the effects they cause. Under displacement of responsibility, people avoid feelings of responsibility for unethical behavior by shifting responsibility for those actions onto someone else.

Diffusion of responsibility occurs in a group of people, where with the increasing number of people, the level of diffusion increases. In this phenomenon, a person has lower inclination towards responsibility as they feel that others are also equally responsible in the group.

40 In Guilford's structure of Intellect Model, obtained abilities have been named in which of the following sequence

1 Operations, Contents and Products
2 Operations, Products and Contents
3 Contents, Operations and Products
4 Products, Contents and Operations

Ans. (1)

Exp. In Guilford's structure of Intellect Model, obtained abilities have been named in following sequence: Operations, contents and products.

Guilford's Structure of Intellect (SOI) Model is a multiple intelligences theory. He believed that intelligence wasn't a monolithic, global attribute but a combination of multiple abilities, that were relatively independent. He applied the factor analytical method to learn these mental abilities.

Operations refer to general intellectual processes. There are six operations namely, cognition, memory recording, memory retention, divergent production, convergent production, and evaluation.

Contents include the broad areas to which human intellect operations are applied. There are five contents namely, symbolic, semantic, behavioural, auditory, and visual.

Products contain results of applying particular operations to specific contents. There are six products namely, units, classes, relations, systems, transformations, and implications.

41 Read each of the following two statements, Assertion (A) and Reason (R), and indicate your answer using codes given below:

Assertion (A) Differences between intelligence levels of monozygotic twins are attributed to environmental influences.

Reason (R) Monozygotic twins have identical genetically determined reaction range.

Codes

1 Both (A) and (R) are true, and (R) is the correct explanation of (A)
2 Both (A) and (R) are true, but (R) is not the correct explanation of (A)
3 (A) is true, but (R) is false
4 (A) is false, but (R) is true

Ans. (1)

Exp. Both (A) and (R) are true, and (R) is the correct explanation of (A).

Differences between intelligence levels of monozygotic twins are attributed to environmental influences. This is true because the environment or the surroundings where they have been brought up contributes to the differences in intelligence levels.

Monozygotic twins have identical genetically determined reaction range is true because monozygotic twins share a common genotype. However, most monozygotic twin pairs are not identical; several types of phenotypic discordance may be observed, such as differences in intelligence. This explains why the differences between intelligence levels are attributed to environmental influences.

42 Match List I with List II and select the correct answer by choosing from the codes given below :

List I (Explanation)	List II (Concept)
A. Remembering meaning of words, properties of objects	I. Sensory memory
B. Helping information to be brought back to mind when it cannot be recalled spontaneously	II. Semantic memory
C. Remembering specific experiences of the past	III. Retrieval cues
D. Retaining representation of sensory input for brief periods of time	IV. Episodic memory

Codes

	A	B	C	D		A	B	C	D
1	I	II	III	IV	2	II	III	IV	I
3	III	II	I	IV	4	IV	II	III	I

Ans. (2)

Exp. The correct matching is A-II, B-III, C-IV and D-I.

Semantic memory is the memory related to remembering meaning of words, properties of objects. It is the memory for general factual knowledge and concepts, of the kind that endows information with meaning and ultimately allows people to engage in such complex cognitive processes.

Retrieval cues are related to helping information to be brought back to mind when it cannot be recalled spontaneously. Retrieval cue is a prompt or stimulus used to guide memory recall.

Episodic memory is the memory related to remembering specific experiences of the past. It is the ability to remember personally experienced events associated with a particular time and place.

Sensory memory is the memory related to retaining representation of sensory input for brief periods of time. It is the brief storage of information from each of the senses, in a relatively unprocessed form beyond the duration of a stimulus, for recoding into another memory (such as short-term memory) or for comprehension.

43 Information in short-term memory enters long-term storage through

1 Selective attention
2 Elaborative rehearsal
3 Learning
4 Information processing

Ans. (2)

Exp. Information in short-term memory enters long-term storage through Elaborative rehearsal.

Elaborative rehearsal is an encoding strategy to facilitate the formation of memory by linking new information to what one already knows. It is a technique to help the short-term memory store thoughts and ideas and pass into the long-term memory. For instance, when trying to remember that someone is named George, one might think of five other things one knows about people named George.

44 Read each of the following two statements, Assertion (A) and Reason (R) and indicate your answer using codes given below:

Assertion (A) A neural membrane is double-layered.

Reason (R) Lipid molecules turn their tails toward each other.

Codes

1 Both (A) and (R) are true and (R) is the correct explanation of (A)
2 Both (A) and (R) are true, but (R) is not the correct explanation of (A)
3 (A) is true, but (R) is false
4 (A) is false, but (R) is true

Ans. (1)

Exp. Both (A) and (R) are true and (R) is the correct explanation of (A).

A neural membrane is double-layered is true. The neural membrane is the site where most processes involved in neural preservation and functioning are triggered. This membrane is composed of two layers of lipid or fat molecules.

Lipid molecules turn their tails toward each other is also true because the inner layer is hydrophobic and outer layer is hydrophilic. The water-repelling tails of these molecules directed toward the middle of the membrane and away from the fluid found outside and inside the cell.

45 The inputs from our sensory receptors are structured by

1 Selective principles
2 Gestalt principles
3 Analytical principles
4 Learning principles

Ans. (2)

Exp. The inputs from our sensory receptors are structured by Gestalt principles.

The sensory receptors transduce the input energy into neural activity, which is transmitted to our brains, where we construct a mental representation of the stimulus (or, in most cases, the multiple related stimuli) called a percept. An ambiguous stimulus may be translated into multiple percepts, experienced randomly, one at a time, in what is called 'multistable perception.' Therefore, the input is said to be structured by Gestalt principles.

Directions (Q. Nos 46 - 50) *Read the following paragraph and answer the questions which are as follows :*

A researcher working in the area of human intelligence wanted to develop a new verbal test of intelligence. For this purpose, he wrote 200 objective multiple-choice items. Each item had four alternatives, one of which was right and the three remaining ones were wrong. He administered this initial version to a sample of 400 subjects. Using P27 and P73 as the cut-off points, he obtained two groups – Low scoring and High scoring respectively.

The item difficulty index and the item discrimination index were computed for each of the 200 items. To assess whether each item significantly discriminates between Low scoring and High scoring groups, appropriate statistical significance tests were also employed. This item analysis process retained 150 items. The final version of 150 items was administered to a fresh sample of 750 subjects. The appropriate measures of internal consistency reliability were obtained. The test norms were developed using normalised T scores (mean = 100, SD = 20) and the Wechsler type deviation IQ scores. To assess the dimensionality of verbal intelligence, the researcher also carried out the factor analysis of item scores.

46 Which one of the following tests of statistical significance can be employed in the above study to evaluate whether the item significantly discriminates between the Low scoring and High scoring groups ?

1 Chi-square
2 Point-biserial correlation
3 T-test
4 Biserial correlation

***Ans.** (2)*

➲ *Exp.* Point-biserial correlation of statistical significance can be employed in the above study to evaluate whether the item significantly discriminates between the Low scoring and High scoring groups.

The Point-Biserial Correlation Coefficient is a correlation measure of the strength of association between a continuous-level variable (ratio or interval data) and a binary variable. Binary variables are variables of nominal scale with only two values.

In this case, test scores are the binary variables which are naturally dichotomous in the form of 0 or 1, and the total test score is the continuous-level variable. Therefore, the point-biserial correlation is used.

47 Which of the following reliability coefficients can be computed in the above study to assess the internal consistency ?

I. Odd-even reliability coefficient
II. Kuder-Richardsen reliability coefficient
III. Cronbach alpha coefficient
IV. Interscorer reliability coefficient

Codes

1 Only I　　2 I and III
3 I, II and III　　4 II, III and IV

***Ans.** (3)*

➲ *Exp.* Odd-even reliability coefficient, Kuder-Richardsen reliability coefficient and Cronbach alpha coefficient are the reliability coefficients that can be computed in the above study to assess the internal consistency.

Odd-even reliability coefficient is a measure of reliability in which a test is split into two parts and an individual's scores on both halves are compared. The items might be divided randomly or using odd-even method.

Kuder-Richardsen reliability coefficient is a measure of internal consistency reliability for measures with dichotomous choices.

Cronbach alpha coefficient is a measure of internal consistency, that is, how closely related a set of items are as a group.

48 For the above test, what is the expected percentile rank for the T-score of 120 ?

1 60　　2 68　　3 75　　4 84

***Ans.** (4)*

➲ *Exp.* The expected percentile rank for the T-score of 120 is 84.

In the given case, the mean is 100, and SD is 20. The corresponding one SD falls near 84.1 in the percentile rank. Therefore, the expected percentile rank is 84.

49 For the above test, a T-score of 80 would correspond to the deviation IQ of

1 68　　2 80
3 85　　4 115

***Ans.** (3)*

➲ *Exp.* For the above test, a T-score of 80 would correspond to the deviation IQ of 85.

The mean for the T-score is 100 and SD is 20. Therefore, the T-score of 80 corresponds to one SD below the mean (100-20).

The standard deviation is a measure of spread, in this case of IQ scores. A standard deviation of 15 means 68% of the norm group has scored between 85 (100 – 15) and 115 (100 + 15). In other words, 68% of the norm group has a score within one standard deviation of the average (100). The deviation IQ corresponding to one SD below the mean will be 85 (100-15).

50 In the above study, which type of correlation can be employed to carry out the factor analysis of the test items ?

1 Biserial correlations
2 Phi coefficients
3 Point-Biserial correlations
4 Rank order correlations

***Ans.** (2)*

➲ *Exp.* Phi coefficients are the type of correlation which can be employed to carry out the factor analysis of the test items.

The Phi coefficient (also referred to as the mean square contingency coefficient) is a measure of association for two binary variables. In this case, the binary variables are the test items. The phi coefficient is the product-moment correlation coefficient when both variables are coded (0, 1).

PAPER III

1 The full form of ROC is

1 Receiver-Operating Characteristic
2 Response-Operating Characteristic
3 Receiver Operating Curve
4 Response Operating Curve

Ans. (1)

Exp. The full form of ROC is Receiver-Operating Characteristic.

Receiver-Operating Characteristic curve is used in signal detection theory. Receiver Operating-Characteristic curve or ROC curve is a graphical plot of specificity vs. sensitivity that illustrates the performance of a binary classifier system as its discrimination threshold is varied. The curve is created by plotting the True Positive Rate (TPR) against the False Positive Rate (FPR) at various threshold settings.

2 Match List I with List II and select the correct answer by choosing from the codes given below :

List I (Concepts)	List II (Explanations)
A. Engram	I. Engaging in conscious recollection
B. Explicit memory	II. Changes in dendrites and in the sensitivity of synapse through repeated stimulation
C. Long-term potentiation	III. Recollecting something without being consciously aware
D. Implicit memory	IV. The physical trace of memory in the brain

Codes

	A	B	C	D
1	I	II	III	IV
2	IV	I	II	III
3	II	III	IV	I
4	III	I	II	IV

Ans. (2)

Exp. The correct matching is A-IV, B-I, C-II and D-III.

Engram is the physical trace of memory in the brain. It is the hypothetical memory trace that is stored in the brain. The nature of the engram, in terms of the exact physiological changes that occur to encode a memory, is as yet unknown.

Explicit memory is the memory which engages in conscious recollection. Explicit memory is also known as declarative memory. It is long-term memory that can be consciously recalled: general knowledge or information about personal experiences that an individual retrieves in response to a specific need or request to do so.

Long-term potentiation is the changes in dendrites and in the sensitivity of synapse through repeated stimulation. It is the enhancement of synaptic transmission, which can last for weeks, caused by repeated brief stimulations of one nerve cell that trigger stimulation of a succeeding cell. The capacity for potentiation has been best shown in hippocampal tissue. LTP is studied as a model of the neural changes that underlie memory formation, and it may be a mechanism involved in some kinds of learning.

Implicit memory is the memory which recollects something without being consciously aware. Implicit memory is also known as procedural memory. For e.g. riding a bicycle. It is the memory for a previous event or experience that is produced indirectly, without an explicit request to recall the event and without awareness that memory is involved.

3 Read each of the following two statements, Assertion (A) and Reason (R) and indicate your answer using codes given below:

Assertion (A) An infant often acts as if objects stop existing when they are moved out of his perceptual range.

Reason (R) The infant has not yet developed the object concept.

Codes

1 Both (A) and (R) are true, and (R) is the correct explanation of (A)
2 Both (A) and (R) are true, but (R) is not the correct explanation of (A)
3 (A) is true, but (R) is false
4 (A) is false, but (R) is true

Ans. (1)

Exp. Both (A) and (R) are true, and (R) is the correct explanation of (A).

An infant often acts as if objects stop existing when they are moved out of his perceptual range. According to Jean Piaget theory of cognitive development infant does not develop the theory of object permanence until 12 months of age. The infant has not yet developed the object concept is also true. It occurs during the sensorimotor stage.

4 Mechanistic view of motivation can be characterised as

I. S-O-R explanation
II. Direction of behaviour is determined by bonds between stimulus and response or habits
III. Probability of elicitation of various habits depend upon prior reinforcement contingencies
IV. Behaviour once elicited persists until the removal of sustaining stimuli

Codes

1 I, II and III
2 I, III and IV
3 II, III and IV
4 I, II and IV

Ans. (3)

Exp. The correct codes are II, III, and IV.

The mechanistic approach assumes that motivational processes are automatic; that is, the organism, human or otherwise, need not understand what it is doing in order for the processes to work. Neither conscious awareness nor intent is assumed to be operative in the mechanistic approach. Researchers taking the mechanistic point of view are often interested in studying internal need states and genetically programmed behaviours.

Mechanistic view of motivation can be characterised as:

Direction of behaviour is determined by bonds between stimulus and response or habits. Direction is what a person wants to achieve, what they intend to do. It implies a target that motivated people try to "hit." That target may be to do well on a test or it may be to perform better than anyone else in a work group.

Probability of elicitation of various habits depend upon prior reinforcement contingencies. Reinforcement is a process of strengthening desirable behaviours, often through the use of rewards. It is based on the concept of "Law of Effect", the behaviour of individual towards positive consequences tends to repeat, but the behaviour of individual towards negative consequences tends not to repeat.

Behaviour once elicited persists until the removal of sustaining stimuli. The removal of motivating stimulus that leads to decrease in motivation but the behaviour persists until it is fully removed.

5 Read each of the following two statements, Assertion (A) and Reason (R) and indicate your answer using codes given below:

Assertion (A) In terms of SOI model, intelligence can be taken as a superset of creativity.

Reason (R) Divergent production is just one of the operations of intellect.

Codes

1 Both (A) and (R) are true, and (R) is the correct explanation of (A)
2 Both (A) and (R) are true, but (R) is not the correct explanation of (A)
3 (A) is true, but (R) is false
4 (A) is false, but (R) is true

Ans. *(1)*

Exp. Both (A) and (R) are true and (R) is the correct explanation of (A).

In terms of SOI model, intelligence can be taken as a superset of creativity is true. This is because Guilford's work on the Structure of Intellect (SOI) implies that creativity is a subset of intelligence where he considered divergent thinking as one of the cognitive operations in the SOI model.

Divergent production is just one of the operations of intellect is true. Convergent production, divergent production, memory recording, memory retention, cognition and evaluation are also the operations of intellect.

6 Which of the following is true of the threshold hypothesis regarding intelligence creativity relationship?

1 There is a 'U' type relationship between intelligence and creativity
2 There is 'inverted U' type relationship between intelligence and creativity
3 The relationship between the two is 'ill-defined' above a specific level of intelligence
4 The relationship between the two is ill defined below a specific level of intelligence

Ans. *(3)*

Exp. The relationship between the two is 'ill-defined' above a specific level of intelligence is true of the threshold hypothesis regarding intelligence creativity relationship.

The basic idea behind the threshold hypothesis is that high creativity requires high or at least above-average intelligence. At this, above-average intelligence is thought to form a necessary but not a sufficient condition for high creativity (Guilford, 1967).

7 Read each of the following two statements, Assertion (A) and Reason (R) and indicate your answer using codes given below:

Assertion (A) According to Rollo May, to grow psychologically, our values must be constantly challenged.

Reason (R) Rollo May proposed that Neurotic anxiety occurs when our values are challenged.

Codes

1 Both (A) and (R) are true, and (R) is the correct explanation of (A)
2 Both (A) and (R) are true, but (R) is not the correct explanation of (A)
3 (A) is true, but (R) is false
4 (A) is false, but (R) is true

Ans. *(3)*

Exp. (A) is true, but (R) is false.

According to Rollo May, to grow psychologically, our values must be constantly challenged. According to Rollo May's theory, healthy people challenge their destiny, cherish their freedom, and live authentically with other people and themselves.

Rollo May proposed that Neurotic anxiety occurs when our values are challenged is false. Neurotic anxiety occurs when it is disproportionate to the threat, does involve repression, or does involve other forms of intrapsychic conflict.

8 Match List I with List II and select the correct answer by choosing from the codes given below

List I (Concept)	List II (Explanation)
A. Monism	I. Brain functions as an undifferentiated whole
B. Dualism	II. Mind and body consists of the same substance
C. Equipotentiality	III. Body is material and mind is non-material
D. Reductionism	IV. Understanding of behavioural phenomenon in terms of biological principles

Codes

	A	B	C	D		A	B	C	D
1	I	II	III	IV	2	II	III	I	IV
3	IV	III	II	I	4	III	I	IV	II

Ans. *(2)*

Exp. The correct matching is A-II, B-III, C-I and D-IV.

Monism is the belief that the mind and body consists of the same substances or entities. It is the position that reality consists of a single substance, whether this is identified as mind (idealistic monism), matter (natural monism), or God (pantheism). In the context of the mind–body problem, monism is any position (such as neutral monism) that avoids dualism. George Berkeley is thè supporter of monism.

Dualism is the belief that the body is the material and mind is non-material. It is the position that reality consists of two separate substances, defined by René Descartes as thinking substance (mind) and extended substance (matter). In the context of the mind–body problem, dualism is the position that the mind and the body constitute two separate realms or substances. Dualistic positions raise the question of how mind and body interact in thought and behaviour. Plato, Aristotle and Rene Descartes are the supporters of dualism.

Equipotentiality is the concept where brain functions as an undifferentiated whole. It is based on Karl S. Lashley's hypothesis that large areas of cerebral cortex have similar potential to perform particular functions, including learning and other complex processes (e.g., maze navigation), so that intact cortical areas may take over functions of damaged or destroyed areas.

Reductionism is the understanding of behavioural phenomenon in terms of biological principles. It is the strategy of explaining or accounting for some phenomenon or construct by claiming that, when properly understood, it can be shown to be some other phenomenon or construct, where the latter is seen to be simpler, more basic, or more fundamental. A common form of reductionism is that in which psychological phenomena are reduced to biological phenomena, so that mental life is presented as merely a function of biological processes.

9 The correlation matrix was factor-analysed by the three methods listed below and the same number of factors were extracted in each case

I. Principal Components Method
II. Maximum Likelihood Method
III. Principal Axes Method

Arrange the above methods in descending order in terms of variance condensed

1 II, III and I
2 II, I and III
3 III, I and II
4 I, III and II

Ans. *(4)*

Exp. The correct sequence of methods in descending order in terms of variance condensed are Principal Components Method, Principal Axes Method, Maximum Likelihood Method.

Principle Components Method or Principal Component Analysis (PCA) is a statistical procedure that uses an orthogonal transformation to convert a set of observations of possibly correlated variables into a set of values of linearly uncorrelated variables called principal components.

Maximum Likelihood Method or Maximum Likelihood Estimation (MLE) is a method of estimating the parameters of a statistical model given observations, by finding the parameter values that maximise the likelihood of making the observations given the parameters.

Principal Axes Method or Principal-Axis Factor Analysis is an extraction method in which the coefficient of multiple determination of one variable with all other variables in the system is used as the initial communality estimate for that variable.

10 Which of the following are lesion techniques?

I. Aspiration Lesions
II. Radioactive frequency lesions
III. Cryogenic Blockade
IV. Bregma

Codes

1 I, II and IV
2 II, III and V
3 I, II and III
4 All of the above

Ans. *(3)*

Exp. Aspiration Lesions, Radioactive frequency lesions and Cryogenic Blockade are lesion techniques.

Aspiration Lesions are the image-guided puncture of a cystic lesion (such as a cyst, an abscess or bruising) or solid lesion (a growth) in order to remove a fluid or tissue sample with a suction needle. The hollow aspiration needles come in different sizes and lengths.

Radioactive frequency Lesions is a procedure in which special needles are used to create lesions along selected nerves. The needles heat the nerve to 80°C.

Cryogenic Blockade is like a reversible lesion where the tissue is temporarily cooled to the point that all neural activity in the vicinity of the probe stops.

11 People tend to be in better physical health and are better able to cope with stress when they are provided with

I. Physical comfort
II. Moral comfort
III. Psychological comfort
IV. Ideological comfort

Codes

1 I and II
2 II and III
3 III and IV
4 I and III

Ans. *(4)*

Exp. People tend to be in better physical health and are better able to cope with stress when they are provided with Physical and Psychological comfort.

Comfort (or being comfortable) is a sense of physical or psychological ease, often characterised as a lack of hardship. Persons who are lacking in comfort are uncomfortable or experiencing discomfort. Most of these universal themes falls under the physical comfort such as contact comfort, comfort food, and thermal comfort. A degree of psychological comfort can be achieved by recreating experiences that are associated with pleasant memories, such as engaging in familiar activities, maintaining the presence of familiar objects, and consumption of comfort foods.

12 Read each of the following two statements, Assertion (A) and Reason (R) and indicate your answer using codes given below:

Assertion (A) Leadership is a process where people merely make an attribution about other individuals.

Reason (R) People regard leader as a change agent.

Codes

1 Both (A) and (R) are true, and (R) is the correct explanation of (A)
2 Both (A) and (R) are true, but (R) is not the correct explanation of (A)
3 (A) is true, but (R) is false
4 (A) is false, but (R) is true

Ans. *(2)*

Exp. Both (A) and (R) are true, but (R) is not the correct explanation of (A).

Leadership is a process where people merely make an attribution about other individuals. This is true as according to the attribution theory of leadership, individuals make inferences about leadership ability by observing and interpreting certain environmental and behavioural cues. Leaders make attributions (try to understand) about the cause of the performance before deciding on the appropriate action to take.

People regard leader as a change agent. This is also true because a leader being an agent of change refers to a person who works tirelessly to make bold ideas a reality in order to create a more equitable, effective system. Regardless of their background or job profession, these trailblazers are making an impact to improve the lives of students across the region and beyond. However, it is based on transformational leadership. Therefore, the reason is correct but it does not explain the attribution theory of leadership.

13 Besides psychology which Behavioural Science contributed in the development of Organisational Psychology as a field of study?

I. Sociology
II. Anthropology
III. Political Science
IV. Social work

Codes

1 I and II   2 I, II and IV
3 II, III and IV   4 I, II and III

Ans. *(4)*

Exp. Besides psychology, Sociology, Anthropology and Political Science are the other behavioural sciences that contributed in the development of Organisational Psychology as a field of study.

Sociology is the study of social behaviours or society, including its origins, development, organizations, networks, institutions which uses various methods of empirical investigation and critical analysis to develop a body of knowledge about social order, disorder, and change.

Anthropology is the study of various aspects of humans within past and present societies. Social anthropology and cultural anthropology study the norms and values of societies. Linguistic anthropology studies how language affects social life.

Political Science is the study of system of governance and the analysis of political thoughts and behaviour. It helped to develop organizational psychology by understanding issues related to exercise of power and authority, nature of political conflict, etc.

14 Which of the following is not a positive symptom of Schizophrenia ?

I. Disorganised speech II. Bizarre behaviour
III. Flat affect IV. Hallucinations

Codes

1 Only IV   2 I and II
3 Only III   4 I and III

Ans. *(3)*

Exp. Flat affect is not a positive symptom of Schizophrenia.

Flat affect is a negative symptom of schizophrenia. A negative symptom is a deficit in the ability to perform the normal functions of living—for example, logical thinking, self-care, social interaction, and planning, initiating, and carrying out constructive actions—as shown in apathy, flat affect, emotional withdrawal, poor rapport, and lack of spontaneity. In flat affect, there is a total or near absence of appropriate emotional responses to situations and events.

A positive symptom is a symptom of schizophrenia that represents an excess or distortion of normal function, as distinct from a deficiency in or lack of normal function. Positive symptoms include hallucinations, disorganised speech and bizarre behaviour.

15 Read each of the following two statements, Assertion (A) and Reason (R) and indicate your answer using codes given below

Assertion (A) People belonging to a particular group have some common perceptual patterns.

Reason (R) Personal experiences influence one's perception.

Codes

1 Both (A) and (R) are true, and (R) is the correct explanation of (A)
2 Both (A) and (R) are true, but (R) is not the correct explanation of (A)
3 (A) is true, but (R) is false
4 (A) is false, but (R) is true

Ans. (1)

Exp. Both (A) and (R) are true and (R) is the correct explanation of (A).

People belonging to a particular group have some common perceptual patterns. The perception of people belonging to a particular group may be affected by two factors: the degree to which a consensual viewpoint among the group can be identified, which is defined as entitativity, and the degree to which the viewpoint is considered trustworthy, which is defined as epistemic trust.

Personal experience influence one's perception is also true because environment and one's community does have an impact on individual perceptual processes but each individual perceives differently.

16 A study shows that children from poor families drew large circles to represent a coin than the children from rich families. This is an example of

1 Perceptual constancy
2 Perceptual distortion
3 Perceptual set
4 Perceptual adaptation

Ans. (3)

Exp. A study shows that children from poor families drew large circles to represent a coin than the children from rich families. This is an example of Perceptual set.

It is a temporary readiness to perceive certain objects or events rather than others. It is a schema or frame that influences the way in which a person perceives objects, events, or people. In this case, the children from poor families perceive large circles as coins because of their perceptual set of considering a larger coin for more money.

17 Match List I with List II and select the correct answer by choosing from the codes given below :

List I	List II
A. Hit	I. Signal is present but response is No
B. Miss	II. Signal is present and response is Yes
C. False Alarm	III. Signal is absent and the response is No
D. Correct Rejection	IV. Signal is absent but the response is Yes

Codes

	A	B	C	D		A	B	C	D
1	IV	I	III	II	2	II	I	IV	III
3	II	I	III	IV	4	IV	III	II	I

Ans. (2)

Exp. The correct matching is A-II, B-I, C-IV and D-III.

Hit is when signal is present and response is Yes. It is the accurate identification of a signal in a signal detection task.

Miss is when signal is present but response is No. It is an incorrect indication by the participant that a signal is absent in a trial when it is actually present.

False Alarm is when signal is absent but the response is Yes. It is an incorrect observation by the participant that a signal is present in a trial when in fact it is absent.

Correct Rejection is when signal is absent and the response is No. It is an accurate decision by the participant that a target stimulus (signal) is not present.

These are all part of a signal detection task. It is a task in which the observer is required to discriminate between trials in which a target stimulus (the signal) is present and trials in which it is not (the noise). Signal detection tasks provide objective measures of perceptual sensitivity.

18 People often cannot remember where they heard what they heard. Sometimes people think they saw things they did not see or heard things they did not hear. This is the case of

1 Bias
2 Misattribution
3 Suggestibility
4 Blocking

Ans. (2)

Exp. People often cannot remember where they heard what they heard. Sometimes people think they saw things they did not see or heard things they did not hear. This is the case of Misattribution.

Misattribution of memory refers to the ability to remember information correctly, but being wrong about the source of that information. It is an incorrect inference as to the cause of an individual's or group's behaviour or of an interpersonal event. For example, misattribution of arousal is an effect in which the physiological stimulation generated by one stimulus is mistakenly ascribed to another source.

19 Memory retrieval is

I. Reconstructive
II. Constructive
III. Unconscious
IV. Symbolic

Codes

1 Only I
2 Only II
3 I and II
4 III and IV

Ans. (3)

Exp. Memory retrieval is both reconstructive and constructive.

Memory retrieval is the process of recovering or locating information stored in memory. It is the final stage of memory, after encoding and retention.

The constructive processing refers to the retrieval of memories in which those memories are altered, revised, or influenced by newer information. In this process, the memories are influenced by the meaning we give to events.

The reconstructive processing is the process of remembering conceived as involving the recreation of an experience or event that has been only partially stored in memory. When a memory is retrieved, the process uses general knowledge and schemas for what typically happens in order to reconstruct the experience or event.

20 Read each of the following two statements, Assertion (A) and Reason (R) and indicate your answer using codes given below:

Assertion (A) Words that are logically connected have been found to be recalled more easily than the words that were concretely connected.

Reason (R) The deeper the level of processing, the higher the level of recall achieved.

Codes

1 Both (A) and (R) are true, and (R) is the correct explanation of (A)
2 Both (A) and (R) are true, but (R) is not the correct explanation of (A)
3 (A) is true, but (R) is false
4 (A) is false, but (R) is true

***Ans.** (1)*

Exp. Both (A) and (R) are true and (R) is the correct explanation of (A).

Words that are logically connected have been found to be recalled more easily than the words that were concretely connected. This is true because it is based on Zinchenko's study where he presented sets of words which were related "logically" and "concretely" and the results indicated that the words were best recalled when they formed the goal of the action or a logical relationship under logical instructions which require deeper level of processing rather than shallow processing.

The deeper the level of processing, the higher the level of recall achieved is true. This is because deeper processing involves elaboration rehearsal which involves a more meaningful analysis (e.g. images, thinking, associations etc.) of information and leads to better recall.

21 Analogical reasoning consists of the following processes

I. Retrieval	II. Mapping
III. Evaluation	IV. Abstraction
V. Predictions	

Codes

1 I, II and IV	2 I, III and IV
3 I, II, IV and V	4 All of these

***Ans.** (4)*

Exp. Analogical reasoning consists of Retrieval, Mapping, Evaluation, Abstraction , Predictions.

Analogical reasoning is a thinking characterised by extrapolations from the familiar to the unfamiliar, rather than by the use of formal logic or consecutive reasoning. It is particularly important in problem solving and learning, in which known similarities between aspects of certain entities are used to make assumptions about other aspects or entities. It consists of :

1. *Retrieval* : In retrieval, a person may be reminded of a prior analogous situation in long-term memory.
2. *Mapping* : It involves a process of aligning the representations and projecting inferences from one analog to the other.
3. *Evaluation* : In evaluation, once an analogical mapping has been done, the analogy and its inferences are judged.
4. *Abstraction* : In abstraction, we may derive a more general understanding based on abstracting the common relational pattern.
5. *Prediction* : In prediction, we make predictions about a future event, or when predicting a scientific outcome by analogy with another domain.

22 Read each of the following two statements, Assertion (A) and Reason (R) and indicate your answer using codes given below:

Assertion (A) Patients with Amygdala damage are unable to recognise fear in others' facial expression.

Reason (R) Looking at fearful faces activates Amygdala.

Codes

1 Both (A) and (R) are true, and (R) is the correct explanation of (A)
2 Both (A) and (R) are true, but (R) is not the correct explanation of (A)
3 (A) is true, but (R) is false
4 (A) is false, but (R) is true

***Ans.** (1)*

Exp. Both (A) and (R) are true and (R) is the correct explanation of (A).

Patients with Amygdala damage are unable to recognise fear in others' facial expression. This is true because the human amygdala is a key structure for processing emotional facial expressions. Subjects who lack a functional amygdala can have a selective impairment in recognising fearful faces.

Looking at fearful faces activates Amygdala. This is true as blood-oxygen-level dependent functional magnetic resonance imaging (BOLD-fMRI) shows activation within the amygdala that is often highest for fearful faces. This explains why patients with amygdale damage are unable to recognize fear in others' facial expression.

23 In Sternberg's triarchic theory, the type of intelligence that involves the ability to think critically and analytically is called

1 Componential intelligence
2 Contextual intelligence
3 Crystallised intelligence
4 Experiential intelligence

***Ans.** (1)*

Exp. In Sternberg's triarchic theory, the type of intelligence that involves the ability to think critically and analytically is called as Componential intelligence.

Componential intelligence (also known as analytical intelligence) is a concept developed by Sternberg in his triarchic theory of intelligence. He proposed that intelligence is comprised of three different processes: practical, componential, and creative. Componential intelligence is the most recognized form of intelligence and is what most IQ tests measure. It includes logic, abstract thinking, verbal skills, and mathematical skills. It is measured by academic problem solving like analogies and puzzles.

24 Who among the following has given Regression Argument to support racial differences in intelligence ?

1 HJ Eysenck
2 MW Eysenck
3 Jensen
4 Burt and Vernon

Ans. (3)

Exp. Jensen has given Regression Argument to support racial differences in intelligence.

Jensen claimed, on the basis of his research, that general cognitive ability is essentially an inherited trait, determined predominantly by genetic factors rather than by environmental conditions. According to Jensen, regression effects can be predicted to differ for blacks and whites if the two races indeed have genetically different population means.

Accordingly, it would be predicted that upper status non-whites children should, on the average, regress downward toward the non-white population mean IQ of about 85, while lower status white children would regress upward toward the white population mean of about 100. In the downward and upward regression, the two groups' means could cross each other, the lower status whites thereby being slightly above the upper status whites. This supported racial difference in intelligence.

25 Creative thinking is a combination of flexibility in thinking and reorganisation in understanding to produce ________ and _________ .

1 new ideas; solutions
2 new ideas; conclusions
3 innovative ideas, conclusions
4 innovative ideas; solutions

Ans. (4)

Exp. Creative thinking is a combination of flexibility in thinking and reorganisation in understanding to produce innovative ideas and solutions.

Creative thinking is a process in which the individual generates a unique, novel and productive solution to a problem. It is defined as personal, imaginative thinking which produces useful solutions. In the book 'The Art of Though' from 1926, Graham Wallas proposed some of the stages of creativity thinking stages which include

(i) Preparation
(ii) Incubation
(iii) Illumination
(iv) Verification.

26 Which of the following components of creativity are scored in the 'Picture construction' sub-test of non-verbal Torrance Test of Creative Thinking (Non-verbal)?

I. Originality
II. Elaboration
III. Fluency
IV. Flexibility

Codes

1 I and II
2 I, II and IV
3 II and IV
4 I, II and III

Ans. (1)

Exp. Originality and Elaboration are the components of creativity which are scored in the 'Picture construction' sub-test of non-verbal Torrance Test of Creative Thinking (Non-verbal).

The Torrance Tests of Creativity Thinking (TTCT) is designed to identify and evaluate creative potential using two parts – a Verbal test and a Figural (non-verbal) test. The Verbal test contains seven subtests – Asking, Guessing Causes, Guessing Consequences, Product Improvement, Unusual Uses, Unusual Questions, and Just Suppose.

The Figural (Non-Verbal) test has three subsets – Picture Construction (from a marked cue), Picture Completion (again with cues), and Parallel Lines. The first of these subtests is scored on originality and elaboration while the remainder are scored on fluency, flexibility, originality, and elaboration.

Originality is the statistical rarity of the responses. Elaboration is the amount of detail in the responses.

27 The fear of one's own potential greatness and the ambivalent feelings toward greatness in others is called

1 Propium striving
2 Self-exonerating mechanism
3 Fluctuating asymmetry
4 Jonah-complex

Ans. (4)

Exp. The fear of one's own potential greatness and the ambivalent feelings toward greatness in others is called Jonah-complex.

Jonah complex, in the humanistic psychology of Abraham Maslow, is the inhibition of becoming fully self-actualised—that is, of fulfilling one's potential—for fear of facing new challenges and situations. It is named for the biblical prophet Jonah, who attempted to evade the mission imposed on him by God.

28 Read each of the following two statements, Assertion (A) and Reason (R) and indicate your answer using codes given below:

Assertion (A) Pituitary gland is frequently referred to as the master gland.

Reason (R) Most of pituitary hormones are tropic hormones.

Codes

1 Both (A) and (R) are true, and (R) is the correct explanation of (A)
2 Both (A) and (R) are true, but (R) is not the correct explanation of (A)
3 (A) is true, but (R) is false
4 (A) is false, but (R) is true

Ans. (1)

Exp. Both (A) and (R) are true and (R) is the correct explanation of (A).

Pituitary gland is frequently referred to as the Master gland. The pituitary gland is often dubbed the 'Master gland' because its hormones control other parts of the endocrine system, namely the thyroid gland, adrenal glands, ovaries and testes.

Most of pituitary hormones are tropic hormones is true because tropic hormones are hormones that have other endocrine glands as their target. Most tropic hormones are produced and secreted by the anterior pituitary.

29 Match List I with List II and select the correct answer by choosing from the codes given below:

List I (Variables)	List II (Explanations)
A. Confirmity	I. Social influence involving direct request from others
B. Compliance	II. Process in which members of extreme groups accept the beliefs and rules in unquestioning way
C. Intense indoctrination	III. Rules indicating how individuals are expected to behave in a specific situation
D. Social norms	IV. Social influence in which individuals change their attitude/behaviour to go along with existing norms

Codes

	A	B	C	D
1	IV	III	II	I
2	I	III	II	IV
3	IV	I	II	III
4	III	I	II	IV

Ans. *(4)*

➲ *Exp.* The correct matching is A-III, B-I, C-II, D-IV.

Conformity refers to the rules indicating how individuals are expected to behave in a specific situation. It is the adjustment of one's opinions, judgements, or actions so that they become more consistent with the opinions, judgements, or actions of other people or the normative standards of a social group or situation.

Compliance is the phenomenon where social influence involving direct request from others. It is submission to the demands, wishes, or suggestions of others. It is a change in a person's behaviour in response to a direct request.

Intense Indoctrination is the process in which members of extreme groups accept the beliefs and rules in unquestioning way. It is the social inculcation of beliefs, especially by individuals in positions of power or authority.

Social Norms refer to the social influence in which individuals change their attitude/behaviour to go along with existing norms. Social norm is any of the socially determined consensual standards that indicate what behaviours are considered typical in a given context (descriptive norms) and what behaviours are considered proper in the context (injunctive norms).

30 Match List I with List II and select the correct answer by choosing from the codes given below:

List I (Concept)	List II (Process)
A. Cohesiveness and conformity	I. Social influence based on individual's desire to be liked by others
B. Norms and social influence	II. Social influence based on individual's desire to be correct-to possess the accurate perceptions of the social world
C. Individuation	III. The need to be distinguishable from others in some respect
D. Information and social influence	IV. Accepting influence of those we like

Codes

	A	B	C	D
1	IV	III	I	II
2	III	IV	II	I
3	II	III	I	IV
4	IV	I	III	II

Ans. *(4)*

➲ *Exp.* The correct matching is A-IV, B-I, C-III and D-II.

Cohesiveness and conformity refer to accepting influence of those we like. The greater the cohesiveness, the greater the influence of the group members to persuade one another to conform to the group norms. The greater the conformity, the greater the identity of the members to the group and the greater the group cohesiveness.

Norms and social influence refer to the social influence based on individual's desire to be liked by others. It is the influence of other people that leads us to conform in order to be liked and accepted by them.

Individuation refers to the need to be distinguishable from others in some respect. It is the process through which a person achieves a sense of individuality separate from the identities of others and begins to consciously exist as a human in the world.

Information and social influence refer to the social influence based on individual's desire to be correct to-possess the accurate perceptions of the social world. It is an influence to accept information from another as evidence about reality. It comes into play when people are uncertain, either because stimuli are intrinsically ambiguous or because there is social disagreement.

31 The degree to which variations in environment can affect the development of individuals with the particular genotype is

1 Canalisation
2 Co-dominance
3 Reaction range
4 Ritualisation

Ans. *(3)*

➲ *Exp.* The degree to which variations in environment can affect the development of individuals with the particular genotype is Reaction range.

In genetics, Reaction range (also known as range of reaction) is when the phenotype (expressed characteristics) of an organism depends both on the organism's genetic characteristics (genotype) and the environment. For instance, two siblings raised together can have radically different IQs and natural talents. Reaction range is a range established by one's genes, between upper and lower boundaries for traits such as intelligence; one's environment determines where, within those limits, one will be.

32 Match List I with List II and select the correct answer by choosing from the codes given below :

List I (Theorist)	List II (Explanation)
A. Piaget	I. Children construct knowledge through social interaction with others.
B. Kohlberg	II. Children are embedded in a number of environmental systems and influences.
C. Bronfenbrenner	III. Children construct knowledge by transforming, organising and reorganising previous knowledge.
D. Vygotsky	IV. Children's moral thoughts are advanced through discussions with others.

Codes

	A	B	C	D		A	B	C	D
1	I	II	III	IV	2	II	IV	III	I
3	III	II	I	IV	4	III	IV	II	I

Ans. (4)

Exp. The correct matching is A-III, B-IV, C-II and D-I.

Jean Piaget introduced Piaget theory of cognitive development which states that children construct knowledge by transforming, organising and reorganising previous knowledge.

Kohlberg introduced Kohlberg theory of moral development which states that children's moral thoughts are advanced through discussions with others.

Bronfenbrenner introduced Ecological systems theory which states that children are embedded in a number of environmental systems and influences.

Vygotsky introduced Sociocultural theory which states that children construct knowledge through social interaction with others.

33 Three groups of subjects were formed with random assignment. Group I was tested under 'No drug' condition, Group II was tested under 'Low drug dosage' condition, and Group-III was tested under 'High drug dosage' condition. Each group was required to learn two lists, a list of CVC trigrams and a list of three-lettered meaningful words. The dependent variable was the number of items recalled after ten minutes after learning each list. This experiment employs

1 Randomised three group design
2 Randomised six group design
3 3×2 mixed factorial design
4 Randomised 3×2 factorial design

Ans. (3)

Exp. The given experiment employs 3×2 mixed factorial design. It means that each variable dependent factor is tested at 3 levels.

A mixed factorial design involves two or more independent variables, of which at least one is a within-subjects (repeated measures) factor and at least one is a between-groups factor. In the simplest case, there will be one between-groups factor and one within-subjects factor.

34 Read each of the following two statements, Assertion (A) and Reason (R) and indicate your answer using codes given below :

Assertion (A) Teachers need to teach children the use of multiple strategies : finding out what works well, when and where.

Reason (R) Most children are not consciously aware of a variety of strategies they can employ while learning.

Codes

1 Both (A) and (R) are true, and (R) is the correct explanation of (A)
2 Both (A) and (R) are true, but (R) is not the correct explanation of (A)
3 (A) is true, but (R) is false
4 (A) is false, but (R) is true

Ans. (1)

Exp. Both (A) and (R) are true and (R) is the correct explanation of (A).

Teachers need to teach children the use of multiple strategies: finding out what works well, when and where. This is true as the children will have experiences in which they solve problems and experience world in more than one way. The multiple strategies are referred to students' ability to solve problems in more than one way.

Most children are not consciously aware of a variety of strategies they can employ while learning. This is true because at times children are not consciously aware of the different strategies they possess to learn, and that is where the role of teacher comes in to guide them and make them aware.

35 Which of the following sequence is correct in case of steps in a goal-setting program for students ?

1 Specify the objectives to be accomplished → Define goal difficulty → Specify the time span for assessment of performance → Discuss goal attainment strategies
2 Discuss goal attainment strategies → Define goal difficulty → Specify the objectives to be accomplished → Specify time span for assessment of performance

3 Specify the time span for assessment of performance → Discuss goal attainment strategies → Specify the objectives to be accomplished → Define goal difficulty
4 Define goal difficulty → Discuss goal attainment strategies → Specify time span for assessment of performance → Specify the objectives to be accomplished

Ans. (1)

Exp. The correct sequence in case of steps in a goal-setting program for students is as follows:

Specify the objectives to be accomplished → Define goal difficulty → Specify the time span for assessment of performance → Discuss goal attainment strategies

Goal setting is a process that establishes specific, time-based behaviour targets that are measurable, achievable, and realistic. Goal setting is effective only if individuals concerned are aware of what is to be accomplished and accept the goals for themselves, believing in their attainability.

Specify the objectives to be accomplished : It requires identifying the objective and laying out a plan that maximises efficiency and execution of the objective.

Define goal difficulty : The goals should be specific, time constrained and difficult. Vague goals reduce limited attention resources; goals require realistic time restrictions, illogically short time limits, intensify the difficulty of the goal outside the intentional level and, disproportionate time limits are not encouraging. Difficult goals should be set ideally at the 90th percentile of performance assuming that motivation and not ability is limiting attainment of that level of performance.

Specify the time span for assessment of performance : It is needed to establish a time frame, when does the goal need to be accomplished and the performance is assessed on a regular basis.

Discuss goal attainment strategies : It should be ensured that the new strategies are used and an additional performance goal could motivate students to actually use the discovered or acquired strategies to attain the desired outcome.

36 The field of Industrial Psychology was created/developed by

1 FB Taylor 2 H Munsterberg
3 Elton Mayo 4 H Mintzberg

Ans. (2)

Exp. The field of Industrial Psychology was created/ developed by H. Munsterberg.

Hugo Münsterberg was a German-American psychologist. He was one of the pioneers in applied psychology, extending his research and theories to industrial/organisational (I/O), legal, medical, clinical, educational and business settings. Münsterberg's works Vocation and Learning (1912) and Psychology and Industrial Efficiency (1913) are usually considered the beginning of what would later become known as industrial psychology.

37 Match List I with List II and select the correct answer by choosing from the codes given below :

List I (Therapy)	List II (Therapist)
A. Systematic desensitisation	I. Albert Bandura
B. Social-Learning Therapy	II. Meichenbaum
C. Cognitive Therapy	III. Joseph Wolpe
D. Cognitive Behaviour Modification	IV. Aaron Beck

Codes

	A	B	C	D
1	I	II	III	IV
2	III	I	IV	II
3	II	III	IV	I
4	IV	III	II	I

Ans. (2)

Exp. The correct matching is A-III, B-I, C-IV and D-II

Systematic desensitisation was introduced by Joseph Wolpe. It is a behavioural therapy used to treat anxiety disorders like PTSD, phobias etc.

Social-Learning Therapy was introduced by Albert Bandura. It emphasise that we learn social behaviour by imitating the behaviour of others.

Cognitive Therapy was introduced by Aaron Beck. This therapy focuses on present thoughts rather than depending upon past.

Cognitive Behaviour Modification was introduced by Donald Meichenbaum. This style of therapy focuses on positive thoughts by discouraging negative thoughts.

38 A procedure that provides information to the learner in small steps, guarantees immediate feedback and allows the learner to determine the pace with which to complete the task. It is called

1 Auto shaping 2 Chaining
3 Programmed learning 4 Continuous contracting

Ans. (3)

Exp. A procedure that provides information to the learner in small steps, guarantees immediate feedback and allows the learner to determine the pace with which to complete the task. It is called as Programmed learning.

Programmed learning is an individualised and systematic instructional strategy for classroom learning and self-learning. Programmed learning received its major impetus from B. F. Skinner and is based on his theory of operant conditioning, according to which learning is best accomplished in small, incremental steps with immediate reinforcement, or reward, for the learner.

Therefore, the learning material is broken down into small chunks of information and is followed by a comprehension question to be answered by the learner, who receives immediate feedback with regard to the correctness of the answer. If the answer is correct, the learner may proceed to the next chunk; otherwise he or she must go back to the previous chunk and try it again. Thus, programmed learning is based on the principles of small steps, self-pacing, and immediate feedback.

39 Behaviour modification by the application of operant conditioning consists of the following

I. Token economy
II. Punishment
III. Time-out
IV. Withdrawal of reinforcement

Codes

1 I and II 2 II and III
3 I and IV 4 I and III

Ans. (4)

Exp. Behaviour modification by the application of operant conditioning consists of Token economy and Time out. *Token Economy* is a system of behaviour modification based on the principles of Operant Conditioning. It is often used by people who practice Applied Behaviour Analysis (ABA). A token economy rewards good deeds with items that can be used to trade for a desirable item later on.

Time-out (also known as social exclusion) is a form of behavioural modification that involves temporarily separating a child from an environment where unacceptable behaviour occurred.

40 Match List I with List II and select the correct answer by choosing from the codes given below :

List I	List II
A. Observational learning	I. Learning where an object is located
B. Place learning	II. A response that can be observed by others
C. Overt responding	III. The process whereby information is acquired by attending to events in the environment
D. Latent learning	IV. Learning that takes place independent of reinforcement

Codes

	A	B	C	D		A	B	C	D
1	II	IV	III	I	2	III	I	II	IV
3	II	I	III	IV	4	III	IV	II	I

Ans. (2)

Exp. The correct matching is A-III, B-I, C-II and D-IV.

Observational learning is the process whereby information is acquired by attending to events in the environment. It is the acquisition of information, skills, or behaviour through watching the performance of others, either directly or via such media as films and videos.

Place learning is the learning where an object is located. It is the learning of locations or physical positions of goals (e.g., where food can be found).

Overt responding is a response that can be observed by others. It is any observable or external reaction, such as pointing to indicate one's preference from among a set of objects or answering yes to a question.

Latent learning is a learning that takes place independent of reinforcement. Edward Tolman was the one who first introduced latent learning. It is the learning that is acquired without conscious effort, awareness, intention, or reinforcement and is not manifested as a change in performance until a specific need for it arises.

41 According to self-determination theory ______ and ____ form the basis for intrinsic motivation.

1 competence ; relatedness 2 competence ; autonomy
3 control ; autonomy 4 control ; competence

Ans. (2)

Exp. According to self-determination theory competence and autonomy form the basis for intrinsic motivation.

Self-determination theory (SDT) is the concept that states that the regulation of behaviour varies along a continuum from externally controlled (e.g., to obtain rewards or avoid punishments) to autonomous or intrinsically motivated (e.g., to have fun or explore interests). The theory emphasises the importance of intrinsic motivation for producing healthy adjustment and asserts that negative outcomes ensue when people feel that they are driven mainly by external forces and extrinsic rewards.

The theory posits that goal directed behaviours are driven by three innate psychological needs: autonomy (the need to feel ownership of one's behaviour), competence (the need to produce desired outcomes and to experience mastery), and relatedness (the need to feel connected to others) in every human being.

42 Match List I with List II and select the correct answer by choosing from the codes given below:

List I (Concept)	List II (Explanation)
A. Fixed Action Pattern	I. When two incompatible response tendencies are simultaneously aroused, the organisms may display behaviours that appear to be irrelevant to the situation
B. Displacement Activity	II. Highly stereotyped responses that are assumed to be genetically programmed reactions that occur in the presence of a particular 'sign' stimulus
C. Hedonic Bias	III. A state in which a person performs an action because the act itself is satisfying or rewarding internally.
D. Intrinsic motivation	IV. Tendency to take more credit for success than to take responsibility for failure

Codes

	A	B	C	D		A	B	C	D
1	I	II	III	IV	2	II	I	IV	III
3	III	IV	II	I	4	IV	III	I	II

Ans. (2)

Exp. The correct matching is A-II, B-I, C-IV and D-III.

Fixed Action Pattern are highly stereotyped responses that are assumed to be genetically programmed reactions that occur in the presence of a particular 'sign' stimulus. It is a stereotyped, genetically pre-programmed, species-specific behavioral sequence that is evoked by a releaser stimulus and is carried out without sensory feedback.

Displacement Activity is done when two incompatible response tendencies are simultaneously aroused, the organisms may display behaviours that appear to be irrelevant to the situation. It is apparently irrelevant activity that is produced as the result of two contradicting instincts in particular situations of conflict or thwarting.

Hedonic Biases are the tendency to take more credit for success than to take responsibility for failure. It refers to when people have a general habit of attributing success to themselves and attributing failure to external factors.

Intrinsic motivation is a state in which a person performs an action because the act itself is satisfying or rewarding internally. It is an incentive to engage in a specific activity that derives from pleasure in the activity itself (e.g., a genuine interest in a subject studied) rather than because of any external benefits that might be obtained (e.g., money, course credits).

43 Match List I with List II and select the correct answer by choosing from the codes given below :

List I (Concept)	List II (Meaning)
A. Dasein	I. Physical, objective world
B. Umwelt	II. Human interactions
C. Eigenwelt	III. Individual as being in the world
D. Mitwelt	IV. Self-awareness

Codes

	A	B	C	D		A	B	C	D
1	I	III	IV	II	2	I	III	II	IV
3	III	I	IV	II	4	III	I	II	IV

Ans. (3)

Exp. The correct matching is A-III, B-I, C-IV and D-II.

Dasein refers to an individual as being in the world. In the thought of German philosopher Martin Heidegger (1889–1976), it is the particular kind of being manifest in humans. It is their being as Dasein that allows humans access to the larger question of being in general, since access to the world is always through what their own being makes possible.

Umwelt refers to the physical, objective world. In the thought of German philosopher Martin Heidegger (1889–1976), it is that aspect of Dasein (being-in-the-world) that is constituted by a person's engagement with the world immediately around him or her.

Eigenwelt refers to self-awareness. In the thought of German philosopher Martin Heidegger (1889–1976), it is that aspect of Dasein (being-in-the-world) that is constituted by a person's relationship to the self.

Mitwelt refers to human interactions. In the thought of German philosopher Martin Heidegger (1889–1976), it is that aspect of Dasein (being-in-the-world) that is constituted by a person's relationships and interactions with other people.

44 A group of 25 subjects were tested on reaction time under three conditions – low stressful, moderately stressful and highly stressful. The data were analysed by suitable ANOVA.

What would be the degrees of freedom for 'stressfulness × subjects' interaction ?

1 2   2 3
3 24   4 48

Ans. (4)

Exp. The degrees of freedom for 'stressfulness × subjects' interaction are 48.

Degree of freedom $= n - 1 = 25 - 1 = 24$

The degrees of freedom for 'stressfulness × subjects' interaction are 24*2=48

45 Read each of the following two statements Assertion (A) and Reason (R) and indicate your answer using codes given below :

Assertion (A) Most experimental studies of lesion effects are studies of bilateral than unilateral lesions.

Reason (R) Behavioural effects of unilateral lesions in all brain structures can be difficult to detect.

Codes

1 Both (A) and (R) are true, and (R) is the correct explanation of (A)
2 Both (A) and (R) are true, but (R) is not the correct explanation of (A)
3 (A) is true, but (R) is false
4 (A) is false, but (R) is true

Ans. (1)

Exp. Both (A) and (R) are true, and (R) is the correct explanation of (A).

Most experimental studies of lesion effects are studies of bilateral than unilateral lesions. This is true as human and animal lesion studies have shown that behaviour can be catastrophically impaired after bilateral lesions but that unilateral damage often produces little or no effect, even controlling for lesion extent.

Behavioural effects of unilateral lesions in all brain structures can be difficult to detect. This is true because unilateral lesions occur in only one part of the brain so detection of behavioural effects becomes difficult. Therefore, most of experimental studies of lesion effects are studies of bilateral than unilateral lesions.

46 An act, that helps or is designed to help others regardless of the helper's motive is called

1 Prosocial Behaviour   2 Altruism
3 Nurturance   4 Social obligation

Ans. (1)

Exp. An act that helps or is designed to help others regardless of the helper's motive is called as Prosocial behaviour.

Prosocial behaviour is a voluntary behaviour intented to benefit another. Thus it includes behaviours such as helping, sharing or providing comfort to another.

47 Difference between what one can accomplish with or without help is called

1 Zone of proximal development
2 Resilience
3 Identity fusion
4 Transition

Ans. (1)

Exp. The difference between what one can accomplish with or without help is called Zone of proximal development.

The Zone of proximal development was introduced in Lev Vygotsky's sociocultural theory. It is the difference between a child's actual level of ability and the level of ability that he or she can achieve when assisted by, or working in cooperation with, older or more experienced partners (e.g., adults or more knowledgeable peers). Vygotsky asserted that what children can do with the assistance of others is even more indicative of their developmental status than what they can do alone.

48 Read each of the following two statements, Assertion (A) and Reason (R) and indicate your answer using codes given below.

Assertion (A) According to Adler, a child's birth order is important in shaping his/her personality.

Reason (R) There are unique experiences associated with birth order of every child.

Codes

1 Both (A) and (R) are true, and (R) is the correct explanation of (A)
2 Both (A) and (R) are true, but (R) is not the correct explanation of (A)
3 (A) is true, but (R) is false
4 (A) is false, but (R) is true

Ans. (1)

Exp. Both (A) and (R) are true and (R) is the correct explanation of (A).

According to Adler, a child's birth order is important in shaping his/her personality. Alfred Adler was one of the first theorists to suggest that birth order influences personality. He argued that birth order can leave an indelible impression on an individual's style of life, which is one's habitual way of dealing with the tasks of friendship, love, and work.

There are unique experiences associated with birth order of every child. According to Adler, firstborns are 'dethroned' when a second child comes along, and this may have a lasting influence on them, causing them to develop a Middle child syndrome. Younger and only children may be pampered and spoiled, which was suggested to affect their later personalities. The reason is true and explains why the child's birth order is important in shaping his/her personality.

49 Punishment given frequently to young students leads to

1 improved interpersonal relationships
2 desirable behaviours
3 better academic performance
4 fear, anger and worry

Ans. (4)

Exp. Punishment given frequently to young students leads to fear, anger and worry.

Punishment is anything that reduces the frequency of unwanted behaviours. In theory, punishment should suppress inappropriate behaviours totally, but this is rarely the actual result. Whether corporal or not, punishment simply teaches children that if they break rules they will suffer negative consequences. Punishment does not necessarily teach children why the rules are in place, why the rules are important or how they can act in accordance of the rules.

Unfortunately, punishment is only effective at deterring inappropriate behaviours in so far as it provokes fear in children. Children come to fear for their possessions privileges preferences and even safety and well being.

50 Persons with genetic 'markers' for schizophrenia have a physical vulnerability to the disorder but will not develop schizophrenia unless they are exposed to critical times in development. This is according to

1 Biological model
2 Social learning model
3 Neurobiological model
4 Stress-vulnerability model

Ans. (4)

Exp. Persons with genetic 'markers' for schizophrenia have a physical vulnerability to the disorder but will not develop schizophrenia unless they are exposed to critical times in development. This is according to Stress-vulnerability model.

In this model, vulnerabilities are enduring, although changeable traits, impacted by factors such as genetics, life events and adverse interpersonal environments. The greater an individual's level of vulnerability, the less stress is required to trigger the symptoms of a mental illness.

51 The influence of surrounding environment on perception is called

1 Hoffding function
2 Priming effect
3 Law of Pragnaz
4 Context effect

Ans. (4)

Exp. The influence of surrounding environment on perception is called as Context effect.

A context effect is an aspect of cognitive psychology that describes the influence of environmental factors on one's perception of a stimulus. The impact of context effects is considered to be part of top-down design. Context effects can impact our daily lives in many ways such as word recognition, learning abilities, memory, and object recognition. It can have an extensive effect on marketing and consumer decisions.

52 Read each of the following two statements, Assertion (A) and Reason (R) and indicate your answer using codes given below :

Assertion (A) Hull proposed that Reaction Potential (SER) is the product of Habit Strength (SHR) and Drive (D) from this some testable prediction can be made about the rate of eye lid conditioning in relation to drive.

Reason (R) Hull's theory is based on Hypothetico-Deductive model which involved deducting testable consequences based on postulates.

Codes

1 Both (A) and (R) are true, and (R) is the correct explanation of (A)
2 Both (A) and (R) are true, but (R) is not the correct explanation of (A)
3 (A) is true, but (R) is false
4 (A) is false, but (R) is true

Ans. (2)

Exp. Both (A) and (R) are true, but (R) is not the correct explanation of (A).

Hull proposed that Reaction Potential (SER) is the product of Habit Strength (SHR) and Drive (D) from this some testable prediction can be made about the rate of eye lid conditioning in relation to drive. Reaction Potential (SER) is the output in Hull's system, which is directly correlated with response strength measures such as reaction latency or amplitude of response. The magnitude of RP is determined by a number of variables but chief among these are Habit strength (SHR) and Drive level (D). Hull assumes that RP is related to Habit Strength (SHR) and to drive according to multiplicative function SER = SHR x D.

Hull's theory is based on Hypothetico-Deductive model which involved deducting testable consequences based on postulates. The hypothetico-deductive method is a method of scientific inquiry in which the credibility or explanatory power of a falsifiable hypothesis is tested by making predictions on the basis of this hypothesis and determining whether these predictions are consistent with empirical observations.

53 Long Term Potentiation mean facilitation of synaptic transmission following

1 High-frequency electrical stimulation applied to pre-synaptic neurons
2 Low-frequency electrical stimulation applied to pre-synaptic neurons
3 High-frequency electrical stimulations applied to post-synaptic neurons
4 Low-frequency electrical stimulation applied to post-synaptic neurons

Ans. (1)

Exp. Long Term Potentiation means facilitation of synaptic transmission follows high-frequency electrical stimulation applied to pre-synaptic neurons.

Long-Term Potentiation (LTP) is a persistent strengthening of synapses based on recent patterns of activity. These are patterns of synaptic activity that produce a long-lasting increase in signal transmission between two neurons. It is one of several phenomena underlying synaptic plasticity, the ability of chemical synapses to change their strength.

54 Which one of the following is not a mnemonic device?

1 Method of Loci 2 Method of reinforcement
3 Categorical clustering 4 Pegword system

Ans. (2)

Exp. Method of reinforcement is not a mnemonic device. Method of loci, Categorical clustering and Pegword system are mnemonic devices.

Mnemonic devices are techniques a person can use to help them improve their ability to remember something.

Method of Loci is a method of memory enhancement which uses visualisations with the use of spatial memory, familiar information about one's environment, to quickly and efficiently recall information.

Categorical clustering is a way of organising information in memory. This strategy can make it easier to remember information and recall it later on.

Pegword system is a strategy that utilises the principle of learning and recalling new information by association with familiar facts.

55 Read each of the following two statements, Assertion (A) and Reason (R) and indicate your answer using codes given below :

Assertion (A) Second order factors can be obtained from promax rotated first order factors.

Reason (R) Promax rotation is a method of oblique rotation.

Codes

1 Both (A) and (R) are true, and (R) is the correct explanation of (A)
2 Both (A) and (R) are true, but (R) is not the correct explanation of (A)
3 (A) is true, but (R) is false
4 (A) is false, but (R) is true

Ans. *(1)*

Exp. Both (A) and (R) are true and (R) is the correct explanation of (A).

Second order factors can be obtained from promax rotated first-order factors. This is true as Promax rotation is an oblique rotation, which allows factors to be correlated. This rotation can be calculated more quickly than a direct oblimin rotation, so it is useful for large datasets.

Promax rotation is a method of oblique rotation. This is true as promax is one of the rotation methods under oblique rotation, along with varimax, direct oblimin, quartimax, and equimax. It explains why second order factors can be obtained from promax rotated first-order factors.

56 **In an experiment one group of subjects was asked to estimate the product of $8 \times 7 \times 6 \times 5 \times 4 \times 3 \times 2 \times 1$ in 5 seconds. The other group was asked to estimate the product of $1 \times 2 \times 3 \times 4 \times 5 \times 6 \times 7 \times 8$ in the same time. The former group attained a larger estimate than the later group. The biasing effect involved in this case is because of**

1 Availability of information
2 Adjustment
3 Representativeness
4 Gambler's fallacy

Ans. *(2)*

Exp. The biasing effect involved in the given case is because of Adjustment.

The anchoring and adjustment heuristic was first theorised by Amos Tversky and Daniel Kahneman. According to this theory, once an anchor is set, people adjust away from it to get to their final answer; however, they adjust insufficiently, resulting in their final guess being closer to the anchor than it would be otherwise. Adjustment is a psychological heuristic that influences the way people intuitively assess probabilities.

57 **Match List I with List II and select the correct answer by choosing from the codes given below:**

List I (Phenomenon)	List II (Explanation)
A. Thinking	I. Process of choosing between two or more alternatives on the basis of information about them
B. Reasoning	II. Processing information in various ways to move towards a desired goal
C. Decision-making	III. Mental activity through which we transform available information in order to reach conclusion
D. Problem solving	IV. An activity that involves the manipulation of mental representation of various features of the external world

Codes

	A	B	C	D		A	B	C	D
1	I	II	III	IV	2	II	III	IV	I
3	III	IV	II	I	4	IV	I	II	III

Ans. *(1)*

Exp. The correct matching is A-I, B-II, C-III and D-IV.

Thinking is the process of choosing between two or more alternatives on the basis of information about them. It is cognitive behaviour in which ideas, images, mental representations, or other hypothetical elements of thought are experienced or manipulated. In this sense, thinking includes imagining, remembering, problem solving, daydreaming, free association, concept formation, and many other processes.

Reasoning is the process of processing information in various ways to move towards a desired goal. It is a type of thinking in which logical processes of an inductive or deductive character are used to draw conclusions from facts or premises.

Decision-Making is the mental activity through which we transform available information in order to reach conclusion. It is the cognitive process of choosing between two or more alternatives, ranging from the relatively clear cut (e.g., ordering a meal at a restaurant) to the complex (e.g., selecting a mate).

Problem solving is an activity that involves the manipulation of mental representation of various features of the external world. It is the process by which individuals attempt to overcome difficulties, achieve plans that move them from a starting situation to a desired goal, or reach conclusions through the use of higher mental functions, such as reasoning and creative thinking.

58 **Read each of the following two statements, Assertion (A) and Reason (R) and indicate your answer using codes given below:**

Assertion (A) In general, members of joint family tend to be low on stress than those of nucleus family.

Reason (R) Social support increases the stress responses.

Codes

1 Both (A) and (R) are true, and (R) is the correct explanation of (A)
2 Both (A) and (R) are true, but (R) is not the correct explanation of (A)
3 (A) is true, but (R) is false
4 (A) is false, but (R) is true

Ans. *(3)*

Exp. (A) is true, but (R) is false.

In general, members of joint family tend to be low on stress than those of nucleus family is true because in joint family people give emotional support, moral support, and financial support to one another. Thus, family members can be very comforting to us when we are faced with a wide range of life stressors, and they can be extremely helpful in our efforts to manage these challenges.

Social support increases the stress responses is false as whenever social support increases your stress level tends to decrease. Social support can be thought of as the soothing impact of friends, family, and acquaintances. Social support is connected to favorable health outcomes because it has several beneficial physiological effects in stressful situations.

59 Rogers use Q-sort technique to identify

1 Internal and external frame of reference
2 Real self and Ideal self
3 Conditional and unconditional positive regard
4 Conditions of worth and worthlessness

Ans. (2)

Exp. Rogers use Q-sort technique to identify real self and ideal self.

'Q-sort' is a self-assessment procedure for measuring congruence between the real self and the ideal self, a state of internal consistency which Carl Rogers saw as an important to healthy personality growth. Carl Rogers believed that for a person to achieve self-actualisation they must be in a state of congruence.

This means that self-actualisation occurs when a person's 'ideal self' is congruent with their actual behaviour.

60 Which of the following are the characteristics of Nomothetic approach to personality ?

I. Emphasis on variations in a person
II. Interpretation of test scores
III. Group norms
IV. General laws of personality

Codes

1 I, III and IV
2 II, III and IV
3 I, II and IV
4 All of these

Ans. (2)

Exp. The characteristics of Nomothetic approach to personality are interpretation of test scores, group norms and general laws of personality.

Nomothetic approach is related to the formulation of general laws as opposed to the study of an individual case. A nomothetic approach involves the study of groups of people or cases for the purpose of discovering those general and universally valid laws or principles that characterise the average person or case. The characteristics are described as follows:

- *Interpretation of test scores* : Nomothetic interpretations tend to be quantitative. They compare the scores of the individual to a relevant comparison group. Placing the results in a relevant context allows the psychologist to distinguish average or typical scores from various types of exceptional scores. Psychometric testing and other quantitative methods are consistent with a nomothetic approach to test interpretation.
- *Group norms* : Psychologists explain the norm group used to interpret the test; they may interpret the results in relation to several norm groups.
- *General laws of personality* : Psychologists who adopt this approach are mainly concerned with studying what we share with others (i.e. similarities between people). Therefore, the nomothetic approach involves establishing laws or generalisations that apply to all people.

61 Sensory-specific satiety takes place in

1 Papillae
2 Thalamus
3 Nucleus of Solitary Tract (NST)
4 Insula

Ans. (3)

Exp. Sensory-specific satiety takes place in Nucleus of Solitary Tract (NST).

Nucleus of Solitary Tract (NST) is a collection of neural cell bodies in the medulla oblongata of the brainstem that relays information from the intermediate nerve, glossopharyngeal nerve, and vagus nerve. Gustatory (taste) neurons project to the anterior division of the nucleus, with touch and temperature afferents immediately lateral and visceral afferents medial and caudal. Gustatory neurons project from the solitary nucleus to control reflexes of acceptance or rejection, to anticipate digestive processes, and to activate higher levels of the taste system.

62 The multiple correlation of academic achievement with Numerical ability, Abstract reasoning, and Verbal ability was found to be 0.6. Which of the following statement/s would be true in this context?

I. None of the three predictors would correlate more than 0.6 with academic achievement.
II. The three predictors together would explain 36 per cent variance in academic achievement.
III. At least, one predictor would correlate 0.6 with academic achievement.
IV. The three predictors would explain 60 per cent of variance in academic achievement.

1 Only II
2 I and II
3 II and IV
4 III and IV

Ans. (2)

Exp. The multiple correlation of academic achievement with Numerical ability, Abstract reasoning, and Verbal ability was found to be 0.6. Statement I and II are true in this context.

None of the three predictors would correlate more than 0.6 with academic achievement. A multiple correlation coefficient (R) yields the maximum degree of liner relationship that can be obtained between two or more independent variables and a single dependent variable.

The three predictors together would explain 36 per cent variance in academic achievement. It is clearly mentioned that multiple correlation with three variables, which are academic achievement, numerical and verbal ability was found to be 0.6. The variance can be calculated by squaring the correlation coefficient and multiplying it by 100. Here, R = 0.6, variance= $R^2 \times 100 = 0.6^2 \times 100 = 36$. Therefore, the variance is 36%.

63 The different schemas had an impact on social cognitive, which refer to

I. Persons II. Groups
III. Roles IV. Events

Codes

1 I, II and III 2 II, III and IV
3 I, II and IV 4 I, III and IV

Ans. *(4)*

Exp. The different schemas had an impact on social cognitive, which refer to persons, roles and events. Social cognition is the area of social psychology that examines how people perceive and think about their social world. It mainly refers to how people deal with own species (members of the same species) or even across species (such as pet) information, which include four stages i.e. encoding, storage, retrieval and processing. In the area of social psychology, social cognition refers to a specific approach in which these processes are studied according to the methods of cognitive psychology and information processing theory.

64 Match List I with List II and select the correct answer by choosing from the codes given below :

List I (Test/Experiment)	List II (Concept)
A. Strange Situation Test	I. Observation Learning
B. Visual-Cliff Test	II. Morality
C. Bodo-Doll Experiment	III. Attachment
D. Heinz Dilemma	IV. Depth perception

Codes

	A	B	C	D		A	B	C	D
1	II	I	IV	III	2	III	I	IV	II
3	III	IV	I	II	4	II	IV	I	III

Ans. *(3)*

Exp. The correct matching is A-III, B-IV, C-I and D-II.

The *Strange Situation Test* explains the concept of attachment. The Strange situation is a standardised procedure devised by Mary Ainsworth in the 1970s to observe attachment security in children within the context of caregiver relationships. It applies to infants between the age of 9 and 18 months. The procedure involves series of eight episodes lasting approximately 3 minutes each, whereby a mother, child and stranger are introduced, separated and reunited.

The *Visual-Cliff Test* explains the concept of depth perception. Eleanor J. Gibson and Richard D. Walk (1960) investigated the ability of newborn animals and human infants to detect depth. Gibson and Walk tested whether youngsters would crawl over an apparent cliff - if the neonates did it could be assumed that the ability to see depth was not inborn. If they did not, this would support a nativist view - that perceptual abilities are innate.

The *Bobo-Doll Experiment* explains the concept of observational learning. Bandura (1961) conducted a controlled experiment study to investigate if social behaviors (i.e., aggression) can be acquired by observation and imitation.

The *Heinz Dilemma* explains the concept of morality. It is a story about an ethical dilemma faced by a character named Heinz that was used by Lawrence Kohlberg to assess the moral reasoning skills of those he asked to respond to it. Having exhausted every other possibility, Heinz must decide whether to steal an expensive drug that offers the only hope of saving his dying wife.

65 Read each of the following two statements, Assertion (A) and Reason (R) and indicate your answer using codes given below:

Assertion (A) According to Vygotsky, human thinking and reasoning are products of social activity.

Reason (R) Every cognitive process appears first on social plane and then on psychological plane after internalisation.

Codes

1 Both (A) and (R) are true, and (R) is the correct explanation of (A)
2 Both (A) and (R) are true, but (R) is not the correct explanation of (A)
3 (A) is true, but (R) is false
4 (A) is false, but (R) is true

Ans. *(1)*

Exp. Both (A) and (R) are true, and (R) is the correct explanation of (A).

According to Vygotsky, human thinking and reasoning are products of social activity. This is true as Vygotsky's sociocultural theory of human learning describes learning as a social process and the origination of human intelligence in society or culture. The major theme of Vygotsky's theoretical framework is that social interaction plays a fundamental role in the development of cognition.

Every cognitive process appears first on social plane and then on psychological plane after internalisation. This is true as the main idea of the theory is that the ways people interact with others and the culture they live in shape their mental abilities. This means that the skills children learn first are related to interactions with others and they then take that information and use it within themselves. Hence, it explains how thinking and reasoning are products of social activity.

66 The most effective way for dealing with bullying in schools is

1 to give harsh punishment to those students who indulge in such behaviour
2 to provide counselling to students who are potential bullies and clearly communicate to them that such behaviour will not be tolerated

3 to isolate such students and ban them from participation in any extra-curricular activity
4 to ignore the problem and continue to focus only on good students

Ans. (2)

Exp. The most effective way for dealing with bullying in schools is to provide counselling to students who are potential bullies and clearly communicate to them that such behaviour will not be tolerated.

Bullying behaviour can take the form of verbal bullying, social bullying, cyber bullying or physical bullying. Bullying behaviour is generally intentional, recurring and an abuse of power. Counselling to a particular person who bullies should be educated with the negative aspects of bullying and the mental health disturbance to the concerned person.

67 Match List I with List II and select the correct answer by choosing from the codes given below :

List I	List II
A. Variable-pay program	I. An incentive plan for the improvement of group productivity linked with total amount of money allocation.
B. Piece-rate pay plan	II. Compensation distribution based on certain formula around company's profitability
C. Profit-sharing plan	III. Workers are paid a fixed sum for each unit of production
D. Gain sharing	IV. Portion of employee's pay based on individual, organisational measure of performance

Codes

	A	B	C	D
1	I	II	III	IV
2	II	III	IV	I
3	III	IV	I	II
4	IV	III	II	I

Ans. (4)

Exp. The correct matching is A-IV, B-III, C-II and D-I.

Variable-pay program is a portion of employee's pay based on individual/organisational measure of performance. It is any number of bonuses, incentives, commissions, and other cash compensation that is dependent on employee performance. It is basically employee compensation that changes.

Piece-rate pay plan is where workers are paid a fixed sum for each unit of production. It can be used by a business that wants to pay its employees based on the number of units of production that they complete. Using this type of pay plan converts compensation into a cost that directly varies with sales, assuming that all produced goods are immediately sold.

Profit-sharing plan is where compensation distribution based on certain formula around company's profitability. It rewards employees for increases in organisational profits. All such plans have a formula specifying how a fixed percentage of organisational profits are divided among employees.

Gain sharing is an incentive plan for the improvement of group productivity linked with total amount of money allocation. It rewards employees for increases in efficiency on some important organisational criteria such as decreasing wastefulness and increasing productivity.

68 McClelland's theory basically focuses on ____ needs whilst Maslow's theory focuses on ____ needs.

1 two ; four
2 three ; four
3 three ; five
4 two ; five

Ans. (3)

Exp. McClelland's theory basically focuses on three needs whilst Maslow's theory focuses on five needs.

McClelland's theory includes need for power, need for achievement and need for affiliation. Maslow theory includes physiological needs, safety needs, belonging needs, esteem needs and actualization needs.

69 Read each of the following two statements Assertion (A) and Reason (R) and indicate your answer using codes given below :

Assertion (A) A large proportion of Down Syndrome cases can be identified in prenatal diagnosis through the use of amniocentesis.

Reason (R) The amniocentesis procedure reveals that the fetus does not have the defect, and the parents are spared months of needless anxiety.

Codes

1 Both (A) and (R) are true and (R) is the correct explanation of (A)
2 Both (A) and (R) are true, but (R) is not the correct explanation of (A)
3 (A) is true, but (R) is false
4 (A) is false, but (R) is true

Ans. (2)

Exp. Both (A) and (R) are true, but (R) is not the correct explanation of (A).

A large proportion of Down Syndrome cases can be identified in prenatal diagnosis through the use of amniocentesis. Amniocentesis (also referred to as Amniotic Fluid Test or AFT) is a medical procedure used in prenatal diagnosis of chromosomal abnormalities and fetal infections, and also for sex determination, in which a small amount of amniotic fluid, which contains fetal tissues, is sampled from the amniotic sac surrounding a developing fetus and then the fetal DNA is examined for genetic abnormalities.

The amniocentesis procedure reveals that the fetus does not have the defect, and the parents are spared months of needless anxiety is true because the most common reason to have an 'amnio' is to determine whether a baby has certain genetic disorders or a chromosomal abnormality, such as Down syndrome. However, it does not explain how Down Syndrome cases can be identified in prenatal diagnosis.

70 Vijay was working as executive manager in a multinational company. His team members always found it difficult to get along with him. Vijay always craved for excessive admiration and attention, took undue advantage of others, was very arrogant and preoccupied with fantasies of unlimited success and power. He seems to be suffering from

1 Borderline personality disorder
2 Narcissistic personality disorder
3 Histrionic personality disorder
4 Schizoid personality disorder

Ans. (2)

Exp. Vijay seems to be suffering from Narcissistic personality disorder.

Narcissistic personality disorder is a mental disorder in which people have an inflated sense of their own importance, a deep need for admiration and a lack of empathy for others.

Directions (Q. Nos. 71 to 75) *Read the following paragraph and answer the questions which are follows :*

Scaling in psychology can be classified into two categories – psychophysical scaling and psychological scaling.

Although psychological scaling had its origin in Fechner's method of first choices and the work on colour preference, the major work in psychological scaling began in 1920's in the context of attitude measurement. Bogardus Social Distance Scale (1925) is one of such first attempts.

A major breakthrough in attitude scaling occurred when Thurstone developed his Law of Comparative Judgement (LCJ) and also proposed the three methods-paired comparison, equal appearing intervals and successive intervals. In the paired comparison, every statement/stimulus is paired with every other statement/stimulus.

The computational methods of paired comparison are most extensively developed, some of them using Thurstone's LCJ directly for this purpose.

Such pairing of statements/stimuli is not involved in methods of Equal Appearing Intervals (EAI) and Successive Intervals (SI).

Moreover, the distributions of the categories, assigned by the judges to each attitude statement in EAI and SI need not be normal; in fact the distributions for several statements are skewed.

This situation requires some computational precautions.

Moreover, the method of succesive intervals was computationally quite laborious in pre-computer era and hence it was not so popular.

In the classical scaling tradition Guttmann developed the scalogram technique and Edwards developed the scale discrimination technique. Likert's development of summated ratings represent an important landmark in attitude measurement. It follows the traditional psychometric model.

Aiken and Groth-Marnatt (2009) concluded that other scaling techniques, less frequently used for attitude measurement, include Osgood's semantic differential, Q-sort, expectancy value rating, magnitude estimation, multidimensional scaling etc.

71 The scale values of the attitude statements, obtained by analysing paired comparison data following Thurstone's LCJ, would yield

1 Nominal scale
2 Ordinal scale
3 Interval scale
4 Ratio scale

Ans. (3)

Exp. The scale values of the attitude statements, obtained by analyzing paired comparison data following Thurston's LCJ, would yield Interval scale.

Interval scale is a scale marked in equal intervals so that the difference between any two consecutive values on the scale is equivalent regardless of the two values selected. Interval scales provide information about order. Interval scales are numeric scales in which we know not only the order, but also the exact differences between the values. The classic example of an interval scale is Celsius temperature.

72 Read each of the following two statements Assertion (A) and Reason (R) and indicate your answer using codes given below :

Assertion (A) The method of paired comparison is not suitable for scaling the large number of attitude statements.

Reason (R) In method of paired comparison, every attitude statement is paired with every other attitude statement.

Codes

1 Both (A) and (R) are true, and (R) is the correct explanation of (A)
2 Both (A) and (R) are true, but (R) is not the correct explanation of (A)
3 (A) is true, but (R) is false
4 (A) is false, but (R) is true

Ans. (1)

Exp. Both (A) and (R) are true and (R) is the correct explanation of (A).

The method of paired comparison is not suitable for scaling the large number of attitude statements. The paired comparison technique is a research design that yields interval-level scaled scores that are created from ratings made by each respondent for all possible pairs of items under consideration.

In method of paired comparison, every attitude statement is paired with every other attitude statement.In this method, there is a comparison of entities in pairs to judge which of each entity is preferred, or has a greater amount of some quantitative property, or whether or not the two entities are identical. This explains why the method of paired comparison is not suitable for scaling the large number of attitude statements.

73 Which one of the following can be used to find the scale values of attitude statements, when method of equal appearing intervals is used ?

1 Mean
2 Standard deviation
3 Median
4 Quartile deviation

Ans. (3)

➲ *Exp.* Median can be used to find the scale values of attitude statements, when method of equal appearing intervals is used.

Median is a simple measure of central tendency. To find the median, we arrange the observations in order from smallest to largest value. If there is an odd number of observations, the median is the middle value. If there is an even number of observations, the median is the average of the two middle values.

74 Fill in the blank with the most appropriate alternative.

It would be desirable to carry out the factor analysis of attitude scales obtained by method of _____.

1 paired comparison
2 equal appearing intervals
3 successive intervals
4 summated ratings

Ans. (4)

➲ *Exp.* It would be desirable to carry out the factor analysis of attitude scales obtained by method of Summated ratings. Summated ratings are a collection of related question that measure underlying constructs.

75 In studying attitudes towards the outgroup, a series of bipolar adjective scales were used. Most probably, the researcher used

1 Bogardus Social Distance Scale
2 Osgood's Semantic Differential
3 Guttmann's Scalogram
4 Attitude Scale obtained by method of equal appearing intervals

Ans. (2)

➲ *Exp.* In studying attitudes towards the out-group, a series of bipolar adjective scales were used. Most probably, the researcher used Osgood's Semantic Differential.

Osgood's Semantic Differential scale is a type of a rating scale designed to measure the connotative meaning of objects, events and concepts. The connotations are used to derive the attitude towards the given object, event or concept.

UGC-NET PSYCHOLOGY

SOLVED PAPER 2016 (July)

PAPER II

1 A procedure that establishes a sequence of responses which lead to a reward following the final response and then working backwards is called

1 Shaping
2 Stimulus control
3 Chaining
4 Stimulus generalisation

Ans. (3)

Exp. A procedure that establishes a sequence of responses which lead to a reward following the final response and then working backwards is called as Chaining.

Chaining is an instructional procedure used in behavioural psychology. It is a psychological method of teaching or reinforcing a skill by breaking it down into a series of smaller tasks that begin from the simplest to the most complex. Each step or link on the line acts as a cue to the next task on the line.

There are two types of chaining (i) forward and (ii) backward chaining. Forward chaining is where one starts from the beginning, linking up tasks to the end, while backward chaining is where one links up tasks from the end backwards to the beginning.

Forward chaining is preferred over backward chaining, but where the subject does not know the end result as a motivation, backward chaining is preferable.

2 In a study on scaling of attitude items, eleven statements were included. What would be the number of pairs of attitude statements?

1 21 2 55 3 110 4 121

Ans. (2)

Exp. Formula for calculating the number of pairs of attitude statements is $n\,(n-1)/2 = 11\,(11-1)/2 = 11(10)/2 = 55$

3 Who first attempted to describe personality traits in terms of Lexican descriptors?

1 Ross Stagner
2 Allport and Odbert
3 RB Cattell
4 Coasta and McCrae

Ans. (2)

Exp. Allport and Odbert were the people who first attempted to describe personality traits in terms of Lexican descriptors.

Lexican descriptors is based on the presumption that personality traits are encoded as words in natural languages and examining those words leads to the scientifically agreeable personality model.

4 Read each of the following two statements, Assertion (A) and Reason (R) and indicate your answer using codes given below:

Assertion (A) Classical conditioning is quick when UCS is presented immediately after CS rather than before.

Reason (R) According to cognitive perspective, classical conditioning occurs because CS provides expectancy about the coming of UCS.

Codes

1 Both (A) and (R) are true and (R) is the correct explanation of (A)
2 Both (A) and (R) are true, but (R) is not the correct explanation of (A)
3 (A) is true, but (R) is false
4 (A) is false, but (R) is true

Ans. (1)

Exp. Both (A) and (R) are true and (R) is the correct explanation of (A).

Classical conditioning is quick when UCS (Unconditioned stimulus) is presented immediately after CS (Conditioned stimulus) rather than before is true because classical conditioning is more effective when the Conditioned stimulus occurs before the Unconditioned stimulus, rather than after it, or during the same time. Thus, the Conditioned stimulus acts as a type of signal or cue for the Unconditioned stimulus.

According to cognitive perspective, classical conditioning occurs because CS provides expectancy about the coming of UCS is also true and it is the correct explanation because cognitive perspective models emphasise the role of cognitive factors such as memory processes and expectancies in the etiology and maintenance of conditioned responses.

5 Which of the following have been explained by Freud in his psycho-analytic theory of motivation?

I. Homeostasis II. Drives

III. Hedonism IV. Instincts

Codes

1 I, II and IV 2 I, III and IV

3 II, III and IV 4 I, II and III

Ans. (2)

Exp. Homeostasis, instincts and hedonism are the concepts that have been explained by Freud in his psycho-analytic theory of motivation.

Freud talks about Homeostasis in his Drive Theory. He says that the human body constantly strives for a homeostatic state. Hedonism is a school of thought that argues that pleasure and happiness are the primary or most important intrinsic goods and the proper aim of human life. In Freudian psychoanalysis, the pleasure principle (German: Lustprinzip) is the instinctual seeking of pleasure and avoiding of pain in order to satisfy biological and psychological needs. Life Instincts sometimes referred to as sexual instincts are those that deal with basic survival, pleasure and reproduction. These instincts are essential for sustaining the life of the individual as well as the continuation of the species.

6 Match List I with List II and select the correct answer by choosing from the codes given below :

	List I (Concept)		List II (Explanation)
A.	Trait	I.	Specific emotional and behavioural qualities of personality that are thought to be biologically based.
B.	Type	II.	A collection of highly interconnected traits or dispositions which determine personality integration.
C.	System	III.	Clustering of many stable and enduring dispositions or qualities.
D.	Temperament	IV.	Consistent pattern of emotional and behavioural reactions a person displays across variety of situations.

Codes

	A	B	C	D		A	B	C	D
1	I	II	III	IV	2	II	I	III	IV
3	III	II	IV	I	4	IV	III	II	I

Ans. (4)

Exp. The correct matching is A-IV, B-III, C-II, D-I.

Traits are the consistent pattern of emotional and behavioural reactions a person displays across variety of situations. The trait approach focuses on the specific psychological attributes along which individuals tend to differ in consistent and stable ways.

Type approach is the clustering of many stable and enduring dispositions or qualities. It attempts to comprehend human personality by examining certain broad patterns in the observed behavioural characteristics of individuals.

System is a collection of highly interconnected traits or dispositions which determine personality integration. The system approach suggests personality as a system of mediating processes, conscious and unconscious, whose interactions are manifested in predictable patterns of situation-behaviour relations.

Temperament is the specific emotional and behavioural qualities of personality that are thought to be biologically based. The temperament approach suggests that temperament is the basic foundation of personality, usually assumed to be biologically determined and present early in life, including such characteristics as energy level, emotional responsiveness, demeanor, mood, response tempo, behavioural inhibition, and willingness to explore.

7 Which of the following is correctly arranged?

1 Encoding – retrieval – storage
2 Encoding – storage – retrieval
3 Storage – encoding – retrieval
4 Retrieval – encoding – storage

Ans. (2)

Exp. Encoding – storage – retrieval is correctly arranged.

Encoding is the process where you tend to process the information from the sensory system into a form which may be visual, acoustic and semantic.

Storage is the process where information is stored as short term or long term depending upon the process of maintenance or elaborative rehearsal.

Retrieval refers to accessing or recalling information from memory store.

8 Which one of the following does not contribute to memory?

1 Interesting/disinteresting learning material
2 Goal behind learning
3 Gender
4 Some rest after learning

Ans. (3)

Exp. Gender does not contribute to memory. Although there are many physiological and psychological gender differences in humans, memory, in general, is fairly stable across the sexes.

Interesting/disinteresting learning material, goal behind learning and some rest after learning are the factors which contribute to memory.

9 In terms of efficiency in scanning information, which one of the following strategies is considered to be the best?

1 Conservative focusing
2 Focus gambling
3 Simultaneous scanning
4 Successive scanning

Ans. (1)

Exp. In terms of efficiency in scanning information, Conservative focusing is considered to be the best. Strategies in concept attainment consist of four stages:

Simultaneous Scanning: In thinking and problem-solving simultaneous scanning is an ideal strategy. In this strategy, the subject uses the information he she possesses to eliminate several hypothesis and rationally thinks through the remaining hypothesis that could be true.

Conservative focusing: It is more efficient technique since the subject uses a correct instance as appoint of reference and selects additional cards to test each attributes value individually.

Focus gambling strategy : As the name suggests, it runs on luck. If someone is lucky, they may hit on the correct concept in fewer trials and if they are unlucky they would require more trials. Therefore, this strategy is to be recommended only when the reward is big in fewer trials and you lose less even if you have to take many trials.

Successive scanning : It tests one hypothesis at a time, narrowing down to the right one. Instead of rationally deducing the number of remaining concepts, this person plays a guessing game. It is not as efficient as simultaneous scanning but it requires less thinking and less memorising of previous cases.

10 In retrograde amnesia, which of the following kind of problem is seen?

1 Problems with recalling previously learned material
2 Problems with face recognition
3 Difficulty finding routes
4 Poor encoding of verbal material

Ans. (1)

Exp. In retrograde amnesia, there are problems with recalling previously learned material.

Retrograde Amnesia (RA) is a loss of memory-access to events that occurred or information that was learned, before an injury or the onset of a disease. It tends to negatively affect episodic, autobiographical and declarative memory while usually keeping procedural memory intact with no difficulty for learning new knowledge.

11 Read each of the following two statements, Assertion (A) and Reason (R) and indicate your answer using codes given below:

Assertion (A) Extraverted individuals are sociable, impulsive and like excitement.

Reason (R) Brains of extraverts react more slowly and weakly to stimuli which cause them to seek excitement by approaching the environment.

Codes

1 Both (A) and (R) are true and (R) is the correct explanation of (A)
2 Both (A) and (R) are true, but (R) is not the correct explanation of (A)
3 (A) is true, but (R) is false
4 (A) is false, but (R) is true

Ans. (1)

Exp. Both (A) and (R) are true and (R) is the correct explanation of (A).

Extraverted individuals are sociable, impulsive and like excitement. It is true as people who are high in extroversion tend to seek out social stimulation and opportunities to engage with others. These individuals are often described as being full of life, energy and positivity.

Brains of extraverts react more slowly and weakly to stimuli which cause them to seek excitement by approaching the environment. According to Hans Eysenck biological based model for extraversion and introversion, the cortical activity in the brain of the extraverts tend to have low arousal and hence they seek excitement by approaching the environment whereas it is vice versa for introverts. Thus, the reason explains why the extraverted individuals are sociable, impulsive and like excitement.

12 Match List I with List II and select the correct answer by choosing from the codes given below

List I (Concepts)	List II (Explanations)
A. Personality Structure	I. Psychological reactions and motives that change dynamically over relatively brief periods.
B. Personality Process	II. Stable and enduring qualities that define the individual and distinguish individuals from one another.
C. Personality Development	III. People sometimes change and sometimes resist change or are unable to change accordingly.
D. Psychopathology and Change	IV. Everybody comes upto be an unique individual by adulthood.

Codes

	A	B	C	D
1	I	II	III	IV
2	II	III	IV	I
3	II	I	IV	III
4	IV	I	II	III

Ans. (3)

Exp. The correct matching is A-II, B-I, C-IV and D-III.

Personality Structure refers to stable and enduring qualities that define the individual and distinguish individuals from one another. It is the organisation of the personality in terms of its basic, enduring components and their relationship to each other.

Personality Process refers to psychological reactions and motives that change dynamically over relatively brief periods. It is the dynamics of personality functioning that change over time and across situations as the individual interacts with different people and events in the environment.

Personality Development is when everybody comes up to be a unique individual by adulthood. It is the gradual development of personality in terms of characteristic emotional responses or temperament, a recognisable style of life, personal roles and role behaviours, a set of values and goals, typical patterns of adjustment, characteristic interpersonal relations and sexual relationships, characteristic traits, and a relatively fixed self-image.

Psychopathology and Change is when people sometimes change and sometimes resist change or are unable to change accordingly. Psychopathology is the scientific study of mental disorders, including their theoretical underpinnings, etiology, progression, symptomatology, diagnosis, and treatment.

13 Match List I with List II and indicate your answer using the codes given below

List I (Concepts)	List II (Explanations)
A. Artificial concepts	I. Representation of objects
B. Natural concepts	II. Clearest objects in the physical world
C. Prototypes	III. Defined by set of rules
D. Visual images	IV. Not based on precise properties

Codes

	A	B	C	D		A	B	C	D
1	II	III	IV	I	2	III	IV	II	I
3	III	II	IV	I	4	IV	III	I	II

Ans. (2)

Exp. The correct matching is A-III, B-IV, C-II, and D-I.

Artificial concepts are defined by set of rules. These are defined by a specific set of characteristics and principles. Various properties of geometric shapes, like squares and triangles, serve as useful examples of artificial concepts.

Natural concepts are not based on precise properties. These are based on the natural or living experience of your own.

Prototypes are the clearest objects in the physical world. These are the best representation of a concept.

Visual images are the representation of the objects. These involve the sense of having 'pictures' in the mind. Such images may be memories of earlier visual experiences or syntheses produced by the imagination.

14 According to Master and Johnson following is the correct sequence of human sexual response

1 Excitement → Orgasm → Plateau → Resolution
2 Excitement → Plateau → Orgasm → Resolution
3 Excitement → Arousal → Orgasm → Resolution
4 Arousal → Excitement → Orgasm → Resolution

Ans. (2)

Exp. The correct order of the stages of Master's and Johnson's sexual response cycle is Excitement → Plateau → Orgasm → Resolution.

Master's and Johnson's human sexual response cycle consists of four phases which are linear and comes one after the other. In the Excitement stage, the body prepares for sexual activity by tensing muscles. In the Plateau stage, breathing becomes more rapid and the muscles continue to tense. In Orgasm state, the vagina begins a series of regular contractions; in the man, the penis also contracts rhythmically to expel the sperm and semen (ejaculation). Finally, the Resolution stage brings a gradual return to the resting state.

15 In graphical representations showing stress levels on X-axis and performance on Y-axis, best performance can be expected at

1 lower end of X-axis
2 middle portion of X-axis
3 higher end of X-axis
4 None of the above

Ans. (2)

Exp. In graphical representations showing stress levels on X-axis and performance on Y-axis, best performance can be expected at middle portion of X-axis.

The Yerkes-Dodson law states that performance increases with increased physiological or mental arousal (stress), but only up to a point. When the level of arousal (stress) becomes too high, performance decreases. Optimal level of stress leads to the optimal performance.

16 Lesions of the ventromedial nuclei in the hypothalamus produce

1 Anorexia
2 Obesity
3 Low level of Leptin
4 Hypoinsulinemia

Ans. (2)

Exp. Lesions of the ventromedial nuclei in the hypothalamus produce obesity.

Lateral hypothalamus is known for feeling of hunger and Ventromedial hypothalamus is known for feeling of fullness. If there is a lesion in Ventromedial hypothalamus it would result in increase in appetite and therefore result in obesity.

17 Match List I with List II and select the correct answer by choosing from the codes given below:

List I (Attitude Scaling Technique)	List II (Computational Feature)
A. Paired comparison	I. Computes median category as scale values
B. Scalogram	II. Computes Z-scores as estimates of scale values
C. Equal appearing intervals	III. Computes coefficient of reproducibility
D. Summated ratings	IV. Computes routine measures of item analysis like item-remainder correlation to select items

Codes

	A	B	C	D		A	B	C	D
1	III	II	I	IV	2	I	IV	II	III
3	II	III	I	IV	4	II	III	IV	I

Ans. (3)

Exp. The correct matching is A-II, B-III, C-I and D-IV.

Paired comparison computes Z-scores as estimates of scale values. In statistics, a paired difference test is a type of location test that is used when comparing two sets of measurements to assess whether their population means differ. For carrying out paired difference tests, Z-scores or Z-test is used where the population standard deviation of the difference is known.

Scalogram computes coefficient of reproducibility. The coefficient of reproducibility is often used as a criterion of scalability when forming an attitude scale by the Guttman scalogram technique. It measures the extent to which an observed set of response patterns agrees with that expected from a perfect scale.

Equal appearing intervals compute median category as scale values. In the equal appearing intervals scale, several statements, whose position on the scale has been determined by judges, is used. The scale-value of a statement is computed as the mean or median position to which it is assigned by the judges.

Summated ratings compute routine measures of item analysis like item-remainder correlation to select items. In the summated ratings scale, multiple items will be combined or summed. The item-remainder coefficient is the correlation of each item with the sum of the remaining items.

18 When the action potential reaches the end of the axon terminals, it causes the release of

1 an electric spark that sets off the next neuron
2 positively charged ions that excite the next cell
3 negatively charged ions that inhibit the next cell
4 neurotransmitters that excite or inhibit the next cell

Ans. (4)

Exp. When the action potential reaches the end of the axon terminals, it causes the release of neurotransmitters that excite or inhibit the next cell.

Action potential in neurons are also known as 'nerve impulses' or 'spikes' and the temporal sequence of action potentials generated by a neuron is called its 'spike train'.

When the action potential reaches the end of the axon (the axon terminal), it causes neurotransmitter-containing vesicles to fuse with the membrane, releasing neurotransmitter molecules into the synaptic cleft.

19 According to Freud following are the characteristics of instinct.

I. A source in some bodily deficit.
II. An aim that focuses on gratification of need.
III. An impetus that propels the person to act.
IV. An object through which instinct achieves its aim.

Codes

1 I and II　　2 I, II and IV
3 II, III and IV　　4 I, II, III and IV

Ans. (4)

Exp. According to Freud, instinct have four basic characteristics, which are as follows:

- *A source in some bodily deficit* : It is region of the body in a state of excitation or tension.
- *An aim that focuses on gratification of need* : It is to seek pleasure by narrowing the state of excitation or tension.
- *An impetus that propels the person to act* : It is amount of force the instinct exerts.
- *An object through which instinct achieves its aim* : It is person or object that can satisfy the aim.

20 Guilford initially started his work extending Thurston's theory of primary abilities but later on diverged on the grounds

I. Obtained factors were not primary (independent) rather related to each other.
II. Thurston's factor analysis was mainly oriented to get simple structure.
III. It was difficult to name the abilities (factors).
IV. Guilford also found second-order and higher-order factors.

Codes

1 I and II　　2 II and III
3 I, II and III　　4 I, II, III and IV

Ans. (4)

Exp. Guilford initially started his work extending Thurstone's theory of primary abilities but later on diverged on the following grounds:

- Obtained factors were not primary (independent) rather related to each other. According to Guildford, there is no such thing as a general intelligence. He divided mental capacities into 120 factors, and each factor is dependent on operations and products.
- Thurstone's factor analysis was mainly oriented to get simple structure. Guilford rejected broad factor groups like that of Thurstone's primary abilities. According to him, intelligence consists of numerous intellectual abilities.
- It was difficult to name the abilities (factors). The structure of intellect defines intelligence as a systematic collection of abilities or functions for processing different kinds of items of information in various ways. Originally the SOI model included 120 factors, with over 100 having been empirically verified. The model also suggests where new abilities may be discovered based on existing abilities.
- Guilford also found second-order and higher-order factors. In later modifications he acknowledged that the first-order factors could be correlated, therefore giving rise to multiple higher-order factors, but he still denied the existence of a general factor.

21 AIDS attack a number of very different population; young gay men, intravenous drug users, haemophiliacs, Haitians, infants and recipients of blood transfusion, but commonly among them is the decrease in T lymphocytes, so it is an example of

1 Inductive reasoning　　2 Deductive reasoning
3 Analogical reasoning　　4 Syllogism

Ans. (1)

Exp. AIDS attack a number of very different population; young gay men, intravenous drug users, haemophiliacs, Haitians, infants and recipients of blood transfusion, but commonly among them is the decrease in T lymphocytes, so it is an example of Inductive reasoning.

Inductive reasoning is a logical process in which multiple premises, all believed true or found true most of the time, are combined to obtain a specific conclusion. Inductive reasoning is often used in applications that involve prediction, forecasting or behaviour. Usually inductive reasoning starts with specific to general examples and hence it is known bottom-up processing. Here it started with young gay men, intravenous drug users, haemophiliacs, Haitians, infants and recipients of blood transfusion and ended with T lymphocytes (specific to general).

22 Match List I with List II and select the correct answer by choosing from the codes given below

List I	List II
A. Reintegrative memory	I. Familiarity that we have met it before
B. Recall	II. There is some residue from the past to learn easily
C. Recognition	III. Activity of some performance learned in the past
D. Relearning	IV. To check details of the recovery of events in the personal past

Codes

	A	B	C	D		A	B	C	D
1	IV	III	I	II	2	IV	I	III	II
3	I	II	IV	III	4	I	IV	II	III

Ans. (1)

Exp. The correct matching is A-IV, B-III, C-I and D-II.

To check details of the recovery of events in the personal past is known as Reintegrative memory. It is the process of recovering or recollecting memories from partial cues or reminders.

Activity of some performance learned in the past is known as Recall. It is the transfer prior learning or past experience to current consciousness: that is, to retrieve and reproduce information; to remember.

Familiarity that we have met it before is known as Recognition. It is a form of remembering in which a situation, event, place, person, or the like provokes a subjective feeling of recognition and is therefore believed to be in memory, although it is not specifically recalled.

There is some residue from the past to learn easily is known as Relearning. It is a way of measuring quantitatively, without relying on an individual's conscious memory i.e., how much learned material is retained.

23 A 40 years old person is having the mental age of 20 years. What would be his IQ?

1 100
2 50
3 80
4 125

Ans. (2)

Exp. Formula for calculating IQ of a person is

$$\frac{\text{Mental age}}{\text{Chronological age}} \times 100 = \frac{20}{40} \times 100 = 50$$

24 Muller-Lyer illusion is likely to occur more in cultures characterised by

1 people living in rectangular and square buildings
2 people living in buildings which are round and have few corners
3 people living in open spaces
4 people living in caves

Ans. (1)

Exp. Muller- Lyer illusion is likely to occur more in cultures characterised by people living in rectangular and square buildings.

The Muller-Lyer illusion is an optical illusion consisting of a set of lines that end in arrowheads. The orientation of the arrowheads affects one's ability to accurately perceive the length of the lines. One of the most popular theories which suggests what causes the Muller-Lyer to take place is the perspective explanation. In the three-dimensional world, we often use angles to judge depth and distance.

This explanation is supported by studies comparing the response to the Muller-Lyer illusion by American children and both rural and urban Zambian children. American children were susceptible to the illusion and the urban Zambian children were more susceptible than the rural Zambian children. Since, the rural Zambian children were much less exposed to rectangular structures.

25 Read each of the following two statements, Assertion (A) and Reason (R) and indicate your answer using codes given below:

Assertion (A) According to Classical Test Theory (CTT), reliability can be conceptualised as the ratio of true score variance to the observed score variance.

Reason (R) According to the CTT, the random error of measurement is assumed to be uncorrelated with the true score.

Codes

1 Both (A) and (R) are true and (R) is the correct explanation of (A)
2 Both (A) and (R) are true, but (R) is not the correct explanation of (A)
3 (A) is true, but (R) is false
4 (A) is false, but (R) is true

Ans. (1)

Exp. Both (A) and (R) are true and (R) is the correct explanation of (A).

According to Classical Test Theory (CTT), reliability can be conceptualised as the ratio of true score variance to the observed score variance. It is true because the reliability is equal to the proportion of the variance in the test scores that we could explain if we knew the true scores. The reliability of test scores becomes higher as the proportion of error variance in the test scores becomes lower and vice versa. The square root of the reliability is the absolute value of the correlation between true and observed scores.

According to the CTT, the random error of measurement is assumed to be uncorrelated with the true score. It is true and explains the assertion as the classical test theory assumes that each person has a *true score*, 'T' that would be obtained if there were no errors in measurement.

26 Match List I with List II and select the correct answer by choosing from the codes given below.

List I (System)	List II (Components)
A. Visual system	I. Hammer, pinna, oval window
B. Auditory system	II. Cornea, vitreous humour, aqueous humour
C. Neural system	III. GABA, Serotonin, Dopamine
D. Messenger system	IV. Glial cells, myelin, neurillemma

Codes

	A	B	C	D		A	B	C	D
1	I	II	III	IV	2	II	III	IV	I
3	III	II	I	IV	4	II	I	IV	III

Ans. (4)

Exp. The correct matching is A-II, B-I, C-IV and D-III.

Visual system consists of Cornea, vitreous humour, aqueous humour. It includes the components of the nervous system and the non-neural apparatus of the eye that contribute to the perception of visual stimulation.

Auditory system consists of Hammer, pinna, oval window (pinna is the outer ear and it is made of three tiny bones hammer, anvil and stirrup). It includes the biological structures and processes responsible for hearing. The peripheral auditory system, or auditory periphery, includes the external, middle, and inner ears and the auditory nerve.

Neural system consists of Glial cells, Myelin and Neurillemma. It is a complex network of nerves and cells that carry messages to and from the brain and spinal cord to various parts of the body.

Messenger system consists of GABA, Serotonin and Dopamine. It includes messengers like extracellular molecules, often hormones or neurotransmitters.

27 Read each of the following two statements, Assertion (A) and Reason (R) and indicate your answer using codes given below:

Assertion (A) Organisms learn to perform responses that produce positive reinforcers.

Reason (R) Positive reinforcement strengthens responses that permit escape from or avoidance of stimulus.

Codes

1 Both (A) and (R) are true and (R) is the correct explanation of (A)
2 Both (A) and (R) are true, but (R) is not the correct explanation of (A)
3 (A) is true, but (R) is false
4 (A) is false, but (R) is true

Ans. (3)

Exp. Organisms learn to perform responses that produce positive reinforcers. It is true because in the operant conditioning, positive reinforcement involves the addition of a reinforcing stimulus following a behaviour that makes it more likely that the behaviour will occur again in the future.

Positive reinforcement does not strengthen responses that permit escape from or avoidance of stimulus. It is the negative reinforcement that strengthens responses that permit escape from or avoidance of stimulus.

28 One prominent class of theorists of deductive reasoning believe that deduction depends on _______ of inference akin to those of _______ .

1 informal rules; logical calculus
2 formal rules; analytical calculus
3 procedural rules; logical calculus
4 formal rules; logical calculus

Ans. (4)

Exp. One prominent class of theorists of deductive reasoning believe that deduction depends on formal rules of inference akin to those of logical calculus.

Deductive reasoning believes that deduction depends on formal rules of inference akin of those of logical calculus. Logical calculus has grammar, semantic and set of rules to understand inference.

Deductive reasoning is a logical process in which a conclusion is based on the concordance of multiple premises that are generally assumed to be true.

29 Read each of the following two statements, Assertion (A) and Reason (R) and indicate your answer using codes given below:

Assertion (A) Ideas lose their original identity on fusion into more complex ideas.

Reason (R) Mind sometimes is analogous to chemical laws.

Codes

1 Both (A) and (R) are true and (R) is the correct explanation of (A)
2 Both (A) and (R) are true, but (R) is not the correct explanation of (A)
3 (A) is true, but (R) is false
4 (A) is false, but (R) is true

Ans. (1)

Exp. Both (A) and (R) are true and (R) is the correct explanation of (A).

Ideas lose their original identity on fusion into more complex ideas. It is true according John Locke, who proposed that the ideas are the objects of thought and understanding. All ideas come from experience and none are innate. Hence, the simple ideas become the materials of reason and knowledge and complex ones because of experiences.

Mind sometimes is analogous to chemical laws. It is true because when many impressions or ideas are operating in the mind together, there sometimes takes place a process of a similar kind to chemical combination. It is proper to say that the simple ideas generate the complex ones. This explains why the ideas lose their original identity on fusion into more complex ideas.

30 What type of cell is responsible for the reproduction of other cells of the body?

I. Blood cells　　II. Stem cells

III. Neurons　　IV. Basal cells

Codes

1 Only I　　2 Only II

3 III and IV　　4 IV and I

Ans. (2)

Exp. Stem cells are the cells that can replicate or differentiate into many types of cells and hence they are responsible for the reproduction of other cells of the body. These are undifferentiated cells of a multicellular organism which is capable of giving rise to indefinitely more cells of the same type and from which certain other kinds of cell arise by differentiation.

31 If the bones of the middle ear begins to deteriorate, the person will suffer difficulty in

I. Loudness

II. Timbre

III. Conduction

IV. Stimulation

Codes

1 Only I　　2 II and III

3 Only III　　4 V and IV

Ans. (3)

Exp. If the bones of the middle ear begin to deteriorate, the person will suffer difficulty in Conduction. The main function of the middle ear is conduction and vibration and the function of inner ear is related to frequency and intensity of sound.

The middle ear is an air-filled, membrane (lined space) located between the ear canal and the Eustachian tube, cochlea and auditory nerve. The cavity also plays a very important role in a person's ability to hear. Inside the middle ear, three small bones (ossicles) form a chain and conduct sound vibrations from the eardrum to the inner ear.

32 What is the correct sequence of products in Guilford's Struct of Intellect Model (SOI)?

1 Unit → Class → System → Relations → Implication → Transformation

2 Class → Unit → Systems → Relation → Transformation → Implication

3 Unit → Class → Relation → System → Transformation → Implication

4 Unit → Relation → Class → System → Transformation → Implication

Ans. (3)

Exp. The correct sequence of products in Guilford's Structure of Intellect Model (SOI) is:

Unit → Class → Relation → System → Transformation → Implication

These come under the Product dimension of Guilford's theory. As the name suggests, this dimension contains results of applying particular operations to specific contents. The SI model includes six products in increasing complexity, which are as follows :

(i) *Units* : Single items of knowledge.

(ii) *Classes* : Sets of units sharing common attributes.

(iii) *Relations* : Units linked as opposites or in associations, sequences or analogies.

(iv) *Systems* : Multiple relations interrelated to comprise structures or networks.

(v) *Transformations* : Changes, perspectives, conversions or mutations to knowledge.

(vi) *Implications*: Predictions, inferences, consequences or anticipations of knowledge.

33 The light passes through the eye in which of the following sequence?

1 Cornea, Pupil, Lens, Retina

2 Cornea, Lens, Pupil, Retina

3 Lens, Cornea, Pupil, Retina

4 Pupil, Cornea, Lens, Retina

Ans. (1)

Exp. The light passes through the eye in following sequence : cornea, pupil, lens and retina.

Light enters the eye through the cornea. From the cornea, the light passes through the pupil. From there, it then hits the lens. This is the clear structure inside the eye that focuses light rays onto the retina.

34 Which one of the following statement is true in the context of item analysis?

1 Item-total correlation is equal to Item-remainder correlation

2 Item-total correlation is greater than or equal to item-remainder correlation

3 Item-total correlation is smaller than or equal to item-remainder correlation

4 Item-total correlation cannot be negative

Ans. (2)

Exp. In the context of item analysis, item-total correlation is greater than or equal to item-remainder correlation.

Item analysis is a process which examines student responses to individual test items (questions) in order to assess the quality of those items and of the test as a whole. Item analysis is especially valuable in improving items which will be used again in later tests, but it can also be used to eliminate ambiguous or misleading items in a single test administration.

35 Match List I with List II and select the correct answer by choosing from the codes given below

List I	List II
A. Mental Age	I. Stern
B. Intelligence Quotient	II. Binet
C. Mental Tests	III. Spearman
D. Tetrad Equation	IV. JM Cattell

Codes

	A	B	C	D		A	B	C	D
1	I	II	III	IV	2	II	I	IV	III
3	III	II	I	IV	4	IV	III	II	I

Ans. (2)

Exp. The correct matching is A-II, B-I, C-IV, D-III.

Mental age was first defined by French psychologist Alfred Binet, who introduced the intelligence test in 1905, with the assistance of Theodore Simon.

Intelligence quotient was given by Stern. He formulated the basic definition of Intelligence Quotient in 1912, when he defined Intelligence Quotient as a ratio of an estimated 'mental age' and 'actual chronological age.'

Mental tests was given by J.M Cattell. He introduced the term 'mental test' as a general term for his set of tests which included measures of sensation, using weights to determine just-noticeable differences, reaction time, human memory span and rate of movement.

Tetrad Equation was given by Spearman. Spearman claimed that testing a person's abilities to complete tasks against expected outcomes could be measured and expressed in a mathematical formula and that mathematical formula is now known as Tetrad equation.

36 The difference in images in the two eyes is greater for objects that are close and smaller for distant objects is an example of

1 Binocular Disparity
2 Convergence
3 Accommodation
4 Relative Size

Ans. (1)

Exp. The difference in images in the two eyes is greater for objects that are close and smaller for distant objects is an example of Binocular Disparity.

It refers to the difference in image location of an object seen by the left and right eyes, resulting from the eyes' horizontal separation (parallax). The brain uses binocular disparity to extract depth information from the two-dimensional retinal images in stereopsis.

37 Read each of the following two statements, Assertion (A) and Reason (R) and indicate your answer using codes given below:

Assertion (A) Information is transferred from STM to LTM.

Reason (R) Information maintained in the rehearsal buffer is prevented from decaying in STM.

Codes

1 Both (A) and (R) are true and (R) is the correct explanation of (A)
2 Both (A) and (R) are true, but (R) is not the correct explanation of (A)
3 (A) is true, but (R) is false
4 (A) is false, but (R) is true

Ans. (2)

Exp. Both (A) and (R) are true, but (R) is not the correct explanation of (A).

Information is transferred from STM to LTM. It is true as information moves from Short-term memory (STM) to Long-term memory (LTM) through rehearsal. It has been viewed as serving to maintain items in STM and transfer information to LTM.

Information maintained in the rehearsal buffer is prevented from decaying in STM. It is true as the information is retained in the rehearsal buffer in STM, but it does not explain why the information is transferred from STM to LTM. Therefore, both the assertion and reason are independently correct and the reason does not explain the given assertion.

38 Arrange the parts of CNS in ascending order.

I. Thalamus
II. Medulla oblongata
III. Spinal cord
IV. Frontal lobe

Codes

1 I, II, III, IV
2 II, I, III, IV
3 IV, II, I, III
4 III, II, I, IV

Ans. (4)

Exp. The correct sequence is III, II, I, IV.

(i) *Spinal Cord* : It is a long, fragile tube like structure that begins at the end of the brain stem and continues down almost to the bottom of the spine (spinal column).

(ii) *Medulla Oblongata* : It is the continuation of the spinal cord within the skull, forming the lowest part of the brainstem and containing control centres for the heart and lungs.

(iii) *Thalamus* : It is a small structure within the brain located just above the brain stem between the cerebral cortex and the midbrain and has extensive nerve connections to both. The main function of the thalamus is to relay motor and sensory signals to the cerebral cortex.

(iv) *Frontal Lobe* : It is located at the front of the brain and is one of the four major lobes of the cerebral cortex in the mammalian brain. It is concerned with motor and higher order executive functions.

39 Shaping in instrumental conditioning means

1 Teaching a complex sequence of behaviours by first shaping the final response in the sequence and then working backwards
2 A continuous reinforcement schedule is used for establishing new behaviours
3 It involves reinforcing successive approximation of the final desired behaviour
4 Consistent occurrence of a behaviour in the presence of discriminative stimulus

Ans. (3)

Exp. Shaping in instrumental conditioning means reinforcing successive approximations of the final desired behaviour.

Shaping involves rewarding successive closer approximations to the target behaviour. Both shaping and chaining are used to attain the desired target behavior. Instrumental conditioning is another term for Operant conditioning, a learning process first described by BF Skinner. In Instrumental conditioning, reinforcement or punishment are used to either increase or decrease the probability that a behaviour will occur again in the future. Shaping is a method of operant conditioning by which successive approximation of a target behaviour is reinforced.

40 According to Trichromatic theory of colour vision, which of the following are the three types of cones?

1 Red, Yellow and Blue
2 Red, Blue and Green
3 Yellow, Blue and Green
4 Yellow, Red and Blue

Ans. (2)

Exp. According to Trichromatic theory of colour vision, Red, Blue and Green are the three types of cones.

The wavelengths of these three colours can be combined to create every colour on the visible light spectrum. This theory was first suggested by Thomas Young and later tested by Hermann Von Helmholtz.

41 Read each of the following two statements, Assertion (A) and Reason (R) and indicate your answer using codes given below

Assertion (A) 'gf' and 'gc' correlate positively across the age levels with moderate magnitude.

Reason (R) 'gf' being neural energy is invested in the cultivation of 'gc' and both are having different growth patterns.

Codes

1 Both (A) and (R) are true and (R) is the correct explanation of (A)
2 Both (A) and (R) are true, but (R) is not the correct explanation of (A)
3 (A) is true, but (R) is false
4 (A) is false, but (R) is true

Ans. (1)

Exp. Both (A) and (R) are true and (R) is the correct explanation of (A).

'gf' and 'gc' correlate positively across the age levels with moderate magnitude. The fluid intelligence (gf) increase up to an age and declines after that age as it is dependent on inherent biological traits, whereas crystallized intelligence (gc) increases with age, experience and exposure. The assertion is true that both 'gf' and 'gc' correlate positively across the age levels, but with moderate magnitude.

'gf' being neural energy is invested in the cultivation of 'gc' and both are having different growth patterns. It is also true because fluid intelligence leads to the cultivation of crystallised intelligence and both have different growth patterns which explains why both 'gf' and 'gc' correlate moderately across the age levels.

42 Read each of the following two statements, Assertion (A) and Reason (R) and indicate your answer using codes given below :

Assertion (A) The creators of three dimensional movies simulate convergence by photographing a scene with two cameras placed a few inches apart.

Reason (R) Convergence is a binocular cue for perceiving depth by the extent to which the eyes converge inwards when looking at an object.

Codes

1 Both (A) and (R) are true and (R) is the correct explanation of (A)
2 Both (A) and (R) are true, but (R) is not the correct explanation of (A)
3 (A) is true, but (R) is false
4 (A) is false, but (R) is true

Ans. (2)

Exp. Both (A) and (R) are true, but (R) is not the correct explanation of (A).

The creators of three dimensional movies simulate convergence by photographing a scene with two cameras placed a few inches apart. It is true as it explains retinal disparity which is the slight difference between the right and left retinal images. When both eyes focus on an object, the different position of the eyes produces a disparity of visual angle, and a slightly different image is received by each retina. The two images are automatically compared and, if sufficiently similar, are fused, providing an important cue to depth perception.

Convergence is a binocular cue for perceiving depth by the extent to which the eyes converge inwards when looking at an object. It is true as it enables the slightly different images of an object seen by each eye to come together and form a single image. The muscular tension exerted is also a cue to the distance of the object from the eyes.

Both the assertion and reason are examples of binocular cues, and are independently correct, but the reason does not explain the assertion.

43 In heightened emotional states, the following functions are not triggered by Sympathetic Nervous System activity.

I. Perspiration II. Heightened pulse rate
III. Digestion IV. Pupillary dilation

Codes

1 Only III 2 III and IV
3 I, II and III 4 I, III and IV

Ans. *(1)*

Exp. Sympathetic Nervous System triggers perspiration, heightened pulse rate and pupillary dilation. However, Sympathetic Nervous System does not triggers digestion.

The Sympathetic Nervous System (SNS) is part of the Autonomic Nervous System (ANS), which also includes the Parasympathetic Nervous System (PNS). The Sympathetic Nervous System activates what is often termed the fight or flight response. Nor- epinephrine and epinephrine are two hormones that are released in response to emergencies within the body. These two hormones often lead to what is common called an 'Adrenaline rush,' which is the feeling of urgency that comes during stressful situations, which results in perspiration, heightened pulse rate and pupillary dilation.

44 Match List I with List II and select the correct answer by choosing from the codes given below :

List I (Type of Conditioning)	List II (Explanation)
A. Delayed conditioning	I. The onset of UCS precedes the onset of the CS and the UCS goes off before CS comes on
B. Trace conditioning	II. The CS and UCS come on and go off at the same time
C. Simultaneous conditioning	III. The onset of CS precedes the onset of the UCS and the CS goes off before the onset of UCS
D. Backward conditioning	IV. The onset of the CS precedes the onset of the UCS and the CS remains on for the initial part of UCS

Codes

	A	B	C	D		A	B	C	D
1	I	II	IV	III	2	IV	II	III	I
3	IV	III	I	II	4	IV	III	II	I

Ans. *(4)*

Exp. The correct matching is A-IV, B-III, C-II and D-I.

Delayed conditioning is when the onset of the CS precedes the onset of the UCS and the CS remains on for the initial part of UCS. It is a procedure in which the conditioned stimulus is presented, and remains present, for a fixed period (the delay) before the unconditioned stimulus is introduced.

Trace conditioning is when the onset of CS precedes the onset of the UCS and the CS goes off before the onset of UCS. It is a procedure in which a conditioned stimulus and an unconditioned stimulus are separated by a constant interval (called the trace interval), with the conditioned stimulus presented first.

Simultaneous conditioning is when the CS and UCS come on and go off at the same time. It is a procedure in which the conditioned stimulus and the unconditioned stimulus are presented at the same time.

Backward conditioning is when the onset of UCS precedes the onset of the CS and the UCS goes off before CS comes on. It is a procedure in which an unconditioned stimulus is consistently presented before a neutral stimulus.

45 Which of the following statement/s is/are true, when the Eysenck Personality Questionnaire (EPQ or EPQ-R) and Costa and McCrae's NEO-PI–3 are compared?

I. EPQ-R Psychoticism (P) scale is uncorrelated with Five-Factor Agreeableness (A) and Consentiousness (C) Scale.

II. P scale is positively correlated with (A) and (C) scales.

III. (P) scale is negatively correlated with (A) and (C) scales.

IV. EPQ-R has Lie scale, NEO-PI–3 has no lie scale.

V. Both EPQ-R and NEO-PI-3 have lie scale.

Codes

1 I and V 2 II and V
3 III and IV 4 I and V

Ans. *(3)*

Exp. Statement III and IV are correct.

(P) scale is negatively correlated with (A) and (C) scales. Researchers have suggested that the Psychoticism (P) personality dimension of the Eysenck Personality Questionnaire is negatively correlated with the agreeableness (A) and conscientiousness (C) constructs of the five-factor model of NEO-PI-3.

EPQ-R has Lie scale; NEO-PI–3 has no lie scale. According to Eysenck and Eysenck (1976), the lie scale included in the Eysenck Personality Questionnaire (EPQ) permits lying to be diagnosed when a set of rarely performed desirable acts are endorsed as being typical of the respondent, and when common non-desirable acts are subsequently denied.

Directions (Q. Nos. 46 to 50) *Read the following paragraph and answer the five questions which follow :*

An environmental psychologist hypothesized that the noise would adversely affect the performance on mental tasks. One hundred and fifty subjects, 75 boys and 75 girls, studying in the twelfth standard, in the age range of 17 to 19 years and in the IQ range of 85 to 115, constituted the initial pool of subjects.

Three groups of equal size were formed by random assignment. Group I performed under high noise condition (75 decibels), Group II performed under moderate noise condition (60 decibels), and Group III performed under silent condition. Each subject was instructed to solve 45 simple numerical problems in the allotted time of 90 minutes. The mean number of correctly solved problems were twenty-four, twenty and fifteen respectively. The intergroup mean differences were statistically significant.

46 The variable 'intelligence', in the above study, can be labelled as

I. Behavioural variable
II. Organismic variable
III. Continuous variable
IV. Controlled variable

Codes

1 I and IV
2 II and III
3 I, III and IV
4 II, III and IV

***Ans.* (4)**

Exp. The variable 'intelligence', in the above study, can be labeled as an Organismic variable, Continuous variable, and Controlled variable.

(i) *Organismic Variable* : It is the internal forces and influences that influence an organism's behaviour.

(ii) *Continuous Variable* : It is a variable that has an infinite number of possible values. In other words, any value is possible for the variable.

(iii) *Controlled Variable* : It is the one element that is not changed throughout an experiment, because its unchanging state allows the relationship between the other variables being tested to be better understood.

47 Which one of the following conclusion can be drawn on the basis of the above study?

1 The researcher's hypothesis has been accepted
2 The researcher's hypothesis has been rejected
3 The researcher's hypothesis has been partially accepted
4 Inadequate data to evaluate researcher's hypothesis

***Ans.* (2)**

Exp. Here the hypothesis is that noise would adversely affect the performance on mental tasks but here the Group I students performed under high noise condition (75 decibels), Group II performed under moderate noise condition (60 decibels), and Group III performed under silent condition. The mean number of correctly solved problems was twenty-four(High noise), twenty (moderate noise) and fifteen(Silent condition) respectively. Hence, the research hypothesis is rejected because Group I students who placed under high noise conditions can able to solve 24 numerical problems.

48 Read each of the following two statements, Assertion (A) and Reason (R) and indicate your answer using codes given below:

Assertion (A) In the above study, the subjects have been randomly assigned to the three groups.

Reason (R) Random assignment of the subjects enables the experimenter to manipulate the independent variable effectively.

Codes

1 Both (A) and (R) are true and (R) is the correct explanation of (A)
2 Both (A) and (R) are true, but (R) is not the correct explanation of (A)
3 (A) is true, but (R) is false
4 (A) is false, but (R) is true

***Ans.* (1)**

Exp. Both (A) and (R) are true and (R) is the correct explanation of (A).

In the above study, the subjects have been randomly assigned to the three groups. It is true because the subjects are randomly assigned to high noise, moderate and silent conditions.

Random assignment of the subjects enables the experimenter to manipulate the independent variable effectively. It is true as random assignment of participants helps to ensure that any differences between and within the groups are not systematic at the outset of the experiment. This ensures that each participant or subject has an equal chance of being placed in any group.

49 Match List I with List II in the context of the above study, select the correct answer by choosing from the codes given below:

List I (Types of Variable)	List II (Variables)
A. Independent variable	I. Subject's education
B. Dependent variable	II. Subject's gender
C. Controlled variable	III. Noise level
D. Discrete variable	IV. Number of numerical problems correctly solved by subject

Codes

	A	B	C	D
1	III	IV	I	II
2	IV	III	I	II
3	IV	III	II	I
4	III	IV	II	I

***Ans.* (1)**

Exp. The correct matching is A-III, B-IV, C-I, D-II.

Noise level is an example of independent variable because noise level has been manipulated as high, moderate and silent condition in the above study.

Number of numerical problems correctly solved by subject is an example of dependent variable because it is the outcome variable in the above study.

Subject's gender is an example of discrete variable since the gender would be either male, female, transgender etc. they are discrete.

Subject's education is an example of a controlled variable which is held constant by the experimenter as all the students belong to twelfth standard.

50 In the above study, the researcher's hypothesis would be labelled as

I. directional
II. non-directional
III. causal
IV. correlational

Codes

1 Only I
2 I and III
3 II and III
4 II and IV

Ans. (2)

Exp. In the above study, the researcher's hypothesis would be labelled as directional and causal.

Causal hypothesis states that changes in one variable causes change in another variable (Change in noise level leads to change in the performance level).

Directional hypothesis is where a researcher thinks the result might go. For example it may be of positive or negative relationship and hence it is called as one tailed hypothesis. In the above passage the hypothesis which mentioned was the noise would adversely affect the performance on mental tasks is directional.

PAPER III

1 Amit met with an accident and later turned into impulsive, irresponsible and less concerned with the consequences of his actions. He must have suffered damage in

1 Parietal lobe
2 Frontal lobe
3 Occipital lobe
4 Temporal lobe

Ans. (2)

Exp. Amit met with an accident and later turned into impulsive, irresponsible and less concerned with the consequences of his actions. He must have suffered damage in Frontal lobe. Damage to the Frontal lobe can lead to many serious and behavioural issues. The Frontal lobes are involved in motor function, problem-solving, spontaneity, memory, language, initiation, judgement etc.

2 Effective teaching may include conceptual scaffolding, which is best described by the following statement.

1 Introducing practice sessions after every module
2 Gradually fading support as student proficiency increases
3 Punishing student for incorrect answers
4 Encouraging brighter students to help weaker students

Ans. (2)

Exp. Effective teaching may include conceptual scaffolding, is best described by gradually fading support as student proficiency increases.

It is the support given during the learning process which is tailored to the needs of the student with the intention of helping the student to achieve his/her learning goals. It is changing the level of support to suit the cognitive potential of the child. Over the course of a teaching session, one can adjust the amount of guidance to fit the child's potential level of performance. More support is offered when a child is having difficulty with a particular task and, over time, less support is provided as the child makes gains on the task.

3 Read each of the following two statements, Assertion (A) and Reason (R) and indicate your answer using codes given below:

Assertion (A) Individuals high in achievement motivation are more attracted to tasks of intermediate difficulty.

Reason (R) Individuals high in achievement motivation are highly motivated to avoid failure.

Codes

1 Both (A) and (R) are true and (R) is the correct explanation of (A)
2 Both (A) and (R) are true, but (R) is not the correct explanation of (A)
3 (A) is true, but (R) is false
4 (A) is false, but (R) is true

Ans. (1)

Exp. Both (A) and (R) are true and (R) is the correct explanation of (A).

Individuals high in achievement motivation are more attracted to tasks of intermediate difficulty is true because they are the ones who prefer intermediate difficulty than people with lower motivation and they do not even prefer easy ones.

Individuals high in achievement motivation are highly motivated to avoid failure is also true because individuals who are high in achievement tends to prefer success to their ability and failure to their lack of effort.

4 A social worker, appointed to assist the psychiatrist, used to administer and interpret Rorschach test. This is an

1 ethically incorrect practice
2 ethically correct practice
3 ethically correct practice provided the results are used only for diagnostic purpose
4 ethically correct practice provided the results are kept confidential and are used only for diagnostic purpose

Ans. (1)

Exp. A social worker, appointed to assist the psychiatrist, used to administer and interpret Rorschach test. This is an ethically incorrect practice.

Social worker is not allowed to administer and interpret Rorschach ink blot test since he/she was appointed to assist the psychiatrist. A test should be handled well with proper set of procedures and evaluation in order to study about the depth of an individual.

5 Facial feedback hypothesis means

I. your facial expression affects other's emotions.

II. other's facial expression affects your emotions.

III. facial expression provides feedback to the brain about emotions.

IV. All the three

Codes

1 Only III 2 I and III
3 I and II 4 Only I

Ans. (2)

Exp. Facial feedback hypothesis means your facial expression affects other's emotions and facial expression provides feedback to the brain about emotions.

The facial feedback hypothesis states that our facial expressions affect our emotions. It suggests that smiling can make us feel happy even when we start out feeling sad. The facial feedback hypothesis is based on the idea that a facial expression not only expresses an emotion, but also that expression and experience are linked in that afferent sensory feedback from the facial action influences the emotional experience.

6 The following instrument cannot be utilised in the measurement of emotions

1 Sphygmomano meter
2 Galvanic skin response
3 Digital thermometer
4 Pupillary measurement camera

Ans. (3)

Exp. Digital thermometer cannot be utilised in the measurement of emotions.

The instruments that can be utilised in the measurement of emotions are Sphygmomanometer, Galvanic skin response and Pupillary measurement camera.

Digital thermometer are mainly used for recording temperature in the mouth or armpit and it is not used for measuring the emotions.

7 Match the items of List I with List II.

List I (Disorder)	List II (Typical Symptoms)
A. PTSD	I. Pill rolling movement
B. Major depressive disorder	II. Flashbacks
C. Parkinson's Disease	III. Echolalia
D. Catatonic Schizophrenia	IV. Appetite loss

Codes

	A	B	C	D		A	B	C	D
1	I	II	III	IV	2	IV	III	II	I
3	III	I	IV	II	4	II	IV	I	III

Ans. (4)

Exp. The correct matching is A-II, B-IV, C-I and D-III.

The typical symptoms of *PTSD* are flashbacks. PTSD (Post-traumatic stress disorder) is a disorder that may result when an individual lives through or witnesses a traumatic event. It involves flashbacks etc.

The typical symptom of *Major depressive disorder* is appetite loss. Major depressive disorder is a mood disorder characterised by persistent sadness and other symptoms of a major depressive episode. Physical symptoms associated with depression include nausea or the sensation of a 'knot in the stomach,' which makes food unappealing, hence resulting in a loss of appetite.

The typical symptom of *Parkinson's disease* is pill rolling movement. Parkinson's disease is a progressive neurodegenerative disease caused by the death of dopamine-producing neurons which controls balance and coordinates muscle movement. The 'pill rolling' movement refers to the tremors of the fingers, usually the thumb plus the other fingers, that makes it look as if the person is rolling a pill in the fingers.

The typical symptom of *Catatonic Schizophrenia* is echolalia. Catatonic schizophrenia is a relatively rare subtype of schizophrenia characterised by abnormal motor activity, specifically motor immobility or excessive motor activity. It involves echolalia which is a mechanical repetition of words and phrases uttered by another individual.

8 Arrange in sequence the stage of personality development according to Rollo May.

1 Innocence → ordinary consciousness of self → rebellion → creative consciousness of self
2 Innocence → rebellion → ordinary consciousness of self → creative consciousness of self
3 Ordinary consciousness of self → innocence → rebellion → creative consciousness of self
4 Rebellion → innocence → ordinary consciousness of self → creative consciousness of self

Ans. (2)

Exp. The stage of personality development according to Rollo May is Innocence → rebellion → ordinary consciousness of self → creative consciousness of self.

Innocence is the pre-egoic state where an individual only do what he knows but he has all the will and drive to satisfy his needs.

Rebellion is the stage where a person wants freedom but he has no understanding in his responsibility.

Ordinary is the stage of normal adult where he finds his responsibility but finds it demanding.

Creative is the stage of authentic adult who is beyond the self actualisation and ready to face the challenges with courage.

9 The rapid change in performance as the size of reinforcement in varied is called

1 Crespi effect
2 Disequilibrium hypothesis
3 Premack principal
4 Programmed learning

Ans. (1)

Exp. The rapid change in performance as the size of reinforcement in varied is called Crespi effect.

Crespi effect is a phenomenon which was observed in classical conditioning in which a conditioned response changes distinctively to an abruptly changed reinforcement and it was observed by American psychologist Leo.P Crespi in 1942.

10 Creativity has been conceptualised in terms of following.

I. Creativity as a product
II. Creativity as a process
III. Creativity as a potential
IV. Creativity as perseverance

Codes

1 I and II
2 II and III
3 I, II and III
4 I, II and IV

Ans. (3)

Exp. Creativity has been conceptualised in terms of creativity as a product, creativity as a process and creativity as a potential.

The product approach to creativity mainly adheres to the aesthetics or creative outcome of products such as art works. Potential approach to creativity involves how capable the creative individual is.

Process approach to creativity involves the general process of creativity thinking which involves associative and divergent thinking. It does not involved in creative and non-creative individuals.

11 In Solomon Asch's study on conformity, subjects conformed to the Group approximately what percent of time?

1 25%
2 35%
3 45%
4 over 50%

Ans. (2)

Exp. In Solomon Asch's study on conformity, subjects conformed to the Group approximately 35% of time. Solomon Asch (1951) conducted an experiment to investigate the extent to which social pressure from a majority group could affect a person to conform. Asch measured the number of times each participant conformed to the majority view. On average, about one third (35%) of the participants who were placed in this situation went along and conformed to the clearly incorrect majority on the critical trials.

12 Perceived fairness of the amount and rewards among individuals refers to ______ while perceived fairness of the ways used for rewards and pays refers to ______

1 Organisational justice, Distributive justice
2 Equity, Organisational justice
3 Distributive justice; Procedural justice
4 Procedural justice; Distributive justice

Ans. (3)

Exp. Perceived fairness of the amount and rewards among individuals refers to distributive justice while perceived fairness of the ways used for rewards and pays refers to procedural justice.

Distributive justice is the belief that rules can be changed and punishments and rewards distributed according to relative standards. Procedural justice is mainly allocated to perceived fairness of the rules and decision making in the result process.

13 Match List I with List II and select the correct answer by choosing from the codes given below:

List I (Verbal Responses)	List II (Explanations)
A. Mand	I. Provides grammatical framework for verbal behaviour
B. Tact	II. Repeating someone else's utterances
C. Echoic behaviour	III. Verbal behaviour of naming things
D. Autoclitic behaviour	IV. Verbal command that is reinforced when the listener carries out the command

Codes

	A	B	C	D
1	IV	III	II	I
2	III	IV	I	II
3	III	IV	II	I
4	IV	III	I	II

Ans. (1)

Exp. The correct matching is A-IV, B-III, C-II and D-I.

Mand is a verbal command that is reinforced when the listener carries out the command. It is a category of utterances in which the speaker makes demands on the hearer, as in 'Listen to me' or 'Pass the salt, please'. According to the behaviourist analysis of language, this form of verbal behaviour is reinforced by the compliance of the listener.

Tact is a verbal behaviour of naming things. It is a term used to describe a verbal operant which is controlled by a non-verbal stimulus (such as an object, event, or property of an object) and is maintained by non-specific social reinforcement (praise).

Echoic behaviour is repeating someone else's utterances. It is a form of verbal behaviour where the speaker repeats the same sound or word that was said by another person, like an echo.

Autoclitic behaviour provides grammatical framework for verbal behaviour. It is a verbal behaviour that modifies the functions of other verbal behaviours.

14 Match List I with List II and select the correct answer by choosing from the codes given below.

List I (Scale)	List II (Test)
A. Structural scales	I. Rorschach Inkblot Test
B. Lambda	II. Zukerman- Kuhlman Personality Questionnaire
C. Abasement	III. California Psychological Inventory
D. Impulsive Sensation Seeking	IV. Thematic Apperception Test

Codes

	A	B	C	D		A	B	C	D
1	I	II	III	IV	2	III	I	IV	II
3	II	III	I	IV	4	IV	I	II	III

Ans. *(2)*

Exp. The correct matching is A-III, B-I, C-IV and D-II.

Structural scales are a part of California Psychological Inventory. These are sociability, likeability, prudence, prudence, adjustment, intellectance and ego control.

Lambda is a part of Rorschach Inkblot test where Lambda = F/(R–F), where 'F' indicates the number of pure form responses, and 'R' indicates the total number of responses.

Abasement is a miscellaneous need in Thematic Apperception Test. It is a miscellaneous need to submit passively to an external force and to accept injury, blame, criticism, punishment, or to feel guilt and inferiority.

Impulsive sensation seeking scale is a part of Zukerman-Kuhlman Personality Questionnaire which involves the impulsive sensation seeking. According to Zukerman, "sensation seeking is a personality trait defined by the search for experiences and feelings that are varied, novel, complex, and intense, and by the readiness to take physical, social, legal, and financial risks for the sake of such experiences."

15 The concept of ________ is vital in the understanding of fractional antedating goal response

1 Drive stimulus reduction
2 Reactive Inhibition
3 Secondary Reinforcement
4 Conditioned Inhibition

Ans. *(3)*

Exp. The concept of Secondary Reinforcement is vital in the understanding of fractional antedating goal response.

In operant conditioning , secondary reinforcement refers to a situation in which a stimulus reinforces a behaviour after it has been associated with a primary reinforcer.

16 Match List I with List II and select the correct answer by choosing from the codes given below :

List I (Term in factor analysis)	List II (Example/Brief explanation)
A. Factor extraction method	I. Correlations among varimax rotated factors
B. Cattell's scree	II. Promax
C. Factor rotation method	III. Principal axes
D. Inter-factor correlation matrix	IV. Correlation among oblique-rotated factors
	V. Method to decide number of factors for rotation.

Codes

	A	B	C	D		A	B	C	D
1	III	V	II	IV	2	III	V	II	I
3	V	III	II	IV	4	II	III	V	IV

Ans. *(1)*

Exp. The correct matching is A-III, B-V, C-II and D-IV.

An example of *Factor extraction method* is Principal axes. A factor extraction method is used to form uncorrelated linear combinations of the observed variables. Prinicpal axes is an extraction method in which the coefficient of multiple determination of one variable with all other variables in the system is used as the initial communality estimate for that variable.

Cattell's scree is a method to decide number of factors for rotation. The Cattell's scree test is a graphical strategy with a non-numerical solution to determine the number of components to retain.

An example of *Factor rotation method* is Promax. Rotations minimise the complexity of the factor loadings to make the structure simpler to interpret. Promax allows factors to be correlated.

Inter-factor correlation matrix is used to find correlation among oblique-rotated factors. A correlation matrix is a table showing correlation coefficients between variables.

17 Which of the following identity status describes the individual who has been exploring but not yet committed to self chosen values and goals?

1 Identity achievement
2 Identity foreclosure
3 Identity diffusion
4 Identity moratorium

Ans. *(4)*

Exp. According to James Marcia identity theory, an individual who has explored themselves but not yet committed is known as Identity moratorium. It describes the individual who has been exploring, but not yet committed to self-choosen values and goal. It is the status of individuals who are in the midst of a crisis, whose commitments are either absent or are only vaguely defined, but who are actively exploring alternatives.

18 Scientific study of Creativity is considered to be started by

1 Galton 2 Guilford 3 Torrance 4 Mednick

Ans. *(2)*

Exp. Scientific study of Creativity is considered to be started by Guilford.

Guilford is one of the leaders of the psychometric school of research on intelligence, creativity and personality. He initiated the development of a system of psychological tests for the study of productive thought and creative abilities of the individual. He was the one who described about the multiple solutions to a problem which is divergent thinking and narrowing a solution to a problem is convergent thinking.

19 Match List I with List II and select the correct answer by choosing from the codes given below :

List I (Concepts)	List II (Explanation)
A. Metacomponents	I. Determining which elements in a set of information are relevant for one's purpose and which are not.
B. Selective Encoding	II. Marshalling emotions in the service of a goal.
C. Motivating Oneself	III. Higher-order mental processes being used to guide problem solving efforts.
D. Practical Intelligence	IV. Using mental components to help one to adapt, shape, or select an environment that is appropriate for oneself.

Codes

	A	B	C	D
1	I	II	III	IV
2	III	I	II	IV
3	II	III	IV	I
4	IV	III	I	II

Ans. *(2)*

Exp. The correct matching is A-III, B-I, C-II and D-IV.

Metacomponents are higher-order mental processes being used to guide problem solving efforts. These are executive processes used in problem solving and decision making that involve the majority of managing our mind.

Selective encoding is determining which elements in a set of information are relevant for one's purpose and which are not. It is distinguishing what is important in a problem and what is irrelevant (i.e. filter).

Motivating oneself is marshalling emotions in the service of a goal. It is an essential component of emotional intelligence for self-motivation.

Practical intelligence is using mental components to help one to adapt, shape, or select an environment that is appropriate for oneself. It is the ability to apply one's intelligence in practical, everyday situations.

20 Culture exerts strong effect on memory through the operation of cultural schema. One's memory is influenced by learning in

1 own culture effect
2 culture effect due to enculturation
3 acculturation effect
4 socialisation effect

Ans. *(1)*

Exp. Culture exerts strong effect on memory through the operation of cultural schema. One's memory is influenced by learning in own culture effect.

People coming from different backgrounds perceive their environment differently and hence, process and store the information in their memory in different ways. The recall and recognition process also differs in different cultures.

Enculturation is defined as a process where individuals learn about and identify with their ethnic group. It is the process of learning our own culture.

21 Evolutionary Social Psychology Research seeks to investigate

1 changes in human behaviour
2 seeks to investigate the potential role of genetic factors on social behaviour
3 interrelationships between people of two groups of different social environment
4 focuses on individual's behaviour

Ans. *(2)*

Exp. Evolutionary Social Psychology Research seeks to investigate the potential role of genetic factors on social behaviour.

Social psychology is the scientific study of how people's thoughts, feelings and behaviours are influenced by the actual, imagined or implied presence of others Genetics play an important role in determining the individual characteristics of a person that make him/her pre-disposed to behave and think a particular manner.

Evolutionary social psychology acclaims that social behaviours developed through genetics and inheritance.

22 Which one of the following is the right explanation of flash bulb memory?

1 New, important, helpful social events
2 Unspecific, important, common events
3 Specific, surprising, unimportant events
4 Unspecific, important, common events

Ans. *(3)*

Exp. Specific, surprising and unimportant events are the part of flashbulb memory which is highly detailed as a particular snapshot of an event.

Flash bulb memories are memories of learning something so shocking or surprising that it creates a strong and seemingly very accurate memory of learning about the event, but not the event itself. The emotional arousal experienced during the time of the event is what makes flash bulb memories so strong. e.g. when a person first learns about the death of a loved one, the sadness felt at that moment is so strong that the memory gets etched in a little deeper than other memories and are stored in the mind forever.

23 Read each of the following two statements, Assertion (A) and Reason (R) and indicate your answer using codes given below :

Assertion (A) Heteronomous children focus on the objective consequences rather than intentions.

Reason (R) Moral development in a heteronomous child is limited.

Codes

1 Both (A) and (R) are true and (R) is the correct explanation of (A)
2 Both (A) and (R) are true, but (R) is not the correct explanation of (A)
3 (A) is true, but (R) is false
4 (A) is false, but (R) is true

Ans. *(1)*

Exp. Both (A) and (R) are true and (R) is the correct explanation of (A).

Heteronomous children focus on the objective consequences rather than intentions. It is true as in Jean Piaget's theory of moral development, heteronomous stage is the stage during which the child, approximately 6 to 10 years of age, equates morality with the rules and principles of his or her parents and other authority figures. That is, the child evaluates the rightness or wrongness of an act only in terms of adult sanctions for or against it and of the consequences or possible punishment it may bring.

Moral development in a heteronomous child is limited. It is true and it is the correct explanation because according to Jean Piaget theory of moral development children belongs to 6 to 10 years of age develop their morality only based on the obedience and in order to avoid punishments from the adults. Hence they focus on object consequences and moral development is also limited.

24 Match List I with List II and select the correct answer by choosing from the codes given below :

List I (Psychologist)	List II (Phenomenon)
A. Ebbinghaus	I. Some tasks to complete
B. Bartlett	II. Short stories Use
C. Murray	III. Use of meaningful words
D. Lewin	IV. Use of non-sense syllables

Codes

	A	B	C	D
1	I	II	III	IV
2	II	III	IV	I
3	III	IV	I	II
4	IV	III	II	I

Ans. *(4)*

Exp. The correct matching is A-IV, B-III, C-II, D-I.

Ebbinghaus is associated with the use of non-sense syllables. Non-sense syllables consisting of two consonants separated by a vowel were originally proposed by Hermann Ebbinghaus as the proper material to be used in the experimental study of verbatim-memory, such material being of uniform difficulty, accurately measurable, available in sufficient quantity.

Bartlett is associated with the use of meaningful words. Bartlett showed that very little of an event is actually perceived at the time of its occurrence but that, in reconstructing the memory, gaps in observation or perception are filled in with the aid of previous experiences.

Murray is associated with short stories use. Morgan and Murray (1935) used story telling technique. It was in the belief that the content of imagined stories would provide clues to the underlying dynamics of a subject's interpersonal relationships and self-attitudes.

Lewin is associated with some tasks to complete. Lewin reasoned that the "intention to carry out a specific task builds a psychological tension, which is released when the intended task is completed".

25 Which of the following sequences is correct with respect to effective teaching?

1 Match students level → specify learning goals → emphasize self comparison → suggest improvements and model problem-solving.
2 Specify learning goals → emphasize self-comparison → suggest improvements and model problem-solving → match student' level.
3 Suggest improvements and model problem solving →match student's level →specify learning goals →emphasize self-comparison.
4 Emphasize self-comparison → match student' level → specify learning goals → suggest improvements and model problem-solving.

Ans. *(1)*

Exp. Match students' level → specify learning goals → emphasize self comparison → suggest improvements and model problem-solving is the correct sequence with respect to effective teaching.

In order to make teaching most effective the teacher must attempt to match the student's level of understanding, specify learning goals in clear language and emphasise self-comparison so that the student performs better than before. The teacher should suggest inprovements and model problem-solving.

26 Which of the following techniques can be used to study activities in a living human brain?

I. Computerised Tomography
II. Ablation and Lesioning
III. Stereotoxic Procedures
IV. Functional Magnetic Resonance Imaging

Select the correct answer using the codes given below

1 I and IV
2 III and IV
3 II, III and IV
4 I, III and IV

Ans. (1)

Exp. Computerised Tomography and Functional Magnetic Resonance Imaging are the techniques which can be used to study activities in a living human brain.

Computerised Tomography falls under the category of structural brain imaging and fMRI falls under the category of functional brain imaging techniques.

Functional Magnetic Resonance Imaging (fMRI) scans are a series of MRIs measuring brain function. fMRI is a functional neuroimaging procedure using MRI technology that measures brain activity by detecting changes associated with blood flow.

Computerised Tomography is an imaging procedure that uses special X-ray equipment to create detailed pictures or scans, of areas inside the body.

27 Read each of the following two statements Assertion (A) and Reason (R) and indicate your answer using codes given below:

Assertion (A) Pre-operational child has irreversible thought.

Reason (R) The pre-operational child fails to perform conservation tasks.

Codes

1 Both (A) and (R) are true and (R) is the correct explanation of (A)
2 Both (A) and (R) are true, but (R) is not the correct explanation of (A)
3 (A) is true, but (R) is false
4 (A) is false, but (R) is true

Ans. (1)

Exp. Both (A) and (R) are true and (R) is the correct explanation of (A).

Pre-operational child has irreversible thought is true because the child believes that action cannot be reversed or done. For example if someone who made a bat using clay and if a boy sees it he would think that the bat cannot be reversed or turn into clay again.

The pre-operational child fails to perform conservation tasks is true because a child in his stage will not come to know that even if the particular quantity is changed to another shape it will remains the same as it is.

28 Sleep disorders can be categorised as

1 Paraphilias and Dysfunctions
2 Insomnia and Hypersomnia
3 Parasomnias and Dyssomnias
4 Serotonergic and Dopaminergic

Ans. (3)

Exp. Sleep disorders can be categorised as Parasomnias and Dyssomnias.

Parasomnias are the disorder which involves unusual physical events that takes place during sleep. Sleep walking, night terror, nightmares are the examples of parasomnia.

Disorder which affects the quality and quantity of your sleep is known as Dyssomnias. It may be either due to lack of sleep or excessive sleep. It includes Insomnia, narcolepsy etc.

29 Match List I with List II and select the correct answer by choosing from the codes given below :

List I (Goals in educational achievement)	List II (Description)
A. Mastery	I. Solving problem at hand gains importance
B. Task involvement	II. Students intend to maximise ability, regardless of short term failure
C. Performance improvement	III. Students focus on how they are judged by others
D. Ego involvement	IV. Students intend to increase competence

Codes

	A	B	C	D
1	II	I	IV	III
2	I	II	III	IV
3	III	IV	II	I
4	IV	III	II	I

Ans. (1)

Exp. The correct matching is A-II, B-I, C-IV and D-III.

Mastery is a goal in educational achievement when students intend to maximise ability, regardless of short term failure. A mastery goal orientation is defined as a focus on mastering new skills, trying to gain increased understanding, and improving competence.

Task involvement is a goal in educational achievement when solving problem at hand gains importance. Individuals who gain a sense of competence from improvements in personal mastery are considered task-involved.

Performance improvement is a goal in educational achievement when students intend to increase competence. A performance goal orientation focuses on demonstrating competence.

Ego involvement is a goal in educational achievement when students focus on how they are judged by others. Individuals who gain a sense of competence from demonstrating superior performance in relation to others are considered to be ego-involved.

30 Which of the following phenomena result from failures in attentional capture?

I. Inattentional blindness
II. Change detection
III. Flicker paradigm

Codes

1 I and III
2 I and II
3 II and III
4 All of these

Ans. (1)

Exp. Inattentional blindness and Flicker paradigm are the phenomena that result from failures in attentional capture.

Inattentional Blindness, also known as perceptual blindness, is a psychological lack of attention that is not associated with any vision defects or deficits. It may be further defined as the event in which an individual fails to recognise an unexpected stimulus that is in plain sight. Flicker paradigm involves the image and the altered image that appear on the screen and the observers are instructed to click the screen as soon as they see the difference.

31 Read each of the following two statements, Assertion (A) and Reason (R) and indicate your answer using codes given below :

Assertion (A) Individuals high in self-esteem have a relatively weak desire for social rewards.

Reason (R) Social anxiety and loneliness are both associated with unrewarding social interactions.

Codes

1 Both (A) and (R) are true and (R) is the correct explanation of (A)
2 Both (A) and (R) are true, but (R) is not the correct explanation of (A)
3 (A) is true, but (R) is false
4 (A) is false, but (R) is true

Ans. (2)

Exp. Both (A) and (R) are true, but (R) is not the correct explanation of (A).

Individuals high in self-esteem have a relatively weak desire for social rewards is true because an individual who is high in their self-esteem feels their subjective worth being, have a strong sense of self and are confident about them. They do not feel the need to be affirmed by others around them and take full responsibility of their thoughts and actions. Their need to seek social rewards tends to be low and have a relatively weak desire for social rewards.

Social anxiety and loneliness are both associated with unrewarding social interactions. It is also true because social anxiety and loneliness can make a person ill confident and unsure about socialising with other people. They either choose not to interact or interact reluctantly, unable to convey communicate effectively. They have immense fear of speaking in public and are unnerved by the thought that how others would be judging them.

Both the statements are independently correct, but the reason does not explain the given assertion.

32 Which of the following statement/s is/are true about culture-fair tests?

I. They attempt to minimise the use of language.
II. Suitable different versions of the test are devised for different cultural groups.
III. They are composed of materials to which all sociocultural groups have been presumably exposed.
IV. They attempt to assess the effects of culture on people's intellectual and creative skills.

Select the correct answer using the codes given below

1 Only I	2 I and III
3 I, II and III	4 II, III and IV

Ans. (2)

Exp. Statement I and III are correct about culture-fair tests.

Culture-fair tests attempt to minimise the use of language and contain less verbal instructions and the questions relate to images or puzzles. As they focus more on logic reasoning, they are better suited for people from different cultures.

They are composed of materials to which all sociocultural groups have been presumably exposed. An example of culture-fair intelligence test is Ravens progressive matrices.

However, research has shown that even these tests are not completely free of cultural bias.

33 Which is the correct sequence of the stages involved in creative thinking?

1 Preparation; orientation; illumination; incubation; verification
2 Preparation; incubation; illumination; orientation; verification
3 Orientation; preparation; incubation; illumination; verification
4 Orientation; preparation; illumination; incubation; verification

Ans. (3)

Exp. Orientation; preparation; incubation; illumination; verification is the correct sequences of stages in creative thinking. This stage of creativity was proposed by Graham Wallas.

Orientation is the stage which involves listing the dimensions of the problem.Preparation is the stage where you gather information for a problem. Incubation is the stage where you allows the mind to wander and prepares the mind to all open ideas. Illumination is the stage of insight of 'aha' experience and the final stage is the verification where you tend to evaluate and analyse the idea happened in illumination.

34 Selective attention in vision and audition respectively have been dubbed as

1 'optic' and 'haptic'
2 'spotlight' and 'gateway'
3 'spatial' and 'acoustic'
4 'central' and 'peripheral'

Ans. (2)

Exp. Selective attentions in vision and audition respectively have been dubbed as 'spotlight' and 'gateway'. Selective attention is the process of focusing on a particular object in the environment for a certain period of time. Attention is a limited resource, so selective attention allows us to tune out unimportant details and focus on what really matters.

35 Match List I with List II and select the correct answer by choosing from the codes given below :

List I (Intervention model)	List II (Used primarily for)
A. Eye Movement Desensitisation and Retraining	I. Ventilation
B. Client Centred Therapy	II. Cognitive Restructuring
C. Rational Emotive Behaviour Therapy	III. Post-traumatic Stress
D. Behaviour Therapy	IV. Desensitisation

Codes

	A	B	C	D		A	B	C	D
1	II	III	IV	I	2	I	II	III	IV
3	III	I	II	IV	4	IV	III	II	I

Ans. (3)

Exp. The correct matching is A-III, B-I, C-II and D-IV.

Eye Movement Desensitisation and Retraining is an intervention model used for Post-traumatic stress. Eye movement desensitisation and reprocessing (EMDR) is a structured therapy that encourages the patient to briefly focus on the trauma memory while simultaneously experiencing bilateral stimulation (typically eye movements), which is associated with a reduction in the vividness and emotion associated with the trauma memories.

Client-Centered therapy is an intervention model for Ventilation. It is a form of psychotherapy developed by Carl Rogers in the early 1940s. According to Rogers, an orderly process of client self-discovery and actualisation occurs in response to the therapist's consistent empathic understanding of, acceptance of, and respect for the client's frame. Ventilation allows a client's full and free expression of feelings or emotions, especially in session.

Rational Emotive Behaviour Therapy is an intervention model for Cognitive Restructuring. It is a form of cognitive behaviour therapy based on the concept that an individual's self-defeating beliefs influence and cause negative feelings and undesirable behaviours. It is a technique used in cognitive therapy and cognitive behaviour therapy to help the client identify his or her self-defeating beliefs or cognitive distortions, refute them, and then modify them so that they are adaptive and reasonable.

Behaviour Therapy is an intervention model for Desensitisation. It is a form of psychotherapy that applies the principles of learning, operant conditioning, and classical conditioning to eliminate symptoms and modify ineffective or maladaptive patterns of behaviour. Desensitisation is a reduction in emotional or physical reactivity to stimuli that is achieved by such means as deconditioning techniques.

36 Which is not the part of 'on the job training'?

1 Orientation training
2 Job instruction training
3 Role playing
4 Apprentice training

Ans. (4)

Exp. Apprentice training is not the part of 'on the job training'. It is a means by which a novice gains practical experience in a trade or profession, often through a formal program of instruction and supervision from an experienced practitioner or a mentor.

Orientation training, job instruction training and role playing come under the part of 'on the job training'.

Orientation Training : Orientation means providing new employees with basic information about the employer. Training programmes are used to ensure that the new employee has the basic knowledge required to perform the job satisfactorily.

Job Instruction Training (JIT) : It is a step-by-step, relatively simple technique used to train employees on the job. It is especially suitable for teaching manual skills or procedures; the trainer is usually an employee's supervisor but can be a co-worker.

Role-Playing Exercises : They are designed to simulate the interpersonal challenges faced when working with others. In the typical role-play, the candidate is given background information regarding the scenario and asked to play a particular role (e.g. team leader, customer service representative). During the exercise, he or she interacts directly with a trained role-player (actor).

37 Match List I with List II and select the correct answer by choosing from the codes given below :

List I	List II
A. Symbolising	I. Employee's belief that how successfully they can accomplish the task in future
B. Forethought	II. Employees process visual experiences that guide for their future actions
C. Self-regulatory	III. Employees plan their actions anticipating their desired performance level
D. Self-reflective	IV. Employees actions by setting internal standards for their performance

Codes

	A	B	C	D		A	B	C	D
1	I	II	III	IV	2	II	III	IV	I
3	III	IV	I	II	4	IV	I	II	III

Ans. (2)

Exp. The correct matching is A-II, B-III, C-IV and D-I.

Employees process visual experiences that guide for their future actions comes under the category of *Symbolising*. By symbolising their experiences, employees give coherence, direction, meaning, and continuity to their lives.

Employees plan their actions anticipating their desired performance comes under *Forethought*. Through the exercise of forethought, employees motivate themselves and guide their actions anticipatorily.

Employee's actions by setting internal standards for their performance are known as *Self-regulatory*. The self-regulation of motivation, affect, and action operates partly through personal standards and evaluative reactions to one's own behavior.

Employee's belief that how successfully they can accomplish the task in future is known as *Self-reflective level*. In verifying the adequacy of thought by self-reflective means, employees generate ideas and act on them or predict occurrences from them.

38 'Pygmalion effect' in educational settings suggests

1 exceptional progress by student as a result of high teacher expectations
2 biases creeping into summative assessment
3 authenticity factors in classroom assessment
4 influences on curricular structure

Ans. (1)

Exp. 'Pygmalion effect' in educational settings suggests exceptional progress by student as a result of high teacher expectations.

'The Pygmalion effect' refers to situations where teacher expectancies of student performance become self-fulfilling prophecies; students perform better or worse than other students based on the way their teacher expects them to perform.

39 Match List I with List II and select the correct answer by choosing from the codes given below :

List I (Psychologist)		List II (Concept/approach)
A. Vygotsky	I.	Ethological approach
B. Piaget	II.	Ecological approach
C. Bronfenbrenner	III.	Zone of proximal development
D. Bowlby	IV.	Epistemological approach

Codes

	A	B	C	D		A	B	C	D
1	III	IV	II	I	2	III	I	II	IV
3	I	IV	III	II	4	IV	I	II	III

Ans. (1)

Exp. The correct matching is A-III, B-IV, C-II and D-I.

Lev Vygotsky developed the zone of proximal development in what a child learns without guidance and a child learns with adult guidance.

Jean Piaget theory of cognitive development is mainly related to the epistemological approach.

Bronfenbrenner ecological theory focuses on context and quality of child environment.

John Bowlby approach was ethological which was in his attachment theory. Ethological approach is an individual's behaviour which is a part of biological component.

40 Which of the following is not a diagnosable sleep disorder?

1 Somnambulism
2 Somniloquy
3 Sleep terror
4 Insomnia

Ans. (4)

Exp. Insomnia is not a diagnosable sleep disorder. It is difficulty falling asleep or staying asleep, even when a person has the chance to do so.

Somnambulism (sleep walking), Somniloquy (sleep talking) and sleep terror are the diagnosable sleep disorder.

Somniloquy or sleep-talking is a parasomnia that refers to talking aloud while asleep. It can be quite loud, ranging from simple mumbling sounds to loud shouts and long frequently inarticulate speeches and can occur many times during a sleep cycle.

Somnambulism is an abnormal condition of sleep in which motor acts (as walking) are performed.

Sleep Terror or Night terror, is a sleep disorder, causing feelings of terror or dread and typically occurs during the first hours of stage 3-4 (NREM) sleep. Night terrors tend to happen during periods of arousal from delta sleep, also known as slow-wave sleep.

41 A field experiment at the Bronx Zoo illustrated the potential importance of ________ indicating that an individual has legitimate authority. Fill in the blank from given below.

1 gender
2 uniforms
3 age
4 an authoritarian personality

Ans. (2)

Exp. A field experiment at the Bronx Zoo illustrated the potential importance of uniforms indicating that an individual has legitimate authority. When the visitors entered the zoo, a person was approached to them to not to touch the handrail of a bird exhibit. Visitors were more often comply with the person who was dressed in uniforms than a person who wore casual clothes.

42 Self-actualisers are characterised as

I. They have more efficient perception of reality than non-actualisers.
II. They show greater acceptance of themselves, others, and nature than do non-actualisers.
III. They tend to be more concerned with undertaking tasks that will benefit themselves.
IV. They also have some weaknesses.

Codes

1 I, II and III	2 I, II and IV
3 II, III and IV	4 I, III and IV

Ans. (2)

Exp. Statement I, II and IV are correct in relation to Self-actualisers. The characteristics of self-actualisers are as follows:

- Self-actualisers have more efficient perception of reality than non-actualisers. They are able to judge situations correctly and honestly. They are very sensitive to the superficial and dishonest.
- They show greater acceptance of themselves, others, and nature than do non-actualisers. Self-actualisers accept their own human nature with all its flaws. The shortcomings of others and the contradictions of the human condition are accepted with humour and tolerance.
- They also have some weaknesses. Being self-actualised does not mean they do not have any weaknesss or shortcomings.
- They do not tend to be more concerned with undertaking tasks that will benefit themselves. Most of Maslow's subjects had a mission to fulfill in life or some task or problem 'beyond' themselves (instead of outside themselves) to pursue.

43 Thinking is a complex set of collaborations between ________ and _______ representations and processes.

1 linguistic; semantic
2 linguistic; verbal
3 semantic; non-linguistic
4 linguistic; non-linguistic

Ans. (4)

Exp. Thinking is a complex set of collaborations between linguistic and non-linguistic representations and processes. Linguistics is the scientific study of the physical, structural, functional, psychological, and social characteristics of human language. A non-linguistic meaning is an actual or possible derivation from sentience, which is not associated with signs that have any original or primary intent of communication. Gestures, symbols pertain to non-linguistic whereas linguistics pertains to language.

44 Match List I with List II and select the correct answer by choosing from the codes given below :

List I	List II
A. Autistic thinking	I. Planning
B. Creative thinking	II. Fantasy
C. Deterministic thinking	III. Illusion
D. Cognitive thinking	IV. Dreams

Codes

	A	B	C	D
1	I	II	III	IV
2	IV	III	II	I
3	IV	I	II	III
4	I	IV	III	II

Ans. (2)

Exp. The correct matching is A-IV, B-III, C-II and D-I.

Dreams involve Autistic thinking. Autistic thinking is narcissistic, egocentric thought processes, such as fantasising and daydreaming that have little or no relation to reality. It is similar to dereistic thinking, but the emphasis is on self-absorption rather than disconnection from reality.

Illusion involves Creative thinking. Creative thinking is the mental processes leading to a new invention, solution, or synthesis in any area. A creative solution may use pre-existing elements (e.g., objects, ideas) but creates a new relationship between them. Products of creative thinking include illusions new machines, social ideas, scientific theories, and artistic works.

Fantasy involves Deterministic thinking. Deterministic thinking is one of the major cognitive distortions. This type of thinking ignores any possibility in making a conclusion about events.

Planning involves Cognitive thinking. Cognitive thinking refers to the use of mental activities and skills to perform tasks such as planning, learning, reasoning, understanding, remembering, and paying attention and more.

45 Signal detection depends upon

1 motivation and expectations
2 signal intensity and noise
3 sensitivity and response criterion
4 absolute and relative thresholds

Ans. (3)

Exp. Signal detection depends upon sensitivity and response criterion.

The initial point for signal detection theory is that nearly all reasoning and decision making takes place in the presence of some unpredictability. Signal detection theory provides an accurate language and graphic notation for analysing decision making in the presence of uncertainty. The general approach of signal detection theory has direct application in terms of sensory experiments.

Signal detection theory states that the detection of a stimulus depends on both the intensity of a stimulus and physical/psychological state of the individual. According to the theory, there are a number of determiners of how a detecting system will detect a signal and where its threshold levels will be.

46 Which of the following does not present with symptoms of mental retardation?

1 Cri du chat syndrome
2 Down's syndrome
3 Fugue
4 Trisomy 21

Ans. (3)

Exp. Fugue is not associated with symptoms of mental retardation.

Fugue comes under the dissociative disorder where a person losses awareness of their identity which usually involves in unexpected travel.

Cri du chat syndrome, Down's syndrome (chromosomal abnormality of trisomy-21) comes under the symptom of mental retardation.

47 Read each of the following two statements, Assertion (A) and Reason (R) and indicate your answer using the codes given below:

Assertion (A) Neurons cannot fire during absolute refractory period.

Reason (R) A neuron can release only one neurotransmitter.

Codes

1 Both (A) and (R) are true and (R) is the correct explanation of (A)
2 Both (A) and (R) are true, but (R) is not the correct explanation of (A)
3 (A) is true, but (R) is false
4 (A) is false, but (R) is true

Ans. (3)

Exp. Neurons cannot fire during absolute refractory period. During the absolute refractory period, the neuron cannot be excited to generate a second action potential (no matter how intense the stimulus).

A neuron can release only one neurotransmitter is false as during the co-transmission stage, neuron can release two or more neurotransmitters.

48 Read each of the following two statements, Assertion (A) and Reason (R) and indicate your answer using the codes given below:

Assertion (A) When method of equal appearing intervals is employed to scale attitude items, median is usually used as an estimate of scale value.

Reason (R) Under normal distribution, mean, median and mode are identical.

Codes

1 Both (A) and (R) are true and (R) is the correct explanation of (A)
2 Both (A) and (R) are true, but (R) is not the correct explanation of (A)
3 (A) is true, but (R) is false
4 (A) is false, but (R) is true

Ans. (2)

Exp. Both (A) and (R) are true, but (R) is not the correct explanation of (A).

When method of equal appearing intervals is employed to scale attitude items, median is usually used as an estimate of scale value. It is true that the median is generally a better measure of the center when there are extreme values or outliers because it is not affected by the precise numerical values of the outliers.

Under normal distribution, mean, median and mode are identical. It is true because the normal distribution is a symmetrical, bell-shaped distribution in which the mean, median and mode are all equal. This, however, does not explain the use of median in equal appearing interval scale. Therefore, the reason does not explain the assertion.

49 Match List I with List II and select the correct answer by choosing from the codes given below :

List I (Book)	List II (Author)
A. Toward a Psychology of Being	I. May
B. A Way of Being	II. Maslow
C. Man's Search for Meaning	III. Rogers
D. Love and Will	IV. Frankl

Codes

	A	B	C	D
1	I	II	III	IV
2	II	III	IV	I
3	III	II	I	IV
4	IV	I	II	III

Ans. (2)

Exp. The correct matching is A-II, B-III, C-IV and D-I.

Toward a Psychology of Being is written by Abraham Maslow. In this compelling book, Maslow uses studies of psychologically healthy people and of the healthiest experiences and moments in the lives of average people to demonstrate that human beings can be loving, noble and creative, that they are capable of pursuing the highest values and aspirations.

A Way of Being is written by Carl Rogers. Psychologist Carl Rogers was the founder of the humanistic psychology movement and father of client-centered therapy.

Man's search for Meaning was written by Victor Frankl. It is a 1946 book by Viktor Frankl chronicling his experiences as a prisoner in Nazi concentration camps during World War II, and describing his psychotherapeutic method, which involved identifying a purpose in life to feel positive about, and then immersively imagining that outcome.

Love and Will was written by Rollo May. May shows how we can attain a deeper consciousness by bringing fresh insight to these concepts.

50 Therapist suggested to Sunil that while trying to give up the habit of washing hands unnecessarily, he should wear a rubber band around his wrist and snap it everytime he feels like washing his hands. What therapy he is using?

1 Systematic desensitisation
2 Aversion therapy
3 Flooding
4 Modelling

Ans. (2)

Exp. Therapist suggested to Sunil that while trying to give up the habit of washing hands unnecessarily, he should wear a rubber band around his wrist and snap it every time he feels like washing his hands. He is using Aversion therapy.

Aversion therapy or aversive therapy is a behavioral intervention treatment which is used to eliminate unwanted or undesirable behaviours in which a person is conditioned to dislike a certain stimulus due to its repeated pairing with an unpleasant stimulus.

51 The need for __________ produces active, controlling social behaviour while need for _______ produces more passive, less controlling social behaviour.

1 affiliation; self-esteem 2 confidence; intimacy
3 affiliation; intimacy 4 intimacy; affiliation

Ans. *(3)*

Exp. The need for affiliation produces active, controlling social behaviour while need for intimacy produces more passive, less controlling social behaviour.

The need for affiliation is a term that was popularised by David McClelland and describes a person's need to feel a sense of involvement and belonging within a social group.

52 According to Triarchic Theory of Intelligence, arrange the correct functional sequence of metacomponents.

1 Identification of problem → defining the givens, goals and obstacles → choosing appropriate strategy → selection of lower order processes → selection of mental representation → allocation of mental resources → monitoring → evaluation.
2 Identification of problem → defining the givens, goals and obstacles → selection of lower order processes → choosing appropriate strategy → selecting a mental representation → allocating mental resources → monitoring → evaluation
3 Identification of problem → choosing appropriate strategy → defining givens, goals and obstacles → allocating mental resources → monitoring → selecting mental representation → evaluation
4 Defining the givens, goals and obstacles → identification of problem → selection of lower order processes → choosing appropriate strategy → selecting a mental representation → allocating mental resources → monitoring → evaluation

Ans. *(2)*

Exp. According to Triarchic Theory of Intelligence, the correct functional sequence of metacomponents are :

Identification of problem → defining the givens, goals and obstacles → selection of lower order processes → choosing appropriate strategy → selection of mental representation → allocation of mental resources → monitoring → evaluation.

Triarchic Theory of Intelligence was given by Robert Sternberg. Metacomponents are higher order mental processes that intelligent people use effectively to guide their problem-solving efforts. These components, which are common to all tasks, include the following:

Identification of problem : It involves recognising the existence of the problem that needs to be solved.

Defining the givens, goals and obstacles : It involves defining the nature of the problem with all the goals, and obstacles of the problem.

Selection of lower order processes : It involves selection of lower order processes that will be needed to solve the problem.

Choosing appropriate strategy : It involves choosing appropriate strategy for solving the problem.

Selecting a mental representation : It involves selecting a mental representation or 'mental map' of the givens, the relations among the givens, and the goals found in the problem.

Allocation of mental resources : It involves allocation of one's own attention and other mental resources for use in solving the problem.

Monitoring : It includes monitoring of how well one is achieving one's goals during problem solving.

Evaluation : It includes the results once a solution has been reached.

53 Match List I with List II and select the correct answer by choosing from the codes given below :

List I (Method of student discipline)	List II (Description)
A. Positive reinforcement	I. Decreasing behaviour by presenting aversive stimulus after it
B. Negative reinforcement	II. Strengthening behaviour by removing aversive stimulus when behaviour occurs.
C. Presentation punishment	III. Decreasing behaviour by removing pleasant stimulus after behaviour occurs.
D. Removal punishment	IV. Strengthening behaviour by presenting desired stimulus after behaviour occurs.

Codes

	A	B	C	D		A	B	C	D
1	I	II	III	IV	2	II	IV	I	III
3	IV	II	I	III	4	III	I	II	IV

Ans. *(3)*

Exp. The correct matching is A-IV, B-II, C-I and D-III.

Strengthening behaviour by presenting desired stimulus after behaviour occurs is known as *Positive reinforcement*. It is the procedure of presenting a positive reinforcer after a response.

Strengthening behaviour by removing aversive stimulus when behaviour occurs is known as *Negative reinforcement*. It is the removal, prevention, or postponement of an aversive stimulus as a consequence of a response, which, in turn, increases the probability of that response.

Decreasing behaviour by removing pleasant stimulus after behavior occurs is known as *Negative punishment*. It is the punishment that results because some stimulus or circumstance is removed as a consequence of a response.

Decreasing behaviour by presenting aversive stimulus after it occurs is known as *Positive punishment*. It is the punishment that results because some stimulus or circumstance is presented as a consequence of a response.

54 Read each of the following two statements, Assertion (A) and Reason (R) and indicate your answer using codes given below:

Assertion (A) The child always carries water bottle with him while he goes to school.

Reason (R) The child wants to satisfy his primary need.

Codes

1 Both (A) and (R) are true and (R) is the correct explanation of (A)
2 Both (A) and (R) are true, but (R) is not the correct explanation of (A)
3 (A) is true, but (R) is false
4 (A) is false, but (R) is true

Ans. *(1)*

Exp. Both (A) and (R) are true and (R) is the correct explanation of (A).

The child always carries water bottle with him while he goes to school. The child wants to satisfy his primary need.

The primary need is an innate need that arises out of biological processes and leads to physical satisfaction, such as the need for water and sleep. Therefore, the child carries a water bottle to satisfy his primary need of thirst.

55 Read each of the following two statements, Assertion (A) and Reason (R) and indicate your answer using codes given below:

Assertion (A) According to Rogers, ideal condition for the development of a healthy self concept and movement toward becoming fully functioning is unconditional positive regard.

Reason (R) With unconditional positive regard there is incongruence between true self and experience.

Codes

1 Both (A) and (R) are true and (R) is the correct explanation of (A)
2 Both (A) and (R) are true, but (R) is not the correct explanation of (A)
3 (A) is true, but (R) is false
4 (A) is false, but (R) is true

Ans. *(3)*

Exp. (A) is true, but (R) is false.

According to Rogers, ideal condition for the development of a healthy self-concept and movement toward becoming fully functioning is unconditional positive regard. Unconditional positive regard is accepting the client as it is in spite of what the client does or says. It is an attitude of caring, acceptance, and prizing that others express toward an individual irrespective of his or her behaviour and without regard to the others' personal standards. Unconditional positive regard is considered conducive to the individual's self-awareness, self-worth, and personality growth. It is, according to Carl Rogers, a universal human need essential to healthy development.

With unconditional positive regard there is incongruence between true self and experience is false because with unconditional positive regard there is congruence between true self and experience.

56 Read each of the following two statements, Assertion (A) and Reason (R) and indicate your answer using codes given below :

Assertion (A) Managers differ across cultures in their interpersonal styles and skills.

Reason (R) Personal values held by a manager shape his perception of a situation.

Codes

1 Both (A) and (R) are true and (R) is the correct explanation of (A)
2 Both (A) and (R) are true, but (R) is not the correct explanation of (A)
3 (A) is true, but (R) is false
4 (A) is false, but (R) is true

Ans. *(2)*

Exp. Both (A) and (R) are true but (R) is not the correct explanation of (A).

Managers differ across cultures in their interpersonal styles and skills. Each manager style of approach is different in respective of cultures. Environment and one's community does have an impact on individual interpersonal styles and skills.

Personal values held by a manager shape his perception of a situation is also true because the values adhered to by the manager will shape his perception of a situation.

57 Which among the following neurotransmitters are found throughout central nervous system?

I. Acetylcholine
II. Norepinephrine
III. Dopamine
IV. Serotonin
V. GABA

Codes

1 I, III and IV
2 III, IV and V
3 II, III and IV
4 I, IV and V

Ans. *(4)*

Exp. Acetylcholine, Serotonin and GABA are the neurotransmitters found throughout central nervous system.

Acetylcholine acts as neuromodulator as well as neurotransmitters which mainly involves to contract smooth muscles. Serotonin is mainly responsible for mood, happiness. GABA is mainly responsible for stress relaxation and acts as a inhibitory neurotransmitter.

58 Read each of the following two statements, Assertion (A) and Reason (R) and indicate your answer using codes given below:

Assertion (A) As per Guilford's SOI model, intelligence can be taken as superset of creativity.

Reason (R) Creativity involves divergent production that is just one of five operations of intellect.

Codes

1 Both (A) and (R) are true and (R) is the correct explanation of (A)
2 Both (A) and (R) are true, but (R) is not the correct explanation of (A)
3 (A) is true, but (R) is false
4 (A) is false, but (R) is true

Ans. (3)

Exp. (A) is true, but (R) is false.

As per Guilford's SOI model, intelligence can be taken as superset of creativity. It is true as Guilford's (1967) work on the Structure of the Intellect (SOI) implies that creativity is a subset of intelligence; he considered divergent thinking as one of the cognitive operations in the SOI model.

Creativity involves divergent production that is just one of five operations of intellect. It is false as there are six operations of intellect instead of five. Operations or general intellectual processes are cognition, memory recording, memory retention, divergent production, convergent production and evaluation.

59 In which one of the following scaling methods, Law of Comparative Judgement is used clearly while computing scale values?

1 Summated ratings
2 Equal appearing intervals
3 JND scales
4 Paired Comparison

Ans. (4)

Exp. In Paired comparison, Law of Comparative Judgement is used clearly while computing scale values.

The Law of Comparative Judgement was conceived by L.L. Thurstone. It is more aptly described as a model that is used to obtain measurements from any process of pairwise comparison. Paired comparison generally is any process of comparing entities in pairs to judge which of each entity is preferred or has a greater amount of some quantitative property or whether or not the two entities are identical.

60 Read each of the following two statements, Assertion (A) and Reason (R) and indicate your answer using codes given below :

Assertion (A) Japanese subjects detect background changes while US subjects detect focal object changes.

Reason (R) Eastern cultures encourage a holistic view, Western cultures de-emphasise context.

Codes

1 Both (A) and (R) are true and (R) is the correct explanation of (A)
2 Both (A) and (R) are true, but (R) is not the correct explanation of (A)
3 (A) is true, but (R) is false
4 (A) is false, but (R) is true

Ans. (1)

Exp. Both (A) and (R) are true and (R) is the correct explanation of (A).

Japanese subjects detect background changes while U.S. subjects detect focal object changes. It is true as East Asians (Japanese) and Westerners (U.S.) perceive the world and think about it in very different ways. Westerners are inclined to attend to some focal object, analysing its attributes and categorising it in an effort to find out what rules govern its behaviour. East Asians are more likely to attend to a broad perceptual and conceptual field, noticing relationships and changes and grouping objects based on family resemblance rather than category membership.

Eastern cultures encourage a holistic view, Western cultures de-emphasise context is also true and it is the correct explanation because western culture emphasise independent autonomy and eastern culture promotes collectivist and holistic approach.

61 The model of memory most frequently cited consists of Short Term Memory (STM) which serve(s) as gateway to Long-Term Memory (LTM). This model was propounded by

1 Ebbinghaus
2 Craik and Lockhart
3 Tulving
4 Atkinson and Shiffrin

Ans. (4)

Exp. The model of memory most frequently cited consists of Short Term Memory (STM) which serve(s) as gateway to Long-Term Memory (LTM). This model was propounded by Atkinson and Shiffrin. The Atkinson–Shiffrin model (also known as the Multi-Store Model) is a model of memory proposed in 1968 by Richard Atkinson and Richard Shiffrin. The model asserts that human memory has three separate components, which are:

(i) Sensory register, where sensory information enters memory.

(ii) Short-term store, also called working memory or short-term memory, which receives and holds input from both the sensory register and the long-term store.

(iii) Long-term store, where information which has been rehearsed in the short-term store is held indefinitely.

62 Which of the following disorders generally show a childhood onset?

I. Delusional disorder
II. Asperger's syndrome
III. Attention-deficit hyperactivity disorder
IV. Mild Cognitive Impairment

Codes

1 III and IV 2 II and III
3 I, II and III 4 II, III and IV

Ans. (2)

Exp. Asperger's syndrome and Attention-deficit hyperactivity disorder are the disorders which generally show a childhood onset.

Asperger Syndrome (AS) is a neurodevelopment disorder characterised by significant difficulties in social interaction and non-verbal communication, alongwith restricted and repetitive patterns of behaviour and interests.

Attention deficit hyperactivity disorder (ADHD) is one of the most common neurodevelopmental disorders of childhood. It is usually first diagnosed in childhood and often lasts into adulthood. Children with ADHD may have trouble paying attention, controlling impulsive behaviours or be overly active.

63 The phenomenon of clinging to one's initial conceptions after the basis on which they were formed and had been discredited refers to

1 Belief bias 2 Belief perseverance
3 Over confidence 4 Framing decisions

Ans. (2)

Exp. The phenomenon of clinging to one's initial conceptions after the basis on which they were formed and had been discredited refers to Belief perseverance.

People tend to hold on to their beliefs even when it appears that they shouldn't. Belief perseverance refers to the tendency that people cling to their initial conceptions even when the evidence proves them wrong or the receiving new information that contradicts or disconfirms the basis of that belief.

64 Long-Term Potentiality involves

1 release of nitric oxide
2 increase in cell bodies
3 increased number of NMDA (N-methyl-d-aspartic acid) receptors
4 increased sensitivity of NMDA (N-methyl-d-aspartic acid) receptors

Ans. (4)

Exp. Long Term Potentiality involves increased sensitivity of NMDA (N-methyl-d-aspartic acid) receptors. NMDA receptors must be activated, and the membrane of the post synaptic neuron must be partially depolarized are the two criteria for long term potentiation to occur.

65 Mechanistic and Cognitive approaches to motivation differ in the extent to which ______ are invoked to account for the initiation, direction, intensity and persistence of goal directed behaviour.

1 dynamic traits 2 higher mental processes
3 drives 4 instincts

Ans. (3)

Exp. Mechanistic and Cognitive approaches to motivation differ in the extent to which drives are invoked to account for the initiation, direction, intensity and persistence of goal directed behaviour.

Drive combines motivation, learning, reinforcement, and habit formation to explain and predict human behaviour. It describes where drives come from, what behaviours result from these drives, and how these behaviours are sustained. The difference between the mechanistic and cognitive approaches is what they believe the source of behaviour is.

The mechanistic approach believes that environmental or homeostatic changes motivate behaviour. The cognitive approach believes that how information is processed has an influence on motivated states. Attributing your failure of being able to complete a task to its difficulty will have different effects on future motivation than attributing it to a lack of skills.

66 Which of the following are the correct explanation of discrimination and stimulus generalisations?

I. Learning to respond to one stimulus but not to the other similar stimuli.
II. Learning to respond to one stimulus but not to the other different stimuli.
III. Stimuli similar to the one used during conditioning also elicit the conditioned response.
IV. Stimuli different to the one used during conditioning also elicit the conditioned response.

Codes

1 I and III 2 I and IV 3 II and III 4 II and IV

Ans. (1)

Exp. Statement I and III are the correct explanation of discrimination and stimulus generalisations.

Discrimination involves the ability to distinguish between one stimulus and similar stimuli. In both cases, it means only responding to certain stimuli but not to those that are similar.

Stimuli similar to the one used during conditioning also elicit the conditioned response. Stimulus generalisation is when stimuli elicit similar responses to previously conditioned stimuli that share certain qualities.

67 Training and development offer competitive advantage to a firm by

I. removing performance deficiency
II. minimising accidents and damage
III. making employees stay long
IV. meeting employees personal needs

Codes

1 I, III and IV	2 II, III and IV
3 I, II and IV	4 I, II and III

Ans. (4)

Exp. Training and development offer competitive advantage to a firm by removing performance deficiency, minimising accidents and damage and make employees stay long. Meeting employee's personal needs is not a part of training and development which does not offer competitive advantage to a firm.

68 Which of the following is the term for describing a child's one word utterances?

1 Over extensions
2 Under extensions
3 Holophrases
4 Telegraphic speech

Ans. (3)

Exp. Holophrases is the term for describing a child's one word utterances.

A holophrase is one of the single-word utterances characteristic of children in the early stages of language acquisition, such as 'dada' or 'yes'. These are considered to involve a speech act going beyond the literal meaning of the single word so that, for example, 'cookie' means 'I want a cookie now.'

69 Read each of the following two statements, Assertion (A) and Reason (R) and indicate your answer using codes given below :

Assertion (A) People have tendency to recall experiences that are consistent with their current moods.

Reason (R) Moods and memories are congruent.

Codes

1 Both (A) and (R) are true and (R) is the correct explanation of (A)
2 Both (A) and (R) are true, but (R) is not the correct explanation of (A)
3 (A) is true, but (R) is false
4 (A) is false, but (R) is true

Ans. (1)

Exp. Both (A) and (R) are true and (R) is the correct explanation of (A).

People have tendency to recall experiences that are consistent with their current moods. It is true as mood-congruent memory is the consistency between one's mood state and the emotional context of memories recalled. During positive mood states, individuals will tend to retrieve pleasant memories, whereas during negative mood states, negative thoughts and associations will more likely come to mind.

Moods and memories are congruent is also true. It explains why people recall experience with their current moods. People try to remember information when their mood is similar (for example happy mood) to the time of encoding is known as mood-congruent memory.

70 Match List I with List II and select the correct answer by choosing from the codes given below:

List I (Approach to perception)	List II (Description)
A. Computational	I. Fragments of sensory information form reality
B. Constructivist	II. Direct reception of information from environment
C. Ecological	III. Separate recognition of visual features
D. Feature analysis	IV. Manipulate incoming signals to understand world

Codes

	A	B	C	D
1	I	II	III	IV
2	IV	I	II	III
3	III	IV	I	II
4	II	III	IV	I

Ans. (2)

Exp. The correct matching is A-IV, B-I, C-II and D-III.

Manipulate incoming signals to understand world comes under the *Computational approach*. The computational approach to perception holds that perception is the result of nervous system activity that modifies and processes raw sensations into reality.

Fragments of sensory information form reality come under *Constructivist approach*. The Constructivist approach to perception holds that we construct reality by putting together raw bits of sensory information. Our expectations of reality influence our perceptions.

Direct reception of information from environment comes under *Ecological approach*. The Ecological approach to perception argues that the environment holds many clues that allow us to perceive our surroundings.

Separate recognition of visual features comes under *Feature analysis*. The ability to perceive form, patterns, and objects not only results from the encoding of stimulus features by visual neurons (feature analysis), but is also under the influence of top-down processes.

Directions (Q. Nos. 71 to 75) *Read the following paragraph and answer the questions which follow :*

An industrial psychologist wanted to study the job efficiency of the company executives in relation to MBA marks, selection test scores, evaluations scores at the end of inhouse training. Job efficiency correlated with MBA marks ($r = 0.40$), selection test scores ($r = 0.50$) and the evaluation scores at the end of inhouse training ($r = 0.60$). All the three correlations were statistically significant. The multiple regression was computed using job efficiency as the criterion and the other three variables as the predictors. The three predictors explained 56.25 percent of variance in the job efficiency.

The industrial psychologist further thought that the communication skills assessment would enhance the predictability of job efficiency. As such, the communication skills of the respondents were also assessed, which correlated with job efficiency by 0.35, again a statistically significant value. However when communication skills were added as the fourth predictor in the multiple regression, the change in R^2 (squared multiple correlation) was found to be insignificant.

71 What percent of variance in job efficiency is explained by evaluation scores at the end of training?

1 36 percent
2 40 percent
3 60 percent
4 64 percent

Ans. (1)

Exp. Correlation for job efficiency was 0.6, $r = 0.6$

Per cent of variance $R^2 = 0.6 * 0.6 = 36$ per cent.

72 What would be the multiple correlation between the job efficiency and the three predictors (MBA marks, selection test scores, and the evaluations scores at the end of inhouse training)?

1 0.50
2 0.65
3 0.75
4 Inadequate data

Ans. (3)

Exp. The multiple correlation between job efficiency and the three predictors (MBA marks, selection test scores, and the evaluations scores at the end of inhouse training) is 0.75. The correlation squared is the percent of variance that is explained by the dependent variable, i.e., job efficiency. The variance for three predictors is 56.25%.

$$\% \text{ Variance} = R^2$$
$$56.25\% = R^2$$
$$56.25/100 = R^2$$
$$0.5625 = R^2$$
$$R = \sqrt{0.5625}$$
$$= 0.75$$

73 Which one of the following conclusion can be drawn on the basis of above study?

I. All the four predictors (MBA marks, selection test scores, evaluation scores at the end of inhouse training, and the communication skills) are individually valid.
II. Out of the above four predictors, all except communication skills, are individually valid.
III. Communication skills assessment has satisfactory incremental validity.
IV. Communication skills assessment has unsatisfactory incremental validity.

Select the correct answer using the codes given below

1 I only
2 I and III
3 I and IV
4 II and IV

Ans. (3)

Exp. All the four predictors (M.B.A. marks, selection test scores, evaluation scores at the end of in house training, and the communication skills) are individually valid and Communication skills assessment has unsatisfactory incremental validity is because even after the introduction of communication skills there is no change in the values and hence this conclusion can also be drawn.

74 The 'b' coefficient obtained in multiple regression is

1 Partial correlation coefficient
2 Correlation coefficient
3 Regression coefficient
4 Partial regression coefficient

Ans. (4)

Exp. The 'b' coefficient obtained in multiple regressions is Partial regression coefficient. If it is linear regression coefficient we call it as regression coefficient. If it is multiple regression coefficients we call it as Partial regression coefficient.

75 Which one of the following conclusion can be drawn on the basis of above paragraph?

1 All the four predictors (MBA marks, selection test scores, evaluation scores at the end of inhouse training and communication skills) are uncorrelated with each other.
2 Out of the four predictors, at least some are correlated with each other.
3 Communication skills scores are uncorrelated with other predictors.
4 The four predictors theoretically appear to be correlated, but we cannot infer about their intercorrelations from the data provided.

Ans. (2)

Exp. Out of the four predictors, at least some are correlated with each other because even after the introduction of communication skills there is no significant change in the amount of variance but some of the predictors are at least correlated with each other.

UGC-NET PSYCHOLOGY

SOLVED PAPER 2015 (December)

PAPER II

1 Motion sickness can occur when

I. one loses his vestibular sense.

II. one relies only on visual information.

III. one's visual information and vestibular system's information are congruent.

IV. one's visual system and vestibular system are in conflict.

Codes

1 Only I
2 I and II
3 Only IV
4 I and IV

Ans. *(3)*

Exp. Motion sickness can occur when one's visual system and vestibular system are in conflict.

Motion sickness is a common syndrome that occurs upon exposure to certain types of motion. It is thought to be caused by conflict between the vestibular, visual, and other proprioceptive systems. Although nausea is the hallmark symptom, it is often preceded by stomach awareness, malaise, drowsiness, and irritability. Many people suffer from this condition if they ride on a roller coaster or other similar amusement park rides.

2 Read each of the following two statements, Assertion (A) and Reason (R) and indicate your answer using the codes given below:

Assertion (A) Iconic store is a discrete visual sensory store.

Reason (R) Because information is believed to be stored in the form of visual codes.

Codes

1 Both (A) and (R) are true and (R) is the correct explanation of (A)
2 Both (A) and (R) are true, but (R) is not the correct explanation of (A)
3 (A) is true, but (R) is false
4 (A) is false, but (R) is true

Ans. *(3)*

Exp. (A) is true, but (R) is false.

Iconic store is a discrete visual sensory store. This is true as iconic memory is the visual sensory memory register pertaining to the visual domain and a fast-decaying store of visual information. It is a component of the visual memory system which also includes Visual Short-term Memory (VSTM) and Long-term Memory (LTM).

Because information is believed to be stored in the form of visual codes. This is false as information is not stored in the form of visual codes only. The information can be stored in the auditory, spatial, and tactile forms. Only iconic memory is stored in the form of visual codes.

3 Backward conditioning occurs when

1 CS and US are presented simultaneously
2 CS is presented first and US is presented before the termination of CS
3 CS is presented first and US is presented after the termination of CS
4 US is presented first and CS is presented after the termination of US

Ans. *(4)*

Exp. Backward conditioning occurs when US is presented first and CS is presented after the termination of US.

Backward conditioning is a type of conditioning in which the presentation of the Unconditioned Stimulus (US) precedes the presentation of the Conditioned Stimulus (CS). This type of conditioning is very ineffective because the CS does not predict the US. From the perspective of an evolutionary psychologist, it is not adaptive, and perhaps maladaptive, to learn something about a neutral stimulus if it predicts nothing that is biologically relevant.

4 Which among the following defines problem space?

I. An initial state

II. A goal state

III. A set of operations

Select the correct answer from the codes given below :

1 I and III
2 I and II
3 II and III
4 I, II and III

Ans. (4)

Exp. An initial state, a goal state and a set of operations define a problem space.

According to the Problem Space Theory, people solve problems by searching in a problem space. The problem space consists of the initial (current) state, the goal state and all possible states in between. The actions that people take in order to move from one state to another are known as operators.

5 The James-Lange Theory and the Cognitive Theory of Emotion disagree on whether

1 specific brain centers are involved in specific emotions
2 bodily feedback determines which emotion is felt
3 individuals can judge their emotions accurately
4 there is no any biological involvement in human emotions

Ans. (2)

Exp. The James-Lange Theory and the Cognitive Theory of Emotion disagree on whether bodily feedback determines which emotion is felt.

The James-Lange theory states that our emotions are caused by our interpretation of bodily reactions. According to the theory, when an event occurs, our body reacts and then we feel emotion after the brain interprets that physiological change.

Rather than being the cause of physiological events, emotions happen as a result of physiological events, such as muscular tension, increased heart rate, perspiration, dry mouth, and running. This theory disagree whether bodily feedback determines which emotion is felt because in case of cognitive theories, the stimulus leads to the arousal that is labelled using the cognition that leads to the emotion.

6 Match List I with List II and select the correct answer from the codes given below :

List I		List II
A. Binet	I.	Intelligent people often have intelligent relatives
B. Broca	II.	Performance based intelligence tests eliminate cultural bias
C. Wechsler	III.	Correlation between intelligence and brain size
D. Galton	IV.	Intelligence is a collection of mental abilities

Codes

	A	B	C	D
1	I	II	III	IV
2	II	III	IV	I
3	III	IV	I	II
4	IV	III	II	I

Ans. (4)

Exp. The correct matching is A-IV, B-III, C-II, D-I.

According to *Binet*, intelligence is a collection of mental abilities. Binet and colleague Theodore Simon developed a series of tests designed to assess mental abilities. Rather than focus on learned information such as math and reading, Binet instead concentrated on other mental abilities such as attention and memory. The scale they developed became known as the Binet-Simon Intelligence Scale.

According to *Broca*, there is a correlation between intelligence and brain size. Broca is known for making contributions towards anthropometry—the scientific approach to measurements of human physical features. He initially thought that the most important aspect was the relative size between the frontal and rear areas of the brain, with Caucasians having a larger frontal area than Negroes.

According to *Wechsler*, performance based intelligence tests eliminate cultural bias. Wechsler designed an entire scale that allowed the measurement of non-verbal intelligence which was known as a performance scale. This scale required a subject to actively do something, such as copying symbols or pointing to a missing detail in a picture, rather than just answering questions. This was an important development, as it attempted to overcome biases that were caused by "language, culture, and education".

According to *Galton*, intelligent people often have intelligent relatives. In 1869, Galton released a compilation of the data he had collected and published it under the title 'Hereditary Genius'. In this book, Galton showed that success seemed to run in families, and that the more closely related a person was to a high-achiever, the more likely they were to become one themselves.

7 Biologically based emotional and behavioural tendencies that are evident in early childhood represent

1 trait
2 type
3 temperament
4 style

Ans. (3)

Exp. Biologically based emotional and behavioural tendencies that are evident in early childhood represent temperament.

Temperament is the behavioural and emotional characteristics that are fairly well established at birth. Researchers have identified three basic temperament styles of infants i.e., easy, difficult and slow to warm up.

8 In Jungian theory, the idea that energy is automatically redistributed in the psyche in order to achieve equilibrium or balance depicts:

1 Principle of equivalence
2 Principle of synchronicity
3 Principle of entropy
4 Principle of opposites

Ans. (3)

Exp. In Jungian theory, the idea that energy is automatically redistributed in the psyche in order to achieve equilibrium or balance depicts Principle of entropy.

According to Jung, the psychic energy operates in three ways following the principles of opposites, equivalence, and entropy. The principle of entropy means that an equal distribution of energy creates balance in personality. It refers to the equalisation of energy differences. The ideal is an equal distribution of psychic energy all over the structures of the personality. Jung borrowed the idea from physics, where 'entropy' refers to the tendency of all physical systems to 'run down,' that is, for all energy to become evenly distributed.

9 After the recent terrorist attacks in France, a psychologist proposed a study wherein he would interview two hundred French citizens to find whether their attitude towards fate as a consequence of the attack. This study can best be labelled as

1 attitude change experiment
2 field experiment
3 ex-post facto study
4 psychometric study

Ans. *(3)*

Exp. The above given study can best be labelled as ex-post facto study, since the study was conducted after the terrorist attacks have already occurred.

Ex-post facto study or after-the-fact research is a category of research design in which the investigation starts after the fact has occurred without interference from the researcher. It is also often applied as a substitute for true experimental research to test hypotheses about cause and effect relationships or in situations in which it is not practical or ethically acceptable to apply the full protocol of a true experimental design.

10 Match List I with List II and select the correct answer from the codes given below :

List I (Cutaneous receptors)		List II (Responds to)	
A.	Free nerve endings	I.	Sudden displacement of skin
B.	Ruffini endings	II.	Gradual skin indentation
C.	Merkel's disks	III.	Gradual skin stretch
D.	Pacinian corpuscles	IV.	Temperature change and pain

Codes

	A	B	C	D		A	B	C	D
1	I	II	III	IV	2	II	III	IV	I
3	III	IV	I	II	4	IV	III	II	I

Ans. *(4)*

Exp. The correct matching is A-IV, B-III, C-II, D-I.

Free nerve endings are associated with temperature change and pain. Free nerve endings can detect temperature, mechanical stimuli (touch, pressure, stretch) or danger (nociception).

Ruffini endings are associated with gradual skin stretch. Ruffini endings are slow adapting, encapsulated receptors that respond to skin stretch and are present in both the glabrous and hairy skin.

Merkel's disks are associated with gradual skin indentation. Merkel's disks are slow-adapting, unencapsulated nerve endings that respond to light touch; they are present in the upper layers of skin that has hair or is glabrous.

Pacinian corpuscles are associated with sudden displacement of skin. Pacinian corpuscles are rapidly-adapting, deep receptors that respond to deep pressure and high-frequency vibration.

11 Read each of the following two statements, Assertion (A) and Reason (R) and indicate your answer using the codes given below :

Assertion (A) A tree shall appear in same perceived size whether one views it from near or far point.

Reason (R) The size of retinal image remains invariant.

Codes

1 Both (A) and (R) are true and (R) is the correct explanation of (A)
2 Both (A) and (R) are true, but (R) is not the correct explanation of (A)
3 (A) is true, but (R) is false
4 (A) is false, but (R) is true

Ans. *(3)*

Exp. (A) is true, but (R) is false.

A tree shall appear in same perceived size whether one views it from near or far point. This is true because of size constancy. Size constancy is one type of visual subjective constancy. Within a certain range, people's perception of one particular object's size will not change, regardless of changes in distance or the video size change on the retina. The perception of image is still based upon the actual size of the perceptual characteristics.

The size of retinal image does not remain invariant. This is because the size of the retinal image changes with the change in distance. The linear size of a retinal image varies inversely with the distance from the eye of the corresponding physical object.

12 Which of the following is correct while comparing classical and operant conditioning?

1 Operant conditioning takes place before reinforcement while classical conditioning takes place after reinforcement
2 Operant conditioning takes place as a result of some voluntary action while classical conditioning takes place without choice
3 In operant conditioning, response is elicited while in classical conditioning it is emitted
4 In operant conditioning magnitude of the response is the index of conditioning while in classical conditioning it is the rate of response

Ans. *(2)*

Exp. Operant conditioning takes place as a result of some voluntary action while classical conditioning takes place without choice.

In Operant conditioning, learning refers to changes in behaviour as a result of experiences that occur after a response. It involves changing voluntary behaviours. A behaviour response is followed by either reinforcement or punishment. Reinforcement following a behaviour will cause the behaviour to increase, but if behaviour is followed by punishment the behaviour will decrease.

In Classical conditioning, learning refers to involuntary responses that result from experiences that occur before a response. Classical conditioning occurs when two different stimuli are associated.

13 Words learned under water are recalled

1 better on land than under water
2 better above land (sky) than on land
3 better above land (sky) than under water
4 better under water than on land

Ans. (4)

Exp. Words learned under water are recalled better under water than on land because of the Context-dependent memory.

Context-dependent memory refers to improved recall of specific episodes or information when the context present at encoding and retrieval are the same. One particularly common example of context-dependence at work occurs when an individual has lost an item (e.g. lost car keys) in an unknown location. Typically, people try to systematically 'retrace their steps' to determine all of the possible places where the item might be located. Based on the role that context plays in determining recall, it is not at all surprising that individuals often quite easily discover the lost item upon returning to the correct context.

14 Read each of the following two statements, Assertion (A) and Reason (R) and indicate your answer using the codes given below:

Assertion (A) People overlook flaws if the overall issue is perceived as important.

Reason (R) People have some biases.

Codes

1 Both (A) and (R) are true and (R) is the correct explanation of (A)
2 Both (A) and (R) are true, but (R) is not the correct explanation of (A)
3 (A) is true, but (R) is false
4 (A) is false, but (R) is true

Ans. (1)

Exp. Both (A) and (R) are true and (R) is the correct explanation of (A).

People overlook flaws if the overall issue is perceived as important. This is true as it explains the halo effect. It is a rating bias in which a general evaluation (usually positive) of a person, or an evaluation of a person on a specific dimension, influences judgements of that person on other specific dimensions. We tend to overlook the flaws if the general evaluation is perceived as important or favorable.

People have some biases. This is also true as individuals have an inclination or predisposition for or against something. Halo effect is a cognitive bias which is a tendency for preference. This explains why people overlook flaws if the overall issue is perceived as important.

15 Simi is totally blind, but she follows a 24-hr day-night cycle like the rest of us and seems comfortably adapted to it. Studies on animals suggest she relies on

I. a built in rhythm in her Supra-Chiasmatic Nucleus (SCN)
II. non-visual receptors in her eyes
III. social activity
IV. clocks

Select the correct answer from the codes given below.

1 Only II
2 Only IV
3 III and IV
4 I, III and IV

Ans. (4)

Exp. In the given case, studies on animals suggest that Simi relies on a built in rhythm in her Supra-Chiasmatic Nucleus (SCN), social activity and clocks.

Several aspects of human physiology and behaviour are dominated by 24-hr circadian rhythms with key impacts on health and well-being. These include mainly the sleep–wake cycle, vigilance and performance patterns, and some hormone secretions. The rhythms are generated spontaneously by an internal 'pacemaker,' the Supra-Chiasmatic Nuclei within the anterior hypothalamus. This master clock has, for most humans, an intrinsic rhythm slightly longer than 24 hr.

16 Flynn effect is

1 high IQ score of a generation in comparison to succeeding generation
2 high IQ score of a generation in comparison to preceding generation
3 a person's increase in accumulated knowledge with increase in age
4 a person's change in accumulated knowledge with increase in age

Ans. (2)

Exp. Flynn effect is high IQ score of a generation in comparison to preceding generation.

It deals with the issue of how the general IQ scores of a population change over time. In his study of IQ tests scores for different populations over the past sixty years, James R Flynn discovered that IQ scores increased from one generation to the next for all of the countries for which data existed (Flynn, 1994). Research shows that IQ gains have been mixed for different countries. In general, countries have seen generational increases between 5 and 25 points.

17 Which of the following sequences is correct?

1 Oral phase → Anal phase → Latency → Phallic → Genital
2 Anal → Oral → Phallic → Latency → Genital
3 Oral → Anal → Phallic → Latency → Genital
4 Oral → Phallic → Anal → Genital → Latency

Ans. (3)

Exp. The correct sequence is Oral → Anal → Phallic → Latency → Genital.

Freud (1905) proposed that psychological development in childhood takes place in a series of fixed stages. These are called psychosexual stages because each stage represents the fixation of libido (roughly translated as sexual drives or instincts) on a different area of the body. As a person grows physically certain areas of their body become important as sources of potential frustration (erogenous zones), pleasure or both. The five stages of development are:

(i) *Oral* (0-1 years of age): During this stage, the mouth is the pleasure center for development.
(ii) *Anal* (1-3 years of age): During this stage, toddlers and pre-school-aged children begin to experiment with urine and feces.
(iii) *Phallic* (3-6 years of age): During this stage, pre-schoolers take pleasure in their genitals and, at this stage, children also begin to discover the differences between males and females.
(iv) *Latency* (6-12 years of age): During this stage, sexual instincts subside, and children begin to further develop the superego or conscience.
(v) *Genital* (12+ years of age): During this stage, sexual impulses re-emerge.

18 Which one of the following is considered as a non-parametric alternative to one-way ANOVA for independent samples?

1 Kruskal-Wallis H-test
2 Mann-Whitney U-test
3 Kolmogorov-Smirnov test
4 Friedman's ANOVA

Ans. (1)

Exp. Kruskal-Wallis H-test is considered as a non-parametric alternative to one-way ANOVA for independent samples.

The Kruskal-Wallis H-test (sometimes also called the 'one-way ANOVA on ranks') is a rank-based non-parametric test that can be used to determine if there are statistically significant differences between two or more groups of an independent variable on a continuous or ordinal dependent variable. It is considered the non-parametric alternative to the one-way ANOVA, and an extension of the Mann-Whitney U-test to allow the comparison of more than two independent groups.

19 Read each of the following two statements, Assertion (A) and Reason (R) and indicate your answer using the codes given below :

Assertion (A) Action potentials normally travel along axons in one direction.

Reason (R) The portions of an axon over which an action potential has just travelled are left momentarily refractory.

Codes

1 Both (A) and (R) are true and (R) is the correct explanation of (A)
2 Both (A) and (R) are true, but (R) is not the correct explanation of (A)
3 (A) is true, but (R) is false
4 (A) is false, but (R) is true

Ans. (1)

Exp. Both (A) and (R) are true and (R) is the correct explanation of (A).

Action potentials normally travel along axons in one direction. This is true and action potential only moves in one direction, though, from the cell body to the presynaptic terminal. The refractory period keeps the action potential from moving backward down the axon.

The portions of an axon over which an action potential has just travelled are left momentarily refractory. This is true as the action potential moves from one Node of Ranvier to the next, the inactivated sodium channels in the previous axon segment prevent the membrane from depolarising again. Therefore, the action potential can only move forward toward axon segments with closed sodium channels ready for rising phase depolarisation.

20 Match List I with List II and select the correct answer from the codes given below :

List I (Cues)	List II (Perceptions)
A. Linear perspective	I. Our two eyes observe objects from slightly different positions
B. Aerial perspective	II. Parallel lines appears to converge at distance
C. Atmospheric perspective	III. Objects below the horizon appear near
D. Retinal disparity	IV. Farther away objects are less distinctly seen

Codes

	A	B	C	D		A	B	C	D
1	I	II	III	IV	2	II	III	IV	I
3	III	IV	I	II	4	IV	III	II	I

Ans. (2)

Exp. The correct matching is A-II, B-III, C-IV, D-I.

Linear perspective is when the parallel lines appears to converge at distance. It is a system of creating an illusion of depth on a flat surface. All parallel lines (orthogonals) in a painting or drawing using this system converge in a single vanishing point on the composition's horizon line.

Aerial perspective is when the objects below the horizon appear near. As we look off into the horizon, closer objects seem more distinct while those in the distance might be obscured by dust, fog, or water vapour.

Atmospheric perspective is when the farther away objects are less distinctly seen. Objects that are farther away seem to be blurred or slightly hazy due to the atmosphere.

Retinal disparity is when our two eyes observe objects from slightly different positions. Retinal disparity refers to the small difference between the images projected on the two retinas when looking at an object or scene. This slight difference or disparity in retinal images serves as a binocular cue for the perception of depth.

21 Read each of the following two statements, Assertion (A) and Reason (R) and indicate your answer using the codes given below.

Assertion (A) A desirable behaviour of an individual can be effectively used as a reference for another less desirable activity.

Reason (R) Premack has suggested that all responses should be thought of as potential reinforcers.

Codes

1 Both (A) and (R) are true and (R) is the correct explanation of (A)
2 Both (A) and (R) are true, but (R) is not the correct explanation of (A)
3 (A) is true, but (R) is false
4 (A) is false, but (R) is true

Ans. *(1)*

➲ *Exp.* Both (A) and (R) are true and (R) is the correct explanation of (A)

A desirable behaviour of an individual can be effectively used as a reference for another less desirable activity. This is true as it is based on the Premack's principle or the relativity theory of reinforcement. It states that more probable or desirable behaviors will reinforce less probable or desirable activities.

Premack has suggested that all responses should be thought of as potential reinforcers. It is correct as the Premack Principle states that preferred behaviours, or behaviours with a higher level of intrinsic reinforcement, can be used as rewards or reinforcements, for less preferred behaviours.

22 Which memory is the result of instrumental/ motor learning processes?

1 Semantic memory
2 Episodic memory
3 Sensory memory
4 Procedural memory

Ans. *(4)*

➲ *Exp.* The memory which is the result of instrumental/motor learning processes is Procedural memory.

Procedural memory is a part of the long-term memory that is responsible for knowing how to do things, also known as motor skills. As the name implies, procedural memory stores information on how to perform certain procedures, such as walking, talking and riding a bike.

23 If you begin with a problem and come up with many different solutions; you are using ______ , which is a form of creative thinking; contrarily sometimes you come up with correct solution by using _______ thinking.

1 convergent, inductive
2 convergent, deductive
3 convergent, divergent
4 divergent, convergent

Ans. *(4)*

➲ *Exp.* If you begin with a problem and come up with many different solutions; you are using divergent, which is a form of creative thinking; contrarily sometimes you come up with correct solution by using convergent thinking.

Divergent thinking is a creative thinking in which an individual solves a problem or reaches a decision using strategies that deviate from commonly used or previously taught strategies. It is used to generate creative ideas by exploring many possible solutions.

Convergent thinking is critical thinking in which an individual uses linear, logical steps to analyse a number of already formulated solutions to a problem to determine the correct one or the one that is most likely to be successful.

24 Select the correct formula to measure Body Mass Index (BMI).

1 Weight in kg squared/Height in meters
2 Weight in kg squared/Height in meters squared
3 Weight in kg/Height in meters
4 Weight in kg/Height in meters squared

Ans. *(4)*

➲ *Exp.* The correct formula to measure Body Mass Index (BMI) is Weight in kg/Height in meters squared. The BMI is an attempt to quantify the amount of tissue mass (muscle, fat and bone) in an individual, and then categories that person as underweight, normal weight, overweight or obese based on that value. Body Mass Index (BMI) is a person's weight in kilograms divided by the square of height in meters. A high BMI can be an indicator of high body fatness.

25 Which of the following are not identified by Thurstone?

I. Induction	II. Spatial
III. Symbolic	IV. Semantic

Select the correct answer from the codes given below.

1 I and II	2 III and IV
3 I and III	4 I, II and III

Ans. *(2)*

➲ *Exp.* Semantic and Symbolic were not identified by Thurstone. These are covered in Guilford's theory in which Symbolic is the information perceived as symbols or signs that stand for something else, e.g. Arabic numerals, the letters of an alphabet or musical and scientific notations. Semantic is concerned with verbal meaning and ideas generally considered to be abstract in nature.

26 Match List I with List II and select the correct answer from the codes given below :

	List I (Concepts)		**List II** (Theorists)
A.	Rational functions	I.	Freud
B.	Impetus	II.	Jung
C.	Masculine protest	III.	Adler
D.	Hyper competitiveness	IV.	Horney

Codes

	A	B	C	D		A	B	C	D
1	I	II	III	IV	2	II	I	III	IV
3	III	II	IV	I	4	IV	III	I	II

Ans. (2)

➲ *Exp.* The correct matching is A-II, B-I, C-III, D-IV.

Rational functions are associated with Jung. The functions of consciousness refer to the different ways in which the conscious mind can apprehend reality. According to Jung, these are sensation, intuition, thinking and feeling. Thinking and feeling are rational functions.

Impetus is associated with Freud. According to Freud, all Instincts have a source, a goal, an object and an impetus. Impetus is the amount of force the instinct exerts.

Masculine protest is associated with Adler. Masculine protest is a concept developed by the psychologist Alfred Adler, the founder of Individual Psychology. It is the suggestion that women reject a feminine identity in order to be valued and compensated in the same manner as men. In men it is typically expressed as a superiority complex.

Hyper competitiveness is associated with Horney. Hyper competitiveness is the indiscriminate need to win at all costs in order to feel superior.

27 Match List I with List II and select the correct answer from the codes given below :

	List I (Types of Variables)		**List II** (Examples)
A.	Continuous variable	I.	Examination results in terms of pass and fail
B.	Real discrete variable	II.	Voice pitch
C.	Artificially discrete variable	III.	Intelligence
D.	Qualitative variable	IV.	Nationality

Codes

	A	B	C	D		A	B	C	D
1	III	IV	I	II	2	III	I	IV	II
3	II	IV	I	II	4	II	I	IV	III

Ans. (1)

➲ *Exp.* The correct matching is A-III, B-IV, C-I, D-II.

An example of a *Continuous variable* is Intelligence. It is a variable whose value is obtained by measuring, i.e. one which can take on an uncountable set of values.

An example of a *Real discrete variable* is Nationality. It is a variable that falls into separate natural categories with no immediate values possible.

An example of an *Artificially discrete variable* is Examination results in terms of pass and fail. It is a variable that falls into separate artificially created categories by the researcher with no immediate values possible.

An example of a *Qualitative variable* is Voice pitch. It is a descriptive characteristic or attribute, that is, one that cannot be numerically ordered.

28 In which lobe of the cerebral cortex, the primary olfactory cortex lies?

1 Frontal lobe
2 Temporal lobe
3 Occipital lobe
4 Parietal lobe

Ans. (2)

➲ *Exp.* The primary olfactory cortex lies in Temporal lobe.

The olfactory cortex is the part of the cerebral cortex that processes olfactory information. It is involved in the sense of smell. The olfactory cortex is located in the uncus, found along the ventral surface of the temporal lobe. Olfaction is the only sensory system that is not routed through the Thalamus.

29 "Factor analysis is used as a means of confirming a structured model than as a means of discovering a structural model". This is true of which theory of intelligence?

1 Spearman
2 Thurstone
3 Jensen
4 Guilford

Ans. (4)

➲ *Exp.* "Factor analysis is used as a means of confirming a structured model than as a means of discovering a structural model". This is true of Guildford's theory of intelligence.

JP Guilford (1961) developed the structure of intellect model on the basis of the factor analysis. He suggested that every mental process or intellectual activity can be described in terms of three basic dimensions or parameters such as operation, content and production. He argued that intelligence consisted 150 different and independent skills. Each of these intellectual abilities or structures is inter-linked.

30 Read each of the following two statements Assertion (A) and Reason (R) and indicate your answer using the codes given below :

Assertion (A) One focuses on the discovery of truth and interests that are empirical, critical and rational.

Reason (R) A person high on economic values focuses on usefulness and practicality.

Codes

1 Both (A) and (R) are true and (R) is the correct explanation of (A)
2 Both (A) and (R) are true, but (R) is not the correct explanation of (A)
3 (A) is true, but (R) is false
4 (A) is false, but (R) is true

Ans. (2)

➲ *Exp.* Both (A) and (R) are true, but (R) is not the correct explanation of (A).

One focuses on the discovery of truth and interests that are empirical, critical and rational. It is true and is based on Allport's theoretical value which emphasises on the interest in the discovery of the truth. The key characteristics of this value are empiricism and intellectualism.

A person high on economic values focuses on usefulness and practicality. It is true and is based on Allport's economic value which emphasises on the interest in the usefulness. The key characteristics of this value are resourcefulness and interest in practical affairs.

The statements are independently correct but do not explain one another.

31 A supervisor, who was asked to rate his subordinates on the basis of his observations, found an employee who did not take a medical leave in that year. On the basis of this observation, the supervisor rated the employee as 'medically fit', 'highly efficient' and 'meticulous'. This is an example of

1 lineancy error
2 constant error
3 tendency to give extreme rating
4 halo effect

Ans. *(4)*

➲ *Exp.* In the given case, this is an example of Halo effect.

Halo effect is a rating bias in which a general evaluation (usually positive) of a person, or an evaluation of a person on a specific dimension, influences judgements of that person on other specific dimensions. For example, in this case, a person who did not take a medical leave in a year was judged as "medically fit", "highly efficient" and "meticulous" by the supervisor. This may or may not be true and is based on only one specific dimension.

32 Which of the following parts of the basal ganglia constitute the striatum?

I. Amygdala	II. Caudate
III. Putamen	IV. Globus pallidus

Select the correct answer from the codes given below.

1 I and II	2 I and III
3 II and III	4 III and IV

Ans. *(3)*

➲ *Exp.* The parts of basal ganglia that constitute the striatum are Caudate and Putamen.

Caudate Nucleus: Each of the brain's hemispheres contains a caudate nucleus, and both are located centrally and near the basal ganglia. They are also situated near the thalamus, which is deep in the brain, close to the midbrain.

Putamen : It is a large structure located within the brain. It is involved in a very complex feedback loop that prepares and aids in movement of the limbs. It is closely intertwined with the caudate nucleus, nucleus accumbens and globus pallidus, which are together known as the corpus striatum.

33 Among the laws of perceptual grouping, the law of simplicity is a tendency to

1 perceive simple patterns in terms of complex shapes
2 perceive complex patterns in terms of simpler shapes
3 perceive simpler shapes only
4 perceive complex shapes only

Ans. *(2)*

➲ *Exp.* Among the laws of perceptual grouping, the law of simplicity is a tendency to perceive complex patterns in terms of simpler shapes.

Law of simplicity or likelihood principle states that an observer will tend to perceive the simplest interpretation (i.e., the one with the shortest description). It is law of perceptual organisation stating that human beings perceive the result of stimulus patterns in the simplest form possible.

34 What is the role of positive and negative reinforcement?

1 To increase the likelihood that responses preceding both will be repeated.
2 To decrease the likelihood that responses preceding negative reinforcement will be repeated.
3 To increase the likelihood that responses preceding only positive reinforcement will be repeated.
4 To ensure that there are no negative consequences following the behaviour.

Ans. *(1)*

➲ *Exp.* The role of positive and negative reinforcement is to increase the likelihood that responses preceding both will be repeated.

Positive reinforcement occurs when a desirable event or stimulus is presented as a consequence of a behavior and the behaviour increases.

In negative reinforcement, a response or behaviour is strengthened by stopping, removing or avoiding a negative outcome or aversive stimulus.

35 Match List I with List II and select the correct answer from the codes given below :

List I	List II
A. Sensory memory	I. Information that passes through a gate and transferred to short-term memory
B. Attention	II. Information subjected to deep processing
C. Short-term memory	III. Temporary storage of sensory information
D. Elaborative rehearsal	IV. Brief storage of information

Codes

	A	B	C	D		A	B	C	D
1	I	II	III	IV	2	III	I	IV	II
3	III	IV	I	II	4	IV	III	II	I

Ans. *(2)*

➲ *Exp.* The correct matching is A-III, B-I, C-IV, D-II.

Sensory memory is a temporary storage of sensory information. Sensory memory is a brief precursor to short-term memory that allows us to process and recall the sensations we take in.

In *Attention*, the information that passes through a gate and transferred to short-term memory. The general attention model assumes that after detection of the target, an attention gate opens briefly to allow information to enter a visual short-term memory.

Short-term memory is a brief storage of information. Short term memory is the capacity to store a small amount of information in the mind and keep it readily available for a short period of time.

In *Elaborative rehearsal*, the information is subjected to deep processing. Deep processing involves elaboration rehearsal which involves a more meaningful analysis (e.g. images, thinking, associations etc.) of information and leads to better recall.

36 While forming a concept one chooses to take one hypothesis and selects many of its features to quickly form the concept at once

1 Successive scanning
2 Conservative focusing
3 Focus gambling
4 Simultaneous scanning

Ans. *(3)*

Exp. While forming a concept one chooses to take one hypothesis and selects many of its features to quickly form the concept at once is Focus gambling.

Focus gambling is a type of concept-discovery task that requires the generation of hypotheses about what combination of features defines a concept, a strategy in which the participant changes more than one feature from one hypothesis to the next. Focus gambling contrasts with the more conservative strategy of varying one feature at a time to determine its relevance to the concept.

37 Which among the following are the final outcome of curiosity?

I. Drives to explore
II. Increases arousal
III. Gains information and resources
IV. Reduction in tension

Select the correct answer from the codes given below.

1 II and III
2 II, III and IV
3 I and IV
4 I, II and III

Ans. *(1)*

Exp. The final outcomes of curiosity are increase in arousal and gaining of information and resources.

Curiosity is a state of increased arousal response promoted by a stimulus high in uncertainty and lacking in information. When compared to existing knowledge, the novel, uncertain, conflicting, or complex properties of external stimuli create a conceptual conflict that arouses the internal state of arousal called curiosity. The defining feature is that curiosity produces an unpleasant sensation (usually labeled arousal) that is reduced by exploratory behaviour. Once curiosity has been aroused, the organism engages in a process of exploration to reduce the state of arousal.

38 Read the statement and select the correct answer out of given options.
"If one hand is placed in a container of hot water and other in cold water. Then both hands are placed in a container of lukewarm water." Most people experience

1 the hand initially placed in hot water feels the lukewarm water as cool whereas hand initially placed in cold water feels it as hot
2 the hand initially placed in hot water feels the lukewarm water as hot whereas hand initially placed in cold water feels it as cold
3 both the hands will have feeling of equal hotness, but more than temperature of lukewarm water
4 both the hands will have feeling of equal coldness lower than temperature of lukewarm water

Ans. *(1)*

Exp. Most people experience the hand initially placed in hot water feels the lukewarm water as cool whereas hand initially placed in cold water feels it as hot.

The 'hot water hand' feels cold and the 'cold water hand' feels hot when it's placed in the room temperature or lukewarm water. It is because the skin has tiny sensors called thermoreceptors that send signals to your brain. There are different types of receptors on skin, some sense pressure, some sense pain, and others sense temperature (hot and cold). When we put our hands in the water, the brain gets information from the thermoreceptors. If we keep our hands in the hot water or cold water long enough, the thermoreceptors get used to the temperature of the water.

The room temperature water is cooler than the hot water, and warmer than the cold water. So, when we switch to the room temperature water, the receptors that got used to the hot water, send signals that sense it as cold; and the receptors that got used to the cold water sense the room temperature water as hot.

39 An accused is harassed and tortured until he confesses to the crime is an example of

1 negative reinforcement
2 punishment
3 primary reinforcement
4 secondary reinforcement

Ans. *(1)*

Exp. An accused is harassed and tortured until he confesses to the crime is an example of negative reinforcement. The police continue to use third degree or brutal methods until the accused makes a confession. Thus, removal of the third-degree torture is reinforcing which makes the culprit confess the crime.

Negative reinforcement is a term described by BF Skinner in his theory of operant conditioning. In negative reinforcement, a response or behaviour is strengthened by stopping, removing or avoiding a negative outcome or aversive stimulus.

40 **Which of the following are not mnemonic devices?**

I. Categorical clustering
II. Pegword system
III. Consolidation
IV. Rehearsal

Select the correct answer from the codes given below.

1 I and II
2 II and III
3 I and III
4 III and IV

Ans. (4)

Exp. Consolidation and Rehearsal are not mnemonic devices.

Consolidation is the neurobiological processes by which a permanent memory is formed following a learning experience. Memory consolidation is a category of processes that stabilize a memory trace after its initial acquisition.

Rehearsal is the repetition of information in an attempt to maintain it longer in memory. According to the dual-store model of memory, rehearsal occurs in short-term memory and may allow a stronger trace to then be stored in long-term memory. Although rehearsal implies a verbal process, it is hypothesized to occur in other modalities as well.

41 **Read each of the following two statements, Assertion (A) and Reason (R) and indicate your answer using the codes given below:**

Assertion (A) Advertising and media campaigns are based frequently on the availability heuristic.

Reason (R) Consumers recall instances of being satisfied and expect this outcome to recur.

Codes

1 Both (A) and (R) are true and (R) is the correct explanation of (A)
2 Both (A) and (R) are true, but (R) is not the correct explanation of (A)
3 (A) is true, but (R) is false
4 (A) is false, but (R) is true

Ans. (1)

Exp. Both (A) and (R) are true and (R) is the correct explanation of (A).

Advertising and media campaigns are based frequently on the availability heuristic. It is true as availability is a common strategy for making judgements about likelihood of occurrence in which the individual bases such judgements on the salience of the information held in his or her memory about the particular type of event. In other words, we often rely on how easy it is to think of examples when making a decision. The number of examples there are is directly dictated by how accessible these examples are. Consequently, we ignore less easily recalled information even if it is statistically (and obviously) more important.

Consumers recall instances of being satisfied and expect this outcome to recur. The availability heuristic can be utilised in marketing through examples of results the product has brought forth; this makes it easier for potential customers to imagine an outcome they could likely achieve if they chose it. This explains why the advertising and media campaigns are based frequently on the availability heuristic.

42 **Match List I with List II and select the correct answer from the codes given below :**

List I (Measures)	List II (Body parts)
A. EMG	I. Sweat glands
B. EEG	II. Iris
C. GSR	III. Muscles
D. Pupillometry	IV. Cortical neurons

Codes

	A	B	C	D
1	I	II	III	IV
2	II	III	IV	I
3	III	IV	I	II
4	IV	III	II	I

Ans. (3)

Exp. The correct matching is A-III, B-IV, C-I, D-II.

EMG is associated with Muscles. An Electromyogram (EMG) is a test that is used to record the electrical activity of muscles.

EEG is associated with Cortical neurons. An Electroencephalogram (EEG) is a test used to find problems related to electrical activity of the brain. An EEG tracks and records brain wave patterns.

GSR is associated with sweat glands. Galvanic Skin Response (GSR) originates from the autonomic activation of sweat glands in the skin.

Pupillometry is associated with Iris. Pupillometry is the measurement of minute fluctuations in pupil diameter in response to a stimulus. This method suggests that pupil responses could be used as an objective measure of visual acuity.

43 **Read each of the following two statements, Assertion (A) and Reason (R) and indicate your answer using the codes given below :**

Assertion (A) Value of h^2 (heritability) derived for a particular population is not the correct estimation for other populations.

Reason (R) Different populations have similar genotypes, but they experience different environment.

Codes

1 Both (A) and (R) are true and (R) is the correct explanation of (A)
2 Both (A) and (R) are true, but (R) is not the correct explanation of (A)
3 (A) is true, but (R) is false
4 (A) is false, but (R) is true

Ans. (1)

Exp. Both (A) and (R) are true and (R) is the correct explanation of (A).

Value of h^2 (heritability) derived for a particular population is not the correct estimation for other populations. Heritability is the proportion of this total variation between individuals in a given population due to genetic variation. Heritability is specific for specific population in a specific area, so it is not the correct estimation for other populations.

Different populations have similar genotypes, but they experience different environment. This is true as different populations may have similar genotypes but they experience different environment, therefore, heritability is specific for a particular population.

44 What is the correct sequence an auditory stimulus takes to reach the primary auditory cortex?

1 Cochlear nuclei, Superior olive, Inferior colliculus, Medial geniculate nucleus
2 Cochlear nuclei, Inferior colliculus, Superior olive, Medial geniculate nucleus
3 Superior olive, Cochlear nuclei, Inferior colliculus, Medial geniculate nucleus
4 Medial geniculate nucleus, Inferior colliculus, Superior olive, Cochlear nucleus

Ans. (1)

Exp. The correct sequence an auditory stimulus takes to reach the primary auditory cortex is Cochlear nuclei, Superior olive, Inferior colliculus, Medial geniculate nucleus.

The information proceeds from the Organ of Corti to spiral ganglion cells and the VIIIth nerve afferents in the ear, to the Cochlear nuclei, many crossing in the trapezoid body to the Superior olive in the brain stem. Then all ascending fibers stop in the Inferior colliculus in the midbrain and the Medial geniculate body in the thalamus, before reaching the cortex in the superior temporal gyrus.

45 Read each of the following two statements Assertion (A) and Reason (R) and indicate your answer using the codes given below.

Assertion (A) Non-equivalent control groups are often encountered in quasi-experimental research.

Reason (R) Quasi-experimental designs are highly useful in policy and program evaluation research.

Codes

1 Both (A) and (R) are true and (R) is the correct explanation of (A)
2 Both (A) and (R) are true, but (R) is not the correct explanation of (A)
3 (A) is true, but (R) is false
4 (A) is false, but (R) is true

Ans. (2)

Exp. Both (A) and (R) are true, but (R) is not the correct explanation of (A).

Non-equivalent control groups are often encountered in quasi-experimental research. Non-equivalent control group design is a quasi-experimental design in which the responses of a treatment group and a control group are compared on measures collected at the beginning and end of the research.

Quasi-experimental designs are highly useful in policy and program evaluation research. Quasi-experiments are subject to concerns regarding internal validity, because the treatment and control groups may not be comparable at baseline. With random assignment, study participants have the same chance of being assigned to the intervention group or the comparison group. Quasi-experiments are used for interventions developed for target populations and highly useful in policy and program evaluation research.

There are three types of quasi-experimental designs – non-equivalent control group, non-equivalent comparison group and time-series design.

Both the statements are independently correct but does not explain one another.

Directions (Q. Nos. 46-50) *Read the following paragraph and answer the questions which follow :*

A psychometrician wanted to develop a new test of Abstract Thinking. He prepared eighty items, presumably assessing abstract thinking. Each item had five alternative answers, one of them being correct. The psychometrician carried out item analysis by using item-remainder correlations.

Item analysis retained sixty items. To examine internal consistency among the items, inter-item correlations were inspected. Then the split-half reliability coefficient, Kuder- Richardson reliability coefficient and Cronbach's alpha coefficient were obtained for the 60 item test.

The analysis yielded the Cronbach's alpha coefficient of 0.90. Since, the test was fairly long and the alpha coefficient was also quite high, an attempt was made to develop two short versions of equal length by randomly dividing the test items. The 60 item version was, then, correlated with the already established abstract reasoning test, using N = 500. The correlation between the new and an established test was 0.24, significant at .01 level.

46 In the above context, which one of the following correlation should be computed to obtain item-remainder correlations?

1 Point biserial correlation
2 Phi-coefficient
3 Rank difference correlation
4 Tetrachoric correlation

Ans. (1)

Exp. In the above context, Point-biserial correlation should be computed to obtain item-remainder correlations. The Point Biserial Correlation coefficient (r_{ph}) is a correlation coefficient used when one variable (e.g. Y) is dichotomous; Y can either be 'naturally' dichotomous, like whether a coin lands heads or tails, or an artificially dichotomized variable. The point-biserial correlation is mathematically equivalent to the Pearson (product moment) correlation.

47 Which one of the following statements would be true in the above context?

1 Kuder-Richardson reliability coefficient would also be .90, but the split-half reliability coefficient may differ from .90
2 Split-half reliability coefficient would also be .90, but the Kuder-Richardson reliability coefficient may differ from .90
3 Both Kuder-Richardson reliability coefficient and split-half reliability coefficient would be .90
4 The correlation between odd and even parts of the test would be .90

Ans. (1)

Exp. Kuder-Richardson reliability coefficient would also be .90, but the split-half reliability coefficient may differ from .90.

Both KR20 and Cronbach's alpha are measures of internal consistency (broadly referred to as coefficient alpha). Under ideal circumstances (e.g., no missing data, unidimensionality of items) and with binary items, KR20 and Cronbach's alpha should essentially be the same. Both split-half and Kuder-Richardson coefficient may differ because in the split-half, we divide the test into two separate tests and then calculate the reliability.

48 To obtain inter-item correlations, which one of the following correlation coefficients should be used in the above analysis?

1 Biserial correlation
2 Point biserial correlation
3 Phi-coefficient
4 Rank difference correlation

Ans. (3)

Exp. To obtain inter-item correlations, Phi-coefficient should be used in the above analysis.

The Phi-coefficient is a statistical measure used to evaluate the strength of association between two dichotomous variables. When the classification is truly discrete and the variables can take only one of two values, the Phi-coefficient is an appropriate measure of correlation.

49 What is the expected Cronbach alpha for the short versions, referred to in the paragraph?

1 0.45 2 0.67
3 0.82 4 0.90

Ans. (3)

Exp. The expected Cronbach alpha for the short versions is 0.82.

It is calculated using the formula, $r = \frac{2x}{1+x}$, where x is the original Cronbach Alpha for the whole test, i.e., 0.90. Putting the value of x in the formula, we get $r = 0.82$.

50 Which one of the following conclusions can be drawn from the data provided above ? The new Abstract Thinking Test has

1 satisfactory convergent validity
2 satisfactory divergent validity
3 satisfactory concurrent validity
4 unsatisfactory concurrent validity

Ans. (4)

Exp. It can be concluded that the new Abstract Thinking Test has unsatisfactory concurrent validity because it is less than 0.5, i.e., 0.24 which is considered a weak correlation.

Concurrent validity refers to the extent to which the results of a particular test, or measurement, correspond to hose of a previously established measurement for the same construct.

PAPER III

1 The factors that influence social behaviour and thoughts in certain ways are called

1 independent variables 2 confounding variables
3 dependent variables 4 mediating variables

Ans. (4)

Exp. The factors that influence social behaviour and thoughts in certain ways are called mediating variables.

A mediating variable explains the relation between the independent (predictor) and the dependent (criterion) variable. It explains how or why there is a relation between two variables.

2 Read each of the following two statements, Assertion (A) and Reason (R) and indicate your answer using the codes given below:

Assertion (A) In pre-conventional stage, children understand morality on the basis of social customs and values.

Reason (R) In pre-conventional stage, children make decisions based on whether they will be rewarded or punished.

Codes

1 Both (A) and (R) are true and (R) is the correct explanation of (A)
2 Both (A) and (R) are true, but (R) is not the correct explanation of (A)
3 (A) is true, but (R) is false
4 (A) is false, but (R) is true

Ans. (4)

Exp. (A) is false, but (R) is true.

In pre-conventional stage, children understand morality on the basis of social customs and values. This is false as throughout the pre-conventional level, a child's sense of morality is externally controlled. In the conventional stage, the child understands the morality on the basis of social customs and values.

In pre-conventional stage, children make decisions based on whether they will be rewarded or punished. This is true as during this pre-conventional stage, children accept and believe the rules of authority figures, such as parents and teachers. A child with pre-conventional morality has not yet adopted or internalised society's conventions regarding what is right or wrong, but instead focuses largely on external consequences that certain actions may bring.

3 Research shows that the following does not contribute to teacher effectiveness

1 Communication skills
2 Use of ICT
3 Years of experience
4 Use of student feedback

Ans. (3)

Exp. Research shows that the years of experience does not contribute to teacher effectiveness.

The number of years a teacher has taught does make a difference but not necessarily make the teaching effective. The teacher might be teaching outdated or inappropriate teaching tools and techniques. The teacher must keep evolving with changing times and requirements of the students.

4 Match List I with List II and select the correct answer from the codes given below :

List I	List II
A. Graphic rating scales	I. Evaluation method where employees are ranked from best to worst
B. Behaviourally anchored rating scales	II. Evaluator rates employees on classification of some qualities
C. Group order ranking	III. Evaluator rates performance factors on an incremental basis
D. Individual ranking	IV. Evaluator rates actual job related behaviour along a continuum

Codes

	A	B	C	D		A	B	C	D
1	I	II	III	IV	2	IV	III	I	II
3	III	IV	II	I	4	II	IV	III	I

Ans. (3)

Exp. The correct matching is A-III, B-IV, C-II, D-I.

In *Graphic rating scales*, an evaluator rates performance factors on an incremental basis. Graphic rating scale is a performance appraisal method in which an employee is rated against a list of traits or behaviours which are deemed important and relevant for effective employee performance and productivity.

In *Behaviourally anchored rating scales*, an evaluator rates actual job related behaviour along a continuum. Behaviourally Anchored Rating Scales (BARS) are scales used to rate performance. It is an appraisal method that aims to combine the benefits of narratives, critical incidents, and quantified ratings by anchoring a quantified scale with specific narrative examples of good, moderate, and poor performance.

In *Group order ranking*, an evaluator rates employees on classification of some qualities. Group Order Ranking method is a process of performance appraisal that requires a manager or supervisor to position his employees into given performance brackets or classes like top one fifth or third quarter etc.

Individual ranking is an evaluation method where employees are ranked from best to worst. Individual ranking method demands the evaluator to rank each employee in the classes from highest to lowest.

5 Read each of the following two statements, Assertion (A) and Reason (R) and indicate your answer using the codes given below:

Assertion (A) Obsessive compulsive disorder is a disorder of thought and is thus classified in the schizophrenia spectrum in DSM-5.

Reason (R) Evidence base shows that a combination of pharmacotherapy and psychotherapy yields good results in OCD therapy.

Codes

1 Both (A) and (R) are true and (R) is the correct explanation of (A)
2 Both (A) and (R) are true, but (R) is not the correct explanation of (A)
3 (A) is true, but (R) is false
4 (A) is false, but (R) is true

Ans. (4)

Exp. (A) is false, but (R) is true.

Obsessive compulsive disorder is a disorder of thought and is thus classified in the schizophrenia spectrum in DSM-5. This is false as Obsessive Compulsive Disorder is not a disorder of thought and is classified in the DSM-5 category of Obsessive-Compulsive and Related Disorders. Obsessive-Compulsive Disorder (OCD) is a common, chronic and long-lasting disorder in which a person has uncontrollable, reoccurring thoughts (obsessions) and behaviours (compulsions) that he or she feels the urge to repeat over and over.

Evidence base shows that a combination of pharmacotherapy and psychotherapy yields good results in OCD. This is true as research has suggested that OCD can be treated using pharmacotherapy, specialised psychotherapy, anatomically targeted treatments, or their combination.

6 Phonemic restoration as we perceive speech in a noisy party is an example of

1 top down processing
2 bottom up processing
3 subliminal perception
4 supraliminal perception

Ans. *(1)*

➲ *Exp.* Phonemic restoration as we perceive speech in a noisy party is an example of top down processing.

Phonemic restoration effect is a perceptual phenomenon where under certain conditions, sounds actually missing from a speech signal can be restored by the brain and may appear to be heard.

The effect occurs when missing phonemes in an auditory signal are replaced with a noise that would have the physical properties to mask those phonemes, creating an ambiguity. When listeners were also able to see the words being spoken, they were much more likely to correctly identify the missing phonemes. Like every sense, the brain will use every piece of information it deems important to make a judgement about what it perceives. Using the visual cues of mouth movements, the brain will engage in top-down processing to make a decision about what phoneme is supposed to be heard.

7 Feeling touchy or hypersensitive following an upsetting experience is a form of

1 imprinting 2 habituation
3 sensitisation 4 reflexive behaviour

Ans. *(3)*

➲ *Exp.* Feeling touchy or hypersensitive following an upsetting experience is a form of sensitisation. Sensitisation is the process whereby an organism is made more responsive to certain aspects of its environment. Sensitisation is a non-associative learning process in which repeated administration of a stimulus results in the progressive amplification of a response. Sensitisation often is characterised by an enhancement of response to a whole class of stimuli in addition to the one that is repeated.

8 Entry of information into long-term memory depends upon

I. maintenance rehearsal
II. elaborative rehearsal
III. method of loci
IV. primary memory

Select the correct answer from the codes given below :

1 I and II 2 I and III
3 II and IV 4 II and III

Ans. *(4)*

➲ *Exp.* Entry of information into long-term memory depends upon elaborative rehearsal and method of loci.

Information moves from STM to LTM when it is encoded in one of three ways: through sound (acoustic encoding), imagery (visual encoding), or meaning (semantic encoding). Encoding in STM tends to be primarily acoustic, secondarily visual, and much less often semantic.

Elaborative rehearsal is generally the best way to encode information in LTM semantically. It involves processing new information in a way that is personally meaningful and which associates the new information with other material that already exists in LTM.

The method of loci is particularly helpful in remembering items in serial order. It requires us to visualise objects/places that we know well in a specific sequence, imagine the objects we want to remember and associate them one by one to the physical locations.

9 Because it has the external features associated with the concept of dog, a wolf is perceived as a dog. This is an example of

1 centration 2 equilibration
3 object permanence 4 prototype

Ans. *(4)*

➲ *Exp.* Because it has the external features associated with the concept of dog, a wolf is perceived as a dog. This is an example of a prototype.

Prototype is the best or average exemplar of a category. It is an object, event, or person that is held to be typical of a category and comes to represent or stand for that category. It is an early model of something that represents or demonstrates its final form.

10 Which of the following is the final destination for much of the brain's information about emotion before action is taken?

1 Amygdala
2 Anterior cingulate cortex
3 Pre-frontal cortex
4 Hypothalamus

Ans. *(3)*

➲ *Exp.* The final destination for much of the brain's information about emotion before action is taken is the Pre-frontal cortex.

The Pre-frontal cortex is a part of the brain located at the front of the frontal lobe. It is implicated in a variety of complex behaviours, including planning, and greatly contributes to personality development.

The Pre-frontal cortex is known not only to be involved in emotional responses, but also to have numerous connections with other parts of the brain that are responsible for controlling dopamine, norepinephrine, and serotonin, three neurotransmitters that are important in mood regulation.

11 Cattell propounded gf-gc Theory of Intelligence mainly based on

1 first order factors of abilities
2 second order factors of abilities
3 third order factors of abilities
4 higher order factors of abilities

Ans. *(2)*

Exp. Cattell propounded gf-gc Theory of Intelligence mainly based on second order factors of abilities.

Cattell used the factor-analytic technique to identify sixteen source traits. He often uses the terms source trait and factor interchangeably. Factor analysis is a statistical technique that determines a number of factors, or clusters, based on the intercorrelation between a number of individual elements.

The Second Order Confirmatory Factor Analysis or CFA is a statistical method employed by the researcher to confirm that the theorised construct in a study loads into certain number of underlying sub-constructs or components. The Second-Order Abilities according to Cattell's Gf-Gc Theory are: Fluid Intelligence (Gf), Crystallised Intelligence (Gc), Short-Term Memory (Gsm), Long-Term Memory (Glr), Processing Speed (Gs), Visual Processing (Gv), Auditory Processing (Ga), and Quantitative Knowledge (Gq). Intelligence (g) represents effects and interactions of numerous abilities working in concert. Gf and Gc viewed as more general abilities that support the others.

12 Which of the following are elements in Carl Roger's person centered Theory of Personality and Psycho-therapy?

I. Ideal self　　II. Congruence
III. Positive regards　　IV. Dissonance

Select the correct answer from the codes given below :

1 I, II and III　　2 II, III and IV
3 I, III and IV　　4 I, II and IV

Ans. (1)

Exp. The elements in Carl Roger's person centered Theory of Personality and Psycho-therapy are Ideal self, Congruence, and Positive regards.

Carl Rogers believed that for a person to achieve self-actualisation they must be in a state of congruence. This means that self-actualisation occurs when a person's 'ideal self' (i.e. who they would like to be) is congruent with their actual behaviour (self-image). Congruence or congruity is an instance or point of agreement or correspondence between the ideal self and the real self. Unconditional positive regard is the basic acceptance and support of a person regardless of what the person says or does, especially in the context of client-centered therapy.

13 Which one of the following statements is true?

1 The 'Global Five' factors in personality refer to the second order factors of 16 PF, latest edition
2 The 'Global Five' factors refer to the factors assessed by the NEO-Five Factor Inventory, latest edition
3 The 'Global Five' factors refer to the factors assessed by Goldberg's bipolar adjectives
4 The 'Global Five' factors are derived from Eysenck Personality Profiler, latest edition

Ans. (1)

Exp. The 'Global Five' factors in personality refer to the second order factors of 16 PF, latest edition.

At the primary level, the 16 PF measures 16 primary trait constructs,with a version of the Big Five secondary traits at the secondary level. These higher-level factors emerged from factor-analysing the 16 x 16 intercorrelation matrix for the sixteen primary factors themselves.

The 16 PF yields scores on primary and second-order "global" traits, thereby allowing a multilevel description of each individual's unique personality profile. The Big Five (BF) trait of Openness seems to be related to 16 PF Openness/ Tough-mindedness, The BF trait of Conscientiousness to the 16 PF Self-Control, the BF Extraversion to the 16 PF Extraversion, the BF Agreeableness/Dis-Agreeableness to the 16 PF Independence/Accommodation, and the BF Neuroticism to the 16 PF Anxiety.

14 Read each of the following two statements, Assertion (A) and Reason (R) and indicate your answer using the codes given below :

Assertion (A) Castration does not eliminate sexual behaviour completely in mammals, including humans, of both sexes.

Reason (R) Hormones do not play role in the regulation of sexual behaviour.

Codes

1 Both (A) and (R) are true and (R) is the correct explanation of (A)
2 Both (A) and (R) are true, but (R) is not the correct explanation of (A)
3 (A) is true, but (R) is false
4 (A) is false, but (R) is true

Ans. (3)

Exp. (A) is true, but (R) is false.

Castration does not eliminate sexual behaviour completely in mammals, including humans, of both sexes. The assertion is true because sexual motivation is influenced by hormones such as testosterone, estrogen, progesterone, oxytocin, and vasopressin.

Hormones do not play role in the regulation of sexual behaviour. This is false as in most mammalian species, sex hormones control the ability to engage in sexual behaviours. However, sex hormones do not directly regulate the ability to copulate in primates (including humans). The hypothalamus is the most important part of the brain for sexual functioning; it produces important sexual hormones that are then secreted by the pituitary gland. Castration alone does not eliminate sexual behaviour completely in mammals, including humans of both sexes.

15 Read each of the following two statements, Assertion (A) and Reason (R) and indicate your answer using the codes given below:

Assertion (A) Helpful individuals perceive the world as fair and predictable in which good behaviour is rewarded and bad behaviour is punished.

Reason (R) People believe in a just world.

Codes

1 Both (A) and (R) are true and (R) is the correct explanation of (A)

2 Both (R) and (R) are true, but (R) is not the correct explanation of (A)

3 (A) is true, but (R) is false

4 (A) is false, but (R) is true

Ans. (1)

Exp. Both (A) and (R) are true and (R) is the correct explanation of (A).

Helpful individuals perceive the world as fair and predictable in which good behaviour is rewarded and bad behaviour is punished. This is true as individuals who are helpful engage in a just-world hypothesis or just-world fallacy. It is the cognitive bias that assumes that "people get what they deserve"-that actions will have morally fair and fitting consequences for the actor. For example, the assumptions that noble actions will eventually be rewarded and evil actions will eventually be punished fall under this hypothesis.

People believe in a just world. This is true as the just-world theory (Lerner, 1980) assumes that people want to believe that they live in a world where good things happen to good people and bad things only to bad ones and where therefore everyone harvests what they sow.

16 Which of the following statements best defines maturation?

1 It is directly based on social-cognitive learning

2 It is an automatic biological development of the body that naturally unfolds over time

3 It does not take place in human beings

4 It is the basis of all physical and psychological developments

Ans. (2)

Exp. Maturation is an automatic biological development of the body that naturally unfolds over time.

Maturation is the biological processes involved in an organism's becoming functional or fully developed. It is naturally occurring time-related changes in a participant (e.g., growth, ageing, fatigue, boredom, attention shifts).

17 Read each of the following two statements, Assertion (A) and Reason (R) and indicate your answer using the codes given below :

Assertion (A) Leaders exert powerful effects on followers through the attributions followers make about them.

Reason (R) Leaders have self-confidence and environmental sensitivity.

Codes

1 Both (A) and (R) are true and (R) is the correct explanation of (A)

2 Both (A) and (R) are true, but (R) is not the correct explanation of (A)

3 (A) is true, but (R) is false

4 (A) is false, but (R) is true

Ans. (2)

Exp. Both (A) and (R) are true, but (R) is not correct explanation of (A).

Leaders exert powerful effects on followers through the attributions followers make about them. This is true and reflects the concept of attribution theory of leadership. It is a model of leadership emergence and evaluation that assumes that individuals make inferences about leadership ability by observing and interpreting certain environmental and behavioural cues.

Leaders have self-confidence and environmental sensitivity. This is true both self confidence and environmental sensitivity are vital ingredients of leadership but it does not explain the attribution theory of leadership.

18 The following disorders are coded on Axis I of a five axis diagnosis.

I. V codes　　II. Personality disorders

III. Clinical conditions　　IV. Intellectual deficit

Select the correct answer from the codes given below :

1 I and III　　2 II and IV

3 I and IV　　4 II and III

Ans. (1)

Exp. V codes and Clinical conditions are coded on Axis I of five axis diagnosis.

V Codes addresses issues that are a focus of clinical attention or affect the diagnosis, course, prognosis, or treatment of a patient's mental disorder. However, these codes are not mental disorders.

Clinical conditions are represented in the Axis I which are the most familiar and widely recognised (e.g. major depressive episode, schizophrenic episode, panic attack). These clinical conditions represent the acute symptoms which needs treatment.

19 Four important elements in the Theory of Signal Detection are

1 errors, hits, speed and accuracy

2 speed, accuracy, power and false alarm

3 hit, miss, correct rejection and false alarm

4 acuity, efficacy, speed and power

Ans. (3)

Exp. Four important elements in the Theory of Signal Detection are hit, miss, correct rejection and false alarm. Signal Detection Theory holds that the detection of a stimulus depends on both the intensity of the stimulus and the physical and psychological state of the individual. To apply Signal Detection Theory to a data set where stimuli were either present or absent, and the observer categorised each trial as having the stimulus present or absent, the trials are sorted into one of four categories: hit (signal present and subject says "yes"), miss (signal present and subject says "no"), false alarm (signal absent and subject says "yes"), and correct rejection (signal absent and subject says "no").

20 In Hullian system, the term 'hierarchy of responses' is used to depict

I. if the first innate response pattern does not alleviate a need, another pattern will occur.
II. if the second innate response pattern does not reduce the need another pattern will occur.
III. if the third innate response pattern does not work, still another pattern will occur and so on.
IV. if none of the innate behaviour pattern is effective in reducing the need, the organism will stop responding.

Codes

1 I, II and III	2 I, III and IV
3 II, III and IV	4 I, II and IV

Ans. (1)

Exp. In Hullian system, the term 'hierarchy of responses' is used to depict if the first innate response pattern does not alleviate a need, another pattern will occur. Also if the second innate response pattern does not reduce the need another pattern will occur. And, if the third innate response pattern does not work, still another pattern will occur and so on. Organisms are born with hierarchy of unlearnt responses. Unlearnt behaviours are triggered first when the need arises. If these behaviours fail organism learns new behaviours to reduce the need.

21 Jia had written a list to do her weekend work, but incidently left it home while going out for her first activity. Trying to remember the list, Jia remembers what was at the beginning of the list and what was at the end but not those things in the middle. This is an example of

1 encoding specificity effect
2 flash bulb memory
3 serial position effect
4 tip-of-the tongue effect

Ans. (3)

Exp. In the given scenario, it is an example of serial position effect.

It is the tendency of a person to recall the first and last items in a series in a better way than the middle items. The term was coined by Hermann Ebbinghaus through studies he performed on himself, and refers to the finding that recall accuracy varies as a function of an item's position within a study list. When asked to recall a list of items in any order (free recall), people tend to begin recall with the end of the list, recalling those items best (the recency effect). Among earlier list items, the first few items are recalled more frequently than the middle items (the primacy effect).

22 How does one select the option with the highest expected utility while making rational decision-making ? Find the correct sequence.

I. Assigning utilities.
II. Weighting/multiplying the utilities by the likelihoods.
III. Evaluating the likelihood of alternatives.
IV. Assessing the consequences.

Select the correct answer from the codes given below :

1 I, IV, II and III	2 I, III, II and IV
3 I, IV, III and II	4 III, IV, I and II

Ans. (2)

Exp. The correct sequence is I, III, II and IV.

The subjective expected utility hypothesis states that person maximises pleasure and minimises pain while making rational decision-making. The person first try to assign utilities, then evaluate the likelihood of alternatives. The person will now weigh or multiply the utilities by the likelihoods and then assess the consequences.

23 Brief stress enhances the activity of immune system as evidenced by the action of ______ .

1 macrophages	2 T cells
3 B cells	4 All of these

Ans. (2)

Exp. Brief stress enhances the activity of immune system as evidenced by the action of T cells.

In contrast to chronic/long-term - stress that suppresses/dysregulates immune function, an acute/ short-term fight-or-flight stress response experienced during immune activation can enhance innate and adaptive immunity. Since T cells are crucial mediators of cell-mediated immunity, the observed stress-induced increase in T cell attracting chemokines and Type 1 cytokines suggested that short-term stress may induce an increase in T cell number/activity which can be quantified in absolute numbers.

24 Torrance Tests of Creative Thinking (TTCT) are mainly indexing

1 creative products
2 creative processes
3 creative personality
4 creative persuation

Ans. (2)

Exp. Torrance Tests of Creative Thinking (TTCT) are mainly indexing creative processes.

Measures of the creative process usually have the person do something to show creative thinking. Most often, these tasks involve thinking of many different ideas, called divergent thinking, or thinking of one appropriate idea, called convergent thinking. The most widely used creativity tests are the Torrance Tests of Creative Thinking (TTCT).

25 Personality assessments in forensic settings use the following psychometric and behavioural measures

I. Galvanic Skin Response (GSR)
II. Millon Clinical Multiaxial Inventory (MCMI)
III. Continuous Performance Test (CPT)
IV. Sixteen Personality Factors Test (16 PF)

Select the correct answer from the codes given below :

1 I and II
2 III and IV
3 I, II and III
4 II, III and IV

Ans. (1)

Exp. Personality assessments in forensic settings use the following psychometric and behavioural measures: Galvanic Skin Response (GSR) and Millon Clinical Multiaxial Inventory (MCMI).

The Galvanic Skin Response (GSR) is defined as a change in the electrical properties of the skin. The signal can be used for capturing the autonomic nerve responses as a parameter of the sweat gland function. Galvanic Skin Response is used to identify how humans respond emotionally towards various stimuli and how these responses are affected by stimulus properties personality characteristics social expectancies ('men are not afraid of the dark!') and the interaction of cultural aspects and individual learning histories.

The Millon Clinical Multiaxial Inventory-III (MCMI-III) instrument provides a measure of 24 personality disorders and clinical syndromes for adults undergoing psychological or psychiatric assessment or treatment.

26 Read each of the following two statements, Assertion (A) and Reason (R) and indicate your answer using the codes given below.

Assertion (A) Paired comparison method is not considered suitable for scaling large number of Attitude scale statements.

Reason (R) For computing scale values, paired comparison method uses Thurstone's law of comparative judgement.

Codes

1 Both (A) and (R) are true and (R) is the correct explanation of (A)
2 Both (A) and (R) are true, but (R) is not the correct explanation of (A)
3 (A) is true, but (R) is false
4 (A) is false, but (R) is true

Ans. (2)

Exp. Both (A) and (R) are true, but (R) is not the correct explanation of (A).

Paired comparison method is not considered suitable for scaling large number of Attitude scale statements. It is true as it is only effective when the number of objects is limited. This is because it requires the direct comparison and with a large number of stimulus objects the comparison becomes cumbersome. The formula for calculating the number of pairs is $\frac{n(n-1)}{2}$ where 'n' is the number of items. Therefore, it is not considered suitable for scaling large number of Attitude scale statements.

For computing scale values, paired comparison method uses Thurstone's law of comparative judgement. It is true as Thurstone first introduced a scientific approach to use pairwise comparisons for measurement, which he referred to as the law of comparative judgement. The law of comparative judgement is used to obtain measurements from any process of pairwise comparison.

Both the statements are independently correct, but do not explain one another.

27 The following are found to be significant factors in educational achievement.

I. Teacher-student ratio
II. Medium of instruction
III. Rehearsal and practice
IV. Environmental stimulation

Select the correct answer from the codes given below :

1 I and II
2 I and III
3 I, III and IV
4 II, III and IV

Ans. (3)

Exp. Teacher – student ratio, Rehearsal and practice, and Environmental stimulation are found to be significant factors in educational achievement.

The *Teacher – student ratio* in a classroom plays a vital role in deciding the effectiveness of teaching and learning. A very big student population will make it difficult for the class teacher to focus on all students and address to their individual needs. This might lead to chaos or inattentiveness in the class and hamper the learning process. The ideal teacher-student ratio is said to be 1:30.

Rehearsal and practice help the students to polish their skills and enhance their learning. It ensures that they will remember what they have learnt for longer duration and in a much better manner.

Environmental stimulation in a classroom setting is an added advantage to the learning process. It breaks the monotony and increases the interest of the students in a particular subject. It gives the students an out of the book perspective and stimulates their creativity and imagination.

28 Which one of the scaling method is more likely to yield multi-dimensional attitude scale?

1 Guttman Scalogram analysis
2 Paired Comparison method
3 Equal Appearing Intervals method
4 Method of Summated Rating

Ans. (4)

Exp. The scaling method which is more likely to yield multi-dimensional attitude scale is Method of Summated Rating.

Summated rating scales are used to measure attitudes commonly consists of numerous items whose scores are summed to yield a total score which combine the scores on each dimension separately.

The Method of Summated Ratings or the Likert scale is a psychometric scale commonly involved in research that employs questionnaires. A Likert item is simply a statement that the respondent is asked to evaluate by giving it a quantitative value on any kind of subjective or objective dimension, with level of agreement/ disagreement being the dimension most commonly used.

29 When is aspiration a method of choice to make a lesion?

1 In a deeper brain area
2 In an area of cerebral cortex
3 An irreversible lesion
4 In underlying white matter

Ans. (2)

Exp. Aspiration in an area of cerebral cortex is a method of choice to make a lesion.

Aspiration biopsy is the removal of living tissue, for microscopic examination, by suction through a fine needle attached to a syringe. The procedure is used primarily to obtain cells from a lesion containing fluid or when fluid is formed in a serious cavity. Aspiration lesions are readily applied to cerebral cortex.

30 Trace the sequence of events turning default female sex of the fetus into male.

I. SRY gene produces SRY protein.
II. Presence of Y chromosome.
III. Testosterone masculanise Wolffian duct into seminal vesicles.
IV. Primitive gonad develop into testes.
V. Mullerian inhibiting hormone defeminizes the fetus.

Select the correct answer from the codes given below :

1 II, I, IV, V, III
2 II, IV, V, I, III
3 II, IV, I, V, III
4 IV, II, I, III, V

Ans. (1)

Exp. The correct sequence is: II, I, IV, V, III.

In humans, half of spermatozoons carry X chromosome and the other half Y chromosome. A single gene (SRY) present on the Y chromosome produces SRY protein that acts as a signal to set the developmental pathway towards maleness.

Presence of this gene starts off the process of virilisation. The primitive gonad develops into testes.

This and other factors like Mullerian inhibiting hormone defeminizes the fetus and testosterone masculanises the Wolffian duct into seminal vesicles, result in the sex differences in humans. The cells in females, with two X chromosomes, undergo X-inactivation, in which one of the two X chromosomes is inactivated. The inactivated X chromosome remains within a cell as a Barr body.

31 A psychologist was administering a projective test which involved a word association task. She tended to nod and smile every time a plural word was given by the respondent.

The following testing bias was seen

1 Favoritism
2 Test wiseness
3 Selective reinforcement
4 Gender of Assessor

Ans. (3)

Exp. The testing bias was Selective reinforcement.

It is a type of behaviour modification which seeks to increase the occurrence of certain behaviours by responding to desired behaviours with a pleasurable stimulus, while seeking to extinguish undesirable behaviours by not responding to those hence, the reinforcing response is said to be selective.

32 Match List I and List II and select the correct answer from codes given below :

List I (Measures of personality assessment)	List II (Scoring elements)
A. MMPI	I. V, X,Y, Z scales
B. MCMI	II. Needs and presses
C. TAT	III. Populars
D. Rorschach inkblots	IV. L, F, K scales

Codes

	A	B	C	D
1	III	II	I	IV
2	II	IV	III	I
3	I	III	IV	II
4	IV	I	II	III

Ans. (4)

Exp. The correct matching is A-IV, B-I, C-II, D-III.

The scoring elements in *MMPI* are L, F, K scales. The L scale is the lie scale which was developed to detect attempts by individuals to present them in a favourable light. The F scale is used to detect attempts at over-reporting. The K scale or defensiveness scale is a more effective and less obvious way of detecting attempts to present oneself in the best possible way by under-reporting.

The scoring elements in *MCMI* are V, X, Y, Z scales. The Validity Scale (V) contains a number of improbable items which may indicate questionable results if endorsed. The three scales: the Disclosure Scale (X), the Desirability Scale (Y) and the Debasement Scale (Z), are used to provide information about a person's response style.

The scoring elements in *TAT* are needs and presses. American psychologist Henry Murray (1893–1988) developed a theory of personality that was organised in terms of motives, presses, and needs.

The scoring elements in *Rorschach Inkblots* are Populars. "Popularity" and "originality" of responses are considered as basic dimensions in the analysis.

33 Read each of the following two statements, Assertion (A) and Reason (R) and indicate your answer using the codes given below:

Assertion (A) Gf and Gc correlate positively with each other with moderate magnitude.

Reason (R) Cattell used second order factor solutions for the identification of Gf and Gc were oblique.

Codes

1 Both (A) and (R) are true and (R) is the correct explanation of (A)
2 Both (A) and (R) are true, but (R) is not the correct explanation of (A)
3 (A) is true, but (R) is false
4 (A) is false, but (R) is true

Ans. (1)

Exp. Both (A) and (R) are true, and (R) is the correct explanation of (A).

Gf and Gc correlate positively with each other with moderate magnitude. Fluid intelligence or fluid reasoning is the capacity to reason and solve novel problems, independent of any knowledge from the past. Crystallized intelligence is the ability to use skills, knowledge, and experience. Both types of intelligence increase throughout childhood and adolescence and are positively correlated with each other across the age levels, but with moderate magnitude.

Cattell used second order factor solutions for the identification of Gf and Gc were oblique. Oblique is used for first and second order factors where the factors are correlated to one another. This is true and explains the correlation between Gf and Gc.

34 The underlying motivation for acts of Aggression is ________ .

1 intent to harm
2 anger
3 retaliation
4 need to exert control

Ans. (4)

Exp. The underlying motivation for acts of Aggression is need to exert control.

Aggression stems from the basic need to control the behaviour of other people. This need is viewed as the major motive underlying a tremendous amount of the physical and psychological harm that people inflict upon one another.

35 Which of the following is a characteristic of Chomsky's Theory?

1 Development of language is between 3 and 5 years of Age
2 Language development is dependent on the reinforcements received by the child
3 Children acquire mistakes in language by observing their parents and others around them
4 Children have an innate mental grammar

Ans. (4)

Exp. According to Chomsky's Theory, children have an innate mental grammar.

Noam Chomsky gave the concept of Universal Grammar (UG). The basic postulate of UG is that language is hard-wired into the brain, it is innate. The theory suggests that linguistic ability becomes manifest without being and that there are properties that all natural human languages share.

It is a matter of observation and experimentation to determine precisely what abilities are innate and what properties are shared by all languages. The theory proposes that there is an innate, genetically determined language faculty that knows these rules, making it easier and faster for children to learn to speak than it otherwise would be.

36 Match List I with List II and select the correct answer from the codes given below :

List I	List II
A. Physical trauma	I. The cognitive and emotional upheaval that follows a highly distressing life
B. Psychological trauma	II. Most of us remember nothing before the age of about 3 to 4 years
C. Infantile amnesia	III. It may cause permanent amnesia if particular areas of the brain are damaged
D. Repression	IV. Distressing mental content is transferred from the conscious to the unconscious level of awareness

Codes

	A	B	C	D		A	B	C	D
1	I	II	III	IV	2	II	III	IV	I
3	III	I	IV	II	4	IV	III	II	I

Ans. (*)

Exp. The correct matching is: A- III, B-I, C-II, D-IV.

Physical trauma may cause permanent amnesia if particular areas of the brain are damaged. Amnesia refers to the loss of memories, such as facts, information and experiences. Brain surgery, head injury or trauma are risk factors for developing amnesia.

Psychological trauma is the cognitive and emotional upheaval that follows a highly distressing life. It is a response to an event that a person finds highly stressful. It can cause a wide range of physical and emotional symptoms.

Infantile amnesia makes most of us remember nothing before the age of about 3 to 4 years. It is the inability of adults to recollect early episodic memories and is associated with the rapid forgetting that occurs in childhood.

Repression causes distressing mental content to transfer from the conscious to the unconscious level of awareness. It is the unconscious blocking of unpleasant emotions, impulses, memories, and thoughts.

37 Match List I with List II and select the correct answer from the codes given below :

List I (Concepts)	List II (Theorists)
A. Vicarious trial and error	I. Skinner
B. Hypothetical deduction	II. Tolman
C. Cumulative recording	III. Hull
D. Reciprocal determination	IV. Bandura

Codes

	A	B	C	D		A	B	C	D
1	I	II	III	IV	2	I	III	IV	II
3	II	III	I	IV	4	IV	I	II	III

Ans. *(3)*

Exp. The correct matching is A-II, B-III, C-I, D-IV.

Vicarious trial and error is associated with Tolman. Vicarious trial-and-error (VTE) is a term that Muenzinger and Tolman used to describe the rat's conflict-like behaviour before responding to choice.

Hypothetical deduction is associated with Hull. According to this description scientific inquiry and research proceeds by means by formulating hypotheses that can be either proved or disproved through experimentation and observation.

Cumulative recording is associated with Skinner. It is a continuous tally or graph to which new data are added. In conditioning, for example, a cumulative record is a graph showing the cumulative number of responses over a continuous period of time.

Reciprocal determination is associated with Bandura. It is the theory set forth by psychologist Albert Bandura which states that a person's behaviour both influences and is influenced by personal factors and the social environment.

38 The centre - surround organisation of ganglion cells that enhance contrast at edges in a visual environment is well illustrated by

1 craik bands
2 mach bands
3 luminance bands
4 optic bands

Ans. *(2)*

Exp. The centre - surround organisation of ganglion cells that enhance contrast at edges in a visual environment is well illustrated by mach bands.

Mach bands is an optimal illusion. It exaggerates the contrast between edges of the slightly differing shades of gray, as soon as they contact one another, by triggering edge-detection in the human visual system. It can be explained by how the sensory neurons that send visual information from the eye to the brain (aka Ganglion cells) process the input from the photoreceptors.

39 Match List I with List II and select the correct answer from the codes given below:

List I (Diagnosis)	**List II** (Axis used in multiaxial system)
A. General medical conditions	I. V
B. GAF (Global Assessment Functioning)	II. I
C. V codes	III. II
D. Personality disorders	IV. III

Codes

	A	B	C	D		A	B	C	D
1	II	III	IV	I	2	III	IV	I	II
3	IV	I	II	III	4	I	II	III	IV

Ans. *(3)*

Exp. The correct matching is A IV, B-I, C-II, D-III.

Axis V is associated with the Global Assessment of Functioning (GAF). The GAF went from 0 to 100 and provided a way to summarize in a single number just how well the person was functioning overall.

Axis I is associated with V codes addresses issues that are a focus of clinical attention or affect the diagnosis, course, prognosis, or treatment of a patient's mental disorder.

Axis II is associated with Personality disorders. Disorders like paranoid, schizoid, schizotypical, antisocial, etc. fall under this axis.

Axis III is associated with General medical conditions. It provided information about any medical conditions that were present which might impact the patient's mental disorder or its management.

40 The growth needs of ERG Theory are represented by various needs in Maslow's Model

1 Physiological and social needs
2 Safety needs and esteem needs
3 Social needs and esteem needs
4 Esteem needs and self-actualisation needs

Ans. *(4)*

Exp. The growth needs of ERG Theory are represented by various needs in Maslow's Model esteem needs and self-actualisation needs.

Alderfer's ERG theory suggests that there are three groups of core needs: Existence (E), Relatedness (R), and Growth (G)—hence the acronym ERG. These groups align with Maslow's levels of physiological needs, social needs, and self-actualisation needs, respectively.

41 In Bloom's taxonomy of educational objectives, the following appear in ascending order.

1 Remember → Understand → Apply → Analyse
2 Apply → Analyse → Understand → Remember
3 Understand→Apply → Remember → Analyse
4 Analyse → Remember → Apply → Understand

Ans. *(1)*

Exp. In Bloom's taxonomy of educational objectives, the following appear in ascending order:

Remember → Understand → Apply → Analyse

There are six levels of cognitive learning according to the revised version of Bloom's Taxonomy. Each level is conceptually different. The six levels are remembering, understanding, applying, analysing, evaluating, and creating.

42 Failure to develop consistent identity results in __________.

1 inferiority
2 role confusion
3 stagnation
4 social isolation

Ans. *(2)*

Exp. Failure to develop consistent identity results in role confusion.

Adolescence is the period of life between childhood and adulthood. According to psychologist Erik Erikson, adolescents go through the psychosocial, crisis of identity versus role confusion, which involves exploring who they are as individuals.

It is the fifth stage and it occurs during adolescence, from about 12-18 years. During this stage, adolescents search for a sense of self and personal identity, through an intense exploration of personal values, beliefs and goals.

43 Helpers respond to the needs of a victim because they want to accomplish something rewarding; this may be referred as

1 negative state-relief model
2 empathic-joy hypothesis
3 empathy-altruism hypothesis
4 pluralistic empathy

Ans. *(2)*

Exp. Helpers respond to the needs of a victim because they want to accomplish something rewarding; this may be referred to as empathic-joy hypothesis.

The hypothesis states that the reason for someone helping another in need are positive feelings associated with the altruistic behaviour. Helping others is a reward in itself because it brings a person happiness and joy when they commit a helping behaviour.

44 The philosophy of Advaita Vedanta in respect of shaping beliefs does not distinguish between

I. self and non-self
II. human and nature
III. human and society

Select the correct answer from the codes given below.

1 I and II　　2 I and III
3 II and III　　4 I, II and III

Ans. *(4)*

Exp. The philosophy of Advaita Vedanta in respect of shaping beliefs does not distinguish between self and non-self, human and nature, and human and society.

Advaita is often translated as 'non-dualism' though it literally means 'non-secondness.' According to Advaita metaphysics, Brahman, which is the ultimate, transcendent and immanent God of the latter Vedas, appears as the world because of its creative energy (maya). The world has no separate existence apart from Brahman.

The experiencing self (jiva) and the transcendental self of the Universe (atman) are in reality identical (both are Brahman), though the individual self seems different as space within a container seems different from space as such. These cardinal doctrines are represented in the anonymous verse 'Brahma satyam jagan mithya; jivo brahmaiva na aparah' (Brahman is alone true, and this world of plurality is an error; the individual self is not different from Brahman).

45 Which is the correct order of the emergence of following psycho-social strengths?

1 Love, Fidelity, Wisdom, Care
2 Care, Fidelity, Love, Wisdom
3 Fidelity, Love, Care, Wisdom
4 Care, Fidelity, Wisdom, Love

Ans. *(3)*

Exp. The correct order of the emergence of psycho-social strengths is Fidelity, Love, Care, Wisdom. Erikson's stage theory characterises an individual advancing through the eight life stages as a function of negotiating their biological and socio-cultural forces. The two conflicting forces each have a psychosocial crisis which characterises the eight stages. If an individual does indeed successfully reconcile these forces (favouring the first mentioned attribute in the crisis), they emerge from the stage with the corresponding virtue.

Hope is the virtue achieved in the 1st stage, Trust vs. Mistrust. Will is the virtue achieved in the 2nd stage, Autonomy vs. Shame/Doubt. Purpose is the virtue achieved in the 3rd stage, Initiative vs. Guilt. Competence is the virtue achieved in the 4th stage, Industry vs. Inferiority. Fidelity is the virtue achieved in the 5th stage, Identity vs. Role Confusion. Love is the virtue achieved in the 6th stage, Intimacy vs. Isolation. Care is the virtue achieved in the 7th stage, Generativity vs. Stagnation. Wisdom is the virtue achieved in the 8th stage, Ego Integrity vs. Despair.

46 From the following list of tools used by the career guidance counsellor, Select the odd one out.

DAT　　2 GATB　　3 DBDA　　4 SVIB

Ans. *(4)*

Exp. The odd one out is the SVIB. The DAT, GATB and DBDA are aptitude tests.

Strong Vocational Interest Blank (SVIB) is an interest inventory used in career assessment. The goal of this assessment is to give insight into a person's interests, so that they may have less difficulty in deciding on an appropriate career choice for themselves. It is also frequently used for educational guidance as one of the most popular career assessment tools.

The Differential Aptitude Tests (DAT) is a battery of tests is designed to measure students' ability to learn or to succeed in a number of different areas.

The General Aptitude Test Battery (GATB) is a professional career aptitude test which measures nine different aptitudes and can be used to help assess the likelihood that you will be successful in specific careers or training programs.

David's Battery of Differential Abilities (DBDA) is a battery consisting of 8 ability tests – verbal ability, numerical ability, spatial ability, closure ability, reasoning ability, mechanical ability, clerical ability and psychomotor ability.

47 Job design comprises of different aspects

I. Job enlargement
II. Job enrichment
III. Job rotation

Select the correct answer from the codes given below :

1 I and II　　2 I and III
3 II and III　　4 I, II and III

Ans. *(4)*

➲ *Exp.* Job design comprises of different aspects as Job enlargement, Job enrichment, and Job rotation.

Job design is the process of creating a job that enables the organisation to achieve its goals while motivating and rewarding the employee.

Job enlargement is adding additional activities within the same level to an existing role.

Job enrichment is a process that is characterised by adding dimensions to existing jobs to make them more motivating.

Job rotation is the systematic movement of employees from one job to another within the organisation to achieve various human resources objectives such as orienting new employees, training employees, enhancing career development, and preventing job boredom or burnout.

48 The following are disorders that are included in the anxiety disorders spectrum.

I. Panic disorder
II. Body dysmorphic disorder
III. PTSD
IV. Fugue

Select the correct answer from the codes given below :

1 I and II
2 I and III
3 I, II and IV
4 II, III and IV

Ans. (2)

➲ *Exp.* Panic disorder and PTSD are the disorders that are included in the anxiety disorders spectrum.

Panic disorder is an anxiety disorder characterised by recurrent unexpected panic attacks. Post Traumatic Stress Disorder (PTSD) is a disorder that develops in some people who have experienced a shocking, scary or dangerous event.

49 Detecting movement in spite of camouflage is easier for people who are

1 field dependent
2 field independent
3 both field dependent and field independent
4 neither field dependent nor field independent

Ans. (2)

➲ *Exp.* Detecting movement in spite of camouflage is easier for people who are field independent.

Some people identify camouflaged objects with ease compared with others. The literature suggests that Field-Independent individuals detect camouflaged object better than their Field-Dependent counterparts. Field independent (relative to field dependent) people have the ability to focus on details despite the clutter of background information. Field dependence and field independence is an area of study in which individual differences in cognitive style have been identified.

50 Read the following statement and decide : "If a rat that had previously learned to traverse a maze or a runway to obtain food is placed directly into a non-empty goal box, it will stop traversing the maze or runway on subsequent trials". What it exemplifies?

1 Latent learning
2 Place learning
3 Response extinction
4 Latent extinction

Ans. (4)

➲ *Exp.* The given statement exemplifies Latent extinction.

Krech and Tolman (1932) used a complicated maze to study how rats used strategies (hypotheses) to reach the goal box. They changed the colors of the doors (dark, light), making them swing or freeze etc. Latent extinction refers to decrease in responses which occur as a result of non-reinforced experience in the goal box.

Rats trained in a maze with reinforcement in goal box, were then placed directly into an empty goal box by the experimenter. Rats when reintroduced into the maze showed hesitant responses to go to the goal box for they did not expect the reinforcement.

51 Match List I with List II and select the correct answer by choosing from the codes given below :

List I	List II
A. Encoding failure	I. Information that is not accessed evades from the storage over a time
B. Proactive interference	II. Information is not attended to encoding
C. Decay	III. Newer information interferes with the retrieval of older information
D. Retroactive interference	IV. Older information already in memory interferes with the learning of new information

Codes

	A	B	C	D
1	I	II	III	IV
2	I	III	IV	II
3	II	III	IV	I
4	II	IV	I	III

Ans. (4)

➲ *Exp.* The correct matching is A-II, B-IV, C-I, D-III.

In *Encoding failure* information is not attended to encoding. Encoding failure refers to a breakdown in the process of getting information into the cognitive system.

In *Proactive interference* older, information already in memory interferes with the learning of new information. Proactive interference refers to the reduction in memory performance for recently learned information resulting from the prior learning of related materials.

In *Decay* information that is not accessed evades from the storage over a time. The Decay theory is a theory that proposes that memory fades due to the mere passage of time.

In *Retroactive interference*, newer information interferes with the retrieval of older information. Retroactive interference happens when an individual is unable to recall old information because new information prevents its retrieval.

52 Read each of the following two statements, Assertion (A) and Reason (R) and indicate your answer using the codes given below:

Assertion (A) Language affects our thought process.

Reason (R) Language affects our ability to store information.

Codes

1 Both (A) and (R) are true and (R) is the correct explanation of (A)
2 Both (A) and (R) are true, but (R) is not the correct explanation of (A)
3 (A) is true, but (R) is false
4 (A) is false, but (R) is true

***Ans.* (2)**

Exp. Both (A) and (R) are true, but (R) is not the correct explanation of (A).

Language affects our thought process. This is true as the main use of language is to transfer thoughts from one mind, to another mind. The bits of linguistic information that enter into one person's mind, from another, cause people to entertain a new thought with profound effects on his world knowledge, inferencing, and subsequent behavior.

Language affects our ability to store information. This is true as the language we speak affects the way we process, store and retrieve information. However, it does not explain how language affects the thought process.

53 Trace the right sequence of hypothetical series of events by McClelland in the context of n-Ach.

I. n-Ach in children
II. Independence training by parents
III. Economic development
IV. Self-reliance values

Select the correct answer from the codes given below :

1 I, II, IV and III
2 IV, II, I and III
3 I, IV, II and III
4 IV, II, III and I

***Ans.* (2)**

Exp. The correct sequence is IV, II, I and III.

Need for Achievement (n-Ach) refers to an individual's desire for significant accomplishment, mastering of skills, control, or high standards. Sources of high n-Ach include parents who encouraged more self-reliance and independence in childhood. Independent training by parents will allow more room for children to grow and learn from their own mistakes. This will lead to higher achievement levels in children which will eventually promote economic growth.

54 Match List I with List II and select the correct answer from the codes given below :

List I (Concepts)	List II (Descriptions)
A. Little-C	I. Everyday creativity
B. Big-C	II. Creativity in eminents
C. Pro-C	III. Creativity in a chosen profession
D. Mini-C	IV. Personal creativity

Codes

	A	B	C	D
1	I	II	III	IV
2	II	I	IV	III
3	III	II	I	IV
4	I	II	IV	III

***Ans.* (1)**

Exp. The correct matching is A-I, B-II, C-III, D-IV.

Dr James C Kaufman and Dr Ronald Beghetto have identified four developmental levels of creativity:

Little-C refers to everyday creativity. With appropriate feedback, advancements are made and what was created might be of value to others.

Big-C refers to creativity in eminent. It includes an evaluation of one's entire career and entire body of work and then evaluates the entire body of work against other great contributors and decides where one fits in.

Pro-C refers to creativity in a chosen profession. At this level, one has the ability to be creative at a professional level and in a professional venue.

Mini-C refers to personal creativity. At this level, what one creates might not be revolutionary but it is new and meaningful to them.

55 Read each of the following two statements, Assertion (A) and Reason (R) and indicate your answer using the codes given below :

Assertion (A) Projective techniques are difficult to standardise and norm.

Reason (R) Projective techniques are not timed tests.

Codes

1 Both (A) and (R) are true and (R) is the correct explanation of (A)
2 Both (A) and (R) are true, but (R) is not the correct explanation of (A)
3 (A) is true, but (R) is false
4 (A) is false, but (R) is true

***Ans.* (2)**

Exp. Both (A) and (R) are true, but (R) is not the correct explanation of (A).

Projective techniques are difficult to standardise and norm. This is true as is very difficult to develop standardised tests and norms for projective tests. Projective test employs ambiguous stimuli, notably inkblots (Rorschach Test) and enigmatic pictures (Thematic Apperception Test) to evoke responses that may reveal facets of the subject's personality by projection of internal attitudes, traits and behaviour patterns upon the external stimuli.

Projective techniques are not timed tests. This is true as the aim of the projective tests is to unveil the true personality and issues of a person they are not timed, instead the person is given ample time to reflect and respond.

Both the statements are independently correct, but the reason does not explain the assertion.

56 A 19 years old boy was administered the Wechsler Intelligence Scale for children by the clerical staff of a busy psychologist who later wrote the test report. a xerox copy of the test material was shared with the child's parents to ensure that he performs well. The following ethical principles of testing were violated

I. Use of age Appropriate test
II. Professional qualification of tester
III. Copyright
IV. Culture fair testing

Select the correct answer from the codes given below :

1 I and III 2 II and III
3 I, II and III 4 All of these

Ans. (3)

Exp. The ethical principles of testing which were violated are: Use of appropriate test, Professional qualification of tester are and Copyright.

The subject is 19 years old boy who administered the Wechsler Intelligence Scale for children. This is a violation of using age appropriate test. The test was administered by the clerical staff which violates the ethical principle of professional qualification of tester. A psychological test should only be administered by a trained and a qualified professional.

The subject is not supposed to be given the test prior to actual assessment for practice. The xerox copy of the test material was shared which violates the ethical principle of copyright. The assessment report has to be written by a trained and a qualified professional and has to be kept confidential, to be shared only with the people concerned.

57 Match List I with List II and select the correct answer by choosing from the codes given below :

List I (Sleep phenomenon)	List II (EEG displays)
A. Stage-1 sleep	I. Single large–ve wave followed by large +ve wave
B. Stage-3 sleep	II. Low voltage high frequency EEG signal
C. Sleep spindle	III. Occasional presence of delta waves
D. K-complex	IV. Waxing and waning burst of 12-14 Hz wave

Codes

	A	B	C	D
1	I	IV	III	II
2	II	III	IV	I
3	III	IV	I	II
4	IV	III	II	I

Ans. (2)

Exp. The correct matching is A-II, B-III, C-IV, D-I.

Stage-1 sleep is associated with low voltage high frequency EEG signal. In terms of brain wave activity, Stage 1 sleep is associated with both alpha and theta waves.

Stage-3 sleep is associated with occasional presence of delta waves. Delta waves are associated with the deep sleep stages: Stage 3 and REM.

Sleep spindle is associated with waxing and waning burst of 12-14 Hz wave. Sleep spindles, a defining characteristic of stage 2 sleep, are brief, powerful bursts of synchronous ~12–15 Hz neuronal firing in thalamocortical networks that occur most frequently late in the night.

K-complex is associated with single large –ve wave followed by large +ve wave. K-complex consists of a brief negative high-voltage peak, usually greater than 100 μV, followed by a slower positive complex around 350 and 550 ms and at 900 ms, a final negative peak.

58 Emergent Stage I sleep is characterised by

I. sleep-spindle
II. electromygraphic changes
III. electro-oculographic changes
IV. K-complex

Select the correct answer from the codes given below :

1 I and II 2 I and IV
3 I, III and IV 4 II, III and IV

Ans. (4)

Exp. Emergent Stage I sleep is characterised by K-complex, electromygraphyic changes and electro-oculographic changes.

After stage four, we begin to go back up the stages, until we reach stage one again. This is sometimes called stage one emergent.

A K-complex is an electroencephalography (EEG) waveform that occurs during Stage 2 of NREM sleep. They are more frequent in the first sleep cycles. In the emergent Stage-1, K-complex can be seenwhen there is a difference of more than 3 minutes between two waves. However, if the difference is between two K-complex is less than 3 minutes, then it is a part of NREM sleep.

During the emergent Stage-1, there is a paralysis of muscle systems in the body which are considered as electromygraphic changes and can be measured by Electromygraphy (EMG). It is a diagnostic procedure to assess the health of muscles and the nerve cells that control them (motor neurons).

During the emergent Stage-1, rapid eye movements are considered as electro-oculogrpahic changes which can be measured using Electro-oculography (EOG/E.O.G.). It is a technique for measuring the corneo-retinal standing potential that exists between the front and the back of the human eye.

59 Self is conceptualised in Western and Eastern perspectives on personality, respectively, as

1 free and deterministic
2 instinctive and learned
3 ideal and real
4 independent and interdependent

Ans. (4)

Exp. Self is conceptualised in Western and Eastern perspectives on personality, respectively, as independent and interdependent.

The Western Culture lays more emphasis on individuality of a person and hence, they have a more independent perspective. The Eastern Culture has more of interdependence and lays more emphasis on group norms and Culture rather than an individual. The Eastern culture is more collectivist while the Western culture is more individualistic.

60 Match the items of List I and List II and select the correct answer from the codes given below :

List I (Scholars)	List II (Concepts)
A. Cattell	I. Assortative mating
B. Jensen	II. Investment hypothesis
C. Sternberg	III. Wisdom
D. Spearman	IV. Positive manifold

Codes

	A	B	C	D		A	B	C	D
1	I	II	III	IV	2	II	I	IV	III
3	III	IV	II	I	4	II	I	III	IV

Ans. (4)

Exp. The correct matching is A-II, B-I, C-III, D-IV.

Cattell is associated with Investment Hypothesis. According to Cattell's (1987) Investment theory individual differences in acquisition of knowledge and skills are partly the result of investment of Fluid Intelligence (Gf) in learning situations demanding insights in complex relations.

Jensen is associated with Assortative mating. Assortative mating is a mating pattern and a formof sexual selection in which individuals with similar phenotypes mate with one another more frequently than would be expected under a random mating pattern.

Sternberg is associated with Wisdom. Sternberg's Balance theory of Wisdom states that the application of tacit knowledge as mediated by values toward the achievement of a common good through a balance among multiple intrapersonal, interpersonal and extra personal interests in order to achieve a balance among adaptation to existing environments, shaping of existing environments and selection of new environments.

Spearman is associated with Positive manifold. Positive manifold is the idea that all the variables are positively correlated. For example, scores on a vocabulary test will correlate positively with scores on a mathematics test.

61 Match List I with List II and select the correct answer from the codes given below :

List I (Tools/Theories)	List II (Features)
A. Kelley's Personal Construct Theory	I. 11 categories of scoring TAT
B. Murray's TAT	II. 6 sub-categories of needs and goals
C. McClelland and Atkinson's Measure of n-Ach	III. 20 needs
D. Rotter's Scale	IV. One postulate and 11 corollaries

Codes

	A	B	C	D		A	B	C	D
1	IV	III	II	I	2	II	III	IV	I
3	III	IV	I	II	4	IV	III	I	II

Ans. (4)

Exp. The correct matching is A-IV, B-III, C-I, D-II.

Kelley's Personal Construct Theory is associated with one postulate and 11 corollaries. The fundamental postulate states that our psychological processes are directed by how we anticipate events. The 11 corollaries are construction, individual, organisation, dichotomy, choice, range, experience, modulation, fragmentation, commonality, and sociality corollary.

Murray's TAT is associated with 20 needs. Murray divides needs into several binary categories: manifest (overt) or latent (covert), conscious or unconscious, and primary (viscerogenic) and secondary (psychogenic) needs.

McClelland and Atkinson's is associated with the measure of n-Ach. The aim of need achievement theory is to explain why certain individuals are more motivated to achieve than others.

Rotter's Scale is associated with 6 sub-categories of needs and goals. Rotter listed six broad categories of needs, with each category representing a group of functionally related behaviours: that is, behaviours that lead to the same or similar reinforcements.

62 Match List I with List II and select the correct answer from the codes given below :

List I (Concepts)	List II (Descriptions)
A. Phonemes	I. Smallest meaningful combination of sounds
B. Syntax	II. Effective and appropriate use of language in social context
C. Morphemes	III. Basic sound of consonants and vowels
D. Pragmatics	IV. Combination of words to make meaningful phrases and sentences

Codes

	A	B	C	D		A	B	C	D
1	I	II	III	IV	2	II	III	IV	I
3	III	IV	I	II	4	IV	III	II	I

Ans. *(3)*

Exp. The correct matching is A-III, B-IV, C-I, D-II

Phonemes are basic sounds of consonants and vowels. It is a speech sound that plays a meaningful role in a language and cannot be analyzed into smaller meaningful sounds, conventionally indicated by slash symbols.

Syntax is the combination of words to make meaningful phrases and sentences. It is the set of rules that describes how words and phrases in a language are arranged into grammatical sentences.

Morphemes are smallest meaningful combination of sounds. It is a unit of meaning that cannot be analysed into smaller such units.

Pragmatics is the effective and appropriate use of language in social context. It is the analysis of language in terms of its functional communicative properties rather than its formal and structural properties.

63 Read each of the following two statements, Assertion (A) and Reason (R) and indicate your answer using the codes given below:

Assertion (A) The forgetting of a memory is caused by the disappearance of its engram over a period of time.

Reason (R) Once the engram has disappeared, the memory no longer exists anywhere in the memory system.

Codes

1 Both (A) and (R) are true and (R) is the correct explanation of (A)
2 Both (A) and (R) are true, but (R) is not the correct explanation of (A)
3 (A) is true, but (R) is false
4 (A) is false, but (R) is true

Ans. *(1)*

Exp. Both (A) and (R) are true and (R) is correct explanation of (A).

The forgetting of a memory is caused by the disappearance of its engram over a period of time. This is true as it is based on decay theory of forgetting which results in disappearance of an engram. An engram is a unit of cognitive information imprinted in a physical substance, theorized to be the means by which memories are stored as biophysical or biochemical changes in the brain or other biological tissue, in response to external stimuli.

Once the engram has disappeared, the memory no longer exists anywhere in the memory system. When the engram disappears, an individual begins to forget things. This is because once the engram has disappeared, the memory no longer exists in the memory system.

64 Which is the correct sequence of Reinforcement schedules in terms of their effectiveness in response rate and resistance to extinction during learning experiments?

1 Variable Ratio → Fixed Ratio → Variable Interval → Fixed Interval → Continuous Reinforcement Schedule
2 Fixed Ratio → Variable Ratio → Fixed Interval → Variable Interval → Continuous Reinforcement Schedule
3 Continuous Reinforcement schedule → Variable Ratio → Fixed Ratio → Variable Interval → Fixed Interval
4 Variable Ratio → Variable Interval → Fixed Ratio → Fixed Interval → Continuous Reinforcement Schedule

Ans. *(4)*

Exp. The correct sequence is: Variable Ratio → Variable Interval → Fixed Ratio → Fixed Interval → Continuous Reinforcement Schedule.

Variable Ratio is a schedule of reinforcement where a response is reinforced after an unpredictable number of responses. This schedule creates a steady, high rate of responding. Gambling and lottery games are good examples of a reward based on a variable ratio schedule.

Variable Interval is where the reinforcement for a certain behaviour comes at random times or variable intervals. This is an example of intermittent reinforcement, which occurs when only some instances of a certain behaviour are rewarded (and not all of them).

Fixed Ratio is a schedule of reinforcement where a response is reinforced only after a specified number of responses. This schedule produces a high, steady rate of responding with only a brief pause after the delivery of the reinforce.

Fixed Interval is a schedule of reinforcement where the first response is rewarded only after a specified amount of time has elapsed. This schedule causes high amounts of responding near the end of the interval, but much slower responding immediately after the delivery of the reinforcer.

Continuous Reinforcement Schedule occurs when reinforcement is delivered after every single target behaviour.

65 When a Background Interference Procedure was used experimentally, the following findings became apparent?

1 Field independent persons did better than field dependent persons
2 Field dependent persons did better than field independent persons
3 Both field dependent and field independent persons did equally well
4 BIP enhanced the performance of all subjects

Ans. *(1)*

Exp. When a Background Interference Procedure was used experimentally, it was apparent that the field independent persons did better than field dependent persons.

Canter's Background Interference Procedure was designed to increase the sensitivity of the Bender test to the discernment of organic brain damage. Field independent (relative to field dependent) people have the ability to focus on details despite the clutter of background information.

66 People with moderate mental retardation would have an IQ in the range of

1 10 to 19 2 35 to 54 3 55 to 70 4 20 to 34

Ans. (2)

Exp. People with moderate mental retardation would have an IQ in the range of 35 to 54.

Profound mental retardation is found between the IQ range of 10 – 19, severe mental retardation is found between the IQ range of 20 – 34, and borderline mental retardation is found between the IQ range of 55 – 70.

67 The following is not typically found in a school guidance counsellor's office

1 Sand pit 2 Lie detector
3 Psychometric tests 4 Puppets and play dough

Ans. (2)

Exp. Lie detector is not typically found in a school guidance counsellor's office.

Polygraph tests are popularly known as lie detector. They are used by police in investigating crime only in exception cases. In most of the cases, it is still illegal in India.

68 The following social factors play a role in educational settings

I. Cooperation II. Competition
III. Peer influence IV. Role modelling

Select the correct answer from the codes given below :

1 I and II 2 II and III
3 III and IV 4 All of these

Ans. (4)

Exp. The social factors which play a role in educational settings are Cooperation, Competition, Peer influence and Role modelling.

In an educational setting, a healthy sense of competition among the students is good for optimum performance and academic excellence. Peer influence can also lead students in a positive direction if applied with correct intentions. Role models play an important role in a student's life. A positive role model can motivate and encourage students to strive and be better in academics and in general as a human being. Cooperative learning is an educational approach which aims to organise classroom activities into academic and social learning experiences.

69 According to Piaget, the children are able to grasp the concept of object permanence and conservation in

1 sensory motor stage
2 pre-operational stage
3 concrete operational stage
4 formal operations stage

Ans. (*)

Exp. According to Piaget, the children are able to grasp the concept of object permanence in the sensorimotor stage (0-2 years). Object permanence refers to when an infant understands that an object still exists, even when they are not able to see, smell, touch, or hear it. The children are able to grasp the concept of conservation in the concrete operational stage (7-11 years). It is the idea that an object, such as water or modeling clay, remains the same even when its appearance changes.

70 Match List I with List II and select the correct answer from the codes given below :

List I	List II
A. Symbolic social influence	I. A form of social influence in which one person orders to perform some action
B. Normative social influence	II. Social influence based on the desire to be correct
C. Informational social influence	III. Social influence based on the desire to be liked
D. Obedience	IV. Social influence resulting from the mental representation of others or our relationship

Codes

	A	B	C	D		A	B	C	D
1	I	II	III	IV	2	II	III	IV	I
3	III	IV	I	II	4	IV	III	II	I

Ans. (4)

Exp. The correct matching is: A-IV, B-III, C-II, D-I.

Symbolic social influence is a social influence resulting from the mental representation of others or our relationship. Psychological presence of others in our mental representation of them influences our behaviour and thought.

Normative social influence is a social influence based on the desire to be liked. It is where a person conforms in order to be accepted and belong to a group.

Informational social influence is social influence based on the desire to be correct. It is an influence to accept information from another as evidence about reality.

Obedience is a form of social influence in which one person orders to perform some action. An individual acts in response to a direct order from another individual, who is usually an authority figure.

Directions (Q.Nos. 71 to 75) *Read the following paragraph and answer the five questions which follow :*

Experimental personality research was extremely popular after 1950 for about three to four decades. In experimental personality research, one of the major focus is to study how the effect of experimentally manipulated independent variable is moderated by personality variable/s.

In one of such study, the researcher wanted to study whether the effect of Interpolated learning (A) is moderated by Anxiety (B). The researcher hypothesised that the interpolated learning would adversely affect the recall of original learning more in high anxious subjects

than low anxious subjects. Using a standardised Anxiety scale, from an initial pool of two hundred subjects, fifty high and fifty low anxious subjects were obtained. Both, high as well as low anxious groups were further divided into two groups—Experimental group and Control group.

The experimental groups first learned List A of CVC trigrams, then learned another List-List (B) of CVC trigrams with similar association values, and then tested for Recall (A) The subjects in control groups learned List (A). Then they received the cancellation task for the specific period (equal to the average time, taken by the corresponding experimental group to learn List (B). The subjects were then tested for the Recall of 1. Groupwise means and standard deviations for recall scores were obtained.

The standard deviations were found comparable across the groups. Treating recall scores as the dependent variable, the appropriate ANOVA was carried out. The main effect of (A) was found significant at 0.05 level. Similarly, the F-ratio, defined as '$MS_{A \times B}/MS_E$' was found statistically significant at 0.01 level.

71 Which one of the following designs is used in the above research?

1 Multigroup design with single I. V.
2 2 × 2 factorial design
3 2 × 2 mixed factorial design
4 Repeated measures design

Ans. (3)

Exp. The design used in the above research is a 2 x 2 mixed factorial design.

A mixed factorial design involves two or more independent variables, of which at least one is a within-subjects (repeated measures) factor and at least one is a between-groups factor. In the simplest case, there will be one between-groups factor and one within-subjects factor. The two variables used in the above research are Interpolated learning (present or absent) and Anxiety (high or low).

72 Which one of the following statements is true in the context of above study?

1 The assumption of homogeneity of variance was satisfied.
2 The assumption of homogeneity of variance was not satisfied.
3 The correction for heterogeneity of variance was required.
4 The data are insufficient to evaluate the assumption of homogeneity of variance.

Ans. (1)

Exp. According to passage 'the assumption of homogeneity of variance was satisfied' is correct.

Since, ANOVA was carried out and the main effect was found significant at 0.05. There are three assumptions that ANOVA assumes, which are:

1. The data is normally distributed.
2. There is homogeneity of variance, which means that the variance among the groups should be approximately equal.
3. The observations are independent of each other.

73 On the basis of the information provided about the main effect of 'A', it can be concluded that

1 interpolated learning had no effect on the recall of 'A'
2 interpolated learning caused retroactive interference
3 interpolated learning caused retroactive facilitation
4 either retroactive interference or retroactive facilitation has occurred

Ans. (4)

Exp. On the basis of the information provided about the main effect of 'A', it can be concluded that either retroactive interference or retroactive facilitation has occurred. Retroactive Interference (RI) is a phenomenon that occurs when newly learned information interferes with and impedes the recall of previously learned information. Retroactive facilitation is facilitation or improvement in the learning or performance of a task caused by positive transfer from training on a different task occurring later in time.

74 What would be the degrees of freedom for the numerator and denominator of the F-ratio defined as '$MS_{A \times B} / MS_E$' ?

1 1 and 96 respectively   2 1 and 98 respectively
3 2 and 97 respectively   4 3 and 96 respectively

Ans. (1)

Exp. The degrees of freedom for the numerator and denominator of the F-ratio defined as '$MS_{A \times B} / M_{SE}$' is 1 and 96 respectively.

The degrees of freedom for the numerator can be calculated using the formula, $df = (2-1)(2-1) = 1$.

The degrees of freedom for the denominator can be calculated using the formula,

$$df = (50 + 50) - (2 + 2) = 100 - 4 = 96.$$

75 Which of the following conclusion/s can be drawn about the researcher's hypothesis?

I. Researcher's hypothesis has been verified.
II. Researcher's hypothesis has not been verified.
III. Full data have not been presented which is necessary to evaluate the researcher's hypothesis.
IV. Anxiety moderated the effect of interpolated learning.

Select the correct answer from the codes given below :

1 Only I   2 I and IV   3 III and IV   4 II and IV

Ans. (3)

Exp. According to researcher's hypothesis: full data have not been presented which is necessary to evaluate the researcher's hypothesis and anxiety moderated the effect of interpolated learning.

UGC-NET PSYCHOLOGY

SOLVED PAPER 2015 (June)

PAPER II

1 Partial reinforcement is considered better than continuous reinforcement because

1 the learning occurs rapidly
2 the learning occurs slowly
3 the extinction occurs rapidly
4 the extinction occurs slowly

***Ans.* (4)**

Exp. Partial reinforcement is considered better than continuous reinforcement because the extinction occurs slowly.

Partial schedules only reinforce the desired behaviour occasionally rather than all the time. This leads to slower learning since it is initially more difficult to make the association between behaviour and reinforcement. However, partial schedules also produce behaviour that is more resistant to extinction. Therefore, the extinction occurs slowly.

2 Match the items of List I with List II and indicate your answer using the codes given below:

List I (Tests)	List II (Dimensions/Traits assessed)
A. EPPS	I. State anxiety
B. EPQ-R	II. Psychoticism
C. NEO-PI-R	III. Achievement motivation
D. STAI	IV. Openness to experience

Codes

	A	B	C	D		A	B	C	D
1	III	II	IV	I	2	I	II	IV	III
3	III	IV	II	I	4	I	IV	II	III

***Ans.* (1)**

Exp. The correct matching is A-III, B-II, C-IV, D-I.

EPPS (Edwards Personal Preference Schedule) assesses Achievement motivation. It is forced choice, objective, non-projective personality inventory. The EPPS was designed to illustrate relative importance to the individual of several significant needs and motives.

It measures Achievement, Deference, Order, Exhibition, Autonomy, Affiliation, Intraception, Succorance, Dominance, Degradation, Nurturance, Change, Endurance, Heterosexuality, and Aggression.

EPQ-R (Eysenck Personality Questionnaire) assesses Psychoticism. It is a measure that assesses individual personality traits that was developed by Hans and Sybil Eysenck. The Eysenck Personality Questionnaire – Revised (EPQ-R) measures three major dimensions of personality: Extraversion/Introversion, Neuroticism, and Psychoticism. The EPQ-R is an excellent assessment tool to measure the personality domain.

NEO-PI-R (Revised NEO Personality Inventory) assesses Openness to experience. It is a personality inventory that involves the Big Five personality traits. It is a revised version of Costa and McCrae's NEO Personality Inventory. The NEO PI-R assesses the Big Five personality traits: Extraversion, Agreeableness, Conscientiousness, Neuroticism and Openness to Experience.

STAI (State-Trait Anxiety Inventory) assesses State anxiety. It is a commonly used measure of trait and state anxiety. It can be used in clinical settings to diagnose anxiety and to distinguish it from depressive syndromes.

3 Which of the following is correctly arranged?

1 Sensory memory, Short-term memory, Forgetting
2 Long-term memory, Sensory memory, Short-term memory
3 Sensory memory, Short-term memory, Long-term memory
4 Episodic memory, Short-term memory, Long-term memory

***Ans.* (3)**

Exp. The correct arrangement is as follows: Sensory memory, Short-term memory, Long-term memory.

The three major memory stages are Sensory, Short-term, and Long-term (Atkinson and Shiffrin, 1968). The information begins in Sensory memory, moves to Short-term memory, and eventually moves to Long-term memory.

Sensory memory refers to the brief storage of sensory information.

Most of the information that gets into sensory memory is forgotten, but information that we turn our attention to, with the goal of remembering it, may pass into Short-term memory. If information makes it past Short term-memory it may enter Long-Term Memory (LTM), memory storage that can hold information for days, months, and years.

4 Arrange the four basic characteristics of instincts as per Freud's Psychoanalytic Theory in terms of sequence.

I. An impetus   II. A source
III. An object   IV. An aim

Codes

1 II, I, IV, III   2 III, II, I, IV
3 II, IV, I, III   4 I, II, III, IV

Ans. *(3)*

Exp. The correct order is II, IV, I, III.

Freud's Psychoanalytic Theory suggests that the drive is based on four components: source, aim, impetus, and object.

Instincts have four basic characteristics:

1. *Source* : It is a bodily deficit or a lack of a physiological need.
2. *Aim* : It is the gratification of the need. The aim is to quite the need caused.
3. *Impetus* : It propels the person to act. It is the force which is acted upon to achieve the need.
4. *Object* : It is through which the instinct achieves its aim. It satisfies the absence of the physiological need.

5 History of Intelligence Testing can be described in following sequence.

1 Galton, JM Cattell, Binet-Simon, Wechsler
2 JM Cattell, Stern-Terman, Binet-Simon, Wechsler
3 Wechsler, Binet-Simon, Spearman, RB Cattell
4 Galton, JM Cattell, Spearman, Wechsler

Ans. *(1)*

Exp. History of Intelligence Testing can be described in following sequence: Galton, JM Cattell, Binet-Simon, Wechsler.

Sir Francis Galton (1822-1911) became one of the first person to study intelligence. He tried to measure physical characteristics of noblemen and created a laboratory to measure their reaction time and other physical and sensory qualities.

James McKeen Cattell (1860-1944) research on individual differences played a significant role in introducing and emphasising the experimental technique and importance of methodology in experimentation in America. Regarding the beginnings of his intelligence tests, in Leipzig, Cattell independently began to measure "simple mental processes".

Alfred Binet and Simon (1857-1911) developed the first test resembling a modern intelligence test. Binet designed a series of questions aimed at distinguishing children who may have learning disabilities or need special help, which he thought children of different ages could answer correctly.

David Wechsler (1896-1981) expanded the idea of assessing adult intelligence using written tests. He developed well-known intelligence scales, such as the Wechsler Adult Intelligence Scale (WAIS) and the Wechsler Intelligence Scale for Children (WISC).

6 Bartlett described memory as a

1 constructive mental process
2 reproductive mental process
3 active mental process
4 a process of retention

Ans. *(1)*

Exp. Bartlett described memory as a constructive mental process.

The constructive mental processes are the processes in which memories are influenced by the meaning we give to events. When we retrieve information, then, the memory that is produced is affected not just by the direct prior experience we have had with the stimulus, but also by our guesses and inferences about its meaning. The notion that memory is based on constructive processes was first put forward by Frederic Bartlett, a British psychologist. He suggested that people tend to remember information in terms of schemas, organised bodies of information stored in.

7 Deterioration Quotient (DQ) was first used in which intelligence tests?

1 Binet-Simon Test
2 Galton-Cattell Test
3 Raven Progressive Matrices
4 Wechsler Adult Intelligence Test

Ans. *(4)*

Exp. Deterioration Quotient (DQ) was first used in Wechsler Adult Intelligence Test.

Wechsler has proposed a measure of deterioration called the Deterioration Quotient (DQ) or Index, which is based on a comparison of two groups of subtests of the scales. Although, Wechsler does not limit deterioration to organic loss, pointing out that prolonged functional illness, as well as senility, may reduce intellectual efficiency, many psychologists associate mental deterioration with organic disease and consider it an irreversible process. Wechsler's DQ or deterioration ratio has therefore been widely used in studies of organic brain damage.

8 According to Hull-Spence Theory, anxiety is emotionally based drive and therefore, it can be hypothesised that high anxious subjects would be faster on eyelid conditioning than the low anxious subjects. Using Taylor Manifest Anxiety Scale (TMAS), a researcher confirmed this hypothesis. This provides evidence for the

I. convergent and discriminant validity of the MAS.
II. validity of the Hull-Spence Theory.
III. generalisability of the MAS.
IV. construct validity of the MAS.

Codes

1 Only II	2 I and II
3 II and III	4 II and IV

Ans. *(4)*

➲ ***Exp.*** According to Hull-Spence Theory, anxiety is emotionally based drive and therefore, it can be hypothesised that high anxious subjects would be faster on eyelid conditioning than the low anxious subjects. Using Taylor Manifest Anxiety Scale (TMAS), a researcher confirmed this hypothesis. This provides evidence for the validity of the Hull-Spence Theory and construct validity of the MAS.

In order to reduce the level of discomfort experienced, an organism creates an action (behaviour) that will allow it to gain a reward, which in this case, is the reduction of its discomfort. According to the theory, people with high anxiety will have faster eyelid conditioning. This hypothesis was confirmed using the Taylor Manifest Anxiety Scale. This provides the evidence for the validity of the Hull-Spence Theory.

It also provides the evidence of construct validity of the MAS as the measure behaves in a way consistent with the theoretical hypotheses. Hull and Spence believed that the notion of drive-reduction is a main contributor to learning and behaviour.

9 The best home environment for intellectual development is one

1 in which child is encouraged to work out problems with guidance and support from parents
2 in which parents dictate the child what to do
3 in which child is left on his own
4 in which father is absent to impose his authority

Ans. *(1)*

➲ ***Exp.*** The best home environment for intellectual development is one in which child is encouraged to work out problems with guidance and support from parents.

The ways in which parent and child interact, can encourage the intellectual development and development of emergent literacy skills in young children. Scaffolding represents the helpful interactions between a parent and child that enable the child to do something beyond his or her independent efforts.

10 According to Interference theory, which one of the following causes forgetting?

1 Failure of storage	2 Failure of encoding
3 Failure of retrieval	4 Response competition

Ans. *(4)*

➲ ***Exp.*** According to Interference theory, Response competition causes forgetting.

Interference theory states that forgetting occurs because memories interfere with and disrupts one another, in other words forgetting occurs because of interference from other memories. Forgetting is due to the failure of retrieval of the information, and this failure is due to the competition between newly acquired information and existing information.

Melton and Irwin (1940) thought interference was due to the interpolated information weakening the original memory traces. McGeoch (1942) proposed another theory of forgetting to account for the interference seen in the laboratory.

His response-competition theory (also referred to as multiple trace hypothesis) predicts that when there are two or more items that are potential responses to a memory query, the strength of the memory trace of each possible response determines which memory trace will be retrieved, in that the strongest trace will be retrieved.

11 The evidence that sleep is a biological motive comes from ________ in lengthy sleep deprived subjects.

1 rebound effect of slow wave sleep
2 rebound effect of REM sleep
3 insomnia
4 enhanced stage I and stage II sleep

Ans. *(1)*

➲ ***Exp.*** The evidence that sleep is a biological motive comes from rebound effect of slow wave sleep in lengthy sleep deprived subjects.

Slow-Wave Sleep (SWS), often referred to as deep sleep, consists of stage three of non-rapid eye movement sleep. Generally, rebound sleep refers to an increased amount of sleep a person receives as a result of being sleep deprived or stressed during waking hours.

Sleep is organised into different stages, which can be broadly categorised into Rapid Eye Movement (REM) and Non-Rapid Eye Movement (NREM). When a person experiences rebound sleep, they can experience an increase in REM sleep, NREM sleep, or both. Like rebound sleep in general, REM rebound sleep usually occurs in response to sleep deprivation or stress. REM rebound can also occur in response to a suppression of REM sleep in particular. A person experiencing REM rebound might sleep more than normal, or sleep a normal amount, but spend a higher proportion of that sleep in a REM stage.

12 On a Wechsler type intelligence scale, the subject has a deviation IQ 115. What would be his T score (Mean = 50, SD = 10)?

1 60	2 65	3 68	4 84

Ans. *(1)*

➲ ***Exp.*** The T score of the subject would be 60.

It can be calculated using Z-scores. In this case, the Z-score would be +1. T-score is calculated considering, Mean=50, SD=10, and using the formula: T score = Mean + SD (Z score) = 50 + 10 (1) = 60.

13 Complex behavioural sequences which are species-typical behaviours are triggered by

1 releasers in the environment
2 learned behaviours
3 needs
4 incentives

Ans. *(1)*

Exp. Complex behavioural sequences which are species-typical behaviours are triggered by releasers in the environment.

Species-typical behaviours are almost always a product of nervous systems, meaning that they're created and influenced by species' genetic code and social and natural environment; this implies that they are strongly influenced by evolution.

Complex behavioural sequence learning is inherent to human ability because it is an integrated part of conscious and non-conscious learning as well as activities. Sequences of information or sequences of actions are used in various everyday tasks: 'from sequencing sounds in speech, to sequencing movements in typing or playing instruments, to sequencing actions in driving an automobile and releasers in the environment.

14 The following areas are involved in human vision

I. Prestriate cortex
II. Striate cortex
III. Inferotemporal cortex
IV. Posterior parietal cortex

Choose the correct option.

1 I and II
2 I, II and III
3 II, III and IV
4 I, II, III and IV

Ans. (4)

Exp. Areas involved in human vision are Prestriate cortex, Striate cortex, Inferotemporal cortex and Posterior parietal cortex.

Prestriate cortex : It is a visually responsive regions in the cerebral cortex outside the striate cortex. On the basis of function and connectivity, the prestriate cortex has been divided into multiple visual areas.

Striate cortex : It is the first region of the cerebral cortex that receives visual input from the thalamus, particularly from the lateral geniculate nucleus.

Inferotemporal cortex : It is a region of the brain on the inferior (lower) portion of the outer layer (cortex) of the temporal lobe that is particularly involved in the perception of form. This visual association cortex contains neurons with very complicated stimulus requirements; lesions in this area impair form and object perception even though visual discrimination thresholds are unchanged.

Posterior parietal cortex : It receives input from the three sensory systems that play roles in the localisation of the body and external objects in space: the visual system, the auditory system, and the somatosensory system. Damage to posterior parietal cortex results in deficits in visual working memory.

15 Which one of the following is not correct in regard of semantic memory?

1 It is relatively stable
2 There is interference in it
3 It is free from acquisition context
4 It has chunking

Ans. (2)

Exp. Semantic memory does not have interference in it. It includes facts, meanings, concepts, and knowledge about the external world and refers to general factual knowledge. In contrast to most memory systems that decline with age, semantic memory tends to remain relatively stable across the life span. Semantic memory reflects our knowledge of the world around us, hence the term 'general knowledge' is often used.

It holds generic information that is more than likely acquired across various contexts and is used across different situations. The goal of semantic chunking is to find semantically contained fragments of a sentence representation that can be processed independently and recombined without loss of information. We anchor its principles in established concepts of semantic theory, in particular event and situation semantics.

16 Self-modelling means

1 a type of learning in which individuals watch themselves behaving in a situationally appropriate manner and then show the same behaviours later on
2 type of learning in which individuals learn new behaviour
3 type of learning in which individuals learn to develop self-beliefs
4 type of learning in which individuals learn through guided-participation from significant others

Ans. (1)

Exp. Self-modelling means a type of learning in which individuals watch themselves behaving in a situationally appropriate manner and then show the same behaviours later on.

In self-modelling, an individual learns productive behaviour by observing himself or herself engaged in positive behaviour from pre-recorded and pre-edited videotapes. With an emphasis on successful behaviour (i.e. exceptions), video self-modelling represents a unique and welcome departure from the more common and demoraliding emphasis on problems and deficiencies. Allowing people to watch themselves engaging in productive, functional behaviours is an empowering and respectful way to help them improve their lives and opportunities.

17 Match List I and List II and indicate your correct choice among the codes given below :

List I (Types of Reinforcer)	List II (Descriptions)
A. Punisher	I. Acquired satisfier
B. Positive reinforcer	II. Removing aversive stimulus
C. Negative reinforcer	III. Presenting reward
D. Secondary reinforcer	IV. Aversive consequence

Codes

	A	B	C	D		A	B	C	D
1	IV	III	II	I	2	I	III	II	IV
3	III	IV	II	I	4	I	II	III	IV

Ans. (1)

Exp. The correct matching is A-IV, B-III, C-II, D-I.

A *Punisher* is any aversive stimulus that is used as a consequence to an action for the purpose of decreasing or extinguishing repeated occurrences of that action.

A *Positive reinforcer* is a reinforcing stimulus that serves to increase the likelihood of the response that produces it. It is a presenting reward.

A *Negative reinforcer* is the removal of an aversive or unpleasant stimulus, which, by removing it, is meant to increase the frequency of a positive behaviour.

A Secondary reinforcer is a stimulus which reinforces a behaviour after being previously associated with a primary reinforcer or a stimulus that satisfies basic survival instinct such as food, drinks, and clothing. It is an acquired satisfier.

18 While travelling in a train, nearby objects appear to move faster in the opposite direction than do far away objects, this phenomena is called

1 phi-phenomena
2 motion parallax
3 autokinetic movement
4 perception of movement

Ans. (2)

Exp. While travelling in a train, nearby objects appear to move faster in the opposite direction than do far away objects, this phenomena is called motion parallax.

Motion parallax is a monocular depth cue in which we view objects that are closer to us as moving faster than objects that are further away from us.

19 Which of the following is correctly arranged?

1 Identify, Set goals, Explore, Alternatives, Select, Evaluate, Implement
2 Identify, Explore, Set goals, Alternatives, Select, Implement, Evaluate
3 Select, Explore, Identify, Set goals, Alternatives, Implement, Evaluate
4 Explore, Identify, Select, Set goals, Alternatives, Evaluate, Implement

Ans. (2)

Exp. The correct arranged sequence is Identify, Explore, Set goals, Alternatives, Select, Implement, Evaluate.

First we identify the problem, and then we explore various ways to solve that particular problem. We have a set goal in mind, and to meet that goal we need a number of alternatives which can be both positive and negative, to meet that particular goal. We will try to select the best alternative and try to implement that alternative to the problem situation. Finally, we will evaluate whether that implementation was able to solve the problem or not.

20 Read each of the following two statements, Assertion (A) and Reason (R) and indicate your answer using the codes given below :

Assertion (A) According to the True Score Model in the Classical Test Theory (CTT), for a population on a large sample, Mean of the obtained scores = Mean of the true scores.

Reason (R) In the CTT, the errors of measurement are assumed to be independently distributed with a mean and variance equal to zero.

Codes

1 Both (A) and (R) are true and (R) is the correct explanation of (A)
2 Both (A) and (R) are true, but (R) is not the correct explanation of (A)
3 (A) is true, but (R) is false
4 (A) is false, but (R) is true

Ans. (1)

Exp. Both (A) and (R) are true and (R) is the correct explanation of (A).

According to the True Score Model in the Classical Test Theory (CTT), for a population on a large sample, Mean of the obtained scores = Mean of the true scores. According to the Classical Test Theory (CTT), the observed score is the sum of true score and error score. In a large sample, we try to eliminate or reduce the error scores as it becomes negligible, so the mean of obtained scores is equal to the mean of true scores. The assertion is therefore correct.

In the CTT, the errors of measurement are assumed to be independently distributed with a mean and variance equal to zero. Since the errors of measurement are assumed to be independent with a mean and variance equal to zero, it is considered negligible and hence can be ignored. This is also true and explains the assertion statement.

21 Match List I and List II and select the correct answer by choosing from codes given below :

List I	List II
A. Libido	I. Human beings strive to return to an inorganic state of balance that preceded life, in which there is no painful struggle to satisfy biological needs
B. Thanatos	II. Psychic and pleasurable feelings associated with gratification of life instincts
C. Suppression	III. A person's refusal to perceive an unpleasant environment in external reality
D. Denial	IV. Individual's active and conscious attempt to stop anxiety provoking thoughts by simply not thinking about them

Codes

	A	B	C	D		A	B	C	D
1	I	II	III	IV	2	III	I	II	IV
3	II	I	IV	III	4	IV	III	II	I

Ans. (3)

Exp. The correct matching is A-II, B-I, C-IV, D-III.

Libido is psychic and pleasurable feelings associated with gratification of life instincts. 'Libido' is a term used in Psychoanalytic theory to describe the energy created by the survival and sexual instinct. The Libido is part of the id and is the driving force of all behaviour.

Thanatos is when human beings strive to return to an inorganic state of balance that preceded life, in which there is no painful struggle to satisfy biological needs. According to Freud, humans have a life instinct (eros) and a death instinct, called thantos. This death instinct compels humans to engage in risky and destructive behaviours that could lead to death (remember, it is an instinct for personal death). Behaviours such as thrill seeking, aggression and risk taking can be considered actions stemming from thantos.

Suppression is individual's active and conscious attempt to stop anxiety provoking thoughts by simply not thinking about them. It is a conscious effort to put disturbing thoughts and experiences out of mind, or to control and inhibit the expression of unacceptable impulses and feelings.

Denial is a person's refusal to perceive an unpleasant environment in external reality. Denial is the refusal to accept reality or fact, acting as if a painful event thought or feeling did not exist. It is considered one of the most primitive of the defense mechanisms because it is characteristic of early childhood development.

22 Read each of the following two statements, Assertion (A) and Reason (R) and indicate your answer using the codes given below.

Assertion (A) Retinal disparity is an important monocular cue in depth perception.

Reason (R) Convergence is a muscular cue in depth perception.

Codes

1 Both (A) and (R) are true and (R) is the correct explanation of (A)
2 Both (A) and (R) are true, but (R) is not the correct explanation of (A)
3 (A) is true, but (R) is false
4 (A) is false, but (R) is true

Ans. (4)

Exp. (A) is false, but (R) is true.

Retinal disparity is an important monocular cue in depth perception. This statement is false because retinal disparity is an important binocular cue in depth perception. It is the slight difference between the right and left retinal images. When both eyes focus on an object, the different position of the eyes produces a disparity of visual angle, and a slightly different image is received by each retina. The two images are automatically compared and, if sufficiently similar, are fused, providing an important cue to depth perception.

Convergence is a muscular cue in depth perception. This statement is true as convergence requires muscles in the process of perception. It is the rotation of the two eyes inward toward a light source so that the image falls on corresponding points on the foveas. Convergence enables the slightly different images of an object seen by each eye to come together and form a single image. The muscular tension exerted is also a cue to the distance of the object from the eyes.

23 As per Schachter and Singer's Theory of Emotions, one shall experience emotions based on situational clues when

I. there is a physiological arousal.
II. there are cognitions/explanations available for arousal.
III. there is no physiological arousal.
IV. there are no proper explanations available for one's arousal.

Choose the correct code.

1 I and II
2 I and IV
3 II and III
4 III and IV

Ans. (1)

Exp. As per Schachter and Singer's Theory of Emotions, one shall experience emotions based on situational clues when there is a physiological arousal and there are cognitions/explanations available for arousal.

The Schachter–Singer theory views emotion as the result of the interaction between two factors: physiological arousal and cognition. According to the Schacter–Singer theory, physiological arousal is cognitively interpreted based on environmental context; this process culminates in emotional experience.

More specifically, this theory claims that physiological arousal is cognitively interpreted within the context of each situation, which ultimately produces the emotional experience. These cognitive interpretations include how a person labels and understands what they are experiencing. These are formed based on the person's past experiences.

24 Spearman Inferred General Intelligence on the basis of

I. positive manifold in inter-correlation matrix.
II. tetrad differences in equation.
III. unequal scores of same subjects on intelligence tests.
IV. reports from the subjects.

Codes

1 I and III
2 II and IV
3 I and II
4 III and IV

Ans. (3)

➲ *Exp.* Spearman Inferred General Intelligence on the basis of positive manifold in inter-correlation matrix and tetrad differences in equation.

Positive manifold in inter-correlation matrix : Spearman (1904) gave persons tests of many different kinds of cognitive ability. When he examined the correlations of these tests with each other, he found that all the correlations were positive, and called this the 'positive manifold.' The positive manifold leads to a large first factor derived from factor analysis, dubbed general intelligence, or g.

Tetrad differences in equation : Spearman used the 'tetrad difference' method to analyse intelligence. This method has been widely used in various psychological investigations; it is represented by the quantity 'F', and it is the difference between the cross products of two opposite coefficients of any four correlation coefficients in a square block.

For example, consider four intellectual activities that are measured in the test, having correlation coefficients R13, R14, R23, R24 in the correlation matrix (nearby four in the correlation matrix), then the mathematical expression of tetrad equation would be, F=(R13)(R24)-(R14)(R23). Spearman observed that the cross multiplication of any two opposite correlation coefficients in the square block (nearby four correlation coefficients) in the correlation matrix was almost equal, i.e., the value of F approximately equals to zero.

25 The parasympathetic nerves project from

1 the lumbar and thoracic regions of the spinal cord
2 the brain and sacral region of the spinal cord
3 the brain and the lumbar region of the spinal cord
4 the lumbar and the sacral regions of the spinal cord

***Ans.** (2)*

➲ *Exp.* The parasympathetic nerves project from the brain and sacral region of the spinal cord.

Parasympathetic nervous system is a part of autonomic nervous system. The parasympathetic nervous system consists of nerves originating either from the brain or sacral region of the spinal cord that project to ganglia usually located either near or in end organs.

Preganglionic neurons from the brain are found in motor nuclei of the oculomotor (Cranial Nerve-III), facial (Cranial Nerve-VII), glossopharyngeal (Cranial Nerve-IX), and vagus (Cranial Nerve-X) nerves. Preganglionic neurons in the sacral region are found in the nucleus pudendus. Parasympathetic neurons in the sacral region innervate reproductive organs, colon, and cloaca. Their fibers form part of the pelvic plexus and project to specific body organs.

26 Read each of the following two statements, Assertion (A) and Reason (R) and indicate your answer using the codes given below:

Assertion (A) People who learn more and more lists of words on successive days have more and more difficulty in learning each new list next day.

Reason (R) People have limited capacity to learn verbal material.

Codes

1 Both (A) and (R) are true and (R) is the correct explanation of (A)
2 Both (A) and (R) are true, but (R) is not the correct explanation of (A)
3 (A) is true, but (R) is false
4 (A) is false, but (R) is true

***Ans.** (2)*

➲ *Exp.* Both (A) and (R) are true, but (R) is not the correct explanation of (A).

People who learn more and more lists of words on successive days have more and more difficulty in learning each new list next day. This statement is true as people have difficulty in retaining new information due to the prior existing information. This is referred to as the phenomenon of interference.

People have limited capacity to learn verbal material. This is true as the working memory is a limited capacity part of the human memory system that combines the temporary storage and manipulation of information in the service of cognition. According to the multi-component model, working memory includes an executive controller that interacts with separate short-term stores for auditory-verbal and visuospatial information. The statement is true but it does not explain the interference phenomenon described in the assertion.

27 Read each of the following two statements, Assertion (A) and Reason (R) and indicate your answer using the codes given below:

Assertion (A) A synapse does not necessarily result into action potential in post-synaptic neuron.

Reason (R) Synapses produce inhibitory post-synaptic potential also in post-synaptic neuron.

Codes

1 Both (A) and (R) are true and (R) is the correct explanation of (A)
2 Both (A) and (R) are true, but (R) is not the correct explanation of (A)
3 (A) is true, but (R) is false
4 (A) is false, but (R) is true

***Ans.** (1)*

➲ *Exp.* Both (A) and (R) are true and (R) is the correct explanation of (A).

A synapse does not necessarily result into action potential in post-synaptic neuron. A neuron communicates with another cell by sending an electrical signal to its finger tips, which causes the fingertips to release chemicals that stimulate a neighbouring cell. This electrical signal is called a post-synaptic potential. This type of potential is a graded depolarisation of the membrane. If it is large enough, it will trigger an action potential. But if it is not large enough, it will not generate action potential in the neighbouring cell. Therefore, the Assertion is true.

Synapses produce inhibitory post-synaptic potential also in post-synaptic neuron. Synapses can either be excitatory or inhibitory. Inhibitory synapses decrease the likelihood of the firing action potential of a cell while excitatory synapses increase its likelihood. Therefore, due to the inhibitory post-synaptic potential, the synapse does not necessarily result into action potential. Therefore, the reason is the correct explanation of the given assertion.

28 Which of the following is not the way we acquire concepts?

1 Naturally acquired
2 By discrimination learning
3 Innate
4 By definition

Ans. (3)

Exp. Innate is not the way we acquire concepts.

Concepts can be acquired naturally, by discrimination learning or by definition. Concepts are not innate. The innate responses are usually known as instincts.

Concepts are mental categories for objects, events, or ideas that have a common set of features. Natural concepts are created "naturally" through your experiences and can be developed from either direct or indirect experiences. Discrimination learning is one example of an associative learning task in which an individual is required to establish an association between a particular stimulus and delivery of a reward, while another stimulus is not associated with a reward.

29 Match List I and List II and select the correct answer by choosing from codes given below :

List I		List II
A. Functional fixedness	I.	A cognitive process that employ appropriate novelty to originality that suits some purpose
B. Back tracking	II.	A problem-solving phenomenon in which people fail to see alternative uses for common objects
C. Creativity	III.	A problem-solving technique that involves keeping track of solving process where in assumptions are made; so they may later be changed
D. Working backward	IV.	A problem-solving technique that identifies the final goals and the steps in reverse order

Codes

	A	B	C	D		A	B	C	D
1	I	II	III	IV	2	II	III	IV	I
3	III	I	II	IV	4	II	III	I	IV

Ans. (4)

Exp. The correct matching is A-II, B-III, C-I, D-IV.

Functional fixedness is a problem-solving phenomenon in which people fail to see alternative uses for common objects. It is the tendency to perceive an object only in terms of its most common use. It limits a person to seeing an object only in the way in which it is traditionally used.

Back tracking is a problem-solving technique that involves keeping track of solving process where in assumptions are made; so they may later be changed. Back tracking is a general algorithmic technique that considers searching every possible combination in order to solve an optimisation problem.

Creativity is a cognitive process that employs appropriate novelty to originality that suits some purpose. It is a phenomenon whereby something new and somehow valuable is formed. The created item may be intangible (such as an idea, a scientific theory, a musical composition, or a joke) or a physical object (such as an invention, a literary work, or a painting).

Working backward is a problem-solving technique that identifies the final goals and the steps in reverse order. The Working backward heuristic is a method of problem solving in which an individual imagines they have already solved the problem they are trying to solve. By imagining the problem is solved they can then work backwards in their mind and eventually visualise a solution to the problem.

30 Visual Cliff is a laboratory method for testing depth perception in

1 infants
2 children
3 adults
4 old-age people

Ans. (1)

Exp. Visual cliff is a laboratory method for testing depth perception in infants.

Visual cliff method involves an apparatus to investigate the development of depth perception in non-verbal human infants and in non-human animals, and in particular, whether depth perception is an innate ability or learned through visuomotor experience. The apparatus consists of a table with a checkerboard pattern, dropping steeply down a "cliff" to a surface with the same pattern some distance below the tabletop.

The apparatus is covered with a transparent surface, and the participant is positioned on this at the border between the tabletop and the cliff. Reluctance to crawl onto the surface covering the cliff is taken as an indication that the participant can discriminate the apparent difference in depth between the two sides of the apparatus. Most infants as young as 6 months of age will not cross to the side over the cliff.

31 Read each of the following two statements, Assertion (A) and Reason (R) and indicate your answer using the codes given below :

Assertion (A) Surface traits are simply a collection of trait elements which obviously go together in many different individuals and circumstances. Intercorrelated trait elements or variables cluster together to form a surface trait.

Reason (R) Source traits are underlying factors that control the variation in surface clusters.

Codes

1 Both (A) and (R) are true and (R) is the correct explanation of (A)
2 Both (A) and R are true, but (R) is not the correct explanation of (A)
3 (A) is true, but (R) is false
4 (A) is false, but (R) is true

Ans. (2)

Exp. Both (A) and R are true, but (R) is not the correct explanation of (A).

Surface traits are simply a collection of trait elements which obviously go together in many different individuals and circumstances. Intercorrelated trait elements or variables cluster together to form a surface trait. The surface trait is comprised of the source traits that can be observed in an individual and are easily observable and common clusters of behaviour. All these traits form part of an individual's personality.

Source traits are underlying factors that control the variation in surface clusters. Source Traits are the building blocks or sources of human personality. All these traits form part of an individual's personality. When the source traits are put together, they make up the Surface Traits, which are the traits we see and think of as personality.

32 Match List I with List II and select the correct answer by choosing the correct code given below :

List I	List II
A. −67 mv	I. Polarised
B. +45 mv	II. Hyperpolarised
C. −70 mv	III. Depolarised
D. −72 mv	IV. Completely depolarised

Codes

	A	B	C	D		A	B	C	D
1	III	II	I	IV	2	III	IV	I	II
3	II	IV	III	I	4	IV	III	I	II

Ans. (2)

Exp. The correct matching is A-III, B-IV, C-I, D-II.

A *depolarised* cell has a membrane potential of–67 mv. An Excitatory Post-Synaptic potential (EPSP) moves the resting membrane potential in a positive direction; that is, it depolarises the neuron (for example, – 67 mV).

A *completely depolarised* cell has a membrane potential of +45 mv. When the cell is completely depolarised it reaches beyond 0 mV and becomes more positive (for example, +45 mV).

A *polarised cell* has a membrane potential of -70 mv. When the neuron is inactive and polarised, it's said to be at its resting potential. The resting potential can vary quite a bit between different types of neurons, but in general, the resting membrane potential is somewhere around –70 millivolts (mV).

A *hyperpolarised cell* has a membrane potential of -72 mv. An Inhibitory Post-Synaptic Potential (IPSP) moves the resting potential in a negative direction; that is, it hyperpolarizes the neuron (for example, –72 mV).

33 Read each of the following two statements, Assertion (A) and Reason (R) and indicate your answer using the codes given below :

Assertion (A) In problem-solving process, people generally evolve/select the optimal solutions of a problem.

Reason (R) A number of solutions are identified to choose from.

Codes

1 Both (A) and (R) are true and (R) is the correct explanation of (A)
2 Both (A) and (R) are true, but (R) is not the correct explanation of (A)
3 (A) is true, but (R) is false
4 (A) is false, but (R) is true

Ans. (1)

Exp. Both (A) and (R) are true and (R) is the correct explanation of (A).

In problem-solving process, people generally evolve/select the optimal solutions of a problem. People select best alternative or optimal solution for the problem. Problem-solving is a mental process that involves discovering, analysing and solving problems. The ultimate goal of problem-solving is to overcome obstacles and find a solution that best resolves the issue. In order to correctly solve a problem, it is important to follow a series of steps. Many researchers refer to this as the problem-solving cycle, which includes developing strategies and organising knowledge.

A number of solutions are identified to choose from. This is also true and explains the assertion as a number of solutions are identified before choosing the best alternative or optimal solution.

34 Sometimes old information facilitates our learning of new information. The phenomenon is known as ________ .

1 consolidation effect
2 transfer effect
3 proactive interference
4 excitatory effect

Ans. (2)

Exp. Sometimes old information facilitates our learning of new information. The phenomenon is known as transfer effect.

Transfer effects are found when learning one task either facilitates (positive transfer) or interferes with (negative transfer) learning the second task.

35 A man judged to be 6 feet tall when standing at 10 feet away has 'X' size of retinal image whereas at 20 feet, it has X/2 retinal size image. How tall shall he be perceived at a distance of 5 feet?

1 6 feet
2 $6 \times \frac{10-5}{2}$ feet
3 $6 \times \frac{10+5}{2}$ feet
4 Size cannot be judged

Ans. (1)

Exp. In perception, we do not perceive things in absolute terms rather we perceive things in relative terms. In the present situation, the man shall be perceived 6 feet which is relative to other objects or surrounding environment.

36 The first attempt to both theories and measure intelligence was made by

1 JM Cattell
2 Galton
3 Binel
4 Spearman

Ans. (2)

Exp. The first attempt to both theories and measure intelligence was made by Galton.

Sir Francis Galton attempted to measure the intelligence of human beings in order to provide evidence for his belief that intelligence is inherited. Galton believed that intelligence could be assessed through measuring reaction times, highest audible tone, head size, visual acuity and colour sense. Although, further study found that these characteristics do not denote intelligence, Galton demonstrated individual differences not only exist but are also able to be objectively measured. As a result of developing practical measures of individual differences, Galton is regarded as the 'Father of mental testing'.

37 Read each of the following two statements, Assertion (A) and Reason (R) and indicate your answer using the codes given below :

Assertion (A) According to Maslow, after the gratification of basic needs, we move in positive direction, but it is not automatic.

Reason (R) We often fear our best side, our talents, our finest impulses, our creativeness.

Codes

1 Both (A) and (R) are true and (R) is the correct explanation of (A)
2 Both (A) and (R) are true, but (R) is not the correct explanation of (A)
3 (A) is true, but (R) is false
4 (A) is false, but (R) is true

Ans. (1)

Exp. Both (A) and (R) are true and (R) is the correct explanation of (A).

According to Maslow, after the gratification of basic needs, we move in positive direction, but it is not automatic. The statement is true as after the gratification of basic needs, we tend to move in a positive direction but it is not automatic as we have a lot of fears which may hinder our movement.

We often fear our best side, our talents, our finest impulses, and our creativeness. The reason explains the assertion as the fears of unknown hinders our positive movement. It is known as Jonah complex in the humanistic psychology of Abraham Maslow. It is inhibition of becoming fully self-actualized that is, of fulfilling one's potential for fear of facing new challenges and situations. Therefore, after the gratification of basic needs, we tend to move in positive direction but it is not automatic.

38 A fifth test was added to an old established selection test battery of four tests. Two multiple correlations, one between a suitable external criterion and three tests of the old battery and the other between the same criterion and four tests of the new battery were computed. The significant change is R^2 would provide an evidence for the

1 predictive validity of the old battery
2 incremental validity of the fifth test
3 predictive validity of the new battery
4 concurrent validity of the fifth test

Ans. (2)

Exp. The significant change is R^2 would provide an evidence for the incremental validity of the fifth test.

Incremental validity is a type of validity that is used to determine whether a new psychometric assessment will increase the predictive ability beyond that provided by an existing method of assessment. A significant change in the R-square statistic (using an F-test to determine significance) is interpreted as an indication that the newly added variable offers significant additional predictive power for the dependent variable over variables previously included in the regression model.

39 Which of the following stages is called the period of problem-solving behaviour?

1 Secondary circular reaction
2 Reflex
3 Tertiary reaction
4 Primary circular reaction

Ans. (3)

Exp. Tertiary reaction is called the period of problem-solving behaviour.

Piaget's sensorimotor stage of development can be broken down into six additional sub-stages including simple reflexes, primary circular reactions, secondary circular reactions, coordination of reactions, tertiary circular reactions, and early symbolic thought.

Tertiary circular reaction refers to an infant's action that creatively alters former schemes to fit the requirements of new situations. Tertiary circular reactions emerge toward the end of the sensorimotor stage, at about the beginning of the 2nd year; they differ from earlier behaviours in that the child can, for the first time, develop new schemes to achieve a desired goal.

40 The rate of responding is found to be higher in the condition of

1 variable internal schedule of reinforcement
2 fixed-ratio schedule of reinforcement
3 variable-ratio schedule of reinforcement
4 Both (2) and (3)

Ans. (4)

Exp. The rate of responding is found to be higher in the condition of fixed-ratio schedule of reinforcement and variable-ratio schedule of reinforcement.

In a fixed-ratio schedule of reinforcement, the reinforcement is delivered after a predictable number of responses (e.g., after 2, 4, 6, and 8 responses). The rate of response is high with pauses after reinforcement. An example could be piecework where a factory worker is getting paid for every 'x' number of items manufactured.

In a variable-ratio schedule of reinforcement, the reinforcement is delivered after an unpredictable number of responses (e.g., after 1, 4, 5, and 9 responses). The rate of response is high and steady, e.g. gambling.

41 Read the following statements and indicate which are correct.

I. Archetypes are themes that have existed in all cultures throughout history.
II. Personal unconscious is the region next to the ego which consists of all the forgotten experiences that have lost their intensity.
III. Masculine archetype in men is called animus.
IV. Persona is a compromise between demands of the environment and necessities of an individual.

Codes

1 I, II and III   2 II, III and IV
3 I, II and IV   4 I, III and IV

Ans. (3)

Exp. Statement I, II and IV are correct.

Archetypes are themes that have existed in all cultures throughout history. Jungian archetypes are defined as universal, primal symbols and images that derive from the collective unconscious. Jung labelled these archetypes the Self, the Persona, the Shadow and the Anima/Animus.

Personal unconscious is the region next to the ego which consists of all the forgotten experiences that have lost their intensity. It is the portion of each individual's unconscious that contains the elements of his or her own experience as opposed to the collective unconscious. The personal unconscious consists of everything subliminal, forgotten, and repressed in an individual's life. It also contains complexes based on the individual's personal experience. In Jung's view, the personal unconscious must be integrated into the conscious ego for individuation to occur.

Persona is a compromise between demands of the environment and necessities of an individual. The persona (or mask) is the outward face we present to the world. It conceals our real self and Jung describes it as the "conformity" archetype.

Masculine archetype in women is called animus, while the feminine archetype in men is called anima. These archetypal images are based upon both what is found in the collective and personal unconscious.

42 Trace the correct sequence of the following events for audition

I. Synapses in primary auditory cortex
II. Synapse in superior olives
III. Synapse in the inferior colliculi
IV. Synapse in the cochlear nuclei
V. Synapse in medial geniculate nucleus

Codes

1 IV, II, III, V, I   2 IV, III, II, V, I
3 II, III, V, IV, I   4 III, II, V, IV, I

Ans. (1)

Exp. The correct sequence is IV, II, III, V, I.

Synapse in the cochlear nuclei : The information proceeds from the Organ of Corti to spiral ganglion cells and the VIIIth nerve afferents in the ear, to the cochlear nuclei.

Synapse in superior olives : From cochler nuclei, there are many crossing in the trapezoid body, and the input moves to the superior olives in the brain stem.

Synapse in the inferior colliculi : Then all ascending fibers stop in the inferior colliculi in the midbrain.

Synapse in medial geniculate nucleus : After inferior colliculi, the input moves to the medial geniculate nucleus in the thalamus, before reaching the cortex in the superior temporal gyrus.

Synapses in primary auditory cortex : The primary auditory cortex receives direct input from the medial geniculate nucleus of the thalamus and thus is thought to identify the fundamental elements of audition.

43 Our brain construct our perceptions because

I. sensations are disassembled into information bits.
II. neuro muscular cues from the greater inward turn when the eyes view a near object.
III. brain reassembles information into its own functional model.
IV. perception is merely projecting the world onto our brain.

Codes

1 I, II and III   2 II, III and IV
3 I, III and IV   4 I, II and IV

Ans. (1)

Exp. Our brain construct our perceptions because sensations are disassembled into information bits. Our brain construct our perceptions because sensations are disassembled into information bits.

Also, the reason behind construction of perception by our mind is neuro muscular cues from the greater inward turn when the eyes view a near object. This is known as convergence. Convergence is when the eyes turn inward to look at an object close up. The closer the object, the more the eye muscles tense to turn the eyes inward.

Information sent from the eye muscles to the brain helps to determine the distance to the object.

Also, brain reassembles information into its own functional model. For unknown reasons, the human brain distinctly separates the handling of images of living things from images of non-living things, processing each image type in a different area of the brain. For years, many scientists have assumed the brain segregated visual information in this manner to optimise processing the images themselves.

44 Match List I and List II and select the correct answer from the codes given below :

List I	List II
A. Self-schema	I. A generalised evaluation of self
B. Self-esteem	II. When a person doubts one's abilities to perform a task
C. Self-presentation	III. Organisation of informations about self
D. Self-handicapping	IV. The way one thinks of presenting oneself before public

Codes

	A	B	C	D		A	B	C	D
1	IV	II	III	I	2	II	III	I	IV
3	III	I	IV	II	4	I	III	II	IV

Ans. (3)

Exp. The correct matching is A-III, B-I, C-IV, D-II.

Self-schema is the organisation of informations about self. The self-schema refers to a long lasting and stable set of memories that summarise a person's beliefs, experiences and generalisations about the self, in specific behavioural domains.

Self-esteem is a generalised evaluation of self. Self-esteem reflects a person's overall subjective emotional evaluation of his or her own worth. It is a judgment of oneself aswell as an attitude toward the self.

Self-presentation is the way one thinks of presenting oneself before public. It refers to how people attempt to present themselves to control or shape how others (called the audience) view them. It involves expressing oneself and behaving in ways that create a desired impression. Self-presentation is part of a broader set of behaviours called impression management.

Self-handicapping is when a person doubts one's abilities to perform a task. It is a cognitive strategy by which people avoid effort in the hopes of keeping potential failure from hurting self-esteem.

45 Which of the following factors reduce the accuracy of eyewitness testimony?

I. Suggestibility
II. Source monitoring errors
III. Interference
IV. Illusion of out group homogeneity

Codes

1 I and II   2 I, II and IV
3 I, III and IV   4 II, III and IV

Ans. (2)

Exp. The factors which reduce the accuracy of eyewitness testimony are Suggestibility, Source monitoring errors and Illusion of out group homogeneity.

When someone witnesses a crime, that person's memory of the details of the crime is very important in catching the suspect. As memory is so fragile, witnesses can be easily (and often accidentally) misled due to the problem of suggestibility.

Suggestibility describes the effects of misinformation from external sources that leads to the creation of false memories.

Outgroup homogeneity is the tendency for members of a group to see themselves as more diverse and heterogeneous than they are seen by an out-group. Individuals may view people belonging to a particular social group (like race, gender, etc.) responsible for a crime hence inaccurately giving eyewitness testimony.

Source-monitoring error is a type of memory error where the source of a memory is incorrectly attributed to some specific recollected experience.

Directions (Q. Nos. 46-50) *Read the following paragraph and answer the questions that follows :*

Psychology, as a scientific study of behaviour, employs several diverse research methods to collect and analyse data. In the early phase of modern psychology, experimental method has been highly popular. The early psychologists, like Fechner and Ebbirghaus, were well-known experimentalists. Experimental method allows the active manipulation of the Independent Variable (IV). Ronald Fisher and others systematised the area of experimental designs.

Due to the success of controlled laboratory experiments, field experiments were also carried out where the IV is manipulated in the natural or field setting. Especially due to the need for policy and program evaluation research, quasi-experimental designs have also been developed. Various non-experimental methods, including surveys and correlational research, are also employed in psychology.

The survey method employs interviews, both structured and unstructured and questionnaires. Both open-end and close-end questions and scale items can be used in interview schedules and questionnaires. Different types of observations, including naturalistic observation, participant and non-participant observation, are also used in certain areas like ethology. In the qualitative research tradition, case studies are widely used.

Special research approaches, e.g. ethnographic research, have been developed for specialised areas like cross-cultural psychology. In addition, psychologists use various measurement techniques including standardised objective tests, projective methods, situational tests and even physiological measures. The use of such diverse methods and measurement techniques has enriched the science of psychology as well as our understanding of human and animal behaviour including the cognitive processes.

46 Which of the following are considered as quasi-experimental designs?

I. Time series designs
II. Regression discontinuity design
III. Survey
IV. Non-equivalent control group design

Codes

1 Only IV
2 I and IV
3 I, II and IV
4 II, III and IV

Ans. *(3)*

Exp. The quasi-experimental designs are Time series design, Regression discontinuity design and Non-equivalent control group design.

The simplest type of *Time Series Design* is the interrupted time series. This design is typically used to evaluate the impact of a population-wide policy or intervention. It involves a single treatment group which is measured many times before and after the start of the intervention.

A *Regression Discontinuity Design* (RDD) is a quasi-experimental pretest-posttest design that elicits the causal effects of interventions by assigning a cut-off or threshold above or below which an intervention is assigned. The one-group pretest-posttest design is called a pre-experimental design or a bad experiment because it has so little internal validity.

In the *non-equivalent control group design*, a treatment group and a comparison group are compared using pretest and posttest measures.

47 Which one of the following is a limitation of case study?

1 It does not provide indepth information of the subject
2 It is difficult to generalise from the case study
3 It is useful only in clinical and counselling psychology
4 It uses diverse methods and sources to collect data about the subject

Ans. *(2)*

Exp. The limitation of a case study is that it is difficult to generalise from the case study. Generalising is difficult or impossible because one person or small group cannot represent all similar groups or situations.

Case studies are in-depth investigations of a single person, group, event or community. Typically, data are gathered from a variety of sources and by using several different methods (e.g. observations and interviews). The research may also continue for an extended period of time, so processes and developments can be studied as they happen. The case study research method originated in clinical medicine (the case history, i.e. the patient's personal history).

48 Read each of the following two statements Assertion (A) and Reason (R) and indicate your answer using the codes given below.

Assertion (A) Experimental method, as compared to other methods, is more suitable for studying cause and effect relationship.

Reason (R) As compared to other methods, experimental method permits more efficient control of extraneous variance.

Codes

1 Both (A) and (R) are true and (R) is the correct explanation of (A)
2 Both (A) and (R) are true, but (R) is not the correct explanation of (A)
3 (A) is true, but (R) is false
4 (A) is false, but (R) is true

Ans. *(1)*

Exp. Both (A) and (R) are true, and (R) is the correct explanation of (A).

Experimental method, as compared to other methods, is more suitable for studying cause and effect relationship. The prime method of inquiry in science is the experiment. The key features are control over variables, careful measurement and establishing cause and effect relationships. An experiment is an investigation in which a hypothesis is scientifically tested.

As compared to other methods, experimental method permits more efficient control of extraneous variance. In an experiment, an independent variable (the cause) is manipulated and the dependent variable (the effect) is measured; any extraneous variables are controlled. An advantage is that experiments should be objective. The views and opinions of the researcher should not affect the results of a study. This is good as it makes the data more valid and less bias. By controlling the extraneous variables, we are able to explain the cause and effect relationships better exhibited by the experiments.

49 The emic-etic distinction is emphasised in

1 quasi-experimental research
2 ethological research
3 case studies
4 ethnographic research

Ans. *(4)*

Exp. The emic-etic distinction is emphasised in ethnographic research.

Ethnography is a research method central to knowing the world from the standpoint of its social relations. It is a qualitative research method predicated on the diversity of culture at home (wherever that may be) and abroad. Emic and etic refer to two kinds of field research done and viewpoints obtained: emic, from within the social group (from the perspective of the subject) and etic, from outside (from the perspective of the observer).

50 In a survey of students, each student was asked to state his views on the relevance of present educational system in not more than 60 words. This is an example of

1 scale item
2 closed-end question
3 check-list item
4 open-end question

Ans. (4)

Exp. In a survey of students, each student was asked to state his views on the relevance of present educational system in not more than 60 words. This is an example of open-end question.

Open-ended questions are questions that cannot be answered with a simple 'yes' or 'no', and instead require the respondent to elaborate on their points. Open-ended questions are questions that allow someone to give a free-form answer.

PAPER III

1 Which of the following is an application of operant conditioning?

1 Aversive conditioning
2 Behaviour modification
3 Systematic desensitisation
4 Transfer of learning

Ans. (2)

Exp. Behaviour modification is an application of operant conditioning.

Behaviour modification is a treatment approach, based on the operant conditioning that replaces undesirable behaviours with more desirable ones through positive or negative reinforcement. Operant conditioning is the process in which behavioural change (i.e., learning) occurs as a function of the consequences of behaviour. Operant conditioning has become a very influential area of psychology, because it has successfully provided practical solutions to many problems in human behaviour.

2 The basic assumptions of humanistic approach

I. People are naturally striving to be creative and happy.
II. It is possible to specify an universal set of values that will provide people with moral anchor enabling them to decide what is right or wrong and good or bad.
III. It believes in uniqueness of individuals and they should be trained to realise their inner potentials.
IV. All the innate potentials and growth mechanisms can be studied scientifically similar to natural success.

Codes

1 I and III	2 II and III
3 II and IV	4 III and IV

Ans. (1)

Exp. Statement I and III are correct in relation to the basic assumptions of humanistic approach.

People are naturally striving to be creative and happy. The humanistic approach assumes that people are basically good, and have an innate need to make themselves and the world better. It emphasises the personal worth of the individual, the centrality of human values, and the creative, active nature of human beings.

It believes in uniqueness of individuals and they should be trained to realise their inner potentials. The humanistic approach assumes that all individuals are unique and are motivated to achieve their potential.

Statement II and IV are incorrect

Humanistic approach views the individual as unique it does not attempt to establish universal laws about the causes of behaviour, it is an idiographic approach.

The approach views the individual as unique it does not believe that scientific measurements of their behaviour are appropriate.

3 Deductive and inductive reasoning refers to

I. universal to universal
II. universal to particular
III. particular to particular
IV. particular to universal

Codes

1 I and II	2 III and I
3 II and IV	4 IV and III

Ans. (3)

Exp. Deductive and inductive reasoning refers to universal to particular and particular to universal respectively.

Deductive reasoning is a logical process in which a conclusion is based on the concordance of multiple premises that are generally assumed to be true. Deductive reasoning is sometimes referred to as top-down logic.

Inductive reasoning is a logical process in which multiple premises, all believed true or found true most of the time, are combined to obtain a specific conclusion. Inductive reasoning is often used in applications that involve prediction, forecasting, or behaviour.

4 According to Wallas, creative performance completes through following sequence.

1 Preparation, Illumination, Incubation, Verification
2 Problem funding, Problem identification, Incubation, Insight

3 Problem identification, Preparation, Incubation, Illumination
4 Preparation, Incubation, Illumination, Verification

Ans. (4)

Exp. According to Wallas, creative performance completes through following sequence:

Preparation : In this stage, the thinker formulates the problem and collects the facts and materials considered necessary for finding new solutions.

Incubation : During this period, some of the ideas that were interfering with the solution will tend to fade. The overt activity and sometimes even thinking about the problem is absent in this stage. But the unconscious thought process involved in creative thinking is at work during this period.

Illumination : Following the period of incubation, the creative ideas occur suddenly. Consequently the obscure thing becomes clear. This sudden flash of solution is known as illumination and is similar to 'aha (eureka)' experience. e.g. Archimedes found solution to the crown problem.

Verification : Though the solution is found in illumination stage, it is necessary to verify whether that solution is correct or not. Hence in this last stage evaluation of the solution is done. If the solution is not satisfactory the thinker will go back to creative process from the beginning. If it is satisfactory, the same will be accepted and if necessary, minor modification may also be made in solution.

5 Read each of the following two statements, Assertion (A) and Reason (R) and indicate your answer using the codes given below :

Assertion (A) Gf and Gc correlate positively with each other across the age levels but with moderate magnitude.

Reason (R) Gf and Gc have different growth patterns. Gc grows rapidly in childhood and adolescence whereas Gf grows rapidly during adulthood.

Codes

1 Both (A) and (R) are true and (R) is the correct explanation of (A)
2 Both (A) and (R) are true, but (R) is not the correct explanation of (A)
3 (A) is true, but (R) is false
4 (A) is false, but (R) is true

Ans. (3)

Exp. (A) is true, but (R) is false.

Gf and Gc correlate positively with each other across the age levels but with moderate magnitude. Fluid abilities (Gf) drive the individual's ability to think and act quickly, solve novel problems and encode short-term memories. Fluid intelligence is grounded in physiological efficiency and is thus relatively independent of education and acculturation. The other factor encompasses crystallised abilities (Gc) and stems from learning and acculturation and is reflected in tests of knowledge, general information, use of language (vocabulary) and a wide variety of acquired skills. Personality factors, motivation and educational and cultural opportunity are central to its development and it is only indirectly dependent on the physiological influences that mainly affect fluid abilities.

Gf and Gc have different growth patterns. Gc does not grow rapidly in childhood and adolescence and Gf does not grow rapidly during adulthood. Gf is believed to peak quite early in life and grow rapidly in childhood whereas Gc tends to peak later in life and grow rapidly in adulthood. Therefore, the reason statement is false.

6 In absorptive phase of energy metabolism, what is the position of insulin and glucagon hormones?

I. High insulin	II. High glucagon
III. Low insulin	IV. Low glucagon

Codes

1 I and II	2 I and IV
3 III and IV	4 I and IV

Ans. (4)

Exp. In absorptive phase of energy metabolism, high insulin and low glucagon is the position of insulin and glucagon hormones.

Distinct mechanisms are in place to facilitate energy storage, and to make stored energy available during times of fasting and starvation. The absorptive state, or the fed state, occurs after a meal when your body is digesting the food and absorbing the nutrients (catabolism exceeds anabolism). Depending on the amounts and types of nutrients ingested, the absorptive state can linger for up to 4 hours.

The ingestion of food and the rise of glucose concentrations in the bloodstream stimulate pancreatic beta cells to release insulin into the bloodstream, where it initiates the absorption of blood glucose by liver hepatocytes, and by adipose and muscle cells. In response to a drop in blood glucose concentration, the hormone glucagon is released from the alpha cells of the pancreas. Glucagon acts upon the liver cells, where it inhibits the synthesis of glycogen and stimulates the breakdown of stored glycogen back into glucose.

7 Pygmalion effect is

1 exceptional fall in the performance of a student as a result of teacher's expectations
2 exceptional progress made by a student as a result of teacher's expectations
3 exceptional fall in the performance of a student because of peer competition
4 exceptional progress made by a student as a result of peer competition

Ans. (2)

Exp. Pygmalion effect is exceptional progress made by a student as a result of teacher's expectations.

The Pygmalion effect, or Rosenthal effect, is a psychological phenomenon wherein high expectations lead to improved performance in a given area. The work of Rosenthal and Jacobsen shows that teacher expectations influence student performance. Positive expectations influence performance positively and negative expectations influence performance negatively. This effect is exceptional progress made by a student as a result of teacher's expectations. When we expect certain behaviours of others, we are likely to act in ways that make the expected behaviour more likely to occur. In terms of teaching, faculties who gripe about students establish a climate of failure, but faculty who value their students' abilities create a climate of success.

8 Which one of the following semantic dimensions are measured by the 'semantic differential scale'?

1 Evaluation and potency
2 Potency and action
3 Evaluation and action
4 Evaluation, potency and action

Ans. (4)

Exp. Evaluation, potency and action are the semantic dimensions which are measured by the 'semantic differential scale'.

Semantic Differential (SD) is a type of a rating scale designed to measure the connotative meaning of objects, event and concepts. The connotations are used to derive the attitude towards the given object, event or concept. Osgood and his colleagues performed a factor analysis of large collections on semantic differential scales and found three recurring attitudes that people use to evaluate words and phrases: evaluation, potency, and action or activity.

Evaluation loads highest on the adjective pair 'good-bad'. The 'strong-weak' adjective pair defines the potency factor. Adjective pair 'active-passive' defines the action or activity factor. These three dimensions of affective meaning were found to be cross-cultural universals in a study of dozens of cultures.

9 Conversion disorder (Hysteria) is now placed in the category of

1 anxiety disorders
2 anxiety related disorders
3 somatoform disorders
4 psychological factors affecting physical conditions

Ans. (3)

Exp. Conversion disorder (Hysteria) is now placed in the category of somatoform disorders.

Somatoform disorders refer to a group of disorders that involve complaints of physical symptoms that have no physiological or biological basis.

Conversion disorder is a somatoform disorder that involves loss of physical function(s) for which no underlying physiological cause can be identified. It involves an actual physical disturbance or problem, but the cause of the problem is purely psychological. With conversion disorder, an individual might suddenly lose a particular body function (for example, eyesight, use of arm) without any underlying physiological cause, and then just as suddenly regain the function.

10 Suppose Merry wants to know if she can learn Spanish by playing some language tapes while she sleeps. Her question concerns the general topic of ________ and according to the text, the answer would most likely be ________ .

1 subliminal perception, may be
2 signal detection, no
3 subliminal perception, no
4 signal detection, may be

Ans. (3)

Exp. Merry question concerns the general topic of subliminal perception and according to the text, the answer would most likely be no.

Subliminal perception is the perception of a series of stimulus which the person is not consciously aware of and gets under the influence involuntarily, in addition to the perception with sensory organs. It is the registration of stimuli below the level of awareness, particularly stimuli that are too weak (or too rapid) for an individual to consciously perceive them.

Learning a new language involves many different layers: recognising the sounds, learning the vocabulary and mastering the grammar. So far, research suggests it may be possible to get familiarised with the tone and accent of a language or even the meaning of words while sleeping, but to a weaker level than what we already do all the time during the day without noticing.

11 Read each of the following two statements Assertion (A) and Reason (R) and indicate your answer using the codes given below :

Assertion (A) In the randomised two group designs, if the mean difference between the two groups is analysed both by t and F tests, F is always larger than t.

Reason (R) In the randomised two groups design, the $t^2 = F$.

Codes

1 Both (A) and (R) are true and (R) is the correct explanation of (A)
2 Both (A) and (R) are true, but (R) is not the correct explanation of (A)
3 (A) is true, but (R) is false
4 (A) is false, but (R) is true

Ans. (4)

Exp. (A) is false, but (R) is true.

In the randomised two-group designs, if the mean difference between the two groups is analysed both by t and F tests, F is not always larger than t. A randomised two-group design is any of various experimental designs in which individual participants are assigned to different conditions (groups) using a purely chance process, such as rolling a die. When the mean differences between the groups are analysed using both t and F, F is not always larger than t. For example, if $t<1$, then the F ratio will be smaller than t. Therefore, the assertion is false.

In the randomised two groups design, the $t^2 = F$. When both t-test and F-test are used on the same data obtained from two groups, the functional relationship between values of t and F if calculated would be $t^2 = F$. The t-test is calculated in terms of mean and F-test is variance which is square of standard deviation and standard is square root of average of square of mean.

12 Which one of the following laid down the social foundation of organisational behaviour?

1 Viteles 2 Munsturberg
3 Taylor 4 Mayo

Ans. (4)

Exp. Mayo laid down the social foundation of organisational behaviour.

Mayo is known for having established the scientific study of what today is called organisational behaviour when he gave close attention to the human, social and political problems of industrial civilisation. Mayo's work helped to lay the foundation for the human relations movement. Mayo developed a matrix which he used to illustrate the likelihood that a given team would be successful. His matrix demonstrates the role that varying combinations of group norms and group cohesiveness play in team effectiveness. Elton Mayo's management theory promotes the hypothesis that workers are motivated by social and relational forces more than financial or environmental conditions.

13 Which theory of personality is considered as third-force-movement in contemporary psychology?

1 Psychoanalysis
2 Behaviouristic
3 Humanistic/Existential
4 Cognitive

Ans. (3)

Exp. Humanistic/Existential theory of personality is considered as third-force-movement in contemporary psychology.

The humanistic approach is thus often called the "third force" in psychology after psychoanalysis and behaviourism (Maslow, 1968). The humanistic approach in psychology developed as a rebellion against what some psychologists saw as the limitations of the behaviourist and psychodynamic psychology. Humanism rejected the assumptions of the behaviourist perspective which is characterised as deterministic, focused on reinforcement of stimulus-response behaviour and heavily dependent on animal research.

Humanistic psychology also rejected the psychodynamic approach because it is also deterministic, with unconscious irrational and instinctive forces determining human thought and behaviour. Both behaviourism and psychoanalysis are regarded as dehumanising by humanistic psychologists. The contributions to humanistic approach are limited to areas such as therapy, abnormality, motivation and personality.

14 Read each of the following two statements, Assertion (A) and Reason (R) and indicate your answer using the codes given below:

Assertion (A) Ego-involved learners are driven by performance goals.

Reason (R) Ego-involved learners are pre-occupied with themselves and are concerned with their evaluation by others.

Codes

1 Both (A) and (R) are true and (R) is the correct explanation of (A)
2 Both (A) and (R) are true, but (R) is not the correct explanation of (A)
3 (A) is true, but (R) is false
4 (A) is false, but (R) is true

Ans. (1)

Exp. Both (A) and (R) are true and (R) is the correct explanation of (A).

Ego-involved learners are driven by performance goals. Ego-involved learners are concerned with the evaluation of their work by others. A student who is ego-involved will be seeking to perform the task to boost their own ego, for the praise that completing the task might attract, or because completing the task confirms their own self-concept e.g. clever, strong, funny etc. Therefore, they are driven by performance goals.

Ego-involved learners are pre-occupied with themselves and are concerned with their evaluation by others. Ego-involved students can become very anxious or discouraged in the face of failure, because such failure challenges their self-concept. Therefore, they are more concerned with their evaluation by others. Hence, this explains the assertion.

15 According to Piaget, which is the primary motivating force behind development?

1 Accommodation
2 Assimilation
3 Equilibration
4 Adaptation

Ans. (3)

Exp. According to Piaget, Equilibration is the primary motivating force behind development.

When a child's existing schemas are capable of explaining what it can perceive around it, it is said to be in a state of equilibrium, i.e. a state of cognitive (i.e. mental) balance.

Piaget emphasised the importance of schemas in cognitive development and described how they were developed or acquired. Equilibration means maintaining balance between assimilation and accommodation. Equilibration is the driving force that moves all development forward. Piaget didn't believe that development progressed steadily. Instead, it moved in leaps and bounds according to experiences.

16 Read each of the following two statements, Assertion (A) and Reason (R) and indicate your answer using the codes given below:

Assertion (A) Method of loci helps keeping memories intact and retrievable.

Reason (R) Familiar loci are already organised in our long-term memories.

Codes

1 Both (A) and (R) are true and (R) is the correct explanation of (A)
2 Both (A) and (R) are true, but (R) is not the correct explanation of (A)
3 (A) is true, but (R) is false
4 (A) is false, but (R) is true

Ans. *(1)*

Exp. Both (A) and (R) are true and (R) is the correct explanation of (A)

Method of loci helps keeping memories intact and retrievable. It is true as the items which are to be remembered are converted into mental images and associated with specific positions or locations. For instance, to remember a shopping list, each product could be imagined at a different location along a familiar street. The method of loci is also known as the memory journey, memory palace, or mind palace technique.

Familiar loci are already organised in our long-term memories. This is true and explains how method of loci helps in keeping memories intact and retrievable. In the method of loci, participants use various strategies well and commit to long-term memory a unique vivid image associated with each item. They have also committed to long-term memory a familiar route with firmly established stop-points or loci.

17 Which one of the following biases play an important role in stereotyping and prejudice?

1 False consensus 2 Illusory correlation
3 Priming 4 Confirmation

Ans. *(2)*

Exp. Illusory correlation plays an important role in stereotyping and prejudice.

Sometimes people believe there is some relationship between events, variables, etc. even though none really exists. This is known as the illusory correlation and it occurs in everyday life as well as science.

18 Which of the following glands does secrete sex steroids that are released by the gonads?

1 Adrenal medulla 2 Anterior pituitary
3 Adrenal cortex 4 Pancreas

Ans. *(3)*

Exp. Adrenal cortex glands do secrete sex steroids that are released by the gonads.

The adrenal glands (also known as suprarenal glands) are endocrine glands that produce a variety of hormones including sex steroids. The innermost layer of the cortex, the zona reticularis, produces androgens that are converted to fully functional sex hormones in the gonads and other target organs. Adrenal androgens male sex hormones are mainly dehydroepiandrosterone (DHEA) and testosterone. All have weak effects, but play a role in early development of the male sex organs in childhood, and in women during puberty. These are involved in creating and maintaining the differences between men and women.

19 Which one of the following was not an assumption of the foundation of 'Scientific Management' propounded by Taylor?

1 Interest of employer and employees are the same
2 Employees mostly want high wages/salary
3 Employer want a low labour cost
4 Management of incentives has great value

Ans. *(3)*

Exp. According to the 'Scientific Management' Theory by Taylor, employees do not want a low labour cost.

Fredrick Winslow Taylor commonly known as 'Father of Scientific Management' conducted various experiments during this process which forms the basis of scientific management. It implies application of scientific principles for studying and identifying management problems.

The basic assumptions of the foundation of 'Scientific Management' propounded by Taylor are as follows:

Interest of employer and employees are the same : Taylor believed that interest of employer and employees should be fully harmonised so as to secure mutually understanding relations between them.

Employees mostly want high wages/salary : The aim of Scientific Management is to see maximum prosperity for employer and employees. It is important only when there is opportunity for each worker to attain his highest efficiency. Maximum output and optimum utilisation of resources will bring higher profits for the employer and better wages for the workers. Both managers and workers should be paid handsomely.

Management of incentives has great value : Taylor's emphasis on wage incentives, led to astounding increase in productivity and also wages for workers.

20 Which one of the following proposed the 'ABX' Theory of Dyadic Attraction?

1 Header 2 Jones
3 Newcomb 4 Lombardo

Ans. *(3)*

Exp. Newcomb proposed the 'ABX' Theory of Dyadic Attraction.

The Newcomb's model or ABX' Theory of Dyadic Attraction was introduced by Theodore. M. Newcomb in 1953. Newcomb gives a different approach of communication process. The main purpose of the theory is to introduce the role of communication in social relationship/society and most vital to maintain social equilibrium within the social system. He does not include the message as a separate purpose of communication showing all communication as a means of sustaining relationship between people.

21 The statement, "Normalcy and Abnormalcy differ in degree not in kind" represents the _____ of abnormalcy.

1 deviance criteria
2 personal discomfort criteria
3 statistical criteria
4 social discomfort criteria

Ans. (3)

➲ *Exp.* The statement, "Normalcy and Abnormalcy differ in degree not in kind" represents the statistical criteria of abnormalcy.

According to the statistical criterion, normality and abnormality only differ in degree. Thus, abnormality and superior merely represent quantitative deviations from the normal or average. Individuals who possess an average amount of intelligence, personality stability and social adaptability are considered normal. Those who possess considerably less than this are abnormals and those who possess considerably more are superior. Therefore, according to this criterion most of the people are normal. The superior is slightly intelligent than the normal and the abnormal shows slightly more maladaptive behaviour than the normal.

22 According to Signal Detection theory, detection of stimuli depends on

I. their physical energy.
II. internal factors like relative costs.
III. absolute threshold.
IV. internal factors like benefits with detecting their presence.

Codes

1 I, II and III	2 II, III and IV
3 III, I and IV	4 I, II and IV

Ans. (4)

➲ *Exp.* According to Signal Detection Theory, detection of stimuli depends on–their physical energy, internal factors like relative costs and internal factors like benefits with detecting their presence.

Detection theory or Signal Detection theory is a means to quantify the ability to discern between information-bearing patterns (called stimulus in living organisms, signal in machines) and random patterns that distract from the information (called noise, consisting of background stimuli and random activity of the detection machine and of the nervous system of the operator).

Signal Detection theory holds that the detection of a stimulus depends on both the intensity of the stimulus and the physical and psychological state of the individual. e.g. when you walk to your car that is parked in an empty parking lot late at night all by yourself, you might be much more aware of noises because the situation is somewhat threatening. In this case, you may hear some slight noises that you might otherwise not hear if you were in a different situation that was not as threatening. Thus, your ability to detect signals or noises has been affected by these factors.

23 Which of the following are the sources of error in social cognition?

I. Counterfactuals thinking
II. Thought suppression
III. Magical thinking
IV. Judging by resemblance

Codes

1 I and II	2 I, II and III
3 I, III and IV	4 III and IV

Ans. (2)

➲ *Exp.* Counterfactuals thinking, Thought suppression and Magical thinking are the sources or error in social cognition.

The sources of error in social cognition are as follows :

- *Counterfactual thinking* is imagining ways in which events in one's life might have turned out differently. This often involves feelings of regret or disappointment (e.g., If only I hadn't been so hasty) but may also involve a sense of relief, as at a narrow escape (e.g., If I had been standing three feet to the left...).
- *Thought suppression* is the attempt to control the content of one's mental processes and specifically to rid oneself of undesired thoughts or images. Ironically, engaging in thought suppression often only serves to make the unwanted thoughts more intrusive.
- *Magical thinking* is the belief that events or the behaviour of others can be influenced by one's thoughts, wishes, or rituals. Magical thinking is typical of children up to 4 or 5 years of age, after which reality thinking begins to predominate.

24 Match items of List I with the items of List II. Select the correct answer by the using codes given below :

List I	List II
A. Latent learning	I. Learning a response to terminate an aversive stimulus
B. Cognitive learning	II. Occurrence of learning is not evident in behaviour until later
C. Escape learning	III. A change in the way of processing informations as a result of experiences
D. Avoidance learning	IV. Learning a response to avoid an aversive stimulus

Codes

	A	B	C	D		A	B	C	D
1	III	II	IV	I	2	II	III	I	IV
3	I	IV	II	III	4	IV	III	I	II

Ans. (2)

➲ *Exp.* The correct matching is A-II, B-III, C-I, D-IV.

Latent learning is when the occurrence of learning is not evident in behaviour until later. Tolman also worked on latent learning, defined as learning which is not apparent in the learner's behaviour at the time of learning, but which manifests later when a suitable motivation and circumstances appear.

Cognitive learning is a change in the way of processing information as a result of experiences. It is concerned with acquisition of problem-solving abilities and with intelligence and conscious thought.

Escape learning is learning a response to terminate an aversive stimulus. Escape learning occurs to terminate an unpleasant stmulus such as annoyance or pain, thereby negatively reinforcing the behaviour.

Avoidance learning is learning a response to avoid an aversive stimulus. Avoidance learning is a behaviourist term that describes when an organism learns a response in order to avoid experiencing an unpleasant stimulus.

25 The diagram below is an example of

The boy	hit	the ball	over the fence

1 constituents
2 linguistic universals
3 morphemes
4 underlying representation

Ans. (1)

Exp. The given diagram is an example of constituents.

A constituent is a linguistic unit that is a component of a larger and more complex unit. It is now mainly associated with the type of constituent analysis practiced in phrase-structure grammar and other forms of generative grammar. In this form of analysis a canonical English sentence, such as 'The man opened a window', is usually said to have the immediate constituents "noun phrase" (NP) and "verb phrase" (VP); the verb phrase can be further subdivided into the constituents "verb" (V) and "noun phrase," and both noun phrases into "determiner" (det) and "noun" (N).

26 Creativity is considered to be grounded in right hemisphere because

I. left hemisphere specialises in sequential and analytical processes.
II. right hemisphere specialises in global, parallel and holistic processes.
III. left hemisphere is involved in generation of novel ideas.
IV. creativity involves divergent thinking that is function of right hemisphere.

Codes

1 I, II and IV
2 II, III and I
3 IV, II and III
4 II, III and IV

Ans. (1)

Exp. Statement I, II and IV are correct in relation to Creativity.

Creativity is considered to be grounded in right hemisphere because left hemisphere specialises in sequential and analytical processes. The left hemisphere of the brain processes information analytically and sequentially. It focuses on the verbal and is responsible for language. It processes from details into a whole picture. The left hemisphere's functions include order and pattern perception as well as creating strategies.

Also, the reason behind considering creativity to be grounded in right hemisphere is that right hemisphere specialises in global, parallel and holistic processes. The right-brain hemisphere is the center of nonverbal, intuitive, holistic modes of thinking.

Aslo, creativity involves divergent thinking that is function of right hemisphere. The right side of the brain is intuitive, imaginative and creative. It is linked with artistic prowess such as singing, painting, composing music, writing poetry and other things that are defined by creativity and art. Divergent thinking is a thought procedure where individuals spontaneously generate innovative, original solutions to problems.

27 Read each of the following two statements, Assertion (A) and Reason (R) and indicate your answer using the codes given below :

Assertion (A) Being awake disrupts the homeostasis of the body.

Reason (R) Sleep is terminated by a return to homeostasis.

Codes

1 Both (A) and (R) are true and (R) is the correct explanation of (A)
2 Both (A) and (R) are true, but (R) is not the correct explanation of (A)
3 (A) is true, but (R) is false
4 (A) is false, but (R) is true

Ans. (2)

Exp. Both (A) and (R) are true, but (R) is not the correct explanation of (A).

Being awake disrupts the homeostasis of the body. Homeostasis, in general, is any internal biochemical system that regulates the body's internal environment, with a view to maintaining properties such as temperature, acidity etc, in a stable and relatively constant condition. Sleep-wake homeostasis, in particular, can be thought of as a kind of internal timer or counter that generates a homeostatic sleep drive or pressure for sleep as a function of the amount of time elapsed since the last adequate sleep episode.

Sleep is terminated by a return to homeostasis. It is quite intuitive in its operation the longer we have been awake, the stronger the desire and need to sleep becomes and the greater the likelihood of falling asleep, the longer we have been asleep the more the pressure to sleep dissipates and the greater the likelihood of awakening.

Both the statements are independently correct, but the reason does not follow the assertion.

28 Which one of the following can be primarily employed to assess creativity?

1 Abstract thinking
2 Convergent thinking
3 Divergent thinking
4 Symbolic thinking

Ans. (3)

Exp. Divergent thinking can be primarily employed to assess creativity.

Divergent thinking is one of the well-studied aspects of creativity. It is the generation of a variety of ideas and alternative solutions to problems. As some of the resulting ideas are original, divergent thinking represents the potential for creative thinking and problem solving.

It refers to a way of solving problems wherein a variety of possible solutions are proposed in an effort to find the best one. Divergent thinking is an important aspect of creative thinking. The creative process doesn't always take your directly to the best solution, but by encouraging a variety of possible solutions, new ideas are more likely to emerge.

29 Which one of the following psychologists first empirically established that social stress distort physical health?

1 Selye
2 Lazarus and Folkman
3 Holmes and Rahe
4 Srivastava and Pestonjee

Ans. (3)

Exp. Holmes and Rahe were the psychologists who first empirically established that social stress distort physical health.

Holmes and Rahe (1967) developed a questionnaire called the Social Readjustment Rating Scale (SRRS) for identifying major stressful life events. Each one of the 43 stressful life events was awarded a Life Change Unit depending on how traumatic it was felt to be by a large sample of participants.

30 Which of the following two styles of leadership were identified in Ohio State Leadership studies?

1 Employees-centered and production-centered
2 Initiating structure and people-oriented
3 Initiating structure and consideration for relationship
4 Authoritarian and democratic

Ans. (3)

Exp. The Ohio State University Leadership Study underscores two different behavioural views on leadership: people-oriented (consideration) and task-oriented (initiating structure).

Initiating structure refers to the extent to which a leader is likely to define and structure his own role as well as the roles of subordinates in the search for goal attainment. It includes behaviour that attempts to organise work, work relationships and goals. The leader characterised as high in initiating structure specifies the task to be performed by each member of his group, sets down deadlines, gives directions and puts pressure on them for its fulfillment.

Consideration refers to the extent to which a leader is likely to have job relationships which are characterised by mutual trust, respect for subordinates' ideas and regard for their feelings. He shows concern for his followers' comfort, well-being, status and satisfaction.

31 Read each of the following two statements, Assertion (A) and Reason (R) and indicate your answer using the codes given below :

Assertion (A) The Recognition By Components (RBC) Model provides a method for recognising three dimensional objects across variations in new points.

Reason (R) Any three dimensional object can be generally described according to its parts and their spatial relations.

Codes

1 Both (A) and (R) are true and (R) is the correct explanation of (A)
2 Both (A) and (R) are true, but (R) is not the correct explanation of (A)
3 (A) is true, but (R) is false
4 (A) is false, but (R) is true

Ans. (1)

Exp. Both (A) and (R) are true, and (R) is the correct explanation of (A).

The Recognition By Components (RBC) Model provides a method for recognising three dimensional objects across variations in new points. The Recognition-By-Components theory, or RBC theory, is a bottom-up process proposed by Irving Biederman in 1987 to explain object recognition. According to RBC theory, we are able to recognize objects by separating them into geons (the object 's main component parts).

Any three dimensional object can be generally described according to its parts and their spatial relations. Biederman suggested that geons are based on basic 3-dimensional shapes (cylinders, cones etc.) that can be assembled in various arrangements to form a virtually unlimited number of objects. Therefore, the reason follows the assertion and explains why we are able to recognise three-dimensional objects.

32 Which one of the following may not be put in the category of 'Absolute Standard' methods of performance appraisal?

1 Critical Incidents method
2 Behaviourally Anchored Rating method
3 Ranking method
4 Checklist method

Ans. (3)

Exp. Ranking method may not be put in the category of 'Absolute Standard' methods of performance appraisal.

Absolute standard is a method of performance appraisal used to evaluate the performance of an employee in comparison to standards established by the firm. Evaluation is done on an individual basis rather than comparing co-workers.

These standards can be set using research on work sampling, production data or expert opinions. Ranking method may not be put in the category of absolute standard method. The following performance appraisal techniques can be categorised under absolute standards:

Critical Incident is a qualitative method whereby behavioural traits exhibited by each employee are documented with the aim to evaluate performance as opposed to personality.

Checklist Appraisal is a simple questionnaire with Yes/No responses in which the appraiser checks off all the tasks that have been successfully completed by the employee.

Behaviourally Anchored Rating Scales (BARS) is a list of descriptive statements of behaviour that are rated against a scale from least to most effective. The appraiser must identify the level of effectiveness for each given statement in order to determine the employee's overall performance.

33 Match List I and List II and select the correct answer from the codes given below:

List I (Designs)	**List II** (Features)
A. Randomised block design	I. Each subject participates under all experimental conditions
B. Factorial design	II. Analyses the data for matched groups
C. Single-factor repeated measures design	III. Suitable for studying the interactions among the independent variables
D. Design with a covariate	IV. Employs statistical control

Codes

	A	B	C	D		A	B	C	D
1	III	II	IV	I	2	III	II	I	IV
3	II	III	I	IV	4	II	III	IV	I

Ans. (3)

Exp. The correct matching is A-II, B-III, C-I, D-IV.

Randomised block design analyses the data for matched groups. With a randomised block design, the experimenter divides subjects into subgroups called blocks, such that the variability within blocks is less than the variability between blocks. Then, subjects within each block are randomly assigned to treatment conditions in the experiment.

Factorial design is suitable for studying the interactions among the independent variables. It is an experimental study in which two or more categorical variables are simultaneously manipulated or observed in order to study their joint influence (interaction effect) and separate influences (main effects) on a separate dependent variable.

Single-factor repeated measures design is used when each subject participates under all experimental conditions. It is an experimental design in which the effects of treatments are seen through the comparison of scores of the same participant observed under the treatment condition.

Design with a covariate employs statistical control. A covariate is a variable that is of no direct interest to the researcher, but one thatmay have an effect on the outcome (the dependent variable). Results of a study can be made more accurate by controlling for the variation in the covariate. Therefore, any design with a covariate can be used to statistically control its effect on the dependent variable.

34 Cultures of honour are characterised by strong norms indicating that aggression is

1 an inappropriate response to insults to one's honour
2 an appropriate response to regards to one's honour
3 an appropriate response to insults to one's honour
4 an inappropriate response to regards to one's honour

Ans. (3)

Exp. Cultures of honour are characterised by strong norms indicating that aggression is an appropriate response to insults to one's honour.

Culture of honour is a cultural norm in a region, nation, or ethnic group prescribing immediate, definitive retribution as the preferred reaction to an insult or other transgression, particularly one that threatens a person's reputation. Ethnographic studies suggest that cultures that subsist by herding typically attach more importance to honor and reputation than do people from agrarian societies, since a person in a herding culture who vociferously defends against threats is less likely to have his or her livelihood taken away by rustlers.

In the culture of honour, the person (usually a man) feels obliged to protect his or her reputation by answering insults, affronts, and threats, oftentimes through the use of violence. The 'culture of honour' places utmost importance on the ability to respond to social insults and economic challenges.

35 Discovery and understanding of our own abilities bring happiness, but also bring fear of new responsibilities and duties. It is called

1 Electra complex
2 Jonah complex
3 Motives conflict
4 Motive to avoid success

Ans. (2)

Exp. Discovery and understanding of our own abilities bring happiness, but also bring fear of new responsibilities and duties. It is called Jonah Complex.

Abraham Maslow posited the existence of a psychological condition inherent in human beings which sabotages their dreams of greatness and relegates them to live in mediocrity and conformity. He called this condition the Jonah Complex. The Jonah Complex is "an evasion of growth and fulfilling one's best talents. It is a 'fear of one's greatness.' It is one of the biggest reasons why people do not bother to find out and actively pursue their purpose in life.

36 Memory for surprising and consequential events (emotional public events) are known as

1 photographic memory
2 flash bulb memory
3 iconic memory
4 implicit memory

Ans. (2)

Exp. Memory for surprising and consequential events (emotional public events) are known as flash bulb memory.

Flash bulb memories are memories of learning something so shocking or surprising that it creates a strong and seemingly very accurate memory of learning about the event-but not the event itself.

37 Intimacy, passion and commitment are the components of

1 romantic love
2 companionate love
3 infatuated love
4 consummate love

Ans. (4)

Exp. Intimacy, passion and commitment are the components of consummate love.

The triangular theory of love explains the topic of love in an interpersonal relationship. Psychologist Robert Sternberg's theory describes types of love based on three different scales: intimacy, passion, and commitment. Consummate love is the complete form of love, which includes all three components, representing the ideal relationship toward which many people strive but which apparently few achieve. Sternberg cautions that maintaining a consummate love may be even harder than achieving it.

38 Which of the following are innate behaviours?

I. Reflexes
II. Taxes
III. Fixed action patterns
IV. Genotype

Codes

1 I and III
2 I, II and III
3 I, III and IV
4 I, II, III and IV

Ans. (2)

Exp. The innate behaviours are Reflexes, Taxes, and Fixed action patterns.

Reflexes are involuntary movements or actions. Some movements are spontaneous and occur as a part of the baby's normal activity. Others are responses to certain actions. Healthcare providers check reflexes to determine if the brain and nervous system are working well. Some reflexes occur only in specific periods of development.

A *taxes* is a response to a stimulus resulting in movement towards or away from the stimulus.

A *fixed action pattern* is a series or sequence of acts that occur behaviourally in animals. This sequence is unchangeable and will be carried out to completion once started, regardless of changes in the original stimulus.

39 Which one of the following proposed the 'Response Inhibition' Theory of Extinction?

1 Hull
2 Guthrie
3 Tolman
4 Deese

Ans. (1)

Exp. Hull proposed the 'Response Inhibition' Theory of Extinction.

According to Hull, whenever any reaction is evoked in an organism there is left a condition or state which acts as a primary negative motivation in that it has an innate capacity to produce a cessation of the activity which produced the state. This cessation leads to the extinction of behaviour.

40 Read each of the following two statements, Assertion (A) and Reason (R) and indicate your answer using the codes given below :

Assertion (A) An infant often acts as if objects stop existing when they are moved out of his perceptual range.

Reason (R) The infant has not yet developed the object concept.

Codes

1 Both (A) and (R) are true and (R) is the correct explanation of (A)
2 Both (A) and (R) are true, but (R) is not the correct explanation of (A)
3 (A) is true, but (R) is false
4 (A) is false, but (R) is true

Ans. (1)

Exp. Both (A) and (R) are true and (R) is the correct explanation of (A).

An infant often acts as if objects stop existing when they are moved out of his perceptual range. It is true and is based on the concept of Object permanence. Object permanence describes a child's ability to know that objects continue to exist even though they can no longer be seen or heard. When an object is hidden from sight, infants under a certain age often become upset that the item has vanished.

In Piaget's theory of cognitive development, infants develop this understanding by the end of the "sensorimotor stage", which lasts from birth to about two years of age. Piaget thought that an infant's perception and understanding of the world depended on their motor development, which was required for the infant to link visual, tactile and motor representations of objects.

According to this view, it is through touching and handling objects that infants develop object permanence.

41 Rollo May's views on personality development can be described in following sequence.

1 Physical dependence, Psychological dependence, Rebellion, Ordinary consciousness of self, Creative consciousness of self.
2 Physical dependence, Rebellion, Ordinary consciousness of self, Self actualisation.
3 Psychological dependence, Physical dependence, Ordinary consciousness of self, Creative consciousness of self.
4 Physical dependence, Psychological dependence, Ordinary consciousness of self, Rebellion, Creative consciousness of self.

Ans. (1)

Exp. Rollo May's views on personality development can be described in following sequence :

Physical dependence : In the Innocence stage, an infant has few drives other than the will to live. They have a physical dependence on objects and people around them.

Psychological dependence : In the Innocence stage, the infant moves from the physical dependency to psychological dependencies which involve dependencies on comfort from the primary caregivers.

Rebellion : In this stage, a developing child seeks freedom but cannot properly care for herself.

Ordinary consciousness of self : This is stage of adulthood. Overwhelmed by its demands, young adults tend to seek protection in conformity and tradition.

Creative consciousness of self: This is a stage which marks a point of productive, creative self-actualization during which a person moves past egotism and self-involvement.

42 We tend to attribute to another's behaviour to external causes when information is of

I. high consensus
II. low distinctiveness
III. high distinctiveness
IV. high consistency

Codes

1 I and II   2 I, III and IV
3 II, III and IV   4 I, II and IV

Ans. (2)

Exp. We tend to attribute to another's behaviour to external causes when information is of high consensus, high distinctiveness and high consistency.

Consensus is the co-variation of behaviour across different people. Distinctiveness refers to how unique the behaviour is to the particular situation. Consistency is the covariation of behaviour across time.

According to Hewstone and Jaspars (1987), we are able to determine whether a person would likely to make a personal (internal), stimulus (external) or circumstantial attribution by assessing the levels of consensus, distinctiveness, and consistency in a given situation:

- Low Consensus, Low Distinctiveness, High Consistency = Personal Attribution
- High Consensus, High Distinctiveness, High Consistency = Stimulus Attribution
- High Consensus, Low Distinctiveness, Low Consistency = Circumstance Attribution

43 According to Kohlberg, ________ and ________ are the major reasons of moral behaviour during the stage of conventional morality.

1 gaining acceptance; getting rewards
2 avoiding censure by others; achieving justice
3 gaining acceptance; avoiding censure by others
4 avoiding censure by others; achieving justice

Ans. (3)

Exp. According to Kohlberg, gaining acceptance and avoiding censure by others are the major reasons of moral behaviour during the stage of conventional morality. Conventional morality is characterised by an acceptance of society's conventions concerning right and wrong.

Gaining acceptance : Stage three of Kohlberg's stages of moral development, i.e. Interpersonal Concordance or "Good Boy-Nice Girl" Orientation suggests that at this level an individual obeys rules and follows society's norms even when there are no consequences for obedience or disobedience. The individuals conform to avoid disapproval, dislike by others. The value of human life is based on the empathy and affection of the needs of its possessor or of other persons.

Avoiding censure : Stage four of Kohlberg's stages of moral development, i.e. the "Law and Order" orientation suggests that individuals conform to avoid censure by legitimate authorities and resultant guilt.

44 Match List I with List II and select the correct answer from the codes given below :

List I		List II	
A.	Sufficient cause	I.	A condition, existence of which guarantee for the genesis of a mental disorder
B.	Reinforcing cause	II.	A condition that tends to maintain maladaptive behaviour that has already occurred
C.	Contributory cause	III.	A condition that occurs relatively in early life and may not show its effect for many years
D.	Distal cause	IV.	A condition that increases the probability of a disorder

Codes

	A	B	C	D		A	B	C	D
1	II	IV	III	I	2	I	II	IV	III
3	IV	III	II	I	4	III	I	IV	II

Ans. (2)

Exp. The correct matching is A-I, B-II, C-IV, D-III.

Sufficient cause is a condition, existence of which guarantee for the genesis of a mental disorder. For example, condition 'X' guarantees the occurrence of a disorder 'Y'.

Reinforcing cause is a condition that tends to maintain maladaptive behaviour that has already occurred. It is a condition that tends to maintain a healthy or maladaptive behavior or behavioral pattern in an individual. An example is when special attention is given to a person who is ill, which can contribute either to a speedy recovery or to a delayed recovery. It is typical, however, to use the term in relation to negative or maladaptive consequences.

Contributory cause is a condition that increases the probability of a disorder. For example, 'X' increases the probability of developing a disorder 'Y' but is neither necessary nor sufficient for the disorder to occur.

Distal cause is a condition that occurs relatively in early life and may not show its effect for many years. It is a cause that underlies or is remote from the more obvious direct cause of a departure from good health. For example, atmospheric contamination with ozone-destroying substances, such as chlorofluorocarbon compounds, is a distal cause of skin cancer due to increased ultraviolet radiation flux.

45 **Match List I with List II and select the correct answer by using the codes given below :**

List I (Names)	List II (Features)
A. Template Matching Model	I. The extent to which spatial relations deviate from the prototype
B. Feature Matching Model	II. Description of three dimensional objects according to their parts and spatial relations
C. Recognition-by-Component Model	III. Visual analysis detects colours and edges
D. Configuration Model	IV. Recognition of bar codes and finger prints

Codes

	A	B	C	D
1	I	II	III	IV
2	I	III	IV	II
3	IV	II	III	I
4	IV	III	I	II

Ans. *(*)*

➲ *Exp.* The correct matching is A-IV, B-III, C-II, D-I.

Template Matching Model is the recognition of bar codes and finger prints. Bar codes and finger prints are made to compare with various stored copies (templates) that are stored in a machine. The attempt is to match against all templates. Template matching works well with computers which have check-sorting machines – number characters are maximally discernible so that computer can make no mistake.

Feature Matching Model is the visual analysis that detects colours and edges. It assumes that stimuli consist of combinations of elementary features, (e.g for the alphabet, features may include horizontal lines, vertical lines, diagonals and curves) and make discriminations based on a small number of characteristics of stimuli distinctive feature components stored in memory.

Recognition-by-Component Model is the description of three dimensional objects according to their parts and spatial relations. According to RBC theory, we are able to recognise objects by separating them into geons (the object's main component parts). Biederman suggested that geons are based on basic 3-dimensional shapes (cylinders, cones, etc.) that can be assembled in various arrangements to form a virtually unlimited number of objects.

Configuration Model is the extent to which spatial relations deviate from the prototype. It is less concerned with individual features, but it is exquisitely sensitive to the overall arrangement in the input.

46 **Which of the following statements are true about the Principal components analysis?**

I. Unities (values of 1) are retained in the diagonal spaces of the correlation matrix.

II. The first principal component explains maximum variance.

III. Principle components analysis follows Common Factor Model.

IV. Principle components analysis yields oblique unrotated factors.

Codes

1 I and II 2 I and IV
3 II and III 4 I, II and IV

Ans. *(1)*

➲ *Exp.* The following statements are true about the Principal components analysis:

- Unities (values of 1) are retained in the diagonal spaces of the correlation matrix.
- The first principal component explains maximum variance.

Principal Component Analysis (PCA) is a technique for reducing the dimensionality of such datasets, increasing interpretability but at the same time minimizing information loss. It does so by creating new uncorrelated variables that successively maximize variance.

47 **Find the correct sequence among the following oxytocin related events.**

I. Carrying down by axons.

II. Contraction of uterine muscles.

III. Synthesis in paraventricular nucleus of hypothalamus.

IV. Secreted by neurosecretory cells in posterior pituitary.

Codes

1 I, IV, III, II 2 III, I, IV, II
3 I, II, IV, III 4 IV, I, III, II

Ans. *(2)*

➲ *Exp.* The correct sequence is III, I, IV, II.

Synthesis in paraventricular nucleus of hypothalamus : Oxytocin in a nine amino acid peptide that is synthesized in hypothalamic neurons.

Carrying down by axons : It is then transported down by the axons of the posterior pituitary.

Secreted by neurosecretory cells in posterior pituitary : It is secreted by neurosecretory cells in posterior pituitary, bloodstream and also within the brain. It is also secreted from a few other tissues, including the ovaries and testes.

Contraction of uterine muscles : During the later stages of gestation, there is an increase in abundance of oxytocin receptors on uterine smooth muscle cells, which is associated with increased 'irritability' of the uterus (and sometimes the mother as well). Oxytocin is released during labour when the fetus stimulates the cervix and vagina, and it enhances contraction of uterine smooth muscle to facilitate parturition or birth.

48 Match List I with List II and select the correct answer by choosing correct code given below :

List I (Concepts)	List II (Explanations)
A. Situated learning	I. Internalise knowledge and skills developed in interaction with others
B. Social negotiation	II. Aspect of learning process that relies on collaboration with others and respect for different perspectives
C. Appropriate	III. Skills are tied to the settings in which they are learned and are difficult to apply in new settings
D. Cognitive apprenticeship	IV. A relationship in which a less experienced learner acquires knowledge and skills in interaction with expert

Codes

	A	B	C	D		A	B	C	D
1	I	II	III	IV	2	III	IV	I	II
3	III	II	I	IV	4	I	IV	III	II

Ans. (3)

Exp. The correct matching is A-III, B-II, C-I, D-IV.

Situated learning is based on skills that are tied to the settings in which they are learned and are difficult to apply in new settings. Situated learning "takes as its focus the relationship between learning and the social situation in which it occurs".

Social negotiation is an aspect of learning process that relies on collaboration with others and respect for different perspectives. Social negotiation is a subset of the first class collaborative element, cultural negotiation, which is itself a subset of information exchange. The amount and type of social negotiation involved in a collaborative process is linked to the characteristics of the collaborative media and the participants.

Appropriate is internalising knowledge and skills developed in interaction with others. It is the process of constructing knowledge from social and cultural sources, and integrating it into pre-existing schemas.

Cognitive apprenticeship is a relationship in which a less experienced learner acquires knowledge and skills in interaction with expert. It supports learning in a domain by enabling students to acquire, develop and use cognitive tools in authentic domain activity.

49 Which one of the following concepts is equivalent to the concept of 'habit family hierarchy' proposed by Hull?

1 Drive reduction
2 Cognitive map
3 Habit strength
4 Means-end remedies

Ans. (2)

Exp. Cognitive map is equivalent to the concept of 'habit family hierarchy' proposed by Hull.

The habit family hierarchy is the concept that several different routes to the same goal are available, each having a particular strength that determines its arrangement in a preferential order and hence its potential for expression.

This was explained by experimentation done by Tolman on cognitive maps. A cognitive map is a type of mental representation which serves an individual to acquire, code, store, recall, and decode information about the relative locations and attributes of phenomena in their everyday or metaphorical spatial environment.

The concept was used to explain the behaviour of rats that appeared to learn the spatial layout of a maze, and subsequently the concept was applied to other animals, including humans. The term was later generalised by some researchers, especially in the field of operations research, to refer to a kind of semantic network representing an individual's personal knowledge or schemas.

50 A psychotic disorder in which a person's functioning is not markedly impaired, whether is behaviour obviously odd or bizarre and free from hallucinations is called

1 Schizo affective disorder
2 Schizophreniform disorder
3 Delusional disorder
4 Shared psychotic disorder

Ans. (3)

Exp. A psychotic disorder in which a person's functioning is not markedly impaired, whether behaviour obviously odd or bizarre and free from hallucinations is called Delusional disorder.

Delusional disorder refers to a condition in which an individual displays one or more delusions for one month or longer. Delusional disorder is distinct from schizophrenia and cannot be diagnosed if a person meets the criteria for schizophrenia. Delusions may seem believable at face value and patients may appear normal as long as an outsider does not touch upon their delusional themes. Also, these delusions are not due to a medical condition or substance abuse.

51 What is not typical of Atkinson and Shiffrin Model of Memory?

1 STM is engaged in complex cognitive activities
2 STM is gateway to LTM
3 It is a sequential model
4 STM controls and enhances information to LTM

Ans. (1)

Exp. STM is engaged in complex cognitive activities is not typical of Atkinson and Shiffrin Model of Memory.

Working memory is engaged in complex cognitive activities. The term working memory is used for the short-term maintenance and manipulation of information necessary for performing complex cognitive tasks such as learning, reasoning, and comprehension.

STM is a gateway to LTM. The classic "modal model" of memory argues that short term memory (STM) serves as the primary gateway for the formation of long term memory (LTM) representations (Atkinson & Shiffrin, 1968).

It is a sequential model. According to this model, information is stored sequentially in three memory systems: sensory memory, short-term memory, and long-term memory.

STM controls and enhances information to LTM. The STM sets into motion control process of maintenance rehearsal to retain the information for as much time as required.

52 According to Erikson, adequate training, sufficient education and good models during the age range 6 to 11 years will lead to

1 initiative
2 identity
3 industriousness
4 autonomy

Ans. (3)

Exp. According to Erikson, adequate training, sufficient education and good models during the age range 6 to 11 years will lead to industriousness.

Industry versus inferiority is the fourth of Erikson's eight stages of psychosocial development, occurring from ages 6 to 11 years, during which the child learns to be productive and to accept evaluation of his or her efforts or becomes discouraged and feels inferior or incompetent. If they succeed in navigating this stage with adequate training, sufficient education and good models, they are able to develop a meaningful social role to give back to society. They will become industrious, namely, productive and contributing members to society as a whole. If they do not succeed at this stage, they may develop low self-esteem, culminating in a sense of inferiority, namely, viewing themselves as unproductive and possibly not fully useful members of society.

53 Read each of the following two statements, Assertion (A) and Reason (R) and indicate your answer using the codes given below.

Assertion (A) People's fantasies would reflect their achievement concerns.

Reason (R) All people strive to succeed by excelling at any task where evaluation is possible.

Codes

1 Both (A) and (R) are true and (R) is the correct explanation of (A)
2 Both (A) and (R) are true, but (R) is not the correct explanation of (A)
3 (A) is true, but (R) is false
4 (A) is false, but (R) is true

Ans. (3)

Exp. (A) is true, but (R) is false.

People's fantasies would reflect their achievement concerns. It is true as need for achievement (N-Ach) is an individual's desire for significant accomplishment, mastering of skills, control, or high standards. It is associated with a range of actions which are "intense, prolonged and repeated efforts to accomplish something difficult".

All people strive to succeed by excelling at any task where evaluation is possible. It is false as it is only seen in individuals who have high need for achievement. They like to receive regular feedback on their progress and achievements.

54 Match List I with List II and select the correct answer by choosing from codes given below.

List I (Methods)	List II (Effects on Behaviour)
A. Electrical stimulation of satiety centre	I. Cessation of eating
B. Electrical stimulation of hunger centre	II. Initiation of eating
C. Lesion of satiety centre	III. Hyperphagia
D. Lesion of hunger centre	IV. Aphagia

Codes

	A	B	C	D
1	II	I	IV	III
2	I	II	IV	III
3	II	I	III	IV
4	I	II	III	IV

Ans. (4)

Exp. The correct matching is A-I, B-II, C-III, D-IV.

Electrical stimulation of satiety centre leads to cessation of eating. The ventromedial nucleus is believed to be a satiety center. Electrical stimulation of the satiety center has been found to cause a cessation of eating.

Electrical stimulation of hunger centre leads to initiation of eating. The lateral nucleus is thought to act as a feeding center. Electrical stimulation of the lateral feeding center causes initiation of eating.

Lesion of satiety centre leads to hyperphagia. Large bilateral electrolytic lesions to the ventromedial hypothalamus produce hyperphagia (excessive eating) and extreme obesity.

Lesion of hunger centre leads to aphagia. Bilateral electrolytic lesions to the lateral hypothalamus produce aphagia—a complete cessation of eating.

55 Which of the following statements are true about simple bivariate linear regression?

I. The b coefficient is a slope of the regression line.
II. The b coefficient denotes change in Y, when X changes by 1 unit.
III. The errors of prediction have a mean and variance of zero.

IV. If the *b* coefficient is significant, the product moment correlation between *X* and *Y* is also significant.

Codes

1 I and II 2 III and IV
3 I, II and III 4 I, II and IV

Ans. *(4)*

Exp. Statement I, II and IV are true about simple bivariate linear regression.

The *b* coefficient is a slope of the regression line. The *b* coefficients refer to the slopes of the regression lines.

The *b* coefficient denotes change in *Y*, when *X* changes by 1 unit. *b* coefficients are interpreted as the amount of change in the dependent variable (Y) that is associated with a change in one unit of the independent variable (X).

If the *b* coefficient is significant, the product moment correlation between *X* and *Y* is also significant. If the beta coefficient is significant, examine the sign of the beta. If the beta coefficient is positive, the interpretation is that for every 1-unit increase in the predictor variable, the outcome variable will increase by the beta coefficient value.

56 People vary in their perceptual-cognitive styles, which may be due to

I. the degree to which their perceptions are flexible
II. aspects of their personality
III. rigid belief
IV. field dependence or independence
V. motives

Codes

1 I, II, III and IV 2 II, III, IV and V
3 III, IV, V and I 4 V, I, II and IV

Ans. *(4)*

Exp. People vary in their perceptual-cognitive styles, which may be due to motives, the degree to which their perceptions are flexible, aspects of their personality and field dependence or independence.

Cognitive styles refer to the preferred way individual processes information. A number of cognitive styles have been identified and studied over the years. Field independence versus field dependence is probably the most well known style. It refers to a tendency to approach the environment in an analytical, as opposed to global, fashion. At a perceptual level, field independent personalities are able to distinguish figures as discrete from their backgrounds compared to field dependent individuals who experience events in an undifferentiated way. In addition, field dependent individuals have a greater social orientation relative to field independent personalities.

57 Which of the following fit into declarative memories?

I. Semantic memory
II. Short-term memory
III. Episodic memory
IV. Procedural memory

Codes

1 I and III 2 II and IV
3 I, II and III 4 All of these

Ans. *(1)*

Exp. Semantic memory and Episodic memory fit into declarative memories.

Long-term memory is not a single store and has two components: declarative (explicit) and non-declarative (implicit). Declarative memory has to do with the storage of facts, and events we have personally experienced. Recalling information from declarative memory involves some degree of conscious effort, as information must be consciously brought to mind and "declared".

Episodic memory and Semantic memory are components of declarative memory. Semantic memory involves the recall of ideas, concepts, and facts commonly regarded as general knowledge. Episodic memory, on the other hand, involves the recollection of personal events or episodes in a person's life, such as birthdays.

58 Read each of the following two statements, Assertion (A) and Reason (R) and indicate your answer using the codes given below :

Assertion (A) In operant conditioning, the rat presses the bar spontaneously.

Reason (R) Shaping is a procedure in which rewards gradually guide an animal's behaviour toward a desired goal.

Codes

1 Both (A) and (R) are true and (R) is the correct explanation of (A)
2 Both (A) and (R) are true, but (R) is not the correct explanation of (A)
3 (A) is true, but (R) is false
4 (A) is false, but (R) is true

Ans. *(4)*

Exp. (A) is false, but (R) is true.

In operant conditioning, the rat presses the bar spontaneously. It is false, because the rat presses the bar deliberately based on the reinforcement (e.g., food on pellet) or punishment (e.g., electric shock) the rat receives.

Shaping is a procedure in which rewards gradually guide an animal's behaviour toward a desired goal.

It is a technique that is used in operant conditioning in which the behaviour is modified by stepwise reinforcement of behaviours that produce progressively closer approximations of the desired behaviour.

59 According to cognitive approach, the role of a teacher is to

I. correct wrong answers
II. correct misconceptions
III. facilitate and supervise
IV. teach effective strategies

Codes

1 I and III 2 I and IV
3 II and III 4 II and IV

Ans. *(4)*

➲ *Exp.* According to cognitive approach, the role of a teacher is to correct misconceptions and teach effective strategies. The Cognitive Learning Theory explains why the brain is the most incredible network of information processing and interpretation in the body as we learn things. When we say the word 'learning', we usually mean 'to think using the brain'.

Cognitive Learning Theory implies that the different processes concerning learning can be explained by analysing the mental processes first.

It posits that with effective cognitive processes, learning is easier and new information can be stored in the memory for a long time. On the other hand, ineffective cognitive processes result to learning difficulties that can be seen anytime during the lifetime of an individual.

60 Match List I and List II and indicate your correct choice by using codes given below:

List I (Theories of Motivation)	List II (Characteristics)
A. Drive theories	I. Pulling by goal
B. Incentive theories	II. Information
C. Opponent process theories	III. Hedonic
D. Cognitive (social)	IV. Pushing toward goal

Codes

	A	B	C	D
1	I	II	III	IV
2	IV	I	III	II
3	II	I	III	IV
4	IV	III	I	II

Ans. *(2)*

➲ *Exp.* The correct matching is A-IV, B-I, C-III, D-II.

Drive theories focus on pushing toward goal. According to the drive theory of motivation, people are motivated to take certain actions in order to reduce the internal tension that is caused by unmet needs.

Incentive theories focus on pulling by goal. The incentive theory of motivation is a behavioural theory that suggests people are motivated by a drive for incentives and reinforcement. It also proposes that people behave in a way they believe will result in a reward and avoid actions that may entail punishment.

Opponent process theories are hedonic in nature. The theory assumes that many hedonic, affective, or emotional states are automatically opposed by Central Nervous system mechanisms which reduce the intensity of hedonic feelings, both pleasant and aversive.

Cognitive (social) theories is based on information. The theory postulates that internal processes lead to behavioural outcomes. The conceptual framework is based on reciprocal interactions between variables.

61 Match List I with List II and select the correct answer from the codes given below :

List I	List II
A. Mitwelt	I. A person exists in a given particular place at a particular time. Being conscious of it, one can choose the direction of one's life
B. Dasein	II. The experiences and meaning we share with others through our relationships
C. Unwelt	III. Unique presence of human beings of self-awareness and self-relatedness
D. Eigenwelt	IV. The biological and natural environment for human beings and animals including biological needs, drives and instincts

Codes

	A	B	C	D
1	I	IV	III	II
2	III	II	I	IV
3	II	I	IV	III
4	IV	II	III	I

Ans. *(3)*

➲ *Exp.* The correct matching is A-II, B-I, C-IV, D-III.

Mitwelt is the experiences and meaning we share with others through our relationships. It is the aspect that is constituted by a person's relationships and interactions with other people.

Dasein is a concept indicating that a person exists in a given particular place at a particular time. Being conscious of it, one can choose the direction of one's life. It is the particular kind of being manifest in humans. It allows humans access to the larger question of being in general, since access to the world is always through what their own being makes possible.

Unwelt is the biological and natural environment for human beings and animals including biological needs, drives and instincts. It is that aspect of Dasein (being-in-the-world) that is constituted by a person's engagement with the world immediately around him or her.

Eigenwelt is the unique presence of human beings of self-awareness and self-relatedness. It is that aspect of Dasein (being-in-the-world) that is constituted by a person's relationship to the self.

62 Intelligence is necessary but not sufficient condition for creativity. It represents

1 Threshold Theory
2 Certification Theory
3 Interference Theory
4 Collaborative Theory

Ans. *(1)*

➲ *Exp.* Intelligence is necessary but not sufficient condition for creativity. It represents the Threshold Theory.

The Threshold Theory, which holds that above a certain level, intelligence doesn't have much effect on creativity: most creative people are pretty smart but they don't have to be that smart, at least as measured by conventional intelligence tests. An IQ of 120, indicating that someone is very smart but not exceptionally so, is generally considered sufficient for creative genius. According to Threshold Theory, not necessarily being in the top 1 per cent of intelligence has no correlation with being fantastically creative. Rather, there is a minimum Threshold of intelligence that you need to have and after that it comes down to a lot of deliberate practice, putting in your reps and developing your skill set.

63 In which of the following disorders, a person has two or more different personalities and either of which is dominant at a time?

1 Dissociative amnesia
2 Split personality
3 Dissociative identity disorder
4 Schizophrenia

Ans. (3)

Exp. In dissociative identity disorder, a person has two or more different personalities and either of which is dominant at a time.

Dissociative Identity Disorder (DID), previously known as Multiple Personality Disorder (MPD), is a mental disorder characterised by at least two distinct and relatively enduring identities or dissociated personality states that alternately show in a person's behaviour, accompanied by memory impairment for important information not explained by ordinary forgetfulness. These symptoms are not accounted for by substance abuse, seizures other medical conditions, nor by imaginative play in children. Diagnosis is often difficult as there is considerable comorbidity with other mental disorders.

64 What is not true of facial feedback hypothesis of emotions?

1 Acting as another acts does not help us feel what another feels
2 Facial expressions influence our emotional experience
3 To be empathic mimic other's emotional expressions
4 Professional actors exhibit expression specific autonomic nervous system changes

Ans. (1)

Exp. Acting as another acts does not help us feel what another feels is not true of facial feedback hypothesis of emotions .

The facial feedback hypothesis is the theory of emotion that assumes that facial expressions provide feedback to the brain concerning the emotion being expressed, which in turn causes and intensifies the emotion. At an inter-person level, facial feedback may be involved in transferring emotional states between people through a process that, via mimicking and facial feedback, results in emotional contagion. The facial feedback hypothesis asserts facial expressions are not only the results of our emotions but are also capable of influencing our emotions. In other words, the act of smiling can itself actually makes you feel happier.

65 Which is not a characteristic symptom of Narcolepsy?

1 Cataplexy
2 Sleep paralysis
3 Nocturnal myoclonus
4 Hypnagogic hallucinations

Ans. (3)

Exp. Nocturnal myoclonus is not a characteristic symptom of Narcolepsy.

The Nocturnal Myoclonus Syndrome (NMS) consists of stereotyped, repetitive jerks of the lower limbs that occur during sleep or wakefulness. NMS is often related with Restless-legs syndrome (RLS) and can cause severe sleep disturbances and daytime sleepiness.

Narcolepsy is a sleep disorder characterised by excessive sleepiness, sleep paralysis, hallucinations, and in some cases episodes of cataplexy (partial or total loss of muscle control, often triggered by a strong emotion such as laughter). In narcolepsy, the normal boundary between awake and asleep is blurred.

66 In a study, 25 subjects performed the same task under three conditions–relaxed, moderately stressed and highly stressed. The suitable analysis of variance was carried out. The degrees of freedom for the conditions *X* subjects interaction (used as an estimate of error variance) would be

1 24   2 48   3 72   4 74

Ans. (2)

Exp. The degrees of freedom would be 48.

The formula for calculating degrees of freedom is, df = (n-1) (m-1), where 'n' is the number of conditions and 'm' is the number of subjects. Putting the values of n =3, m =25 in the formula, df = (3-1) (25-1) = 2 x 24 = 48.

67 Which one of the following is not included in Hackman and Oldham's Job characteristics model of work motivation?

1 Variety of skill
2 Significance of the task
3 Quality of job life
4 Autonomy

Ans. (3)

Exp. Quality of job life is not included in Hackman and Oldham's Job characteristics model of work motivation.

The Job characteristics model, designed by Hackman and Oldham, is based on the idea that the task itself is key to employee motivation. Specifically, a boring and monotonous job stifles motivation to perform well, whereas a challenging job enhances motivation. Variety, autonomy and decision authority are three ways of adding challenge to a job. Job enrichment and job rotation are the two ways of adding variety and challenge. It states that there are five core job characteristics (i.e., skill variety, task identity, task significance, autonomy and feedback).

68 Which is the correct sequence of stages involved in creative thinking?

1 Preparation, Orientation, Illumination, Verification , Incubation
2 Preparation, Incubation, Illumination, Orientation Verification
3 Orientation, Preparation, Incubation, Illumination, Verification
4 Orientation, Preparation, Illumination, Incubation, Verification

Ans. (3)

Exp. The correct sequence of stages involved in creative thinking are explained below:

1. *Orientation* : In this stage, the individual identifies the problem that must be solved. After identification, the problem is defined that involves producing as many questions as possible.
2. *Preparation* : In this stage, the individual defines the problem and gathers information in order to solve it. Failing to solve the problem, the thinker turns away from it initiating next stage.
3. *Incubation* : This is a time of solitude and relaxation, where idea associations take place at a subconscious level. During this period some of the ideas that were interfering with the solution will tend to fade. The overt activity and sometimes even thinking about the problem is absent in this stage.
4. *Illumination*: The process once again becomes conscious in the stage of ideation, with the generation of further ideas, which are not necessarily judged or assessed. The individual then experiences an illumination or insight (Eureka!) with the emergence of an idea, an image or a solution.
5. *Verification* : In this stage, new ideas are tested and verified, leading to the elaboration of a solution and to its production.

69 Which of the following is not correct for the Piaget's theory?

1 Disequilibrium terminates in structural change
2 Individual stages of development cannot be skipped or omitted from the sequence
3 Stages of equilibrium do not last as long as stages of disequilibrium
4 Later stages are independent of the elements and experiences of early stages

Ans. (4)

Exp. Later stages are not independent of the elements and experiences of early stages is not correct about Piaget's theory. The later stages evolve from the previous stage.

Disequilibrium terminates in structural change : The structure change places the organism in a position of stability, but the stability lasts for only a short period.

Individual stages of development cannot be skipped or omitted from the sequence : An individual cannot progress from an earlier stage of development to a later one without going through any intermediate stages.

Stages of equilibrium do not last as long as stages of disequilibrium : If the process of equilibrium or equilibration is the primary motivator, one might theorise that the organism spends more time in a state of imbalance than in a state of stability. Certain periods of growth (such as adolescence) are characterised by abrupt changes. These changes, however, are usually preceded by periods of some stability.

70 Match the List I with List II and select the correct answer by choosing from the codes given below :

List I	List II
A. Knowing one's emotions	I. Having skills in managing emotions of others
B. Motivating oneself	II. Handling feelings and emotions so they are appropriate
C. Managing emotions	III. Marshalling emotions in service of goal
D. Handling relationships	IV. Monitoring feelings from moment to moment

Codes

	A	B	C	D		A	B	C	D
1	IV	III	II	I	2	I	II	III	IV
3	I	III	IV	II	4	II	III	I	IV

Ans. (1)

Exp. The correct matching is A-IV, B-III, C-II, D-I.

Knowing one's emotions is monitoring feelings from moment to moment. Psychologists Salovey and Mayer defined emotional intelligence as the "ability to monitor one's own and others' feelings and emotions, to discriminate among them, and to use this information to guide one's thinking and actions."

Motivating oneself is marshalling emotions in service of goal. Goleman defined emotional intelligence as "Marshalling emotions in the service of a goal is essential for paying attention, for self-motivation and mastery, and for creativity".

Managing emotions is handling feelings and emotions so they are appropriate. According to Goleman, 'Management of Emotions' component of Emotional Intelligence includes handling feelings, so that they are appropriate, ability to soothe oneself and the ability to shake off rampant anxiety, gloom or irritability.

Handling relationships is having skills in managing emotions of others. Reuven's Bar-On's conceptual model describes an array of interrelated emotional and social competencies that determine how effective individuals are at understanding and expressing themselves, understanding others and interacting with them as well as coping with daily demands and challenges.

Directions (Q. Nos. 71-75) *Read the following paragraph and answer the questions that follows :*

The most popular method of measuring attitudes is to administer the attitude scale. Although, Bogardus Social Distance Scale (1925) is one of the first attitude scales, a major breakthrough in attitude scaling was made by LL Thurstone who developed the Law of Comparative Judgement (LCJ) and also proposed the three scaling methods—paired comparison, equal appearing intervals and successive intervals. In the paired comparison, every statement/stimulus is paired with every other statement/stimulus.

The computational methods of paired comparison are most extensively developed and use Thurstone's LCJ directly for this purpose. Since, the paired comparison method has limitations in scaling large number of statements/stimuli, the two other methods-equal appearing intervals and successive intervals-were developed by Thurstone. The method of successive intervals was computationally labourious in the pre-computer era and hence, it was not so popular. In the classical scaling tradition, Guttmann developed the scalogram technique and Edwards developed the scale discrimination technique.

Likert's development of summated ratings represent an important landmark in attitude measurement. It follows the traditional psychometric model.

Aiken and Groth-Marnatt (2009) pointed out that other scaling techniques, less frequently used for attitude assessment, include Osgood's semantic differential, Q-sort, magnitude estimation, expectancy value scaling, facet analysis, multi-dimensional scaling etc.

71 If eleven attitude statements are to be scaled by the method of paired comparison, what would be the number of pairs?

1 11   2 55
3 110   4 121

Ans. (2)

Exp. If eleven attitude statements are to be scaled by the method of paired comparison 55 will be the number of pairs.

The numbers of pairs can be calculated using the formula, $\frac{n[n-1]}{2}$, where n is the number of items. Here, $n = 11$.

Number of pairs $= \frac{11-[10]}{2} = 55$

72 In which of the scaling method, item-remainder correlations are frequently calculated?

1 Equal appearing intervals
2 Paired comparison
3 Successive intervals
4 Summated ratings

Ans. (4)

Exp. Item-remainder correlations are frequently calculated in Summated ratings.

The item-remainder coefficient is the correlation of each item with the sum of the remaining items. For a scale with 10 items, the item-remainder for Item 1 would be calculated by correlating responses to Item 1 with the sum of responses to Items 2 through 10.

Summated rating is a type of assessment instrument comprising a series of statements measuring the same construct or variable to which respondents indicate their degree of agreement or disagreement. A Likert scale is the most commonly used summated rating scale.

73 Read each of the following two statements, Assertion (A) and Reason (R) and indicate your answer using the codes given below:

Assertion (A) In method of equal appearing intervals, median is often used as a measure of scale value.

Reason (R) In normal distribution mean, median and mode are equal.

Codes

1 Both (A) and (R) are true and (R) is the correct explanation of (A)
2 Both (A) and (R) are true, but (R) is not the correct explanation of (A)
3 (A) is true, but (R) is false
4 (A) is false, but (R) is true

Ans. (2)

Exp. Both (A) and (R) are true, but (R) is not the correct explanation of (A).

In equal appearing intervals, any attitude involves a continuum ranging from the strongest possible appreciation of a value at one extreme to the strongest possible depreciation of that value at the other. Thurstone devised a scaling procedure which attempted to divide any given attitude into a number of equal appearing intervals, and so give respondents a scale-value according to their responses to the statements in a particular attitude or value-set. In case of equal appearing intervals, we take median and quartiles. Hence, the Assertion is true.

In normal distribution mean, median and mode are equal. It is true but it does not explain why we use median as a measure of scale value in method of equal appearing intervals.

74 Which one of the following techniques usually yields multi-dimensional attitude scales?

1 Summated ratings
2 Paired comparison
3 Equal appearing intervals
4 Scalogram

Ans. (1)

Exp. Summated ratings technique usually yields multi-dimensional attitude scales.

Many constructs are quite broad and may contain multiple aspects or dimensions. Attitudes toward complex things (such as government, jobs, families, and life in general) can contain many facets. To adequately express their attitudes and opinions, people may need multiple dimensions, reflected in multiple subscales. For the same purpose, summated rating technique can be used.

75 Which of the following techniques is/are well-known for being associated with cumulative scales?

I. Bogardus Social Distance Scales
II. Likert's Summated Ratings
III. Guttman's Scalogram Analysis
IV. Osgood's Semantic Differential

Codes

1 Only I	2 I and II
3 I and III	4 II, III and IV

Ans. (3)

Exp. The following techniques is/are well-known for being associated with cumulative scales:

Borgadus Social Distance Scales is a psychological testing scale created by Emory S. Bogardus to empirically measure people's willingness to participate in social contacts of varying degrees of closeness with members of diverse social groups, such as racial and ethnic groups.

Guttman's Scalogram Analysis is also sometimes known as cumulative scaling or scalogram analysis. The purpose of Guttman scaling is to establish a one-dimensional continuum for a concept to be measured. This is typically done in a 'Yes/No' dichotomous format.

UGC-NET PSYCHOLOGY

SOLVED PAPER 2014 (December)

PAPER II

1 The California F-Scale measures

1 the qualities associated with feminine characteristics
2 the tendency for seeking sensation
3 a person's proneness to being rigid and authoritarian
4 the qualities of extrovertion

Ans. (3)

Exp. The California F-Scale measures a person's proneness to being rigid and authoritarian.

The California F-scale is a 1947 personality test, designed by Theodor W. Adorno and others to measure the 'authoritarian personality'. The F-scale measures responses on several different components of authoritarianism, such as conventionalism, authoritarian aggression, anti-intraception, superstition, destructiveness, cynicism, projectivity, etc.

2 Raven's Standard Progressive Matrices is presumed to measure

1 Crystallised Intelligence
2 Convergent Thinking
3 General Intelligence
4 Spatial Reasoning

Ans. (3)

Exp. Raven's Standard Progressive Matrices is presumed to measure General intelligence.

Raven's Standard Progressive Matrices is a non-verbal test typically used to measure general human intelligence and abstract reasoning and is regarded as a non-verbal estimate of fluid intelligence. The test covers two main types of intelligence: educative ability (existing knowledge) and reproductive ability (ability to remember, retain and reproduce).

3 A projection apparatus used to show visual stimuli for very brief durations is called

1 Visual cliff
2 Tachistoscope
3 EEG Apparatus
4 Trapezoidal window

Ans. (2)

Exp. A projection apparatus used to show visual stimuli for very brief durations is called Tachistoscope.

It is an instrument used for exposing objects to the eye for a very brief measured period of time. It can be used to increase recognition speed, to show something too fast to be consciously recognised or to test which elements of an image are memorable.

4 Match List I with List II and select the correct answer by choosing from the codes given below :

List I (Authors)	List II (Concepts)
A. Cattell	I. General and specific factors
B. Spearman	II. Fluid and crystallised intelligence
C. Gardner	III. Triarchic theory of intelligence
D. Sternberg	IV. Multiple Intelligence theory

Codes

	A	B	C	D
1	I	III	IV	II
2	II	I	IV	III
3	III	IV	II	I
4	IV	III	II	I

Ans. (2)

Exp. The correct matching is A-II, B-I, C-IV, D-III.

Cattell is associated with the concept of fluid and crystallised intelligence. Fluid intelligence refers to the application of intellectual abilities to new situations, which is tested through tasks such as completing mazes, solving puzzles and analysing relationships. Crystallised intelligence refers to the knowledge and information acquired through education and experience, which is tested through tasks such as vocabulary, general information and reading comprehension.

Spearman is associated with the concept of General and specific factors. Charles Spearman (1927) argued that intelligence is a general ability that is applied to all kinds of tasks. He called this general cognitive ability the 'g' factor. Though Spearman recognised some specific abilities, which he called's' factor, he emphasised the role of general intellectual ability in influencing performance on intellectual tasks.

Gardner is associated with the concept of Multiple Intelligence theory. Howard Gardner (1999) proposed a theory of multiple intelligences in which he identified eight distinct types of intelligence: Linguistic Ability, Spatial Ability, Bodily-kinesthetic Ability, Intrapersonal Ability, Musical Ability, Interpersonal Ability, Logical/mathematical Ability, and Naturalistic Ability.

Sternberg is associated with the concept of Triarchic theory of intelligence. Robert Sternberg (1985) proposed a Triarchic theory of intelligence in which he identified three types of intelligence: analytical, practical and creative.

5 Match List I with List II and select the correct answer by choosing from the codes given below :

List I (Parts of Human Brain)		List II (Functions)
A. Thalamus	I.	Plays a special role in memory
B. Medulla	II.	Involved in mediating emotions
C. Hippocampus	III.	Helps in control sleeps and wakefulness
D. Amygdala	IV.	Helps the organism to maintain upright position

Codes

	A	B	C	D
1	III	IV	I	II
2	IV	III	I	II
3	IV	I	II	III
4	I	IV	III	II

Ans. *(1)*

Exp. The correct matching is A-III, B-IV, C-I, D-II.

Thalamus helps in control sleeps and wakefulness. It has several functions, such as the relaying of sensory signals, including motor signals to the cerebral cortex, and the regulation of consciousness, sleep, and alertness.

Medulla helps the organism to maintain upright position. Medulla plays a role in proprioception (or kinesthesia) which is the sense through which we perceive the position and movement of our body, including our sense of equilibrium and balance.

Hippocampus plays a special role in memory. It is involved in processing new information and storing new memories. It plays an integral role in learning.

Amygdala is involved in mediating emotions. It governs initial emotional reactions to events, particularly fear and aggression.

6 Some factors that influence the effectiveness of rewards are

I. Magnitude of the reward

II. Reward delay

III. Successive approximation

IV. Need

Codes

1 I, II and IV   2 II and IV

3 I and II   4 II, III and IV

Ans. *(1)*

Exp. Magnitude of the reward, reward delay and need are the factors that influence the effectiveness of rewards.

Magnitude of reward refers to the proportion of the amount of effort that one puts into a task compared to the proportion of the expected outcome or reward. If the reward is less than the effort, then the person would be less motivated to do the task.

Reward delay refers to the process associated with resisting a smaller but more immediate reward in order to receive a larger or more enduring reward later.

Need of a person also a plays an important role. It refers to the extent to which the person perceives the reward as being useful to his or her needs, the more the person would be motivated to achieve it.

7 Which of the following descriptions are correct?

I. Weber's Ratio means that greater the magnitude of a stimulus, smaller the change required for a difference to be detected.

II. The ability to detect, resolve and perceive fine details of a visual display is called visual acuity.

III. Stimulation of a succession of neighbouring retinal loci is called the image retina movement system.

IV. Adaptation refers to the proportion of incident light that is reflected.

Select the correct answer using the codes given below :

1 I and IV are correct   2 II and I are correct

3 IV and III are correct   4 II and III are correct

Ans. *(4)*

Exp. Statement II and III are correct.

The ability to detect, resolve and perceive fine details of a visual display is called visual acuity. Visual acuity is a measure of the ability of the eye to distinguish shapes and the details of objects at a given distance.

Stimulation of a succession of neighbouring retinal loci is called the image retina movement system. It is a subsystem of the visual system, based on direction-sensitive neurons, that computes the movement of objects from the movement of images across the retina, but that is unable on its own to distinguish between retinal movements caused by movements in the environment.

Statement I and IV are incorrect.

Weber's Ratio means that greater the magnitude of a stimulus, greater is the change required for a difference to be detected.

Adaptation occurs when sensory receptors reduce their responsiveness to a stimulus after repeated or continuous exposure. Reflectance refers to the proportion of incident light that is reflected.

8 Read each of the following two statements, Assertion (A) and Reason (R) and indicate your answer using the codes given below :

Assertion (A) Both, context dependent memory and state dependent retrieval refer to the ease with which one can recall information in a similar context or state as when it was acquired.

Reason (R) According to encoding specificity principle retrieval of information is successful to the extent that the retrieval cues match the cues the learner used during the learning phase.

Codes

1 Both (A) and (R) are true and (R) is the correct explanation of (A)
2 Both (A) and (R) are true, but (R) is not the correct explanation of (A)
3 (A) is true, but (R) is false
4 (A) is false, but (R) is true

Ans. (1)

Exp. Both (A) and (R) are true and (R) is the correct explanation of (A).

Both, context dependent memory and state dependent retrieval refer to the ease with which one can recall information in a similar context or state as when it was acquired. Cognitive psychologists point out that when information is encoded, features of the context surrounding the information are also encoded (for example, where the information was, who provided the information and so on). These same features of context can be used later to aid in retrieval of stored information.

According to encoding specificity principle retrieval of information is successful to the extent that the retrieval cues match the cues the learner used during the learning phase. In 1983, Tulving proposed the Encoding Specificity hypothesis, which states that memory of information is improved if the cues present during learning are also present at the time of retrieval because those cues can be used to facilitate retrieval.

9 Cognition refers to the mental activity associated with ____ , understanding and _____ information.

1 processing; sending
2 passing; sending
3 processing; communicating
4 passing; communicating

Ans. (3)

Exp. Cognition refers to the mental activity associated with processing, understanding and communicating information.

Congnition refers to the mental processes involved in gaining knowledge and comprehension. These processes include thinking, knowing, remembering, judging and problem-solving. These are higher-level functions of the brain and encompass language, imagination, perception and planning. Cognitive psychology is the study of mental processes such as attention, language use, memory, perception, problem-solving, creativity and thinking.

10 The left hemisphere is more skilled at

1 seeing the forest not the trees
2 interpreting speech and language
3 analysing the melodies
4 judging the symmetry in a photograph

Ans. (2)

Exp. The left hemisphere is more skilled at interpreting speech and language.

In general, the left hemisphere or side of the brain is responsible for language and speech. Because of this, it has been called the 'dominant' hemisphere. There is an area in the frontal lobe of the left hemisphere called Broca's area. If this area is destroyed, a person will have difficulty producing the sounds of speech, because of the inability to move the tongue or facial muscles to form words. There is a region in the left temporal lobe called Wernicke's area. Damage to this area causes Wernicke's aphasia in which an individual can make speech sounds, but they are meaningless (receptive aphasia) because they do not make any sense. The right hemisphere plays a large part in interpreting visual information and spatial processing.

11 The perception that one is worse off relative to those with whom one compares oneself refers to

1 Constant deprivation
2 Continuous deprivation
3 Marginal deprivation
4 Relative deprivation

Ans. (4)

Exp. The perception that one is worse off relative to those with whom one compares oneself refers to Relative deprivation.

It is the experience of being deprived of something to which one believes to be entitled. It refers to the discontent people feel when they compare their positions to others and realise that they have less of what they believe themselves to be entitled than those around them.

12 On a Wechsler type intelligence scale Arish has a deviation IQ of 115. If the norms of this test are expressed in terms of normalised T scores (mean = 50, SD = 10), what would be the T score of Arish?

1 40   2 60   3 65   4 84

Ans. (2)

Exp. The T score of Arish will be 60.

Deviation IQ are a standard score with mean of 100 and a standard deviation of 15.

The formula for calculating Deviation IQ is

Deviation IQ = 100 + 15 (Z)

Putting the value of Deviation IQ = 115, we can calculate the value of Z.

$$115 = 100 + 15\,(Z)$$
$$Z = 1$$

The formula for calculating T score is

$$T \text{ score} = 50 + 10\,(Z)$$

Putting $Z = 1$, we can calculate T score.

T score $= 50 + 10(1)$

T score $= 60$

13 Read each of the following two statements, Assertion (A) and Reason (R) and indicate your answer using the codes given below :

Assertion (A) The squared correlation between the true score and the obtained score is called reliability index.

Reason (R) According to the Classical Reliability theory, the mean of the true scores and the mean of the obtained scores are equal.

Codes

1 Both (A) and (R) are true and (R) is correct explanation of (A)
2 Both (A) and (R) are true, but (R) is not the correct explanation of (A)
3 (A) is true, but (R) is false
4 (A) is false, but (R) is true

***Ans.* (3)**

Exp. (A) is true, but (R) is false.

The squared correlation between the true score and the obtained score is called reliability index. The index of reliability is a statistic that provides a theoretical estimate of the correlation between actual scores of a psychometric test and the assumed true scores. Reliability is the (squared) correlation between observed scores and true scores error scores $R_{xx} = r^2$.

According to the Classical Reliability theory, the mean of the true scores and the mean of the obtained scores are equal. This is false, because it occurs only when the error is considered to be zero.

14 Read each of the following two statements, Assertion (A) and Reason (R) and indicate your answer using the codes given below :

Assertion (A) Creative people usually have a broad range of knowledge about lot of subjects and are good at using mental imagery.

Reason (R) Creative people are often unconventional and value their autonomy.

Codes

1 Both (A) and (R) are true and (R) is correct explanation of (A)
2 Both (A) and (R) are true, but (R) is not the correct explanation of (A)
3 (A) is true, but (R) is false
4 (A) is false, but (R) is true

***Ans.* (2)**

Exp. Both (A) and (R) are true, but (R) is not the correct explanation of (A).

Creative people usually have a broad range of knowledge about lot of subjects and are good at using mental imagery. According to Csikszentmihalyi (1997), creative people usually have a broad range of knowledge about a lot of subjects and are good at using mental imagery. Mental imagery refers to mental images that are representations for objects or events used in mental activities and are interacted with in similar ways as physical objects (e.g., scanning a map or rotating an object).

Creative people are often unconventional and value their autonomy. Csikszentmihalyi (1997) also stated that creative people value their independence and are often unconventional in their work, but not otherwise. The reason statement is true, but it does not explain the given assertion.

15 Which of the following are problems with punishment?

I. The effect of punishment is often temporary.
II. Severe punishment creates fear and anxiety.
III. Mild punishment is paired with reinforcement of the correct behaviour.
IV. Aggressive punishment can model aggressive behaviour.

Codes

1 I and IV
2 II and III
3 II, III and IV
4 I, II and IV

***Ans.* (4)**

Exp. Statement I, II and IV contains the problems with punishment.

The effect of punishment is often temporary. Any behaviour changes that result from punishment are often temporary. Punished behaviour is likely to reappear after the punitive consequences are withdrawn.

Severe punishment creates fear and anxiety. Many studies have shown that severe punishment can lead to negative and adverse outcomes like fear, anxiety, increased aggression, antisocial behaviour, physical injury and mental health problems.

Aggressive punishment can model aggressive behaviour. Punishment over a long period of time can lead to learning of aggressive behaviour and the victim in turn can become aggressive too.

Mild punishment is paired with reinforcement of the correct behaviour. This is not a problem with punishment. It is a procedure involving the response-contingent presentation of a mild aversive stimulus, reinforcement of alternative behaviours, and training for stimulus control.

16 A numerical ability test with 50 items has a Cronbach alpha of .80. If the test is randomly divided into two halves of the some length, the expected correlation between the two halves would be

1 0.40
2 0.56
3 0.67
4 0.80

***Ans.* (3)**

Exp. The expected correlation between the two halves would be 0.67.

Cronbach's alpha is a measure of internal consistency, that is, how closely related a set of items are as a group. It is considered to be a measure of scale reliability.

Cronbach's alpha can be calculated by the formula:

$$\alpha = \frac{k \cdot r}{1 + (k-1) \cdot r}$$

where, $k = 50$, $\alpha = 0.80$

$$\alpha = \frac{50 \times r}{1 + 49 \times r}$$

$$0.8 = \frac{50r}{1 + 49r}$$

$$r = 0.074$$

When the test is divided into two equal halves, the value of k becomes 25.

$\therefore$ New Cronbach $\alpha = \dfrac{25 \times r}{1 + (25 - 1)\, r}$

Putting the value of $r = 0.074$

$$\alpha = \frac{25 \times 0.074}{1 + 24 \times 0.074} = 0.664 \sim 0.67$$

17 Organising items into familiar, manageable units, often automatically, is termed

1 Priming
2 Chunking
3 Shaping
4 Encoding

Ans. (2)

Exp. Organising items into familiar, manageable units, often automatically, is termed as Chunking.

Chunking is the strategy that can be used to improve a person's short-term memory. It involves reducing long strings of information that can be difficult to remember down into shorter, more manageable chunks.

18 Match List I with List II and select the correct answer by choosing from the codes given below :

List I (Memory Modules)	List II (Descriptions)
A. Episodic memory	I. Memory system that retains information we cannot readily express verbally.
B. Semantic memory	II. Memory for factual information that we acquired at a specific time.
C. Autobiographical memory	III. Memory system that stores general abstract knowledge about the world.
D. Procedural memory	IV. Memory for information about events in our own life.

Codes

	A	B	C	D
1	III	IV	I	II
2	IV	II	III	I
3	II	III	IV	I
4	I	II	IV	III

Ans. (3)

Exp. The correct matching is A-II, B-III, C-IV, D-I.

Episodic memory is memory for factual information that we acquired at a specific time. Episodic memory stores information about personal life experiences and events.

Semantic memory is memory system that stores general abstract knowledge about the world. It is the memory for general factual knowledge and concepts, of the kind that endows information with meaning.

Autobiographical memory is memory for information about events in our own life. It is the memory for events and facts related to one's personal life story.

Procedural memory is memory system that retains information we cannot readily express verbally. Procedural memory stores information about skills and how to do things such as how to ride a bike, how to drive and how to type.

19 Match List I with List II and select the correct answer by choosing from the codes given below :

List I (Scaling Techniques)	List II (Features)
A. Paired comparison	I. Assesses unidimensionality of the scale.
B. Equal appearing intervals	II. Suitable for assessing multi-dimensional attitudes.
C. Scalogram analysis	III. Suitable for scaling a large number of attitude items.
D. Summated ratings	IV. Employs Z scores as the measure of scale values.

Codes

	A	B	C	D
1	IV	III	II	I
2	III	IV	I	II
3	II	III	I	IV
4	IV	III	I	II

Ans. (4)

Exp. The correct matching is A-IV, B-III, C-I, D-II.

Paired comparison employs Z scores as the measure of scale values. It is a procedure in which magnitudes between pairs of stimuli are adjusted so that the differences between stimuli within each pair are perceived as equal.

Equal appearing intervals is suitable for scaling a large number of attitude items. It is a systematic procedure for comparing a set of stimuli or other items. A pair of stimuli is presented to an individual, who is asked to compare them on a particular dimension, such as size, loudness, or brightness; the process is continued until every item in the set has been compared with every other item.

Scalogram analysis assesses unidimensionality of the scale. It is a type of attitude measure that consists of multiple verbal statements ordered to reflect increasing levels of positive evaluation. Endorsement of a particular statement implies endorsement of all statements less extreme than that statement.

Summated ratings is suitable for assessing multi-dimensional attitudes. It is a type of assessment instrument comprising a series of statements measuring the same construct or variable to which respondents indicate their degree of agreement or disagreement. The response values for individual items may be summed to obtain a total or average score that reflects a person's general attitude toward the construct of interest.

20 Among the following concepts which are related to Alfred Adler's theory of personality?

I. Organ inferiority II. Psychoticism
III. Archetypes IV. Masculine protest

Codes

1 I and IV 2 II and III
3 I and II 4 IV and III

Ans. *(1)*

Exp. Concepts related to Alfred Adler's theory of personality are Organ inferiority and Masculine protests.

In one of his earliest and most famous publications, 'Study of Organ Inferiority and its Physical Compensation,' Adler outlined the basics for what would be the beginning foundation of his personality theory.

Organ inferiority was a term coined by Alfred Adler, to describe how people who found themselves born with certain physical defects develop feelings of inferiority and start taking actions to compensate for their weaknesses.

Alfred Adler created the term Masculine protest to describe the behaviour of women who reject traditional feminine roles in favour of more masculine ones. And one big reason that women (and men, too) reject roles is because they want to gain power and feel more dominant in a situation.

21 Which of the following are true of short-term memory?

I. Limited capacity
II. Brief storage of information
III. Unlimited capacity
IV. Duration of storage less than twenty seconds

Codes

1 I, III and IV
2 III and IV
3 I, II and IV
4 II and IV

Ans. *(3)*

Exp. Limited capacity, brief storage of information and duration of storage less than twenty seconds are true of short-term memory.

Short-term memory is the capacity for holding, but not manipulating, a small amount of information in mind in an active, readily available state for a short period of time. According to Atkinson and Shiffrin (1971) items can be kept in short-term memory by repeating them verbally (acoustic encoding), a process known as rehearsal. The duration of Short-Term Memory seems to be between 15 and 30 seconds and the capacity about 7 items.

22 Match List I with List II and select the correct answer by choosing from the codes given below :

List I (Theories)	List II (Descriptions)
A. James-Lange	I. Triggering the feeling of pleasure and pain simultaneously.
B. Cannon-Bard	II. Emotional experience comprise of the physiological arousal and its cognitive labelling.
C. Opponent- process	III. Emotion arising stimulus simultaneously triggers physiological responses and the subjective experience of emotion.
D. Two-factor	IV. Emotional experience refers to our awareness of our physiological responses to emotion arousing stimuli.

Codes

	A	B	C	D
1	IV	III	II	I
2	IV	II	III	I
3	III	II	IV	I
4	III	IV	I	II

Ans. *(*)*

Exp. The correct matching is A-IV, B-III, C-I, D-II.

James-Lange theory states that emotional experience refers to our awareness of our physiological responses to emotion arousing stimuli. It argues that the physiological changes in the body that accompany arousing events lead us to experience a particular emotion.

Cannon-Bard theory states that emotion arising stimulus simultaneously triggers physiological responses and the subjective experience of emotion. According to this theory, physiological arousal and the emotional experience occur simultaneously following activation of brain regions responsible for processing emotionally arousing experiences.

Opponent-process theory states that triggering the feeling of pleasure and pain occurs simultaneously. Richard Solomon developed a motivational theory based on opponent processes. Basically he states that every process that has an affective balance (i.e. pleasant or unpleasant) is followed by a secondary, 'opponent-process'.

Two-factor theory states that emotional experience comprise of the physiological arousal and its cognitive labelling. In their cognitive arousal theory (two-factor theory), Schachter and Singer (1962) proposed that two things have to happen before emotion occurs: the physical arousal and a labelling of the arousal based on cues from the surrounding environment.

23 A view of memory suggesting that the greater the effort expended in processing information will be recalled later represents

1 Neural network models of memory
2 Levels of processing model of memory
3 Multiple components model of memory
4 Three stage model of memory

Ans. *(2)*

Exp. A view of memory suggesting that the greater the effort expended in processing information will be recalled later represents levels of processing model of memory.

The Levels of processing model of memory states that encoding into memory and therefore subsequent retention depend on the depth of cognitive elaboration that the information receives and that deeper encoding improves memory. In early critical experiments, depth was achieved by processing the meaning of to-be-remembered words rather than focusing on shallower dimensions, such as the sound of the words.

24 Match List I with List II and select the correct answer by choosing from the codes given below :

List I (Concepts)		List II (Descriptions)
A. Morpheme	I.	The set of rules by which we derive meanings from morphemes, words and sentences.
B. Grammar	II.	The rules for combining words into grammatically sensible sentences.
C. Semantics	III.	The system of rules that enables us to communicate with and understand others.
D. Syntax	IV.	The smallest unit that carries meaning, may be a word or a part of word.

Codes

	A	B	C	D		A	B	C	D
1	I	II	III	IV	2	II	III	IV	I
3	III	IV	II	I	4	IV	III	I	II

Ans. *(4)*

Exp. The correct matching is A-IV, B-III, C-I, D-II.

Morpheme is the smallest unit that carries meaning, may be a word or a part of word. It is not identical to a word, and the principal difference between the two is that a morpheme may or may not stand alone, whereas a word, by definition, is freestanding.

Grammar is the system of rules that enables us to communicate with and understand others. It is the system of rules governing the structure and use of a language.

Semantics is the set of rules by which we derive meanings from morphemes, words and sentences. It is primarily the smallest grammatical unit in a language. In other words, it is the smallest meaningful unit of a language.

Syntax is the rules for combining words into grammatically sensible sentences. It is the set of rules, principles and processes that govern the structure of sentences in a given language, specifically word order. The term syntax is also used to refer to the study of such principles and processes.

25 During resting potential, cell membrane is

I. almost permeable to sodium.
II. almost permeable to potassium.
III. almost impermeable to sodium.
IV. almost impermeable to potassium.

Codes

1 I and IV
2 II and III
3 I and II
4 III and IV

Ans. *(2)*

Exp. During resting potential, cell membrane is almost permeable to potassium and almost impermeable to sodium.

The cell membrane is almost permeable to potassium. The membrane is most permeable to potassium at rest, and this leads to potassium efflux. The potassium ions leak through the membrane at a greater rate than sodium enters. There is loss of positively charged ions from the inner part of the cell membrane. The inner part of the membrane carries a relatively more negative charge than the outer part of the cell membrane.

The cell membrane is almost impermeable to sodium. The resting potential is maintained because the channels for sodium ions are closed. The membrane remains impermeable to sodium ions in the rest state.

26 Read each of the following two statements, Assertion (A) and Reason (R) and indicate your answer using the codes given below:

Assertion (A) Females score higher than males with respect to verbal activities, while males tend to score higher on visual-spatial abilities.

Reason (R) Gender differences in different abilities are due to interplay of heredity and environment.

Codes

1 Both (A) and (R) are true and (R) is the correct explanation of (A)
2 Both (A) and (R) are true, but (R) is not the correct explanation of (A)
3 (A) is true, but (R) is false
4 (A) is false, but (R) is true

Ans. *(1)*

Exp. Both (A) and (R) are true and (R) is the correct explanation of (A).

Females score higher than males with respect to verbal activities, while males tend to score higher on visual-spatial abilities. Research findings have traditionally indicated that sex differences favouring males appear in non-verbal abilities (e.g. Voyer, Voyer, & Bryden, 1995), while sex differences favouring females appear in verbal abilities (Hyde & Linn, 1988). Meta-analyses have consistently reported males to be more spatially skilled than females (Linn and Petersen, 1985; Hedges and Nowell, 1995; Voyer and Saunders, 2004; Halpern et al., 2007). So, the Assertion statement is true.

Gender differences in different abilities are due to interplay of heredity and environment. Though, the difference in both the cases was found to be almost negligible, the role of nature and nurture does play a crucial role in showing differences in the abilities of males and females. The Reason is true and explains the Assertion.

27 Mental grouping of similar objects, events or people is called

1 Cognition
2 Concept
3 Prototype
4 Thinking

Ans. (2)

Exp. Mental grouping of similar objects, events or people is called concept.

Concept is an idea that represents a class of objects or events or their properties, such as cats, walking, honesty, blue, or fast. It is a mental grouping of similar things, events and people that is used to remember and understand what things are, what they mean and what categories or groups they belong to. According to Merril and Wood, 1974, "a concept consists of a set of objects, symbols or events (referents) which have been grouped together because they share some common characteristics".

28 Read each of the following two statements, Assertion (A) and Reason (R) and indicate your answer using the codes given below :

Assertion (A) A neuron without an Axon cannot transmit information even to other neurons immediately adjacent to it.

Reason (R) Dendrite receives information from other neurons and Axons transmit it forward.

Codes

1 Both (A) and (R) are true and (R) is the correct explanation of (A)
2 Both (A) and (R) are true, but (R) is not the correct explanation of (A)
3 (A) is true, but (R) is false
4 (A) is false, but (R) is true

Ans. (4)

Exp. (A) is false, but (R) is true.

A neuron without an Axon cannot transmit information even to other neurons immediately adjacent to it. This is false as there are neurons, which do not possess axon and are still able to transmit information to other neurons via dendrites. An anaxonic neuron is a type of neuron where there is no axon or it cannot be differentiated from the dendrites.

Dendrite receives information from other neurons and Axons transmit it forward. The dendrites are covered with synapses formed by the ends of axons from other neurons. To achieve long distance, rapid communication, neurons have evolved special abilities for sending electrical signals (action potentials) along axons. This mechanism, called conduction, is how the cell body of a neuron communicates with its own terminals the axon. Communication between neurons is achieved at synapses by the process of neurotransmission.

29 A form of conditioning in which the onset of the Conditioned Stimulus (CS) precedes the onset of the Unconditioned Stimulus (UCS) and the presentation of CS and UCS does not overlap is termed as

1 Backward conditioning
2 Delayed conditioning
3 Trace conditioning
4 Simultaneous conditioning

Ans. (3)

Exp. A form of conditioning in which the onset of the Conditioned Stimulus (CS) precedes the onset of the Unconditioned Stimulus (UCS) and the presentation of CS and UCS does not overlap is termed as Trace conditioning.

It is a form of associative learning that can be induced by presenting a Conditioned stimulus (CS) and an Unconditioned Stimulus (UCS) following each other, but separated by a temporal gap. During trace conditioning, the CS and UCS do not overlap, instead the CS begins and ends before the UCS is presented.

30 Match List I with List II and select the correct answer by choosing from the codes given below :

	List I (Procedures)		List II (Behavioural Outcomes)
A.	Positive reinforcement	I.	Learn to perform responses that produce pleasant outcome.
B.	Negative reinforcement	II.	Learn to suppress responses that lead to unpleasant outcome.
C.	Positive punishment	III.	Learn to suppress responses that lead to loss or postponement of desired stimulus.
D.	Negative punishment	IV.	Learn to perform responses that permit to avoid or escape an unpleasant event.

Codes

	A	B	C	D
1	IV	III	I	II
2	I	II	IV	III
3	II	I	III	IV
4	I	IV	II	III

Ans. (4)

Exp. The correct matching is A-I, B-IV, C-II, D-III.

In *Positive reinforcement*, an individual learns to perform responses that produce pleasant outcome. It refers to the introduction of a desirable or pleasant stimulus after a behaviour. The desirable stimulus reinforces the behaviour, making it more likely that the behaviour will reoccur.

In *Negative reinforcement*, an individual learns to perform responses that permit to avoid or escape an unpleasant event. It is the encouragement of certain behaviours by removing or avoiding a negative outcome or stimuli.

In *Positive punishment*, an individual learns to suppress responses that lead to unpleasant outcome. It is adding something to the mix that will result in an unpleasant consequence. The goal is to decrease the likelihood that the unwanted behaviour will happen again in the future.

In *Negative punishment*, an individual learns to suppress responses that lead to loss or postponement of desired stimulus. It involves taking something good or desirable away to reduce the occurrence of a particular behaviour.

31 Match List I (Terms) with List II (Descriptions) and indicate your answer with the help of the codes given below :

List I (Terms)		List II (Descriptions)
A. Accommodation	I.	Certain minimum frequency of intermittent light necessary to be perceived as continuous.
B. Critical fusion frequency	II.	Refers to the level of vision formed by the target on the retina.
C. Visual angle	III.	Discrimination between lights of different wavelength compositions
D. Colour perception	IV.	Variable refractive capacity of the lens of the eye.

Codes

	A	B	C	D
1	III	II	I	IV
2	IV	II	III	I
3	II	III	IV	I
4	IV	I	II	III

Ans. (4)

Exp. The correct matching is A-IV, B-I, C-II, D-III.

Accommodation refers to variable refractive capacity of the lens of the eye. It is the ability of the eye to change the focal length of the lens by changing the curvature of the eye lens. It allows the eye to automatically adjust focus from seeing things at a distance and 'tune' it to seeing nearer objects.

Critical fusion frequency (CFF) refers to certain minimum frequency of intermittent light necessary to be perceived as continuous. It is the transition point for an intermittent light of increasing temporal frequency, where the flickering ceases and the light is perceived as continuous. If the light's modulation depth is high, then CFF is the temporal equivalent of a visual acuity measurement.

Visual angle refers to the level of vision formed by the target on the retina. It is the angle a viewed object subtends at the eye, usually stated in degrees of arc. It also is called the object's angular size.

Colour perception refers to discrimination between lights of different wavelength compositions. It is a feature of visual perception. It is an ability to perceive differences between light composed of different wavelengths independently of light intensity.

32 Match the items of List I (Concepts) with List II (Originators) and indicate your answer with the help of the codes given below :

List I (Concepts)		List II (Originators)
A. Locus of Control	I.	CG Jung
B. Learned Helplessness	II.	Abraham Maslow
C. Deficiency Needs	III.	Martin Seligman
D. Archetypes	IV.	Julian Rotter

Codes

	A	B	C	D
1	I	II	III	IV
2	III	II	I	IV
3	IV	III	II	I
4	III	I	IV	II

Ans. (3)

Exp. The correct matching is A-IV, B-III, C-II, D-I.

Locus of Control is associated with Julian Rotter. It is a psychological concept that refers to how strongly people believe they have control over the situations and experiences that affect their lives.

Learned Helplessness is associated with Martin Seligman. It is a basic principle of behavioural theory, demonstrating that prior learning can result in a drastic change in behaviour and seeking to explain why individuals may accept and remain passive in negative situations despite their clear ability to change them.

Deficiency Needs is associated with Abraham Maslow. These are the biological and physiological needs - air, food, drink, shelter, warmth, sex, sleep in Maslow's theory of Need Hierarchy.

Archetypes are associated with CG Jung. The contents of the collective unconscious are called archetypes.

33 Read each of the following two statements, Assertion (A) and Reason (R) and indicate your answer using the codes given below :

Assertion (A) Shaping and chaining can be used to establish any form of behaviour in any organism.

Reason (R) 'Instinctive drift' is a tendency to return to the type of behaviour the organism displays under natural conditions.

Codes

1 Both (A) and (R) are true and (R) is correct explanation of (A)
2 Both (A) and (R) are true, but (R) is not the correct explanation of (A)
3 (A) is true, but (R) is false
4 (A) is false, but (R) is true

Ans. (4)

Exp. (A) is false, but (R) is true.

Shaping and chaining can be used to establish any form of behaviour in any organism. Shaping is a procedure in which reinforcement is provided for a correct response and reinforcement is withheld for responses that are not in the class of the target behaviour. Chaining is a sequences of responses in which each response produces a stimulus change that functions as conditioned reinforcement for that response and as discriminative stimulus for the next response in the chain. However, all behaviours in any organism can not be developed through these two techniques. Both shaping and chaining have certain conditions which needs to be fulfilled before establishing and learning a new behaviour. Both shaping and chaining cannot be used to establish any kind of behaviour.

'Instinctive drift' is a tendency to return to the type of behaviour the organism displays under natural conditions. Very often conditioned behaviour is easily over taken by the instinctual or the natural behaviour. Instinctive drift, alternately known as instinctual drift, is the tendency of an animal to revert to unconscious and automatic behaviour that interferes with learned behaviour from operant conditioning. Instinctive drift is a phenomenon where such conditioning erodes and an animal reverts to its natural behaviour. Hence, the reason statement is true.

34 Read each of the following two statements, Assertion (A) and Reason (R) and indicate your answer using the codes given below :

Assertion (A) Motion Parallax is the relative apparent motion of objects in the visual field as the viewer moves his head.

Reason (R) Motion Parallax is a monocular spatial cue.

Codes

1 Both (A) and (R) are true and (R) is correct explanation of (A)
2 Both (A) and (R) are true, but (R) is not the correct explanation of (A)
3 (A) is true, but (R) is false
4 (A) is false, but (R) is true

Ans. (2)

Exp. Both (A) and (R) are true, but (R) is not the correct explanation of (A).

Motion Parallax is the relative apparent motion of objects in the visual field as the viewer moves his head. Motion parallax refers to the fact that objects moving at a constant speed across the frame will appear to move a greater amount if they are closer to an observer (or camera) than they would if they were at a greater distance.

Motion Parallax is a monocular spatial cue. Monocular cues require only one eye and include signals about the state of the ciliary muscles, atmospheric perspective, linear perspective, and occlusion of distant objects by near objects. Motion parallax is a monocular spatial cue that results from our motion. The reason statement is true but it does not explain why motion parallax is the relative apparent motion of objects.

35 Major connections in the visual system of the brain are

I. optic chiasm
II. lateral geniculate nucleus of thalamus
III. medial geniculate nucleus
IV. superior colliculus
V. inferior colliculus

Codes

1 I, II and IV
2 I, II and V
3 I, III and IV
4 II, III and IV

Ans. (1)

Exp. Major connections in the visual system of the brain are optic chiasm, lateral geniculate nucleus of thalamus, and superior colliculus.

The *optic chiasm* or optic chiasma is an X-shaped space just infront of the pituitary gland where optic nerve fibers pass through to the brain. Crucial to vision, the left and right optic nerves intersect at the chiasm.

The *Lateral Geniculate Nucleus (LGN) of thalamus* is a relay center in the thalamus for the visual pathway. It receives a major sensory input from the retina. The LGN is the main central connection for the optic nerve to the occipital lobe.

The *Superior colliculus* helps in the control of eye movements. It has a general role in the control of gaze, including combined movements of the eyes and head.

36 Ceci's Bioecological theory proposes that there are ____ rather than a single underlying ____ intelligence.

1 multiple cognitive potentials, general
2 metacomponents; perceptual
3 performance components, heritable
4 knowledge components, environmental

Ans. (1)

Exp. Ceci's Bioecological theory proposes that there are multiple cognitive potentials, rather than a single underlying general intelligence.

The Biocological model of development is a theoretical model of gene–environment interactions in human development. This model, first proposed by Urie Bronfenbrenner and Stephen J. Ceci, in 1994, is an extension of Bronfenbrenner's original theoretical model of human development, called ecological systems theory. Bioecological Theory of Intelligence discusses how society shapes intelligence. This theory recognises the role of society and the environment in shaping human intelligence. In fact, intelligence may be a biological disposition which develops within the environment.

37 Match the items in List I with List II and mark your answer with the help of codes given below :

List I (Classifications of Development Delay)	List II (Ranges of IQ Scores)
A. Mild	I. 25-40
B. Profound	II. 55-70
C. Severe	III. Below 25
D. Moderate	IV. 40-55

Codes

	A	B	C	D		A	B	C	D
1	IV	II	I	III	2	II	III	I	IV
3	III	I	IV	II	4	II	I	III	IV

Ans. (2)

Exp. The correct matching is A-II, B-III, C-I, D-IV.

Developmental delay can range in degree from Mild (IQ scores between 55 and 70), Moderate (IQ scores between 40 and 55), Severe (IQ scores between 25 and 40) and Profound (IQ scores below 25).

38 According to ethological theory, species-specific behaviour has following characteristics.

I. Fixed-action pattern
II. Instinctive
III. Unlearned
IV. Innate

Codes

1 I, III and IV
2 II, III and IV
3 I, II and III
4 All of these

Ans. (4)

Exp. According to ethological theory, species-specific behaviour has following characteristics: Fixed-action pattern, Instinctive, Unlearned and Innate.

The ethological concept of species-specific behaviour is based on the premise that certain behavioural similarities are shared by almost all members of a species. Some of these behaviours are unique to certain species, but to be 'species-specific,' they do not have to be unique—they simply have to be characteristic of that species.

It is the behaviour that is specific to the members of a species and is unlearned. While some species-specific behaviour is learned from parents, it's also sometimes the product of a fixed action pattern, also known as an Innate Releasing Mechanism (IRM). In these instances, a neural network is 'programmed' to create a hard-wired, instinctive behaviour in response to an external stimulus.

39 Read the following two statements, Assertion (A) and Reason (R). Indicate your answer using the codes given below :

Assertion (A) Operant conditioning emphasised the study of overt, observable behaviour, environmental conditions and the processes which determine behaviour.

Reason (R) Operant conditioning deals with the function of behaviour rather than the structure of personality. It is deterministic theory in which there is no free will.

Codes

1 Both (A) and (R) are true and (R) is the correct explanation of (A)
2 Both (A) and (R) are true, but (R) is not the correct explanation of (A)
3 (A) is true, but R is false
4 (A) is false, but (R) is true

Ans. (1)

Exp. Both (A) and (R) are true and (R) is the correct explanation of (A).

Operant conditioning emphasised the study of overt, observable behaviour, environmental conditions and the processes which determine behaviour. Operant conditioning is the theory of BF Skinner which is based upon the idea that learning is a function of change in overt behaviour. Changes in behaviour are the result of an individual's response to events (stimuli) that occur in the environment.

Operant conditioning deals with the function of behaviour rather than the structure of personality. It is deterministic theory in which there is no free will. Operant conditioning is based on the idea that behaviour is 'learnt' simply through the process of reinforcement. This has led critics to label Skinner's ideas as deterministic which states that the operant conditioning assumes that environmental factors beyond a person's control are responsible for their behaviour. This explains why the operant conditioning emphasised the study of overt and observable behaviour, environmental conditions and processes.

40 Which of the following statements are true about the EPQ-R (Revised Eysenck Personality Questionnaire) and the NEO-PI-R (Revised NEO Personality Inventory)?

I. Both the tests measure Openness to Experience.
II. The Psychoticism scale of the EPQ-R correlates negatively with the Agreeableness and the Conscientiousness scales of the NEO-PI-R.
III. EPQ-R has a Lie scale; NEO-PI-R does not have a Lie scale.
IV. Extraversion and Neuroticism scales of the EPQ-R positively correlate with the corresponding NEO-PI-R scales.

Codes

1 I and II 2 II and IV
3 III and IV 4 II, III and IV

Ans. (4)

Exp. Statement II, III and IV are true about the EPQ-R (Revised Eyesenck Personality Questionnaire) and the NEO-PI-R (Revised NEO Personality Inventory).

The Psychoticism scale of the EPQ-R correlates negatively with the Agreeableness and the Conscientiousness scales of the NEO-PI-R. Psychoticism encompasses egocentricity, lack of interpersonal warmth, lack of empathy, and impulsiveness. This domain is fairly similar to the low pole of the Big Five Agreeableness and Conscientiousness dimension.

EPQ-R has a Lie scale; NEO-PI-R does not have a Lie scale. Eysenck Personality Questionnaire (EPQ) includes a lie-scale which indicates social acquiescence or self-insight.

Extraversion and Neuroticism scales of the EPQ-R positively correlate with the corresponding NEO-PI-R scales. There are significant positive correlations between Extraversion of EPQ-R and Extraversion of NEO-PI-R scale (0.727) and between Neuroticism of EPQ-R and Neuroticism of NEO-PI-R scale (0.709). The neuroticism dimension describes a trait opposed to emotional stability, and defines the degree to which a person is predisposed to experience negative affect. Extraversion is the second dimension included in the model and depicts sociable, carefree, friendly, convivial, easygoing, and impulsive individuals.

Both the tests do not measure Openness to Experience. Only NEO-PI-R measures Openness to Experience. It is a dimension of the Big Five personality model and the five-factor personality model that refers to individual differences in the tendency to be open to new aesthetic, cultural, or intellectual experiences.

41 Match the items List I (Theories) with List II (Theorists) and mark your answer with the help of codes given below :

List I (Theories)	List II (Theorists)
A. Dialectical humanism	I. JB Watson
B. Avoidance-Avoidance conflict	II. Gordon Allport
C. Behaviourism	III. Erich Fromm
D. Functional autonomy	IV. Dollard and Miller

Codes

	A	B	C	D
1	I	II	IV	III
2	IV	III	I	II
3	III	IV	I	II
4	IV	III	II	I

Ans. (3)

Exp. The correct matching is A-III, B-IV, C-I, D-II.

Dialectical humanism is associated with Erich Fromm. Erich Fromm is generally classified as a neo-Freudian by students of personality theory. Fromm called his theory dialectical humanism because he used a form of reasoning called 'dialectics' to explain the development of human beings and societies.

Avoidance-Avoidance conflict is associated with Dollard and Miller. This conflict involves choosing between undesirable alternatives or outcomes in which a person tends to avoid. For instance, a person who dislikes his job but fears on quitting and unemployment.

Behaviourism is associated with JB Watson. He is famous for having founded classical behaviourism, an approach to psychology that treated behaviour (both animal and human) as the conditioned response of an organism to environmental stimuli and inner biological processes and that rejected as unscientific all supposed psychological phenomena.

Functional autonomy is associated with Gordon Allport. Allport was one of the first researchers to draw a distinction between Motive and Drive. The idea that drives can become independent of the originalmotives for a given behaviour is known as functional autonomy.

42 Mr *A* goes out one frosty morning and finds that his car is covered with a thick layer of frost. He needs to get to work and looks for his ice scraper.

Unable to find it, he thinks a moment, goes into the house and returns with a hard plastic spatula from the kitchen. In using the spatula as a make shift ice scraper Mr *A* has overcome

1 confirmation fixedness
2 confirmation bias
3 creativity bias
4 functional fixedness

Ans. (4)

Exp. Mr. A has overcome functional fixedness.

It is a cognitive bias that can sometimes prevent us from thinking of novel or creative solutions to problems. It is the inability to think about or use an object in a way other than the way it is commonly used.

43 Read each of the following two statements, Assertion (A) and Reason (R) and indicate your answer using the codes given below :

Assertion (A) Radiant energy is propagated in a continuous wave form, which can be described by its wavelength.

Reason (R) Radiant energy also behaves as if it is emitted as discrete quanta of energy.

Codes

1 Both (A) and (R) are true and (R) is the correct explanation of (A).
2 Both (A) and (R) are true, but (R) is not the correct explanation of (A)
3 (A) is true, but (R) is false
4 (A) is false, but (R) is true

Ans. (2)

➲ *Exp.* Both (A) and (R) are true, but (R) is not the correct explanation of (A).

Radiant energy is propagated in a continuous wave form, which can be described by its wave length. Radiant energy is the energy of electromagnetic waves. It is a form of energy that can travel through space. The assertion statement is about the structure of waves and is true.

Radiant energy also behaves as if it is emitted as discrete quanta of energy. Radiant energy is the energy of electromagnetic and gravitational radiation. It behaves as if it is emitted as discrete quanta of energy. The reason statement is about the particles and is true but does not explain the assertion.

44 Byrne believed sexual motivation results from the inter-play of ______ environment and ____ .

1 genes; experience
2 genes; imagination
3 physiology; imagination
4 physiology; lust

Ans. (3)

➲ *Exp.* Byrne believed sexual motivation results from the inter-play of physiology, environment and imagination.

Sexual Motivation is the subjective drive or force that generates our level or sexual interest at any given time. It compels us to seek out through direct sexual activity with another individual or self gratification, drives our sexual fantasies, and regulates our sexual arousal. Sexual motivation can be stimulated by both internal (physiology) and external (environment) cues and relies heavily on imagination and visual stimulation.

45 Read each of the following two statements, Assertion (A) and Reason (R) and indicate your answer using the codes given below :

Assertion (A) Lazarus believes our cognitive appraisal of a situation always precedes emotion.

Reason (R) Emotions influence thinking.

Codes

1 Both (A) and (R) are true and (R) is the correct explanation of (A)
2 Both (A) and (R) are true, but (R) is not the correct explanation of (A)
3 (A) is true, but (R) is false
4 (A) is false, but (R) is true

Ans. (2)

➲ *Exp.* Both (A) and (R) are true, but (R) is not the correct explanation of (A)

Lazarus believes our cognitive appraisal of a situation always precedes emotion. According to Lazarus, the appraisal of the situation would come before both the physical arousal and the experience of emotion.

Emotions influence thinking. Thoughts and emotions have a complex relationship. Just as thoughts can influence emotions, emotions can also influence thoughts. For example, an irritable mood leads to negative thoughts related to inconveniences or annoyances. It is true but it does not explain why our cognitive appraisal precedes emotions.

Directions (Q. Nos. 46-50) *Read the passage given below and answer the questions that follow :*

The research process usually begins with the identification and formulation of research problem. Once, the problem is identified, the appropriate hypotheses are developed.

The hypotheses are tentative solutions to the problem and represent the conjectural statements of relationship among two or more variables. The hypotheses could be classified in various ways, such as directional vs non-directional, correlational vs causal etc. Edwards classified the variables in psychological research as stimulus variables, organismic variables and behavioural variables. The variables are classified as the continuous variables and discrete variables, the latter having two subtypes-the real discrete variables and artificially discrete variables. The variables in research need to be properly operationalised. Robinson classified the psychological studies in four categories : Laboratory experiments, Field experiments, Ex-post facto field studies and Ex-post facto analysis of experiment (slightly modified). The fourth category, on its own, is accorded less respect but is essential for the advancement of Science.

46 Which of the following hypothesis are non-directional hypotheses?

I. Males and females differ on anxiety.
II. Intelligence and academic achievement are negatively related.
III. Anxiety disrupts academic performance of the students.
IV. Stress and work output are related.

Codes

1 Only II	2 I and III
3 III and IV	4 I and IV

Ans. (4)

➲ *Exp.* Following hypothesis are non-directional hypotheses:

- Males and females differ on anxiety.
- Stress and work output are related.

A non-directional hypotheses is a hypotheses that one experimental group will differ from another without specification of the expected direction of the difference. In the first hypothesis, it is hypothesised that males and females differ on anxiety, but it does not tell which gender group will have more anxiety. The second hypothesis suggests that stress and work output are related, but it does not tell in which direction stress and work output are related.

47 Which one of the following is an example of Artificially discrete organismic variable?

1 Examination result as pass or fail
2 Nationality
3 Classification of students as low, average and high intelligent
4 Gender

Ans. (3)

Exp. Classification of students as low, average and high intelligent is an example of an Artificially discrete organismic variable.

Organismic variables refer to the physiological and psychological features of the organism that influence behaviour. A discrete variable is a variable that has distinct, discrete values but no precise numerical flow. For example, gender can be thought of as a discrete variable with two possible values, male or female. A distinction can be drawn between naturally and artificially discrete variables (e.g., the male/female dichotomy of sex is natural, while the classification of students as low, average and high is artificial).

48 Which one of the following cannot be employed as the dependent variable in a psychological experiment?

I. Heart rate　　II. Learning rate
III. Reaction time　　IV. Age

Codes

1 Only IV　　2 I and II
3 III and IV　　4 I, II and IV

Ans. (1)

Exp. Age cannot be employed as the dependent variable in a psychological experiment.

A dependent variable is a measure of the behaviour of the participant that reflects the effects of the independent variable. A dependent variable is what you measure in the experiment and what is affected during the experiment. The dependent variable responds to the independent variable. It is called dependent because it 'depends' on the independent variable. Since, age of a person cannot be altered using any variable it cannot be a dependent variable.

49 Arrange the following three types of investigation in ascending order in terms of the researcher's ability (usually) to control secondary variance.

I. Laboratory experiments
II. Field experiments
III. Ex-post facto field studies

Codes

1 III, I, II　　2 I, II, III
3 III, II, I　　4 II, III, I

Ans. (3)

Exp. The correct order is III, II, I.

Ex-post facto study is a systematic empirical inquiry in which the scientist does not have direct control of independent variables because their manifestations have already occurred or because they are inherently not manipulated.

Field experiments are done in the everyday (i.e. real life) environment of the participants. The experimenter still manipulates the independent variable, but in a real-life setting (so cannot really control extraneous variables).

Laboratory experiments is an experiment conducted under highly controlled conditions. The variable which is being manipulated by the researcher is called the independent variable and the dependent variable is the change in behaviour measured by the researcher. The experimenter has maximum control over the variables.

50 After the catastrophic earthquake, the researcher interviewed a group of subjects to understand whether the earthquake has changed their attitude towards fate. This can best be labelled as an example of

1 Ex-post facto field study
2 Field experiment
3 Attitude change experiment
4 Ethological study

Ans. (1)

Exp. After the catastrophic earthquake, the researcher interviewed a group of subjects to understand whether the earthquake has changed their attitude towards fate. This can best be labelled as an example of Ex-post facto field study.

Since the study was done post the occurrence of the event, it is a case of Ex-post facto study. An ex-post facto research is the one that examines past occurrences in order to understand a current state. Although this type of design involves both a dependent variable and an independent variable, the investigator cannot manipulate the latter. In this case, the catastrophic earthquake is an independent variable which cannot be manipulated by the researcher.

PAPER III

1 Among the following descriptions of major defense mechanisms, which one describes 'projection'?

1 Assigning logical or socially desirable motives to that we do
2 Directing a motive that cannot be gratified in one form into another channel
3 Denying that an unpleasant reality exists
4 Assigning our own undesirable qualities to others

Ans. *(4)*

Exp. Projection is assigning our own undesirable qualities to others.

Projection is the mis-attribution of a person's undesired thoughts, feelings or impulses onto another person who does not have those thoughts, feelings or impulses. Projection is used especially when the thoughts are considered unacceptable for the person to express or they feel completely ill at ease with having them. e.g. a spouse may be angry at their significant other for not listening, when in fact it is the angry spouse who does not listen. Projection is often the result of a lack of insight and acknowledgement of one's own motivations and feelings.

2 Match the items of List I (Theories) with List II (Explanations) and mark your answer with the help of the codes given below :

List I (Theories)		List II (Explanations)
A.	Doctrine of specific nerve energies	I. The basilar membrane vibrates as a whole to the frequency of the sound wave.
B.	Frequency theory	II. The sensation elicited by stimulus depends primarily on the nerve excited and secondarily on the stimuli.
C.	Purkinje effect	III. Refers to the tendency to perceive the simplest and the most stable figure of all possible alternatives.
D.	Law of Pragnanz	IV. The illumination decreases owing to the shift from photopic cone vision to scotopic rod vision.

Codes

	A	B	C	D
1	II	I	IV	III
2	III	IV	I	II
3	II	I	III	IV
4	III	IV	II	I

Ans. *(1)*

Exp. The correct matching is A-II, B-I, C-IV, D-III.

Doctrine of specific nerve energies state that the sensation elicited by stimulus depends primarily on the nerve excited and secondarily on the stimuli. Each sensory receptor organ and its nerve fiber receive and transmit just one modality of sensation, regardless of how it is stimulated.

Frequency theory states that the basilar membrane vibrates as a whole to the frequency of the sound wave. The way it works is, that sound waves cause the entire basilar membrane to vibrate at different rates, which, in turn, causes the neural impulses to be transmitted at different rates.

Purkinje effect says that the illumination decreases owing to the shift from photopic cone vision to scotopic rod vision. The Purkinje effect is the tendency for the peak luminance sensitivity of the eye to shift toward the blue end of the color spectrum at low illumination levels as a part of dark adaptation. In consequence, reds will appear darker relative to other colors as light levels decrease.

Law of Pragnanz refers to the tendency to perceive the simplest and the most stable figure of all possible alternatives. People will perceive and interpret ambiguous or complex images as the simplest forms possible.

3 Engram involves many physical changes. They are

I. change in number of receptor sites.
II. change in the transmission system.
III. changes in the sensitivity of the synapse through repeated stimulation.
IV. changes in the dendrites.
V. changes in the neuron structure.

Codes

1 I, III and IV
2 III and V
3 I, II and IV
4 II and IV

Ans. *(1)*

Exp. Engram involves many physical changes like change in number of receptor sites, changes in the sensitivity of the synapse through repeated stimulation and changes in the dendrites.

In neuropsychological terms, a memory trace is an engram, a hypothetical means by which information is stored as biophysical or biochemical change in the brain (and other neural tissue) in response to external stimuli. The engram is the representation of a memory in the brain. A retrieval cue induces a pattern of activity; if this pattern is similar to a previously encoded pattern you remember the event.

4 Match List I with List II and indicate your answer with the help of codes given below :

List I (Counselling skills)	List II (Features)
A. Self-disclosure	I. Telling the client to view the problem from an alternate perspective.
B. Directive	II. Explaining to the client the logical outcomes of sequential thinking.
C. Reframing	III. Counsellor discloses about personal experiences from the past.
D. Logical consequences	IV. Telling the client how to go about solving the problem/crisis.

Codes

	A	B	C	D		A	B	C	D
1	IV	III	II	I	2	III	IV	I	II
3	II	I	III	IV	4	I	III	IV	III

Ans. (2)

➲ *Exp.* The correct matching is A-III, B-IV, C-I, D-II.

Self-disclosure is a process of communication by which the counsellor discloses about personal experiences from the past about himself or herself to the client. The information can be descriptive or evaluative and can include thoughts, feelings, aspirations, goals, failures, successes, fears and dreams, as well as one's likes, dislikes and favourites.

Directive counselling involves telling the client how to go about solving the problem/crisis. The counsellor plays a more active role than the client. The client makes the decision but the counsellor tries to direct the thinking of the counselee by informing, explaining, interpreting and advising. Eg. Career counselling.

Reframing involves telling the client to view the problem from an alternate perspective. It is a technique used by counsellors to shift a client's view of a particular problem, event, or person. It is based on the assumption that when clients are able to view a situation from another perspective, opportunities for finding alternative, acceptable solutions to their problems increase.

Logical consequences involve explaining to the client the logical outcomes of sequential thinking. A logical consequence is an imposed consequence given by an adult that is related to the behaviour. For breaking the toy, a logical consequence might be that the child must earn money to buy a newtoy or that the childwill not be allowed to play with breakable toys.

5 Read each of the following two statements, Assertion (A) and Reason (R) and indicate your answer using the codes given below :

Assertion (A) Freud's theory holds that many behaviours are caused by unconscious motivation. Personality is determined by biological drives of sex and aggression.

Reason (R) Personality differences results from variations in learning experiences.

Codes

1 Both (A) and (R) are true and (R) is the correct explanation of (A)
2 Both (A) and (R) are true, but (R) is not the correct explanation of (A)
3 (A) is true, but (R) is false
4 (A) is false, but (R) is true

Ans. (2)

➲ *Exp.* Both (A) and (R) are true, but (R) is not the correct explanation of (A).

Freud's theory holds that many behaviours are caused by unconscious motivation. Personality is determined by biological drives of sex and aggression. Sigmund Freud was the first psychologist to propose the notion that much of behaviour and personality are influenced by unconscious forces including unconscious impulses, instincts, conflicts and drives. According to Freud, we come into this world with certain instincts and impulses (especially sexual and aggressive impulses) already driving our behaviour. So, the assertion statement is true.

Personality differences results from variations in learning experiences. Learning experiences are considered an important intervening construct between person inputs, including personality. The reason statement is also true but it does not explain why behaviours are caused by unconscious motivations.

6 Match the items in List I with List II and mark your answer using the given codes :

List I (Therapies)	List II (Clinical conditions)
A. Cognitive Behaviour Therapy	I. Anxiety disorders
B. Exposure techniques	II. Post-traumatic stress disorder
C. Dialectic Behaviour Therapy	III. Depression
D. Eye-movement desensitisation and reprocessing	IV. Borderline personality disorder

Codes

	A	B	C	D		A	B	C	D
1	III	I	IV	II	2	IV	II	III	I
3	II	IV	I	III	4	I	III	II	IV

Ans. (1)

➲ *Exp.* The correct matching is A-III, B-I, C-IV, D-II.

Cognitive Behaviour Therapy is used in the treatment of depression. It is one of the most evidence-based psychological interventions for the treatment of several psychiatric disorders such as depression.

Exposure techniques is used in the treatment of Anxiety disorders. It is a psychological treatment that was developed to help people confront their fears. The exposure to the feared objects, activities or situations in a safe environment helps reduce fear and decrease avoidance. Exposure therapy has been scientifically demonstrated to be a helpful treatment or treatment component for a range of problems like anxiety.

Dialectic Behaviour Therapy (DBT) is used in the treatment of Borderline Personality Disorder. It is a type of psychotherapy which is used to treat Borderline Personality Disorder (BPD). DBT is a form of Cognitive Behavioural Therapy (CBT), meaning it's a therapy that focuses on the role of cognition, which refers to thoughts and beliefs, and behaviour, or actions, in the development and treatment of BPD.

Eye-movement desensitisation and reprocessing is used in the treatment of Post-traumatic stress disorder. It is an interactive psychotherapy technique used to relieve psychological stress. It is a treatment for trauma and Post-Traumatic Stress Disorder (PTSD).

7 Which of the following are the physiological reactions to stress?

I. Decrease in metabolic rate
II. Dilation of pupils
III. Lower blood pressure
IV. Increased heart rate

Codes

1 II and IV　　2 I, II and IV
3 I, III and IV　　4 II, III and IV

Ans. (2)

Exp. The physiological reactions to stress include a decrease in metabolic rate, dilation of pupils and increased heart rate.

Stress is a biological and psychological response experienced on encountering a threat that we feel we do not have the resources to deal with. The sympathetic division of the autonomic division mobilises the body in times of stress, danger or intense emotional arousal. Activation of the sympathetic division results in a number of physiological changes in the body, including dilation of pupils, increased heart rate, rapid breathing, increased perspiration and heightened physiological arousal.

8 According to Albert Bandura, any behaviour produces two sets of consequences. They are

I. Inhibition　　II. Self-evaluation
III. External outcomes　　IV. Habit

Codes

1 I and II　　2 III and IV
3 II and III　　4 I and IV

Ans. (3)

Exp. According to Albert Bandura, any behaviour produces two sets of consequences. They are self-evaluation and external outcomes.

Bandura's Social Cognitive Theory (SCT) recognises physical, social and self-evaluative outcome expectations. Particularly the latter have a central place in motivation. It posits that people learn from one another, observation, imitation and modelling. People learn through observing others' behaviour, attitudes and outcomes of those behaviours. It explains human behaviour in terms of continuous reciprocal interaction between cognitive, behavioural and environmental influences.

9 The degree to which one can control an event ______ the stress and inability to predict the occurrence of an event usually ______ the stress.

1 increases, increases
2 increases, decreases
3 decreases, increases
4 decreases, decreases

Ans. (3)

Exp. The degree to which one can control an event decreases the stress and inability to predict the occurrence of an event usually increases the stress.

Previous research suggests that controllability is a key factor in the impact of stress on behaviour. It suggests that learning how to control stressors buffers people from the negative effects of stress on subsequent cognitively demanding tasks. Predictability is also an important factor in the effects of stress. For example, animals given the opportunity to determine whether shocks delivered to them will be signaled or unsignaled, typically choose to spend their time in the signaled conditions regardless of whether the shock is escapable or inescapable.

10 Match List I (Studying Motivations) with that of List II (Explanations) and mark your answer with the help of the codes given below :

List I (Studying motivations)		List II (Explanations)	
A.	Behaviouristic approach	I.	Interpersonal relations with community.
B.	Humanistic approach	II.	Incentives rewards and punishment.
C.	Cognitive approach	III.	Actualising needs.
D.	Socio-cultural approach	IV.	Behaviour is determined by our thinking and attribution.

Codes

	A	B	C	D		A	B	C	D
1	II	III	IV	I	2	III	II	IV	I
3	I	II	IV	III	4	I	III	II	IV

Ans. (1)

Exp. The correct matching is A-II, B-III, C-IV, D-I.

Behaviouristic Approach includes incentives like rewards and punishment. Incentives in the environment determine organisms' behaviour. It places emphasis on the importance of the environment in influencing behaviour. An organism is more likely to continue a behaviour if the consequences are positive.

Humanistic Approach focuses on actualising needs. Maslow proposed a hierarchy of needs or drives in order of decreasing priority or potency but increasing sophistication: physiological needs, safety, belongingness and love, esteem, and self-actualisation.

Cognitive Approach suggests that behaviour is determined by our thinking and attribution. Cognitive psychologists try to build up cognitive models of the information processing that goes on inside people's minds, including perception, attention, language, memory, thinking, and consciousness. Attribution is concerned with how individuals interpret events and how this relates to their thinking and behaviour.

Socio-cultural Approach involves interpersonal relations with community. It is used to describe awareness of circumstances surrounding individuals and how their behaviours are effected specifically by their surrounding, social and cultural factors.

11 Read each of the following two statements, Assertion (A) and Reason (R) and indicate your answer using the codes given below :

Assertion (A) People with external locus of control are prone to learned helplessness.

Reason (R) People with internal locus of control believe that intelligence is changeable and they work at developing new strategies.

Codes

1 Both (A) and (R) are true and (R) is the correct explanation of (A)
2 Both (A) and (R) are true, but (R) is not the correct explanation of (A)
3 (A) is true, but (R) is false
4 (A) is false, but (R) is true

Ans. *(2)*

Exp. Both (A) and (R) are true, but (R) is not the correct explanation of (A).

People with external locus of control are prone to learned helplessness. External locus of control is the belief that one's behaviour will not lead to valued reinforcement that is available in the environment and therefore not under one's control. Learned helplessness is a state that occurs after a person has experienced a stressful situation repeatedly. They come to believe that they are unable to control or change the situation, so they do not try even when opportunities for change become available. So, the statement is true because people when unable to control their environment become prone to develop learned helplessness.

People with internal locus of control believe that intelligence is changeable and they work at developing new strategies. People with a high internal locus of control believe in their own ability to control themselves and influence the world around them. Their belief in their ability to change things may well make them more confident and they will hence, seek information that will help them influence people and situations. The statement is also true, but it tries to explain how people with internal locus of control are different from people with external locus of control. So it does not explain the assertion.

12 According to Problem Space theory, a problem solver generally operates through three states; ______, the goal state and all possible ______ .

1 Pre state; final state
2 First state; outcome state
3 Initial state; outcome state
4 Initial state; intermediate state

Ans. *(4)*

Exp. According to Problem Space theory, a problem-solver generally operates through three states; initial state, the goal state and all possible intermediate state.

Problem Space refers to the entire range of components that exist in the process of finding a solution to a problem. This range starts with an initial state where individuals engage in 'defining the problem,' then proceeds to the intermediate stage of 'identifying and testing possible solutions' and ends with the final stage of goal state of 'choosing and implementing a solution'. So, it includes all of the smaller steps that exist between these identified stages.

13 According to self-determination theory of motivation given by Ryan and Deci, the three inborn and universal needs are

1 Autonomy, Symmetry and Competence
2 Symmetry, Competence and Relatedness
3 Autonomy, Competence and Relatedness
4 Competence, Relatedness and Order

Ans. *(3)*

Exp. According to self-determination theory of motivation given by Ryan and Deci, the three inborn and universal needs are Autonomy, Competence and Relatedness.

Self-Determination Theory (SDT) is an important theory of motivation that addresses issues of extrinsic and intrinsic motivation. People have innate psychological needs (i) Competence : Need to stay ahead (ii) Relatedness : Need for love and Belonging (iii) Autonomy: Need for Independence. If these universal needs are met, the theory argues that people will function and grow optimally. To actualise their inherent potential, the social environment needs to nurture these needs.

14 Physiological psychologists distinguish between ______ thirst and ____ thirst which result from an increase in the concentration of solutes and low blood pressure respectively.

1 Osmotic, Hypovolumic
2 Osmotic, Hypervolumic
3 Hypovolumic, Osmotic
4 Hypervolumic, Osmotic

Ans. *(1)*

Exp. Physiological psychologists distinguish between Osmotic thirst and Hypovolumic thirst which result from an increase in the concentration of solutes and low blood pressure respectively.

Osmotic thirst, or intracellular dehydration (water deficit), is activated in response to increases in tonicity when compensatory mechanisms are unsuccessful in conserving sufficient water to decrease serum osmolality and restore fluid balance. Hypovolumic thirst, occurs when the volume of your blood is reduced due to fluid loss from sweating.

15 Sternberg's Triarchic theory identifies _____ types of components; _____ are used to plan, control and monitor in problem solving.

1 three, meta components
2 four, performance
3 problem solving, knowledge
4 several, acquisition components

Ans. *(1)*

Exp. Sternberg's Triarchic theory identifies three types of components; meta components are used to plan, control and monitor in problem-solving.

Sternberg associated the workings of the mind with a series of components. He labelled these components as the metacomponents, performance components, and knowledge-acquisition components. The metacomponents are executive processes used in problem solving and decision making that involve the majority of managing our mind. The performance components, are the processes that actually carry out the actions the metacomponents dictate. The knowledge-acquisition components, are used in obtaining new information.

16 Read each of the following two statements, Assertion (A) and Reason (R) and indicate your answer using the codes given below:

Assertion (A) Environments that influence educational and cultural opportunities enhance crystallised intelligence.

Reason (R) Crystallised intelligence is developed through stimulating fluid intelligence.

Codes

1 Both (A) and (R) are true and (R) is the correct explanation of (A)
2 Both (A) and (R) are true, but (R) is not the correct explanation of (A)
3 A is true, but R is false
4 A is false, but R is true

Ans. *(1)*

Exp. Both (A) and (R) are true and (R) is the correct explanation of (A).

Environments that influence educational and cultural opportunities enhance crystallised intelligence. Crystallised intelligence involves knowledge that comes from prior learning and past experiences. Situations that require crystallised intelligence include reading comprehension and vocabulary exams. Crystallised intelligence is a product of educational and cultural experiences which interact with fluid intelligence. So, the assertion statement is true that such environments enhance crystallised intelligence.

Crystallised intelligence is developed through stimulating fluid intelligence. Fluid Intelligence is the capability to reason out and solve novel problems independent of past experiences. It is being able to think and reason abstractly and solve problems. When the fluid intelligence is stimulated, the crystallised intelligence also develops. The reason is true as it correctly explains how crystallised intelligence can be enhanced.

17 Read each of the following two statements, Assertion (A) and Reason (R) and indicate your answer using the codes given below:

Assertion (A) We use mental short-cuts to solve problems.

Reason (R) Problem-solving includes thinking.

Codes

1 Both (A) and (R) are true and (R) is the correct explanation of (A)
2 Both (A) and (R) are true, but (R) is not the correct explanation of (A)
3 (A) is true, but (R) is false
4 (A) is false, but (R) is true

Ans. *(2)*

Exp. Both (A) and (R) are true, but (R) is not the correct explanation of (A).

We use mental short-cuts to solve problems. A heuristic is a mental shortcut that allows people to solve problems and make judgements quickly and efficiently. These rule-of-thumb strategies shorten decision-making time and allow people to function without constantly stopping to think about their next course of action. It is true as we use heuristics or mental short-cuts to solve our problems.

Problem-solving includes thinking. Problem-solving refers to a way of reaching a goal from a present condition, where the present condition is either not directly moving toward the goal, is far from it, or needs more complex logic in order to find steps toward the goal. It is considered the most complex of all intellectual functions, since it is a higher-order cognitive process that requires the modulation and control of basic skills. This suggests that problem-solving involves the thinking process.

18 Match the items of List I (Concepts) with List II (Originators) and mark your answer with the help of codes given below :

List I (Concepts)	**List II** (Originators)
A. Personology	I. George Kelly
B. Individual psychology	II. HJ Eysenck
C. Personal Construct Theory	III. Henry Murray
D. Biological Trait Theory	IV. Gordon Allport

Codes

	A	B	C	D		A	B	C	D
1	III	IV	I	II	2	I	II	III	IV
3	II	III	I	IV	4	IV	I	II	III

Ans. (1)

➲ *Exp.* The correct matching is A-III, B-IV, C-I, D-II.

Personology was given by Henry Murray. It is a trend within personality psychology created by Henry A. Murray in the 1930s. It is an idiographic approach to personality, focusing on the interaction between psychological needs and presses coming from the individual's environment.

Individual Psychology was given by Gordon Allport. He was one of the first modern trait theorists. He organised these traits into a hierarchy of three levels: cardinal, central and source traits.

Personal Construct Theory was given by George Kelly. According to him, personality is composed of the various mental constructs through which each person views reality.

Biological Trait Theory was given by HJ Eysenck. He was a personality theorist who focused on temperament—innate, genetically based personality differences. He believed personality is largely governed by biology and he viewed people as having two specific personality dimensions extroversion introversion and neuroticism stability.

19 Which of the following are the characteristics of NREM sleep?

I. Decrease in heart rate.
II. Increase in breathing rate.
III. Muscles are relaxed.
IV. Increase in brain's metabolic rate.

Codes

1 I and III are correct
2 II and III are correct
3 I and IV are correct
4 II, III and IV are correct

Ans. (1)

➲ *Exp.* The characteristics of NREM sleep are decrease in heart rate and relaxation of muscles.

NREM (Non-Rapid Eye Movement) sleep is dreamless sleep. During NREM, the brain waves on the electroencephalographic (EEG) recording are typically slow and of high voltage, the breathing and heart rate are slow and regular, the blood pressure is low, and the sleeper is relatively still.

20 Match the following with the help of codes given below :

List I (Concepts/Phenomenons)	List II (Examples/Descriptions)
A. Morpheme	I. Adjective before the noun
B. Phoneme	II. Conclusion of statements
C. Syntax	III. Break
D. Syllogism	IV. 'D' or 'A'

Codes

	A	B	C	D
1	III	IV	I	II
2	III	IV	II	I
3	IV	III	II	I
4	IV	II	III	I

Ans. (1)

➲ *Exp.* The correct matching is A-III, B-IV, C-I, D-II.

Morphemes are the smallest meaningful elements of a language. This signifies that morphemes cannot be segmented into smaller parts as it will discard the meaning. The example of morpheme is break.

Phonemes are the basic units of speech of a language. These are put together to create morphemes and words. The main difference between a morpheme and phoneme is that while a morpheme carries a meaning, a phoneme itself does not carry any meaning. It is merely a unit of speech. The example of phoneme is 'D' or 'A'.

Syntax/Syntactical is the organisation of words in a sentence; the rules and principles that govern the sentence structure of any language. The example of syntax is adjective before the noun.

Syllogism is the deductive reasoning; an extremely subtle, sophisticated or deceptive argument; a formal argument in logic that is formed by two statements and a conclusion which must be true if the two statements are true. The example of syllogism is conclusion of statements.

21 The 30 × 30 correlation matrix, representing the correlation among the thirty facet scales of the NEO-PI-3 were factor analysed by three methods

I. Principal components method
II. Maximum likelihood method
III. Principal axes method and the five factors were extracted in each case.

Usually the variance explained by the factor solution would be in the following ascending order :

Codes

1 II, III, I
2 I, III, II
3 II, I, III
4 III, II, I

Ans. (1)

➲ *Exp.* The correct order is II, III, I.

Maximum Likelihood method is a popular statistical method used for fitting a mathematical model to some data. The modelling of real world data using estimation by maximum likelihood offers a way of tuning the free parameters of the model to provide a good fit.

Principal axes method is an extraction method in which the coefficient of multiple determination of one variable with all other variables in the system is used as the initial communality estimate for that variable. Both Maximum likelihood method and Principal axes method are exploratory factor analysis methods.

Principal component method represents the directions of the data that explain a maximal amount of variance. Principal Components Analysis (PCA) is one of a family of techniques for taking high-dimensional data, and using the dependencies between the variables to represent it in a more tractable, lower-dimensional form, without losing toomuch information. PCA is one of the simplest and most robust ways of doing such dimensionality reduction.

22 Pituitary gland is called master gland because

1 hormones secreted by posterior pituitary regulate the activities of other glands
2 hormones secreted by anterior pituitary regulate the activities of other glands
3 hormones secreted by both posterior and anterior pituitary regulate the activities of other glands
4 it is located in the Central Nervous System

Ans. (2)

➲ *Exp.* Pituitary gland is called master gland because hormones secreted by anterior pituitary regulate the activities of other glands.

The pituitary gland is sometimes called the 'master' gland of the endocrine system because it controls the functions of many of the other endocrine glands. The pituitary gland is no larger than a pea, and is located at the base of the brain. The gland is attached to the hypothalamus (a part of the brain that affects the pituitary gland) by nerve fibers and blood vessels.

The pituitary gland itself consists of 2 major structures: Anterior and Posterior glands. The anterior pituitary gland produces the adrenocorticotropic hormone, which stimulates the adrenal glands to secrete steroid hormones and cortisol, a growth hormone, which regulates growth, metabolism and body composition, and releases them into the bloodstream.

23 Using Sternberg's theory as the reference, match List I with List II and choose the correct code :

List I (Components)		List II (Types)	
A.	Experiential	I.	Analytic
B.	Contextual	II.	Creative
C.	Componential	III.	Practical
		IV.	Successful

Codes

	A	B	C		A	B	C
1	III	IV	II	2	II	III	I
3	II	IV	III	4	II	I	III

Ans. (2)

➲ *Exp.* The correct matching is A-II, B-III, C-I.

The *Experiential component* is associated with Creative intelligence. It is a subtheory in the triarchic theory of intelligence specifying the kinds of experience to which the components of intelligence are applied. According to the experiential subtheory, people are creatively intelligent to the extent that they can cope with relative novelty and automatise routine aspects of tasks so as to devote more resources to novel stimuli in their environment.

The *Contextual component* is associated with Practical intelligence. It is a part of the triarchic theory of intelligence according to which factors in the environment affect both an individual's intelligence and what constitutes an intelligent response to a given situation. The subtheory postulates that people are intelligent in context to the extent that they effectively adapt to, shape, and select environments.

The *Componential component* is associated with analytic intelligence. It is a subtheory in the triarchic theory of intelligence that specifies three kinds of information-processing components in human intelligence. The three components are (a) metacomponents, which are used to plan, monitor, and evaluate problem solving and decision making; (b) performance components, which are actually used to solve the problems or make the decisions; and (c) knowledge-acquisition components, which are used to learn how to solve the problems or make the decisions in the first place.

24 A study employed two groups, matched on intelligence, each group with 30 subjects. Each subject was required to learn a list of CVC trigrams and the number of trials required to learn the list was the dependent variable. What would be the degrees of freedom if a suitable t-test is used to evaluate the mean difference?

1 29 2 30 3 58 4 60

Ans. (1)

➲ *Exp.* In the given situation degree of freedom is 29, if a suitable t-test is used to evaluate the mean difference.

For a matched design, the degrees of freedom can be calculated using the formula, df = n-1 where 'n' is the number of subjects in each group.

Each group has 30 subjects, so 'n' = 30 and df = (30-1) = 29.

25 _____ states that allocating_______rewards for behaviours previously _____ rewarded decreases level of motivation.

1 Two factor theory; extrinsic; not
2 Theory X; monetary; intrinsically
3 Cognitive evaluation theory; extrinsic; intrinsically
4 Theory Y; financial; selectively

Ans. (3)

➲ *Exp.* Cognitive evaluation theory states that allocating extrinsic rewards for behaviours previously intrinsically rewarded decreases level of motivation. It is a theory in psychology that is designed to explain the effects of external consequences on internal motivation.

Intrinsic motivation may decrease over time due to repetitive actions. This is to say that the motivation was not undermined by an external force but was decreasing because of doing the same action over and over. Material rewards contingent on superior performance incentivize employee efforts. In this way, the reward or the external event controls employee behaviour at workplace. At the same time the external events provide feedback to the employee on his or her competence in dealing with the assigned task. Consequently, events that further greater perceived competence will strengthen intrinsic motivation, whereas those that further lower perceived competence will weaken intrinsic motivation.

26 Read each of the following two statements, Assertion (A) and Reason (R) and indicate your answer using the codes given below :

Assertion (A) The orbital frontal cortex and the basal ganglia, especially the caudate nucleus, are the brain structures most often implicated in obsessive compulsive disorder.

Reason (R) Reduced metabolic activity has been found in both the orbital frontal cortex and the caudate nucleus in people with obsessive compulsive disorder.

Codes

1 Both (A) and (R) are true and (R) is the correct explanation of (A)
2 Both (A) and (R) are true, but (R) is not the correct explanation of (A)
3 (A) is true, but (R) is false
4 (A) is false, but (R) is true

Ans. *(3)*

Exp. (A) is true, but (R) is false

The orbital frontal cortex and the basal ganglia, especially the caudate nucleus, are the brain structures most often implicated in obsessive compulsive disorder. Imaging, surgical, and lesion studies suggest that the prefrontal cortex (orbitofrontal and anterior cingulated cortexes), basal ganglia, and thalamus are involved in the pathogenesis of Obsessive-compulsive disorder (OCD). So, the assertion statement is true.

Reason (R) is false as there is an increased metabolic activity in both the orbital frontal cortex and the caudate nucleus in people with OCD.

27 A 17 years old woman has been binging on large quantities of food above and beyond, what most people would eat under similar circumstances. She then engages in purging behaviour as often as 3 or 4 times a week. She feels she has no control over it. The results of her physical examination are normal and she is of normal weight.

She is most likely suffering from

1 Anorexia nervosa
2 Bulimia nervosa
3 Binge-eating disorder
4 Eating disorder not otherwise specified

Ans. *(2)*

Exp. The woman is most likely suffering from Bulimia nervosa.

Bulimia Nervosa is a psychological and severe life-threatening eating disorder described by the ingestion of an abnormally large amount of food in short time period, followed by an attempt to avoid gaining weight by purging what was consumed. Methods of purging include forced vomiting, excessive use of laxatives or diuretics, and extreme or prolonged periods of exercising. Often, in these binge/purge episodes, a woman or man suffering from this disorder will experience a loss of control and engage in frantic efforts to undo these feelings.

28 Which of the following are characteristics of Charismatic leaders?

I. Vision and articulation
II. Risk taking behaviour
III. Volatile moods
IV. Sensitivity to followers' needs

Codes

1 II, III and IV
2 I, II and IV
3 I, III and IV
4 I and IV

Ans. *(2)*

Exp. The characteristics of Charismatic leaders are:

Vision and articulation : Charismatic leaders have a vision – expressed as a idealised goal – that proposes a future better than the status quo, and are able to clarify the importance of the vision in terms that are understandable to others.

Risk taking behaviour : They are willing take on high personal risk, incur high costs and engage in self sacrifice to achieve the visions.

Sensitivity to followers' needs : They are perceptive of others' abilities and responsive to their needs and feelings.

29 What would be the degrees of freedom for the second-order interaction effect in a 3 × 3 × 2 factorial design?

1 2
2 4
3 9
4 18

Ans. *(2)*

Exp. The degrees of freedom for the second-order interaction effect in a $3 \times 3 \times 2$ factorial design are 4.

The $3 \times 3 \times 2$ factorial design includes 3 variables with 3 levels, 3 levels and 2 levels respectively. A second-order interaction effect is an effect in which three independent variables combine to have a non-additive influence on a dependent variable.

The degrees of freedom for second-order interaction can be calculated using the formula:

$df = (j-1)(k-1)(l-1)$, where j, k and l refer to the levels of each variable. Putting the values of $j = 3$, $k = 3$, $l = 2$,

$df = (3-1)(3-1)(2-1) = 4$

30 Which of the following are features of Borderline Personality Disorder?

I. Affective instability
II. Lack of remorse
III. Impulsivity
IV. Self-mutilation
V. Over concern with order and rules

Codes

1 I, II and III
2 I, III and IV
3 I, II, IV and V
4 II, III, IV and V

Ans. *(2)*

➲ *Exp.* The features of Borderline Personality Disorder are Affective instability, Impulsivity and Self-mutilation.

Borderline Personality Disorder is an illness marked by an ongoing pattern of varying moods, self-image, and behaviour. These symptoms often result in impulsive actions and problems in relationships. Affective instability, defined as repeated, rapid, and abrupt shifts in mood, is considered the core pathology in borderline personality disorder. Typical expressions of impulsivity in individuals with the disorder include substance abuse, spending sprees, gambling, reckless driving, risky sexual behaviour, sudden relationship break-ups (e.g., treatment dropout), and non-suicidal self-injury (NSSI, e.g., cutting or burning). Self-mutilation involves intentional self-injury or self-harm which is considered a pervasive problem in several psychopathologies, and especially in Borderline Personality Disorder (BPD).

31 Read each of the following two statements, Assertion (A) and Reason (R) and indicate your answer using the codes given below :

Assertion (A) A major function of the perceptual system is to keep the appearance of objects the same inspite of change in the stimuli.

Reason (R) The posterior brain system selects objects on the basis of location, shape or colour and the anterior system is responsible for guiding the process.

Codes

1 Both (A) and (R) are true and (R) is the correct explanation of (A)
2 Both (A) and (R) are true, but (R) is not the correct explanation of (A)
3 A is true, but (R) is false
4 A is false, but (R) is true

Ans. *(2)*

➲ *Exp.* Both (A) and (A) are true, but (R) is not the correct explanation of (R)

A major function of the perceptual system is to keep the appearance of objects the same inspite of change in the stimuli. A perceptual system is a computational system (biological or artificial) designed to make inferences about properties of a physical environment based on senses. A sensory organ (biological or artificial) is used to capture this information. Therefore, any perceptual system must incorporate input from at least one sensory organ. Examples of perceptual systems include: visual system, auditory system, olfactory system, and somatosensory system. The major function of the perceptual system is to keep the appearance of the objects same despite the changing nature of stimuli. So, the Assertion is true.

The posterior brain system selects objects on the basis of location, shape or colour and the anterior system is responsible for guiding the process. It is true that posterior part of brain system is responsible for the location, shape and colour of objects and anterior system is responsible for guiding the perceptual process, but it does not explain the given assertion.

32 Social Psychology focuses on _______ and their ________ .

1 Individuals; feelings
2 Groups; experiences
3 People; feelings
4 People; thoughts

Ans. *(2)*

➲ *Exp.* Social Psychology focuses on groups and their experiences.

As defined by Gordon W. Allport, Social Psychology is the study of how an individual's thoughts, feelings, and actions are affected by the actual, imagined, or symbolically represented presence of other people. Social psychologists are interested in the impact that the social environment and group interactions have on attitudes and behaviours.

33 Arrange the following stages of friendship in the order given by Selman.

I. Two-way fair-weather cooperation
II. Momentary playmateship
III. Autonomous interdependence
IV. Intimate, mutually shared relationship
V. One-way assistance.

Codes

1 II, IV, V, III, I
2 I, III, V, IV, II
3 II, V, I, IV, III
4 V, I, IV, III, II

Ans. *(3)*

➲ *Exp.* The correct order is II, V, I, IV, III.

Following are the five stages that children go through as they learn to make and keep friends:

Level 0 Friendship: Momentary Playmates (Approximate ages: 3-7 years) : Children at this stage view friends as momentary playmates and their friendships are all about having fun together. Their friends are kids who are conveniently nearby and who do the same things they like to do.

Level 1 Friendship : One-Way Assistance (Approximate ages: 4-9 years) : At this level, children understand that friendship goes beyond whatever their current activity is, but they still think in very pragmatic terms. They define friends as children who do nice things for them-such as sharing a treat, saving them a seat on the bus or giving them nice presents.

Level 2 Friendship: Two-Way, Fair Weather Cooperation (Approximate ages: 6-12 years) : These children are able to consider a friend's perspective in addition to their own, but not at the same time. So what this means is that they understand turn taking, but they can't really step back and get an observer's perspective that would allow them to see patterns of interaction in their relationships.

Level 3 Friendship: Intimate, Mutually Shared Relationships (Approximate ages: 11-15 years) : At this stage, friends help each other solve problems and confide thoughts and feelings that they don't share with anyone else. They know how to compromise and they do kind things for each other without 'keeping score,' because they genuinely care about each other's happiness.

LEVEL 4 Friendship Autonomous interdependence (Approximate ages: 12 years to adulthood) : At this stage, children place a high value on emotional closeness with friends. They can accept and even appreciate differences between themselves and their friends.

34 Memory problem that people with dementia, including Alzheimer's, typically have is called

1 Psychogenic amnesia
2 Reterograde amnesia
3 Reteroactive amnesia
4 Anterograde amnesia

Ans. *(4)*

Exp. Memory problem that people with dementia, including Alzheimer's, typically have is called Anterograde amnesia.

Alzheimer's disease also known as just Alzheimer's or AD is a progressive, degenerative and ultimately fatal brain disease, in which cell to cell connections in the brain are lost. It is the most common cause of dementia. Anterograde amnesia is characterised by the inability to store, retain or recall new knowledge after the event that triggers the onset of amnesia. Patients in this state often cannot remember what they ate for their last meal or events from the immediate past. They may fill in gaps in their memory with fabricated events (confabulation).

35 Problem-solving comprise of different stages which refer to the sequence of

1 Preparation; illumination; incubation; verification
2 Incubation; preparation; illumination; verification
3 Preparation, incubation; illumination, verification
4 Preparation, incubation, verification, illumination

Ans. *(3)*

Exp. Problem-solving comprise of different stages which are:

(i) *Preparation* : In this stage, the thinker formulates the problem and collects the facts and materials considered necessary for finding new solutions.

(ii) *Incubation* : During this period some of the ideas that were interfering with the solution will tend to fade. The overt activity and sometimes even thinking about the problem is absent in this stage. But the unconscious thought process involved in creative thinking is at work during this period.

(iii) *Illumination* : Following the period of incubation the creative ideas occur suddenly. Consequently the obscure thing becomes clear. This sudden flash of solution is known as illumination and is similar to 'aha (eureka)' experience.

(iv) *Verification* : Though the solution is found in illumination stage, it is necessary to verify whether that solution is correct or not. Hence in this last stage evaluation of the solution is done.

36 Which one of the following theories predicts that work motivation will be low if employee perceives that increased effort will have little or no effect on his/her performance?

1 Just World Theory
2 Need Drive Theory
3 Expectancy Theory
4 Normative Theory

Ans. *(3)*

Exp. Expectancy Theory predicts that work motivation will be low if employee perceives that increased effort will have little or no effect on his/her performance.

Expectancy theory proposes that individuals decide to act in a behaviour certain way because they are motivated to select a behaviour over other behaviours based on their expectation of the result. The individual chooses based on estimates of how well the expected results of a given behaviour are going to match up with the desired results. Expectancy theory explains the behavioural process of why individuals are motivated to choose one behavioural option over another. It also explains how they make decisions to achieve the outcome that they perceive as most valuable.

37 In which of Piaget's stages of development would a child be when he has just developed object permanence?

1 Sensorimotor
2 Pre-operational
3 Concrete operational
4 Formal operational

Ans. *(1)*

Exp. A child will develop object permanence in the Sensorimotor stage of Piaget's stages of development. According to psychologist Jean Piaget, children progress through a series of four critical stages of cognitive development. Each stage is marked by shifts in how kids understand the world. During the Sensorimotor stage, infants and toddlers acquire knowledge through sensory experiences and manipulating objects. Piaget believed that developing object permanence or object constancy, the understanding that objects continue to exist even when they cannot be seen, was an important element at this point of development.

38 Read each of the following two statements, Assertion (A) and Reason (R) and indicate your answer using the codes given below.

Assertion (A) Individuals who display disexecutive syndrome are unable to take decisions, are easily distracted and show tendency towards perseveration.

Reason (R) Individuals with extensive injuries to the temporal lobes show deficits in their executive functions.

Codes

1 Both (A) and (R) are true and (R) is the correct explanation of(A)
2 Both (A) and (R) are true, but (R is not the correct explanation of (A)
3 (A) is true, but (R) is false
4 (A) is false, but (R) is true

Ans. (3)

Exp. (A) is true, but (R) is false.

Individuals who display disexecutive syndrome are unable to take decisions, are easily distracted and show tendency towards perseveration. Dysexecutive Syndrome (DES) consists of a group of symptoms, usually resulting from brain damage, that fall into cognitive, behavioural and emotional categories and tend to occur together. The term was introduced by Alan Baddeley to describe a common pattern of dysfunction in executive functions, such as planning, abstract thinking, flexibility and behavioural control. Perseveration is also often seen in patients with DES. Perseveration is the repetition of thoughts, behaviours, or actions after they have already been completed. The Assertion is true.

Reason (R) is false as individual with extensive injuries to the frontal lobes show deficits in their executive functions. The frontal lobes also subsume what is collectively referred to as executive skills. These functions include attention, reasoning, judgment, problem solving, creativity, emotional regulation, impulse control and awareness of aspects of one's and others' functioning.

39 A psychologist wanted to study marital love between husbands and wives in arranged and love marriages. Fifty arranged marriage couples and fifty love marriage couples were randomly choosen and both the husbands and wives, were administered Marital Love Scale. The data should be analysed by

1 Factorial ANOVA for independent groups
2 Factorial ANOVA for repeated measures
3 Mixed factorial ANOVA
4 Randomised one-way ANOVA

Ans. (3)

Exp. The given data should be analysed by Mixed factorial ANOVA. There are two factors in the study: type of marriage (love and arrange) and sex (husbands and wives). The present study is of 2 x 2 factorial design.

A Mixed factorial ANOVA compares the mean differences between groups that have been split on two 'factors' (also known as independent variables), where one factor is a 'within-subjects' factor and the other factor is a 'between-subjects' factor. The primary purpose of a mixed ANOVA is to understand, if there is an interaction between these two factors on the dependent variable.

40 Match List I with List II and indicate your answer with the help of the codes given below :

List I (Roles)	List II (Descriptions)
A. Liaison	I. Transmits information to different members of the organisation.
B. Disseminator	II. Responsible for representing the organisation at major transactions.
C. Negotiator	III. Maintains a network of outside contacts who provide favours and information to the organisation.
D. Entrepreneur	IV. Searches around for opportunities and also starts innovative projects.

Codes

	A	B	C	D		A	B	C	D
1	III	I	II	IV	2	IV	II	I	III
3	I	II	IV	III	4	II	I	III	IV

Ans. (1)

Exp. The correct matching is A-III, B-I, C-II, D-IV.

As a *Liaison*, a manager maintains a network of outside contacts who provide favours and information to the organisation. He/She must communicate with internal and external contacts.

As a *Disseminator*, a manager transmits information to different members of the organisation. He/She must know how to share information and outside views effectively, which means that good communication skills are vital.

As a *Negotiator*, a manager is responsible for representing the organisation at major transactions. He/She may be needed to take part in, and direct, important negotiations within your team, department, or organisation.

As an *Entrepreneur*, a manager searches around for opportunities and also starts innovative projects. He/She creates and controls change within the organisation. This means solving problems, generating new ideas, and implementing them.

41 According to Negative State Relief Model, people provide help to others because

I. People provide help to others to regulate their moods.
II. Helping is a means to momentarily boost emotion.
III. People provide help due to the fear of the consequences of help.
IV. It bolsters their spirit over long periods.

Select the correct answer using the codes given below :

1 I, II and III
2 II, III and IV
3 I, II and IV
4 I, III and IV

Ans. (3)

Exp. Statement I, II, and IV are correct in relation to Negative State Relief Model.

People provide help to others to regulate their moods. The negative-state relief model states that human beings have an innate drive to reduce negative moods. They can be reduced by engaging in any mood-elevating behaviour, including helping behaviour, as it is paired with positive value such as smiles and thank you. Thus, negative mood increases helpfulness because helping others can reduce one's own bad feelings.

Helping is a means to momentarily boost emotion. Under the negative state relief model, individuals are made to believe that their induced mood was fixed temporarily. Specifically, this theory predicts that at least under certain circumstances, a temporary feeling of sadness is likely to result in an increased willingness to help others.

It bolsters their spirit over long periods. Specifically, people have been socialized in such a way that they are rewarded for helping other people. Over time, people internalise this and find helping others rewarding.

42 Which is the one that is not a 'Big Five' factor of personality?

1 Extraversion
2 Psychoticism
3 Conscientiousness
4 Agreeableness

Ans. (2)

Exp. Psychoticism is not a 'Big Five' factor of personality.

The Big Five personality traits is a suggested taxonomy, or grouping, for personality traits. The theory identifies five factors: extraversion (outgoing/energetic vs. solitary/reserved), agreeableness (friendly/compassionate vs. critical/rational), openness to experience (inventive/curious vs. consistent/cautious), conscientiousness (efficient/organised vs. extravagant/careless), and neuroticism (sensitive/nervous vs. resilient/confident).

43 Read each of the following two statements, Assertion (A) and Reason (R) and indicate your answer using the codes given below :

Assertion (A) Transpersonal psychotherapy views man as a spiritual being, views consciousness as central to therapy and emphasises emotions, feelings and experimental aspects of the client.

Reason (R) Self-acceptance, flexibility, recognition and awareness are some important concepts of Rational Emotive Behaviour Therapy.

Codes

1 Both (A) and R are true and (R)is the correct explanation of (A)
2 Both (A) and (R) are true, but (R) is not the correct explanation of (A)
3 (A) is true, but (R) is false
4 (A) is false, but (R) is true

Ans. (2)

Exp. Both (A) and (R) are true, but (R) is not the correct explanation of (A).

Transpersonal psychotherapy views man as a spiritual being, views consciousness as central to therapy and emphasises emotions, feelings and experimental aspects of the client. Transpersonal psychotherapy enhances the study of mind-body relations, spirituality, consciousness, and human transformation. Experts disagree as to the specific model and margins of this form of therapy, however the three key areas that are considered through transpersonal psychotherapy are combined/holistic and natural psychology, transformative psychology, and ego-transcended psychology.

Self-acceptance, flexibility, recognition and awareness are some important concepts of Rational Emotive Behaviour Therapy. Rational Emotive Behaviour Therapy, also known as REBT, continually work on recognising our irrational beliefs, disputing them, changing our irrational "musts," and transforming negative emotions into more positive ones. In REBT rational beliefs are defined as beliefs that are flexible, non-extreme, and logical. REBT places emphasis on self acceptance and self-awareness which involves trying to avoid self-judgment and recognising that humans can and will make mistakes.

Both the statements are independently correct and explaining two different therapies, so they are not mutually related.

44 Read each of the following two statements, Assertion (A) and Reason (R) and indicate your answer using the codes given below:

Assertion (A) Organisational justice is perception of what is fair in the workplace composed of distributive, procedural and interactional justice.

Reason (R) Employees have greater tolerance of overpayment inequities than underpayment inequities as part of distributive justice.

Codes

1 Both (A) and (R) are true and (R) is the correct explanation of (A)
2 Both (A) and (R) are true, but (R)is not the correct explanation of (A)
3 (A) is true, but (R) is false
4 (A) is false, but (R) is true

Ans. (2)

Exp. Both (A) and (R) are true, but (R) is not the correct explanation of (A).

Organisational justice is perception of what is fair in the workplace composed of distributive, procedural and interactional justice. Organisational justice refers to employee perceptions of fairness in the workplace. Distributive justice reflects perceptions regarding fairness of outcomes, while procedural justice reflects perceptions of processes that lead to these outcomes. Interactional justice focuses on the way in which an individual is treated when decisions are made; individuals feel they are being treated fairly when employers provide explanations for decisions and treat employees with dignity, respect, and sensitivity.

Employees have greater tolerance of overpayment inequities than underpayment inequities as part of distributive justice. Employees can tolerate overpayment inequities, i.e., to earn more than they deserve rather than underpayment inequities, i.e., not getting what they actually deserve. This is a part of distributive justice. The statement is correct but it does not explain Organisational justice, rather explains one of the types of justice.

45 A strategy designed to gain favourable response to a small request at first, with the intent of making the person more likely to agree later to a larger request is known as

1 Compliance
2 Door-in the face
3 Foot-in the door technique
4 Obedience

Ans. (3)

Exp. Foot-in-the-door Technique is a strategy designed to gain favourable response to a small request at first, with the intent of making the person more likely to agree later to a larger request.

It is a compliance tactic that involves getting a person to agree to a large request by first setting them up by having that person agree to a modest request.

46 The Visual Placement tests conducted by Held and Hein were specifically intended to study

1 Development of depth perception
2 Relationship between sensory feedback resulting from self-initiated movement and perceptual development
3 Motor development
4 Discrimination learning

Ans. (2)

Exp. The Visual Placement tests conducted by Held and Hein were specifically intended to study relationship between sensory feedback resulting from self-initiated movement and perceptual development.

Held and Hein were interested in the development of perception. They decided to test whether being moved around (by someone or something else) while experiencing visual changes was enough to develop visually-guided behaviour, or whether the individual needed to move themselves around in order to learn such skills.

47 Which one of the following is not a correct elaboration of reading strategy in the field of literature?

1 C for careful reading
2 A for aim of reading
3 P refers to problem identification
4 S refers to solution of the problem

Ans. (1)

Exp. C for careful reading is not a correct elaboration of reading strategy in the field of literature.

Reading strategies involve various strategies that need to be followed to improve reading ability.

48 Read each of the following two statements, Assertion (A) and Reason (R) and indicate your answer using the codes given below:

Assertion (A) The objective of mastery goals in students is to improve, learn, seek challenges and persist inspite of difficulties.

Reason (R) Teachers can stimulate mastery goal orientation through the techniques of self-monitoring, self-improvement and deeper understanding of subject.

Codes

1 Both (A) and (R) are true and (R) is the correct explanation of (A)
2 Both (A) and R are true, but (R) is not the correct explanation of (A)
3 (A) is true, but (R) is false
4 (A) is false, but (R) is true

Ans. (2)

Exp. Both (A) and (R) are true, but (R) is not the correct explanation of (A).

The objective of mastery goals in students is to improve, learn, seek challenges and persist inspite of difficulties. There are two types of goals: mastery goals and performance goals. Mastery goals are aimed at attaining a standard of competence defined by self-improvement or skill development. Individuals who hold mastery goals either seek task-related self-improvement or strive to gain task mastery. So, the Assertion is true.

Teachers can stimulate mastery goal orientation through the techniques of self-monitoring, self-improvement and deeper understanding of subject. Teachers can stimulate mastery goal orientation through different techniques. Self-monitoring shows how much people monitor their self-presentations, expressive behaviour, and non-verbal affective displays. Self-improvement is the improvement of one's knowledge, status, or character by one's own efforts. It is the quest to make ourselves better in any and every facet of life. Mastery learning is a set of group-based, individualised, teaching and learning strategies based on the premise that students will achieve a high level of understanding in a given domain if they are given enough time. The reason statement is true, but it does not explain the objective of mastery goals rather it states how teachers can stimulate the mastery goal orientation.

49 Temporary support that parents provide to a child to do a task until the child can do it alone, is termed as

1 Ageism
2 Induction
3 Scaffolding
4 Power assertion

Ans. (3)

Exp. Temporary support that parents provide to a child to do a task until the child can do it alone, is termed as Scaffolding.

It refers to a process in which teachers model or demonstrate how to solve a problem and then step back, offering support as needed. Psychologist and instructional designer Jerome Bruner first used the term 'Scaffolding' in this context back in the 1960s. The theory is that when students are given the support they need while learning something new, they stand a better chance of using that knowledge independently. Bruner recommends positive interaction and three modes of representation during teaching: actions, images and language.

50 Read each of the following two statements, Assertion (A) and Reason (R) and indicate your answer using the codes given below :

Assertion (A) Children of permissive-indulgent parents tend to the impulsive, aggressive, inconsiderate and demanding.

Reason (R) Permissive-indulgent parents are high on warmth, discipline and control.

Codes

1 Both (A) and (R) are true and (R) is the correct explanation of (A)
2 Both (A) and (R) are true, but (R) is not the correct explanation of (A)
3 (A) is true, but (R) is false
4 (A) is false, but (R) is true

Ans. *(3)*

Exp. (A) is true, but (R) is false

Children of permissive-indulgent parents tend to the impulsive, aggressive, inconsiderate and demanding. Permissive-indulgent parents are very responsive to the child's emotional needs. But they don't set limits or are very inconsistent in enforcing boundaries. They do not control or regulate their children's behaviour. So their children are less aware of the limits of acceptable behaviour. They also exhibit worse impulse control and have more behavioural problems. When facing stressfulsituations, they are more likely to resort to using Aggression. So, the assertion statement is true.

Permissive-indulgent parenting is a parenting style characterised by high responsiveness and low demandingness. So, the reason statement is false.

51 Rogers in his Person Centred Counselling approach emphasises ______ and ______ .

1 empathy; sympathy
2 experiential focussing; unconditional positive regard
3 congruence; sympathy
4 unconditional positive regard; empathy

Ans. *(4)*

Exp. Rogers in his Person Centred Counseling approach emphasises unconditional positive regard and empathy.

Person Centred Counseling is a form of counseling developed by psychologist, Carl Rogers beginning in the 1940s and extending into the 1980s. It seeks to facilitate a client's self-actualising tendency, "an inbuilt proclivity toward growth and fulfillment", via acceptance (unconditional positive regard), therapist congruence (genuineness), and empathic understanding. The counselor accepts the client unconditionally, without judgement, disapproval, or approval. He/She experiences an empathic understanding of the client's internal frame of reference. Accurate empathy on the part of the counselor helps the client believe the counselor's unconditional regard for them.

52 According to the frequency of their occurrence, arrange the following in ascending order.

I. Alpha waves | II. Beta waves
III. Theta waves | IV. Delta waves

Codes

1 IV, III, I, II
2 III, IV, I, II
3 II, I, III, IV
4 II, I, IV, III

Ans. *(1)*

Exp. The correct ascending order is IV, III, I, II.

Delta waves : It is the lowest frequency brain wave recorded in electroencephalography. Delta waves are large, regular-shaped waves that have a frequency of 1 to 3 Hz. They are associated with deep sleep.

Theta waves : It is a type of regular brain wave with a frequency of 4 to 7 Hz. Theta waves occur during REM sleep in non-human animals, Stage 2 NREM sleep in humans, and the drowsy state prior to sleep onset in newborn infants, adolescents, and adults.

Alpha waves : It is a type of low-amplitude brain wave (frequency 8–12 Hz) that typically occurs when the eyes are closed or unfocused and no deliberate mental tasks are taking place; it is associated with a wakeful but relaxed state.

Beta waves : It is the type of brain wave (frequency 13–30 Hz) associated with alert wakefulness and intense mental activity.

53 Match the items of List I (Theories) with List II (Descriptions) and mark your answer with the help of the codes given below :

	List I (Theories)		List II (Descriptions)
A.	Theory of Signal Detection	I.	Sensory subjective magnitude grows in proportion to the intensity of the stimulus raised to a power.
B.	The Fechner Law	II.	The minimal amount of stimulus energy required for a detection of a stimulus.
C.	Absolute Threshold	III.	Evaluation of the separate effects of the observer's sensory capacity and response bias.
D.	Stevens Power Law	IV.	Larger and larger inputs in stimulus energy are required to obtain a corresponding sensory effect.

Codes

	A	B	C	D		A	B	C	D
1	I	II	III	IV	2	I	II	IV	III
3	III	IV	II	I	4	III	II	I	IV

Ans. *(3)*

Exp. The correct matching is A-III, B-IV, C-II, D-I.

Theory of Signal Detection is the evaluation of the separate effects of the observer's sensory capacity and response bias. It is a means to measure the ability to differentiate between information-bearing patterns and random patterns that distract from the information.

The Fechner's Law suggests that larger and larger inputs in stimulus energy are required to obtain a corresponding sensory effect. It states that the subjective sensation is proportional to the logarithm of the stimulus intensity. According to this law, human perceptions of sight and sound work in the following manner: the perceived loudness/brightness is proportional to logarithm of the actual intensity measured with an accurate nonhuman instrument.

Absolute Threshold is the minimal amount of stimulus energy required for a detection of a stimulus. It is the smallest level of energy required by an external stimulus to be detectable by the human senses, including vision, hearing, taste, smell and touch. It is more precisely defined as the degree of intensity of a stimulus necessary to correctly detect that stimulus 50% of the time. Stimuli at or above the absolute threshold - those which can be detected-are called supraliminal.

Stevens Power Law suggests that sensory subjective magnitude grows in proportion to the intensity of the stimulus raised to a power. It is a proposed relationship between the magnitude of a physical stimulus and its perceived intensity or strength.

54 Match List I with List II and select the correct answer using the codes given below :

List I (Hypothalamic areas)	List II (Effects of lesion)
A. Lateral pre-optic area	I. Deficit in physiological mechanisms of temperature regulation.
B. Pre-optic area	II. Deficit in drinking.
C. Ventromedial hypothalamus	III. Under eating, weight loss and low insulin level.
D. Lateral hypothalamus	IV. Increased meal frequency, weight gain and high insulin level.

Codes

	A	B	C	D		A	B	C	D
1	IV	III	I	II	2	III	IV	II	I
3	II	I	IV	III	4	I	II	III	IV

Ans. *(3)*

Exp. The correct matching is A-II, B-I, C-IV, D-III.

Lesions in *Lateral pre-optic area* causes deficit in drinking. Lesion of the lateral preoptic area (LPO) of the rat were used to study the participation of this area in drinking behaviour and it was found that there was a significant reduction in water intake.

Lesions in *Pre-optic area* causes deficit in physiological mechanisms of temperature regulation. The pre-optic region, in and near the rostral hypothalamus, contains neurons that are sensitive to subtle changes in hypothalamic or core temperature.

Lesions in *Ventromedial hypothalamus* causes increased meal frequency, weight gain and high insulin level. VMH is the important center for satiety and adiposity and could be the ultimate pathway for control of food intake and obesity.

Lesions in *Lateral hypothalamus* causes under eating, weight loss and low insulin level. The lesions of the lateral hypothalamus prevented spontaneous feeding, resulting in starvation.

55 Down syndrome is associated with which of the causal factor?

1 Trisomy 18
2 Trisomy 12
3 Trisomy 21
4 Trisomy 14

Ans. *(3)*

Exp. Down syndrome is associated with Trisomy 21.

Trisomy 21 is also known as Down syndrome. It is a genetic disorder that involves birth defects, intellectual disabilities, and characteristic facial features. Additionally, it often involves heart defects, visual and hearing impairments and other health problems. Sometimes, an error occurs when the 46 chromosomes are being divided in half and an egg or spermcell keeps both copies of the 21 chromosome instead of just one copy.

56 Salient features of classical conditioning are

I. Responses are voluntary.
II. Based on principle of association by contiguity.
III. Antecedent stimuli are important in forming association.
IV. Goal is to increase the rate of an already occurring response.
V. Goal is to create a new response to stimulus.

Codes

1 II, III and V
2 I, III and IV
3 II, III, IV and V
4 I, III, IV and V

Ans. *(1)*

Exp. Statement II, III and IV are correct in relation to salient features of classical conditioning.

Classical conditioning theory involves learning a new behaviour along with the process of association. In simple terms two stimuli are linked together to produce a new learned response in a person or animal.

Salient features of classical conditioning are as follows :

(i) *Based on principle of association by contiguity* : A principle that posits that classical conditioning is effective only when the conditioned stimulus and unconditioned stimulus are contiguous (i.e. follow one another closely in time).

(ii) *Antecedent stimuli are important in forming association* : An antecedent is a stimulus that cues an organism to perform a learned behaviour.

(iii) *Goal is to create a new response to stimulus* : The goal of classical conditioning is determined when two stimuli are linked together to produce a new learned response in a person or animal.

57 In which part of the brain does classical conditioning take place?

1 Reticular formation 2 Amygdala
3 Cerebellum 4 Hypothalamus

Ans. (3)

Exp. Classical conditioning takes place in Cerebellum.

The main regions of the brain associated with classical conditioning are the cerebellum, which coordinates motor and bodily functions. The cerebellum and its associated circuitry constitutes the entire essential neuronal system for classical conditioning of eye-blink and other discrete responses (e.g. limb flexion) learned with an aversive Unconditioned Stimulus (US) using the standard delay paradigm where the Conditioned Stimulus (CS) and the US co-terminate.

58 Read each of the following two statements, Assertion (A) and Reason (R) and indicate your answer using the codes given below:

Assertion (A) Conditioning fails to occur when unconditioned stimulus and conditioned stimulus are paired in a random order.

Reason (R) Cognitive processes involving expectation play an important role in classical conditioning.

Codes

1 Both (A) and (R) are true and (R) is the correct explanation of (A)
2 Both (A) and (R) are true, but (R) is not the correct explanation of (A)
3 (A) is true, but (R) is false
4 (A) is false, but (R) is true

Ans. (1)

Exp. Both (A) and (R) are true and (R) is the correct explanation of (A).

Conditioning fails to occur when unconditioned stimulus and conditioned stimulus are paired in a random order. It is true because when the stimuli are not matched in a sequence, conditioning will fair to occur.

Cognitive processes involving expectation play an important role in classical conditioning. Conditioning is beneficial because it's helped us create expectations to prepare for future events. The cognitive processes play a role in creating expectations in classical conditioning. However, the expectations occur only when the unconditioned stimulus and conditioned stimulus are paired in a random order.

59 Arrange the following in order of sequence of career planning and decision-making.

I. Educational awareness
II. Career exploration
III. Self-awareness
IV. Career awareness

Codes

1 III, IV, I, II 2 III, I, IV, II
3 I, III, II, IV 4 II, IV, I, III

Ans. (2)

Exp. The correct sequence is III, I, IV, II.

The career planning and decision-making process has four steps :

Step 1 Self-awareness : It is a vital and often overlooked step in planning one's career paths. This involves taking a careful inventory of your current values, interests, skills and personal qualities.

Step 2 Educational awareness : It is about the education and training needed to achieve career goals.

Step 3 Career awareness : It involves exploring different careers. This involves researching these in detail and the opportunities in these areas.

Step 4 Career exploration : It involve decisions that are made which may involve narrowing down the options. One might need to gain some relevant work experience or work shadowing or gain some experience via voluntary activities.

60 Match List I with List II and indicate your answer using the codes given below :

List I (Models of memory)	List II (Theorists)
A. Levels of processing	I. Atkinson and Shiffrin
B. Working memory	II. Tulving
C. Modal model	III. Craik and Lockhart
D. Multistore model	IV. Baddeley and Hitch

Codes

	A	B	C	D
1	IV	III	II	I
2	II	I	III	IV
3	I	II	IV	III
4	III	IV	I	II

Ans. (4)

Exp. The correct matching is A-III, B-IV, C-I, D-II.

The *Levels of processing* approach was given by Craik and Lockhart. They suggested that information needed to be processed in order to be transferred from Short term to long-termmemory. Deep processing increased the chance that the information would be preserved, compared to shallow processing.

The *Working memory* approach was given by Baddeley and Hitch. It is an alternative to the multi-store model of memory. It is based upon the findings of the dual-task study and suggests that there are four separate components to our working memory.

The *Modal model* was given by Atkinson and Shiffrin. They proposed that memory consisted of three stores: a sensory register, Short-term memory (STM) and Long-term memory (LTM).

The *Multistore model* was given by Tulving. He proposed a distinction between memories for general knowledge and memories for events. He argued that Long-term memory is made of two different yet interacting systems: semantic memory and episodic memory. Semantic memory is memory for meanings and facts. Episodic memory contains information about one's own personal experiences.

61 According to Tolman, the three parts of learning that work together as Gestalt are

I. Significant
II. Habit strength
III. Sign
IV. Means-end-relationship
V. Drive strength

Codes

1 II, III and V
2 III, IV and V
3 I, II and III
4 I, III and IV

Ans. (4)

Exp. According to Tolman, the three parts of learning that work together as Gestalt are significant, sign, and means-end-relationship.

In order to facilitate the learning process, Tolman proposes three basic components to be employed: (1) the significant, that is the desired outcome, goal, or behavior, (2) the sign, referring to the stimuli that prompts learners to take action, and (3) means-end relations, referring to a learner's internal thought process or relationships. According to Tolman, these 'sign gestalts' collectively form a 'cognitive map'. This cognitive map is also influenced by environment factors, which influences the learner's behaviour and prompts them to choose specific gestalts.

62 Match the items in List I with items in List II and mark your answer with the help of the codes given below :

List I (Attachment style)	List II (Attachment characteristics)
A. Avoidant attachment	I. Infant, after separation from primary caregiver, shows contradictory behaviour upon his or her return.
B. Secure attachment	II. Infant rarely cries when separated from the primary caregiver and does not make contact upon his or her return.
C. Disorganised-disoriented attachment	III. Infant cries when primary caregiver leaves and actively seek the caregiver upon his or her return.
D. Ambivalent (resistant) attachment	IV. Infant becomes anxious before the primary caregiver leaves, is upset during the absence and seeks at the same time avoids contact on his or her return.

Codes

	A	B	C	D
1	I	III	II	IV
2	III	II	IV	I
3	IV	I	III	II
4	II	III	I	IV

Ans. (4)

Exp. The correct matching is A-II, B-III, C-I, D-IV.

In *Avoidant attachment* style, an infant rarely cries when separated from the primary caregiver and does not make contact upon his or her return. They do not look at the stranger or the mother and reacted very little to her absence or her return, seeming to have no interest or concern.

In *Secure attachment* style, an infant cries when primary caregiver leaves and actively seek the caregiver upon his or her return. Infants labelled as secure were willing to get down from their mother's lap soon after entering the room with their mothers. They explored happily, looking back at their mothers and returning to them every now and then (sort of like "touching base"). When the mother left, the infants got upset. When the mother returned, the infants approached her, were easily soothed, and were glad to have her back.

In *Disorganised-Disoriented attachment* style, an infant after separation from primary caregiver, shows contradictory behaviour upon his or her return. These disorganised–disoriented infants would approach her but with their eyes turned away from her, as if afraid to make eye contact. In general, these infants seemed fearful and showed a dazed and depressed look on their faces.

In *Ambivalent (resistant) attachment* style, an infant becomes anxious before the primary caregiver leaves, is upset during the absence and seeks at the same time avoids contact on his or her return. The word 'ambivalent' means to have mixed feelings about something. Ambivalent babies were clinging and unwilling to explore, very upset by the stranger regardless of the mother's presence, protested mightily when the mother left, and were hard to soothe. When the mother returned, these babies would demand to be picked up but at the same time push the mother away or kick her in a mixed reaction to her return.

63 Which one of the following is not a correct way of stimulating creative thinking?

1 Brainstorming
2 Keep a diary
3 Mind mapping
4 Offering money

Ans. (4)

Exp. Offering money is not a correct way of stimulating creative thinking.

Creative thinking is a way of looking at problems or situations from a fresh perspective that suggests unorthodox solutions (which may look unsettling at first). Creative thinking can be stimulated both by an unstructured process such as brainstorming and by a structured process such as lateral thinking. Often, creativity in this sense involves what is called lateral thinking or the ability to perceive patterns that are not obvious. Creative people can devise new ways to carry out tasks, solve problems, and meet challenges. They bring a fresh and sometimes unorthodox perspective to their work and can help departments and organisations to move in more productive directions.

Mind Mapping is a form of visual thinking which allows you to explore a subject or idea using keywords, which trigger associations in the brain to spark further ideas. Visual thinking is known for the powerful way in which it can boost our memory, productivity and creativity.

64 Short-term memories are stored in which part of the brain?

1 Cerebellum
2 Amygdala
3 Hippocampus
4 Prefrontal cortex

Ans. (4)

Exp. Short-term memories are stored in Prefrontal cortex.

The cerebral cortex plays a key role in memory, attention, perceptual awareness, thought, language and consciousness. It is divided into four main regions or lobes, which cover both hemispheres. The frontal lobe involved in conscious thought and higher mental functions such as decision-making, particularly in that part of the frontal lobe known as the prefrontal cortex and plays an important part in processing short-term memories and retaining longer term memories which are not task-based.

65 Match List I with List II and indicate your answer using the codes given below :

List I (Concepts)	List II (Descriptions)
A. Heuristics	I. Judgements made on the basis of specific kind of information that can be brought to mind.
B. Representative Heuristics	II. Tendency to use a number of value as a starting point to whom one adopts.
C. Availability Heuristics	III. Simple rules for drawing inferences in a rapid and effortless manner.
D. Anchoring and Adjustment Heuristics	IV. Judgements made on the basis of resemblance of current stimuli to other stimuli.

Codes

	A	B	C	D
1	III	I	IV	II
2	III	IV	II	I
3	III	IV	I	II
4	IV	III	I	II

Ans. (3)

Exp. The correct matching is A-III, B-IV, C-I, D-II

Heuristics are simple rules for drawing inferences in a rapid and effortless manner. It is a mental shortcut that helps us to make decisions and judgements quickly without having to spend a lot of time in researching and analyzing information.

Representative Heuristics are judgements made on the basis of resemblance of current stimuli to other stimuli. It is a mental shortcut that helps us make a decision by comparing information to our mental prototypes.

Availability Heuristics are judgements made on the basis of specific kind of information that can be brought to mind. It is a mental shortcut that helps us to make a decision based on how easy it is to bring something to mind.

Anchoring and Adjustment Heuristic is a tendency to use a number of value as a starting point to whom one adopts. It is also known as focalism, refers to the human tendency to accept and rely on, the first piece of information received before making a decision. That first piece of information is the anchor and sets the tone for everything that follows.

66 A readiness to make a particular perceptual response or class of responses to particular organisations of stimuli is called

1 Perceptual vigilance
2 Perceptual constancy
3 Perceptual set
4 Perceptual style

Ans. (3)

Exp. A readiness to make a particular perceptual response or class of responses to particular organisations of stimuli is called Perceptual set.

A Perceptual set is a temporary readiness to perceive certain objects or events rather than others. For example, a person driving a car has a perceptual set to identify anything in the car or on the road that might affect his or her safety. It is a schema or frame that influences the way in which a person perceives objects, events, or people. It is a tendency to perceive or notice some aspects of the available sensory data and ignore others.

67 In a 2 × 2 factorial design, with A and B as the two IVs, the F ratio '$MS_{A \times B} / MS_E$' is statistically significant. It implies that

1 there is cross-over interaction
2 there is disordinal interaction
3 there is either cross-over or disordinal interaction
4 there are both disordinal and cross-over interactions

Ans. (3)

Exp. In a 2 x 2 factorial design, with A and B as the two IVs, the F ratio '$MS_{A \times B} / MS_E$' is statistically significant. It implies that there is either cross-over or disordinal interaction.

A cross-over interaction (also referred to as ordinal non-independence), of course, exists when the ordering of the data points corresponding to the levels of one independent variable depends on the level of the other independent variable. When two or more group means switch or cross, a disordinal interaction occurs.

68 **Read each of the following two statements, Assertion (A) and Reason (R) and indicate your answer using the codes given below :**

Assertion (A) Inaccuracy among eye-witness occurs with the passage of time between witnessing an event and testifying about what was seen and heard.

Reason (R) Witnesses are always exposed to misleading postevent information from police, news stories and statements made by others.

Codes

1 Both (A) and (R) are true and (R) is the correct explanation of (A)
2 Both (A) and (R) are true, but (R) is not the correct explanation of (A)
3 (A) is true, but (R) is false
4 (A) is false, but (R) is true

Ans. (1)

Exp. Both (A) and (R) are true and (R) is the correct explanation of (A).

Inaccuracy among eye-witness occurs with the passage of time between witnessing an event and testifying about what was seen and heard. Eye-witness testimony is a situational account of a witness of what is typically a crime or an accident. The inaccuracy among eye-witness increases with the passage of time. Therefore, the Assertion statement is true.

Witnesses are always exposed to misleading post event information from police, news stories and statements made by others. Cognitive and memory research has shown that eye-witness accounts can be influenced and incorrect due to a number of factors such as stress, outside influences such a leading questioning, or misattribution of memory. This explains why inaccuracy occurs among eye-witness with the passage of time.

69 **From among the following who theorised mostly on the concept of 'achievement motivation'?**

1 Rogers, CR
2 Julian Rotter
3 David Mc Clelland
4 Frankl, VE

Ans. (3)

Exp. David Mc Clelland theorised mostly on the concept of 'achievement motivation'.

Achievement motivation is the desire to perform well and be successful. In this sense, the term often is used synonymously with need for achievement. It is the desire to overcome obstacles and master difficult challenges. High scorers in achievement motivation are likely to set higher standards and work with greater perseverance than equally gifted low scorers. David McClelland found a significant relationship between high achievement motivation and early independence in childhood; in addition, there is a positive correlation between high achievement motivation and actual achievement in later life.

70 **Concepts that closely matches the defining characteristics of a concept are known as**

1 formal concepts
2 natural concepts
3 prototype
4 subordinate concepts

Ans. (3)

Exp. Concepts that closely matches the defining characteristics of a concept are known as Prototype.

Prototype is the best or average exemplar of a category. For example, the prototypical bird is some kind of mental average of all the different kinds of birds of which a person has knowledge or with which a person has had experience. More generally, it is an object, event, or person that is held to be typical of a category and comes to represent or stand for that category. It is an early model of something that represents or demonstrates its final form.

Directions (Q. Nos. 71-75) *Read the passage given below and answer the questions that follows :*

An anxiety researcher, working in the interaction model of Anxiety, wanted to factor analyse anxiety-producing situations.

He had a hunch that anxiety-producing situations would broadly belong to two categories inter personal evaluative and physically threatening. His tool, assessing situation-specific anxiety had 14 situations. For each situation, the subject was required to indicate on 11 five-point rating scales as to how he or she would respond in that situation. Thus, for each situation scale, the minimum score would be 11 and the maximum score would be 55. The correlation matrix among the 14 situation scales was formed.

Two factor analyses were carried out on this correlation matrix. In the first factor analysis, unities were retained in the diagonal spaces of the correlation matrix and the un-rotated factors were extracted. Using Cattell's scree plot, three factors were retained for rotation. The rotated factors had small or moderate inter-factor correlations. In the second factor analysis, appropriate communality estimates were inserted in the diagonal spaces of the correlation matrix and the three factors were rotated using the same rotation method, used in the same factor analysis.

71 **Cattell's scree plot is a**

1 plot of the order of Eigen values on X-axis and the actual Eigen values of the reduced correlation matrix on Y-axis
2 plot of the order of Eigen values on X-axis and the actual Eigen values of the unreduced correlation matrix on Y-axis
3 plot displaying variables using the first two factor as axis
4 plot of the order of the factors on X-axis and the factor loading on Y-axis

Ans. (2)

➲ *Exp.* Cattell's scree plot is a plot of the order of Eigen values on X-axis and the actual Eigen values of the unreduced correlation matrix on Y-axis.

Cattell's scree plot in exploratory factor analysis, is a graphic that shows (in descending order) the eigen values of the communality-adjusted correlation matrix. The X-axis shows the amount of factors and the Y-axis shows the eigen values.

72 In the first factor analysis, while factor analysing the 14 × 14 correlation matrix, which one of the following four factor extraction method, has probably been used?

1 Maximum likelihood method
2 Principal axes method
3 Principal components method
4 Confirmatory factor analysis method

Ans. (3)

➲ *Exp.* In the first factor analysis, while factor analysing the 14 x 14 correlation matrix, Principal components method is used. This is because the unities are retained and unreduced correlation matrix is obtained. The Principal component analysis involves finding the linear combination of a set of variables that has maximum variance and removing its effect, repeating this successively.

73 Out of the following four factor rotation methods, which method/s can yield the above results?

I. Oblimin rotation
II. Varimax rotation
III. Promax rotation
IV. Quartimax rotation

Codes

1 Only I
2 I and II
3 I and III
4 III and IV

Ans. (3)

➲ *Exp.* Out of the given four factors rotation methods, Oblimin rotation and Promax rotation methods can yield the results.

There are five factors of rotation divided into two categories: Orthogonal (varimax, quartimax and equimax) and Oblique (oblimin and promax). Oblique factor rotation assumes that the factors are correlated whereas orthogonal assumes that factors are uncorrelated. In the paragraph, it has been mentioned that there is a small or moderate inter-factor correlations, so oblique rotation will be used to yield the required results. Therefore, oblimin and promax rotation will be used.

74 Which one of the following statements is true?

1 The first factor analysis used component model; the second factor analysis used common factor model
2 The first factor analysis used common factor model; the second factor analysis used principal component model
3 Both, the first and second factor analyses used component model
4 Both, the first and second factor analyses used common factor model

Ans. (2)

➲ *Exp.* Accoding to the paragraph the first factor analysis used common factor model; the second factor analysis used principal component model is true.

75 Which one of the following statements is true?

1 The second factor solution would explain more percent of variance
2 The second factor solution would explain less percent of variance
3 Both factor solutions would explain same percent of variance
4 Such prediction is not possible

Ans. (2)

➲ *Exp.* The second factor solution would explain less percent of variance is true.

The initial estimation of factor analysis produces an unrotated solution where each successive factor explains less variance than the prior factor, but rotation redistributes the variance among factors. Thus, the amount of variance accounted for by a factor will differ before and after rotation, but neither the total amount of explained variance nor the communalities of the measured variables will change. The first factor solution is based on principal component analysis which explains higher variance as compared to the second factor solution which is based on principal axis method.

UGC-NET PSYCHOLOGY

SOLVED PAPER 2014 (June)

PAPER II

1 Autonomic Nervous System is concerned with the regulation of

I. smooth muscles II. skeletal muscles
III. cardiac muscles IV. glands

Codes

1 I and II 2 I, II and III
3 I, III and IV 4 I, II, III and IV

Ans. (3)

Exp. Autonomic Nervous System is concerned with the regulation of smooth muscles, cardiac muscles and glands.

Autonomic Nervous System controls the glands and the smooth muscles that comprise the heart, blood vessels and the lining of the stomach and intestines. These muscles are called smooth because microscopic examination shows that they lack the striated appearance characteristics of skeletal muscles. Cardiac muscle (heart muscle) is an involuntary, striated muscle that is found in the walls and histological foundation of the heart, specifically the myocardium. Glands are organ in the human or animal body which secretes particular chemical substances for use in the body or for discharge into the surroundings.

2 What would be the total number of pairs in a study scaling the twelve attitude items by the method of paired comparison?

1 132 2 72 3 66 4 60

Ans. (3)

Exp. The total number of pairs in a study scaling the twelve attitude items by the method of paired comparison is 66. The formula for calculating the number of pairs is:

n(n-1)/2, where n is the number of number items

= 12 (12–1)/2 = 12*11/2 = 66

3 Match the List I and List II and indicate your answer with the help of codes given below :

List I (Theorist)	List II (Motivational Concept)
A. Hull	I. Instinct
B. Cannon	II. Drive
C. Tinbergen	III. Homeostatic
D. McDougall	IV. Fixed Action Pattern

Codes

	A	B	C	D
1	II	III	IV	I
2	III	IV	II	I
3	IV	I	II	III
4	I	II	III	IV

Ans. (1)

Exp. The correct matching is A-II, B-III, C-IV, D-I.

Hull is associated with Drive. He created his own learning theory sometimes referred to as Drive theory or Systematic behaviour theory. He believed that drive reduction is a major cause of learning and behaviour.

Cannon is associated with Homeostatic. It is a self-regulating process by which biological systems maintain stability while adjusting to changing external conditions. This concept explains how an organism can maintain more or less constant internal conditions that allow it to adapt and to survive in the face of a changing and often hostile external environment.

Tinbergen is associated with Fixed Action Pattern. A Fixed Action Pattern is the courtship and aggression behaviour of the male three-spined stickleback during the mating season, described in a series of studies by Niko Tinbergen.

McDougall is associated with Instinct. He was one of the first to write about the Instinct theory of motivation. He suggested that instinctive behaviour was composed of three essential elements i.e., perception, behaviour and emotion.

4 Match the List I and List II and indicate your answer with the help of codes given below :

List I (Psychologist)	List II (Concept of Personality)
A. Kelly	I. Mandala
B. Erickson	II. Corollary
C. Adler	III. Fidelity
D. Jung	IV. Compensation

Codes

	A	B	C	D
1	II	IV	III	I
2	I	III	IV	II
3	II	III	IV	I
4	I	IV	III	II

Ans. (3)

Exp. The correct matching is A-II, B-III, C-IV, D-I

Kelly is associated with the concept of Corollary. Kelly's personality theory is known as Personal Construct Theory and is presented in a scientific format, organised into a fundamental postulate and 11 corollaries. The 11 corollaries are: construction, individual, organisation, dichotomy, choice, range, experience, modulation, fragmentation, commonality and sociality.

Erickson is associated with the concept of Fidelity. Erikson's stages of psychosocial development are a comprehensive psychoanalytic theory that identifies a series of eight stages that a healthy developing individual should pass through from infancy to late adulthood. Fidelity is the ability to sustain loyalties freely pledged in spite of the inevitable contradictions and confusions of value systems.

Adler is associated with the concept of Compensation. In one of his earliest and most famous publications, 'Study of Organ Inferiority and Its Physical Compensation,' Adler outlined the basics for what would be the beginning foundation of his personality theory. The article focuses mainly on the topics of organ inferiority and compensation. Organ inferiority is when one organ, or portion of the body, is weaker than the rest. Adler postulated that the body's other organs would work together in order to compensate for the weakness of this "inferior" organ. When compensation occurs, other areas of the body make up for the function lacking in the inferior portion.

Jung is associated with the concept of Mandala. Mandala is a graphical representation of the center (the Self by Jung). It can appear in dreams and visions or it can be created spontaneously as by drawing. It is present in the cultural and religious representations.

5 Read each of the following two statements, Assertion (A) and Reason (R) and indicate your answer using the codes given below:

Assertion (A) The level at which we first categorise an object is the basic in the hierarchy of concepts.

Reason (R) Concepts are related to one another.

Codes

1 Both (A) and (R) are true and (R) is the correct explanation of (A)
2 Both (A) and (R) are true, but (R) is not the correct explanation of (A)
3 (A) is true, but (R) is false
4 (A) is false, but (R) is true

Ans. *(2)*

Exp. Both (A) and (R) are true, but (R) is not the correct explanation of (A).

The level at which we first categorise an object is the basic in the hierarchy of concepts. This means that to understand any concept, we must first categorise it. A hierarchy is a system or organisation in which people or groups are ranked one above the other according to status or authority. It is an arrangement of items (objects, names, values, categories etc) in which the items are represented as being above, below or at the same level as one another.

Concepts are related to one another. A concept is an idea that represents a class of objects or events or their properties, such as cats, walking, honesty, blue, or fast. Two different concepts can be related to each other. E.g., Teaching and Learning. This does not explain the need to categorise an object in the hierarchy of concepts.

6 Which set of processes is involved in storing of information in long-term memory?

I. Chunking
II. Long-term potentiation
III. Consolidation
IV. Monitoring

Codes

1 II and III
2 I, II and IV
3 III and IV
4 I, III and IV

Ans. *(1)*

Exp. The set of processes involved in storing of information in Long-term memory are Long-term potentiation and Consolidation.

Long-Term Potentiation (LTP) is a persistent increase in synaptic strength following high-frequency stimulation of a chemical synapse. It is the long-lasting enhancement of the neural signals, which helps in storing information for long.

Consolidation is the neurobiological processes by which a permanent memory is formed following a learning experience.

7 An oil painting itself can include all of the following cues to depth perception except

1 linear perspective
2 retinal disparity
3 texture gradient
4 relative image size

Ans. *(2)*

Exp. An oil painting itself can include all of the given cues to depth perception except retinal disparity.

Linear perspective one of the monocular depth cues, arising from the principle that the size of an object's visual image is a function of its distance from the eye. Thus, two objects appear closer together as the distance from them increases, as seen in the tracks of a railroad that appear to converge on the horizon.

Texture gradient is the progressive decline in the resolution of textures as the viewer moves away from them.

Relative image size refers to the fact that the more distant an object, the smaller its image will be on the retina. Therefore, if there are two identical objects, the one that is farther away will be the one that has a smaller image on the retina.

Retinal disparity is a binocular cue which requires integration of information from both the eyes. It is important in gauging how far away objects are. The more difference (or greater disparity) between the image each eye has of the same object, the closer it is to you. The farther away an object is, on the other hand, the more similar it looks from viewing it with each eye alone.

8 Read each of the following two statements, Assertion (A) and Reason (R) and indicate your answer using the codes given below:

Assertion (A) Everyday people face situations wherein they have to choose one alternative to the exclusion of others and they make use of the concurrent schedules of reinforcement effectively.

Reason (R) The matching law suggests that we choose between response alternatives in such a way so as to maximise the reinforcement we receive from the chosen alternative.

Codes

1 Both (A) and (R) are true and (R) is the correct explanation of (A)
2 Both (A) and (R) are true, but (R) is not the correct explanation of (A)
3 (A) is true, but (R) is false
4 (A) is false, but (R) is true

Ans. *(1)*

Exp. Both (A) and (R) are true and (R) is the correct explanation of (A).

Everyday people face situations wherein they have to choose one alternative to the exclusion of others and they make use of the concurrent schedules of reinforcement effectively. In operant conditioning, concurrent schedules of reinforcement are schedules of reinforcement that are simultaneously available to an individual, so that they can respond on either schedule. We face different situations on the daily basis and we choose one alternative on the basis of concurrent schedules of reinforcement.

The matching law suggests that we choose between response alternatives in such a way so as to maximise the reinforcement we receive from the chosen alternative. Based on the matching law, we tend to choose alternatives which have a higher chance of being reinforced. This explains why people choose one alternative to the exclusion of others.

9 Which of the following is/are example(s) of continuous organismic variable?

I. Gender
II. Heart beats per minute
III. Trials required to learn a list of CVC trigrams
IV. Intelligence

Codes

1 Only I
2 Only IV
3 II and IV
4 II, III and IV

Ans. *(3)*

Exp. The examples of continuous organismic variable are Heart beats per minute and Intelligence.

Organismic variable is a factor considered in behavioural assessment which refers to the physiological and psychological features of the organism that influence behaviour. It is any characteristic of the research participant/individual under study that can be used for classification.

10 Arrange the following in correct sequence through which the sound waves reach the receptors.

I. Oval window
II. Incus
III. Stapes
IV. Malleus
V. Tympanic membrane

Codes

1 V, IV, II, III, I
2 V, IV, III, II, I
3 V, IV, I, III, II
4 V, III, II, IV, I

Ans. *(1)*

Exp. The correct sequence is V, IV, II, III, I

The correct sequence through which the sound waves reach the receptors can be described as follows:

Tympanic membrane is the ear drum. It divides the external ear from the middle ear. Sound waves travel along the auditory canal and strike the tympanic membrane, causing it to vibrate. This vibration results in movement of the three ossicles, namely malleus, incus, and stapes.

Malleus or hammer, is a hammer-shaped small bone or ossicle of the middle ear.

Incus, also known as the "anvil," is the middle of three small bones in the middle ear.

Stapes is the third of three tiny bones in the middle ear and the one closest to the inner ear. Because of its shape, it's sometimes called the stirrup. As the ossicles move, the stapes presses into a thin membrane of the cochlea known as the oval window.

Oval window, also known as the Fenestra ovalis, is a connective tissue membrane which is located at the end of the middle ear and the beginning of the inner ear.

11 Arrange the following into correct sequence as per James-Lange Theory.

I. Emotion producing situation
II. Feeling of emotion
III. Elicitation of emotional responses
IV. The brain receives sensory feedback from the muscles and other organs

Codes

1 I, II, III, IV
2 I, IV, II, III
3 II, III, IV, I
4 I, III, IV, II

Ans. *(4)*

Exp. The correct sequence is I, III, IV, II.

The James-Lange Theory of emotion proposes that emotions occur as a result of physiological reactions to events. There is an emotion-producing situation which elicits emotional responses. The brain receives sensory feedback from the muscles and other organs and a specific pattern of autonomic nervous system arousal is observed. This arousal leads to feeling of emotions. For example, if you were to encounter a venomous snake in your backyard, your sympathetic nervous system (responsible for activating your fight-or-flight response) would initiate physiological arousal, making your heart race and increasing your breathing rate. According to the James–Lange theory of emotion, you would experience a feeling of fear only after this physiological arousal had taken place. Different arousal patterns would be associated with different feelings.

12 Read each of the following two statements, Assertion (A) and Reason (R) and indicate your answer using the codes given below :

Assertion (A) Ego defense mechanisms help to protect the person from overwhelming anxiety.

Reason (R) Major psychodynamic functions of anxiety are to help the individual avoid conscious recognition of acceptable instinctual impulses and to allow impulse qualification only indirectly.

Codes

1 Both (A) and (R) are true and (R) is the correct explanation of (A)
2 Both (A) and (R) are true, but (R) is not the correct explanation of (A)
3 (A) is true, but (R) is false
4 (A) is false, but (R) is true

Ans. *(3)*

Exp. (A) is true, but (R) is false.

Ego defense mechanisms help to protect the person from overwhelming anxiety. Ego defense mechanisms (or factors), defined by Freud are unconscious resources used by the ego to reduce conflict between the id and superego, are a reflection of how an individual deals with conflict and stress.

Reason (R) is false, as in anxiety we do not avoid conscious recognition of acceptable instinctual impulses. This happens in fearful situations.

13 Continuum of 'Birth Weight' is the basis of studying

1 the effect of biological factors on intellectual development
2 the effect of genetics on intellectual development
3 the effect of genetic and socio-cultural factors on intellectual development
4 the effect of biological and socio-cultural factors on intellectual development

Ans. *(1)*

Exp. Continuum of 'Birth Weight' is the basis of studying the effect of biological factors on intellectual development.

Birth weight is the body weight of a baby at its birth. The growth curve of a child is tracking the birth weight of the child at different time periods, and it is assumed to be increasing with increase in time.

Although babies born at the lower end of the birth weight continuum have greater mortality risks, there are maternal and infant risks for birth weights that are on the higher end of the continuum. These births are known as high birth weight or macrosomia (large body). This is nothing related to genetic factors.

14 Which of the following are methods of solving problems?

I. Trial and error
II. Mental set
III. Algorithm
IV. Heuristics
V. Functional fixedness

Codes

1 I, II and III	2 I, IV and V
3 I, III and IV	4 III, IV and V

Ans. *(3)*

Exp. The methods of solving problems are Trial and error, Algorithm and Heuristics.

Trial and error is a fundamental method of problem-solving. It is characterised by repeated, varied attempts which are continued until success or until the agent stops trying.

Algorithms are mental processes which relate to how people understand, diagnose, and solve problems, mediating between a stimulus and response. A mathematical formula is a good example of an algorithm, as it has a straightforward and step-by-step way of being solved.

Heuristics are action-oriented mental shortcuts that use what we know and are familiar with to try something, hoping for a positive response. They can save a lot of time, because we don't usually need a complex and comprehensive procedure for the various actions we take in our lives.

15 Read each of the following two statements, Assertion (A) and Reason (R) and indicate your answer using the codes given below :

Assertion (A) In a memory experiment participants, were found to use both verbal and visual encoding while performing the given task.

Reason (R) Episodic buffer, a component of working memory, is used to integrate and to store briefly the information from phonological loop and visuo-spatial sketch-pad.

Codes

1 Both (A) and (R) are true and (R) is the correct explanation of (A)
2 Both (A) and (R) are true, but (R) is not the correct explanation of (A)
3 (A) is true, but (R) is false
4 (A) is false, but (R) is true

Ans. *(1)*

Exp. Both (A) and (R) are true and (R) is the correct explanation of (A).

In a memory experiment the participants, were found to use both verbal and visual encoding while performing the given task. Evidence suggests that working memory uses two different systems for dealing with visual and verbal information. A visual processing task and a verbal processing task can be performed at the same time.

Episodic buffer, a component of working memory, is used to integrate and to store briefly the information from phonological loop and visuo-spatial sketch-pad. Working memory is a multi-component system which includes the central executive, visuospatial sketchpad, phonological loop, and episodic buffer. The episodic buffer acts as a 'backup' store which communicates with both long-term memory and the components of working memory.

Episodic buffer was assumed to be a temporary store of limited capacity that was capable of combining a range of different storage dimensions, allowing it to collate information from perception, from the visuo-spatial and verbal subsystems. It was assumed to do so by representing them as multidimensional chunks or episodes, which were assumed to be available to conscious awareness. This explains why the participants were able to encode both verbal and visual information while performing the given task.

16 Put the steps involved in observational learning in sequence of its occurrence.

I. Reproduction
II. Attention
III. Motivation for later use
IV. Retention codes

Codes

1 IV, II, I, III   2 I, IV, III, II
3 II, IV, I, III   4 III, I, II, IV

Ans. *(3)*

Exp. The correct sequence is II, IV, I, III.

Observers cannot learn unless they pay attention to what's happening around them, then must not only recognise the observed behaviour but also remember it at some later time.

One must be physically and/intellectually capable of producing the act and for the production, the motivation is important. Bandura formulated his findings in a four-step pattern which combines a cognitive view and an operant view of learning.

Attention is noticing the behaviour to implement observational learning.

Retention is how well the behaviour is remembered.

Reproduction is the ability to execute the model's behaviour.

Motivation is having a reason, desire or will for imitating the behaviour.

17 Which set of following conditions indicate failure of recognition?

I. Associative agnosia
II. Constructional apraxia
III. Prosopagnosia
IV. Pure alexia
V. Ataxia

Codes

1 I, II and V   2 II, III and IV
3 I, III and IV   4 II, III and V

Ans. *(3)*

Exp. The conditions which indicate the failure of recognition are Associative agnosia, Prosopagnosia and Pure alexia.

Associative agnosia is a form of visual agnosia. It is impairment in recognition or assigning meaning to a stimulus that is accurately perceived and not associated with a generalised deficit in intelligence, memory, language or attention.

Prosopagnosia, also called face blindness, is a cognitive disorder of face perception in which the ability to recognise familiar faces, including one's own face (self-recognition), is impaired, while other aspects of visual processing and intellectual functioning remain intact.

Individuals who have *Pure alexia* suffer from severe reading problems while other language-related skills such as naming, oral repetition, auditory comprehension or writing are typically intact.

18 Read each of the following two statements, Assertion (A) and Reason (R) and indicate your answer using the codes given below :

Assertion (A) A positive charge applied to the inside of the membrane of the neuron produced depolarisation.

Reason (R) Inside of the membrane was positively charged.

Codes

1 Both (A) and (R) are true and (R) is the correct explanation of (A)
2 Both (A) and (R) are true, but (R) is not the correct explanation of (A)
3 (A) is true, but (R) is false
4 (A) is false, but (R) is true

Ans. *(3)*

Exp. (A) is true, but (R) is false.

A positive charge applied to the inside of the membrane of the neuron produced depolarisation. Polarisation is the existence of opposite electrical charges on either side of a cell membrane. Depolarisation is a change within a cell, during which the cell undergoes a shift in electric charge distribution, resulting in less negative charge inside the cell compared to the outside.

Inside of the membrane was positively charged. It is false as the inside of the neural membrane of the neuron at rest is negatively charged, and the outside is positively charged.

19 What would be the degrees of freedom for a chi-square based on 4 x 5 contingency table?

1 5   2 9   3 12   4 20

Ans. *(3)*

Exp. The degrees of freedom for a chi-square based on 4×5 contingency table are 12.

The formula for calculating degrees of freedom is:

df = (r-1) (c-1), where 'r' is the number of rows and c is the number of columns.

Here, r = 4, c = 5, df = (4-1) (5-1) = 12.

20 Which one of the following events is critical for the development of internal sex organs in males during 3rd month of gestation?

1 Activation of 'sry gene'
2 Presence of anti-mullerian hormone
3 Presence of dihydrotestosterone
4 Development of testes

Ans. (2)

Exp. The event critical for the development of internal sex organs in males during 3rd month of gestation is the presence of anti-mullerian hormone.

Anti-Müllerian hormone is a protein hormone which is important in the development of the reproductive tract in a male foetus and is also produced (before birth) by the testes and ovaries. About eight weeks after conception the human foetus has two sets of ducts, one of which can develop into the male reproductive tract and the other into the female reproductive tract. If the foetus is genetically male (XY chromosomes) then the embryonic testes will produce Anti-Müllerian hormone.

This causes the Müllerian (female) ducts to disappear – hence the term anti-Müllerian hormone, whilst testosterone produced by the testes causes the male (Wolffian) ducts to survive. The Wolffian ducts go on to develop into the different parts of the male reproductive system: the epididymis, the vas deferens, the seminal vesicles and the prostate gland. In a female fetus (XX chromosomes) the Wolffian ducts disappear (because of the lack of testosterone) and the Müllerian ducts develop into the fallopian tubes, uterus (womb), cervix and the upper part of the vagina.

21 Children of affluent and educated parents tend to score higher on tests of ability than children of parents living in poverty and who are not well educated. This relationship between socio-economic status and scores on ability tests is because of conditions indicate failure of

I. genetic differences in ability between different social classes.
II. differences in the adequacy of the biological and environmental factors in nutrition and health care.
III. differences in the cultural and learning experiences provided for children from different social classes.

Codes

1 I and III　　2 II and III
3 I and II　　4 All of these

Ans. (4)

Exp. The given relationship between socio-economic status and scores on ability tests is becouse of the conditions indicate the failure of all of the following factors :

Genetic differences in ability between different social classes : The socio-economic status influences comprise of environmental variance and the association of socio-economic status and children's cognitive growth is likely to be partially mediated by genetic factors.

Differences in the adequacy of the biological and environmental factors in nutrition and health care : People with high Socio-economic Status (SES) are more likely to have healthier food habits, whereas people with low SES have dietary profiles less consistent with nutritional recommendations or dietary guidelines, hence contributing to their poorer health status.

Differences in the cultural and learning experiences provided for children from different social classes : It is plausible that children from higher SES families experience greater opportunities for and support in cognitive engagement and learning than children from more disadvantaged homes. Differences in the availability of learning opportunities, support and resources are thought to accentuate individual differences in cognitive ability.

22 In reasoning when the premises are true, _____ cannot be false.

1. conclusion　　2. argument
3. thoughts　　4. prepositions

Ans. (1)

Exp. In reasoning when the premises are true, conclusion cannot be false.

If both the premises are true, the obtained conclusion must be true. A deductive argument is to provide a guarantee of the truth of the conclusion provided that the argument's premises are true. This point can be expressed also by saying that, in a deductive argument, the premises are intended to provide such strong support for the conclusion that, if the premises are true, then it would be impossible for the conclusion to be false.

23 Arrange the following stages of memory in order of their occurrence.

I. Chunking
II. Sensory register
III. Consolidation
IV. Elaborative rehearsal
V. Selective attention

Codes

1 V, II, I, IV, III　　2 III, II, V, I, IV
3 I, V, II, IV, III　　4 II, I, V, III, IV

Ans. (1)

Exp. The correct order of stages of occurrence is V, II, I, IV, III.

The stages of memory in order of their occurrence are: Selective attention, Sensory register, Chunking, Elaborative Rehearsal and Consolidation.

Selective attention refers to the ability to pay attention to a limited array of all available sensory information.

Selectively attended sensory information is initially held in the sensory registers.

Sensory register is the memory store where information first comes in through the senses. There are separate sensory registers for each sense: the iconic store codes visual information and the echoic store codes auditory information.

Chunking is grouping together items or words so that they can be stored or processed as single concepts. It is a process by which individual pieces of information are bound together into a meaningful whole.

Elaborative rehearsal is a memory technique that involves thinking about the meaning of the termto be remembered, as opposed to simply repeating the word over and over.

Consolidation is a neurological process that involves gradually converting information from Short-term memory into Long-term memory.

24 Arjun gets annoyed when his mother nags him to do his homework. When he finally does it, his mother stops nagging. Now, he does the homework without any nagging. Here 'nagging' has served as a

1 punishment by application
2 positive reinforcement
3 negative reinforcement
4 punishment by removal

Ans. *(3)*

Exp. Here 'nagging' has served as a negative reinforcement.

In negative reinforcement, a response or behaviour is strengthened by stopping, removing or avoiding a negative outcome or aversive stimulus. Negative reinforcement involves the removal of a negative condition to strengthen a behaviour.

25 Read each of the following two statements, Assertion (A) and Reason (R) and indicate your answer using the codes given below:

Assertion (A) Larger the image of an object on the retina, the closer it is judged to be. In addition, if an object is larger than other objects, it is often perceived as closer.

Reason (R) Retinal disparity provides an important cue for depth perception.

Codes

1 Both (A) and (R) are true and (R) is the correct explanation of (A)
2 Both (A) and (R) are true, but (R) is not the correct explanation of (A)
3 (A) is true, but (R) is false
4 (A) is false, but (R) is true

Ans. *(2)*

Exp. Both (A) and (R) are true, but (R) is not the correct explanation of (A).

Larger the image of an object on the retina, the closer it is judged to be. When an object is far away, its retinal image size becomes small, and when the object is near, its retinal image size becomes big. It is true as nearer objects seem to be larger in size and the larger the size of the object, the closer it is perceived.

Retinal disparity provides an important cue for depth perception. Retinal disparity refers to the small difference between the images projected on the two retinas when looking at an object or scene. This slight difference or disparity in retinal images serves as a binocular cue for the perception of depth. The reason statement is true but it does not explain why the larger objects are perceived closer.

26 Which of the following cells do produce myelin in the Central Nervous System?

1 Schwann cells
2 Astrocytes
3 Microglia
4 Oligodendrocytes

Ans. *(4)*

Exp. The cells which produce myelin in the Central Nervous System are Oligodendrocytes.

Oligodendrocytes are a type of non-neuronal Central Nervous System cell that forms myelin sheaths around axons. Myelin is formed by oligodendrocytes in the Central Nervous System (CNS). Each oligodendrocyte forms multiple sheaths (up to 30 or more) around different axons.

Myelin is formed by Schwann cells in the peripheral nervous system (PNS) and each Schwann cell forms a single myelin sheath around an axon.

Astrocyte is a star-shaped non-neuronal Central Nervous System cell with numerous extensions that run in all directions. Astrocytes provide structural support for the brain, are responsible for many homeostatic controls, and may isolate receptive surfaces.

Microglia is an extremely small type of non-neuronal Central Nervous System cell that removes cellular debris from injured or dead cells.

27 After the general election in a country, a social psychologist interviewed 200 voters to study their attitudes towards the winning party. This is an example of

1 field experiment
2 attitude change experiment
3 correlational study
4 ex post-facto research

Ans. *(4)*

Exp. After the general election in a country, a social psychologist interviewed 200 voters to study their attitudes towards the winning party. This is an example of ex-post facto research. It is also called after-the-fact research. It is a category of research design in which the investigation starts after the fact has occurred without interference from the researcher. It is also often applied as a substitute for true experimental research to test hypotheses about cause-and-effect relationships or in situations in which it is not practical or ethically acceptable to apply the full protocol of a true experimental design.

28 Read each of the following two statements, Assertion (A) and Reason (R) and indicate your answer using the codes given below :

Assertion (A) Low levels of serotonin release are associated with aggression and other forms of antisocial behaviour.

Reason (R) Serotonergic neurons play an inhibitory role in human aggression.

Codes

1 Both (A) and (R) are true and (R) is the correct explanation of (A)
2 Both (A) and (R) are true, but (R) is not the correct explanation of (A)
3 (A) is true, but (R) is false
4 (A) is false, but (R) is true

Ans. (1)

Exp. Both (A) and (R) are true and (R) is the correct explanation of (A).

Low levels of serotonin release are associated with aggression and other forms of anti-social behaviour. Low serotonin has been linked to impulsive aggression. Aggression, unlike impulsivity, is not a personality trait, but a behaviour wherein one injures or harms others. It is thought by some to be oriented towards survival, but when it is constant and excessive, it injures both at individual and community levels. Lower serotonin levels in the brain are also thought to be linked to poor orbitofrontal cortex function, which is in turn seen to be present in people with anti social behaviour. It is true as low serotonin levels are associated either high aggression or antisocial behaviour.

Serotonergic neurons play an inhibitory role in human aggression. The serotonergic system seems to be involved in various inhibitory responses throughout the Central Nervous System. The decrease of the level of serotonin generated by the action of enzyme monoaminooxide is associated with violent behaviour and anti-social personality disorder. This explains why low levels of serotonin are associated with aggression and anti-social behaviour.

29 Constructive Alternativism refers to

1 a person's mental processes are psychologically channelised by the ways in which he anticipates events
2 all present interpretations of the universe are subject to revision or replacement
3 it is a category of thought by which the individual construes or interprets his personal world of experience
4 it is a process by which a person predicts and controls personal experiences by construing their replications

Ans. (2)

Exp. Constructive Alternativism refers to all present interpretations of the universe are subject to revision or replacement.

In the Personality Construct Theory of George A. Kelly, Constructive Alternativism is the capacity to view the world from multiple perspectives, that is, to envision a variety of alternative constructs.

With his theory of Constructive Alternativism, George Kelly posited that our experiences of the world around us, including events that take place or our understanding of people, including ourselves, are open to an immense variety of interpretations. Kelly argued that no one construct is a final or definitively accurate way of grasping the world. Instead, we can always create alternative constructs to better explain or represent that which we observe.

30 Which of the following is not a consequence of Spearman's Theory?

1 The correlation between different measures of intelligence will be positive
2 The correlation between two measures of intelligence will be equal to $r_{1g} \times r_{2g}$ where 1 and 2 represent the two different measures and 'g' represents general factor
3 The correlation between two measures of intelligence will be equal to $r_{1g} \times r_{2g}$ where 1 and 2 represent the two different measures and 'g' represents general factor
4 The law of tetrad difference will hold for four measures of intelligence

Ans. (3)

Exp. Statement 3 is not a consequence of Spearman's Theory.

Spearman tried to correlate different measures of intelligence and found that the correlation is positive. The measures of intelligence are related to common general intellectual functioning. The general cognitive ability is measured or expressed in numerical terms.

There are four measures of intelligence and these four measures are collectively known as Law of Tetrad Difference, which states that $r_{12} \times r_{34} = r_{13} \times r_{24}$. The above formula has a multiplicative element and not an additive element, which makes the Statement 3 as an incorrect choice.

31 A test involves presenting a pair of words like father-daughter and the subject is required to list as many ways in which the pair is related. In this measure which of the abilities are given by Guilford?

1 Divergent production of symbolic relations
2 Divergent production of semantic relations
3 Convergent production of symbolic relations
4 Divergent production of semantic systems

Ans. (2)

Exp. The abilities given by Guilford are Divergent production of semantic relations.

Divergent production is the creative generation of multiple answers to a set problem. Divergent production abilities are in connection with creative thinking, where many ideas need to be brought to light with ease. Semantic relation focuses on the relationship between signifiers—like words, phrases signs, and symbols—and what they stand for, their denotation.

32 Match the List I and List II and indicate your answer with the help of codes given below:

Unit I (Phenomenon)	Unit II (Description)
A. Thoughts	I. Properties that best exemplify the concept
B. Concept	II. Process of assigning an object to a concept (class)
C. Prototype	III. Language of the mind
D. Categorisation	IV. Represents an entire class

Codes

	A	B	C	D		A	B	C	D
1	III	II	I	IV	2	III	IV	I	II
3	I	II	III	IV	4	IV	III	II	I

Ans. (2)

Exp. The correct matching is A-III, B-IV, C-I, D-II.

Thoughts are language of the mind. It is an idea, image, opinion, or other product of thinking.

Concept represents an entire class. It is an idea that represents a class of objects or events or their properties.

Prototype is the property that best exemplify the concept. It is the best or average exemplar of a category. More generally, it is an object, event, or person that is held to be typical of a category and comes to represent or stand for that category.

Categorisation is the process of assigning an object to a concept (class). It is the process by which objects, events, people, or experiences are grouped into classes on the basis of characteristics shared by members of the same class and features distinguishing the members of one class from those of another.

33 Match the List I and List II and indicate your answer with the help of codes given below :

List I (Phenomenon)	List II (Condition)
A. Loss of memory of events that occurred prior to a loss inducing event	I. Mental contamination
B. Loss of memory of events that occurs after a loss inducing event	II. Retrograde amnesia
C. Blocking of information in memory we don't try to remember, produced by our retrieval of other related information	III. Anterograde amnesia
D. Mental processing that is not readily under our control, influence our judgements, emotions or behaviour	IV. Retrieval inhibition

Codes

	A	B	C	D		A	B	C	D
1	IV	I	III	II	2	I	III	IV	II
3	II	I	IV	III	4	II	III	IV	I

Ans. (4)

Exp. The correct matching A-II, B-III, C-IV, D-I.

Mental contamination is the mental processing that is not readily under our control, influence our judgements, emotions or behaviour. It occurs when individuals experience feelings of internal dirtiness and distress in the absence of physical contact with a contaminant.

Retrograde amnesia is the loss of memory of events that occurred prior to a loss inducing event. It is a loss of memory-access to events that occurred or information that was learned in the past.

Anterograde amnesia is the loss of memory of events that occurs after a loss inducing event. It is a condition in which a person is unable to create new memories after an amnesia-inducing event.

Retrieval inhibition is the blocking of information in memory we don't try to remember, produced by our retrieval of other related information. As we learn new information to replace old information, retrieval access to the old information becomes inhibited.

34 After several visits to the doctor for chemotherapy, Anita finds that she begins to feel nauseous just sitting in the waiting room. According to classical conditioning, Anita's feeling of nausea in the absence of chemotherapy is

1 an unconditioned stimulus
2 an unconditioned response
3 a conditioned stimulus
4 a conditioned response

Ans. (4)

Exp. According to classical conditioning, Anita's feeling of nausea in the absence of chemotherapy is a conditioned response. Whenever Anita is given chemotherapy, she feels nauseated. This means that feeling of nausea is an unconditioned response. But when the same response is felt by just sitting in the waiting room without the absence of chemotherapy, the same feeling of nausea becomes a conditioned response.

During acquisition the Conditioned Stimulus (CS) and Unconditioned Stimulus (US) are paired as described (waiting room and chemotherapy). This repeated number of chemotherapy increases the strength and/or frequency of the CR (nausea) gradually.

A conditioned response (CR) in classical conditioning, is the learned or acquired response to a conditioned stimulus.

35 Which of the following do not belong to laws of perceptual grouping?

I. Law of figure and ground
II. Law of good continuation
III. Law of common fate
IV. Law of closure
V. Law of proximity

Codes

1 I and V 2 II and IV
3 III and V 4 I and III

Ans. *(4)*

Exp. Law of figure and ground and law of common fate do not belong to laws of perceptual grouping.

The Law of figure and ground states that we can distinguish an object (the figure of the rule) from its background (the ground). It suggests that when we perceive a visual image, we tend to simplify it by separating in the figure and the ground. The figure is the object that we perceive. The ground is everything in the background.

The Law of Common Fate observes that when objects point in the same direction,we see themas a related group.

Perceptual grouping refers to the process of determining which regions and parts of the visual scene belong together as parts of higher order perceptual units such as objects or patterns. There are four laws of perceptual grouping: similarity, proximity, closure and continuation.

The Law of Good Continuation means that figures with edges that are smooth are more likely seen as continuous than edges that have abrupt or sharp angles.

The Law of Proximity states that humans perceive stimuli that are close to each other by grouping them and recognising them as part of the same object.

The Law of Closure states that the brain tends to perceive forms and figures in their complete appearance despite the absence of one or more of their parts, either hidden or totally absent.

The Law of Similarity states that that elements that are similar to each other tend to be perceived as a unified group.

36 Match the List I and List II and indicate your answer with the help of codes given below :

List II (Number)	List I (Structure)
A. 31	I. Lobes of cerebrum
B. 7	II. Cranial nerves
C. 12	III. Cervical vertebrae
D. 4	IV. Spinal nerves

Codes

	A	B	C	D		A	B	C	D
1	IV	II	III	I	2	IV	III	II	I
3	II	III	IV	I	4	III	I	II	IV

Ans. *(2)*

Exp. The correct matching is A-IV, B-III, C-II, D-I.

There are 4 *lobes of cerebrum* - the frontal lobe, parietal lobe, temporal lobe, occipital lobe.

There are 12 *cranial nerves.* In higher vertebrates (reptiles, birds, mammals), the 12 pairs of cranial nerves are: olfactory (CN I), optic (CN II), oculomotor (CN III), trochlear (CN IV), trigeminal (CN V), abducent (or abducens; CN VI), facial (CN VII), vestibulocochlear (CN VIII), glossopharyngeal (CN IX), vagus (CN X), accessory (CN XI), and hypoglossal (CN XII).

There are 7 *cervical vertebrae.* The cervical spine has 7 stacked bones called vertebrae, labelled C1 through C7. The top of the cervical spine connects to the skull, and the bottom connects to the upper back at about shoulder level.

There are 31 pairs of *spinal nerves.* These spinal nerves control motor, sensory, and other functions. These nerves are located at the cervical, thoracic, lumbar, sacral, and coccygeal levels.

37 Read each of the following two statements, Assertion (A) and Reason (R) and indicate your answer using the codes given below :

Assertion (A) Non-equivalent control groups are often pencountered in quasi-experimental studies, as compared to experimental studies.

Reason (R) In quasi-experimental studies, as compared to experimental studies, secondary variance is less efficiently controlled.

Codes

1 Both (A) and (R) are true and (R) is the correct explanation of (A)
2 Both (A) and (R) are true, but (R) is not the correct explanation of (A)
3 (A) is true, but (R) is false
4 (A) is false, but (R) is true

Ans. *(2)*

Exp. Both (A) and (R) are true, but (R) is not the correct explanation of (A).

Non-equivalent control groups are often encountered in quasi-experimental research studies, as compared to experimental studies. A quasi-experimental research is research that resembles experimental research but is not true experimental research. Although the independent variable is manipulated, participants are not randomly assigned to conditions or orders of conditions. When participants are not randomly assigned to conditions, the resulting groups are likely to be dissimilar in some ways. For this reason, researchers consider them to be non-equivalent. A non-equivalent groups design is a between-subjects design in which participants have not been randomly assigned to conditions. Therefore, the assertion is true.

In quasi-experimental studies, as compared to experimental studies, secondary variance is less efficiently controlled. Secondary variance results from extraneous, outside factors that the experimenter did not recognise and/or control for. These extraneous variables may have an effect on the dependent variable, but the experimenter may not be interested in selecting these variables for an independent variable. In a quasi-experimental research, secondary variance is less likely to be controlled as compared to experimental research. The reason statement is also true, but it does not explain why the non-equivalent control groups are used in quasi-experimental studies.

38 Self Determination Theory (humanistic view of motivation) focuses on which of the following needs?

I. Autonomy
II. Competence
III. Esteem
IV. Self-actualisation
V. Relatedness

Codes

1 I, III and IV
2 II, IV and V
3 I, II and V
4 III, IV and V

Ans. (3)

Exp. Self Determination Theory (humanistic view of motivation) focuses on Autonomy, Competence and Relatedness.

Self-determination theory is a theory of human motivation and personality which suggests that people are able to become self-determined when their needs for competence, relatedness, and autonomy are fulfilled. Competence is the need to be effective in dealing with the environment. Relatedness is the need to have close, affectionate relationships. Autonomy is the need to feel self-governing and independent.

39 What is an Ipsative test?

1 for an individual examinee, the high scores on some sub-scales are accompanied by low scores on other sub-scales
2 a test that measures one or more clearly defined, but relatively heterogeneous segments of ability
3 a test in which the average of the sub-scales is always the same for every examinee
4 a test which gives an estimate of how much of the total variance in a given trait is due to genuine factors

Ans. (3)

Exp. An Ipsative test is a test in which the average of the sub-scales is always the same for every examinee.

It is a scale in which the points distributed to the various different items must sum to a specific total. In such a scale, all participants will have the same total score but the distribution of the points among the various items will differ for each individual.

40 Which of the following are correct for self-concept?

I. Self-concept includes not only one's perceptions of what one is like, but also what one thinks one ought to be.
II. Self-concept follows the general laws and principles of perception established in experimental psychology.
III. Self-concept represents an organised, coherent and integrated pattern of self related perceptions.
IV. Development of self-concept follows a specific time table of critical stages.

Codes

1 I, III and IV
2 II, III and IV
3 I, II and IV
4 I, II and III

Ans. (4)

Exp. Statement I, II and III are correct for self-concept.

Self-concept includes not only one's perceptions of what one is like, but also what one thinks one ought to be. It includes both one's perception of self and thought processes.

Self-concept follows the general laws and principles of perception established in experimental psychology. Some non-human animals, including chimpanzees, orangutans, and perhaps dolphins, have at least a primitive sense of self. We know this because of some interesting experiments that have been done with animals. Therefore, self-concept follows general laws and principles applicable to human beings as a result of experimental psychology.

Self-concept represents an organised, coherent and integrated pattern of self related perceptions. Self-concept is defined as an "overall vision (as an integrated, coherent, and stable individuality) transcending the experiential and event content of self-awareness".

The development of concept is influenced by parental attitudes and behaviour. When the parents are supportive the child's internalisation of the parents' own attitudes toward success and failure, helps in development of self-concept. Therefore, it does not depend on specific time table of critical stages.

41 Which of the following is/are not a product in Guilford's model?

I. Convergent production
II. Divergent production
III. Transformation
IV. Implication

Codes

1 I and II
2 III and IV
3 I, II and IV
4 I, II and IV

Ans. (1)

Exp. Convergent production and Divergent production are not products in Guilford's Model.

In Guilford's Structure of Intellect (SI) theory, intelligence is viewed as comprising operations, contents, and products. Convergent and divergent productions are kinds of operations. Convergent production is the ability to deduce a single solution to a problem; also known as rule-following or problem-solving. Divergent production is the ability to generate multiple solutions to a problem; also known as creativity.

The products in Guilford's model are Units, Classes, Relations, System, Implications and Transformation.

42 The process of expanding our level of awareness and allowing us to observe ourselves engaged in the problem-solving process is termed as

1 representativeness heuristic
2 algorithm
3 anchoring and adjustment heuristic
4 metacognitive processing

Ans. (4)

Exp. The process of expanding our level of awareness and allowing us to observe ourselves engaged in the problem-solving process is termed as metacognitive processing.

Metacognitive processesing include people's monitoring and control of their cognitions. Even though self-regulation itself does not require that regulators are conscious of their ongoing efforts, we assume that individuals engage in self-awareness and reflection which are explicit metacognitive processes. Metacognition is an awareness of one's own thought processes and an understanding of the patterns behind them. It can take many forms, such as reflecting on one's own ways of thinking and knowing when and how to use particular strategies for problem-solving.

43 A network of associated facts and concepts that make out general knowledge of the world is referred to as

1 Episodic memory
2 Explicit memory
3 Implicit memory
4 Semantic memory

Ans. (4)

Exp. A network of associated facts and concepts that make out general knowledge of the world is referred to as semantic memory.

Semantic memory is the memory for general factual knowledge and concepts, of the kind that endows information with meaning and ultimately allows people to engage in such complex cognitive processes as recognising objects and using language.

44 Match the List I and List II and indicate your answer with the help of codes given below:

List I (Temporal Arrangement of)		List II (Form of UCS and CS Conditioning)
A. Onset of the Unconditioned Stimulus (UCS) occurs while the Conditioned Stimulus (CS) is still present	I.	Trace conditioning
B. Onset of the Conditioned Stimulus (CS) precedes the onest of the Unconditioned Stimulus (UCS)	II.	Simultaneous conditioning
C. The Conditioned Stimulus (CS) and the Unconditioned Stimulus (UCS) begin and end at the same time	III.	Backward conditioning
D. Unconditioned Stimulus (UCS) precedes the Conditioned Stimulus(CS)	IV.	Delay conditioning

Codes

	A	B	C	D		A	B	C	D
1	I	III	II	IV	2	IV	I	II	III
3	III	I	IV	II	4	II	IV	I	III

Ans. (2)

Exp. The correct matching is A-IV, B-I, C-II, D-III.

In the *Trace conditioning*, the onset of the Conditioned Stimulus (CS) precedes the onset of the Unconditioned Stimulus (UCS). The onset of CS precedes the onset of UCS and the presentation of the CS and UCS does not overlap.

In the *Simultaneous conditioning*, the Conditioned Stimulus (CS) and the Unconditioned Stimulus (UCS) begin and end at the same time. CS and UCS presented together. e.g the bell begins to ring at the same time the food is presented. Both begin, continue and end at the same time.

In the *Backward conditioning*, the Unconditioned Stimulus (UCS) precedes the Conditioned Stimulus (CS). e.g. the food is presented, and then the bell rings.

In the *Delayed conditioning*, the onset of the Unconditioned Stimulus (UCS) occurs while the Conditioned Stimulus (CS) is still present. CS is presented before the UCS and it (CS) stays on until the US is presented. e.g. a bell begins to ring and continues to ring until food is presented.

45 Phi phenomena is the principle behind

1 illusion of brightness
2 illusion of distance
3 illusion of size
4 illusion of movement

Ans. (4)

Exp. Phi phenomena is the principle behind illusion of movement.

The Phi phenomenon is an illusion of movement that arises when stationary objects e.g. light bulbs, are placed side by side and illuminated rapidly one after another. The effect is frequently used on theatre marquees to give the impression of moving lights.

Directions (Q. Nos. 46-50) *Read the passage given below and answer the questions that follows :*

A psychologist wanted to develop a numerical ability test for the student population. She wrote eighty multiple-choice items, each item with five alternatives. The item analysis was carried out by finding discrimination index and item-remainder correlation for each item. Sixty items were retained in item analysis. The new version, with finally retained sixty items was administered to a new sample (N = 400) twice with a time gap of eight weeks. The test-retest correlation was found to be 0.22, significant at 0.01 level. The data obtained at the first administration of the sixty item version was also used for computing split-half reliability.

The correlation between scores based on odd items and the scores based on even items was found to be 0.60. The split-half reliability coefficient was obtained after applying Spearman-Brown correction.

The scores obtained by the students were correlated with their marks in Mathematics in their annual examination which took place three months after the data collection. The product-moment correlation of 0.6 was obtained between test scores and mathematics. Norms were developed for the test. The normative sample yielded a mean of 40 and standard deviation of 8. The data were found to be normally distributed. As norms, percentile ranks were obtained.

46 Which of the following correlation is suitable while computing item-remainder correlation in the above analysis?

1 Phi-coefficient
2 Point-biserial correlation
3 Spearman rank difference correlation
4 Multiple correlation

Ans. *(2)*

Exp. Point-biserial correlation is suitable while computing item-remainder correlation in the above analysis. It is used to measure the strength and direction of the association that exists between one continuous variable and one dichotomous variable. The phi-coefficient is used to evaluate the strength of association between two dichotomous variables.

47 What inference can you draw about the reliability of the text?

1 The test has unsatisfactory 'test-retest reliability'
2 The test has satisfactory test-retest reliability
3 The test has satisfactory internal consistency and test-retest reliability
4 The rest has satisfactory test-retest reliability, but unsatisfactory internal consistency

Ans. *(1)*

Exp. 'Test-retest reliability' refers to the degree to which test results are consistent over time. In order to measure test-retest reliability, we must first give the same test to the same individuals on two occasions and correlate the scores. Since, the test-retest reliability is 0.22, it has poor reliability. Therefore, the test has unsatisfactory 'test-retest reliability'.

48 What would be the percentile rank for a score of 48?

1 16 2 60 3 68 4 84

Ans. *(4)*

Exp. The percentile rank for a score of 48 is 84.

According to the paragraph, the mean is 40 and standard deviation is 8. One SD means 40 (+8) = 48. Therefore, the Percentile corresponding to 1 SD = 84.1% ~ 84 %

49 What would be the split-half reliability coefficient after Spearman-Brown correction?

1 16 2 60 3 68 4 85

Ans. *(3)*

Exp. The split-half reliability coefficient after Spearman-Brown correction is 0.75.

The formula for calculating split-half reliability coefficient is 2r/1+r, where r is the product-moment correlation. According to the paragraph, r = 0.6.

= 2 x 0.6/ 1+ 0.6 = 0.75.

50 What evidence has been obtained for the validity of the above test?

1 Satisfactory predictive validity
2 Unsatisfactory predictive validity
3 Satisfactory concurrent validity
4 Unsatisfactory concurrent validity

Ans. *(1)*

Exp. Predictive validity is the extent to which a score on a test predicts the score on some criterion measure. Here, the scores were predicted on the basis of Mathematics annual examination which is a criterion measure.

The product-moment correlation of 0.6 was obtained between test scores and mathematics. The test has satisfactory predictive validity.

PAPER III

1 Using the multiaxial system of DSM-IV-TR paranoid personality disorder and borderline personality disorder would be coded on

1 Axis I 2 Axis II
3 Axis III 4 Axis IV

Ans. *(2)*

Exp. Using the mutiaxial system of DSM-IV-TR paranoid personality disorder and borderline personality disorder would be coded on Axis II.

Multiaxial assessment is a system or method of evaluation, grounded in the biopsychosocial model of assessment that considers multiple factors in mental health diagnoses, for example, multiaxial diagnosis is characterised by five axes in the DSM-IV-TR; American Psychiatric Association, 2000.

Axis I provided information about clinical disorders. Any mental health conditions, other than personality disorders or mental retardation, would have been included here. Axis II provided information about personality disorders and mental retardation.

Axis III provided information about any medical conditions that were present which might impact the patient's mental disorder or its management.

Axis IV was used to describe psychosocial and environmental factors affecting the person.

Axis V was a rating scale called the Global Assessment of Functioning; the GAF went from 0 to 100 and provided a way to summarise in a single number just how well the person was functioning overall.

2 Match the List I and List II and indicate your answer with the help of codes given below :

List I (Author)	List II (Statement)
A. Herbert Spencer	I. "Discovery consists of seeing what everybody has seen and thinking what nobody has thought"
B. Albert Von	II. "It is human nature to hate those whom we have injured"
C. Karl Marx	III. "Opinion is ultimately determined by the feelings and not the intellect"
D. Tacitus Agricola	IV. 'Mere social contact begets ... a stimulation of animal spirits that heightens the efficiency of each individual workman'

Codes

	A	B	C	D		A	B	C	D
1	III	II	IV	I	2	III	I	IV	II
3	II	I	III	IV	4	II	III	I	IV

Ans. **(2)**

Exp. The correct matching is A-III, B-I, C-IV, D-II.

Herbert Spencer said, "Opinion is ultimately determined by the feelings and not the intellect." Herbert Spencer is famous for his doctrine of social Darwinism, which asserted that the principles of evolution, including natural selection, apply to human societies, social classes, and individuals as well as to biological species developing over geologic time.

Albert Von said, "Discovery consists of seeing what everybody has seen and thinking what nobody has thought". In the 1920s and 1930s, Dr. Albert Szent-Györgyi, a Hungarian professor of medicinal chemistry, made some very important discoveries that help us to understand basic nutrition.

Karl Marx said, "Mere social contact begets...a stimulation of animal spirits that heightens the efficiency of each individual workman." Marxism is a social, political, and economic theory originated by Karl Marx that focuses on the struggle between capitalists and the working class. Marx wrote that the power relationships between capitalists and workers were inherently exploitative and would inevitably create class conflict.

Tacitus Agricola said "It is human nature to hate those whom we have injured." Publius Tacitus was a Roman orator, lawyer, and senator. He is considered one of antiquity's greatest historians.

3 Which of the following are the features of behavioural assessment?

I. Researcher can collect self reported samples of behaviour from respondents as they live their daily lives.

II. Researcher devises explicit coding system that contains behavioural categories of interest.

III. It requires high level of interjudge reliability in using the coding categories to record behaviour.

IV. It is applied to record behaviour in live settings, but not in video taped behaviour.

Codes

1 II, III and IV
2 I, II and III
3 I, II and IV
4 All of these

Ans. **(2)**

Exp. Statement I, II and III contains the features of behavioural assessment.

Behavioural assessment is a method used in the field of psychology to observe, describe, explain, predict and sometimes correct behaviour. It can be useful in clinical, educational and corporate settings. There are many different tools that are useful in behavioural assessment and allow for a deeper understanding of why behaviour is occurring.

Behavioural assessment consists of self-reported samples of behaviour from individuals. Researchers can use codes to record behaviour. Behavioural assessment also requires high level of interjudge reliability to measure the behaviour in terms of codes. However, behavioural assessment is not necessary done to record behaviour in live settings and the same conclusions can be drawn from video-tapes. Therefore, Statement IV is not applicable and not considered as a feature of behavioural assessment.

4 The concept of 'creative intelligence' was given by

1 Gardner
2 Guilford
3 Torrance
4 Sternberg

Ans. **(4)**

Exp. The concept of 'creative intelligence' was given by Sternberg.

Instead of one intelligence, Robert Sternberg proposed a Triarchic theory of intelligence including analytical, creative and practical intelligence. Creative intelligence involves reacting successfully to new situations and being able to successfully produce new ideas.

5 Which one of the following appropriately represents the 'equity' theory of work motivation?

1 Input of A = Output of A
2 Output of A = Output of B
3 Input of A = Input of B
4 $\frac{\text{Output of A}}{\text{Input of A}} = \frac{\text{Output of B}}{\text{Input of B}}$

Ans. **(4)**

Exp. Output of A/Input of A = Output of B/Input of B appropriately represents the 'equity' theory of work motivation.

In the equity theory of motivation, employee's motivation depends on their perception of how fair is the compensation and treatment for their work input. Equity theory states that the employees perceive what they get from a job situation (outcomes) about what they put into it (inputs) and then compare their inputs-outcomes ratio with the inputs- outcomes ratios of others.

6 People who do well on embedded-figure tests are characterised to have_________ perceptual cognitive style.

1 constricted
2 flexible
3 field-independent
4 field-dependent

Ans. (3)

Exp. People who do well on embedded-figure tests are characterised to have field-independent perceptual cognitive style.

Embedded figures are the figures hidden inside the other figure. An Embedded Figures Test (EFT) is a test used to measure cognitive functioning and style in an individual by having them find geometric shapes within a larger complex image. This test can also be used to look at analytical style, social behaviours, problem solving style and defense mechanisms.

A field-independent learning style is defined by a tendency to separate details from the surrounding context. It can be compared to a field-dependent learning style, which is defined by a relative inability to distinguish detail from other information around it. Since embedded figure test involves a non-verbal reasoning, a person with field independent learning tend to rely less on the teacher or other learners for support.

7 Match the List I and List II and indicate your answer with the help of codes given below :

List I (Concept)	List II (Theorist)
A. Shaping and Chaining	I. Tolman
B. Law of Effect	II. Skinner
C. Cognitive Map	III. Bandura
D. Modeling	IV. Thorndike

Codes

	A	B	C	D		A	B	C	D
1	I	III	IV	II	2	II	III	I	IV
3	II	IV	I	III	4	III	IV	II	I

Ans. (3)

Exp. The correct matching is A-II, B-IV, C-I, D-III.

The concept of *Shaping and Chaining* was given by Skinner. These terms are related to Operant Conditioning proposed by him. Shaping involves reinforcing successive approximations of a desired behaviour. Chaining involves one response leading to the occurrence of another response.

The concept of *Law of Effect* was given by Thorndike. The law of effect principle suggested that responses closely followed by satisfaction will become firmly attached to the situation and therefore more likely to reoccur when the situation is repeated.

The concept of *Cognitive Map* was given by Tolman. A cognitive map is a type of mental representation which serves an individual to acquire, code, store, recall, and decode information about the relative locations and attributes of phenomena in their everyday or metaphorical spatial environment.

The concept of *Modeling* was given by Bandura. Modeling is a social approach that exaggerates on how important it is to be aware of attitudes and the result of emotional responses. It focuses on learning by observing others. It is used to uncover evolved behaviour.

8 An experimenter wishes to chemically stimulate the brain area of the animal by two substances, what are the choices among the following?

I. GABA   II. Glutamic acid
III. Glycine   IV. Kainic acid

Codes

1 I and III   2 II and IV
3 III and IV   4 I and II

Ans. (2)

Exp. The substances to chemically stimulate the brain area of the animal are Glutamic Acid and Kainic Acid.

Excitatory neurotransmitter have excitatory effects on the neuron, meaning they increase the likelihood that the neuron will fire an action potential. These excitatory neurotransmitters are used to chemically stimulate the brain area of the animals in various experiments.

Glutamic Acid is an excitatory neurotransmitter, in fact the most abundant one, in the vertebrate nervous system. *Kainic acid* is a potent neuroexcitatory amino acid agonist that acts by activating receptors for glutamate, the principal excitatory neurotransmitter in the central nervous system.

9 Explaining language development Jerome Bruner proposed

1 Developmental Time Table
2 Language Acquisition System
3 Language Acquisition Support System
4 Language Processing System

Ans. (3)

Exp. Explaining language development Jerome Bruner proposed the Language Acquisition Support System.

The Language Acquisition Support System (LASS) refers to the importance of a child's social support network, which works in conjunction with innate mechanisms to encourage or suppress language development. It argues that children do have an innate ability to learn and acquire language, but also require the interaction of other users of the same language to excel in their learning.

10 Read each of the following two statements, Assertion (A) and Reason (R) and indicate your answer using the codes given below:

Assertion (A) Promax-rotated factors cannot be subjected to higher-order factor analysis.

Reason (R) Promax rotation results in oblique factors.

Codes

1 Both (A) and (R) are true and (R) is the correct explanation of (A)

2 Both (A) and (R) are true, but (R) is not the correct explanation of (R)

3 (A) is true, but (R) is false

4 (A) is false, but (R)s true

Ans. (4)

Exp. (A) is false, but (R) is true.

Promax-rotated factors cannot be subjected to higher-order factor analysis. This is false as higher-order factors are all factors except primary factors, and are in fact extracted from the primary factors. Promax rotated factors can be subjected to higher-order factor analysis. Therefore, the Assertion is false.

Promax rotation results in oblique factors. In oblique method, the factors are correlated. One of the methods of carrying out oblique rotation is promax. Therefore, the reason is correct that promax rotation results in oblique factors.

11 While McClelland used TAT based on pictures to measure achievement motivation, what winter used to measure power motivation?

1 TAT pictures

2 Verbal material

3 Performance test

4 Line drawings

Ans. (2)

Exp. Winter used verbal material to measure power motivation.

Power motivation is the theory that some people are motivated by a desire for prestige and reputation or the ability to influence others and be in a position of power. People express their desire for power in different ways. They may take risks and use prestige to motivate others.

Winter used verbal material in the nPower system to measure a specific type of power orientation, which is associated with a moderate sense of security and a moderately defensive style of power-seeking. Winter developed a technique for scoring power motivation directly from any type of verbal material without the need of ambiguous pictures or story construction.

12 Match the List I and List II and indicate your answer with the help of codes given below :

List I (Theorist)	List II (Theory/Hypothesis of Emotion)
A. Tomkins	I. Dimensional appraisal
B. Schacter and Singer	II. Personal meaning
C. Smith and Ellsworth	III. Facial feedback hypothesis
D. Lazarus	IV. Unexplained arousal and appraisal of situations

Codes

	A	B	C	D		A	B	C	D
1	III	IV	I	II	2	III	I	II	IV
3	IV	III	I	II	4	I	II	III	IV

Ans. (1)

Exp. The correct matching is A-III, B-IV, C-I, D-II.

Tomkins proposed the Facial feedback hypothesis. It is based on the idea that a facial expression not only expresses an emotion, but also that expression and experience are linked in that afferent sensory feedback from the facial action influences the emotional experience.

Schacter and Singer proposed the theory of Unexplained arousal and appraisal of situations. According to this theory, emotion results from the interaction between two factors: physiological arousal and cognition. More specifically, this theory claims that physiological arousal is cognitively interpreted within the context of each situation, which ultimately produces the emotional experience.

Smith and Ellsworth proposed the theory of Dimensional appraisal. They identified eight dimensions on emotional perception in facial expressions, out of which pleasantness and arousal are the most studied dimensions.

Lazarus proposed the concept of Personal meaning. According to him, primary appraisals are evaluations of the personal significance of a person–environment encounter. If the individual evaluates that there is no harm to their well-being, the situation is appraised as irrelevant. However, if the person–environment interaction is appraised as harming, threatening, or challenging the well-being of the individual, the situation is appraised as stressful.

13 Defence attorneys often protest prosecutor's use of eyewitness testimony because

1 eyewitnesses are more prone to forgetting

2 a confident witness is usually right

3 source errors may cause an eyewitness to make a false identification

4 poor eyesight of eyewitnesses tends to invalidate their testimony

Ans. (3)

Exp. Defence attorneys often protest prosecutor's use of eyewitness testimony because source errors may cause an eyewitness to make a false identification.

Eyewitness testimony is an evidence given under oath in a court of law by an individual who claims to have witnessed the facts under dispute. Psychological research on the accuracy of eyewitnesses examines two areas of eyewitness error: memory for events (recall) and identification errors (facial recognition) which may result in false identification.

14 Match the List I and List II and indicate your answer with the help of codes given below :

List I (Description)	**List II** (Nomenclature)
A. Number of new cases that occur over a given period of time	I. Epidemiology
B. Study of the distribution of diseases or health related behaviours in a given population	II. Syndrome
C. Number of active cases in a population in a given period of time	III. Incidence
D. A group or cluster of symptoms that occur together	IV. Prevalence

Codes

	A	B	C	D
1	II	I	III	IV
2	IV	II	I	III
3	III	I	IV	II
4	I	IV	III	II

Ans. (3)

Exp. The correct matching is A-III, B-I, C-IV, D-II.

Epidemiology is the study of the distribution of diseases or health related behaviours in a given population. It is the study of the incidence and distribution of specific diseases and disorders.

Syndrome is a group or cluster of symptoms that occur together. It is a set of symptoms and signs that are usually due to a single cause (or set of related causes) and together indicate a particular physical or mental disease or disorder.

Incidence is the number of new cases that occur over a given period of time. It is the rate of occurrence of new cases of a given event or condition (e.g., a disorder, disease, symptom, or injury) in a particular population in a given period.

Prevalence is the number of active cases in a population in a given period of time. It is the total number or percentage of cases (e.g., of a disease or disorder) existing in a population, either at a given point in time (point prevalence) or during a specified period (period prevalence).

15 Read each of the following two statements, Assertion (A) and Reason (R) and indicate your answer using the codes given below :

Assertion (A) People maintain buffer zone around their bodies.

Reason (R) The extent of personal space depends on the familiarity with others near to them.

Codes

1 Both (A) and (R) are true and (R) is the correct explanation of (A)
2 Both (A) and (R) are true, but (R) is not the correct explanation of (A)
3 (A) is true, but (R) is false
4 (A) is false, but (R) is true

Ans. (2)

Exp. Both (A) and (R) are true, but (R) is not the correct explanation of (A).

People maintain a buffer zone around their bodies. The body buffer zone is the physical distance of a person prefers to maintain between him or herself and one or more other individuals to avoid feeling uncomfortable. This zone varies depending on the relationship with the others; it is smaller, for example, when there is a close relationship. Therefore, the Assertion is true.

The extent of personal space depends on the familiarity with others near to them. Personal space is the region surrounding a person which they regard as psychologically theirs. Most people value their personal space and feel discomfort, anger, or anxiety when their personal space is encroached. Entering somebody's personal space is normally an indication of familiarity and sometimes intimacy. The reason is also true but it does not explain why people develop buffer zone, rather it states the factors affecting the personal space.

16 Subjects in Milgram's experiment who gave large shocks rationalised that they were not personally responsible for their actions. This arises questions about one's willingness to commit in human acts. It was as a result of

1 coercive power
2 expert power
3 obedience to legitimate authority
4 conformity to group pressure

Ans. (3)

Exp. Subjects in Milgram's experiment who gave large shocks rationalised that they were not personally responsible for their actions. This arises questions about one's willingness to commit in human acts. It was as a result of obedience to legitimate authority.

Obedience is compliance with commands given by an authority figure. In the 1960s, the social psychologist Stanley Milgram did a famous research study called the obedience study. It showed that people have a strong tendency to comply with authority figures. He examined justifications for acts of genocide were based on obedience-which they were just following orders from their superiors.

17 The Id, according to Freud, is driven by aggressive and sexual instincts. This corresponds to Jung's archetype called

1 shadow
2 persona
3 evil force
4 sun

Ans. (1)

Exp. The Id, according to Freud, is driven by aggressive and sexual instincts. This corresponds to Jung's archetype called shadow.

In Jungian psychology, 'shadow' may refer to an unconscious aspect of the personality which the conscious ego does not identify in itself. The shadowis the dark side. According to Jung, the shadow, in being instinctive and irrational, is prone to psychological projection. It may be one's link to more primitive animal instincts just what Freud talked about Id.

18 In Jensen's distinction between Level I and Level II abilities, which one of the following is not a characteristic of Level I ability?

1 It involves neural registration and consolidation of stimulus inputs
2 It involves relatively little transformation of input
3 It is abstract and is measured by tests which are 'culture reduced'
4 It is relatively homogeneously distributed among different racial group

Ans. (3)

Exp. According to Jensen, intelligence consists of two levels of abilities. The Level I ability is associative learning, which consists of Short-Term Memory (STM), rote learning, attention and simple associative skills. The Level II is called cognitive learning, which consists of abstract thinking, symbolic thought, conceptual learning, and use of language in problem-solving.

Level I ability involves neural registration and consolidation of stimulus inputs so whatever the stimulus inputs is coming, it will be retained. It involves relatively little transformation of input. It involves rote memorisation of simple facts and skills so little to no transformation of inputs is seen at the Level I ability.

He argued that Level I ability, i.e. associative learning is equally distributed across all racial and national groups but on the contrary, Level II, i.e. cognitive learning is concentrated more the middle class Anglo-American populations than in the lower class black populations. Therefore, Level I ability is relatively homogeneously distributed among different racial group.

According to him, genetic differences in intelligence exist among people coming from different races, nationalities and social classes. So, it cannot be said that the Level I ability is culturally reduced.

19 Efficiency of a work organisational most appropriately refers to

1 attainment of organisational goals
2 maximum use of scarce and valued resources of the organisation
3 capability to produce a maximum quantity and quality output
4 higher level of initiative, flexibility, development and adjustment to changes

Ans. (2)

Exp. Efficiency of a work organisation most appropriately refers to maximum use of scarce and valued resources of the organisation. Organisational efficiency examines how to increase the output an organisation can achieve, using a specific amount of resources. The more output delivered using those same resources, the more efficient the organisation is. Efficiency of a work organisation is maximum utilisation of scarce and valued resources of the organisation to satisfy as many wants as possible.

20 Arrange the following five main step of a behavioural self-regulation programme from start to its end.

I. Collect the baseline data.
II. Develop a plan of intervention to modify antecedents and/ or consequences.
III. Specify the problem behaviour.
IV. Implement the programme and keep measuring behaviour.
V. Identify antecedents and consequences.

Codes

1 III, I, V, II, IV
2 I, III, IV, II, V
3 III, II, IV, I, V
4 II, III, I, V, IV

Ans. (1)

Exp. The correct sequence is III, I, V, II, IV.

The five main steps of a behavioural self-regulation programme from start to its end are as follows:

(i) *Specify the problem behaviour* : The identification and specification of the problem, behaviour is the first step in behavioural self-regulation programme.
(ii) *Collect the baseline data* : Once the problem behaviour is analysed, the data is collected at the baseline level.
(iii) *Identify antecedents and consequences* : After baseline data collection, the antecedents and consequences of problem behaviour are identified.
(iv) *Develop a plan of intervention to modify antecedents and/or consequences* : Based on the identified antecedents and consequences, a plan of intervention is developed.
(v) *Implement the program and keep measuring behaviour* : Once the intervention is planned, the program is implemented and evaluation of behaviour is done by measuring behaviour.

21 Arrange the following stages of language development in order of their occurrence.

I. Semantic development.
II. Production of meaningful speech.
III. Phonological development.
IV. Grammar/Syntax.

Codes

1 III, I, IV, II
2 I, IV, III, II
3 III, I, II, IV
4 I, III, IV, II

Ans. (1)

➲ *Exp.* The correct sequence of stages of language development is III, I, IV, II.

(i) *Phonological development* : It refers to forming and using speech sounds to clearly communicate language. As more sounds of a language are acquired, language becomes clearer and pronunciation, fluency and intonation all improve.

(ii) *Semantic Development* : It is the gradual acquisition of words and the meanings they carry. First words are usually produced at around the first year of birth. It is a slow but a gradual process in which a child, perhaps, learns a couple of words a week.

(iii) *Grammar/Syntax* : It refers to the rules used to combine words to make sentences.

(iv) *Production of meaningful speech* : It is the process by which thoughts are translated into speech.

22 Which of the following statements is/are true about principle components analysis?

I. While computing unities are retained in the diagonal spaces of correlation matrix.

II. The first principle component condenses maximum variance.

III. The subsequently extracted principle component is uncorrelated with the previously extracted principle component.

IV. The principle component cannot be subjected oblique rotation.

Codes

1 I and IV   2 I and III
3 II and III   4 I, II and III

Ans. (4)

➲ *Exp.* Statement I, II and III are true about principle components analysis.

While computing unities are retained in the diagonal spaces of correlation matrix. With PCA, unities are used in the diagonal of the correlation matrix computationally implying that all the variance is common or shared.

The first principle component condenses maximum variance. Factor model explores a reduced correlation matrix. That is, communalities (r^2) are inserted on the diagonal of the correlation matrix, and the extracted factors are based only on the common variance, with specific and error variances excluded.

The subsequently extracted principle component is uncorrelated with the previously extracted principle component. With this method, correlated variables are converted into uncorrelated principal components which permit to save the largest variance among features.

The principle component can be subjected to both oblique and orthogonal rotation.

23 Match the List I and List II and indicate your answer with the help of codes given below :

List I (Function of Perception)	List II (Perceptual Issue)
A. Attention	I. Where is the something (object)?
B. Localisation	II. What do characterise that thing (the object)?
C. Recognition	III. Is there something?
D. Abstraction	IV. What is that thing?

Codes

	A	B	C	D
1	IV	I	III	II
2	II	I	III	IV
3	II	I	IV	III
4	III	I	IV	II

Ans. (4)

➲ *Exp.* The correct matching is A-III, B-I, C-IV, D-II.

The perceptual issue in *Attention* is "Is there something?" Attention is a state in which cognitive resources are focused on certain aspects of the environment rather than on others and the central nervous system is in a state of readiness to respond to stimuli.

The perceptual issue in *Localisation* is "Where is the something (object)?" *Localisation* is the ability to determine the physical position or spatial location of a stimulus in any sensory modality.

The perceptual issue in Recognition is "What is that thing?" *Recognition* is a sense of awareness and familiarity experienced when one encounters people, events, or objects that have been encountered before or when one comes upon material that has been learned in the past.

The perceptual issue in *Abstraction* is "What do characterize that thing (the object)?" Abstraction is the formation of general ideas or concepts by extracting similarities from particular instances. The precise cognitive processes by which this occurs remain a subject of investigation.

24 Which one of the following is generally not a measure in polygraph test for Guilt knowledge/Lie detection?

1 Heart Rate (HR)
2 Electro Dermal Response (EDR)
3 Muscle Tone (EMG)
4 Blood Pressure (BP)

Ans. (3)

➲ *Exp.* The only thing which we do not measure in polygraph test for Guilt knowledge is the Muscle Tone (EMG). Muscle tone is the amount of tension (or resistance to movement) in muscles. No study has been done which establishes the EMG to identify lying patterns.

When a person takes a polygraph test, four to six sensors are attached to him. A polygraph is a machine in which the multiple ('poly') signals from the sensors are recorded on a single strip of moving paper ('graph'). The sensors usually record: the person's breathing rate, Heart Rate (HR), person's pulse rate, Blood Pressure (BP), perspiration, skin conductivity (Electro Dermal Response, EDR), etc. In general, a significant change (such as a faster heart rate, higher blood pressure, increased perspiration) indicates that the person is lying.

25 Arrange the following events of the process of memory in order of their occurrence.

I. Sprouting
II. Formation of cell assembly
III. Consolidation
IV. Reverberation
V. Long-term pontentiation

Codes

1 II, III, I, IV, V　　2 I, II, III, V, IV
3 IV, I, II, III, V　　4 II, IV, V, I, III

Ans. (4)

Exp. The correct sequence of process of memory in order of their occurrence is following: II, IV, V, I, III.

(i) *Formation of cell assembly* : Cell assemblies are groups of highly interconnected neurons. The locus of memory is the particular set of neurons comprising a cell assembly or phase sequence connected by synapses which are activated and modified by experience.

(ii) *Reverberation* : It is the interpretation of the persistent activity can exist in recurrently connected networks.

(iii) *Long-term pontentiation* : It is the enhancement of synaptic transmission last for weeks, caused by repeated brief stimulations of one nerve cell that trigger stimulation of a succeeding cell.

(iv) *Sprouting* : It is the growth of new bushier nerve fibers with more branches to make new connections. Sprouting and rerouting enable the growth and formation of entirely new neural connections at the synapse to compensate for the loss of the function due to brain injury.

(v) *Consolidation* : It is the neurobiological processes by which a permanent memory is formed following a learning experience.

26 In ________ the teacher does not have ________ role, students pose and answer their own questions.

1 Discussion; specific
2 Discussion; dominant
3 Conversation; dominant
4 Conversation; specific

Ans. (2)

Exp. In discussion the teacher does not have dominant role, students pose and answer their own questions.

The method of conversation is commonly used for all talk between two individuals, whereas the method of discussion is for talk concerning a precise subject. The teacher plays the role of an advisor rather than authority. The teacher is in charge of organizing the lessons, encouraging pupils' work, setting appropriate tasks, sharing the pupils' joy over their discoveries, and mediating their discussions. He or she also plans and supervises lessons such that each pupil has appropriate work to do.

27 Match the List I and List II and indicate your answer with the help of codes given below:

List I (Author)	List II (Statement)
A. Carol Gilliyan	I. Decisions are based on morality of caring and a concern with justice
B. Kohlberg	II. Decisions of females are preferable based on care orientation
C. Skoe	III. Decision are based on commitment to specific individuals and relationship
D. Walker	IV. Decisions are based on universal principles of justice and fairness

Codes

	A	B	C	D
1	III	IV	II	I
2	II	III	IV	I
3	III	I	II	IV
4	II	III	I	IV

Ans. (1)

Exp. The correct matching is A-III, B-IV, C-II, D-I.

According to *Carol Gilliyan*, the decisions are based on commitment to specific individuals and relationship. She proposed three stages in her Ethics of Care theory is pre-conventional, conventional and post-conventional. Within each stage, there are goals and specific transition points that move the individual through the stages.

According to *Kohlberg*, the decisions are based on universal principles of justice and fairness. Consistent with Piaget, Kohlberg proposed that children form ways of thinking through their experiences which include understandings of moral concepts such as justice, rights, equality and human welfare. This theory made us understands that morality starts from the early childhood years and can be affected by several factors.

According to *Skoe*, the decisions of females are preferable based on care orientation. Skoe investigated the possibility that sex-role orientation is a better predictor of care-oriented moral development than gender for both men and women. The relationship between sex-role orientation and care-oriented moral reasoning was found to be stronger than that between gender and moral reasoning. However, this finding was accounted for largely by differences among women.

According to *Walker*, the decisions are based on morality of caring and a concern with justice. She focused on the effects of social inequalities on the way morality is understood in ethics and everyday life.

28 Which of the following do/does not describe an obsession?

I. Continually reliving a traumatic event.

II. An unwanted thought that a person finds intrusive and distressing.

III. A behaviour or mental act that a person feels compelled to perform.

IV. Something a person enjoys doing and talking about constantly.

Codes

1 I, II and IV
2 II and IV
3 II, III and IV
4 I, III and IV

Ans. (4)

Exp. Statement I, III and IV does not describe an obsession.

Obsesson is an wanted thought that a person that a person finds intrusive and distressing. It is a persistent thought, idea, image, or impulse that is experienced as intrusive or inappropriate and results in marked anxiety, distress, or discomfort.

The response to an obsession is often an effort to ignore or suppress the thought or impulse or to neutralise it by a compulsion. Compulsions are recurrent actions. It is a behaviour or mental act that a person feels compelled to perform which describe a compulsion and not an obsession. Continually reliving a traumatic event and something a person enjoys doing and talking about constantly, do not describe an obsession

29 The ability to consult and rely on one's experiences and feelings as the basis for making important decisions is called

1 self-actualising tendency
2 organismic valuing process
3 experiential freedom
4 organismic trusting

Ans. (4)

Exp. The ability to consult and rely on one's experiences and feelings as the basis for making important decisions is called organismic trusting.

A person with organismic trust (also called the "organismic valuing process") relies on inner experience at each moment to guide behavior. The person perceives inner needs and emotions and various aspects of the social situation without distortion. Dysfunction comes when a person loses touch with inner feelings and values. The individual integrates all these facets of experience and comes to an inner sense of what is right for him or her. This sense is trustworthy; it is not necessaiy to depend on outside authorities to say what is right.

30 Read each of the following two statements, Assertion (A) and Reason (R) and indicate your answer using the codes given below :

Assertion (A) Environments that affect educational and cultural opportunities influence crystallised intelligence directly and fluid intelligence indirectly.

Reason (R) Crystallised intelligence is developed through the investment of fluid intelligence in cultural settings.

Codes

1 Both (A) and (R) are true and (R) is the correct explanation of (A)
2 Both (A) and (R) are true, but (R) is not the correct explanation of (A)
3 (A) is true, but (R) is false
4 (A) is false, but (R) is true

Ans. (4)

Exp. (A) is false, but (R) is true.

Environments that affect educational and cultural opportunities influence crystallised intelligence directly and fluid intelligence indirectly. Fluid Intelligence is the capability to reason out and solve novel problems independent of past experiences. It is being able to think and reason abstractly and solve problems. Crystallised intelligence involves knowledge that comes from prior learning and past experiences. Situations that require crystallised intelligence include reading comprehension and vocabulary exams. Crystallised intelligence is a product of educational and cultural experiences which interact with fluid intelligence. So, the assertion statement is incorrect that such environments affect fluid intelligence indirectly.

Crystallised intelligence is developed through the investment of fluid intelligence in cultural settings. Fluid intelligence is culture free in nature as it does not vary from culture to culture. On the other hand, crystallized intelligence is culture dependent. This ability is considered dependent on learning, experience and education. As we age and accumulate new knowledge and understanding, crystallized intelligence becomes stronger. The reason is true because the crystallised intelligence is developed through acquired fluid intelligence in cultural settings.

31 Arrange the following events that occurred in historical development of industrial and organisational psychology in correct chronological order.

I. Scientific management (Taylor)

II. Hawthorne studies (Elton Mayo)

III. 'Humanisation' of job (Munsterberg)

IV. Time and motion (Gilbreth)

Codes

1 I, III, IV, II
2 II, III, I, IV
3 I, II, III, IV
4 IV, III, II, I

Ans. (1)

Exp. The correct chronological order is I, III, IV, II.

1. *Scientific management (Taylor)* : Taylor began the theory's of development in the United States during the 1880s and 1890s within manufacturing industries, especially steel. Its peak of influence came in the 1910s.

2. *'Humanisation' of job (Munsterberg)* : Münsterberg's works 'Vocation and Learning' (1912) and 'Psychology' and 'Industrial Efficiency' (1913) are usually considered the beginning of what was later came to known as industrial psychology.
3. *Time and motion (Gilbreth)* : The Gilbreth developed a method of time-and-motion study that systematically investigated and analysed the mechanics and timing of specific tasks, and their research resulted in the publication of Motion Study in 1914-15.
4. *Hawthorne studies (Elton Mayo)*: The Hawthorne studies were conducted on workers at the Hawthorne plant of the Western Electric Company by Elton Mayo and Fritz Roethlisberger in the 1920s. The Hawthorne studies were part of a refocus on managerial strategy incorporating the socio-psychological aspects of human behaviour in organisations.

32 Gardner's Theory of Multiple Intellgence refers to an individual's eight separate abilites, logical mathematical, verbal, spatial, interpersonal, ______ and naturalistic.

Codes

1 bodily-kinesthetic, mechanical, intrapersonal
2 mechanical, bodily-kinesthetic, intrapersonal
3 mental, bodily-kinesthetic, cognitive
4 musical, bodily-kinesthetic, intrapersonal

***Ans.* (4)**

Exp. Gardner's Theory of Multiple Intelligence refers to an individual's eight separate abilities, logical mathematical, verbal, spatial, interpersonal, musical, bodily-kinesthetic, intrapersonal and naturalistic.

1. *Logical-mathematical intelligence* is the ability to think conceptually and abstractly, and capacity to discern logical and numerical patterns.
2. *Verbal-linguistic intelligence* refers to the well-developed verbal skills and sensitivity to the sounds, meanings and rhythms of words.
3. *Spatial-visual intelligence* is the capacity to think in images and pictures, to visualize accurately and abstractly.
4. *Interpersonal intelligence* is the capacity to detect and respond appropriately to the moods, motivations and desires of others.
5. *Musical intelligences* is the ability to produce and appreciate rhythm, pitch and timber.
6. *Bodily-kinesthetic intelligence* is the ability to control one's body movements and to handle objects skillfully.
7. *Intrapersonal* is the capacity to be self-aware and in tune with inner feelings, values, beliefs and thinking processes.
8. *Naturalist intelligence* is the ability to recognise and categorise plants, animals and other objects in nature.

33 A parent deliberately ignores a child's temper tantrums in an attempt to discourage them. The parent's strategy is in accordance with

1 negative reinforcement
2 extinction
3 operant escape
4 operant avoidance

***Ans.* (2)**

Exp. The parent's strategy is in accordance with extinction. Ignoring the child's temper will help to slowly and gradually extinct the behaviour. In extinction, the reinforcement is discontinued, that is, the reinforcing stimulus is no longer presented. The result of this procedure is a decline in the rate of the formerly reinforced response.

34 Arrange the following five events in order from top to bottom.

I. Stimulation of anterior pituitary
II. Stimulation of ovaries
III. Stimulation of neurosecretory cells
IV. Release of Gondotropic hormone
V. Release of Gonadotropic releasing hormone

Codes

1 III, V, I, IV, II
2 II, IV, I, V, III
3 I, V, III, II, IV
4 IV, V, III, IV, I

***Ans.* (1)**

Exp. The correct arrangement is III, V, I, IV, II.

1. *Stimulation of neurosecretory cells* : A neurosecretory cell is a type of neuron, or nerve cell, whose function is to translate neural signals into chemical stimuli. The hypothalamus contains two distinct neurosecretory systems: the magnocellular system and the parvicellular system. The cells which control the release of the pituitary gonadotrophic hormones are located in the preoptic area, just rostral to the hypothalamus.
2. *Release of Gonadotropic releasing hormone* : Gonadotrophic-releasing hormone is produced and secreted by specialised nerve cells in the hypothalamus of the brain. Gonadotropin-releasing hormone (GnRH) is a decapeptide produced in the hypothalamus which is released into tiny blood vessels that carry this hormone from the brain to the pituitary gland.
3. *Stimulation of anterior pituitary* : The Anterior Pituitary is an endocrine gland controlled by the hypothalamus. It is the largest part of the pituitary gland, and is responsible for synthesis and release of most pituitary hormones. The stimulation of anterior pituitary causes the release of gonadotrophic hormones.
4. *Release of Gonadotropic hormone* : Gonadotropic hormones are any of several hormones that stimulate functions of the gonads. These includes follicle-stimulating hormone and luteinizing hormone, produced by the anterior pituitary gland in response to gonadotropin-releasing hormone, and chorionic gonadotropin, which is produced by the placenta.
5. *Stimulation of ovaries* : Luteinizing hormone (LH) and *Follicle-Stimulating Hormone* (FSH) stimulate the gonads-in males, the testes, and in females, the ovaries. They are not necessary for life, but are essential for reproduction.

35 Which of the following strategies facilitate problem-solving?

I. Algorithms II. Mental set
III. Planning fallacy IV. Heuristics
V. Analogy

Codes

1 I, II and IV 2 II, III and IV
3 I and V 4 I, IV and V

Ans. (4)

Exp. Algorithms, Heuristics and Analogy are the strategies that facilitate problem-solving.

An Algorithm is a set of step-by-step procedures that provides the correct answer to a particular problem.

A Heuristic is an experience-based strategy for solving a problem or making a decision that often provides an efficient means of finding an answer but cannot guarantee a correct outcome.

An Analogy is an abstract parallel between two quite different things. It is the accessing and transferring of elements from familiar categories or situations to the current problem.

36 Match the List I and List II and indicate your answer with the help of codes given below :

List I (Attitude Scaling Technique)		List II (Feature)
A. Equal appearing scale	I.	Checks unidimensionality of the intervals
B. Paired comparison	II.	Employs 'Z' as a measure of scale value
C. Scalogram	III.	Can assess multidimensional attitudes
D. Summated ratings	IV.	Suitable for scaling large number of items

Codes

	A	B	C	D		A	B	C	D
1	IV	II	I	III	2	II	IV	I	III
3	IV	II	III	I	4	III	I	IV	II

Ans. (1)

Exp. The correct matching is A-IV, B-II, C-I, D-III.

Equal appearing scale is suitable for scaling large number of items. It is a procedure in whichmagnitudes between pairs of stimuli are adjusted, so that the differences between stimuli within each pair are perceived as equal.

Paired comparison employs 'Z' as a measure of scale value. It is a systematic procedure for comparing a set of stimuli or other items. A pair of stimuli is presented to an individual, who is asked to compare them on a particular dimension, such as size, loudness, or brightness; the process is continued until every item in the set has been compared with every other item.

Scalogram checks unidimensionality of the intervals. It is a type of attitude measure that consists of multiple verbal statements ordered to reflect increasing levels of positive evaluation. Endorsement of a particular statement implies endorsement of all statements less extreme than that statement.

Summated ratings can assess multidimensional attitudes. It is a type of assessment instrument comprising a series of statements measuring the same construct or variable to which respondents indicate their degree of agreement or disagreement. The number of response options for each item varies, often from 5 to 7 points (e.g., from strongly agree to strongly disagree). The response values for individual items may be summed to obtain a total or average score that reflects a person's general attitude toward the construct of interest.

37 A social worker, with a training of Master of Social Work (MSW), who was appointed as an assistant to a psychiatrist, use to administer and interpret Rorschach test. This is an

1 ethically incorrect practice
2 ethically correct practice
3 ethically correct practice provided the result are kept confidential
4 ethically correct practice provided the result are used only for diagnostic purpose

Ans. (1)

Exp. This is an ethically incorrect practice.

An ethically incorrect practice is not conforming to approved standards of social or professional behavior. The social worker administering and interpreting the Rorschach test is an ethically incorrect practice because the Rorschach test is only conducted and interpreted by a professional psychologist or psychiatrist.

38 Learned helplessness may appear when stress causes

I. Anxiety
II. Anger and aggression
III. Withdrawal and apathy
IV. Feeling of uncontroliability

Codes

1 I and II 2 II and III
3 II and IV 4 III and IV

Ans. (4)

Exp. Learned helplessness may appear when stress causes Withdrawal, Apathy and Feeling of Uncontrollability.

Learned helplessness is a phenomenon in which repeated exposure to uncontrollable stressors results in individuals failing to use any control options that may later become available. Essentially, individuals are said to learn that they lack behavioral control over environmental events, which, in turn, undermines the motivation to make changes or attempt to alter situations. In the literature of learned helplessness, passive behaviors like withdrawal and apathy arise from feelings of uncontrollability. Learned helplessness creates motivational, cognitive and emotional deficiencies, which make it difficult for people to learn new things, take initiative and cope with adversities.

39 Read each of the following two statements, Assertion (A) and Reason (R) and indicate your answer using the codes given below :

Assertion (A) In case of anxiety disorder, people become inclined to make negative evaluation of themselves, their world and their future.

Reason (R) People acquire a relatively stable set of cognitive structures or schemas that contain dysfunctional beliefs.

Codes

1 Both (A) and (R) are true and (R) is the correct explanation of (A)
2 Both (A) and (R) are true, but (R) is not the correct explanation of (A)
3 (A) is true, but (R) is false
4 (A) is false, but (R) is true

Ans. *(4)*

Exp. (A) is false, but (R) is true.

In case of anxiety disorder, people become inclined to make negative evaluation of themselves, their world and their future. Anxiety disorder is a group of disorders that have as their central organising theme the emotional state of fear, worry, or excessive apprehension. Fear of negative evaluation (FNE) was originally defined as a trait related to "apprehension about others' evaluations, distress over their negative evaluations, avoidance of evaluative situations and the expectation that others would evaluate oneself negatively". Social anxiety is, in part, a response to perceived negative evaluation by others. Therefore, the Assertion statement is false.

People acquire a relatively stable set of cognitive structures or schemas that contain dysfunctional beliefs. People acquire a relatively stable set of cognitive structures or schemas that contain dysfunctional beliefs. An early maladaptive schema is a pervasive self-defeating or dysfunctional theme or pattern of memories, emotions, and physical sensations, developed during childhood or adolescence and elaborated throughout one's lifetime, that often has the form of a belief about the self or the world. So, the reason statement is true.

40 ________ arises when one is simultaneously having two inconsistent ________ .

1 Stress; thoughts
2 Stress; approaches
3 Anxiety; cognitions
4 Tension; cognitions

Ans. *(4)*

Exp. Tension arises when one is simultaneously having two inconsistent cognitions.

Cognitive dissonance is the perception of contradictory information. Relevant items of information include a person's actions, feelings, ideas, beliefs, and values, and things in the environment. Cognitive dissonance is typically experienced as psychological stress when persons participate in an action that goes against one or more of those things. According to this theory, when two actions or ideas are not psychologically consistent with each other, people do all in their power to change them until they become consistent.

41 Arrange the following events in the order of their occurrence in Panic circle.

I. Apprehension or worry
II. Body sensations
III. Perceived threat
IV. Interpretation of sensations as catastrophic
V. Trigger stimulus

Codes

1 I, III, II, V, IV
2 V, II, III, I, IV
3 V, III, I, II, IV
4 III, V, I, II, IV

Ans. *(3)*

Exp. The correct arrangement is V, III, I, II, IV.

Clark (1996) focused on the importance of the repetitive nature of panic attacks which is called Panic Circle.

1. *Trigger stimulus* : This can be started off either by an external trigger or by an internal trigger: an initial, relatively small variation in bodily sensations.
2. *Perceived threat* : In Clark's theory the only antecedent cause is the learned threat and this is caused by some previously occurring critical event.
3. *Apprehension or worry* : A panic attack is a sudden and intense feeling of terror, fear, or apprehension, without the presence of actual danger.
4. *Body sensations* : It is common for panic disorder to cause feelings of numbness and tingling. This can occur almost anywhere on the body but is most commonly felt on the face, hands, arms, feet and legs.
5. *Interpretation of sensations as catastrophic* : Catastrophic thinking can be defined as ruminating about irrational worst-case outcomes.

42 Read each of the following two statements, Assertion (A) and Reason (R) and indicate your answer using the codes given below :

Assertion (A) A person's responses on MMPI were disregarded because he has scored very high on frequency sub-scale.

Reason (R) Frequency sub-scale indicates the style of an individual to respond in a typical way.

Codes

1 Both (A) and (R) are true and (R) is the correct explanation of (A)
2 Both (A) and (R) are true, but (R) is not the correct explanation of (A)
3 (A) is true, but (R) is false
4 (A) is false, but (R) is true

Ans. *(1)*

Exp. Both (A) and (R) are true and (R) is the correct explanation of (A).

A person's responses on MMPI were disregarded because he has scored very high on frequency sub-scale. The Minnesota Multiphasic Personality Inventory (MMPI) is a psychological test that assesses personality traits and psychopathology. The MMPI-2 is designed with 10 clinical scales which assess ten major categories of abnormal human behaviour, and four validity scales, which assess the person's general test-taking attitude and whether they answered the items on the test in a truthful and accurate manner. The F scale or Infrequency or Frequency scale is intended to detect unusual or a typical ways of answering the test items, like if a person were to randomly fill out the test. Therefore, the assertion is true.

Frequency sub-scale indicates the style of an individual to respond in a typical way. Frequency sub-scale indicates the style of an individual to respond in a typical way. Frequency sub-scale taps a number of strange thoughts, peculiar experiences, feelings of isolation and alienation and a number of unlikely or contradictory beliefs, expectations and self-descriptions. If a person answers too many of the F and Fb scale items incorrectly, it will invalidate the entire test. Hence, the reason is true and explains the assertion.

43 Which of the following are the components of emotional intelligence, according to Mayer and Salovey model?

I. Perceiving emotions
II. Using emotions to facilitate thoughts
III. Understanding emotions
IV. Managing emotions

Codes

1 I and III
2 I and IV
3 I, III and IV
4 All of these

Ans. *(4)*

Exp. According to Mayer and *Salovey* model, the components of emotional intelligence are:

Perceiving emotions: It refers to the ability to perceive and correctly express their emotions and other people's.

Using emotions to facilitate thoughts: It refers to the ability to use emotions in a way that facilitates thought.

Understanding emotions: It refers to the capacity to understand emotions, emotional language, and emotional signals.

Managing emotions: It refers to the ability to manage their emotions in order to achieve goals.

44 Read each of the following two statements Assertion (A) and Reason (R) and indicate your answer using the codes given below

Assertion (A) There exists an inverted 'U' shape relationship between job stress and performance.

Reason (R) Experience of job stress generates arousal and motivation for making effort.

Codes

1 Both (A) and (R) are true and (R) is the correct explanation of (A)
2 Both (A) and (R) are true, but (R) is not the correct explanation of (A)
3 (A) is true, but (R) is false
4 (A) is false, but (R) is true

Ans. *(1)*

Exp. Both (A) and (R) are true and (R) is the correct explanation of (A).

There exists an inverted 'U' shape relationship between job stress and performance. According to the Yerkes-Dodson law, performance increases with physiological or mental arousal (stress) but only up to a point. When the level of stress becomes too high, performance decreases. So, there is a 'U' shape relationship between stress and performance.

Experience of job stress generates arousal and motivation for making effort. The experience of job stress leads to more arousal which is enough to make efforts for performance. This is also true and explains why there is an inverted 'U' shape relationship between job stress and performance.

45 Read each of the following two statements, Assertion (A) and Reason (R) and indicate your answer using the codes given below :

Assertion (A) The body ages as a result of accumulated damage to the system beyond the body's ability to repair it.

Reason (R) Ageing also involves damage due to environmental assaults on Biological System.

Codes

1 Both (A) and (R) are true and (R) is the correct explanation of (A)
2 Both (A) and (R) are true, but (R) is not the correct explanation of (A)
3 (A) is true, but (R) is false
4 (A) is false, but (R) is true

Ans. *(2)*

Exp. Both (A) and (R) are true, but (R) is not the correct explanation of (A).

The body ages as a result of accumulated damage to the system beyond the body's ability to repair it. The programmed theories imply that ageing follows a biological timetable (regulated by changes in gene expression that affect the systems responsible for maintenance, repair and defense responses).

Ageing also involves damage due to environmental assaults on Biological System. The damage or error theories emphasise environmental assaults to living organisms that induce cumulative damage at various levels as the cause of ageing.

Both the statements are true and explained by two different theories of ageing but these are not related.

46 In a signal detection task, the liberal observer shall having

I. bias to make more yes responses.
II. lesser expectations that signal is present.
III. high hit rate and low false alarm rate.
IV. high hit rate as well high false alarm rate.
V. equally likely to make yes or no responses.
VI. greater expectations that signal is present.

Codes

1 I, II and V 2 I, IV and VI
3 II, III and V 4 IV, V and VI

Ans. *(2)*

Exp. The correct options are I, IV and VI.

In a signal detection task, the liberal observer shall having:

Bias to make more yes responses : Bias is the perceiver's propensity to categorise stimuli as targets vs. foils and is described as liberal, neutral, or conservative. A liberal observer has a lower criterion for judging that a target is present, which means they will make a bias to make more yes responses.

High hit rate as well high false alarm rate : A liberal observer minimises missed detections but increases exposure to false alarms, which means they have a high hit rate as well high false alarm rate.

Greater expectations that signal is present : A liberal observer feels there is always a signal which is present, so they have a greater expectations that signal is present.

47 Which of the following characterises slow-wave sleep?

1 State 1 to 4 and REM sleep
2 Stage 3 and 4
3 NREM and REM sleep
4 Stage 1 to 4

Ans. *(2)*

Exp. Stage 3 and 4 characterises slow-wave sleep.

Stage 3 and stage 4 are described as slow-wave sleep that is marked by a predominance of delta waves. Stage 3 sleep is also known as deep sleep, and it is harder to wake someone up if they are in this phase. Muscle tone, pulse, and breathing rate decrease in N3 sleep as the body relaxes even further. In Stage 4, brain activity picks up, nearing levels seen when you're awake. At the same time, the body experiences atonia, which is a temporary paralysis of the muscles, with two exceptions: the eyes and the muscles that control breathing.

48 Read each of the following two statements, Assertion (A) and Reason (R) and indicate your answer using the codes given below :

Assertion (A) Damage to anterior third ventricle area results into adipsia.

Reason (R) Stimulation of anterior Third Ventricle (AV3V) inhibits drinking.

Codes

1 Both (A) and (R) are true and (R) is the correct explanation of (A)
2 Both (A) and (R) are true, but (R) is not the correct explanation of (A)
3 (A) is true, but (R) is false
4 (A) is false, but (R) is true

Ans. *(3)*

Exp. (A) is true, but (R) is false.

The anterior third ventricle is associated with intake of water. If there is a damage, the intake of water will decrease. Any severe damage may cause adipsia. Adipsia is a disease characterised by the absence of thirst even in the presence of body water depletion or salt excess. It is a rare condition that typically presents as hypernatremic dehydration. Therefore, the Assertion statement is true.

Stimulation of anterior Third Ventricle (AV3V) inhibits drinking is false as any damage and not stimulation, to anterior third ventricle inhibits drinking.

49 Read each of the following two statements, Assertion (A) and Reason (R) and indicate your answer using the codes given below :

Assertion (A) Subliminal perception implies detection of a stimulus with a magnitude for below the absolute threshold.

Reason (R) Receptors always receive information and that is always perceived.

Codes

1 Both (A) and (R) are true and (R) is the correct explanation of (A)
2 Both (A) and (R) are true, but (R) is not the correct explanation of (A)
3 (A) is true, but (R) is false
4 (A) is false, but (R) is true

Ans. *(3)*

Exp. (A) is true, but (R) is false.

Subliminal perception implies detection of a stimulus with a magnitude for below the absolute threshold. Subliminal stimuli or "above threshold", are any sensory stimuli below an individual's threshold for conscious perception. Subliminal perception is the perception of a series of stimulus which the person is not consciously aware of and gets under the influence involuntarily, in addition to the perception with the five sense organs. Therefore, the Assertion is true.

Receptors always receive information and that is always perceived. Receptors always receive information is true but we cannot always say that all the information received by the receptors are perceived.

50 Which of the following are not the function of working memory?

I. Storing declarative memories
II. Executive functions

III. Sensory register
IV. Constructive process
V. Chunking.

Codes

1 II, IV and V 2 I and III
3 II and V 4 I, III and IV

Ans. *(4)*

Exp. Storing declarative memories, Sensory register, Constructive process are not the function of working memory :

Working memory is a multi-component system which includes the central executive, visuospatial sketchpad, phonological loop, and episodic buffer.

Storing declarative memories : Whereas working memory maintains information in the order of seconds, declarative and procedural memory support long-term knowledge, and can store information for years. Therefore, working memory is unable to store declarative memories.

Sensory register : Information from sensory memory has the shortest retention time, ranging from mere milliseconds to five seconds. In sensory memory, no manipulation of the incoming information occurs as it is transferred quickly to working memory. The amount of information is greatly reduced during this transfer because the capacity of working memory is not large enough to cope with all the input coming from our sense organs.

Constructive process : Constructive process refers to remembering conceived as involving the use of general knowledge stored in one's memory to construct a more complete and detailed account of an event or experience by changing or filling in various features of the memory.

Working memory has executive functions carried out by the central executive which is responsible for monitoring and coordinating the operation of the other systems (i.e., visuospatial sketchpad and phonological loop) and relates them to long term memory (LTM). Chunking is the recoding of smaller units of information into larger, familiar units. Chunking is often assumed to help bypassing the limited capacity of working memory (WM).

51 Read each of the following two statements, Assertion (A) and Reason (R) and indicate your answer using the codes given below :

Assertion (A) Children with learning disability are allowed to type or tape record their assignments.

Reason (R) Omitting handwriting as a criterion for evaluating reports/copies is a way of helping children with learning diability.

Codes

1 Both (A) and (R) are true and (R) is the correct explanation of (A)
2 Both (A) and (R) are true, but (R) is not the correct explanation of (A)
3 (A) is true, but (R) is false
4 (A) is false, but (R) is true

Ans. *(1)*

Exp. Both (A) and (R) are true and (R) is the correct explanation of (A).

Learning disabilities are neurologically-based processing problems. These processing problems can interfere with learning basic skills such as reading, writing and/or math. The assertion is true as typing and tape recording of assignments can be done by students with learning disabilities.

Omitting handwriting as a criterion for evaluating reports/copies is a way of helping children with learning disability. It will help focus on the content of the study matter and it will increase the chances of getting more score. The reason is also correct as it explains the reason behind the typing and tape recording of assignments.

52 Match the List I and List II and indicate your answer with the help of codes given below :

List I (Concept)	List II (Description)
A. Planning fallacy	I. Tendency to adhere to bad decisions even if the losses increases
B. Confirmation bias	II. Tendency to evaluate events by thinking about alternatives to them
C. Counter-factual thinking	III. Tendency to underestimate the resources needed to achieve a goal
D. Escalation of commitment	IV. Tendency to pay attention primarily to information that confirms existing views

Codes

	A	B	C	D		A	B	C	D
1	IV	II	I	III	2	III	IV	II	I
3	I	III	IV	II	4	II	I	III	IV

Ans. *(2)*

Exp. The correct matching is A-III, B-IV, C-II, D-I.

Planning fallacy is the tendency to underestimate the resources needed to achieve a goal. It is a phenomenon in which predictions about how much time will be needed to complete a future task display an optimism bias and underestimate the time needed.

Confirmation bias is the tendency to pay attention primarily to information that confirms existing views. It is the tendency to search for, interpret, favour and recall information in a way that confirms one's pre-existing beliefs or hypotheses.

Counterfactual thinking is the tendency to evaluate events by thinking about alternatives to them. It involves the human tendency to create possible alternatives to life events that have already occurred; something that is contrary to what actually happened. Counterfactual thinking is, as it states: "counter to the facts".

Escalation of commitment is the tendency to adhere to bad decisions even if the losses increase. It is a human behaviour pattern in which an individual or group facing increasingly negative outcome from a decision, action, or investment nevertheless continues the behaviour instead of altering course.

53 Cattell's Culture Fair Intelligence Test (CFIT) is presumed to measure

1 Crystallised intelligence
2 Fluid intelligence
3 Verbal fluency
4 Convergent thinking

***Ans.* (2)**

Exp. Cattell's Culture Fair Intelligence Test (CFIT) is presumed to measure the Fluid intelligence. It was constructed by Raymond B Cattell in an attempt to produce a measure of cognitive abilities that accurately estimated intelligence devoid of socio-cultural and environmental influences. Since, Fluid intelligence measures the ability of one to solve problem and use logic. It is the capability to reason out and solve novel problems, independent of past experiences. It is being able to think and reason abstractly and solve problems.

54 Read each of the following two statements, Assertion (A) and Reason (R) and indicate your answer using the codes given below :

Assertion (A) Lesions of the amygdala decrease people's emotional responses.

Reason (R) Memory of frightening event is poor in people with damaged amygdala.

Codes

1 Both (A) and (R) are true and (R) is the correct explanation of (A)
2 Both (A) and (R) are true, but (R) is not the correct explanation of (A)
3 (A) is true, but (R) is false
4 (A) is false, but (R) is true

***Ans.* (2)**

Exp. Both (A) and (R) are true, but (R) is not the correct explanation of (A).

The amygdala has been implicated in emotional processes. Patients with amygdala lesions that provides a rich source of information on cognitive and emotional functioning after damage to this structure. So, the Assertion statement is true.

Patients with amygdala damage have been reported to display less intense negative, compared to positive, emotions, to be impaired at recognising facial expressions of negative emotions, to show deficits in episodic or autobiographical emotion-related memories and to evidence reduced emotional potentiation of memory. This is correct but does not explain why the lesions of the amygdala causes a decrease in emotional responses.

55 Match the List I and List II and indicate your answer with the help of codes given below :

List I (Explanation)	List II (Model)
A. Matching the whole image to a stored representations of the whole object	I. Recognition by components model
B. Extracting discriminating features from the images and match these model with known features of objects	II. Template matching model
C. Three-dimensional structure of objects by specifying their parts and the spatial relations among the parts	III. Configurable model
D. Distinguishing among objects that share the same basic parts and model overall structure with the prototype	IV. Feature matching model

Codes

	A	B	C	D		A	B	C	D
1	II	III	IV	I	2	III	IV	II	I
3	IV	I	II	III	4	I	II	III	IV

***Ans.* (*)**

Exp. The correct matching is: A-II, B-IV, C-I, D-III.

Recognition by components model involves three-dimensional structure of objects by specifying their parts and the spatial relations among the parts. It is a process proposed by Irving Biederman in 1987, to explain object recognition. According to RBC theory, we are able to recognise objects by separating them into geons.

Template matching model involves matching the whole image to a stored representation of the whole object. In this model, the pattern recognition proceeds by comparing an incoming sensory stimulation pattern to mental images or representations of patterns (templates) until a match is found.

Configurable model involves distinguishing among objects that share the same basic parts and overall structure with the prototype. It hypothesises that people form a unified overall impression of other people; the unifying forces shape individual elements to bring them in line with the overall impression. The pressure toward unity changes the meaning of the individual elements to fit better in context.

Feature matching model involves extracting discriminating features from the images and match these with known features of objects. It proposes that we decompose visual patterns into a set of critical features, which we then try to match against features stored in memory.

56 Match the List I and List II and indicate your answer with the help of codes given below :

List I (Process)	List II (Principle)
A. Imaginations inflation	I. Mnemonics
B. Effortful processing	II. False memories
C. Method of Loci	III. Encoding specificity principle
D. Context dependent memory	IV. Intentional encoding

Codes

	A	B	C	D		A	B	C	D
1	II	I	III	IV	2	I	III	IV	II
3	II	IV	I	III	4	III	II	I	IV

Ans. *(3)*

Exp. The correct matching is A-II, B-IV, C-I, D-III.

The process of *Imagination inflation* is associated with the principle of false memories. Imagination inflation is a type of memory distortion that occurs when imagining an event that never happened increases confidence in the memory of the event. Imagining a false event increases familiarity and people mistake this familiarity for evidence that they have experienced the event.

The process of *Effortful processing* is associated with the principle of intentional encoding. Effortful operations, such as rehearsal and elaborative mnemonic activities, require considerable capacity, interfere with other cognitive activities also requiring capacity, are initiated intentionally, and show benefits from practice.

The *Method of Loci* is associated with the mnemonics. The method of loci is a mnemonic device that relies on spatial relationships between "loci" (e.g., locations on a familiar route or rooms in a familiar building) to arrange and recollect memorial content.

The process of *Context dependent memory* is associated with the encoding specificity principle. The encoding specificity principle is the general principle that matching the encoding contexts of information at recall assists in the retrieval of episodic memories. This principle plays a significant role in both the concept of context-dependent memory and the concept of state-dependent memory.

57 Which one of the following incorrect regarding the causes of origin of prejudice?

1 Perception of threat self esteem or/ and group interest
2 Competition for scarce resources
3 Categorising ourselves as a member of a group and others as members of group
4 Unfavourable or negative actions directed towards members of other group

Ans. *(4)*

Exp. Statement 4 is incorrect regarding the causes of origin of prejudice. It is the definition of prejudice, rather than causes of origin of prejudice.

Prejudice is an unjustified or incorrect attitude (usually negative) towards an individual based solely on the individual's membership of a social group. Prejudice is preconceived opinion that is not based on reason or actual experience and unfavourable or negative directed towards members of other group but does not count any actions upon it. Prejudice is an unjustified or incorrect attitude (usually negative) towards an individual based solely on the individual's membership of a social group.

58 Match the List I and List II and indicate your answer with the help of codes given below :

List I (Meta Need)	List II (Meta Pathology)
A. Truth	I. Hatred
B. Perfection	II. Anger
C. Justice	III. Hopelessness
D. Goodness	IV. Mistrust

Codes

	A	B	C	D		A	B	C	D
1	IV	II	III	I	2	IV	III	II	I
3	I	II	III	IV	4	I	III	II	IV

Ans. *(2)*

Exp. The correct matching is A-IV, B-III, C-II, D-I.

Metamotivation is what motivates and impels an individual toward self-actualisation and excellence. Maslow describes a meta need as any need for knowledge, beauty, or creativity. Meta needs are involved in self-actualisation and constitute the highest level of needs, coming into play primarily after the lower level needs have been met. Meta pathology is the thwarting of self-development related to failure to satisfy the meta needs. Metapathology prevents self-actualisers from expressing, using and fulfilling their potential.

The meta need of *Truth* is associated with the meta pathology of mistrust.

The meta need of *Perfection* is associated with the meta pathology of hopelessness.

The meta need of *Justice* is associated with the meta pathology of anger.

The meta need of *Goodness* is associated with the meta pathology of hatred.

59 According to Sternberg's Theory, which of the following are associated with 'performance component' of the cognitive processes?

I. Perceptual processing
II. Retrieval from long-term memory
III. Storage of information in memory
IV. Problem sloving skills

V. Formulation of strategies for problem-solving

Codes

1 I and II
2 I, II, and III
3 II, III and IV
4 III and IV

Ans. *(2)*

Exp. According to Sternberg's theory, perceptual processing, retrieval from long-term memory, and storage of information in memory are associated with 'performance component' of the cognitive processes.

Performance components carry out the directions of the metacomponents. It is performance components that allow us to store information in short-term memory, compare two concepts, compare solutions to the task, etc.

(i) *Perceptual processing* : It involves perceiving problems in our long-term memory, perceiving relations between objects, and applying relations to another set of terms.

(ii) *Retrieval from long-term memory* : It involves retrieving information stored in the long-term memory.

(iii) *Storage of information in memory* : It involves holding information for retrieval.

60 Match the List I and List II and indicate your answer with the help of codes given below :

List I (Leadership Theory)	List II (Proposer)
A. Cognitive Resource Theory	I. Hersey and Blanchard
B. Situational Leadership Theory	II. Robert House
C. Path-goal Theory	III. Fiedler and Garcia
D. Normative Decision Theory	IV. Vroom and Yetton

Codes

	A	B	C	D		A	B	C	D
1	I	II	III	IV	2	III	I	II	IV
3	II	III	I	IV	4	IV	III	II	I

Ans. *(2)*

Exp. The correct matching is A-III, B-I, C-II, D-IV.

Hersey and Blanchard proposed the Situational Leadership Theory. The theory suggests that no single leadership style is best. Instead, it depends on which type of leadership and strategies are best-suited to the task.

Robert House proposed the Path-goal Theory. The theory states that a leader's behaviour is contingent to the satisfaction, motivation and performance of their employees.

Fiedler and Garcia proposed the Cognitive Resource Theory. The theory states the influence of the leader's resources on his or her reaction to stress.

Vroom and Yetton proposed the Normative Decision Theory. The theory models the most ideal decision for a given situation.

61 Read each of the following two statements, Assertion (A) and Reason (R) and indicate your answer using the codes given below:

Assertion (A) Scientists found activation in pre-frontal cortex neurons involved in planning motor actions whenever a monkey in their experiment saw a picture of a peanut.

Reason (R) The mirror neurons respond to actions that the animal plans and performs itself and also to actions performed by others. These are likely to play in learning by observation.

Codes

1 Both (A) and (R) are true and (R) is the correct explanation of (A)
2 Both (A) and (R) are true, but (R) is not the correct explanation of (A)
3 (A) is true, but (R) is false
4 (A) is false, but (R) is true

Ans. *(4)*

Exp. (A) is false, but (R) is true.

Scientists found activation in pre-frontal cortex neurons involved in planning motor actions whenever a monkey in their experiment saw a picture of a peanut. This is false as the activation was not found in pre-frontal cortex neurons, rather it was found in the inferior frontal gyrus (region F5) and the inferior parietal lobule.

The mirror neurons respond to actions that the animal plans and performs itself and also to actions performed by others. These are likely to play in learning by observation. Mirror neurons allow us to learn through imitation. They enable us to reflect body language, facial expressions, and emotions. Mirror neurons play an essential part in our social life. These are important for the child development, as well as relationships and education. So, this statement is true.

62 Which of the following concepts are not used by Clark Hull in his theory?

I. Reaction potential
II. Sign-significant
III. Effective reaction potential
IV. Habit strength
V. Contiguity

Codes

1	I, III and V	2	I, and IV
3	II and V	4	II, III and IV

Ans. *(3)*

Exp. The concepts not used by Clark Hull in his theory are Sign-Significant and contiguity.

Hull suggested that all motivation arises as a result of these biological needs. In his theory, Hull used the term 'drive' to refer to the state of tension or arousal caused by biological or physiological needs. Thirst, hunger and the need for warmth are all examples of drives. A drive creates an unpleasant state; a tension that needs to be reduced. Hull talked about unlearned behaviour, habit strength, reaction potential, and effective reaction potential.

Ferdinand de Saussure talked about sign-significant, is something that can be interpreted as having a meaning that is something other than itself, and therefore can communicate information to the one interpreting or decoding the sign. Edwin Ray Guthrie spoke about Contiguity; association by contiguity is the principle that ideas, memories and experiences are linked when one is frequently experienced with the other.

63 Match the List I and List II and indicate your answer with the help of codes given below :

List I (Neuron System)	List II (Areas of Brain)
A. The Acetyl Cholinergic	I. Raphe nuclei system
B. The Noraderenergic System	II. Lateral hypothalamus
C. The Serotonergic System	III. Pons and basal fore brain
D. The Hypocretinergic System	IV. Locus coeruleaus

Codes

	A	B	C	D		A	B	C	D
1	I	II	III	IV	2	III	I	IV	II
3	IV	III	I	II	4	III	IV	I	II

Ans. (4)

Exp. The correct matching is A-III, B-IV, C-I, D-II.

The Acetyl Cholinergic is associated with pons and basal forebrain. Acetylcholine serves a variety of important functions in the brain. A major projection from the basal forebrain lateral to the hypothalamus into the cerebral cortex is believed to have a role in cortical activation, learning, memory, and cortical plasticity.

The Noraderenergic System is associated with Locus coeruleaus. The locus coeruleaus is the major source of noraderenergic innervation in the brain and sends widespread connections to rostral (cerebral cortex, hippocampus, hypothalamus) and caudal (cerebellum, brainstem nuclei) brain areas.

The Serotonergic System is associated with Raphe nuclei system. The raphe nuclei are distributed near the midline of the brainstem along its entire rostro-caudal extension. The serotonergic neurons are their main neuronal components, although a proportion of them lie in subdivisions of the lateral reticular formation.

The Hypocretinergic System is associated with Lateral hypothalamus. The hypocretins are neuropeptides of related sequence derived from the same precursor whose expression is restricted to a few thousand neurons of the lateral hypothalamus.

64 Read each of the following two statements, Assertion (A) and Reason (R) and indicate your answer using the codes given below

Assertion (A) Researchers have shown that language may play an important role in shaping important aspects of cognition.

Reason (R) 'Linguistic relativity' hypothesis suggests that language shapes or determines our thoughts and the way we think.

Codes

1 Both (A) and (R) are true and (R) is the correct explanation of (A)
2 Both (A) and (R) are true, but (R) is not the correct explanation of (A)
3 (A) is true, but (R) is false
4 (A) is false, but (R) is true

Ans. (2)

Exp. Both (A) and (R) are true, but (R) is not the correct explanation of (A).

The assertion is true as because language is a powerful tool in shaping thought about abstract domains and one's native language plays an important role in shaping habitual thought (e.g., howone tends to think about time).

The 'Linguistic relativity hypothesis' holds that the structure of human language effects the way in which an individual conceptualises their world. Every human language reflects the values of the place and culture where it originated and this effects and shapes the mentality of the persons who speak those different languages. The reason is also true but there is no explanation why and how language shapes the cognition.

65 Which of the following are reasoning as proposed by Kohlberg?

I. Obedience, self-interest and conformity.
II. Law and order, self-interest and purpose.
III. Law and order, human rights and universal human ethics.
IV. Conformity, identity and competence.

Codes

1 I and II　　2 I and III
3 I and IV　　4 II and III

Ans. (2)

Exp. The reasoning proposed by Kohlberg is

(i) Obedience, self-interest and conformity.
(ii) Law and order, human rights and universal human ethics.

Kohlberg's six stages can be more generally grouped into three levels of two stages each: pre-conventional, conventional and post-conventional.

Level 1 (Pre-Conventional)

1. Obedience and punishment orientation
(How can I avoid punishment?)

2. Self-interest orientation
   (What's in it for me?)
   (Paying for a benefit)

Level 2 (Conventional)

3. Interpersonal accord and conformity
   (Social norms)
   (The good boy/girl attitude)
4. Authority and social-order maintaining orientation
   (Law and order morality)

Level 3 (Post-Conventional)

5. Social contract orientation
6. Universal ethical principles
   (Principled conscience)

66 Making 'riskier' decision during adolescence may be correlated with

1 lack of peer contact
2 protective parenting
3 slower frontal lobe development
4 delays in reaching puberty

Ans. (3)

➲ *Exp.* Making 'riskier' decision during adolescence may be correlated with slower frontal lobe development. Slow development of the prefrontal cortex explains teenagers' seemingly impulsive and risky behaviour. The function of the frontal lobe involves the ability to project future consequences resulting from current actions, the choice between good and bad actions, the over-ride and suppression of socially unacceptable responses, and the determination of similarities and differences between things or events.

67 In which case the sensitivity 'd' shall be high in a signal detection task?

1 When proportion of hit responses exceeds the proportion of false alarm responses a lot
2 When proportion of false alarm responses exceeds the proportion of hit responses a lot
3 When proportion of hit responses and the proportion of false alarm responses are equal
4 When proportion of hit responses exceeds the proportion of false alarm responses a little

Ans. (1)

➲ *Exp.* When proportion of hit responses exceeds the proportion of false alarm responses a lot, the sensitivity 'd' shall be high in a signal detection task. According to the signal detection theory, there are a number of determiners of how a detecting system will detect a signal, and where its threshold levels will be.

The theory can explain how changing the threshold will affect the ability to discern, often exposing how adapted the system is to the task, purpose or goal at which it is aimed. The sensitivity index or d 'provides the separation between the means of the signal and the noise distributions, compared against the standard deviation of the signal or noise distribution. It will be high. When proportion of hit responses exceeds the proportion of false alarm responses a lot.

68 Read each of the following two statements, Assertion (A) and Reason (R) and indicate your answer using the codes given below:

Assertion (A) Information reaching the meaning level of processing and elaboration the best chance of being retained.

Reason (R) According to information processing theories of memory, information is transferred from stage to stage until some of it is finally lodged in long-term memory.

Codes

1 Both (A) and (R) are true and (R) is the correct explanation of (A)
2 Both (A) and (R) are true, but (R) is not the correct explanation of (A)
3 (A) is true, but (R) is false
4 (A) is false, but (R) is true

Ans. (2)

➲ *Exp.* Both (A) and (R) are true, but (R) is not the correct explanation of (A).

Information reaching the meaning level of processing and elaboration the best chance of being retained. The levels of processing model (Craik and Lockhart, 1972) focuses on the depth of processing involved in memory, and predicts the deeper information is processed, the longer a memory trace will last. Deep processing involves elaboration rehearsal which involves a more meaningful analysis (e.g. images, thinking, associations etc.) of information and leads to better recall. For example, giving words a meaning or linking them with previous knowledge. The Assertion is true.

According to information processing theories of memory, information is transferred from stage to stage until some of it is finally lodged in long-term memory. Information processing is how individuals perceive, analyse, manipulate, use, and remember information. In order for a memory to go into storage (i.e., long-term memory), it has to pass through three distinct stages: Sensory Memory, Short-Term Memory, and finally, Long-Term Memory. The reason statement is true but it does not explain the assertion.

69 Understanding about one's own use of language systematically is referred as

1 metalinguistic awareness
2 pragmatics
3 pronunciation
4 syntax

Ans. (1)

➲ *Exp.* Understanding about one's own use of language systematically is referred as metalinguistic awareness. It refers to the ability to objectify language as a process as well as an artifact. The concept of metalinguistic awareness is helpful in explaining the execution and transfer of linguistic knowledge across languages (e.g. code switching as well as translation among bilinguals).

70 Bandura's Social Learning Theory had the main focus on

1 moral emotion
2 moral reasoning
3 moral behaviour
4 moral emotion and reasoning

Ans. (3)

Exp. Bandura's Social Learning Theory had the main focus on moral behaviour.

Albert Bandura also believes that moral development is best understood by considering a combination of social and cognitive factors, especially those involving self-control. Bandura argues that in developing a moral self, individuals adopt standards of right and wrong that serve as guides and restraints for conduct. In this self-regulatory process, people monitor their conduct and the conditions under which it occurs, judge it in relation to moral standards, and regulate their actions by the consequences they apply to themselves.

Directions (Q. Nos. 71-75) *Read the passage given below and answer the questions that follow* :

A researcher wanted to study the effect of a specific drug on the activity of rats. He suspected if the effect of the drug is moderated by temperature. He varied drug dosage three levels-no drug (placebo), low drug dosage (Smglkg body-weight) and high drug dosage (I Omg/kg body-weight). He varied temperature 2 at two levels -2SOC and 39°C. Fifteen rats were randomly assigned to each of the six groups. The activity scores for each rate were obtained through activity wheel. The cell means and standard deviations for activity scores were obtained for the six cells. All the cells had comparable standard deviations.

A suitable analysis of variance was carried out using the activity scores as the dependent variable. One of the interesting finding in this research was that the F ratio defined as '$MS_{A \times B} / MS_E$' was statistically significant at 0.01 level.

71 From the above paragraph, it can be inferred that the assumption of homogeneity of variance

1 has been violated
2 has been satisfied
3 cannot be evaluated in the absence of relevant data
4 suggests square-root transformation of data in this case

Ans. (2)

Exp. The assumption of homogeneity of variance has been satisfied. It is that the variance within each of the populations is equal. This is an assumption of analysis of variance (ANOVA). ANOVA works well even when this assumption is violated except in the case where there are unequal numbers of subjects in the various groups. From the above paragraph, it can be inferred that the assumption of homogeneity of variance has been satisfied.

72 What would be the degrees of freedom for error variance?

1 83   2 84   3 89   4 90

Ans. (2)

Exp. The degrees of freedom for error variance can be calculated by subtracting (N-1) and (k-1), where 'N' = total number of rats and 'k' = number of groups.

Here, df = 89-5 = 84

84 will be the degrees of freedom for error variance.

73 From the significant F ratio '$MS_{A \times B} / MS_E$', it can be inferred that

1 the main effect of drug dosage is significant
2 the main effect of temperature is significant
3 the effect of drug dosage is moderated by temperature
4 the main effect of drug dosage, the main effect of temperature and the interaction effect of the two, all are significant

Ans. (3)

Exp. From the significant F ratio '$MS_{A \times B} / MS_E$', it can be inferred that the effect of drug dosage is moderated by temperature. The interaction effect of drug dose and temperature is significant. Interaction effects occur when the effect of one variable depends on the value of another variable.

74 What would be the degrees of freedom for the interaction term?

1 2   2 3
3 5   4 6

Ans. (1)

Exp. The degrees of freedom for the interaction term can be calculated by the formula,

$df = dfa \times dfb$

$dfa = (r-1) = 3-1 = 2$, where r is the number of levels of drug dosage

$dfb = (c-1) = 2-1 = 1$, where c is the number of levels of temperature

$df = 2 \times 1 = 2$

2 is the degrees of freedom for the interaction term.

75 Since the F ratio, defined as '$MS_{A \times B} / MS_E$' is significant it would be desirable to carry out

1 post-hoc comparisons for the three levels of A
2 post-hoc comparison for the two levels of 8
3 compute x multivariate ANOVA
4 simple effects analysis

Ans. (4)

Exp. Since the F ratio, defined as '$MS_{A \times B} / MS_{SE}$' is significant it would be desirable to carry out simple effects analysis.

Simple effects analysis tests are follow-up tests when the interaction is significant. They explore the nature of the interaction by examining the difference between groups within one level of one of the independent variables. It can be defined as '$MS_{A \times B} / MS_E$'.

UGC-NET PSYCHOLOGY

SOLVED PAPER 2013 (December)

PAPER II

1 The visible spectrum wavelength ranges from

1 380 to 760 nanometres
2 200 to 700 nanometres
3 400 to 1000 nanometres
4 100 to 1000 nanometres

Ans. (1)

Exp. The visible spectrum wavelength ranges from 380 to 760 nanometres.

Visible spectrum is the portion of the whole spectrum of light that is visible to the human eye. It is a distribution of electromagnetic energy displayed by decreasing wavelength. In the case of the visible spectrum, it is the series of visible colors (with wavelengths in the range 400–700 nm) produced when white light is refracted through a prism.

2 Shyam does not like to be in family gatherings, but his mother has asked him to attend it. He decides to tell a lie that he has examination on that day however, he finds it very distasteful. Shyam is experiencing

1 double avoidance conflict
2 double approach conflict
3 approach-avoidance conflict
4 double approach-double avoidance conflict

Ans. (1)

Exp. Shyam is experiencing a Double avoidance conflict. Double Avoidance Conflict is when a person is simultaneously repelled by two goals (objects, actions, or whatever) and obliged to select one. It is also called Avoidance-Avoidance conflict.

3 Given below are the two statements, one labelled as Assertion (A) and the other labelled as Reason (R). Indicate your answer using the codes given below :

Assertion (A) Computational approach involves a rigorous, mathematically oriented analysis of certain aspects of visual perception derived largely from computer simulation and artificial intelligence.

Reason (R) Neurophysiological approach argues that sensory and perceptual phenomena are best explained by known neural and physiological mechanisms serving sensory structures.

Codes

1 Both (A) and (R) are true and (R) is the correct explanation of (A)
2 Both (A) and (R) are true, but (R) is not the correct explanation of (A)
3 (A) is true, but (R) is false
4 (A) is false, but (R) is true

Ans. (2)

Exp. Both (A) and (R) are true, but (R) is not the correct explanation of (A).

Computational approach involves a rigorous, mathematically oriented analysis of certain aspects of visual perception derived largely from computer simulation and artificial intelligence.

Computational approach is mathematically oriented and views the visual system like a computer that is programmed to perceive objects. According to this theory, there are a series of processing stages leading to a final form that can be perceived.

Neurophysiological approach argues that sensory and perceptual phenomena are best explained by known neural and physiological mechanisms serving sensory structures.

The physiological approach is concerned with the relationship between the stimulus and the neural mechanisms that process them. An example of this approach is the use of neuroimaging technologies (e.g. fMRI, PET) to examine the neural mechanisms that underlie stimulus processing. This does not explain the computational approach.

4 Having seen or heard a stimulus once may facilitate our recognising it on a latter occasion, even if we are not aware that this is happening. This phenomena is referred to as

1 Primacy effect
2 Recency effect
3 Practice effect
4 Priming effect

Ans. (4)

Exp. The given phenomena is referred to as Priming effect.

Priming effect is the effect in which recent experience of a stimulus facilitates or inhibits later processing of the same or a similar stimulus. It is an implicit memory effect in which exposure to one stimulus (i.e. perceptual pattern) influences the response to another stimulus. In repetition priming, presentation of a particular sensory stimulus increases the likelihood that participants will identify the same or a similar stimulus later in the test. In semantic priming, presentation of a word or sign influences the way in which participants interpret a subsequent word or sign.

5 Given below are the two statements, one labelled as Assertion (A) and the other labelled as Reason (R). Indicate your answer using the correct codes given below :

Assertion (A) Naturalistic observation is the highly preferred method in ethological research.

Reason (R) Naturalistic observation is free from observer bias.

Codes

1 Both (A) and (R) are true and (R) is the correct explanation of (A)
2 Both (A) and (R) are true, but (R) is not the correct explanation of (A)
3 (A) is true, but (R) is false
4 (A) is false, but (R) is true

Ans. (3)

Exp. (A) is true, but (R) is false.

Naturalistic observation is the highly preferred method in ethological research. Ethological research is the scientific and objective study of animal behaviour, usually with a focus on behaviour under natural conditions and viewing behaviour as an evolutionarily adaptive trait. Naturalistic observation is an observational method that involves observing people's behaviour in the environment in which it typically occurs. Thus, naturalistic observation is a type of field research (as opposed to a type of laboratory research).

Naturalistic observation is free from observer bias is false as in Naturalistic observations, observer may be biased. The primary limitation with this approach is that the mere presence of the observer could affect the behaviour of the people being observed. If the researcher acts as a participant observer there can be concerns with biases resulting from developing relationships with the participants. Concretely, the researcher may become less objective resulting in more experimenter bias.

6 There are various kinds of cells in human body. Which one of the following is not a neuron?

1 Sensory
2 Glia
3 Inter
4 Motor

Ans. (2)

Exp. Glia is not a neuron. The glia cells surround neurons and provide support for and insulation between them.

Sensory neurons carry signals from the outer parts of your body into the central nervous system.

Motor neurons carry signals from the central nervous system to the outer parts (muscles, skin, glands) of your body.

Interneurons connect various neurons within the brain and spinal cord.

7 Given below are the two statements, one labelled as Assertion (A) and the other labelled as Reason (R). Indicate your answer using the codes given below :

Assertion (A) During action potential, there is change in polarisation of ions across neuronal membrane.

Reason (R) All the negative ions are transported outside the neuronal membrane.

Codes

1 Both (A) and (R) are true and (R) is the correct explanation of (A)
2 Both (A) and (R) are true, but (R) is not the correct explanation of (A)
3 (A) is true, but (R) is false
4 (A) is false, but (R) is true

Ans. (3)

Exp. (A) is true, but (R) is false.

During action potential, there is change in polarisation of ions across neuronal membrane. Polarisation is a difference in electric potential between two surfaces or two sides of one surface because of chemical activity. Polarisation occurs normally in living cells, such as neurons and muscle cells, which maintain a positive charge on one side of the plasma membrane and a negative charge on the other.

All the negative ions are transported outside the neuronal membrane. This is false because action potentials are caused when different ions cross the neuronal membrane. A stimulus first causes sodium channels to open. As there are many more sodium ions on the outside, and the inside of the neuron is negative relative to the outside, sodium ions rush into the neuron. Remember, sodium has a positive charge, so the neuron becomes more positive and becomes depolarised. It takes longer for potassium channels to open. When they do open, potassium rushes out of the cell, reversing the depolarisation.

8 Individual differences in intelligence are due to

1 Only genetic factors
2 Only environmental factors
3 genetic and economic factors
4 many factors including genetic and environmental

Ans. (4)

Exp. Individual differences in intelligence are due to many factors including genetic and environmental. Genetic factors are important in determining one's intelligence. Individual differences occur on the basis of stimulation received by his or her external environment. This may include family status, peer group, economic level etc.

9 Put the parts of the brain in sequence, going from higher to lower level of brain.

I. Metencephalon II. Mesencephalon
III. Diencephalon IV. Telencephalon
V. Myelencephalon

Codes

1 I, II, III, IV, V 2 II, IV, I, III, V
3 IV, III, II, I, V 4 III, II, I, V, IV

***Ans.* (3)**

➲ *Exp.* The correct order is IV, III, II, I, V.

Each brain is divided into five anatomical units i.e., Telencephalon; Diencephalon; Mesencephalon; Metencephalon and Myelencephalon.

The Telencephalon eventually form the cerebral hemispheres, and the Diencephalon form the thalamic and hypothalamic brain regions that receive neural input from the retina. Indeed, the retina itself is a derivative of the Diencephalon. The Mesencephalon does not become subdivided, and its lumen eventually becomes the cerebral aqueduct. The Myelencephalon eventually becomes the medulla oblongata, whose neurons generate the nerves that regulate respiratory, gastrointestinal, and cardiovascular movements. The Metencephalon gives rise to the cerebellum, the part of the brain responsible for coordinating movements, posture, and balance.

10 Arrange the following layers of retina in order of light travelling from environment to back of the eyeball.

I. Ganglion cells II. Cone receptors
III. Horizontal cells IV. Bipolar cells

Codes

1 I, II, III, IV 2 II, III, IV, I
3 IV, II, III, I 4 I, IV, III, II

***Ans.* (4)**

➲ *Exp.* The correct order is I, IV, III, II.

Layers of retina is order of light travelling from environment to back of the eyeball are Ganglion cells, Bipolar cells, Horizontal cells, Cone receptors.

Ganglion cell is the only type of neuron in the retina that sends signals to the brain resulting from visual stimulation. Retinal ganglion cells receive input from retinal bipolar cells and amacrine cells. The axons of retinal ganglion cells form the optic nerve.

Bipolar cell is a neuron with only two extensions—an axon and a dendrite—that run from opposite sides of the cell body. Retinal bipolar cell is any of various neurons in the inner nuclear layer of the retina that receive input from the photoreceptors (retinal rods and retinal cones) and transmit signals to retinal ganglion cells and amacrine cells. Rods and cones are served by different populations of retinal bipolar cells, called rod bipolars and cone bipolars.

Horizontal cells are the laterally interconnecting neurons having cell bodies in the inner nuclear layer of the retina of vertebrate eyes. They help integrate and regulate the input from multiple photoreceptor cells. Horizontal cells provide inhibitory feedback to rod and cone photoreceptors.

Cone receptors, or cones, are photoreceptor cells in the retinas of vertebrate eyes including the human eye. They respond differently to light of different wavelengths, and thus responsible for colour vision, and function best in relatively bright light, as opposed to rod cells, which work better in dim light.

11 The resting potential of a neuron is

1 - 95 mV 2 + 85 mV
3 -70 mV 4 + 70 mV

***Ans.* (3)**

➲ *Exp.* The resting membrane potential of a neuron is about –70 mV, this means that the inside of the neuron is 70 mV less than the outside. At rest, there are relatively more sodium ions outside the neuron and more potassium ions inside that neuron.

12 The chi-square, computed for a contingency table, was based on six degrees of freedom. If the contingency table had three rows, how many columns would it have?

1 2 2 3 3 4 4 6

***Ans.* (3)**

➲ *Exp.* If the contingency table had three rows, the number of columns will be four.

The degrees of freedom is calculated using the formula $df = (r-1)\ (c-1)$

By putting the values of $df = 6$ and $r = 3$ in the formula above, we get the value of $c = 4$

13 Given below are the two statements, one labelled as Assertion (A) and the other labelled as Reason (R). Indicate your answer using the codes given below :

Assertion (A) Test-retest reliability of psychometric tests is more than that of projective tests.

Reason (R) Trait approach presumes consistency of personality.

Codes

1 Both (A) and (R) are true and (R) is the correct explanation of (A)
2 Both (A) and (R) are true, but (R) is not the correct explanation of (A)
3 (A) is true, but (R) is false
4 (A) is false, but (R) is true

***Ans.* (2)**

➲ *Exp.* Both (A) and (R) are true, but (R) is not the correct explanation of (A).

Test-retest reliability of psychometric tests is more than that of projective tests.

Psychometric tests are a standard and scientific method used to measure individual's mental capabilities and behavioural style. The calculation of scores have a standardised procedure so the chances of subjectivity will be less. Projective test is a personality test designed to let a person respond to ambiguous stimuli, presumably revealing hidden emotions and internal conflicts projected by the person into the test. The subjectivity in the interpretation of the results will lower the reliability.

Trait approach presumes consistency of personality. Traits predispose one to act in a certain way, regardless of the situation. This means that traits should remain consistent across situations and over time, but may vary between individuals. It is presumed that individuals differ in their traits due to genetic differences. This does not explain why the test-retest reliability of the psychometric tests is more than that of projective tests.

14 Match List I with List II and indicate your answer with the help of the codes given below :

List I (Measure of Intelligence)	List II (Psychologist)
A. EEG	I. Binet
B. Reaction Time	II. Eysenck
C. Culture Fair Test	III. Galton
D. Verbal Test	IV. Horn

Codes

	A	B	C	D		A	B	C	D
1	I	II	III	IV	2	III	I	II	IV
3	II	III	IV	I	4	IV	II	I	III

Ans. *(3)*

Exp. The correct matching is A-II, B-III, C-IV, D-I.

Eysenck suggested that differences in extraversion are reflected in the basal level of cortical arousal, hypothesising that extraverts possess a lower basal level compared to introverts. Traditionally, cortical arousal is measured as alpha power in the electroencephalogram. (EEG) Eysenck himself regarded EEG, and particularly alpha power, as the 'standard measure of cortical arousal.'

Sir Francis Galton attempted to measure intelligence through Reaction Time (RT) tests.

Cattell and Horn used factor analysis to study the structure of intelligence. They argued that general intelligence exists and consists of two factors: fluid intelligence and crystallized intelligence. Abbreviated as Gf, Fluid intelligence is a largely non-verbal and relatively culture-reduced form of mental efficiency. It is related to a person's inherent capacity to learn and solve problems. Thus, fluid intelligence is used when a task requires adaptation to a new situation. For these reasons, Cattell believed that measures of fluid intelligence were culture-free. Based on this assumption, he devised the Culture Fair Intelligence test in an attempt to eliminate cultural bias in testing.

Alfred Binet was commissioned to identify students who needed educational assistance that the first intelligent quotient (IQ) tests were born. Binet's Verbal IQ test is well-known around the world as a way to compare intelligence.

15 After the recent heavy catastrophic floods in a given state, a psychologist interviewed 120 participants to understand the psychological consequences of the event. This is an example of

1 Ex post facto field research
2 Field experiment
3 Controlled experiment
4 Psychometric research

Ans. *(1)*

Exp. After the recent heavy catastrophic floods in a given state, a psychologist interviewed 120 participants to understand the psychological consequences of the event. This is an example of Ex post facto field research.

Ex post facto study or after-the-fact research is a category of research design in which the investigation starts after the fact has occurred without interference from the researcher. It is also often applied as a substitute for true experimental research to test hypotheses about cause-and-effect relationships or in situations in which it is not practical or ethically acceptable to apply the full protocol of a true experimental design.

16 Match List I with List II and indicate your answer with the help of the codes given below :

List I (Parts of the Eye)	List II (Descriptions)
A. Rods and Cones	I. Stable and unique in individual and can be used for identification better than finger prints
B. Iris	II. Photoreceptors in retina
C. Ciliary muscles	III. The optic disc where optic nerve fibres leave the eye enroute to the brain
D. Blind spot	IV. Control its curvature which varies depending on the distance of the object focussed

Codes

	A	B	C	D		A	B	C	D
1	IV	I	II	III	2	II	I	IV	III
3	I	II	III	IV	4	III	IV	I	II

Ans. *(2)*

Exp. The correct matching is A-II, B-I, C-IV, D-III

Rods and cones are photoreceptors in retina. There are two types of photoreceptors in the human retina, rods and cones. Rods are responsible for vision at low light levels (scotopic vision). Cones are active at higher light levels (photopic vision), are capable of color vision and are responsible for high spatial acuity.

Iris are stable and unique in individual and can be used for identification better than fingerprints. Iris recognition is an automated method of biometric recognition.

Ciliary muscles are the muscles that adjust the shape of the lens to accommodate objects of varying distance away. Ciliary muscles control its curvature which varies depending on the distance of the objects focussed.

Blind spot is the location on the retina known as the optic disc, where the optic nerve fibre exit the back of the eye. The optic disc is where optic nerve fibres leave the eye enroute to the brain.

17 Match List I with List II and indicate your answer with the help of the codes given below :

List I (Visual Variables)	List II (Explanations)
A. Colour	I. The effect of intensity of light on the observer
B. Illuminance	II. The intensity of light reflected from an illuminated surface
C. Luminance	III. The amount of incident light
D. Brightness	IV. The subjective or psychological effect that different wavelengths of light on the observer

Codes

	A	B	C	D		A	B	C	D
1	I	II	III	IV	2	IV	III	II	I
3	II	I	III	IV	4	I	IV	II	III

Ans. (2)

Exp. The correct matching is A-IV, B-III, C-II, D-I

Colour is the subjective or psychological effect that different wavelengths of light on the observer. It is the quality of visible light that corresponds to wavelength as perceived by retinal receptors. It is thus the subjective experience of a physical entity. Colour is characterised by the three separate attributes of hue, saturation, and luminous intensity, but in general usage the term refers to hue only.

Illuminance is the amount of incident light. It is the light (luminous flux) falling on a unit area of a surface. The standard unit of illuminance is the lux.

Luminance is the intensity of light reflected from an illuminated surface. It is the amount of light reflected or emitted from an object as measured in candelas per square meter.

Brightness is the effect of intensity of light on the observer. It is the perceptual correlate of light intensity. The brightness of a stimulus depends on its amplitude (energy), wavelength, the adaptation state of the observer, and the nature of any surrounding or intervening stimuli.

18 Given below are the three types of psychological investigations

I. Field experiments,

II. Laboratory experiments

III. Ex post facto field studies

If the above investigations are arranged in descending order in terms of researcher's ability to control secondary variance, the typical order would be

1 II, I, III 2 III, I, II 3 II, III, I 4 III, II, I

Ans. (1)

Exp. The correct order is II, I, III.

In *Laboratory experiments,* the researcher has maximum control over the variables and the environment. The researcher can manipulate the conditions to the maximum degree.

Field experiments are done in the everyday (i.e. real life) environment of the participants. The experimenter still manipulates the independent variable, but since its in a real-life setting, controlling the extraneous variables is difficult and at times not possible.

Ex post facto study or after-the-fact research is a category of research design in which the investigation starts after the fact has occurred without interference from the researcher. It is also often applied as a substitute for true experimental research to test hypotheses about cause-and-effect relationships or in situations in which it is not practical or ethically acceptable to apply the full protocol of a true experimental design.

19 What is the correct sequence of events for hunger motivation?

I. Energy level to its set point

II. A bout of eating

III. Presence of an energy deficit

IV. Satiation

V. Hunger

Codes

1 I, II, III, IV, V 2 III, V, II, I, IV

3 II, I, III, V, IV 4 V, IV, III, I, II

Ans. (2)

Exp. The correct sequence is III, V, II, I, IV.

The correct sequence of events for hunger motivation is (i) Presence of an energy deficit (ii) Hunger (iii) A bout of eating (iv) Energy level of its set point (v) Satiation.

What is usually meant by hunger is the urge to eat arising from an energy deficit. The 'normal hunger' or appetite for food is the product of having an empty, or less than full, upper gut together with the anticipation of the pleasure of eating. In other words, usually when a (well-nourished) person says they are 'hungry,' or even 'starving,' what they are really experiencing and communicating is a momentary desire for food reward.

A food's energy (macronutrient) content, and not its fillingness, should determine its reward value, as energy content is of primary biological value and satiety limits further energy intake. These reward effects (of nutrients) appear separate from the satiating actions of nutrients, which may actually reduce food reward. In humans, 'satiety index,' that is, the satiating capacity (kJ) for kJ of foods, is inversely related to their palatability.

20 Persons high in achievement motivation tend to prefer tasks that are

1 very easy
2 extremely difficult
3 moderately difficult
4 all types of task

Ans. (3)

Exp. Persons high in achievement motivation tend to prefer tasks that are moderately difficult.

People with a high need for achievement tend to prefer moderately difficult tasks. Such tasks allow people to succeed and to see themselves as competent for having succeeded. Very difficult tasks tend to prevent success and very easy tasks don't allow people to feel competent when they succeed.

21 Match List I with List II and indicate your answer with the help of the codes given below :

List I (Definition)	List II (Memory System)
A. Memory for factual information that we acquired at a specific time	I. Procedural memory
B. Memory for general abstract knowledge that we cannot remember acquiring at a specific time	II. Episodic memory
C. Memory for information necessary to perform skilled motor activity	III. Autobiographical memory
D. Memory for events in our own life	IV. Semantic memory

Codes

	A	B	C	D
1	II	IV	I	III
2	IV	I	III	II
3	III	II	IV	I
4	I	III	II	IV

Ans. (1)

Exp. The correct matching is A-II, B-IV, C-I, D-III.

Procedural memory is the memory for information necessary to perform skilled motor activity. It is responsible for knowing how to do things, also known as motor skills. It stores information on how to perform certain procedures, such as walking, talking and riding a bike.

Episodic memory is the memory for factual information that we acquired at a specific time. It is the memory of autobiographical events times, places, associated emotions and other contextual who, what, when, where, why knowledge that can be explicitly stated or conjured. It is the collection of past personal experiences that occurred at a particular time and place.

Autobiographical memory is the memory for events in our own life. It is a memory system consisting of episodes recollected from an individual's life, based on a combination of episodic (personal experiences and specific objects, people and events experienced at particular time and place) and semantic (general knowledge and facts about the world) memory.

Semantic memory is the memory for general abstract knowledge that we cannot remember acquiring at a specific time. It processes ideas and concepts that are not drawn from personal experience e.g. common knowledge, such as the names of colours, the sounds of letters, the capitals of countries and other basic facts acquired over a lifetime.

22 Match List I with List II and indicate your answer with the help of the codes given below :

List I (Phenomenon)	List II (Psychologist)
A. Observational learning	I. Skinner
B. Cognitive Map	II. Vygotsky
C. Association of different stimuli	III. Bandura
D. Learning pulls to cognitive development	IV. Pavlov

Codes

	A	B	C	D
1	II	I	III	IV
2	III	I	IV	II
3	III	I	II	IV
4	II	III	I	IV

Ans. (2)

Exp. The correct matching is A-III, B-I, C-IV, D-II.

The phenomenon of *Observational learning* was given by Bandura. Albert Bandura explained that behaviour is learned from the environment through the process of observational learning.

The phenomenon of *Cognitive Map* was given by Skinner. Skinner carried out experiment on Cognitive Map. It is a type of mental representation which serves an individual to acquire, code, store, recall and decode information about the relative locations and attributes of phenomena in their everyday or metaphorical spatial environment.

The phenomenon of *Association of different stimuli* was given by Pavlov. It is a type of learning in which an initially neutral stimulus—the Conditioned Stimulus (CS)—when paired with a stimulus that elicits a reflex response—the unconditioned stimulus (US)—results in a learned, or Conditioned Response (CR) when the CS is presented.

The phenomenon of *Learning pulls to cognitive development* was given by Vygotsky. Lev Vygotsky explained that the role of culture and social interactions are imperative to cognitive development.

23 Given below are the two statements, one labelled as Assertion (A) and the other labelled as Reason (R). Indicate your answer using the codes given below :

Assertion (A) The minimum flicker rate of a light source that results in a perceptual shift from apparent flicker to apparent steady continuous light is known as Critical Flicker Frequency (CFF).

Reason (R) The CFF marks the border between seeing flicker and seeing fusion.

Codes

1 Both (A) and (R) are true and (R) is the correct explanation of (A)
2 Both (A) and (R) are true, but (R) is not the correct explanation of (A)
3 (A) is true, but (R) is false
4 (A) is false, but (R) is true

Ans. (2)

Exp. Both (A) and (R) are true, but (R) is not the correct explanation of (A).

The minimum flicker rate of a light source that results in a perceptual shift from apparent flicker to apparent steady continuous light is known as Critical Flicker Frequency (CFF). Critical Flicker Frequency (CFF) threshold is defined as the frequency at which a flickering light is indistinguishable from a steady, non-flickering light. CFF is useful for assessing the temporal characteristics of the visual system. We may not appreciate this fact because under normal conditions the visual system cannot discriminate or appreciate the fact that these sources are in fact going on and off.

The CFF marks the border between seeing flicker and seeing fusion. The flicker fusion threshold, or flicker fusion rate, is a concept in the psychophysics of vision. It is defined as the frequency at which an intermittent light stimulus appears to be completely steady to the average human observer. Flicker fusion threshold is related to persistence of vision. This does not explain the Critical Flicker Frequency (CFF).

24 A person rattles the box of dog's biscuits before giving the biscuit to dog. As the person rattles the box the dog begins to salivate. Thus, rattling of box is ..... and the salivation of dog is a kind of ....

1 CS; CR
2 CS; UCR
3 UCS; CR
4 UCS; UCR

Ans. (1)

Exp. The rattling of box is CS and the salivation of dog is a kind of CR.

In classical conditioning, the Conditioned Stimulus(CS) is a previously neutral stimulus that, after becoming associated with the unconditioned stimulus, eventually comes to trigger a conditioned response.

In classical conditioning, the Conditioned Response (CR) is the learned response to the previously neutral stimulus. The previously neutral stimulus will then evoke the response all on its own. At this point, the response becomes known as the conditioned response.

25 In operant conditioning a schedule of reinforcement that reinforces a response at unpredictable time intervals is the case of

1 fixed - ratio schedule
2 variable - ratio schedule
3 fixed - interval schedule
4 variable - interval schedule

Ans. (4)

Exp. In operant conditioning a schedule of reinforcement that reinforces a response at unpredictable time intervals is the case of Variable-interval schedule. A variable interval schedule is a type of operant conditioning reinforcement schedule in which reinforcement is given after an unpredictable amount of time has passed (an unpredictable amount of time) but this amount of time is on a changing/variable schedule.

26 Given below are the two statements, one labelled as Assertion (A) and the other labelled as Reason (R). Indicate your answer using the codes given below :

Assertion (A) Learning refers to the modification of behaviour as a result of past experience.

Reason (R) Experience is achieved through observation.

Codes

1 Both (A) and (R) are true and (R) is the correct explanation of (A)
2 Both (A) and (R) are true, but (R) is not the correct explanation of (A)
3 (A) is true, but (R) is false
4 (A) is false, but (R) is true

Ans. (2)

Exp. Both (A) and (R) are true, but (R) is not the correct explanation of (A).

Learning refers to the modification of behaviour as a result of past experience. Learning is often defined as a relatively lasting change in behaviour that is the result of experience. The process of learning new things is not always the same. Learning can happen in a wide variety of ways. Learning through association, reward, punishment, observation or reading enriches experiences.

Experience is achieved through observation. It is true but does not explain the given Assertion.

27 A person had a blue car that was in the shop more than it was out. Since, then the person could not think of owning a blue or green coloured car. The person's aversion even to green cars is an example of

1 discrimination
2 generalisation
3 latent learning
4 the over justification effect

Ans. (2)

Exp. The person's aversion even to green cars is generalisation. It involves the elicitation of a response to a stimulus that resembles the discriminative stimulus. It is useful in that it facilitates the transfer of behaviour across similar situations. e.g. a secretary who can type on a typewriter can also type on a computer keyboard.

28 Which of the following best describes the serial position curve?

1 Greater accuracy of recall of words in the beginning of the list and in the middle of the list
2 Greater accuracy of recall of words in the beginning of the list and gradual diminished accuracy by the end of the list
3 Greater accuracy of recall of words in beginning and at end of the list
4 Greater accuracy of recall of words in the middle and at the end of the list

Ans. (3)

Exp. Greater accuracy of recall of words in beginning and at end of the list best describes the serial position curve.

Serial position curve is a 'U' shaped learning curve that is normally obtained while recalling a list of words due to the greater accuracy of recall of words from the beginning and end of the list than words from the middle of list.

29 The degree to which construct system allows new information to enter that will allow construct system to change is called

1 Individual corollary
2 Permeability
3 Loose construing
4 Constructive alternativism

Ans. (2)

Exp. The degree to which construct system allows new information to enter that will allow construct system to change is called Permeability.

It is a degree to which a construct's range of convenience can be altered. A construct is permeable if it admits newly perceived elements to its context. It is impermeable if it rejects elements on the basis of their newness.

30 Who among the following has developed a test for personality assessment where the subject has to choose between a pair of jokes?

1 McCafe
2 McCall
3 JM Cattell
4 RB Cattell

Ans. (4)

Exp. RB Cattell developed a test for personality assessment where the subject has to choose between a pair of jokes. He constructed a test that was published by Institute of Personality and Ability Testing. IPAT has two forms. Form 'A' has 8 pair of jokes for 13 factors. Form 'B' comprised of 10 items per factor to be rated independently.

31 Given below are the two statements, the first labelled as Assertion (A) and the other labelled as Reason (R). Indicate your answer using the codes given below :

Assertion (A) Working memory can hold a large amount of information even though it can retain only 7 to 9 items.

Reason (R) Items in working memory contain several separate bits of information grouped together called chunks.

Codes

1 Both (A) and (R) are true and (R) is the correct explanation of (A)
2 Both (A) and (R) are true, but (R) is not the correct explanation of (A)
3 (A) is true, but (R) is false
4 (A) is false, but (R) is true

Ans. (1)

Exp. Both (A) and (R) are true and (R) is the correct explanation of (A).

Working memory can hold a large amount of information even though it can retain only 7 to 9 items. Working memory is a cognitive system with a limited capacity that is responsible for temporarily holding information available for processing. Working memory is important for reasoning and the guidance of decision making and behaviour. Working memory is generally considered to have limited capacity.

Items in working memory contain several separate bits of information grouped together called chunks. Chunking in psychology is a process by which individual pieces of information are bound together into a meaningful whole. A chunk is defined as a familiar collection of more elementary units that have been inter-associated and stored in memory repeatedly and act as a coherent, integrated group when retrieved. Chunking is the process of storing information and it explains how working memory can only retain 7 to 9 items.

32 Who has emphasised the linguistic relativity hypothesis?

1 Noam Chomsky
2 Jean Piaget
3 Steven Pinker
4 Whorf BL

Ans. (4)

Exp. Whorf BL emphasized the linguistic relativity hypothesis.

The Linguistic Relativity Hypothesis, popularly known as the Sapir-Whorf hypothesis, or as Whorfianism, holds that the structure of human language effects the way in which an individual conceptualises their world. Working from the position that every language describes and conceptualises the world in its own unique way, it holds that a person's native language limits their cross-cultural understanding.

33 Telegraphic speech is typical of the _____ stage.

1 Babbling
2 One-word
3 Two-word
4 Three-word

Ans. (3)

Exp. Telegraphic speech is typical of the two-word stage. Telegraphic speech, according to linguistics and psychology, is speech during the two-word stage of language acquisition in children, which is laconic and efficient. The name derives from the fact that someone sending a telegram was generally charged by the word.

34 The sentence 'Blue Jeans wear false smiles' has correct .... , but incorrect ....

1 morphemes; phonemes
2 phonemes; morphemes
3 semantics; syntax
4 syntax; semantics

***Ans.** (4)*

Exp. The sentence 'Blue Jeans wear false smiles' has correct syntax, but incorrect semantics.

In linguistics, syntax is the set of rules, principles and processes that govern the structure of sentences in a given language, specifically word order. The term 'syntax' is also used to refer to the study of such principles and processes. Semantics is primarily the linguistic, and also philosophical. These are rules for determining the meaning of words and sentences.

35 Given below are the two statements, the first as Assertion (A) and the other labelled as Reason (R). Indicate your answer using the codes given below :

Assertion (A) In deduction, conclusion is derived from a premise.

Reason (R) People reason by using deduction as well as induction.

Codes

1 Both (A) and (R) are true and (R) is the correct explanation of (A)
2 Both (A) and (R) are true, but (R) is not the correct explanation of (A)
3 (A) is true, but (R) is false
4 (A) is false, but (R) is true

***Ans.** (2)*

Exp. Both (A) and (R) are true but (R) is not the correct explanation of (A).

In deduction, conclusion is derived from a premise. Deductive reasoning is a logical process in which a conclusion is based on the concordance of multiple premises that are generally assumed to be true. Deductive reasoning is sometimes referred to as top-down logic. Its counterpart, inductive reasoning, is sometimes referred to as bottom-up logic. Inductive reasoning is a logical process in which multiple premises, all believed true or found true most of the time, are combined to obtain a specific conclusion. Inductive reasoning is often used in applications that involve prediction, forecasting, or behaviour.

People reason by using deduction as well as induction. This is true but it does not explain how conclusion is derived from a premise in deduction.

36 Match List I with List II and indicate your answer with the help of the codes given below :

List I (Phenomenon)		List II (Psychological name)
A. Smallest unit that carries meaning	I.	Grammar
B. Rules to communicate and understand others	II.	Semantics
C. Rules for desiring meanings	III.	Morphemes
D. Rules for combining words	IV.	Syntax

Codes

	A	B	C	D		A	B	C	D
1	III	I	IV	II	2	III	II	IV	I
3	III	I	II	IV	4	III	II	I	IV

***Ans.** (3)*

Exp. The correct matching is A-III, B-I, C-II, D-IV.

Grammar refers to the rules to communicate and understand others. It is the system of rules governing the structure and use of a language.

Semantics refers to the rules for desiring meanings. They are rules for determining the meaning of words and sentences. Sentences, for example, can have the same semantic meaning while having different syntax: "Johny hit the ball" and "The ball was hit by Johny."

Morphemes are the smallest unit that carries meaning. These are the smallest units of meaning within a language. For morphemes example, the word 'playing' consists of two morphemes, 'play' and 'ing'.

Syntax refers to the rules for combining words. It is a system of rules for combining words and phrases to form grammatically correct sentences.

37 Three types of feature detector cells are

1 Simple cells, Glial cells, T-cells
2 Simple cells, Complex cells, Glial cells
3 Sensory cells, Hypercomplex cells, T-cells
4 Simple cells, Complex cells, Hypercomplex cells

***Ans.** (4)*

Exp. Three types of feature detector cells are Simple cells, Complex cells and Hypercomplex cells.

Simple cells have narrow, elongated excitatory and inhibitory zones that have a specific axis of orientation. These cells are 'line detectors'. Their receptive fields can be built from the convergent connections of lateral geniculate nucleus cells.

Complex cells have large receptive fields without clear excitatory or inhibitory zones. They respond best to a moving edge of specific orientation and direction of motion. These direction selective neurons are powerful 'motion detectors'. Their receptive fields could be built from the convergent connections of simple cells.

Hypercomplex cells have very large receptive fields that may combine complex cells' signals. Many of them respond best to an oriented edge that is stopped, i.e., its end does not extend beyond a specific part of the receptive field. Neurons with such a pattern of response act as angle detectors. The glial cells surround neurons and provide support for and insulation between them and a T cell, or T lymphocyte, is a type of lymphocyte (a subtype of white blood cell) that plays a central role in cell-mediated immunity).

38 Given below are the two statements, the first as Assertion (A) and the other labelled as Reason (R). Indicate your answer using the codes given below :

Assertion (A) Sleep fulfills a critical biological function.

Reason (R) Sleep is required to restore the homeostatis.

Codes

1 Both (A) and (R) are true and (R) is the correct explanation of (A)
2 Both (A) and (R) are true, but (R) is not the correct explanation of (A)
3 (A) is true, but (R) is false
4 (A) is false, but (R) is true

Ans. *(1)*

Exp. Both (A) and (R) are true and (R) is the correct explanation of (A).

Sleep fulfills a critical biological function. Sleep plays a vital role in good health and well-being throughout your life. Getting enough quality sleep at the right times can help protect your mental health, physical health, quality of life and safety. Studies also show that sleep deficiency alters activity in some parts of the brain. If you're sleep deficient, you may have trouble making decisions, solving problems, controlling your emotions and behaviour and coping with change.

Sleep is required to restore the homeostatis. The homeostatic process is the drive to sleep that is influenced by the duration of wakefulness. The circadian process transmits stimulatory signals to arousal networks to promote wakefulness in opposition to the homeostatic drive to sleep. Therefore, sleep is considered to fulfill a critical biological function.

39 Choose the odd one for pattern of sympathetic activation during emotions

1 increased heart rate 2 pupil constriction
3 lowered skin resistance 4 increased breathing rate

Ans. *(2)*

Exp. The odd one for pattern of sympathetic activation during emotions is pupil constriction.

The Sympathetic Nervous System (SNS) is part of the Autonomic Nervous System (ANS), which also includes the Parasympathetic Nervous System (PNS). The Sympathetic Nervous System activates what is often termed the fight or flight response. It is, however, constantly active at a basic level to maintain homeostasis. Its stimulation causes vasoconstriction of most blood vessels, including many of those in the skin, the digestive tract and the kidneys and so it leads to increased heart rate, pupil dilation, lowered skin resistance and increased breathing rate.

40 Out of following who has not divided intelligence into two general components?

1 Cattell JM 2 Jensen
3 Hebb 4 Thurstone

Ans. *(4)*

Exp. Thurstone has not divided intelligence into two general concepts. Thurstone argued that 'g' was a statistical artifact resulting from the mathematical procedures used to study it. Thurstone using factor analysis found that intelligent behaviour does not arise from a general factor, but rather emerges from seven independent factors that he called primary abilities, word fluency, verbal comprehension, spatial visualisation, number facility, associative memory, reasoning and perceptual speed.

Cattell has studied intelligence in depth. He developed a model based on two central factors: fluid intelligence (Gf) and Crystallized Intelligence (Gc). Cattell's model differs from Spearman's conception of intelligence as a single unit.

Jensen accepts Spearman's idea of a general factor in human intelligence, and his own theory divides intelligence into two distinct sets of abilities: Level I abilities account for memory functions and simple associative learning, and Level II abilities comprise abstract reasoning and conceptual thought.

Hebb's ideas of intelligence 'A' and 'B' is that the intellectual development includes two distinct things: (A) direct intellectual power, by neural maturation, and (B) the development of qualitative modifications of perception and behavior. The first factor is what reaches a peak somewhere around the beginning of adolescence, declining slowly thereafter; the second is the product of the first factor

41 Number of different factors as specified by Spearman to explain the performance on some tests

1 one 's' factor and many 'g' factors
2 many 's' factors and many 'g' factors
3 one 's' factor and one 'g' factor
4 many 's' factors and one 'g' factor

Ans. *(4)*

Exp. Spearman specified the use of many 's' factors and one 'g' factor to explain the performance on some tests.

Spearman proposed that his two-factor theory has two components. The general intelligence, 'g', influences the performance on all mental tasks, while, 's', influences abilities on a particular task. Spearman saw individuals as having more or less general intelligence, while 's' varied from person-to-person on a task. The interaction between these two different abilities would drastically change how individual differences and cognition are understood in psychology, possibly creating the basis for wisdom.

42 Which set of three approaches is more relevant to study the impact of Genetic factors on intelligence?

I. Correlation between siblings.

II. Correlation between identical twins reared apart.

III. Adopted child studies.

IV. Correlation between parents and children.

Codes

1 I, II and III 2 II, III and IV
3 I, II and IV 4 I, III and IV

Ans. *(3)*

Exp. The correct codes are I, II, and IV

Siblings who were raised together in the same environment have more similar IQs than those of adopted children who were brought up in the same household.

Twin studies suggest that the variance in IQ is linked to genetics. This research suggests that genetics may play a larger role than environmental factors in determining individual IQ.

Kong reports that, "Nurture has a genetic component, i.e. alleles in the parents affect the parents' phenotypes and through that influence the outcomes of the child." These results were obtained through a meta-analysis of educational attainment and polygenic scores of non-transmitted alleles. Although the study deals with educational attainment and not IQ, these two are strongly linked.

43 Match List I with List II and indicate your answer with the help of the codes given below :

List I (Psychologist)	List II (Concept)
A. Adler	I. Basic anxiety
B. Bandura	II. Triadic Reciprocal causation
C. Jung	III. Fictional Finalism
D. Horney	IV. Principle of Equivalence

Codes

	A	B	C	D		A	B	C	D
1	II	IV	III	I	2	I	III	II	IV
3	III	II	IV	I	4	III	IV	II	I

Ans. *(3)*

Exp. The correct matching is A-III, B-II, C-IV, D-I.

Adler gave the concept of Fictional Finalism. Fictional Finalism proposes that people act as much from accepted ideals as they do from observed reality. Whatever the sub-conscious mind accepts as true, it acts as if it is true whether it is or not - it does not have the benefit of the conscious mind's ability to observe independently and check with real experience.

Bandura gave the concept of Triadic Reciprocal causation. According to him, reciprocal determinism is a model composed of three factors that influence behaviour: the environment, the individual, and the behaviour itself. Essentially, Bandura believes that an individual's behaviour influences and is influenced by both the social world and personal characteristics.

Jung gave the concept of Principle of Equivalence. The Principle of Equivalence is the energy available to the opposing thoughts is equal, but one is fulfilled and the other is not. If you acknowledge your opposite thought, the energy is used to help your psyche grow; if you deny it, the energy goes into a complex that develops around an archetype.

Horney gave the concept of Basic anxiety. She developed one of the best known theories of neurosis. Horney believed that neurosis resulted from basic anxiety caused by interpersonal relationships. Her theory proposes that strategies used to cope with anxiety can be overused, causing them to take on the appearance of needs.

44 Researchers have found different ways in which an individual's genotype shapes his or her environment. Which of the following is not one of them?

1 The genotype has a passive effect on environment resulting from genetic similarity between parents and children

2 The child's genotype evokes particular kinds of reactions from social and physical environment

3 The child's genotype plays an active role in shaping the environment

4 People with different genotypes are differentially sensitive or susceptible to their environment

Ans. *(4)*

Exp. Statement 4 is not one of the ways in which an individual's genotype shapes his or her environment.

The genotype of an organism is the inherited map it carries within its genetic code. Not all organisms with the same genotype look or act the same way because appearance and behaviour are modified by environmental and developmental conditions. Likewise, not all organisms that look alike necessarily have the same genotype. Your genotype is your complete heritable genetic identity; it is your unique genome that would be revealed by personal genome sequencing.

45 Match List I with List II and indicate your answer with the help of the codes given below :

List I (Types of Variable)	List II (Example)
A. Continuous	I. Selection test outcomes in terms of selected rejected
B. Real discrete	II. Voice pitch
C. Artificially discrete	III. Intelligence
D. Qualitative	IV. Gender

Codes

	A	B	C	D		A	B	C	D
1	IV	I	II	III	2	II	IV	I	III
3	III	I	IV	II	4	III	IV	I	II

Ans. *(4)*

Exp. The correct matching is A-III, B-IV, C-I, D-II.

Continuous variable is a variable that can take any value between two numbers. It can be measured but not numbered. The example of continuous variable is Intelligence.

A discrete variable is one that falls into separate categories with no intermediate values possible (e.g., male/female, alive/dead, French/Dutch, flying/walking). Discrete variables are also categorical in form. A distinction can be drawn between naturally and artificially discrete variables (e.g., the male/female dichotomy of sex is natural, while the young/old dichotomy of age is artificial). The example of *Real discrete* variable is gender. The example of *Artificially* discrete variable is selection test outcomes in terms of selected/rejected.

Qualitative variable is a variable that cannot be ordered on a numerical scale in statistics so it is assigned to nominal scales. Nominal scale is where data is assigned to a category. The example of qualitative variable is Voice Pitch.

Directions (Q. Nos. 46-50) *Read the passage given below and answer the questions that follow :*

The Classical Test Theory assumes that every obtained score is a sum of the true score and the error of measurement. The earlier versions of the CTT, in their reliability conceptualisation, ambitiously addressed the random errors of measurement.

Accordingly, reliability can be conceptualised as a consistency between the true score and the obtained score. Reliability can be studied through various perspectives. In the test construction phase, internal consistency reliability is given heavy emphasis. Various reliability coefficients such as split-half reliability, Kuder-Richardson reliability, Cronbach alpha etc have been developed for this purpose. One of the earlier development in CFT is the Spearman-Brown formula. The other important types of reliabilities include test-retest reliability and interscorer reliability. In addition to reliability, psychologists emphasise test validity. Content validity, concurrent validity, predictive validity, construct validity are some of the important types of validities in psychometric studies.

Factor analysis has also been employed in evaluating the test validity. Once the reliability and validity are well established, the test constructor attempts to establish the representative and comprehensive norms.

46 Reliability is conceptualised as

1 $\frac{\text{Obtained Variance}}{\text{True Variance}}$

2 $\frac{\text{True Variance}}{\text{True Variance} + \text{Error Variance}}$

3 $\frac{\text{True Variance}}{\text{Error Variance}}$

4 $\frac{\text{Obtained Variance}}{\text{Error Variance}}$

Ans. (2)

Exp. Reliability is conceptualised as True Variance/ True Variance + Error Variance.

"The reliability of any set of measurements is logically defined as the proportion of their variance that is true variance. We think of the total variance of a set of measures as being made up of two sources of variance: true variance and error variance. The true measure is assumed to be the genuine value of whatever is being measured. The error components occur independently and at random"

Observed Variance = "True" Variance + Error Variance

Reliability = "True" Variance / Observed Variance

47 Cronbach alpha is

I. larger than split half reliability coefficient.
II. smaller than reliability coefficient.
III. average of all possible split-half reliability coefficients.
IV. equal to Kuder-Richardson reliability for dichotomous items.

Codes

1 Only I 2 Only II 3 III and IV 4 I and IV

Ans. (3)

Exp. Cronbach's alpha is average of all possible split-half reliability coefficients and equal to Kuder-Richardson reliability for dichotomous items.

Coefficient alpha is the most commonly used internal consistency reliability coefficient. Alpha is the mean of all possible k-split alphas if the items are divided into 'k' parts of equal size.

The Kuder and Richardson Formula 20 test checks the internal consistency of measurements with dichotomous choices. It is equivalent to performing the split-half methodology on all combinations of questions and is applicable when each question is either right or wrong. A correct question scores 1 and an incorrect question scores 0.

48 The interscorer reliability is especially important for

I. projective tests
II. achievement tests with short answers
III. multiple choice tests
IV. judgements by multiple raters

Codes

1 Only I 2 II and III
3 I and IV 4 I, II and IV

Ans. (4)

Exp. The interscorer reliability is especially important for projective tests, achievement tests with short answers, and judgements by multiple raters.

A psychological test in which words, images, or situations are presented to a person and the responses analysed for unconscious expression of elements of personality that they reveal and judgement by multiple raters will bias the results by the subjectivity of the raters. Since, there is no standardised way of concluding of a score so the interscorer reliability is important for the results to be accepted.

49 Consider that a newly developed test for assessing abstract reasoning and a well established test of abstract reasoning are administered to a sample of 350 and a correlation of 0.25, significant at .01 level is obtained. It will be inferred that the new test has

1 unsatisfactory concurrent validity
2 satisfactory concurrent validity
3 unsatisfactory predictive validity
4 satisfactory predictive validity

Ans. (1)

Exp. The new test has unsatisfactory concurrent validity.

Concurrent validity pertains to the extent to which the measurement tool relates to other scales measuring the same construct and that have already been validated. The given test has a low correlation with the already established test.

50 Factor analysis is best suited for studying

1 concurrent validity
2 predictive validity
3 content validity
4 construct validity

Ans. (4)

Exp. Factor analysis is best suited for studying construct validity.

A commonly used method to investigate construct validity is Confirmatory Factor Analysis (CFA). CFA is a tool that a researcher can use to attempt to reduce the overall number of observed variables into latent factors based on commonalities within the data. Construct validity is 'the degree to which a test measures what it claims, or purports, to be measuring, how well a test or tool measures the construct that it was designed to measure.

PAPER III

1 Match List I with List II and indicate your answer with the help of the codes given below :

List I (Type of Love)	List II (Explanation)
A. Eros	I. A type of unselfish love characterised by devotion to the welfare of others
B. Agape	II. A type of love that incorporates all other types of love
C. Authentic love	III. A type of procreative love that is savouring and experiential
D. Philia	IV. Brotherly love

Codes

	A	B	C	D		A	B	C	D
1	III	I	II	IV	2	III	IV	II	I
3	IV	I	III	II	4	II	IV	I	III

Ans. (1)

Exp. The correct matching is A-III, B-I, C-II, D-IV.

Eros is a type of procreative love that is savouring and experiential. It is a psychological desire that seeks procreation or creation through an enduring union with a loved one. It is making love and a wish to establish a lasting union.

Agape is a type of unselfish love characterised by devotion to the welfare of others. It is defined as "esteem for the other, the concern for the other's welfare beyond any gain that one can get out of it; disinterested love, typically, the love of God for man". It is altruistic love.

Authentic love is a type of love that incorporates all other types of love.

Philia is a type of brotherly love. It is an intimate non-sexual friendship between two people. Examples of philia would be the slowly evolving love between siblings or between lifelong friends.

2 Out of the following, who has not explained intelligence in terms of psychometric approach?

1 Jensen
2 Cattell
3 Sternberg
4 Thurstone

Ans. (3)

Exp. Sternberg has not explained intelligence in terms of psychometric approach.

Sternberg's Triarchic theory of intelligence is based on a broader definition of intelligence than is typically used. In this theory, intelligence is defined in terms of the ability to achieve success in life based on one's personal standards–and within one's sociocultural context. The ability to achieve success depends on the ability to capitalize on one's strengths and to correct or compensate for one's weaknesses. Success is attained through a balance of analytical, creative, and practical abilities–a balance that is achieved in order to adapt to, shape, and select environments.

3 Select one of the levels and one of the stages given below as envisaged by Kohlberg in the Theory of Development of Moral Reasoning.

I. Two levels
II. Three levels
III. Four levels
IV. Five stages
V. Six stages
VI. Eight stages

Codes

1 I and V　　2 II and IV
3 II and V　　4 III and VI

Ans. (3)

Exp. Kohlberg identified three distinct level of moral reasoning and each level has two sub-stages in the Theory of Development of Moral Reasoning. In total there are six stages.

Level 1. Preconventional Morality : Preconventional morality is the earliest period of moral development. There are two stages within this level:

Stage 1. Obedience and Punishment : The earliest stages of moral development, obedience and punishment are especially common in young children, but adults are also capable of expressing this type of reasoning.

Stage 2. Individualism and Exchange : At the individualism and exchange stage of moral development, children account for individual points of view and judge actions based on how they serve individual needs.

Level 2. Conventional Morality : The next period of moral development is marked by the acceptance of social rules regarding what is good and moral. There are two stages at this level of morality:

Stage 3. Developing Good Interpersonal Relationships : Often referred to as the "good boy-good girl" orientation, this stage of the interpersonal relationship of moral development is focused on living up to social expectations and roles.

Stage 4. Maintaining Social Order : This stage is focused on ensuring that social order is maintained.

Level 3. Postconventional Morality : At this level of moral development, people develop an understanding of abstract principles of morality. The two stages at this level are:

Stage 5. Social Contract and Individual Rights : The ideas of a social contract and individual rights cause people in the next stage to begin to account for the differing values, opinions, and beliefs of other people.

Stage 6. Universal Principles : Kohlberg's final level of moral reasoning is based on universal ethical principles and abstract reasoning.

4 Match List I with List II and indicate your answer with the help of the codes given below :

List I (Style)	List II (Description)
A. Impulsive cognitive style	I. Responding slowly, carefully and accurately
B. Reflective cognitive style	II. Memorising,but not understanding the learning material
C. Deep processing	III. Responding quickly, but often learning style inaccurately
D. Surface processing	IV. Understanding the underlying learning style concepts and meaning of learning material

Codes

	A	B	C	D		A	B	C	D
1	I	II	III	IV	2	III	I	IV	II
3	II	IV	I	III	4	IV	III	II	I

Ans. (2)

Exp. The correct matching is A-III, B-I, C-IV, D-II.

Impulsive cognitive style involves responding quickly, but often learning style inaccurately. In impulsive cognitive style, a person reacts quickly, but as a result makes comparatively more errors.

Reflective cognitive style involves responding slowly, carefully and accurately. In reflective cognitive style, the person reacts more slowly and therefore makes fewer errors.

Deep processing involves understanding the underlying learning style concepts and meaning of learning material. It is the cognitive processing of a stimulus that focuses on its meaningful properties rather than its perceptual characteristics.

Surface processing involves memorising, but not understanding the learning material. It is the cognitive processing of a stimulus that focuses on its superficial, perceptual characteristics rather than its meaning.

5 Which of the following is not a factor for poor academic performance among low socio-economic status students?

1 Resistance culture　　2 Tracking
3 Learned helplessness　　4 Family size

Ans. (4)

Exp. Family size is not a factor for poor academic performance among low socio-economic status students.

Cultural resistance is the broad use of arts, literature, and traditional practices to challenge or fight unjust or oppressive systems and/or power holders within the context of non-violent actions, campaigns and movements.

Tracking is separating pupils by academic ability into groups for all subjects or certain classes and curriculum within a school. It may be referred to as streaming or phasing in certain schools.

Learned helplessness is a mental state in which an organism forced to bear aversive stimuli, or stimuli that are painful or otherwise unpleasant, becomes unable or unwilling to avoid subsequent encounters with those stimuli, even if they are 'escapable,' presumably because it has learned that it cannot control the situation.

6 What are the attitudes, goals and strategies of failure avoiding students?

1 High fear of failure, very high or very low goals and self-defeating strategies
2 Expectations of failure, very high or very low goals and self-defeating strategies
3 High fear of failure, very high or very low goals and learned helplessness
4 High fear of failure, no goals, learned helplessness

Ans. (1)

➲ *Exp.* The attitudes, goals and strategies of failure avoiding students should be high fear of failure, very high or very low goals and self-defeating strategies.

Failure avoiding students don't expect to succeed – they just want to avoid failing. In order to do so, they frequently make excuses, procrastinate or simply don't participate. In order to avoid failure, they have a high fear of failure. They have very high or very low goals and adopt self-defeating strategies.

Fear of failure is a persistent and irrational anxiety about failing to measure up to the standards and goals set by oneself or others. This may include anxiety over academic standing, losing a job, sexual inadequacy, or loss of face and self-esteem. Fear of failure may be associated with perfectionism and is implicated in a number of psychological disorders, including eating disorders and some anxiety disorders.

Self-defeating strategies are repetitive actions by an individual that invite failure or misfortune and thus prevent him or her from attaining goals or fulfilling desires.

7 Hunger is caused by

I. expectation of food
II. deficiency of energy
III. homeostatic disturbance
IV. deficiency of oxygen

Codes

1 Only I 2 I and II
3 I, II and III 4 All of these

Ans. (3)

➲ *Exp.* Hunger is caused by expectation of food, deficiency of energy and homeostatic disturbance.

What is usually meant by hunger is the urge to eat arising from an energy deficit. The 'normal hunger' or appetite for food is the product of having an empty, or less than full, upper gut together with the anticipation of the pleasure of eating. In other words, usually when a (well-nourished) person says they are 'hungry,' or even 'starving,' what they are really experiencing and communicating is a momentary desire for food reward.

A food's energy (macronutrient) content, and not its fillingness, should determine its reward value, as energy content is of primary biological value and satiety limits further energy intake. 'These reward effects (of nutrients) appear separate from the satiating actions of nutrients, which may actually reduce food reward'. In humans, 'satiety index,' that is, the satiating capacity kJ for kJ of foods, is inversely related to their palatability.

8 Arrange the developmental stages of language given by Vygotsky in correct sequence given below.

I. Potential Concept stage
II. Vague Syncretic stage
III. Mature Concept stage
IV. Complex stage

Codes

1 III, I, IV, II 2 II, IV, I, III
3 I, III, II, IV 4 IV, II, III, I

Ans. (2)

➲ *Exp.* The correct sequence is II, IV, I, III.

Vygotsky agrued that there are four stages in the formation of concept. They are :

Vague Syncretic stage: In this stage, the children failed to use systematic strategies and showed little understanding of the concept.

Complex stage: In this stage, non-random strategies were used, but these strategies were not useful in finding the main features of the concept.

Potential concept stage: In this stage, systematic strategies were used but were limited to focusing on one feature at a time.

Mature concept stage: In this stage, systematic strategies relation to more than one feature at a time were used and let to successful formation of the concept.

9 Given below are the two statements, the first as Assertion (A) and the other labelled as Reason (R). Indicate your answer using the correct codes given below :

Assertion (A) Labour Unions Act collectively to protect employee's interests.

Reason (R) Labour unions have little influence on employee competence.

Codes

1 Both (A) and (R) are true and (R) is the correct explanation of (A)
2 Both (A) and (R) are true, but (R) is not the correct explanation of (A)
3 (A) is true, but (R) is false
4 Both (A) and (R) are false

Ans. (3)

➲ *Exp.* (A) is true, but (R) is false.

Labour Union Act collectively to protect employee's interest but they don't have any influence on employee competence.

Labour unions have strong influence on employee competence.

10 A person while intrinsically motivated does not seek when performing

I. enjoyment II. reward
III. challenge IV. avoidance of punishment

Codes

1 I and II 2 II and III
3 II and IV 4 III and IV

Ans. (3)

➲ *Exp.* A person while intrinsically motivated does not seek when performing reward and avoidance of punishment.

Intrinsic motivation is the act of doing something without any obvious external rewards. One does it because it's enjoyable and interesting, rather than because of an outside incentive or pressure to do it, such as a reward or deadline/punishment.

11 Imagine becoming a renowned painter some day. I am engaging in

1 divergent thinking 2 prospective thinking
3 creative thinking 4 autistic thinking

Ans. (4)

Exp. Imagine becoming a renowned painter some day. I am engaging in autistic thinking.

It is narcissistic, egocentric thought processes, such as fantasising and daydreaming, that have little or no relation to reality. It is comprised of inner thoughts and individual reality. Daydreaming and fantasies are common elements of autistic thinking.

12 The known stimulus elicits the _______ while the unknown stimulus elicits the _______ .

1 operant behaviour; respondent behaviour
2 operant behaviour; conditioned behaviour
3 conditioned behaviour; operant behaviour
4 respondent behaviour; operant behaviour

Ans. (4)

Exp. The known stimulus elicits the respondent behaviour while the unknown stimulus elicits the operant behaviour.

Respondent behaviours are elicited by antecedent stimuli. Respondent conditioning occurs through stimulus-stimulus pairing procedures. Respondent behaviours include reflexes, such as an eye blink to clean the eye. Respondent behaviours are considered "ready-made" behaviours where no "learning" is required.

On the other hand, operant behavior is any behaviour whose future frequency is determined by its history of consequences. Operant behaviours are defined by their effects, not by the form of the behaviour. Operant conditioning is an automatic process that refers to the selective effects of consequences on behavior. Operant conditioning includes both reinforcement, the effect of which is a behavior increase; and punishment, the effect of which is a behavior decrease. The term positive refers to the presentation of a stimulus event. The term negative refers to the removal of a stimulus event.

13 Match List I with List II and indicate your answer with the help of the codes given below :

List I (Kind of Effect of Stress)	List II (Effects)
A. Physiological effects	I. Reduced work performance
B. Emotional effects	II. Expansion of air passages in lungs
C. Cognitive effects	III. Feeling of anxiety
D. Behavioural effects	IV. Increased distractibility

Codes

	A	B	C	D		A	B	C	D
1	II	III	IV	I	2	IV	III	I	II
3	III	IV	II	I	4	I	II	IV	III

Ans. (1)

Exp. The correct matching is A-II, B-III, C-IV, D-I.

Reduced work performance is an example of Behavioural effects. Behavioural symptoms of stress include: Changes in appetite-either not eating or eating too much, procrastinating and avoiding responsibilities, increased use of alcohol, drugs, or cigarettes, exhibiting more nervous behaviours, such as nail biting, fidgeting, and pacing, etc.

Expansion of air passages in lungs is an example of Physiological effects. It consists of two divisions, the parasympathetic and the sympathetic. It is the sympathetic nervous system (the "fight-or-flight" system) that reacts when the human body is subjected to stress: Heart rate increases, digestion slows or shuts down, and energy is sent to the muscles to help deal with whatever action the stressful situation requires. The parasympathetic system returns the body to normal, day-to-day functioning after the stress is ended.

Feeling of anxiety is an example of emotional effects. Emotional symptoms of stress include: Becoming easily agitated, frustrated, and moody, feeling overwhelmed, like you are losing control or need to take control, having difficulty relaxing and quieting your mind, feeling bad about yourself (low self-esteem), lonely, worthless, and depressed and avoiding others.

Increased distractibility is an example of cognitive effects. Cognitive factors, such as how an individual interprets a stressful event, can affect the impact of stress.

14 Escape learning involves

1 instrumental conditioning with positive reinforcement
2 classical conditioning with positive reinforcement
3 classical conditioning with negative reinforcement
4 instrumental conditioning with negative reinforcement

Ans. (4)

Exp. Escape learning involves instrumental conditioning with negative reinforcement.

Escape learning occurs to terminate an unpleasant stimulus such as annoyance or pain, thereby negatively reinforcing the behaviour. For example, to persuade a rat to jump from a platform into a pool of water, you might electrify the platform to mildly shock the rat. The rat jumps due to escape learning, since it jumps into the water to escape the electric shock.

15 Given below are the two statements, the first as Assertion (A) and the other labelled as Reason (R). Indicate your answer using the codes given below :

Assertion (A) Subliminal or below threshold perception exerts an observable influence on various response parameters is not a controversial question.

Reason (R) Subliminally presented emotional stimuli activate cortical areas that mediate emotional experiences.

Codes

1 Both (A) and (R) are true and (R) is the correct explanation of (A)
2 Both (A) and (R) are true, but (R) is not the correct explanation of (A)
3 (A) is true, but (R) is false
4 (A) is false, but (R) is true

Ans. (4)

Exp. (A) is false, but (R) is true.

Subliminal or below threshold perception exerts an observable influence on various response parameters is not a controversial question. Perception without awareness is not the same thing as subliminal perception. Subliminal perception is supposed to occur when a stimulus is too weak to be perceived yet a person is influenced by it. According to Schmeidler and the vast majority of psychologists studying subliminal phenomena, a threshold is the point at which a stimulus is perceived 50% of the time.

Subliminally presented emotional stimuli activate cortical areas that mediate emotional experiences. Cortical, subcortical and peripheral sensory nerve potentials are involved in the subliminal perception.

16 Which are the concepts mainly used by Sternberg in his Theory of Intelligence?

I. Meta components
II. Performance components
III. Factor analysis
IV. Selective encoding

Codes

1 I, II and III
2 II, III and IV
3 I, II and IV
4 I, III and IV

Ans. (3)

Exp. The concepts mainly used by Sternberg in his Theory of Intelligence are Meta components, Performance concepts and Selective encoding.

Sternberg associated the workings of the mind with a series of components. These components he labelled the Meta components, Performance components and Selective encoding. The Meta components are executive processes used in problem solving and decision making that involve the majority of managing our mind.

The Performance components, are the processes that actually carry out the actions the meta components dictate. These are the basic processes that allow us to do tasks, such as perceiving problems in our long-term memory, perceiving relations between objects and applying relations to another set of terms.

Selective encoding is used in the knowledge-acquisition components which are used in obtaining new information. These components complete tasks that involve selectively choosing relevant information from a mix of information, some of it relevant and some of it irrelevant. These components can also be used to selectively combine the various pieces of information they have gathered.

17 Given below are the two statements, the first as Assertion (A) and the other labelled as Reason (R). Indicate your answer using the correct codes given below :

Assertion (A) Total variance of test score is the sum of True variance and Error variance

Reason (R) True score and error score are independent of each other.

Codes

1 Both (A) and (R) are true and (R) is the correct explanation of (A)
2 Both (A) and (R) are true, but (R) is not the correct explanation of (A)
3 (A) is true, but (R) is false
4 (A) is false, but (R) is true

Ans. (1)

Exp. Both (A) and (R) are true and (R) is the correct explanation of (A).

Total variance of test score is the sum of True variance and Error variance. The reliability of any set of measurements is logically defined as the proportion of their variance that is true variance. We think of the total variance of a set of measures as being made up of two sources of variance: True variance and Error variance.

True score and error score are independent of each other. The true measure is assumed to be the genuine value of whatever is being measured. The error components occur independently and at random. The true score is the mean that would be approached as the number of trials increases indefinitely. It is a theory of testing based on the idea that a person's observed or obtained score on a test is the sum of a true score (error-free score) and an error score. Both the true and error score are independent of each other which explain the total variance obtained.

18 While evaluating the Personnel Selection Programme, job performance was found to have a multiple correlation of 0.6 with the four predictors in the selection test battery. This means that the four predictors explain

1 36% variance in job performance
2 40% variance in job performance
3 60% variance in job performance
4 64% variance in job performance

Ans. (1)

Exp. The four predictors explain 36% variance in job performance.

In statistics, the coefficient of multiple correlation is a measure of how well a given variable can be predicted using a linear function of a set of other variables. It is the correlation between the variable's values and the best predictions that can be computed linearly from the predictive variables. The squared coefficient of multiple correlation can also be computed as the fraction of variance of the dependent variable that is explained by the independent variables.

19 The standardised regression coefficient (β) in bivariate regression indicates

1 change in Y scores when X scores change by 1
2 change in Y scores when X scores change by 1
3 change in Z scores of Y when X scores change by 1
4 change in Z scores of Y when X scores change by 1

Ans. (4)

Exp. The standardised regression coefficient (β) in bivariate regression indicates change in Z scores of Y when X scores change by 1 SD.

The standardised regression coefficient, found by multiplying the regression coefficient b_i by S_{Xi} and dividing it by S_Y, represents the expected change in Y (in standardised units of S_Y where each 'unit' is a statistical unit equal to one standard deviation) due to an increase in x_i of one of its standardised units (i.e., S_{Xi}), with all other X variables unchanged.

20 In a single group pre-test and post-test design, which one of the following statistical method can be best employed to evaluate the mean differences of pre and post-tests?

1 Mann-Whitney U test
2 Randomised ANOVA
3 Chi-Square
4 Repeated measures ANOVA

Ans. (4)

Exp. Repeated measures ANOVA can be best employed to evaluate the mean differences of pre and post-tests.

Repeated measures ANOVA is the equivalent of the one-way ANOVA, but for related, not independent groups and is the extension of the dependent t-test. A repeated measures ANOVA is also referred to as a within-subjects ANOVA or ANOVA for correlated samples. All these names imply the nature of the repeated measures ANOVA, that of a test to detect any overall differences between related means.

The Mann–Whitney U test is a non-parametric test of the null hypothesis that it is equally likely that a randomly selected value from one sample will be less than or greater than a randomly selected value from a second sample.

One-way ANOVA (in Randomized Blocks) covers the simplest form of randomized-block design. The experimental units are grouped into sets, known as blocks, with the aim that units in the same set will be more similar to each other than units in different blocks.

A chi Square (X2) statistic is used to investigate whether distributions of categorical variables differ from one another. Basically categorical variable yield data in the categories and numerical variables yield data in numerical form.

21 Ideas interfering with the correct solution of a problem fade during this stage of creative thinking. This stage is

1 Evaluation
2 Revision
3 Illumination
4 Incubation

Ans. (4)

Exp. Ideas interfering with the correct solution of a problem fade during this stage of creative thinking. This stage is called incubation.

In psychology, 'incubation' refers to the unconscious processing of problems, when they are set aside for a period of time, that may lead to insights. It was originally proposed by Graham Wallas in 1926 as one of his four stages of the creative process: Preparation, Incubation, Illumination, and Verification.

22 Which of the following strategies do not help improve memory?

1 Use of mnemonics
2 Minimise interference
3 Mass learning
4 Elaborative rehearsal

Ans. (3)

Exp. Mass Learning does not help to improve memory. Massed practice, which describes studying that is done less frequently, but for large periods of time.

A mnemonic device, or memory device is any learning technique that aids information retention in the human memory. Mnemonics make use of elaborative encoding, retrieval cues and imagery as specific tools to encode any given information in a way that allows for efficient storage and retrieval.

Interference occurs in learning when there is an interaction between the new material and transfer effects of past learned behaviour, memories or thoughts that have a negative influence in comprehending the new material.

Elaborative rehearsal is a memory technique that involves thinking about the meaning of the term to be remembered, as opposed to simply repeating the word to yourself over and over.

23 Explicit or Declarative memory consist of which of the following types of memories ?

I. Procedural memory
II. Episodic memory
III. Semantic memory
IV. Autobiographical memory

Codes

1 I and II
2 II and IV
3 II, III and IV
4 I, II and IV

Ans. (3)

Exp. Explicit or Declarative memory consists of Episodic, Semantic and Autobiographical memory.

Declarative (explicit) memory is a type of long-term memory containing information that is conscious and known. There are two types of declarative long-term memories, semantic and episodic. One type of declarative memory is general knowledge that anyone has the ability to know.

Most of this information is what is learned in school or by reading. This kind of LTM is called Semantic memory. The word 'Semantic' refers to meaning, so this kind of knowledge is the awareness of the meanings of words, concepts, and terms as well as names of objects, math skills, and so on. The other kind of factual memory is the personal knowledge that each person has of his or her daily life and personal history, a kind of autobiographical memory. Memories of what has happened to people each day, certain birthdays, anniversaries that were particularly special, childhood events, and so on are called episodic memory, because they represent episodes from their lives.

Procedural memory or Implicit memory is the unconscious memory of skills and how to do things, particularly the use of objects or movements of the body.

24 Given below are the two statements, the first as Assertion (A) and the other labelled as. Reason (R). Indicate your answer using the correct codes given below :

Assertion (A) We can process information very quickly and perform complex tasks quickly and accurately.

Reason (R) Brain processes information in a serial fashion.

Codes

1 Both (A) and (R) are true and (R) is the correct explanation of (A)
2 Both (A) and (R) are true, but (R) is not the correct explanation of (A)
3 (A) is true, but (R) is false
4 (A) is false, but (R) is true

***Ans.* (2)**

Exp. Both (A) and (R) is true, but (R) is not the correct explanation of (A)

We can process information very quickly and perform complex tasks quickly and accurately. The information processing approach is based on a number of assumptions, including: (1) information made available by the environment is processed by a series of processing systems (e.g. attention, perception, short-term memory); (2) these processing systems transform or alter the information in systematic ways; (3) the aim of research is to specify the processes and structures that underlie cognitive performance; (4) information processing in humans resembles that in computers.

Brain processes information in a serial fashion. The idea of information processing was adopted by cognitive psychologists as a model of how human thought works.

25 Match List I with List II and indicate your answer with the help of the codes given below:

List I	List II
A. Converting information from temporary to more permanent memory and spatial memory	I. Temporal lobes
B. Working memory	II. Hippocampus
C. Semantic memory	III. Neuro fibrillary tangles
D. Alzheimer's disease	IV. Frontal lobes

Codes

	A	B	C	D
1	II	IV	I	III
2	I	II	III	IV
3	IV	III	II	I
4	III	I	IV	II

***Ans.* (1)**

Exp. The correct matching is A-II, B-IV, C-I, D-III.

The *Temporal lobes* plays a role in semantic memory. It mainly revolves around hearing and selective listening. It receives sensory information such as sounds and speech from the ears. It is also a key to being able to comprehend, or understand meaningful speech.

The *Hippocampus* converts information from temporary to more permanent memory and spatial memory. It not only assists with the storage of long-term memories, but is also responsible for the memory of the location of objects or people.

The *Neuro-fibrillary tangles* plays a role in Alzheimer's disease. Neuro-fibrillary tangles (NFTs) are aggregates of hyperphosphorylated tau protein that are most commonly known as a primary marker of Alzheimer's disease.

The *Frontal lobes* play a role in working memory. It is also where our personality is formed and where we can carry out higher mental processes such as planning. In addition, the frontal lobe is necessary to being able to speak fluently (without fault) and meaningfully.

26 Which of the following parts of the brain are related to the recognition of the facial expression of emotions?

I. Hypothalamus
II. Prefrontal cortex
III. Amygdala
IV. Hippocampus

Codes

1 I and II
2 II and III
3 II and IV
4 I, II and III

***Ans.* (2)**

Exp. Prefrontal cortex and Amygdala are related to the recognition of the facial expression of emotions.

The human amygdala has long been associated with recognising faces and facial emotions. Subjects who lack a functional amygdala can have a selective impairment in recognising fearful faces and blood-oxygen-level dependent on functional magnetic resonance imaging (BOLD-fMRI) shows activation within the amygdala that is often highest for fearful faces.

While the large majority of work has focused on fearful faces, the human amygdala is also responsive to neutral or happy faces measured using BOLD-fMRI and single-neuron recordings. Indeed, in some studies the amygdala responds to some extent to all facial expressions.

Disruption of processing within medial prefrontal cortex with transcranial magnetic stimulation produces longer reaction times in response to morphs of angry facial expressions, but not in response to happy facial expressions. A role for prefrontal cortex in the recognition of anger is also supported by the finding of increased activation in orbitofrontal and anterior cingulate cortex, when subjects were shown facial expressions of anger, but not of sadness.

27 Which of the following is most appropriate for the assessment of Self-actualisation?

1 Myers-Briggs Type Indicator
2 Personal Orientation Inventory
3 Rosenberg Self-esteem Inventory
4 Edwards Personal Preference Scale

Ans. (2)

Exp. Personal Orientation Inventory (POI) is most appropriate for the assessment of self-actualisation.

It measures the attitudes and values of normal to high-functioning adults in terms of the concept of 'self-actualizing.' When used in counseling or as a pre and post-therapy measure, the POI provides a picture of an individual's level of positive mental health. In addition to therapeutic applications, the POI is useful in research, employee development, and studies of consumer behaviour.

28 There is a gradual acceleration of responses just before the provision of reinforcement in a fixed interval schedule. This acceleration is referred to as

1 the Fixed - Interval gradient
2 the Fixed - Interval variant
3 the Fixed - Interval caper
4 the Fixed - Interval scallop

Ans. (4)

Exp. This acceleration is referred to as the Fixed-Interval scallop.

A Fixed-interval schedule often produces a scallop: a gradual increase in the rate of responding, with responding occurring at a high rate, just before reinforcement is available. No responding occurs for some time after reinforcement. This pattern of gradual acceleration of responding from beginning to end of each interval produces a fluted or 'scalloped' pattern, which has been labelled the fixed-interval scallop.

29 When the individual attributes failure to the beliefs that everyone would fail in solving the problem and that the failure results from external causes, the state is described as

1 personal helplessness
2 hopelessness
3 learned optimism
4 universal helplessness

Ans. (4)

Exp. When the individual attributes failure to the beliefs that everyone would fail in solving the problem and that the failure results from external causes, the state is described as Universal helplessness.

Universal helplessness is in which the individual attributes failure to the beliefs that everyone would fail in solving the problem, and that the failure results from external causes.

30 Given below are the two statements, the first as Assertion (A) and the other labelled as Reason (R). Indicate your answer using the correct codes given below :

Assertion (A) Our facial expressions influence our emotional experience.

Reason (R) We can exert complete voluntary control over our facial muscles during emotional expressions.

Codes

1 Both (A) and (R) are true and (R) is the correct explanation of (A)
2 Both (A) and (R) are true, but (R) is not the correct explanation of (A)
3 (A) is true, but (R) is false
4 (A) is false, but (R) is true

Ans. (3)

Exp. (A) is true, but (R) is false.

Our facial expressions influence our emotional experience.

The facial feedback hypothesis asserts that facial expressions are capable of influencing our emotions. According to the facial feedback hypothesis, facial expressions are not only the results of our emotions but are also capable of influencing our emotions. In other words, the act of smiling can itself actually makes you feel happier. Research investigating the facial feedback hypothesis has found that suppressing facial expressions of emotion may decrease how intensely those emotions are experienced.

Emotion is displayed not only through facial expression but also through tone of voice, behaviour and body language. Therefore, we cannot exert complete voluntary control over our facial muscles during emotional expressions.

31 The mental representation of what one wants to say comprises the

1 surface : phrase structure
2 central : phrase structure
3 primary : phrase structure
4 deep : phrase structure

Ans. (4)

Exp. The mental representation of what one wants to say comprises the deep : phrase structure.

Deep structure and surface structure (also D-structure and S-structure, although these abbreviated forms are sometimes used with distinct meanings) concepts are used in linguistics, specifically in the study of syntax in the Chomskyan tradition of transformational generative grammar.

The Deep structure of a linguistic expression is a theoretical construct that seeks to unify several related structures. For example, the sentences 'Pat loves Chris' and 'Chris is loved by Pat' mean roughly the same thing and use similar words. Some linguists, Chomsky in particular, have tried to account for this similarity by positing that these two sentences are distinct surface forms that derive from a common (or very similar) deep structure.

32 The Law of Pragnanz or Law of Good Figure refers to

1 tendency to read an ambiguous stimulus in accordance with an expectation
2 viewing under suboptimal conditions such as an object is shaded or overlapped
3 the tendency to perceive the simplest and most stable figure of all possible perceptual alternatives
4 the ability to recognise and identify common objects

Ans. (3)

Exp. The Law of Pragnanz or Law of Good Figure refers to the tendency to perceive the simplest and most stable figure of all possible perceptual alternatives.

Law of Pragnanz (good figure, law of simplicity) says that people will perceive and interpret ambiguous or complex images as the simplest form(s) possible. This is the fundamental principle of gestalt. The most general Gestalt principle, which states that the simplest organisation, requiring the least cognitive effort, will emerge as the figure. Pragnanz shares a common root with pregnant, and so it carries the idea of a 'fully developed figure.' That is, our perceptual system prefers to see a fully developed Gestalt, such as a complete circle as opposed to a broken circle.

33 What behaviour can be emitted is basically

1 a psychotherapist determined phenomenon
2 a reward determined capacity
3 a species-typical capacity
4 a procedure determined phenomenon

Ans. (3)

Exp. What behaviour can be emitted is basically a species-typical capacity.

The ethological concept of species-typical behaviour is based on the premise that certain behavioural similarities are shared by almost all members of a species. Some of these behaviours are unique to certain species, but to be 'species-typical,' they do not have to be unique—they simply have to be characteristic of that species.

To understand the importance of species-typical behaviour, think about an animal that looks exactly like a dog, but meows, refuses to play fetch, and climbs trees. It's not surprising that humans would find this animal confusing; we expect an animal that looks a certain way to act a certain way, and we associate those behaviours with that animal (e.g. we associate the practice of meowing with cats).

34 Memory can be distorted by being influenced by the individual's expectations rather than what has actually happened. This is termed as

1 mood dependent memory
2 mood congruence effect
3 flash bulb memory
4 confirmation bias

Ans. (4)

Exp. Memory can be distorted by being influenced by the individual's expectations rather than what has actually happened. This is termed as confirmation bias. It is also called confirmatory bias or myside bias.

It is the tendency to search for, interpret, favour and recall information in a way that confirms one's pre-existing beliefs or hypotheses.

35 Given below are the two statements, the first as Assertion (A) and the other labelled as Reason (R). Indicate your answer using the correct codes given below :

Assertion (A) Psychometric and cognitive (information processing) approaches to study intelligence are complimentary to each other.

Reason (R) Psychometric theories deal with intelligence primarily in its structural aspects, cognitive theories deal with it primarily in its processing aspects.

Codes

1 Both (A) and (R) are true and (R) is correct explanation of (A)
2 Both (A) and (R) are true, but (R) is not the correct explanation of (A)
3 (A) is true, but (R) is false
4 (A) is false, but (R) is true

Ans. (1)

Exp. Both (A) and (R) are true and (R) is correct explanation of (A).

Psychometric and cognitive (information processing) approaches to study intelligence are complimentary to each other. This is true as the psychometric approach to studying intelligence involves obtaining scores from many people on a variety of tests. The results are factor analysed in order to describe the pattern of correlations between the tests, and the factors are named according to the tests that load on them. Hence, the information processing approach characterises thinking as the environment providing input of data, which is then transformed by our senses. The information can be stored, retrieved and transformed using 'mental programs', with the results being behavioural responses.

Psychometric theories deal with intelligence primarily in its structural aspects, cognitive theories deal with it primarily in its processing aspects. This explains both psychometric approach to intelligence and the cognitive approach to intelligence.

36 Which one of the following is a cause of permanent lesion?

1 Cryogenic blockade
2 Radio frequency
3 Electrical stimulation
4 Transcranial magnetic stimulation

Ans. (2)

Exp. Radio Frequency (RF) is the cause of permanent lesion. It is a rate of oscillation in the range of around 3Â kHz to 300Â GHz, which corresponds to the frequency of radio waves, and the alternating currents which carry radio signals. RF usually refers to electrical rather than mechanical oscillations.

37 Some Psychologist stated that the relationship between intelligence and creativity is not the same throughout the range of Intelligence Quotient (IQ). Which out of the following is appropriate explanation of the relationship between these at different levels of IQ?

1 Below that critical level of IQ, the relationship is negative and above that it is positive
2 Below that critical level of IQ, it is zero and above that it is positive
3 Below that critical level of IQ, the relationship is positive and above that it is negative
4 Below that critical level of IQ, the relationship is positive and above that level zero relationship

Ans. (4)

Exp. Below that critical level of IQ, the relationship is positive and above that level is zero relationship.

Threshold Theory states that intelligence is a necessary, but not sufficient condition for creativity. There is a moderate positive relationship between creativity and intelligence until IQ ~120.

Intelligence is classically defined as 'the ability to acquire and utilise knowledge.' In testing circumstances, an Intelligence Quotient (IQ) is gauged by one's ability to utilise information that gained historically. Creativity is the ability to come up with new ideas through a mental process of connecting existing concepts. The ideas don't have to be revolutionary (which is a common misconception many people have about creative thinking), they just have to be new for the thinker. Creativity is the ability to go beyond the intelligence frame and capitalise on seemingly random connections of concepts.

38 Which of the following pairs is not the negative symptom of Schizophrenia?

1 Emotional flattening and Asociality
2 Anhedonia and Amotivation
3 Poverty of speech and Apathy
4 Hallucinations and Bizarre behaviour

Ans. (4)

Exp. Hallucinations and Bizarre behaviour are not negative symptoms of Schizophrenia.

Schizophrenia is a serious mental disorder in which people interpret reality abnormally. It may result in some combination of hallucinations, delusions, and extremely disordered thinking and behaviour that impairs daily functioning, and can be disabling.

Negative symptoms of Schizophrenia are those which are abnormally absent. Examples include loss or a decrease in the ability to initiate plans, speak, express emotion or find pleasure.

Hallucinations are the experience of hearing, seeing, smelling, tasting, or feeling things that are not there. They are vivid and clear with an impression similar to normal perceptions. Auditory hallucinations, "hearing voices," are the most common in schizophrenia and related disorders.

Bizzare/Disorganised or abnormal motor behaviour are movements that can range from childlike silliness to unpredictable agitation or can manifest as repeated movements without purpose. When the behaviour is severe, it can cause problems in the performance of activities of daily life. It includes catatonia, when a person appears as if in a daze with little movement or response to the surrounding environment.

39 Match List I with List II and indicate your answer with the help of the codes given below :

List I	List II
A. Pituitary gland	I. Estrogens
B. Gonads	II. Prolactin
C. Adrenal gland	III. Thyroxin
D. Thyroid gland	IV. Corticosterone

Codes

	A	B	C	D
1	I	II	III	IV
2	II	I	IV	III
3	IV	III	II	I
4	III	I	II	IV

Ans. (2)

Exp. The correct matching is A-II, B-I, C-IV, D-III.

Pituitary gland produces Prolactin. It is a hormone produced by your pituitary gland which sits at the bottom of the brain. It causes breasts to grow and develop and causes milk to be made after a baby is born. Normally, both men and women have small amounts of prolactin in their blood.

Gonads produce Estrogens. These hormones – nearly always synonymous with gonadal steroids – are hormones produced by the gonads, and include both steroid and peptide hormones. The major steroid hormones include estradiol and progesterone from the ovaries, and testosterone from the testes.

Adrenal gland produces Corticosterone. Corticosteroids (adrenal cortical steroids) are natural hormones made by the adrenal cortex which are important in maintaining good health. There are two types of corticosteroids, the glucocorticoids and the mineralocorticoids.

Thyroid gland produces thyroxin. It is the main hormone secreted into the bloodstream by the thyroid gland. It is the inactive form and most of it is converted to an active form called triiodothyronine by organs such as the liver and kidneys.

40 Match List I with List II and indicate your answer with the help of the codes given below :

List I (Accomplishment)	List II (Cognitive Developmental Stage)
A. Egocentric thought	I. Sensorimotor
B. Object permanence	II. Formal operational
C. Abstract reasoning	III. Pre-operational
D. Conservation reversibility	IV. Concrete operational

Codes

	A	B	C	D		A	B	C	D
1	II	III	IV	I	2	III	I	II	IV
3	IV	II	I	III	4	I	IV	III	II

Ans. *(2)*

Exp. The correct matching is A-III, B-I, C-II, D-IV.

Egocentric thought is observed in pre-operational stage. The preoperational stage (ages 2–7) is a time of developing language and concepts. Egocentrism is the inability to see the world through anyone else's eyes but one's own. For the pre-operational child, everyone else must see what the child sees, and what is important to the child must be important to everyone else.

Object permanence is observed in sensorimotor stage. The sensorimotor stage is the first of Piaget's stages. It concerns infants from birth to age 2. By the end of the sensorimotor stage, infants have fully developed a sense of object permanence, the knowledge that an object exists even when it is not in sight.

Abstract reasoning is observed in formal operational stage. In the last of Piaget's stages, formal operations (age 12 to adulthood), abstract thinking becomes possible. Individuals need formal-operational thinking that require critical thinking, problem-solving abilities, and abstract thinking based on formal-operational skills.

Conservation reversibility is observed in concrete operational stage. In this stage (ages 7–12), children finally become capable of conservation and reversible thinking.

41 Given below are the two statements, the first as Assertion (A) and the other labelled as Reason (R). Indicate your answer using the codes given below :

Assertion (A) Solution to any problem generally requires making reason from long-term goal to short-term goals and so on.

Reason (R) Generating short-term goals are necessary for finding the most suitable solution to the problem.

Codes

1 Both (A) and (R) are false
2 (A) is true, but (R) is false
3 Both (A) and (R) are true, but (R) is not the correct explanation of (A)
4 Both (A) and (R) are true and (R) is the correct explanation of (A)

Ans. *(4)*

Exp. Both (A) and (R) are true and (R) is the correct explanation of (A).

Solution to any problem generally requires making reason from long-term goal to short-term goals and so on. Any solution of the problem requires a larger objective which needs to be broken down into short-term achievable goals.

Generating short-term goals are necessary for finding the most suitable solution to the problem. It is important to generate short-term goals as these are necessary to find the most suitable and appropriate solution of the problem. This explains why there is a need to make reason from long-term to short-term goals.

42 Given below are the two statements, the first as Assertion (A) and the other labelled as Reason (R). Indicate your answer using the correct codes given below :

Assertion (A) People tend to be more aggressive when they consume less alcohol.

Reason (R) Alcohol impairs higher order cognitive functioning.

Codes

1 Both (A) and (R) are true and (R) is the correct explanation of (A)
2 Both (A) and (R) are true, but (R) is not the correct explanation of (A)
3 (A) is true, but (R) is false
4 (A) is false, but (R) is true

Ans. *(2)*

Exp. Both (A) and (R) are true, but (R) is not the correct explanation of (A)

People tend to be more aggressive when they consume less alcohol. According to the World Health Organisation, the use of alcohol is more closely associated with aggressive behaviour than any other type of psychotropic substance. Important issue that should be taken into account in the treatment of alcohol-induced aggression is the fact that people who abuse alcohol are inclined to take less account of future gratification (e.g. avoiding damage to health or social considerations) than of immediate gratification (e.g. alcohol consumption, immediate release of aggression).

Alcohol impairs higher order cognitive functioning which means it is more difficult to problem-solve, control anger, and make good decisions when drinking. Decreased cognitive function also means it's more likely for someone to misread a situation and overreact. This is true, but it does not explain why people tend to be more aggressive when they consume less alcohol.

43 Match List I with List II and indicate your answer with the help of the codes given below :

List I (Term)	List II (Explanation)
A. Social influence	I. The term refer to the audience effect and coaction effects
B. Social cognitive theory	II. Part of the self-concept derives from group membership
C. Social facilitation	III. Any process whereby a person's attitudes, opinions, beliefs or behaviour are altered
D. Social identity	IV. An approach to social learning incorporating findings from learning

Codes

	A	B	C	D		A	B	C	D
1	I	II	III	IV	2	IV	II	I	III
3	III	IV	I	II	4	IV	I	III	II

Ans. (3)

Exp. The correct matching is A-III, B-IV, C-I, D-II.

Social influence is any process whereby a person's attitudes, opinions, beliefs or behaviour are altered. It takes many forms and can be seen in conformity, socialisation, peer pressure, obedience, leadership, persuasion, sales and marketing.

Social cognitive theory is an approach to social learning incorporating findings from learning. It holds that portions of an individual's knowledge acquisition can be directly related to observing others within the context of social interactions, experiences and outside media influences.

Social facilitation is the term that refers to the audience effect and coactions effects. Social facilitation, or the audience effect, is the tendency for people to perform differently when in the presence of others than when alone. Compared to their performance when alone, when in the presence of others, they tend to perform better on simple or well-rehearsed tasks and worse on complex or new ones.

Social identity is a part of the self-concept derives from group membership. It is a person's sense of who they are based on their group membership(s).

44 According to .... Theory, thoughts and feeling change because people are motivated to justify emotions that would otherwise seem hypothetical. This theory was proposed by ....

1 Dissonance; Festinger
2 Cognitive dissonance; Festinger
3 Cognitive dissonance; Baron
4 Normative social influence; Baron

Ans. (2)

Exp. According to Cognitive Dissonance theory, thoughts and feeling change because people are motivated to justify emotions that would otherwise seem hypothetical. This theory was proposed by Festinger.

It states that a powerful motive to maintain cognitive consistency can give rise to irrational and sometimes maladaptive behaviour. According to Festinger, we hold many cognitions about the world and ourselves; when they clash, a discrepancy is evoked, resulting in a state of tension known as cognitive dissonance. As the experience of dissonance is unpleasant, we are motivated to reduce or eliminate it, and achieve consonance (i.e. agreement).

45 The well known study on obedience to authority was done by

1 Stanley Milgram
2 Solomon Asch
3 Latane and Darley
4 Zimbardo

Ans. (1)

Exp. The well known study on obedience to authority was done by Stanley Milgram.

Stanley Milgram conducted an experiment focusing on the conflict between obedience to authority and personal conscience. He examined justifications for acts of genocide offered by those accused at the World War II, Nuremberg War Criminal Trials.

46 Somatic Nervous System does not activate which one of the following?

1 Glands
2 Eyes
3 Ears
4 Skeletal muscles

Ans. (1)

Exp. Somatic Nervous System does not activate glands.

The nervous system is the part of an animal 's body that co-ordinates its actions and transmits signals to and from different parts of its body. It consists of two main parts, the Central Nervous System (CNS) and the Peripheral Nervous System (PNS). Skeletal muscle is one of three major muscle types, the others being cardiac muscle and smooth muscle. It is a form of striated muscle tissue which is under the 'voluntary' control of the somatic nervous system.

Glands are an organ in the human or animal body which secretes particular chemical substances for use in the body or for discharge into the surroundings. Autonomic Nervous System (ANS) innervates glands, neurons of the gastrointestinal tract, and cardiac and smooth muscles of glandular tissue.

47 Three mountains task was used by Piaget to study .... in children.

1 centration
2 conservation
3 egocentrism
4 reversibility

Ans. (3)

Exp. Three mountains task was used by Piaget to study egocentrism in children.

In Piaget's Three-Mountain Task, e.g. children in the concrete operational stage can describe how a mountain scene would look to an observer seated opposite them. Conservation, equal amounts of liquid are poured into two identical containers.

The liquid in one container is then poured into a different shaped cup, such as a tall and thin cup or a short and wide cup. Children are then asked which cup holds the most liquid.

Despite seeing that the liquid amounts were equal, children almost always choose the cup that appears fuller. One of the most important developments in this stage is an understanding of reversibility, or awareness that actions can be reversed.

48 Receiver Operating Characteristic Curve describes

1 the smallest difference between two stimuli necessary to detect them as different
2 the relationship between the proportion of hits and false alarms for a constant stimulus intensity
3 detection of a change in a stimulus is related to the magnitude of the stimulus
4 as the number of sensation units grows arithmetically, the stimulus intensity increases geometrically

Ans. (2)

Exp. Receiver Operating Characteristic Curve describes the relationship between the proportion of hits and false alarms for a constant stimulus intensity.

A Receiver Operating Characteristic Curve, or ROC curve, is a graphical plot that illustrates the performance of a binary classifier system as its discrimination threshold is varied. The curve is created by plotting the True Positive Rate (TPR) against the False Positive Rate (FPR) at various threshold settings. The true-positive rate is also known as sensitivity, recall or probability of detection in machine learning. The false-positive rate is also known as the fall-out or probability of false alarm and can be calculated as (1 - specificity). The ROC curve is thus the sensitivity as a function of fall-out.

49 As compared to primary school students, middle school students use more of

I. Rehearsal II. Elaboration
III. Metacognition

Codes

1 I and II 2 I and III
3 II and III 4 All of these

Ans. (4)

Exp. As compared to primary school students, middle school students use more of Rehearsal, Elaboration and Metacognition.

Elaborative rehearsal is a memory technique that involves thinking about the meaning of the term to be remembered, as opposed to simply repeating the word to yourself over and over.

Elaboration is the process of adding more information to existing, relatively simple information to create a more complex, emergent whole. It involves developing an idea by incorporating details to amplify the original simple idea.

The term 'metacognition' refers to the act of thinking about thinking, or the cognition of cognition. It is the ability for you to control your own thoughts. It really is the knowledge and regulation of cognitive phenomena which means, you can control your own thoughts.

50 Match List I with List II and indicate your answer with the help of the codes given below :

	List I (Phenomenon)		List II (Psychologist)
A.	Explanation of creativity in terms of product	I.	Getzels and Jackson
B.	Explanation of creativity in terms of process	II.	Gordon
C.	Explanation of creativity in terms of personality characteristics	III.	Torrance
D.	Explanation of creativity in terms of motivational factors	IV.	Rogers

Codes

	A	B	C	D		A	B	C	D
1	I	II	III	IV	2	III	IV	II	I
3	IV	II	III	I	4	IV	III	I	II

Ans. (4)

Exp. The correct matching is A-IV, B-III, C-I, D-II.

Getzels and Jackson explain creativity in terms of personality characteristics. Studies by them indicated that the correlation between creativity and intelligence tends to drop when IQ scores are higher than 120 (Getzels & Jackson, 1962). Conversely, other studies reported that creative artists, scientists, mathematicians, and writers all tend to score higher than average on IQ tests.

Gordon explains creativity in terms of motivational factors.

Torrance explains creativity in terms of process. Torrance Test of Creativity and Thinking test measures creative thinking using picture-based and word-based exercises to assess fluency, flexibility (number of different categories of response), originality, and elaboration (amount of detail).

Rogers explains creativity in terms of product. Rogers suggests that the creative process has three elements: [1] It must produce an observable result, which "must be acceptable to some group at some point in time". [2] The product has to be novel and "this novelty grows out of the unique qualities of the individual in his interaction with the materials of experience". [3] "There is no fundamental difference in the creative process" across different fields of activity.

51 Match List I with List II and indicate your answer with the help of the codes given below :

	List I (Phenomenon)		List II (Psychological Term)
A.	Tendency to stick to one's own pre-conceptions	I.	Mental set
B.	Inability to judge a problem from alternative perspective	II.	Confirmation bias
C.	Tendency to judge a problem and find its solution from previous results	III.	Functional fixedness
D.	Tendency to think about things only in respect of their usual functions	IV.	Fixation

Codes

	A	B	C	D		A	B	C	D
1	I	II	IV	III	2	II	IV	III	I
3	II	IV	I	III	4	II	I	III	IV

Ans. (3)

Exp. The correct matching is A-II, B-IV, C-I, D-III.

Mental set is the tendency to judge a problem and find its solution from previous results. It is the tendency for people to persist in using problem-solving patterns that have worked for them in the past.

Confirmation bias is the tendency to stick to one's own pre-conceptions. It is the tendency to search for evidence that fits one's beliefs while ignoring any evidence to the contrary.

Functional fixedness is the tendency to think about things only in respect of their usual functions. It is a block to problem solving that comes from thinking about objects in terms of only their typical functions.

Fixation is the inability to judge a problem from alternative perspective.

52 Arrange the following treatment methodologies in order in which they got known.

I. Client Centered therapy
II. Psychoanalytic therapy
III. Reciprocal Inhibition technique
IV. Reinforcement contingency

Codes

1 I, II, III, IV
2 II, I, III, IV
3 II, I, IV, III
4 III, IV, I, II

Ans. *(3)*

Exp. The correct order is II, I, IV, III.

The *Psychoanalytic therapy* came to full prominence in the last third of the twentieth century as part of the flow of critical discourse regarding psychological treatments after the 1960s, long after Freud's death in 1939.

Client-centered therapy was developed by Carl Rogers in the 1940s. This type of therapy diverged from the traditional model of the therapist as expert and moved instead toward a nondirective, empathic approach that empowers and motivates the client in the therapeutic process.

The *Reinforcement contingency* or three-term contingency (also known as the ABC contingency) in operant conditioning or contingency management describes the relationship between a behavior, its consequence, and the environmental context. The three-term contingency was first defined by B. F. Skinner in the early 1950s.

Reciprocal inhibition was a foundation for initial psychological theories that formed the basis for systematic desensitisation as a treatment for anxiety. Wolpe (1954) applied the concept of reciprocal inhibition by proposing that one cannot be simultaneously anxious and relaxed. Therefore, an antagonistic response to counter anxiety would be a state of relaxation. From this, the technique of systematic desensitisation for treatment of anxiety was borne.

53 Arrange the following tests in decreasing order of their projective ability

I. Rorschach's Ink Blot test.
II. Thematic Apperception test.
III. Rosenzweig's Picture Frustration scale.
IV. Sack's Sentence Completion test.

Codes

1 I, II, III, IV
2 IV, III, II, I
3 III, II, I, IV
4 II, III, I, IV

Ans. *(1)*

Exp. The correct order is I, II, III, IV.

The *Rorschach Inkblot Test* is a projective psychological test consisting of 10 inkblots printed on cards (five in black and white, five in colour) created in 1921. The Rorschach is what psychologists call a projective test.

The *Thematic Apperception Test,* or TAT, is a projective measure intended to evaluate a person's patterns of thought, attitudes, observational capacity, and emotional responses to ambiguous test materials. In the case of the TAT, the ambiguous materials consist of a set of cards that portray human figures in a variety of settings and situations.

The *Rosenzweig's Picture Frustration scale* consists of 24 cartoon pictures, each portraying two persons in a frustrating situation. Each picture contains two 'speech balloons,' a filled one for the 'frustrator' or antagonist, and a blank one for the frustrated person, or protagonist. The subject is asked to fill in the blank balloon with his or her response to the situation and the responses are scored in relation to a number of psychological defense mechanisms.

The *Sack's Sentence Completion Test* (SSCT) is a 60-item test that asks respondents to complete 60 questions with the first thing that comes to mind across four areas: Family, Sex, Interpersonal, Relationships and Self-concept.

54 Match List I with List II and indicate your answer with the help of the codes given below :

List I	List II
A. Authoritarian and unloving parents	I. Conflicted and irritable children
B. Permissive and loving parents	II. Moody and conduct disordered children
C. Neglectful and uninvolved parents	III. Friendly and competitive children
D. Authoritative and loving parents	IV. Impulsive and aggressive children

Codes

	A	B	C	D		A	B	C	D
1	I	II	III	IV	2	III	IV	II	I
3	I	III	IV	II	4	II	I	IV	III

Ans. *(4)*

Exp. The correct matching is A-II, B-I, C-IV, D-III.

Authoritarian and unloving parents are associated with moody and conduct disordered children. Authoritarian parenting is where parents establish the rules and expect that children will follow them without exception. Children have little to no involvement in problem-solving challenges or obstacles. Instead, parents expect that children will follow all of the rules all the time.

Permissive and loving parents are associated with conflicted and irritable children. Permissive parents don't offer much discipline. They tend to be lenient and may only step in when there is a serious problem. There may be few consequences for misbehaviour because parents have an attitude of 'kids will be kids.'

Neglectful and uninvolved parents are associated with impulsive and aggressive children. Uninvolved parents tend to be neglectful. They often do not meet their children's basic needs and may expect children to raise themselves. Sometimes this is due to a parent's mental health issues or substance abuse problems. They may also lack knowledge about parenting and child development or may feel overwhelmed by life's other problems.

Authoritative and loving parents are associated with Friendly and competitive children. Authoritative parents also have rules that children are expected to follow, however, they allow some exceptions to the rule. They often tell children the reasons for the rules and they are more willing to consider a child's feelings when setting limits.

55 Given below are the two statements, the first as Assertion (A) and the other labelled as Reason (R). Indicate your answer using the codes given below :

Assertion (A) The most important neurotransmitter implicated in schizophrenia is Dopamine.

Reason (R) Clinical evidence suggests that drugs which reduce the level of dopamine in the brain also give rise to psychotic states like schizophrenia.

Codes

1 Both (A) and (R) are true and (R) is the correct explanation of (A)
2 Both (A) and (R) are true, but (R) is not the correct explanation of (A)
3 (A) is true, but (R) is false
4 (A) is false, but (R) is true

Ans. *(3)*

Exp. (A) is true but (R) is false.

The most important neurotransmitter implicated in schizophrenia is dopamine. Dopamine was first suspected when amphetamine users began to show schizophrenia-like psychotic symptoms. One of the side effects of amphetamine usage is to increase the release of dopamine in the brain. Drugs used to treat schizophrenia decrease the activity of dopamine in areas of the brain responsible for some of the positive symptoms.

Clinical evidence suggests that drugs which reduce the level of dopamine in the brain also give rise to psychotic states like schizophrenia. This is not true.

56 Given below are the two statements, the first as Assertion (A) and the other labelled as Reason (R). Indicate your answer using the correct codes given below :

Assertion (A) Long-term potentialism is related to neural mechanism of learning and memory.

Reason (R) There is facilitation of synaptic transmission following high frequency electrical stimulation.

Codes

1 Both (A) and (R) are true and (R) is the correct explanation of (A)
2 Both (A) and (R) are true, but (R) is not the correct explanation of (A)
3 (A) is true, but (R) is false
4 (A) is false, but (R) is true

Ans. *(2)*

Exp. Both (A) and (R) are true, but (R) is not the correct explanation of (A).

Long-term potentialism is related to neural mechanism of learning and memory. Long Term Potentialism (LTP) is a long lasting strengthening response of the postsynaptic nerve cell when the stimulation athwart the synapse which occurs in repeated stimulation. It involves the long term and learning memory. This is also the capacity of brain cells to hold on how recurrent they deliver signals in some brain cells. Aside from that, it is an everlasting improvement in transmitting signals in the middle of two neurons that usually results from stimulating them synchronously.

There is facilitation of synaptic transmission following high frequency electrical stimulation. This is long term potentiation. This is true but does not explain why long term potentialism is related to neural mechanism of learning and memory.

57 Given below are the two statements, the first as Assertion (A) and the other labelled as Reason (R). Indicate your answer using the codes given below :

Assertion (A) Information processing is a mode of attention that concerns the non-temporal information processing demands of a task.

Reason (R) Subliminal perception is a form of perception in which stimuli are not detected or consciously perceived.

Codes

1 Both (A) and (R) are true and (R) is the correct explanation of (A)
2 Both (A) and (R) are true, but (R) is not the correct explanation of (A)
3 (A) is true, but (R) is false
4 Both (A) and (R) are false

Ans. *(2)*

Exp. Both (A) and (R) are true, but (R) is not the correct explanation of (A).

Information processing is a mode of attention that concerns the non-temporal information processing demands of a task.

Information processing is how individuals perceive, analyse, manipulate, use, and remember information. Improvements are seen in selective attention (the process by which one focuses on one stimulus while tuning out another), as well as divided attention (the ability to pay attention to two or more stimuli at the same time).

Subliminal perception is a form of perception in which stimuli are not detected or consciously perceived. Subliminal messages and perception are linked to the idea of mind control, and the roots of this are placed very far back in our history. Mind control is where an individual or group of individuals can be controlled without their awareness. It is perception below the individual's/group's threshold. It is also the idea that people can be made to do things they would not ordinarily do. Subliminal is a two part word consisting of the prefix 'sub' and the root word 'limen'. Sub-means below and limen means threshold. Thus, subliminal comes to mean below threshold.

58 Match List I with List II and indicate your answer with the help of the codes given below :

List I (Charismatic Leader)		List II (Characteristic)
A. Personal risk	I.	Engages in behaviours that are perceived as novel and counter to norms
B. Environmental sensitivity	II.	Willing to take on high personal risk, incur high costs and engage in self-sacrifice to achieve the vision
C. Sensitivity to follower needs	III.	Able to make a realistic assessments of the environmental constraints and resources needed to bring about change
D. Unconventional behaviour	IV.	Perceptive of other's abilities and responsive to their needs and feelings

Codes

	A	B	C	D		A	B	C	D
1	II	III	IV	I	2	I	IV	III	II
3	II	IV	III	I	4	III	II	I	IV

Ans. *(1)*

Exp. The correct matching is A-II, B-III, C-IV, D-I.

A charismatic leader takes *personal risk*. It is the willingness to take on high personal risk, incur high costs and engage in self-sacrifice to achieve the vision.

A charismatic leader has *environmental sensitivity*. It means being able to make a realistic assessments of the environmental constraints and resources needed to bring about change.

A charismatic leader has *sensitivity to follower needs*. It means being perceptive of other's abilities and responsive to their needs and feelings.

A charismatic leader has an *unconventional behavior*. It means engaging in behaviours that are perceived as novel and counter to norms.

59 Vestibule Training utilises equipment which are closely ________ to the actual ones, used ________

1 resemble; on the job
2 similar; on the job
3 resemble; off the job
4 similar; off the job

Ans. *(1)*

Exp. Vestibule Training utilises equipment which is closely resemble to the actual ones, used on the job.

Vestibule Training is a term for near-the-job training, as it offers access to something new (learning). It is a form of training in which new employees learn the job in a setting that approximates as closely as is practicable to the actual working environment. An example is the training of airline pilots in a simulated cockpit.

60 The perspectives of motivation that identify specific needs

1 Content Theories
2 Process Theory of Motivation
3 Equity Theory and OB mode Theory
4 Expectancy Theories

Ans. *(1)*

Exp. The perspectives of motivation that identify specific needs are Content theories.

Content theories argue that we direct and sustain our behaviour towards meeting unmet needs. Maslow argues that we seek to meet basic needs (such as shelter, food, and warmth—known as deficiency needs) before being motivated by higher-order or 'growth' needs (satisfying work, personal self-fulfilment).

61 Out of the following statements, find out the one which is wrong according to social psychological research

1 Situational forces have tremendous power to shape human behaviour rather than personality or character
2 Both humans and animals respond more quickly when in the presence of other members of their species
3 A by stander in an emergency situation is likely to intervene or help in a group than if alone
4 The uninhibited aggressive behaviour sometimes shown by mobs and crowds may be the result of deindividuation

Ans. *(3)*

Exp. The incorrect statement is that a bystander in an emergency situation is likely to intervene or help in a group than if alone.

The bystander effect, or bystander apathy, is a social psychological phenomenon that refers to cases in which individuals do not offer any means of help to a victim when other people are present.

The probability of help is inversely related to the number of bystanders. It refers to an approach to behaviour which holds that general traits do not exist (perhaps apart from Intelligence). Behaviour, then, is seen as being influenced by external, situational factors rather than internal traits or motivations. Situationist based their claims on experiments in which traits such as extraversion were estimated based on behaviour in different situations. They found that a particular person's ratings in one situation were not highly predictive of that person's score in another situation

62 Who among the following is credited with developing Logo therapy?

1 Fritz Perls   2 Eric Burne
3 Victor Frankel   4 Rollo May

Ans. (3)

➲ *Exp.* Victor Frankl is credited with developing Logo therapy. Logo therapy is a term derived from 'logos,' a Greek word that translates as meaning,' and therapy, which is defined as treatment of a condition, illness, or maladjustment. Developed by Victor Frank, the theory is founded on the belief that human nature is motivated by the search for a life purpose.

63 Match List I with List II and indicate your answer with the help of the codes given below :

List I (Perceptual Theory)	List II (Explanation)
A. Signal Detection	I. The detection of change in a stimulus is relative to the magnitude of the stimulus
B. Stevens' Power Law	II. The ability to detect a weak stimulus varies from moment to moment as per response bias
C. Fechner's Law	III. The magnitude of a sensation is a logarithmic function of the stimulus
D. Weber's Fraction	IV. Sensory magnitude grows in proportion to the physical intensity of the stimulus raised to a power

Codes

	A	B	C	D
1	III	IV	I	II
2	IV	III	II	I
3	I	II	III	IV
4	II	IV	III	I

Ans. (4)

➲ *Exp.* The correct matching is A-II, B-IV, C-III, D-I.

Signal Detection theory is the ability to detect a weak stimulus varies from moment to moment as per response bias.

Detection theory or signal detection theory is a means to quantify the ability to discern between information-bearing patterns (called stimulus in living organisms, signal in machines) and random patterns that distract from the information (called noise, consisting of background stimuli and random activity of the detection machine and of the nervous system of the operator).

Stevens' Power Law states that when sensory magnitude grows in proportion to the physical intensity of the stimulus raised to a power. Stevens' power law is a proposed relationship between the magnitude of a physical stimulus and its perceived intensity or strength.

Fechner's Law is the magnitude of a sensation is a logarithmic function of the stimulus. It states that the subjective sensation is proportional to the logarithm of the stimulus intensity. According to this law, human perceptions of sight and sound work as follows: Perceived loudness/brightness is proportional to logarithm of the actual intensity measured with an accurate nonhuman instrument.

Weber's Fraction is the detection of change in a stimulus is relative to the magnitude of the stimulus. Weber's Law, also sometimes known as the Weber-Fechner Law, suggests that the just noticeable difference is a constant proportion of the original stimulus. For example, imagine that you presented a sound to a participant and then slowly increased the decibel levels.

64 Match List I with List II and indicate your answer with the help of the codes given below :

List I (State of Attachment)	List II (Description)
A. Privation	I. The state of a child who has never formed a close attachment with anyone
B. Anaclitic depression	II. A condition or disorder found among juvenile delinquents involving a lack of guilt and remorse
C. Deprivation	III. A condition experienced by some children who are poorly cared for having loss of appetite and feeling of helplessness
D. Affectionless psychopathology	IV. The state of a child who has formed a close relationship to someone, but is later separated from that person

Codes

	A	B	C	D
1	I	III	IV	II
2	IV	II	I	III
3	IV	III	I	II
4	I	II	IV	III

Ans. (1)

Exp. The correct matching is A-I, B-III, C-IV, D-II.

Privation is the state of a child who has never formed a close attachment with anyone. Privation is failure to Form an Attachment.

Anaclitic depression is a condition experienced by some children who are poorly cared for having loss of appetite and feeling of helplessness. Hospitalism (or anaclitic depression in its sublethal form) was a pediatric diagnosis to describe infants who wasted away while in hospital. The symptoms could include retarded physical development and disruption of perceptual-motor skills and language.

Deprivation is the state of a child who has formed a close relationship to someone, but is later separated from that person. Deprivation might be defined as losing something in which a person once had, whereas privation might be defined as never having something in the first place.

Affectionless psychopathology is a condition or disorder found among juvenile delinquents involving a lack of guilt and remorse. It describes individuals who cannot exhibit caring behaviours, concern, or affection for other people. They don't have empathy for others. They show no or very little remorse, guilt, shame, or contrition for their bad deeds.

65 Select the pair of poles of dimensions for 'permissive parenting style' as proposed by Maccoby and Martin.

I. Demanding II. Responsive
III. Unresponsive IV. Undemanding

Codes

1 I and III 2 I and II
3 III and IV 4 II and IV

Ans. (4)

Exp. The dimensions for 'permissive parenting style' as proposed by Maccoby and Martin are Responsive and Undemanding. The three parenting styles, as argued later by Maccoby and Martin, corresponded to high and low values on the responsiveness (warmth) and demandingness (control) dimensions. The permissive style (characterised by high responsiveness and low demandingness) was associated with child behaviour characterised by low self-control and low self-reliance.

The authoritative style (characterized by high levels of both responsiveness and demandingness) was associated with assertive, self-reliant child behavior.

The authoritarian style (low responsiveness and high demandingness) was associated with discontented, withdrawn child behavior; and the permissive style (characterized by high responsiveness and low demandingness) was associated with child behavior characterized by low self-control and low self-reliance.

Maccoby and Martin also described a fourth parenting style that was low on both responsiveness and demandingness that they labeled the uninvolved style.

66 Match List I with List II and indicate your answer with the help of the codes given below:

	List I (Psychological Term)		List II (Phenomena)
A.	Acquisition	I.	The reappearance, after a rest period, of an extinguished conditioned response
B.	Extinction	II.	The tendency, once a response has been conditioned, for stimuli similar to the conditioned stimulus to evoke similar responses
C.	Spontaneous recovery	III.	The diminishing of conditioned response, occurs in classical conditioning when an Unconditioned Stimulus (UCS) does not follow as a Conditioned Stimulus (CS) occurs in operant conditioning when a response is no longer reinforced
D.	Generalisation	IV.	The initial stage of learning during which a response is established and gradually strengthened. In classical conditioning, it is the phase in which a stimulus comes to evoke a conditioned response. In operant conditioning, a reinforced response is strengthened

Codes

	A	B	C	D		A	B	C	D
1	IV	III	I	II	2	IV	III	II	I
3	I	II	III	IV	4	I	II	IV	III

Ans. (1)

Exp. The correct matching is A-IV, B-III, C-I, D-II.

Acquisition is the initial stage of learning during which a response is established and gradually strengthened. In classical conditioning, it is the phase in which a stimulus comes to evoke a conditioned response. In operant conditioning, a reinforced response is strengthened. Acquisition refers to the first stages of learning when a response is established. In classical conditioning, it refers to the period when the stimulus comes to evoke the conditioned response.

Extinction is the diminishing of conditioned response, occurs in classical conditioning when an Unconditioned Stimulus (UCS) does not follow as a Conditioned Stimulus (CS) occurs in operant conditioning when a response is no longer reinforced. Extinction is used to stop the behaviour from not occurring so ignoring is believed to work best. Extinction is observed in both operantly conditioned and classically conditioned behaviour. When operant behaviour that has been previously reinforced no longer produces reinforcing consequences the behaviour gradually stops occurring.

Spontaneous recovery is the reappearance, after a rest period, of an extinguished conditioned response. Spontaneous recovery is a phenomenon of learning and memory that was first named and described by Pavlov in his studies of classical conditioning. In that context, it refers to the re-emergence of a previously extinguished conditioned response after a delay.

Generalisation is the tendency, once a response has been conditioned, for stimuli similar to the conditioned stimulus to evoke similar responses. Generalisation is the tendency to respond in the same way to different but similar stimuli. e.g. a dog conditioned to salivate to a tone of a particular pitch and loudness will also salivate with considerable regularity in response to tones of higher and lower pitch.

67 What would be the degrees of freedom for error variance in a five group randomised ANOVA, with twelve subjects per group?

1 54 2 55
3 59 4 60

Ans. *(2)*

Exp. The degrees of freedom for error variance in a five group randomised ANOVA, with twelve subjects per group is 55.

SSE is the error sum of squares, with associated degrees of freedom $kx(m-1)$

Degrees of freedom $= 5 \times 1\ (12-1) = 5 \times 11 = 55$

68 ARIMA (Autoregressive Integrated Moving Averages) model is especially useful in analysing the data obtained through

1 factorial designs
2 randomised block designs
3 time series designs
4 quasi-experimental designs with non-equivalent control groups

Ans. *(3)*

Exp. ARIMA model is especially useful in analysing the data obtained through time series designs.

In statistics and econometrics, and in particular in time series analysis, an autoregressive integrated moving average model is a generalisation of an autoregressive moving average model. Both of these models are fitted to time series data either to better understand the data or to predict future points in the series

69 Which of the following is correct of the Rorschach Ink Blot Cards?

1 Five chromatic and five achromatic
2 Two chromatic and eight achromatic
3 Three chromatic and seven achromatic
4 Three chromatic, five achromatic and two unstructured

Ans. *(1)*

Exp. There are five chromatic and five achromatic inkblots.

The Rorschach inkblot test is a popular performance-based personality test developed by Hermann Rorschach (1884–1922). The test consists of 10 inkblots: 5 are achromatic and 5 include chromatic colours. Respondents are asked what the inkblots "might be." Their responses are coded, tabulated, and compared with norms for interpretation. In the mid 1900s, several Rorschach systems emerged in the United States.

The Rorschach test is a psychological test in which subjects' perceptions of inkblots are recorded and then analysed using psychological interpretation, complex algorithms, or both. Some psychologists use this test to examine a person's personality characteristics and emotional functioning. It has been employed to detect underlying thought disorder, especially in cases where patients are reluctant to describe their thinking processes openly.

70 Selection is the process of differentiating between _______ in order to identify those with a greater likelihood of _________ in a job.

1 applicants; good performance
2 candidates; good performance
3 applicants; success
4 candidates; success

Ans. *(3)*

Exp. Selection is the process of differentiating between applicants in order to identify those with a greater likelihood of success in a job.

Selection is the process of choosing an item (e.g., an individual, an object, a measurement) from a larger universe of units for a purpose, such as study, testing, classifying, or working (hiring employees). Selection is the process of actually bringing talent in the company. Structured interviews, personality tests, knowledge tests, and work samples are tools that I-O psychologists help design to ensure the right talent is selected.

Directions (Q.Nos. 71-75) *Read the following passage and answer the questions that follow :*

The Wechsler Adult Intelligence Scale (WAIS) was administered to a sample of 300 subjects. The intercorrelations among all the sub-scales were obtained. Unities were retained in the diagonal spaces of the correlation matrix and it was factor analysed. Cattell's scree indicated two factor solution. The two factors were subjected to Varimax Rotation. The two rotated factors were named as Verbal intelligence and Performance Intelligence. The two factors, together, explained 62percent of variance.

71 Which one of the following method of factor extraction is likely to have been employed in the present work?

1 Principal component analysis
2 Principal axis factoring
3 Maximum likelihood
4 Unweighted least squares

Ans. *(1)*

➲ *Exp.* Principal component analysis is likely to have been employed in the present work.

Principal component analysis isa method of analysis which involves finding the linear combination of a set of variables that has maximum variance and removing its effect, repeating this successively.

72 The inter-factor correlation between the two rotated factors obtained in this analysis, will be

1 greater than zero
2 smaller than zero
3 zero
4 zero or greater than zero

Ans. (3)

➲ *Exp.* The inter-factor correlation between the two rotated factors obtained will in this analysis be zero.

Inter-factor correlations are obtained when researchers extract more than one factor and implement an oblique rotation, and they reveal the degree to which the dimensions underlying the observed variables are themselves associated with each other.

73 Cattell's scree is a

1 plot displaying variables using the first two factors as axes
2 plot of the order of unrotated factors on X axis and eigenvalues on Y axis
3 plot of the order of unrolated factors on X axis and the communalities on the Y axis
4 eigenvalues on X axis and communalities on Y axis

Ans. (2)

➲ *Exp.* Cattell's scree is a plot of the order of unrotated factors on X axis and eigenvalues on Y axis.

The Cattell's scree test is a graphical strategy with a non-numerical solution to determine the number of components to retain. Cattell's (1966) scree test is another factor estimation technique reliant on eigenvalues. Also known as the 'above the elbow' approach, it uses relative, rather than absolute eigenvalues. Factors have their eigenvalues plotted alongside each other (y-axis) in order of magnitude. Insignificant factors explaining little variance (and therefore low eigenvalues) will form a near-straight line towards the right of the graph.

74 The Factor Analytic Model followed in the above analysis can be best labelled as

1 Common Factor Model
2 Confirmatory Factor Analysis Model
3 Oblique Factor Analysis Model
4 Component Model

Ans. (4)

➲ *Exp.* The Factor Analytic Model followed in the above analysis can be best labelled as Component model. Cmponent Model, primarily, Principal Component Analysis, or PCA, is a dimensionality-reduction method that is often used to reduce the dimensionality of large data sets, by transforming a large set of variables into a smaller one that still contains most of the information in the large set.

75 In this research, the factor analysis has

1 established the predictive validity of the WAIS
2 explored the dimensionality of the WAIS sub-scales
3 provided evidence in favour of Spearman's two-factor Model
4 demonstrated that all the WAIS sub-scales are highly internally consistent

Ans. (2)

➲ *Exp.* In this research, the factor analysis has explored the dimensionality of the WAIS sub-scales.

Factor analysis is one of the unsupervised machine learning algorithms which is used for dimensionality reduction. This algorithm creates factors from the observed variables to represent the common variance i.e. variance due to correlation among the observed variables. The Wechsler scales, like the Binet and other tests, measure intellectual performance as a multi-dimensional construct.

This means that, rather than conceptualising intelligence as a single characteristic, the tests contain numerous scales assessing qualitatively different types of intellectual functioning. The WAIS-III contains the following scales : Verbal Scales-Information, Comprehension, Arithmetic, Similarities: Digit Span: Vocabulary Letter-Number Sequencing Performance Scales- Digit Symbol: Picture Completion: Block Design, Picture Arrangement: Matrix Reasoning, Object Assembly, Symbol Search.

UGC-NET PSYCHOLOGY

SOLVED PAPER 2013 (June)

PAPER II

1 Substantially higher performance scores than verbal scores on the subtests of Wechsler Adult Intelligence Scale (WAIS) indicates

1 Gender differences 2 Learning difficulties
3 Genetic influences 4 Cultural biases

Ans. (2)

Exp. Substantially higher performance scores than verbal scores on the subtest of Wechsler Adult Intelligence Scale (WAIS) indicate learning difficulties.

Wechsler designed an entire scale that allowed the measurement of non-verbal intelligence which was known as a Performance scale. This was an important development, as it attempted to overcome biases that were caused by language, culture, and education. Further, this scale also provided an opportunity to observe a different type of behaviour, because something physical was required. Clinicians were able to observe how a participant reacted to the 'longer interval of sustained effort, concentration, and attention' that the performance tasks required. As the Wechsler–Bellevue scale was the first to effectively use the performance scale, it also introduced the 'possibility of directly comparing an individual's verbal and non-verbal intelligence'. This was possible as 'the results of both scales were expressed in comparable units'. The WAIS test is also used to measure cognitive abilities relevant to assessing and identifying specific learning difficulties such as dyslexia and dyscalculia, as well as a child's cognitive development with respect to their chronological age.

2 Ruchi remembers that, when she was eight year old she was whimsical. This memory of Ruchi is called

1 episodic memory 2 semantic memory
3 sensory memory 4 amnesic memory

Ans. (1)

Exp. Ruchi remembers that when she was eight year old she was whimsical. This memory of Ruchi is called episodic memory. In the given question, Richa's memory of childhood is an example of episodic memory, and not semantic or sensory or amnesic. Episodic memory is the type of declarative memory containing the personal information which is not readily available to others, such as daily activities and events.

3 Which is the most basic and common obstacle to problem solving?

1 Confirmation bias 2 Fixation
3 Functional fixedness 4 Mental set

Ans. (2)

Exp. The most basic and common obstacle to the problem solving is Fixation.

Fixation involves the process of getting stuck on a particular way of thinking about something. e.g., sometimes solution to a problem remains out of reach because the elements of the problem are not arranged properly or because people get stuck in certain ways of thinking that acts barriers to solving the problem. This is termed as fixation, which occurs more or less automatically, influencing the attempts to solve the problem without any conscious awareness of that influence.

Functional fixedness is actually a kind of mental set, defined as tendency of people to persist in using the patterns that have worked for them in past. While confirmation bias is the tendency to search for the evidence that fits one's belief while ignoring the evidence that does not fits one's belief.

Although, all the options are an example of obstacle to the problem solving but option (2) would be the best possible out of it.

4 The child who says 'Milk gone' is engaging in _______. This type of utterance demonstrates that children are actively experimenting with rules of _______ .

1 babbling; syntax
2 telegraphic speech; syntax
3 babbling ; semantics
4 telegraphic speech; semantics

Ans. (2)

Exp. The child who says 'Milk gone' is engaging in telegraphic speech. This type of utterance demonstrates that children are actively experimenting with rules of syntax.

Telegraphic speech is a condensed or abbreviated speech in which only the most central words, carrying the highest level of information, are spoken. Syntax is set of rules that describe how words and phrases in a language are arranged into grammatical sentences, or the branch of linguistics that studies such rules. Research suggests that 18-month-old infants are capable of representing abstract non-local dependencies, suggesting that a core property of syntax emerges early in development.

5 Problem solving comprises of four stages. Choose the correct sequence of stages

1 Incubation, preparation, verification, illumination
2 Preparation, incubation, illumination, verification
3 Incubation, preparation, illumination, verification
4 Preparation, illumination, incubation, verification

Ans. (2)

Exp. Problem solving comprises of four basic stages which was outline by Wallas (1958). The stages in their correct sequence is as follows :

Preparation: During the preparation stage, the problem is "investigated in all directions" as the thinker readies the mental soil for the sowing of the seeds. It's the accumulation of intellectual resources out of which to construct the new ideas.

Incubation: Next comes incubation stage, which is a period of unconscious processing, during which no direct effort is exerted upon the problem at hand—this is where the "combinatory play" that marked Einstein's thought takes place.

Illumination: Following Incubation is the Illumination stage, which Wallas based on French polymath Henri Poincaré's concept of "sudden illumination" — that flash of insight that the conscious self can't will and the subliminal self can only welcome once all elements gathered during the Preparation stage have floated freely around during Incubation and are now ready to click into an illuminating new formation.

Verification: The last stage, unlike the second and the third, shares with the first a conscious and deliberate effort in the way of testing the validity of the idea and reducing the idea itself to an exact form.

6 Match the List I with List II and select the correct answer from the codes given below :

List I (Author)	List II (Focus/Emphasis)
A. Kagan and Haveman, 1979	I. Mental manipulation
B. Silverman, 1978	II. Solution of problem
C. Whittaker, 1970	III. Mediating process
D. Humphrey, 1963	IV. Goal-directed process

Codes

	A	B	C	D		A	B	C	D
1	I	II	IV	III	2	I	II	III	IV
3	I	III	II	IV	4	I	IV	III	II

Ans. (1)

Exp. The correct match is: A-I, B-II, C-IV, D-III.

Kagan and Haveman (1979) focused on mental manipulation. According to them, thinking can best be described as the mental manipulation of images, symbols, concepts, rules and other meditational units.

Silverman (1978) focused on solution of problem. According to him, thinking is a process that entitles us to find solutions to problem by using symbolic representation of stimuli and events.

Whittaker (1970) focused on goal-directed process. According to him, thinking is mostly goal directed and one desires to reach the goal by planning.

Humphrey (1963) focused on mediating process. According to him, mediation is seen as a process of gaining insights. The cognitive mediation theory describes mediation as a cognitive process. It assumes that the parties must gain insights, since they are not able to find a solution at the beginning of the procedure, but at its end. They need to gain insights when suddenly empowered to do so. More precisely, they do not just need to be enlightened during the mediation but also before, when taking decisions to conflict resolution.

7 Given below are two statements, one is labelled as Assertion (A) and the other labelled as Reason (R).

Assertion (A) Thinking about objects brings change in attitudes.

Reason (R) Attitudes toward complex issues and objects are typically a mixture of positive and negative feelings.

Codes

1 Both (A) and (R) are true and (R) is the correct explanation of (A)
2 Both (A) and (R) are true, but (R) is not the correct explanation of (A)
3 (A) is true, but (R) is false
4 (A) is false, but (R) is true

Ans. (1)

Exp. Both (A) and (R) are true and (R) is the correct explanation of (A).

Thinking about objects brings change in attitudes. It is true as thoughts about the attitude object or message are largely favorable or unfavorable. By examining the ratio of positive to negative thoughts, the likely amount of attitude change produced can be approximated. If there is a greater proportion of favorable than unfavorable thoughts, your attitude will change in a positive direction. The opposite is true if there are a greater proportion of negative thoughts. Hence, thinking about objects brings change in attitudes.

Attitudes toward complex issues and objects are typically a mixture of positive and negative feelings. All definitions of attitudes agree that an attitude is a state of the mind, a set of views, or thoughts, regarding some topic (called the 'attitude object'), which have an evaluative feature (positive, negative or neutral quality), accompanied by an emotional component and a thought component. The evaluative feature represents the feelings. Therefore, it is true that attitudes toward complex issues and objects are typically a mixture of positive and negative feelings, and it explains the assertion.

8 Match the List I with List II and select the correct answer from the codes given below:

List I (Memory Phenomena)	List II (Brief Description)
A. Semantic memory	I. Memory for events that occur in a particular time, place or context.
B. Priming	II. Memory for skills and habits.
C. Episodic memory	III. Memory for general knowledge and facts about the world.
D. Procedural memory	IV. Information that people already have in storage is activated to help them remember new information better and faster.

Codes

	A	B	C	D		A	B	C	D
1	III	II	IV	I	2	IV	III	II	I
3	III	IV	I	II	4	II	IV	III	I

Ans. (3)

Exp. The correct matching is A-III, B-IV, C-I, D-II

Semantic memory is memory for general knowledge and facts about the world.The word 'semantic' refers to the meaning, so this is kind of knowledge of awareness of meanings of words, concepts and terms as well as the names of objects, skills etc.

Priming is the information that people already have in storage and is activated to help them remember new information better and faster. It is the tendency to remember information that is presented at the beginning of a body of information better than the information that follows.

Episodic memory is memory for events that occur in a particular time, place or context. For e.g. Your first day experience at your first job.

Procedural memory is memory for skills and habits. It is also called non-declarative memory and it is the type of long term-memory for skills, procedure, habits and conditioned responses. These memories are not conscious but are implied to exist because they affect conscious behaviour. For e.g. tying up the shoelaces.

9 A subject is presented four non-sense syllabus one-by-one each for two seconds. After presentation of the four items, the subject is asked to count backward aloud by threes from some number for 15 seconds and after that he/she is asked to recall the non-sense syllabus. What memory storage is being measured in this experiment?

1 Sensory memory storage
2 Working memory storage
3 Short-term memory storage
4 Long-term memory storage

Ans. (3)

Exp. The memory storage being measured in this experiment is Short-term memory storage.

Short-term memory is the memory system in which information is held for brief period of time while being used. It holds about 7± 2 chunks of information and lasts about 30 seconds. Short-term memory is the reproduction, recognition, or recall of a limited amount of material after a period of about 10 to 30 seconds. In the case, the subject was asked to recall the non-sense syllables after 15 seconds. Therefore, the STM storage is used here.

10 When the previously learned task affects the retention of task being currently acquired, the phenomenon is referred to as

1 retroactive interference
2 proactive interference
3 retroactive effect
4 proactive effect

Ans. (2)

Exp. When the previously learned task affects the retention of task being currently acquired, the phenomenon is referred to as proactive interference.

Proactive Interference is the interference in new learning due to previous learning of similar or related material. It occurs when we cannot learn a new task because of an old task that had been learnt. When what we already know interferes with what we are currently learning – where old memories disrupt new memories.

11 Given below are two statements, one is labelled as Assertion (A) and the other labelled as Reason (R).

Assertion (A) Positive psychology draws its strength from humanistic psychology.

Reason (R) Both humanistic and positive psychology believe in positive human qualities.

Codes

1 Both (A) and (R) are true and (R) is the correct explanation of (A)
2 Both (A) and (R) are true, but (R) is not the correct explanation of (A)
3 (A) is true, but (R) is false
4 (A) is false, but (R) is true

Ans. (2)

Exp. Both (A) and (R) are true, but (R) is not the correct explanation of (A).

Positive psychology draws its strength from humanistic psychology. Positive psychologists rightly see humanistic psychology as one among several historical foundations leading to the creation of positive psychology and not the most important among its progenitors. Therefore, the assertion is true that positive psychology draws its strength from humanistic psychology.

Both humanistic and positive psychology believes in positive human qualities. It is true and depicts the commonality between humanistic and positive psychology, but does not explain the assertion. The conceptual ideas of human nature did influence the development of positive psychology. The previous waves of psychology focused on human flaws, overcoming deficiencies, avoiding pain, and escape from unhappiness, positive psychology focuses on well-being, contentment, excitement, cheerfulness, the pursuit of happiness, and meaning in life. The humanistic movement wanted to look at what drives us to want to grow and achieve fulfillment.

12 The basic difference between classical conditioning and instrumental learning is of

1 presentation of stimulus
2 emitting of response
3 temporal contiguity
4 mechanism

Ans. (4)

Exp. The basic difference between classical conditioning and instrumental learning is of mechanism.

Mechanism of learning is the way the behaviour is conditioned. In classical conditioning, a neutral stimulus is paired with a conditioned response. In operant conditioning, a desired behaviour is paired with a consequence.

Classical conditioning is a type of learning in which an initially neutral stimulus—the conditioned stimulus (CS)—when paired with a stimulus that elicits a reflex response—the unconditioned stimulus (US)—results in a learned, or conditioned, response (CR) when the CS is presented. Instrumental learning is any form of conditioning in which the correct response is essential for reinforcement. Instrumental conditioning is similar to operant conditioning and usually involves complex activities in order to reach a goal.

13 Major criticisms of Thurston' s theory of intelligence are based on

I. use of subjective measures.
II. restricted heterogeneity in sample.
III. method of factor analysis.

Which of the statements given above is/are correct?

1 I and II
2 I and III
3 II and III
4 All of these

Ans. (3)

Exp. Major criticisms of Thurston's theory of intelligence are based on restricted heterogeneity in sample and method of factor analysis.

Restricted heterogeneity in sample : Extreme sample heterogeneity, especially with respect to age and educational attainment, tends to amplify the size of the general factor, but very likely by contaminating g with uncontrolled developmental and experiential effects. In this regard, some theorists even interpret the first general factor explicitly as a reflection of sample heterogeneity rather than g (Kelley, 1928; Oleron, 1957).

Method of factor analysis : Many cognitive psychologists, downplay factor-analytic results on the grounds that the rotation and placement of factor axes and hence their interpretation in terms of shared intellective processes judged to underlie marker test performances are mathematically arbitrary.

14 Given below are two statements, labelled as Assertion (A) and the other labelled as Reason (R).

Assertion (A) Heritability of intelligence explains variations due to genetics for individuals within a given population.

Reason (R) Earlier the children from deprived families were adopted, the higher their intelligence score will be.

Codes

1 Both (A) and (R) are true and (R) is the correct explanation of (A)
2 Both (A) and (R) are true, but (R) is not the correct explanation of (A)
3 (A) is true, but (R) is false
4 (A) is false, but (R) is true

Ans. (2)

Exp. Both (A) and (R) are true, but (R) is not the correct explanation of (A).

Heritability of intelligence explains variations due to genetics for individuals within a given population. Many of these studies have focused on similarities and differences in IQ within families, particularly looking at adopted children and twins. These studies suggest that genetic factors underlie about 50 percent of the difference in intelligence among individuals. Therefore, the assertion is true.

Earlier the children from deprived families were adopted, the higher their intelligence score will be. The importance of home environment is also shown in studies of children who are remove from deprived environment and placed in middle or upper class adoptive homes. Typically, children when removed from deprived families show a gradual increase in IQ on the order of 10-12 points (Sherr and Weinberg, 1977) when deprived children remain in their impoverished environment, either they show no improvement in IQ or they actually deteriorate intellectually overtime (Serpell, 2010). As per the research, the assertion is correct but reason is not particularly the suitable explanation.

15 Given below are two statements, the labelled as Assertion (A) and the other labelled as Reason (R).

Assertion (A) Psychoactive drugs affects the nervous systems to cause change in perception or mood.

Reason (R) Reticular activating system is related to perception and mood.

Codes

1 Both (A) and (R) are true and (R) is the correct explanation of (A)
2 Both (A) and (R) are true, but (R) is not the correct explanation of (A)
3 (A) is true, but (R) is false
4 (A) is false, but (R) is true

Ans. *(3)*

Exp. (A) is true, but (R) is false.

Psychoactive drugs affects the nervous systems to cause change in perception or mood. It is true as psychoactive drugs alter communication between brain cells. Individual brain cells (neurons) communicate with one another through a series of biological messengers called neurotransmitters. These neurotransmitters are released from the neuron sending the message and bind to receptors on the neuron receiving the message. Some psychoactive substances are able to mimic the effects of neurotransmitters. Others interfere with normal brain function by blocking it, or by altering the way neurotransmitters are stored, released, and removed.

Reticular activating system is a part of the reticular formation thought to be particularly involved in the regulation of arousal, alertness, and sleep–wake cycles. It is not related to perception and mood.

16 Match the List I with List II and select the correct answer from the codes given below

List I (Glands)		List II (Hormons)
A. Pituitary	I.	Melatonin
B. Adrenal Cortex	II.	Adrenaline
C. Pineal	III.	Prolactin
D. Adrenal Medulla	IV.	Corticosteroids

Codes

	A	B	C	D
1	II	I	III	IV
2	I	III	II	IV
3	IV	III	I	II
4	III	IV	I	II

Ans. *(4)*

Exp. The correct matching is A-III, B-IV, C-I, D-II.

Pituitary gland is associated with Prolactin. It is master gland, which produces many hormones. The anterior pituitary gland (or adenohypophysis) is a lobe of gland which secretes prolactin. It is also known as lactogenic hormone. Prolactin is mainly used to help women produce milk after the child birth. It is secreted from the pituitary gland in response to eating, mating, estrogen treatment, ovulation and nursing. It is secreted in pulses in between these events. It plays an essential role in metabolism, regulation of the immune system and pancreatic development.

Adrenal cortex is associated with Corticosteroids. Corticosteroids are a class of steroid hormones that are produced in the adrenal cortex of vertebrates as well as the synthetic analogies of these hormones.

Pineal gland is associated with Melatonin. Melatonin helps control your sleep and wake cycles.

Adrenal medulla is associated with adrenaline. Adrenal medulla is the inner portion of adrenal gland. It makes epinephrine (adrenaline) and norepinephrine (noradrenaline). Epinephrine is secreted in response to low blood levels of glucose as well as exercise and stress.

17 What is the correct sequence of ear parts given below ?

1 Eardrum, Hammer, Anvil, Stirrup, Oval window
2 Oval window, Hammer, Eardrum, Anvil, Stirrup
3 Eardrum, Anvil, Stirrup, Hammer, Oval window
4 Oval window, Anvil, Hammer, Stirrup, Eardrum

Ans. *(1)*

Exp. The correct sequence of ear part is Eardrum, Hammer, Anvil, Stirrup, Oval window.

Ears are important for hearing and for controlling a sense of position and balance. The ear can be separated into multiple sections. The outer ear includes the pinna, which is the visible part of the ear that protrudes from our heads, the auditory canal, and the tympanic membrane, or eardrum. The middle ear contains three tiny bones known as the ossicles, which are named the malleus (or hammer), incus (or anvil), and the stapes (or stirrup). The inner ear begins with the oval window.

Sound waves travel along the auditory canal and strike the tympanic membrane, causing it to vibrate. This vibration results in movement of the three ossicles. As the ossicles move, the stapes presses into a thin membrane of the cochlea known as the oval window.

18 We can cope with stress by becoming aware of our irrational, upsetting thoughts and replacing them with rational, calming thoughts. This view represents.

1 Cognitive behavioural approach
2 Psychoanalytical approach
3 Socio-cultural approach
4 Bio-social approach

Ans. *(1)*

Exp. We can cope with stress by becoming aware of our irrational, upsetting thoughts and replacing them with rational, calming thoughts. The view represents Cognitive behavioral approach.

Cognitive behavioral approach is any theory deriving from general behavioral theory that considers cognitive or thought processes as significant mediators of behavioral change. A central feature in the theoretical formulations of the process is that people respond primarily to cognitive representations of their environments rather than to the environments themselves. The theory has led to popular therapeutic procedures that incorporate cognitive behavior techniques to effect changes in self-image as well as behaviors.

19 An instrumental response is conditioned only when organism interprets the reinforcement as being controlled by its response. This view is supported by

1 Tolman 2 Skinner
3 Seligman 4 Beck

Ans. *(3)*

Exp. An instrumental response is conditioned only when organism interprets the reinforcement as being controlled by its response. The view is supported by Seligman.

Seligman gave the concept of learned helplessness, the tendency to fail to act to escape from a situation because of a history of repeated failures in the past. In other words, an instrumental its response is conditioned only when organism interprets the reinforcement is being controlled by its' response, otherwise the response is not elicited.

20 When a child gets two chocolates once every week for its performance in the class it is an instance of

1 fixed ratio, variable interval
2 fixed ratio, fixed interval
3 variable ratio, fixed interval
4 variable ratio, variable interval

Ans. *(2)*

Exp. When a child gets two chocolates once every week for its performance in the class it is an instance of fixed ratio, fixed interval.

Fixed Ratio Schedule of Reinforcement: It is the schedule of reinforcement in which the number of response required for reinforcement is always the same. e.g. the child gets two chocolates once every week.

Fixed Interval Schedule of Reinforcement: It is the schedule of reinforcement in which the interval of time that must pass before the reinforcement becomes possible is always the same. e.g. child gets two chocolate every week for its performance in the class.

21 Match the List I with List II and select the correct answer from the codes given below:

List I (Learning term)	List II (Brief explanation)
A. Positive reinforcement	I. Removal of a pleasant or appetitive stimulus after a behavioural response
B. Classical conditioning	II. Delivery of a pleasant or appetitive stimulus that follows a behavioural response
C. Punishment	III. Presenting a neutral stimulus after a stimulus that usually elicits a specific response
D. Omission training	IV. Presentation of an unpleasant or aversive stimulus after a behavioural response

Codes

	A	B	C	D		A	B	C	D
1	II	III	IV	I	2	IV	I	III	II
3	I	IV	II	III	4	III	IV	I	II

Ans. *(1)*

Exp. The correct matching is A-II, B-III, C-IV, D-I.

Positive reinforcement is delivery of a pleasant or appetitive stimulus that follows a behavioural response. It is an increase in the probability of occurrence of some activity because that activity results in the presentation of a stimulus or of some circumstance. It is the procedure of presenting a positive reinforcer after a response.

Classical conditioning is presenting a neutral stimulus after a stimulus that usually elicits a specific response. It is a type of learning in which an initially neutral stimulus—the conditioned stimulus (CS)—when paired with a stimulus that elicits a reflex response—the unconditioned stimulus (US)—results in a learned, or conditioned, response (CR) when the CS is presented.

Punishment is presentation of an unpleasant or aversive stimulus after a behavioural response. It is the process in which the relationship, or contingency, between a response and some stimulus or circumstance results in the response becoming less probable.

Omission training is removal of a pleasant or appetitive stimulus after a behavioural response. It is a method in behaviorism used to stop undesirable behaviours. It is used when something that the subject (the person/animal being trained) enjoys is taken away as punishment for an action or behaviour. This is done in the hope to prevent the action/behaviour from occurring again.

22 Match the List I with List II and select the correct answer from the codes given below:

List I (Name of Psychologist)	List II (Name of Test)
A. JB Rotter	I. NEO-Personality inventory
B. C Robert Cloninger	II. Hardy Personality
C. Suzanne Kobasa	III. Locus of control
D. PT Costa	IV. Temperament and character inventory

Codes

	A	B	C	D
1	I	II	III	IV
2	III	IV	II	I
3	III	IV	I	II
4	III	IV	IV	I

Ans. *(2)*

Exp. The correct matching is A-III, B-IV, C-II, D-I.

J.B. Rotter is associated with the development of Locus of Control test. The Locus of control personality test is used to assess the extent to which an individual possesses internal or external reinforcement beliefs.

C. Robert Cloninger is associated with Temperament and Character Inventory. The Temperament and Character Inventory (TCI) is an instrument for personality assessment that was developed by C. Robert Cloninger to provide a comprehensive biopsychosocial model of personality as it develops within individuals

Suzanne Kobasa is associated with Hardy Personality test. Kobasa described a pattern of personality characteristics that distinguished managers and executives who remained healthy under life stress, as compared to those who developed health problems.

P.T Costa is associated with NEO-Personality Inventory. It is a personality inventory that examines a person's Big Five personality traits (openness to experience, conscientiousness, extraversion, agreeableness, and neuroticism). Costa and McCrae renamed their instrument the NEO Personality Inventory (NEO PI). In this version, 'NEO' was now considered part of the name of the test and was no longer an acronym. The assessment at this time included six facet sub-scales for the three original factors (N, E, & O).

23 In a study on 'Career Aspirations of Students', the respondents were required to state their career aspirations in about sixty words. This would be an example of

1 fixed-alternative item
2 scale item
3 open-end item
4 checklist item

Ans. (3)

Exp. In a study on 'Career Aspirations of Students', the respondents were required to state their career aspirations in about sixty words. This would be an example of open-end item.

An open-end item does not come with any multiple-choice options for the respondent. It is a question that encourages the respondent to answer freely in his or her own words, providing as much or as little detail as desired.

24 Given below are two statements, one is labelled as Assertion (A) and the other labelled as Reason (R).

Assertion (A) In Ponzo illusion and Muller-Lyer illusion, linear perspective is misapplied to the display.

Reason (R) According to Gregory perception is only a function of stimulus characteristics.

Codes

1 Both (A) and (R) are true and (R) is the correct explanation of (A)
2 Both (A) and (R) are true, but (R) is not the correct explanation of (A)
3 (A) is true, but (R) is false
4 (A) is false, but (R) is true

Ans. (1)

Exp. Both (A) and (R) are true and (R) is the correct explanation of (A).

In Ponzo illusion and Muller-Lyer illusion, linear perspective is misapplied to the display. Ponzo illusion is a visual illusion in which the upper of two parallel horizontal lines of equal length appears to be longer than the bottom of the two lines when they are flanked by oblique lines that are closer together at the top than they are at the bottom. Müller-Lyer illusion is a geometric illusion in which a difference is perceived in the length of a line depending on whether arrowheads at either end are pointing toward each other or away from each other. Pressey and his colleagues (Pressey et al., 1971; Pressey & Epp, 1992) proposed that the Ponzo illusion is caused by the same mechanism that causes the Müller-Lyer illusion.

According to Gregory, perception is only a function of stimulus characteristics. Psychologist Richard Gregory (1970) argued that perception is a constructive process which relies on top-down processing. Stimulus information from our environment is frequently ambiguous so to interpret it, we require higher cognitive information either from past experiences or stored knowledge in order to makes inferences about what we perceive. According to him, the formation of incorrect hypotheseswill lead to errors of perception like in illusions.

25 Match the List I with List II and select the correct answer from the codes given below :

List I (Law)	List II (Meaning)
A. Closure	I. Elements close together are grouped together
B. Proximity	II. Patterns are perceived in the most basic, direct manner possible
C. Similarity	III. Groupings are made in terms of complete figures
D. Simplicity	IV. Elements similar in appearance are grouped together

Codes

	A	B	C	D
1	I	IV	II	III
2	II	III	I	IV
3	IV	II	III	I
4	III	I	IV	II

Ans. (4)

Exp. The correct matching is A-III, B-I, C-IV, D-II.

Closure is when groupings are made in terms of complete figures. It is one of the Gestalt principles of organisation. It states that people tend to perceive incomplete forms (e.g., images, sounds) as complete, synthesising the missing units so as to perceive the image or sound as a whole—in effect closing the gap in the incomplete forms to create complete forms.

Proximity is when elements close together are grouped together. It states that people tend to organise objects close to each other into a perceptual group and interpret them as a single entity.

Similarity is when elements similar in appearance are grouped together. It states that people tend to organise objects with similar qualities into a perceptual group and interpret them as a whole.

Simplicity is when patterns are perceived in the most basic, direct manner possible. The Gestalt Principle of Simplicity states that we perceive the simplest shape possible, even when it is made up of several different shapes.

26 Which of the following is not one of the Big Five personality factors ?

1 Submissiveness
2 Agreeableness
3 Extroversion
4 Openness to experience

Ans. *(1)*

Exp. The factor which is not one of the Big Five Personality factors is Submissiveness.

The Big Five Personality Factors are usually labeled extroversion, neuroticism, agreeableness, conscientiousness, and openness to experience. The Big five factor theory is the model of personality traits that describes five basic trait dimensions. It is a model of the primary dimensions of individual differences in personality.

Agreeableness is the tendency to act in a cooperative, unselfish manner. Extroversion is characterised by an orientation of one's interests and energies toward the outer world of people and things rather than the inner world of subjective experience. Openness to experience refers to individual differences in the tendency to be open to new aesthetic, cultural, or intellectual experiences. Neuroticism is characterised by a chronic level of emotional instability and proneness to psychological distress. Conscientiousness is the tendency to be organized, responsible, and hardworking.

27 Given below are two statements, one is labelled as Assertion (A) and the other labelled as Reason (R).

Assertion (A) The level of arousal for optimal performance varies for different tasks.

Reason (R) Too little arousal can be non-motivating, too high arousal can be disruptive.

Codes

1 Both (A) and (R) are true and (R) is the correct explanation of (A)
2 Both (A) and (R) are true, but (R) is not the correct explanation of (A)
3 (A) is true, but (R) is false
4 (A) is false, but (R) is true

Ans. *(2)*

Exp. Both (A) and (R) are true, but (R) is not the correct explanation of (A).

The level of arousal for optimal performance varies for different tasks. It is true and is based on the Yerkes-Dodson law, which is a model of the relationship between stress and task performance. It proposes that an individual reaches his/her peak level of performance with an intermediate level of stress, or arousal. For optimal performance, the arousal levels can vary from one task to the next. Researchers have found that different tasks require different levels of arousal for optimal performance. For example, difficult or intellectually demanding tasks may require a lower level of arousal (to facilitate concentration), whereas tasks demanding stamina or persistence may be performed better with higher levels of arousal (to increase motivation).

Too little arousal can be non-motivating, too high arousal can be disruptive. It is true as too little or too much arousal results in poorer performance. Too little arousal doesn't provide much in the way of motivation. Too much arousal is disruptive as it causes a stronger stress reaction that can hamper performance. That optimal level of arousal differs from person to person, according to factors like the specific task, degree of skill, and confidence level. This doesn't explain why the levels of arousal vary for different tasks.

28 Match the List I with List II and select the correct answer from the codes given below

List I (Behaviour)	List II (Expression Mode)
A. Tone	I. Facial
B. Crying	II. Glandular
C. Laugh	III. Verbal
D. Eyebrow	IV. Muscular

Codes

	A	B	C	D		A	B	C	D
1	III	II	IV	I	2	I	IV	III	II
3	II	IV	III	I	4	II	I	III	IV

Ans. *(1)*

Exp. The correct matching is A-III, B-II, C-IV, D-I.

Tone is associated with verbal expression. The tone of voice in communication is defined as 'the way a person speaks to someone'.

Crying is associated with glandular expression. Tears are clear liquid secreted by lacrimal glands (tear glands) found in the eyes.

Laugh is associated with muscular expression. During laughter, muscles in diaphragm, abdomen and face actively flex and release.

Eyebrow is associated with facial expression. People raise their eyebrows to express surprise, doubt, disbelief, exasperation, exaggeration, or unconsciously when giving orders, making demands, or arguing important points.

29 A slow graded electrical potential produced by a receptor cell in response to a physical stimulus is

1 receptor potential
2 generator potential
3 transduction
4 arousal

Ans. (1)

➲ *Exp.* A slow graded electrical potential produced by a receptor cell in response to a physical stimulus is receptor potential.

It is the transmembrane potential difference produced by activation of a sensory receptor. A receptor potential is often produced by sensory transduction.

30 This area contains 'Somato Sensory Cortex'

1 Parietal lobe
2 Frontal lobe
3 Temporal lobe
4 Occipital lobe

Ans. (1)

➲ *Exp.* The area that contains 'Somato Sensory Cortex' is the Parietal lobe.

The Parietal lobes are at the top and back of the brain. This area contains the Somato Sensory Cortex, an area of neurons running down the front of the parietal lobes on either side of the brain. This area processes information from the skin and internal body receptors for touch, temperature and body position.

31 Give the correct sequence of the location of following glands in human body from top to bottom

1 Thyroid, Adrenal, Pancreas, Pituitary
2 Thyroid, Pancreas, Pituitary, Adrenal
3 Pituitary, Adrenal, Thyroid, Pancreas
4 Pituitary, Thyroid, Adrenal, Pancreas

Ans. (4)

➲ *Exp.* The correct sequence is: Pituitary, Thyroid, Adrenal, Pancreas.

The *Pituitary gland* is located below the brain. Usually no larger than a pea, the gland controls many functions of other endocrine glands.

The *Thyroid gland* is located in front of the neck, below the larynx (voice box). The thyroid plays an important role in the body's metabolism.

An *Adrenal gland* is located on top of each kidney. Like many glands, the adrenal glands work hand-in-hand with the hypothalamus and pituitary gland. The adrenal glands make and release corticosteroid hormones and epinephrine that maintain blood pressure and regulate metabolism.

The *Pancreas* is located across the back of the abdomen, behind the stomach. The pancreas plays a role in digestion, as well as hormone production. Hormones produced by the pancreas include insulin and glucagon, which regulate levels of blood sugar.

32 A complex behaviour that is rigidly patterned throughout a species and is unlearned is called

1 imprinting   2 instinct
3 emotion   4 feeling

Ans. (2)

➲ *Exp.* A complex behaviour that is rigidly patterned throughout a species and is unlearned is called instinct. An instinct is an innate, species-specific biological force that impels an organism to do something, particularly to perform a certain act or respond in a certain manner to specific stimuli.

33 Our tendency to perceive objects as unchanging despite changes in sensory input is an illustration of

1 figure-ground relationship 2 perceptual constancy
3 binocular cues   4 linear perspective

Ans. (2)

➲ *Exp.* Our tendency to perceive objects as unchanging despite changes in sensory input is an illustration of perceptual constancy.

Perceptual constancy is the phenomenon in which an object or its properties (e.g., size, shape, color) appear unchanged despite variations in the stimulus itself or in the external conditions of observation, such as object orientation or level of illumination. Examples of perceptual constancy include brightness constancy, color constancy, shape constancy, and size constancy.

34 Given below are two statements, one is labelled as Assertion (A) and the other labelled as Reason (R).

Assertion (A) As compared to other methods of psychological research, experimental method is usually considered to be best suited for studying cause and effect relationship.

Reason (R) Secondary variance is more efficiently controlled in experimental method.

Codes

1 Both (A) and (R) are true and (R) is the correct explanation of (A)
2 Both (A) and (R) are true, but (R) is not the correct explanation of (A)
3 (A) is true, but (R) is false
4 (A) is false, but (R) is true

Ans. (1)

➲ *Exp.* Both (A) and (R) are true and (R) is the correct explanation of (A).

As compared to other methods of psychological research, experimental method is usually considered to be best suited for studying cause and effect relationship. The experimental method involves manipulating one variable to determine if changes in one variable cause changes in another variable. This method relies on controlled methods, random assignment and the manipulation of variables to test a hypothesis.

The experimental method is a systematic and scientific approach to research in which the researcher manipulates one or more variables and controls and measures any change in other variables. Experiment establishes cause and effect, by keeping other variable as constant. Therefore, the assertion is true.

Secondary variance is more efficiently controlled in experimental method. Secondary variance results from extraneous, outside factors that the experimenter did not recognise and/or control for. These extraneous variables may have an effect on the dependent variable, but the experimenter may not be interested in selecting these variables for an independent variable. Once the potential sources of secondary variance are identified, they should either be eliminated or held constant. Holding constant means maintaining consistency across all the experimental sessions. The reason statement is true and it explains the assertion.

35 Arrange these typical investigations in descending order in terms of the researcher's ability to control secondary variance.

I. Field experiment

II. Laboratory experiment

III. Ex-post facto study

Codes

1 III, I and II   2 II, I and III
3 III, II and I   4 I, II and III

Ans. (2)

Exp. The correct order is II, I and III.

Controlling secondary variance is one of the most important aspects of good research methodology. Once the potential sources of secondary variance are identified, they should either be eliminated or held constant. Holding constant means maintaining consistency across all the experimental sessions. Essentially, all participants are treated exactly the same, with only the independent variable varying between them. Holding extraneous, secondary variables constant means that all the participants, in all the conditions, are exposed to them in the same way.

Laboratory experiments are a research method by which researchers create controllable environments to test hypotheses. The degree of control over secondary variance is most in the experimental research.

The *Field experiments* are done in the everyday environment of the participants. The experiment still manipulates the independent variable but in a real life setting. Since, the presence of extraneous variables may affect the research more in a field experiment; there is less control over secondary variance.

Ex-post facto study is a method in which groups with qualities that already exist are compared or some dependent variable. Also known as 'after the fact' research, an ex-post facto design is considered quasi- experiment because the subjects are not randomly assigned and they are grouped based on particular characteristic or trait. In an ex-post facto study, there is least control over the secondary variance.

36 What is the correct sequence of development of the following personality tests

I. Maudsley Personality Inventory

II. Minnesota Multiphasic Personality Inventory-2

III. Millon Clinical Multiaxial Inventory

IV. NEO PI-3

Codes

1 I, II, III and IV   2 IV, III, II and I
3 II, IV, I and III   4 I, III, II and IV

Ans. (4)

Exp. The correct sequence is I, III, II, and IV.

Maudsley Personality Inventory (MPI) has been developed by Jensen and Eysenck in 1958. It is a self-reported instrument intended for adult populations and designed to measure the two major personality dimensions of extraversion-introversion (E) and neuroticism (N) as they are defined in Eysenck's dimensional theory.

The *Million Clinical Multiaxial Inventory* is a psychological assessment tool intended to provide information on psychopathology, including specific disorders outlined in the IV, it is intended for adults (18 and over) with at least an 8th grade reading level who are currently seeking mental health services. The original version of the MCMI was published in 1977.

The *Minnesota Multiphasic Personality Inventory*-2 (MMPI-2) is one of the most frequently used personality tests in mental health. It was revised in the year of 1989. MMPI-2 is a psychological test that assesses personality traits and psychopathology. It is primarily intended to test people who are suspected of having mental health or other clinical issues.

The Revised NEO Personality Inventory 3 or NEO PI-3, is a psychological personality inventory; a 240 item measure o the Big Five Personality traits; Extraversion, Agreeableness, Conscientiousness, Neuroticism and openness to experience. The NEO PI-3 and NEO-FFI were updated in 2010 in a manual called the NEO Inventories for the NEO Personality-3.

37 Perceiving one thing in relation, to another when both are presented simultaneously is called

1 Simultaneous perception
2 Figure-ground perception
3 Consecutive perception
4 Successive perception

Ans. (2)

Exp. Perceiving one thing in relation to another when both are presented simultaneously is called Figure-ground perception.

Figure-ground perception refers to the tendency of the visual system to simplify a scene into the main object that we are looking at (the figure) and everything else that forms the background (or ground). While the concept of figure-ground perception is an important principle in Gestalt psychology, it is usually not identified as one of the laws of perceptual organization.

38 Verbal behaviour that is reinforced when someone else's verbal response is repeated verbation is called

1 autoclitic behaviour   2 echoic behaviour
3 reinforced behaviour   4 operant behaviour

Ans. (2)

Exp. Verbal behaviour that is reinforced when someone else's verbal response is repeated verbation is called Echoic behaviour.

Echoic behaviour is a form of verbal behaviour where the speaker repeats the same sound or word that was said by another person, like an echo. Infants and children absorb vast amounts of information through the imitation of others. When they imitate vocally, we call this echoic behavior. In typically developing infants and children vocal imitation skills emerge early in development and occur naturally.

39 Which of the following are essential to Spearman's methodology of theory development ?

I. Tetral equation
II. Tetral difference
III. Specific factor
IV. Neurological basis of intelligence

Select the correct answer using the codes given below

1 I, II and III 2 I, III and IV
3 II, III and IV 4 I, II and IV

Ans. (1)

Exp. Tetrad equation, Tetrad difference and Specific factor are essential to Spearman's methodology of theory development.

Tetrad equation: Spearman considered four intellectual activities that are measured in the intelligence test, having correlation coefficients R13, R14, R23, R24 in the correlation matrix (nearby four in the correlation matrix), then the mathematical expression of tetrad equation would be, F=(R13)(R24)-(R14)(R23). In this form they became known as the tetrad difference equations.

Tetrad difference: Spearman used the 'tetrad difference' method to analyze intelligence. This method has been widely used in various psychological investigations; it is represented by the quantity F, and it is the difference between the cross products of two opposites coefficients of any four correlation coefficients in a square block.

Specific factor: The variation in measured intelligence that was not explainable in terms of this general factor or 'g' was attributed by Spearman to specific factors or 's'. There were many different specific factors. All intellectual tasks require some amount of 'g.' according to Spearman, the more highly the two functions were correlated, the more highly saturated they were with 'g.' Tests that are thought to have high 'g' loadings involve abstract reasoning, comprehension, and problem solving.

40 Dissociable sub-systems operate simultaneously in each hemisphere and help us recognise similarity at one level and differences at another level in the perceived pattern. This system consists of

I. top-down processing system
II. abstract category sub-system
III. bottom-up processing system
IV. specific-exemplar sub-system

Select the correct answer using the codes given below

1 I and II 2 III and IV
3 II and IV 4 I and IV

Ans. (3)

Exp. The given system consists of abstract category sub-system and specific-exemplar sub-system.

Abstract category sub-system: An abstract category subsystem encodes the visual category to which an input stimulus belongs. It uses C JMarsolek, a features-based strategy in which relatively invariant features of shapes can be used to indicate that different visual inputs belong to the same abstract category.

Specific-exemplar sub-system: In contrast, a specific-exemplar subsystem encodes the visual exemplar to which an input stimulus corresponds. It uses a whole-based strategy in which complex distributed representations can be used to indicate that even visually similar inputs correspond to different exemplars (Marsolek, 2003, 2004).

41 Based on Eysenkian theory of personality, what is the correct sequence levels of personality from bottom to top ?

I. Habit level II. Trait level
III. Type level IV. SR level

Codes

1 I, II, III and IV 2 IV, III, II and I
3 IV, I, II and III 4 II, IV, I and III

Ans. (3)

Exp. The correct sequence is IV, I, II and III.

Eysenck (1947, 1994) recognised a four-level hierarchy of behaviour organisation. Based on Eysenkian theory of personality, the correct sequence levels of personality are as follows:

SR level: At the lowest level are specific acts or cognitions (SR or specific responses), individual behaviors or thoughts that may or may not be characteristic of a person.

Habit level: At the second level are the habitual acts or cognitions, that is, responses that recur under similar conditions. As opposed to specific responses, habitual responses must be reasonably reliable or consistent.

Trait level: Several related habitual responses form a trait—the third level of behavior. Eysenck (1981) defined traits as "important seem-permanent personality dispositions".

Type level: The fourth level is that of types or superfactors. A type is made up of several interrelated traits. For example, persistence may be related to inferiority, poor emotional adjustment, social shyness, and several other traits, with the entire cluster forming the introverted type.

42 Speed and power tests cannot be differentiated on the basis of

I. time limit II. verbal content
III. non-verbal content IV. difficulty level

Codes

1 I and IV 2 II and IV
3 II and III 4 I, III and IV

Ans. (3)

Exp. Speed and power tests cannot be differentiated on the basis of its verbal content and non-verbal content.

In a speed test, there is a time limit within which the test taker is required to answer all the items. Power test assesses the underlying ability (or power) of the individuals by allowing them sufficient time, i.e. these tests do not have any time limit. Speed and power tests can be differentiated on the basis of time limit and difficulty level. In a speed test, all the items are of the same degree of difficulty. In a power test, the items are generally arranged in an increasing order of difficulty.

43 According to two factors of Retroactive Interference, RI is caused by two factors. One is unlearning of the first task during the time one is engaged in the second task. What is the second factor?

1 Unlearning of the responses of second task
2 Competition of the first task responses with the second task responses that inhibits the recall responses of the first task at the time of recall
3 Inability to recall responses from first task
4 Decaying of memory-traces of responses of first task

Ans. (2)

Exp. The second factor is competition of the first task responses with the second task responses that inhibits the recall responses of the first task at the time of recall.

Retroactive interference occurs when newly acquired information interferes with the ability to recall info learnt at an earlier time. It happens because it takes for the brain to convert short-term memories into long term memories, when new information is entered into the system or due to competition among retrieval cues. When different memories become associated with similar or identical cues, confusion can result and accusing a cue may call up the wrong memory.

44 One of the difficulty with the survey method is

1 inability to examine changes over time
2 that subjects may give dishonest or inaccurate responses
3 the relatively small number of subjects used
4 the impossibility of getting a representative sample

Ans. (2)

Exp. One of the difficulties with the survey method is that the subjects may give dishonest or inaccurate responses.

A survey is an attempt to provide a compressive perspective on same topic. It is used to collect information about people's attitudes, beliefs and behaviour.

In a survey unlike what is in an observation method, it is very difficult for the investigator to know for sure whether the response given by the respondent is true or not.

45 A cell in a contingency table had an obtained frequency of 16 and an expected frequency of 25. What would be the contribution of this cell to the total chi-square value?

1 3.24 2 5.06 3 9.00 4 81.00

Ans. (1)

Exp. Square $X_c^2 = \Sigma \frac{(0_i - E_i)^2}{E_i}$

$$X^2 = \frac{(25-16)^2}{25} = \frac{9\times 9}{25} = \frac{81}{25} = 3.24$$

Directions (Q. Nos. 46-50) *Read the passage given below and answer the questions that follow.*

The notion of true score is at the heart of classical reliability theory. This model proposes that the obtained score on a variable is a sum of true score and the random error of measurement, the two components being independent. Using this model, various ways of computing reliability have been developed. One of the way of examining the reliability of a test is to test the homogeneity of test items or the internal consistency. The most widely used method of estimating the reliability is split-half technique, also called as odd-even reliability. In this context, Spearman Brown correction is important. Kuder-Richardson reliability and Chronbach Alpha are the two other methods of studying internal consistency.

Another important type of reliability is the interscorer reliability. This reliability is not useful for objective tests, but for certain types it is quite important. There are also other types of reliability such as parallel form reliability and test-retest reliability, the latter concerned with temporal stability of the test results.

46 Reliability can be defined as

1 $\frac{\text{True score variance}}{\text{Total variance}}$
2 $\frac{\text{Error variance}}{\text{Total variance}}$
3 $\frac{\text{True score variance}}{\text{Error variance}}$
4 $\frac{\text{Error variance}}{\text{Total score variance}}$

Ans. (1)

Exp. Reliability can be defined as True score variance/Total variance.

Test reliability is always established for a defined population; reliability of a test in one population may not be the same as in other populations.

Test variance is central to reliability. Since a test score (X) consists of true and error components, the total variance (σ_x^2) of a test administered to a group consists of true score variance (σ_t^2) and error variance (σ_e^2):

$$\sigma_x^2 = \sigma_t^2 + \sigma_e^2$$

Test Variance = True Score Variance + Error

Test reliability (Rxx) is calculated from these variances:

$$R_{xx} = \frac{\text{Total Variance - Error Variance}}{\text{Total Variance}}$$

$$= \frac{\text{True score variance}}{\text{Total variance}}$$

47 For a newly developed test, the scores on odd and even part correlated by 0.4. After applying Spearman-Brown formula

1 The corrected reliability would by 0.8
2 The corrected reliability would be 0.4
3 The corrected reliability would be greater than 0.4 and lesser than 0.8
4 The corrected reliability would be lesser than 0.4

Ans. (3)

Exp. The corrected reliability would be greater than 0.4 and lesser than 0.8.

The Spearman–Brown prediction formula, also known as the Spearman–Brown prophecy formula, is a formula relating psychometric reliability to test length and used by psychometricians to predict the reliability of a test after changing the test length. The formula for calculate reliability is: r full = 2 (r half)/ 1 + r half

$r = 2 \times 0.4 / 1 + 0.4 = 0.8 / 1.4 = 0.57$.

The corrected reliability was calculated as 0.57, which is greater than 0.4 and lesser than 0.8.

48 Which of the following statement is true for tests with dichotomous items ?

1 Chronbach Alpha is greater than Kuder-Richardson reliability
2 Chronbach Alpha is smaller than Kuder-Richardson reliability
3 Chronbach Alpha and Kuder-Richardson reliability are equal
4 Chronbach Alpha may be greater or smaller than Kuder-Richardson reliability

Ans. (3)

Exp. Cronbach Alpha and Kuder-Richardson reliability are equal.

Both Kuder-Richardson (KR20) and Cronbach's alpha are measures of internal consistency. Internal consistency is the degree of interrelationship or homogeneity among the items on a test, such that they are consistent with one another and measuring the same thing.

Kuder–Richardson formula 20 (K-R 20) and Kuder–Richardson formula 21 (K-R 21) is used for assessing the internal consistency reliability of a test or subtest made up of dichotomous variables. Cronbach's alpha is a measure of the average strength of association between all possible pairs of items contained within a set of items. Under ideal circumstances (e.g., no missing data, unidimensionality of items) and with dichotomous or binary items, KR20 and Cronbach's alpha should essentially be the same.

49 For which of the following types of tests interscorer reliability is relevant ?

I. Objective personality inventories
II. Projective tests
III. Achievement tests with descriptive items
IV. Intelligence tests

Select the correct answer using the codes given below.

1 I and II   2 II and IV
3 I and III   4 II and III

Ans. (4)

Exp. The interscorer reliability is relevant in Projective tests and Achievement tests with descriptive items.

Interscorer or interrater reliability is the extent to which independent evaluators produce similar ratings in judging the same abilities or characteristics in the same target person or object. It is often expressed as a correlation coefficient. If consistency is high, a researcher can be confident that similarly trained individuals would likely produce similar scores on targets of the same kind. If consistency is low, there is little confidence that the obtained scores could be reproduced with a different set of raters.

Projective tests purportedly expose certain aspects of the personality of individuals that are impossible to measure by means of an objective test and are much more reliable at uncovering 'protected' or unconscious personality traits or features.

An achievement test is a standardised test that is designed to measure an individual's level of knowledge in a particular area. Unlike an aptitude test which measures a person's ability to learn something, an achievement test focuses specifically on how much a person knows about a specific topic or area such as Math, Geography, or Science.

50 If two groups are administered the same test with a time gap of eight weeks, we would be able to compute

1 Test-retest reliability
2 Parallel form reliability
3 Interscorer reliability
4 None of the above reliabilities can be computed

Ans. (4)

Exp. If two groups are administered the same test with a time gap of eight weeks, we would not be able to compute any of the given reliability test.

Test retest reliability used to assess the consistency of a measure from one term to another. In fact interval between test-retest normally should be not less than 15 days. However, as per the literature available in most of the studies normally it is between 15 to 30 days. The sample size and its type may affect the decision on interval. For older people and children it may be shorter as they easily forget.

Parallel forms reliability used to assess the consistency of the results of two tests constructed in the same way from the same content domain. It is administered simultaneously one after the other. There is no time gap.

Interscorer reliability used to assess the degree to which different raters give constant estimates of same phenomenon. The time gap of 8 weeks is not required in this test.

PAPER III

1 Three A's - Achievement, Affiliation and Aggression are reflected in

1 emotion
2 motivation
3 ambition
4 expectation

Ans. (2)

Exp. Three A's – Achievement, Affiliation and Aggression is reflected in motivation.

Motivation is the impetus that gives purpose or direction to behavior and operates in humans at a conscious or unconscious level. Motives are frequently divided into (a) physiological, primary, or organic motives, such as hunger, thirst, and need for sleep; and (b) personal, social, or secondary motives, such as affiliation, competition, and individual interests and goals.

Achievement motives : It is the desire to perform well and be successful and to overcome obstacles and master difficult challenges.

Affiliation motives : It is the need to be with other people which is revealed through one's attraction to others through friendship, sociability or group membership.

Aggression motives : It is the intense frustrations after high expectations. Verbal and nonverbal insults, fear, and anxiety lead to aggression.

2 A fifth test was added to an established selection test battery of four tests. The old and new versions were correlated to an external criterion of job proficiency. The significant change in R^2 was noted. This provided an evidence for

1 internal consistency of the fifth test with the earlier four tests
2 construct validity of the fifth test
3 reliability of the selection test battery of five tests
4 incremental validity of the fifth test

Ans. (4)

Exp. A fifth test was added to an established selection test battery of four tests. The old and new versions were correlated to an external criterion of job proficiency. The significant change in R 2 was noted. This provided an evidence for incremental validity of the fifth test.

Incremental validity is the type of validity that is used to determine whether a new psychometric assessment will increase the predictive ability beyond that provided by an existing method of assessment. Here, the old and new versions were correlated where significant change in R2 was noted, that increased the predictive validity beyond the existing method of assessment.

3 Which of the following scaling method/s has/have been proposed by LL Thurstone ?

I. Cumulative scale
II. Paired Comparison Method
III. Scale Discrimination Technique
IV. Equal Appearing Intervals

Select the correct answer using the codes given below

1 Only II
2 II and III
3 II and IV
4 I, II and IV

Ans. (3)

Exp. The scaling methods proposed by LL Thurstone are Paired Comparison Method and Equal Appearing Intervals.

Paired Comparison Method: Paired comparison method involves pair wise comparison i.e. comparing entities in pair to judge which is preferable or has a certain level of some property.

Equal Appearing Intervals: Equal Appearing Intervals is a technique of attitude measurement. On the assumption that any attitude involves a continuum ranging from the strongest possible appreciation of value at one extreme to the strongest possible deprecation of that value at the others.

4 The kind of brain cells involved in observational learning are known as

1 Glial Cells
2 Myelin Sheath
3 Mirror Neuron
4 Golgi body

Ans. (3)

Exp. The brain cells involved in observational learning are known as Mirror neurons.

Mirror neuron is a type of cell in the brains of certain animals (including humans) that responds in the same way to a given action (e.g., grasping an object) whether the animal performs the action itself or sees another animal (not necessarily of the same species) perform the action.

5 Given below are two statements, one is labelled as Assertion (A) and the other labelled as Reason (R).

Assertion (A) Memory for autobiographical information and for life experiences is called autobiographical memory.

Reason (R) It relates to the knowledge about where and when one is born, his/her educational history and places one lived in.

Codes

1 Both (A) and (R) are true and (R) is the correct explanation of (A)
2 Both (A) and (R) are true, but (R) is not the correct explanation of (A)
3 (A) is true, but (R) is false
4 (A) is false, but (R) is true

Ans. (2)

➲ *Exp.* Both (A) and (R) are true, but (R) is not the correct explanation of (A)

Memory for autobiographical information and for life experiences is called autobiographical memory. It is a person's memory for episodes or experiences that occurred in his or her own life. Autobiographical memory can consist of information stored in episodic memory (i.e., of events experienced at a particular time and place), semantic memory (i.e., of knowledge of general facts and concepts that give meaning to information), or a mix of the two.

It relates to the knowledge about where and when one is born, his/her educational history and places one lived in. This is true and explains the autobiographical information is called autobiographical memory, but does not explain why the memory for life experiences is called autobiographical memory. So this is partially explained.

6 Neural network model of memory suggests the following

I. Inter connectedness of neural units.

II. Information is processed quickly.

III. Information in memory is not located in specific parts of brain.

Codes

1 I and II

2 I and III

3 II and III

4 I, II and III

Ans. (4)

➲ *Exp.* Neural network model of memory suggests the following:

Inter connectedness of neural units: The neural network model assumes that neurons form a complex network with other neurons, forming a highly interconnected network; each neuron is characterized by the activation value (how much energy it takes to activate that neuron), and the connection between two neurons is characterized by the weight value (how strong the connection between those neurons is).

Information is processed quickly: The parallel distributed processing (PDP) model is an example of a network model of memory. "Parallel processing" is a computing term; unlike serial processing (performing one operation at a time), parallel processing allows hundreds of operations to be completed at once—in parallel. Therefore, the information is processed quickly in the neural network model of memory.

Information in memory is not located in specific parts of brain: Neural network model of memory is a technique for modeling the neural changes in the brain that underlie cognition and perception in which a large number of simple hypothetical neural units are connected to one another. These neural units are not located in specific parts of the brain.

7 Match the List I with List II and select the correct answer from the codes given below:

List I (Memory phenomena)	List II (Descriptions)
A. Method of Loci	I. Reducing what is to be remembered to a few key points and then encoding these with an acronym.
B. Elaboration mnemonic	II. Concepts are presented by the nodes of a network and relationship between concepts by link between the nodes.
C. Associative network	III. Visualising a walk through the rooms in a 'memory theatre', leaving one of the key topics at each location.
D. Reduction mnemonic	IV. Remembering something by associating each item with each line of rhyme.

Codes

	A	B	C	D		A	B	C	D
1	III	IV	I	II	2	III	IV	II	I
3	IV	II	III	I	4	I	II	IV	III

Ans. (2)

➲ *Exp.* The correct matching is A-III, B-IV, C-II, D-I.

Method of Loci is visualising a walk through the rooms in a 'memory theatre', leaving one of the key topics at each location. It is an effectivemnemonic device, or a trick to aid in memory storage and retrieval.

Elaborative mnemonic is remembering something by associating each item with each line of rhyme. Mnemonics are useful tools for memorising factual information. The 12 cranial nerves, in order, are olfactory, optic, oculomotor, trochlear, trigeminal, abducens, facial, auditory, glossopharyngeal, vagus, sensory (accessory), and hypoglossal.

Associative network is when concepts are presented by the nodes of a network and relationship between concepts by link between the nodes. Associative networks are cognitive models that incorporate long-known principles of association to represent key features of human memory.

Reduction mnemonic is reducing what is to be remembered to a few key points and then encoding these with an acronym. It can be used for remembering lists by creating an easily remembered acronym, or, taking each of the initial letters of the list members, create a memorable phrase in which the words with the same acronym as the material.

8 Which of the following strategies is classified as 'problem- focused' rather than 'emotion focused'?

1 Engaging in cognitive reappraisal
2 Learning techniques of relaxation
3 Seeking social support
4 Engaging in physical exercise

Ans. (1)

Exp. Engaging in cognitive reappraisal is classified as 'problem-focused' rather than 'emotion-focused'.

Problem-focused is a stress-management strategy in which a person directly confronts a stressor in an attempt to decrease or eliminate it. This may involve generating possible solutions to a problem, confronting others who are responsible for or otherwise associated with the stressor, and other forms of instrumental action.

Cognitive reappraisal suggests that cognitive evaluation is involved in the generation of each and every emotion. Evaluation includes both a primary appraisal and a secondary appraisal. The primary appraisal is the initial evaluation of a situation's relevance to one's moral norms and personal preferences and to the likelihood of reaching one's goals. It is followed by second appraisal which is one's evaluation of his or her ability to cope with the consequences of an interaction with the environment.

9 Match the List I with List II and select the correct answer from the codes given below

List I (Motivational concept)	List II (Example)
A. Existence need	I. Expectancy
B. Hygiene factor	II. Recognition
C. Motivators	III. Security
D. Process theories	IV. Working conditions

Codes

	A	B	C	D
1	IV	III	II	I
2	IV	III	I	II
3	III	IV	II	I
4	III	IV	I	II

Ans. (3)

Exp. The correct matching is A-III, B-IV, C-II, D-I.

Existence needs concern our basic material requirements for living. These include what Maslow categorised as physiological needs and safety-related needs. The example of existence need is Security.

Hygiene factors, or extrinsic motivators, tend to represent more tangible, basic needs—i.e., the kinds of needs included in the existence category of needs in the ERG theory or in the lower levels of Maslow's hierarchy of needs. The example of hygiene factor is Working condition.

Motivation factors, or intrinsic motivators, tend to represent less tangible, more emotional needs—i.e., the kinds of needs identified in the "relatedness" and "growth" categories of needs in the ERG theory and in the higher levels of Maslow's hierarchy of needs. Intrinsic motivators include challenging work, recognition, relationships, and growth potential. Managers need to recognize that while these needs may fall outside the more traditional scope of what a workplace ought to provide, they can be critical to strong individual and team performance. The example of Motivators is Recognition.

Process theories of motivation try to explain why behaviours are initiated. These theories focus on the mechanism by which we choose a target, and the effort that we exert to 'hit' the target. The example of process theories is Expectancy theory.

10 A person after seeing the different colours of water in the sea of Kanyakumari has written a poem. This may be due to

1 Heuristics
2 Imaginal thought
3 Motoric thought
4 Prepositional thought

Ans. (4)

Exp. A person after seeing the different colours of water in the sea of Kanyakumari has written a poem. This may be due to Prepositional thought.

The affordances of prepositions in creative thinking is called 'prepositional thinking'. It begins with Ross Gibson's assertion that the experience of creative research is dynamic and complex: involving immersion, exertion, and reflection. It involve a set of working examples, as to how to think with, in, through prepositions, how to use these small words productively and creatively in writing and research. How to reach for and play with prepositions 'in order to write our way across/over/through bodies, places, times, and wounds'. Prepositions give us language of thought, of process, they reveal what we do not know; but they also are an invitation.

11 One of the following types of love does not belong to Rollo May's classification of love

1 Eros
2 Philia
3 Agape
4 Narcissism

Ans. (4)

Exp. The type of love that does not belong to Rollo May's classification of love is Narcissism.

Rollo Reece May was an American existential psychologist. He was the author of the influential book 'Love and Will', which was published in 1969. May's thoughts on love is documented mainly through his book 'Love and Will', which focuses on love and sex in human behaviour. He specifies 5 particular types of love, however, he believes that they should not be separate, but society has separated love and sex into two different ideologies. The five types of love are:

Sex– lust, tension release

Eros – procreative love, savouring, experiential

Philia – brotherly love, liking

Agape – uselfish love, devotion to the welfare of others

Authentic love – incorporates all other types of love.

12 A psychologist employed in the school, at the instruction of school authorities, administered an IQ test to the school children and displayed the scores on the notice board.
This is an

1 ethically incorrect practice, since it violates confidentiality.
2 ethically incorrect practice, since it violates informed consent.
3 ethically correct practice in view of the transparent policies of the school.
4 ethically correct practice provided the IQ scores are not taken into consideration, while giving grades.

Ans. (1)

Exp. A psychologist employed in the school, at the instruction of school authorities, administered an IQ test to the school children and displayed the scores on the notice board. This is an ethically incorrect practice, since it violates confidentiality.

Confidentiality is a principle of professional ethics requiring providers of mental health care or medical care to limit the disclosure of a patient's identity, his or her condition or treatment, and any data entrusted to professionals during assessment, diagnosis, and treatment.

Similar protection is given to research participants and survey respondents against unauthorised access to information they reveal in confidence.

13 Given below are two statements, one is labelled as Assertion (A) and the other labelled as Reason (R).

Assertion (A) The method of paired comparison is especially suited for scaling the large number of stimuli.

Reason (R) The method of paired comparison usually employs law of comparative judgements for getting scale values.

Codes

1 Both (A) and (R) are true and (R) is the correct explanation of (A)
2 Both (A) and R are true, but (R) is not the correct explanation of (A)
3 (A) is true, but (R) is false
4 (A) is false, but (R) is true

Ans. (4)

Exp. (A) is false, but (R) is true.

The method of paired comparison is especially suited for scaling the large number of stimuli is not true. This is because it can avoid observers to compare every possible pairs since the number of paired comparisons for n stimuli is $n(n-1)/2$ which becomes prohibitive for large values of n.

The method of paired comparison usually employs law of comparative judgements for getting scale values. The law of comparative judgement was conceived by L. L. Thurstone. The essential idea behind the LCJ is that it can be used to scale a collection of stimuli based on simple comparisons between stimuli two at a time: that is, based on a series of paired comparisons. Therefore, the reason statement is true.

14 Which of the following is/are the process theories of work motivation?

I. Mc Clelland's theory of needs.
II. Herzberg's two-factor theory of work motivation.
III. Porter-Lawler's performance satisfaction theory.
IV. Vroom's expectancy theory.

Codes

1 Only IV   2 I and III
3 II and IV   4 III and IV

Ans. (4)

Exp. The correct codes are III and IV.

Process theories of motivation try to explain why behaviors are initiated. These theories focus on the mechanism by which we choose a target, and the effort that we exert to 'hit' the target.

The following are the process theories of work motivation:

Porter-Lawler's performance satisfaction theory: The Porter and Lawler theory of motivation is based on the assumption that rewards cause satisfaction and that sometimes performance produces reward. They hypothesize that the relationship between satisfaction and performance is linked by another variable rewards.

Vroom's expectancy theory: Vroom's expectancy theory assumes that behavior results from conscious choices among alternatives whose purpose it is to maximize pleasure and to minimize pain. Vroom realized that an employee's performance is based on individual factors such as personality, skills, knowledge, experience and abilities.

15 The technique involved in guidance which is called 'The heart of the guidance programme' is

1 the case study   2 the interview
3 the cumulative record   4 aptitude test

Ans. (4)

Exp. Aptitude test is 'The heart of guidance programme'. Without it, guidance is incomplete. It helps students to resolve their educational as well as personal and vocational problems.

It makes an effective use of the information collected about the individual or the group to provide insight into the problems for a better guidance programme. It may be viewed as an applied art that seeks deliberately to change the behaviour of an individual.

16 Match the List I with List II and select the correct answer from the codes given below

List I (Types of Development)	List II (Change in Person)
A. Social development	I. Changes in body structure and function overtime.
B. Emotional development	II. Changes in mental processes become more complex and differentiated
C. Physical development	III. Changes overtime in the way we relate to others.
D. Cognitive development	IV. Changes in hormones that takes place as one grows.

Codes

	A	B	C	D		A	B	C	D
1	II	IV	III	I	2	III	IV	I	II
3	II	III	IV	I	4	III	I	II	IV

Ans. (2)

Exp. The correct matching is A-III, B-IV, C-I, D-II.

Social development refers to changes overtime in the way we relate to others. It is about improving the well-being of every individual in society so they can reach their full potential.

Emotional development is changes in hormones that take place as one grows. While the changes that occur during puberty can be seen on the outside, adrenarche is mainly a period of psychological and emotional development.

Physical development is changes in body structure and function overtime. It also involves brain development, which not only enables childhood motor coordination but also greater coordination between emotions and planning in adulthood, as our brains is not done developing in infancy or childhood.

Cognitive development is changes in mental processes become more complex and differentiated. It includes mental processes, thinking, learning, and understanding, and it doesn't stop in childhood.

17 Given below are two statements, one is labelled as Assertion (A) and the other labelled as Reason (R).

Assertion (A) Teacher is effective, when her students had good achievement/score well in the examination.

Reason (R) The teacher does not practices / gives corporeal punishment to her students.

Codes

1 Both (A) and (R) are true and (R) is the correct explanation of (A)
2 Both (A) and (R) are true, but (R) is not the correct explanation of (A)
3 (A) is true, but (R) is false
4 (A) is false, but (R) is true

Ans. (3)

Exp. (A) is true, but (R) is false.

Teacher is effective, when her students had good achievement/score well in the examination. If the teacher is effective the students will have good achievements and if students perform well, the teacher would not punish.

The teacher does not practice / gives corporeal punishment to her students. This is false, as in some cases the teacher gives corporeal punishment to her students, which is ethically and morally wrong.

18 Given below are two statements, one is labelled as Assertion (A) and the other labelled as Reason (R).

Assertion (A) Signal detection theory measures two components of a person's ability to detect signals - perceptual sensitivity and decision criterion.

Reason (R) Studies of vigilance have revealed that the ability to detect an event is dependent on various factors such as training and expectations.

Codes

1 Both (A) and (R) are true and (R) is the correct explanation of (A)
2 Both (A) and (R) are true, but (R) is not the correct explanation of (A)
3 (A) is true, but (R) is false
4 (A) is false, but (R) true

Ans. (2)

Exp. Both (A) and (R) are true, but (R) is not the correct explanation of (A).

Signal detection theory measures two components of a person's ability to detect signals - perceptual sensitivity and decision criterion. The ability to identify a stimulus when it is embedded in a distracting background is called signal detection theory. Whether a stimulus is consciously perceived is determined by the strength of sensory processing and top-down factors such as expectations and attention.

Signal detection theory (SDT) provides a framework for decomposing perceptual performance into two statistics: d', the perceptual sensitivity or the sensitivity of the system to signal occurrence in signal-to-noise ratio (SNR) units, and a decision criteria or an overall bias to report signal presence, modelled as the criterion, c.

Studies of vigilance have revealed that the ability to detect an event is dependent on various factors such as training and expectations. This is true because when the detecting system is a human being, characteristics such as training, experience, expectations, physiological state (e.g., fatigue) and other factors can affect the threshold applied. However, it does not explain why the signal detection theory measures perceptual sensitivity and decision criteria.

19 Match the List I with List II and select the correct answer from the codes given below

List I (Theory)	List II (Characteristics)
A. Humanistic theory	I. We may acquire money because it protects us.
B. Cognitive theory	II. People are motivated by the conscious desire for personal growth.
C. Drive-reduction theory	III. People represent their worlds mentally.
D. Psychoanalytic theory	IV. Behaviour depends upon instinctual forces.

Codes

	A	B	C	D		A	B	C	D
1	III	II	IV	I	2	IV	I	III	II
3	II	III	I	IV	4	I	II	III	IV

Ans. (3)

Exp. The correct matching is A-II, B-III, C-I, D-IV.

Humanistic theory states that people are motivated by the conscious desire for personal growth. It derives largely from ideas associated with existentialism and phenomenology and focuses on individuals' capacity to make their own choices, create their own style of life, and actualize themselves in their own way.

Cognitive theory states that people represent their worlds mentally. It is the theory of mind that focuses on mental activities, such as perceiving, attending, thinking, remembering, evaluating, planning, language, and creativity, especially a theory that suggests a model for the various processes involved.

Drive reduction theory states that we may acquire money because it protects us. It is a major theory of motivation in the behaviorist learning theory tradition. "Drive" is defined as motivation that arises due to a psychological or physiological need. It works as an internal stimulus that motivates an individual to sate the drive.

Psychoanalytic theory states that behaviour depends upon instinctual forces. It is the diverse complex of assumptions and constructs underlying the approach known as psychoanalysis. Classically, the term refers specifically to the formulations of Sigmund Freud.

20 According to Elizabeth Kubler-Ross most people experience predictable stages, when they face impending death. Which is the correct sequence of the stages ?

1 Anger, Sadness, Bargaining, Denial, Acceptance
2 Bargaining, Anger, Denial, Sadness, Acceptance
3 Acceptance, Anger, Bargaining, Denial, Sadness
4 Denial, Anger, Bargaining, Sadness, Acceptance

Ans. (4)

Exp. The correct sequence of the stages is Denial, Anger, Bargaining, Sadness, Acceptance.

Kübler-Ross originally developed stages to describe the process patients with terminal illness go through as they come to terms with their own deaths; it was later applied to grieving friends and family as well, who seemed to undergo a similar process. The stages include:

Denial : The first reaction is denial. In this stage, individuals believe the diagnosis is somehow mistaken, and cling to a false, preferable reality.

Anger : When the individual recognizes that denial cannot continue, they become frustrated, especially at proximate individuals.

Bargaining : The third stage involves the hope that the individual can avoid a cause of grief. Usually, the negotiation for an extended life is made in exchange for a reformed lifestyle.

Sadness/Depression : During the fourth stage, the individual despairs at the recognition of their mortality. In this state, the individual may become silent, refuse visitors and spend much of the time mournful and sullen.

Acceptance : In this last stage, individuals embrace mortality or inevitable future, or that of a loved one, or other tragic event. People dying may precede the survivors in this state, which typically comes with a calm, retrospective view for the individual, and a stable condition of emotions.

21 Match the List I with List II and select the correct answer from the codes given below:

List I (Disorders)	List II (Description)
A. Prosopagnosia	I. Ignoring one half of visual space and not perceiving objectes in that field
B. Unilateral visual neglect	II. Inability to recognise faces
C. Agnosia	III. Impairment in realistic self appraisal
D. Anosognosia	IV. Failure to recognise objects

Codes

	A	B	C	D		A	B	C	D
1	I	IV	III	II	2	III	II	I	IV
3	III	I	IV	II	4	II	I	IV	III

Ans. (4)

Exp. The correct matching is A-II, B-I, C-IV, D-III.

Prosopagnosia is the inability to recognise faces. It is also called face blindness. It is a cognitive disorder of face perception in which the ability to recognise familiar faces, including one's own face (self-recognition), is impaired, while other aspects of visual processing (e.g., object discrimination) and intellectual functioning (e.g., decision-making) remain intact.

Unilateral visual neglect is ignoring one half of visual space and not perceiving objects in that field. It is an attention disorder that arises as a result of injury to the cerebral cortex. It is also commonly known as contralateral neglect, hemispatial neglect, visuospatial neglect, spatial neglect, or hemineglect.

Agnosia is failure to recognise objects. It is a neurological condition in which a patient is unable to recognise and identify objects, persons, or sounds using one or more of their senses in spite of normally functioning senses. It is a sensory disorder as person is unable to process sensory information.

Anosognosia is impairment in realistic self-appraisal. It is a lack of ability to perceive the realities of one's own condition. It's a person's inability to accept that they have a condition that matches up with their symptoms or a formal diagnosis.

22 Match the List I with List II and select the correct answer from the codes given below:

List I (Types of Attention)	List II (Description)
A. Focused attention	I. Attention can be attention shifted internally and which does not require changes in orientation or eye movements
B. Overt attention	II. Attention dealing attention with some specific inputs and exclude others
C. Divided attention	III. Attention that is attention dependent on orienting responses and eye movements
D. Covert attention	IV. Attention shared between more than one simultaneous tasks

Codes

	A	B	C	D		A	B	C	D
1	II	IV	I	III	2	III	IV	II	I
3	I	II	IV	III	4	II	III	IV	I

Ans. (4)

Exp. The correct matching is A-II, B-III, C-IV, D-I.

Focused attention is the attention dealing with some specific inputs and exclude others. Focused attention is the brain's ability to concentrate its attention on a target stimulus for any period of time. It is a type of attention that makes it possible to quickly detect relevant stimuli.

Over attention is the attention that is dependent on orienting responses and eye movements. Overt attention is the characteristic activity of a perceptual system, not a processing of data coming in over a channel of sense. Perhaps the clearest example of this is the ability to look at one object in the environment but pay attention to another or others.

Divided attention is the attention shared between more than one simultaneous tasks. Divided attention is a type of simultaneous attention that allows us to process different information sources and successfully carry out multiple tasks at a time

Covert attention is the attention that can be shifted internally and which does not require changes in orientation or eye movements. Covert attention is attention directed to a location that is different from that on which the eyes are fixated.

23 Which of the following is the correct sequence of describes the cognitive triad of depression ?

1 Helplessness, Sleeplessness, Worthlessness
2 Thoughtlessness, Worthlessness, Sleeplessness
3 Hopelessness, Worthlessness, Thoughtlessness
4 Hopelessness, Worthlessness, Helplessness

Ans. (4)

Exp. The correct sequence is: Hopelessness, Worthlessness, Helplessness

Beck proposed that depression was the result of a cognitive triad of negative thoughts including hopelessness (e.g., 'It will always be this way'), worthlessness (e.g., 'I don't deserve to be happy'), and helplessness (e.g., 'There is nothing I can do to make it better').

24 The speech delivered by Ex-Prime Minister of India at UN was enjoyed by delegates. The speech consisted of the formation as

1 Phonemes, Words, Morphemes, Phrases
2 Phonemes, Morphemes, Words, Phrases
3 Morphemes, Phonemes, Words, Phrases
4 Morphemes, Phonemes, Phrases, Words

Ans. (2)

Exp. The speech delivered by Ex-Prime Minister of India at UN was enjoyed by delegates. The speech consisted of the formation as Phonemes, Morphemes, Words, Phrases.

A Phoneme is a basic unit of a language's phonology, which is combined with other phonemes to form meaningful units such as words or morphemes.

Morpheme is the smallest unit of meaning but will not necessarily stand on its own.

In linguistics, a word is the smallest element that may be uttered in isolation with semantic or pragmatic content (with literal or practical meaning).

In everyday speech, a phrase may refer to any group of words. In linguistics, a phrase is a group of words (sometimes a single word) that form a constituent and so function as a single unit in the syntax of a sentence.

25 Many responses are possible in any learning situation. That response, which brings about reinforcement rapidly with least amount of effort is most likely to occur first. If that is blocked, the animal will prefer the next shortest route and so on. This is known as

1 habit strength
2 generalised habit strength
3 habit family hierarchy
4 frustration drive stimulus

Ans. (3)

Exp. Many responses are possible in any learning situation. That response, which brings about reinforcement rapidly with least amount of effort is most likely to occur first. If that is blocked, the animal will prefer the next shortest route and so on. This is known as habit family hierarchy.

Habit family hierarchy is the concept that several different routes to the same goal—or more generally, responses to the same stimulus—are available, each having a particular strength that determines its arrangement in a preferential order and hence its potential for expression.

26 Different item functioning probably reveals

1 administration bias
2 construct bias
3 interpretation bias
4 predictive bias

Ans. (2)

Exp. Different item functioning probably reveals construct bias.

Different item functioning is a statistical characteristic of an item that shows the extent to which the item might be measuring different abilities for members of separate subgroups. It refers to differences in the functioning of items across groups, oftentimes demographic, which are matched on the latent trait or more generally the attribute being measured by the items or test. Test items need to accurately tap into the construct of interest in order to derive meaningful ability level groups.

Construct bias refers to whether a test accurately measures what it was designed to measure. Construct bias occurs when the construct measured is not identical across cultures or when behaviours that characterise the construct are not identical across cultures. This type of bias can stem from several sources; for example the definition of a construct may show an incomplete overlap across cultures.

27 Immunity system's functioning is most likely to increase when

1 People just share about their problems
2 They are taught represser coping styles
3 They practice effective stress management techniques
4 The general adaptation syndrome begins

Ans. (3)

Exp. Immunity system's functioning is most likely to increase when they practice effective stress management techniques.

The immune system is a collection of billions of cells that travel through the bloodstream. They move in and out of tissues and organs, defending the body against foreign bodies (antigens), such as bacteria, viruses and cancerous cells. Stress can also have an indirect effect on the immune system as a person may use unhealthy behavioural coping strategies to reduce their stress, such as drinking and smoking. Stress is linked to headaches; infectious illness (e.g. 'flu); cardiovascular disease; diabetes, asthma and gastric ulcers. By practicing effective stress management techniques, immunity system's functioning can be enhanced. Research has suggested that using stress management strategies like engaging in positive emotions as a strong faith, social support and other stress reduction strategies seem able to retard or even reverse the ill-effects of stress on immune system.

28 Which of the following methods of probing increases the probability of eliciting increased information from eyewitness ?

1 Direct probing
2 Open-ended questions
3 Cognitive interview
4 Prompted recollection of events

Ans. (3)

Exp. Cognitive Interview (CI) is the method of probing which increases the probability of eliciting increased information from eyewitness.

It is a method of interviewing in which eyewitnesses and victims report what they remember from a crime scene. Using four retrievals, the primary focus of the cognitive interview is to make witnesses and victims of a situation aware of all the events that transpired.

The CI aids in minimising misinterpretation together with uncertainty that is otherwise seen in the questioning process of a standard police interview. Cognitive interview reliably enhances the process of memory retrieval and has been found to elicit memories without generating inaccurate accounts of information or confabulations.

29 Situations in which each person can increase his/her individual gains by acting in a certain way, but if all (or most) persons act that same way, the outcomes experienced by all is reduced. This phenomenon is known as

1 Social loafing
2 Social dilemmas
3 Reciprocity
4 Conflict

Ans. (2)

Exp. Situations in which each person can increase his/her individual gains by acting in a certain way, but if all (or most) persons act that same way, the outcomes experienced by all is reduced. This phenomenon is known as Social dilemmas.

Social dilemmas are situations in which collective interests are at odds with private interests. Such situations arise when faced with prioritising either short-term selfish interests or the long-term interests of a group, organisation, or society. Many of the most challenging issues, from the interpersonal to the intergroup, are at their core social dilemmas.

30 Which of the following beliefs does not underly a person's ability to regulate his/her feelings in order to lessen negative effect of stressful conditions ?

1 People can have the most pleasure if they give up short-term pleasures
2 People should strive to experience emotions that are pro-individual and prosocial
3 People should strive to experience no emotion
4 The best emotions to feel are those that are appropriate to the situation, including painful ones

Ans. (3)

Exp. People should strive to experience no emotion does not underlie a person's ability to regulate his/her feelings in order to lesson negative effect of stressful conditions.

'Emotion regulation' is a term generally used to describe a person's ability to effectively manage and respond to an emotional experience. People unconsciously use emotion regulation strategies to cope with difficult situations many times throughout each day. Regulating one's feelings in order to lesson negative effects of stressful conditions is known as self-regulation. Successful emotion regulation is often reflected in higher levels of positive emotions than negative emotions.

This does not mean the complete elimination of negative emotions. The negative effect (as a subjective experience of negative emotions) is necessary and adaptive in certain situations. For example, fear motivates a person to participate in safer behaviors; frustration may be necessary when working toward difficult goals. Successful emotion regulation processes may also involve, paradoxically, the triggering of negative emotions, as well as concurrent positive and negative emotions. Nonetheless, in general, reports of higher affective well-being indicate more successful emotion regulation

31 In treating which of the following conditions 'mand' is used as the central principle of behaviour modification?

1 Anxiety
2 Autism
3 Anhedonia
4 ADHD

Ans. (2)

Exp. In Autism, 'mand' is used as the central principle of behaviour modification. The mand repertoire is essential for early language learners and is therefore of clinical importance.

Mands increase the probability of obtaining access to specific items, activities, actions, information, etc., when access to those stimuli is delivered or controlled by another person. In addition, manding helps establish the reciprocal speaker and listener roles that are essential for increasing verbal competence.

Children with autism frequently present with limited interests and often do not readily learn to emit mands without specific teaching. Furthermore, children with autism do not readily acquire mands as a result of tact or receptive discrimination training alone.

As a result, the development of a mand repertoire and its relevance to early language training for children with language delays and disorders, specifically those with autism, has been documented in the behaviour analytic literature. The benefits of mand training for children with autism often include a reduction in maladaptive behaviour, an increase in social initiations, and an increase in spontaneous language.

32 Match the List I with List II and select the correct answer from the codes given below

List I (Styles of Interrogati)	List II (Brief Descriptions)
A. Counseling style	I. Helpful, ingratiating and fatherly approach as a way to obtain a confession
B. Dominant style	II. Brusque, factual and formal attempt to gather evidence
C. Collusive Style	III. A friendly, unemotional and non-judgmental effort to obtain accurate evidence
D. Business like style	IV. Impatient and emotional attempt to get the suspect to confess

Codes

	A	B	C	D		A	B	C	D
1	I	IV	II	III	2	II	III	IV	I
3	III	IV	I	II	4	IV	II	III	I

Ans. (3)

Exp. The correct matching is A-III, B-IV, C-I, D-II.

Counseling style is a friendly, unemotional and non-judgmental effort to obtain accurate evidence. It is characterised as cooperative, unemotional and non-judgmental effort aimed at securing evidence.

Dominant style is impatient and emotional attempt to get the suspect to confess. It is characterised as confrontational, impatient and emotional effort aimed at securing a confession.

Collusive style is helpful, ingratiating and fatherly approach as a way to obtain a confession. It is characterised as cooperative, helpful, ingratiating, paternalistic, and problem solving approach aimed at securing a confession.

Business like style is brusque, factual and formal attempt to gather evidence. It is characterised as confrontational, brusque, factual and formal approach aimed at securing evidence.

33 Match the List I with List II and select the correct answer from the codes given below :

List I (Concept)	List II (Psychologist)
A. Four A's of Schizophrenia	I. Anna Freud
B. Theory of Ego-defence Mechanism	II. E Blenler
C. Separation Anxiety	III. H Selye
D. General Adaptation Syndrome	IV. Otto Rank

Codes

	A	B	C	D		A	B	C	D
1	II	I	IV	III	2	II	IV	I	III
3	IV	I	III	II	4	IV	II	III	I

Ans. *(1)*

Exp. The correct matching is A-II, B-I, C-IV, D-III

Four A's of Schizophrenia was given by Eugene Bleuler. The fundamental symptoms, which are virtually present through all the course of the disorder, are also known as the famous Bleuler's four A's: Alogia, Autism, Ambivalence, and Affect blunting.

Theory of Ego-defense Mechanism was given by Anna Freud. Anna Freud identified and discussed ten defense mechanisms as being commonly recognized in the field of psychoanalysis: regression, repression, reaction-formation, isolation, undoing, projection, introjection, turning against the self, reversal, and sublimation.

Separation Anxiety was given by Otto Rank. Between 1924 and 1939 Otto Rank put forward three major elements of a comprehensive theoretical edifice that has yet to be fully articulated. These are conceptually linked by the fundamental importance of person-environment mergence and separation. Rank's theory of emotions highlights anxiety as the affect of separation, and guilt as the feeling that binds the individual to others.

General Adaptation Syndrome was given by Hans Selye. General adaptation syndrome (GAS) is a term that describes the physiological changes the body automatically goes through when it responds to stress. First developed by Hans Selye in 1936, GAS is considered to be a pioneering modern biological formulation of stress.

34 Which one of the following does not belong to the mechanism of operant learning?

1 Events that follow an action
2 Involuntary response
3 Process that weakens or suppresses behaviour
4 Use of consequences to streng then behaviour

Ans. *(2)*

Exp. Involuntary response does not belong to the mechanism of operant learning.

Operant conditioning is a type of learning in which an individual's behaviour is modified by its consequences; the behaviour may change in form, frequency, or strength. Operant conditioning is a term that was coined by BF Skinner in 1937. The word operant refers to, 'an item of behaviour that is initially spontaneous, rather than a response to a prior stimulus, but whose consequences may reinforce or inhibit recurrence of that behaviour.'

35 The art of establishing trust, respect and cooperation in a relationship is referred to as

1 personal distance
2 continuation behaviour
3 use of humor
4 rapport

Ans. *(4)*

Exp. Rapport refers to the art of establishing trust, respect and cooperation in a relationship.

Rapport occurs when two or more people feel that they are in sync or on the same wavelength because they feel similar or relate well to each other. Rapport is theorised to include three behavioural components i.e. mutual attention, mutual positivity and coordination.

36 Given below are two statements, one is labelled as Assertion (A) and the other labelled as Reason (R).

Assertion (A) Individuals take high risk in mountaineering.

Reason (R) Intrinsic motivation is the desire to be effective and to perform a behaviour for its own sake.

Codes

1 Both (A) and (R) are true and (R) is the correct explanation of (A)
2 Both (A) and (R) are true, but (R) is not the correct explanation of (A)
3 (A) is true, but (R) is false
4 (A) is false, but (R) is true

Ans. *(1)*

Exp. Both (A) and (R) are true and (R) is the correct explanation of (A).

Individuals take high risk in mountaineering. Individual take high risk in mountaineering only when the person wants to climb it. No one from the outside world can motivate him/her to climb up. He/ she only climb if there is actual desire or internal motive.

Intrinsic motivation is the desire to be effective and to perform a behaviour for its own sake. Intrinsic motivation is motivation that comes from within. That doesn't depend on any extrinsic reward. This explains why individuals take high risk in mountainerring.

37 The procedure called 'semantic priming' is used to study, which of the following phenomena?

1 Signal detection ability
2 Field dependence -independence
3 Locus of control
4 Subliminal perception

Ans. *(4)*

Exp. The procedure called 'semantic priming' is used to study Subliminal Perception.

Subliminal perception is the registration of stimuli below the level of awareness, particularly stimuli that are too weak (or too rapid) for an individual to consciously perceive them.

38 Given below are two statements, one is labelled as Assertion (A) and the other labelled as Reason (R).

Assertion (A) Ingratiation is a technique for gaining compliance from other person in which requester first introduces himself/herself to the target person as an authority and then asks to comply his/her order.

Reason (R) Ingratiation induces liking in target person for requester and attempts to change target person's behaviour in one's favour.

Codes

1 Both (A) and (R) are true and (R) is the correct explanation of (A)
2 Both (A) and (R) are true, but (R) is not the correct explanation of (A)
3 (A) is true, but (R) is false
4 (A) is false, but (R) is true

Ans. (4)

Exp. (A) is false, but (R) is true.

Ingratiation is not a technique for gaining compliance from other person in which requester first introduces himself/herself to the target person as an authority and then asks to comply his/her order. This technique is known as obedience.

Ingratiation induces liking in target person for requester and attempts to change target person's behaviour in one's favour. Ingratiation is using efforts to win the liking and approval of other people, especially by deliberate impression management. Ingratiation is usually regarded as strategic, insincere, and manipulative.

Integration is a psychological technique in which an individual attempts to influence, manipulate or control another by becoming more attractive or likeable to their target. Therefore the assertion is false. The term ingratiation refers to behaviours that a person illicitly enacts to make others like him or her or think well of his or her qualities as a person.

There are many ways in which people can ingratiate themselves. One that is frequently used is to show interest in another person; ask questions, pay attention and single out the person so that you make him or her feel special. A second strategy is do favours or to help or assist a person. Thus R is true but A is false.

39 One of the following tests do not belong to self-concept instrumentation

1 Rosenberg Self-esteem Scale
2 Coppersmith self-esteem inventories
3 The Self-perception Inventory
4 Body-image Questionnaire

Ans. (4)

Exp. Body-image Questionnaire does not belong to self-concept instrumentation.

The Rosenberg Self-Esteem Scale is a tool for assessing global self-esteem. Psychologists and sociologists are common users for this instrument. Also, the instrument is a vital part of self-esteem measure in social science research and is mainly used adolescents.

The Coppersmith Self-Esteem Inventories (CSEI) have been taken by thousands of individuals. Findings from the two forms demonstrate the relationship of academic achievement to personal satisfaction in school and adult life. Normative data is available in both the Adult and School forms. The CSEI can be used for individual diagnosis, classroom screening and pre-post evaluation.

The Belbin Team Inventory is a behavioural test, also called the Belbin Self-Perception Inventory, Belbin Team Role Inventory, SPI or BTRSPI. It was devised by Meredith Belbin to measure preference for nine Team Roles, he had identified eight of those whilst studying numerous teams.

40 Our expectancies, learning, past experiences and cultural factors play a critical role in shaping our perception. This is well explained by

1 Information processing approach
2 Bottom-up processing approach
3 Top-down processing approach
4 Hierarchical processing approach

Ans. (3)

Exp. Our expectancies, learning, past experiences and cultural factors play a critical role in shaping our perception. This is well explained by Top-down processing approach. Top down processing can be seen as processing what one is perceiving using past information. It occurs when someone infers from a generalisation, law etc. to conclude something about a particular example, instance, case etc. Top-down processing is information processing in which an overall hypothesis about or general conceptualization of a stimulus is applied to and influences the analysis of incoming stimulus data.

41 Match the List I with List II and select the correct answer from the codes given below :

List I		List II	
A.	Inductive Reasoning	I.	Analysis and combination of thoughts
B.	Bottom-up Processing	II.	Interpretation of ideas and concepts
C.	Deductive Reasoning	III.	Developing a general principle
D.	Top-down Processing	IV.	Using a principle for conclusion

Codes

	A	B	C	D		A	B	C	D
1	I	III	IV	II	2	II	I	III	IV
3	III	I	IV	II	4	IV	II	III	I

Ans. (4)

Exp. The correct matching is A-IV, B- II, C-III, D-I.

Inductive Reasoning is using a principle for conclusion. It works the other way, moving from specific observations to broader generalizations and theories. Informally, we sometimes call this a "bottom up" approach. In inductive reasoning, we begin with specific observations and measures, begin to detect patterns and regularities, formulate some tentative hypotheses that we can explore, and finally end up developing some general conclusions or theories.

Bottom-up Processing is the interpretation of ideas and concepts. It is the information processing in which incoming stimulus data initiate and determine the higher level processes involved in their recognition, interpretation, and categorization.

Deductive Reasoning is developing a general principle. Sometimes this is informally called a "top-down" approach. We narrow down even further when we collect observations to address the hypotheses. This ultimately leads us to be able to test the hypotheses with specific data – a confirmation (or not) of our original theories.

Top-down Processing is analysis and combination of thoughts. It is the information processing in which an overall hypothesis about or general conceptualization of a stimulus is applied to and influences the analysis of incoming stimulus data.

42 Which of the following is not correct about the two hemispheres of the brain ?

1 The two hemispheres of human brain are connected by a complex network of neurons called the corpus callosum
2 The left hemisphere, in most people, is involved in verbal and analytic behaviour and is more dominant
3 The right hemisphere, in most people, is more involved in non-verbal thinking such as spatial problem-solving and is less dominant
4 The brain has two hemispheres in human being only

***Ans.** (4)*

Exp. Statement(4) is not true as more recently, animal studies have highlighted that fishes, reptiles, amphibians and mammals also possess left and right hemispheres that differentially control certain behaviors. The divided behaviors of these animals provide a window into our ancestral past, telling the story of our shared evolutionary history with early vertebrates.

The brain can thus be described as being divided into left and right cerebral hemispheres. Each of these hemispheres has an outer layer of grey matter, the cerebral cortex that is supported by an inner layer of white matter.

43 Recent researches show that creativity is correlated with

I. intelligence and cognition
II. psychoticism
III. openness to experience
IV. agreeableness codes

Select the correct answer using the codes given below

1 Only I
2 I and IV
3 I, III and IV
4 I, II and III

***Ans.** (4)*

Exp. The correct options are I, II and III.

Creativity is the ability to come up with new ideas through a mental process of connecting existing concepts. The ideas don't have to be revolutionary (which is a common misconception many people have about creative thinking), they just have to be new for the thinker.

The relationship between intelligence and creativity has been subject to empirical research for decades. Nevertheless, there is yet no consensus on how these constructs are related. One of the most prominent notions concerning the interplay between intelligence and creativity is the threshold hypothesis, which assumes that above-average intelligence represents a necessary condition for high-level creativity.

Eysenck (1993) went into lengthy detail about the different ways to test the correlation of psychoticism and creativity, and ultimately finds five different ways of supporting the psychoticism-creativity model. First, he stated that persons genetically related to diagnosed psychotics are unusually creative. He cited genetic studies that corroborate this view as well as a previously made hypothesis which contends "that there is a common genetic basis for great potential in creativity and for psychological deviation."

The second supporting criterion is that psychoticism is related to tested creativity (also referred to as originality). The third supporting study relates psychoticism to creative achievement.

Openness to experience, the drive for cognitive exploration of inner experience, is the personality trait most consistently associated with creativity.

44 Which of the following theorists hold the deterministic assumption of human nature ?

I. Erickson
II. Murray
III. Adler
IV. Maslow

Select the correct answer using the codes given below

1 I and II
2 III and IV
3 I and III
4 II and III

***Ans.** (1)*

Exp. Erickson and Murray hold the deterministic assumption of human nature

The determinist approach proposes that all behavior has a cause and is thus predictable. Free will is an illusion, and our behavior is governed by internal or external forces over which we have no control.

One of the main assumptions of the humanistic approach is that humans have free will; not all behavior is determined. Personal agency is the humanistic term for the exercise of free will. Personal agency refers to the choices we make in life, the paths we go down and their consequences. For humanistic psychologists such as Maslow (1943) and Rogers (1951) freedom is not only possible but also necessary if we are to become fully functional human beings.

45 According to Piaget changes in schemes occur due to the following processes

I. Organisation
II. Circular reaction
III. Adaptation
IV. Mental representation

Select the correct answer using the codes given below
1 I and II
2 I and III
3 II, III and IV
4 I, III and IV

Ans. (2)

Exp. According to Piaget changes in schemes occur due to the Organisation and Adaptation.

The concept of cognitive structure in humans is central to Piaget's theory. Cognitive structures are patterns of physical or mental action that underlie specific acts of intelligence. These patterns correspond with stages of child development. Piaget based his theory on two biological tendencies: organisation and adaptation.

Humans are designed to organise their experiences in to logical sets of meanings. Organisation defines how experiences are related to each other. The organisation of information and experiences makes the human thinking process more efficient. Adaptation is the tendency to adjust to the environment. It is the process by which humans match the original experience and the new experience and this may not fit together.

Directions (Q. Nos. 46-50) *Read the following passage and answer the five questions that follows.*

An experiment was performed varying 'modality of presentation' 1 at two levels and 'retention interval' 2 at three levels. Recall scores were used as the dependent variable. Each cell contained randomly assigned 15 subjects. After the experiment was over, cell-wise means and standards deviations were computed. The cell-wise standard deviations were approximately equal. The data were analysed by following suitable ANOVA model. One of the interesting finding was that the F ratio, computed as ($MS_{A \times B}$ / MS_E) was significant at .01 level.

46 How many subjects were employed in the above experiment ?

1 30 2 45
3 75 4 90

Ans. (4)

Exp. In the above experiment, 90 subjects were employed.

Each cell contained randomly assigned fifteen subjects. The experiment was performed varying modality of presentation at two levels and retention interval at three levels , therefore 90 subjects were employed.

47 Which one of the following statements appears to be correct for the above data?

1 The assumption of homogeneity of variance is violated
2 The assumption of homogeneity of variance is satisfied
3 Means and variances are proportional
4 No data are provided about the assumption of homogeneity of variance

Ans. (2)

Exp. The assumption of homogeneity of variance is satisfied.

The assumption of homogeneity of variance is that the variance within each of the populations is equal. This is an assumption of analysis of variance (ANOVA). ANOVA works well even when this assumption is violated except in the case where there are unequal numbers of subjects in the various groups. If the variances are not homogeneous, they are said to be heterogeneous.

48 The main effect of retention interval would be associated with ________ degrees of freedom.

1 2 2 3 3 5 4 6

Ans. (1)

Exp. The main effect of retention interval would be associated with 2 degrees of freedom.

The df for interaction equals (Number of columns-1) (Number of rows - 1), so for this example is (2-1)*(3-1)=2.

49 Which of the following conclusion/s can be drawn from the above data ?

I. Main effect of modality of presentation is significant.
II. Main effect of retention interval is significant.
III. The interaction effect is significant.
IV. Neither the main effect nor interaction effect is significant.

Select the correct answer using the codes given below
1 Only III 2 Only IV
3 I and II 4 I, II and III

Ans. (1)

Exp. The interaction effect is significant is the correct conclusion.

Interaction effect in a factorial design, is the joint effect of two or more independent variables on a dependent variable above and beyond the sum of their individual effects: The independent variables combine to have a different (and multiplicative) effect, such that the value of one is contingent upon the value of another. This indicates that the relationship between the independent variables changes as their values change. For example, if a researcher is studying how gender (female vs. male) and dieting (Diet A vs. Diet B) influence weight loss, an interaction effect would occur if women using Diet A lost more weight than men using Diet A.

50 Which of the following statement/s is/are correct about the experimental design in the above study ?

I. It is a balanced factorial design.
II. It is an unbalanced factorial design.
III. It is a 2 x 3 factorial design.
IV. It is a between-groups design.

Select the correct answer using the codes given below :
1 Only III 2 I and III
3 II and III 4 I, III and IV

Ans. (4)

Exp. The correct options are I, III and IV.

In ANOVA and Design of Experiments, a balanced design has an equal number of observations for all possible level combinations.

This is a 2 (modality of presentation) x 3 (retention level) mixed factorial design. Recall scores were used as the dependent variable. Each cell contained randomly assigned 15 subjects.

In the design of experiments, a between-group design is an experiment that has two or more groups of subjects each being tested by a different testing factor simultaneously.

51 Match the List I with List II and select the correct answer from the codes given below :

List I	List II
A. Identity diffusion	I. Individuals who are exploring alternatives in an effort to find values and goals to guide their life
B. Identity foreclosure	II. Individuals who have explored and committed themselves to self-chosen values and occupational goals
C. Identity achievement	III. Individuals who do not have firm commitments to values and goals and are not actively trying to reach them
D. Moratorium	IV. Individuals who have accepted ready-made values that authority figures have chosen for them

Codes

	A	B	C	D		A	B	C	D
1	IV	III	I	II	2	III	IV	I	II
3	IV	III	II	I	4	III	IV	II	I

Ans. *(4)*

Exp. The correct matching is A-III, B-IV, C-II, D-I.

Identity diffusion occurs when individuals do not have firm commitments to values and goals and are not actively trying to reach them. Identity confusion/diffusion occurs when adolescents neither explore nor commit to any identities.

Identity foreclosure occurs when individuals have accepted ready-made values that authority figures have chosen for them. It occurs when an individual commits to an identity without exploring options.

Identity achievement occurs when individuals have explored and committed themselves to self-chosen values and occupational goals. Individuals who have explored different options, discovered their purpose, and have made identity commitments are in a state of identity achievement.

Moratorium occurs when Individuals have explored and committed themselves to self-chosen values and occupational goals. It is a state in which adolescents are actively exploring options but have not yet made commitments.

52 Cognitive change occurs because of

1 Cognitive self regulation
2 Cognitive complexity
3 Cognitive conflict
4 Cognitive maturity

Ans. *(3)*

Exp. Cognitive change occurs because of Cognitive conflict.

Cognitive conflict is a psychological state involving a discrepancy between cognitive structures and experience, or between various cognitive structures. This discrepancy occurs when simultaneously active, mutually incompatible representations compete for a single response. The detection of cognitive conflict is thought to trigger compensatory adjustments in executive control processes, which serve to reduce and prevent subsequent instances of similar cognitive conflict.

53 Which components of creativity can be measured in the picture construction activity of Torrance Test of Creative Thinking?

I. Elaboration II. Fluency
III. Flexibility IV. Originality

Select the correct answer using the codes given below

1 I and II 2 III and IV
3 I and IV 4 II and III

Ans. *(3)*

Exp. The components of creativity that can be measured in the picture construction activity of Torrance Test of Creative Thinking are Elaboration and Originality.

Building on JP Guilford's work and created by Ellis Paul Torrance Tests of Creative Thinking (TTCT), a test of creativity, originally involved simple tests of divergent thinking and other problem- solving skills, which were scored on four scales:

Originality is the statistical rarity of the responses.

Elaboration is the amount of detail in the responses.

Fluency is the total number of interpretable, meaningful, and relevant ideas generated in response to the stimulus.

Flexibility is the number of different categories of relevant responses.

54 Match the List I with List II and select the correct answer from the codes given below

List I (Phenomenon)	List II (Psychologist)
A. Sense of powerlessness	I. Abraham Maslow
B. Free will	II. Rollo May
C. Becoming one's self	III. Victor Frankl
D. Esteem needs	IV. Car Rogers

Codes

	A	B	C	D		A	B	C	D
1	II	III	IV	I	2	III	IV	II	I
3	I	III	IV	II	4	IV	II	III	I

Ans. (1)

Exp. The correct match is A-II, B-III, C-IV, D-I

Sense of powerlessness is associated with Rollo May. Rollo May identified powerlessness and anxiety as two of the fundamental existential problems faced by individuals in the modern world. May described powerlessness as a debilitating feeling of importence or helplessness in the face of overwhelming problems in our society.

Free will is associated with Victor Frankl. Frankl expresses human experience thusly "As we see it, an analogous relationship between the realm of human freedom and a realm superior to man is quite imaginable, so that man is endowed with free will in spite of the plans.

Becoming one's self is associated with Carl Rogers. Carl Rogers (1959) believed that humans have one basic motive, that is the tendency to self-actualise - i.e. to fulfill one's potential and achieve the highest level of 'human-beingness' we can.

Esteem Needs are associated with Abraham Maslow. Maslow believed people move through different stages of five needs that motivate our behaviour. He called these needs physiological, safety, love and belonging (social), esteem and self-actualisation. Maslow believed each stage of need had to be met before progression to the next stage of need could occur.

55 The memory which contains factual information is called

1 Semantic memory 2 Declarative memory
3 Procedural memory 4 Episodic memory

Ans. (2)

Exp. The memory which contains factual information is Declarative memory.

Declarative memory is one of two types of long term human memory. Declarative memory refers to memories which can be consciously recalled such as facts and knowledge. Declarative memory's counterpart is known as non declarative or procedural memory, which refers to unconscious memories such as skills (e.g. learning to ride a bicycle).

56 Given below are two statements, is a labelled as Assertion (A) and the other labelled as Reason (R).

Assertion (A) Playing chess requires higher level of cognitive strategy.

Reason (R) Winning any game needs ability and tricks.

Codes

1 Both (A) and (R) are true and (R) is the correct explanation of (A)
2 Both (A) and (R) are true, but (R) is not the correct explanation of (A)
3 (A) is true, but (R) is false
4 (A) is false, but (R) is true

Ans. (2)

Exp. Both (A) and (R) are true, but (R) is not the correct explanation of (A).

Playing chess requires higher level of cognitive strategy.

A talks about playing chess requires higher level of cognitive strategy but

Winning any game needs ability and tricks.

R talks about winning the game and not about what are those specific skills that are used during the game and how higher level of cognitive strategy can help in winning. Therefore option 2 is correct.

57 Which is the correct sequence of emergence of virtues?

1 Hope, Willpower, Purpose, Competency
2 Willpower, Hope, Purpose, Competency
3 Purpose, Competency, Willpower, Hope
4 Competency, Willpower, Purpose, Hope

Ans. (1)

Exp. The correct sequence of emergence of virtues is: Hope, Willpower, Power, Competency.

Hope is the expectation that one will have positive experiences or that a potentially threatening or negative situation will not materialize or will ultimately result in a favorable state of affairs. Willpower is the ability to carry out one's intentions. Purpose is the reason for which something is done or for which something exists. It is a mental goal or aim that directs a person's actions or behavior.

It is persistence or resolution in pursuing such a goal. Competency is the capability to apply or use the set of related knowledge, skills, and abilities required to successfully perform 'critical work functions' or tasks in a defined work setting.

58 Which of the following are the negative symptoms of Schisophrenia ?

I. Hallucinations and Apathy
II. Asociality and Apathy
III. Anhedonia and Poverty of speech
IV. Poverty of speech and Delusions.

Select the correct answer using the codes given below.

1 I and III 2 II and III
3 III and IV 4 II and IV

Ans. (2)

Exp. The negative symptoms of Schizophrenia are asociality, apathy, anhedonia and poverty of speech.

Asociality refers to the lack of motivation to engage in social interaction, or a preference for solitary activities. Asociality may be associated with avolition, but it can, moreover, be a manifestation of limited opportunities for social relations.

Apathy is defined as a loss of interest in relation to social or emotional situations (a state of indifferent mood). Apathy is presented as a lack of feeling, interest or any particular concern about a specific situation, or life in general.

Anhedonia is one of the core negative symptoms of schizophrenia and is traditionally defined as the inability to experience pleasure or reduced hedonic capacity.

Poverty of speech is a common symptom of schizophrenia, and may co-occur with poverty of content–a symptom in which a person provides extensive verbal feedback that contains little useful information. Poverty of speech is also common in people experiencing emotional distress, particularly depressed people.

59 A competent and well-performing female middle-level manager did not consider herself as suitable for the position of senior manager thinking that females are not suitable for such high positions. This is a typical example of

1 Glass-ceiling phenomenon
2 Gender discrimination
3 High motivation to avoid failure
4 High motivation to approach success

Ans. (1)

Exp. This is a typical example of glass-ceiling phenomenon.

The concept of a glass ceiling is an inequality. Most often this inequality is due to either gender or race, or a combination of both. The inequalities involve an effect that is taking place with relation to employment and occupation. Hence option 1 is correct. Whereas Discrimination based on gender (or sex) is a common civil rights violation that takes many forms, including sexual harassment, pregnancy discrimination and unequal pay for woman who do the same jobs as men.

60 Leaders who exert profound effects on their followers and who establish special types of relationships with their followers are usually considered as

1 Democratic leaders
2 Transformational leaders
3 Normative leaders
4 Consultative leaders

Ans. (2)

Exp. Leaders who exert profound effects on their followers and who establish special types of relationships with their followers are usually considered as Transformational leaders.

Transformational leaders motivate others to do more than they originally intended and often even more than they thought possible.

They set more challenging expectations and typically achieve higher performance. The leader shares the problems and relative information with a specific group of subordinates individually and then makes a decision that may or not be suggested by subordinates.

The leader gets recommendations and ideas from subordinates through arranging a group gathering where the leader makes the decision by self. Hence, option 2 is correct.

61 Match the List I with List II and select the correct answer from the codes given below :

List I (Hemispheric Involvement)		List II (Task Condition)	
A.	Left	I.	Those which minimise response bias
B.	Right	II.	Those which involve speaking or writing
C.	No difference	III.	Those which involve use of hands in three dimensional space
		IV.	Those which involve olfaction

Codes

	A	B	C
1	II	III	IV
2	I	II	III
3	II	III	I
4	IV	I	II

Ans. (3)

Exp. The correct matching is A-II, B-III, C-I.

Left hemisphere is involved with tasks which involve speaking or writing.

Right hemisphere is involved with tasks which involve use of hands in three dimensional space.

No difference: is involved with tasks which minimise response bias.

62 Match the List I with List II and select the correct answer from the codes given below

List I (Disorder)	List II (Symptoms)
A. Dyssomnias	I. Abnormal behaviour that occur during sleep
B. Insomnia	II. Sleeplessness
C. Parassomnias	III. It involve problems in getting to sleep or getting sufficient high quality sleep
D. Hypersomnia	IV. Excessive sleep

Codes

	A	B	C	D
1	II	IV	III	I
2	I	II	III	IV
3	III	II	I	IV
4	I	III	II	IV

Ans. (3)

Exp. The correct matching is A-III, B-II, C-I, D-IV.

Dyssominas involve problems in getting to sleep or getting sufficient high quality sleep. These are disorders that produce either excessive sleepiness or difficulty in initiating or maintaing sleep. Some of the most common dyssomnias include obstructive sleep apnea, restless legs syndrome and conditions of the biological clock such as shift work sleep disorder, and delayed sleep phase syndrome.

Insomnia is sleeplessness. It is difficulty falling asleep or staying asleep, even when a person has the chance to do so. People with insomnia can feel dissatisfied with their sleep and usually experience one or more of the following symptoms: fatigue, low energy, difficulty concentrating, mood disturbances and decreased performance in work or at school.

Parasomnias are abnormal behaviours that occur during sleep. These are clinical disorders that are not abnormalities of the processes that govern our sleep/wake states. Instead, parasomnias consist mainly of inappropriate physical behaviours that intrude predominantly during sleep.

Hypersomnia is excessive sleep. It refers to either excessive daytime sleepiness or excessive time spent sleeping, is a condition in which a person has trouble staying awake during the day.

63 Given below are two statements, one is labelled as Assertion (A) and the other labelled as Reason (R).

Assertion (A) A person's self concept is partly rooted in the feedback of other people.

Reason (R) The reactions of others are based on 'looking-glass self' effect as an internalisation of others reactions to self concept.

Codes

1 Both (A) and (R) are true and (R) is the correct explanation of (A)
2 Both (A) and (R) are true, but (R) is not the correct explanation of (A)
3 (A) is true, but (R) is false
4 (A) is false, but (R) is true

Ans. (1)

Exp. Both (A) and (R) are true and (R) is the correct explanation of (A)

A person's self concept is partly rooted in the feedback of other people. This is explained by the reactions of others are based on 'looking-glass self' effect as an internalisation of others reactions to self concept. We see over self as what others believe we are. That is we create our self concept based on other's feedback. We internalise the image that we create in the social world. Hence, a person's self is partly rooted in the feedback of other people.

64 Given below are two statements, one is labelled as Assertion (A) and the other labelled as Reason (R).

Assertion (A) The anticipatory anxiety that people develop about having another panic attack is thought to arise from activity in the hippocampus of the limbic system.

Reason (R) According to one theory, panic attacks arise from abnormal activity in the amygdala.

Codes

1 Both (A) and (R) are true and (R) is the correct explanation of (A)
2 Both (A) and (R) are true, but (R) is not the correct explanation of (A)
3 (A) is true, but (R) is false
4 (A) is false, but (R) is true

Ans. (2)

Exp. Both (A) and (R) are true, but (R) is not the correct explanation of (A)

The anticipatory anxiety that people develop about having another panic attack is thought to arise from activity in the hippocampus of the limbic system. Anticipatory anxiety is where a person experiences increased levels of anxiety by thinking about an event or situation in the future. Rather than being a specific disorder in its own right, anticipatory anxiety is a symptom commonly found in a number of anxiety related conditions.

It can be extremely draining for people as it can last for months prior to an event. The worries people experience specifically focus on what they think might happen, often with catastrophic predictions about an event. The nature of negative predictions about the event will be the difference between an anxiety level that is incapacitating or merely uncomfortable. According to one theory, panic attacks arise from abnormal activity in the amygdala. But this does not explain the assertion.

65 Which of the following options is true regarding the relationship between thinking and language ?

1 Real thinking requires the use of language
2 A thought that cannot be expressed in a particular language cannot occur to speakers of that language
3 People sometimes think in images rather than in words
4 A thought is never expressed in language

Ans. (3)

Exp. People sometimes think in images rather than in words is true regarding the relationship between thinking and language. The relationship between language and thinking is important. Most agree that language (i.e., words), plays an important role in memory and thinking, but Whorf suggested that language determines the way we think. Whorf's critics argue that language reflects rather than determines thinking. Studies with deaf children and individuals with Williams syndrome have demonstrated that thinking and language are not completely dependent on one another.

66 Which of the following models accepts that the more deeply information is processed, the more likely it is to be retained?

1 Level of processing model
2 Retrieval cues model
3 Atkinson and Shiffrin model
4 Trace model

Ans. (1)

Exp. Level of processing model accepts that the more deeply information is processed, the more likely it is to be retained. The levels of processing model (Craik and Lockhart, 1972) focuses on the depth of processing involved in memory and predicts the deeper information is processed, the longer a memory trace will last.

67 Which of the following is the best description of Cattail's Concept of Fluid Intelligence?

1 One's ability to reason speedily and abstractly and it tends to decrease with age in the range of 25-35 years
2 One's ability to reason speedily and abstractly and it tends to increase with age in the range of 25-35 years
3 Specific mental abilities, which are measured by every task in an intelligence test and increases with age in the range of 5-15 year
4 Specific mental abilities, which are measured by every task in an intelligence test and decrease with age in the range of 5-15 years

***Ans.** (1)*

Exp. One's ability to reason speedily and abstractly and it tends to decrease with age in the range of 25-35 years. Fluid intelligence peaks at around age 20 and then gradually declines. This decline may be related to local atrophy of the brain in the right cerebellum, a lack of practice, or the result of age-related changes in the brain.

Cattell–Horn theory of intelligence is a theory proposing that there are two main kinds of intellectual abilities nested under general intelligence: g-c, or crystallized intelligence (or ability), which is the sum of one's knowledge and is measured by tests of vocabulary, general information, and so forth; and g-f, or fluid intelligence (or ability), which is the set of mental processes that is used in dealing with relatively novel tasks and is used in the acquisition of g-c. In later versions of the theory, other abilities were added, such as g-v, or visual intelligence (or ability), which is the set of mental processes used in handling visual-spatial tasks (e.g., mentally rotating a geometric figure or visualizing what pieces of paper would look like if folded).

68 Given below are two statements, one is labelled as Assertion (A) and the other labelled as Reason (R).

Assertion (A) Many amputees experience phantom limb syndrome where in they continue to feel their missing limbs after surgery.

Reason (R) The image of one's body's boundaries continue to function even after parts of the body are removed.

Codes

1 Both (A) and (R) are true and (R) is the correct explanation of (A)
2 Both (A) and (R) are true, but (R) is not the correct explanation of (A)
3 (A) is true, but (R) is false
4 (A) is false, but (R) is true

***Ans.** (1)*

Exp. Both (A) and (R) are true and (R) is the correct explanation of (A)

Many amputees experience phantom limb syndrome where in they continue to feel their missing limbs after surgery.

Phantom limb syndrome is the ability to feel sensations and even pain in a limb or limbs that no longer exist. The image of one's body's boundaries continue to function even after parts of the body are removed. This explains the experience of phantom limb syndrome.

Phantom limb syndrome is characterised by both non-painful and painful sensations. Non-painful sensations can be divided into the perception of movement and the perception of external sensations (exteroception), including touch, temperature, pressure, vibration and itch. Pain sensations range from burning and shooting pains to feelings of tingling 'pins and needles.' While phantom limb syndrome occurs only in amputees, phantom sensations may be perceived in people who have survived strokes but lost function of certain body parts or who have spinal cord injury or peripheral nerve injury.

69 A person who excels in zeroing in on what information is crucial in a given situation and combining seemingly unrelated facts is high on

I. Componential II. Experiential
III. Contextual

Codes

1 Only I 2 Only II
3 I and II 4 II and III

***Ans.** (2)*

Exp. A person who excels in zeroing in on what information is crucial in a given situation and combining seemingly unrelated facts is high on experiential intelligence. Experiential intelligence is one component (experiential-creative) of the Triarchic theory of intelligence that was put forward by researcher Steinberg in 1985. This theory holds that there are multiple components of intelligence that he referred to as metacomponents, performance components, and knowledge-acquisition components.

These components are theorized to combine in various combinations to perform intellectual tasks such as perceiving problems in our long-term memory, perceiving relations between objects, and applying relations to another set of terms. The experiential-creative component deals chiefly with how well a task is performed with regard to how familiar it is.

70 Given below are two statements. One is labelled as Assertion (A) and the other is labelled as Reason (R).

Assertion (A) Emotional intelligence is the set of skills that underlie accurate assessment, evaluation, expression and regulation of situations.

Reason (R) Emotional intelligence is the basis of empathy for others, self awareness and social skills.

Codes

1 Both (A) and (R) are true and (R) is the correct explanation of (A)
2 Both (A) and (R) are true, but (R) is not the correct explanation of (A)

3 (A) is true, but (R) is false
4 (A) is false, but (R) is true

Ans. (2)

Exp. Both (A) and (R) are true, but (R) is not the correct explanation of (A)

Emotional intelligence is the set of skills that underlie accurate assessment, evaluation, expression and regulation of situations.

Emotional intelligence is the ability to identify and manage your own emotions and the emotions of others.

Emotional intelligence is the basis of empathy for others, self awareness and social skills. It is generally said to include three skills: emotional awareness; the ability to harness emotions and apply them to tasks like thinking and problem solving; and the ability to manage emotions, which includes regulating your own emotions and cheering up or calming down other people. This is true but does not really explain the assertion.

71 The pituitary gland is the master endocrine gland because

1 it produces the largest number of different hormones
2 it controls the secretion of several other endocrine glands
3 it is responsible for functioning of the autonomic nerve system
4 it controls the thinking and amount of body growth

Ans. (2)

Exp. The pituitary gland is called the 'master' gland of the endocrine system because it controls the functions of many of the other endocrine glands.

It controls the secrection of several other endocrine glands.

The pituitary gland is no larger than a pea, and is located at the base of the brain. The gland is attached to the hypothalamus (a part of the brain that affects the pituitary gland) by nerve fibers and blood vessels. The pituitary gland itself consists of 2 major structures: Anterior lobe and Posterior lobe.

72 Hinduism and Buddhism differ regarding the existence of a

1 social dimension of self
2 physical dimension of self
3 psychological dimension of self
4 transcendental dimension of self

Ans. (4)

Exp. Hinduism and Buddhism differ regarding the existence of a transcendental dimension of self. Hinduism is about understanding Brahma, existence, from within the Atman, which roughly means "self" or "soul," whereas Buddhism is about finding the Anatman — "not soul" or "not self."

In Hinduism, attaining the highest life is a process of removing the bodily distractions from life, allowing one to eventually understand the Brahma nature within. In Buddhism, one follows a disciplined life to move through and understand that nothing in oneself is "me," such that one dispels the very illusion of existence. In so doing, one realizes Nirvana.

73 In a recent version of the 16 PF (5th edition) the second-order factor analysis of 16 PF scales is reported yielding five second order factors. They are referred to as

1 global factors
2 big five
3 five-factor model
4 universal personality factors

Ans. (3)

Exp. The five second order factors are referred to as global factors.

16 PF stands for the 16 Personality Factors or 'source traits' that were identified by Raymond Cattell in the 1930s as being the main set of factors whereby a person can be classified. These were derived from an analysis of personality-describing words. There are 16 Primary Factors, which have also been grouped into five global factors.

74 Given below are two statements, one is labelled as Assertion (A) and the other labelled as Reason (R).

Assertion (A) In a maze learning experiment rats who were of reinforced from the beginning and those, which were not is reinforced until the eleventh day of the experiment, did not show the any difference in learning and performance.

Reason (R) It is possible for learning to remain dormant for a considerable length of time before it is manifested in behaviour.

Codes

1 Both (A) and (R) are true and (R) is the correct explanation of (A)
2 Both (A) and (R) are true, but (R) is not the correct explanation of (A)
3 (A) is true, but (R) is false
4 (A) is false, but (R) is true

Ans. (1)

Exp. Both (A) and (R) are true and (R) is the correct explanation of (A)

In a maze learning experiment rats who were of reinforced from the beginning and those, which were not is reinforced until the eleventh day of the experiment, did not show the any difference in learning and performance.

Maze learning is a learning process which involves circumnavigating a subject being presented with a variety of false routes into the core subject.

It is possible for learning to remain dormant for a considerable length of time before it is manifested in behaviour. Over time the learner, if successful, can reach the end goal or aim in the least amount of time by applying their previously held knowledge.

75 Match the List I with List II and select the correct answer from the codes given below :

List I (Stress related term)	List II (Brief explanations)
A. Stress	I. External internal obstacles
B. Frustration	II. Events like competition
C. Eustress	III. Tragic circumstances like funerals
D. Distress	IV. Situation that challenges coping

Codes

	A	B	C	D
1	IV	III	II	I
2	IV	I	II	III
3	IV	II	I	III
4	II	III	I	IV

Ans. *(2)*

Exp. The correct matching is A-IV, B-I, C-II, D-III.

Stress is the situation that challenges coping. Stress generally refers to two things the psychological perception of pressure, on the one hand, and the body's response to it, on the other, which involves multiple systems, from metabolism to muscles to memory.

Frustration is external internal obstacles. Frustration is a feeling of anger or annoyance caused by being unable to do something.

Eustress is events like competition. Eustress is the good stress that motivates you to continue working.

Distress is tragic circumstances like funerals. Distress is when the good stress becomes to much to bear or cope with. Tension builds, there is no longer any fun in the challenge, there seems to be no relief, no end in sight.

UGC-NET PSYCHOLOGY

SOLVED PAPER 2012 (December)

PAPER II

1 In an experiment, the stimuli were presented to the subjects in certain order and after the presentation of stimuli their order was disturbed. In the test phase, the subjects were needed to set them in the presented order.

Which of the following methods was used in this experiment ?

1 Recognition
2 Relearning
3 Reconstruction
4 Recall

Ans. (3)

Exp. In the experiment, the stimuli were presented to the subjects in certain order and after the presentation of stimuli their order was disturbed. In the test phase the subjects were needed to set them in the presented order. Under this experiment reconstruction is used. Reconstruction is the logical recreation of an experience or event that has been only partially stored in memory.

Reconstructive memory refers to the process of assembling information from stored knowledge when a clear or coherent memory of specific events does not exist. e.g. an interviewer may work with crime victim to assemble a memory of the traumatic events surrounding a crime.

2 Given below are two statements, one labelled as Assertion (A) and the other labelled as Reason (R). Read the statements and choose the correct answer using the codes given below.

Assertion (A) If your teacher embarrasses you for asking a question in class, it is less likely that you would ask questions in class in future.

Reason (R) Negative reinforcement reduces the occurrence of a behaviour.

Codes

1 Both (A) and (R) are true and (R) is the correct explanation of (A)
2 Both (A) and (R) are true, but (R) is not the correct explanation of (A)
3 (A) is true, but (R) is false
4 (A) is false, but (R) is true

Ans. (3)

Exp. (A) is true but (R) is false.

If your teacher embarrasses you for asking a question in class, it is less likely that you would ask questions in class in future. The teacher is adding insult and at the same time reducing the likelihood of occurrence of behavior of asking questions in the class. This is an example of positive punishment.

Negative reinforcement reduces the occurrence of a behaviour is false. Negative reinforcement does not reduce the occurrence of a behavior, rather removes an aversive stimulus to strengthen a behavior. In negative reinforcement, a response or behaviour is strengthened by stopping, removing or avoiding a negative outcome or aversive stimulus. Negative reinforcement involves the removal of a negative condition to strengthen a behaviour.

3 Which of the following is in the correct sequence of sympathetic and parasympathetic division?

1 Thoracic, Sacral, Cranial, Cervical, Lumbar
2 Cranial, Lumbar, Thoracic, Cervical, Sacral
3 Sacral, Cervical, Thoracic, Cranial, Lumbar
4 Sacral, Cranial, Cervical, Thoracic, Lumbar

Ans. (*)

Exp. The correct sequence of sympathetic and parasympathetic division is Cranial, Sacral, Cervical, Thoracic and Lumbar.

The parasympathetic division has craniosacral outflow, meaning that the neurons begin at the cranial nerves (CN3, CN7, CN9, CN10) and sacral (S2–S4) spinal cord. The sympathetic division (thoracolumbar outflow) consists of cell bodies in the lateral horn of the spinal cord (intermediolateral cell columns) from T1 to L2. These cell bodies are GVE (general visceral efferent) neurons and are the preganglionic neurons.

There are several locations where preganglionic neurons create synapses with their postganglionic neurons. The paravertebral ganglia of the sympathetic chain (these run on either side of the vertebral bodies), cervical ganglia, thoracic ganglia, rostral lumbar ganglia, caudal lumbar ganglia, and pelvic ganglia.

4 The human ear can generally hear sounds ranging from

1 20 -1000 Hz
2 10 -2000 Hz
3 20 - 2000 Hz
4 1000 -5000 Hz

Ans. (*)

Exp. The human ear can generally hear sounds ranging from 20-20000 Hz.

Hearing range describes the range of frequencies that can be heard by humans or other animals, though it can also refer to the range of levels. Humans can detect sounds in a frequency range from about 20 Hz to 20 kHz. Individual hearing range varies according to the general condition of a human's ears and nervous system.

5 Match the List I with List II and select the correct answer from the codes given below :

	List I (Personality Theories)		List II (Focus)
A.	Behaviourists	I.	Self-concepts
B.	Psychodynamic	II.	Habits
C.	Biological	III.	Childhood fixations
D.	Humanistic	IV.	Inheritance of genes

Codes

	A	B	C	D
1	I	III	IV	II
2	II	IV	III	I
3	II	III	IV	I
4	I	IV	II	III

Ans. (3)

Exp. The correct matching is A-II, B-III, C-IV, D-I.

Behaviourists focus on habits. They consider habit as repeated behaviour that is established through learning. The early behaviorist John Watson described habits as behavioral patterns formed through the repeated association of stimulus and response pairs.

Psychodynamic Personality Theories focus on childhood fixations. A fixation is a persistent focus on an earlier psychosexual stage. Until this conflict is resolved, the individual will remain "stuck" in this stage. A person who is fixated at the oral stage, for example, may be over-dependent on others and may seek oral stimulation through smoking, drinking, or eating.

Biological Personality Theories focus on inheritance of genes. Biological psychology, also called physiological psychology, is the study of the biology of behavior; it focuses on the nervous system, hormones and genetics. Biological theories examine the relationship between mind and body, neural mechanisms, and the influence of heredity and genes on behavior.

Humanistic Personality Theories focus on self-concepts. Self-concept is one's description and evaluation of oneself, including psychological and physical characteristics, qualities, skills, roles and so forth. Self-concepts contribute to the individual's sense of identity over time.

6 The chronological age that most typically corresponds to a given level of performance is called

1 Intelligence Quotient
2 Maturation
3 Mental age
4 None of these

Ans. (3)

Exp. The chronological age that most typically corresponds to a given level of performance is called Mental age.

Mental age (MA) is a numerical scale unit derived by dividing an individual's results in an intelligence test by the average score for other people of the same age. Thus, a 4-year-old child who scored 150 on an IQ test would have a mental age of 6 (the age-appropriate average score is 100; therefore, MA = $(150/100) \times 4 = 6$). The MA measure of performance is not effective beyond the age of 14. Mental age is a concept in relation to intelligence, expressed as the age at which a child is performing intellectually. The mental age of the child that is tested is the same as the average age at which normal children achieve a particular score.

7 The role of unconscious in creative thinking is known as the process of

1 Verification
2 Illumination
3 Inoculation
4 Incubation

Ans. (4)

Exp. The role of unconscious in creative thinking is known as the process of Incubation.

Incubation process is the gradual generation of a solution to a problem at a nonconscious or semiconscious level, often after an attempt at a conscious, deliberate solution has failed. During the incubation process, some of the ideas that were interfering with the solution will tend to fade. The overt activity and sometimes even thinking about the problem is absent in this stage. But the unconscious thought process involved in creative thinking is at work during this period.

8 Which factor is not much related to happiness ?

1 High self-esteem
2 Educational level
3 Close friendship or satisfactory marriage
4 Meaningful religious faith

Ans. (2)

Exp. The factor which is not much related to happiness is educational level.

In Maslow's hierarchy of needs, also known as 'pyramid of happiness', the five levels of needs are: physiological, safety, love and belonging, self-esteem, and self-actualization.

The PERMA model given by Martin Seligman represents five core elements of happiness and well being. PERMA stands for Positive Emotion, Engagement, Relationships (Close friendship or satisfactory marriage), Meaning, and Accomplishments. An individual leading a life of meaning belongs to and serves something that is bigger than him. These large entities could be family, religion, community, country, or even ideas.

9 Which is the correct order of 'Products' given by Guilford ?

1 Units, Relations, Classes, Systems, Implications, Transformations
2 Units, Classes, Systems, Relations, Implications, Transformations
3 Units, Classes, Relations, Systems, Transformations, Implications
4 Units, Classes, Systems, Relations, Transformations, Implications

Ans. (3)

Exp. The correct order of 'Products' given by Guilford:

Units, Classes, Relations, Systems, Transformations, Implications

In Guilford's Structure of Intellect (SI) theory, intelligence is viewed as comprising operations, contents and products. There are five kinds of operations (cognition, memory, divergent production, convergent production, evaluation), 6 kinds of products (units, classes, relations, systems, transformations, and implications) and five kinds of contents (visual, auditory, symbolic, semantic, behavioural). Since, each of these dimensions is independent, there are theoretically 150 different components of intelligence.

10 Which is not the obstacle to problem-solving ?

1 Confirmation bias
2 Fixation
3 Mental Set
4 Heuristics

Ans. (4)

Exp. Heuristics is not the obstacle to problem-solving.

Problem solving is the process by which individuals attempt to overcome difficulties, achieve plans that move them from a starting situation to a desired goal, or reach conclusions through the use of higher mental functions, such as reasoning and creative thinking.

Heuristics in cognition, is an experience-based strategy for solving a problem or making a decision that often provides an efficient means of finding an answer but cannot guarantee a correct outcome. A heuristic is a general problem-solving framework (Tversky and Kahneman, 1974). You can think of these as mental shortcuts that are used to solve problems. A "rule of thumb" is an example of a heuristic. Such a rule saves the person time and energy when making a decision, but despite its time-saving characteristics, it is not always the best method for making a rational decision.

11 Given below are two statements, one labelled as Assertion (A) and the other labelled as Reason (R). Read the statements and choose the correct answer using the codes given below.

Assertion (A) Algorithm is a logical rule that guarantees solving a particular problem.

Reason (R) One can find the solution even to complex problems by following step by step procedure.

Codes

1 Both (A) and (R) are true and (R) is the correct explanation of (A)
2 Both (A) and (R) are true, but (R) is not the correct explanation of (A)
3 (A) is true, but (R) is false
4 (A) is false, but (R) is true

Ans. (2)

Exp. Both (A) and (R) are true, but (R) is not the correct explanation of (A).

Algorithm is a logical rule that guarantees solving a particular problem. When solving a problem, choosing the right approach is often the key to arriving at the best solution. In psychology, one of these problem-solving approaches is known as an algorithm. An algorithm is a defined set of step-by-step procedures that provides the correct answer to a particular problem.

One can find the solution even to complex problems by following step by step procedure. This is true as problem solving is the process by which individuals attempt to overcome difficulties, achieve plans that move them from a starting situation to a desired goal, or reach conclusions through the use of higher mental functions, such as reasoning and creative thinking. However, this does not explain why algorithm guarantees solving a particular problem.

12 Which of the following statements concerning reinforcement is correct ?

1 Learning is most rapid with partial reinforcement, but continuous reinforcement produces the greatest resistance to extinction.
2 Learning is most rapid with continuous reinforcement, but partial reinforcement produces the greatest resistance to extinction.
3 Learning is the fastest and resistance to extinction is the greatest after continuous reinforcement.
4 Learning is the fastest and resistance to extinction is the greatest following partial reinforcement.

Ans. (2)

Exp. Learning is most rapid with continuous reinforcement, but partial reinforcement produces the greatest resistance to extinction is correct.

In continuous reinforcement schedules, reinforcement is provided every single time after the desired behavior. Due to the behavior reinforced every time, the association is easy to make and learning occurs quickly. However, this also means that extinction occurs quickly after reinforcement is no longer provided.

In partial or intermittent reinforcement, the response is reinforced only part of the time. Learned behaviours are acquired more slowly with partial reinforcement, but the response is more resistant to extinction.

13 The sentence 'Blue Jeans wear false smiles' has correct _______ , but incorrect _______ .

1 morphemes; phonemes
2 phonemes; morphemes

3 semantics; syntax
4 syntax; semantics

Ans. (4)

Exp. The sentence 'Blue Jeans wear false smiles' has correct syntax but incorrect semantics. In linguistics, syntax is the set of rules, principles and processes that govern the structure of sentences in a given language, specifically word order. The term syntax is also used to refer to the study of such principles and processes.

Semantics is primarily the linguistic and also philosophical, study of meaning—in language, programming languages, formal logics, and semiotics. It focuses on the relationship between signifiers —like words, phrases, signs, and symbols—and what they stand for, their denotation.

14 Match the List I with List II and select the correct answer from the codes given below :

List I (Types of Thinking)	List II (Characteristics)
A. Autistic thinking	I. Reasoning
B. Realistic thinking	II. Drawing facts
C. Convergent thinking	III. Unusual uses
D. Creative thinking	IV. Fantasy

Codes

	A	B	C	D		A	B	C	D
1	I	III	IV	II	2	III	I	II	IV
3	II	I	III	IV	4	IV	I	II	III

Ans. (4)

Exp. The correct matching is A-IV, B-I, C-II, D-III.

Autistic thinking is associated with fantasy. It is narcissistic, egocentric thought processes, such as fantasizing and daydreaming that have little or no relation to reality. It is similar to dereistic thinking, but the emphasis is on self-absorption rather than disconnection from reality.

Realistic thinking is associated with reasoning. It is based or focused on the objective qualities and requirements that pertain in different situations. Realistic thinking permits adjustment of thoughts and behavior to the demands of a situation; it depends on the ability to interpret external situations in a fairly consistent, accurate manner.

Convergent thinking is associated with drawing facts. It is critical thinking in which an individual uses linear, logical steps to analyze a number of already formulated solutions to a problem to determine the correct one or the one that is most likely to be successful.

Creative thinking is associated with unusual uses. Creative or divergent thinking is concerned with innovative ideas, unusual ways of solving problems and with something that is not traditional.

15 The main function of autoclitic behaviour is to

I. qualify responses
II. express relations
III. providing a grammatical framework for verbal behaviour

Select the correct answer using the codes given below :

1 Only I   2 II and III
3 I and III   4 All of these

Ans. (4)

Exp. The main functions of autoclitic behaviour are. (i) qualify responses (ii) express relations (iii) providing a grammatical framework for verbal behaviour.

Autoclitics are verbal responses that modify the effect on the listener of the primary operants that comprise B F Skinner's classification of verbal behavior. An autoclitic is a verbal behavior that modifies the functions of other verbal behaviors. The main functions are described as follows:

Qualify responses : Qualifying autoclitics modify the listener's behavior in their qualification of tacts in its intensity or direction.

Express relations : Relational autoclitics describe the relation between verbal operants, and modify the listener's behavior in that way.

Providing a grammatical framework for verbal behaviour : Skinner describes grammatical manipulations, such as the order or grouping of responses, as autoclitic.

16 The phi-phenomenon, stroboscopic motion, induced motion and autokinetic motion are all

1 Pictorial cues
2 Apparent motion
3 Double images
4 Non-verbal cues

Ans. (2)

Exp. The phi-phenomenon, stroboscopic motion, induced motion and autokinetic motion are all Apparent motion.

Apparent motion is an illusion of motion or change in size of a visual stimulus.

The phi-phenomenon is an illusion that is visual in nature, which causes an observer or viewer to distinguish and perceive movement in stationary objects. It is a perceptual illusion in which people see motion that is produced by a succession of immobile images.

Stroboscopic illusion is the apparent motion of a series of separate stimuli occurring in close consecutive order, as in motion pictures. It is the apparent motionlessness or reverse motion of a moving object, such as a rotating fan, produced by illuminating it with a series of intermittent light flashes.

Induced motion is an illusion of movement that occurs when a small stationary stimulus is surrounded by a large moving stimulus. The small object appears to move, while the large object appears to be still. An example is the haunted swing illusion.

Autokinetic effect is the illusion of seeing a static spot of light moving in a dark room. The autokinetic effect has been used in certain psychological experiments, for example, investigating suggestibility or the establishment of group norms.

17 Which one of the following is the most important feature of the defence mechanism of rationalisation ?

1 Going back to an earlier stage of development
2 Justifying one's actions
3 Magically atoning for certain acts that give rise to guilt
4 Attributing one's emotions to other persons

Ans. (2)

Exp. The most important feature of the defence mechanism of rationalisation is justifying one's actions.

Rationalisation is a defense mechanism identified by Freud. According to Freud, when people are not able to deal with the reasons they behave in particular ways, they protect themselves by creating self-justifying explanations for their behaviours. e.g., if I flunk out of school because I didn't study properly it might be so hard for me to deal with that I rationalise my behaviours by saying that I simply didn't have enough time to study because I have a full-time job, a baby at home and so many other demands on my time.

18 'People control basic anxiety by moving toward, away from and against others.' Which group of personality psychologists theorised this statement ?

1 Psychoanalytic
2 Neo-Freudian
3 Social learning
4 Cognitive

Ans. (2)

Exp. Neo-Freudian personality psychologists theorised this statement, 'People control basic anxiety by moving toward, away from and against others.'

The Neo-Freudian denotes an approach that derives from the classical psychoanalysis of Sigmund Freud but with modifications and revisions that typically emphasize social and interpersonal elements over biological instincts.

Karen Horney was a Neo-Freudian psychologist known for her theory of neurotic needs. She identified three ways of dealing with the world that are formed by an upbringing in a neurotic family: Moving Toward People, Moving Against People and Moving Away From People.

19 A psychotic person would probably score the highest on which MMPI-2 scale?

1 Depression
2 Hysteria
3 Schizophrenia
4 Mania

Ans. (3)

Exp. A psychotic person would probably score the highest on Schizophrenia MMPI-2 scale.

The Minnesota Multiphasic Personality Inventory (MMPI) is a psychological test that assesses personality traits and psychopathology. It is primarily intended to test people who are suspected of havingmental health or other clinical issues. Scale 8 of MMPI, also known as Schizophrenia is a 78-item scale is intended to show whether a person has, or is likely to develop, a schizophrenia disorder. It considers whether someone is experiencing hallucinations, delusions, or bouts of extremely disorganized thinking.

20 Match the List I with List II and select the correct answer from the codes given below :

List I (Part of eye)		List II (Function)	
A.	Pupil	I.	Focus images on the retina
B.	Iris	II.	Begin the processing of visual information
C.	Lens	III.	Allows light to enter
D.	Retina	IV.	Controls the size of the pupil

Codes

	A	B	C	D
1	I	II	III	IV
2	III	IV	I	II
3	I	III	IV	II
4	IV	II	I	III

Ans. (2)

Exp. The correct matching is A-III, B-IV, C-I, D-II.

The *pupil* allows light to enter. It is the aperture through which light passes on entering the eye. It is located immediately in front of the lens.

The *iris* controls the size of the pupil. The size of the opening of pupil is controlled by a circle of muscle called the iris innervated by fibers of the autonomic nervous system.

The *lens* focuses images on the retina. It is a transparent, biconvex structure in the anterior portion of the eyeball (just behind the iris) that provides the fine, adjustable focus of the optical system on the retina.

The *retina* begins the processing of visual information. It is the light-sensitive inner surface of the eye. A layer of neurons lines the inner surface of the back of the eye and provides the sensory signals required for vision. It processes the signals of the photoreceptors and convey an output signal to the brain by way of the optic nerve.

21 Learning by imitating others' behaviour is called _______ learning. The researcher best known for studying this type of learning is

1 Observational : Bandura
2 Secondary : Pavlov
3 Observational : Watson
4 Secondary : Skinner

Ans. (1)

Exp. Learning by imitating other's behaviour is called Observational learning. The researcher best known for studying this type of learning is Bandura.

Observation learning is the acquisition of information, skills, or behavior through watching the performance of others, either directly or via such media as films and videos. Observational learning was illustrated during the famous Bobo Doll Experiment by Albert Bandura. Social learning theory, proposed by Albert Bandura, emphasizes the importance of observing, modelling, and imitating the behaviors, attitudes, and emotional reactions of others.

22 As we enter a movie theatre from bright light the visual sensitivity increases and within 5-10 minutes, we are able to see under low levels of illumination. This is due to

1 Visual acuity
2 Dark adaptation
3 Saturation
4 Transduction

Ans. (2)

Exp. Dark Adaptation is the process by which our eyes adjust to darkness after being exposed to light. e.g. when we move from a bright, sunny area outside to a relatively dark room inside, it is difficult to see at first. But gradually our eyes recover and become more sensitive to the dim light indoors. Dark adaptation is made possible by the dilation of our pupils and changes in the rods and cones of our retinas. Rods detect form and motion and cones detect colour. So in darkness, our rods kick into high gear while the cones take a backseat.

23 Which of the following internal conditions determine perceptual process ?

I. Intelligence
II. Emotion
III. Motivation
IV. Information

Select the correct answer using the codes given below

1 I and II
2 II and III
3 II and IV
4 I and IV

Ans. (2)

Exp. The correct codes are II and III.

Perception is the process whereby people select, organise and interpret sensory stimulations into meaningful information. Perception lies at the base of every individual behaviour. Perception is the process whereby people select, organise, and interpret sensory stimulations into meaningful information. Emotion and motivation are internal conditions determine perceptual process.

Emotions routinely affect how and what we see. Fear, for example, can affect low-level visual processes, sad moods can alter susceptibility to visual illusions, and goal-directed desires can change the apparent size of goal-relevant objects.

Motivation or motivational factors increase the individual's sensitivity to those stimuli which he considers as relevant to the satisfaction of his needs in view of his past experience with them.

24 Wechsler Adult Intelligence Scale has eleven subtests out of which

1 five are verbal and six are performance
2 six are verbal and five are performance
3 seven are verbal and four are performance
4 four are verbal and seven are performance

Ans. (2)

Exp. Wechsler Adult Intelligence Scale has eleven subtests out of six are verbal and five are performance. The Wechsler scales, like the Binet and other tests, measure intellectual performance as a multidimensional construct. This means that, rather than conceptualising intelligence as a single characteristic, the tests contain numerous scales assessing qualitatively different types of intellectual functioning.

The WAIS-R, a revised form of the WAIS, was released in 1981 and consisted of six verbal and five performance subtests. The verbal tests were: Information, Comprehension, Arithmetic, Digit Span, Similarities, and Vocabulary. The Performance subtests were: Picture Arrangement, Picture Completion, Block Design, Object Assembly, and Digit Symbol. A verbal IQ, performance IQ and full scale IQ were obtained.

25 Arrange the following in correct sequence of memory processes.

I. Encoding
II. Storage
III. Attention
IV. Retrieval

Codes

1 III, I, II, IV
2 II, III, I, IV
3 I, III, II, IV
4 III, II, I, IV

Ans. (1)

Exp. The correct sequence of memory processes is (i) Attention (ii) Encoding (iii) Storing (iv) Retrieval

Attention: the filter through which we experience the world

Encoding: how we process what our attention admits into the mind

Storage: what happens once information enters the brain

Retrieval: the recall of that information or behaviour

Memory is essentially the capacity for storing and retrieving information. Three processes are involved in memory: encoding, storage, and retrieval. All three of these processes determine whether something is remembered or forgotten. It is actually a complex process that allows us to learn and recall vast amounts of information every moment of every day.

26 Match the List I with List II and select the correct answer from the codes given below :

List I (Cues)		List II (Explanation)
A. Relative size	I.	Straight lines seem to join together as they become more distant
B. Linear Perspective	II.	An object changes position on the retina as the head moves
C. Motion Parallax	III.	If two objects are of same size, the one producing the smaller retinal image is farther away
D. Texture gradient	IV.	The texture of a surface appears smoother as distance increases

Codes

	A	B	C	D
1	III	I	II	IV
2	I	III	IV	II
3	IV	II	III	I
4	II	IV	I	III

Ans. (1)

Exp. The correct matching is A-III, B-I, C-II, D-IV.

Relative size is defined as if two objects are of same size, the one producing the smaller retinal image is farther away. It is a perceptual clue which allows you to determine how close objects are to an object of known size.

Linear Perspective is when straight lines seem to join together as they become more distant. It is a type of monocular cue in which parallel lines appear to converge at some point in the distance.

Motion Parallax is when an object changes position on the retina as the head moves. It is a monocular depth cue in which we view objects that are closer to us as moving faster than objects that are further away from us.

Texture gradient is when the texture of a surface appears smoother as distance increases. It is a gradual change in appearance of objects from coarse to fine - some objects appear closer because they are coarse and more distinct, but gradually become less and less distinct (and more fine) which makes the objects appear to get further and further away.

27 Given below are two statements, one labelled as Assertion (A) and the other labelled as Reason (R). Read the statements and choose the correct answer using the codes given below.

Assertion (A) Biderman's 'recognition by components' theory states that objects can be thought of as being composed of basic building blocks called Geons.

Reason (R) The relationship between features and geons does not exist. Geons are not composed of features such as edges, corners etc.

Codes

1 Both (A) and (R) are true and (R) is the correct explanation of (A)
2 Both (A) and (R) are true, but (R) is not the correct explanation of (A)
3 (A) is true, but (R) is false
4 (A) is false, but R is true

Ans. *(3)*

Exp. (A) is true but (R) is false.

Biderman's 'recognition by components' theory states that objects can be thought of as being composed of basic building blocks called Geons. Biderman's 'recognition by components' theory states that objects can be thought of as being composed of basic building blocks called Geons. Geons are composed of features such as edges and corners. The Recognition-By-Components theory or RBC theory, is a bottom-up process proposed by Irving Biderman in 1987 to explain object recognition. According to RBC theory, we are able to recognise objects by separating them into geons (the object 's main component parts).

The relationship between features and geons does not exist. Geons are not composed of features such as edges, corners etc is false as Biderman suggested that geons are based on basic 3-dimensional shapes (cylinders, cones etc.) that can be assembled in various arrangements to form a virtually unlimited number of objects. Geons can be determined from the features or the contours that mark the edges and corners at orientation and depth discontinuities of an image of an object, i.e., the contours that specify a good line drawing of the object's shape or volume.

28 Given below are two statements, one labelled as Assertion (A) and the other labelled as Reason (R). Read the statements and choose the correct answer using the codes given below.

Assertion (A) People just coldly store and retrieve bits of data.

Reason (R) Psychologists recognise that people reconstruct their own version of the past.

Codes

1 Both (A) and (R) are true and (R) is the correct explanation of (A)
2 Both (A) and (R) are true, but (R) is not the correct explanation of (A)
3 (A) is true, but (R) is false
4 (A) is false, but (R) is true

Ans. *(4)*

Exp. (A) is false but (R) is true.

People just coldly store and retrieve bits of data. This is false as schema theory accurately predicts that people do not always coldly store and retrieve bits of data in a computer-like fashion. The mind can distort an event as it encodes and stores impressions of reality.

Psychologists recognise that people reconstruct their own version of the past. This is true as according to the 'narrative' conception, memory 'is not meant to represent the past as we experienced it to be the case. Instead, the function of memory is to reconstruct the past in order to help us build a smooth and robust narrative of our lives'.

29 Ventromedial nucleus, a central area on the underside of the hypothalamus, lead to

1 excessive eating
2 stop eating
3 stop sex
4 excessive obesity

Ans. *(2)*

Exp. Ventromedial nucleus, a central area on the underside of the hypothalamus, lead to stop eating.

The ventromedial nucleus (also known as ventromedial hypothalamus) is located inside the hypothalamus. It is known as a nucleus because it is a distinct grouping of neurons within the hypothalamus.

The ventromedial nucleus is responsible for the feeling of satiation, or fullness after eating, in organisms. It tells us when we have eaten enough and to stop eating. Lesions on the ventromedial nucleus can cause over eating and obesity in organisms because they are not getting the information that they are full. The ventromedial nucleus is also involved in mammalian sexuality like presenting behaviours in female members of a species and scent-marking behaviours in males.

30 **Given below are two statements, one labelled as Assertion (A) and the other labelled as Reason (R). Read the statements and choose the correct answer using the codes given below.**

Assertion (A) According to interference theory of forgetting, forgetting is caused due to the intervening task, which occurs between original task and its recall.

Reason (R) The intervening task weaken the memory trace.

Codes

1 Both (A) and (R) are true and (R) is the correct explanation of (A)
2 Both (A) and (R) are true, but (R) is not the correct explanation of (A)
3 (A) is true, but (R) is false
4 (A) is false, but (R) is true

Ans. *(2)*

Exp. Both (A) and (R) are true, but (R) is not the correct explanation of (A).

According to interference theory of forgetting, forgetting is caused due to the intervening task, which occurs between original task and its recall. This is true as interference theory states that forgetting occurs because memories interfere with and disrupt one another, in other words forgetting occurs because of interference from other memories.

The intervening task weaken the memory trace. It was assumed that memory can be disrupted or interfered with by what we have previously learned or by what we will learn in the future. This idea suggests that information in long-term memory may become confused or combined with other information during encoding thus distorting or disrupting memories. Therefore, an intervening task weaken the memory trace.

31 **Match the List I with List II and select the correct answer from the codes given below**

List I (Emotion)		List II (Nerves Activity)	
A.	Fear	I.	Parasympathetic arousal
B.	Anger	II.	Sympathetic arousal
C.	Depression	III.	Sympathetic and parasympathetic arousal

Codes

	A	B	C		A	B	C
1	II	III	I	2	I	II	III
3	II	I	III	4	III	II	I

Ans. *(1)*

Exp. The correct matching is A-II, B-III, C-I.

Fear is associated with Sympathetic arousal. It is a sympathetic reaction. Fearful stimuli increase sympathetic nerve activity, which influences our physiological state, such as palpitation, peripheral vasoconstriction, decreased peripheral temperature, increased blood pressure, increased blood flow to the skeletal muscles, and increased trunk temperature.

Anger is associated with Sympathetic and parasympathetic arousal. It is a strong reaction of both the sympathetic and parasympathetic branches of the autonomic nervous systems.

Depression is associated with Parasympathetic arousal. It is seen as a parasympathetic arousal as patterns of parasympathetic nervous system (PNS) activity are related to depression symptoms and the use and effectiveness of regulatory responses to dysphoric affect.

32 **Given below are two statements, one labelled as Assertion (A) and the other labelled as Reason (R). Read the statements and choose the correct answer using the codes given below.**

Assertion (A) The high achievement motivation displayed by children has emotional roots.

Reason (R) Highly motivated children often have parents who encourage their independence from an early age and praise and reward them for their successes.

Codes

1 Both (A) and (R) are true and (R) is the correct explanation of (A)
2 Both (A) and (R) are true, but (R) is not the correct explanation of (A)
3 (A) is true, but (R) is false
4 (A) is false, but (R) is true

Ans. *(1)*

Exp. Both (A) and (R) are true and (R) is the correct explanation of (A).

The high achievement motivation displayed by children has emotional roots. This is true as achievement motivation is the need for excellence and significant accomplishment, despite what rewards may be offered after the achievement has been met. People high in achievement motivation; try to achieve high level of success in their lives.

Highly motivated children often have parents who encourage their independence from an early age and praise and reward them for their successes. This is true as McClelland and associates (1953) suggested that achievement motivation is an important acquired motive and children who have high achievement motivation were those whose families pressurises for achievement. Both the tendency to work towards success and tendency to approach success are provoked from socialisation and past experiences. Therefore, it explains that the high achievement motivation displayed by children has emotional roots.

33 A person, otherwise limited in mental ability, has amazing specific skills. This is because of

1 academic under-achievement
2 practical intelligence
3 academic over-achievement
4 savant syndrome

Ans. (4)

Exp. A person, otherwise limited in mental ability, has amazing specific skills. This is because of savant syndrome.

Savant syndrome is a condition in which a person with limited mental ability has amazing specific skills. The skills in which savants excel are generally related to memory. It may include rapid calculation, artistic ability, musical ability or map making. Most of the people with savant syndrome are associated with autism and known as autistic savants.

A savant is a person with an intellectual disability or an autism spectrum disorder (autistic savant) who demonstrates exceptional, usually isolated, cognitive abilities, such as rapid calculation, identifying the day of the week for any given date, or musical talent. The term idiot savant initially was used to denote such a person but has been discarded as pejorative.

34 A man borrows money and forgets to pay it back because paying back is painful. This is an example of

1 Repression
2 Reaction formation
3 Regressia
4 Rationalisation

Ans. (1)

Exp. A man borrows money and forgets to pay it back because paying back is painful. This is an example of Repression.

Repression is an unconscious mechanism employed by the ego to keep disturbing or threatening thoughts from becoming conscious. Thoughts that are often repressed are those that would result in feelings of guilt from the superego. e.g., in the Oedipus complex, aggressive thoughts about the same sex parents are repressed.

Repression banishes unacceptable ideas, fantacies, affects or impulses from consciousness or that keeps out of consciousness what has never been conscious. Although not subject to voluntary recall, the repressed material may emerge in behaviour in disguised form.

35 Whenever daughter performs well in her studies, she receives a chocolate from parents, but her brother is given a chocolate only, when he gets the highest marks in the class. This is a paradigm of

1 Positive and negative reinforcement
2 Primary and secondary reinforcement
3 Continuous and secondary reinforcement
4 Continuous and partial reinforcement

Ans. (4)

Exp. Whenever daughter performs well in her studies, she receives a chocolate from parents, but her brother is given a chocolate only, when he gets the highest marks in the class. This is a paradigm of Continuous and partial reinforcement.

Continuous reinforcement is when humans or animals are positively reinforced every time a specific behaviour occurs e.g. every time a lever is pressed a pellet is delivered and then food delivery is shut off. Continuous reinforcement in operant and instrumental conditioning, is the reinforcement of every correct (desired) response.

Partial or intermittent reinforcement in operant or instrumental conditioning, is any pattern of reinforcement in which only some responses are reinforced.

36 The location of the optic nerve exit point from the retina of the eye is called as

1 bipolar cell
2 fovea
3 blind spot
4 cone

Ans. (3)

Exp. The location of the optic nerve exit point from the retina of the eye is called as blind spot.

Blind spot, small portion of the visual field of each eye that corresponds to the position of the optic disk also known as the optic nerve head within the retina. There are no photoreceptors, i.e. rods or cones in the optic disk and, therefore, there is no image detection in this area.

The blind spot of the right eye is located to the right of the centre of vision and in the left eye. With both eyes open, the blind spots are not perceived because the visual fields of the two eyes overlap. Indeed, even with one eye closed, the blind spot can be difficult to detect subjectively because of the ability of the brain to 'fill in' or ignore the missing portion of the image.

37 For an intelligence test, while computing item-remainder correlations for item analysis, we compute

1 phi-coefficient
2 spearman rho
3 tetrachoric correlation
4 point-biserial correlation

Ans. (4)

Exp. For an intelligence test, while computing item-remainder correlations for item analysis, we compute point-biserial correlation.

The point biserial correlation coefficient, is a special case of pearson's correlation coefficient. It measures the relationship between two variables: One continuous variable (must be ratio scale or interval scale) and one naturally binary variable. The item remainder value is a decimal value which is correlated with a nominal or categorical value.

38 Which of the following personality psychologist does not fall in the group of humanistic approaches of personality ?

1 Carl Rogers
2 Rollo May
3 Martin Seligman
4 Abraham Maslow

Ans. (3)

Exp. Martin Seligman does not fall in the group of humanistic approaches of personality.

Martin Seligman is a pioneer of Positive Psychology (the term itself was coined by Abraham Maslow), not simply because he has a systematic theory about why happy people are happy, but because he uses the scientific method to explore it. Through the use of exhaustive questionnaires, Seligman found that the most satisfied, upbeat people were those who had discovered and exploited their unique combination of signature strengths, such as humanity, temperance and persistence.

Humanistic psychology, also often referred to as humanism, emerged during the 1950s as a reaction to the psychoanalysis and behaviourism that dominated psychology at the time. Psychoanalysis was focused on understanding the unconscious motivations that drive behaviour while behaviourism studied the conditioning processes that produce behaviour. The early development of humanistic psychology was heavily influenced by the works of a few key theorists, especially Abraham Maslow, Carl Rogers, Rollo May and Erich Fromm.

39 A subject has a T score (Mean = 50; SD = 10) of 40 on an abstract reasoning test. The corresponding percentile rank would be

1 16 2 34
3 40 4 84

Ans. (1)

Exp. A subject has a T score (Mean = 50; SD = 10) of 40 on an abstract reasoning test. The corresponding percentile rank would be 16.

A t score is a scaled score, its mean is 50, and the standard deviation is 10. Thus, a student with a T-score of 60 is one standard deviation above the mean.

A percentile is a measure that gives us information to know how many scores fall under a specific cut (the percentage number). The fixed percentages allow us to convert standard deviation units to percentiles. For example, (-2) SD equals to a percentile rank of 2; that is, two percent of the cases fall below this point. Each point on the base line of the figure can be equated to the following percentiles.

(−2) SD = 2%

(−1) SD = 16% (2 + 14)

0 SD = Mean = 50% (16 + 34)

Therefore, a mean of 50 reflects 16 percentile.

40 Which of the following tests are considered to be culture-fair tests of intelligence?

I. Cattell's Culture-Fair Test of Intelligence
II. Raven's Progressive Matrices
III. Wechsler's Intelligence Scale for Children
IV. Goodenough-Harris Test

Select the correct answer using the codes given below :

1 Only I 2 I and II
3 I, II and III 4 I, II and IV

Ans. (4)

Exp. The following tests are considered to be culture fair tests of intelligence :

Cattell's Culture-Fair Test of Intelligence : The Cattell's Culture Fair Intelligence Test (CFIT) was constructed by Raymond B Cattell, in an attempt to produce a measure of cognitive abilities that accurately estimated intelligence devoid of socio-cultural and environmental influences.

Raven's Progressive Matrices : Raven's Progressive Matrices (often referred to simply as Raven's Matrices) or RPM is a non-verbal group test typically used in educational settings. It is usually a 60-item test used in measuring abstract reasoning and regarded as a non-verbal estimate of fluid intelligence.

Goodenough-Harris Test : The Draw-a-Person test (DAP test, or Goodenough– Harris Draw-a-Person test) is a psychological projective personality or cognitive test used to evaluate children and adolescents for a variety of purposes. The purpose of the test is to assist professionals in inferring children's cognitive developmental levels with little or no influence of other factors such as language barriers or special needs.

41 The information in terms of sound is maintained in

1 Semantic code 2 Acoustic code
3 Iconic code 4 Information code

Ans. (2)

Exp. The information in terms of sound is maintained by Acoustic code.

Acoustic code is the information stored in terms of sound rather than the meaning of what is said. Acoustic encoding is the process of remembering and comprehending something that is heard. Repetition of words or putting information into a song or rhythm uses acoustic encoding. Learning the multiplication table, for instance, can be an acoustic process.

42 Which of the following personality tests are considered to be the projective in nature ?

I. Thematic Apperception Test
II. Kent-Rosenoff Word Association Test
III. NEO Five-Factor Inventory
IV. Rotter's Incomplete Sentence Blank

Select the correct answer using the codes given below :

1 Only I 2 I and II
3 I, II and IV 4 II, III and IV

Ans. (3)

Exp. The correct codes are I, II and IV.

The following personality tests are considered to be projective in nature :

Thematic Apperception Test : It is a projective measure intended to evaluate a person's patterns of thought, attitudes, observational capacity, and emotional responses to ambiguous test materials. In the case of the TAT, the ambiguous materials consist of a set of cards that portray human figures in a variety of settings and situations.

Kent-Rosenoff Word Association Test : It is a test of personality and mental function in which the subject is required to respond to each of a series of words with the first word that comes to mind or with a word of a specified class of words (such as antonyms).

Rotter's Incomplete Sentence Blank : It is a projective psychological test developed by Julian Rotter and Janet E rafferty in 1950. It comprises 40 incomplete sentences which the subject has to complete as soon as possible but the usual time taken is around 20 minutes, the responses are usually only 1–2 words long such as I regret ... 'Mostly girls...'. the test can be administered both individually and in a group setting.

NEO Five-Factor Inventory is not a projective test of personality. The NEO Five Factor Inventary assesses the Big five personality traits: Extraversion, Agreeableness, Conscientiousness, Neuroticism and Openness to Experience.

43 Given below are two statements, one labelled as Assertion (A) and the other labelled as Reason (R). Read the statements and choose the correct answer using the codes given below.

Assertion (A) Thalamus and Hypothalamus play an important role in emotions.

Reason (R) Thalamus and Hypothalamus anatomically lie close each other.

Codes

1 Both (A) and (R) are true and (R) is the correct explanation of (A)
2 Both (A) and (R) are true, but (R) is not the correct explanation of (A)
3 (A) is true, but (R) is false
4 (A) is false, but (R) is true

Ans. *(3)*

Exp. (A) is true but (R) is false.

Thalamus and Hypothalamus play an important role in emotions. The thalamus and hypothalamus are located within the diencephalon (or "interbrain"), and are part of the limbic system. They regulate emotions and motivated behaviours like sexuality and hunger.

Thalamus and Hypothalamus anatomically lie close each other. This is false as the thalamus lies superior to the hypothalamus, separated from it by the hypothalamic sulcus.

44 Taylor conceptualised anxiety as a drive and hypothesised that subjects scoring higher on her anxiety scale would be conditioned faster than the low-scoring subjects. The experimental studies confirmed this hypothesis for eyelid conditioning. The results provide evidence for the

1 predictive validity of the anxiety scale
2 construct validity of the anxiety scale
3 concurrent validity of the anxiety scale
4 content validity of the anxiety scale

Ans. *(2)*

Exp. The results provide evidence for the construct validity of anxiety scale.

Construct validity is ' the degree to which a test measures what it claims, or purports, to be measuring, how well a test or tool measures the construct that it was designed to measure.'

Predictive validity is the extent to which performance on a test is related to later performance that the test was designed to predict. Predictive validity is determined by calculating the correlation coefficient between the results of the assessment and the subsequent targeted behaviour.

Concurrent validity refers to the extent to which the results of a measure correlate with the results of an established measure of the same or a related underlying construct assessed within a similar time frame.

Content validity (also known as logical validity) refers to the extent to which a measure represents all facets of a given construct. Content validity refers to how accurately an assessment or measurement tool taps into the various aspects of the specific construct in question.

45 Given below are two statements, one labelled as Assertion (A) and the other labelled as Reason (R). Read the statements and choose the correct answer using the codes given below.

Assertion (A) According to Flynn, performance on IQ tests has substantially increased around the world at all age levels.

Reason (R) Performance on IQ tests is because of the interaction between genetics and environment.

Codes

1 Both (A) and (R) are true and (R) is the correct explanation of (A)
2 Both (A) and (R) are true, but (R) is not the correct explanation of (A)
3 (A) is true, but (R) is false
4 (A) is false, but (R) is true

Ans. *(2)*

Exp. Both (A) and (R) are true, but (R) is not the correct explanation of (A).

According to Flynn, performance on IQ tests has substantially increased around the world at all age levels. Flynn effect is the gradual cross-cultural rise in raw scores obtained on measures of general intelligence. These increases have been roughly 9 points per generation (i.e., 30 years). The gains have been unequally distributed across the different kinds of abilities, with fluid abilities showing substantially greater gains than crystallized abilities.

Performance on IQ tests is because of the interaction between genetics and environment. Environment and intelligence research investigates the impact of environment on intelligence. This is one of the most important factors in understanding human group differences in IQ test scores and other measures of cognitive ability. It is estimated that genes contribute about 20–40% of the variance in intelligence in childhood and about 80% in old age. Thus, the environment and its interaction with genes account for a high proportion of the variation in intelligence seen in groups of young children and for a small proportion of the variation observed in groups of mature adults. However, it does not explain the rise of IQ scores around the world at all age levels.

Directions (Q. Nos. 46-50) *Read the following paragraph carefully and answer the questions that follow* :

The concept of variable is of central importance in research. In psychological research, variables can be classified in several ways. Edwards has classified variables in three types - stimulus variables, behavioural variables and organismic variables. From another perspective, variables have been classified into two types - the continuous variables and discrete variables. The discrete variables are further sub-classified as real discrete variables and artificially discrete variables.

The variables in research can be defined in various ways, the two common types of definitions being-constitutive definitions and operational definitions.

The operationalisation of variables is of crucial importance in carrying out actual research. The tentative statements of expected relationship between two or more variables are called hypotheses. The research hypotheses may be directional or non-directional. Needless to say that the hypotheses constitute to be the powerful tools in psychological research.

46 Which of the following variable(s) can be labelled as organismic variable(s)?

I. Task complexity
II. Intelligence
III. Errors made while learning task
IV. Heart rate

Select the correct answer using the codes given below :

1 Only IV
2 II and IV
3 I, II and IV
4 II, III and IV

Ans. (2)

Exp. The correct codes are II and IV.

The variables which can be labelled as organismic variables are Intelligence and Heart rate.

An organismic variable is any relatively stage physical characteristic of an organism such as gender, eye color, height, weight, body build, as well as characteristics like intelligence, educational level, neuroticism, and prejudices. Organismic variable is a variable inside an organism or a process or an operation that occurs internally but is hypothesized to play a casual role in determining overt responding.

47 Which one of the following is an example of an artificially discrete variable ?

1 Number of children in a family
2 Nationality
3 Sex
4 Examination results in terms of pass and fail

Ans. (4)

Exp. Examination results in terms of pass and fail is an example of an artificially discrete variable.

A variable is a quantity that has changing values. A discrete variable is a variable that can only take on a certain number of values. In other words, they don 't have an infinite number of values. Continuous variables can take on an infinite number of possibilities.

A distinction can be drawn between naturally and artificially discrete variables (e.g., the male/female dichotomy of sex is natural, while the young/old dichotomy of age is artificial). It is generally not a good idea to create artificially discrete variables because it decreases the variance of the variable (i.e., range restriction). Furthermore, the conceptual basis for the distinction and differences between the various categorical levels can be very tenuous at best (e.g., 39 is young; but 40 is old; 90% is an A; but 89% and 80% are both Bs [typical course grading scheme]).

48 Which of the following is/are operational definitions of intelligence ?

I. Intelligence ratings by an observing psychologist.
II. Intelligence as an ability to think critically, solve problems and adapt to the novel situations.
III. Intelligence as a score on Raven's progressive matrices.

Select the correct answer using the codes given below :

1 Only II
2 Only III
3 I and III
4 I, II and III

Ans. (3)

Exp. Operational definitions of intelligence are (i) Intelligence rating by an observing psychologist. (ii) Intelligence as a score on Raven's progressive matrices. In the options I and III, intelligence has been defined as ratings and scores respectively.

An operational definition is a description of something in terms of the operations (procedures, actions, or processes) by which it could be observed and measured. For example, the operational definition of anxiety could be in terms of a test score, withdrawal from a situation, or activation of the sympathetic nervous system. The process of creating an operational definition is known as operationalization.

49 'Males are more extraverted than females' is an example of

1 Null hypothesis
2 Non-directional hypothesis
3 Directional hypothesis
4 Unverifiable hypothesis

Ans. (3)

Exp. 'Males are more extraverted than females' is an example of Directional hypothesis.

Hypothesis is a tentative and formal prediction about the relationship between two or more variables in the population being studied and the hypothesis translates the research question into a prediction of expected outcomes. A hypothesis is a statement about the relationship between two ormore variables thatwe set out to prove or disprove in our research study.

Directional hypothesis are usually derived from theory. They may imply that the researcher is intellectually committed to a particular outcome. They specify the expected direction of the relationship between variables i.e. the researcher predicts not only the existence of a relationship but also its nature.

50 Which of the following represent(s) stylistically correct version(s) of a hypothesis ?

I. To study the relationship between intelligence and academic achievement.

II. Is there a relationship between intelligence and academic achievement ?

III. Intelligence and academic achievement are positively correlated.

IV. Intelligence and academic achievement are unrelated.

Select the correct answer using the codes given below :

1 Only I
2 Only III
3 I and II
4 III and IV

Ans. (4)

Exp. The correct codes are III and IV.

The hypotheses are written in specific rather than vague descriptions and explanations. The details are used accurately to provide adequate information so readers can follow the development of the study.

The following represent(s) stylistically correct versions of a hypothesis:

Intelligence and academic achievement are positively correlated.

Intelligence and academic achievement are unrelated.

PAPER III

1 Match the List I with List II and select the correct answer from the codes given below :

List I (Stages)	List II (Cognitive Development)
A. Operational concrete	I. Mature adult thought emerges, thinking by deductive logic, abstract thought
B. Pre-operational	II. Develops conservation concepts, classify object in series
C. Sensorimotor	III. Represent the world mentally, thought egocentric, child shows animism
D. Formal operational	IV. Lacks of language, does not use symbol, internal behaviour begins

Codes

	A	B	C	D
1	I	II	IV	III
2	II	I	IV	III
3	II	III	IV	I
4	I	III	IV	II

Ans. (3)

Exp. The correct matching is A-II, B-III, C-IV, D-I.

In the *concrete operational stage*, a child develops conservation concepts and classify object in series. The children mentally 'operate' on concrete objects and events. As children continue into elementary school, they become able to represent ideas and events more flexibly and logically. Conservation is the belief that an amount or quantity stays the same even if it changes apparent size or shape. Classification is the ability to identify the properties of categories, to relate categories or classes to one another, and to use categorical information to solve problems.

In the *pre-operational stage*, a child represents the world mentally, thought egocentric and shows animism. The children use their new ability to represent objects in a wide variety of activities, but they do not yet do it in ways that are organized or fully logical. Egocentrism in early childhood refers to the tendency of young children to think that everyone sees things in the same way as the child. Animism is the belief that inanimate objects are capable of actions and have lifelike qualities.

In the *sensorimotor stage*, a child lacks of language, does not use symbol, and internal behaviour begins. It is the first stage, and is defined as the period when infants "think" by means of their senses and motor actions. As every new parent will attest, infants continually touch, manipulate, look, listen to, and even bite and chew objects.

In the *formal operational stage*, a mature adult thought emerges, thinking by deductive logic, abstract thought. It is the last of the Piagetian stages in which the child becomes able to reason not only about tangible objects and events, but also about hypothetical or abstract ones. Hypothetico deductive reasoning is the ability to think scientifically through generating predictions, or hypotheses, about the world to answer questions. The individual can think about hypothetical and abstract concepts they have yet to experience. Abstract thought is important for planning regarding the future.

2 Children learn to add new words through a process called

1 Fast mapping
2 New mapping
3 Extensions
4 Inspiration

Ans. (1)

Exp. Children learn to add new words through a process called Fast mapping.

Fast mapping is the ability of young children to learn new words quickly on the basis of only one or two exposures to these words. Fast mapping is the term used for the hypothesised mental process whereby a new concept is learned (or a new hypothesis formed) based only on a single exposure to a given unit of information. It is the process of rapidly learning a new word by contrasting it with a familiar word.

3 The perception of a stimulus that is below the threshold for conscious experience is termed as

1 just noticeable difference
2 differential threshold
3 signal detection
4 subliminal perception

Ans. *(4)*

Exp. The perception of a stimulus that is below the threshold for conscious experience is termed as subliminal perception.

It is the presumed ability to perceive a stimulus that is below the threshold for conscious experience. It occurs when the stimulus is too weak to perceive yet a person is influenced by it. Subliminal perception is supposed to occur when a stimulus is too weak to be perceived yet a person is influenced by it.

4 Inspite of passing of many years you have little trouble in remembering where you were when you discovered the 'Taj Tragedy' of 26/11 in Mumbai. What this memory is called?

1 Implicit memory
2 Flash bulb memory
3 Episodic memory
4 Non-declarative memory

Ans. *(2)*

Exp. Under Flash bulb memory, 'Inspite of passing of many years you have little trouble in remembering where you were when you discovered the 'Taj Tragedy' of 26/11 in Mumbai'.

A flash bulb memory is a highly detailed, exceptionally vivid 'snapshot' of the moment and circumstances in which a piece of surprising and consequential (or emotionally arousing) news was heard.

5 Which of the following explains the typical intelligence-creativity relationship?

1 U-shaped relationship
2 Inverted U-shaped relationship
3 Linear negative relationship
4 None of the above

Ans. *(4)*

Exp. Creativity and intelligence are positively correlated because high ability is component of creativity but up to a certain level and after that there is no relationship. Intelligence and creativity is related to one another when IQ is found to be between 110 and 120. This is the critical level but after this level, creativity and intelligence are independent of one another and no relationship can be seen between the two constructs.

The U-shaped curve usually refers to the non-linear relationship between two variables, in particular, a dependent and an independent variable.

The relationship between changes in arousal and motivation is often expressed as an inverted-U function (also known as the Yerkes-Dodson law). The basic concept is that, as arousal level increases, performance improves, but only to a point, beyond which increases in arousal lead to a deterioration in performance.

A linear relationship means that you can represent the relationship between two sets of variables with a line (the word 'linear' literally means 'a line'). In other words, a linear line on a graph is where you can see a straight line with no curves.

So, on the basis on above relation we know that none of them explains intelligence creativity relationship.

6 Perceptive auditory receptors in the cochlea are identified as

1 basilar cells
2 hair cells
3 malleus cells
4 glial cells

Ans. *(2)*

Exp. Perceptive auditory receptors in the cochlea are identified as hair cells.

In mammals, the auditory hair cells are located within the spiral organ of Corti on the thin basilar membrane in the cochlea of the inner ear. They derive their name from the tufts of stereocilia called hair bundles that protrude from the apical surface of the cell into the fluid-filled cochlear duct.

7 A realistic understanding of death concept is based on the following ideas

I. Permanence
II. Universality
III. Mortality
IV. Non-functionality

Select the correct answer using the codes given below :

1 I and II
2 II, III and IV
3 III and IV
4 I, II and IV

Ans. *(4)*

Exp. A realistic understanding of death concept is based on Permanence, Universality and Non-functionality ideas.

Permanence : Permanence or irreversibility refers to the understanding that once the physical body dies it cannot be made alive again. In offering this definition the question of whether there is some sort of noncorporeal continuation after death of the body (e.g., concepts such as reincarnation and resurrection) is left open. It has also been useful to distinguish the irreversibility of death of the physical body from the question of whether any kind of life functions continue after death.

Universality : Universality refers to the understanding that all living things must eventually die.

Non-functionality : Non-functionality refers to the understanding that once a living thing dies all of the typical life-defining capabilities of the living physical body (e.g., walking, eating, hearing, seeing, thinking, and learning) cease. Here again, specifying the person's physical body distinguishes this aspect of the concept of death from the issue of whether some noncorporeal aspect of a person, such as the spirit, is capable of any life-like functions (e.g., loving, helping) after death.

8 The neurotransmitters called as feel good hormones are known as

1 dopamine
2 endorphins
3 acetylcholine
4 GABA

Ans. (2)

Exp. The neurotransmitters called as feel good hormones are known as endorphins. One group of hormones is nicknamed the "feel-good hormones" because of the happy and, sometimes, euphoric feelings they produce. They're also considered neurotransmitters, which means they carry messages across the spaces between nerve cells. The four feel-good hormones are:

Dopamine, serotonin, endorphins, and oxytocin. Endorphins are the body's natural painkillers. Endorphins are released by the hypothalamus and pituitary gland in response to pain or stress, this group of peptide hormones both relieves pain and creates a general feeling of well-being.

9 Which of the following is/are the content theories of work motivation ?

I. Alderfer's ERG theory
II. Herzberg's two-factor theory
III. Maslow's theory of need hierarchy
IV. Porter and Lawler's performance satisfaction theory

Select the correct answer using the codes given below :

1 Only II
2 II and III
3 I, II and III
4 II, III and IV

Ans. (3)

Exp. The content theories of work motivation are (i) Alderfer's ERG theory. (ii) Herzberg's two-factor theory. (iii) Maslow's theory of need hierarchy.

Alderfer's ERG theory : Alberger's ERG theory prioritises in terms of the categories' concreteness. Existence needs are the most concrete, and easiest to verify. Relatedness needs are less concrete than existence needs, which depend on a relationship between two or more people. Finally, growth needs are the least concrete in that their specific objectives depend on the uniqueness of each person.

Herzberg's two-factor theory : Herzberg labelled factors causing dissatisfaction of workers as 'hygiene' factors because these factors were part of the context in which the job was performed, as opposed to the job itself. Hygiene factors included company policies, supervision, working conditions, salary, safety and security on the job. In contrast, motivators are factors that are intrinsic to the job, such as achievement, recognition, interesting work, increased responsibilities, advancement and growth opportunities. According to Herzberg's research, motivators are the conditions that truly encourage employees to try harder.

Maslow's theory of need hierarchy : Abraham Maslow posited that there are some needs that are basic to all human beings, and in their absence nothing else matters. As we satisfy these basic needs, we start looking to satisfy higher order needs. In other words, once a lower level need is satisfied, it no longer serves as a motivator.

Porter and Lawler's performance satisfaction theory is a process theory of work motivation.

10 Each individual is different from every other because of which one of the following reason?

1 Chromosomes from the two parents randomly pair up in each child
2 The female germ cells and the male germ cells contain varying numbers of chromosomes
3 The male body cells and female body cells have different numbers of chromosomes
4 The fertilisation of the egg takes place at different times and days in different individuals

Ans. (1)

Exp. Each individual is different from every other because chromosomes from the two parents randomly pair up in each child.

Chromosomes are the microscopic thread like part of the cell that carries hereditary information in the form of genes. Chromosomes are bundles of tightly coiled DNA located within the nucleus of almost every cell in our body. Humans have 23 pairs of chromosomes. As the genetic material passes from parents to child, the chromosomes are responsible for containing the instructions that make the offspring unique while still carrying traits from the parent.

In most organisms, one chromosome is inherited from the mother and the other is inherited from the father; to ensure that offspring carry traits from both parents. It's crucial that certain cells, like reproductive cells, have the correct number of chromosomes in order to function properly.

11 Match the List I with List II and select the correct answer from the codes given below :

List I (Concepts)		List II (Explanations)	
A.	Person schemas	I.	A schema consisting of an organised collection of beliefs and feelings about ourself.
B.	Role schemas	II.	Mental schemas suggesting that certain traits and behaviours go together and that individuals having them represent certain type.

List I (Concepts)	List II (Explanations)
C. Self-schemas	III. The schemas containing information about how persons playing specific roles generally act and what they are like.
D. Scripts	IV. Schemas that indicate what is expected to happen in a given setting

Codes

	A	B	C	D		A	B	C	D
1	II	III	I	IV	2	I	III	II	IV
3	IV	III	I	II	4	III	I	IV	II

Ans. *(1)*

Exp. The correct matching is A-II, B-III, C-I, D-IV.

Person schemas are mental schemas suggesting that certain traits and behaviours go together and that individuals having them represent certain type. Person schemas are focused on specific individuals. For example, your schema for your friend might include information about her appearance, her behaviors, her personality, and her preferences.

Role schemas are the schemas containing information about how persons playing specific roles generally act, and what they are like. Role schema is norms and expected behavior from people with a specific role in society. It includes both achieved roles and ascribed roles.

Self-schemas are a schema consisting of an organised collection of beliefs and feelings about ourself. Self-schema is described as knowledge one accumulates about themselves by interacting with the natural world and human beings around them.

Scripts are schemas that indicate what is expected to happen in a given setting. It is a cognitive schematic structure—a mental road map—containing the basic actions (and their temporal and causal relations) that comprise a complex action.

12 Match the List I with List II and select the correct answer from the codes given below :

List I (Psychologists)	List II (Memory Concepts)
A. George Miller	I. Three memory system
B. Atkinson and Shiffrin	II. Working memory
C. Bartlett	III. Magical number > ± 2
D. Alan Baddeley	IV. Constructive memory

Codes

	A	B	C	D		A	B	C	D
1	I	II	III	IV	2	II	III	I	IV
3	IV	II	I	III	4	III	I	IV	II

Ans. *(4)*

Exp. The correct matching is A-III, B-I, C-IV, D-II.

George Miller is associated with magical number > ± 2. Miller set out to measure the amount of information that can be held in short-term memory. Miller used experimental findings from several different studies to support his idea that on average, short-term memory can hold seven plus or minus two (five to nine) chunks or bits of information. This was popularly known as magical number.

Atkinson and Shiffrin are associated with Three memory system. The Atkinson-Shiffrin model is a theory of human memory that could be broken down into three different memory stores: Sensory Memory, Short-Term Memory and Long-Term Memory.

Bartlett is associated with Constructive memory. Bartlett is associated with reconstructive memory. Reconstructive memory is the process of remembering conceived as involving the recreation of an experience or event that has been only partially stored in memory. When a memory is retrieved, the process uses general knowledge and schemas for what typically happens in order to reconstruct the experience or event.

Alan Baddeley is associated with Working memory. Alan Baddeley showed that people remembered more short words than long words in a recall test. Working memory refer primarily to the model including phonological loop for temporarily manipulating and storing speech-based information and a visuospatial sketchpad that performs a similar function for visual and spatial information. Both are supervised by a limited capacity central executive, a control system responsible for the distribution of attention and general coordination of ongoing processes.

13 Paradoxical Intention is based on which of the following ?

1 Negative practice
2 Logo therapy
3 Existential therapy
4 Reciprocal inhibition

Ans. *(2)*

Exp. Paradoxical Intention is based on Logo therapy.

Within the framework of Logotherapy, two techniques have been developed: 'paradoxical intention' and 'dereflection.' Paradoxical intention is a technique that invites you to wish for the thing that you fear most. This was originally suggested for use in the case of anxiety or phobias, in which humor and ridicule can be used when fear is paralyzing. The Paradoxical intention is to create a paradox against the intrinsic fears and attempts to break the vicious cycle of anticipated anxiety.

14 Given below are two statements, one labelled as Assertion (A) and the other labelled as Reason (R). Read the statements and choose the correct answer using the codes given below.

Assertion (A) People rebel against the norms of their group.

Reason (R) People desire to be liked and to be right.

Codes

1 Both (A) and (R) are true and (R) is the correct explanation of (A)
2 Both (A) and (R) are true, but (R) is not the correct explanation of (A)
3 (A) is true, but (R) is false
4 (A) is false, but (R) is true

Ans. *(4)*

Exp. (A) is false but (R) is true.

People rebel against the norms of their group. Group norms are the expectations and behaviours associated with a social group, such as a nationality, an organization, or a sports team. Group norms can emerge during group interaction as group members are exposed to the opinions, or observe the actions, of fellow group members. People tend to follow the norms of their group. Therefore, the assertion is false.

People desire to be liked and to be right. This is true as the need to belong, also often referred to as belongingness, refers to a human emotional need to affiliate with and be accepted by members of a group. It is instead centered on gaining acceptance, attention and support from members of the group as well as providing the same attention to other members. The need to belong is an intrinsic motivation to affiliate with others and be socially accepted. This need plays a role in a number of social phenomena such as self-presentation and social comparison.

15 My friend is doing Masters Course in Management after completing a degree course in engineering. This act refers to the case of

1 Autistic thinking 2 Convergent thinking
3 Divergent thinking 4 Evaluative thinking

Ans. *(3)*

Exp. My friend is doing Masters course in management after completing a degree course in engineering. This acts refers to the case of Divergent thinking.

Divergent thinking refers to a way of solving problems wherein a variety of possible solutions are proposed in an effort to find one that works. This is in contrast to convergent thinking, which relies on focusing on a finite number of solutions rather than proposing multiple solutions. Divergent thinking takes its name from the idea that a theoretically limitless number of sometimes even unrelated solutions can be generated in an effort to find the best one.

16 Arrange the correct sequence for controlling irrational thoughts given below.

I. Evaluate the accuracy
II. Reward your self for effective change
III. Prepare incompatible thoughts
IV. Develop awareness

Codes

1 IV, II, I, III 2 II, IV, I, III
3 IV, I, III, II 4 III, II, I, IV

Ans. *(3)*

Exp. The correct sequence for controlling irrational thoughts given as follows (i) Develop awareness (ii) Evaluate the accuracy (iii) Prepare incompatible thoughts (iv) Reward your self for effective change

17 How many interactions can be studied in a 2 × 3 × 5 factorial design?

1 4 2 5 3 29 4 30

Ans. *(1)*

Exp. 4 interactions can be studied in a 2 x 3 x 5 factorial design.

In the given factorial design, there are three independent variables which have 2, 3 and 5 levels respectively. There is one three-way interaction among all the variables. There are three two-way interactions between variable 1 and variable 2, variable 2 and variable 3, and variable 3 and variable 1. So, in total there are four interactions which can be studied.

18 Which of the following is not an error in eye witness testimony ?

1 Suggestibility
2 Illusion of outgroup homogeneity
3 Source monitoring
4 Forgetting

Ans. *(4)*

Exp. Forgetting is not an error in eye witness testimony. The errors in eye witness testimony are: suggestibility, illusion of outgroups homogeneity and source monitoring.

Eyewitness testimony is a legal term. It refers to an account given by people of an event they have witnessed. e.g. they may be required to give a description at a trial of a robbery or a road accident someone has seen. This includes identification of perpetrators, details of the crime scene etc. Eyewitness testimony is an important area of research in cognitive psychology and human memory.

19 Which of the following factors help in making faster recovery from illness and helps in coping physical adversity more effectively ?

1 Stress
2 Optimism
3 'Type A' behaviour
4 Ingratiation

Ans. *(2)*

Exp. Optimism helps in making faster recovery from illness and helps in coping physical adversity more effectively.

Optimism is the attitude that good things will happen and that people's wishes or aims will ultimately be fulfilled. Optimists are people who anticipate positive outcomes, whether serendipitously or through perseverance and effort, and who are confident of attaining desired goals. Most individuals lie somewhere on the spectrum between the two polar opposites of pure optimism and pure pessimism but tend to demonstrate sometimes strong, relatively stable or situational tendencies in one direction or the other.

20 The essential unity of the individual self-sense with that of the universe principle is the central argument of

1 Jainism
2 Advaita Vedanta
3 Yoga
4 Buddhism

Ans. (2)

Exp. The essential unity of the individual self-sense with that of the universe principle is the central argument of Advaita Vedanta.

Advaita Vedanta is a school of Hindu philosophy and religious practice giving a unifying interpretation of the whole body. The term Advaita (literally, "non-duality") refers to the idea that Brahman alone, pure consciousness, is ultimately real, while the transient phenomenal world is an illusory appearance (maya) of Brahman, and the true self, atman, which is self-luminous pure awareness, is identical with Brahman. In this view, jivanatman or individual self is a mere reflection of singular Atman in a multitude of apparent individual bodies. Advaita refers to the identity of the true self (Atman) which is pure consciousness and the ultimate world principle (Brahman) which is also pure consciousness.

21 The abstract, idealised representations that capture an average or typical notion of members of the category is known as

1 Network
2 Exemplar
3 Prototype
4 Category presentation

Ans. (3)

Exp. The abstract, idealised representations that capture an average on typical notion of members of the category is known as Prototype.

Prototype is what is perceived to be a complete image of something with all expected qualities and characteristics present. It refers to graded categorisation where some members of a category are more central, or more perfect, than others. This means that although some things may belong to a certain category of elements, they still may be perceived as unequal.

22 Because of the lightening speed, computers can retrieve and manipulate stored data faster than people can, but the human brain beats the computer hands down when it comes to

1 using heuristics
2 following algorithms
3 serial processing
4 simultaneous processing

Ans. (4)

Exp. During simultaneous processing, human brain can beat the computer.

It is the mental process of combining discrete/separate bits of information or stimuli into a whole. Also known as parallel processing, it is information processing in which two or more sequences of operations are carried out simultaneously by independent processors. A capacity for parallel processing in the human brain would account for people's apparent ability to carry on different cognitive functions at the same time, such as driving a car while also listening to music and having a conversation. The term is usually reserved for processing at a higher, symbolic level, as opposed to the level of individual neural units described in models of parallel distributed processing.

23 The final decisions reached by groups can often be predicted quite accurately by relatively simple rules. What these rules are known as?

1 Thumb rules
2 Logistic rules
3 Cognitive decision schemas
4 Social decision schemas

Ans. (4)

Exp. The final decisions reached by groups can often be predicted quite accurately by relatively simple rules. These rules are known as Social decision schemas.

The basic elements of Social Decision Scheme (SDS) theory are individual preferences, group preference compositions (distinguishable, distributions), patterns of group influence (decision schemes, social combination rules) and collective responses (group decisions, judgements, solutions and the like).

24 Children are taught names of objects, animals, people, etc., by binding the relation between names and form. According to Skinner _______ functions as a verbal operant.

1 sign
2 symbol
3 tact
4 mand

Ans. (3)

Exp. Children are taught names of objects, animals, people, etc., by binding the relation between names and form. According to Skinner tact functions as a verbal operant.

Tact is a term that BF Skinner used to describe a verbal operant which is controlled by a non-verbal stimulus (such as an object, event, or property of an object) and is maintained by non-specific social reinforcement (praise). A tact may be pure or impure. e.g. if the environmental stimulus evokes the response, the tact would be considered pure. If the tact is evoked by a verbal stimulus the resulting tact would be considered impure.

25 Match the List I with List II and select the correct answer from the codes given below :

List I	List II
A. Cerebellum	I. Sleep
B. Reticular Formation	II. Emotions
C. Medulla	III. Reflexive activites
D. Limbic system	IV. Motor control

Codes

	A	B	C	D
1	I	IV	II	III
2	III	II	I	IV
3	I	II	III	IV
4	IV	I	III	II

Ans. (4)

Exp. The correct matching is A-IV, B-I, C-III, D-II.

Cerebellum is associated with Motor control. The cerebellum receives information from the sensory systems, the spinal cord and other parts of the brain and then regulates motor movements. The cerebellum coordinates voluntary movements such as posture, balance, coordination, and speech, resulting in smooth and balanced muscular activity.

Reticular Formation is associated with Sleep. The reticular formation has projections to the thalamus and cerebral cortex that allow it to exert some control over which sensory signals reach the cerebrum and come to our conscious attention. It plays a central role in states of consciousness like alertness and sleep.

Medulla is associated with Reflexive activities. The medulla oblongata helps regulate breathing, heart and blood vessel function, digestion, sneezing, and swallowing. This part of the brain is a center for respiration and circulation. Sensory and motor neurons (nerve cells) from the forebrain and midbrain travel through the medulla.

Limbic system is associated with Emotions. The primary structures within the limbic system include the amygdala, hippocampus, thalamus, hypothalamus, basal ganglia and cingulate gyrus. The amygdala is the emotion centre of the brain, while the hippocampus plays an essential role in the formation of new memories about past experiences.

26 A motivation to defy the confirmity in order to protect one's sense of freedom and self-efficacy is called

1 asserting one's uniqueness
2 coercion
3 disobedience
4 reactance

Ans. (4)

Exp. A motivation to defy the confirmity in order to protect one's sense of freedom and self-efficacy is called reactance.

Reactance is a motivational reaction to offers, persons, rules, or regulations that threaten or eliminate specific behavioural freedoms. Reactance occurs when a person feels that someone or something is taking away his or her choices or limiting the range of alternatives.

27 Given below are two statements, one labelled as Assertion (A) and the other labelled as Reason (R). Read the statements and choose the correct answer using the codes given below.

Assertion (A) Projective testing would be of the greatest interest to psychodynamic personality psychologist.

Reason (R) Projective testing is designed to uncover unconscious thoughts, feelings and conflicts.

Codes

1 Both (A) and (R) are true and (R) is the correct explanation of (A)
2 Both (A) and (R) are true, but (R) is not the correct explanation of (A)
3 (A) is true, but (R) is false
4 (A) is false, but (R) is true

Ans. (1)

Exp. Both (A) and (R) are true and (R) is the correct explanation of (A).

Projective testing would be of the greatest interest to psychodynamic personality psychologist. This is true as a projective test is a type of personality test in which an individual offers responses to ambiguous scenes, words, or images. The goal of such tests is to uncover the hidden conflicts or emotions that the individual projects onto the test with the hope that these issues can then be addressed through psychotherapy or other appropriate treatments. This type of test emerged fromthe psychoanalytic school of thought, which suggested that people have unconscious thoughts or urges.

Projective testing is designed to uncover unconscious thoughts, feelings and conflicts. This is true as projective tests were intended to uncover feelings, desires and conflicts that are hidden from conscious awareness. By interpreting the responses to ambiguous cues, psychoanalysts hope to uncover these unconscious feelings thatmight be causing problems in a person's life.

28 Leaders who adjust their style, from one that is task oriented and directive to one that is more relations oriented and less directive, are following the principles of

1 Democratic leadership theory
2 Situational leadership theory
3 Consultative leadership theory
4 Equity leadership theory

Ans. (2)

Exp. Leaders who adjust their style, from one that is task oriented and directive to one that is more relations oriented and less directive are following the principles of Situational Leadership Theory.

Situational Leadership Theory is a leadership style that has been developed and studied by Kenneth Blanchard and Paul Hersey. Situational leadership refers to when the leader or manager of an organisation must adjust his style to fit the development level of the followers he is trying to influence.

29 Match the List I with List II and select the correct answer from the codes given below :

	List I		List II
A.	Mixed Model	I.	Creativity
B.	Regression	II.	Type I and II Intelligence
C.	Elaboration	III.	Structure of Intellect
D.	Divergent thinking	IV.	Emotional Intelligence

Codes

	A	B	C	D		A	B	C	D
1	II	I	IV	III	2	I	II	IV	III
3	IV	II	I	III	4	III	II	IV	I

***Ans.* (*)**

Exp. The correct matching is A-IV, B-III, C-I, D-II.

Mixed Model is associated with Emotional Intelligence. Developed by Daniel Goleman, this model of Emotional Intelligence is heavily focused on defining Emotional Intelligence using a vast array of skills and competencies that affect leadership performance. The Mixed Model outlines five essential Emotional Intelligence constructs: Self-awareness, Self-regulation, Social scale, Empathy and Motivation.

Regression is associated with Structure of Intellect. In regression equations; the Structure of Intellect contributed only to the predictions for an annual evaluation of academically gifted students or other academic variables.

Elaboration is associated with Creativity. Elaboration is a dimension in creativity. It is part of fleshing out the ideas in a group of collaborators, carrying an idea to fruition, and adding the details to make something real, understandable, or aesthetically pleasing. Elaboration takes an inspiring or original idea and completes it.

Divergent Thinking is associated with Type I and II intelligence. Guilford (1967) associated the properties of divergent thinking with four main characteristics: fluency (the ability to rapidly produce a large number of ideas or solutions to a problem); flexibility (the capacity to consider a variety of approaches to a problem simultaneously); elaboration (the ability to think through the details of an idea and carry it out); and originality (the tendency to produce ideas different from those of most other people).

30 According to epidemiology, different types of measures of epidemiology of mental illness are

I. prevalence II. point prevalence
III. incidence IV. percentage

Select the correct answer using the codes given below :

1 I, II and IV 2 I, III and IV
3 II, III and IV 4 I, II and III

***Ans.* (4)**

Exp. According to epidemiology, different types of measures of epidemiology of mental illness are prevalence, point prevalence and incidence.

Prevalence: Prevalence is the total number or percentage of cases (e.g., of a disease or disorder) existing in a population.

Point prevalence: Point prevalence is the total number or percentages of cases at a given point in time.

Incidence: Incidence is the rate of occurrence of new cases of a given event or condition (e.g., a disorder, disease, symptom, or injury) in a particular population in a given period. An incidence rate is normally expressed as the number of cases per some standard proportion (1,000 or 100,000 are commonly used) of the entire population at risk per year.

31 Given below are two statements, one labelled as Assertion (A) and the other labelled as Reason (R). Read the statements and choose the correct answer using the codes given below.

Assertion (A) Encoding specificity states that a retrieval cue is successful only, if it is present at the time of encoding.

Reason (R) When participants are given category names as retrieval it enables the participant of the experiment to remember, which were previously presented to them to remember.

Codes

1 Both (A) and (R) are true and (R) is the correct explanation of (A)
2 Both (A) and (R) are true, but (R) is not the correct explanation of (A)
3 (A) is true, but (R) is false
4 (A) is false, but (R) is true

***Ans.* (2)**

Exp. Both (A) and (R) are true, but (R) is not the correct explanation of (A).

Encoding specificity states that a retrieval cue is successful only, if it is present at the time of encoding. This is true as the encoding specificity principle is the general principle that matching the encoding contexts of information at recall assists in the retrieval of episodic memories. It provides a framework for understanding how the conditions present while encoding information relate to memory and recall of that information.

When participants are given category names as retrieval it enables the participant of the experiment to remember, which were previously presented to them to remember. This is true because when a person uses information stored in their memory it is necessary that the information is accessible. The accessibility is governed by retrieval cues, these cues are dependent on the encoding pattern; the specific encoding pattern may vary from instance to instance, even if nominally the item is the same, as encoding depends on the context. This conclusion was drawn from a recognition-memory task. However it does not explain the assertion.

32 Match the List I with List II and select the correct answer from the codes given below :

	List I		List II
A.	Meaning of words	I.	Morpheme
B.	Rules that govern the order of words	II.	Phoneme
C.	Smallest unit of sound	III.	Semantics
D.	Smallest unit of meaning	IV.	Syntax

Codes

	A	B	C	D		A	B	C	D
1	III	IV	II	I	2	I	II	III	IV
3	I	III	IV	II	4	IV	II	III	I

Ans. (1)

Exp. The correct matching is A-III, B-IV, C-II, D-I.

The *meaning of words* is referred to as Semantics. Semantics is primarily the linguistic and also philosophical, study of meaning—in language, programming languages, formal logics and semiotics. It focuses on the relationship between signifiers—like words, phrases, signs, and symbols—and what they stand for, their denotation.

The rules that govern the order of words are referred to as Syntax. In linguistics, syntax is the set of rules, principles and processes that govern the structure of sentences in a given language, specifically word order. The term syntax is also used to refer to the study of such principles and processes.

The *smallest unit of sound* is referred to as Phoneme. A phoneme is one of the units of sound or gesture in the case of sign languages, that distinguish one word from another in a particular language.

The *smallest unit of meaning* is referred to as Morpheme. In linguistics, a morpheme is the smallest grammatical unit in a language. In other words, it is the smallest meaningful unit of a language. A morpheme is not identical to a word, and the principal difference between the two is that a morpheme may or may not stand alone, whereas a word, by definition, is freestanding.

33 Given below are two statements, one labelled as Assertion (A) and the other labelled as Reason (R). Read the statements and choose the correct answer using the codes given below.

Assertion (A) Entrepreneurs prefer to take moderate risks, as a result of skill and not chance.

Reason (R) Entrepreneurs usually have innovative ideas and they persistently work to implement those ideas.

Codes

1 Both (A) and (R) are true and (R) is the correct explanation of (A)
2 Both (A) and R are true, but (R) is not the correct explanation of (B)
3 (A) is true, but (R) is false
4 (A) is false, but (R) is true

Ans. (2)

Exp. Both (A) and (R) are true, but (R) is not the correct explanation of (A).

Entrepreneurs prefer to take moderate risks, as a result of skill and not chance. This is true because for entrepreneurs, taking risks and business growth go hand in hand. Entrepreneurs take risks on a regular basis, no matter how big or small they may be. This is not to say that entrepreneurs take risks just for the sake of it – successful risks are calculated and based on an underlying motivator.

Entrepreneurs usually have innovative ideas and they persistently work to implement those ideas. This is true as the entrepreneurs have the ability to think newer, better and more economical ideas of business organisation and management. However, this does not explain why entrepreneurs take moderate risks.

34 Building an environment of acceptance and appreciation of all students for supporting students' motivation to learn is the objective of

1 grouping
2 evaluation
3 recognition
4 responsibility

Ans. (1)

Exp. Building an environment of acceptance and appreciation of all students for supporting students' motivation to learn is the objective of grouping.

Teachers who create warm and accepting yet business-like atmospheres will promote persistent effort and favorable attitudes toward learning. This strategy will be successful in children and in adults. Interesting visual aids, such as booklets, posters, or practice equipment, motivate learners by capturing their attention and curiosity.

People enjoy having their work and learning achievement appreciated and recognized by others (Malone & Lepper, 1983). When students are provided channels to display their work, motivation increases. Vygotsky (1978) theorized that communication and collaborative group work can enhance individuals' thinking and learning. Students can share learning strategies and perspectives with each other through social interaction. Collaboration seems to work best when students depend on each other to reach a desired goal, when there are rewards for group performance, and when students know how to work together effectively.

35 A positive or negative environmental stimulus that motivates behaviour

1 reinforcement
2 punishment
3 incentive
4 learning

Ans. (1)

Exp. A positive or negative environmental stimulus that motivates behaviour is called reinforcement.

Reinforcement is a process in which the frequency or probability of a response is increased by a dependent relationship, or contingency, with a stimulus or circumstance. It is the procedure that results in the frequency or probability of a response being increased in such a way.

In positive reinforcement, there is an increase in the probability of occurrence of some activity because that activity results in the presentation of a stimulus or of some circumstance.

In negative reinforcement, there is removal, prevention, or postponement of an aversive stimulus as a consequence of a response, which, in turn, increases the probability of that response.

36 The seat of emotion is to be found in the

1 reticular formation 2 hind brain
3 limbic system 4 fore brain

Ans. (3)

Exp. The seat of emotion is to be found in the limbic system. The limbic system is the area of the brain most heavily implicated in emotion and memory. Its structures include the hypothalamus, thalamus, amygdala, and hippocampus. The hypothalamus plays a role in the activation of the sympathetic nervous system, which is a part of any emotional reaction.

The thalamus serves as a sensory relay center; its neurons project signals to both the amygdala and the higher cortical regions for further processing. The amygdala plays a role in processing emotional information and sending that information on to cortical structures. The hippocampus integrates emotional experience with cognition.

37 If a manager gives Kavita a positive appraisal on her first evaluation as an employee because he thought that she had been a 'top-notch' performer in her job interview, he may be making an error based on

1 halo effect 2 attributional errors
3 leniency error 4 self-serving bias

Ans. (1)

Exp. If a manager gives Kavita a positive appraisal on her first evaluation as an employee because he thought that she had been a 'top-notch' performer in her job interview, he may be making an error based on halo effect.

The halo effect is a rating bias in which a general evaluation (usually positive) of a person, or an evaluation of a person on a specific dimension, influences judgments of that person on other specific dimensions. For example, a person who is generally liked might be judged as more intelligent, competent, and honest than he or she actually is. The halo effect is a type of cognitive bias in which our overall impression of a person influences how we feel and think about his or her character. Essentially, your overall impression of a person ('He is nice!') impacts your evaluations of that person's specific traits ('He is also smart!').

38 The most common cause of severe intellectual and emotional impairment in older individuals is

1 Parkinson's disease 2 Multiple sclerosis
3 Alzheimer's disease 4 Senile psychosis

Ans. (3)

Exp. The most common cause of severe intellectual and emotional impairment in older individuals is Alzheimer's disease.

Alzheimer's disease is a progressive neurodegenerative disease characterized by cortical atrophy, neuronal death, synapse loss, and accumulation of amyloid plaques and neurofibrillary tangles, causing dementia and a significant decline in functioning. Early features include deficits in memory (e.g., rapid forgetting of new information, impaired recall and recognition), anomia, executive dysfunction, depressive symptoms, and subtle personality changes such as decreased energy, social withdrawal, indifference, and impulsivity. As the disease progresses, there is global deterioration of cognitive capacities with intellectual decline, aphasia, agnosia, and apraxia as well as behavioral features, including apathy, emotional blunting, mood-dependent delusions, decreased sleep and appetite, and increased motor activity (e.g., restlessness, wandering).

39 Match the List I with List II and select the correct answer from the codes given below.

List I (Designs)	List II (Features)
A. Block design	I. Each subject participates under all experimental conditions
B. Factorial design	II. Experiments with more than two independent variables
C. Single-factor repeated measures design	III. Subjects matched on some extraneous variable related to the dependent variable
D. Time series design	IV. Studies the same set of experimental units on several occasions
	V. Suitable for studying the interactions among the independent variables

Codes

	A	B	C	D		A	B	C	D
1	V	III	I	II	2	III	V	IV	I
3	III	II	I	IV	4	III	V	I	IV

Ans. (4)

Exp. The correct matching is A-III, B-V, C-I, D-IV.

A *Block design* is the one in which subjects are matched on some extraneous variable related to the dependent variable. With a block design, the experimenter divides participants into subgroups called blocks, such that the variability within blocks is less than the variability between blocks. Then, participants within each block are randomly assigned to treatment conditions. Because this design reduces variability and potential confounding, it produces a better estimate of treatment effects.

A *Factorial design* is the one which is suitable for studying the interactions among the independent variables. A factorial design experiment is an experiment whose design consists of two or more factors, each with discrete possible values or 'levels', and whose experimental units take on all possible combinations of these levels across all such factors.

A *Single-factor repeated measures design* is the one in which each subject participates under all experimental conditions. The single-factor repeated measures is performed in designs with one independent variable, two or more levels, and the participants undergo all conditions or levels of the study. The dependent variable is distributed normally, and variances are similar for each condition.

A *Time series design* is the one which studies the same set of experimental units on several occasions. Time-series design is a type of quasi-experimental design where a series of periodic measurements is taken from one group of test units, followed by a treatment, then another series of measurements.

40 Given below are two statements, one labelled as Assertion (A) and the other labelled as Reason (R). Read the statements and choose the correct answer using the codes given below.

Assertion (A) Mansi wants to be superior, winning and being the best in any work she does.

Reason (R) A personal intention to seem competent or perform well in the eyes of others.

Codes

1 Both (A) and (R) are true and (R) is the correct explanation of (A)
2 Both (A) and (R) are true, but (R) is not the correct explanation of (A)
3 (A) is true, but (R) is false
4 (A) is false, but (R) is true

Ans. *(1)*

➲ *Exp.* Both (A) and (R) are true and (R) is the correct explanation of (A).

Mansi wants to be superior, winning and being the best in any work she does. A personal intention to seem competent or perform well in the eyes of others.

41 The research findings indicate that job satisfaction and performance usually have

1 weak negative correlation
2 no correlation
3 weak positive correlation
4 strong positive correlation

Ans. *(3)*

➲ *Exp.* The research findings indicate that job satisfaction and performance usually have weak positive correlation.

The relationship between job satisfaction and job performance has a long and controversial history. Research results of Iaffaldano and Muchinsky (1985) have found a weak connection, approximately 0.17, between job satisfaction and job performance. Judge, Thoreson, Bono, and Patton (2001) discovered that after correcting the sampling and measurement errors of 301 studies, the correlation between job satisfaction and job performance increased to 0.30.

42 Which of the following is not a 'critical situation' in the learning theory of personality development?

1 Feeding
2 Sex Training
3 Language Training
4 Anger Training

Ans. *(3)*

➲ *Exp.* Language Training is not a 'critical situation' in the learning theory of personality development.

Coming from a behavioral and psychodynamic school of thought, John Dollard and Neal Miller attempted to combine the two. Dollard and Miller supported the idea of four situations as a child, in which learning shapes one's personality.

The first situation is the feeding situation, which has to do with how a parent feeds their child. The second situation is cleanliness training, or how parents teach potty training. The third situation is early sex training, and it's when parents teach children about the avoidance of taboos when it comes to sex such as masturbation or homosexuality, thus instilling a learned sense of anxiety for years to come. Lastly, the fourth situation is anger-anxiety conflicts.

43 Match the List I with List II and select the correct answer from the codes given below :

List I (Disorders)	List II (Explanations)
A. Depression	I. Classical conditioning
B. Schizophrenia	II. Negative attribution style
C. Phobia	III. Alcoholism
D. Korsakoff's syndrome	IV. Dopamine hypothesis

Codes

	A	B	C	D		A	B	C	D
1	III	II	IV	I	2	II	IV	I	III
3	I	III	II	IV	4	II	I	IV	III

Ans. *(2)*

➲ *Exp.* The correct matching is A-II, B-IV, C-I, D-III.

Depression is associated with Negative attribution style. The role of attribution in psychopathology has been investigated most systematically within the depression context. The presumption which makes people depressive consists, to an excessive degree, of internal, stable and global attributions to negative occurrences. Negative attributions for unpleasant events are associated with the loss of self-respect which follows.

Schizophrenia is associated with Dopamine hypothesis. The dopamine hypothesis of schizophrenia suggests that a dysregulated dopamine system contributes to positive, negative, and cognitive symptoms of the disease. The dopamine hypothesis of schizophrenia postulates that hyperactivity of dopamine D2 receptor neurotransmission in subcortical and limbic brain regions contributes to positive symptoms of schizophrenia, whereas negative and cognitive symptoms of the disorder can be attributed to hypofunctionality of dopamine D1 receptor neurotransmission in the prefrontal cortex.

Phobia is associated with Classical conditioning. Classical conditioning can be studied in the development of phobias. Watson and Raynor presented Little Albert with a white rat and he showed no fear. Watson then presented the rat with a loud bang that startled Little Albert and made him cry. After the continuous association of the white rat and loud noise, Little Albert was classically conditioned to experience fear at the sight of the rat.

Korsakoff's syndrome is associated with Alcoholism. Korsakoff's syndrome is a disorder that primarily affects the memory system in the brain. It usually results from a deficiency of thiamine (vitamin B1), which may be caused by alcohol abuse, dietary deficiencies, prolonged vomiting, eating disorders, or the effects of chemotherapy.

44 Feature Detector neurons consist of

I. complex cells II. simple cells

III. glial cells IV. hyper complex cells

Select the correct answer using the codes given below :

1 I and II 2 II, III and IV

3 I, II and IV 4 III and IV

Ans. *(3)*

Exp. Feature detector neurons consist of complex cells, simple cells, and hyper complex cell.

Complex cells : Complex cells have large receptive fields without clear excitatory or inhibitory zones. They respond best to a moving edge of specific orientation and direction of motion.

Simple cells : Simple cells have narrow, elongated excitatory and inhibitory zones that have a specific axis of orientation. These cells are 'line detectors'. Their receptive fields can be built from the convergent connections of lateral geniculate nucleus cells.

Hyper complex cells : Hypercomplex cells have very large receptive fields that may combine complex cells' signals. Many of them respond best to an oriented edge that is stopped, i.e. its end does not extend beyond a specific part of the receptive field. Neurons with such a pattern of response act as 'angle detectors'. These direction selective neurons are powerful 'motion detectors'. Their receptive fields could be built from the convergent connections of simple cells.

Glial cells : are non-neuronal tissue in the nervous system that provides structural, nutritional, and other kinds of support to neurons.

45 One of the Neo-Freudian psychologists combines the humanistic, existential and psychoanalytic perspectives in which of the following concepts ?

1 Personality Development

2 Positive Psychology

3 Theory of Love

4 None of the above

Ans. *(3)*

Exp. One of the Neo-Freudian psychologists combines the humanistic, existential and psychoanalytic perspectives in Theory of Love.

Rollo May is a prolific writer who has penned many books on various topics that touch on psychology and existentialism. One of his most famous books on love is "Love and Will" (1969) where his seminal ideas on the interdependence of love and will are discussed. He is a humanistic existential psychologist, that means his view of humanity is more or less on the positive end of the spectrum. He believed that society separated love and sex into two different ideologies when they should be classified as one. May identified five types of love: libido, eros, philia, agape and manic.

Directions (Q. Nos. 46-50) *Read the following passage carefully and answer the questions that follow :*

A researcher in personality and psychometry, after a thorough scrutiny of human characteristics, located eighty personality scales which presumably provide a comprehensive description of human personality. He administered these scales to a sufficiently large sample (N = 1000) and obtained the intercorrelations among the eighty scales. The researcher wanted to factor analyse these scales. Retaining unities in the diagonal spaces of the 80 × 80 correlation matrix, the unrotated factors were extracted. Using various criteria for deciding the number of factors for rotation, 15 factors were retained.

The 15 factors together explained 70% of the total variance. These 15 factors were rotated by following a suitable method and the resulting inter-correction matrix was examined. Several of the inter-factor correlations were fairly high. Second-order factor analysis was then carried out which yielded five, nearly orthogonal factors.

46 While factor-analysing the 80 × 80 correlation matrix, out of the following 4 factor extraction methods, which one has probably been employed in the above work?

1 Least square method

2 Confirmatory factor analysis method

3 Principal axes method

4 Principal components method

Ans. *(4)*

Exp. While factor-analysing the 80 x 80 correlation matrix, principal components analysis probably has been employed in the above work.

Retaining unities in the diagonal spaces of the 80 x 80 correlation matrix, the unrotated factors were extracted. The correlation matrix, which is used for principal components analysis, retains unities in themain diagonal. Principal components analysis yields one or more composite variables that capture much of the information originally contained in a larger set of items. The components, moreover, are defined as weighted sums of the original items. That is, principal components are linear transformations of the original variables. They are grounded in actual data and are derived from the actual items. They are merely a reorganization of the information in the actual items.

47 Which one of the following, is not the criterion for deciding the number of factors for rotation?

1 Cattell's Scree

2 Guttmann's root ≥ 1 criterion

3 Percentage of total variance explained by the factor solution

4 Wilks' criterion

Ans. *(4)*

➲ *Exp.* The only criterion not used for deciding the number of factors for rotation is Wilk's criterion.

Wilks's lambda distribution (named for Samuel S.Wilks), is a probability distribution used in multivariate hypothesis testing, especially with regard to the likelihood-ratio test and Multivariate Analysis of Variance (MANOVA). Wilks' lambda is a measure of how well each function separates cases into groups. It is equal to the proportion of the total variance in the discriminant scores not explained by differences among the groups. Smaller values of Wilks' lambda indicate greater discriminatory ability of the function. The associated chi-square statistic tests the hypothesis that the means of the functions listed are equal across groups. The small significance value indicates that the discriminant function does better than chance at separating the groups.

48 Out of the following 4 factor rotation methods, which method(s) can yield the above reported results?

I. Oblimin rotation
II. Varimax rotation
III. Promax rotation
IV. Quartimax rotation

Select the correct answer using the codes given below :

1 I and II
2 I and III
3 II and III
4 II and IV

Ans. (2)

➲ *Exp.* Out of the following 4 factor rotation methods, the methods which yield the above reported results are oblimin and promax. Both oblimin and promax are used for non-orthogonal (oblique) rotation of factors.

Oblimin rotation: It is a method for oblique (nonorthogonal) rotation. When delta equals 0 (the default), solutions are most oblique. As delta becomes more negative, the factors become less oblique. To override the default delta of 0, enter a number less than or equal to 0.8.

Promax rotation: It is an oblique rotation, which allows factors to be correlated. This rotation can be calculatedmore quickly than a direct oblimin rotation, so it is useful for large datasets.

Varimax and Quartimax are used for orthogonal rotation of factors.

49 Which of the following conditions are necessary for carrying out second-order factor analysis ?

I. It is hypothesised that there are a few orthogonal second-order factors.

II. The first-order factors should have been obliquely rotated.

III. At least, some of the inter-factor correlations should be fairly high.

Which of the statements given above are correct?

1 I and II
2 I and III
3 II and III
4 All of these

Ans. (3)

➲ *Exp.* The following conditions are necessary for carrying out second-order factor analysis:

The first-order factors should have been obliquely rotated. Oblique rotation is a transformational system used in factor analysis when two or more factors (i.e., latent variables) are correlated. Oblique rotation reorients the factors so that they fall closer to clusters of vectors representing manifest variables, thereby simplifying the mathematical description of the manifest variables.

At least, some of the inter-factor correlations should be fairly high. A second-order factor is a latent construct that emerges from a further factor analysis (i.e., a second-order factor analysis) of the primary dimensions derived from correlations among a set of items or variables. The higher order dimensions so derived are held to generate the first-order factors that in turn generate observed responses at the level of the individual item or scale.

Orthogonal rotation is a transformational system used in factor analysis in which the different underlying or latent variables are required to remain separated from or uncorrelated with one another.

50 The two factors are said to be orthogonal, when the angle of separation between the two factors is

1 90 degrees
2 lesser than 90 degrees
3 greater than 90 degrees
4 in between 0 to 180 degrees

Ans. (1)

➲ *Exp.* The two factors are said to be orthogonal, when the angle of separation between the two factors is 90 degrees. Two lines or planes are orthogonal if they are at right angles (90°) to each other.

51 Difficulty in deployment of attention can occur, in which of the following states?

I. Engagement
II. Distraction
III. Disengagement
IV. Shifting

Select the correct answer using the codes given below :

1 I and III
2 I, II and IV
3 I, III and IV
4 II, III and IV

Ans. (3)

➲ *Exp.* The correct codes are I, III and IV.

According to Posner and Petersen (1990), spatially selective attention involves three components. The difficulty in deployment of attention can occur in: engagement, Disengagement and Shifting.

Engagement: Engagement is the beginning of preferential processing.

Disengagement: Disengagement is the end of preferential processing.

Shifting: Shifting is the movement of attention.

52 Match the List I with List II and select the correct answer from the codes given below :

List I (Types)	List II (Examples)
A. Emotional	I. Feedback from others about how one is doing
B. Instrumental	II. Listening to people's problems, caring, reassurance
C. Appraisal	III. Simple conversation, recreation, going shopping
D. Socialising	IV. Material supports, low interest loan, medicine etc

Codes

	A	B	C	D		A	B	C	D
1	I	III	II	IV	2	II	I	IV	III
3	II	IV	I	III	4	I	IV	III	II

Ans. *(3)*

➲ *Exp.* The correct matching is A-II, B-IV, C-I, D-III.

An example of *emotional support* is listening to people's problems, caring, and reassurance. Emotional support is talking about personal problems, displays of encouragement, attachment, etc.

An example of *instrumental support* is listening to material supports, low interest loan, medicine etc. Material support/instrumental support includes direct material aid, care and favors, etc.

An example of *appraisal* is feedback from others about how one is doing. Appraisal has three basic functions: (1) to provide adequate feedback to each person on his or her performance; (2) to serve as a basis for modifying or changing behavior toward more effective working habits; and (3) to provide data to managers with which they may judge future job assignments and compensation.

An example of *socialising* is simple conversation, recreation, going shopping. Socialising is the action or practice of participating in social activities or mixing socially with others.

53 Match the List I with List II and select the correct answer from the codes given below :

List I (Type of correlation)	List II (Brief explanation)
A. Phi-coefficient	I. Correlation of a variable with a set of other variables
B. Spearman rho	II. Correlation between a dichotomous variable and a continuous variable
C. Partial correlation	III. Correlation between two variables measured on or transformed to ordinal scale
D. Point biserial correlation	IV. Correlation between two variables after removing the influence of extraneous variable(s)
	V. Correlation between two dichotomous variables

Codes

	A	B	C	D		A	B	C	D
1	V	III	IV	II	2	II	III	IV	V
3	V	III	I	IV	4	III	V	IV	I

Ans. *(1)*

➲ *Exp.* The correct matching is A-V, B-III, C-IV, D-II.

Phi-coefficient is the correlation between two dichotomous variables. The phi correlation coefficient (phi) is one of a number of correlation statistics developed to measure the strength of association between two variables. The phi is a nonparametric statistic used in cross-tabulated table data where both variables are dichotomous. Dichotomous means that there are only two possible values for a variable.

Spearman rho is the correlation between two variables measured on or transformed to ordinal scale. Spearman correlation coefficient is a nonparametric measure of statistical dependence between two variables that were measured on an ordinal scale; that is, the individual observations (cases) can be ranked into two ordered series. It is also called Spearman's rank correlation coefficient and Spearman's rho.

Partial correlation is the correlation between two variables after removing the influence of extraneous variable(s). Partial correlation is the association between two variables, x and y, with the influence of one or more other variables (z1, z2) statistically removed, controlled, or held constant; the effect of the z variable is removed from both x and y.

Point biserial correlation is the correlation between a dichotomous variable and a continuous variable. The Point Biserial Correlation coefficient is a special case of Pearson 's correlation coefficient. It measures the relationship between two variables: One continuous variable (must be ratio scale or interval scale) and one naturally binary variable.

54 Match the List I with List II and select the correct answer from the codes given below :

List I (Personality Approaches)	List II (Phenomenon)
A. Analytical Psychology	I. Peak experience
B. Individual Psychology	II. Transference neurosis
C. Humanistic Psychology	III. Will to Power
D. Psychoanalysis	IV. Archetypes

Codes

	A	B	C	D		A	B	C	D
1	II	IV	I	III	2	IV	III	I	II
3	I	III	IV	II	4	IV	II	III	I

Ans. *(2)*

Exp. The correct matching is A-IV, B-III, C-I, D-II.

Analytical Psychology involves Archetypes. Analytical psychology is a theory of mind that emphasises the importance of wholeness for each individual. Archetype is any one of a set of symbols representing aspects of the psyche that derive from the accumulated experience of humankind.

Individual Psychology involves Will to Power. Individual psychology is the psychological theory of Alfred Adler, which is based on the idea that throughout life individuals strives for a sense of mastery, completeness, and belonging and is governed by a conscious drive to overcome their sense of inferiority by developing to their fullest potential, obtaining their life goals, and creating their own styles of life. Will to Power is the determination to strive for superiority and domination, which he believed to be particularly strong in men who feel a need to escape the feelings of insecurity and inferiority that they associate with femininity.

Humanistic Psychology involves Peak experience. Humanistic psychology is a psychological perspective that emphasises the study of the whole person. Peak experience is a moment of awe, ecstasy, or sudden insight into life as a powerful unity transcending space, time, and the self.

Psychoanalysis involves Transference. Psychoanalysis was founded by Sigmund Freud (1856-1939). Freud believed that people could be cured by making conscious their unconscious thoughts and motivations, thus gaining insight. Transference is a patient's displacement or projection onto the analyst of those unconscious feelings and wishes originally directed toward important individuals, such as parents, in the patient's childhood.

55 Given below are two statements, one labelled as Assertion (A) and the other labelled as Reason (R). Read the statements and choose the correct answer using the codes given below.

Assertion (A) Thyroid over-secretion leads to a condition known as 'Grave's disease'.

Reason (R) Grave's disease is characterised by accelerated metabolic processes.

Codes

1. Both (A) and (R) are true and (R) is the correct explanation of (A)
2. Both (A) and (R) are true, but (R) is not the correct explanation of (A)
3. (A) is true, but (R) is false
4. (A) is false, but (R) is true

Ans. *(2)*

Exp. Both (A) and (R) are true, but (R) is not the correct explanation of (A)

Thyroid over-secretion leads to a condition known as 'Grave's disease'. It is as Grave's disease is a type of autoimmune problem that causes the thyroid gland to produce too much thyroid hormone, which is called hyperthyroidism. Graves' disease is often the underlying cause of hyperthyroidism. In Graves' disease, your immune systemcreates antibodies that cause the thyroid to grow and make more thyroid hormone than your body needs. These antibodies are called Thyroid Stimulating Immunoglobulins (TSIs). The TSIs bind to thyroid cell receptors, which are normally 'docking stations' for thyroid-stimulating hormone (TSH—the hormone responsible for telling the thyroid to produce hormones). The TSIs then trick the thyroid into growing and producing too much thyroid hormone, leading to hyperthyroidism.

Grave's disease is characterised by accelerated metabolic processes. Increased basal metabolic rate or resting energy expenditure has been observed in patients with hyperthyroidism, but that does not explain the over-secretion of thyroid hormone.

56 Which of the following emerges, when self-control replaces parental-control?

1 Ego 2 Super ego
3 Identity Achievement 4 Identity Diffusion

Ans. *(2)*

Exp. Super ego emerges, when self-control replaces parental control.

The super ego incorporates the values and morals of society which are learned from one's parents and others. It develops around the age of 3 – 5 during the phallic stage of psychosexual development. The superego's function is to control the id's impulses, especially those which society forbids, such as sex and aggression. It also has the function of persuading the ego to turn to moralistic goals rather than simply realistic ones and to strive for perfection.

57 In a repeated measures ANOVA, with twenty subjects, each subject was tested under all 3 experimental conditions, the conditions X subjects variance (also used as an estimate of error variance) would be based on ____ degrees of freedom.

1 3 2 19 3 38 4 57

Ans. *(3)*

Exp. In a repeated measures ANOVA, with twenty subjects, each subject was tested under all 3 experimental conditions, the conditions X subjects variance (also used as an estimate of error variance) would be based on 38 degrees of freedom.

In the given question,

k = 3 (three experimental conditions are given)

n = 20 (number of subjects)

degrees of freedom of subjects = k-1

In repeated measures ANOVA, the error degrees of freedom can be calculated using the formula, df = (n-1)(k-1)

Therefore, df = 38

58 Arrange the following correlations in descending order in terms of the strength of relationship between the two variables

I. 0.8 II. – 0.5
III. 0.4 IV. – 0.9

Codes

1 IV, II, III, I 2 IV, I, II, III
3 I, III, II, IV 4 III, II, I, IV

Ans. (2)

Exp. Arrangement of correlations in descending order in terms of the strength of relationship between the two variables is -0.9, 0,8, -0.5, 0.4.

Correlation strength is measured from -1.00 to +1.00. The correlation coefficient, often expressed as r, indicates a measure of the direction and strength of a relationship between two variables. When the r value is closer to +1 or -1, it indicates that there is a stronger linear relationship between the two variables. A correlation of -0.9 is a strong negative correlation while a correlation of 0.4 would be a weak positive correlation. A correlation of -0.5 is weaker than -0.9, and a correlation of 0.8 is stronger than 0.4.

59 Hypnagogic images occur during drowsy state i.e. between ...... and ...... whereas hypnopompic images occur between ...... and ....

1 waking, sleeping; waking, sleeping
2 sleeping, waking; waking, sleeping
3 waking, sleeping; sleeping, waking
4 sleeping, waking; sleeping, waking

Ans. (3)

Exp. Hypnagogic images occur during drowsy state i.e. between waking and sleeping whereas hypnopompic images occur between sleeping and waking .

Hypnagogic or hypnopompic hallucinations are visual, tactile, auditory, or other sensory events, usually brief but occasionally prolonged, that occur at the transition from wakefulness to sleep (hypnagogic) or from sleep to wakefulness (hypnopompic). There is a tendency for hypnagogic and hypnopompic hallucinations associated with narcolepsy to be associated with certain HLA phenotypes.

Hypnagogic is describing or relating to the drowsy state that occurs in the transition from wakefulness to sleep. A transient, dreamlike image experienced while falling asleep is called a hypnagogic hallucination.

Hypnopompic is describing or relating to the transitional state between sleep and wakefulness. An imaginary sensory perception occurring just prior to full wakefulness is called a hypnopompic hallucination.

60 Learning is knowledge acquisition through cognitive processing of information. Who among the following holds this view?

1 Dollard and Miller 2 Edward Tolman
3 Albert Bandura 4 Michael Posner

Ans. (3)

Exp. Learning is knowledge acquisition through cognitive processing of information. This is the view of Albert Bandura.

Social learning theory, proposed by Albert Bandura, emphasizes the importance of observing, modelling, and imitating the behaviors, attitudes, and emotional reactions of others. Social learning theory considers how both environmental and cognitive factors interact to influence human learning and behavior.

61 Match the List I with List II and select the correct answer from the codes given below :

List I (Psychologists)	List II (Theoretical Model)
A. Broadbent	I. Late selection model
B. Deutsch and Deutsch	II. Attenuation model
C. Treisman	III. Capacity model
D. Kahneman	IV. Filter model

Codes

	A	B	C	D		A	B	C	D
1	II	IV	III	I	2	IV	I	II	III
3	I	III	IV	II	4	III	II	I	IV

Ans. (2)

Exp. The correct matching is A-IV, B-I, C-II, D-III.

Broadbent is associated with Filter model. Broadbent (1958) proposed that physical characteristics of messages are used to select one message for further processing and that all others are lost. Information from all of the stimuli presented at any given time enters an unlimited capacity sensory buffer. One of the inputs is then selected on the basis of its physical characteristics for further processing by being allowed to pass through a filter.

Deutsch and Deutsch are associated with Late selection model. The late selection or response selection model proposed by Deutsch and Deutsch (1963) suggests that all information in the unattended ear is processed on the basis of meaning, not just the selected or highly pertinent information.

Treisman is associated with Attenuation model. Treisman (1964) agrees with Broadbent's theory of an early bottleneck filter. However, the difference is that Treisman's filter attenuates rather than eliminates the unattended material. Attenuation is like turning down the volume so that if you have 4 sources of sound in one room (TV, radio, people talking, baby crying) you can turn down or attenuate 3 in order to attend to the fourth. This means that people can still process the meaning of the attended message(s).

Kahneman is associated with Capacity model. Capacity theory is the theoretical approach that pulled researchers from Filter theories with Kahneman's published 1973 study, Attention and Effort positing attention was limited in overall capacity, that a person's ability to perform simultaneous tasks depends on how much "capacity" the jobs require.

62 The process of organic and intellectual self-regulation is called

1 equilibration
2 equilibrium
3 assimilation
4 accommodation

Ans. (1)

Exp. The process of organic and intellectual self-regulation is called equilibration.

According to Piaget, development is driven by the process of equilibration. Equilibration encompasses assimilation (i.e., people transform incoming information so that it fits within their existing thinking) and accommodation (i.e, people adapt their thinking to incoming information). When a child's existing schemas are capable of explaining what it can perceive around it, it is said to be in a state of equilibrium, i.e. a state of cognitive (i.e. mental) balance. Piaget emphasised the importance of schemas in cognitive development, and described how they were developed or acquired.

63 Which of the following dimension(s) given by Guilford in his structure of intellect model explains the concept of creativity?

I. Operations
II. Contents
III. Products

Select the correct answer using the codes given below :

1 Only I
2 Only II
3 I and II
4 II and III

Ans. (1)

Exp. The dimension Operations given by Guilford in his structure of intellect model explains the concept of creativity.

In Guilford's Structure of Intellect (SI) theory, intelligence is viewed as comprising operations, contents, and products. There are 6 kinds of operations (cognition, memory recording, memory retention, divergent production, convergent production, evaluation), 6 kinds of products (units, classes, relations, systems, transformations, and implications), and 5 kinds of contents (visual, auditory, symbolic, semantic, behavioral). Since each of these dimensions is independent, there are theoretically 180 different components of intelligence. Parenthetically, it is interesting to note that a major impetus for Guilford's theory was his interest in creativity (Guilford, 1950). The divergent production operation identifies a number of different types of creative abilities.

64 "Any activity can be a reinforce, if a contingency schedule constraints an animal's access to that activity." This is known as

1 Instinctual drift
2 Disequilibrium hypothesis
3 Premack principle
4 Concurrent reinforcement schedule

Ans. (2)

Exp. "Any activity can be reinforcer if a contingency schedule constraints an animal's access to that activity". This is known as Disequilibrum hypothesis.

Disequilibrium, then, refers to our inability to fit new information into our schema. When you come across information or experiences that do not fit into your current knowledge base, this is where disequilibrium begins.

65 Token economy is a behaviour modification technique based on the following learning principles

I. Discrimination learning
II. Contingency contracting
III. Positive reinforcement
IV. Classical conditioning

Select the correct answer using the codes given below :

1 I and III
2 II and IV
3 II and III
4 III and IV

Ans. (3)

Exp. Token economy is a behaviour modification technique based on the following learning principles:

Contingency contracting : A contingency contract is a mutually agreed-upon statement between a teacher and student, a parent and child, or a client and therapist regarding the change or changes desired, typically specifying behaviors and their positive and negative consequences.

Positive reinforcement : Positive reinforcement involves the addition of a reinforcing stimulus following a behaviour that makes it more likely that the behaviour will occur again in the future. When a favourable outcome, event, or reward occurs after an action, that particular response or behaviour will be strengthened.

66 Given below are two statements, one labelled as Assertion (A) and the other labelled as Reason (R). Read the statements and choose the correct answer using the codes given below.

Assertion (A) When asked about his religious beliefs, Ram expressed 'I do not know. I just don't see how there can be God and yet so much evil in the world'.

Reason (R) Identity-foreclosed individuals have committed themselves to values and goals without exploring alternatives.

Codes

1 Both (A) and (R) are true and (R) is the correct explanation of (A)
2 Both (A) and (R) are true, but (R) is not the correct explanation of (A)
3 (A) is true, but (R) is false
4 (A) is false, but (R) is true

Ans. (2)

Exp. Both (A) and (R) are true but (R) is not the correct explanation of (A).

When asked about his religious beliefs, Ram expressed 'I do not know. I just don't see how there can be God and yet so much evil in the world'. In the given example, Ram is not yet sure about believing in God. He might have explored his options which suggest that God may not be present because of the evil persistent in the world.

Identity-foreclosed individuals have committed themselves to values and goals without exploring alternatives. This is true as Identity foreclosure occurs when people think they know who they are, but they have not even explored their options yet. Perhaps they grew up in a Christian home, attended Christian schools, and associated primarily with others in the faith. They may identify as a Christian without ever questioning their belief system. Then they leave home and meetmore diverse groups of people or study world religions in school and decide to reevaluate their religious beliefs. However, this does not explain Ram beliefs.

67 Match the List I with List II and select the correct answer from the codes given below :

List I (Learning Concepts)	List II (Explanations)
A. Drive	I. The learner must do something
B. Cue	II. The learner must attend something
C. Response	III. The learner's behaviour must get him/her something he/she wants
D. Reinforcement	IV. The learner must want something

Codes

	A	B	C	D
1	I	II	III	IV
2	II	III	IV	I
3	IV	II	I	III
4	III	IV	I	II

Ans. (3)

Exp. The correct matching is A-IV, B-II, C-I, D-III.

Drive is when the learner must want something. A drive, such as hunger or thirst, motivates the organism to act in ways that will reduce the tension. Drive is a generalized state of readiness precipitating or motivating an activity or course of action. Drive is hypothetical in nature, usually created by deprivation of a needed substance (e.g., food), the presence of negative stimuli (e.g., pain, cold), or the occurrence of negative events.

Cue is when the learner must attend something. Cues are internal or external events which have a signaling significance to an organism which subsequently affects learning and behaviour. The cue may be verbal of non-verbal. Psychologists tend to manipulate cues in studies of memory perception etc.

Response is when the learner must do something. Response is any glandular, muscular, neural, or other reaction to a stimulus. A response is a clearly defined, measurable unit of behavior discussed in terms of its result (e.g., pressing a lever, indicating yes vs. no on a survey item) or its physical characteristics (e.g., raising an arm).

Reinforcement is when the learner's behaviour must get him/her something he/she wants. The term reinforce means to strengthen, and is used in psychology to refer to anything stimulus which strengthens or increases the probability of a specific response.

68 Given below are two statements, one labelled as Assertion (A) and the other labelled as Reason (R). Read the statements and choose the correct answer using the codes given below.

Assertion (A) Children have remarkable ability to create mental representations of the world in the form of language.

Reason (R) Reasoning and problem solving are the ways of manipulating the ideas.

Codes

1 Both (A) and (R) are true and (R) is the correct explanation of (A)
2 Both (A) and (R) are true, but (R) is not the correct explanation of (A)
3 (A) is true, but (R) is false
4 (A) is false, but (R) is true

Ans. (2)

Exp. Both (A) and (R) are true, but (R) is not the correct explanation of (A).

Children have remarkable ability to create mental representations of the world in the form of language. This is true as Piaget claimed that cognitive development is at the center of the human organism, and language is contingent on knowledge and understanding acquired through cognitive development. According to Piaget, children are born with a very basic mental structure (genetically inherited and evolved) on which all subsequent learning and knowledge is based.

Reasoning and problem solving are the ways of manipulating the ideas. This is true as thinking is a complex mental process through which we manipulate information (either acquired or stored). However, this does not explain children's ability to create mental representations of the world in the form of language.

69 Given below are two statements, one labelled as Assertion (A) and the other labelled as Reason (R). Read the statements and choose the correct answer using the codes given below.

Assertion (A) Increased metabolic activity in frontal cortex and the caudate nucleus has been implicated in Obsessive Compulsive Disorder.

Reason (R) Current evidence suggests that increased serotonin activity and increased sensitivity of some brain structures to serotonin are involved in Obsessive Compulsive Symptoms.

Codes

1 Both (A) and (R) are true and (R) is the correct explanation of (A)
2 Both (A) and (R) are true, but (R) is not the correct explanation of (A)
3 (A) is true, but (R) is false
4 (A) is false, but (R) is true

***Ans.** (2)*

Exp. Both (A) and (R) are true, but (R) is not the correct explanation of (A).

Increased metabolic activity in frontal cortex and the caudate nucleus has been implicated in Obsessive Compulsive Disorder. Obsessive-Compulsive Disorder (OCD) is an anxiety disorder characterised by uncontrollable, unwanted thoughts and repetitive, ritualised behaviours you feel compelled to perform. Functional imaging studies have reported with remarkable consistency hyperactivity in the Orbitofrontal Cortex (OFC), Anterior Cingulate Cortex (ACC), and caudate nucleus of patients with Obsessive-Compulsive Disorder (OCD).

Current evidence suggests that increased serotonin activity and increased sensitivity of some brain structures to serotonin are involved in obsessive compulsive symptoms. The functional imagining findings have often been interpreted as evidence that abnormalities in cortico-basal ganglia-thalamo-cortical loops involving the OFC and ACC are causally related to OCD. This interpretation remains controversial, however, because such hyperactivity may represent either a cause or a consequence of the symptoms.

Both are true, but the reason does not follow the assertion.

70 Given below are two statements, one labelled as Assertion (A) and the other labelled as Reason (R). Read the statements and choose the correct answer using the codes given below.

Assertion (A) Cattell used the term 'Ergs' to explain the source of motivation.

Reason (R) Ergs were regarded by Cattell as static and secondary units of personality.

Codes

1 Both (A) and (R) are true and (R) is the correct explanation of (A)
2 Both (A) and (R) are true, but (R) is not the correct explanation of (A)
3 (A) is true, but (R) is false
4 (A) is false, but (R) is true

***Ans.** (1)*

Exp. Both (A) and (R) are true, and (R) is the correct explanation of (A).

Cattell used the term 'Ergs' to explain the source of motivation. Erg is a term used by Raymond B. Cattell, in preference to drive or instinct, to denote a type of innate dynamic trait that directs an individual toward a goal and provides the motivational energy to obtain it. Examples include curiosity, self-assertion, gregariousness, protectiveness, and hunger.

Ergs were regarded by Cattell as static and secondary units of personality. Erg is a constitutional trait, it is a permanent or static structure of the personality. It may strengthen or weaken but it cannot disappear.

71 Age related changes in intelligence are best explained by

1 Cattell's theory
2 Jensen's theory
3 Sternberg's theory
4 Guilford's theory

***Ans.** (1)*

Exp. Age related changes in intelligence are best explained by Cattell's theory.

Cattell–Horn theory of intelligence is a theory proposing that there are two main kinds of intellectual abilities nested under general intelligence: g-c, or crystallized intelligence (or ability), which is the sum of one's knowledge and is measured by tests of vocabulary, general information, and so forth; and g-f, or fluid intelligence (or ability), which is the set of mental processes that is used in dealing with relatively novel tasks and is used in the acquisition of g-c.

In later versions of the theory, other abilities were added, such as g-v, or visual intelligence (or ability), which is the set of mental processes used in handling visual-spatial tasks (e.g., mentally rotating a geometric figure or visualizing what pieces of paper would look like if folded). This theory was originated by Raymond B. Cattell in the 1940s; subsequently developed by U.S. psychologist John L. Horn (1928–2006) beginning in the 1960s.

72 Given below are two statements, one labelled as Assertion (A) and the other labelled as Reason (R). Read the statements and choose the correct answer using the codes given below.

Assertion (A) Vigilance refers to a person attending to a field of stimulation over a prolonged period of time in which the person seeks to detect the appearance of a particular target stimulus.

Reason (R) Signal Detection Theory suggests that detection of stimuli depends on their physical energy and on internal factors.

Codes

1 Both (A) and (R) are true and (R) is the correct explanation of (A)
2 Both (A) and (R) are true, but (R) is not the correct explanation of (A)
3 (A) is true, but (R) is false
4 (A) is false, but (R) is true

Ans. (2)

Exp. Both (A) and (R) are true, but (R) is not the correct explanation of (A).

Vigilance refers to a person attending to a field of stimulation over a prolonged period of time in which the person seeks to detect the appearance of a particular target stimulus. Vigilance is a state of extreme awareness and watchfulness directed by one or more members of a group toward the environment, often toward potential threats (e.g., predators, intruders, enemy forces in combat). In a military context, vigilance tasks (e.g., sentry duty, ship and air traffic control, antiaircraft and missile defense tracking) demand maximum physiological and psychological attention and readiness to react, characterized by an ability to attend and respond to stimulus changes for uninterrupted periods of time. This level of vigilance can produce significant cognitive stress and occasional physiological stress reactions.

Signal Detection Theory suggests that detection of stimuli depends on their physical energy and on internal factors. Signal detection theory (SDT) has provided a valuable theoretical framework for describing perceptual and other aspects of cognition and for quantitatively relating psychophysical phenomena to findings from sensory physiology. A key notion of SDT is that human performance in many tasks is limited by variability in the internal representation of stimuli due to internal or external noise. Both are true, but the reason does not follow the assertion.

73 Match the List I with List II and select the correct answer from the codes given below

List I (Thinking Style)	List II (Developmental Stage)
A. Egocentric thought	I. Sensorimotor
B. Object permanence	II. Formal operational
C. Abstract reasoning	III. Pre-operational
D. Conservation, reversibility	IV. Concrete operational

Codes

	A	B	C	D
1	II	III	IV	I
2	III	I	II	IV
3	IV	II	I	III
4	III	I	IV	II

Ans. (2)

Exp. The correct matching is A-III, B-I, C-II, D-IV.

Egocentric thought is a part of Pre-operational stage. At this stage, kids learn through pretend play but still struggle with logic and taking the point of view of other people. Egocentrism refers to the child's inability to see a situation from another person's point of view. The egocentric child assumes that other people see, hear, and feel exactly the same as the child does.

Object permanence is a part of Sensorimotor stage. During this stage, infants and toddlers acquire knowledge through sensory experiences and manipulating objects. Piaget believed that developing object permanence or object constancy, the understanding that objects continue to exist even when they cannot be seen, was an important element at this point of development. Object permanence is the knowledge of the continued existence of objects even when they are not directly perceived.

Abstract reasoning is a part of Formal operational stage. The final stage of Piaget's theory involves an increase in logic, the ability to use deductive reasoning, and an understanding of abstract ideas.

Conservation and reversibility is a part of Concrete operational stage. Kids at this point of development begin to think more logically, but their thinking can also be very rigid. They tend to struggle with abstract and hypothetical concepts. Conservation is the belief that an amount or quantity stays the same even if it changes apparent size or shape. Reversibility takes conservation one step further.

74 Given below are two statements, one labelled as Assertion (A) and the other labelled as Reason (R). Read the statements and choose the correct answer using the codes given below.

Assertion (A) Damage to the temporal lobe can result in psychological blindness.

Reason (R) The temporal lobe forms and stores visual and verbal memory.

Codes

1 Both (A) and (R) are true and (R) is the correct explanation of (A)
2 Both (A) and (R) are true, but (R) is not the correct explanation of (A)
3 (A) is true, but (R) is false
4 (A) is false, but (R) is true

Ans. (4)

Exp. (A) is false, but (R) is true.

Damage to the temporal lobe can result in psychological blindness. This is false as research has shown that in patients with lesions to the parietal cortex fail to respond to and report stimuli presented on the side of space contralateral to damage. That is, they appear to be functionally blind to a range of stimuli since such lesions do not result in any sensory deficits, shortcomings have been explained in terms of a lack of attentional processing, for which the parietal cortese plays a large role.

The temporal labe forms and stores visual and vermal memory is true.

The temporal lobes are highly associated with memory skills. Left temporal lesions result in impaired memory for verbal material. Right side lesions result in recall of non-verbal material, such as music and drawings.

75 Given below are two statements, one labelled as Assertion (A) and the other labelled as Reason (R). Read the statements and choose the correct answer using the codes given below.

Assertion (A) The size of differences in the intelligence scores between fathers and sons explains the group differences in intelligence.

Reason (R) In Jensen's views, the sons' tend to be higher or lower in intelligence than their fathers who are very low and high on intelligence, respectively.

Codes

1 Both (A) and (R) are true and (R) is the correct explanation of (A)

2 Both (A) and (R) are true, but (R) is not the correct explanation of (A)

3 (A) is true, but (R) is false

4 (A) is false, but (R) is true

Ans. (1)

Exp. Both (A) and (R) are true and (R) is the correct explanation of (A).

The size of differences in the intelligence scores between fathers and sons explains the group differences in intelligence. Jensen (1969) proposed two level-theories of mental abilities and demonstrated clear-cut genetic differences in the average intelligence of races and social classes. According to Jensen, observations like very bright parents can have an intellectually mediocre child or that rather dull parents can have an exceptionally bright child have often pointed to mistakenly as evidence that intelligence is not inherited. But the fact is that genetic theory predicts precisely that we should find such discrepancies between parents and their offspring.

In Jensen's views, the sons' tend to be higher or lower in intelligence than their fathers who are very low and high on intelligence, respectively. A parent with a high IQ will usually, but by no means always, have children whose IQs are somewhat lower than his own but are still above the average for the general population. A parent with a low IQ, on the other hand, will usually, but not always, have children whose IQs are somewhat higher than his own but are still below the average of the population. This phenomenon, discovered by Sir Francis Galton, is called "regression toward the mean," and it holds true for height and other inherited physical traits as well as for IQ. Therefore, such discrepancies explain the differences in intelligences between parents and offspring.

UGC-NET PSYCHOLOGY SOLVED PAPER 2012 (June)

PAPER II

1 We sometimes attempt to solve problems by applying the techniques that worked in similar situations in the past. What type of method are we using?

1 Trial and error 2 Analogy
3 Algorithms 4 Heuristics

Ans. (2)

Exp. Analogy is an attempt to solve problems by applying the techniques that worked in similar situations in the past.

A problem is said to be analogous if it is similar to the previous problem. This method to problem solving involves using an old solution to solve a new problem and find a new solution. In other words, a previous problem is solved effectively and the content learned from the old problem is incorporated into the new problem to find a new solution. In order to use an old solution for a new problem, one must be able to distinguish the basic foundation of the problem at hand and draw a correlation from the new problem to the old problem.

2 The fact that a nearer object may obscure a more distant object from the view is due to

1 figure and ground 2 proximity
3 interposition 4 closure

Ans. (3)

Exp. The fact that a nearer object may obscure a more distant object from the view is due to interposition.

Interposition occurs in instances where one object overlaps the other, which causes us to perceive depth. Interposition or overlapping is a type of monocular cue in which one object partially covers another. It creates the appearance that the object that is being covered or overlapped, is the one that is further away.

3 Match List I with List II and indicate your answer with the help of codes given below.

List I (Phenomenon)	List II (Psychologist)
A. Learned helplessness	I. Bandura
B. Cognitive map	II. Seligman
C. Observational learning	III. Wolpe
D. Systematic desensitisation	IV. Tolman

Codes

	A	B	C	D
1	II	IV	I	III
2	III	IV	II	I
3	I	III	IV	II
4	IV	II	III	I

Ans. (1)

Exp. The correct match is A-II, B-IV, C-I, D-III.

Learned helplessness was proposed by Seligman. Learned helplessness is a state that occurs after a person has experienced a stressful situation repeatedly. They come to believe that they are unable to control or change the situation, so they do not try — even when opportunities for change become available.

Cognitive map was proposed by Tolman. A cognitive map is a mental picture or image of the layout of one's physical environment. Cognitive maps can help us navigate unfamiliar territory, give directions and learn or recall information. When we create cognitive maps, we often omit information that is irrelevant to the task at hand.

Observational learning was proposed by Bandura. Observational learning is concerned with the acquisition of attitudes, values and styles of thinking and behaving through observation of the examples provided by others. The importance of observational learning lies in helping individuals, especially children, to acquire new responses by observing others' behavior.

Systematic desensitisation was proposed by Wolpe. Systematic desensitization is a type of behavioral therapy based on the principle of classical conditioning for the treatment or therapy for phobias, fears and aversions that people have. The premise is to reduce a person's anxiety responses through counter-conditioning - a person who learned to be afraid of something is associating fear with that object or behaviour and the way to eliminate this is to teach the person to replace the feelings of anxiety with feelings of relaxation when the object or behaviour is present.

4 In a 3×4 contingency table, using chi-square test, the degrees of freedom associated with the chi-square will be

1 12 2 9
3 7 4 6

Ans. (4)

Exp. In a 3 × 4 contingency table, using chi-square test, the degrees of freedom associated with the chi-square will be

The degrees of freedom is calculated using the formula:

$df = (r-1)(c-1)$, where r is the number of rows and c is the number of columns. Here r = 3, c = 4.

The degrees of freedom is $(3-1)(4-1) = 6$.

5 Match List I and List II and indicate your answer with the help of codes given below.

List I (Function)	List II (Area of the Brain)
A. Visuo-spatial function	I. Hypothalamus
B. Social norms	II. Cerebellum
C. Releasing factors	III. Orbito-frontal cortex
D. Balance	IV. Parietal cortex

Codes

	A	B	C	D
1	II	I	IV	III
2	I	II	III	IV
3	IV	III	II	I
4	IV	III	I	II

Ans. (4)

Exp. The correct match is A-IV, B-III, C-I, D-II.

The *Hypothalamus* controls the releasing factors. It is a section of the brain responsible for the production of many of the body's essential releasing factors like corticotrophin-releasing factor, prolactin-releasing factor and the somatotropin-releasing factor. These releasing factors stimulate the pituitary gland which in turn release hormones, or chemical substances that govern physiologic functions such as temperature regulation, thirst, hunger, sleep, mood, sex drive and the release of other hormones within the body.

The *Cerebellum* controls the balance. It receives information from the sensory systems, the spinal cord and other parts of the brain and then regulates motor movements and helps in maintaining balance. It is also important for learning motor behaviours.

The *Orbito-frontal cortex* controls the social norms. It is extensively connected with diverse neural areas that underlie its participation in social norms, i.e., what to do and what not to do. It receives extensive sensory input and sends output to areas important for social regulation. Any damage to the orbito-frontal cortex selectively impairs the ability to modify interpersonal behavior in reference to social norms.

The *Parietal cortex* controls the visuo-spatial function. It controls functions like control of spatial attention-shifting attention between visual field locations or sustaining attention to one location. As a part of the cortex, it has a lot of responsibilities and has to be able to process sensory information within seconds. The parietal lobe is where sensory information such as vision, taste, temperature and touch are integrated or processed.

6 Read each of the following two statements Assertion (A) and Reason (R) and indicate your answer using the codes given below.

Assertion (A) In Edwards Personal Preference Schedule (EPPS), forced choice format is used.

Reason (R) Forced choice format reduces acquiescence response set.

Codes

1 Both (A) and (R) are true and (R) is the correct explanation of (A)
2 Both (A) and (R) are true, but (R) is not the correct explanation of (A)
3 (A) is true, but (R) is false
4 (A) is false, but (R) is true

Ans. (3)

Exp. (A) is true, but (R) is false.

In Edwards Personal Preference Schedule (EPPS), forced choice format is used. Edwards Personal Preference Schedule (EPPS) is a forced choice, objective, non-projective personality inventory. The target audience in between the ages of 16-85 and takes about 45 minutes to complete. Edwards derived the test content from the human needs system theory proposed by Murray, which measures the rating of individuals in fifteen normal needs or motives. The EPPS was designed to illustrate relative importance to the individual of several significant needs and motives. So, A is true.

Forced choice format reduces acquiescence response set is false. Acquiescence response set is the tendency of a test responder to agree or say 'yes' to the presented items. Forced choice format instead increases acquiescence bias.

7 Why do individuals with high need for achievement quit early when faced by very difficult task?

1 Get tired easily
2 Have poor perseverance
3 Have high anxiety
4 Have high need for efficiency

Ans. (4)

Exp. Individuals with high need for achievement quit early when faced by very difficult task because they have a high need for efficiency.

The need for achievements refers to an individual's desire for significant accomplishment, mastering of skills, seeking control or achieving high standards. The need for achievement is greatest for those individuals who have a strong desire to excel. Achievers seek neither power nor approval; rather, their only focus is on success. Achievers prefer work that has a moderate chance for success (about 50/50) and tend to avoid situations that are low-risk and those that are high-risk.

Low-risk situations are avoided because of the presumed ease of accomplishment related to low-risk activities and the belief that things which come easy are not a true measure of success. High-risk situations are avoided by achievers because of the fear that success might be more related to luck than actual effort. Achievers need to be able to see the correlation between the level of effort they exert and the success that results.

8 Read each of the following two statements Assertion (A) and Reason (R) and indicate your answer using the codes given below.

Assertion (A) According to RB Cattell, source traits are important in the understanding of personality.

Reason (R) Oblique rotation is used for uncovering source traits.

Codes

1 Both (A) and (R) are true and (R) is the correct explanation of (A)
2 Both (A) and (R) are true, but (R) is not the correct explanation of (A)
3 (A) is true, but (R) is false
4 (A) is false, but (R) is true

Ans. *(1)*

Exp. Both (A) and (R) true and (R) is the correct explanation of (A).

According to RB Cattell, source traits are important in the understanding of personality. Cattell theorised that there are 16 source traits that are the building blocks of personality. All these traits form the part of an individual's personality. When all the source traits are taken together along with other variables in the environment they make up the surface traits, which are the traits we see and think of as personality. Therefore source traits are topological and are the inter-correlation among source traits which results in surface traits. Surface traits are considered one construct of multiple traits that go together.

Oblique rotation is used for uncovering source traits. Oblique rotation method is used to analyse information from a factor analysis. Factor analysis is a type of statistical procedure that is conducted to identify clusters or groups of related items (called factors) on a test. Rotation methods simplify factors and make results more reliable and easier to interpret. Rotation methods in which correlations between the factors are allowed are oblique. Oblique rotation is used for uncovering source traits as these source traits are important in understanding of personality.

9 Which of the following represents the Tetrad equation as given by Spearman?

1 $r_{12} \times r_{34} = r_{14} \times r_{23}$
2 $r_{13} \times r_{24} = r_{14} \times r_{23}$
3 $r_{14} \times r_{23} = r_{13} \times r_{24}$
4 All of these

Ans. *(4)*

Exp. The Tetrad equation as given by Spearman is $r_{ap} \times r_{bq} = r_{aq} \times r_{bp}$.

All the four equations r_1, r_2, r_3 and r_4 can be used once on both sides without repetition in different combinations.

10 What among the following define a problem space?

I. An initial state
II. A goal state
III. A set of operations

Codes

1 I and III
2 I and II
3 II and III
4 I, II and III

Ans. *(4)*

Exp. Initial state, goal state and set of operations define a problem space.

A problem space refers to the entire range of components that exist in the process of finding a solution to a problem. This range starts with 'defining the problem,' then proceeds to the intermediate stage of 'identifying and testing possible solutions' and ends with the final stage of 'choosing and implementing a solution'. It also includes all of the smaller steps that exist between these identified stages.

The Problem Solving Theory is composed of three equally different states, first initial state, which is the current state we are in, all the states in between and the final which is the goal state. We could compare this idea to a person who has to go through labyrinth and explore many different ways to find the exit. The mental operators help us enter different states of exploration of the same issue.

11 A generalised picture or model of an object or event, learned in the past and stored in memory, is

1 perceptual constancy
2 memory trace
3 prototype
4 cognitive map

Ans. *(3)*

Exp. A generalised picture or model of an object or event, learned in the past and stored in memory is Prototype.

A prototype is the best example or cognitive representation of something within a certain category. Prototypes are used to enhance memory and recall, since you can keep a prototype of something and then match new, similar things to the prototype in order to identify, categorise or store this new thing.

Perceptual constancy is the tendency of animals and humans to see familiar objects as having standard shape, size, colour, or location regardless of changes in the angle of perspective, distance, or lighting.

Memory trace also known as an engram is a unit of cognitive information imprinted in a physical substance, theorized to be the means by which memories are stored as biophysical or biochemical changes in the brain or other biological tissue, in response to external stimuli.

A cognitive map is a mental picture or image of the layout of one's physical environment. The term was first coined by a psychologist named Edward Tolman in the 1940s. Cognitive maps can help us navigate unfamiliar territory, give directions and learn or recall information. When we create cognitive maps, we often omit information that is irrelevant to the task at hand. This means that they can differ from the actual environment we are mapping.

12 Read each of the following two statements Assertion (A) and Reason (R) and indicate your answer using the codes given below.

Assertion (A) We are able to recognise the similarity and differences of two objects.

Reason (R) Dissociable sub-systems operate simultaneously in each cerebral hemisphere.

Codes

1 Both (A) and (R) are true and (R) is the correct explanation of (A)
2 Both (A) and (R) are true, but (R) is not the correct explanation of (A)
3 (A) is true, but (R) is false
4 (A) is false, but (R) is true

Ans. *(1)*

Exp. Both (A) and (R) true and (R) is the correct explanation of (A).

We are able to recognise the similarity and differences of two objects.

The dissociable neural subsystems operate in parallel (not in sequence) to underlie visual object recognition: An abstract-category subsystem operates more effectively than a specific-exemplar subsystem in the left hemisphere, and a specific-exemplar subsystem operates more effectively than an abstract-category subsystem in the right hemisphere.

13 What is the correct sequence of events given below?

I. Releasing of neurotransmitters
II. Post synaptic potential
III. Binding on receptor sites
IV. Synthesis of neurotransmitters

Codes

1 I, II, III, IV
2 IV, III, II, I
3 IV, I, III, II
4 II, IV, I, III

Ans. *(3)*

Exp. The correct sequence of events is arranged as follows:

Synthesis of neurotransmitters: Neurotransmitters are synthesized by neurons and are stored in vesicles, which are typically located in the axon's terminal ends.

Releasing of neurotransmitters: When an impulse arrives at a synapse from an activated neuron (also called presynaptic neuron), a chemical substance called a neurotransmitter is released.

Binding on receptor sites: The neurotransmitters released from the pre synaptic neuron will now bind to the receptors of the post synaptic neurons.

Post synaptic potential: The binding on the receptor sites leads to the opening of channel-shaped molecules in the membrane of the resting neuron (also called post synaptic neuron). Post Synaptic Potential (PSP) is a temporary change in the electric polarisation of the membrane of a nerve cell (neuron). The result of chemical transmission of a nerve impulse at the synapse (neuronal junction), the post synaptic potential can lead to the firing of a new impulse.

14 Read each of the following two statements Assertion (A) and Reason (R) and indicate your answer using the codes given below.

Assertion (A) The amplitude of the action potential in a neuron does not go beyond + 40 mV.

Reason (R) Neurons function on 'all or none' basis.

Codes

1 Both (A) and (R) are true and (R) is the correct explanation of (A)
2 Both (A) and (R) are true, but (R) is not the correct explanation of (A)
3 (A) is true, but (R) is false
4 (A) is false, but (R) is true

Ans. *(2)*

Exp. Both (A) and (R) true, but (R) is not the correct explanation of (A).

The amplitude of the action potential in a neuron does not go beyond + 40 mV. An action potential occurs when a neuron sends information down to an axon, away from the cell body. The action potential is an explosion of electrical activity that is created by a depolarising current. This means that some event (a stimulus) causes the resting potential to move toward 0 mV. When the depolarisation reaches about −55 mV a neuron will fire an action potential. This is the threshold. Additional sodium rushes in, and the membrane of the stimulated cell actually reverses its polarity so that the outside of the membrane is negative relative to the inside. Eventually, the cell potential reaches +40 mV, or the action potential. If the neuron does not reach this critical threshold level, then no action potential will fire.

Neurons function on 'all or none' basis. When the threshold level is reached, an action potential of a fixed size will always fire. For any given neuron, the size of the action potential is always the same. There are no big or small action potentials in one nerve cell as all action potentials are the same size. Therefore, the neuron either does not reach the threshold or a full action potential is fired - this is the 'all or none' principle. This is true but does not explain why the amplitude of the action potential in a neuron does not go beyond + 40 mV.

15 A man reflects his anger from his boss to his child, is an example of

1 projection
2 reaction formation
3 displacement
4 regression

Ans. (3)

Exp. A man reflects his anger from his boss to his child, is an example of displacement.

Displacement is the transfer of feelings or behavior from the original object to another person or thing. In psychoanalytic theory, displacement is considered to be a defense mechanism in which the individual discharges tensions associated with, for example, hostility and fear by taking them out on a less threatening target. Thus, a man might transfer his anger from his boss towards his child.

16 Speed and power tests can be distinguished on the basis of

I. time limit
II. difficulty level
III. verbal/non-verbal content

Codes

1 I and II　　2 I and III
3 II and III　　4 I, II and III

Ans. (1)

Exp. The correct codes are I and II.

Speed and power tests can be distinguished on the basis of:

Time limit: In a speed test, there is a time limit within which the test taker is required to answer all the items. Such a test evaluates the individual on the basis of time taken to answer the items accurately. The power test assesses the underlying ability of the individuals by allowing them sufficient time. It does not have a time limit.

Difficulty level: In a speed test, all the items are of the same degree of difficulty. In a power test, the items are generally arranged in an increasing order of difficulty.

17 Natural concepts are based on

1 prototypes
2 a set of rules/properties
3 schemas
4 propositions

Ans. (1)

Exp. Natural concepts are based on prototype. A member of the natural concept that might possess all or most of those characteristic features is called a prototype. A prototype is an example that embodies the most common and typical features of a concept.

A concept is a mental category used to represent a class or group of objects, people, organisations, events, situations or relations that share common characteristics or attributes. Formal concept that is clearly defined by a set of rules, a formal definition or a classification system; also known as an artificial concept. A Natural concept is acquired not from a definition but through everyday perceptions and experiences; also known as a fuzzy concept. People form natural concepts as the result of their experience in the real world.

18 Match List I and List II and indicate your answer with the help of codes given below.

List I (Presentation of reinforcement)	List II (Type of reinforcement)
A. An unpleasant stimulus is presented to decrease behaviour	I. Positive reinforcement
B. An unpleasant stimulus is removed to increase behaviour	II. Negative reinforcement
C. A pleasant stimulus is presented to increase behaviour	III. Positive punishment
D. A pleasant stimulus is removed to decrease behaviour	IV. Negative punishment

Codes

	A	B	C	D
1	I	II	III	IV
2	II	III	IV	I
3	IV	I	III	II
4	III	II	I	IV

Ans. (4)

Exp. The correct match is A-III, B-II, C-I, D-IV.

Positive reinforcement is when a pleasant stimulus is presented to increase behaviour. A positive reinforcement is a pleasant stimulus which is presented to increase or strengthen a behavior by providing a consequence an individual finds rewarding.

Negative reinforcement is when an unpleasant stimulus is removed to increase behaviour. A negative reinforcement is the removal of an unpleasant reinforcer or an adverse stimulus which is 'rewarding' to the animal or personwhich can also strengthen behaviour.

Positive punishment is when an unpleasant stimulus is presented to decrease behaviour. It is a punishment that results because some stimulus or circumstance is presented as a consequence of a response to decrease the likelihood of behaviour.

Negative punishment is when a pleasant stimulus is removed to decrease behaviour. It is a punishment that results because some stimulus or circumstance is removed as a consequence of a response to decrease the likelihood of behaviour

19 Short-term memory is capable of holding approximately how many items of unrelated information?

1 one　　2 two to four
3 five to nine　　4 ten to twelve

Ans. (3)

Exp. Short-term memory is capable of holding approximately five to nine items of unrelated information.

Short-Term Memory (STM) is the second stage of the multi-store memory model proposed by the Atkinson-Shiffrin. The duration of STM seems to be between 15 and 30 seconds and the capacity about 7 items. The Magic number 7 (plus or minus two) provides evidence for the capacity of short-term memory. Most adults can store between 5 and 9 items in their short-term memory.

This idea was put forward by Miller (1956) and he called it the magic number 7. He thought that short-term memory could hold 7 (plus or minus 2 items) because it only had a certain number of 'slots' in which items could be stored.

20 Learning of fears is best explained by

1 Operant conditioning
2 Classical conditioning
3 Observational learning
4 Latent learning

Ans. *(2)*

Exp. Learning of fears is best explained by Classical conditioning.

Fears are reflexes, most of which are in-built but can be trained using classical conditioning. It was first proposed and studied by Ivan Pavlov. Classical conditioning is one form of learning in which an organism 'learns' through establishing associations between different events and stimuli. e.g. when a neutral stimulus (such as a bell) is paired with an unconditioned stimulus (such as food) which produces some involuntary bodily response all on its own (such as salivating), the neutral stimulus begins to trigger a response by the organism similar (some salivation) to that produced by the unconditioned stimulus. In this way, the organism has 'learned' that the neutral stimulus equals something good (just like the unconditioned stimulus).

21 Arrange the following theories of emotion in correct sequence according to their emergence.

I. James-Lange
II. Cannon-Bard
III. Schachter and Singer
IV. Darwin

Codes

1 I, III, II, IV
2 IV, III, II, I
3 IV, I, II, III
4 I, II, III, IV

Ans. *(3)*

Exp. The correct sequence is IV, I, II, III.

The theories of emotion in correct sequence according to their emergence are arranged as follows:

Charles Darwin proposed that emotions evolved because they had adaptive value. e.g. fear evolved because it helped people to act in ways that enhanced their chances of survival. Darwin believed that facial expressions of emotion are innate (hard-wired). He pointed out that facial expressions allow people to quickly judge someone's hostility or friendliness and to communicate intentions to others.

According to James-Lange theory, people experience emotion because they perceive their bodies' physiological responses to external events. According to this theory, people don't cry because they feel sad. Rather, people feel sad because they cry and, likewise, they feel happy because they smile. This theory suggests that different physiological states correspond to different experiences of emotion.

Cannon-Bard theory states that the experience of emotion happens at the same time that physiological arousal happen. Neither one causes the other. The brain gets a message that causes the experience of emotion at the same time that the autonomic nervous system gets a message that causes physiological arousal.

Stanley Schachter and Jerome Singer proposed a different theory to explain emotion. They said that people's experience of emotion depends on two factors: physiological arousal and the cognitive interpretation of that arousal. When people perceive physiological symptoms of arousal, they look for an environmental explanation of this arousal. The label people give an emotion depends on what they find in their environment.

22 What is true of drives?

I. Internal states
II. Aroused by tension
III. Underlying need
IV. Guided by external stimuli

Codes

1 I, II and IV
2 I, II and III
3 II, III and IV
4 I, II, III and IV

Ans. *(2)*

Exp. The correct codes are I, II, and III.

The following are true of drives:

Internal states: The drive refers to the state of tension or arousal caused by internal states which are defined by biological or physiological needs.

Aroused by tension: A drive creates an unpleasant state and a tension that needs to be reduced. An aroused state of psychological tension typically arises from a need.

Underlying need: A drive is an urgent basic underlying need pressing for satisfaction, usually rooted in some physiological tension, deficiency, or imbalance (e.g., hunger and thirst) and impelling the organism to action.

23 Intellectual functioning is mainly in the domain of which lobe of the cortex?

1 Occipital lobe
2 Frontal lobe
3 Parietal lobe
4 Temporal lobe

Ans. *(2)*

Exp. Intellectual functioning is mainly in the domain of frontal lobe of the cortex.

Frontal Lobe is located in front of the central sulcus. It is concerned with reasoning, planning, parts of speech and movement (motor cortex), emotions and problem-solving. It is concerned with intellectual and executive functioning, which includes higher level cognitive processes of planning, decision making, problem solving, action sequencing, task assignment and organization, effortful and persistent goal pursuit, inhibition of competing impulses, flexibility in goal selection, and goal-conflict resolution. These often involve the use of language, judgment, abstraction and concept formation, and logic and reasoning.

24 A nerve cell that responds to a vertical line, but not to horizontal line is an example of

1 linear perspective system
2 feature detector
3 pattern analyser
4 selection and organisation process

Ans. (2)

Exp. A nerve cell that responds to a vertical line, but not to horizontal line is an example of feature detector.

Feature detection theory proposes that the nervous system sorts and filters incoming stimuli to allow the human (or animal) to make sense of the information. In the organism, this system is made up of feature detectors, which are individual neurons, or groups of neurons, that encode specific perceptual features. The theory proposes an increasing complexity in the relationship between detectors and the perceptual feature. The most basic feature detectors respond to simple properties of the stimuli.

Further along the perceptual pathway, higher organized feature detectors are able to respond to more complex and specific stimuli properties. When features repeat or occur in a meaningful sequence, we are able to identify these patterns because of our feature detection system.

One source of evidence for feature matching comes from Hubel and Wiesel's research, which found that the visual cortex of cats contains neurons that only respond to specific features (e.g. one type of neuron might fire when a vertical line is presented, another type of neuron might fire if a horizontal line moving in a particular direction is shown).

25 The visual signals from each retina reach striate cortex via which of the following?

1 Lateral geniculate nucleus
2 Medical geniculate nucleus
3 Infero-temporal cortex
4 Posterior parietal cortex

Ans. (1)

Exp. The visual signals from each retina reach striate cortex via the lateral geniculate nucleus of the thalamus.

The axons of the retina's ganglion cells pass through the optic nerve, the optic chiasm and the optic tractus. They wrap around the midbrain and cross the medial surface of the temporal lobe and 80% of them then terminate in a synaptic relay called the Lateral Geniculate Nucleus (LGN), located in the dorsal part of the thalamus. The LGN is thus the major target for each optic tract.

The distribution of the LGN's neurons into various layers suggests that some distinct aspects of the visual information from the retina may be processed separately in this synaptic relay. And that is exactly what has been demonstrated experimentally. Because the right LGN processes all of the visual signals from the left visual field (and for the left LGN), it receives axons from the left nasal retina and the right temporal retina.

Medical geniculate nucleus, Infero-temporal cortex and Posterior parietal cortex are parts of auditory pathway.

26 Observational learning involves

I. attention and retention
II. attention and reinforcement
III. production processes and motivation
IV. reinforcement and motivation

Codes

1 I and III	2 II and IV
3 III and IV	4 I and II

Ans. (1)

Exp. The correct codes are I and III.

Observational learning involves the following factors

Attention and retention: Observers cannot learn unless they pay attention to what is happening around them. This process is called attention and is influenced by characteristics of the model, as well as how much the observer likes or identifies with the model. It is also influenced by characteristics of the observer, such as the observer's expectations or level of emotional arousal. Observers have to not only recognise the observed behaviour, but also remember it. This process is called retention and it depends on the observer's ability to code or structure the information so that it is easily remembered.

Production processes and motivation: Observers must be physically and intellectually capable of producing the act. This process is called production process. In many cases, the observer possesses the necessary responses, but sometimes reproducing the observed actions may involve skills the observer has not yet acquired. An observer must be motivated to reproduce the actions they have seen. This process is called production motivation.

27 Which of the following factors reduce the accuracy of eyewitness testimony?

I. Suggestibility
II. Source monitoring errors
III. Interference
IV. Decay of memory traces
V. Illusion of outgroup homogeneity

Codes

1 I, II and III	2 I, III and IV
3 I, II and V	4 II, III and V

Ans. (3)

Exp. The correct codes are I, II, and V.

The following factors reduce the accuracy of eyewitness testimony:

Suggestibility: Suggestibility describes the effects of misinformation from external sources that leads to the creation of false memories. When someone witnesses a crime, that person's memory of the details of the crime is very important in catching the suspect. Because memory is so fragile, witnesses can be easily (and often accidentally) misled due to the problem of suggestibility.

Source monitoring errors: A source-monitoring error is a type of memory error where the source of a memory is incorrectly attributed to some specific recollected experience.

Illusion of outgroup homogeneity: Outgroup homogeneity is the tendency for members of a group to see themselves as more diverse and heterogeneous than they are seen by an out-group. Thus, for example, whereas Italians see themselves as quite diverse and different from one another, Americans view Italians as more similar to each other, or more alike. Individuals may view people belonging to a particular social group (like race, gender, etc.) responsible for a crime hence inaccurately giving eyewitness testimony.

28 Microsleep occurs mainly due to one of the following

1 Sleep disorder
2 Drugged state
3 Sleep deprivation
4 Dreaming state

Ans. (3)

Exp. Microsleep frequently occurs as a result of Sleep deprivation.

A microsleep is a short episode of sleep that can last anywhere from 1 second to 30 seconds. They occur during times of sleepiness, generally without warning. It's a very light sleep. Often the person having the microsleep won't even be aware they had just nodded off.

Sleep deprivation is caused by what's called sleep debt. The longer you stay awake, the more sleep debt you acquire. The more sleep debt you have, the more sleepy you become and the easier it will be to fall asleep. Sleep debt can only be paid off with sleep. A good night's sleep will pay off all your sleep debt, while a bad night's sleep will only pay some of it off, bringing some sleep debt with you into the next day. A few bad nights sleep in a row will create a large accumulation of sleep debt, making you feel sleep deprived and susceptible to microsleep.

29 Self-efficacy is

1 a person's mental model of his or her ability and attitudes
2 a generalised evaluative attitude toward the self that influences both moods and behaviour
3 the process by which a person comes to know or perceive the personal attributes
4 a set of beliefs that one can perform adequately in a particular situation

Ans. (4)

Exp. Self-efficacy is not a model, attitude or a process. According to Albert Bandura, self-efficacy is 'the belief in one's capabilities to organise and execute the courses of action required to manage prospective situations.' In other words, self-efficacy is a person's belief in his or her ability to succeed in a particular situation. Bandura described these beliefs as determinants of how people think, behave and feel. These beliefs begin to form in early childhood as children deal with a wide variety of experiences, tasks and situations. However, the growth of self-efficacy does not end during youth but continues to evolve throughout life as people acquire new skills, experiences and understanding.

30 Which one of the following is a product in Guilford's model?

1 Evaluation
2 Cognition
3 Transformation
4 Symbols

Ans. (3)

Exp. Transformation is a product in Guilford's model.

Guilford's model is a model of intelligence that postulates five operations (cognition, memory, divergent production, convergent production, evaluation), six products (units, classes, relations, systems, transformations, implications), and five contents (symbolic, semantic, behavioral, auditory, visual).

The Product dimension contains results of applying particular operations to specific contents. Transformation refers to changes, perspectives, conversions, or mutations to knowledge.

Directions (Q. Nos. 31-34) *Read the following passage and answer the four questions that follow.*

A researcher wanted to test the hypothesis that a given drug would adversely affect the rate of learning. A group of 40 subjects was employed in the research. Each subject was required to learn a task upto two errorless trials. Then, each subject was given a specified drug dosage (1mg/body weight in kilogram) and 30 minutes after, the subject was required to learn another equated learning task upto two errorless trials.

The number of trials required to learn each task followed a normal distribution. The mean number of trials required to learn the tasks were 24 and 20 only for normal and 'drugged conditions', respectively. The two conditions had comparable standard deviations. The mean difference was tested by a suitable statistical test and the difference was found to be significant at .01 level.

31 What can you conclude about the researcher's hypothesis?

1 The hypothesis has been verified
2 The hypothesis has been rejected
3 The hypothesis has been partially verified
4 The data are inadequate to evaluate researcher's hypothesis

Ans. (2)

Exp. The researcher hypothesised that the drug would adversely affect the rate of learning. Results suggested that number of trials required to learn the task was more in normal conditions, as compared to the drugged conditions. This indicates that the rate of learning increased with the introduction of drugs, affecting the rate of learning.

The hypothesis is, therefore, rejected. A hypothesis is a specific, testable prediction. It describes in concrete terms what you expect will happen in a certain circumstance. A hypothesis is used in an experiment to define the relationship between two variables. The purpose of a hypothesis is to find the answer to a question.

32 What statistical test appears to be suitable for evaluating mean differences?

1 Independent samples t-test
2 One-way ANOVA for independent groups
3 Paired sample t-test
4 Chi-square test

Ans. (3)

Exp. Paired sample t-test is used when differences between two scores on the same group is measured. One score is taken before the introduction of independent variable (in this case, drug) and the other score is taken after the introduction of independent variable. A paired sample t-test is used to compare two population means where you have two samples in which observations in one sample can be paired with observations in the other sample.

ANOVA test is a way to find out if survey or experiment results are significant. In other words, they help you to figure out if you need to reject the null hypothesis or accept the alternate hypothesis. Basically, you 're testing groups to see if there's a difference between them.

Chi-Square test of Independence is used to determine if there is a significant relationship between two nominal (categorical) variables. The frequency of one nominal variable is compared with different values of the second nominal variable. The independent t-test, also called the two sample t-test, independent-samples t-test or student's t-test, is an inferential statistical test that determines whether there is a statistically significant difference between the means in two unrelated groups.

33 The dependent variable in this experiment is

1 drug dosage
2 trials required to learn the task
3 body weight
4 time interval between the drug administration and learning the second task

Ans. (2)

Exp. The dependent variable in this experiment is trials required to learn the task. A dependent variable is what you measure in the experiment and what is affected during the experiment. The dependent variable responds to the independent variable. It is called dependent because it 'depends' on the independent variable. In a scientific experiment, you cannot have a dependent variable without an independent variable.

Example You are interested in how stress affects heart rate in humans. Your independent variable would be the stress and the dependent variable would be the heart rate. You can directly manipulate stress levels in your human subjects and measure how those stress levels change heart rate.

34 The above information suggests that

I. parametric model should be followed in data analysis.
II. non-parametric model should be followed in data analysis.
III. the scores under two conditions appear to have homogeneity of variance.
IV. the scores under two conditions appear to be heterogeneous for variance.

Codes

1 I and III
2 I and IV
3 II and III
4 II and IV

Ans. (1)

Exp. The correct codes are I and III.

Parametric model should be followed in data analysis: A parametric model is the that makes assumptions about the parameters (defining properties) of the population distribution(s) from which one's data are drawn, while a non-parametric test is one that makes no such assumptions.

The scores under two conditions appear to have homogeneity of variance: Homogeneity of variance is an assumption underlying both t tests and F tests (analyses of variance, ANOVAs) in which the population variances (i.e., the distribution, or "spread," of scores around the mean) of two or more samples are considered equal.

35 Railroad tracks that seem to draw closer together as they recede into the distance are an example of

1 linear perspective
2 relative size
3 binocular vision
4 feature detection

Ans. (1)

Exp. Railroad tracks that seem to draw closer together as they recede into the distance is an example of linear perspective.

Linear perspective is a system of creating an illusion of depth on a flat surface. All parallel lines (orthogonal) in a painting or drawing using this system converge in a single vanishing point on the composition's horizon line. Linear perspective is an artistic or visual term that refers to the eye's sense of depth and distance perception. This is why two identical items will appear to vary in size with the amount of distance involved and why roads appear to narrow with distance.

36 Memory for particular events is called

1 semantic
2 sensory
3 episodic
4 procedural

Ans. (3)

Exp. Memory for particular events is called episodic memory.

Episodic memory is the ability to remember personally experienced events associated with a particular time and place. It includes recollecting the three 'Ws' of an event—what, where, and when. It also include a sense of self-awareness and a subjective conscious experience as well (termed autonoetic consciousness). In other words, in addition to recalling the facts of a past event, an individual has to engage in "mental time travel" and remember that he or she was the one who lived the event.

37 A test of abstract thinking had the norms in terms of normalised T scores (Mean = 50, SD = 10). If the subject received a T score of 60, what would be his percentile rank?

1 16 2 60 3 66 4 84

Ans. (4)

Exp. The percentile rank would be 84.

A T-score is a scaled score, its mean is 50, and the standard deviation is 10. Thus, a student with a T-score of 60 is one standard deviation above the mean. A percentile is a measure that gives us information to know how many scores fall under a specific cut (the percentage number). The fixed percentages allow us to convert standard deviation units to percentiles.

For example, (−2) SD equals to a percentile rank of 2; that is, two percent of the cases fall below this point. Each point on the base line of the figure can be equated to the following percentiles. (−2) SD = 2% (−1) SD = 16% (2 + 14) 0 SD = Mean = 50% (16 + 34) +1 SD = 84% (50 + 34) +2 SD = 98% (84 +14).

Therefore, one standard deviation above the mean reflects 84 percentile.

38 Match List I and List II and indicate your answer with the help of codes given below.

List I (Childhood experience)	List II (Personality characteristic)
A. Little gratification in oral stage	I. Overly dependent
B. Excessive gratification in oral stage	II. Impulsive
C. Overly harsh toilet training in anal stage	III. Hostile
D. Relieved toilet training in anal stage	IV. Compulsive

Codes

	A	B	C	D		A	B	C	D
1	II	IV	III	I	2	I	III	IV	II
3	I	IV	II	III	4	II	III	I	IV

Ans. (2)

Exp. The correct matching is A-I, B-III, C-IV, D-II.

Little gratification in oral stage results in overly dependent personality.

Excessive gratification in oral stage results in hostile personality.

Overly harsh toilet training in anal stage results in compulsive personality.

Relieved toilet training in anal stage results in impulsive personality.

39 Multiple Abstract Variance Analysis is used to study the effect of

1 one independent variable on more than one dependent variables

2 more than one independent variables on one dependent variable

3 more than one independent variables on more than one dependent variables

4 None of the above

Ans. (4)

Exp. Multiple Abstract Variance Analysis (MAVA) is a statistical technique used to estimate the proportion of variance in a phenotypic trait due to genetic and environmental factors.

Cattell developed technique to analyse the effects of hereditary and environment based on data from relatives and non-relatives to investigate nature nurture question statistically. The study of gene-environmental conditions that alter human personality behaviour is expressed largely as behavioural genetics. A major part of behavioural genetics is the study of quantitative genetics such as IQ, competitiveness, mental inclinations and extra/introversion. By observing and comparing such human traits, scientists are able to note the individual genetic differences. One way to measure the individual differences is by using Cattell 's MAVA or multiple abstract variance analysis.

The MAVA allows scientists to compare individuals within a family dynamic, whether it is twins or an adopted individual. Tests like the MAVA have revealed that an individual's genes, along with environments, influence behaviour. Overall it is believed that genetic influences can intermingle with environmental influences to produce a hypothesised behaviour.

40 Match List I and List II and indicate your answer with the help of codes given below.

List I (Brief description)	List II (Type of Reinforcement)
A. reinforcement occurs after a set time period	I. Fixed ratio
B. reinforcement occurs after a set number of responses	II. Variable interval
C. reinforcement occurs after a varying time period	III. Fixed interval
D. reinforcement occurs after a varying number of responses	IV. Variable ratio

Codes

	A	B	C	D		A	B	C	D
1	III	I	II	IV	2	I	IV	III	II
3	IV	III	I	II	4	II	IV	III	I

Ans. (1)

Exp. The correct matching is A-III, B-I, C-II, D-IV

There are four schedules of partial reinforcement:

Fixed-ratio schedules are those where reinforcement occurs after a set number of responses. This schedule produces a high, steady rate of responding with only a brief pause after the delivery of the reinforcer. An example of a fixed-ratio schedule would be delivering a food pellet to a rat after it presses a bar five times.

Variable-interval schedules occur when reinforcement occurs after varying time period. This schedule produces a slow, steady rate of response. An example of this would be delivering a food pellet to a rat after the first bar press following a one-minute interval, another pellet for the first response following a five-minute interval and a third food pellet for the first response following a three-minute interval.

Fixed-interval schedules are those where reinforcement occurs after a set time period. This schedule causes high amounts of responding near the end of the interval, but much slower responding immediately after the delivery of the reinforcer. An example of this in a lab setting would be reinforcing a rat with a lab pellet for the first bar press after a 30-second interval has elapsed.

Variable-ratio schedules occur when reinforcement occurs after a varying number of responses. This schedule creates a high steady rate of responding. Gambling and lottery games are good examples of a reward based on a variable ratio schedule. In a lab setting, this might involve delivering food pellets to a rat after one bar press, again after four bar presses and a third pellet after two bar presses.

41 Which of the following effectors is mainly responsible for instrumental (motor) response?

1 Smooth muscles
2 Cardiac muscles
3 Skeletal muscle
4 Adrenal gland

Ans. *(3)*

Exp. The effector which is mainly responsible for instrumental (motor) response is Skeletal muscle.

Skeletal muscle is one of three major muscle types, the others being cardiac muscle and smooth muscle. It is a form of striated muscle tissue which is under the 'voluntary' control of the somatic nervous system. An effector is a peripheral tissue at the outer end of an efferent neural path (one leading away from the central nervous system).

42 A process following learning during which a memory becomes more firmly established is called

1 over-learning
2 consolidation
3 transfer period
4 constructive processing

Ans. *(2)*

Exp. A process following learning during which a memory becomes more firmly established is called consolidation.

Consolidation is a neurological process that involves gradually converting and solidifying the short-term memory making it a long-term memory by giving it an engram, or a proper place in the memory. Over-learning, according to Hermann Ebbinghaus, is just practice which is only done after something is already in the long-term memory.

43 Read each of the following two statements Assertion (A) and Reason (R) and indicate your answer using the codes given below.

Assertion (A) A large body of research indicates that violence and aggression is learned through observation.

Reason (R) Learning through observation takes place due to exposure to similar situation and experienced reinforcement.

Codes

1 Both (A) and (R) are true, and (R) is the correct explanation of (A)
2 Both (A) and (R) are true, but (R) is not the correct explanation of (A)
3 (A) is true, but (R) is false
4 Both (A) and (R) are false

Ans. *(3)*

Exp. (A) is true but (R) is false.

A large body of research indicates that violence and aggression is learned through observation.

'Observational learning', also referred to as modeling or social learning, occurs by observing, retaining and replicating behaviour seen in others. The individuals performing the imitated behaviour are called models. While this type of learning can take place at any stage in life, it is thought to be particularly important during childhood, when authority is important.

Learning through observation takes place only due to exposure to similar situation and not through experienced reinforcement, which is a feature of operant conditioning. In the observational learning, the model's behavior is imitated whether the behavior is reinforced or not.

44 Some steps in test construction are listed below

I. Internal consistency assessment
II. Item analysis
III. Test-retest reliability
IV. Item writing

Usually, the above steps are carried out in the following sequence.

Codes

1 IV, II, I, III
2 IV, I, III, II
3 II, IV, I, III
4 IV, III, II, I

Ans. *(1)*

Exp. The correct codes are IV, II, I, IIII.

The steps in test construction are carried out in the following sequence:

Item writing : It includes written statements for tests. Item writing refers to the process of constructing the items required for a given test or assessment.

Item analysis : It involves the process where the statements are checked whether they are good enough to measure the construct. It also includes discrimination and difficulty level of the items.

Internal consistency assessment : It is checked if the items are correlated with one another, or asking the similar thing.

Test-retest reliability : It is checked if the whole test is giving us consistent results.

45 What is the correct order of the following conflicts occurring in an individual's life?

I. Autonomy Vs. Self-doubt
II. Identity Vs. Role confusion

III. Competence Vs. Inferiority
IV. Intimacy Vs. Isolation

Codes

1 I, II, III, IV 2 II, I, IV, III
3 I, III, II, IV 4 III, II, IV, I

Ans. *(3)*

➲ *Exp.* The order of conflicts occurring in an individual's life is I, III, II, IV.

Autonomy Vs. Self-doubt: The second stage of Erikson's thcory of psychosocial development takes place during early childhood and is focused on children developing a greater sense of personal control. Children who successfully complete this stage feel secure and confident, while those who do not are left with a sense of inadequacy and self-doubt.

Competence vs Inferiority: The fourth psychosocial stage takes place during the early school years from approximately ages 5 to 11. Through social interactions, children begin to develop a sense of pride in their accomplishments and abilities. Successfully finding a balance at this stage of psychosocial development leads to the strength known as competence, in which children develop a belief in their abilities to handle the tasks set before them.

Identity vs Role confusion: The fifth psychosocial stage takes place during the often turbulent teenage years. This stage plays an essential role in developing a sense of personal identity which will continue to influence behavior and development for the rest of a person's life. Success leads to an ability to stay true to yourself, while failure leads to role confusion and a weak sense of self.

Intimacy vs Isolation: Young adults need to form intimate, loving relationships with other people. Success leads to strong relationships, while failure results in loneliness and isolation. This stage covers the period of early adulthood when people are exploring personal relationships.

46 Which of the following attitude scaling method(s) has/have been proposed by LL Thurstone?

I. Paired comparison
II. Summated ratings
III. Scalogram
IV. Equal appearing intervals

Codes

1 Only II 2 Only IV
3 I and IV 4 II and III

Ans. *(3)*

➲ *Exp.* LL Thurstone has proposed the following attitude scaling method(s):

Paired comparison: Paired comparison is any process of comparing entities in pairs to judge which of each entity is preferred or has a greater amount of some quantitative property or whether or not the two entities are identical.

Equal appearing intervals: The method of equal-appearing intervals or the Thurstone scale is used to measure attitudes of people. It allows us to use a scale tomeasure an indicator.

This kind of scale is used to measure people's attitude towards a fairly clear and unidimensional concept, using a number of statements that vary in how they express a positive or negative opinion about themain concept. Equal appearing intervals devised a scaling procedure which attempted to divide any given attitude into a number of equal appearing, any attitude involves a continuum ranging from the strongest possible appreciation of a value at one extreme to the strongest possible depreciation of that value at the other trained on it with years of experience.

47 Match List I and List II and indicate your answer with the help of codes given below.

List I (Validity type)	List II (Brief description)
A. Predictive validity	I. Covering all the important areas in a given course of study
B. Concurrent validity	II. Yielding theoretically consistent results
C. Construct validity	III. High relationship between the new test and the established test of same trait
D. Content validity	IV. Forecasting some significant behaviour on the basis of test scores

Codes

	A	B	C	D		A	B	C	D
1	III	IV	II	I	2	IV	III	I	II
3	II	I	IV	III	4	IV	III	II	I

Ans. *(4)*

➲ *Exp.* The correct matching is A-IV, B-III, C-II, D-I

Predictive validity is used for forecasting some significant behaviour on the basis of test scores. Predictive validity is the extent to which performance on a test is related to later performance that the test was designed to predict.

Predictive validity is determined by calculating the correlation coefficient between the results of the assessment and the subsequent targeted behaviour.

Concurrent validity represents high relationship between the new test and the established test of same trait. Concurrent validity is a type of evidence that can be gathered to defend the use of a test for predicting other outcomes and predictive validity is the extent to which a score on a scale or test predicts scores on some criterion measure.

Construct validity is 'the degree to which a test measures what it claims or purports, to be measuring, how well a test or tool measures the construct that it was designed to measure. Construct validity gives theoretically consistent results.

Content validity (also known as logical validity) refers to the extent to which a measure represents all facets of a given construct. Content validity refers to how accurately an assessment or measurement tool taps into the various aspects of the specific construct in question or important areas in a given course of study.

48 During emotions skin conductance changes occur due to the activity of some of the following

I. Sweat glands
II. Adrenal glands
III. Parasympathetic nervous system

Codes

1 I and II	2 I and III
3 II and III	4 I, II and III

***Ans.* (1)**

Exp. Skin conductance refers to the phenomenon that the skin momentarily becomes a better conductor of electricity when either external or internal stimuli occur that are physiologically arousing. During emotions skin conductance changes occur due to the activity of some of the following :

Sweat glands : Sweat glands release sweat which increases the skin conductance.

Adrenal glands : Adrenal glands gets activated when the sympathetic nervous system is stimulated. Skin conductance is not under conscious control. Skin conductance is not under conscious control. Instead, it is modulated autonomously by sympathetic activity which drives human behaviour, cognitive and emotional states on a subconscious level.

49 What among the following is true for mental set?

I. It can enhance the quality and speed of perceiving and problem-solving under some conditions.
II. It can enhance the quality and speed of perceiving and problem-solving in new situations.
III. It may inhibit or distort the quality of mental activities in new situations.
IV. It may inhibit or distort the quality of mental activities under same conditions.

Codes

1 I and II	2 II and III
3 I and III	4 III and IV

***Ans.* (3)**

Exp. Statement I and III is true for mental set.

A mental set is a framework for thinking about a problem. It can be shaped by habit or by desire.

Mental set can enhance the quality and speed of perceiving and problem-solving under some conditions. Some mental set can enhance the quality and speed of perceiving and problem solving under some conditions. Mental sets can make it easy to solve a class of problem, but attachment to the wrong mental set can inhibit problem-solving and creativity.

Mental set may inhibit or distort the quality of mental activities in new situations. In newer situations, individuals mindlessly apply these procedures to solve new problem types—even when these strategies are no longer efficient or correct. Hence, mental set may inhibit or distort the quality of mental activities in new situations.

50 Match List I and List II and indicate your answer with the help of codes given below.

List I		List II
A. Thinking	I.	Mental activity through, which we transform available information in order to reach conclusions
B. Reasoning	II.	An activity that involves the manipulation of mental representation of various features of the external world
C. Decision-making	III.	Processing information in various ways in order to move toward desired goals
D. Problem-solving	IV.	The process of choosing between two or more alternatives on the basis of information about them

Codes

	A	B	C	D		A	B	C	D
1	IV	III	II	I	2	II	I	IV	III
3	III	IV	II	I	4	II	III	I	IV

***Ans.* (2)**

Exp. The correct matching is A-II, B-I, C-IV, D-III

Thinking is an activity that involves the manipulation of mental representation of various features of the external world. It is the human process of using knowledge and information to make plans, interpret and model the world and constructively interact with and make predictions about the world in general.

Reasoning is a mental activity through, which we transform available information in order to reach conclusions. It is the human ability to use facts, logic, science, math etc. to find solutions to practical and intellectual problems. As an example, humans had for centuries dreamed of the ability to fly, but finally in the early 20th century, two bicycle mechanics were able to use reasoning to build the first airplane by combining this dream with physics, mathematics and engineering.

Decision making is the process of choosing between two or more alternatives on the basis of information about them. Individuals make choices based on their personal preferences, values and goals. Every decision has an outcome and involves risk. e.g. when deciding which college or university to attend, a student must weigh the costs and benefits of each school and come to a decision that maximizes his benefits and minimises his costs, compared to other choices.

Problem solving is processing information in various ways in order to move toward desired goals. It is a mental process that involves discovering, analysing and solving problems. The ultimate goal of problem-solving is to overcome obstacles and find a solution that best resolves the issue.

PAPER III

1 Match List I and List II and indicate your answer with the help of codes given below.

List I (Task)		List II (Type of memory)	
A.	Free recall and recognition	I.	Semantic memory
B.	Sentence verification task	II.	Sensory memory
C.	Priming	III.	Episodic memory
D.	Scanning task	IV.	Implicit memory

Codes

	A	B	C	D		A	B	C	D
1	IV	II	I	III	2	II	I	III	IV
3	I	IV	II	III	4	III	I	IV	II

Ans. (4)

Exp. The correct matching is A-III, B-I, C-IV, D-II.

Free recall and recognition is associated with Episodic memory. Free-recall and recognition has been a paramount experimental paradigm in unraveling mechanisms of episodic memory. In free-recall, participants are presented with a list of items (typically words) and are subsequently required to retrieve them in any order. Successful recall requires an active, self-initiated, search process for the items, with no external retrieval cues.

Sentence verification task is associated with Semantic memory. Sentence verification task is a procedure in which participants are briefly presented with simple sentences and asked to make quick judgments about them. The sentence-verification task most commonly is used in cognitive research on semantic memory and verbal comprehension.

Priming is associated with Implicit memory. Priming is another, smaller subset of implicit memory. It involves using pictures, words or other stimuli to help someone recognize another word or phrase in the future.

Scanning task is associated with Sensory memory. In the Sternberg scanning paradigm, participants are presented with a brief list of study items (the memory set), followed by a test item (the probe). The task is to judge, as rapidly as possible while minimizing errors, whether the probe is a member of the memory set. Sternberg's classic result was that mean response time was an approximately linearly increasing function of memory set size. Sensory memory is used in this task.

2 Development of Superego, according to Freud is a result of

1 identification with the opposite sex parent
2 resolution of oedipus/electra complex
3 age advancement
4 anatomical superiority

Ans. (2)

Exp. Development of Superego, according to Freud, is a result of resolution of oedipus/electra complex.

The Oedipal complex is a term used by Sigmund Freud in his theory of psychosexual stages of development, and is the generic term for both Oedipus and Electra complexes. The Oedipal complex occurs during the Phallic stage of development (ages 3-6) in which the source of libido (life force) is concentrated in the erogenous zones of the child's body.

During this stage, children experience an unconscious feeling of desire for their opposite-sex parent and jealousy and envy toward their same-sex parent. The Oedipus complex is successfully resolved when the boy begins to identify with his father as an indirect way to have the mother. The father becomes a role model rather than a rival. Through this identification with the aggressor, boys acquire their superego and the male sex role. The boy substitutes his desire for his mother with the desire for other women.

3 Which of the following dimensions do not belong to Costa and McCrae's NEO-PI-R?

I. Conscientiousness II. Psychoticism
III. Agreeableness IV. Lie scale

Codes

1 Only II 2 II and IV
3 I, III and IV 4 II, III and IV

Ans. (2)

Exp. Psychoticism and Lie scale do not belong to Costa and McCrae's NEO-PI-R

The following dimensions do not belong to Costa and McCrae's NEO-PI-R:

Psychoticism: It is a dimension of personality in Eysenck's dimensions characterized by aggression, impulsivity, aloofness, and antisocial behavior, indicating a susceptibility to psychosis and psychopathic disorders.

Lie scale: It is a set of items within a psychological instrument (particularly a personality assessment) used to indicate whether a respondent has been truthful in answering. It is a part of Eysenck's Personality Questionnaire (EPQ).

4 When information currently being adversely affects the retention of information acquired previously, the phenomenon is referred to as

1 Distortion
2 Retroactive interference
3 Proactive interference
4 Retrieval failure

Ans. (2)

Exp. When information currently being adversely affects the retention of information Acquired previously, the phenomenon is referred to as Retroactive interference.

Retroactive interference is the interference that occurs when new learning or exposure to new information impairs the ability to remember material or carry out activities previously learned, especially if the two sets of material are similar.

Directions (Q. No 5-6) *In the questions given below are two statements labelled as Assertion (A) and other as Reason (R). Indicate your anser using the codes given below.*

Codes

1 Both (A) and (R) are true and (R) is the correct explanation of (A)
2 Both (A) and (R) are true, but (R) is not the correct explanation of (A)
3 (A) is true, but (R) is false
4 (A) is false, but (R) is true

5 Assertion (A) Median is used as a measure of scale value in method of equal appearing intervals.

Reason (R) In normal distribution mean, median and mode are identical.

Ans. (2)

Exp. Both (A) and (R) are true but (R) is not the correct explanation of (A).

Median is used as a measure of scale value in method of equal appearing intervals. The median is used to describe skewed distributions and for data measured on an ordinal scale. A skewed distribution is a distribution of data with outliers or scores that fall substantially above or below most other scores in a data set.

In normal distribution mean, median and mode are identical and are equal. When measurements produce a normal distribution, certain things are predictable.

6 Assertion (A) Research suggests that delay conditioning is generally the most effective method for establishing a conditioned response.

Reason (R) Conditioned stimulus helps predict forthcoming presentation of the unconditioned stimulus.

Ans. (1)

Exp. Both (A) and (R) are true, and (R) is the correct explanation of (A).

Research suggests that delay conditioning is generally the most effective method for establishing a conditioned response. In delayed conditioning the conditioned stimulus (CS) is presented before the unconditioned stimulus (US) and CS stays on until the US is presented. This is generally the best, especially when the delay is short. e.g. a bell begins to ring and continues to ring until food is presented. There is an overlap of CS and UCS just for some time (about 2 seconds) which builds a very strong association. Therefore, (A) is true, i.e. it is the most effective method for establishing conditioned response.

Conditioned stimulus helps predict forth coming presentation of the unconditioned stimulus. It is true as the most important aspect of the conditioning stimulus is that it helps the organism predict the coming of the unconditional stimulus. Thus, it explains how delay conditioning is the most effective method for establishing a conditioned response.

7 Which of the following is not a cause of forgetting?

1 Interference
2 Decay
3 Selective attention
4 Retrieval inhibition

Ans. (3)

Exp. Selective attention is not a cause of forgetting.

Selective attention refers to the processes that allow an individual to select and focus on particular input for further processing while simultaneously suppressing irrelevant or distracting information. It is the concentration on certain stimuli in the environment and not on others, enabling important stimuli to be distinguished from peripheral or incidental ones. Selective attention is typically measured by instructing participants to attend to some sources of information but to ignore others at the same time and then determining their effectiveness in doing this.

8 Which of the following attributions of an event with positive outcome shall be optimistic (non depressogenic)?

1 Internal, stable and specific causes
2 External, unstable and global causes
3 Internal, stable and global causes
4 External, unstable and specific causes

Ans. (3)

Exp. The following attributions of an event with positive outcome shall be optimistic : internal, stable and global.

In an internal or dispositional, attribution, people infer that an event or a person's behaviour is due to personal factors such as traits, abilities, or feelings.

When people make a stable attribution, they infer that an event or behaviour is due to stable, unchanging factors.

When making a global attribution, individual tends to generalize and relate to many other areas of life. For a pessimistic person, the attribution would be external, unstable and specific.

9 A child was classified as a case of mental retardation. On DSM IV / IV (TR), this diagnosis would be recorded on

1 Axis I 2 Axis II 3 Axis III 4 Axis IV

Ans. (2)

Exp. A child was classified as a case of mental retardation. On DSM IV / IV (TR), this diagnosis would be recorded on Axis II.

Axis II provided information about personality disorders and mental retardation. The DSM-IV uses a multiaxial or multi-dimensional approach to diagnosing because rarely do other factors in a person's life not impact their mental health. Disorders which would have fallen under this axis include: Paranoid Personality Disorder, Schizoid Personality Disorder, Schizotypal Personality Disorder, Antisocial Personality Disorder, Borderline Personality Disorder, Histrionic Personality Disorder, Narcissistic Personality Disorder, Avoidant Personality Disorder,

10 Awareness of one's own thought processes enabling effective learning through correction is called

1 Algorithm 2 Analogies
3 Meta cognition 4 Constructive process

Ans. (3)

Exp. Awareness of one's own thought processes enabling effective learning through correction is called Meta cognition.

Meta cognition refers to higher order thinking which involves active control over the cognitive processes engaged in learning. Activities such as planning how to approach a given learning task, monitoring comprehension and evaluating progress toward the completion of a task are metacognitive in nature.

11 How many subjects would be required in a $3 \times 3 \times 2$ factorial design with ten subjects per cell?

1 10 2 18 3 90 4 180

Ans. (4)

Exp. 3 x 3 x 2 factorial design is a three-way ANOVA design. Let us assume we need to find out the effect on performance of three variables. The first variable is sex (three levels: Male, Female and Trans), second variable is stress level (three levels: High, Medium and Low) and the third variable is the light under which they work (two levels: Low Light and High Light). For the third variable, we will get 9 groups for each variable (Low Light: Male-High stress, Male-Medium stress, Male- Low stress, Female- High stress, Female-Medium stress, Female- Low stress, Trans- High stress, Trans-Medium stress, Trans-Low stress, etc.). The number of groups in both the light situation will be 18. If there are 10 subjects in each group, we will have 180 subjects in total.

12 Mechanistic model of growth focuses on

I. role of environmental input and behaviour output
II. evolutionary origin
III. quantitative increase in learned responses

Codes

1 I and II 2 I and III
3 II and III 4 I, II and III

Ans. (2)

Exp. The correct codes are I and III.

Mechanistic model of growth focuses on following factors:

Role of environmental input and behaviour output : A mechanistic model of growth focuses on role of environmental input (stimulus) and behavior output (response). Mechanistic models are based on an understanding of the behavior of a system's components.

Quantitative increase in learned responses : It also focuses on quantitative increase in learned responses. A mechanistic model assumes that a complex system can be understood by examining the workings of its individual parts and the manner in which they are coupled.

Mechanistic model does not believe in evolutionary origin which means whatever we learn is in-built and we adapt slowly. According to mechanistic model, if there is no reward or reinforcement, we do not learn anything. Empirical models are based on direct observation, measurement and extensive data records.

13 Selye largely ignored the contribution of one of the following in stress

1 Adrenal Medulla
2 Anterior pituitary
3 Adrenal cortex
4 Chronic psychological factors

Ans. (1)

Exp. Selye largely ignored the contribution of Adrenal Medulla. Selye emphasised the role of hormones released from the adrenal cortex rather than those produced by the adrenal medulla.

Selye noticed that the body has been adapting to external stressors in terms of a biological pattern that is actually predictable, so that the internal balance or homeostasis, would be restored and maintained. In its attempt to retain homeostasis, the body makes use of its hormonal system, also known as the fight or flight response. With this response, you would notice how the body wants things to be resolved fast and easy, that's why it already resorts to releasing hormones that would enable you to combat stress in the most immediate way possible.

This struggle of the body against stress is the main theme of the General Adaptation Syndrome. Another observation that Selye discovered was that even if one's body wants to control or reduce the stress, it still has its limits. The limited supply of body's energy to adapt to the stressful environment is even more compromised when the body is exposed to the stressor continuously.

14 Which of the following clinical procedure(s) is/are not based on classical conditioning?

I. Flooding
II. Transference
III. Client centred therapy
IV. Systematic desensitisation

Codes

1 Only I 2 II and III
3 I, II and III 4 I, III and IV

Ans. (2)

Exp. The correct codes are II and III.

The following clinical procedures are not based on classical conditioning:

Transference : Transference is a phenomenon where patients undergoing clinical therapy begin to transfer their feelings of a particular person in their lives to the therapist. e.g. the patient may begin to feel the same feelings towards his or her therapist as the patient does for his or her lover. These types of feelings may be positive or negative. The therapist must be aware of this phenomenon and may even be able to use it to help the patient. e.g. role playing with the patient.

Client-centered therapy : Client-centred therapy is a humanistic approach that deals with the ways in which individuals perceive themselves consciously rather than how a counsellor can interpret their unconscious thoughts or ideas.

15 Annual or semi-annual ratings of each employee's performance, coupled with feedback about the ratings they receive are referred to as

1 performance appraisals
2 rating inventories
3 behaviourally anchored rating scales
4 graphic rating scales

Ans. (1)

Exp. Annual or semi-annual ratings of each employee's performance, coupled with feedback about the ratings they receive are referred to as performance appraisals.

A Performance Appraisal (PA), also referred to as a performance review, performance evaluation, (career) development discussion, or employee appraisal is a method by which the job performance of an employee is documented and evaluated.

16 Match List I and List II and indicate your answer with the help of codes given below.

List I (Hormones)	List II (Synthesised form)
A. Steroidal hormones	I. An amino acid
B. Peptide hormones	II. Long chain of amino acids
C. Protein hormones	III. Fat molecule
D. Amino acid derivates	IV. Short chain of amino acids

Codes

	A	B	C	D		A	B	C	D
1	IV	III	I	II	2	IV	I	II	III
3	IV	III	II	I	4	III	II	I	IV

Ans. (3)

Exp. The correct matching is A-III, B-IV, C-II, D-I

The synthesized form of *Steroidal hormones* is fat molecule. The primary hormones derived from lipids are steroids. Steroid hormones are derived from the lipid cholesterol. For example, the reproductive hormones testosterone and the estrogens—which are produced by the gonads (testes and ovaries)—are steroid hormones. The adrenal glands produce the steroid hormone aldosterone, which is involved in osmoregulation, and cortisol, which plays a role in metabolism. Like cholesterol, steroid hormones are not soluble in water (they are hydrophobic). Because blood is water-based, lipid-derived hormones must travel to their target cell bound to a transport protein. This more complex structure extends the half-life of steroid hormones much longer than that of hormones derived from amino acids.

The synthesized form of *Peptide hormones* is long chain of amino acids. Examples of peptide hormones include antidiuretic hormone (ADH), a pituitary hormone important in fluid balance, and atrial-natriuretic peptide, which is produced by the heart and helps to decrease blood pressure.

The synthesized form of *Protein hormones* is short chain of amino acids. Some examples of protein hormones include growth hormone, which is produced by the pituitary gland, and follicle-stimulating hormone (FSH), which has an attached carbohydrate group and is thus classified as a glycoprotein. FSH helps stimulate the maturation of eggs in the ovaries and sperm in the testes.

The synthesized form of *Amino acid derivates* is an amino acid. The amino acid-derived hormones are relatively small molecules that are derived from the amino acids tyrosine and tryptophan. If a hormone is amino acid-derived, its chemical name will end in "-ine". Examples of amino acid-derived hormones include epinephrine and norepinephrine, which are synthesized in the medulla of the adrenal glands, and thyroxine, which is produced by the thyroid gland. The pineal gland in the brain makes and secretes melatonin which regulates sleep cycles.

17 Arrange the following needs in accordance with Maslow's hierarchy.

I. Esteem needs
II. Love-belongingness
III. Physiological needs
IV. Safety needs
V. Self-actualisation

Codes

1 III, II, I, IV, V
2 III, II, IV, I, V
3 III, IV, I, II, V
4 III, IV, II, I, V

Ans. (4)

Exp. The needs can be arranged in accordance with Maslow's hierarchy in the following order: Physiological needs, Safety needs, Love-belongingness, Esteem needs and Self-actualisation.

Maslow stated that people are motivated to achieve certain needs and that some needs take precedence over others. Our most basic need is for physical survival and this will be the first thing that motivates our behaviour. Once that level is fulfilled the next level up is what motivates us and so on. Biological and Physiological Needs Air, food, drink, shelter, warmth, sex, sleep.

Safety Needs Protection from elements, security, order, law, stability, freedom from fear. Love and Belongingness Needs Friendship, intimacy, trust and acceptance, receiving and giving affection and love. Affiliating, being part of a group (family, friends, work). Esteem Needs Achievement, mastery, independence, status, dominance, prestige, self-respect, respect from others. Self-Actualisation Needs Realising personal potential, self-fulfillment, seeking personal growth and peak experiences.

18 What is true for the contention that we are normally driven to eat by the anticipated pleasure of eating?

1 Set point theory
2 Negative feedback system
3 Positive incentive theory
4 Homeostatis

Ans. (3)

Exp. Positive incentive theory is true for the contention that we are normally driven to eat by the anticipated pleasure of eating. Positive incentive value is the anticipated pleasure involved in the performance of a particular behaviour, such as eating a particular food or drinking a particular beverage. It is a key element of the positive-incentive theories of hunger.

A set point is a theory that states everyone's body has a genetically determined range of weight and temperature that their body will try to maintain to stay at optimal health.

Negative feedback is the process of feeding back to the input a part of a system 's output, so as to reverse the direction of change of the output. This tends to keep the output from changing, so it is stabilising and attempts to maintain homeostasis. Humans seek balance in their lives. When things are out of order or imbalanced, it tends to cause problems. This is true particularly with regard to our internal state or well-being.

Homeostasis refers to this tendency to maintain a balanced or constant internal state that is optimal for functioning.

19 What does reduce the problem distance between starting point and the goal?

1 Normative - utilitarian
2 Means - end analysis
3 Normative - logical
4 Heuristic - shortcuts

Ans. (2)

Exp. Means-end analysis reduce the problem distance between starting point and the goal. In means-ends analysis, the problem solver begins by envisioning the end, or ultimate goal and then determines the best strategy for attaining the goal in his current situation.

Utilitarianism is a normative ethical theory that places the locus of right and wrong solely on the outcomes (consequences) of choosing one action/policy over other actions/policies.

A logic problem is a general term for a type of puzzle that is solved through deduction. Given a limited set of truths and a question, we step through the different scenarios until an answer is found. While these problems rarely involving coding, they require problem-solving and the ability to articulate plausible outcomes.

A heuristic is a mental shortcut that allows people to solve problems and make judgements quickly and efficiently. These rule-of-thumb strategies shorten decision-making time and allow people to function without constantly stopping to think about their next course of action. Heuristics are helpful in many situations, but they can also lead to cognitive biases.

20 In an experiment, if a light is repeatedly presented just before the electric shock is given the animal learns.

1 Operant escape and then operant avoidance
2 Operant avoidance and then operant escape
3 Only operant escape
4 Only operant avoidance

Ans. (3)

Exp. In an experiment, if a light is repeatedly presented just before the electric shock is given, the animal learns only operant escape.

In escape behaviour the occurrence of the behaviour terminates the aversive stimulus. In other words, the dog escapes the stimulus by doing another behaviour and that behaviour is then strengthened.

21 The contention that our facial expressions influence our emotional experience, attests to which of the following hypothesis?

1 Universality hypothesis of facial expressions
2 Emotional specificity hypothesis of ANS activity
3 Emotional generality hypothesis of ANS activity
4 Facial feedback hypothesis

Ans. (4)

Exp. The contention that our facial expressions influence our emotional experience, attests to facial feedback hypothesis.

The Facial Feedback theory holds that facial movement and expressions can influence attitude and emotional experience. For instance, when a person attends a function and is required to smile for the duration of the function, they will actually have a better experience of the function.

The facial feedback theory of emotion concerns the relationship between emotional experience and facial expression. The theory argues that emotional experience (feelings) can be managed by producing different or opposite facial expressions. It also suggests that people do not experience emotions directly; instead, they infer or 'read' their emotions from the expressions that appear on their faces.

22 Match List I and List II and indicate your answer with the help of codes given below.

	List I (Cognitive Process/ System)		List II (Process/ Locale)
A.	Feature based processing	I.	Right cerebral hemisphere
B.	Whole based processing	II.	Top down processing
C.	Abstract category system	III.	Bottom-up processing
D.	Specific exemplar subsystem	IV.	Left cerebral hemisphere

Codes

	A	B	C	D
1	I	III	IV	II
2	III	II	IV	I
3	II	IV	I	III
4	IV	I	III	II

Ans. *(2)*

Exp. The correct matching is A-III, B-II, C-IV, D-I

Feature based processing features uses bottom-up processing (for example, image edges, corners, and other structures well localized in two dimensions) and tracks these as they move from frame to frame. Bottom-up processing is an explanation for perceptions that start with an incoming stimulus and working upwards until a representation of the object is formed in our minds. This process suggests that our perceptual experience is based entirely on the sensory stimuli that we piece together using only data that is available from our senses.

Whole based or Holistic processing uses top-down processing. It is said to characterize expert face recognition, but the extent to which whole-word processes contribute to word recognition is unclear, particularly as word recognition is thought to proceed by a component-based process. In top-down processing, perceptions begin with the most general and move toward the more specific. These perceptions are heavily influenced by our expectations and prior knowledge.

Abstract category system uses left cerebral hemisphere. The dissociable neural subsystems theory (Marsolek, 1999, 2003) posits that an abstract-category (AC) subsystem recognizes the visual category to which an object stimulus belongs (e.g., piano, cat, pen, etc.). AC processing takes place only in left hemisphere visual areas.

Specific exemplar system uses right cerebral hemisphere. A specific-exemplar (SE) subsystem identifies the individuated visual exemplar to which an object stimulus corresponds (e.g., a calico cat, a different calico cat, a grand piano, etc.). SE processing takes place only in right hemisphere visual areas.

23 Match List I and List II and indicate your answer with the help of codes given below.

	List I (Symptom)	List II (Disorder)
A.	Waxy flexibility	I. Agoraphobia
B.	Rapid speech and flight of ideas	II. Schizophrenia
C.	Excessive fear of crowded places	III. Narcolepsy
D.	Cataplexy	IV. Manic

Codes

	A	B	C	D		A	B	C	D
1	III	IV	I	II	2	III	II	IV	I
3	IV	II	I	III	4	II	IV	I	III

Ans. *(4)*

Exp. The correct matching is A-II, B-IV, C-I, D-III

Agoraphobia is an anxiety disorder that often develops after one or more panic attacks. Symptoms include excessive fear and avoidance of crowded places and situations that might cause feelings of panic, entrapment, helplessness or embarrassment.

Schizophrenia is characterised by thoughts or experiences that seem out of touch with reality, disorganised speech or behaviour and decreased participation in daily activities. Difficulty with concentration and memory may also be present. Waxy flexibility is a psychomotor symptom of catatonia as associated with schizophrenia which leads to a decreased response to stimuli and a tendency to remain in an immobile posture.

Narcolepsy causes sudden attacks of sleep. Sudden loss of muscle tone and hallucinations might occur. Cataplexy is a sudden, brief loss of voluntary muscle tone triggered by strong emotions such as laughter. The condition is most commonly associated with narcolepsy, a sleep disorder.

Mania is a condition in which you display an over-the-top level of activity or energy, mood or behaviour. This elevation must be a change from our usual self and be noticeable by others. Symptoms include rapid speech and flight of ideas.

24 In the two-way ANOVA, with A and B as the independent variables, if the F ratio computed as $MS_{A \times B}/MS_W$ is significant, it can be concluded that

I. Main effect of A is significant.

II. Main effect of B is significant.

III. Interaction effect is significant.

Codes

1 Only III 2 I and II
3 II and III 4 I, II and III

Ans. *(1)*

Exp. In two-way ANOVA, if $MS_{A \times B}/MS_W$ is significant, A*B refers to the interaction effect of both the variables A and B is significant.

Interaction effect the joint effect of two or more independent variables on a dependent variable above and beyond the sum of their individual effects: The independent variables combine to have a different (and multiplicative) effect, such that the value of one is contingent upon the value of another. This indicates that the relationship between the independent variables changes as their values change. So the interaction effect is significant. We cannot say about the main effect of A and main effect of B.

25 Which among the following is a reversible lesion?

1 Cryogenic lesion
2 Aspiration lesion
3 Radio-Frequency lesion
4 Knife cut lesion

Ans. *(1)*

Exp. Cryogenic lesion is a reversible lesion.

Cryotherapy or cryogenic is used to treat a variety of benign and malignant tissue damage, medically called lesions. The term 'cryotherapy' comes from the Greek cryo meaning cold and therapy meaning cure. The most prominent use of the term refers to the surgical treatment, specifically known as cryosurgery. It is a reversible method as it can be caused by using extreme temperatures.

26 Match List I and List II and indicate your answer with the help of codes given below.

List I (Type of Bias)		List II (Decision)
A. Anchoring	I.	Making estimates from an initial value
B. Hindsight	II.	Adjusting past events by current knowledge
C. Framing	III.	Phrasing of situation guides biased decision
D. Representativeness	IV.	Most stereo typical exemplars are selected

Codes

	A	B	C	D		A	B	C	D
1	II	I	IV	III	2	I	III	II	IV
3	II	III	IV	I	4	I	II	III	IV

Ans. *(4)*

Exp. The correct matching is A-I, B-II, C-III, D-IV

Anchoring bias is used in making estimates from an initial value. The Anchoring Heuristic, also known as focalism, refers to the human tendency to accept and rely on, the first piece of information received before making a decision. That first piece of information is the anchor and sets the tone for everything that follows.

Hindsight bias is used in adjusting past events by current knowledge. Hindsight bias, also known as the knew-it-all-along effect or creeping determinism, is the inclination, after an event has occurred, to see the event as having been predictable, despite there having been little or no objective basis for predicting it.

Framing bias is phrasing of situation that guides biased decision. The framing effect is an example of cognitive bias, in which people react to a particular choice in different ways depending on how it is presented; e.g. as a loss or as a gain. People tend to avoid risk when a positive frame is presented but seek risks when a negative frame is presented. Gain and loss are defined in the scenario as descriptions of outcomes (e.g. lives lost or saved, disease patients treated and not treated, lives saved and lost during accidents, etc).

In representativeness bias most stereo typical exemplars are selected. A representativeness heuristic is a cognitive bias in which an individual categorises a situation based on a pattern of previous experiences or beliefs about the scenario. It can be useful when trying to make a quick decision, but it can also be limiting because it leads to close-mindedness such as in stereotypes.

27 Arrange different types of 'Play' in an increasing order of cognitive complexity.

I. Constructive II. Dramatic
III. Functional IV. Games

Codes

1 II, I, III, IV 2 II, III, I, IV
3 I, II, III, IV 4 I, III, II, IV

Ans. *(2)*

Exp. The correct order is II, III, I, IV.

According to Piaget, children engage in types of play that reflect their level of cognitive development: dramatic (symbolic/fantasy) play, functional play, constructive play. and games with rules.

Dramatic or Symbolic/Fantasy play is role playing or make-believe play, such as pretending to be a baby, firefighter, superhero, or monster, and make believe actions, such as driving a car by moving a pretend steering wheel, or using a block of wood as a cell phone.

Functional play is the use of bodily movements, with or without objects, such as running and jumping, sliding, gathering and dumping, manipulating and stacking objects, and informal games without rules.

Constructive play uses objects—blocks, Legos, Tinkertoys, or different materials (sand, modeling clay, paint, blocks) —in an organized, goal-oriented way to make something.

Games with rules are games with peers that are controlled by pre-established rules, such as tag, Mother-May-I, checkers, Duck-Duck-Goose, and so on.

28 Some people believe that certain objects bring luck and help them in being successful. Such superstitions may be the result of

1 insight
2 a program of behaviour modification
3 autoshaping
4 token economy systems

Ans. *(3)*

Exp. Some people believe that certain objects bring luck and help them in being successful. Such superstitions may be the result of autoshaping.

Autoshaping is a form of conditioning in which a subject that has been given reinforcement following a stimulus, regardless of its response to that stimulus, consistently performs an irrelevant behavior.

Insight occurs when a solution to a problem presents itself quickly and without warning. It is the sudden discovery of the correct solution following incorrect attempts based on trial and error.

Behaviour modification is a treatment approach, based on the principles of operant conditioning that replaces undesirable behaviours with more desirable ones through positive or negative reinforcement.

A token economy is a system of contingency management based on the systematic reinforcement of target behaviour. The reinforcers are symbols or 'tokens' that can be exchanged for other reinforcers.

29 Read each of the following two statements Assertion (A) and Reason (R) and indicate your answer using the codes given below.

Assertion (A) Fear or stress prior to surgery has been associated with slower post surgical recovery, including delays in wound healing.

Reason (R) Psychological factors can influence physical illness.

Codes

1 Both (A) and (R) are true and (R) is the correct explanation of (A)
2 Both (A) and R are true, but (R) is not the correct explanation of (A)
3 (A) is true, but (R) is false
4 (A) is false, but (R) is true

Ans. *(2)*

Exp. Both (A) and (R) are true, but (R) is not the correct explanation of (A).

Fear or stress prior to surgery has been associated with slower post surgical recovery, including delays in wound healing. Psychological stress can extend the time required to heal wounds by 25 per cent or more. Studies in which we and other researchers have created small wounds about the size of a pencil-eraser and then measured the rate of healing, show that stress slows closure. e.g. dental students took an average of 40 per cent longer to heal a small, standardised wound made prior to exams, compared to an identical wound made during their summer vacation. In contrast to the relatively mild and predictable stress of academic examinations, surgery is a high-stakes stressor and people's anxiety levels before surgery are often very high. After surgery, anxiety and depression can make pain worse—and pain is certainly another stressor that can slow your healing.

Psychological factors can influence physical illness, which is also true. But surgery is not a physical illness, rather a treatment to illness.

30 The way in which a child's efforts to master a new or challenging task is supported in a flexible and contingent way by teachers, parents or more competent persons is called

1 Scaffolding
2 Social influence
3 Social mediation
4 Social referencing

Ans. *(1)*

Exp. The way in which a child's efforts to master a new or challenging task is supported in a flexible and contingent way by teachers, parents or more competent persons is called Scaffolding.

Scaffolding is an instructional method in which teachers demonstrate the process of problem-solving for their students and explain the steps as they go along. After a few initial explanations the instructor will then remove themselves from the students and only offer help when needed. Scaffolding is slowly withdrawing or knowing when to withdraw support by a more knowledgeable other.

Social referencing is a process where the infant takes cues from other people in the environment, about which emotions and actions are appropriate in a certain context or situation. Infants observe the behaviour of others and emulate their actions and behaviours. As a substitute to Piaget's constructivism, he argues that knowledge is internalisation of social activity.

Mediation refers to people intentionally interject items between their environment and themselves, so that they are able to modify it and gain specific benefits.

Social influence occurs when a person 's emotions, opinions or behaviours are affected by others. Social influence takes many forms and can be seen in conformity, socialisation, peer pressure, obedience, leadership, persuasion, sales and marketing.

31 Which one of the following pairs is not correctly matched?

	Term in factor analysis		Meaning / Example
1	Factor extraction method	:	Principle axes
2	Factor rotation method	:	Promax
3	Inter factor correlation	:	Correlation between orthogonal factors
4	Cattell's scree	:	Plot to decide number of factors retain for interpretation

Ans. *(3)*

Exp. The pairs which is not correctly matched is Inter factor correlation : Correlation between orthogonal factors.

Interfactor correlations are obtained when researchers extract more than one factor and implement an oblique rotation, and they reveal the degree to which the dimensions underlying the observed variables are themselves associated with each other. Orthogonality means "uncorrelated." An orthogonal model means that all independent variables in that model are uncorrelated.

32 Choose the right sequence for stages of a sleep bout

1 II, III, IV, REM
2 III, II, REM, II
3 REM, II, III, I
4 I, II, III, REM

Ans. *(2)*

Exp. The right sequence for stages of a sleep bout is III, II, REM, II.

There are five stages of sleep. Stages 1-4 are non-REM sleep, followed by REM sleep.

Stage 1 is light sleep where you drift in and out of sleep and can be awakened easily. In this stage, the eyes move slowly and muscle activity slows. During this stage, many people experience sudden muscle contractions preceded by a sensation of falling.

In *Stage 2*, eye movement stops and brain waves become slower with only an occasional burst of rapid brain waves. The body begins to prepare for deep sleep, as the body temperature begins to drop and the heart rates slows.

When a person enters *Stage 3*, extremely slow brain waves called delta waves are interspersed with smaller, faster waves. This is deep sleep. It is during this stage that a person may experience sleepwalking, night terrors, talking during one's sleep and bedwetting. These behaviours are known as parasomnias and tend to occur during the transitions between non-REM and REM sleep.

In *Stage 4*, deep sleep continues as the brain produces delta waves almost exclusively. People roused from this state feel disoriented for a few minutes.

During REM (rapid eye movement) sleep, brain waves mimic activity during the waking state. The eyes remain closed but move rapidly from side-to-side, perhaps related to the intense dream and brain activity that occurs during this stage.

33 Child using whole arm movement in writing before he uses his fingers in holding a pen or pencil is indicative of

1 Proximo - Distal principle
2 Cephalo - Caudal principle
3 Specific movement
4 Neural control

Ans. (1)

Exp. Child using whole arm movement in writing before he uses his fingers in holding a pen or pencil is indicative of Proximo-distal principle.

The Proximo-distal principle also describes the direction of development. This principle states that development proceeds from the centre of the body outward. Think of a fertilised egg. This one tiny cell divides and expands outward to become an embryo. The spinal cord forms first and development progress outward to become a fetus. The limbs of the body forms before the hands and feet and the hands and feet develop before the finger and the toes.

The Cephalo-caudal principle states that development proceeds from top to bottom. According to this principle, a child will gain physical control of their head first. After this, physical control will move downward to the arms and lastly to the legs.

Functional movement usually involves gross motor movement involving the core, which refers to the muscles of the abdomen and spine, such as segmental stabilisers.

The neural circuitry that controls this process is complex and highly distributed: it involves pathways at many levels of the brain, the spinal cord and the peripheral nervous system and is mediated by multiple neurotransmitters.

34 Principle stating that a more preferred activity can be used to reinforce a less preferred activity is referred to as

1 Trace conditioning
2 Hull's principle
3 Principle of stimulus generalisation
4 Premack Principle

Ans. (4)

Exp. Principle stating that a more preferred activity can be used to reinforce a less preferred activity is refered to as Premack principle.

According to Premack principle, some behaviour that happens reliably can be used as a reinforcer for a behaviour that occurs less reliably. e.g. most children like to watch television--this is a behaviour that happens reliably (they learn to like TV all on their own and it is something they will do willingly without any interference from their parents) and parents often use this behaviour to reinforce something children like to do less such as washing dishes. So, some parents might condition children to wash dishes by rewarding dish washing with watching television.

35 According to Atkinson and Shiffrin, model of human memory which of the following sequence of events is correct?

1 Attention–sensory memory–short-term memory–long-term memory–elaborative rehearsal
2 Sensory memory–attention–short-term memory–elaborative rehearsal–long-term memory.
3 Attention–short-term memory–sensory memory–elaborative rehearsal–long-term memory
4 Sensory memory–short-term memory–attention, long-term memory–elaborative rehearsal

Ans. (2)

Exp. The multistore model of memory was proposed by Atkinson and Shiffrin (1968) and is a structural model. They proposed that memory consisted of three separate stores: Sensory memory, Short-Term Memory (STM) and Long-Term Memory (LTM).

Attention is the first step in remembering something, if a person's attention is focused on one of the sensory stores then the data from sensory memory is transferred to STM. If the information is given meaning (elaborative rehearsal) it is passed on to the LTM.

Elaborative rehearsal involves the process of linking new information in a meaningful way with information already stored in long-term memory.

36 Attribution, the process by which we determine the causes behind other's behaviour, involves focusing on which aspects of behaviour?

1 Consensus, distinctiveness and attraction
2 Distinctiveness, consistency and influence
3 Consensus, consistency and distinctiveness
4 Distinctiveness, influence and attraction

Ans. (3)

Exp. Attribution is the process by which we determine the causes behind others' behaviour. It involves focusing consensus, consistency and distinctiveness. Kelley's (1967) covariation model is the best known attribution theory. He developed a logical model for judging whether a particular action should be attributed to some characteristic (internal) of the person or the environment (external). Kelley believed that there were three types of causal information which influenced our judgements.

(i) Consensus- The extent to which other people behave in the same way in a similar situation. e.g. Alison smokes a cigarette when she goes out for a meal with her friend. If her friend smokes, her behaviour is high in consensus. If only Alison smokes it is low.

(ii) Consistency- The extent to which the person behaves like this every time the situation occurs. If Alison only smokes when she is out with friends, consistency is high. If she only smokes on one special occasion, consistency is low.

(iii) Distinctiveness- The extent to which the person behaves in the same way in similar situations. If Alison only smokes when she is out with friends, her behaviour is high in distinctiveness. If she smokes at any time or place, distinctiveness is low.

37 Deliberate application of known strategies to tasks, planning their use in advance, monitoring them in action, evaluating their output and modifying subsequent behaviour on the basis of performance is called

1 self-regulated learning 2 implicit learning
3 deductive reasoning 4 cognitive learning

***Ans.* (1)**

Exp. Deliberate application of known strategies to tasks, planning their use in advance, monitoring them in action, evaluating their output and modifying subsequent behaviour on the basis of performance is called Self-regulated learning.

Self-regulated learning is a cyclical process, wherein the student plans for a task, monitors their performance and then reflects on the outcome. The cycle then repeats as the student uses the reflection to adjust and prepare for the next task. The process is not one-size-fits-all; it should be tailored for individual students and for specific learning tasks.

38 At what level do we understand the complete meaning and sense of a language structure?

1 Phonemes 2 Syntax
3 Prosodic contour 4 Morphemes

***Ans.* (3)**

Exp. At prosodic contour level, we understand the complete meaning and sense of a language structure.

Syllogism or Prosodic Contour is the deductive reasoning. It is an extremely subtle, sophisticated or deceptive argument and a formal argument in logic that is formed by two statements. It is also a conclusion which must be true if the two statements are true.

Phonemes are the basic units of speech of a language. Phonemes are put together to create morphemes and words. The main difference between a morpheme and phoneme is that while a morpheme carries a meaning, a phoneme itself does not carry any meaning. It is merely a unit of speech. Syntax/Syntactical is the organisation of words in a sentence. It refers to the rules and principles that govern the sentence structure of any language.

Morphemes are the smallest meaningful elements of a language. This signifies that morphemes cannot be segmented into smaller parts as it will discard the meaning. e.g. if we take words such book, pencil, cup, eraser, box, none of these can be segmented further.

39 In terms of the percentage of common variance shared by the two variables, arrange the following co-relations in descending order.

I. 0.60 II. – 0.50
III. – 0.70 IV. 0.40

Codes

1 III, I, II, IV 2 I, IV, III, II
3 I, IV, II, III 4 I, III, IV, II

***Ans.* (1)**

Exp. The correct sequence will be: III, I, II, IV i.e, –0.70, 0.60, –0.50, 0.40.

First the given correlations will be converted to percentage of common variance: 36%, 25%, 49%, 16%. Arranging the percentages in descending order, we will get: 49%, 36%, 25%, 16%.

The squared correlation describes the proportion of variance in common between the two variables. If we multiply this by 100 we then get the percent of variance in common between two variables. That is: $r^2 jk \times 100$ = percent of variance in common between Xj and Xk.

40 What do characterise Rapid Eye Movement sleep?

I. Delta waves
II. Loss of muscle tone
III. Low voltage-high frequency waves
IV. Higher cerebral activity

Codes

1 I, II and III 2 I, II and IV
3 II, III and IV 4 I, II, III and IV

***Ans.* (3)**

Exp. The correct codes are II, III, and IV.

Rapid Eye Movement sleep is characterised by following factors :

Loss of muscle tone: Rapid eye movement sleep or REM, is one of the five stages of sleep that most people experience nightly. It is characterised by quick, random movements of the eyes and paralysis of the muscles.

Low voltage-high frequency waves: REM sleep is defined by the presence of desynchronized (low-voltage, mixed-frequency) brain wave activity, muscle atonia, and bursts of rapid eye. "Sawtooth" wave forms, theta activity (3 to 7 counts per second), and slow alpha activity also characterize REM sleep. During the initial cycle, the REM period may last only 1 to 5 minutes; however, it becomes progressively prolonged as the sleep episode progresses.

Higher cerebral activity: Cerebral activity is characterized by many different activities of the brain accessible to neuro-imaging techniques. Functional processes are normally those occurring over short timescales from small fractions of a second to minutes. They support or are associated with information processing or the transmission and reception of signals in the brain.

41 Threshold hypothesis indicates

1 positive correlation between intelligence and creativity upto a particular level of intelligence
2 negative correlation between intelligence and creativity upto a particular level of intelligence
3 curvilinear relationship between intelligence and creativity after a particular level of intelligence
4 negative correlation between intelligence and creativity after a particular level of intelligence

Ans. (1)

Exp. Threshold hypothesis indicates positive correlation between intelligence and creativity upto a particular level of intelligence (ranging from 100-120 IQ) after which a zero correlation may exist, but not a negative correlation.

The threshold hypothesis is a hypothesis concerning second language acquisition set forth in a study by Cummins that stated that a minimum threshold in language proficiency must be passed before a second-language speaker can reap any benefits from language. It indicates positive correlation between intelligence and creativity upto a particular level of intelligence. It also states that, in order to gain proficiency in a second language, the learner must also have passed a certain and age appropriate level of competence in his or her first language.

42 Match List I with List II and indicate your answer with the help of codes given below.

List I (Components)	List II (Type)
A. Experiential	I. Analytic
B. Contextual	II. Creative
C. Componential	III. Practical
	IV. Successful

Codes

	A	B	C		A	B	C
1	III	IV	II	2	II	III	I
3	IV	II	III	4	II	I	III

Ans. (2)

Exp. The correct matching is A-II, B-III, C-I.

Experiential component is associated with Creative intelligence. According to the experiential subtheory, people are creatively intelligent to the extent that they can cope with relative novelty and automatize routine aspects of tasks so as to devote more resources to novel stimuli in their environment.

Contextual component is associated with Practical intelligence. The subtheory postulates that people are intelligent in context to the extent that they effectively adapt to, shape, and select environments.

Componential component is associated with Analytic intelligence. It specifies three kinds of information-processing components in human intelligence. The three components are (a) metacomponents, which are used to plan, monitor, and evaluate problem solving and decision making; (b) performance components, which are actually used to solve the problems or make the decisions; and (c) knowledge-acquisition components, which are used to learn how to solve the problems or make the decisions in the first place.

43 Match List I with List II and indicate your answer with the help of codes given below

List I (Type of Memory)	List II (Type of Information)
A. Echoic memory	I. Episodic information
B. Iconic memory	II. Auditory information
C. Auto-biographical memory	III. Visual information
D. Implicit memory	IV. Priming

Codes

	A	B	C	D		A	B	C	D
1	IV	I	III	II	2	II	III	I	IV
3	III	IV	II	I	4	IV	II	I	III

Ans. (2)

Exp. The correct matching is A-II, B-III, C-I, D-IV

Echoic memory is one of the sensory memory registers; a component of Sensory Memory (SM) that is specific to retaining auditory information. The sensory memory for sounds that people have just perceived are the form of echoic memory.

Iconic memory is the visual Sensory Memory (SM) register pertaining to the visual domain and a fast-decaying store of visual information. It is a component of the visual memory system which also includes Visual Short-Term Memory (VSTM) and Long-Term Memory (LTM).

Auto-biographical memory is a memory system consisting of episodes recollected from an individual's life, based on a combination of episodic (personal experiences and specific objects, people and events experienced at particular time and place) and semantic (general knowledge and facts about the world) memory.

Implicit memory is one of the two main types of long-term human memory. It is acquired and used unconsciously and can affect thoughts and behaviours. One of its most common forms is procedural memory, which helps people performing certain tasks without conscious awareness of these previous experiences. Priming is another, smaller subset of implicit memory. It involves using pictures, words or other stimuli to help someone recognize another word or phrase in the future. Examples include using green to remember grass and red to remember apple.

44 Which of the following illnesses caused by long-term abuse of alcohol often involves profound retrograde amnesia?

1 Alzheimer's disease
2 Parkinson's disease
3 Huntington's disease
4 Korsakoff's disease

Ans. (4)

Exp. Korsakoff's disease is caused by long-term abuse of alcohol often involves profound retrograde amnesia.

Korsakoff's disease is a syndrome occurring primarily in cases of severe, chronic alcoholism. It is caused by thiamine (vitamin B1) deficiency and damage to the mammillary bodies. Patients with Korsakoff's syndrome demonstrate dense anterograde and retrograde amnesia, which is thought to be due to lesions in the anterior or dorsomedial nuclei (or both) of the thalamus. Other symptoms include confabulation, lack of insight, apathy, and impoverished conversation.

The selective and acute nature of the memory disorder in Korsakoff's syndrome sets it apart from alcoholic dementia (see alcohol-induced persisting dementia), a syndrome characterized by more global impairments in intellectual functioning that evolve gradually over time. Korsakoff's syndrome often follows an episode of Wernicke's encephalopathy (see Wernicke– Korsakoff syndrome).

45 Applied behaviour analysis involves four steps. Which of the following two pairs are included?

I. Define and observe
II. Enumerate and reward
III. Observe and reinforce
IV. Intervene and test

Codes

1 I and II 2 I and IV
3 II and IV 4 III and IV

Ans. (2)

Exp. Applied behaviour analysis involves two pairs which are as follows (i) Define and observe (ii) Intervene and test.

Applied Behaviour Analysis (ABA) is the application of the principles of learning and motivation from behaviour analysis and the procedures and technology derived from those principles, to the solution of problems of social significance. The term ABA stands for Applied Behaviour Analysis. It's an approach that was derived from learning theory. In ABA, a socially significant behaviour is targeted, such as a child learning to make request. And then an environmental alteration is introduced, such as teaching instructions and a reward for a correct response. And then the change in the targeted behaviour is objectively measured.

46 Match List I and List II and indicate your answer with the help of codes given below.

List I (Route)	List II (Processing)
A. Central route to persuasion	I. Heuristic processing
B. Peripheral route to persuasion	II. Elaboration likelihood processing
C. Distinct routes to persuasion	III. Cognitive dissonance
D. Attitude behaviour discrepancies	IV. Systematic processing

Codes

	A	B	C	D
1	IV	I	II	III
2	III	II	IV	I
3	I	II	IV	III
4	II	IV	III	I

Ans. (1)

Exp. The correct matching is A-IV, B-I, C-II, D-III

Heuristic processing uses peripheral route to persuasion. The peripheral route to Persuasion is when people do not elaborate on a persuasive argument and instead are swayed by surface characteristics that are peripheral to the message. When using this route, peripheral cues enable the individual to use mental shortcuts, accepting or rejecting the argument based on superficial factors instead of actively thinking about the issue. Attitude change resulting from the peripheral route is typically temporary and susceptible to additional change.

Elaboration likelihood processing uses Distinct routes to persuasion. The elaboration likelihood model proposes two distinct routes for information processing: a central route and a peripheral route. The central route is used when the message recipient has the motivation as well as the ability to think about the message and its topic. When people process information centrally, the cognitive responses, or elaborations, will be much more relevant to the information, whereas when processing peripherally, the individual may rely on heuristics and other rules of thumb when elaborating on a message.

Systematic processing uses Central route to persuasion. The central route to persuasion is when people elaborate on a persuasive argument, listening carefully and thinking about the logic behind the message. There are times when people are motivated to pay attention to the facts during a speech or other persuasive communication and during those times are persuaded the most by a strong logical argument. If a person believes the persuasion to be reliable, convincing and well-constructed, he or she will typically be receptive to a change in attitude that is long-lasting.

Cognitive dissonance is Attitude behaviour discrepancies. Cognitive dissonance is typically experienced as psychological stress when persons participate in an action that goes against one or more of those things. According to this theory, when two actions or ideas or action and behavior are not psychologically consistent with each other, people do all in their power to change them until they become consistent.

Directions (Q. Nos. 47-50) *Read the following passage and answer the four questions that follow.*

A psychologist developed a new Anxiety Inventory of 25 items. The Cronbach alpha for the inventory was found to be 0.80. The inventory was administered to a group of 50 anxiety disorder patients before beginning their psychotherapy. The patients had a significantly higher mean than the normative group of normals.

The same group of patients was retested after 12 weeks of psychotherapy. The post-test mean was significantly lesser than the pre-test mean. The new Anxiety Inventory was correlated with an established anxiety inventory and the correlation turned out to be 0.20. The norms of the inventory were developed in terms of normalised T scores.

47 What would be the median T score for the new Anxiety Inventory?

1 50 2 100
3 120 4 Inadequate data on median T score

Ans. (1)

Exp. The median T score for the new Anxiety Inventory will be 50.

T-scores are standardized scores on each dimension for each type. A score of 50 represents the mean of the scores. Since the T scores are normalized, the mean and median are equal. Hence the median of the new inventory is 50.

48 The above data indicate that the new inventory has

1 satisfactory parallel form reliability
2 unsatisfactory parallel form reliability
3 satisfactory concurrent validity
4 unsatisfactory concurrent validity

Ans. (4)

Exp. The given data indicate that the new inventory has unsatisfactory concurrent validity.

The new Anxiety Inventory was correlated with an established anxiety inventory and the correlation turned out to be low, i.e., 0.20.

Concurrent validity is a type of evidence that can be gathered to defend the use of a test for predicting other outcomes and predictive validity is the extent to which a score on a scale or test predicts scores on some criterion measure. Concurrent validity and predictive validity are two types of criterion-related validity. The difference between concurrent validity and predictive validity rests solely on the time at which the two measures are administered. Concurrent validity applies to validation studies in which the two measures are administered at approximately the same time.

49 What can you infer about the internal consistency reliability of the new inventory?

1 Satisfactory internal consistency reliability
2 Unsatisfactory internal consistency reliability
3 Split-half reliability needs to be computed first to infer about internal consistency
4 Inadequate data in the above passage to infer about internal consistency

Ans. (1)

Exp. Internal consistency reliability defines the consistency of the results delivered in a test, ensuring that the various items measuring the different constructs deliver consistent scores.

Cronbach's alpha is a measure of internal consistency, that is, how closely related a set of items are as a group. The Cronbach alpha for the inventory was found to be 0.80, which means a high internal consistency. So the internal consistency reliability of the new inventory is Satisfactory internal consistency reliability.

50 The above data indicate that the new inventory has

1 unsatisfactory construct validity
2 satisfactory construct validity
3 unsatisfactory test-retest reliability
4 satisfactory test-retest reliability

Ans. (2)

Exp. The above data indicate that the new inventory has satisfactory construct validity.

The present inventory aims to measure anxiety. The inventory was administered to a group of 50 anxiety disorder patients before beginning their psychotherapy. The patients had a significantly higher mean than the normative group of normals indicating high anxiety for anxiety disorder patients. The same group of patients was retested after 12 weeks of psychotherapy. The post-test mean was significantly lesser than the pre-test mean. Construct validity is the degree to which a test measures what it claims, or purports, to be measuring, how well a test or tool measures the construct that it was designed to measure.

51 Which one of the following theories predicts that work motivation will be low if an employee perceives that an increased effort will have little, or no effect on his/her performance?

1 Just-World theory
2 Need-Drive theory
3 Expectancy theory
4 Normative theory

Ans. (3)

Exp. Vroom's Expectancy theory will predict that the work motivation will be low if an employee perceive that an increased effort will have little or no effect on his/her performance.

Vroom's Expectancy theory assumes that behaviour results from conscious choices among alternatives whose purpose it is to maximise pleasure and to minimise pain. Vroom realised that an employee's performance is based on individual factors such as personality, skills, knowledge, experience and abilities.

An employee's motivation is an outcome of how much an individual wants a reward (valence), the assessment that the likelihood that the effort will lead to expected performance (expectancy) and the belief that the performance will lead to reward (instrumentality).

52 Read each of the following two statements Assertion (A) and Reason (R) and indicate your answer using the codes given below.

Assertion (A) If higher order factor analysis is to be carried out, first order factors should not be subjected to varimax rotation.

Reason (R) Varimax rotation provides oblique factors.

Codes

1 Both (A) and (R) are true and (R) is the correct explanation of (A)
2 Both (A) and (R) are true, but (R) is not the correct explanation of (A)
3 (A) is true, but (R) is false
4 (A) is false, but (R)is true

Ans. (3)

Exp. (A) is true, but (R) is false

If higher order factor analysis is to be carried out, first order factors should not be subjected to varimax rotation.

Varimax rotation does not provide oblique factors. Varimax rotation provides orthogonal factors.

Varimax rotation is a statistical technique used at one level of factor analysis as an attempt to clarify the relationship among factors. Generally, the process involves adjusting the coordinates of data that result from a principal components analysis. The adjustment, or rotation, is intended to maximize the variance shared among items. By maximizing the shared variance, results more discretely represent how data correlate with each principal component. To maximize the variance generally means to increase the squared correlation of items related to one factor, while decreasing the correlation on any other factor. In other words, the varimax rotation simplifies the loadings of items by removing the middle ground and more specifically identifying the factor upon which data load.

A Varimax rotation is used to simplify the expression of a particular sub-space in terms of just a few major items each. The actual coordinate system is unchanged. It is the orthogonal basis that is being rotated to align with those coordinates. The sub-space found with principal component analysis or factor analysis is expressed as a dense basis with many non-zero weights which makes it hard to interpret. Varimax is so called because it maximises the sum of the variances of the squared loadings (squared correlations between variables and factors). Preserving orthogonality requires that it is a rotation that leaves the sub-space invariant.

53 Where are oxytocin and vasopressin hormones synthesised?

1 Posterior pituitary
2 Anterior pituitary
3 Gonads
4 Hypothalamus

Ans. *(4)*

➲ *Exp.* The oxytocin and vasopressin hormones synthesised in Hypothalamus.

Oxytocin and arginine vasopressin (AVP) are neuropeptides synthesized in the hypothalamus and secreted from the posterior pituitary gland. Oxytocin was first described for its important role in stimulating uterine contractions and milk let down after birth, while AVP is central to water homeostasis by regulating urine concentration at the level of the kidney. In addition to these physiologic functions, both peptides are now understood to mediate numerous social behaviors in mammals. The role of the oxytocin and vasopressin systems in social functioning has developed out of a large body of animal research, focusing primarily on rodents.

54 Match List I and List II and indicate your answer with the help of codes given below.

List I (Concept)	List II (Psychologist)
A. Parenting styles	I. Bowlby
B. Attachment	II. Piaget
C. Reciprocal determinism	III. Bandura
D. Centration	IV. Baumrind

Codes

	A	B	C	D		A	B	C	D
1	II	I	IV	III	2	II	IV	I	III
3	IV	I	III	II	4	IV	II	III	I

Ans. *(3)*

➲ *Exp.* The correct matching is A-IV, B-I, C-III, D-II

Bowlby's Evolutionary theory of attachment suggests that children come into the world biologically pre-programmed to form attachments with others, because this will help them to survive. A child has an innate (i.e. inborn) need to attach to one main attachment figure.

Piaget in his theory of cognitive development talks about pre-operational stage of cognitive development. Centration is a behaviour often demonstrated in the pre-operational stage. Centration is the tendency to focus on one salient aspect of a situation and neglect other, possibly relevant aspects.

According to *Albert Bandura*, reciprocal determinism is a model composed of three factors that influence behaviour: the environment, the individual and the behaviour itself. Essentially, Bandura believes that an individual's behaviour influences and is influenced by both the social world and personal characteristics.

Diana Baumrind, a developmental psychologist, identified four main types of parenting styles, sometimes called the Baumrind parenting styles. These 4 parenting styles are now commonly recognised and studied by pediatricians and psychologists. (i) Authoritative parenting (ii) Authoritarian parenting (iv) Permissive parenting (v) Neglectful parenting

55 Which of the following is not a component of Emotional Intelligence as described by Mayer and Salovey?

I. The ability to use emotions to facilitate thinking.
II. The ability to perceive, appraise and express emotions accurately.
III. The ability to perceive, appraise and express emotions appropriately.
IV. The ability to adapt to new and different contexts, select appropriate contexts and effectively shape one's environment to suit one's needs.

Codes

1 Only IV
2 I and IV
3 I, II and IV
4 I, III and IV

Ans. *(1)*

➲ *Exp.* The ability to adapt to new and different contexts, select appropriate contexts and effectively shape one's environment to suit one's needs is not a component of Emotional Intelligence as described by Mayer and Salovey

Mayer and Salovey proposed that Emotional Intelligence was a cognitive ability which is separate but also associated to, general intelligence. This model consists of four different abilities (or branches) including, perception of emotion, emotional facilitation, understanding emotions and management of emotions. These branches are ordered from basic to higher-order abilities which develop as an individual matures. Emotion perception is the ability to perceive emotions in yourself and others. It also includes perceiving non-verbal signals and emotion in stimuli such as landscapes and art. Mayer and Salovey have a 16 step developmental model of emotional intelligence from childhood to adulthood. It comprises four branches.

(i) The ability to perceive emotions in oneself and others accurately.
(ii) The ability to use emotions to facilitate thinking.
(iii) The ability to understand emotions, emotional language and the signals conveyed by emotions.
(iv) The ability to manage emotions so as to attain specific goals.

56 Which of the following are the characteristics of Cattell's Culture Fair Intelligence Test?

I. Speed
II. Power
III. Non-verbal
IV. Performance

Codes

1 I and III
2 I, II and III
3 I, II and IV
4 I and II

Ans. (2)

Exp. The characteristics of Cattell's Culture Fair Intelligence Test are Speed, Power and Non-verbal. A culture-fair test is test designed to be free of cultural bias, as far as possible, so that no one culture has an advantage over another. The test is designed to not be influenced by verbal ability, cultural climate, or educational level. The Culture Fair Intelligence Test (CFIT) was conceived by Raymond B. Cattell in 1920s. It is a non-verbal instrument to measure your analytical and reasoning ability in the abstract and novel situations. The test includes mazes, classifications, conditions and series. Such problems are believed to be common with all cultures. That's the reason that the testing industry claims it free from all cultural influences. Cattell's Culture-fair tests were developed to reduce cultural bias. There are two types of culture-fair tests. In a speed test, the scope of the questions is limited and the methods you need to use to answer them is clear. Taken individually, the questions appear relatively straightforward. Speed test are concerned with how many questions you can answer correctly in the allotted time. A power test on the other hand will present a smaller number of more complex questions. Speed tests contain more items than power tests although they have the same approximate time limit. Speed tests tend to be used in selection at the administrative and clerical level. Power tests tend to be used more at the graduate, professional or managerial level.

57 Technique of shaping is based on which of the following principle?

1 Reciprocal inhibition
2 Response inhibition
3 Stimulus discrimination
4 Successive approximation

Ans. (4)

Exp. The technique of shaping is based on successive approximation.

Shaping (also known as successive approximation) is a teaching technique that involves a teacher rewarding a child as she or he successfully improves the acquisition of a target skill. Shaping is considered an essential process in teaching because behavior cannot be rewarded unless it first occurs. Shaping is intended to lead children in the direction of appropriate complex behavior, and then reward them as they complete each successive step. Successive approximation is a series of rewards that provide positive reinforcement for behaviour changes that are successive steps towards the final desired behaviour.

58 What did Chomsky not argue about language development?

1 There is a universal grammar
2 It is genetically wired
3 There is an innate modular
4 It is based on reinforced learning

Ans. (4)

Exp. Chomsky not argue about language development is based on reinforced learning. Chomsky argued about language acquisition device, not language acquisition support system. Language acquisition support system was proposed by Jerome Bruner.

American-born linguist Noam Chomsky, being a Cartesian and nativist, believes that we are born with a predisposition to learn language. Language development is something that is genetically wired. The essence of his theories of language acquisition state that human beings are pre-wired to learn language and in fact are born with the basic rules for language intact.

Chomsky believes that there is an innate modular language which means a pre-programming in our brain to understand and learn language.

Many of the unique details of any specific language structure are heavily influenced by the environment, but according to Chomsky, the human brain is ready made to quickly acquire language at specific stages in the developmental process. Prior to Chomsky, it was widely agreed that language acquisition was mostly a learned process. For instance, many believed that language skills were developed solely through watching and learning our parents and other people in our environment. Chomsky's notion that the brain is pre-wired for language was quite a contrast to the accepted beliefs of the time.

59 What are the two types of declarative memory given by Edel Tulving?

1 Episodic and semantic
2 Semantic and procedural
3 Reconstructive and semantic
4 Procedural and reconstructive

Ans. (1)

➲ *Exp.* The two types of declarative memory given by Edel Tulving are episodic and semantic.

Declarative memory contains knowledge, ideas, information, stories. It is a type of memory that is consciously inspectable, which means that one can verbally report his/her declarative memory. According to Tulving (1989), there are two types of declarative memory: semantic, and episodic memory. Semantic memory is memory for meanings and facts. This memory contains what one knows. Semantic information cannot be temporally dated. Episodic memory contains information about one's own personal experiences. Episodic information can be temporally dated, this means that it is stored with some information about when was learned.

60 Read each of the following two statements Assertion (A) and Reason (R) and indicate your answer using the codes given below.

Assertion (A) Illusions are instances in which perception yields false interpretation of physical reality.

Reason (R) Theory of misapplied constancy suggests that when looking at illusions, we interpret certain cues as suggesting that some parts are farther than others because of our powerful tendency toward size constancy.

Codes

1 Both (A) and (R) are true and (R) is the correct explanation of (A)
2 Both (A) and (R) are true, but (R) is not the correct explanation of (A)
3 (A) is true, but (R) is false
4 (A) is false, but (R) is true

***Ans.* (1)**

➲ *Exp.* Both (A) and (R) are true and (R) is the correct explanation of (A).

Instances in which perception yields false interpretations of physical reality (or errors). Illusions due to distortion of physical conditions include mirages, in which you perceive things that aren't really there - like the water you often seem to see on the dry road ahead of you. Theory of illusions suggesting that the underlying elicitor is the improper utilisation of cues which typically permit correct comprehension of these properties as size and shape. The illusion occurs because of a misapplication of size constancy scaling.

In most cases, size constancy allows us to perceive objects in a stable way by taking distance into account. In the three-dimensional world, this principle allows us to perceive a tall person as tall whether they are standing next to us or off in the distance. When we apply this same principle to two-dimensional objects, Gregory suggests, errors can result. Size constancy is an aspect of perceptual constancy in which an object will appear to be the same size to an observer despite of changes in light, rotation, distance, perspective etc. This skill is so important that is appears in an infant only a couple of weeks old.

61 Match List I with List II and indicate your answer with the help of codes given below.

List I (Psychologist)	List II (Measure)
A. Buss	I. Aggression machine
B. Milgram	II. Picture frustration study
C. Rosenzweig	III. State-trait anger Inventory
D. Spielberger	IV. Obedience laboratory-shock generator

Codes

	A	B	C	D		A	B	C	D
1	I	II	III	IV	2	I	III	IV	II
3	II	IV	III	I	4	IV	I	II	III

***Ans.* (*)**

➲ *Exp.* The correct matching is A-I, B-IV, C-II, D-III

Buss aggression machine (shock box) is a machine that allows an experimenter to record a subject's level of state aggression in terms of the duration and intensity of an electric shock that the subject is prepared to give an accomplice. No shock is actually given, but the accomplice behaves as if he or she has received a shock.

Stanley Milgram conducted an experiment focusing on the conflict between obedience to authority and personal conscience. The learner (a confederate called Mr. Wallace) was taken into a room and had electrodes attached to his arms, and the teacher and researcher went into a room next door that contained an electric shock generator and a row of switches marked from 15 volts (Slight Shock) to 375 volts (Danger: Severe Shock) to 450 volts (XXX).

Rosenzweig picture frustration study developed for adults by Saul Rosenzweig is a projective test administered to assess personality characteristics, in which the subject is shown scenes depicting moderately frustrating situations and asked what the frustrated person depicted would probably do, or how the subject would react in such situations. The Rosenzweig Picture Frustration test consists of 24 cartoon pictures, each portraying two persons in a frustrating situation. Each picture contains two "speech balloons," a filled one for the "frustrator" or antagonist, and a blank one for the frustrated person, or protagonist.

Speilberger developed the State-Trait Anger Expression Inventory (STAXI; Speilberger, 1996). It is a 44-item instrument designed to measure anger both as an emotional situational response and a dispositional quality.

62 Components of empathy are

1 Perceiving and advancing
2 Advancing and interpreting
3 Judging and communicating
4 Perceiving and communicating

Ans. (4)

Exp. Components of empathy are perceiving and communicating.

Empathy is a multidimensional construct and requires the ability to perceive, understand, and feel the emotional states of others.

According to most models empathy consists of at least three core components: (1) The ability to recognize emotions in oneself and others via different communicative cues such as facial expressions, speech, or behavior; (2) a cognitive component, also referred to as perspective taking or theory of mind, describing the competency to take over the perspective of another person, though maintaining the essential distinction between self and other; and (3) an affective component, that is, sharing of emotional states with others or the ability to experience similar emotions as others.

63 Read each of the following two statements Assertion (A) and Reason (R) and indicate your answer using the codes given below.

Assertion (A) Paper-pencil self-report personality inventories are very useful in personnel selection.

Reason (R) In selection situation, paper-pencil, self-report inventories are sensitive to impression management.

Codes

1 Both (A) and (R) are true and (R) is the correct explanation of (A)
2 Both (A) and (R) are true, but (R) is not the correct explanation of (A)
3 (A) is true, but (R) is false
4 (A) is false, but (R) is true

Ans. (3)

Exp. (A) is false, but (R) is true.

Paper-pencil self-report personality inventories are useful in personnel selection. This is false as Self-report inventories are more widely used than any form of personality assessment. These are paper-and-pencil test that ask people to respond to questions concerning their traits, values, attitudes, motives, feelings, interests, abilities. In assessment involving self-reports, this objective is invariably haunted by the possibility of misrepresentation. Thus it seems dangerous to ignore the possibility that at least some respondents systematically misrepresent their own personality. Therefore, paper-and-pencil self-report inventories are not much useful in personnel selection.

In selection situation, such test are sensitive to impression management. This is true as people do not always respond accurately when asked questions in such tests. To the extent that people motivated to make a good impression provide inaccurate responses, the validity of self-reports is questionable.

64 Which of the following statements would be false about multiple correlation?

I. It ranges from – 1.00 to 1.00 only.
II. It ranges from 0 to 1.00 only.
III. It ranges from $-\infty$ to $+\infty$.
IV. It ranges from –1.00 to 0 only.

Codes

1 Only I
2 Only II
3 III and IV
4 I, III and IV

Ans. (4)

Exp. Statements I, III, and IV are false about multiple correlation:

The coefficient of multiple correlation is a measure of how well a given variable can be predicted using a linear function of a set of other variables. It is the correlation between the variable 's values and the best predictions that can be computed linearly from the predictive variables.

The coefficient of multiple correlation takes values between 0 and 1; a higher value indicates a better predictability of the dependent variable from the independent variables, with a value of 1 indicating that the predictions are exactly correct and a value of 0 indicating that no linear combination of the independent variables is a better predictor than is the fixed mean of the dependent variable.

65 Which of the following components have been proposed by Torrance?

I. Divergent thinking
II. Elaboration
III. Transformation
IV. Flexibility

Codes

1 I and II
2 II and III
3 II and IV
4 I, II and IV

Ans. (3)

Exp. The following components have been proposed by Torrance are Elaboration and Flexibility.

When offering art activities to young children, we are encouraged to think about 'The Four Components of Creativity' as described by Psychologist Ellis P Torrance Elaboration, Flexibility, Fluency and Originality

(i) *Elaboration* is the ability to extend ideas. Give children new ways of doing old ideas and activities. For instance, providing pipe cleaner and other items to stick into play dough would allow children to elaborate in their play.

(ii) *Flexibility* is the ability to approach different situations and develop solutions from a number of different perspectives. Foster flexibility by allowing plenty of opportunities to explore and experiment. Allowing children to experiment and make mistakes unleashes their creative thinking and a sense of wonder.

(iii) *Fluency* is the ability to produce a number of different ideas. To promote fluency provide children with plenty of opportunities that stimulate the thought process. Ask open ended questions and questions that ask the child's opinion.

(iv) *Originality* is the ability to have a new or novel idea. To promote originality, provide a variety of supplies and experiences in which children can use their imagination and create. By painting or constructing something out of play dough they are creating something out of nothing.

66 Which of the following strategies are used to gain compliance?

I. Ingratiation and commitment
II. Reciprocity and obedience
III. Reciprocity and scarcity
IV. Respect and ingratiation

Codes

1 I and II 2 II and IV
3 III and IV 4 I and III

Ans. *(4)*

Exp. Ingratiation and commitment and Reciprocity and scarcity are strategies used to gain compliance.

Compliance is a response—specifically, a submission—made in reaction to a request. The request may be explicit (e.g., foot-in-the-door technique) or implicit (e.g., advertising). The target may or may not recognize that they are being urged to act in a particular way.

Ingratiating is a psychological technique in which an individual attempts to influence another person by becoming more likeable to their target. This term was coined by social psychologist Edward E. Jones, who further defined ingratiating as "a class of strategic behaviors illicitly designed to influence a particular other person concerning the attractiveness of one's personal qualities." This attempt to obtain compliance involves gaining someone's approval so they will be more likely to appease your demands. Edward E. Jones discusses three forms of ingratiation: flattery, opinion conformity and self-presentation (presenting one's own attributes in a manner that appeals to the target).

Commitment is an obligation or devotion to a person, relationship, task, cause, or other entity or action.

The principle of reciprocity simply means you are more likely to comply with a request if it comes from someone who has previously done something for you. For example, when the Hare Krishna religion was struggling to raise money they found a solution. They would give passersby a book, a magazine, or a flower. Under no circumstances would the giver accept its return. Instead they would ask for a few dollars. It was wildly successful–they raised millions of dollars.

Another principle of persuasion is scarcity — we are more likely to want something the less it's available. This is even more persuasive when something is newly scarce.

67 Which is not the component of Kluver-Bucy syndrome following the removal of anterior temporal lobes?

1 Rejection of anything that is edible
2 A tendency to investigate objects with the mouth
3 Lack of fear
4 Increased sexual activity often directed at inappropriate

Ans. *(1)*

Exp. The components of Kluver-Bucy syndrome following the removal of anterior temporal lobes are tendency to investigate objects with the mouth, Lack of fear and Increased sexual activity often directed at inappropriate.

Kluver-Bucy syndrome is a very rare cerebral neurological disorder associated with damage to both temporal lobes resulting in abnormalities in memory, social and sexual functioning and idiosyncratic behaviours.

The list of symptoms generally include the following:

Docility, characterized by exhibiting diminished fear responses or reacting with unusually low aggression. This has also been termed "placidity" or "tameness".

Dietary changes and hyperphagia, characterized by eating inappropriate objects (pica), or overeating, or both.

Hyperorality, described by Ozawa et al. as "an oral tendency, or compulsion to examine objects by mouth".

Hypersexuality is characterized by a heightened libido or a tendency to seek sexual stimulation from unusual or inappropriate objects. Visual agnosia is characterized by an inability to recognize familiar objects or people.

68 Arrange the following tests in increasing order of their saturation on projective criteria.

I. Thematic Apperception test
II. Differential Aptitude test
III. Rorschach Ink Blot test
IV. Incomplete Sentence blank

Codes

1 III, I, II, IV 2 II, IV, III, I
3 III, I, IV, II 4 II, IV, I, III

Ans. *(4)*

Exp. Increasing order of the testes and their saturation on projective criteria is Differential Aptitude test, Incomplete Sentence blank, Thematic Apperception test and Rorschach Ink Blot test.

Differential Aptitude Tests (DAT) is a battery of tests designed for use in the educational and vocational counseling of students in grades 7 to 12 as well as adults. The battery—which measures abstract reasoning, mechanical reasoning, verbal reasoning, language usage, numerical ability, spatial relations, and perceptual speed and accuracy—pinpoints mental strengths and weaknesses and predicts success both in school and in the workplace.

The Rotter Incomplete Sentences Blank is a projective psychological test developed by Julian B. Rotter. It comes in three forms (for different age groups) and comprises 40 incomplete sentences usually only 1–2 words long, such as "I regret ..." and "Mostly girls ...". As with other sentence completion tests, the subject is asked to complete the sentence.

Thematic Apperception Test (TAT) is a projective test, developed by Henry Alexander Murray and his associates, in which participants are held to reveal their attitudes, feelings, conflicts, and personality characteristics in the oral or written stories they make up about a series of ambiguous black-and-white pictures. Prior to administering the test, the examiner assures the participant that there are no right or wrong answers and indicates that the narratives should have a beginning, middle, and ending. At the end, the stories are discussed to elucidate themes and patterns. Systematic coding schemes, with demonstrated reliability and validity, have been developed to assess different aspects of personality functioning derived from TAT stories, including motivation for achievement, power, affiliation, and intimacy; gender identity; defense mechanisms; and mental processes influencing interpersonal relations. The TAT is one of the most frequently used and researched tests in psychology, particularly in clinical settings for diagnosing disorders, describing personality, and assessing strengths and weaknesses in personality functioning.

Rorschach Inkblot Test is a projective technique in which the participant is presented with 10 unstructured inkblots (half in black and gray and half including color) and is asked "What might this be?" The examiner classifies the responses according to such structural and thematic (content) factors as color (C), movement (M), detail (D), whole (W), popular or common (P), animal (A), form (F), and human (H). Various scoring systems, either qualitative or quantitative, are used.

The object is to interpret the participant's personality structure in terms of factors such as emotionality, cognitive style, creativity, impulse control, and various defensive patterns. Perhaps the best known—and certainly one of the most controversial—assessment instruments in all of psychology, the Rorschach is widely used and has been extensively researched, with results ranging from those that claim strong support for its clinical utility (e.g., for selecting treatment modalities or monitoring patient change or improvement over time) to those that demonstrate little evidence of validity.

69 A listener totally rejects the conclusion that the death penalty is justified for the purpose of preventing further social evil despite he cannot readily refute the premises the speaker is presenting for his conclusion. His reasoning is biased. Why?

1 Due to his mood states
2 Due to his beliefs
3 Confirmation bias
4 Hindsight

Ans. *(2)*

Exp. His reasoning is biased due to his beliefs. Belief bias is one of the most common forms of cognitive bias. It has probably altered your acceptance of arguments more than you would like to admit. Belief bias is a type of cognitive bias wherein we are more likely to accept the outcome of something if it matches our belief system. You may be thinking, well, that's self-explanatory. Not so fast. Belief bias also states that if a person produces an argument that we cannot follow, or that makes no logical sense to us, we are still more likely to accept it because the final premise matches what we also believe — it "makes sense." In other words, you are likely to accept a conclusion as true because it is believable to you, rather than examining whether the conclusion is logically valid. Here are two syllogisms, or logical arguments that require deductive reasoning.

The conclusion (final statement) is inferred from a major premise (the first part of the argument), and a minor premise (the second part of the argument). A confirmation bias is a type of cognitive bias that involves favouring information that confirms previously existing beliefs or biases. e.g. imagine that a person holds a belief that left-handed people are more creative than right-handed people.

Whenever this person encounters a person that is both left-handed and creative, they place greater importance on this 'evidence' supporting their already existing belief. This individual might even seek 'proof' that further backs up this belief while discounting examples that do not support this idea.

Hindsight bias, also known as the knew-it-all-along effect or creeping determinism, is the inclination, after an event has occurred, to see the event as having been predictable, despite there having been little or no objective basis for predicting it.

70 Jensen uses regression argument to account for

1 genetic contribution in abilities
2 context specific abilities
3 group differences in intelligence
4 age related changes in intelligence

Ans. *(3)*

Exp. Jensen uses regression argument to account for group differences in intelligence.

Individual differences refer to distinctiveness and variations among people's characteristics and behavior patterns. Intelligence is the global capacity to understand the world, think rationally, and use available resources effectively when faced with challenges. Intelligence tests provide a global measure of a person's general cognitive competence.

Arthur Jensen proposed a hierarchical model of intelligence consisting of abilities operating at two levels, called Level I and Level II. Level I is the associative learning in which output is more or less similar to the input (e.g., rote learning and memory). Level II, called cognitive competence, involves higher-order skills as they transform the input to produce an effective output.

71 Read each of the following two statements Assertion (A) and Reason (R) and indicate your answer using the codes given below.

Assertion (A) Working memory involves both storage capacity and the capacity to process information held in the memory system.

Reason (R) The serial position effect provides evidence for the existence of two distinct memory systems, working memory and long-term memory.

Codes

1 Both (A) and (R) are true and (R)is the correct explanation of (A)
2 Both (A) and (R) are true, but (R) is not the correct explanation of (A)
3 (A) is true, but (R) is false
4 (A) is false, but (R) is true

***Ans.** (1)*

Exp. Both (A) and (R) are true and (R) is the correct explanation of (A).

Working memory involves both storage capacity and the capacity to process information held in the memory system. The serial position effect provides evidence for the existence of two distinct memory systems, working memory and long term memory.

The Atkinson and Shiffrin model of memory assumes that the processes of moving information from the sensory store to short-term and then long-term memory takes place in discrete stages. At any of these stages information can be lost through interference or decay. Another assumption of this model is that information processing has to start in the sensory register and be attended to, then move to STM and then to LTM with rehearsal.

The serial position effect (split into the primacy and recency effects) is that the first few and last few items in a word list, e.g. are the easiest to remember. A graph of this effect would be roughly parabolic (i.e. U-shaped). The primacy effect occurs because people have time to rehearse the first few items until the STM capacity is reached. The recency effect occurs because the last items are still in STM and have not decayed yet so they are easy to remember.

72 In the multiple components model of working memory, the Central Executive supervises and coordinates the functioning of which of the components?

I. Episodic information and procedural information.
II. Phonological loop and visuospatial sketch pad.
III. Procedural information and abstract semantic information.
IV. Semantic information and episodic information.

Codes

1 I and II
2 I and IV
3 II and III
4 II and IV

***Ans.** (3)*

Exp. Statement II and III are correct about the multiple components model of working memory.

Atkinson's and Shiffrin's (1968) multi-store model was extremely successful in terms of the amount of research it generated. According to the Multi-Store Model, STM holds limited amounts of information for short periods of time with relatively little processing. It is a unitary system. This means it is a single system (or store) without any subsystems whereas working memory is a multi-component system (auditory, and visual).

73 Bio feedback therapy is based on which of the following?

1 Classical conditioning
2 Observational learning
3 Operant conditioning
4 Cognitive learning

***Ans.** (3)*

Exp. Bio feedback theraphy is based on Operant conditioning.

Biofeedback is a treatment technique in which people are trained to improve their health by using signals from their own bodies. Physical therapists use biofeedback to help stroke victims regain movement in paralysed muscles. Psychologists use it to help tense and anxious clients learn to relax.

Specialists in many different fields use biofeedback to help their patients cope with pain. The word 'biofeedback' was coined in the late 1960s to describe laboratory procedures then being used to train experimental research subjects to alter brain activity, blood pressure, heart rate and other bodily functions that normally are not controlled voluntarily. At the time, many scientists looked forward to the day when biofeedback would give us a major degree of control over our bodies.

74 Read each of the following two statements Assertion (A) and Reason (R) and indicate your answer using the codes given below.

Assertion (A) People go out of their way to maintain self-esteem and to sustain the integrity of their self-concept.

Reason (R) 'Self-handicapping' is a deliberate attempt to sabotage one's performance so as to have a readymade excuse for failure.

Codes

1 Both (A) and (R) are true and (R) is the correct explanation of (A)
2 Both (A) and (R) are true, but (R) is not the correct explanation of (A)
3 (A) is true, but (R) is false
4 (A) is false, but (R) is true

***Ans.** (2)*

Exp. Both (A) and (R) are true, but (R) is not the correct explanation of (A)

People go out of their way to maintain self-esteem and to sustain the integrity of their self-concept. 'Self-handicapping' is a deliberate attempt to sabotage one's performance so as to have a readymade excuse for failure.

Self-handicapping is when someone makes excuses for a potential failure or anticipated poor performance. e.g. if a student says, "I'm not going to do well on the Psychology test because I'm sick," then if they get a bad grade they can blame it on illness instead of their lack of skill or preparation. Self-handicapping is a way of preserving self-esteem, but it is a self-defeating behaviour in that the person is avoiding effort and responsibility.

Self-handicapping refers to actions or statements we make that allow us to avoid effort or responsibility for potential failures that could damage our self-esteem. It is much more embarrassing and harmful to our self-esteem to put forth effort and fail than it is to self-handicap and have excuses as to why we failed. When we self-handicap, our decisions and actions provide us with a way to internalise success while externalising failure. In other words, self- handicapping lets us take the credit for our successes, while blaming other external factors for our failures.

75 According to Freud, different types of anxiety are

I. Neurotic anxiety
II. State anxiety
III. Moral anxiety
IV. Reality anxiety

Codes

1 I, II and III
2 I, II and IV
3 I, III and IV
4 II, III and IV

Ans. *(3)*

Exp. According to Freud, different types of anxiety are: neurotic anxiety, moral anxiety and reality anxiety.

Moral anxiety: A fear of violating our own moral principles.

Neurotic anxiety: The unconscious worry that we will lose control of the id's urges, resulting in punishment for inappropriate behavior.

Reality anxiety: Fear of real-world events. The cause of this anxiety is usually easily identified. For example, a person might fear a dog bite when they are near a menacing dog. The most common way of reducing this anxiety is to avoid the threatening object.

PRACTICE SETS (1-5)

UGC-NET PSYCHOLOGY

PRACTICE SET 1

PAPER II

1 Self-actualisation is a process of

I. separating your real needs from your leashed needs.
II. learning how to motivate yourself.
III. expecting yourself to perform well when your arousal is low.
IV. achieving and developing your true potential.

Choose the correct answer from the options given below

1 I and II
2 II and IV
3 Only IV
4 III and IV

2 The decrease in sensitivity of the visual system under light stimulation is known as

I. light adaptation
II. dark adaptation
II. painful adaptation
IV. visual adaptation

Choose the correct answer from the options given below:

1 I and II
2 Only II
3 III and IV
4 Only IV

3 Habituation and sensitisation both refer to a change in response as a result of learning. Which of the following statements best expresses the relationship between the types of changes in response denoted by the two terms?

I. The two terms refer to the same type of change in response
II. The two terms refer to similar kinds of changes in response
III. The two terms refer to different sorts of changes in response
IV. The two terms refer to opposite changes in response

Choose the correct answer from the options given below

1 Both I and II are true
2 Both III and IV are true
3 I is true, but III is false
4 IV is true

4 What is 'the tendency of a stimulus situation to be perceived in approximately the same way under varying circumstances' called?

I. Perceptual invariance
II. Perceptual vigilance
III. Perceptual constancy
IV. Perceptual defense

Choose the correct answer from the options given below

1 I and III
2 Only III
3 III and IV
4 Only IV

5 When a patient develops maladaptive habits and the key focus of psychotherapy is on changing specific observable response pattern identified as a problem, the therapy is known as

1 psychoanalytic therapy
2 behaviour therapy
3 humanistic therapy
4 family therapy

6 Which one set of the following is the correct sequence of events in creative problem-solving?

1 Illumination, Incubation, Verification, Preparation
2 Preparation, Verification, Illumination, Incubation
3 Preparation, Incubation, Illumination, Verification
4 Incubation, Illumination, Preparation, Verification

7 Match the following List I with List II.

List I (Factors Causing Forgetting)	List II (Psychologists)
A. Lack of adequate retrieval cues	I. Atkinson and Shiffrin
B. Learned material to getting the opportunity to persevere and consolidate	II. Craik and Lockhart
C. Single process of displacement of learned material	III. Muller and Pilzecker
D. Dual process of transfer for learned material from STM to LTM	IV. Tulving

Codes

	A	B	C	D		A	B	C	D
1	IV	III	II	I	2	III	IV	I	II
3	IV	III	I	II	4	III	IV	II	I

8 Trait approach to personality asserts that traits are

1 adjectives describing behaviour.
2 discrete and discontinuous categories of people.
3 generalised systems which ensure consistency in behaviour of individuals.
4 psychological categories of temperament associated with specific body physique.

9 Consider the following Statements.

I. Median is preferred method for highly systematic distributions.
II. The mode is most used measure of central tendency.

Which among the above is are correct?

1 Only I 2 Only II
3 Both I and II 4 None of these

10 Arrange the following steps in descending order of problem-solving.

I. Problem
II. Evaluation
III. Formulating of hypothesis
IV. Assembling the tools
V. Revising the solution

Codes

1 V, IV, II, III, I 2 V, II, IV, III, I
3 V, IV, II, I, III 4 IV, V, II, III, I

11 Given below are two statements, one is labelled as Assertion (A) and the other Reason (R). In the light of the above statements, choose the most appropriate answer from the options given below :

Assertion (A) Recognition of the presence of only one attributes or a few attributes eliminates the need of additional attributes redundancy.
Reason (R) Attribute redundancy facilitates the concept identification.

Codes

1 Both (A) and (R) are true and (R) is the correct explanation of (A).
2 Both (A) and (R) are true, but (R) is not the correct explanation of (A).
3 (A) is true, but (R) is false.
4 (A) is false, but (R) is true.

12 According to Cannon-Bard theory,

1 the thalamus plays a central role in producing emotions.
2 the cerebellum must give the go head for emotion.
3 activity in the occipital and parietal lobes happens simultaneously to produce emotion.
4 the sympathetic and para sympathetic nervous systems work in context.

13 Give the sequence of Identity Formation in Adolescents.

I. Consolidation II. Exploration
III. Rapprochement IV. Differentiation

Codes

1 II, IV, III, I 2 IV, II, I, III
3 IV, II, III, I 4 III, I, II, IV

14 Consider the following statements.

I. According to Adler, a Person's final goal is shaped by heredity and environment.
II. Adler insisted that personality is shaped by early childhood experiences.
III. According to Adler, ideas that have no real existence yet influence individuals as if they really existed are called hypothesis.
IV. The doctrine that motivation should be considered according to its final purpose or aim is called teleology.

Which of the statements given above is/are correct?

1 I and II 2 II, III and IV
3 Only IV 4 All of these

15 How do the theory of Planned Behaviour and the theory of Reasoned Action differ?

I. The theory of Planned Behaviour adds the perception of control to the theory of reasoned action
II. The theory of Reasoned Action adds the perception of control to the theory of planned behaviour

III. The theory of Reasoned Action considers self-efficacy, whereas the theory of planned behaviour does not

IV. The theory of Planned Behaviour considers health behaviours whereas the theory of Reasoned Action does not

Choose the most appropriate answer from the options given below:

1 Only I
2 II and IV
3 IV and I
4 III and II

16 Match the following List I with List II.

List I	List II
A. Social learning theory	I. Affects the willingness of others to perform the behaviours they learned
B. Vicarious reinforcement and Vicarious punishment	II. Emphasises the ability to learn by observing a model
C. Observational (or Vicarious) learning	III. The ability to become increasingly more effective in solving problems
D. Learning set	IV. Learning by observing other people's behaviour

Codes

	A	B	C	D
1	I	III	II	IV
2	IV	III	II	I
3	II	I	IV	III
4	I	II	III	IV

17 Which of the following is true of MC4 receptors?

I. MC4-receptor activation stimulates eating

II. A targeted mutation against the MC4-receptor leads to aphagia and death

III. MC4-receptors are highly concentrated in the stomach and duodenum

IV. AGRP stimulates eating by blocking MC4-receptors

Choose the most appropriate answer from the options given below:

1 I and II
2 III and IV
3 II and I
4 Only IV

18 Criticism of recovered memories has centered on the fact that

1 it is reasonable to suspect hidden abuse when a person is depressed has low self-esteem or sexual problem.
2 most victims of sexual abuse rarely remember having been molested.
3 a patient guided by an incompetent therapist might confuse dreams with memories.
4 personally important or traumatic memories can't be created through suggestion.

19 Given below are two statements:

Statement I Human behaviour is a result of interactions between the environment and the person.

Statement II People cannot anticipate events in deciding how to behave.

Select the correct answer using the codes given below:

1 Both I and II are true.
2 Both I and II are false.
3 I is true, but II is false
4 I is false, but II is true

20 A rat is placed on a grid in which an electric charge is introduced which gradually increases until in the midst of its random jumping etc, it happens to press a bar which terminates the shock. Few exposures to such a situation made the animal to learn bar pressing to discontinue the painful shock. This type of training is called

1 avoidance training
2 omission training
3 punishment training
4 escape training

21 Seligman found many similarities between his 'helpless' dogs and people suffering from

1 aggressive behaviour syndrome
2 mental illness
3 schizophrenia
4 depression

22 From research which is essential for short-term memory, which one is essential for LTM respectively?

1 Temporal lobes, parietal lobes
2 Hippocampus, hypothalamus
3 Prefrontal lobes, hippocampus
4 Frontal lobes, parietal lobes

23 Match the following List I with List II.

List I (Condition/Situation)	List II (Principal/Author)
A. A mother allows a child to go out to play only after he has finished his homework	I. Premack principle
B. Conditioning of autonomic behaviour	II. Guthrie
C. Whenever a response occurs that response is immediately and completely associated with all stimuli present at that instant.	III. Neal Miller
D. Partial reinforcement in conditioning	IV. Retardation in extinction

Codes

	A	B	C	D		A	B	C	D
1	III	I	IV	II	2	I	III	II	IV
3	I	III	IV	II	4	III	I	II	IV

24 Given below are two statements, one is labelled as Assertion (A) and the other as Reason (R). In the light of the above statements, choose the most appropriate answer from the options given below :

Assertion (A) Penfield does not suggest that the interpretive cortex is the seat of memory.

Reason (R) Surgical removal of temporal lobe abolish an individual's memory.

Codes

1 Both (A) and (R) are true and (R) is the correct explanation of A
2 Both (A) and (R) are true, but (R) is not the correct explanation of (A)
3 (A) is true, but (R) is false
4 (A) is false, but (R) is true

25 Which one of the following best support the heuristic approach of problem-solving?

1 Trying different responses until one works
2 Following a rule that guarantees a solution to a specific type of problem
3 Applying solutions that were previously successful with other problems similar in underlying structure
4 Employing rules of thumb suggested by our experience that are often used to solve problems

26 In terms of efficiency in scanning information, which one of the following selection strategies is consider to be best?

1 Simultaneous scanning 2 Successive scanning
4 Conservative focusing 4 Focus gambling

27 Professor Eliot told his students that if his door was open, it meant that he was available to them and would gladly answer any questions they might have. But if his door was pushed almost completely shut, it meant that he was busy and would prefer not to answer question at that time. Professor Eliot's door being open was appropriate for which of the following condition?

I. Discriminative stimulus ; asking question
II. Discriminative stimulus ; not asking question
III. Discriminative response ; asking question
IV. Discriminative response ; not asking questions

Choose the correct answer from the options given below:

1 Only I 2 II and III
3 Only III 4 Only IV

28 The most convincing evidence that depth perception is native to humans (and possibly other species) is its

1 importance in adaptive activity
2 early emergence as a perceptual skill
3 integration with motor skill
4 reliance on monocular and binocular cues

29 Delayed reaction tests are used to measure recall of

I. adults, adolescents and infants
II. adolescents and adults
III. adolescents and animals
IV. animals and infants

Choose the correct answer from the options given below:

1 Only I 2 II and III
3 II and IV 4 Only IV

30 Hearing impaired people are less likely to take advantage of new technology to help them hear, if they

1 have been hearing impaired since, birth.
2 were born able to hear for a time.
3 Still remember what it was like to hear.
4 see their impairment as a disability rather than a difference.

31 Reintegration means

I. recalling the whole event by a fraction of ones stimulating phenomenon.
II. recalling the past situation, if it had been associated with a specific colour.
III. recalling the past situation, if it had been verbally presented.
IV. recall and recognition taken together.

Choose the correct answer from the options given below:

1 Only I 2 II and III
3 III and IV 4 Only IV

32 Which of the following are true regarding Broca's area?

I. It is located in the frontal lobe.
II. Its function is speech production.
III. Understanding and processing aspects of language are associated with it.
IV. It helps people using sign language.

Choose the correct answer from the options given below :

1 I and II
2 III and IV
3 I, II and III
4 I, II, III and IV

33 **Which of the following characterises Cognitive Dissonance?**

I. Dissonance often occurs in situations involving forced compliance
II. Attempts to resolve dissonance are reflected in increased cortical activity
III. Dissonance cannot be reduced directly but only by adding cognitions that justify our behaviours
IV. Dissonance is stronger when we have little justification for our attitude–inconsistent behaviour

Choose the correct answer from the options given below :

1 I, II and III
2 I, II and IV
3 II, III and IV
4 I, II, III and IV

34 **A cheetah scrambling up a rocky slope in Montana is likely to be perceived as a mountain lion because**

1 perception is guided by expectations.
2 figure and ground have been confused.
3 contiguity is a powerful influence on perception.
4 the setting provided an ideal camouflage.

35 **Match the following List I with List II.**

List I (Substances)	List II (Functions)
A. DNA	I. Carries hereditary characters
B. Glial cell	II. Protein synthesis
C. Protein	III. Catalyst for bio-chemical reactions
D. RNA	IV. Structural support to neurons

Codes

	A	B	C	D
1	I	III	IV	II
2	II	IV	III	I
3	I	IV	III	II
4	II	III	IV	I

36 **Which one of the following is a nearest parametric alternative to Kruskal–Wallis test?**

1 Independent samples t-test
2 Paired samples t-test
3 One-way ANOVA for independent groups
4 One-way ANOVA for repeated measures

37 **Consider the following statements.**

I. Guilford classify mental abilities the same way chemical element classified in periodic table.
II. Mednick said that true creativity is the ability to think a remote idea.

Which of the statements given above is/are correct?

1 Both I and II are correct
2 Both I and II are not correct
3 I is correct, but II is not correct
4 I is not correct, but II is correct

38 **Given below are two statements, one is labelled as Assertion (A) and the other as Reason (R). In the light of the above statements, choose the most appropriate answer from the options given below :**

Assertion (A) People are sometimes more susceptible to persuasion when they are distracted by extraneous events.

Reason (R) Persuasion can be enhanced by messages that arouse strong emotions.

Codes

1 Both (A) and (R) are true and (R) is the correct explanation of A
2 Both (A) and (R) are true, but (R) is not the correct explanation of (A)
3 (A) is true, but (R) is false
4 (A) is false, but (R) is true

39 **Consider the following statements regarding the physiological bases emotion.**

I. High concentration of adrenaline is associated with emotional arousal.
II. Low concentration of non-adrenaline is related with emotional arousal.
III. Certain areas in the brain are directly anatomically related with desire and aversion.
IV. Emotions are largely under the control of left hemisphere of the brain.

Which of the statements given above are correct?

1 I, II and III
2 I, III and IV
3 II and IV
4 I and III

40 **Cattell proposed his theory of fluid and crystallised intelligences on the basis of which of the following?**

1 First order factors of abilities
2 Second order factors of abilities
3 Third order factors of abilities
4 Higher order factors of abilities

41 **Match the following List I with List II.**

List I (Mental Process)	List II (Thinking Pattern)
A. Controlled and constructive revival of past experiences as images at the ideational level	I. Free association
B. Controlled but unreal images directed towards a theme or pleasure of the moment	II. Hallucination
C. Uncontrolled and irrational perceptions without any wordly sensory stimulation	III. Fantasy
D. Random appearances of uncontrolled and unreal images	IV. Imagination

Codes

	A	B	C	D		A	B	C	D
1	II	I	IV	III	2	IV	III	II	I
3	II	III	IV	I	4	IV	I	II	III

42 Which one of the following provides correct description of the term 'flashbulb memories'?

1 Vivid memory of what happens to us all of a sudden
2 Memories of what we were doing at the time of an emotion-provoking event
3 Remembering a thing of past experiences by certain current revelation
4 memory occurring in the most tranquil moments of life at once

43 What is meant by fixed-ratio schedule of positive reinforcement?

1 Reinforcement is given after a variable number of responses
2 The response must occur a certain number of times before reinforcement is given
3 Reinforcement is given for every occurrence of a particular response
4 No reinforcement is given until a certain interval of time has elasped

44 Which of the following is not a problem with punishment?

1 The effect of punishment is often temporary
2 Severe punishment creates fear and anxiety
3 Mild punishment can be paired with reinforcement of the correct behaviour
4 Aggressive punishment can model aggressive behaviour for the child

45 A change in the axon membrane potential from -70 mV to -90 mV would be termed a(n)

1 repolarisation 2 threshold potential
3 action potential 4 hyperpolarisation

46 Stimulus motives differ from primary motives in that they

1 are unlearned and necessary for survival
2 appear to be innate, but are not necessary for survival
3 are acquired through various forms of conditioning and learning
4 include needs for security, status, approval and achievement

47 Match the following List I with List II.

List I	List II
A. A Skinner and Ferster	I. Drive reduction theory
B. Watson and Raynor	II. Frustration response theory
C. Hull and Spence	III. Schedules of reinforcement
D. Amsell and Rousell	IV. Classical conditioning

Codes

	A	B	C	D		A	B	C	D
1	IV	III	II	I	2	III	IV	II	I
3	IV	III	I	II	4	III	IV	I	II

48 Which one of the following procedures is likely to increase social interaction in severely withdrawn school children?

I. Showing them a film which depicts interaction between children being positively reinforced.
II. Showing them a film, which depicts withdrawn children being positively reinforced.
III. Showing them a film which depicts interaction between children.
IV. Showing them a film which depicts both withdrawn and interacting children being positively reinforced.

Codes

1 Only I 2 II and III
3 Only IV 4 II and IV

49 Rational concept is that which involves

1 a combination of several attributes
2 relationship among elements in a situation
3 at least one element from a number of elements
4 all the elements

50 Which one of the following pairs is correctly matched?

1 Linguistic relativity : Whorf
2 Language acquisition device : Wittgenstein
3 Semantic differential : Chomsky
4 Family resemblance structures : Osgood

51 Consider the following statements.

I. By early adulthood, most people have moved far beyond this level and judge moral right and wrong on the basic of less immediate outcomes.
II. The implications of behaviour for relationships between people or the extent to which the behaviour is consistent with general principles of right and wrong.
III. They consider stealing to be wrong because of the harm it does to others or the violation of their principles of ethics.

Which of the statements given above is/are correct?

1 Only I 2 I and II
3 II and III 4 None of these

52 Which one of the following intelligence tests is also used for diagnostic clinical purpose?

1 Stanford-Binet intelligence scales
2 Wechsler's intelligence scales
3 Thurstone's primary mental ability test
4 Differential aptitude tests of Bennett, Seashore and Wesman

53 Match the following List I with List II.

List I (Instrument)	List II (Psychologist)
A. Random Dot stereogram	I. Sir Charles Wheat Stone
B. Mirror stereoscope	II. Bela Julesz
C. Prism stereoscope	III. Tuler and Clarke
D. Auto stereogram	IV. Sir David Brewster

Codes

	A	B	C	D
1	I	IV	II	III
2	I	II	III	IV
3	IV	I	III	II
4	II	I	IV	III

54 Evoked potentials are larger, quicker and more complex in people with

1 low IQ
2 average IQ
3 high IQ
4 hearing impairment

55 Consider the following statements.

I. The semi interquartile range measures the spread of the middle 50% of scores.

II. Standard deviation is the measure of dispersion of results from the mean result.

Which among the above statements is/are correct?

1 Only I
2 Only II
3 Both I and II
4 None of these

56 Researchers who use narrative records seek to provide a verbal summary of observations and to develop a theory that explains behaviour in the narrative records. This approach to data analysis represents.

1 Qualitative data analysis with comprehensive recording of behaviour.
2 Qualitative data analysis with selective recording of behaviour.
3 Quantitative data analysis with comprehensive recording of behaviour.
4 Quantitative data analysis with selective recording to behaviour.

57 A problem with using memory trace decay theory to explain forgetting from long-term memory is that

1 older memories always get lost, while newer memories always remain.
2 older people cannot remember events in their childhood.
3 older people can still remember things from their early years.
4 there is no physical change in the brain when forming long-term memories.

58 Which of the following could account for a major personality change in middle adulthood?

1 Moving to a new city
2 Changing your looks
3 Making new friends
4 A personal tragedy

59 A cardinal assumption of stimulus generalisation theory of Pavlov is that

1 locus of generalisation gradients is in the testing rather then in the training phase.
2 generalisation gradients might be the result of variations in discriminative thresholds.
3 a process that develops automatically during conditioning along with the spread of associative strength.
4 stimulus generalisation occurs due to "failure of association".

60 Which one of the following statements regarding field experiments is not true?

1 Field experiments require investigators, who are specially skilled for intervening in social situation.
2 The greatest difficulty in field experiments lies in the randomisation and manipulatin of the independents variable.
3 Field experiments are concerned with casual relationship, but not with the direction of relationship.
4 Field experiments are carried out in natural setting.

61 Naturalistic observation is the major method of study used by

1 psychonalaysts, ehtologists, anthropologists and Gestalt psychologists
2 psychonalysts and Gestalt psychologists
3 ethologists, anthropologists and Gestalt psychologists
4 psychonalysts, anthropologists and Gestalt psychologists

62 Field independence refers to

1 a personality dimension, which reflects a persons preference for depending on external sources of information in perceptual situation.
2 reflection of a person's preference for depending on external sources of information in perceptual situation.
3 social orientation, which reflects a persons dependence on society.
4 cluster of information arising from the field surrounding the perceiver.

63 Which one of the following is the correct sequence of neural structures involved in saccadic eye movement generation from the lowest to the highest?

1 Brainstem-visual cortical colliculus areas-superior colliculus -frontal eye field area 8.
2 Frontal eye field are 8-superior colliculus-visual cortical area-Brainstem.
3 Brainstem-superior colliculus-frontal eye field area 8-visual cortical areas.
4 Superior colliculus-frontal eye field area 8-brainstem visual cortical area.

64 The main difference between field studies and laboratory studies is that

1 Field study is less expensive, while laboratory study is more expensive.
2 field study is less explorative, while laboratory study is more explorative.
3 field study has limited scope to control the variables, while laboratory study has adequate scope to rigorously control the variables.
4 Field study can be conducted without sufficient professional experience, while laboratory study cannot be conducted without sufficient professional experience.

65 Consider the following statements.

I. George sperling developed tachisto scope to study the properties of iconic memory.
II. Sperling discovered that the fleeting image of the iconic memory was stay for a long time.

Which of the statements given above is/are correct?

1 Only I
2 Only II
3 Both I and II
4 None of the above

66 In terms of Gestaltist, which of the following is incorrect?

1 Organised material has stable memory
2 The good figure is more susceptible to forgetting
3 A learning is never truly forgotten
4 None of the above

67 Given below are two statements : One is labelled as Assertion (A) and the other as Reason (R). In the light of the above statements, choose the most appropriate answer from the options given below :

Assertion (A) Wilcoxon sign test signed rank test is closely related to dependent sample t-test.

Reason (R) The dependent samplest t-tests analysis if the average difference of two repeated measures is zero.

Codes

1 Both (A) and (R) are true and (R) is the correct explanation of A
2 Both (A) and (R) are true, but (R) is not the correct explanation of (A)
3 (A) is true, but (R) is false
4 (A) is false, but (R) is true

68 Match the following.

List I	List II
A. Felt emotion is based on the interpretation of the reasons for bodily arousal.	I. Cannon-Bard
B. Felt emotions of a person are due to his/her perception of bodily reaction to stimuli.	II. Richard-Lazarus
C. Felt emotions result from appraisal about the environmental situation arising out of memories, dispositions, thought and states of body.	III. James-Lange
D. Felt emotions and bodily reactions emotions are independent of each other and triggered simultaneously by activity of lower brain area.	IV. Schachter-Singer

Codes

	A	B	C	D		A	B	C	D
1	I	II	III	IV	2	IV	III	II	I
3	I	III	II	IV	4	IV	II	III	I

69 Consider the following statements 'Defence mechanism is an irrational form of coping strategy' because defence mechanism

I. is used by psychopaths.
II. hinders learning of rational means of coping.
III. originates out of unconscious motivation.

Which of the statements given above are correct?

1 I and II
2 I and III
3 II and III
4 All of these

70 As per Socrates' Greek Philosophy, which of the following is NOT true about eudaimonia?

1 It means living well or flourishing
2 It is more than merely attaining pleasure
3 Being virtuous is almost identical to eudaimonia
4 Being virtuous does not guarantee eudaimonia

71 Match the following List I with List II.

List I (Theories of Intelligence)	List II (Theorists)
A. Sampling theory	I. RL Thorndike
B. Hierarchical theory	II. LL Thurstone
C. Group Factor theory	III. G Thomson
D. Multifactor theory	IV. C Burt and PE Vernon

Codes

	A	B	C	D
1	IV	III	II	I
2	III	IV	I	II
3	III	IV	II	I
4	IV	III	I	II

72 Which one of the following postulates supports adult. IQ constancy over the life span?

1 Normal distribution of IQ scores in different age groups.
2 With increasing chronological age, there is also an increase in 'functional units' of abilities.
3 'Deviation IQ' remains constant with age group differentials.
4 With increase in chronological age, there is a greater influence of environment than of heredity.

73 Which problem occurs, when respondents react to measurement by reporting what they think they should say, rather than what they actually believe?

1 Socially desirable responding
2 An incorrect causal inference based on correlational data
3 A large margin of error
4 A biased sample

74 Given below are two statements, one is labelled as Assertion (A) and the other is labelled as Reason (R).

Assertion (A) In fixed interval schedule of reinforcement behaviour is reinforced in a fixed time period.

Reason (R) When students get feedback intermittently their level of performance increases

In the light of the above statements, choose the most appropriate answer from the options given below :

1 Both (A) and (R) are correct and (R) is the correct explanation of (A)
2 Both (A) and (R) are correct, but (R) is not the correct explanation of (A)
3 (A) is correct, but (R) is not correct
4 (A) is not correct, but (R) is correct

75 Peter is sitting in a bar at a table in front of his date, Caroline, who is sitting with her back to a mirror. During the conversation, Peter is constantly forced to look directly into the mirror, thereby viewing himself. According to self-awareness theory, which would be a shape up response to reduce his discomfort in this situation?

1 Leave the bar
2 Change sitting position
3 Remove the mirror
4 Act more politely

76 Consider the following statements about Noam Chomsky.

I. He called himself a cartesian linguist.
II. He analysed syntax.
III. He wrote about transformational grammar.
IV. He developed an artificial language called Yerkish.

Which of the statements given above are correct?

1 I and II
2 I and IV
3 I, II and III
4 II, III and IV

77 Which of the following is true about motivation?

I. It activates and directs behaviour.
II. It is accompanied by physiological arousal of the autonomic nervous system produced in response to a stimulus.
III. It involves the cognitive interpretation of body arousal.
IV. It involves a positive or negative conscious experience.

Choose the correct answer from the options given below:

1 Only I
2 I and II
3 III and IV
4 Only II

78 Intrinsic motivation occurs when

I. obligations or approval are factors.
II. there is no obvious external reward for one's behaviour.
III. there are obvious external factors controlling behaviour.
IV. extrinsic motivation is also high.

Choose the correct answer from the options given below:

1 I and II
2 Only II
3 III and IV
4 IV and I

79 What is the level of the brain where sensory information is processed (decoded) as a threat or a non-threat and where cognition takes place ?

1 Neo-cortex
2 Hypothalamus
3 Thalamus
4 Septal area

80 Interference theory of forgetting proposes two processes through which interference produces a detrimental effect on memory. These processes are

I. unlearning and response similarity.
II. response chaining and response competition.
III. response similarity and response chaining.
IV. response competition and unlearning.

Choose the correct answer from the options given below

1 I, II, III
2 Only II and III
3 Only III
4 Only IV

81 The High School Personality Questionnaire, the Children's Personality Questionnaire, the Early School Personality, and the Pre-school. Personality Questionnaire are all downward extensions of the

1 Adult Personality Questionnaire
2 Edwards Personality Questionnaire
3 Eysenck Personality Questionnaire
4 Personality Factor Questionnaire

82 In the short-term memory experiment of Peterson and Peterson, recall is a

I. linearly increasing function of time interval
II. linearly decreasing function of time interval
III. positively acceleration function of time interval
IV. negatively acceleration function of time interval

Choose the correct answer from the options given below

1 I and II 2 III and I
3 IV and II 4 Only IV

83 Consider the following statements.

I. The anterior stream of the human auditory system performs analysis of loudness.
II. The posterior stream provides analyses of perception of form.

Which of the statements given above is/are correct?

1 Only I
2 Only II
3 Both I and II
4 None of the above

84 An effective method of stimulating creativity in classroom situations involves

1 emphasis on children's divergent thinking
2 supportive behaviour of the teacher
3 emphasis on convergent behaviour
4 giving sufficient freedom to the students

85 Which theory determines poverty as a psychological problem of separated classes in society?

1 Attribution theory
2 Depletable self–control theory
3 Distancing theory
4 Multiple factor theory of poverty

Directions (Q. Nos. 86-90) *Read the passage given below and answer the following questions.*

The Wilcoxon sign test signed rank test is closely related to dependent sample t-test. Because the dependent samples t-tests analyses if the average difference of two repeated measures is zero; it require metric (interval or ratio) and normally distribution data; the Wilcoxon sign test uses ranked or ordinal data. Thus, it is a common alternative to the dependent samples t-test when its assumption are not met. The Wilcoxon signed rank test relics on the W statistics. For large samples with n>10 paired observations the W-statistics is a non parametric test, thus, it does not need multivariate normality in the data.

Wilcoxon signed rank is used when comparing two related samples or repeated measurements on a single sample to assess whether their population mean ranks differ.

This procedure known as the Wilcoxon Signed Ranks Test, may be choosen over its respective classical counterpart -the one sample 't' test or the paired difference 't' test, when the researcher is able to obtain data measured at a higher level than an ordinal scale, but does not believe that the assumptions of the classical procedure are sufficiently met. When the assumptions of the 't' test are violated, the Wilcoxon producure (which makes fewer and less stringent assumptions than does the 't' test) is likely to be more powerful in detecting the existence of significant differences than its corresponding classical counterpart. Moreover, even under conditions appropriate to the classical 't'-test, the Wilcoxon Signed ranks test has proven to be almost as powerful.

86 Wilcoxon sign test signed rank test is closely related to

1 Independent sample t-test
2 Dependent sample t-test
3 Paired sample t-test
4 None of these

87 The Wilcoxon signed rank test relies on the W-statistics. For large sample it require

1 n>20 2 n<10
3 n>10 4 n<20

88 Which test does not require multivariate normality in the data?

1 Mann-Whitney test
2 Wilcoxon singed rank test
3 Friedman Rank Test
4 Kruskal Wallis test

89 Consider the following about Wilcoxon signed rank test

I. It is used when comparing two related samples.
II. It is also used when comparing two repeated measurements on a single sample.

Which among the above is /are correct?
1 Only I
2 Only II
3 Both I and II
4 None of the above

90 Consider the following
I. Wilcoxon signed ranks test has proven unsuccessful in classical t-test
II. When the assumptions of t-test is violated, Wilcoxon procedure becomes more powerful.

Which among the above is/are correct?
1 Only I
2 Only II
3 Both I and II
4 None of the above

91 According to the concept of 'learning to learn', which one of the following facilitates the maximum transfer of earning?
I. Learner's level of motivation
II. Learner's current perception of the task
III. Learner's mastery of skills and principles involved in the task
IV. Repetitive practice with the task on the part of the learner. It helps in Problem solving

Choose the correct answer from the options given below.
1 I and II
2 II and IV
3 Only III
4 Only IV

92 Which of the following is not correct regarding classical conditioning?
1 Generalisation is due to spread of excitation over cortex
2 Without reinforcement spontaneous recovery diminishes
3 Exinction is due to abolition of original response
4 None of the above

93 'Skaggs and Robinson hypothesis' implicates that
I. retention increases with similarity between original and interpolated activity
II. retention decreases with similarity between original and interpolated activity
III. retention is not affected
IV. retention fluctuates

Choose the correct answer from the options given below:
1 I and IV
2 Only II
3 III and IV
4 Only III

94 Frank lost a contact lens in the kitchen, he is searching for it by examining each linoleum tile in turn to see, if the lens is contained within the square.
Gemma similarly lost a lens in the kitchen; she is looking for it near the base of the fridge and around the stove, the two appliances she remembers using when she was last in the kitchen. Which statement best describes the problem-solving strategies of these two individuals?
1 Both Frank and Gemma are using algorithms.
2 Both Frank and Gemma are using heuristics.
3 Frank is using a heuristic, whereas Gemma is using an algorithm.
4 Frank is using an algorithm, whereas Gemma is using a heuristic.

95 Given below are two statements, one is labelled as Assertion (A) and the other as Reason (R). In the light of the above statements, choose the most appropriate answer from the options given below:
Assertion (A) The sign test is a non-paramentric test that is used to test whether two groups are equally sized or not.
Reason (R) The sign test is used when dependent samples are ordered in pairs, where the bivariate random variables are mutually independent.

Codes
1 Both (A) and (R) are true and (R) is the correct explanation of A
2 Both (A) and (R) are true, but (R) is not the correct explanation of (A)
3 (A) is true, but (R) is false
4 (A) is false, but (R) is true

Directions (Q. Nos. 96-100) *Read the passage given below and answer the following questions.*

A focus group is a form of qualitative research in which group of people are asked about their attitude towards a product, concept, advertisement, idea or packaging. Questions are asked in an interactive group setting where participants are free to talk with other group members. In the world of marketing, focus groups are an important tool for acquiring feedback regarding new products as well as various topics.

In the social science and urban planning, focus groups allow interviewers to study people in a more natural setting than a one to-one interview. In combination with participant observation, they can be used for gaining access to various cultural and social groups, selecting sites to study, sampling of such sites and raising unexpected issues for exploration.

Focus groups have a high approach validity since the idea is easy to understand the results are believable. Also, they are low in cost, one can get results relatively, quickly and they can increase the sample size of a report by talking with several folks at once.

Used alone or in combination with other methods, the conventional aims of focus groups is to capture content in the form of understanding, perspective, stories, discourses and experiences not otherwise meaningful expressed by number. The focus group can be used either as a primary means of data collection or as a supplement to multi-method approach depending on how it fits into the overall research plan.

96 **Focus group is a form of**

1 qualitative research
2 quantitative research
3 mixed method research
4 None of these

97 **Which among the following is correct about focus group method?**

1 Questions are asked in interactive group setting.
2 Participants are free to talk with other group members.
3 It allow interviewers to study people in natural setting.
4 All of the above.

98 **The significance of focus group method is that**

1 idea is easy to understand
2 low in cost
3 Both (1) and (2)
4 None of the above

99 **The conventional aim of focus group method is to**

1 Capture content in form of stories
2 Capture content in form of discourses
3 Capture content in form of understanding
4 All of the above

100 **Which method can be used as a primary means of data collection or as a supplement to a multi method approach?**

1 Cross-cultural method
2 Focus group
3 Experimental research
4 Ethnography

ANSWERS

1. (3)	**2.** (4)	**3.** (1)	**4.** (2)	**5.** (2)	**6.** (2)	**7.** (1)	**8.** (3)	**9.** (4)	**10.** (4)
11. (4)	**12.** (1)	**13.** (3)	**14.** (2)	**15.** (4)	**16.** (1)	**17.** (1)	**18.** (2)	**19.** (3)	**20.** (3)
21. (1)	**22.** (2)	**23.** (3)	**24.** (3)	**25.** (4)	**26.** (3)	**27.** (1)	**28.** (4)	**29.** (1)	**30.** (1)
31. (1)	**32.** (1)	**33.** (2)	**34.** (4)	**35.** (3)	**36.** (3)	**37.** (2)	**38.** (2)	**39.** (1)	**40.** (2)
41. (2)	**42.** (4)	**43.** (4)	**44.** (3)	**45.** (4)	**46.** (4)	**47.** (1)	**48.** (2)	**49.** (3)	**50.** (2)
51. (3)	**52.** (3)	**53.** (4)	**54.** (3)	**55.** (4)	**56.** (3)	**57.** (3)	**58.** (3)	**59.** (1)	**60.** (1)
61. (1)	**62.** (3)	**63.** (2)	**64.** (1)	**65.** (1)	**66.** (3)	**67.** (2)	**68.** (2)	**69.** (1)	**70.** (4)
71. (4)	**72.** (1)	**73.** (4)	**74.** (3)	**75.** (4)	**76.** (1)	**77.** (4)	**78.** (2)	**79.** (4)	**80.** (4)
81. (1)	**82.** (1)	**83.** (2)	**84.** (1)	**85.** (3)	**86.** (1)	**87.** (1)	**88.** (4)	**89.** (3)	**90.** (1)
91. (2)	**92.** (2)	**93.** (1)	**94.** (4)	**95.** (2)	**96.** (1)	**97.** (4)	**98.** (3)	**99.** (1)	**100.** (4)

UGC-NET PSYCHOLOGY

PRACTICE SET 2

PAPER II

1. The shape of the sigmoid curve of learning is indicated where

I. the number of wrong responses is greater in the beginning of training.
II. the number of correct responses is greater in the beginning of training.
III. the number of wrong responses is greater in the end of training.
IV. the number of wrong responses is greater in the middle of training.

Choose the correct answer from the options given below

1 I and II
2 III and IV
3 Only III
4 IV and I

2. Arrange the sequence of factors in the order of importance that alter the effectiveness of consequences in learning.

I. Satiation, Immediacy, Size, Contingency
II. Contingency, Size, Satiation, Immediacy
III. Size, Satiation, Contingency, Immediacy
IV. Immediacy, Contingency, Size, Satiation

Choose the correct answer from the options given below

1 Only I
2 II and IV
3 III and IV
4 Only IV

3. Match the following List I with List II.

List I		List II
A. Pavlov	I.	Trial and error learning
B. Skinner	II.	Insightful learning
C. Thorndike	III.	Classical conditioning
D. Kohler	IV.	Operant conditioning

Codes

	A	B	C	D
1	III	IV	II	I
2	IV	III	I	II
3	III	IV	I	II
4	IV	III	II	I

4. Assertion (A) In problem-solving Artificial Intelligences (AI), uses all algorithmic means, but can never adopt non-algorithmic strategy.

Reason (R) AI lacks the faculty of experience and comprehension.

Codes

1 Both (A) and (R) are true and (R) is the correct explanation of A
2 Both (A) and (R) are true, but (R) is not the correct explanation of (A)
3 (A) is true, but (R) is false
4 (A) is false, but (R) is true

5. In Schatcher and Singer's classic study, participants were physically aroused by

1 exposure to a happy man
2 exposure to an angry man
3 receiving epinephrine
4 watching an excited film

6. Using both positive and negative instances in developing a concept is advantageous because

1 we can lengthen the post feedback interval.
2 we increase the precision or defining limits of concept.
3 we can counterbalance positive and negative instance.
4 we can downplay the role of memory.

7. The optimal arousal theory states that individuals are motivated to

1 increase stimulation in order to increase arousal.
2 decrease stimulation in order to decrease arousal.
3 maintain neither too much nor too little stimulation and arousal.
4 maintain whatever is the current level of stimulation and arousal.

8. What can high-achieving adoptive parents do for the intellectual development of a low SES child?

1 They have little impact on change in the childs intelligence, because IQ is genetically determined.
2 They may be able to help increase a child's IQ score over time.
3 They can impede the child's intellectual development because their values and attitudes are likely to be different than those of the child.
4 They may negatively affect the child's achievement motivation in school.

9. Which one of the following is the most eclectic classification of the motive ?

1 Inniate and acquired motives
2 Physiological, psychological and mixed motives
3 Primary, secondary and personal motives
4 Physiological, personal and social motives

10. Consider the following statements.

I. Helmholtz was first to attempt to solve the problem of differentiating observer from object motion.
II. He postulated some type of unconscious computation or feedback from eye position or body position.
III. These changes can be subtracted from the retinal displacement.

Which of the above statements are correct?

1 I and II 2 II and III
3 I, II and III 4 None of these

11. Amar received his paper back from his English teacher, Ms Taylor. She informed him that adverbs follow the verbs they modify in sentence order. What level of language analysis does this represent?

1 Syntax 2 Semantics
3 Morphology 4 Pragmatics

12. Match the following List I with List II.

List I (Phenomenon)	List II (Explanation)
A. Premack's principle	I. Readiness of the organism to respond to a specific stimulus is a function of drive and habit strength.
B. Excitatory potential	II. The just noticeable increment to any stimulus bears a constant ratio to that stimulus.
C. Zeigarnick effect	III. More probable behaviours will reinforce less probable behaviours.
D. Weber's law	IV. Tendency to recall more uncompleted tasks than completed tasks.

Codes

	A	B	C	D		A	B	C	D
1	I	III	IV	II	2	III	I	IV	II
3	I	III	II	IV	4	III	I	II	IV

13. According to the interference theory of forgetting,

1 memory capacity is limited, so when new information is brought in, older memories must be removed.
2 new learning can inhibit the retrieval of stored memory and *vice-versa.*
3 forgetting is directly related to the complexity and meaningfulness of the incoming information.
4 cues present at the time of learning interfere with memory retrieval.

14. Give below are two statements.

Statement I Proactive interference occurs when old memories block out new memories.

Statement II Meaningless materials are more likely to be forgotten than meaningful materials.

1 Both I and II are true
2 Both I and II are false
3 I is false, but II is true
4 I is true, but II is false

15. Which one of the following statements about source trait is correct?

I. They appear to be influenced by genetic endowment
II. They describe superficial attributes
III. They refer only to temperamental characteristics
IV. They were discovered by Eysenck

Which among the above is are correct?

1 Only I 2 Only II 3 I and IV 4 Only IV

16. Any discriminative stimulus can serve as a reinforcer for the behaviour that precedes it, which of the following sequence is correct ?

1 S (String), R(String pull), S(Light), R(Bar press), S (Food)
2 S (Light), R (Bar press), S (Food), S (String), R (String pull)
3 S (Food), S (String), R (String pull), S (Light), R (Bar press)
4 R (Bar press), S (Food), S (String), R (String pull), S (Light)

17. Which of the following statements are correct regarding extinction and spontaneous recovery?

I. If reinforcement is delayed during acquisition trials, subsequent resistance to extinction will tend to increase.
II. As the effort required to produce a response increases, resistance to extinction decreases.

III. Resistance to extinction decreases as the amount of reinforcement used during acquisition trials increases.

IV. The amount of spontaneous recovery depends upon the time interval; the shorter the interval the greater the spontaneous recovery.

Select the correct answer using the codes given below:

1 I, II and IV 2 I, III and IV
3 II and III 4 I, II and III

18. Which of the following pairs are correctly matched?

I. The process of allowing frustrated subjects to express their feelings by talking over. – Catharsis

II. Aslam always has a lot of medical complaints. –Repressors

III. Kamala's son is retarded, she insists that his mischief is a sign of his intelligence. – Denial of Reality

IV. Meena feels frustrated by housework, but tells everyone including herself how happy she is with housework. – Projection

Codes

1 I and II 2 I and III
3 II and IV 4 I and IV

19. Given below are two statements, one is labelled as Assertion (A) and the other is labelled as Reason (R).

Assertion (A) In fixed interval schedule of reinforcement behaviour is reinforced in a fixed time period.

Reason (R) When students get feedback intermittently their level of performance increases.

In the light of the above statements, choose the most appropriate answer from the options given below :

1 Both (A) and (R) are correct and (R) is the correct explanation of (A)
2 Both (A) and (R) are correct but (R) is not the correct explanation of (A)
3 (A) is correct but (R) is not correct
4 (A) is not correct but (R) is correct

20. Which one of the following pairs is correctly matched?

1 Perceptual vigilance : Sensitivity to all stimuli
2 Perceptual illusion : Perceiving all information as positive
3 Perceptual set : Seeking attitude supportive information
4 Perceptual defence : Misperceiving or avoiding attitude discrepant information

21. According to a majority of developmental psychologists, basic elements in development would comprise

1 equilibration, maturation and experience
2 maturation, experience and social transmission
3 experience, social transmission and equilibration
4 reciprocation, maturation and utilisation

22. Four temperaments is a proto-psychological interpretation of the ancient medical concept of humorism, arrange them in sequential order.

1 Phlegmatic, Sanguine, Melancholic, Choleric
2 Sanguine, Choleric, Melancholic, Phlegmatic
3 Melancholic, Phlegmatic, Sanguine, Choleric
4 Sanguine, Melancholic, Choleric, Phlegmatic

23. Which one of the following statements indicates true relationship between intelligence and creativity ?

1 Intelligence and creativity have high correlation
2 Intelligence and creativity have low correlation
3 Intelligence and creativity are moderately correlated
4 Intelligence and creativity have higher correlation at lower levels than at higher levels of intelligence

24. Arrange the following stages of brain storming in correct sequence.

I. Idea generation II. Scrutiny
III. Evaluation

Codes

1 I, II, III 2 III, II, I
3 III, I, II 4 I, III, II

25. Which one of the following statements is correct?

I. Retroactive and proactive interference are less than that in recall.

II. Retroactive and proactive interference are more than that in recall.

III. Retroactive interference is less, but proactive interference is more than that in recall.

IV. Retroactive interference is more, but proactive interference is less than that in recall.

Choose the most appropriate answer from the options given below:

1 I and II 2 II and IV
3 Only III 4 IV and I

26. Rogers therapy is the relational climate created by the therapist's attitude to their client, the process that is followed based on the success of the conditions are

1 congruence : unconditional positive regard : empathy
2 unconditional positive regard : empathy : congruence
3 empathy : unconditional positive regard : congruence
4 All of the above

27. Early personality inventories were designed primarily to

1 assist in the prediction of academic and vocational success.
2 identify and analyse psychopathological disorders.
3 study the structure and development of normal personality.
4 test certain proposition of psychoanalytic thinking.

28. The Thematic Apperception Test involves

1 following the individual pictures and analysing the responses to study personality in relation to environment.
2 asking a person to complete a complex task and watching the level of arousal induced.
3 observing how a subject interprets his physiological change in an emotional situation.
4 showing a subject a stress inducing movie and playing denial tapes, while it is being watched.

29. Assertion (A) In creative thinking, certain imageless elements may appear in the process.

Reason (R) Linguistic relativity suggests that language peculiarities determine content of thought.

Codes

1 Both (A) and (R) are true and (R) is the correct explanation of A
2 Both (A) and (R) are true, but (R) is not the correct explanation of (A)
3 (A) is true, but (R) is false
4 (A) is false, but (R) is true

30. Illusions differ from hallucination in that

1 illusions are based on perceptions that have no external reality.
2 hallucinations are simply misjudgements of sensory information.
3 illusions are based on perceptual learning.
4 hallucinations are the result of past experience.

31. Match the following List I with List II.

List I (Developmental Stages)	List II (Events)
A. Anal	I. Thumb sucking
B. Oral	II. Castration anxiety
C. Latency	III. Adult sexual concern
D. Phallic	IV. Toilet training
	V. Overture with regard to sex

Codes

	A	B	C	D
1	IV	V	III	II
2	II	I	V	IV
3	IV	I	V	II
4	II	V	III	IV

32. Match the following List I with List II.

List I	List II
A. Grouping people into discrete behavioural categories	I. Social learning theory
B. Relative difference between one person and another on a continuous dimension	II. Psychoanalysis
C. Emphasis on the importance of environmental determinants of behaviour	III. Trait theories
D. Analysis of the unconscious motives that direct behaviour	IV. Type theories

Codes

	A	B	C	D
1	IV	III	I	II
2	III	IV	II	I
3	IV	III	II	I
4	III	IV	I	II

33. Consider the following statements.

Statement I There are two principles of organisation, temporal and thematic.

Statement II People organise their memory in terms of the associated emotions.

Which of the statements given above is/are correct?

1 I is true, but II is false
2 Both I and II are true
3 Both I and II are false
4 II is true, but I is false

34. Which one set of the following is the correct sequence of vicarious learning process meant for behaviour modelling practice?

1 Motivation, Motoric Production, Retention, Attention
2 Attention, Motoric Production, Retention, Motivation
3 Attention, Retention, Motoric Production, Motivation
4 Retention, Attention, Motivation, Motoric Production

35. Although, the markings in the ceiling titles are of all different shapes and sizes, you notice that larger, spots seem to stand out against a background made up of smaller, lighter ones. Which principle of perceptual grouping explains this distinction?

1 The principle of closure
2 The law of common fate
3 The law of Pragananz
4 The law of similarity

36. In an experiment, two groups of 10 years old children, one from rich families and the other from poor families, were required to estimate the physical sizes of different coins by manipulating a knob, which produced a circular light on a glass-screen. The result was that poor children over-estimated the size of every coin to a greater degree than the rich children did. Which one of the following determinants, explains the above result?

1 Personality
2 Socio-economic status
3 Values
4 Emotional states

37. Consider the following statements.

I. According to Adler, human personality is shaped by people's interpretations of their experiences.
II. The ultimate goal of Adlerian therapy is to increase social interest.
III. Research suggests that early recollections may change during the course of psychology.
IV. A major weakness of Adler's theory is that it is not easily falsifiable.

Which of the statements given above are correct?

1 I and II
2 II and III
3 II, III and IV
4 All of these

Directions (Q. Nos 38-39) *In the questions given below are two statements as Assertion (A) and Reason (R). In the context of two statements, which one of the following is correct?*

Codes

1 Both (A) and (R) are true and (R) is the correct explanation of A
2 Both (A) and (R) are true, but (R) is not the correct explanation of (A)
3 (A) is true, but (R) is false
4 (A) is false, but (R) is true

38. Assertion (A) Effectiveness of reinforcement depends on internal, cognitive factors.

Reason (R) People have a subjective expectation of the outcome of behaving in a certain way.

39. Assertion (A) Each person differs with respect to reinforcement value and finds reinforcement of different values in different situations.

Reason (R) Reinforcement value comes from past experience where past reinforcement from situations is associated with the present situations or behavioural options.

40. Definition of the nature of human personality is bases on

I. Human behaviour is complex.
II. Behaviour is not always what is appears to be
III. We are not always in control of the factors determining our behaviour.

Which of the assumptions given above is/are correct?

1 I, II and III
2 I and II
3 I and III
4 II and IV

41. Match the following List I with List II.

List I	List II
A. Plutchik	I. Felt emotions and bodily changes are independent.
B. Lazarus	II. Certain primary emotions derived from evolutionary process can be arranged in orderly way to bring out realities.
C. Cannon-Bard	III. Emotion we felt results from appraisals of information coming from environment situation and from within the body.
D. Schachter-Singer	IV. Emotion we feel is due to our interpretation of aroused bodily state.

Codes

	A	B	C	D
1	I	IV	III	II
2	II	III	I	IV
3	IV	I	II	III
4	III	IV	I	II

42. Graham Wallach articulated the traditional view of the creative process as four ordered stages. Which one of the following is the correct order of these states?

1 Incubation, Illumination, Preparation, Verification
2 Illumination, Preparation, Verification, Incubation
3 Preparation, Incubation, Illumination, Verification
4 Preparation, Incubation, Verification, Illumination

43. In applied behaviour analysis,

I. skills are broken down into their smallest steps and then reinforced.
II. punishment by application is often used to control behaviour.
III. researchers develop new theories of learning rather than actually solving problems.
IV. the basic form of learning used is classical conditioning.

Choose the correct answer from the options given below

1 Only I
2 III and II
3 I and II
4 IV and I

44. Learning is

I. any temporary change in behaviour.
II. a change in behaviour due to maturation.
III. any permanent change in behaviour brought about by experience.
IV. any permanent change in behaviour due to maturation.

Choose the correct answer from the options given below:

1 I and II
2 Only III
3 II and IV
4 IV and I

45. According to Tesser's (1988) self-evaluation maintenance model, what is the most likely outcome of a self-other comparison in which there is a better performance by and close relationship with the other as well as a low relevance of performance to self-definition?

1 Improvement of own performance
2 Reduced closeness of relationship
3 Reduced importance of performance
4 Basking in reflected glory

46. Consider the following statements.

I. Atkinson was the first to recognise a distinction between short-term and long-term memory.

II. William James developed a model that capture the distinction between LTM and STM.

Which of the statements given above is/are correct?

1 Only I
2 Only II
3 Both I and II
4 None of these

47. In the experiments on size constancy, different conditions are used, which one of the following is the correct sequence of the following conditions in the decreasing order of the constancy values?

1 Monocular with tunnel-Monocular with artificial pupil- Monocular-Binocular
2 Binocular-Monocular-Monucular with artificial pupil- Monocular with tunnel
3 Monocular with tunnel -Binocular-Monocular with artificial pupil-Monocular
4 Binocular-Monocular with tunnel -Monocular with artificial pupil-Monocular

48. Projective measures, particularly inkblot tests, index which of the following?

1 Novelty context of creativity
2 Meaning context of creativity
3 Domain specific creativity
4 General creative potential

49. Consider the following statements.

I. Pavlov performed research with tones that differed in frequency. If one tone served as the CS paired with a US, whereas the other tone was presented without the US, the dog learned to make CRs. only to the tone paired with the US. This is an example of generalisation.

II. The 'misbehaviour' of animals shows that some behaviours are difficult to condition because they interfere with natural appetitive behaviours.

Which of the statements given above is/are correct?

1 Only I
2 Only II
3 Both I and II
4 Neither I nor II

50. On which of the following personality inventories has research in sport psychology revealed the so-called 'iceberg profile?'

1 Essence personality inventory
2 Hogan personality inventory
3 NEO five-factor inventory
4 Profile of mood states

51. Match the following List I with List II.

List I	List II
A. SM Mohsin	I. Draw a man test
B. RR Swami	II. Performance test of intelligence
C. Pramila Pathak	III. Adaption of Wechsler adult performance intelligence scale
D. CM Bhatia	IV. Bihar test of intelligence

Codes

	A	B	C	D
1	II	I	IV	III
2	I	II	III	IV
3	III	I	II	IV
4	IV	III	I	II

52. Which of the following are the types of descriptive research?

I. Field study
II. Case study
III. Ex-post facto
IV. Survey research
V. Content analysis
VI. Ethnographic study

Select the correct answer using the codes given below:

1 I, II, III and IV
2 II, III, IV and V
3 II, III, V and VI
4 All of these

53. Which one of the following behaviours is typically reinforced on a variable ratio schedule?

1 Inserting coins into a gambling machine
2 Checking the mail box to see if mail has arrived
3 Studying for surprise or unexpected quizzes
4 Inserting coins into a vending machine to get a candy bar

54. Which of the following pairs are correctly matched?

A. Aliasing	:	A type signal distortion occurs in too low rate for signal frequency.
B. Stroboscopic apparent movement	:	Apparent movement seen in patterns briefly flashed in different spatial position.
C. Placid	:	A pattern of criss-crossing stripes, created by adding together two sine-wave grating at different orientation.

Codes

1 I and II
2 II and III
3 I and III
4 All of these

55. Which one of the following statements is a precise scientific explanation of the cause of forgetting?

1 Increased retention interval obliterates neurological traces of learning.
2 Active repression results in forgetting.
3 An association once learned is permanently stored and forgetting is due to declining accessibility and retrieval from the storehouse.
4 Lapse of time leads to autonomous decay.

56. In the experiments on memory, nonsense syllables are used

I. because it is difficult to learn meaningless things
II. in order to provide stimuli of low associative value
III. in order to provide novel stimuli to the subjects
IV. because Ebbinghaus used them

Choose the correct answer from the options given below.

1 Only I and II
2 II and IV
3 Only III
4 IV and I

57. A procedure, in which several trials containing the same list of items are successively given and subjects are asked to recall items in any order they wish to on each trial, is called

I. repetitive free recall method
II. single trial free recall method
III. multi-trial free recall method
IV. continuous free recall method

Choose the correct answer from the options given below

1 I is correct
2 IV and II is correct
3 I and III is correct
4 III is correct

58. The term personality refers to

I. the hereditary aspects of one's emotional nature
II. unique and enduring behaviour patterns
III. favourable and unfavourable personal characteristics
IV. charisma, character or temperament

Choose the correct answer from the options given below

1 Only I
2 III and IV
3 Only II
4 Only III

Directions (Q. Nos. 59-63) *Read the passage given below and answer the following questions.*

Gestalt therapy by Fritz Perls, is heavily based on existentialist principles and significantly Zen Buddhism. Gestalt therapy also works on whole person and encourage right mindfulness, similarly as Buddhism. Similarly Client Centered therapy by Carl Rogers works on the principle that therapist does not direct the process of therapy, but patient has the resources to deal with their own 'cure' and 'self growth', provided the environment is safe for them. Like the Buddha this non-authoratative approach suggests that the 'patient can be a light to themselves.'

Thus, we can say that Buddha was a unique Psychotherapist and his teachings, writing and wisdom helped millions of people throughout the centuries. Today even the Western world has reals the psychological essence of Buddhism. In short, the Psychotherapeutic models described by Buddhism or great value and have applications at all times.

59. Gestalt therapy by Fritz Perls is heavily based on

1 existentialist principles
2 hypothetical construct
3 biological behaviours
4 None of the above

60. Client Centered Therapy was proposed by

1 Fritz Perls
2 Carl Rogers
3 Buddha
4 Aurobindo

61. Which among the following is correct about Client Centered Therapy?

1 Patients can be a light to themselves
2 self growth
3 Both 1 and 2
4 None of the above

62. Who is considered as an unique Psychotherapist?

1 Carl Roger
2 Fritz Perls
3 Buddha
4 Krishna

63. Consider the following statements.

1. Client Centered therapy is a non-authoritative approach.
2. Gestalt therapy works on whole person and encourage right mindfulness.

Which among the above is/are correct?

1 Only 1
2 Only 2
3 Both 1 and 2
4 None of these

64. Systematic decay of the memory traces

1 do not seem to increase with the mere passing of time.
2 account for most of what we forget.
3 increase greatly with the passage of time.
4 are attributable to repression in most instances.

65. During the absorptive phase of metabolism,

1 blood glucose levels are lowered
2 it has been some time since, the person last ate food
3 the pancreas secretes glucagon rather than insulin
4 blood glucose levels rise, which triggers the release of insulin by the pancreas

66. Which of the following individuals is engaged in problem-solving, as your text defines the term?

1 Celina who is determining, which of several of used cars is least likely to present a maintenance headache.
2 Das, who is concluding that a particular model of used car is a poor investment over the longer term, based on her ideas regarding the re-sale values of different types of cars.

3 Esther, who is writing down a shopping list because he knows the number of items on the list is probably greater than the number of items he could simply remember.
4 Farooq, who is planning to pick-up some extra shifts so, he can buy a used car he has his eye on.

67. A researcher, interested in studying the psychological functioning of the group, becomes a member of the group and lives with the group members for a stipulated time period. This is an example of which one of the following?

1 Naturalistic observation
2 Participant observation
3 Scientific observation
4 Controlled observation

68. Assertion (A) Incubation period allows people to recover from the fatigue associated with problem-solving.

Reason (R) During incubation period, people forget old, unsuccessful solution to a problem.

Codes

1 Both (A) and (R) are true and (R) is the correct explanation of A
2 Both (A) and (R) are true, but (R) is not the correct explanation of (A)
3 (A) is true, but (R) is false
4 (A) is false, but (R) is true

69. Which of the following statements about the sex drive is correct ?

1 The sex drive in females is closely tied to the menstrual cycle.
2 The sex drive in humans is completely liberated from the influence of hormones.
3 The sex drive in humans can be aroused at virtually any time by almost anything.
4 Recent sexual activity prevents sexual desire from occurring again after a certain amount of time.

70. The function of a _______ in a giant squid physiology experiment is to

I. microelectrode; inject potassium ions into the axon
II. voltmeter; stimulate the interior of the axon
III. microelectrode; compare the electric charge of the interior with that of the exterior
IV. voltmeter; compare the electric charge of the interior with that of the exterior

Choose the correct answer from the options given below

1 Only I　　2 III and I
3 II and IV　　4 Only IV

71. A person suffers damage to the occipital lobe in the right hemisphere of brain during an accident. What will be the effect of this damage on the person?

I. He will suffer loss of vision in the left visual field
II. He will lose ability to understand spoken words
III. He will lose ability to write
IV. He will lose ability to read

Choose the correct answer from the options given below

1 Only I　　2 III and I
3 II and IV　　4 IV and III

72. Which is true regarding the influence of cultural values on eating behaviours?

I. They are the primary cause of innate taste aversion
II. They greatly affect the incentive value of various food
III. They determine a person's set point for various food
IV. They have a homeostatic influence on amount of food consumed

Choose the correct answer from the options given below

1 I and IV　　2 Only III
3 III and II　　4 IV and III

73. Which of the following is a true statement about biological regulation of thirst in the brain?

1 The brain has a 'drink system,' but does not have a 'stop drinking system'.
2 The brain has a 'stop drinking system,' but does not have a 'drink system'.
3 The brain has both a 'drink system' and a 'stop drinking system,' and these control centers use the same neurotransmitters as the control centers for hunger.
4 The brain has both a 'drink system' and a 'stop drinking system,' but these control centers use different neurotransmitters as the control centers for hunger.

74. Match the following List I with List II.

List I	List II
A. Identification	I. Children incorporate their parents' values into their developing superegos
B. Gender Identity	II. One's sense of being male or female
C. Fixation Pleasure	III. Seeking energies at an earlier psychosexual stage

Codes

	A	B	C		A	B	C
1	III	I	I	2	III	II	I
3	I	II	III	4	II	I	III

75. Match the following List I with List II.

List I (Low Scores Characteristic)	List II (Factor Ocean)
A. Conventional, Sown-to-Earth and uncreative	I. Conscientiousness
B. Unreliable, lazy and careless negligent and spontaneous	II. Openness
C. Reserved and comfortable being alone	III. Agreeableness
D. Rude, uncooperative and irritable aggressive and competitive	IV. Extraversion

Codes

	A	B	C	D		A	B	C	D
1	II	III	IV	I	2	II	I	IV	III
3	I	IV	II	III	4	I	II	IV	III

76. Match the following List I with List II.

List I (Socio-cultural Processes)	List II (Labels)
A. Similarities in behaviour between a child and model, child's motive to be like the model and the process of taking on the attributes of the model.	I. Cultural sanctions
B. In an experiment, a man is found to be willing to deliver severe shocks to a male opponent, but not to female opponent.	II. Effect of moderator variables
C. After a certain age, males are not rewarded for displaying, dependency, but similar dependent behaviour may be acceptable in females.	III. Vicarious reinforcement
D. The child in an impoverished neighbourhood sees that tough looking gangsters have status, power and other nice things and appreciates them.	IV. Identification

Codes

	A	B	C	D		A	B	C	D
1	IV	II	III	I	2	IV	II	I	III
3	II	IV	I	III	4	II	IV	III	I

77. Which one of the following statements regarding the sensation seeking motives is correct ?

1 The optimum level of arousal for peak performance will depend upon the nature of the task.
2 The need to explore the environment and the need for sensory stimulation both include sensation seeking motives.
3 Relationship between physiological process such as hormone production and psycho-social processes such as early socialisation explain sensation seeking behaviour.
4 The sensation seeking behaviour recorded in the first person's account reflects both a general state of negativity and the specific feeling of intense anger.

78. Which statement about colour blindness is true?

1 There are more men who are colour blind than woman.
2 All colour-blind people see only in black and white.
3 Some colour blind people see only in blue.
4 Some colour-blind people see only in blue and red.

79. Rushhy (1979) used a four paradigm classification of Computer Assisted Learning (CAL). Which one is not the paradigm as suggested by Rushhy?

I. The instructional paradigm
II. The revelatory paradigm
III. The conjectural paradigm
IV. The anticipatory paradigm

Choose the most appropriate answer from the options given below

1 I and IV
2 Only IV
3 Only II
4 III and II

80. Recall for specific traits or behaviours is better when

I. subjects attempt to memorise lists of traits as behaviours.
II. subjects attempt to form a unified impression.
III. subjects do not attempt to organise or think about the traits.
IV. subjects avoid confusion by not attempting to think about possible inconsistencies in their impression of the person given in the trait list.

Choose the most appropriate answer from the options given below

1 II and III
2 I and IV
3 Only II
4 III and IV

81. Maslow argued that self-actualisation is achieved only after the satisfaction of several other important, but lesser needs, arrange the lesser needs in order.

I. Physiological needs, Safety Needs, Attachment needs, Esteem needs
II. Esteem needs, Physiological needs, Safety needs, Attachment needs
III. Attachment needs, Esteem needs, Physiological needs, Safety needs
IV. None of the above

Choose the most appropriate answer from the options given below:

1 Only I
2 Only III
3 Only II
4 Only IV

82. Intelligence has been defined as "The aggregate or global capacity of the individual to act purposefully, to think rationally and to deal effectively with his environment", by

1 Alfred Binet
2 D Wechsler
3 T Simon
4 LL Thurstone

83. The pitch of a sound stimulus is related to the physical characteristic

1 vibration amplitude
2 the distance between the sound source and the detector
3 sound wave complexity
4 frequency of vibration

84. In experiments with animals when the amount of reinforcement increases, the performance in relation to conditioning is found to have

1 positively accelerated function
2 negatively accelerated function
3 inverted U type function
4 constant function

85. Katherine is trying to hold the names of the students, she just met in her psychology class in short-term memory. According to studies, these short-term memories will be stored in which part of the brain?

1 Cerebellum
2 Hippocampus
3 Amygdala
4 Prefrontal lobes

86. Which one of the following reactions cannot be considered as an expression of emotions ?

1 Electrical conductance of the skin as measured through galvanic skin response
2 Heart rate as measured through electrocardiogram
3 Knee jerk response
4 Pupil dilation

87. Researchers had participants working in a room either by themselves or with two strangers. When smoke was pumped into the room through a vent, the solitary participant

1 noticed the smoke quicker than those in groups
2 was less likely to act
3 thought the smoke was a fire
4 finished the task quickly

88. Which of the following is not one of the reasons for doubting the diagnosis of 'Rebika' as a true multiple personality?

1 Rebika had an abusive early childhood
2 Her doctors made suggestions to her about her personalities
3 Her doctor used hypnosis and drugs, which may have created a very suggestive state in 'Rebika'
4 The author of the book told a psychiatrist that the book would only sell 'if 'Rebika' was labelled a multiple personality.

89. In SPSS, where will you find an alternative to the independent sample 't'-test?

1 Non-parametric test-legacy dialogs- 'U'-test
2 Compare means - 'U'-test
3 Non-parametric tests-legacy dialogs-independent samples
4 Compare means- independent samples

90. The Muller-Lyer illusion exists in cultures, in which there are

1 more men than women
2 more women than men
3 lots of free
4 buildings with lots of corners

91. The receptor on our taste buds work most like

1 receptor in the ears
2 receptor in the eyes
3 receptor sites on olfactory neurons
4 receptor in the skin

92. Seeing subjective contours in a Kaniza figure

1 is a uniquely human trait
2 has no physiological basis
3 indicates that brain damage has occurred
4 suggests that the brain is fabricating a more likely interpretation of the figure

93. A Pigeon is placed in a cage with two pellets containing grains. One to the pellets is round in shape and the other is square. If the pigeon pecks the round pellet it is given a mild shock, but it can eat the grains from the square pellet. Soon if learns to peck only the square pellet.

The above experiment is an example of

1 classical conditioning
2 escape behaviour
3 stimulus discrimination
4 stimulus generalisation

94. Which one of the following theoretical foundations considers intelligence to be a 'genetic potentiality' ?

1 Intelligence B of Hebb
2 Crystallised Intelligence of Cattell
3 Fluid Intelligence of Cattell
4 'g' factor of Spearman

95. **Sternberg's research on short-term memory has a focus on the processes involving**

1 classical or instrumental
2 parallel or serial
3 primary or secondary
4 discriminative or non-discriminative

Directions (Q. Nos. 96-100) *Read the passage given below and answer the following questions.*

Cognitive Revolution in psychology is mostly a response to behaviourism which emphasised on the objectivity and focussed on the overt behaviour for studying human psyche. The focus on the principles of behaviourism had pulled away the attention of psychologists from the mind for a prolonged period of time. Humanistic psychologists emphasised on studying human being as a whole and as a conscious and self aware being.

In 1950s, new disciplinary fields like linguistics, neuroscience and computer science again revived interest in mind as focus of scientific enquiry. This particular perspective was known as the Cognitive Revolution. There were numerous publications by psychologists which further triggered the Cognitive Revolution, Geore Miller's 1956 article 'The Magical Number Seven, Plus or Minus Two' linguist Noam Chornski's rejection of the behaviourist approach in his 1959 review of BF Skinner's Verbal Behaviour (1957)', foundational works in the field of artificial intelligence by John McCarthy, Marvin Minsky, Allen Newell and Herbert Simon in the 1958 article 'Elements of a Theory of Human Problem Solving' and Ulric Neisser's 1967 book 'Cognitive psychology', which served as a core text in cognitive psychology courses were the landmark contribution. Noam Chomski, argued in favour of cognitive studies saying that psychology focusses on behaviour is short sighted and field had to incorporate mental functioning if it has to offer any meaningful contribution in understanding human behaviour.

96. **Cognitive Revolution in psychology is a response to**

1 Functionalism
2 Structuralism
2 Behaviourism
4 None of these

97. **Humanistic psychologists emphasised on studying human being as**

1 a whole
2 as a conscious
3 self aware
4 All of these

98. **The article 'The Magical Number Seven, Plus or Minus Two' was written by**

1 Noam Chomski
2 George Miller
3 Ulric Neisser
4 None of the above

99. **The book 'Cognitive Psychology' was written by**

1 Noam Chomski
2 Ulric Neisser
3 George Miller
4 None of these

100. **'Verbal Behaviour'** (1957) **was written by**

1 John McCarthy
2 Marvin Minsky
3 Allen Newell
4 All of the abvoe

ANSWERS

1. (3)	**2.** (1)	**3.** (3)	**4.** (3)	**5.** (3)	**6.** (2)	**7.** (3)	**8.** (2)	**9.** (1)	**10.** (3)
11. (1)	**12.** (2)	**13.** (2)	**14.** (1)	**15.** (1)	**16.** (1)	**17.** (2)	**18.** (2)	**19.** (2)	**20.** (4)
21. (2)	**22.** (2)	**23.** (4)	**24.** (4)	**25.** (3)	**26.** (1)	**27.** (2)	**28.** (1)	**29.** (2)	**30.** (3)
31. (3)	**32.** (1)	**33.** (1)	**34.** (3)	**35.** (4)	**36.** (3)	**37.** (4)	**38.** (1)	**39.** (1)	**40.** (1)
41. (2)	**42.** (1)	**43.** (1)	**44.** (2)	**45.** (1)	**46.** (4)	**47.** (2)	**48.** (2)	**49.** (2)	**50.** (4)
51. (4)	**52.** (4)	**53.** (1)	**54.** (4)	**55.** (3)	**56.** (3)	**57.** (1)	**58.** (3)	**59.** (1)	**60.** (2)
61. (3)	**62.** (3)	**63.** (3)	**64.** (3)	**65.** (4)	**66.** (4)	**67.** (2)	**68.** (2)	**69.** (3)	**70.** (4)
71. (1)	**72.** (2)	**73.** (4)	**74.** (3)	**75.** (2)	**76.** (2)	**77.** (2)	**78.** (1)	**79.** (3)	**80.** (3)
81. (1)	**82.** (2)	**83.** (4)	**84.** (1)	**85.** (4)	**86.** (3)	**87.** (1)	**88.** (1)	**89.** (3)	**90.** (4)
91. (3)	**92.** (4)	**93.** (3)	**94.** (4)	**95.** (2)	**96.** (3)	**97.** (4)	**98.** (2)	**99.** (2)	**100.** (4)

UGC-NET PSYCHOLOGY

PRACTICE SET 3

PAPER II

1. Match the following List I with List II.

List I (Personality)	List II (Nature)
A. Sanguine	I. Short-tempered and irritable
B. Melancholic	II. Hopeful and excitable
C. Choleric	III. Sadness and depression
D. Phlegmatic	IV. Calmness and apathy

Codes

	A	B	C	D
1	I	III	II	IV
2	I	IV	III	II
3	II	I	IV	III
4	II	III	I	IV

2. Consider the following statements.

I. Learning a road route from a map, understanding a general scientific principle by reading book involve specific factor of intelligence.

II. According to Spearman, apprehension of a new experience, analysing the relationship among the various elements of the experience involves general factor of intelligence.

Which of the statements given above is/are correct?

1 Only I
2 Only II
3 Both I and II
4 Neither I nor II

3. In the experiment by Peterson and Peterson on short-term memory, counting backward in steps of three was used to prevent

1 retroactive interference
2 proactive interference
3 rehearsal interference
4 consolidation of memory traces

4. Which of the following was suggested as an advantage associated with myelination?

1 Myelin changes the height of the action potential
2 Myelin increases the energy requirements of the nerve cell
3 Myelin slows down conduction speed
4 Myelin reduces the threshold for induction of an action potential

5. Arrange the following processes involved in information processing model of memory in correct chronological order.

I. Sensory input
II. Long-term storage
III. Retrieval
IV. Rehearsal buffer

Codes

1 I, III, II, IV
2 I, II, III, IV
3 I, III, IV, II
4 I, IV, II, III

6. Consider the following principles

I. Law of effect
II. Law of contiguity
III. Law of reinforcement
IV. Law of vicarious reinforcement

The correct sequence in which these principles were postulated is

1 I, II, IV, III
2 II, I, IV, III
3 II, I, III, IV
4 I, II, III, IV

7. Which one of the following is the key concept in Banduras theory?

1 Self-defence and self -actualisation
2 Self-reinforcement and self-defence
3 Self-actualisation and self-efficiency
4 Self-efficacy and self-reinforcement

8. Match the following List I with List II.

List I (Phenomenon)	List II (Concept)
A. Apparent motion of a small spot of light against a completely dark background in a completely dark room	I. Stroboscopic movement
B. Small jerky eye movements which occur when a person is fixing on an object	II. Ciliary movement
C. A type of apparent movement without a moving stimulus	III. Auto Kinetic movement
D. Movement of eyeballs	IV. Saccadic movement

Codes

	A	B	C	D
1	II	IV	I	III
2	II	I	IV	II
3	III	I	IV	II
4	III	IV	I	III

9. In Bandura's research, it was found that boys had a higher mean number of aggressive acts than girls. How is the mean calculated?

1 By finding the midpoint in a group of scores.
2 By finding the most commonly occurring number in a group of scores.
3 By subtracting the lowest from the highest score.
4 By adding all the scores up and dividing by the number of scores.

10. The perceived size an after image is directly proportional to the distance of the surface, on which the after image is viewed. This is known as

1 Garcia law
2 Emmert's law
3 Weber's law
4 Fechner's law

11. Which one of the following is the most important characteristic of sensory memory?

I. It can hold all incoming information for a very short period.
II. It can hold only a limited amount of visual information, but unlimited amount of auditory information.
III. It holds its contents only iconically.
IV. It alters the incoming information with the passage of time.

Choose the most appropriate answer from the options given below

1 Only I
2 II and III
3 IV and I
4 Only II

12. Which of the following is the correct sequence for the motivational process?

1 Reinforcement, Need, Behavioural response
2 Need, Drive, Behavioural response
3 Drive, Behavioural response, Need
4 Behavioural response, Drive, Need

13. Choose the correct option about on spontaneous recovery

I. Spontaneous recovery can never be extinguished.
II. Spontaneous recovery is a slow process.
III. Spontaneous recovery occurs before extinction.
IV. Spontaneous recovery can be extinguished with certain unreinforced trials.

Choose the correct answer from the options given below:

1 I and II
2 II and IV
3 III and I
4 Only IV

14. Arrange the following steps involved in test construction in chronological order

I. specifying construct of interest
II. evaluating reliability and validity of test
III. choosing a method
IV. deciding test's function
V. designing item content

Codes

1 I, IV, III, V, II
2 I, III, IV, V, II
3 I, IV, III, II, V
4 I, III, IV, II, V

15. Which of the following was not a finding of Bandura's work on the influence of observational learning on children?

1 Children who viewed a model being punished showed significantly more aggressive acts than those, who saw a model receive no consequences
2 Children who viewed a model being punished showed less aggressive acts than those, who saw a model receive no consequences
3 Children who viewed a model being punished showed more aggressive acts than those, who saw a model being rewarded
4 All of the above

16. Match the following List I with List II.

List I	List II
A. Preparation	I. Ideas are ascertained, checked and reassured by themselves and by other confirming the validity of their hypothesis
B. Incubation	II. 'Happy thoughts' do not occur to lazy persons; they arise in well prepared and well stocked minds
C. Illumination	III. The climax of the process of creative thinking dawns the saving-guiding idea, which is the forerunner of the final solution
D. Verification	IV. The 'hatching' period in creative thought process is characterised by restlessness and poorly coordinated activity accompanied by a feeling of unease and frustration through unconscious thought processes

Codes

	A	B	C	D		A	B	C	D
1	II	IV	III	I	2	II	III	IV	I
3	III	II	I	IV	4	III	IV	I	II

17. Each colour that a human being is capable of experiencing can vary in

1 hue, reflection and brightness
2 hue, reflection and saturation
3 reflection, brightness and saturation
4 hue, brightness and saturation

18. Consider the following statements.

I. A masochist receives sexual pleasure from receiving pain inflected by other.
II. Freud called the mouth, anus and genitals erogenous zones.
III. Moral, the guilt a person experiences after violating personal standard of conduct is called anxiety.
IV. According to Freud, anxiety caused by the super ego.

Which of the statements given above are correct?

1 I and II 2 II, III and IV
3 I and IV 4 II and IV

19. Connie and Sue are identical twins reared apart and recently reunited. Carl and Fred are unrelated students at a major university. Which of the following statements is true of these pairings?

1 Connie and Sue will probably show a long list of amassing similarities, while Carl and Fred will only share a couple of similarities.
2 Connie and Sue will probably share many similarities; Carl and Fred may share many similarities, but are probably not motivated enough to discover them.
3 Connie and Sue will not share as many similarities as Carl and Fred will share.
4 Connie and Sue will have more differences than will Carl and Fred.

20. Compared with normal subjects, amnesias

1 do not improve their performance as quickly in perceptual or motor skills
2 perform equally well on tests of explicit memory
3 perform equally well on tests of implicit memory
4 All of the above

21. Which one of the following is the correct sequence of stages of memory?

1 Storage-organisation-recall
2 Recall-encoding-decoding
3 Encoding-decoding-storage
4 Encoding-storage-retrieval

22. Evidence that newborn infants perceive depth comes from

I. experiments on shape constancy
II. experiments on size constancy
III. experiments on movement constancy
IV. None of the above

Choose the correct answer from the options given below:

1 I and II only 2 Only II
3 III and I only 4 Only IV

23. Of the following, which is the best example of intrinsic motivation?

I. Scuba diving as part of a rescue mission
II. Scuba diving to find sunken treasure
III. Scuba diving because your husband wants you to learn to scuba dive
IV. Scuba diving with delight in underwater scenery

Choose the correct answer from the options given below:

1 I and II 2 II and III
3 III and I 4 Only IV

24. Each of the following is a reason to use a heuristic rather than an algorithm, except

I. Sometimes no algorithm is available to solve a particular problem.
II. Heuristics often require less time and effort to apply than do algorithms.
III. Heuristics produce successful problem solutions with sufficient frequency to justify their use.
IV. Heuristics yield the single best solution to a problem.

Choose the correct answer from the options given below:

1 Only IV
2 I and II
3 Only III
4 IV and I

25. Which type of problem may be solved successfully by the application of an algorithm?

1 Well-defined problems only
2 Ill-defined problems only
3 Both well- and ill-defined problems
4 Neither well- nor ill-defined problems; algorithms apply only to decision-making

26. Consider the following statements regarding the geneses of personality theories
The Personality Theorists

I. look their primary ideas from their clinical experiences.
II. owed much to the medical profession and practice.
III. rebelled against conventional ideas and methods of study.

Which of the statements given above is/are correct?

1 Only I
2 II and III
3 I and III
4 All of these

27. Match the following List I with List II.

List I (Proceses)	List II (Types)
A. Thinking under condition of information deficiency	I. Free association
B. Thinking following random sequence of information	II. Conceptualisation
C. Thinking following classified information	III. Problem solving
D. Thinking to arrange systematically all information to attain a desired outcome	IV. Imagination

Codes

	A	B	C	D		A	B	C	D
1	I	IV	II	III	2	IV	I	III	II
3	I	IV	III	II	4	IV	I	II	III

28. Absorptive phase of energy mobilisation involves the following events. Arrange them in the correct sequence.

I. Glucose increases.
II. Parasympathetic activation.
III. Pancreas secretes insulin.
IV. Glucose enters the body cells.
V. Glucose is stored in liver and muscles as glycogen.
VI. Fat stored in adipose cells as triglycerides.

Codes

1 I, II, III, V, IV, VI
2 I, II, III, IV, V, VI
3 I, III, II, IV, VI, V
4 I, IV, II, VI, V, III

29. Assertion (A) According to Thorndike's law of effect, behaviours that result in unpleasantness are more likely to occur again.

Reason (R) He drew on Gestalt psychology to argue that animals could learn the connections between stimuli and did not need any explicit biologically significant event to make learning occur.

Codes

1 Both (A) and (R) are true and (R) is the correct explanation of (A)
2 Both (A) and (R) are true, but (R) is not the correct explanation of (A)
3 (A) is true, but (R) is false
4 (A) is false, but (R) is true

30. Match the following List I with List II.

List I	List II
A. Expectancy × (Motive × Incentive)	I. JB Rotter
B. Subjective probability × Utility	II. J W Atkinson
C. Potency × Valence	III. W Edwards
D. Expectancy, Reinforcement value	IV. K Lewin

Codes

	A	B	C	D		A	B	C	D
1	III	II	I	IV	2	II	III	IV	I
3	II	IV	I	III	4	III	II	IV	I

31. In group counselling, what is the correct sequence of stages of group development?

I. Forming
II. Norming
III. Mourning
IV. Storming
V. Performing

Codes

1 II, III, I, V, IV
2 I, IV, II, V, III
3 I, III, V, II, IV
4 IV, I, II, III, V

32. Which of the following in learning environment are considered to be true about school success?

I The self image is vital to learning
II Very high goal setting is necessary to motivate and study
III Success experience is a function of challenge more than repetition
IV Child's spiritual identity is vital to learning

Choose the correct answer from the options given below:

1 I and IV 2 II and III
3 I, III and IV 4 II, III and IV

33. Which of the following is the best explanation for why you would be unable to remember the correct answers, if you panic during an exam?

1 anxiety causes extraneous thoughts that interfere with retrieval
2 you have repressed them because the test anxiety was unbearable
3 the answers are actively blocked by the subconscious
4 the capacity of your long-term memory has been reduced

34. Which of the following pairs is/are correctly matched?

1 Positive Reinforcement: If you clean your room, I'll get you a pizza tonight
2 Negative Punishment : If you hit your little brother again, you'll get no dessert
3 Negative Reinforcement: If you go into the office over there, the doctor will remove the thorn from your leg
4 All of the above

35. Which of the following statements about the sex drive is correct?

1 The sex drive is greatly affected by hormone levels in humans
2 The sex drive is necessary for individual survival
3 The sex drive is homeostatic
4 The influence of hormones decreases as we ascend the biological scale

36. Naturalistic observation is the major method of study used by

1 psychoanalysts, ethologists, anthropologists and Gestalt psychologists
2 psychoanalysts and Gestalt psychologists
3 ethologists, anthropologists and Gestalt psychologists
4 psychoanalysts, anthropologist and Gestalt psychologists

37. Consider the following statements.

Statement I In higher order conditioning, a conditioned stimulus functions as, if it were a (n) conditioned stimulus.

Statement II Classical conditioning is a form of learning in which responses come to be controlled by their consequences.

Which of the statements given above is/are correct?

1 Both I and II are true
2 Both I and II are false
3 I is true, but II are false
4 I is false, but II is true.

38. A circadian rhythm refers to a cycle

1 of sexual receptivity caused by hormone cycles
2 of bodily activity approximately 24 hours in length
3 of emotional arousal
4 during which various bodily system are in phase

39. An intelligence test is considered culturally biased if

1 ethnic and racial questions are excluded from the test
2 when all factors are held constant, the content of the test is more difficult for one group than it is for another groups
3 it is administered by someone, who is prejudices towards cultural groups
4 someone with a culturally impoverished background is required to take the test

40. The same fire, which melts butter hardens eggs. With respect to personality development, this statement implies that

1 all individuals react in same way to same environment
2 all individual react differently to same environment
3 all individuals react in same way to different enviroments
4 individuals do not react to environment

41. Assertion (A) A creative solution to a problem depends on mental process of individual.

Reason (R) Contextual factor has no role in the solution.

Codes

1 Both (A) and (R) are true and (R) is the correct explanation of (A)
2 Both (A) and (R) are true, but (R) is not the correct explanation of (A)
3 (A) is true, but (R) is false
4 (A) is false, but (R) is true

42. Which one of the following is not the characteristic of type-A personality?

1 Excessive compulsion for time keeping
2 Meticulous analysis of problems
3 Sleeplessness
4 Always in a hurry

43. Consider the following statements.

I. Different behaviours in different cultures are considered as intelligent.

II. A preference for mental manipulation rather than physical manipulation is the characteristics of intelligent behaviour in non-Western societies.

Which of the statements given above is/are correct?

1 Only I 2 Only II
3 Both I and II 4 None of these

44. **Among the following, which one is quite different from the rest?**

1 Linear perspective
2 Retinal disparity
3 Texture gradient
4 Interposition of object

45. **Consider the following statements.**

Decrease in the likelihood of the response R is contingent upon

I. positive reinforcement if R occurs.
II. omission of reinforcement if R occurs.
III. omission of reinforcement if R does not occur.
IV. punishment if R occurs.

Which of the statements given above is/are correct?

1 I and II
2 III and IV
3 I and III
4 II and IV

46. **Which one of the following pairs is not correctly matched ?**

1	Displacement	:	Direction energy towards another object when the original object is inaccessible
2	Rationalisation	:	Manufacturing good reasons to explain away a bruised ego
3	Reaction formation	:	Behaving in way that is directly opposite to unconscious wishes
4	Fixation	:	Retreating to an earlier phase of development where demands are not so great

47. **Assertion** (A) If the cognitions about an event are present, but arousal is absent, then emotion will still be experienced.

Reason (R) Perceived emotion is a joint function of arousal appraisal and labelling of cognition.

Codes

1 Both (A) and (R) are true and (R) is the correct explanation of (A)
2 Both (A) and (R) are true, but (R) is not the correct explanation of (A)
3 (A) is true, but (R) is false
4 (A) is false, but (R) is true

48. **Consider the following statements.**

I. Rehearsal is a method of storing information in long-term memory.
II. Maintenance rehearsal is sufficient to keep the information in short-term memory, but insufficient to move it into long-term memory.

Which of the statements given above is/are correct?

1 Only I
2 Only II
3 Both I and II
4 None of these

49. **Cognitive theory of learning developed on the basis of experiments designed to test the relative role of motor habits versus sign learning. Under which of the following headings can the experiments be placed?**

I. Place learning
II. Role of drive
III. Latent learning
IV. Whole versus Part learning
V. Reward expectancy

Select the correct answer using the codes given below:

1 I, II, III and IV
2 I, II and V
3 I, III and V
4 II, III, IV and V

50. **Consider the following statements.**

I. Sailors are high on spatial intelligence.
II. Componential intelligence covers the aspects of intelligence measured by standard intelligence test.

Which of the statements given above is/are correct?

1 Only I
2 Only II
3 Both I and II
4 None of these

51. **Ethnocentrism occurs when**

I. researchers falsify their research findings to benefit a particular group.
II. psychological research occurs in a historical context.
III. reports of psychological research are reported incorrectly in the media.
IV. researchers attempt to understand a different culture from their own culture's framework.

Choose the correct answer from the options given below:

1 I and IV
2 Only I
3 II and III
4 Only IV

52. **Ed noticed that whenever he use his electric can opener, his cat would come into the kitchen and act hungry-drooling and mewing pitiably. The reasoned is that because he use the can opener to open the cat's food, the sound of the can opener has become a(n)**

I. unconditioned stimulus
II. conditioned stimulus
III. unconditioned response
IV. conditioned response

Choose the correct answer from the options given below

1 I and IV
2 Only II
3 III and I
4 IV and II

Directions (Q. Nos 53-57) *Read the passage given below and answer the following questions.*

Kasparov's unique brain, together with his years of experience, allowed him to play chess using heuristics. Heuristics are rules of thumb or clever and creative mental shortcuts, that reduce the number of operations and allow one to solve problems easily and quickly. In the late 1990s, Kasparov's clever and creative shortcuts or heuristics, had given him the advantage over the fixed and not so creative algorithms of computer programs. However, computers now have been programmed ,with new algorithms that increase their speed of 'thinking' from analysing 100000 chess moves per second to 2.5 million.

As a result of this increased speed, human chess grand masters, whose thinking focuses on using clever heuristics, no longer have a clear advantage over a computer's 'thinking' ability (Boyce, 2002). Besides being used to solve chess problems, heuristics are often used in daily life to make decisions or draw conclusions (Bailensonet al, 2000).

A commonly used heuristic is called the availability heuristic. The availability heuristic says that we rely on information that is more prominent or easily recalled and overlook other information that is available, but less prominent or notable. e.g. the murder rate in the United States actually decreased in the late 1990s.

However, during this time, network coverage of homicides increased 473%, which made news of murders more available and according to the availability heuristic, led people to conclude that murder rates had become epidemic (Comarow, 2001).

Using the availability heuristic to make a decision means taking a mental shortcut. Although heuristics allow us to make quick decisions, they may result in bad decisions, since we make them using shortcuts, which limits the amount of information we use (F Bower, 1997).

53. Which of the following most likely makes use of heuristics?

1 A chemical equation for the synthesis of sulphuric acid.
2 A recipe for making cookies on the back of a box of cornflakes.
3 An article by a Nobel Prize winner titled 'How to Succeed in Science'.
4 A computer program for keeping track of inventory at a department store.

54. A rule that guarantees the solution to a problem when it is correctly applied is termed as

1 heuristic
2 mental set
3 algorithm
4 schema

55. Consider the following statements.

I. The use of heuristics is a 'best guess' that does not guarantee a solution.
II. Using the availability heuristic to make a decision means taking a mental shortcut.

Which of the statements given above is/are correct?

1 Only I　　2 Only II
3 Both I and II　　4 Neither I nor II

56. Frank lost a contact lens in the kitchen, he is searching for it by examining each linoleum tile in turn to see, if the lens is contained within the square. Gemma similarly lost a lens in the kitchen; she is looking for it near the base of the fridge and around the stove, the two appliances she remembers using when she was last in the kitchen. Which statement best describes the problem-solving strategies of these two individuals?

1 Both Frank and Gemma are using algorithms.
2 Both Frank and Gemma are using heuristics.
3 Frank is using a heuristic, whereas Gemma is using an algorithm.
4 Frank is using an algorithm, whereas Gemma is using a heuristic.

57. After being robbed by a boy recently the shopkeeper says "beware of teenagers in our community". Which of the following explains his reactions?

1 Algorithm
2 Availability Heuristic
3 Representative Heuristic
4 Gambler's fallacy

58. Pattern of familial transmission of intelligence from one generation to other is investigated in which of the following?

1 Linkage analysis studies
2 Adoption studies
3 Association studies
4 Segregation analysis studies

59. A neuroscientist applies an electric shock to sea slugs' tails. After a varying interval, she touches the slugs' tails lightly. Which of the following alternatives correctly names and identifies the variables in this experiment?

1 Independent variable - length of interval; dependent variable - withdrawal response
2 Dependent variable - length of interval; independent variable - withdrawal response
3 Experimental variable -- length of interval; control variable - withdrawal response
4 Control variable - length of interval; experimental variable - withdrawal response

60. Ruby was listening to a tape recording of a famous speech that was played backward. She just heard gibberish until a classmate said the phrase 'meet me in St Louis' was clearly spoken. The tape was rewound and as Ashlynn listened this time, she also clearly heard the same phase. Ruby's ability to detect the phrase the second time through the tape illustrates

I. the opponent-process model of perception
II. the top-down processing model of perception
III. the bottom-up processing model of perception
IV. the electric model of perception

Choose the correct answer from the options given below

1 I, II and III 2 II and I
3 III and IV 4 Only II

61. Concept formation refers to

I. the organisation of phonemes and morphemes into meaningful thought
II. the application of transformation rules to basic sentence
III. inductive as opposed to deductive thinking
IV. organising experiences into meaningful categories

Choose the correct answer from the options given below

1 Only I 2 IV and I
3 II and III 4 Only IV

62. Goal gradient hypothesis states that

I. errors are committed more as animal reaches near the goal
II. errors are committed less as the animal reaches the goal
III. the learning would be more effective the closer the animal is to the goal
IV. None of the above

Choose the most appropriate answer from the options given below:

1 Only I 2 Only III
3 Only II 4 Only IV

63. Which one of the following hypothesis emphasises the role of language in thinking?

I. Thinking is active imagination carried on in words.
II. Process of thinking is sun-vocal talking or implicit speech when the larynx is in a state of low tonus.
III. Linguistic relativity determines the nature of thinking.
IV. Thinking can occur without words as we can thinking about things, for which we do not have name.

Choose the correct answer from the options given below:

1 I and II 2 II and IV
3 Only III 4 IV and I

64. Consider the following statements.

I. Meta components control, monitor and evaluate cognitive processing.
II. Performance components execute strategies assembled by meta components.

Which of the statements given above is/are correct?

1 Only I 2 Only II
3 Both I and II 4 None of these

65. Consider the following statements.

I. Perceptual thinking depends on perception of actual or concrete objects and events.
II. Relaxation theory is also called as 'surplus energy theory'.
III. Gathering information is first step of decision-making.

Which of the statements given above is/are correct?

1 I and II 2 I and III
3 Only I 4 All of these

66. By providing information on the functioning of involuntary systems such as heart rate and stomach contraction a person can be trained to regulate them. This is called

1 systematic desensitisation
2 bio-feedback
3 self-reinforcement
4 para systematic chain-reaction

67. Consider the following statements.

I. In non-directive therapy, 74% of therapists interpret and take direct action with regard to the client.
II. Person centered therapy is a non-directive insight therapy developed by Carl Rogers.

Which of the statements given above is/are correct?

1 Only I
2 Only II
3 Both I and II
4 Neither I nor II

68. Assertion (A) According to trace change theory of forgetting one's memory of what he has seen tends to change in specific ways.

Reason (R) Change in memory are brought about by different principles.

Codes

1 Both (A) and (R) are true and (R) is the correct explanation of (A)
2 Both (A) and (R) are true, but (R) is not the correct explanation of (A)
3 (A) is true, but (R) is false
4 (A) is false, but (R) is true

69. Match the following List I with List II.

List I (Psychologists)	List II (Tests)
A. R Cattell	I. MMPI
B. Hathaway	II. Big five
C. Costa and Mc Rae	III. 16 PF
D. Murray	IV. TAT

Codes

	A	B	C	D		A	B	C	D
1	III	I	IV	II	2	I	III	IV	II
3	I	III	II	IV	4	III	I	II	IV

70. The Seashore Test is used to measure

1 Clerical aptitude
2 musical aptitude
3 mechanical aptitude
4 different aptitude

71. After visual input has been processed in the primary visual cortex, signals are proceed further along a number of pathways. The dorsal stream processes information about

1 form and colour
2 motion and depth
3 brightness and contours
4 complexity and contrast

72. Match the following List I with List II.

List I	List II
A. Social learning theory	I. Emphasises the ability to learn by observing a model
B. Vicarious reinforcement and vicarious punishment	II. Affects the willingness of others to perform the behaviours they learned
C. Observational (or vicarious) learning	III. Learning by observing other people's behaviour
D. Learning set	IV. The ability to become increasingly more effective in solving problem.

Codes

	A	B	C	D		A	B	C	D
1	I	III	II	IV	2	IV	III	II	I
3	II	I	IV	III	4	I	II	III	IV

73. Consider the following statements.

I. Gardner has proposed seven kinds of interrelated intelligences.
II. Solving logical puzzles requires bodily kinesthetic intelligence.

Which of the statements given above is/are correct?

1 Only I
2 Only II
3 Both I and II
4 None of these

74. 'Head factors' in satiety

1 are restricted to the taste of food being eaten
2 permit an animal to learn to adjust the amount consumed of food containing different amounts of calories
3 produce long-lasting suppression of eating
4 include activation of stretch receptors within the stomach

75. Suppose you are asked to determine one's potentiality for a post requiring higher intellectual abilities. Which of the following coefficients of validity would you consider as more important in the psychological tests you chose to administer?

I. Construct validity
II. Convergent validity
III. Predictive validity
IV. Discriminative validity

Select the correct answer using the codes given below

1 II and III
2 I and IV
3 III and IV
4 I and III

76. Match the following List I with List II.

List I (Scholar)	List II (Idea)
A. Edward de Bono	I. Divergent thinking
B. Hudson	II. Brain storming
C. Osborn	III. Lateral thinking
D. Trewartrha and Newport	IV. Decision-making

Codes

	A	B	C	D
1	III	I	II	IV
2	III	II	I	IV
3	II	III	IV	I
4	I	III	II	IV

77. Which of the following pairs is/are correctly matched?

I. Aron Beck : Cognitive Therapy
II. Personal Construct Theory : Kelly
III. Constructive Alternativism : Victor Frank

Codes

1 Only I
2 I and II
3 II and III
4 All of these

78. To what extent are attention deficit disorders associated with dyslexia and dyscalculia, if indeed they are?

1 Attention deficit disorders are not related to dyslexia and dyscalculia
2 Attention deficit disorders are negatively associated with dyslexia and dyscalculia
3 Attention deficit disorders are positively associated with dyslexia and dyscalculia
4 Attention deficit disorders are perfectly correlated with dyslexia and dyscalculia

79. On which of the following personality inventories are items arranged in forced-choice format?

1 Edwards personal preference schedule
2 Eysenck personal preference schedule
3 Sixteen personality factor questionnaire
4 Guilford Zimmerman temperament survey

80. Which of the following alternative correctly classifies the major types of learning described in your text?

1 Associative learning : classical conditioning and sensitisation; non-associative learning: operant conditioning and habituation
2 Associative learning : classical conditioning; non-associative learning : operant conditioning
3 Associative learning: habituation and desensitisation; non-associative learning : classical and operant conditioning
4 Associative learning: classical and operant conditioning; non-associative learning: habituation and sensitisation

81. Generally, institutionalised children show a slower rate of languages development compared to those growing up in normal home conditions. This is most likely because the institutionalised children have

1 somewhat lower IQ scores than normal children scores
2 relative deprivation of social reinforcement
3 low level of cognitive development often limited to the concrete pre-operational stage
4 abstracting the rules of language

82. Gingko Biloba extract is supposed to help memory because it

1 increases the flow of blood to brain
2 clears out the plaques and tangles associated with Alzheimer's
3 lowers cholesterol
4 speeds up the neural firing mechanisms of the brain

83. Which of the following models produced the highest amount of aggression in children when the model was rewarded, according to Bandura's experiments on observational learning?

1 A real life model
2 A video recording of a model
3 A cartoon model
4 They all produced equally high amounts of aggression

84. Saltatory conduction is rapid because

I. cable properties carry the signal under the myelin sheath
II. myelinated cells have more leakage through the membrane
III. myelinated axons are larger in diameter
IV. myelinated cells have more ion channels per unit area than do non-myelinated cells

Choose the correct answer from the options given below:

1 Only I
2 II and III
3 IV and II
4 Only III

85. The Young–Helmholtz theory of colour vision states that

I. black and white are true colour qualities and not just the presence or absence of light
II. the human eye contains three kinds of cones, each kind being sensitive to one of the three primary colours
III. the retina contains two kinds of receptor, one being sensitive to colours and the other being not sensitive to colours
IV. the visual system reaches a state of equilibrium when no external visual stimulus is present

Choose the correct answer from the options given below:

1 I and IV
2 Only II
3 Only III
4 II and I

86. The first step in multicultural education is for the education personal to

1 become immersed in the cultures of their students
2 invite the parents for show and tell
3 say 'hello' in the language of their student
4 learn about the cultures of their students

87. Which hypothesis is probably the most reasonable regarding the potential influence of massed *vs* spaced practice on the relationship between the number of hours spent studying and the degree to which material is learned?

1 The correlation between hours of study and degree of learning should be higher for massed than for spaced practice.
2 The correlation between hours of study and degree of learning should be negative for massed practice, but positive for spaced practice.
3 The correlation between hours of study and degree of learning should be zero for massed practice but positive for spaced practice.
4 The correlation between hours of study and degree of learning should be lower for massed than for spaced practice.

88. What is the most important difference between short- term memory and long-term memory experiments?

1 There is no rehearsal in short-term memory, but rehearsal is essential in long-term memory experiments.
2 The exposure time per item is at least double in long-term memory as compared to short-term memory experiments.
3 The time between exposure of an item and recall is very limited in short-term memory, but in long-term memory experiments it is substantially long.
4 The material used in short-term memory experiments is meaningless, but the material used in long-term memory experiments is meaningful.

89. Forgetting in LTM may occur due to

1 encoding failure
2 semantic failure
3 retrieval failure
4 failure arising out of phonemic similarity

90. Reasoning involves the operation of reading (the recognition, knowledge, memory of words), the contents of the passage being read (the meanings of the words themselves) and the products of the reading (the understanding that the passage provides). This approach is most probably based on the intelligence theory known as

1 Sternberg's triarchic theory
2 Vernon's three kinds of intelligence : A, B and C
3 Thurstone's theory of primary mental abilities
4 Guilford's structure of intelligence model

91. In Robert Plutchik's descriptive theory of basic emotions, the relationship between emotions is differentiated by

1 intensity and proximity
2 intensity, similarity and polarity
3 intensity, similarity and proximity
4 similarity and proximity

92. Match the following List I with List II.

List I (Concepts)	List II (Mental Strategies)
A. Repression	I. Substituting 'good' reasons for 'bad' ones in order to make one's behaviour appear more ethical than it really is
B. Sublimation	II. Pushing of unacceptable impulses back into unconscious region
C. Rationalisation	III. The expression of an unacceptable impulse in a socialised form
D. Projection	IV. Putting the responsibilities of negative personal characteristic to something other than self

Codes

	A	B	C	D		A	B	C	D
1	I	IV	II	III	2	II	III	I	IV
3	I	III	II	IV	4	II	IV	I	III

93. Research with animals such as rats and monkeys with concept attainment problems indicates that

I. animals can learn concepts even though they do not have the ability to use language
II. animals higher up on the phylogenetic scale can learn concepts, those lower on the scale cannot
III. it is impossible without the use of language to learn to abstract a common property
IV. animals think and communicate with language

Choose the correct answer from the options given below:

1 Only I 2 Only III 3 Only IV 4 Only II

94. What is the correct sequence of arrangement of the experimental conditions in an experiment on proactive interference?

1 Learn task 'A', Learn task 'B', Retention interval, Measure recall of task 'A'
2 Learn task 'A', Retention interval, Learn task 'B', Measure recall of task 'B'
3 Learn task 'A', Learn task 'B', Retention interval, Measure recall of task 'B'
4 Learn task 'A', Retention interval, Learn task 'B', Measure recall of task 'A'

95. Which one of the following statements regarding hypothalamic regulation of water intake is correct?

1 Osmoreceptors are influenced by the release of Anti Diuretic Hormone (ADH), which controls the water in take.
2 There are no clearly defined nerve cells in the hypophysis, which respond specifically to dehydration.

3 Water deficit increases the volume of blood and fluid surrounding the body cell.
4 Water deficit increases the concentration of certain chemicals, primarily sodium, in the fluid surrounding the body cell.

Directions (Q. Nos. 96-100) *Read the passage given below and answer the questions that follow:*

The Whorf hypothesis is the view that language shapes cognition i.e. concepts and ways of thinking depend on language. People who speak significantly different languages, then, view the world differently.

Also called the hypothesis of linguistic relativity or the Sapir-Whorf hypothesis, the Whorf hypothesis was named after the early 20th century linguist "Benjamin Whorf, who claimed that, because the Hopi language expressed statements about time in importantly dissimilar ways than other languages, the Hopi held a different conception of time than other peoples. Related to linguistic relativity is linguistic determinism, the view that language necessitates how one thinks (thinking outside the bounds of one's language is impossible).

Some psychologists believe the Whorf hypothesis helps explain cognition; like linguistic determinism, however, it is highly controversial. e.g. Whorf reasoned that because the Inuit (Eskimos) have many names for snow, they must be able to perceive many more kinds of snow than Americans, for whom snow conditions are less important. On the basis of these kinds of observations, Whorf formulated the theory of linguistic relativity.

96. **Which of the following statements best expresses the linguistic relativity hypothesis?**
1 Language is equivalent to thought
2 Language influences thought
3 Thought determines language
4 Language is unrelated to thought

97. **According to a common myth, Eskimos have multiple words for 'snow' that influence the complexity of their thoughts about it. Which hypothesis addresses this myth?**
1 confirmation bias
2 functional fixedness
3 congnitive control
4 linguistic relativity

98. **Which of the following is incorrect about linguistic relativity?**
1 Evidence for the linguistic relativity hypothesis has been derived from cross-cultural studies
2 The Whorf hypothesis is the view that language shapes thought
3 Both 1 and 2
4 Neither 1 nor 2

99. **Which of the following is correct from the following statements?**
1 Linguistic relativity opens the window to the realisation that all languages do not translate do each other.
2 Linguistic categories limit and determine cognitive categories is the weak part of the hypothesis.
3 Linguistic categories and usage influence though and certain kinds of non-linguistic behaviour is the strong part.
4 None of the above

100. **Who proposed the linguistic relativity hypothesis?**
1 Sapir and Whorf
2 Eric Lenneberg
3 Noam Chomsky
4 Steven Pinker

ANSWERS

1. (4)	2. (2)	3. (3)	4. (4)	5. (4)	6. (4)	7. (4)	8. (4)	9. (4)	10. (2)
11. (1)	12. (2)	13. (4)	14. (1)	15. (2)	16. (1)	17. (4)	18. (1)	19. (2)	20. (3)
21. (4)	22. (2)	23. (4)	24. (1)	25. (1)	26. (4)	27. (4)	28. (2)	29. (3)	30. (2)
31. (2)	32. (3)	33. (1)	34. (4)	35. (4)	36. (3)	37. (1)	38. (2)	39. (2)	40. (2)
41. (3)	42. (2)	43. (1)	44. (2)	45. (4)	46. (4)	47. (4)	48. (3)	49. (1)	50. (3)
51. (4)	52. (2)	53. (3)	54. (1)	55. (3)	56. (4)	57. (3)	58. (1)	59. (1)	60. (4)
61. (4)	62. (2)	63. (3)	64. (3)	65. (3)	66. (2)	67. (2)	68. (2)	69. (4)	70. (2)
71. (2)	72. (4)	73. (4)	74. (2)	75. (1)	76. (1)	77. (2)	78. (3)	79. (1)	80. (4)
81. (2)	82. (4)	83. (1)	84. (1)	85. (2)	86. (4)	87. (4)	88. (3)	89. (3)	90. (4)
91. (2)	92. (2)	93. (1)	94. (3)	95. (4)	96. (2)	97. (4)	98. (4)	99. (1)	100. (1)

UGC-NET PSYCHOLOGY

PRACTICE SET 4

PAPER II

1 A qualitative approach sees social reality between people in the real world as

1 mutually constructed
2 mutually exclusive
3 matter of perspective
4 None of the above

2 Learning sex-appropriate behaviour is greatly influenced by

1 self-reinforcement and resolution of unconscious conflicts
2 identification and imitation
3 toilet training and early feeding contacts
4 valuing and self-regard

3 Who said, 'Psychology has a long past but only a short history'?

1 Hermann Ebbinghaus
2 Skinner
3 Aristotle
4 Watson

4 Who said that by expanding self awareness people can acquire freedom of action?

1 Rogers
2 Maslow
3 May
4 Frankl

5 Vouyerstic and exhibitionistic disorders are included in which of the following in DSM-5?

1 Sexual dysfunctions
2 Paraphillic disorders
3 Other conditions that focus on clinical attention
4 Disruptive impulse control and conduct disorders

6 A study to draw the features of a particular individual's situation or a group perfectly is known as

1 Diagnostic research
2 Formulative research
3 Descriptive research
4 Hypothesis testing research

7 Guilford had originally divided intelligence at second order level into

1 two parts
2 120 parts
3 more than a dozen parts
4 seven parts

8 The Reliability coefficient 'r' alway's lie between

1 1-100 2 0-1.00
3 1-10 4 1-50

9 Correlation between X and Y is 0.80. Its *X* and *Y* have common variation of

1 80% 2 20%
3 36% 4 64%

10 Among the following which one is not a theory of intelligence?

1 Coci's biological theory
2 Anderson's theory
3 James-Lange theory
4 Gardner's theory

11 Match the following List I with List II.

List I (Psychologist)	List II (Contributions)
A. Viktor Frankl	I. Shadow
B. Rollo May	II. Logotherapy
C. Fritz Pearls	III. Existential Psychology
D. Carl Jung	IV. Gestalt therapy

Codes

	A	B	C	D
1	I	II	III	IV
2	II	III	IV	I
3	III	II	IV	I
4	III	I	II	IV

12 **Which kind of territory is the space owned by individuals or primary groups, controlled relatively on a permanent basis by them?**

1 Primary territory 2 Secondary territory
3 Public territory 4 Body territory

13 **Milly generally likes to go home to visit her family during vacation. How, after her father tells her she must be home during spring vacation, Milly decides to remain at college. We can probably best understand MIlly's behaviour in terms of**

1 reaction formation
2 regression
3 psychological reactance
4 self-serving bias

14 **In which type of scan strong magnetic fields and radio waves are used?**

1 EEG 2 MRI
3 PET 4 None of these

15 **Short-term memory lasts approximately for**

1 less than two seconds 2 3 to 10 seconds
3 15 to 20 seconds 4 1 to 2 minutes

16 **Which of the following approaches to psychology did not exist at the same time with the others?**

1 Socio-cultural 2 Structuralism
3 Functionalism 4 Psychoanalysis

17 **In Asch's study of perceptual judgement involving the length of lines, naive participants conformed .... of the time to the false judgements of the confederates.**

1 10 percent 2 37 percent
3 68 percent 4 92 percent

18 **Which potential is defined as the difference in electrical charge between the inside and the outside of an undisturbed axon membrane?**

1 resting membrane 2 local
3 action 4 None of these

19 **Match the following List I with List II.**

List I (Measures)		**List II** (Objectives)
A. Mode	I.	Purpose of the test
B. Quartile deviation	II.	Consistency of test scores
C. Reliability	III.	Measure of variability
D. Validity	IV.	Measure of central tendency

Codes

	A	B	C	D		A	B	C	D
1	III	IV	II	I	2	IV	III	II	I
3	III	IV	I	II	4	IV	III	I	II

20 **What is considered statistically 'abnormal' for a person to score in an IQ Test?**

1 Below 55 2 Above 145
3 Both 1 and 2 4 None of these

21 **What are the 'inputs' according to 'GAM' model of bullying in committing cyber-bullying?**

I. Personal factors
II. Situational factors
III. Present internal states
IV. Arousal

Codes

1 I and II 2 II and III
3 III and IV 4 I and IV

22 **Consider the following statements.**

I. Behaviourism originated around 1910.
II. The major and the most radical viewpoint about human behaviour was presented by Sigmund Freud.

Which among the above is/are correct?

1 Only I
2 Only II
3 Both I and II
4 None of the above

23 **According to 2012 survey, what percentage of population lives below poverty line in India?**

1 14% 2 15%
3 12% 4 10%

24 **Which of the following is an example of counter balancing design?**

1 Within design
2 Time series design
3 Latin square design
4 Expost facto design

25 **Glial cells are found throughout the**

1 CNS 2 PNS
3 Both 1 and 2 4 None of these

26 **What statistic is used to check the significance of the Kruskal-Wallis 'H'-test?**

1 Chi-squared 2 Partial n^2
3 'T' 4 Mean rank

27 **What does 'GRIT' (Osgood) stands for?**

1 Graduated and Reciprocal Initiatives in Tension reduction
2 Graduated and Reciprocal Inclination in Trauma reduction
3 Graduated and Reciprocal Initiative in Total peace
4 None of the above

28 Bizzare and illogical dreams occur in
1 REM sleep
2 SWS sleep
3 Both 1 and 2
4 None of these

29 Arrange the following steps of decision-making in order
I. Developing and weighing the options
II. Plan and execute
III. Take follow up action
IV. Choosing least possible option

Codes
1 I, II, III, IV
2 II, III, IV, I
3 I, IV, II, III
4 IV, II, III, I

30 Consider the following statements.
I. Overall, it appears that we perceive changing stimuli better than constant ones.
II. The wavelength of light mainly affects our perception of brightness.

Which of the following statements given above is/are correct?
1 Only I
2 Only II
3 Both I and II
4 Neither I nor II

31 Consider the following statements.
I. Language can be spoken, signed or written.
II. Humans make new sentences each time they speak. This refers to the concept that language is creative.

Which of the statements given above is/are correct?
1 Only I
2 Only II
3 Both I and II
4 Neither I nor II

32 Which of the following regulates homeostatic pressure to sleep?
1 Orexin
2 Melatonin
3 Adenosine
4 All of these

33 Consider the following statements.
I. Concept can be learned only when we can discriminate the appropriate feature.
II. Thinking is some sort of inner speech.

Which of the statements given above is/are not correct?
1 Only I
2 Only II
3 Both I and II
4 None of these

34 The ease or difficulty of concept learning depends on
I. complexity of the stimuli
II. nature of strategies played
III. conditions present during course of learning

Codes
1 Only I
2 I and III
3 II and III
4 All of these

35 Which of the following strategies facilitate problem solving?
I. Algorithms
II. Mental set
III. Planning fallacy
IV. Heuristics
V. Analogy
1 I, II and IV
2 II, III and IV
3 I and V
4 I, IV and V

36 Which among the following is/are included under Pervasive Development Disorder?
1 Autistic disorder
2 Asperger's disorder
3 Rett's disorder
4 All of these

37 Who proposed a psychological analysis of poverty in Indian context?
1 Pareek
2 Ajit K Dalal
3 Anand Lakshmi
4 Dr Girishwar Mishra

38 Which of the following neurous of cortex produce most EEG?
1 Pyramidal
2 Cuboidal
3 Tabular
4 Cylindrical

39 Who gave the concept of happy life?
1 Martin Seligman
2 Carol Ryff
3 Diener
4 Easterlin

40 Jensen's Level I and Level II abilities can be best understood in terms of which of the following?
I. Difficulty and complexity of tasks
II. SES Differences
III. Racial Differences
IV. Gender Differences

Choose the most appropriate answer from the options given below:-
1 I and II
2 III and IV
3 I, II and III
4 II, III and IV

41 What strategies government can use to decrease poverty?
1 Tax avoidence
2 Debt
3 Loan
4 Wages

42 Which of the following is a correct sequence of conditioned emotional response becoming phobia?
I. Stimulus generalisation and higher-order conditioning
II. Desensitisation

III. Amygdala producing fear
IV. Conditional emotional response

Codes

1 I, II, III, IV　　2 II, III, IV, I
3 IV, III, I, II　　4 I, III, II, IV

43 Structure of the intellect model was given by

1 Jensen　　2 Spearman
3 Thurstone　　4 Guilford

44 Consider the following statements.

I. Pre-menstrual dysphoric disorder is marked by anxiety and depression.
II. This category is similar to pre-menstrual syndrome.

Which of the statements given above is/are correct?

1 Only I　　2 Only II
3 Both I and II　　4 Neither I nor II

45 Match the following.

List I (Methods)	List II (Concepts)
A. Command style	I. Most efficient
B. Consult style	II. Majority decision
C. Vote style	III. Advice from stakeholder
D. Consensus style	IV. Authoritarian in nature

Codes

	A	B	C	D
1	IV	III	II	I
2	II	I	IV	III
3	II	I	III	IV
4	IV	III	I	II

46 Ability is transmitted in humans by

1 zygote　　2 gene
3 chromosome　　4 hormone

47 A change in the axon membrane potential from 70 mv to 90 mv would be termed as

1 Repolarisation
2 Threshold potential
3 Action potential
4 Hyperpolarisation

48 Arrange the following theories in order of proposal.

I. Classical Conditioning (Pavlov)
II. Social Development Theory (Vygotsky)
III. Stage Theory of Cognitive Development (Piaget)
IV. Erikson's Stages of Development (Erikson)

Codes

1 II, I, III, IV　　2 I, II, III, IV
3 IV, III, II, I　　4 III, II, IV, I

49 Which of the following sets of interaction distances is in correct chronological order distance wise?

I. Personal Distance　　II. Public Distance
III. Intimate Distance　　IV. Social Distance

Codes

1 I, II, III, IV　　2 IV, III, II, I
3 II, IV, I, III　　4 III, I, IV, II

50 Consider the following statements.

I. Micro electrode always monitor a complex cell.
II. After visual information is processed in the primary visual cortex, it is routed through what and where path way.

Which of the statements given above is/are not correct?

1 Only I　　2 Only II
3 Both I and II　　4 Neither I nor II

51 Given below are two statements, one is labelled as Assertion (A) and the other is labelled as Reason (R).

Assertion (A) Lewin asserted that avoidance – avoidance conflicts are relatively more stable.

Reason (R) Opposing forces tend to remain in a state of disequilibrium.

In the light of the above statements, choose the most appropriate answer from the options given below :

1 Both (A) and (R) are correct and (R) is the correct explanation of (A)
2 Both (A) and (R) are correct but (R) is not the correct explanation of (A)
3 (A) is correct, but (R) is not correct
4 (A) is not correct, but (R) is correct

52 Consider the following statements.

I. Information made available by the environment is processed by a series of processing systems.
II. The aim of research is to specify the processes and structures that underlie cognitive performance.

Which of the statements given above is/are correct?

1 Only I　　2 Only II
3 Both I and II　　4 None of these

53 Loftus and Pickrell (1995) asked people to read and think about events which had happened to them in childhood and also instructed to write a description of one event which was actually fictitious. About one third of the participants described the fictitious events as having really happened to them. This is called

I. Eyewitness memory
II. False memory
III. Flash bulb memory
IV. Autobiographical memory

Choose the correct answer from the options given below :

1 I and II
2 Only II
3 II and III
4 Only I

54 Match the following List I with List II.

	List I (Stages of Trans-Theoretical Model)		List II (Description)
A.	Pre-contemplation	I.	Ready
B.	Contemplation	II.	Not ready
C.	Preparation	III.	Modification Behaviour
D.	Action	IV.	Getting Ready

Codes

	A	B	C	D
1	II	IV	I	III
2	IV	III	II	I
3	II	I	III	IV
4	I	II	IV	III

55 What is the estimated number of poor people according to World Bank?

1 296 millions
2 300 millions
3 292 millions
4 276 millions

56 Emotions like pride and awe constitute which element of PERMA theory by Seligman?

1 Engagement
2 Meaning
3 Accomplishments
4 Positive emotions

57 Put the following in correct sequence on the basis of emergence.

I. Interal Yoga
II. Sufism
III. Buddhism
IV. Bhagavad Gita

Codes

1 II, III, IV, I
2 I, II, III, IV
3 IV, I, III, II
4 IV, III, II, I

58 What are the ways which are used by cyber bullies to bully others?

I. Stealing
II. Exclusion
III. Fake news
IV. Accidents

Codes

1 I and II
2 II and III
3 I, II and III
4 IV and III

59 Which of the following should be considered in item writing?

I. Adaptable difficulty level
II. Clarity
III. Avoid inter-locking items
IV. Use of stereotyped words
V. Use of irrelevant clues

Codes

1 IV and V
2 I, II and III
3 I, IV and V
4 II, III and IV

60 What will happen with the continuous stress?

1 Stage of exhaustion
2 Body resources drained
3 Stress hormones depleted
4 All of the above

61 The physical, environmental and social causes of the stress state are termed as

1 Stress
2 Stressors
3 Distress
4 None of these

62 Which of the following options was not a field that contributed to early understandings of psychological thought?

1 Biology
2 Physiology
3 Astronomy
4 Philosophy

63 Simon and Chabris (1999) demonstrated that which type of attention can result in missing potentially interesting information?

1 Focused
2 Tactile
3 Parallel
4 Distributed

64 Which of the following is correct for the Pheromones?

1 Biochemicals found within the brain which effect a person's behaviour
2 Biochemicals which play an important role in transmitting information from neuron to neuron
3 Chemical messengers found in the Central Nervous System
4 Chemical substances emitted by the person into the environment affecting the behaviour of others

65 Which of the following statements are correct regarding primary research?

I. It is also known as field research.
II. It can be in numerous form that includes questionnaires and telephone interviews.

Select the correct answer using the codes given below:

1 Only I
2 Only II
3 Both I and II
4 Neither I nor II

66 Consider the following statements.

I. Item difficulty index is measured using $\frac{U_P - L_P}{U}$

II. Item discrimination index is measured using $\frac{U_P + L_P}{U + L}$

Which of the above statement is/are correct?

1 Only II
2 Only I
3 Both I and II
4 None of the above

67 James (1890) differentiated between which types of attention?

1 Various forms of top-down attention
2 Auditory (top-down) and visual (bottom-up)
3 Various forms of bottom-up attention
4 Active (top-down) and passive (bottom-up)

68 Which tests would be used to assess whether there is a significant difference between the mean ranks of two conditions?

1 Spearman's Rho 2 Friedman
3 Kruskal-Wallis 4 Wilcoxon

69 The concept of magical number 7 ± 2 was proposed by

1 EL Schwartz 2 J Brown
3 BJ Underwood 4 GA Miller

70 Short-term memory can hold information up to

1 10-15 Seconds 2 20-35 Seconds
3 50-60 Seconds 4 30-45 Seconds

71 Which psychologist was influenced by the science of 'Hermeneutics'?

1 Sigmund Freud 2 William James
3 Wilhelm Dilthey 4 Ebbinghaus

72 In business organisation

I. Psychological testing is done in pre employment state.
II. Psychological testing can be done as performance appraisal tool.

Codes

1 Only I 2 Only II
3 Both I and II 4 None of these

73 Consider the following statements.

I. Guilford's concept of intellect is not just an ability, but a major functional unit of the mind.
II. Intellect is a part of functional unit of the mind which deals with problems like perceptual thinking, learning, problem solving etc.

Which of the statements given above is/ are correct?

1 Only I
2 Only II
3 Both I and II
4 Neither I nor II

74 Write in chronological order

I. Moving Embeded Figures Test
II. Minnesota Child Development Inventory
III. Columbia Mental Maturity Scale
IV. Perceptual Acuity Test

Codes

1 III, II, I, IV 2 II, I, III, IV
3 IV, III, I, II 4 III, I, IV, II

75 Which among these is correct for Cyber bullying?

I. It involves disinhibition
II. Lesser role of Bystanders
III. Ability of targets to retaliate is more
IV. No evidence left behind

Choose the correct answer from the options given below:

1 I and II
2 I, II and III
3 II, III and IV
4 I, II and IV

76 Consider the following statements.

I. Psychological test assess a variety of mental abilities and attributes.
II. Psychological test can be taken in limited format.

Codes

1 Only I 2 Only II
3 Both I and II 4 None of these

77 Consider the following statement.

I. Definition of health is limited to physical mental and social well-being.
II. Three stage strategy is applicable for various counselling.

Codes

1 Only I
2 Only II
3 Both I and II
4 None of the above

78 When was the Journal of Conflict Resolution initiated?

1 1948 2 1957
3 1962 4 1961

79 Consider the following statements.

I. Considered by some educators to be the most useful and flexible of all tests forms, multiple choice items can be used in tests for most school subjects.

II. As children develop, they advance from associative play to cooperative play.

Which of the statements given above is/are correct?

1 Only I
2 Only II
3 Both I and II
4 Neither I nor II

80 Frankl did not argue for a particular meaning to life or a particular set of values, he suggested three ways in which meaning can be created in life, arrange them in order

I. Achievement

II. Transcendent experience

III. Attitude toward unavoidable suffering

Codes

1 II, III and I
2 II, I and III
3 I, II and II
4 I, II and III

81 As study to test a hypothesis of a casual relationship between two or more variables is known as

1 Hypothesis testing research
2 Formulative research
3 Descriptive research
4 Diagnostic research

82 Arrange the following in correct chronological order

I. Rendering guidance

II. Follow-up programme

III. Collecting data

Codes

1 I, II and III
2 III, II and I
3 II, I and III
4 III, I and II

83 Who gave the concept of Eudemonic well-being?

1 Socrates
2 Aristotle
3 Plato
4 Aristippus

84 What are the 'Proximal Processes' in GAM?

I. Primary appraisal

II. Thoughtful action

III. Interaction of internal states

IV. Impulsive action

Codes

1 I and II
2 II and III
3 I, II and IV
4 I and IV

85 What are the characteristics of people with Type A behaviour?

I. Hostility
II. Relaxed
III. Loud speaking
IV. Energetic

Codes

1 I, II and III
2 II, III and IV
3 I, III and IV
4 I and IV

86 Which of the following pairs is/are correctly matched?

I. Guilford : Divergent production model

II. Mednick : Remote associates test

III. Poin care : Illumination test

Codes

1 Only I
2 II and III
3 I and II
4 I and III

87 Which among the following intensity is high in role conflict?

1 Mutual
2 Economic
3 Emotional
4 Developmental

88 Consider the following statements.

I. Environmental influences, as well as attitudes and interests acquired by an individual in the course of life have no influence on the breadth of a person's intelligence.

II. Attitude factor of intelligence is more innate and less dependent on environmental influences.

Which of the statements given above is/are correct?

1 Only I
2 Only II
3 Both I and II
4 Neither I nor II

89 Consider the following statements.

I. In terms of cognitive development, middle childhood is characterised by the child's attainment of the stage of concrete operations.

II. During middle childhood, self concept and academic performance are negatively correlated.

Which of the statements given above is/are correct?

1 Only I
2 Only II
3 Both I and II
4 Neither I nor II

90 $R_{ABCD \ldots K}$ is used to represent

1 Multiple correlation
2 Partial correlation
3 Rank order
4 Product method

91 Arrange the steps of progression on sexual addiction by Dr. Victor Clive.

I. Desensitisation
II. Addiction
III. Acting out
IV. Escalation

Codes

1 III, II, IV, I 2 I, IV, III, II
3 II, I, IV, III 4 III, IV, II, I

92 Who wrote 'Buddhist manual of Psychological Ethics'?

1 Rhys Davids 2 Carl Rogers
3 Eric Fromm 4 DT Suzuki

93 Which of the statement given below is/are correct?

I. A concept referring to a objective having atleast one of a number of feature is a conjunctive.
II. Going from general principles to specific situations is called deductive thought.

Select the correct answer using the codes given below:

1 Only I 2 Only II
3 Both I and II 4 None of these

94 The formula for the Kruskal- Wallis is based upon

1 Ranks 2 Categories
3 Means 4 Deviations

95 Which of the following is an important tool of item analysis, in item difficulty and item discrimination?

1 ICT 2 ICP
3 ICC 4 IDC

96 Consider the following statements.

I. Item analysis makes it possible to shorten a test
II. Item analysis decreases test's validity and reliability.

Which of the above statement is/are correct?

1 Only I 2 Only II
3 Both I and II 4 None of these

97 Which amongst the following is a basic belief system and theoretical framework to our understanding of the reality?

1 Ontology 2 Epistemology
3 Methodology 4 Paradigm

98 Social perception consist of which of the following component?

I. Non-verbal communication
II. Attitude
III. Attribution
IV. Pro-social behaviour

Codes

1 I and II 2 I, II and III
3 I and III 4 All of these

99 What did Martin Seligman considered most important to attain a happy and satisfied life?

1 Engagement with work
2 Purpose
3 Using of signature strengths
4 Accomplishments

100 Arrange the following in the correct sequence of histology.

I. Embedded tissue is cut using microtome
II. Tissue is fixed using formalin
III. Tissue is stained
IV. Tissue is embeded in paraffin

Codes

1 III, II, I, IV 2 II, IV, I, III
3 I, III, II, IV 4 III, I, II, IV

ANSWERS

1. (1)	**2.** (2)	**3.** (1)	**4.** (3)	**5.** (2)	**6.** (3)	**7.** (2)	**8.** (2)	**9.** (4)	**10.** (3)
11. (2)	**12.** (1)	**13.** (3)	**14.** (2)	**15.** (3)	**16.** (1)	**17.** (2)	**18.** (1)	**19.** (2)	**20.** (3)
21. (1)	**22.** (3)	**23.** (3)	**24.** (1)	**25.** (3)	**26.** (4)	**27.** (1)	**28.** (1)	**29.** (3)	**30.** (1)
31. (3)	**32.** (3)	**33.** (4)	**34.** (4)	**35.** (4)	**36.** (4)	**37.** (1)	**38.** (1)	**39.** (3)	**40.** (3)
41. (3)	**42.** (3)	**43.** (4)	**44.** (1)	**45.** (1)	**46.** (2)	**47.** (4)	**48.** (2)	**49.** (3)	**50.** (2)
51. (3)	**52.** (2)	**53.** (2)	**54.** (1)	**55.** (4)	**56.** (4)	**57.** (4)	**58.** (1)	**59.** (2)	**60.** (4)
61. (2)	**62.** (3)	**63.** (1)	**64.** (4)	**65.** (3)	**66.** (4)	**67.** (4)	**68.** (2)	**69.** (1)	**70.** (2)
71. (3)	**72.** (3)	**73.** (3)	**74.** (4)	**75.** (2)	**76.** (1)	**77.** (2)	**78.** (2)	**79.** (2)	**80.** (4)
81. (1)	**82.** (4)	**83.** (2)	**84.** (3)	**85.** (3)	**86.** (3)	**87.** (3)	**88.** (2)	**89.** (1)	**90.** (1)
91. (3)	**92.** (1)	**93.** (2)	**94.** (1)	**95.** (3)	**96.** (1)	**97.** (4)	**98.** (3)	**99.** (4)	**100.** (2)

UGC-NET PSYCHOLOGY

PRACTICE SET 5

PAPER II

1 **In motivational cycle, first stage refers to**
1 Need 2 Goal
3 Incentive 4 Drive

2 **When was the Indian Association of Clinical Psychologists started?**
1 1975 2 1974
3 1972 4 1968

3 **Who among the following divided the human life span into 10 periods?**
1 Baumrind
2 Bee and Mitchell
3 Piteumas
4 Sigmund Freud

4 **What does the international conflict deal with?**
1 Global level conflict
2 Countries boundaries
3 Political issues conflict
4 Mechanical propaganda

5 **The biology of human behaviour is known as**
1 Zoology 2 Ethology
3 Etiology 4 Cosmology

6 **Surveys play an important role in a type of research that is intended to assess the covariation of naturally occurring variables. This general type of research is called**
1 Experimental research
2 Correlational research
3 Analytical research
4 Qualitative research

7 **Which among the following is right about 'Development'?**
1 It reflects the qualitative changes
2 Progressive series of orderly changes
3 Coherent changes
4 All of the above

8 **Bhagavad Gita emphasises the importance of**
1 emotional intelligence
2 visuo-spatial intelligence
3 naturalistic intelligence
4 spatial intelligence

9 **What two psychological approaches dominated psychology from the 1920s to the 1950s?**
1 The cognitive perspective and structuralism
2 Monism and evolutionary psychology
3 Gestalt psychology and functionalism
4 Behaviourism and the psychodynamic approach

10 **What does MRI measure?**
1 Signal from proton
2 Signal from electron
3 Signal from neutron
4 None of the above

11 **Ontology is the nature of our beliefs about**
1 research 2 subjects
3 reality 4 world

12 **Classical conditioning is based on the work of which person?**
1 Freud 2 Pavlov
3 Bandura 4 None of these

13 **Who introduced 'DBT' (Dialectical Behavioural Technique) based on Principles of Buddhism?**
1 Steven C Hayes 2 Jon Kabat Zinn
3 Marsha M Linehan 4 Eric Fromm

14 **In the two group design with a continuous dependent variable, which of the following measures of effect size can be employed?**
I. Cohen's d
II. Point biserial correlation
III. Eta square
IV. Partial eta square

Choose the most appropriate answer from the options given below:-
1 Only I
2 II and III
3 I, II and III
4 I, II and IV

15 Match the following.

List I (Scholars)	List II (Theory)
A. Carl Rogers	I. Extrinsic motivation
B. Skinner	II. Competition
C. Chapman	III. Intrinsic motivation
D. Hurlock	IV. Cooperation

Codes

	A	B	C	D		A	B	C	D
1	I	II	III	IV	2	I	II	IV	III
3	III	I	II	IV	4	II	IV	III	I

16 Which of the following statements is wrong?
1 Body's requirement of sleep varies with age
2 Tertiary prevention is action taken to identify and treat an illness or injury early with an aim of stopping or reversing the problem
3 Endorphins are released during exercise
4 Excessive alcohol consumption leads to shrinking of frontal lobe of the brain.

17 Adams (1967), suggested certain distinction between STM and LTM. Which one of the following statements is incorrect?
1 STM has a smaller storage capacity than LTM.
2 Acoustic interference is primarily responsible for STM, but not for LTM.
3 Semantic interference is also equally responsible for forgetting in STM.
4 Due to certain lesions in hippocampal region individual fails to transfer information from STM to LTM.

18 The radioactive tracer reported in Alzheimer's disease is
1 florbetapir F18
2 flulemetamol F18
3 florbetaben F18
4 All of the above

19 Charles Darwin proposed that natural selection leads to the development of characteristics most suited to the survival and reproduction of a species. His theory has most influenced which branch of psychology?
1 Humanism
2 Evolutionary Psychology
3 Cognitive Psychology
4 Behaviourism

20 What was the focus of attentional research in the late 1980s?
1 Evolutionary theory and biology
2 Controlled processes and verbal reports
3 Cognitive neuroscience, patient date and computer modeling
4 Humans as single channel processors

21 'The most important thing a psychologist can study is how a behaviour or thought helps a person navigate the world, rather than how that thought comes to be or what it is made of'
This viewpoint probably comes from somebody who believes in what historical theoretical approach?
1 Structuralism
2 Functionalism
3 Gestalt
4 Psychoanalysis

22 What percentage of participants fully obeyed the experimenter's command to deliver a 450-volt shock to the learner in the experiment detailed in the text?
1 5%
2 20%
3 35%
4 65%

23 Cyber pornography consumption is mostly
I. International
II. Accidental
III. Out of curiosity
IV. To enhance one's knowledge

Codes
1 I and II
2 II and III
3 I, II and III
4 I, II, III and IV

24 Consider the following statements.
I. Spearman and Thurstone were measurement psychologist.
II. Cattle had a more inclusive and total perspective view of human behaviour.

Which of the statements given above is/are correct
1 Only I
2 Only II
3 Both I and II
4 Neither I nor II

25 In which of the following approach brain imaging used?
1 Psychological approach
2 Biological approach
3 Behavioural approach
4 Psychodynamic approach

26 Consider the following statements.

I. Gestalt psychology emerged in Germany as a reaction to the structuralism of Wundt.

II. Gestalt means 'form' or 'Configuration'.

Which among the above is/are correct?

1 Only I
2 Only II
3 Both I and II
4 None of the above

27 Arrange the phases of Cooperative Inquiry in sequence of their occurrence.

I. Experiences leading to new fields

II. Reframe

III. Reflection   IV. Action

Codes

1 I, II, III, IV   2 IV, III, II, I
3 III, IV, I, II   4 I, III, II, IV

28 Maturation involves within it

1 quantitative changes
2 qualitative changes
3 Both (1) and (2)
4 None of the above

29 Expectancy-value theory falls under which of the following approach?

1 Ethological   2 Cognitive
3 Self-regulation   4 Humanistic

30 Consider the following statements.

I. According to Jensen, 'Intelligence' is essentially another activity or function of the individual like blood pressure, temperature, etc.

II. Intelligence test provides accurate result.

Which of the statements given above is/are correct?

1 Only I
2 Only II
3 Both I and II
4 Neither I nor II

31 Which of the following statements is/are correct regarding naturalistic observation?

I. Carried out in a controlled conditions.

II. An obstrusive observation procedures are used.

III. Popularised by ethologist, who study animal behaviour in its natural habitats.

Select the correct answer using codes given below

1 Only I
2 II and III
3 All of these
4 None of the above

32 Consider the following statements.

I. DIPR only deals with the research on military psychology.

II. Department of Psychiatry have post graduate programmes.

Select the incorrect statement using the codes given below

1 Only I   2 Only II
3 Both I and II   4 None of these

33 Consider the following statements

I. Test retest reliability indicates repeatability of test score with the passage of time.

II. Alternate form of reliability indicates now consistent test scores are likely to be if a person takes two or more form of test.

Which of the above statement is/are correct?

1 Only I
2 Only II
3 Both I and II
4 None of the above

34 Which amongst the following are characteristics of negative stress?

1 It causes anxiety
2 If feels unpleasant
3 It decreases performance
4 All of the above

35 Which model of Conflict Resolution was proposed by Charles E Osgood?

1 Mediation model
2 Affiliation Model
3 GRIT Model
4 No-Arms Model

36 What is/are not a feature of digital learning?

I. Adaptive learning

II. Learning objects

III. Real teacher

IV. Textbooks

Codes

1 I and II   2 II and III
3 I and III   4 III and IV

37 Which of the following is involved in Type 'a' processes of thinking as described by Wertheimer?

1 Grouping and reorganisation
2 Assimilation and conditioning
3 Blind trial and error
4 Partially productive methods

38 Which of the following describes the enduring facilitation of synaptic transmission that occurs following activation of synapses by high intensity and high frequency stimulation of pre-synaptic neurons?

1 Action potential
2 Absolute refractory period
3 Relative refractory period
4 Long term potentiation

39 Match the following.

List I (Social Concepts)	**List II** (Explanations)
A. Elaboration Likelihood Model	I. Gender stereotypes
B. Realistic Conflict Theory	II. Central and peripheral route to persuasion
C. Glass Cliff	III. Idealogical change in core aspect of a group
D. Schism	IV. Intergroup competition as a source of prejudice

Choose the correct answer from the options given below :

	A	B	C	D
1	I	III	II	IV
2	III	IV	I	II
3	II	I	IV	III
4	II	IV	I	III

40 Consider the following statements.

I. Students attributions are totally the result of their previous success and failure experience.
II. Teacher must be careful when they attribute either success or failure to effort.

Which of the statements given above is/are true?

1 Only I
2 Only II
3 Both I and II
4 Neither I nor II

41 Major concepts of Health Promoting Model are

I. Personal factor
II. Real Barrier
III. Activity Related affect
IV. Situational affect

Codes

1 I and II
2 I, II and III
3 I, II and IV
4 I, III and IV

42 Consider the following statements.

I. Guilford classifies mental abilities the same way chemical element classified in periodic table.
II. Mednick said that true creativity is the ability to think a remote idea.

Which of the statements given above is/are correct?

1 Only I
2 Only II
3 I and II
4 None of these

43 Arrange the following in ascending order in terms of control

I. Field experiment
II. Lab experiment
III. Quasi-experiment
IV. Ex-post facto

Codes

1 I, II, III, IV
2 IV, III, I, II
3 IV, I, III, II
4 III, IV, I, II

44 What are the type/types of strain in General Strain Theory?

I. Anticipated presentation of negative value stimuli
II. Anticipated presentation of positive value stimuli
III. Anticipated removal of positive value stimuli
IV. Anticipated failure to achieve positive value stimuli

Codes

1 I, II and III
2 II, III and IV
3 I, III and IV
4 I and IV

45 When cholinergic agonist is injected into ...., it increases REM sleep.

1 GTF
2 LTN
3 PTN
4 PGO

46 Group size affects perceived conformity pressure in that, the .... the group, the ....pressure is exerted.

1 larger, more
2 more compliant, less
3 smaller, more
4 more cohesive, less

47 The Health belief model has been developed to explain why people fail to perform .... behaviours such as or screening tests.

1 reflective, orientations
2 casual, dance
3 healthy, diet oriented
4 preventive, vaccinations

48 Participants' tendencies to obey the experimenter's commands to shock a victim were highest when the experimenter was .... and the victim was ....

1 close; distant
2 close; close
3 distant; distant
4 distant; close

49 Consider the following statements.

I. During adolescence, self-esteem is at its lowest, when the child enters middle school or junior high school.

II. Using flash cards for review is developmentally appropriate for adolescents.

Which of the statements given above is/are correct?

1 Only I
2 Only II
3 Both I and II
4 Neither I nor II

50 Arrange the following in correct sequence.

I. End of cannula to be inserted is cut at an angle.
II. Cannula is inserted in right angle.
III. Other end of cannula is sealed.
IV. A small hole is drilled into skull.

Codes

1 I, II, III, IV   2 II, III, I, IV
3 III, I, II, IV   4 I, III, IV, II

51 Put in sequence the stage of Hans Selye GAS model of stress?

I. Body adapts to stressor
II. Body breaks down
III. Changes in immune system
IV. Body is initial response

Codes

1 IV, I, II, III   2 III, I, II, IV
3 III, II, I, IV   4 IV, II, I, III

52 Which of the following are correct for the Biopsychosocial Model of health?

I. Close interaction between body and mind, though they are separate entities
II. Active participation of the patient
III. Health and illness are on the same continuum
IV. Treatment process involves medication, surgery and radiation

Choose the most appropriate answer from the options given below:

1 I, II and III   2 I, II and IV
3 II, III and IV   4 I, II, III and IV

53 Consider the following statements.

I. A key concept to pre-school education is readiness training.

II. Research on kindergarten indicates that kindergarten promotes readiness and achievement in the first and second grade, but these effects disappear by the third or fourth grade.

Which of the statements given above is/are correct?

1 Only I   2 Only II
3 Both I and II   4 Neither I nor II

54 Common sign and symptom of diabetes are

I. fatigue
II. frequent urination
III. decreased thirst
IV. weight loss

Codes

1 I and III   2 I, II and III
3 I, II and IV   4 All of these

55 Consider the following statements Adrenal insufficiency causes

I. increased blood volume
II. decreased plasma K level
III. hyperglycaemia
IV. reduce excretion of 17 ketosteroids

Which of the options given above are correct?

1 I and IV   2 I, II and III
3 II, III and IV   4 II and III

56 Arrange the steps in order in Pavlov's experiment

I. Selecting stimulus and response
II. Establishing classical conditioning
III. Testing for conditioning

Codes

1 I, II, III   2 III, I, II
3 II, I, III   4 I, III, II

57 Arrange the following in sequence

I. Pre-Contemplation
II. Preparation
III. Action
IV. Maintenance

Codes

1 IV, III, II and I
2 I, II, III and IV
3 III, II, I and IV
4 II, I, III and IV

58 Attitude is made up of different component, which includes

I. Cognitive   II. Affective
III. Behaviourial   IV. Attribution

Codes

1 I and II
2 I, II and III
3 II and IV
4 All of the above

59 **Depending upon the task characteristics, there is a gradual transition from simpler forms of learning to the level of higher complex ones. These different forms are**

I. Establishment of simple S-R relationships
II. Acquiring motor and verbal skills
III. Concept formation
IV. Problem-solving

The correct order of learning sequence is

1 I, IV, II, III
2 I, II, III, IV
3 II, IV, I, III
4 II, III, IV, I

60 **Which of the following procedures are useful in the process of problem solving?**

I. Algorithms
II. Heuristics
III. Sub-goaling
IV. Restructuring

Select the correct answer using the codes given below:

1 I, II, III and IV
2 II and III
3 I and IV
4 II, III and IV

61 **Consider the following statements.**

I. DSM-IV-TR attempts to enhance cultural sensitivity by providing a general framework for evaluating the role of culture.
II. Caffeine withdrawal syndromes associated with headache, fatigue.

Which of the statements given above is/are correct?

1 Only I
2 Only II
3 Both I and II
4 Neither I nor II

62 **Arrange the following steps of problem-solving in order**

I. Defining the problem
II. Identifying the problem
III. Allocating resources
IV. Monitoring progress

Codes

1 IV, III, II, I
2 II, I, III, IV
3 I, II, III, IV
4 III, IV, II, I

63 **What among the following define a problem space?**

I. An inital state
II. A goal state
III. A set of operations

Codes

1 I and III
2 I and II
3 II and III
4 I, II and III

64 **The tendency to believe that a task will take less time than it really will, is known as:**

1 Magical thinking
2 Planning Fallacy
3 Optimistic Bias
4 Fundamental Attribution Error

65 **In which phase of Enright's model of psychological forgiveness, individual gains a cognitive understanding of the offender in a new light that brings a positive change in view about the offender, self and the relationship?**

1. Uncovering phase
2. Decision phase
3. Work phase
4. Deepening phase

66 **Arrange the following in correct sequence to control irrational thoughts.**

I. Develop awareness
II. Self Reward
III. Evaluate
IV. Prepare compatible thoughts

Codes

1 I, III, IV, II
2 I, II, III, IV
3 II, IV, I, III
4 II, I, III, IV

67 **Integration of cognitive aspects of learning with the emotional aspects of experience and learning is known as:**

1 Integrated approach to learning
2 Confluent education
3 Feeling class approach to education
4 Motivational approach to learning

68 **Consider the following statements.**

I. Clinical disorder contains the disorder that brings most people to the attention of a psychological professional.
II. Personality disorder seems to exist from birth and are relatively stable and enduring.

Which of the statements given above is/ are correct?

1 Only I
2 Only II
3 Both I and II
4 Neither I nor II

69 **Arrange in order the scientific thoughts according to their emergence.**

I. Rationalism
II. Positivism
III. Critical research
IV. Post-positivism

Codes

1 I, II, III, IV 2 IV, I, II, III
3 I, II, IV, III 4 II, I, IV, III

70 Who made the distinction between the direct and structural form of violence?

1 Johan Galtung 2 Christine
3 Winger 4 AR Wagner

71 Which among the following is a study to evaluate the frequency with which something occurs or with which it is associated with something else?

1 Diagnostic research
2 Hypothesis research
3 Formulative research
4 None of the above

72 Functionalism influenced which two major areas in psychology?

1 Emotion and cognition
2 Thinking and reasoning
3 Learning and motivation
4 Perception and learning

73 Who said these words, 'Research is a systematic investigation to find answers to a problem'.

1 Kerlinger 2 John W Creswell
3 Burns 4 Earl Robert Bobbie

74 Given below are two statements, one is labelled as Assertion (A) and the other is labelled as Reason (R).

Assertion (A) Lewin asserted that avoidance – avoidance conflicts are relatively more stable.

Reason (R) Opposing forces tend to remain in a state of disequilibrium.

In the light of the above statements, choose the most appropriate answer from the options given below :

1 Both (A) and (R) are correct and (R) is the correct explanation of (A)
2 Both (A) and (R) are correct, but (R) is not the correct explanation of (A)
3 (A) is correct, but (R) is not correct
4 (A) is not correct, but (R) is correct

75 Match the following.

List I (Health Belief)	List II (Description)
A. Attitude towards others	I. Beliefs of significant
B. Subjective norms	II. Related to past behaviour
C. Cue to action	III. Trigger
D. Behavioural control	IV. Evaluation

Codes

	A	B	C	D
1	I	II	III	IV
2	IV	I	III	II
3	IV	III	I	II
4	II	III	I	IV

76 Who coined the term 'Resource Dilemma'?

1 Wades 2 Dawes
3 Stefen 4 None of these

77 In which schools of Indian thought about yoga, 'Prakrti' remains isolated as a principle of ultimate reality into self and is active only in the presence and service of 'Purusa'?

1 Integral yoga philosophy
2 Vedanta
3 Samkhya
4 Sahaj yoga

78 A nerve cell carrying information from your eyes, ears, fingers etc, toward the CNS is called a/an

1 Motor neuron
2 Effector cell
3 Connector neuron
4 Sensory neuron

79 Sensation seeking theory has been given by

1 David McClelland
2 Freud
3 Marvin Zuckerman
4 Boyatzis

80 We are more likely to experience which of the following during adolescence than at any other time in our lives?

1 Moodiness
2 Parent-child conflicts
3 Risky behaviour
4 All of the above

81 Which one set of the following psychologists developed a theory that early experiences affect adult behaviour?

1 Freud, Watson and Harlow
2 Freud and Harlow
3 Watson and Freud
4 Harlow and Watson

82 Which ligand is introduced in body during PET scan?

1 Chlorine-4
2 Helium - 20
3 Fluorine-18
4 All of the above

83 Which among the following chemical ions are involved in the generation of action potential?

1 Na^+ 2 Cl^-
3 K^+ 4 All of these

84 Multivariate Analysis of Variance (MANOVA) is best suited for making groupwise comparisons for several dependent variables. Which of the following are these?

1 Uncorrelated
2 Moderately correlated
3 Very highly correlated
4 Either uncorrelated or have small negative correlations

85 As per Socrates' Greek Philosophy, which of the following is NOT true about eudaemonia?

1 It means living well or flourishing
2 It is more than merely attaining pleasure
3 Being virtuous is almost identical to eudaemonia
4 Being virtuous does not guarantee eudaemonia

86 Attribution of one's own motive to others is called

1 identification
2 projection
3 association
4 reaction formation

87 Which of the following factors influence developmental process?

1 Normative influences
2 Education and Training
3 Hereditary factors
4 All of the above

88 Bandura first became interested in clinical psychology when he

1 entered graduate school at Stanford University.
2 worked on the Alaska highway after graduation from high school.
3 met Skinner at the 1972 APA convention.
4 entered graduate school at the University of Iowa.

89 Match the following.

	List I	List II
A.	Cognitive Assessment System	I. Dass
B.	Hold and Dout Hold Tests	II. Wechsler
C.	Cognitive Assessment Battery	III. Cattell
D.	Differential Ability Test	IV. Elliot

Choose the correct answer from the options given below :

	A	B	C	D
1	I	II	III	IV
2	II	I	IV	III
3	III	IV	I	II
4	IV	III	II	I

90 For computing inter-item correlations, which one of the following is suitable?

1 Point biserial correlation
2 Biserial correlation
3 Rank difference correlation
4 Phi-coefficient

91 Arrange the following in chronological order about the stages in language development

I. Phonemes II. Morphemes
III. Pragmatism IV. Syntax

Codes

1 I, II, III, IV 2 II, I, III, IV
3 II, III, IV, I 4 I, II, IV, III

92 Match the following.

	List I (Concepts)	List II (Specifics)
A.	Digital Content	I. Robert Angrew
B.	Digital Etiquette	II. High Speed
C.	GAM Model	III. Cursing
D.	GST Theory	IV. Bushman, Anderson

Codes

	A	B	C	D		A	B	C	D
1	IV	I	III	II	2	I	II	III	IV
3	I	III	II	IV	4	II	III	IV	I

93 What is 'Jiva' in Indian Psychology?

1 Witness 2 Non-participant
3 Experiential self 4 Objective

94 There are five sub-tests in the performance battery of WAIS. Identify the correct order in which they are administered.

1 DS, PC, BD, OA, PA
2 PC, BD, OA, PA, DS
3 DS, PC, BD, PA, OA
4 OS, PC, PA, BD, DA

95 Cherry (1953) investigated which phenomenon?

1 Focused auditory attention
2 Cocktail party phenomenon
3 Visual disparity
4 Focused visual attention

96 Increasing the size of the group from .... is likely to produce, the greatest increase in conformity.

1 1000 to 2000
2 50 to 100
3 2 to 5
4 5 to 10

97 How many well known psychologists came together by close of World War Second for manifesto human nature and peace?

1 11
2 15
3 13
4 17

98 Which among the following is also known as 'Analysis of Covariance'?

1 ANCOVA
2 MANOVA
3 ANOVA
4 None of these

99 Where does the unipolar axon proceed from one region to another without branching?

1 CNS
2 PNS
3 Spinal cord
4 Brain

100 Match the following List I with List II.

List I (Concept)	List II (Description)
A. Turiyavastha	I. Transcognitive realisation
B. Aparvidya	II. Highest state of consciousness
C. Paravidya	III. Transcendental knowledge
D. Nididhasan	IV. Empirical knowledge

Choose the correct answer from the options given below :

	A	B	C	D
1	I	III	II	IV
2	II	III	IV	I
3	II	I	III	IV
4	III	II	IV	I

ANSWERS

1. (1)	**2.** (4)	**3.** (3)	**4.** (1)	**5.** (2)	**6.** (2)	**7.** (4)	**8.** (1)	**9.** (4)	**10.** (1)
11. (3)	**12.** (2)	**13.** (3)	**14.** (3)	**15.** (3)	**16.** (2)	**17.** (3)	**18.** (4)	**19.** (2)	**20.** (3)
21. (2)	**22.** (4)	**23.** (3)	**24.** (3)	**25.** (2)	**26.** (3)	**27.** (3)	**28.** (3)	**29.** (2)	**30.** (4)
31. (2)	**32.** (4)	**33.** (3)	**34.** (4)	**35.** (3)	**36.** (4)	**37.** (1)	**38.** (4)	**39.** (4)	**40.** (3)
41. (4)	**42.** (3)	**43.** (2)	**44.** (3)	**45.** (1)	**46.** (1)	**47.** (4)	**48.** (1)	**49.** (1)	**50.** (2)
51. (1)	**52.** (4)	**53.** (3)	**54.** (3)	**55.** (3)	**56.** (1)	**57.** (2)	**58.** (2)	**59.** (2)	**60.** (1)
61. (3)	**62.** (2)	**63.** (4)	**64.** (2)	**65.** (3)	**66.** (1)	**67.** (2)	**68.** (3)	**69.** (3)	**70.** (1)
71. (1)	**72.** (3)	**73.** (3)	**74.** (2)	**75.** (2)	**76.** (2)	**77.** (3)	**78.** (4)	**79.** (3)	**80.** (4)
81. (2)	**82.** (3)	**83.** (4)	**84.** (2)	**85.** (4)	**86.** (1)	**87.** (4)	**88.** (2)	**89.** (1)	**90.** (4)
91. (4)	**92.** (4)	**93.** (3)	**94.** (1)	**95.** (2)	**96.** (3)	**97.** (3)	**98.** (1)	**99.** (1)	**100.** (2)